AMERICAN HISTORY

THE EARLY YEARS TO 1877

AMERICAN HISTORY

THE EARLY YEARS TO 1877

DONALD A. RITCHIE

ALBERT S. BROUSSARD

GLENCOE

McGraw-Hill

New York, New York   Columbus, Ohio   Mission Hills, California   Peoria, Illinois

Authors

★★★

Donald A. Ritchie is Associate Historian of the United States Senate Historical Office. Dr. Ritchie received his doctorate in American history from the University of Maryland after service in the U.S. Marine Corps. He has taught American history at various levels, from high school to university. He edits the Historical Series of the Senate Foreign Relations Committee and is the author of several books, including *Press Gallery: Congress and the Washington Correspondents*, which received the Organization of American Historians Richard W. Leopold Prize. Dr. Ritchie has served as president of the Oral History Association and as a council member of the American Historical Association.

Albert S. Broussard is Associate Professor of History at Texas A&M University. Before joining the Texas A&M faculty, Dr. Broussard was Assistant Professor of History and Director of the African American Studies Program at Southern Methodist University. Among his publications is the book *Black San Francisco: The Struggle for Racial Equality in the West, 1900–1954*. The many articles he has published include "Local History and Beyond: Black Urban Communities Revisited" for *Locus, Regional and Local History of the Americas*. Dr. Broussard has also served as president of the Oral History Association.

Glencoe/McGraw-Hill

A Division of The **McGraw·Hill** *Companies*

Printed in the United States of America

Send all inquiries to:
Glencoe/McGraw-Hill
936 Eastwind Drive
Westerville, Ohio 43081

ISBN 0-02-822495-7 (Student Edition)
ISBN 0-02-822501-5 (Teacher's Wraparound Edition)

2 3 4 5 6 7 8 9 027/046 02 01 00 99 98

Academic Consultants

★★

Carol Berkin
Professor of History
Baruch College, CUNY
New York, New York

Richard G. Boehm
Professor of Geography
Southwest Texas State University
San Marcos, Texas

Carlton Jackson
Professor of History
Western Kentucky University
Bowling Green, Kentucky

K. Austin Kerr
Professor of History
The Ohio State University
Columbus, Ohio

Teacher Reviewers

★★

Ken Darlage
Teacher
Central Middle School
Columbus, Indiana

Thomas E. Gray
Social Studies Teacher and
   Department Chair
DeRuyter Central School
DeRuyter, New York

Hattie Jones
American History Teacher
Marion Junior High School
Marion, Arkansas

Peter Russ LoGiudice
Social Studies Department Chair
General Wayne Middle School
Malvern, Pennsylvania

Daniel Michael McClenahen
Principal
Armagh, Brown, and
   Union Elementary Schools
Milroy, Pennsylvania

Margaret Ann Miller
Teacher
Sissonville Middle School
Sissonville, West Virginia

Joe Padilla
Teacher
Ahwahnee Middle School
Fresno, California

Kent Edgar Riley
Social Studies Teacher
Perry Meridian Middle School
Indianapolis, Indiana

JoAnn B. Seghini
Director of Curriculum
   and Staff Development
Jordan School District
Sandy, Utah

Robert Paul Sprague
Social Studies Department Chair
Great Valley High School
Malvern, Pennsylvania

Contents

UNIT FOUR
Early Years of the Republic
1789–1830

★ ★

UNIT FIVE
The Nation Expands 1820-1860

★ ★

UNIT SIX
Rift and Reunion 1820–1877

★ ★

UNIT SEVEN
Modern America Emerges
1877–Present

★ ★ ★ ★ ★ ★ ★ ★ ★ ★ ★ ★ ★ ★ ★ ★ ★ ★ ★

APPENDIX

★ ★ ★ ★ ★ ★ ★ ★ ★ ★ ★ ★ ★ ★ ★ ★ ★ ★ ★

Features

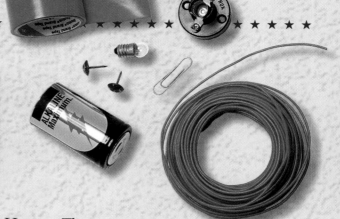

HANDS-ON HISTORY
LAB ACTIVITY

Features

Cultural Kaleidoscope

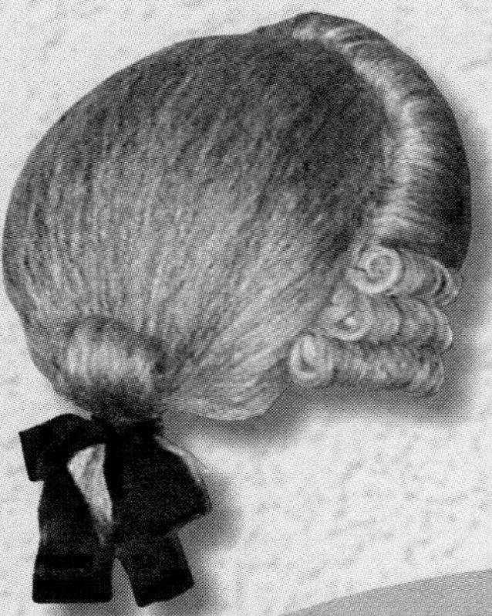

Features

Linking Past and Present

Features

History AND MATH

History AND THE ARTS

History AND SCIENCE

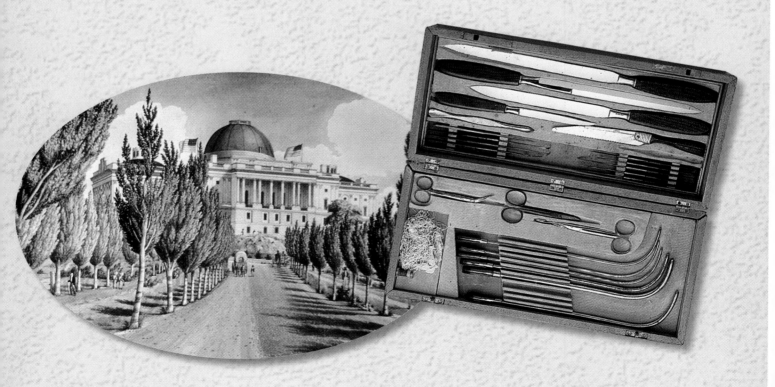

History AND GEOGRAPHY

Major United States River Systems

History AND ECONOMICS

Features

American Literary Heritage

Features

★ ★

Biography ★ ★ ★ ★

Features

Footnotes to History

Features

★ ★

★★★ AMERICA'S FLAGS ★★★

BUILDING SKILLS

Social Studies Skills

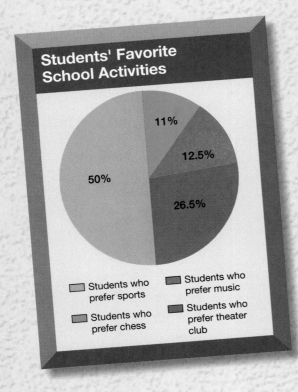

Critical Thinking Skills

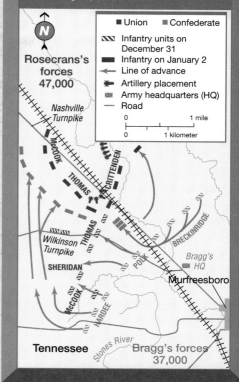

Battle of Stones River (Murfreesboro), December 31, 1862– January 2, 1863

N

Rosecrans's forces 47,000

Union
Confederate
Infantry units on December 31
Infantry on January 2
Line of advance
Artillery placement
Army headquarters (HQ)
Road

0   1 mile
0   1 kilometer

Nashville Turnpike

McCOOK

THOMAS

CRITTENDEN

Wilkinson Turnpike

THOMAS

SHERIDAN

POLK

BRECKINRIDGE

Bragg's HQ

McCOOK

HARDEE

Murfreesboro

Tennessee   Stones River   Bragg's forces 37,000

Study and Writing Skills

★ ★

Cause-and-Effect Charts

CAUSES

- Quebec Act allows French settlers in Ohio Valley
- British quarter soldiers in Boston colonists' homes
- Committees of Correspondence unite colonial opinion
- Coercive Acts close the port of Boston

• Meeting of First Continental Congress

EFFECTS

- Colonies approve protests in Boston
- Colonies ban trade with Great Britain
- Congress appeals directly to King George III for relief
- Delegates agree to meet again the next year

CAUSES

- Easy bank loans encourage land speculation
- Jackson requires specie for government land purchases
- Speculators lose money and cannot repay bank loans

• Bank Panic of 1837

EFFECTS

- Economic crisis deepens throughout the land
- Federal government ends deposits in private banks
- Government creates federal treasury to store its funds

CAUSES

- Military dictatorships in Germany, Italy, and Japan
- Germany invades Poland and Western Europe
- Japan invades the Asian mainland and islands of the Pacific
- Japan attacks American naval base in Hawaii

• World War II

EFFECTS

- United Nations formed
- United States and the Soviet Union become world superpowers
- Cold war develops between Western democracies and Eastern Communist countries

Maps, Charts, Graphs, and Tables

Maps

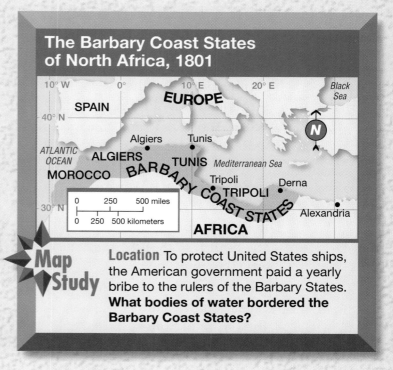

The Barbary Coast States of North Africa, 1801

Map Study

Location To protect United States ships, the American government paid a yearly bribe to the rulers of the Barbary States. **What bodies of water bordered the Barbary Coast States?**

Seceding States, 1860–1861

Wash. Territory
Oregon
40° N
Nevada Territory
Utah Terr.
Calif.
PACIFIC OCEAN
30° N
New Mexico Territory
20°

Dakota Territory
Minn.
Nebraska Territory
Wis.
Iowa
Colorado Territory
Kansas
Ill.
Mo.
Ind.
Indian Terr.
Ark.
Texas
Miss.
La.

N.H.
Vt.
Maine
Mich.
N.Y.
Mass.
R.I.
Conn.
Ohio
Pa.
W. Va.*
N.J.
Ky.
Va.*
Del.
Md.
Tenn.
N.C.
Ala.
S.C.
Ga.
Fla.

ATLANTIC OCEAN

130° W · 120° W · 110° W · 100° W · 90° W · 80° W · 70° W · 60° W

*West Virginia seceded from Virginia in 1861 and was admitted to the Union in 1863.

Union free state
Union slave state
Slave state seceding before Ft. Sumter, April 1861
Slave state seceding after Ft. Sumter, April 1861
Confederate states

0 200 400 miles
0 200 400 kilometers

Map Study

Region After the attack on Fort Sumter, four more Southern states joined the seven that had already seceded from the Union. **Which slave states remained in the Union?**

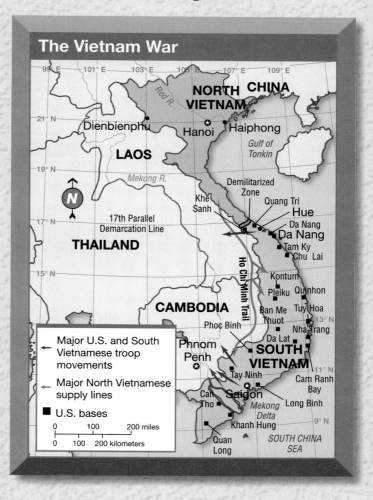

Charts, Graphs, and Tables

Founding the Thirteen Colonies

Colony	Date Founded	Reasons Founded	Founders or Leaders
New England Colonies			
Massachusetts Plymouth Mass. Bay Colony	1620 1630	Religious freedom Religious freedom	John Carver, William Bradford, John Winthrop
New Hampshire	1622	Profit from trade and fishing	Ferdinando Gorges, John Mason
Rhode Island	1636	Religious freedom	Roger Williams
Connecticut	1636	Profit from fur trade, farming; religious and political freedom	Thomas Hooker
Middle Colonies			
New York	1624	Expand trade	Dutch settlers
Delaware	1638	Expand trade	Swedish settlers
New Jersey	1664	Profit from selling land	John Berkeley, George Carteret
Pennsylvania	1681	Profit from selling land; religious freedom	William Penn
Southern Colonies			
Virginia	1607	Expand trade	John Smith
Maryland	1632	Profit from selling land; religious freedom	Cecil Calvert
North Carolina	1663	Profit from trade and selling land	Group of eight aristocrats
South Carolina	1663	Profit from trade and selling land	Group of eight aristocrats
Georgia	1732	Religious freedom; protection against Spanish Florida; safe home for debtors	James Oglethorpe

Chart Study

The 13 colonies were founded over a span of 125 years. **What were the two most common reasons for founding these colonies?**

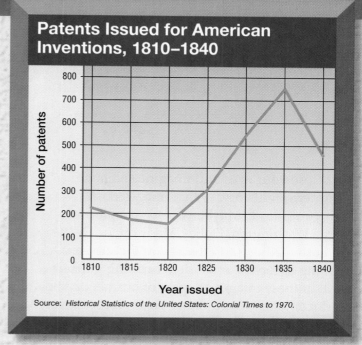

Patents Issued for American Inventions, 1810–1840

Source: *Historical Statistics of the United States: Colonial Times to 1970.*

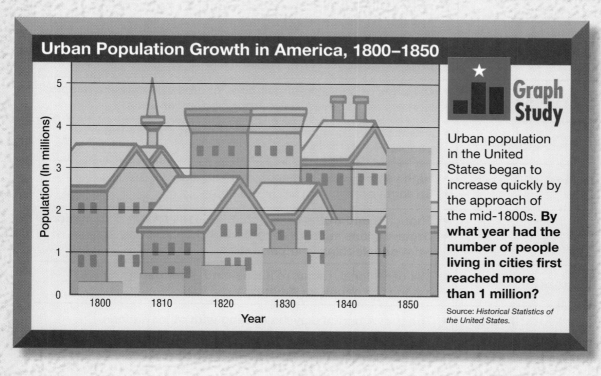

Urban Population Growth in America, 1800–1850

Graph Study

Urban population in the United States began to increase quickly by the approach of the mid-1800s. **By what year had the number of people living in cities first reached more than 1 million?**

Source: *Historical Statistics of the United States.*

Themes in American History

★ ★

Close your eyes and imagine someone says, "American history." What images flash through your mind? Maybe you see people such as George Washington, Dolley Madison, or Dr. Martin Luther King, Jr. Perhaps you picture senators making speeches or soldiers carrying guns or flags. All of these images are part of our history. So are books, documents, works of art, steam locomotives, and countless other things. By themselves, these things tell us little about American history. In order to mean anything, they have to somehow fit together.

Historians help explain the meaning of history by organizing it around themes. A theme is a concept, or big idea, that keeps coming up again and again. This book is organized around 10 recurring themes that will help you study and understand our nation's history.

Theme	Definition
American Democracy	• Form of government in which the people rule themselves, either directly or indirectly
Civil Rights and Liberties	• Privileges and freedoms to which all citizens are entitled under the law
Economic Development	• Process in which people use the nation's resources to provide for their needs and wants
Geography and the Environment	• Land, minerals, climate, space, and all other parts of the physical setting in which people live
Conflict and Cooperation	• Disputes or fights among nations or among a nation's people • Agreement and harmony among nations or people
Influence of Technology	• Advances in science and inventions that change the way people live
The Individual and Family Life	• High value placed on each and every citizen • Strength drawn from life in the home
Ideas, Beliefs, and Institutions	• Thoughts and truths on which Americans founded the nation • Organizations such as schools and churches that uphold what people think is important
Cultural Diversity	• Mix of national, racial, religious, and other backgrounds among the people of America
U.S. Role in World Affairs	• The part America plays in dealing with other nations

★ American Democracy

In a democracy, the people rule themselves. This can mean that people hold meetings where they write their own laws. The United States, however, is too large to hold such meetings. Therefore, the people elect representatives who write the laws and carry them out.

Abraham Lincoln and Stephen A. Douglas both wanted to represent the people of Illinois in the United States Senate. After listening to the candidates debate and give their views, the voters made their choice. They elected Stephen Douglas.

► Lincoln-Douglas debates, 1858

★ Civil Rights and Liberties

American democracy is often called an experiment in freedom. The experiment began when American colonists objected to British rule and demanded certain rights. Colonists often made public protests, such as putting up "liberty poles" in towns or villages. Americans have carried forward the experiment by safeguarding such civil rights and liberties as freedom of speech, freedom of religion, and the right to vote.

▼ "Protecting the Liberty Pole," a colonial symbol of freedom

★ Economic Development

In the beginning, the United States was mostly a nation of farms and farmers. Trade and manufacturing were small but important parts of the total economy. Individual opportunity and political freedom helped Americans expand their economic base. By the end of the 1800s, the economy included modern industry, large cities, and advanced transportation and communication.

▼ **Rural town of Bethlehem, Pennsylvania, mid-1800s**

▶ *Miners in the Sierra* by **Charles Nahl and Frederick August Wenderoth, 1851–1852**

★ Geography and the Environment

Americans used the vast open spaces and resources of the land to build their rich economy. They harnessed running water in eastern streams to get power for early factories. They cleared forests and grasslands to create fields of grain on the central prairies and plains. From the western mountains, they extracted minerals to build giant industries.

★ Conflict and Cooperation

In 1775 and again in 1812, Americans took up arms against the British. These conflicts resulted in gained independence, land, and international respect for the new nation. Thereafter the United States and Great Britain cooperated. They settled their disagreements by treaties rather than war.

▶ **Americans burning stamps to protest Britain's Stamp Act, 1765**

★ Influence of Technology

New technology, or the use of science and machines, has often changed the nation and the lives of its people. After the invention of steam engines and steel rails, railroads revolutionized transportation. Rail cars carried goods much faster than boats and traveled to places where boats could not go. New settlers moving West after 1860 traveled by train.

▼ *Across the Continent* **by Currier and Ives, 1868**

★ The Individual and Family Life

Responsible individuals have often stepped forward to help lead the nation. America's strong family values helped create such individuals. These values spring in part from earlier times when the home was the center of many activities, including work, education, and daily worship.

◄ Early American family shopping at home from items carried by a traveling Yankee peddler of the 1850s

★ Ideas, Beliefs, and Institutions

Strong social, political, and religious beliefs have shaped the nation. Americans from the beginning believed that citizens have certain privileges, such as freedom of speech or the right to trial by jury. Some of the earliest European settlers came to America for the right to worship as they pleased. Freedom of religion and religious beliefs played a large role in the founding of the nation.

▼ **Old Bruton Church, colonial Virginia** as painted by A. Wordsworth Thompson in the 1800s

★ Cultural Diversity

E pluribus unum, a Latin phrase, appears on all United States coins. It means "from the many, [comes] one." The phrase describes American society well. Since earliest times, people from all parts of the world have come to live in the United States. Despite their different backgrounds, people have come together under the American flag and all that it stands for.

▶ **Fourth of July Celebration in Center Square, Philadelphia by John Lewis Krimmel, 1819**

◀ **President James Monroe discussing the Monroe Doctrine with other American leaders, 1823**

★ U.S. Role in World Affairs

When the thirteen colonies won independence from Great Britain, other countries did not take the new nation very seriously. The world began to change its mind as America grew in economic and military strength. When President James Monroe issued the Monroe Doctrine forbidding European nations to interfere in North or South America, the world respected his warning.

Geography in History

★ ★

All history happens somewhere. Geography explains what the "somewheres" are like. It also tells us about the people who live there and how they relate to one another and to the environment.

Like history, geography takes in countless facts. To make sense of them, geographers organize the information around five themes. Understanding the themes of geography will help you see how geography and history often come together.

▼ The continental United States from space

Themes in Geography

Theme	Definition
Location	• Position of a certain place, such as a mountain or a city, on the earth's surface
Place	• Physical or human characteristics that make a certain area on the earth's surface different from all other areas
Movement	• Contact that people in one area have with people in other areas through activities such as trade, migration and travel, or communication
Human/Environment Interaction	• How people use and influence their natural surroundings • How people's natural surroundings influence them
Region	• An area where common physical or human characteristics are shared

 Location

"Where is it?" The geography theme of *location* answers this question about a country, state, city, river, mountain, or any place on Earth. Places have absolute and relative locations. Absolute location is one exact spot on Earth. Relative location tells where a place is compared with one or more other places.

▲ *A View of New Orleans* by John L. Boqueta de Woiseri, 1803

► The city of New Orleans grew at an absolute location at the mouth of the Mississippi River. Because it has a relative location near the Gulf of Mexico, the city became a shipping center.

 # Place

"What makes this point or area on Earth special, or different from all others?" The geography theme of *place* gives us the answer. It describes physical characteristics, such as landforms, climate, and plant or animal life. Place also tells about people in the area and how they work with the physical environment.

▲ Ridges and streams in the Rocky Mountains

◄ Known for their rugged peaks and beautiful scenery, the Rocky Mountains make up the largest mountain chain in North America. In the 1800s, the Rocky Mountains made travel difficult for people and goods headed West. As a result, some settlers traveled by sea.

 **Movement**

"How do people in one area relate to people in other areas?" Geographers answer this question with the theme of *movement*. People, ideas, goods, and information move from place to place. In this way, people stay in contact with others in their own country and in different parts of the world.

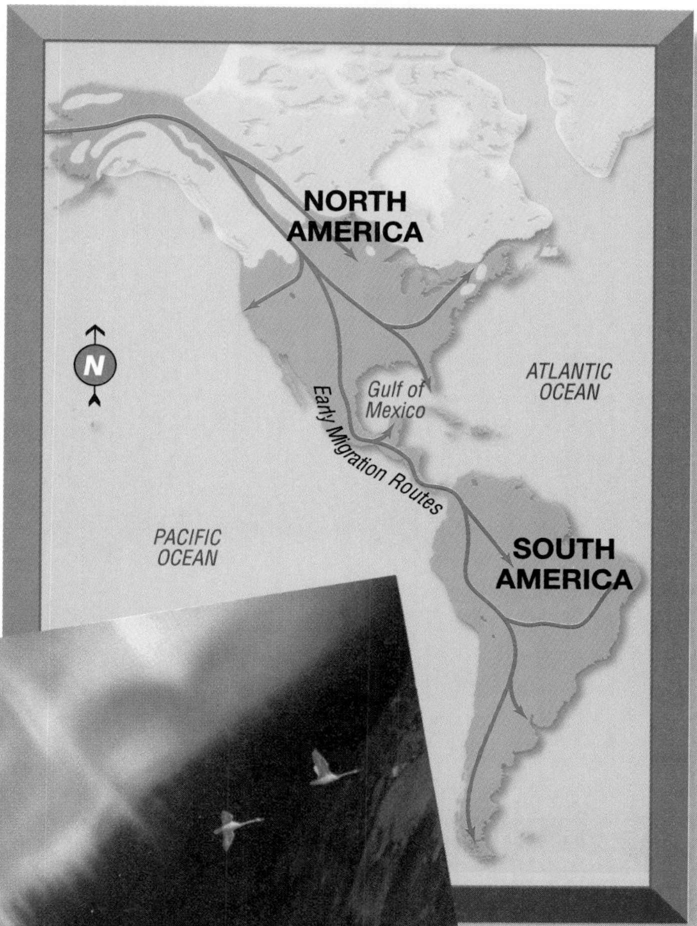

► The story of America began with the movement of ancient people from Asia to North America. Other groups began arriving later. A steady flow of goods and ideas helped create a richly diverse nation.

NORTH AMERICA

ATLANTIC OCEAN

N

Gulf of Mexico

Early Migration Routes

PACIFIC OCEAN

SOUTH AMERICA

▼ Ancient people arriving from Asia

▲ Logging in a forest
in the Northwest

PACIFIC
OCEAN

Northwest
forests

United
States

ATLANTIC
OCEAN

Gulf of
Mexico

N

Human/Environment Interaction

"How does the relationship between people and their natural surroundings influence the way they live?" This is the question that the geography theme of *human/environment interaction* answers. The theme includes how people use the environment and how their actions affect the environment. It also describes how the environment influences the way people live.

▲ European settlers in America cleared away many forestlands to make room for fields, towns, cities, and roads. Vast forests still exist in America's Northwest. Modern Northwest loggers preserve the forests by planting young trees to replace the trees they remove.

Region

"What common characteristics does a certain area share?" The answer to this question deals with the theme of *region.* An area can be called a region because it has the same climate, landforms, or other physical features throughout. Common human traits, such as language, religion, or government, can also form a region.

▼ Farm in the Midwest region

◄ Americans have created different kinds of farms all across the country. The Midwest has been a major farming area since the first European settlers plowed its fertile soil. Its rolling grain fields, scattered farmhouses, and often treeless landscape help make it a region.

UNIT ONE
AMERICA'S BEGINNINGS
PREHISTORY–1700

★★

CHAPTER 1	CHAPTER 2	CHAPTER 3	CHAPTER 4
The Geography of the Americas	The First Americans Prehistory–1492	Explorers Reach the Americas 1000–1535	European Empires in the Americas 1500–1700

MAIZE PLANT

History AND ART
Europeans Encountering Indians
unknown artist

This oil-on-canvas painting depicts an early meeting between Europeans and Native Americans in the fifteenth or sixteenth century.

SETTING THE SCENE

Prehistoric hunters from Asia and their descendants—the Native Americans—were the first humans to see the great variety of land and use the natural resources of the Americas. After many centuries, Europeans also began to settle the Americas. They brought many changes for both the land and its diverse peoples.

▼ NORTHWEST NATIVE AMERICAN VILLAGE

Themes

★ Geography and the Environment
★ Influence of Technology
★ Conflict and Cooperation

Key Events

★ Ice Age hunters and their descendants populate the Americas
★ The Anasazi and Mound Builders develop early Native American cultures
★ Christopher Columbus lands in the Bahamas
★ Spain builds an American empire
★ France claims Canada and Mississippi Valley

Major Issues

★ Native Americans developed a great variety of cultures in diverse geographic settings.
★ Spanish treatment of Native Americans destroyed many Native American populations and cultures.
★ Settlement by the French, Dutch, and Swedes introduced further cultural changes in the Americas.

▲ INCAN TEXTILE

◀ MAYAN JADE MASK

Portfolio Project

As you read the unit, select five events that you think are especially important in the early history of the Americas. For each event write an account from the viewpoint of a Native American who might have been present at the time.

The Magnetic Compass: Going From Here to There

Background

Before sailors had the compass, they relied on the sun, stars, and landmarks along the shore to find their way at sea. Imagine their problems on cloudy days or when they sailed beyond the sight of land!

Chinese sailors probably made the earliest compass—a magnetic device—about 900 years ago. One end of a compass needle always points toward the earth's magnetic north pole. The other end points toward the earth's magnetic south pole. In this activity, you will create a model of an early magnetic compass—a tool that helped European explorers find their way to America in the late 1400s.

▼ NORTH POLE

Believe It OR NOT! The magnetic poles move several miles every few years. Today the north magnetic pole is on an island in northern Canada about 870 miles (1,400 km) from the geographic North Pole. The south magnetic pole is off the coast of Antarctica about 1,700 miles (2,750 km) from the geographic South Pole.

Materials

- large sewing needle
- bar magnet
- slice of cork, about 1 inch in diameter and ¼-inch thick
- sheet of plain paper
- pen
- scissors
- small nonmetal bowl
- water
- magnetic compass
- thimble
- hammer

What To Do

A. Cut a ring of paper to place around the outside of the bowl.

B. On the paper ring, mark the compass directions N, E, S, and W.

C. Fill the bowl about half full with water.

D. Magnetize the sewing needle by stroking it across the south pole of the magnet 25 to 50 times. Be sure to stroke from the middle of the needle toward the point. Always stroke in the same direction.

E. Now that the needle is temporarily magnetized, pass it through the cork horizontally so that it balances when you float the cork in water. SAFETY CHECK: You may want to wear a thimble when placing the needle in the cork.

F. Float the cork and needle in the bowl.

G. Use the compass to determine which end of your needle is pointing north.

H. Rotate the paper ring around the bowl so that the north point of your needle is in line with the N on the paper ring. You now have a floating compass, much like ones used by early sailors.

I. Turn your compass to face each of your room's four walls. Read your compass to determine the north, south, east, and west sides of your classroom.

J. Tip the compass bowl slightly from side to side, being careful not to spill any water. Observe the compass needle.

Lab Activity Report

1. How did the cork and needle react when you pointed your compass to different locations in the room?

2. How did the cork and needle react when you disturbed the water in the bowl of your compass?

3. Why do you think the early sailors floated their compass needles on water?

4. *Drawing Conclusions* What advantages did a magnetic compass provide to early sailors?

GO A STEP FURTHER

ACTIVITY

Iron carried in the hulls of early wooden ships could make compasses read incorrectly. Because the iron was slightly magnetic, compass needles were pulled away from their north-south position. To demonstrate this effect, place the magnet on the outside of the bowl near your floating compass. Does the needle still point north? Now, place the hammer near the bowl. How does this affect the needle?

CHAPTER 1

★★★

The Geography of the Americas

SETTING THE SCENE

Focus

The story of our nation begins with geography—the study of the earth in all of its variety. Geography tells you about the earth's land, water, and plant and animal life. It tells you about the people who live on the earth, the places they have created, and how these places differ. The United States is a land of startling physical differences. It is also a nation of diverse groups of people. A study of geography can help you see how the United States acquired its diversity.

Concepts to Understand

★ Why **geography and the environment** are important to the study of history
★ How geography is related to **cultural diversity** in the United States

Read to Discover . . .

★ how geographers study the earth.
★ the variety of landforms, climates, and resources in the United States.

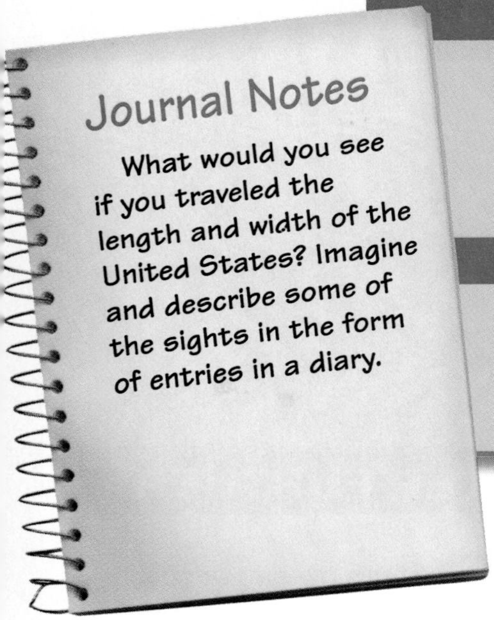

Journal Notes

What would you see if you traveled the length and width of the United States? Imagine and describe some of the sights in the form of entries in a diary.

▶ MODERN GLOBE

Americas			
	Prehistory Native Americans populate the Americas		**1600s** Immigrants, including enslaved African Americans, settle in the Americas
Prehistory–1400s		**1500s**	**1600s**
World	**1400s** The Inca and Aztec flourish in South America	**1500s** Europeans explore the Americas	**1600s** European and American trade routes established

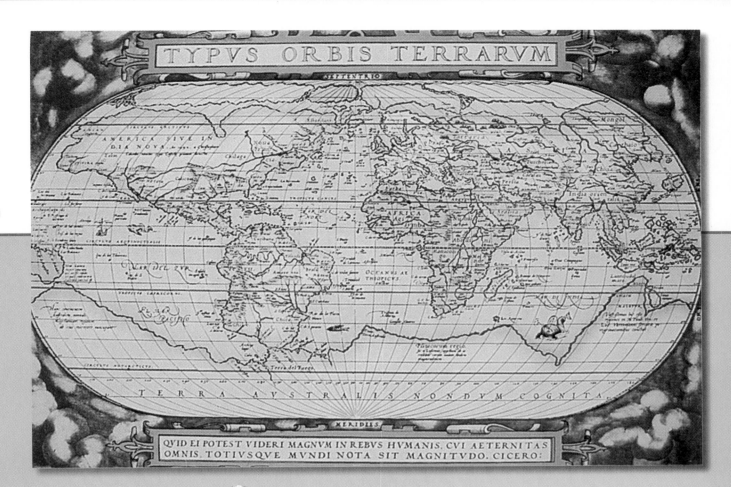

TYPVS ORBIS TERRARVM

QVID EI POTEST VIDERI MAGNVM IN REBVS HVMANIS, CVI AETERNITAS
OMNIS, TOTIVSQVE MVNDI NOTA SIT MAGNITVDO. CICERO:

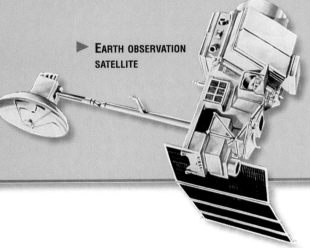

► EARTH OBSERVATION
SATELLITE

History AND ART

World Map
Dutch, 1570

The geography of the world plays a major role in the study of history. This hand-drawn map gave an accurate view of the world as known by Europeans in the sixteenth century.

1776 Declaration of Independence adopted

1700s

1800s Americans move westward
1832 Schoolcraft reaches source of the Mississippi

1800s

1800s Immigrants continue to settle in the United States

1900s LANDSAT satellites map the earth from space

1900s

1900s Protecting the environment raises global concerns

★★

Themes in Geography

SETTING THE SCENE

Read to Learn . . .

★ how the five themes of geography help organize information about the earth and its people.
★ how geography and history are linked.

Terms to Know

★ geography
★ environment
★ immigrant
★ region

Places to Locate

★ Philadelphia
★ Delaware River
★ Schuylkill River

► EARTH RISING OVER MOON

Our word geography comes from the Greek word *geographia,* meaning "earth description." What would you include in a description of the earth? You might give details about the earth's land and water. To give a complete picture of our planet, however, you would also have to describe Earth's life-forms, including its people.

Geographers have organized details about the earth around five themes of geography. These themes, or topics, include **location, place, human/environment interaction, movement,** and **region.** Geographers use these five themes to study and classify all parts of the earth. They also use them to explain connections between the past and the present and to study how the earth has changed over time.

★ Location

The United States was established with the adoption of the Declaration of Independence in 1776, in the city of **Philadelphia,** Pennsylvania. Geographically, you could give two different location descriptions of Philadelphia—its absolute location or its relative location.

Absolute Location

Absolute location describes the exact position of a place on the earth. Think of it as a kind of global address. To write this address, geographers use the numbers on a set of grid lines drawn on a map or globe. These grid lines measure distances north or south of the **Equator,** and east and west of the **Prime Meridian.** The measurements of distances are given in numbers of degrees.

Lines north and south of the Equator show **latitude.** Lines east and west of the Prime Meridian show **longitude.**

For example, the absolute location, or global address, of Philadelphia is 40°N, 75°W. This means that Philadelphia lies about 40 degrees (°) north of the Equator and 75 degrees (°) west of the Prime Meridian.

Relative Location

Relative location tells where a place is in relation to other places. To describe Philadelphia's relative location, geographers could say that it lies between the **Delaware** and **Schuylkill Rivers,** near the western border of New Jersey, and in the southeastern corner of Pennsylvania.

Although relative location is less exact than absolute location, it often gives more clues about the historical happenings at a certain location. Philadelphia, for example, had a central location when compared with other cities early in the nation's history. Thus, it was a convenient meeting place for leaders who traveled from other parts of the country.

★ Place

No two places on the earth are exactly alike. Different locations have different **physical** and **cultural** characteristics. Physical features are those that occur naturally. Cultural features are created by the human beings who live there.

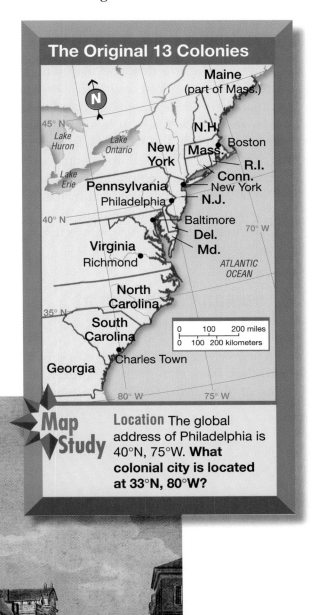

The Original 13 Colonies

Map Study

Location The global address of Philadelphia is 40°N, 75°W. **What colonial city is located at 33°N, 80°W?**

▲ EARLY PHILADELPHIA, 1750

Physical Features

What might the physical features of a place include? Land and water forms, plant and animal life, soil conditions, and climate are all physical features. Think about the city of Philadelphia. Its physical features include a mild climate, fertile soil, and a river that leads into the Delaware Bay.

Cultural Features

How would you describe the cultural features of a place? You could tell about its people, their ideas, languages and religions, and a wide range of related human activities. In early Philadelphia, for example, its founder—William Penn—welcomed people of all national backgrounds and religions to settle in his colony. Diversity among the population thus became one of Philadelphia's outstanding cultural features.

★ Human/Environment Interaction

Wherever humans have lived or traveled, they have changed the natural features of the earth, or the environment.

Human interaction with the land, natural resources, and other natural features of the United States has affected its history a great deal. An English visitor to Philadelphia in 1774 wrote:

 It is not one hundred years since the first tree was cut where the city now stands, and already it consists of more than three thousand and six hundred houses.

Cutting down forests to build homes is only one way that settlers altered the environment of North America. They also hunted wildlife in the forests and fished the lakes and streams. To build towns, they dammed up rivers. With basic tools—and later with advanced technology—human beings have continuously changed the environment of America.

★ Movement

Of all of the geographic themes, movement has affected our nation's history most. For thousands of years, immigrants—people who enter a country to settle—have traveled to this land.

Picturing History

▲ PHYSICAL AND CULTURAL FEATURES Different physical and cultural characteristics help to define what a place is like. **What is one physical characteristic of the Teton Mountains (left)? What is one cultural characteristic of the school classroom (right)?**

Ancestors of the Native Americans arrived in North America first. Then came European explorers. Aboard some European ships came enslaved Africans traveling to the Americas against their will. Political and world economic hardships brought more settlers to America. All the immigrants brought with them their ideas and customs. Their movement shaped the country, just as people moving to the United States today continue to contribute new skills and ideas.

★ Region

The theme of region helps us to see more of the big picture of the world. Geographers generally divide the world into large **regions,** or areas that have something in common. This makes the world easier to study. It also helps us see what relationships exist among different parts of the world.

To describe a region, geographers look at physical characteristics such as location, size, landforms, climate, soil, and natural vegetation. They also look at cultural characteristics, which could include such things as the people's language, religion, government, history, and more.

Sometimes a region is identified by both its physical and cultural characteristics.

Picturing History ▲ **IMMIGRANTS AT CASTLE GARDEN, NEW YORK** The movement of different groups of people to the United States has given our nation a culture rich in diversity. **Who were the first people to arrive in North America?**

During the colonial times, Philadelphia, for example, lay in a physical region known as the Middle Colonies. The cultural background of its settlers also set this area apart as a region. What traits do you think define the area in which you live as a region?

★ SECTION 1 REVIEW ★

Checking for Understanding

1. **Identify** Philadelphia, Delaware River, Schuylkill River.

2. **Define** geography, environment, immigrant, region.

3. **How** do geographers use the five themes of geography?

4. **What** details about Philadelphia helped to define it as a region?

Critical Thinking

5. **Identifying Relationships** Why does the theme of movement have such a strong connection to history in the United States?

ACTIVITY

6. Create a diagram to show important physical features of the place where you live. Then describe how these features have shaped life in your community.

★★★

The Tools of Geography

SETTING THE SCENE

Read to Learn . . .

★ how globes and maps are alike and different.
★ how geographers have divided the earth using a line grid.
★ why geographers have developed map projections.

Terms to Know

★ cartographer
★ latitude
★ parallel
★ longitude
★ meridian
★ coordinates
★ hemisphere
★ map projection

People to Meet

★ Paolo dal Pozzo Toscanelli
★ Christopher Columbus
★ Martin Behaim
★ Gerardus Mercator

Places to Locate

★ Equator
★ Prime Meridian

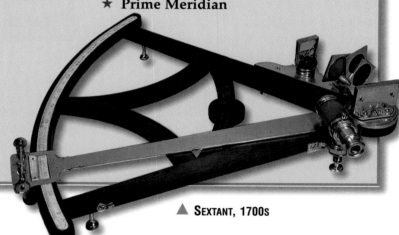

▲ SEXTANT, 1700S

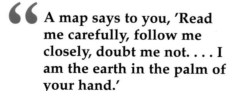

❝A map says to you, 'Read me carefully, follow me closely, doubt me not. . . . I am the earth in the palm of your hand.'❞

With these words, British pilot Beryl Markham—the first woman to fly solo over Africa—expressed her wonder of maps. She was not, however, the first explorer to appreciate maps.

A map drawn by Italian cartographer, or mapmaker, **Paolo dal Pozzo Toscanelli** guided **Christopher Columbus** across the Atlantic in the late 1400s. Maps drawn by Columbus and other daring sea captains guided explorers who came to America later.

Today people use maps to locate places, plot routes, and judge distances. Maps can also display useful information about the world's people.

★ Globes

Photographs from space show the earth in its true form—a great ball spinning around the sun. The only accurate way to draw Earth is as a sphere, or round form.

Behaim's Globe

In 1492 a German geographer named **Martin Behaim** constructed one of the first round maps of the world and called it a globe. Although it contained errors, Behaim's globe was the first plotting of the earth as a sphere.

One advantage of a globe is that it gives a true picture of the size and shape of landmasses and bodies of water. Globes also show the true distances and true direction between places.

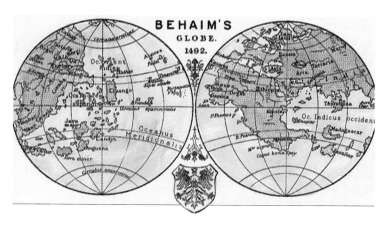

▲ BEHAIM'S GLOBE

Latitude and Longitude

As you read in Section 1, to determine distance and direction on a globe, geographers developed a grid of crisscrossed lines of latitude and longitude. Each line on the grid is measured in degrees (°) and minutes (').

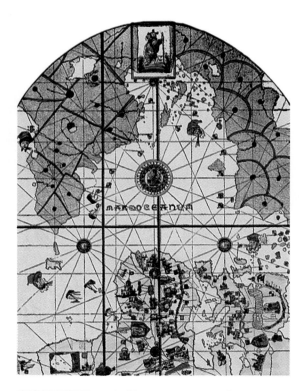

Picturing History

▲ EARLY MAP OF THE AMERICAS
This chart, drawn by a navigator for Christopher Columbus, is one of the earliest-known maps of the American mainland. **What is another name for a cartographer?**

The starting point for measuring lines of latitude, also known as parallels, is the **Equator** located at 0° latitude. Lying parallel to the Equator, lines of latitude measure degrees of distance north or south of the Equator. The letter *N* or *S* following the degree symbol tells you if the location is north or south of the Equator. The latitude farthest north, at the North Pole, is 90°N (North). The latitude farthest south, nearest the South Pole, is 90°S (South).

Lines of longitude, also known as meridians, run north and south from the North Pole to the South Pole. Lines of longitude measure distances east and west of the **Prime Meridian,** which lies at 0° longitude. The letters *E* or *W* tell you if the location is east or west of the prime Meridian. The meridian lying opposite the Prime Meridian is at 180°. It is called the International Date Line.

Grid System

How does this grid help geographers locate places? Each place on the earth has an address on the grid. This grid address is the place's coordinates—its degrees of latitude and longitude. These coordinates identify what lines of latitude and longitude cross closest to the location. Earlier in the chapter you learned that the coordinates of Philadelphia are 40°N and 75°W.

The Global Grid

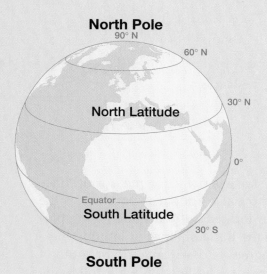

North Pole
90° N

60° N

North Latitude

30° N

0°

Equator
South Latitude

30° S

South Pole

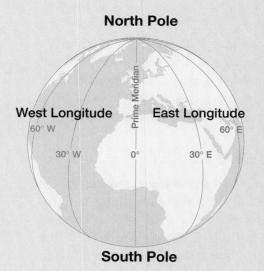

North Pole

Prime Meridian

West Longitude   East Longitude

60° W   60° E

30° W   0°   30° E

South Pole

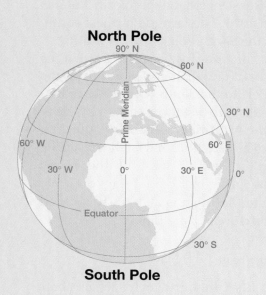

North Pole
90° N

60° N

Prime Meridian

30° N

60° W

60° E

30° W   0°   30° E   0°

Equator

30° S

South Pole

Map Study

Location The earth does not have a natural system of grid lines. Geographers set up a system of imaginary lines that crisscross the globe to locate places. These lines are also used as navigation aids by ship captains and airplane pilots. **At what latitude is the North Pole located?**

Hemispheres and Continents

The Equator and Prime Meridian slice the earth into different hemispheres, or halves. The Northern Hemisphere is all of the earth lying north of the Equator. All area south of the Equator is the Southern Hemisphere. The Prime Meridian divides the earth into the Western and Eastern Hemispheres. Do you live in the Northern or Southern Hemisphere? In the Eastern or Western Hemisphere?

Geographers divide most of the land surface of the earth into seven large land-masses called **continents.** They are **North America, South America, Africa, Europe, Asia, Australia,** and **Antarctica.** Asia is the largest continent, and Australia is the smallest.

North and South America are in the Western Hemisphere. Australia and Asia are in the Eastern Hemisphere. Most of Europe and Africa are in the Eastern Hemisphere, but a small part of their western areas are in the Western Hemisphere. Antarctica is in both the Eastern and Western hemispheres.

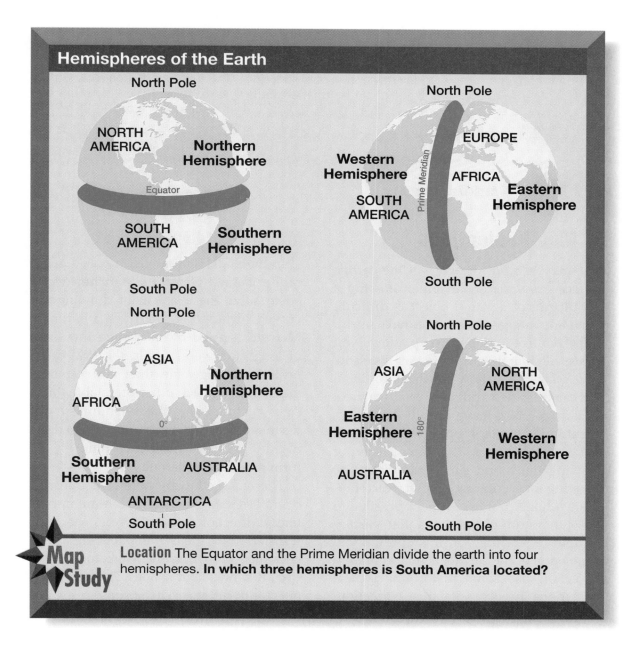

Hemispheres of the Earth

Map Study

Location The Equator and the Prime Meridian divide the earth into four hemispheres. **In which three hemispheres is South America located?**

★★★★★★★★★★★★★★★★★★★★★★ ★★★★★★★★★★★★★★★★★★★★★

Navigational Help From the Sky

"Land Ho!" Whether or not Columbus or his sailors actually shouted these words each time they reached new lands, they were usually glad they had arrived. The tools that early explorers used to sail the uncharted seas were much different from the technology used today.

Then_____

The Astrolabe and the Stars

One early, but dependable, navigation tool was the astrolabe. A sailor held the astrolabe vertically, located a star through its sights, and measured the star's elevation above the horizon. In this way a ship's approximate location could be identified.

Now_____

Out in Space

Today navigation satellites do the work of an astrolabe—and more!

The first navigation satellite system—the Transit system—was launched in 1960. The latest satellites, the NAVSTAR Global Positioning System (GPS), were launched by the United States in 1993. Their signals offer navigational information to make air and surface transportation more efficient. From out in space the GPS can track the location of a vehicle on the earth to within a few meters of its actual position.

▲ NAVIGATION SATELLITE

★★★

◀ ASTROLABE, ITALY 1500S

★ Map Projections

A map is a flat drawing of the earth's surface. As you can imagine, drawing a flat picture of a round object is difficult. What advantages does a map have over a globe? Unlike a globe, a map allows you to see all four hemispheres at the same time. Maps also show much more detail and can be folded and more easily carried.

Cartographers have drawn many different kinds of maps, or projections. Each map projection is a different way of showing the round earth on a flat map. Drawing an accurate map gives cartographers a huge problem. It is impossible to draw a round planet on a flat surface without distorting, or misrepresenting, some parts of the earth. Each kind of map projection has some distortion. Typical distortions involve distance, direction, shape, and/or area.

Mercator Projection

In the mid-1500s, a well-traveled geographer named **Gerardus Mercator** decided to solve the problem of drawing the curved surface of the earth on a flat map. Mercator started by imagining that lines of longitude were cuts in the rind of an ordinary orange. He then laid the segments next to each other on a table. Mercator pictured the major landmasses of Earth on these segments and stretched the narrow points to meet each other in the form of a large rectangle.

This enlarged them somewhat, but their overall shape remained true. More importantly, direction remained true. Mercator transferred his ideas onto paper and created a map known as the **Mercator projection.** It shows land shapes accurately, but not size or distance. Distortions are greater the farther you are from the Equator.

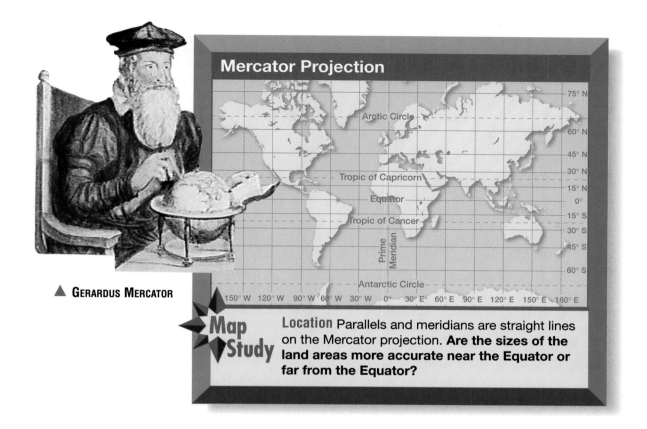

Mercator Projection

▲ GERARDUS MERCATOR

Map Study

Location Parallels and meridians are straight lines on the Mercator projection. **Are the sizes of the land areas more accurate near the Equator or far from the Equator?**

Other Projections

Other geographers followed Mercator's model but developed their own map projections. One type—an **interrupted projection**—shows Mercator's world as a cut-up sphere that has not been stretched and joined together. Although this projection shows the size of landmasses more accurately, the interruptions make it difficult to calculate distances.

Most geographers today use the **Robinson projection.** This projection slices off

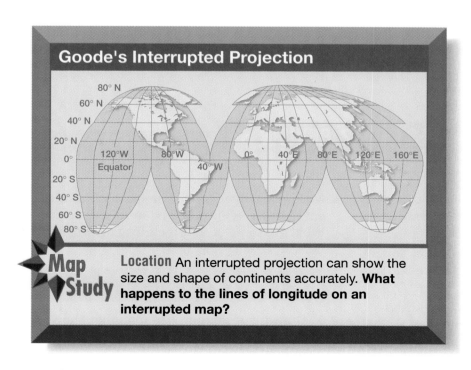

Goode's Interrupted Projection

Map Study

Location An interrupted projection can show the size and shape of continents accurately. **What happens to the lines of longitude on an interrupted map?**

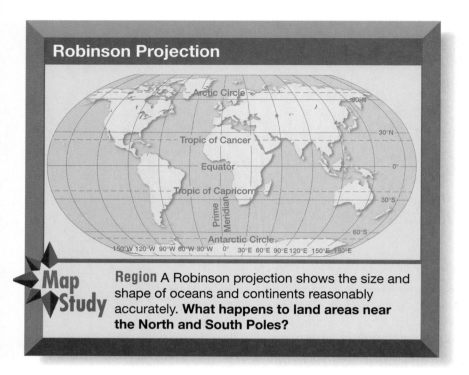

Robinson Projection

Arctic Circle

60°N

Tropic of Cancer

30°N

Equator

0°

Tropic of Capricorn

30°S

Prime Meridian

Antarctic Circle

60°S

150°W 120°W 90°W 60°W 30°W 0° 30°E 60°E 90°E 120°E 150°E 180°E

Map Study

Region A Robinson projection shows the size and shape of oceans and continents reasonably accurately. **What happens to land areas near the North and South Poles?**

LANDSAT photographic satellites orbiting the earth, are pictures of huge expanses of our planet. With LANDSAT images scientists can study whole mountain ranges, oceans, and geographic regions. Changes to the earth's environment can also be tracked using the satellite information.

★ Types of Maps

How often do you use a map? Maps fill our daily lives. Maps of many different kinds are used in this book to help you see the connection between the geography of the United States and its history.

Maps that show a wide range of general information about an area are called **general-purpose** maps. Two of the most common types are physical and political maps. **Physical maps** show natural features, such as rivers and mountains. **Political maps** show places that people have created, such as cities or the boundaries of states and nations.

Special-purpose maps show information on specific topics such as land use, climate, or vegetation. Human activities also appear on special-purpose maps. Exploration, westward movement, or a war's battle sites might be shown.

the tips of Mercator's orange rind and pulls the segments together in a flat-topped oval. Although distortion occurs at the northern and southern edges of the map, the projection gives a fairly accurate view of most sizes and shapes and direction. It also provides a fairly accurate picture of the relationship between landmasses and water.

Today scientific technology has improved the process for mapping the earth even more. LANDSAT maps, created by

---

★ SECTION 2 REVIEW ★

Checking for Understanding

1. **Identify** Paolo dal Pozzo Toscanelli, Christopher Columbus, Martin Behaim, Gerardus Mercator, Equator, Prime Meridian.

2. **Define** cartographer, latitude, parallel, longitude, meridian, coordinates, hemisphere, map projection.

3. **What** are some of the advantages or disadvantages of globes? Of maps?

Critical Thinking

4. **Making Comparisons** Compare the different map projections named in this section. What are some of the strengths and weaknesses of each projection?

ACTIVITY

5. Draw a special-purpose map that shows one of the places in your community that many people visit.

★★

Landscape of the Americas

SETTING THE SCENE

Read to Learn . . .

★ what geographic factors unite North and South America.

★ what major landforms and bodies of water exist in the Western Hemisphere.

★ what physical regions characterize the United States.

Terms to Know

★ isthmus
★ topography
★ elevation
★ relief
★ foothills
★ mesa
★ tributary

Places to Locate

★ Central America
★ Rocky Mountains
★ Andes Mountains
★ Mississippi River
★ Amazon River
★ Death Valley
★ Sierra Madre

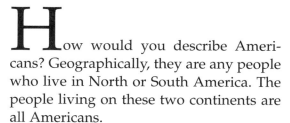

▶ MOUNT SAINT HELENS

How would you describe Americans? Geographically, they are any people who live in North or South America. The people living on these two continents are all Americans.

Many differences and similarities exist among the peoples of North and South America. A number of physical features, however, unite these two continents as a region. As you read this section, decide how physical geography both joins and separates the peoples of the Americas.

★ Identifying Physical Regions

Along with islands in the Caribbean, North and South America occupy most of the Western Hemisphere. Together they stretch from the Arctic Ocean in the Northern Hemisphere almost as far south as the continent of Antarctica in the Southern Hemisphere.

The two continents also share several bodies of water and **landforms**—physical

▲ COSTA RICAN HIGHLANDS The Central Highlands in Costa Rica reach an elevation of 5,000 feet or 1,500 meters above sea level. **What are four landforms that help make up the topography of an area?**

features that help define them as a physical region. The Americas border on two broad oceans—the Pacific Ocean in the west and the Atlantic Ocean in the east. A huge string of mountain ranges snakes down the west coast of both continents.

An isthmus, or narrow strip of land, acts as a continental bridge between North and South America. This region—sometimes called **Central America**—is actually part of North America.

★ Landforms

On a physical map, geographers identify the topography, or the physical features of the earth's surface. One part of the land's topography is its elevation—the height of land above sea level. Another part of the land's topography is relief—the overall differences in height.

Four major landforms also help to make up the topography. Geographers identify these landforms as **mountains, hills, plains,** and **plateaus.**

Mountains and Hills

Mountains are generally the highest, most rugged landforms on Earth. They usually occur in ranges, or groups. In both North and South America, the highest peaks and mountain ranges lie in the West.

The **Rocky Mountains** stretch from Alaska in North America to Mexico. Farther south, the **Andes Mountains** of South America boast the tallest peak in the Western Hemisphere—Mount Aconcagua—at a height of 22,834 feet (6,960 m).

Most mountain areas remain thinly settled. One exception is the Andes Mountains of Peru, where descendants of the Inca—an ancient Native American people— still make their home. Most people of South America, however, choose to settle in valleys or in the foothills of mountains.

These foothills, or low hills at the base of a mountain, receive water from the streams and melting snows that spill off the higher peaks. The well-watered land at lower elevations makes excellent farmland. During the United States's colonial era, the foothills of the Appalachian Mountains drew land-hungry settlers from Europe to North America.

Plains and Plateaus

Plains and plateaus have flat or gently rolling land. The two can differ greatly in elevation, however. Plains are broad areas of land usually close to sea level. Plateaus are high, flat landforms, sometimes several thousand feet high.

Large inland and coastal plains exist in both North and South America. Unlike mountains, these areas tend to be densely populated. Plateaus can also be heavily populated. Some of the earliest farmers in North America built their gardens on top of mesas—small, steep-sided plateaus—in what is now the southwestern United States.

★ Bodies of Water

About 70 percent of the earth's surface is covered with water. Geographers identify bodies of water by their shapes and sizes. The four major types include **oceans, seas, rivers,** and **lakes.**

Oceans and Seas

Oceans and seas, almost all of which contain salt water, are the largest bodies of water on Earth. The major oceans of the world include the Atlantic, Pacific, Indian, and Arctic Oceans. Seas, usually smaller than oceans, are often landlocked, or surrounded by land on all sides. An exception is the Caribbean Sea, which opens into the Atlantic Ocean.

Oceans and seas can affect the development of a region in many ways. They encourage fishing and trade, and can influence the migration and settlement of people. Oceans also affect weather, climate, and the living conditions of people.

Lakes and Rivers

Lakes and rivers crisscross the Americas. They supply freshwater, energy, and valuable transportation routes. In some cases, they serve as boundaries between nations and states. The Great Lakes, for example, form part of the boundry between Canada and the United States. The Rio Grande is a river that separates Texas from Mexico.

In North America, the largest river system is the **Mississippi River** and its tributaries, or smaller rivers and streams. Reaching from Montana to New York, this river system draws water from about 41 percent of the continental United States. Another major river system lies in South America. The **Amazon River** system drains almost 3 million square miles (7 million sq. km).

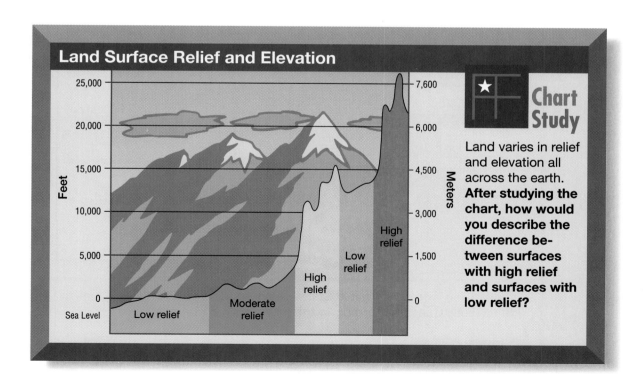

Land Surface Relief and Elevation

★ Chart Study

Land varies in relief and elevation all across the earth. **After studying the chart, how would you describe the difference between surfaces with high relief and surfaces with low relief?**

★ Regions of the United States

Geographers define the United States as a region within the Americas. Political borders, history, and other human traits set it apart from Canada and Mexico. The United States is a large area to study, however, so geographers often divide it into smaller regions.

Geographers identify eight major physical regions of the United States. The physical features found include snow-capped mountains in the west; fertile, rolling plains in the center; and smoothly formed mountains in the east.

Hawaiian Islands

To find one of the nation's westernmost physical regions, you must look outside the mainland of the Americas. About 2,400 miles (3,862 km) west of California lies the state of Hawaii, a cluster of 8 large islands and many smaller islands. These islands grew out of volcanoes that pushed their way up from the floor of the Pacific Ocean. Some volcanoes, such as Mauna Kea, which is 13,766 feet (4,196 m) high, are still active. Most of the islands have white sand beaches. Black sand, which formed when molten lava flowed into the ocean, covers other beaches.

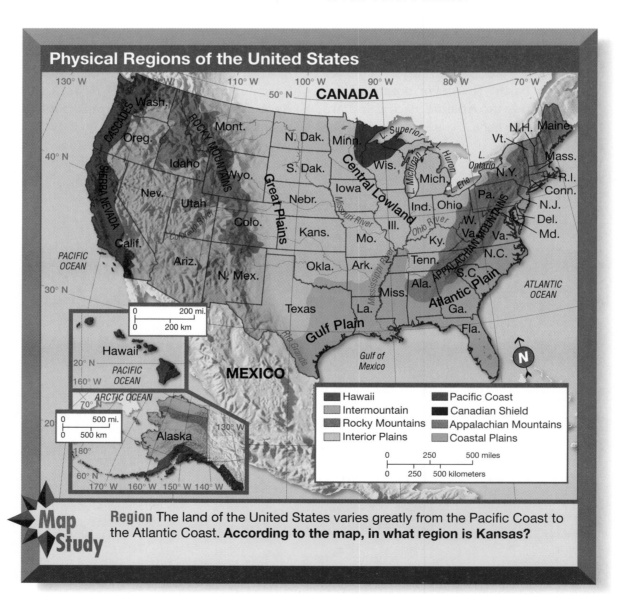

Physical Regions of the United States

Legend:
- Hawaii
- Intermountain
- Rocky Mountains
- Interior Plains
- Pacific Coast
- Canadian Shield
- Appalachian Mountains
- Coastal Plains

Map Study

Region The land of the United States varies greatly from the Pacific Coast to the Atlantic Coast. **According to the map, in what region is Kansas?**

▲ HI-MAUI, MOLOKAI ISLAND Hawaii has many distinctive features, such as its climate and topography, that make it unique among the 50 states. **How were the Hawaiian Islands formed?**

Pacific Coast

A dramatic landscape can be found along the United States's Pacific Coast. Here a series of rugged mountain ranges run from Alaska south to Mexico. They include the Coast Mountains, the Cascade Range, and the Sierra Nevadas. Their majestic peaks include the tallest mountains on the continent—California's Mount Whitney at 14,494 feet (4,418 m), Washington's Mount Rainier at 14,410 feet (4,392 m), and Alaska's Mount McKinley at 20,320 feet (6,194 m).

Intermountain Region

As you head eastward from the Pacific Coast you enter the Intermountain region, where the land unfolds in a gigantic plateau. In the northern half of the region, the Great Basin hollows out the plateau like a huge bowl. The largest body of water found here is Utah's Great Salt Lake.

To the south of the Great Basin, dry deserts sprawl across the Intermountain region. Years of erosion by wind and rain and the constant flow of rivers have carved the desert plateau into a web of canyons. One of the outstanding features of the Intermountain region is **Death Valley.** Tucked along the southern borders of California and Nevada, it is the lowest and hottest place in the United States.

Rocky Mountains

At the eastern edge of the Intermountain region, the elevation soars upward into the Rocky Mountains. Running southward from northern Alaska, the mountains extend all the way to Mexico. Here they take on a new name—the **Sierra Madre,** or "mother range."

The Rockies stand like a great wall across much of the continent. Throughout the 1800s, they posed a serious obstacle to the non-Native American settlers who headed west. "It's not a trip for the fainthearted," remarked one woman pioneer. "Perhaps only the foolhardy try [to cross them]."

Interior Plains

East of the Rockies, the land opens into a huge level to rolling expanse known as the Interior Plains. The open land seemed so vast to non-Native Americans of the 1800s that English author Charles Dickens called it "a sea without water." Because so few trees grew on the dry grasslands at the western end of the Interior Plains, settlers called it the Great American Desert. Geographers call these western lands the Great Plains.

The eastern part of the Interior Plains, called the Central Lowland, looked richer to farmers of the last century. Many settled and prospered there. Today this area, known as the Middle West, still forms the nation's "breadbasket," or major grain-producing region.

Canadian Shield

This region covers a large part of Canada but extends over a small area in the north central United States. This lowland area lacks rich soil for farming. Its wealth of buried minerals, particularly iron ore, has been heavily mined.

Appalachian Mountains

The eastern Interior Plains end at the Appalachian Mountains. This mountain range is old enough to be the grandfather of the Rockies. The Appalachian peaks are much lower than the Rockies due to years of weathering. The highest peak—North Carolina's Mount Mitchell—stands 6,684 feet (2,037 m) tall. To settlers in the 1700s, however, the Appalachians posed a great barrier to new, uncrowded lands. There were no paved roads or interstate highways to make crossing the mountains easier.

Coastal Plains

Most of the settlers who crossed the Appalachians in the 1700s were leaving the heavily populated Atlantic Plain. This lowland along the east coast of the United States begins as a narrow band in Massachusetts and gradually expands into the broad lowlands of the Southeast. Its rich, fertile soil and many Atlantic ports contrast sharply with the mountainous Pacific Coast.

To the south, around the rim of the Gulf of Mexico, a second coastal plain unfolds like a giant fan. This Gulf Plain includes the mouth of the Mississippi River and major port cities.

★ SECTION 3 REVIEW ★

Checking for Understanding

1. **Identify** Central America, Rocky Mountains, Andes Mountains, Mississippi River, Amazon River, Death Valley, Sierra Madre.

2. **Define** isthmus, topography, elevation, relief, foothills, mesa, tributary.

3. **What** draws people to settle in foothills rather than in mountains?

4. **How** do geographers identify physical regions?

5. **What** are the eight major physical regions in the United States? In which of these regions do you live?

Critical Thinking

6. **Comparing and Contrasting** Choose a region in the United States other than the one in which you live. What physical characteristics of the other region might make you want to live there? What physical features of your region do you like?

ACTIVITY

7. Make flash cards showing each type of landform and body of water mentioned in this chapter. On the back of each card, name regions where these physical features might be found.

BUILDING SKILLS
Social Studies Skills

Reading a Land Profile

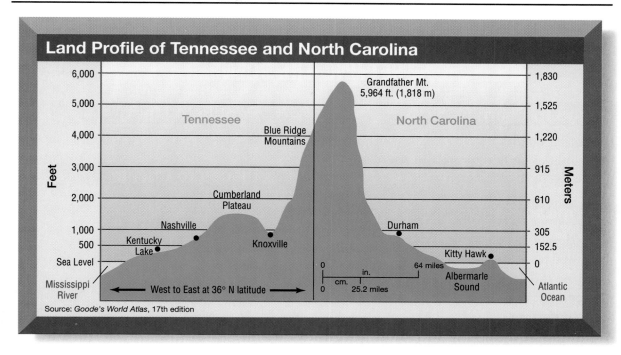

Land Profile of Tennessee and North Carolina

Tennessee

North Carolina

Grandfather Mt.
5,964 ft. (1,818 m)

Blue Ridge
Mountains

Cumberland
Plateau

Nashville

Durham

Kentucky
Lake

Knoxville

Kitty Hawk

Sea Level

Albermarle
Sound

Mississippi
River

← West to East at 36° N latitude →

Atlantic
Ocean

Feet: 6,000 · 5,000 · 4,000 · 3,000 · 2,000 · 1,000 · 500 · Sea Level

Meters: 1,830 · 1,525 · 1,220 · 915 · 610 · 305 · 152.5 · 0

in. 0 — 64 miles
cm. 0 — 25.2 miles

Source: *Goode's World Atlas*, 17th edition

Suppose you are comparing two photographs of the same person's face. In one photo the face looks straight into the camera. In the other you see the side, or profile. The first photograph gives an overall view of the face, while the profile shows the outline. In the same way, a land profile shows the outline of the physical features of a land region.

Learning the Skill

A **land profile** is a diagram that shows the cross section of a geographic region. What is a cross section? If you slice a loaf of bread, each slice is a cross section of the whole loaf. Suppose you hold the slice with the flat side facing you and then trace the outline of the top of the slice. Is it flat or curved? Either way, the line formed by the top of the slice shows the profile of the whole loaf.

Now imagine slicing through a stretch of land as if it were a loaf of bread. Each slice would be a cross section, or a land profile. Because a land profile shows height above sea level, it is also called an *elevation profile*.

Practicing the Skill

Use the land profile to answer the following questions.

1. What are the most western and most eastern points of this land profile?
2. What is the latitude of the profile?
3. What is the highest point on the profile? In which state is it located?
4. Which state has areas below sea level?

APPLYING THE SKILL

5. Suppose you are on a committee to choose a site for a new soccer field in your community. Sketch a land profile of the kind of area you think would be suitable.

★★★

Climate and Resources

SETTING THE SCENE

Read to Learn . . .

★ what factors help determine climate.
★ what climate regions and resources exist in the United States.

Terms to Know

★ climate
★ weather
★ precipitation
★ current
★ timberline

People to Meet

★ Henry Rowe Schoolcraft

Places to Locate

★ Mount Waialeale
★ Sierra Nevadas

▶ BEAR ON THE ALASKAN TUNDRA

In 1852, 17-year-old Samuel Clemens—American author Mark Twain—set out to see the United States. Over the next decade, Clemens visited the Atlantic Coast, the Pacific Coast, and the Gulf Coast. "Why, I've counted one hundred and thirty-six different kinds of weather inside of four and twenty hours," boasted Clemens at one point in his travels.

★ Climate and Weather Patterns

Weather and *climate* do not mean the same thing. Climate is the usual weather pattern of an area over a long period of time. Weather is the condition of the earth's atmosphere over a short period of time.

What Affects Climate?

Two main ingredients in climate are temperature and precipitation, or moisture that falls as rain, snow, or sleet. Some other major factors affect climate. One of these is latitude. Climates get hotter near the Equator and colder near the North and South Poles. Another factor affecting climate is elevation. Higher elevations generally have cooler temperatures than lower elevations. Mountains also affect the amount of moisture the land receives.

Other factors affecting climate are the influence of ocean currents and wind currents. Currents are constantly moving forces of air and water that can be warm or cold.

★ Climate Regions in North America

You can find most of the earth's climate regions somewhere in North America. The United States itself experiences many different climates.

Tropical

Southern Florida and Hawaii, although many miles apart, have something in common. They both have a tropical climate. Florida and Hawaii are closer to the Equator than any other states. Both experience hot, humid weather for much of the year. That provides ideal growing conditions for crops such as citrus fruits and pineapple. Hawaii's **Mount Waialeale** (wy•AH•lay•AH•lay), on the island of Kauai, is one of the wettest spots on the earth, receiving more than 460 inches (1,168 cm) of rain a year.

Mediterranean

The only place in North America where you can find a Mediterranean climate is in the state of California. Areas with Mediterranean climates tend to have

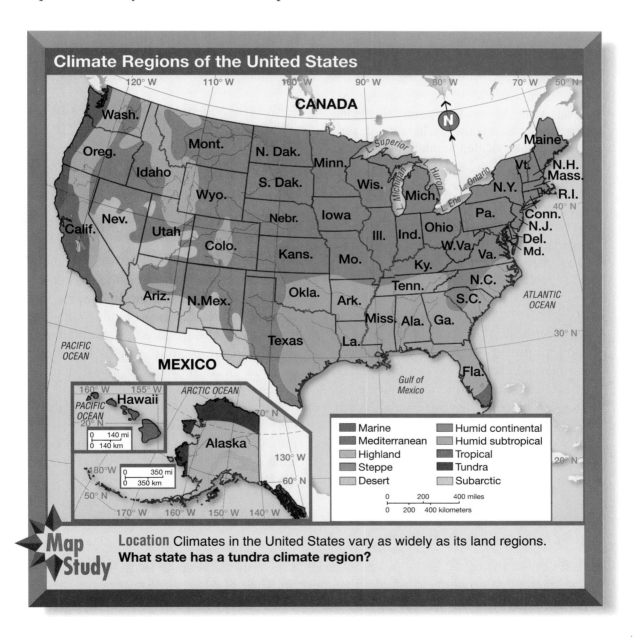

Climate Regions of the United States

Legend:
- Marine
- Mediterranean
- Highland
- Steppe
- Desert
- Humid continental
- Humid subtropical
- Tropical
- Tundra
- Subarctic

0 — 200 — 400 miles
0 — 200 — 400 kilometers

Map Study

Location Climates in the United States vary as widely as its land regions. **What state has a tundra climate region?**

▲ ZABRISKIE POINT, DEATH VALLEY Deserts such as Death Valley have hot days and cold nights and receive little or no rain. **Where are desert climate regions located in the United States?**

Washington and Oregon receive from 60 to 80 inches (152 to 203 cm) of rain a year. Farther north along the coast, portions of Alaska receive rainfall just as heavy.

Highland

Elevation influences the climate in the highland regions such as the Cascades, **Sierra Nevadas,** and Rocky Mountains. Here, temperatures tend to be cool for most of the year, and snow remains on many summits. Even if a highland area is close to the Equator, it will have a cool climate. In Hawaii, for instance, Mauna Kea is often cool enough in winter to provide snow for skiers.

Steppe

East of the Rockies, in both the United States and Canada, sprawl the dry grasslands of the steppe. These regions covered in bushes and short grasses receive little rainfall. They also experience extremes in temperature with the blazing sun in the summer months and blizzards in the winter.

Desert

Desert climates receive the least rainfall of any climate region. In deserts, less than 10 inches (25 cm) of rain fall in an entire year. Desert climates can be found mostly in lands southeast of the Sierra Nevada and in the southwest United States.

Because these areas lack rainfall, farmers have used irrigation, bringing water to the land. Ancestors of Native Americans, such as the Zuni and Hopi, dug irrigation ditches to make the deserts bloom.

mild, wet winters and dry, hot summers. As a result, farmers here can grow crops year-round. California produces an abundance of fruit and vegetables for America's markets.

Marine

Marine means "relating to the sea." So as you might expect, this often moist and rainy climate occurs most commonly near a coast. In North America, marine climates can be found in the Pacific Northwest, a strip of land extending from southern Alaska to northern California. There, coastal mountains force rain-filled clouds to release their moisture. Coastal

Footnotes to History

To the Capital by Air or Sea   Juneau, Alaska, is the only state capital in the United States that cannot be reached by automobile. There are no roads leading into or out of the city to connect it with other Alaskan cities.

Natural Resources of the United States

Legend:
- Aluminum
- Chromium
- Coal
- Cobalt
- Copper
- Gold
- Iron ore
- Lead
- Magnesium
- Natural gas
- Oil
- Silver
- Sulfur
- Tin
- Uranium
- Zinc
- Fish
- Forests

Map Study

Place Forests, fertile soils, fish, and a wide variety of minerals help give the United States its great wealth of natural resources. **What mineral resource is most common in Texas?**

Tundra and Subarctic

The barren lands of northwest Alaska and upper Canada face cold climates—the tundra and subarctic—nearly year-round. The tundra is a vast rolling plain without trees. Summers are brief and warm with temperatures rising above freezing. Winters are cold and snow-filled. The lower layers of soil in the tundra are known as permafrost because they stay permanently frozen.

Humid Continental and Humid Subtropical

The humid continental and humid subtropical climate regions cover nearly half of the United States. In the humid continental region, people enjoy mild summers and cold winters and receive more precipitation than those living in the steppe.

The lower latitudes of the southeastern United States produce warm and humid subtropical climates. As you might expect, this region can supply food and other crops, such as cotton, for the nation throughout much of the year.

★ Vegetation

Before the arrival of non-Native American settlers, evergreen and deciduous forests covered almost half of the United States and Canada. Over the past two centuries, people have permanently cleared more than one-half million square miles (3,354,050 sq. km) of original forestland. Vast forests still span subarctic Canada up to the western mountain ranges until they reach the timberline, or elevation above which trees cannot grow. A wide variety of other vegetation from prairie grasses to cactus to tropical palm trees can be found in North America.

★ North America's Natural Resources

The wealth of natural resources of North America astonished European explorers when they first arrived on the continent. The area's waterways, minerals, fish, wildlife, and timber created the rich backdrop to early settlement. Many expeditions were sent out by early colonial leaders to map some of these resources and the expanse of the land itself. The map on page 29 shows many of the natural resources.

Biography ★★★★

Schoolcraft Finds the Source of the Mississippi

In 1820 explorer **Henry Rowe Schoolcraft** joined an expedition sponsored by the federal government to search for the source of the Mississippi River. That expedition failed.

Twelve years later, in 1832, the federal government sent Schoolcraft and a group of soldiers on another search. Schoolcraft, who by that time was working as an Indian agent in the territories around the Great Lakes, got some Chippewa to act as guides. On July 13 the group came to a clear body of water in a weedy opening. They were looking upon Lake Itasca in central Minnesota, the source of the Mississippi.

Schoolcraft, who was born in Albany County, New York, in 1793, was a geologist, author, politician, and anthropologist, in addition to being a government agent. He became a recognized expert on Native American cultures and settled many disputes in his territory. ★★★

★ SECTION 4 REVIEW ★

Checking for Understanding

1. **Identify** Henry Rowe Schoolcraft, Mount Waialeale, Sierra Nevadas.
2. **Define** climate, weather, precipitation, current, timberline.
3. **How** do latitude and elevation affect climate?
4. **Where** in the United States can you find a Mediterranean climate? How does such a climate benefit America's markets?
5. **What** climate regions exist in the United States? In which climate region do you live?

Critical Thinking

6. **Making Generalizations** Write four valid, or true, generalizations about the physical features and landscape of our nation.

ACTIVITY

7. Draw a map of Minnesota, showing where the Mississippi River flows through it. At the northern end of the river, draw a tiny lake. Label it "Lake Itasca, Source of the Mississippi River."

You and America's Natural Resources

Did you know that by the year 2000 the average person in the United States is expected to produce 4.5 pounds (2 kg) of trash a day? That means you can expect to create about 1,643 pounds (746 kg) of trash a year! Currently only about 20 percent of our country's trash is recycled. Where does all that trash come from and where will it go?

Almost every item in a garbage bin comes from a natural resource. We use petroleum to make all kinds of "throw-away" plastic items. We use aluminum for "throw-away" cans. We use the wood from trees to make "throw-away" catalogs, newspapers, and millions of tons of other paper products.

Much of the world calls America the "throw-away" society. Unfortunately, Americans don't really throw away garbage. We bury it in landfills, try to burn it, or dump it off our coastlines into the world's oceans.

Burning trash pollutes the atmosphere. Unless a landfill is lined with plastic, the garbage can pollute the soil and seep into underground water supplies. Garbage and refuse thrown into the oceans pollute the water and kill plants and animals.

To solve the trash problem, the federal government's Environmental Protection Agency (EPA) has recommended that Americans practice the three R's of environmental protection. *Reduce* the waste that we create. Choose products packaged in recyclable materials. This includes packages made of paper, glass, aluminum, or cardboard. *Reuse* items instead of throwing them away. Look for products in refillable containers. *Recycle* garbage into new forms. If you don't, the

▲ TEENS RECYCLING

next century's environmentalists will be cleaning up this century's garbage. Try using the three R's and join the movement to save our environment.

Making the Geography Connection

1. How much trash is a person expected to create by the year 2000?

2. How does trash threaten our natural resources?

3. Why is it nearly impossible to "throw away" the trash problem?

ACTIVITY

4. The largest portion of our garbage comes from paper. More than 40 percent of all the trash in landfills originally came from trees, the source of paper-making materials. Turn some paper trash into a recycling reminder. Create a sculpture or a collage out of egg cartons, junk mail, pizza boxes, newspapers, and so on. Give your work of art a title.

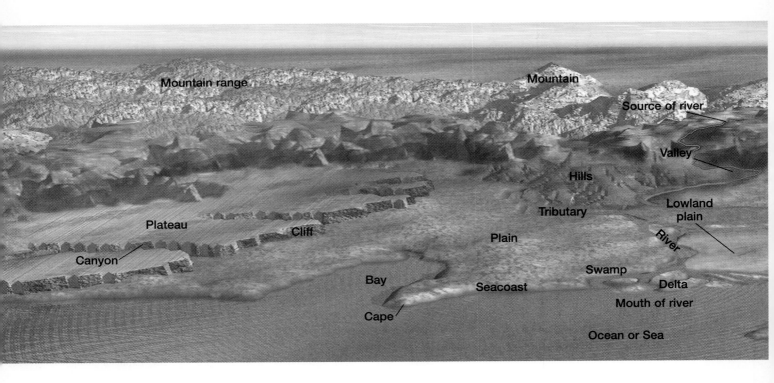

Mountain range • Mountain • Source of river • Valley • Hills • Lowland plain • Plateau • Cliff • Tributary • River • Canyon • Plain • Swamp • Bay • Seacoast • Delta • Cape • Mouth of river • Ocean or Sea

A Dictionary of Geographic Terms

As you read about America's geography and history, you will meet most of the terms listed and explained here. Many of the terms are pictured in the diagram above. Others you learned earlier in this chapter.

absolute location–exact position of a place on the earth, described by global coordinates

basin–area of land drained by a given river and its branches; area of land surrounded by lands of higher elevations

bay–part of a large body of water that extends into a coastline

canyon–deep and narrow valley with steep walls

cape–point of land surrounded by a body of water

channel–deep, narrow body of water that connects two larger bodies of water; deep part of a river or other waterway

cliff–steep, high wall of rock, earth, or ice

continent–one of the seven large landmasses on the earth

cultural feature–characteristic that humans have created in a place, such as language, religion, and history

delta–land built up from soil carried downstream by a river and deposited at its mouth

divide–stretch of high land that separates river basins

downstream–direction in which a river or stream flows from its source to its mouth

elevation–height of land above sea level

Equator–imaginary line that runs around the earth halfway between the North and South Poles; used as the starting point to measure degrees of north and south latitude

glacier–large, thick body of slowly moving ice, found in mountains and polar regions

globe–sphere-shaped model of the earth

gulf–part of a large body of water that extends into a shoreline, larger than a bay

harbor–a sheltered place along a shoreline where ships can anchor safely

highland–elevated land area such as a hill, mountain, or plateau

hill–elevated land with sloping sides; smaller than a mountain

island–land area, smaller than a continent, completely surrounded by water

isthmus–narrow stretch of land connecting two larger land areas

lake–a sizable inland body of water

latitude–distance north or south of the Equator, measured in degrees and minutes

longitude–distance east or west of the Prime Meridian, measured in degrees and minutes

lowland–land, usually level, at a low elevation

map–drawing of all or part of the earth shown on a flat surface

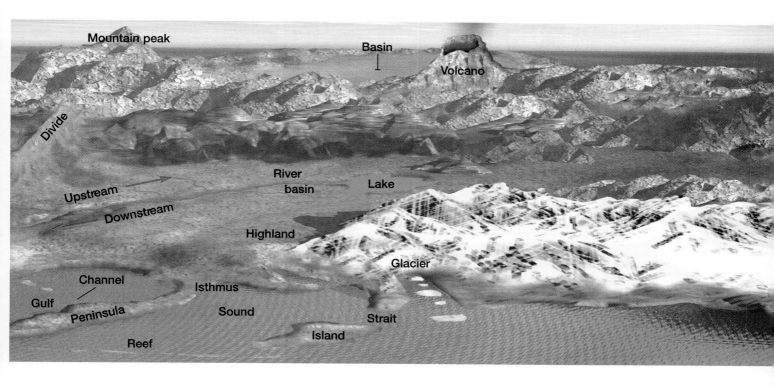

meridian–one of many lines on the global grid running from the North Pole to the South Pole, used to measure degrees of longitude

mesa–area of raised land with steep sides; smaller than a plateau

mountain–land with steep sides that rises sharply from surrounding land; larger and more rugged than a hill

mountain peak–pointed top of a mountain

mountain range–a series of connected mountains

mouth (of a river)–place where a stream or river flows into a larger body of water

ocean–one of the four major bodies of salt water that surround the continents

ocean current–stream of either cold or warm water that moves in a definite direction through an ocean

parallel–one of many lines on the global grid that circle the earth north or south of the Equator; used to measure degrees of latitude

peninsula–body of land almost surrounded by water

physical feature–characteristic of a place occurring naturally, such as a landform, body of water, climate pattern, or resource

plain–area of level land, usually at a low elevation

plateau–area of flat or rolling land at a high elevation

Prime Meridian–line of the global grid running from the North Pole to the South Pole at Greenwich, England; used as the starting point for measuring degrees of east and west longitude

relative location–position of a place on the earth in relation to other places

relief–changes in elevation, either few or many, that occur over a given area of land

river–large stream of water that runs through the land

sea–large body of water completely or partly surrounded by land

seacoast–land lying next to a sea or ocean

sea level–average level of an ocean's surface

sound–body of water between a coastline and one or more islands off the coast

source–(of a river) place where a river or stream begins, often in high lands

strait–narrow stretch of water joining two larger bodies of water

tributary–small river or stream that flows into a large river or stream; a branch of a river

upstream–direction opposite the flow of a river; toward the source of a river or stream

valley–area of low land between hills or mountains

volcano–mountain created as liquid rock or ash are thrown up from inside the earth

Using Key Vocabulary

Match the numbered items in Column A with their definitions in Column B.

Column A
1. longitude
2. climate
3. elevation
4. immigrant
5. timberline

Column B

a. the height of a landmass above sea level

b. the point at which trees can no longer grow

c. imaginary lines that run north and south between the earth's poles

d. usual weather pattern over a long period of time

e. person who enters a country to settle there

Reviewing Facts

1. **Name** the kinds of historical information absolute and relative location can provide.

2. **List** the physical characteristics of a region geographers use to describe it.

3. **Tell** about some of the problems with mapping the earth.

4. **Describe** the difference between a plain and a plateau.

5. **Name** the two greatest extremes in climate in North America.

Understanding Concepts

Geography and the Environment

1. Why is the study of geography important to the study of history?

2. How do people adapt to and change their environment?

3. How did early settlers alter the environment of the United States?

Cultural Diversity

4. How does the geographic theme of movement help to explain the variety of cultures found in the United States?

5. Why is the name "Americans" not limited to people in the United States?

History and Geography

Physical Regions of the United States

Study the map of physical regions of the United States. Then answer the following questions.

1. **Location** Which regions lie along bodies of water?

2. **Region** What region covers the largest area of the United States? The second largest part?

3. **Movement** Which regions would have been a barrier to settlers moving from east to west?

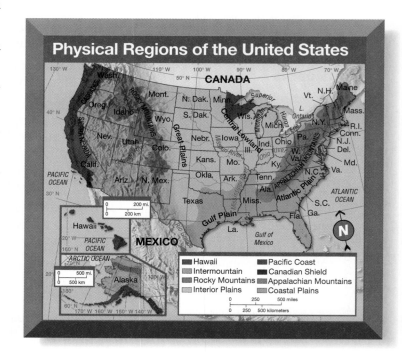

Physical Regions of the United States

Legend:
- Hawaii
- Intermountain
- Rocky Mountains
- Interior Plains
- Pacific Coast
- Canadian Shield
- Appalachian Mountains
- Coastal Plains

Critical Thinking

1. **Determining Cause and Effect** Death Valley is the driest, hottest spot in the United States. How do you think the Rocky Mountains, to its west, have affected its climate?

2. **Identifying Relationships** How does the location of the Interior Plains help to make it America's breadbasket?

3. **Making Comparisons** Compare the advantages and disadvantages of using globes and maps.

4. **Identifying Relationships** The theme of movement has a strong connection to history in the United States. Explain why.

Practicing Skills

Reading a Land Profile

Look carefully at the land profile of South America. Then answer the following questions. Review "Reading a Land Profile" on page 25 if you need to.

1. What are the highest and lowest elevations shown on this land profile?

2. What landform has the highest elevation?

3. What physical features lie closest to sea level?

4. What is the latitude of the profile?

5. What are the most western and eastern points of this land profile?

Cooperative Learning | Interdisciplinary Activity: Geography

Working in groups, explore American rivers by creating a river system map on a large sheet of paper. First, have one member of the group draw the outline of the United States and each of the 48 continental states. Have another member label each state. Then draw and label the Mississippi, Missouri, Ohio, St. Lawrence, Rio Grande, and Colorado Rivers. Locate and label major cities along each river. Draw pictures or cut photographs out of magazines to represent important events, features, or a historical significance of each river. Paste the images in the appropriate place on your map.

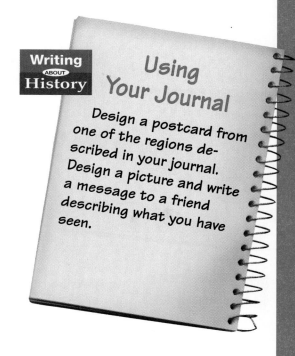

Writing ABOUT History

Using Your Journal

Design a postcard from one of the regions described in your journal. Design a picture and write a message to a friend describing what you have seen.

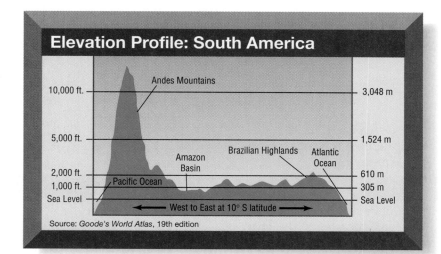

Elevation Profile: South America

10,000 ft.	Andes Mountains — 3,048 m
5,000 ft.	1,524 m
	Brazilian Highlands Atlantic Ocean
	Amazon Basin
2,000 ft.	610 m
1,000 ft.	Pacific Ocean — 305 m
Sea Level	Sea Level

← West to East at 10° S latitude →

Source: *Goode's World Atlas*, 19th edition

CHAPTER 2

★★

The First Americans
Prehistory to 1492

SETTING THE SCENE

Focus

The story of the Americas began thousands of years ago on a land bridge swept by icy winds. On one side of the bridge was northeast Asia, where bands of hunters lived. On the other side was North America—a land with no people at all. Over a long period of time, some of the Asians wandered across the land bridge and entered North America. Those people probably had no idea they were leaving one continent and entering another.

Concepts to Understand

★ How **geography and environment** influenced the lives of early Americans and their descendants

★ How different ways of life among Native American societies led to **cultural diversity**

Read to Discover . . .

★ how the earliest Native Americans lived.

★ what three large civilizations developed in Central and South America before the arrival of Europeans.

▶ BACK OF PERUVIAN MIRROR

Journal Notes

Imagine you are writing a television script for a show about the first Americans. As you read the chapter, jot down ideas in your journal about what you think would make an interesting scene.

Americas	At least 27,000 years ago Asian hunters enter North America	1085 Anasazi build pueblos in North America	
	Prehistory	1000s	1100s
World	About 2,500 years ago Rome founded	1095 Pope Urban II calls for Crusades to the Holy Land	

▲ ARROWHEAD, NORTHEAST WOODLANDS

History AND ART

Pawnee Village
unknown artist

The Pawnee were one of many Native American nations living in North America before the arrival of Europeans.

1300s Aztec build Tenochtitlán in present-day Mexico

1400s Incan empire at its height in South America
1492 Columbus lands in the Americas

1200s

1300s

1400s

1210 Genghis Khan establishes control in China and Southwest Asia

1300s Europeans begin manufacturing gunpowder

1422 Joan of Arc defeats English at French town of Orleans

★★★

The First Americans

SETTING THE SCENE

Read to Learn . . .

★ why people crossed a land bridge to come to the Americas.

★ how the first Americans spread out to inhabit North and South America.

★ what early Native American cultures developed in the present-day United States.

Terms to Know

★ archaeologist
★ maize
★ culture
★ Mound Builders
★ artifact
★ cliff dwellers
★ pueblo
★ adobe

People to Meet

★ C.R. Harrington
★ Peter Lord

Places to Locate

★ Alaska
★ Bering Strait
★ Cahokia

▲ SUBARCTIC WOVEN BASKET

The wind blew in icy sheets, cutting through the hunters' fur robes. In better times, the people would have stayed in the shelter of their caves, waiting for the weather to clear. They had not made a kill for many days, however, and the people needed food. The hunters' only choice was to follow the herds of bison and caribou into the storm.

Luck was with the hunters. In the distance they saw a giant mammoth stuck in a snow bank, trying to free itself. The hunters ran forward, shaking their spears and shouting with excitement. First 1, then 2, then 10 spears hit their target. The beast sank slowly into the snow. The hunt was over. The hunters would have food for many days.

Such a story could possibly have taken place in North America many thousands of years ago. Americans today can only imagine what life might have been like for the earliest Americans. Scientists, however, can tell us much about the earth and climate of the time and about the traces of early people they have found.

★ People Arrive in the Americas

From about 2 million to 10,000 years ago, the earth was in the grip of the Ice Age. The northern half of the world was covered with glaciers. In some places the glaciers were 1 to 2 miles thick.

The 56-mile (90-km) strip of water that now separates **Alaska** from northeastern Asia was the site of a land bridge called Beringia. Because so much of the earth's water froze into ice, the ocean level dropped. This exposed the strip of land between the two continents. Today that land is covered by the waters of the **Bering Strait.**

Large herds of mammoth, bison, and caribou wandered across the land bridge in search of grazing land. Gradually, small groups of Asian hunters who depended on these animals for food followed them into the Americas. Over the years, both the animals and the people made their way into the grasslands at the southern edges of the glaciers.

Living in the Americas

The first Americans stayed on the move in search of food. They killed mammoths, musk oxen, saber-tooth cats, bison, and other large animals. They also tracked smaller animals such as deer, fox, bear, and turkeys. To add to their diets, they gathered seeds, berries, nuts, and the roots and bulbs of plants. Thus they are called **hunter-gatherers.**

The hunter-gatherers made their own tools and weapons. They shaped pieces of stone and bone to make tools for chopping and scraping. They used wooden poles as spears and hardened the tips by placing them in fire. They made animal hides into clothing and tents.

Archaeologists, scientists who search for traces of peoples from the past, believe that these bands of hunter-gatherers grad-

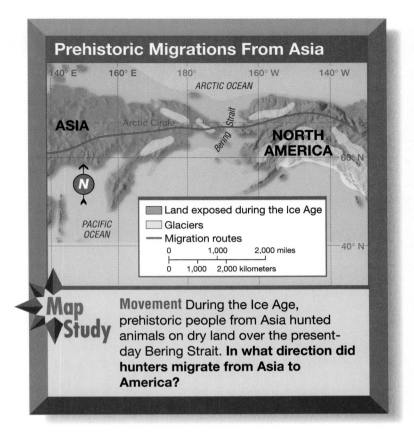

Prehistoric Migrations From Asia

Land exposed during the Ice Age
Glaciers
Migration routes

Map Study

Movement During the Ice Age, prehistoric people from Asia hunted animals on dry land over the present-day Bering Strait. **In what direction did hunters migrate from Asia to America?**

ually spread south in a movement that lasted about 15,000 years. By about 8,000 years ago, groups of people were living throughout both North America and South America.

Responding to Warmer Climates

About 10,000 years ago, the Ice Age ended. The earth's temperatures gradually warmed, the ice melted, and the glaciers shrank. Surface levels of the oceans rose, and the waters of the Bering Strait covered Beringia. No more people would come to the Americas on foot.

The large animals of the Ice Age began to become extinct, or die out. Some scientists think the change in climate may have been responsible. As the climate grew warmer and drier, grasslands where the animals once grazed became desert. Lakes and streams dried up. As their source of food and water disappeared, so did the animal herds.

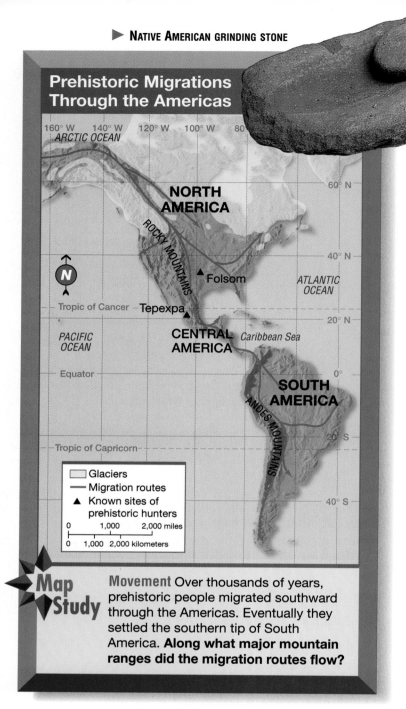

Prehistoric Migrations Through the Americas

160° W 140° W 120° W 100° W 80°

ARCTIC OCEAN

NORTH AMERICA

ROCKY MOUNTAINS

60° N

N

▲ Folsom

40° N

ATLANTIC OCEAN

Tropic of Cancer Tepexpa ▲

20° N

PACIFIC OCEAN

CENTRAL AMERICA Caribbean Sea

Equator

0°

SOUTH AMERICA

ANDES MOUNTAINS

20° S

Tropic of Capricorn

40° S

☐ Glaciers
— Migration routes
▲ Known sites of prehistoric hunters

0   1,000   2,000 miles
0   1,000 2,000 kilometers

Map Study

Movement Over thousands of years, prehistoric people migrated southward through the Americas. Eventually they settled the southern tip of South America. **Along what major mountain ranges did the migration routes flow?**

The hunter-gatherers adjusted to the changes around them in a number of ways. As always, their first concern was food. They fished and hunted smaller animals instead of the large animals of earlier times. The areas over which they hunted and gathered grew smaller. Over time, they settled down to live in one place for long periods of time. They built sturdy, permanent shelters and stored food to make it last longer.

★ The First Farmers

Sometime after about 9,000 years ago, some settled groups began experimenting with the plants in their environment. They probably planted seeds from the best plants and tended them in simple gardens. These garden keepers became the first American farmers.

Later, people in present-day Mexico developed an important grain plant from certain wild grasses growing in the highlands. The grain was maize, the first corn. The practice of growing maize soon spread from Mexico to Central America and South America. By about 2,000 years ago, some groups in North America were growing maize, too. Early American farmers also learned to grow beans, squash, and many other crops.

★ Examining the Evidence

Archaeologists search for remains of tools, weapons, jewelry, artwork, building materials, or any other items used by early Americans. Studying such traces gives scientists clues about how the people lived.

Stone Spearheads

Stone spearheads once tied to the spears of early hunters have been found throughout North America. Spearheads found in 1932 in a cave at Clovis, New Mexico, are about 11,000 years old. Scientists have used that clue to help establish when humans first lived in the American Southwest.

Carved Bone at Old Crow River

In the summer of 1966, scientist **C.R. Harrington** visited a village of Native Americans called the Loucheau in northwestern Canada. Harrington believed this would be a good location for finding evidence of early settlers in the Americas. **Peter Lord,** a Loucheau who lived in the village, agreed to help Harrington.

Walking along the valley of the Old Crow River, Lord discovered a large animal bone that had been carved and shaped. Lord thought it might be a tool that people had made and used thousands of years earlier. Later scientific tests revealed that the carved bone was about 27,000 years old. The age of the bone thus told scientists that people have been living in the Americas for at least 27,000 years. Other archaeological finds suggest that people might have been living on the continent even earlier.

The Native Americans

There are many mysteries still to be solved about the earliest Americans. Scientists believe the evidence does show, however, that the Native Americans are descendants of the hunters who came to the Americas from Asia thousands of years ago. As the Native Americans spread out over the two continents of the Americas, they developed a variety of rich cultures. A culture is a total way of life a people follow to satisfy their needs and wants.

By at least 2,000 years ago, there were two major Native American cultures living in the present-day United States—the **Mound Builders** and the **Anasazi.** *Anasai* is a Navajo word for "Ancient Ones." We do not know what the people called themselves. Their traditions laid the foundation for many later Native American cultures.

▲ PUEBLO FOOD BOWL

▲ APACHE GATHERING BASKET

★ The Mound Builders

The Mound Builders began settling in the Midwest and Southeast about 2,700 years ago. They take their name from the monuments of earth and dirt that they built. The mounds took many different shapes. Some were circular and some were rectangular. They ranged from just a few feet to 100 feet (30 m) high. One of the larger mounds covered a base of 16 acres (6 ha). Sometimes long, winding earthworks surrounded the mounds like protective fences.

Mystery of the Mounds

The mounds were a mystery for people who saw them many years later. Archaeologists have uncovered many artifacts, or items that people had created, inside the mounds. They believe the Mound Builders buried these artifacts for the dead to use in an afterworld. The artifacts include such items as stone pipes, copper tools, and mirrors made of the mineral mica. Archaeologists also know now that some mounds were built for religious ceremonies, not as burial sites.

Footnotes to History

Dog Companions   Dogs were part of Native American life from the very beginning. They came along with the peoples migrating from Asia and may have been trained to help in tracking and hunting game animals. The site of a bison kill in Colorado included the remains of a dog that date back 10,000 years.

The Adena

The Adena were a mound-building people who settled in the southern part of present-day Ohio and western West Virginia. Their culture flourished from about 2,700 to 1,800 years ago. They grew some crops such as sunflowers, pumpkins, and tobacco. They were mainly hunter-gatherers, however, rather than farmers. Plentiful game and wild plants supplied most of their food needs. Because food was always nearby, they could build permanent houses and stay in one location.

The Hopewell

The Hopewell Mound Builders were spread over a wide area that included present-day West Virginia, Ohio, Indiana, Illinois, Iowa, Missouri, Wisconsin, and Michigan. Their culture was at its height between 2,100 and 1,500 years ago.

In contrast to the neighboring Adena, the Hopewell relied heavily on farming for food. Their earthworks were larger, their art more advanced, and their religious ceremonies more organized.

Items found at Hopewell sites reveal that the people participated in a large trading network. Archaeologists have found shells from the Atlantic Ocean, silver from Canada, alligator skulls from Florida, and volcanic glass from Wyoming.

Around A.D. 500, both the Hopewell and the Adena declined and disappeared. No one knows what happened to them, but scientists have suggested that illness, war, or a change in climate may have played a role in their decline.

The Mississippian Culture

The Mississippian mound-building culture developed around the year 700, soon after the disappearance of the Hopewell and the Adena. The most advanced of all the Mound Builders, the Mississippians are also known as **Temple Mound Builders.** Many of their mounds had high, level tops, on which they built temples and homes for their important leaders.

The Mississippians settled near rivers, where they practiced advanced farming methods. They grew large crops of corn, beans, squash, pumpkin, and tobacco. They also kept livestock. Most archaeologists think the Mississippians traded for other goods with Native Americans in present-day Mexico and Central America.

Mississippian villages had large populations. The largest was **Cahokia,** along the Illinois River in present-day Illinois. Estimates place Cahokia's population at about 40,000. Its temple and burial mounds numbered more than 100.

Mississippian villages began to disappear by about 1500. European explorers found only one group after they reached North America.

Picturing History

▲ MOUND BUILDERS The Mound Builders constructed thousands of mounds, such as The Great Serpent Mound of Ohio, as burial and religious sites for their people. **What are two artifacts archaeologists have found in the mounds?**

★ The Cliff Dwellers

Many groups of Native Americans, called cliff dwellers, built houses on the walls of canyons and under the overhangs of caves. The Anasazi were one such group. They lived in the rugged land of present-day Arizona, New Mexico, Colorado, and Utah from about 100 to 1300.

Anasazi Pueblos

The Anasazi built homes that the Spanish explorers of the 1500s called *pueblos,* meaning "villages" in Spanish. The pueblos were built of stone, timber, and adobe bricks. Adobe is a building material made of earth and straw. The pueblos were made up of small apartment-like homes stacked on top of one another. Many were four or five stories high and connected by ladders.

At first the Anasazi built their pueblos on the canyon floor. Later, they began to build them on the sides of cliffs. Archaeologists think it may have been for protection from invaders.

Whatever the reason, it definitely made life more difficult. Farmers with fields at the base of the cliff or on the mesa above it had to spend much of their time climbing.

At the height of their development, the Anasazi grew corn, squash, beans, tobac-

Picturing History

▲ CLIFF PALACE The remains of the Cliff Palace in Colorado's Mesa Verde National Park is an example of an Anasazi cliff dwelling. **Why do archaeologists believe the Anasazi built their homes in cliff walls?**

co, and cotton. They also raised turkeys. Anasazi artists crafted pottery and jewelry from stone, shell, and metal. Some materials found at Anasazi sites reveal that they traded with other Native Americans who lived as far away as Mexico.

No one knows why the Anasazi began to leave their cliff dwellings in about 1300. There may have been a drought, or an enemy may have invaded. Whatever the reason, much of the Anasazi culture was passed to generations of Native Americans who later inhabited the area.

★ SECTION 1 REVIEW ★

Checking for Understanding

1. **Identify** C.R. Harrington, Peter Lord, Alaska, Bering Strait, Cahokia.
2. **Define** archaeologist, maize, culture, Mound Builders, artifact, cliff dwellers, pueblo, adobe.
3. **How** did the first Americans get to North America?
4. **What** was the purpose of the mounds built by the Mississippians?

Critical Thinking

5. **Drawing Conclusions** Think about Peter Lord's discovery and the spearheads found at Clovis, New Mexico. How might they prove that people settled in Canada earlier than in the American Southwest?

ACTIVITY

6. Imagine that you are an early cliff dweller. Draw a plan for a large pueblo.

BUILDING SKILLS
Critical Thinking Skills

Understanding Cause and Effect

To understand events in the past, it is useful to know why and how things happened. When you look for why or how an event or a chain of events took place, you are using the skill of understanding causes and effects.

Learning the Skill

The early bands of Asian hunters were looking for food. That is why they followed herds of Ice Age animals across the Beringia land bridge into North America. Hunting for food was the *cause* that led Asian bands to follow the animals. Crossing the land bridge into North America was the *effect*, or result. The chart shows how one event—the **cause,** led to another—the **effect.**

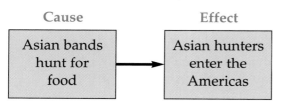

Cause	Effect
Asian bands hunt for food	Asian hunters enter the Americas

As you read, you sometimes can identify cause-and-effect relationships from clue words or terms in sentences. Such written clues include:

because	resulted in	in order to
due to	thus	for this reason
so that	led to	as a result
therefore	produced	brought about

In a chain of historical events, an event often becomes the cause of other events. This chart shows such a chain of events. First the climate warmed, causing grasslands and lakes to disappear. Then the disappearance of the grasslands and lakes caused large Ice Age animals to become extinct.

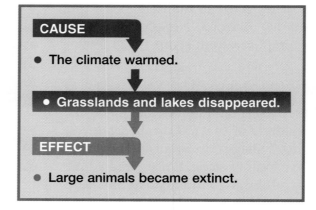

CAUSE
- The climate warmed.

- Grasslands and lakes disappeared.

EFFECT
- Large animals became extinct.

Practicing the Skill

Make a chart showing which events are causes and which are effects in these sentences.

1. Because so much of the earth's water froze during the Ice Age, a land bridge between Asia and North America was uncovered.

2. Archaeologists could estimate when farming began in the Americas because they had discovered the remains of ancient corncobs in a cave in Mexico.

3. The threat of invasion may have been one reason some Native American groups built houses on the sides of cliffs.

4. Climate, illness, war, or invasion may have led to the disappearance of Native American culture groups that once lived in the Middle West.

APPLYING THE SKILL

5. Read an account of a recent event in your community reported in a local newspaper. Determine at least one cause and one effect of that event. Show the chain of events in a chart.

44

★★★

Native American Culture Groups

SETTING THE SCENE

Read to Learn . . .

★ about similarities among Native American cultures.

★ how people in different physical environments developed different cultures.

★ where the most densely populated area was.

Terms to Know

★ shaman
★ totem pole
★ potlatch
★ tepee
★ Iroquois League

People to Meet

★ Hiawatha

Places to Locate

★ Arctic
★ Subarctic
★ Aleutian Islands
★ Alaska Peninsula
★ Cascade Mountains

▶ PRECOLUMBIAN STONE TOOLS

When Europeans first arrived in America in 1492, the Native American population north of Mexico was about 15 to 20 million. Among these millions, there were at least 2,000 different groups, or nations.

Over time these different groups of Native Americans had formed many rich and diverse ways of life. Some of the culture groups developed into large and elaborate empires, while others remained simple in their organization.

To study the many different Native American groups, it is helpful to divide North America into larger culture areas. People who lived in the same culture area often shared many similar cultural traits. The map on page 46 shows 10 major North American culture areas that had developed by the 1400s.

★ A Variety of Lifestyles

During the thousands of years that Native Americans lived in North America, they developed many different ways to get food, build homes, practice religion, and enforce their laws. They spoke more than 1,000 different languages.

Similarities Among Cultures

There were no typical Native Americans, but there were some similarities among their cultures. A nation of Native Americans was usually made up of people who spoke the same language and shared other cultural traits. The most important division in a nation was the clan. The people who belonged to the clan were related to one another by a common ancestor.

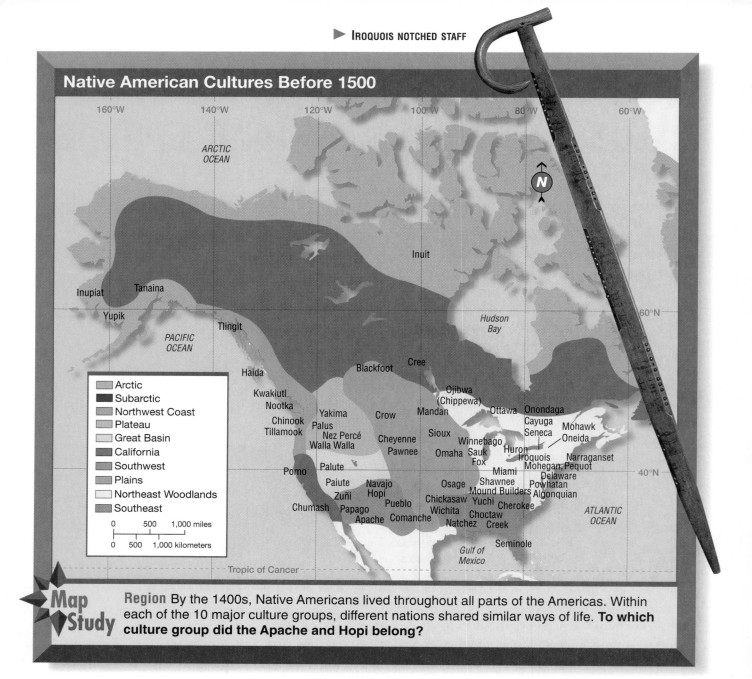

Native American Cultures Before 1500

Legend:
- Arctic
- Subarctic
- Northwest Coast
- Plateau
- Great Basin
- California
- Southwest
- Plains
- Northeast Woodlands
- Southeast

0   500   1,000 miles
0   500   1,000 kilometers

Map Study

Region By the 1400s, Native Americans lived throughout all parts of the Americas. Within each of the 10 major culture groups, different nations shared similar ways of life. **To which culture group did the Apache and Hopi belong?**

Each nation usually had several leaders who made decisions for the entire group. Among some groups, the leaders inherited their positions. Among other groups, the leaders were elected on the basis of their achievements. In some nations, all of the people—not just the leaders—participated in group decision making.

Beliefs

Most Native Americans believed in the power of spirits found in nature. Some believed that spirits dwelled in the sun, moon, wind, rain, and animals. Religious leaders, called shamans, were thought to have close contact with the spirit world.

Native Americans tried to live in harmony with nature and the land. They believed no one person could own land. Land was shared by all members of a nation—not bought, sold, or passed down through inheritance. Many Native American beliefs and related traditions are still observed by Native American groups today and are shared by other Americans as well.

★ The Arctic

The people of the **Arctic** and **Subarctic** areas settled farther north than any other culture. People in these two regions had to adapt to bitterly cold winters and short summers.

The land of the Arctic extends along the northern borders of Alaska and Canada. The two main Native American cultures in this area were the Aleuts and the Inuit.

The Aleuts

Most Aleuts settled on the **Aleutian Islands** of the **Alaska Peninsula.** The Aleuts were mainly hunters but they also gathered clams and berries. They hunted in boats made of whale skin stretched over a frame of whale ribs. They used harpoons and nets to snare their prey.

Aleut villages usually had from 50 to 150 residents. Many of the homes were made from driftwood, whalebone, sod, and animal skins.

Men and women usually wore long parkas made from otter or bird skins, furs, or animal intestines. Women sewed the clothing together with needles made from tiny bird bones and thread made of fish parts.

The Inuit

The Inuit moved farther inland and populated northern Canada. Like the Aleuts, many lived near the sea and hunted seal, walruses, and whales. In summer, they moved inland to hunt caribou and fish in the lakes and rivers.

▶ **MANUFACTURED MOCCASINS**

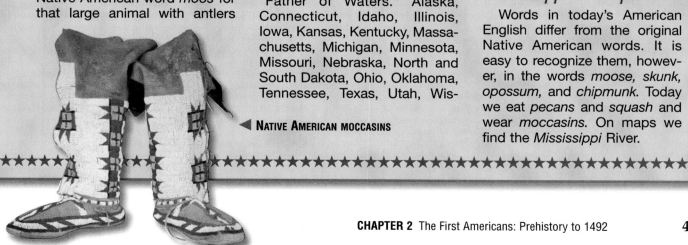

Linking Past and Present

Word History

English settlers arriving in America needed names for things they had never seen before. What did they do? They borrowed words from the Native Americans.

Then

Misi Sipi and *Apasaum*

English settlers took the Native American word *moos* for that large animal with antlers they had learned to hunt. They trapped animals the Native Americans called *squnck, apasaum, and chitmunk.* The settlers also ate *paccans* and *askwash* and wore *mohkussins.* Some sailed along the *Misi Sipi* River.

Settlers also borrowed Native American words to name territories and states. For example, *Mississippi* is a Choctaw word meaning "Great Water" or "Father of Waters." Alaska, Connecticut, Idaho, Illinois, Iowa, Kansas, Kentucky, Massachusetts, Michigan, Minnesota, Missouri, Nebraska, North and South Dakota, Ohio, Oklahoma, Tennessee, Texas, Utah, Wis-

◀ **NATIVE AMERICAN MOCCASINS**

consin and Wyoming all take their names from Native American languages.

Now

Mississippi and *Opossum*

Words in today's American English differ from the original Native American words. It is easy to recognize them, however, in the words *moose, skunk, opossum,* and *chipmunk.* Today we eat *pecans* and *squash* and wear *moccasins.* On maps we find the *Mississippi* River.

Nothing was wasted in the Inuit culture. Anything not used for food was made into clothing, shelter, sleds, weapons, or fuel for heating. Wood was extremely rare on these ice covered, treeless plains. For homes, they built skin tents or sod houses.

★ The Subarctic

The climate of the Subarctic was also harsh, but much of the land was covered with forests and lakes. Like the people of the Arctic, Subarctic people traveled from place to place hunting, fishing, and gathering food.

The caribou was their most important source of meat. They also hunted moose, deer, beaver, and rabbit. Because wood was plentiful, it was used with sod and other material to build homes.

★ The Northwest Coast

The misty, forested coast of the Pacific Northwest supported many Native American nations. The environment teemed with animal, sea, and plant life. Food was so abundant that the people who lived here had no need to farm. Salmon made up a large part of the diet along with sea otters, seals, bear, and moose.

Most villages in the Northwest were near the ocean or rivers. Wood was plentiful, and most groups used it to make large houses, tools, and

◀ NORTHWEST NATIVE AMERICAN GRAVE TOTEM

▲ CANOE BY HAIDA CARVER

weapons. The soft inner bark of trees was used for weaving baskets and for making clothing.

Large canoes that could hold more than 50 people were built by digging out or burning out the inside of giant redwood trees. Like their early ancestors, these people also made large totem poles—tall, wooden posts with carvings of faces.

Among most groups of the Northwest, the wealthiest families made the decisions. To show their wealth, leaders often hosted potlatches. A potlatch was a feast at which the host family gave valuable gifts to members of the community.

★ California

The mild climate and plentiful resources of the California area supported a large population of at least 100 groups of Native Americans. On the coast fish, shellfish, and wild plants were plentiful. Away from the coast, people such as the Pomo hunted small forest game and gathered acorns to pound into meal. They made a kind of mush from the acorn meal.

The Chumash lived on the southern coast and were master ocean fishers. They built long, wooden canoes and traveled many miles out to sea. Simple harpoons and nets made from grass and weighted with stones were used to catch fish.

★ The Plateau

The Plateau culture area was just east of the Northwest Coast. It was bordered by the **Cascade Mountains** on the west and the Rocky Mountains on the east.

The Plateau is a land of many rivers. Salmon was the main source of food for the people who lived here along with bulbs, roots, and berries. The rivers also served as routes for travel and trade.

To protect themselves from winter's cold, many people built homes that were partly underground. In summer, they lived under wooden frames covered with mats.

Although this area was not as populated as the Northwest Coast, it supported more than 20 Native American groups, including the Nez Perce and the Yakima.

★ The Great Basin

The Great Basin was home to the Shoshone, Paiute, and Utes. In this dry desert area, temperatures can soar to more than 100 degrees. Sagebrush and grasses are the only plants, except for the evergreens in the surrounding mountains.

People who lived here were called "diggers" because they had to dig in the ground for most of their food. Seeds, berries, roots, snakes, lizards, insects, and rodents were the main diet for these people who spent most of their time in search of food and water.

★ The Southwest

The people of the Southwest had two basic lifestyles. They were either farmers or hunter-gatherers. Like their cliff-dwelling ancestors, most lived in pueblos.

One of the largest nations, called the Pueblos, included the Hopi and Zuni. The Pueblos were skilled farmers. The land was dry, so they built irrigation canals to grow corn, squash, beans, and tobacco. Corn was ground into meal and made into flat cakes and bread. Surplus or extra food was traded to other nations.

The Pueblos' settled way of life was not always shared by all groups in the Southwest. The Apache and Navajo came to the area around 1500. They roamed the mountains and deserts hunting. When hunting was poor, they raided villages and farms for food. Later the Navajo became farmers like the Pueblos, but the Apache continued their hunting and wandering way of life.

 ▲ PUEBLO FARMING The Pueblos had to be skilled farmers in order to grow crops in their dry climate. **What kinds of crops did the Pueblos grow?**

★ The Plains

The area of the Plains culture stretched west from the Mississippi River to the Rocky Mountains. Large herds of buffalo, antelope, and elk grazed on the treeless grasslands of the Great Plains.

Some of the Native Americans who lived in the Plains area were the Sioux, Pawnee, Crow, Cheyenne, and Comanche. They lived in villages along streams and rivers, where they built homes of sod and farmed the riverbanks. Their crops included corn, beans, squash, tobacco, and sunflowers. During the summer, they left the villages to hunt buffalo herds that roamed the plains. Native Americans used all parts of the buffalo. The people ate the buffalo meat and used the hides for clothing and cone-shaped tents, called tepees. They also used the buffalo bones for tools, cooking utensils, and ceremonial purposes.

The lives of the Plains groups changed dramatically after the Europeans brought horses to North America. The first horses probably reached the Plains in the 1600s. Hunters no longer had to hunt on foot.

They could travel long distances at greater speeds on horseback.

After the people of the Plains acquired horses, they gave up most of their farming and focused on hunting. Instead of settling in one area, they followed the herds.

★ The Northeast Woodlands

The Northeast Woodlands area had dense forests, fertile river valleys, and rushing streams. It supported at least 40 groups of Native Americans. Some groups were constantly on the move in search of food. Others settled in villages, where they built more permanent homes.

The Iroquois and the Algonquin

The Iroquois and Algonquin were the two main cultures in the Northeast Woodlands. There were many different bands within these groups, but most spoke a form of either the Iroquois or Algonquin language.

The Iroquois League

Of the two cultures the Iroquois was the more powerful. For many years, five nations among the Iroquois were constantly at war. These nations were the Cayuga, the Mohawk, the Onondaga, the Oneida, and the Seneca. To bring an end to the bloodshed, a Mohawk leader named **Hiawatha** suggested that the nations band together. They agreed and formed what was known as the Iroquois League. Later they added a sixth member, the Tuscarora. The Iroquois League has been called the first true representative form of government in North America.

★ The Southeast

Of all the Native American culture areas, the Southeast was the most densely populated. The people living here developed a variety of cultures and spoke many different languages. The Cherokee, Creek, Choctaw, Seminole, and Natchez were just a few among the many Native American peoples.

For meat and skins, the men in the Southeast hunted buffalo, deer, and bear; they also fished in streams. Most groups in the Southeast, however, relied heavily on farming. The women planted and harvested corn, beans, squash, and sweet potatoes. Women had a high standing in Southeastern cultures. Some were members of war councils and a few became warriors as well.

★ SECTION 2 REVIEW ★

★★★★★★★★★★★★★★★★★★★★   ★★★★★★★★★★★★★★★★★★★★

Checking for Understanding

1. **Identify** Hiawatha, Arctic, Subarctic, Aleutian Islands, Alaska Peninsula, Cascade Mountains.
2. **Define** shaman, totem pole, potlatch, tepee, Iroquis League.
3. **What** beliefs about land and nature did most Native Americans share?
4. **How** did horses affect the lives of the Native Americans of the Plains?

Critical Thinking

5. **Hypothesizing** If the Inuit had been able to farm in their environment, how do you think it might have changed their culture?

ACTIVITY

6. Choose 1 of the 10 Native American culture areas. Think about the area's physical environment. Draw a scene that shows that environment.

Native American Arts

Artwork of Native Americans reflected the environments in which they lived. From lakes and streams in the eastern woodlands, people gathered thousands of freshwater clam shells. They used the shells to make disc-shaped white and purple beads. Then they strung the beads on threadlike strips of animal tendon. Called *wampum*, this highly prized beadwork was used for gifts, good luck charms, and in exchange for goods.

People in the Southwest created colorful sandpaintings in their *kivas*, or religious rooms. They made the paintings by spreading sand and finely ground flower petals and leaves on the walls.

Southwest Native American people also designed distinctive clay pottery and sculptures. Unique designs painted on the pots, dishes, and ceremonial pieces identified the creators and the groups to which they belonged.

Women of the Plains colored porcupine quills with dyes made from ground-up vegetables and minerals. They stitched or wove the quills into animal skins, which they used for decoration.

In the Northwest, artists used cedar bark, mountain goat wool, and dog hair to weave designs into capes. The designs showed the rank of the wearer.

Walrus tusks, whalebone, antlers, and stone were popular materials for Inuit artists of the Arctic. From these materials they carved buttons, ceremonial knives, masks, and religious charms. Much of their art featured pictures of animals that were important to their survival.

► WAMPUM

▼ NAVAJO SAND PAINTING

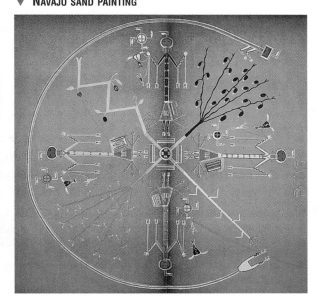

Making the Arts Connection

1. How did the environment affect the art of Native American cultures?

2. What purposes did wampum serve?

3. What do you think you might learn about cultures of the Southwest and the Arctic by studying their artwork?

ACTIVITY

4. On a sheet of paper, design a piece of "environmental" jewelry. Label your design with the types of materials you would use to make the jewelry. List only natural materials that are found in the state where you live.

★★

Empires of the South

SETTING THE SCENE

Read to Learn . . .

★ about the achievements of the Maya in science and mathematics.
★ how trade and conquest made the Aztec a powerful empire.
★ how Inca leaders unified the people of their empire.

Terms to Know

★ civilization
★ specialized worker
★ terrace
★ hieroglyph
★ causeway
★ aqueduct
★ tribute

People to Meet

★ Montezuma

Places to Locate

★ Tenochtitlán
★ Mexico City
★ Cuzco

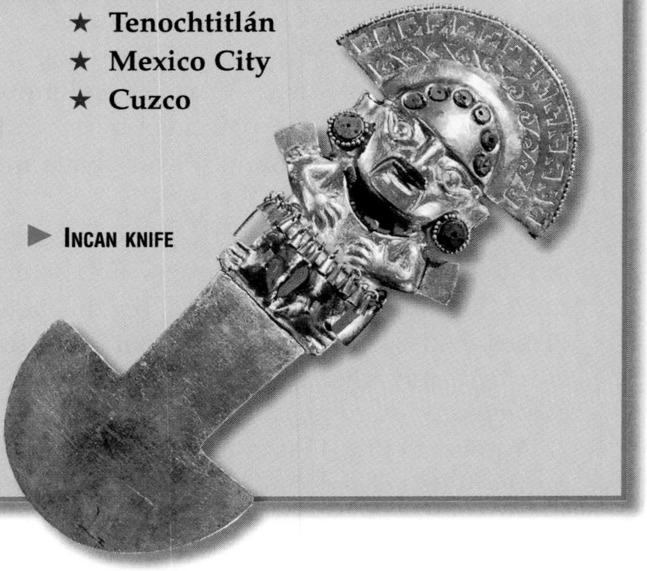

► INCAN KNIFE

❝ There are in the city many large and beautiful houses [with] large . . . rooms and . . . very pleasant gardens of flowers both on the upper and lower floors. . . . Along one of the causeways to this great city run two aqueducts [through which] good fresh water . . . flows into the heart of the city and from this they all drink. **❞**

The person who wrote these words was a Spanish explorer and soldier who came to the Americas in the early 1500s. The scene he described was the city Tenochtitlán (tay•NAWCH•teet•LAHN). In awe of such a beautiful, well-built city, the Spaniard wanted to report what he had seen to rulers in Spain.

Tenochtitlán was the capital of the Aztec empire, a Native American civilization that developed in present-day Mexico. A civilization is a group of people with an advanced culture. In addition to hunting and farming, it usually has some form of writing or method of keeping records, an organized government and religion, cities, and social classes. It also has specialized workers, or those who do only one kind of work such as teaching or jewelry making.

The Aztec were only one of at least three great civilizations that grew up in

Mexico, Central America, and South America. The Mayan civilization, for example, existed long before the Aztec.

★ The Maya

About 3,000 years ago, a small group of farmers began clearing land in the southern part of present-day Mexico and the northern part of Central America. With only simple tools, they cleared thick jungles swarming with insects and snakes.

The villages the farmers created prospered. By the year A.D. 250, they had expanded into an empire that covered nearly 120,000 square miles (310,800 sq. km) and included 200 cities. The population had soared to more than 10 million.

Skilled Farmers

Much of the Maya's growth resulted from their skill in farming. Applying knowledge passed down from their ancestors, they grew corn, beans, squash, sweet potatoes, and avocados. They drained marshes to create more farmland. They built terraces—leveled off strips of land—so they could farm hillsides. They hauled rich soil from riverbanks and river bottoms to make their fields more productive. They also raised turkeys and kept honeybees.

The Maya produced so much food that they had plenty to trade. They also traded salt, honey, and jaguar pelts for jade, brightly colored feathers, and cacao beans. Cacao beans were used as a type of money throughout the empire.

City Builders

The Maya were master builders. At the centers of most of their cities were tall pyramids built of limestone blocks. Atop the pyramids were temples where Mayan priests conducted religious ceremonies.

Rulers and priests lived in the cities' large stone palaces. Most Mayan people, however, lived in simple one-room houses near their fields in the countryside. They visited the cities only to attend religious ceremonies or to exchange goods in the large markets. Before returning home from such a visit, a family might attend a ball game played on one of the large stone courts in the city.

Religion and Science

Priests, many of whom were also rulers, were the most important people in the Mayan empire. The priests helped the Maya please the gods. Gods were thought to control the sun, rain, and other forces of nature. The Maya believed that if the gods

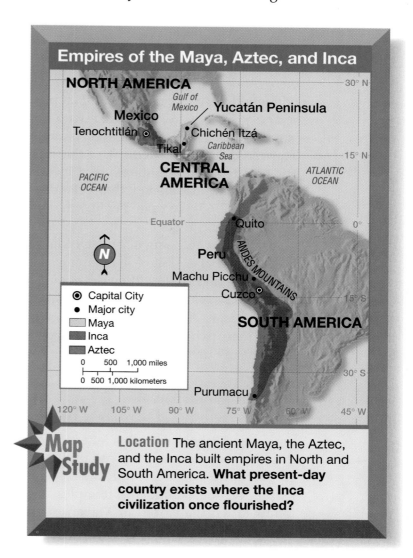

Empires of the Maya, Aztec, and Inca

NORTH AMERICA
Gulf of Mexico
Mexico
Tenochtitlán
Yucatán Peninsula
Chichén Itzá
Tikal
Caribbean Sea
CENTRAL AMERICA
PACIFIC OCEAN
ATLANTIC OCEAN
Equator
Quito
Peru
ANDES MOUNTAINS
Machu Picchu
Cuzco
SOUTH AMERICA
Purumacu

- ◎ Capital City
- • Major city
- Maya
- Inca
- Aztec

0 500 1,000 miles
0 500 1,000 kilometers

120° W   105° W   90° W   75° W   60° W   45° W
30° N   15° N   0°   15° S   30° S

Map Study Location The ancient Maya, the Aztec, and the Inca built empires in North and South America. **What present-day country exists where the Inca civilization once flourished?**

History AND ART

▲ *A MAYAN SEACOAST VILLAGE* by unknown artist The Maya painted beautiful scenes on the walls of their tombs and temples, such as this mural found on the walls of a temple for warriors. **What cultural achievement helped the Maya to tell stories about their rulers and priests?**

were pleased they would favor the people with good weather and bountiful crops.

The priests were fascinated with the stars, the sky, and the passage of time. They studied the movement of the stars and made accurate maps of the star groups. They developed two calendars. One was a 365-day calendar like the one we use today.

In addition to being scientists, Mayan priests were also skilled mathematicians. Using dots and dashes, they developed a system of numbers before anyone else in the Americas. They had a symbol to represent zero, which some advanced civilizations in Europe did not.

Cultural Achievements

The Maya developed a system of writing using symbols instead of letters. These symbols or pictures are called **hieroglyphs.** The Maya carved their hieroglyphs on the columns of temples and tombs to tell the stories of Mayan rulers and priests.

Colorful paintings, created by highly skilled artists, decorated the walls of tombs. Metalsmiths made jewelry from jade, gold, and shells, and weavers created beautifully designed fabrics.

The Mayan Decline

The Mayan empire was at its height from about 250 to 900. By 900, however, the people began deserting their cities and moving to other areas. Archaeologists think the people may have moved away because of drastic climate changes or because the farmland was no longer fertile. There may have been an invasion of outsiders. By the mid-1500s, the Spaniards had taken over all the Mayan strongholds.

The Mayan culture still survives, however. Today, more than 2 million descendants of the Maya live in Mexico and Central America.

★ The Aztec

The Aztec built their empire between 1300 and 1520. Their center in present-day Mexico was west and north of where the Mayan empire had been.

A Message From the Gods

The early Aztec were wandering hunter-gatherers. According to Aztec legend, they were instructed by a god to find a permanent place to settle. The god said an eagle perched on a cactus would mark the place where they should build their home.

The people found the eagle on a marshy island in Lake Texcoco, at the site of present-day **Mexico City.** On this site they built their capital city, which later became home to more than 100,000 people. They named the city Tenochtitlán, meaning "Place of the Prickly Pear Cactus."

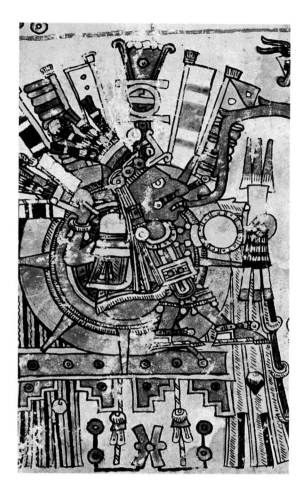

▲ THE RELIGION OF THE AZTEC
Religion played an important role in Aztec society. The Aztec made sacrifices to their gods, such as the sun god Tonatiuh. **What god was the most sacred to the Aztec?**

The Greatness of Tenochtitlán

The Aztec constructed three large causeways, or raised highways over water, to connect their island capital with the mainland around the lake. They also built a system of aqueducts, channels or big pipes for flowing water, to bring freshwater from the mountains. As you read at the beginning of this section, these structures greatly impressed the Spaniards in the early 1500s.

Aztec workers built stone pyramids in Tenochtitlán for the priests. The city also had large, well-stocked outdoor markets, parks, schools, barbershops, and a zoo.

To grow food on the wet, swampy land, farmers built floating gardens. They first anchored mats to the bottom of the swamp and then piled soil on them. The strips of land thus created were more than 100 feet (30 m) long and 15 to 30 feet (5 to 9 m) wide. Farmers tending the gardens moved around in boats. Corn, squash, beans, tomatoes, sweet potatoes, and chili peppers were important crops.

Conquest and Trade

The Aztec built their wealth and power on trade and conquest. Their warriors were fierce and well trained. They took thousands of prisoners in battle.

Conquered peoples became members of Aztec society, but were forced to pay tribute. Tribute was like a tax that could be paid in goods or in services. As more people were conquered, wealth flowed into the empire and its capital.

Aztec society had a rigid class system. Nobles, at the top, inherited their positions. Government officials, priests, and warriors were all nobles. Below them on the social scale were commoners, peasant farmers, and enslaved persons. Many of the people who were conquered were enslaved, but their children were born free. Of the three lowest classes, only commoners could own land. All classes except the nobles had to pay tribute.

▼ CEREMONIAL AZTEC SHIELD

The Aztec traveled great distances to trade. Brightly colored feathers, gold, and other items were exchanged for blue turquoise, chocolate, and other goods not available within the empire. Some Native Americans in the Southwest and Southeast of the present-day United States traded with the Aztec.

Priests and Religion

Religion was very important to the Aztec. The most sacred god was the god of sun and war, but the Aztec worshiped at least 1,000 others.

In addition to religious duties, the priests kept a history of the Aztec people. Information about the gods, important events, and other records were kept in books filled with bark pages. Priests were also teachers. They taught children history, craft making, and religious traditions.

Biography ★★★★

Montezuma and the Aztec Decline

> ❝ [He has] all the things to be found under the heavens . . . fashioned in gold and silver and jewels and feathers . . . jewels so fine that it is impossible to imagine with what instruments they were cut. ❞

These words—from the same Spaniard who reported on Tenochtitlán—described the Aztec emperor **Montezuma II** in the early 1500s. (His name is also spelled Moctezuma.) Montezuma, a 35-year-old priest, came to the throne in 1502. He replaced his uncle, the ninth Aztec ruler. The Aztec were at the height of their power at this point.

From all accounts, Montezuma liked to be surrounded with riches and honor. Before people could approach him, he made them remove their shoes and their jewelry and keep their eyes to the ground. He insisted on eating alone, separating himself from others with a wooden screen.

Montezuma was not a popular emperor. Many of his people resented him for demanding tribute. Records reveal that some Aztec predicted the downfall of the empire under Montezuma. Montezuma

▲ **MONTEZUMA AND CORTÉS**

himself feared that a white god was coming to seize his throne.

In 1520 his fears became fact. The Aztec empire was under attack, and Montezuma was killed in his palace. The conqueror, however, was not a god. It was instead Hernán Cortés, a Spaniard who had come to seize the riches of the Aztec empire.

Although Montezuma had welcomed Cortés when he entered Tenochtitlán in 1519, the Spaniards took him captive. They then looted the city of gold and silver. Eight months later, Montezuma was killed by a stone thrown by an Aztec during a revolt against the Spanish.   ★★★

★ The Inca

The largest empire in the Americas was the one created in South America by the Inca. The Inca began to expand their rule over others about 1200. By the 1400s their empire stretched 2,500 miles (4,023 km) along the Andes Mountains—through present-day Ecuador, Peru, Bolivia, and parts of Argentina and Chile.

The Incan empire was extremely well organized. Unlike the Aztec, the Inca conquered many of their subjects by peaceful means. Before sending soldiers, the Incan ruler would send ambassadors to persuade the people to surrender. Often, those who surrendered were allowed to keep their own rulers.

Incan armies stationed throughout the empire maintained peace. To further unify the empire, newly conquered people were required to learn the Incan language and practice the Incan religion.

The Incan ruler governed from the capital city of **Cuzco,** high in the Andes. His palace—with its hundreds of rooms and thousands of servants—was itself like a town. His bodyguards wore gold armor.

The ruler held great power over the people of his empire. He controlled all of the goods and services they produced and made decisions for them.

The Inca were farmers. They terraced the steep hillsides and built irrigation canals to grow crops. They grew corn, beans, cotton, and squash in the valleys. In the mountains they grew potatoes and raised herds of llama and alpaca for meat and wool.

The government owned all the food that was grown. Some of it was kept in government storehouses for use during wars or other emergencies.

Picturing History

▲ **INCAN BRIDGES** The Inca built straw rope bridges to connect their system of roads. Descendants of the Inca continue to use the same construction for these bridges, replacing them every year. **How many miles long was the road system used to connect the Incan empire?**

Most people had to work on projects for the government. One project was a 10,000-mile (16,090-km) road system to connect the far reaches of the Incan empire. Workers cleared trees, moved huge boulders, dug tunnels, and built bridges to create a stone-covered road.

In the early 1500s, the Incan ruler died, and there was a bitter fight for the throne. In the following years, unrest spread throughout the empire. Thus when invaders from across the Atlantic arrived in the 1500s, they found the Incan civilization in a weakened condition.

★ **SECTION 3 REVIEW** ★

Checking for Understanding

1. **Identify** Montezuma, Tenochtitlán, Mexico City, Cuzco.
2. **Define** civilization, specialized worker, terrace, hieroglyph, causeway, aqueduct, tribute.
3. **What** were two important contributions of the Maya?
4. **How** did the Aztec empire acquire wealth and power?

Critical Thinking

5. **Determining Cause and Effect** How did efficient farming contribute to the cultures of the Maya, Aztec, and Inca?

ACTIVITY

6. Use symbols and pictures to create your own hieroglyphs. Use the hieroglyphs to relate an interesting fact about the Maya, Aztec, or Inca.

Using Key Vocabulary

On a separate sheet of paper, write the vocabulary word that best completes each sentence.

> **maize**
> **shaman**
> **civilization**
> **terrace**
> **tribute**

1. A Native American _____ was believed to have contact with the spirit world.

2. Leveled farmland on a hillside is a _____.

3. People conquered by the Aztec were required to pay _____.

4. Because the Maya had a method of keeping records, they were considered to be a _____.

5. Early farmers in Mexico developed a corn plant called _____.

Reviewing Facts

1. **Tell** why the first Americans came to the Americas.

2. **Describe** the two major Native American cultures that existed in the present-day United States 2,000 years ago.

3. **Name** the leader responsible for founding the Iroquois League.

4. **Describe** how horses brought by Europeans helped to change the lives of the peoples in the Plains culture area.

5. **Describe** how the Inca enlarged their empire.

Understanding Concepts

Geography and Environment

1. How did the end of the Ice Age change the lives of the early Americans?

2. How did the environment of the Northeast Woodlands culture area differ from that of the Southwest culture area?

Cultural Diversity

3. What role did farming play in the cultures of the Maya, the Aztec, and the Inca?

4. How were the cultures of the Adena, the Hopewell, and the Mississippians related to one another?

History and Geography

Sites of Mound Builder Settlements

Study the map of the Mound Builder sites. Then answer the questions at the top of page 59.

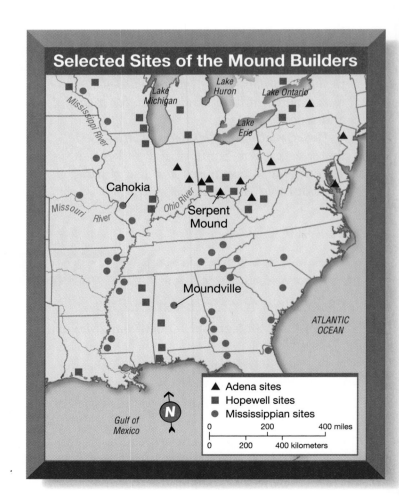

Selected Sites of the Mound Builders

▲ Adena sites
■ Hopewell sites
● Mississippian sites

0   200   400 miles
0   200   400 kilometers

1. **Location** Along what two major rivers did many of the Mound Builders settle?

2. **Place** Near which river did the Adena build most of their settlements?

3. **Movement** Of the Adena, Hopewell, and Mississippian cultures, which settled the farthest north? Which settled the farthest east?

Critical Thinking

1. **Comparing and Contrasting** How did the Incan empire and method of building compare with the Aztec empire and method of building?

2. **Drawing Conclusions** Why is trade important in the development of a culture?

Cooperative Learning Interdisciplinary Activity: Science

As a group, do library research to learn more about the farming methods of the Aztec. Then prepare an illustrated pamphlet to present your findings.

Divide the pamphlet into three small sections. In one section, include written descriptions and drawings to show how the Aztec created farmland in lakes, swamps, and highlands. In another section of the pamphlet, describe and illustrate the crops the farmers grew. In the final section, show how the Aztec used specific crops and how people today may or may not use the same crops.

Practicing Skills

Understanding Cause and Effect

Each sentence below contains a cause-and-effect relationship. On a separate sheet of paper, write the cause and the effect in each sentence. A sentence may have more than one cause or effect.

1. The cold climate of the Ice Age caused oceans to freeze, which made sea levels drop more than 400 feet (122 m).

2. As ice sheets moved slowly southward carrying boulders and debris, they gouged out large holes, carved valleys, and pushed up ridges.

3. Due to the lower sea levels, new areas of land appeared, including a land bridge linking Asia and North America.

4. As the land bridge gradually changed from marsh to grassland, it attracted large herds of mammals such as camels and mammoths.

5. Hunters followed these herds and so crossed the land bridge into the Americas.

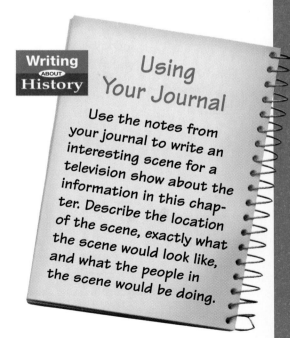

Writing ABOUT History

Using Your Journal

Use the notes from your journal to write an interesting scene for a television show about the information in this chapter. Describe the location of the scene, exactly what the scene would look like, and what the people in the scene would be doing.

CHAPTER 3

★★

Explorers Reach the Americas
1000–1535

SETTING THE SCENE

Focus

About 1,000 years ago sailors from Northern Europe briefly explored the shores of Canada. It would be another 500 years before any other Europeans set foot in the Americas.

Concepts to Understand

★ How a desire to control trade affected **economic development** in Europe and sparked a period of exploration

★ How **technology influenced** European exploration

Read to Discover . . .

★ why European nations wanted to explore the Americas.

★ how the explorers treated Native Americans.

► **WEST AFRICAN ARMLETS**

Journal Notes

As you read the chapter, imagine you are a newspaper editor. In your journal write headlines announcing the important journeys and voyages of travelers described in this chapter.

Americas	1009 Norse make settlement in North America	1179 Mayan capital destroyed	1200 Pueblo culture begins to decline
	1000s	**1100s**	**1200s**
World	1096 First Crusade to the Holy Land	1150 Southeast Asian temple of Angkor Wat is completed	1295 Marco Polo returns to Italy from China

COMPASS, 1500S

> **History AND ART**
>
> ***Departure of Columbus***
> Unknown artist
>
> As shown in this painting, Christopher Columbus set sail from Palos, Spain, in 1492. His history-making voyage would be the subject of many paintings of the 1500s.

1300s	1400s	1500s

1492 Columbus lands in the Bahamas
1497 John Cabot sails to Newfoundland

1513 Balboa crosses the Isthmus of Panama
1535 Cartier claims Canada for France

1300s European Renaissance begins

1419 Prince Henry founds navigation school
1488 Dias rounds southern tip of Africa

1500 Songhai Empire rises in Africa
1522 Magellan's crew completes first world voyage

★★

A Changing Europe

SETTING THE SCENE

Read to Learn . . .

★ about Europeans who reached the Americas before Columbus did.

★ how Europeans lived during the Middle Ages and the Renaissance.

★ why Europeans wanted to find an ocean route to Asia.

Terms to Know

★ saga
★ Middle Ages
★ monarch
★ manor
★ feudal system
★ serf
★ Crusades
★ Renaissance

People to Meet

★ Leif Eriksson
★ Marco Polo
★ Michelangelo
★ Leonardo da Vinci

Places to Locate

★ Greenland
★ Newfoundland

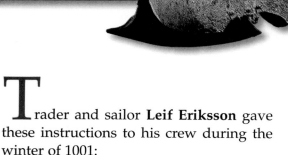

◀ VIKING HELMET

Trader and sailor **Leif Eriksson** gave these instructions to his crew during the winter of 1001:

> **On alternate days we must gather grapes and cut vines, and then fell trees, to make a cargo for my ship.**

Eriksson was a **Norse,** as Northern Europeans from present-day Sweden, Norway, and Denmark were known. He and his crew were camped somewhere along the eastern coast of mainland North America—a land that was new to them.

★ The Norse in North America

Eriksson left his camp in the spring—with a "full cargo of timber" and a "towboat . . . filled with grapes." He returned to his home on the North Atlantic island of **Greenland.** The Norse had been sailing far into the Atlantic for centuries.

By 985, they had settled both Iceland and Greenland.

The Vinland Settlement

When Eriksson returned home to Greenland, he gave glowing reports of the land he had visited. He told of lush grasses so sweet that in the morning he would wet his hands in the grass and put the dew in his mouth. Eriksson described streams filled with plump salmon, and vines bent with the weight of juicy grapes. He called the land **Vinland,** which meant "land of wine."

Eriksson's enthusiasm convinced other Norse to go to Vinland. In 1009, about 100 Norse men and women landed on the North American coast. They brought livestock with them and built a small village of earthen-walled houses.

The settlement ended in disappointment, however. Although the Norse traded for furs with nearby Native Americans, the two groups often fought. After five years of conflict, the Norse left Vinland, never to return.

Remembering the Norse

The Norse did not create maps or write reports of where they had been. The only records of their journeys were Norse legends, known as sagas. For centuries, many educated people thought of the sagas as just exaggerated stories. In the 1960s, however, archaeologists found traces of a Norse settlement on the island of **Newfoundland** in present-day Canada. The sagas had in fact recorded true history.

★ Europe and the Middle Ages

When the Norse were visiting the shores of North America, Western and Southern Europeans were just ending a period of isolation known as the Middle Ages. Few people in other parts of Europe ever heard the Norse sagas or learned of their voyages and settlements.

The fall of the Roman Empire in the year 476 marked the beginning of the Middle Ages in Europe. When Roman rule disappeared, Europe broke up into hundreds of small kingdoms. The power of the kings and queens—or monarchs—who headed the kingdoms was very weak. They often competed with large landowners—called **lords**—in their own kingdoms.

The Feudal System

The lords were mostly free of any control. They ruled their lands, or manors, like tiny independent kingdoms. They made laws for all who lived on their manors and collected taxes and fines. They raised their own armies and sometimes fought one another.

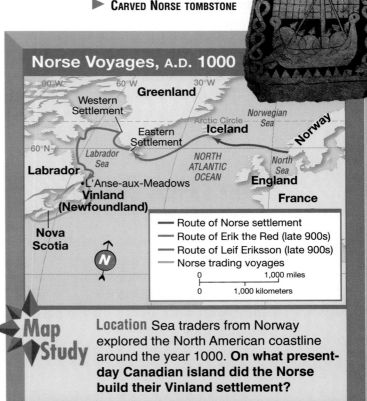

▶ CARVED NORSE TOMBSTONE

Norse Voyages, A.D. 1000

Western Settlement
Greenland
Eastern Settlement
Iceland
Norwegian Sea
Arctic Circle
Norway
Labrador Sea
NORTH ATLANTIC OCEAN
North Sea
Labrador
L'Anse-aux-Meadows
Vinland (Newfoundland)
England
France
Nova Scotia
N

— Route of Norse settlement
— Route of Erik the Red (late 900s)
— Route of Leif Eriksson (late 900s)
--- Norse trading voyages

0   1,000 miles
0   1,000 kilometers

Map Study

Location Sea traders from Norway explored the North American coastline around the year 1000. **On what present-day Canadian island did the Norse build their Vinland settlement?**

At the heart of a manor was the castle, where the lord and family members lived. The castles had walls 2 or 3 feet (61–91 cm) thick to help guard against attackers. Many had the extra protection of **moats,** or waterways, that surrounded the castles. Homes, fields, gardens, and mills were spread out over the manor.

People who lived on a manor performed services for the lord. In exchange the lord promised to protect them. This system of managing the land and its people is called the feudal system. Many small farmers and landowners turned over all their land to a feudal lord in exchange for protection. Some agreed to be soldiers in the lord's army.

Landless peasants, or serfs, who lived and worked on a manor farmed small plots and shared their harvests with the lord. Serfs were considered part of the manor and remained with the land even if a new lord took over a manor.

For 500 years manors provided for most of the people's needs. People living on different manors had little contact with one another, except perhaps in times of battle between lords.

Trade, travel, and cities that had thrived under Roman rule declined. There was little opportunity for people to communicate or exchange new ideas.

★ Decline of the Feudal System

Beginning around the year 1000—about the same time that Leif Eriksson visited North America—several changes began taking place in Europe. Many workers who had been tied to the manors were not happy with their lives. They longed for more freedom.

Life in Towns

Some people managed to leave their manors and move to towns to earn their own livings. There they became craft workers or started businesses. Some became traders.

Moving to a town did not always make life more comfortable. The towns at this time were very crowded and dirty. Garbage was tossed into the streets and diseases spread quickly.

Between 1347 and 1352 a deadly disease spread throughout Europe, killing more than one-fourth of its population. Called the Black Death, the disease was carried by fleas on rats. This disaster broke down what remained of the feudal system.

The New Middle Class

As Europe slowly recovered from the Black Death, towns began to grow again. People became less separated and isolated as increasing trade brought them into contact with one another. At the same time, a new social class—the middle class—began to develop. The **middle class** was made up mostly of merchants who bought and sold goods for a living. It also included lawyers, doctors, and some government officials. Unlike the lords of the manors, people of the middle class were not interested in land and farming. They focused instead on business and trade.

★ Crusades to the Holy Land

Religion played an important role in the changes that took place in Europe during this time. As early as 1096, a series of wars fought for religious reasons helped to open the eyes of Western Europeans to the rest of the world.

Christian and Muslim Conflict

The religious wars were fought in Palestine, a land in Southwest Asia along the eastern edge of the Mediterranean

Linking Past and Present

Hanging in the Sky

People dreamed of flying or floating in the sky long before anyone figured out how to do it.

Then

Just a Sketch

The idea for the first parachute came from

▶ DA VINCI'S PARACHUTE SKETCH

Renaissance artist, scientist, and inventor Leonardo da Vinci. His sketch, drawn in about 1495, showed a fabric parachute in the shape of a large, hollow pyramid.

Now

Safety and Sport

Almost 300 years after Da Vinci, Sebastien Lenormand made the first parachute jump from a tower. Later, parachutes saved the lives of pilots and others whose balloons or airplanes were headed for a crash. They also served as brakes to stop landing aircraft.

Today, parachutes let skydivers jump from heights of as much as 3 miles (5 km) and float freely before opening their parachutes.

▶ MODERN SKYDIVER

Sea. Palestine was the Holy Land for both Christians and Muslims. Europe's Christians considered Palestine and its city of Jerusalem sacred, or holy. Muslims, followers of the religion of Islam, also considered Palestine a sacred city.

In 1071 a group of Turkish Muslims took over Jerusalem and closed it to all Christians. The Catholic Church was outraged. It called for warriors to free the Holy Land from the Turks. Christians all over Europe answered the call. Between 1096 and 1270, Christians from Europe fought a series of wars, called the Crusades.

During the **First Crusade,** Christians captured the city of Jerusalem. Although the Christians held the city for about the next 100 years, the Muslims eventually recaptured it.

Returning Crusaders

The Crusades had an enormous impact on Europeans. Thousands of soldiers went off to these wars, never to return home. Many of those who did return brought back riches from the markets of Southwest Asia. Spices, silk, porcelain, ivory, jewels, soap, and perfumes filled their knapsacks. Some Crusaders also brought back new ideas. They had learned about new medicines to cure the sick and new ways to use spices to prevent food from spoiling.

The Crusaders got the new ideas and products from Muslim markets of Southwest Asia. Muslim merchants regularly traded with India, China, Japan, and other Asian countries. As Europeans learned of the products available from the East, they wanted to buy them.

★ The Rise of Nations in Europe

Europe's middle-class merchants saw an opportunity to make money by trading with the Muslim markets in Southwest Asia. They aided strong rulers in Europe

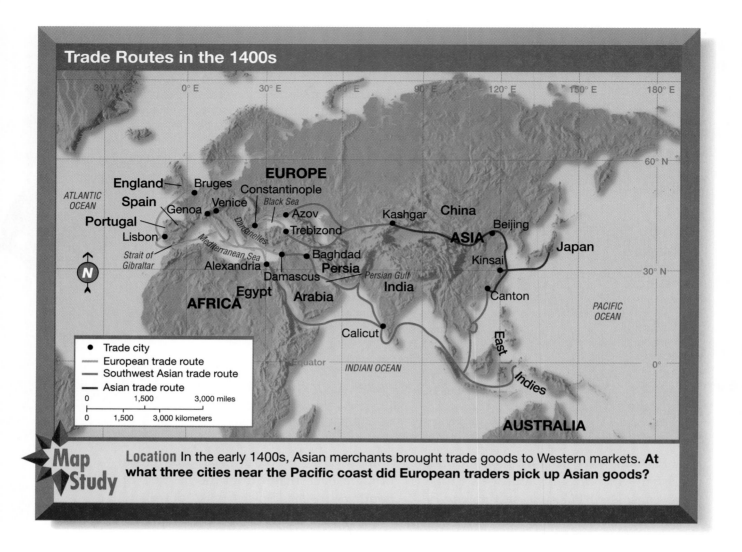

Trade Routes in the 1400s

Map Study

Location In the early 1400s, Asian merchants brought trade goods to Western markets. **At what three cities near the Pacific coast did European traders pick up Asian goods?**

in ending the wars among the feudal lords. Ending the fighting made it safe for them to travel to and from the Southwest Asian markets. Starting in the 1200s, European monarchs gained enough strength to begin forming nations, such as France, England, Spain, Portugal, and others.

In Italy, wealthy middle-class merchants gained a monopoly, or total control, over trade with the Muslim markets. In addition to trade goods, the Italian traders gained new knowledge from the Muslims. They learned about the magnetic compass, the astrolabe, and other sailing improvements. Europeans also shared the Muslim system of mathematics and styles of architecture.

Biography ★★★

Marco Polo Reports Wonders

Italy's **Marco Polo,** born into a family of wealthy merchants, grew up in Venice, Italy. In 1271 when Marco was 17, he accompanied his uncle and father on a trading journey to the East Asian land of Cathay, or present-day China. The merchants—traveling on camels for three-and-a-half years—crossed almost 7,000 miles (11,263 km) of Central Asian mountains and deserts. Finally they reached the palace of Cathay's ruler, called the Khan.

Marco Polo spent 17 years in service to the Khan. He saw and learned much. The people of Cathay had an advanced culture.

▲ MARCO POLO

★ A Rebirth of Learning

Despite the criticism Marco Polo received, many people read his book, *Description of the World.* It helped make more and more Europeans curious about the world beyond their city walls. That curiosity sparked a period of renewed interest in learning and knowledge called the Renaissance. Europe's Renaissance began in the middle 1300s and lasted until about 1600.

Renaissance Art and Science

The Renaissance was a time of creativity and experimentation. Artists began to present their subjects more realistically than in the past. Artists, such as **Michelangelo** and **Leonardo da Vinci,** created beautiful paintings and drawings to show nature and people as they really looked. Writers such as William Shakespeare also produced many great poems and plays.

Renaissance scientists worked toward a better understanding of the human body and how it functions. They studied the movement of the planets and set up exeriments using new scientific instruments they had invented.

They read printed books, used paper money, and even had city fire departments. Their large, well-organized cities had canals, orderly road systems, and hot water.

In 1295, when the Polos returned to Italy, Marco told others about the riches he had found and the people he had met. He reported that there were more than 7,000 islands in the Sea of China that he called the "Indies." He talked of incredible "black stones"—or coal—that fueled fires and of rubies the size of a man's arm. ★★★

★ SECTION 1 REVIEW ★

Checking for Understanding

1. **Identify** Leif Eriksson, Marco Polo, Michelangelo, Leonardo da Vinci, Greenland, Newfoundland.

2. **Define** saga, Middle Ages, monarch, manor, feudal system, serf, Crusades, Renaissance.

3. **Why** did the Norse want to travel to North America following Eriksson's voyage?

4. **How** did the Crusades lead to increased trade?

Critical Thinking

5. **Formulating Questions**   If people in Renaissance Europe had been able to talk to the Norse, what two questions do you think they might have asked?

ACTIVITY

6. Find five items at home or in your classroom that were made in other countries. On an outline map of the world, write the names of those items on the countries they came from.

Reading a Time Line

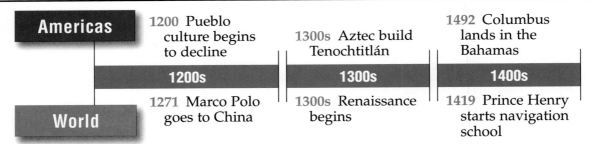

Americas			
1200 Pueblo culture begins to decline	1300s Aztec build Tenochtitlán	1492 Columbus lands in the Bahamas
1200s	**1300s**	**1400s**
1271 Marco Polo goes to China	1300s Renaissance begins	1419 Prince Henry starts navigation school
World			

When you read a time line, you not only see when an event took place but you also see what events took place before and after it. A time line can show you if Columbus sailed to North America before or after the Crusades. It can tell you if the Crusades began before or after the Renaissance.

Learning the Skill

A **time line** is a kind of chart that can be presented on a horizontal or vertical line. It lists events that occurred between specific dates. The number of years between these dates is called the **time span.** For example, a time line that begins in 1400 and ends in 1500 would have a time span of 100 years. A time line that begins in 1490 and ends in 1500 would have a 10-year time span.

Time lines are usually divided into smaller segments, or **time intervals.** If you look at the two time lines below, you'll see that the first time line has a 30-year time span divided into 10-year time intervals. The second time line has a 6-year time span divided into 2-year time intervals.

1400	1410	1420	1430

1490	1492	1494	1496

Sometimes a time line shows events that occurred during the same time period but in two different parts of the world. For example, the time line above shows some important happenings in the Americas and the rest of the world during the same time span.

Practicing the Skill

Use the time line above to answer these questions.

1. What time span and intervals appear on this time line?

2. What events appear above the line? What events appear below the line?

3. After Marco Polo's trip to China, how many years passed before Prince Henry started his navigation school?

4. Did Columbus's voyage to the Bahamas occur before or after the Renaissance began in Europe?

5. How many years before Columbus's voyage did Marco Polo set out for China?

APPLYING THE SKILL

6. Create a time line of your family's history. Interview family members to identify at least 8 to 10 important family events. Place them across the top of your time line. Across the bottom of your time line, place at least five important national or world events that occurred during the same time span.

★★

Portugal and the Age of Exploration

SETTING THE SCENE

Read to Learn . . .

- ★ how Prince Henry led Portugal into the Age of Exploration.
- ★ how trade contributed to the growth of three large empires in Africa.
- ★ about the achievements of Portuguese sea captains.

Terms to Know

- ★ navigation
- ★ caravel
- ★ Age of Exploration
- ★ enslaved person

People to Meet

- ★ Prince Henry
- ★ Mansa Musa
- ★ Bartholomeu Dias
- ★ Vasco da Gama

Places to Locate

- ★ Portugal
- ★ Cape of Good Hope
- ★ India

◀ PRINCE HENRY
THE NAVIGATOR

In the early 1400s, Europeans had no idea what lay in the ocean waters south of **Portugal.** That would change with **Prince Henry** of Portugal. Henry had no wife or family. As the third son of King John I of Portugal, he had little hope of ever being king. Henry had one driving interest, however. That idea was to make Portugal the world's leading sea power.

★ Prince Henry of Portugal

Prince Henry of Portugal was deeply affected by the spirit of learning during the Renaissance. He was also a very religious man. For the Catholic Church he wanted to spread the Christian faith around the world.

Two special goals for his country guided Henry. One goal was to find an ocean route around Africa to Asia. The other goal was to locate the source of the gold that came from lands far to the south in Africa.

Europeans were familiar with areas of North Africa along the Mediterranean Sea. The rest of the continent, however, was largely unknown to them. The African gold that Europeans received

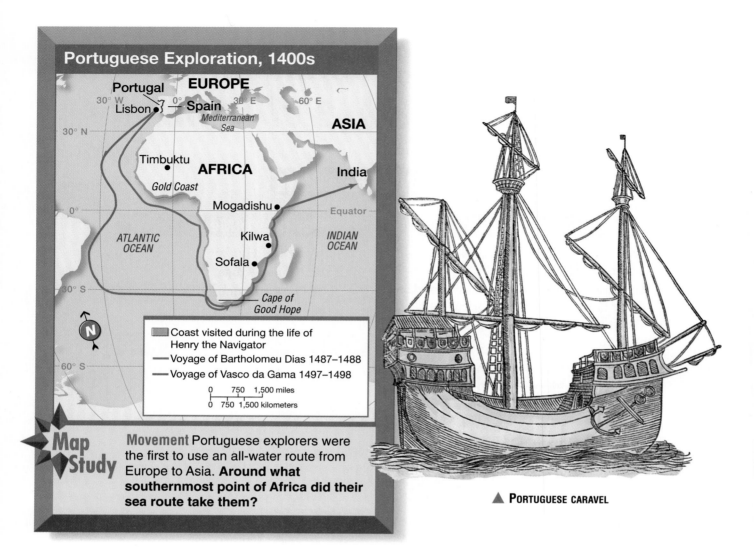

Portuguese Exploration, 1400s

Map legend:
- ▭ Coast visited during the life of Henry the Navigator
- — Voyage of Bartholomeu Dias 1487–1488
- — Voyage of Vasco da Gama 1497–1498

0 750 1,500 miles
0 750 1,500 kilometers

Map Study — **Movement** Portuguese explorers were the first to use an all-water route from Europe to Asia. **Around what southernmost point of Africa did their sea route take them?**

▲ PORTUGUESE CARAVEL

through trade came from Muslim traders who traveled overland and brought the gold to the northern shores of Africa.

To accomplish his goals, Henry realized that Portuguese sailors needed to know more about navigation—the science of piloting ships. He also knew that the Portuguese needed better ships. Henry's first step was to bring together mapmakers, astronomers, and shipbuilders from throughout the Mediterranean world to study and plan voyages of exploration. These experts pooled their talents to uncover knowledge about the seas and to extend the art of navigation.

Portuguese shipbuilders designed a sturdy ship called the caravel. The caravel used triangular sails, fashioned after those

first developed by Arab seafarers. These ships could easily sail against the wind and work their way in and out along coastlines. The caravel was easy to navigate for Portuguese sailors exploring the west coast of Africa.

The Age of Exploration

Prince Henry, who would later be called **Prince Henry the Navigator,** never commanded a ship. Rarely did he even sail on one. Although he would not live to see all that his sailors accomplished, his dream of making Portugal a leading sea power was to come true.

As expeditions returned, Henry's mapmakers corrected and improved their sailing charts. Bit by bit, expedition after expedition, the Portuguese inched their way down the coast of Africa.

Portugal led the rest of Europe into the great Age of Exploration. The Age of Exploration occurred during the 1400s and 1500s. During this period, sea captains and explorers from many different European countries sailed the oceans and mapped the world more accurately than ever had been done before.

For 40 years, one Portuguese expedition after another set out to explore the Atlantic Ocean and the west coast of Africa. In the 1430s the Portuguese sailed more than 1,000 miles (1,600 km) west into the Atlantic and landed on the Azores Islands.

★ Three African Empires

By 1460, the year of Henry's death, the Portuguese had sailed about one-fourth of the way down the west coast of Africa, looking for a way around it. Their voyages showed them that Africa was not the small peninsula they had believed it to be. It was, instead, a huge landmass. Their stops along the coast also showed them that Africa was a place with many peoples, languages, cultures, and a long history of wealth and power.

During Europe's Middle Ages, large, wealthy kingdoms with important cities of trade and learning developed in West Africa. Three large kingdoms—Ghana, Mali, and Songhai—controlled trade routes that ran from North Africa to the West African coast. Gold, salt, ivory, leather, iron, and other goods passed back and forth through their markets.

Most West Africans traded directly with Muslims from North Africa. Muslim merchants made the 1,200-mile (1,931-km) journey south across the **Sahara** in large camel caravans to West African markets.

Picturing History

▲ **PORTUGUESE HARBOR** The growing Portuguese trade began to compete with that of other European countries. **What goods did trading ships bring back to Portugal?**

Ghana

Between 700 and 1050, the empire of Ghana flourished in West Africa. In the markets of Ghana's capital, Kumbi, merchants traded large amounts of gold and salt. Dates, ivory, cloth, and honey also changed hands.

Because most of the traders in Ghana were Muslim, the capital city had a large Muslim pop-

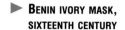

▶ **BENIN IVORY MASK, SIXTEENTH CENTURY**

ulation. Many Islamic houses of worship, called mosques, were built. The people of Ghana adapted many Muslim ideas, including a writing and numbering system.

Mali

By the 1200s the empire of Ghana was replaced by the empire of Mali. The Mali trading city of **Timbuktu** became a leading center of Islamic culture. **Mansa Musa,** the most powerful of the Mali kings, persuaded some of Islam's finest scholars and architects to work in Timbuktu. They built large buildings and several universities. Students from across Africa came to study at the universities. When Mansa Musa died, the kingdom of Mali weakened. By 1500, a third large empire was reaching its height and replaced Mali.

Songhai

The Songhai empire grew rich from trade in gold and ivory. Under Askia Muhammad, who ruled the empire from 1493 to 1528, Songhai rose to the height of its power. As with the Mali empire, Muslim merchants had a strong influence on the culture. They built many mosques and schools and instructed the local people in the ways of the Islamic faith.

Songhai, larger than either the Ghana or Mali empire, extended across a large portion of West Africa. It stood until 1591, when North African soldiers armed with guns invaded and defeated it.

★ Portugal's Search for Riches

Portuguese sea captains stopping along the West African coast heard of the inland trading kingdoms. Such stories of wealth encouraged the Portuguese. Surely they were coming closer to meeting Prince Henry's goal of finding the source of African gold.

Picturing History

▲ **THE SLAVE TRADE** King Affonso of the Kongo, tried unsuccessfully to stop the European slave trade. The rulers of Benin and the Gold Coast also tried to resist the Europeans. **Where did Portugal develop a trade in human beings?**

As the Portuguese pushed south and rounded the bulge of Africa, they gave names to the lands they visited. The names reflected the products widely traded in each area. The Portuguese called one coastal area the **Ivory Coast,** for example, and another place the **Gold Coast.** There was also an area the Portuguese called the **Slave Coast.**

Enslavement of Africans

It was on the Slave Coast that the Portuguese developed a trade in human beings. They brought Africans back to Portugal and sold them at a public auction as enslaved persons. An enslaved person is one forced to serve another person in ways decided by the slaveholder. Enslaved persons have no freedom, and slaveholders think of them as their property.

★ A Passage to India

The Portuguese continued to take what they found of value in Africa. By the mid-1400s, the Portuguese had met Prince Henry's goal of finding riches and profits. They still had not found a way around Africa and on to Asia.

Year after year, Portuguese sailors continued to inch their way south along the coast of Africa. Then, in 1488, explorer **Bartholomeu Dias** (DEE•AHSH) sailed as far south as present-day South Africa. A storm blew his three ships farther out to sea. When the storm ended nearly two weeks later, Dias realized that it had blown his ships around the southern tip of Africa and into the Indian Ocean.

Too tired to push ahead, Dias and his crew returned to Portugal. The Portuguese king was so encouraged by Dias's report that he named the southern tip of Africa the **Cape of Good Hope.** The king felt sure that he would soon realize his hope of reaching **India** by sailing around Africa.

Crossing the Indian Ocean

The king had to wait about 10 more years. In the summer of 1497 another Portuguese explorer, **Vasco da Gama,** headed south along the coast of Africa. He rounded the Cape of Good Hope in November and then set a course across the Indian Ocean. In May of 1498, Da Gama landed on the west coast of India. Before returning to Portugal, he filled his ships with spices, silks, jewels, glassware, and other Asian trade goods.

★ SECTION 2 REVIEW ★

Checking for Understanding

1. **Identify** Prince Henry, Mansa Musa, Bartholomeu Dias, Vasco da Gama, Portugal, Cape of Good Hope, India.

2. **Define** navigation, caravel, Age of Exploration, enslaved person.

3. **What** two special goals did Prince Henry have for Portugal?

4. **What** products were traded throughout West African kingdoms?

5. **Why** were the voyages of Bartholomeu Dias and Vasco da Gama important?

Critical Thinking

6. **Analyzing Information** Why do you think Portuguese seafarers made their voyages of discovery *after* the Renaissance, and not *before* this period?

ACTIVITY

7. Use the scale on the world map in the Reference Atlas in the back of the book to figure out about how many miles the Portuguese sailed to reach the Cape of Good Hope and the west coast of India. Draw a map showing the routes. Put mileage information on the routes.

Motives for Exploration

▲ NEW EUROPEAN MARKETS

▼ CHINESE PORCELAIN

Have you ever wanted to buy something, but thought the price was just too high? Do you know what made that item so costly? Maybe it comes from far away and the cost of transporting it is high. Perhaps the item is scarce. Gold is expensive because the world supply is short. Buyer demand could also be a factor. If many people want to buy the item, the price will probably be high.

Wealthy Europeans of the 1400s wanted to buy fine porcelain, jewels, silk, and spices from East Asia. Because the Turkish Muslims controlled all the trade routes to Asia, they could also control the prices of goods that traveled along those routes. As Europeans demanded more and more Asian goods, the Muslim merchants raised their prices.

To get these goods for less, Europeans wanted to find a way to go around the Muslim traders altogether. The solution they settled on was to find their own route to East Asia by sea.

Making the Economics Connection

1. Name three things that can affect the price of an item.

2. Why did Turkish Muslim traders think they could get the high prices they charged for Asian goods?

3. What was Europe's solution to paying high prices for Asian goods?

ACTIVITY

4. Think of a costly item you have seen in a store. Imagine that you are a merchant who sells the item. Create a newspaper advertisement convincing people to buy the item despite its cost.

★★

Columbus Reaches the Americas

SETTING THE SCENE

Read to Learn . . .

★ why Christopher Columbus believed he could reach Asia by sailing west.
★ what places in the Americas Columbus visited.

Terms to Know

★ mutiny
★ Taino
★ colony

People to Meet

★ Christopher Columbus
★ Queen Isabella
★ King Ferdinand
★ Amerigo Vespucci

Places to Locate

★ San Salvador
★ Bahamas
★ Cuba
★ Hispaniola
★ Santo Domingo

▶ **EXPLORER'S LOG BOOK**

More than 150 years after Marco Polo's death, a young Italian sea captain—**Christopher Columbus**—sat down to read Polo's *Description of the World*. While many scholars still didn't take Polo seriously, the young captain believed every word he read.

★ Marco Polo's Geography

Columbus was especially interested in what Polo had to say about the islands of Cipango. What Polo called Cipango is present-day Japan. According to Polo,

Cipango lay some 1,500 miles (2,414 km) off the eastern shore of Asia.

Polo's geography was not accurate. The islands of Japan are actually less than 500 miles (805 km) from the coast of Asia.

Columbus pondered Polo's report. Because the earth is round, Columbus reasoned, a person should be able to sail west from Europe and reach Asia. Furthermore, if Cipango was 1,500 miles off the coast of Asia, it was actually much closer to Europe than anyone thought. Armed with this misinformation, Christopher Columbus began his lifelong quest to reach Asia by sailing west.

▲ *KOLUMBUS IN FRONT OF FERDINAND AND ISABELLA OF ARAGON IN SANTA FE* by V. Prozik, 1884 With careful attention to detail the artist shows the serious discussion held concerning the planned voyage of Columbus. **For how many years did Columbus try to gain the support of Spain?**

★ Columbus's Vision

Like many Italians of his time, Columbus went to sea at an early age. Then, at 26, he sailed with an Italian fleet along the coast of Portugal.

For several years, Columbus lived in Portugal. The Portuguese taught Columbus new sailing skills and theories about geography. He made several voyages on Portuguese ships to Africa and sailed as far north as Iceland. In the process, he became an expert navigator.

The Portuguese Say "No"

By the early 1480s, Columbus felt ready to make his own trip of exploration. He asked Portugal's King John for money to supply a westward voyage to Asia. Columbus argued that this route would be shorter and easier than the eastward passage around Africa that the Portuguese were looking for. Dias and Da Gama had not yet sailed around Africa when Columbus made his appeal.

Portuguese experts discussed Columbus's plan. They agreed that he could probably get to Asia by sailing west, but they thought he had misjudged the distance. King John agreed. He refused Columbus's request and claimed that Portugal would continue trying to reach Asia by sailing around Africa.

The Spanish Say "Yes"

By now, Columbus was deeply in debt. He did not give up, however. He left Portugal and went to Spain in 1485 to ask the Spanish monarchs **Queen Isabella** and **King Ferdinand** to finance his voyage.

For seven years, Columbus tried to gain support from the Spanish rulers. Each time he asked, experts studied the matter and refused his plan. Finally, just as Columbus was ready to give up, Queen Isabella consented to give him the backing he needed for the voyage.

★ Voyage Across the Atlantic

On August 3, 1492, Columbus left Spain with three small ships. The largest ship, his flagship, was named the *Santa María.* The other two were the *Pinta* and *Niña*.

Columbus and a crew of 90 men and boys first sailed south to the Canary Islands. There the small fleet took on supplies, refilled water casks, and repaired sails. Then, in the early morning hours of September 6, Columbus set out westward across the Atlantic Ocean.

Winds and Weather

At first the voyage went smoothly. The weather was calm, and winds pushed the three ships steadily westward. Columbus had discovered the sea route with the most favorable winds.

After about another month of smooth sailing, the crew became impatient. They had never been away from land this many days. They demanded that Columbus

turn back. If not, they would mutiny, or seize the captain and officers and take control of the ship.

★ "Tierra! Tierra!"

Columbus promised his worried crew to sail home if land was not found in another three days. Just two days later the crew began to see drifting tree branches in the water around the ships—a sign that land was nearby. Columbus promised a reward to the first crew member who sighted land.

Landing in the Bahamas

At 2 o'clock the next morning, the look-out sailor on the *Pinta* suddenly shouted, *"Tierra! Tierra!"*—Land! Land! On October 12, 1492, after 70 days and 2,400 miles

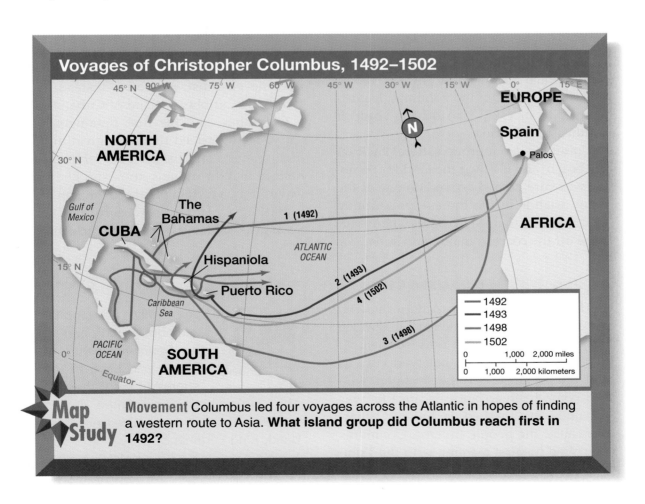

Voyages of Christopher Columbus, 1492–1502

Map Study

Movement Columbus led four voyages across the Atlantic in hopes of finding a western route to Asia. **What island group did Columbus reach first in 1492?**

▲ COLUMBUS REACHES LAND Columbus and his crew had sailed for more than two months when they reached San Salvador. **For what country did they claim this island?**

" I . . . gave to some of them red caps, and glass beads to put round their necks, and many other things of little value, which gave them great pleasure, and made them so much our friends that it was a marvel to see. They afterwards came to the ship's boats where we were, swimming and bringing us parrots, cotton threads, . . . darts, and many other things. "

Columbus quickly noticed the small gold jewelry the Taino wore. He was curious about the source of the gold. One of his goals in sailing to distant lands was to bring back proof of the riches that could be found there.

(3,862 km) of sailing, Columbus had found land.

At dawn the three ships neared an island with a beautiful, white coral beach. Columbus named the island **San Salvador** which meant "Holy Savior." Today, this island is part of the **Bahamas,** located about 50 miles (80 km) off the coast of southeastern Florida.

Columbus led a group ashore, knelt on the beach, and claimed the land for Spain. He was sure he had arrived on one of the many islands in the Indies—present-day East Indies—that Marco Polo had said were off the coast of mainland China.

Meeting With Native Americans

The Taino, the Native Americans who lived on the island, watched the strange large ships that brought bearded men. At first they held back, but they were curious and finally ran to see the strangers who had come to their land. Because he was certain he had reached the Indies, Columbus called the people Indians. Columbus described his first meeting with the Taino in his log:

★ Exploring the Caribbean

With six Taino as guides, Columbus left San Salvador to search for Cipango, which he believed must be nearby. Instead, he found the Caribbean island of **Cuba.**

Columbus saw his first flamingos in Cuba. He described them as "great birds like cranes, but bright red." He also noticed that the Indians smoked rolled-up leaves from a certain plant growing on the island. The plant was tobacco, but the Spaniards called it *tabaco,* which they

★★★ AMERICA'S FLAGS ★★★

Spain, 1492 Christopher Columbus proudly carried the Spanish banner of Castile and Leon to the shores of the Bahamas. The flag's castle represented Queen Isabella. The lion symbolized her husband, King Ferdinand.
★★★★★★★★★★★★★★★★★★★★★★★★

probably took from a Native American word. Columbus and later explorers eventually introduced tobacco to Europe.

Hispaniola

Columbus left Cuba to continue his search for the mainland of Asia—and the source of more gold. He found his way to an island he named **Hispaniola.** Today this island is divided into the countries of Haiti and the Dominican Republic. In Hispaniola, Columbus was sure he had found the source of the Indians' gold because all the people wore gold jewelry.

Columbus and his crew met with their first disaster on Hispaniola. On Christmas Eve, while Columbus and most of the crew were sleeping, the *Santa María* ran aground and was wrecked on a sandbar.

Columbus saw this as a sign that he should have some of his men set up a settlement while he went on to explore further. His crew then used wood from the shipwrecked *Santa María* to build a fort.

★ A Hero's Welcome

On March 4, 1493, after three months of exploring the Caribbean, Columbus set sail for home. He returned to Spain in triumph. His news was received with great excitement, and people were eager to hear his tales of the "Indies."

Columbus reported to the Spanish king and queen, escorted by six Native Americans carrying parrots in cages. He brought gold jewelry and spices as proof that he had found what he still believed to be the Indies.

The Spanish monarchs were curious about the people, but they were more interested in the stories of gold. Eager for riches, they were ready to finance more voyages for Columbus.

★ Later Voyages

Columbus sailed to the Americas three more times between 1493 and 1502. He stopped at many of the islands in the Caribbean Sea including present-day Jamaica. He also landed on the coast of present-day Venezuela and sailed along the coast of Central America.

First Spanish Colony

On his second voyage in 1496, Columbus founded **Santo Domingo** on Hispaniola. It was the first permanent European colony in the Western Hemisphere. A colony is a settlement made in another land by people who are ruled by their home countries. Columbus and two of his brothers governed the colony on Hispaniola over the next four years.

▲ COLUMBUS RETURNS Upon returning to Spain, Columbus shared some of the treasures he had brought back with the Spanish king and queen. **Why were the Spanish monarchs eager for Columbus to make another voyage?**

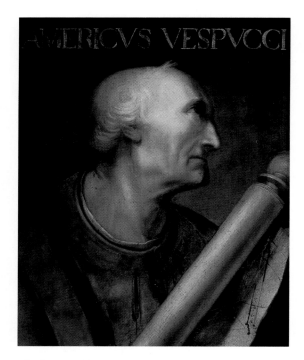
▲ AMERIGO VESPUCCI

Meaning of Columbus's Voyages

Columbus's discoveries brought little gold to Spain. Columbus also did a poor job of governing the Spanish colony at Hispaniola. As a result, he gradually slipped out of favor with the Spanish court. He returned from his last voyage in 1504. Columbus died in 1506, unaware that he had arrived at two uncharted continents.

Other Europeans, however, were quick to recognize that Columbus had sailed to lands that they had never imagined. Soon after Columbus's voyages, other Europeans sailed to the Americas. Still other European sea captains would continue the Age of Exploration with more voyages into uncharted seas. The countries of Spain, France, Portugal, Italy, England, and the Netherlands would all send expeditions searching for new lands and a shorter route to Asia.

★ America, Not Columbia

Amerigo Vespucci (veh•SPOO•chee) was the Italian explorer for whom America was named. Why did Europeans not name America after Columbus?

Vespucci sailed to North America a few years after Columbus. Sailing for Spain and Portugal, he explored the Atlantic coast of South America between 1497 and 1504. Vespucci was one of the first explorers to realize that he had reached uncharted lands. Unlike Columbus, Vespucci wrote that he had come to "a new world," not the East Indies—as the Asian islands were called later. Vespucci published his claims in a booklet that a German mapmaker read in 1507. When the mapmaker drew a map of the two continents, he chose the name "America," based on Vespucci's name.

★ SECTION 3 REVIEW ★

Checking for Understanding

1. **Identify** Christopher Columbus, Queen Isabella and King Ferdinand, Amerigo Vespucci, San Salvador, Bahamas, Cuba, Hispaniola, Santo Domingo.

2. **Define** mutiny, Taino, colony.

3. **What** was Columbus's plan for reaching Asia by sea?

4. **What** islands did Columbus explore on his first two voyages to the Americas?

Critical Thinking

5. **Interpreting Information** Think about what was achieved by Columbus and other explorers during the Age of Exploration. What other name or title could have been given to this period of time?

ACTIVITY

6. Sketch a freehand historical map of the world using the knowledge available at the time of Columbus.

★★

Early European Claims to the Americas

SETTING THE SCENE

Read to Learn . . .

★ how Spain took control of the Caribbean area.
★ about the voyages and claims of Spanish, English, and French explorers.

Terms to Know

★ plantation
★ Columbian Exchange
★ strait
★ Northwest Passage

People to Meet

★ Vasco Núñez de Balboa
★ Ferdinand Magellan
★ John Cabot
★ Giovanni da Verrazano
★ Jacques Cartier

Places to Locate

★ Isthmus of Panama
★ Strait of Magellan
★ Philippine Islands

▶ DRAKE'S TROPHY

> " They have no arms [weapons], and are without warlike instincts; they . . . are so timid that a thousand would not stand before three of our men. So that they are good to be ordered about. . . . "

This was one of Columbus's descriptions of Native Americans he met in the Caribbean. In his logs, Columbus made it clear that he saw the Native Americans as servants to the Spaniards.

★ Spain Conquers the Caribbean

After Columbus set up his colony in Hispaniola, Spain sent more ships and explorers to the Caribbean Islands. In addition to Hispaniola, the Spanish conquered Cuba, Puerto Rico, and Jamaica in their search for riches.

Treatment of Native Americans

Native Americans soon came to fear the Spaniards. Using guns, which Native Americans had never seen before, the Spaniards killed thousands of people. Those who survived were enslaved.

By 1510 most of the gold in the Caribbean Islands had been mined, so the Spaniards turned to agriculture. They raised cattle and horses brought with them from Spain. They also set up plantations, or large farms that usually produce only one crop to be sold. On the plantations the Spaniards grew sugarcane, cotton, and other crops. Enslaved Native

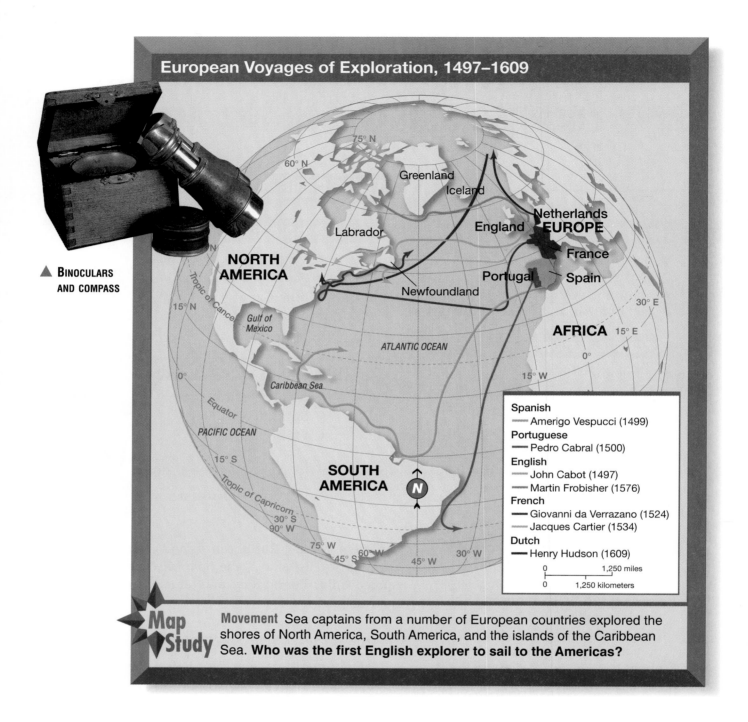

European Voyages of Exploration, 1497–1609

75° N
60° N
Greenland
Iceland
Labrador
Netherlands
England **EUROPE**
NORTH AMERICA
France
Portugal Spain
Newfoundland
Tropic of Cancer
15° N
Gulf of Mexico
30° E
AFRICA 15° E
ATLANTIC OCEAN
0°
15° W
Caribbean Sea
0°
Equator
PACIFIC OCEAN
15° S
SOUTH AMERICA
N
Tropic of Capricorn
30° S
90° W
75° W 60° W 45° W 30° W
45° S
45° W

Spanish
— Amerigo Vespucci (1499)
Portuguese
— Pedro Cabral (1500)
English
— John Cabot (1497)
— Martin Frobisher (1576)
French
— Giovanni da Verrazano (1524)
— Jacques Cartier (1534)
Dutch
— Henry Hudson (1609)

0   1,250 miles
0   1,250 kilometers

▲ **BINOCULARS AND COMPASS**

Map Study **Movement** Sea captains from a number of European countries explored the shores of North America, South America, and the islands of the Caribbean Sea. **Who was the first English explorer to sail to the Americas?**

Americans worked the plantations. When the Spaniards needed more workers, they brought enslaved Africans to the islands. Hundreds of Native Americans were also loaded onto ships and taken back to Spain to be sold into slavery.

The exchange of goods and ideas and people between Europe and the Americas came to be called the **Columbian Exchange,** named after Christopher

Columbus. The most deadly part of the exchange came with the passing of disease from Europeans to the Native Americans.

Spanish Priests in the Caribbean

The Spaniards felt it was also their duty to bring the Catholic faith to the Native Americans. They sent priests and missionaries along with the soldiers and explorers.

Some Spanish priests tried to defend the Native Americans against the harsh treatment of the soldiers.

One priest, **Bartolomé de Las Casas,** worked among the Native Americans for 50 years. He appealed to the Spanish government to help them. The government in Spain did establish rules for their protection. However, rules made in Europe were difficult to enforce thousands of miles across the ocean in the Caribbean.

★ Balboa and the Pacific

It took about 30 years for European explorers to realize that even after crossing the Atlantic, they were still a long way from Asia. They finally recognized, too, that North and South America were blocking their way. They did not give up the goal of finding a western sea route to Asia, however. They believed they could find a route through or around the two continents.

Spanish explorer **Vasco Núñez de Balboa** was the first European to discover a way across the Americas. His route, however, was a land route. Balboa first sailed to the **Isthmus of Panama,** the thin strip of land that joins North and South America. Then, in 1513 with the help of several hundred Native Americans and 190 crew members, he crossed the isthmus on foot.

The 45-mile (72-km) crossing was very difficult and took about a month to complete. Some reports said the treetops over the soldiers' heads were so dense that the sky was blocked out for days. Balboa's crew had to walk overland through thick plant growth in severe heat. They hacked their way through with large knives, fighting off insects, snakes, and fever.

At last Balboa saw an expanse of water ahead. In full armor, he rushed into the water to claim it and all the land it touched for Spain. Although he did not know it at the time, the waters Balboa claimed were another ocean—the **Pacific Ocean.**

★ Magellan Sails Around the World

After Balboa arrived at the Pacific Ocean, European explorers still had to cross an ocean to reach Asia. No one realized how large that ocean was, but **Ferdinand Magellan,** a Portuguese sea captain sailing for Spain, would be the first to find out.

Magellan was convinced he could find a way around the tip of South America, across the sea that Balboa had discovered, and on to Asia. He began his journey in 1519 with five ships and 241 sailors. His list of supplies included 2,800 pounds (1,271 kg) of cheese, 1,300 pounds (590 kg) of honey, 10,000 sardines, 800 pounds (363 kg) of flour, and 250 strings of garlic bulbs.

Naming the Pacific

Once Magellan reached southeastern South America, it took his fleet several months to travel down the coast. He stopped for supplies, to make repairs, and

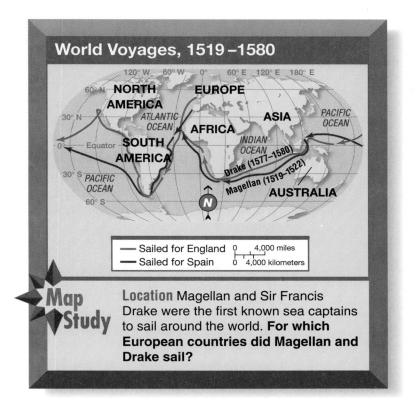

World Voyages, 1519–1580

Sailed for England
Sailed for Spain
0   4,000 miles
0   4,000 kilometers

Map Study

Location Magellan and Sir Francis Drake were the first known sea captains to sail around the world. **For which European countries did Magellan and Drake sail?**

▲ FERDINAND MAGELLAN

was often delayed by bad weather. Wherever he went ashore, he claimed the land for Spain.

When Magellan approached the southern tip of South America, he sailed into a rocky, treacherous strait—a narrow channel of water. The strait was filled with many tiny islands and narrow, curving channels that came to dead ends. For six long weeks, the ships inched their way through the strait.

Finally, on the western side of South America, the ships came into a vast, calm ocean. Magellan named the waters "Pacific," which means "peaceful." Compared with the stormy Atlantic, the Pacific Ocean looked still and quiet. The dangerous strait through which his ships had just passed would later be called the **Strait of Magellan.**

To the Philippines and Spain

Magellan expected to reach Asia in just a few weeks after rounding South America. After months of sailing, however, there was still no sight of land.

Finally in the spring of 1521, after a brief stop on the island of Guam, Magellan landed in the **Philippine Islands.** It would be his final stop. Only three ships remained, and many crew members had died. Magellan was killed when he became involved in a war among the islanders.

In 1522 the *Victoria*—the last of Magellan's original five ships—returned to Spain. The *Victoria* was the first ship ever to circle the world, an important accomplishment. Of the 241 men who set out on the 3-year, 50,000-mile (80,450-km) voyage, only 18 completed the trip.

★ The English Sail West

Although Spain led the way in the exploration of the Americas, other European countries were also interested in the lands to the west. England was the first country to send an expedition to the Americas after Columbus's voyages for Spain.

John Cabot's First Voyage

An Italian sea captain, born Giovanni Cabotto, led England's first voyage to America. In the 1480s, Cabotto moved to England and changed his name to **John Cabot.** Hearing of Columbus's voyages, he convinced England's King Henry VII to send him across the Atlantic in search of Asia.

Cabot made his first trip in 1497 and returned with news of a large landmass north of where Columbus had landed. Cabot had landed off the coast of Canada, on present-day Newfoundland. According to one account—in which he was most likely describing the Inuit—Cabot reported:

    The people of [the land] are dressed in the skins of animals; they use in their wars bows and arrows, lances and darts, and certain clubs of wood, and slings.

Like Columbus, Cabot assumed he had reached Asia. He thought if he traveled along the coast he would eventually reach China and the Indies.

Cabot's Second Voyage

The following year, Cabot made another voyage across the North Atlantic with five ships. After exploring the coast of North America, one ship turned back to England after a bad storm. The others never returned, disappearing without a trace. Cabot's fate is still a mystery.

The English put aside any further interest in the Americas after Cabot's disappearance. His voyages, however, gave England its first claim to land in North America.

★ The French and the Northwest Passage

Neither Balboa nor Magellan had revealed a route through or around the American continents. Other Europeans wondered if there might be a sea route farther north. They even gave such a possible waterway a name—the Northwest Passage.

The French began a search for the Northwest Passage in 1524. They hired Italian sailor **Giovanni da Verrazano** for their first explorations.

Verrazano explored the eastern coast of North America between present-day North Carolina and Nova Scotia. He was the first European to sail into the harbor of present-day New York City. Verrazano was unable to find a water route through North America to Asia, however.

The French tried to find the Northwest Passage again 10 years later. In 1534 and 1535, the French navigator **Jacques Cartier** (kahr•TYAY) made two voyages. He sailed partway up the St. Lawrence River and claimed present-day Canada for France. Like many more explorers who came after him, Cartier had no luck finding a water passage to Asia.

The Spaniards meanwhile took little interest in the idea of a Northwest Passage. They continued to focus on the more southern regions of the Americas.

Footnotes to History

Northwest Passage Found A Northwest Passage does exist—in the cold and ice-jammed waters around the islands of northern Canada. Explorers found the route during the 1800s. Norwegian explorer Roald Amundsen, however, was the first to successfully make an all-water trip through the Northwest Passage. His voyage lasted three years, from 1903 to 1906.

★ SECTION 4 REVIEW ★

Checking for Understanding

1. **Identify** Vasco Núñez de Balboa, Ferdinand Magellan, John Cabot, Giovanni da Verrazano, Jacques Cartier, Isthmus of Panama, Strait of Magellan, Philippine Islands.
2. **Define** plantation, Columbian Exchange, strait, Northwest Passage.
3. **What** did Balboa set out to find?
4. **Why** was Magellan's voyage important?

Critical Thinking

5. **Comparing Points of View** Why might other European countries have felt more of a need to develop a Northwest Passage than Spain did?

ACTIVITY

6. See if you can figure out a possible Northwest Passage. Sketch your route on an outline map of North America.

Using Key Vocabulary

Match the numbered items in Column A with their definitions in Column B.

Column A
1. feudal system
2. monarch
3. navigation
4. colony
5. plantation

Column B
a. territory governed and often settled by another country
b. science of sailing and piloting ships
c. large farm that usually grows only one crop meant to be sold
d. system for managing land during the Middle Ages
e. king or queen of a country

Reviewing Facts

1. **Explain** how the feudal system in Europe limited people's contact with one another.
2. **Describe** how the Crusades heightened European interest in trade.
3. **Identify** the first permanent European colony in the Western Hemisphere and when it was founded.
4. **Explain** how the Age of Exploration led to slaveholding in Europe and America.
5. **List** the achievements of explorers Balboa, Magellan, and Cartier.

Understanding Concepts

Economic Development

1. What changes brought about a growth in trade in Western Europe beginning around 1000?

2. Why did Spain continue exploring the Americas even though Columbus had not found much gold?

Influence of Technology

3. How did the development of skills and crafts by manor workers influence the feudal system?
4. How did Prince Henry of Portugal help to improve navigation?
5. What were some of the things that scientists were interested in during the Renaissance?

Critical Thinking

1. **Making Inferences**   Why do you think Western Europe did not try to find a sea route to Asia until after the 1400s?
2. **Analyzing Information**   Which of the voyages discussed in this chapter do you think had the greatest impact on the history of the United States? Explain your answer.

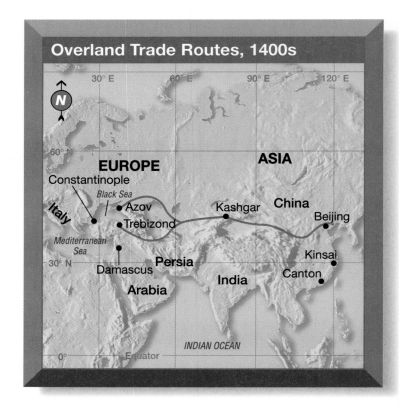

Overland Trade Routes, 1400s

CHAPTER 3 ★ REVIEW

1480–1499	1500–1519	1520–1539
1488 Dias sails around the Cape of Good Hope	**1513** Balboa reaches the Pacific Ocean	**1522** Magellan's world voyage completed
1492 Columbus arrives in the Bahamas	**1518** Spaniards bring enslaved Africans to America	**1534** Cartier explores Canada
1498 Columbus begins third voyage to America		
1498 Da Gama reaches India		

History and Geography

Overland Trade Routes

Study the map of overland trade routes in the 1400s shown on page 86. Then answer the following questions.

1. **Location**   What Chinese city was at the eastern end of the route across Asia?

2. **Place**   At what body of water in the west did the overland routes end?

3. **Movement**   Through what continents did the overland routes pass?

4. **Location**   What cities shown on this map would prosper more from trade routes over water rather than trade routes over land?

Practicing Skills

Reading a Time Line

Study the time line above. Then answer the following questions.

1. What is the time span on this time line?

2. How far apart are the intervals on this time line?

3. Which two events occurred in 1498?

4. How many years were there between Columbus's voyage to the Bahamas and the completion of Magellan's world voyage?

Cooperative Learning Interdisciplinary Activity: Language Arts

As a group, choose an explorer discussed in this chapter. Use library sources to research the explorer's life and achievements. Prepare an interview with that explorer. Plan the questions to ask and the answers you would expect the explorer to give. Include questions relating to the explorer's life as well as the explorations. Write the interview as a magazine article.

If you prefer, make a taped interview in which one member of your group speaks as the explorer and the other members ask questions.

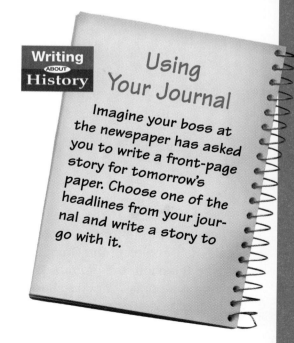

Writing ABOUT History

Using Your Journal

Imagine your boss at the newspaper has asked you to write a front-page story for tomorrow's paper. Choose one of the headlines from your journal and write a story to go with it.

Cultural Kaleidoscope

Early Homes in America

*H*omes for Native Americans meant dwellings adapted to their cultures and to the resources of their environments. To European settlers, building a home meant using the same resources while often adding a touch of the cultures they brought with them to America.

▼
In a Southwest Farming Village

Living in the desert called for houses airy enough to catch daytime breezes yet snug enough to give shelter from cool nights. The Yuma, Pagago, and other Native Americans used reeds and mud from riverbanks to build such houses. They used the reeds to construct a frame and the mud to plaster over the frame.

▲
Around the Great Lakes

Where there were forests, there were plentiful resources for home building. Peoples of the Great Lakes forests cut tall young trees and staked them into the ground. Then they fastened the tops together to create a dome- or cone-shaped frame. Over the frame, they tied sheets of bark that overlapped like shingles.

"Iroquois of the Longhouse"

The Iroquois in the Northeast Woodlands were known for the size and detail of their dwellings, called longhouses. Sheets of bark stripped from elm trees fit closely over domed pole frames, often reaching lengths of 100 feet (30 m). Inside, most longhouses were divided into separate sections for housing several families.

A Touch of Spain

Spaniards built houses with long porches and courtyards like those in Spain. The oldest Spanish house in America resides in St. Augustine, Florida. It reminds us that Spaniards settled there some four centuries ago.

Log Cabins

Swedish settlers in 1638 cut logs to build homes and trading posts along the Delaware River. The Swedes were not the first, however, to build log cabins in America. English settlers who came in the 1620s built houses by standing logs upright to form walls. The Swedes, however, laid logs horizontally to create the cabins popular among settlers in later years.

CHAPTER 4

★★

European Empires in the Americas 1500–1700

SETTING THE SCENE

Focus

After arriving in the Caribbean, the Spaniards continued their exploration of North and South America. Drawn by stories of gold, they conquered both the Aztec and Inca and seized their wealth. In the early 1600s, the French and Dutch also started American colonies.

Concepts to Understand

★ How America's resources contributed to the **economic development** of Spain, France, the Netherlands, and Sweden

★ How **conflict and cooperation** affected relations between Native Americans and European settlers

Read to Discover . . .

★ how the Spaniards settled and governed the lands they conquered.

★ what drew French, Dutch, and Swedish settlers to North America.

▶ Fᴜʀ ᴛʀᴀᴅɪɴɢ ᴄᴀᴍᴘ

Journal Notes

Imagine that the monarchs of Europe have asked you to help them attract settlers to the Americas. As you read this chapter, take notes on things you think might convince Europeans to leave their home countries and come to the Americas.

Americas

1521 Aztec surrender to the Spaniards
1540 Coronado begins exploring the Southwest

1560s Spaniards begin missions in borderlands

1500–1549	1550–1599

1517 Protestant Reformation begins in Germany
1534 England separates from the Roman Catholic Church

1568 Mercator publishes map of the Americas

World

QUETZALCOATL, AZTEC GOD

History AND ART

De Soto Discovering the Mississippi, 1541
by O.F. Barninghaus, 1920

The great explorations of the United States were common subjects for American artists. This painting of De Soto was created by American artist O.F. Barninghaus in 1920.

1608 Champlain founds Quebec
1609 Hudson explores Hudson River
1626 Dutch buy Manhattan Island

1655 Dutch take over New Sweden

1600–1649

1650–1699

1606 Portuguese explorers reach Australia

1653 Taj Mahal completed in India
1689 Russia and China establish boundaries

★★

The Fall of Two Empires

SETTING THE SCENE

Read to Learn . . .

★ how the Spaniards conquered the Aztec and the Inca.
★ how Spanish conquests changed Mexico and South America.

Terms to Know

★ conquistador
★ Nahuatl

People to Meet

★ Montezuma
★ Hernán Cortés
★ Malintzin
★ Francisco Pizarro
★ Atahualpa

Places to Locate

★ Gulf of Mexico
★ Veracruz
★ Lima

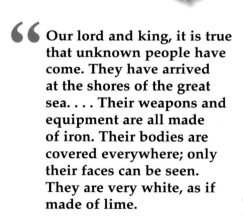

◀ SPANISH BOWL, SIXTEENTH CENTURY

> ❝ Our lord and king, it is true that unknown people have come. They have arrived at the shores of the great sea. . . . Their weapons and equipment are all made of iron. Their bodies are covered everywhere; only their faces can be seen. They are very white, as if made of lime. ❞

An Aztec messenger delivered this message to his emperor, **Montezuma** (MAHN•tuh•ZOO•muh) in his palace at Tenochtitlán (tay•NAWCH•teet•LAHN) in 1519. For some time, the Aztec had heard rumors that there were strangers to the east, along the shores of the "great sea," or present-day **Gulf of Mexico.** The messenger had been sent to find out if the rumors were true.

★ Strangers on the Coast

Montezuma heard the news with a deepening sense of fear. If Aztec legend was correct, the god Quetzalcoatl (KWEHT•suhl•kuh•WAH•tuhl), the Feathered Serpent, had returned to the Aztec empire to reclaim his throne. "If he comes . . . he strikes at kings," the legend warned.

The emperor had many doubts. Was the ancient pale-skinned god of legend truly among the strangers on the coast? On the other hand, could these be humans who had come to harm the Aztec?

Montezuma decided to treat the strangers and their leader as if they were gods. He sent five men to the coast with gifts and an invitation to visit him at Tenochtitlán. His gifts included golden masks inlaid with turquoise, headdresses made of brightly colored feathers, gold jewelry, and shields.

Cortés the Conqueror

When the Aztec messengers arrived at the coast, they presented Montezuma's gifts to the leader of the pale-faced strangers. He was **Hernán Cortés** (kawr•TEHZ). Instead of a god, Cortés was a Spanish conquistador, a Spanish term for *conqueror.*

Cortés was not pleased with Montezuma's messengers. He looked at the gifts with scorn and asked, "And is this all? Is this your gift of welcome?" He placed Montezuma's messengers in chains and fired a cannon nearby to frighten them. He told the messengers, "I and my friends suffer from a disease of the heart which can be cured only by gold."

Cortés Arrives in Mexico

Cortés had been in the Caribbean since 1511 managing his estate. As a reward for helping Spain conquer Cuba, he had received a large land grant on the island. Like other Spaniards, Cortés had heard tales about magnificent cities of gold on the mainland of North America across the Gulf of Mexico. He was eager to find those riches.

In 1518 the governor of Spain's colony in Cuba asked Cortés to set up a post on the Mexican mainland to claim land, look for gold, and begin trading with the Native Americans. Sensing the ambitions of Cortés, the governor changed his mind at the last minute. Cortés decided to disobey the governor and go anyway.

He had outfitted 11 ships for his trip and enlisted the help of 600 Spanish soldiers and 200 Cubans. He loaded the ships with horses, cannons, muskets, and specially trained war dogs dressed in their own armor.

Malintzin the Interpreter

Cortés had crossed the Gulf of Mexico and landed on the **Yucatán Peninsula** by March of 1519. He spent a few weeks sailing along the coast and learning as much as he could from the Maya. Although the great Mayan civilization was gone, Maya descendants still lived and farmed in the region. One Mayan chieftain introduced Cortés to a Native American princess named **Malintzin.**

As a child, Malintzin had been sold into slavery during a time of famine. She spoke both Nahuatl (NAH•WAH•tuhl), the language of the Aztec, and the Mayan language. Before long, she also learned Spanish. Malintzin became Cortés's interpreter, translating Native American languages into Spanish.

Like many people in the coastal areas, Malintzin hated the Aztec. She told Cortés about their wealth and their belief in the pale-skinned god Quetzalcoatl.

Cortés Marches Inland

By April, Cortés decided to journey inland toward the Aztec capital. Before leaving the coast, however, he founded a colony and named it **Veracruz.** In so doing, he claimed Mexico for Spain and the Roman Catholic Church. Sensing that the march would be dangerous and difficult, Cortés also destroyed his ships. He wanted to prevent his soldiers from retreating to Cuba.

Meanwhile, Montezuma became more and more fearful. He sent sacks of gold to the approaching Spaniards, hoping to satisfy them and convince them to turn back. The gifts, however, only made the Spaniards more eager to reach the Aztec capital and its riches.

★ Cortés in Tenochtitlán

Cortés arrived at the entrance to Tenochtitlán on November 8, 1519. There Montezuma, perhaps still uncertain about who the Spaniards were, gave him a grand welcome. That same day he gave the Spaniards their own quarters in the palace and presented them with many precious gifts. Finally, speaking through Malintzin, he offered Cortés the Aztec empire to command.

Cortés sensed that Montezuma feared him. He also saw that he and his troops were in a dangerous position. Montezuma could be leading him into a trap. Aztec warriors were everywhere. If they drew up the bridges leading into the city, the Spaniards would have no escape.

Cortés decided that the best way to control the Aztec would be to seize Montezuma and hold him captive. Montezuma remained a prisoner of the Spaniards in his own palace for months.

Meanwhile, the Spaniards ransacked all the gold or other treasures they could find in the capital. They piled gold jewelry and other items into large heaps and started fires to melt them into gold bars. The bars were easier to carry away. Today the gold that Cortés took from the Aztec would be worth more than $8 million.

A New Spanish Ally: Disease

During the months that Montezuma was held captive by the Spaniards, he became unpopular among the Aztec people. He was killed by a stone thrown by an Aztec during a revolt against the Spanish.

After Montezuma's death, however, the Aztec united and drove the Spaniards from Tenochtitlán. Fleeing Spaniards—many slowed down with the weight of the treasure they carried—were hunted down and killed.

The Aztec had little chance to enjoy their victory, however. One Aztec account told that:

6 6 **After the Spaniards had left the city of Mexico, and before they had made any preparations to attack us again, there came amongst us a great sickness, a general plague. . . .** **9 9**

Picturing History

▲ **INTERPRETER FOR CORTÉS** Malintzin's people, the Maya, lived on the east coast of Mexico. **What colony did Cortés found there?**

Linking Past and Present

Spanish Treasure Ships

Throughout the 1500s and 1600s, hundreds of Spanish treasure ships carried tons of American gold, silver, and jewels to Spain.

Then

Lost at Sea

In 1622 the Spanish ship *Atocha* departed Cuba for Spain. The unlucky crew soon realized that they had sailed into an Atlantic hurricane. The *Atocha* ran into a jagged reef and sank to the ocean floor, taking its treasure and more than 100 crew members with it.

▶ **SPANISH GALLEON**

Now

Treasure Hunt

In 1985, modern treasure hunter and underwater diver Mel Fisher found the *Atocha*'s wooden hull covered with sand off the coast of the Florida Keys. Still buried with it were more than 3,000 emeralds; 30 tons of silver; and hundreds of gold bars, chains, and coins. Some estimate that the treasure is worth $300 million to $1 billion.

The "great sickness" the Aztec wrote about was probably smallpox or measles. These diseases were deadly because the Aztec had never been exposed to them before. The diseases brought by the Spaniards turned into a deadly weapon.

The Final Conquest

Cortés returned to Tenochtitlán 10 months later. With mounted soldiers in the lead, thousands of Native Americans and at least 1,000 Spanish soldiers attacked the capital. The Aztec fought on foot without horses or guns. Their stone knives, copper shields, and cloth armor were no match for the iron weapons and heavy cannons of the Spaniards.

The Aztec surrendered to Cortés on August 13, 1521. It had taken only two years for the Spaniards to destroy the mighty Aztec empire. Tenochtitlán lay in ruins and the golden treasures of the Aztec now belonged to Cortés and to Spain.

Cortés ordered that a new city be built on the site of Tenochtitlán. It would be the new Spanish capital, renamed **Mexico City.**

★ Pizarro and the Inca

Thirteen years after the conquest of the Aztec, the Inca also faced the strength of the Spaniards. The leader of the attack against the Inca was the Spanish conquistador **Francisco Pizarro.**

Like Cortés, Pizarro had heard many stories of the great wealth in the lands of South America. He made several expeditions along the coast to look for the treasure. It was not until 1526, however, when one of his ships spotted an Incan trading boat loaded with silver and gold, that he believed the stories were true.

Pizarro ordered his men to capture the ship. He trained some of the Incan crew to be interpreters, then planned his assault on the Incan empire.

▲ ATAHUALPA BEFORE PIZARRO The Incan ruler Atahualpa was captured by Pizarro. **What later happened to Atahualpa?**

A Broken Promise

In 1531 Pizarro led 180 soldiers across the Isthmus of Panama and then sailed southward along the west coast of South America. When Pizarro's small Spanish army landed in the coastal city of Cajamarco, it learned that the Incan ruler **Atahualpa** (AH•tuh•WAHL•puh) was resting after a bitter civil war with his half-brother. After killing thousands of Inca, the Spaniards marched to Atahualpa's summer home. Like Cortés among the Aztec, Pizarro thought the best way to control the Inca was through their emperor. He took Atahualpa captive.

To gain their leader's freedom, the Inca were ordered to pay a ransom. They collected enough gold and silver to fill the room where their emperor was kept prisoner. At today's prices the roomful of precious metals would be worth more than $65 million. Pizarro promised to free Atahualpa when the ransom was paid, but instead had the Incan leader killed.

The Fall of an Empire

Pizarro then sent soldiers up the mountains to capture the Incan capital of Cuzco. By 1535 most of the Incan empire had fallen. Pizarro set up his capital in **Lima,** Peru. From there he sent expeditions to take control of most of the rest of South America outside Portuguese-held **Brazil.** The Portuguese had held claim to Brazil since 1494.

Unlike the Aztec, who fell to Cortés in only 2 years, parts of the Incan empire held out against the Spaniards for 40 years. The Inca's system of rule encouraged loyalty among its many subjects and the empire was much better unified than the Aztec Empire.

The Spaniards found far more gold in South America than in Mexico. The former Incan empire became Spain's richest colony.

★ SECTION 1 REVIEW ★

Checking for Understanding

1. **Identify** Montezuma, Hernán Cortés, Malintzin, Francisco Pizarro, Atahualpa.
2. **Define** conquistador, Nahuatl.
3. **What** weapons did the Spanish have that the Aztec and Inca did not have?
4. **Why** was the city of Lima important to Pizarro?

Critical Thinking

5. **Drawing Conclusions** Why do you think Montezuma believed that Cortés was the god Quetzalcoatl?

ACTIVITY

6. Imagine you are an Aztec messenger warning the Inca that the Spanish are coming to attack them. Draw a series of five pictures telling them what to expect.

BUILDING SKILLS
Social Studies Skills

Understanding Latitude and Longitude

For more than 17 centuries, mapmakers have used lines of latitude and longitude from the global grid to pinpoint locations on maps and globes.

Learning the Skill

The imaginary horizontal lines that circle the globe from east to west are lines of **latitude.** Because the distance between the lines of latitude is always the same, they are also called **parallels.** The imaginary vertical lines that intersect the parallels are lines of **longitude,** also called **meridians.**

Parallels and meridians are numbered in degrees. The **Equator,** located halfway between the North and South Poles, is 0°. Moving north or south of the Equator, the number of degrees increases until reaching 90°N or S latitude at the poles. St. Augustine, Florida, at 29°N latitude, is 29° north of the Equator. Cuzco, Peru, at 13°S latitude is 13° south of the Equator.

The **Prime Meridian** is 0° longitude. Moving east or west of the Prime Meridian, the number of degrees E or W increases up to 180°. The 180° line of longitude is located on the opposite side of the globe from the Prime Meridian. It is called the **International Date Line.**

The point at which parallels and meridians intersect are the **coordinates** of an exact location. The coordinates for St. Augustine are 29°N and 81°W. The coordinates for Cuzco are 13°S and 71°W.

Spanish Colonies in the Americas

Practicing the Skill

1. What are the approximate coordinates of Santo Domingo on Hispaniola?

2. Is the Isthmus of Panama located about 8°N or 8°S latitude?

3. What city at 19°N and 99°W did the Spaniards conquer?

4. What Spanish capital was built at 12°S and 76°W?

APPLYING THE SKILL

5. Use your Atlas to help you sketch a map of the east coast of the United States and the Atlantic Ocean. On your map draw a small circle at about 32°N and 75°W. Imagine the circle represents a hurricane traveling due west. Label the state the hurricane will probably strike.

97

Spain Builds a Vast Empire

SETTING THE SCENE

Read to Learn . . .

★ what life was like in the Spanish colonies.
★ what areas of the present-day United States the Spaniards explored.
★ how Spain settled the American Southwest.

Terms to Know

★ borderlands
★ viceroy
★ pueblo
★ mission
★ presidio
★ peninsulare
★ creole
★ mestizo

People to Meet

★ Juana Inés de la Cruz
★ Bartolomé de Las Casas
★ Francisco Vásquez de Coronado
★ Hernando de Soto

Places to Locate

★ Peru
★ New Spain
★ St. Augustine

◀ GOLD CRUCIFIX

In 1523 three barefoot men in tattered brown robes got off a Spanish ship at the newly built port of Veracruz on the Gulf of Mexico. Then they walked more than 200 miles (320 km) over rugged trails to reach Mexico City.

Outside the city, Cortés—now ruler of Mexico—met the three men. Thousands of Native Americans watched in amazement as Cortés knelt down before the men and begged forgiveness for his treatment of the Native Americans.

Who were these simply dressed, barefoot men? Why did they have such power over the mighty Hernán Cortés? The men were friars, members of a Catholic religious order. Their influence over Cortés was just one sign of the important role religion played as Spain went on to strengthen and enlarge its empire in the Americas.

★ Spain's American Empire

Spain used the wealth gained from its conquest of the Aztec and Inca to enlarge its army and navy. It was able to finance more explorations and settlements in the Americas. As the most powerful nation in Europe, Spain faced little interference from other European countries.

Ruling the Empire

Spain divided its American empire into two parts. The southern part was made up of its claims in South America and was called **Peru.** The northern part, named **New Spain,** took in all the land north of South America. It included the Caribbean Islands, Central America, Mexico, and all the lands bordering Mexico and the Gulf of Mexico. These lands along the northern edges of Spanish territory were the Spanish **borderlands.**

Spain put a governing official called a viceroy in charge of each part of its empire, one in New Spain and one in Peru. The main responsibility of the viceroy was to produce wealth for Spain. For many years, this was not difficult to do. New, rich deposits of silver were found northwest of Mexico City. These mines produced tons of silver for shipment to Spain. Cotton, sugarcane, and other crops grown on plantations were also shipped to Spain.

Despite the distance across the Atlantic, rulers in Spain succeeded in keeping tight control over their American colonies.

Viceroys and lesser officials sent regular, lengthy reports back to Spain. Likewise officials in Spain sent many rules and regulations to the colonies.

Three Kinds of Settlements

Spanish law called for three kinds of settlements in the Americas—pueblos, missions, and presidios. Pueblos, or towns, were established as centers of trade. Most pueblos were built around a central square that included a church and government buildings. Many towns in Mexico and South America still reflect the style of the Spanish pueblos.

Missions were religious communities that usually included a small town, surrounding farmland, and a church. They were started by Catholic religious workers called missionaries.

Life in a mission centered around the church. Priests taught Native Americans about the Roman Catholic religion and various crafts and skills. Usually a presidio, or fort, was built near a mission. Spanish soldiers stationed at a presidio protected the missions from invaders.

▲ SPANISH MISSION The priests raised crops to feed the many people who lived at the mission. **What were the three types of Spanish settlements?**

Sor Juana Writes Poetry

The life of **Juana Inés de la Cruz** reflects how opportunities for women were limited in New Spain. Men held all the important positions. Women had two choices: to marry and put themselves under the control of their husbands, or to join a convent and put themselves under the control of the church.

Juana Inés de la Cruz was born in a tiny village near Mexico City in 1651. At 17 Juana chose to enter a convent to become a nun, or religious sister. She believed the convent would allow her the time and opportunity to write poetry and study.

Religious leaders soon became angry that Juana wrote poetry about such worldly subjects as love and the rights of women. A Catholic bishop wrote her a letter of warning.

Inside the convent other nuns shunned Sor Juana. Few people from the outside dared to visit her. Finally in 1694 Juana gave in. She reaffirmed her vows as a nun. Her library was removed from her room.

A year later when an epidemic swept through Mexico City, Juana insisted on staying in the convent to tend to the nuns who were ill. At age 43 she died of cholera. Today, many scholars regard Sor Juana as the Americas' first great poet. ★★★

▲ JUANA INÉS DE LA CRUZ

★ Social Classes in New Spain

The people of Spain's American colonies formed a structured society where position was determined mostly by birth.

Peninsulares and Creoles

Peninsulares, or people born in Spain, had the highest positions in Spanish colonial society. Peninsulares held the best jobs in government and in the church. They also owned much of the land and ran the large estates on which the Native Americans worked. They controlled most of the wealth and power.

Creoles were below the peninsulares on the social ladder. These colonists had Spanish parents but had been born in New Spain. Although they could not rise as high as the peninsulares, they still held important positions in the government, church, army, and business.

Mestizos

By the late 1500s, there were about 60,000 peninsulares and creoles in New Spain. They were greatly outnumbered, however, by **mestizos,** people of mixed Spanish and Native American descent. Most mestizos worked on farms and ranches. In towns they worked as carpenters, bakers, tailors, and soldiers.

Treatment of Native Americans

Native Americans made up the largest group of people in Spain's empire. They were forced to work in the mines and on plantations under cruel conditions. Most were paid so little that they had to borrow from landowners just to buy food. They could not change jobs until all their debts were paid. As a result, they were trapped in a system that was close to slavery.

Bartolomé de Las Casas devoted his life to trying to change the Spaniards' abuse of the Native Americans. Las Casas first came to the Caribbean Islands with Columbus in 1502 and later became a priest. In 1542, Spain passed laws meant to end the system of forced labor altogether. Las Casas often found the laws impossible to enforce, however.

★ The Spanish Borderlands

Even before the conquest of the Aztec, Spanish explorers had turned their attention to the borderlands. Their first goal was always to find gold.

Settlement in Florida

As early as 1513, explorer Juan Ponce de León visited Florida, searching for riches—and according to legend—a fountain that promised eternal youth. He found neither, and in 1521 lost his life in a conflict with Native Americans.

In 1565, a group of French people landed in Florida intending to start a settlement. To keep out the French, the Spaniards built a fort and settlement of their own along the east coast of Florida. They called their settlement **St. Augustine.** Founded in 1565, St. Augustine today is the oldest city in the United States started by Europeans.

A Lost Expedition

In 1528 a large Spanish expedition went to Florida looking for gold. The Spaniards lost their way, however, and retreated to Florida's west coast.

The men built rafts and tried to sail across the Gulf of Mexico. Of the 300 men who started the trip, only 4 survived. Those 4 were washed ashore near present-day Galveston, Texas. One of them was a noble named Alvar Núñez Cabeza de Vaca (kuh•BAY•zuh duh VAH•kuh). Another was an African who had been enslaved, named Esteban (ehs•TAY•bahn).

Picturing History ▲ PONCE DE LEÓN The island of Puerto Rico was conquered by Ponce de León in 1509. **What was Ponce de León hoping to find in Florida?**

For nearly nine years the men wandered through the borderlands of southwest North America trying to find their way to Mexico. When they finally reached Spanish territory in 1536, they had walked halfway across the continent.

Coronado in the Southwest

De Vaca claimed that Native Americans had told him of seven cities in a land called Cibola that had huge stockpiles of gold, silver, and precious jewels. **Francisco Vásquez de Coronado** organized a large expedition to the Southwest to find the fabled Seven Cities of Cibola in 1540.

Coronado traveled for almost three years through lands of the present-day southwestern United States. He passed cliff dwellings abandoned by the ancient Anasazi and explored settlements of the Zuni, Hopi, Apache, and Navajo.

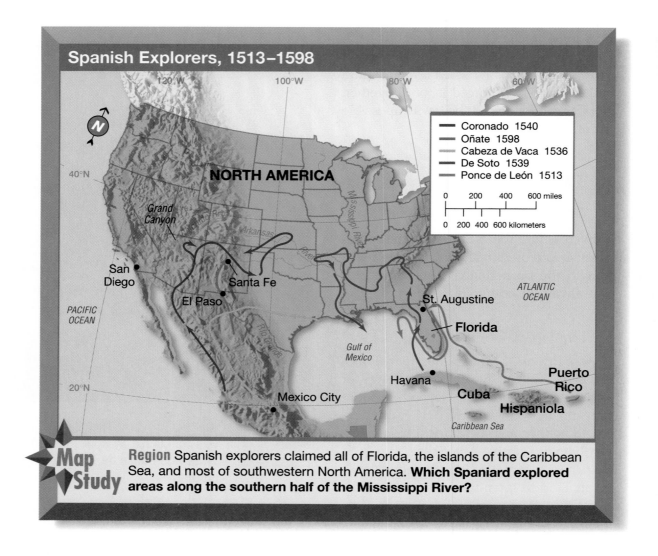

Spanish Explorers, 1513–1598

Legend:
- Coronado 1540
- Oñate 1598
- Cabeza de Vaca 1536
- De Soto 1539
- Ponce de León 1513

Map Study

Region Spanish explorers claimed all of Florida, the islands of the Caribbean Sea, and most of southwestern North America. **Which Spaniard explored areas along the southern half of the Mississippi River?**

To his disappointment Coronado found no splendid cities of gold. From the European point of view, however, his expedition gave Spain claim to lands far to the north of Mexico.

De Soto and the Mississippi River

In 1539 another Spanish expedition—led by **Hernando de Soto**—went in search of the seven cities of gold. De Soto started his journey in Florida. For the next 2 years, he and 600 men made their way through present-day South Carolina, Georgia, Alabama, Mississippi, and Tennessee.

De Soto died of a fever while his group traveled south along the Mississippi River. His men lowered his body into the Mississippi River for burial. Although he had failed to find gold, he gave Spain a claim to all the land he had explored.

★ Borderland Missions

For many years Spanish settlers paid little attention to the northern borderlands. The Spanish government, however, wanted to attract settlers to the area to discourage other countries from making claims. Instead of soldiers, the government sent missionaries to start new settlements.

Knowing how badly the Native Americans of the Caribbean and Mexico had been treated, government officials in Spain thought that missionaries would be able to develop kinder relationships with the people who lived in the borderlands. From the 1560s to the 1820s, Spain set up hundreds of missions in present-day New Mexico, Arizona, Texas, California, Florida, and Georgia.

Life on a Mission

Spanish missions met many of the Native Americans' basic needs. In return, the Native Americans were expected to accept the Catholic religion, practice Spanish customs, and work at the mission.

Most of the missions were made up of one-story, adobe buildings that surrounded a courtyard. Missions usually provided dining areas, schools, workshops, and a church. Some had living quarters where the Native Americans could stay with their families. In the workshops, Native Americans could learn needlework, carpentry, and metalworking skills.

Native American Responses

Some Native Americans enjoyed the benefits that missions provided. Others did not like the restrictions placed on them by the missions. They could not leave without permission, and each day they had scheduled activities that they were forced to attend. The new religion also required them to give up their own religious beliefs and traditions.

Many Native Americans rebelled. Some attacked the missions, killing missionaries and tearing down the mission buildings. Others simply left the missions to go back to their own lives.

Stopping the Russians in California

Upper California was the last borderland Spain settled. The Spaniards had claimed this territory in 1542 when they sailed along the Pacific Coast and explored the site of present-day San Diego. However, they ignored Upper California until the 1760s, when they became alarmed at the activities of traders from Russian-held Alaska. From time to time, the Russians went ashore to hunt and gather furs.

Spanish officials sent an expedition to California in 1769. Their first goal was to establish a chain of missions and military posts along the California coast. The Spaniards began a settlement they called **San Diego.** This was the first of 21 missions built between San Diego and San Francisco.

★ SECTION 2 REVIEW ★

★★★★★★★★★★★★★★★★★★★★ ★★★★★★★★★★★★★★★★★★★★

Checking for Understanding

1. **Identify** Juana Inés de la Cruz, Bartolomé de Las Casas, Francisco Vásquez de Coronado, Hernando de Soto, Peru, New Spain, St. Augustine.

2. **Define** borderlands, viceroy, pueblo, mission, presidio, peninsulare, creole, mestizo.

3. **What** social class of New Spain was the largest? Why?

4. **What** was the basis for Spain's claims to the American Southwest?

5. **Why** did Spain send missionaries to the borderlands?

Critical Thinking

6. **Determining Cause and Effect** What earlier Spanish experiences in the Americas might have encouraged Coronado to believe in the seven cities of gold?

ACTIVITY

7. Create a diagram to illustrate the differences among social classes in New Spain.

An Age of Mercantilism

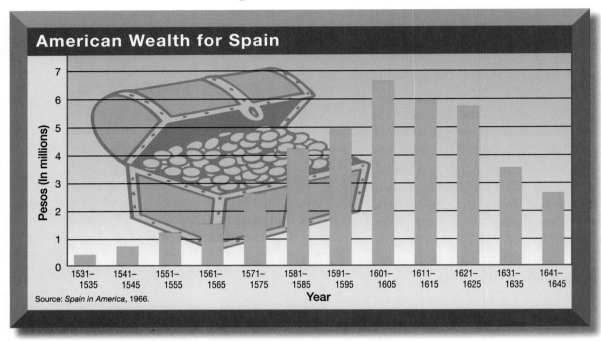

American Wealth for Spain

Pesos (in millions)

Year

Source: *Spain in America*, 1966.

Between the 1400s and 1700s, European countries adopted an economic system called **mercantilism.** According to the theory of mercantilism, a country could be rich only if wealth continually flowed into its economy and its government treasury.

Colonies were one source of wealth. It was always the colonists' duty to ship most of the gold, silver, or other resources found in the colony back to their home country in Europe.

Spain was the first European country in the Americas to profit from mercantilism. Just one ship leaving Cuba carried more than 900 bars of silver, 160 bars of gold, 580 bars of copper, 225,000 gold coins, and 300 popcorn-sized emeralds.

As other European countries set up colonies in the Americas, they too followed mercantilism. For about 300 years, most of the natural resources gathered in the Americas were sent to Europe.

Making the Math Connection

Use the graph to answer the following questions.

1. During which two five-year periods did the value of resources fail to reach 1 million pesos?

2. During which three five-year periods did wealth sent to Spain reach peak amounts?

3. About how much more wealth was gained during the period from 1601–1605 than from 1641–1645?

ACTIVITY

4. Create a chart of American goods you think could have been shipped to Spain during the 1500s and 1600s. List the names of the items and a possible value, such as "tobacco—3,000 pesos." When you have finished, add up the total value of the ship's cargo.

★★★★★★★★★★★★★★★★★★★★★★★★★★★★★★★★

French, Dutch, and Swedish Colonies

SETTING THE SCENE

Read to Learn . . .

★ about French colonization in North America.
★ why the Dutch established New Netherland.

People to Meet

★ Samuel de Champlain
★ Louis Joliet
★ Jacques Marquette
★ Robert de La Salle

Places to Locate

★ Quebec
★ Great Lakes
★ Louisiana
★ New Amsterdam

► EUROPEAN BEAVER HAT

When French explorer **Jacques Cartier** had arrived in eastern Canada in 1534, his sailors planted a 30-foot (9-m) wooden cross on the shore. Cartier himself formally claimed the land for France. Nearby, a group of Native Americans had gathered to watch this strange ceremony. They seemed angry as they pointed to the cross and spoke.

The French had no need to be concerned about the Native Americans for a number of years. Neither Cartier's first voyage in 1534 nor his two later voyages promised a new route to Asia or gold and silver. As a result, the French king had little interest in what the North American continent had to offer.

In addition, France in the mid-1500s was fighting wars in Europe. It had little money or energy for exploring new lands. In 1589, however, the wars in France ended. The French monarch began to take a closer look at the lands Cartier had claimed along the St. Lawrence River.

★ Establishing New France

Cartier had reported to a group of French fur companies that there were a great many furbearing animals in northern North America. These fur companies paid for the first major attempt the French made to settle America. They hired **Samuel de Champlain** to lead the effort.

Major European Explorers, 1487–1682

Explorer	Dates of Voyages	Accomplishments
For Portugal		
Bartolomeu Dias	1487-1488	Sailed around the southern tip of Africa
Vasco da Gama	1497-1499	Sailed around Africa to India
Pedro Alvares Cabral	1500	Sailed to Brazil
For Spain		
Christopher Columbus	1492-1504	Explored the islands of the Caribbean Sea
Juan Ponce de León	1508-1509, 1513	Explored Puerto Rico Explored Florida
Ferdinand Magellan	1519-1522	First to sail around the world
Cabeza de Vaca	1530	Explored Spanish northern Mexico and Brazil
Francisco Coronado	1540-1542	Explored southwestern North America
Hernando de Soto	1516-1520, 1539-1543	Explored Central America Led expedition to the Mississippi River
Juan Cabrillo	1542-1543	Explored the west coast of North America
For England		
John Cabot	1497-1501	Rediscovered Newfoundland (east coast of North America)
Henry Hudson	1610-1611	Explored Hudson Strait and Hudson Bay
For the Netherlands		
Henry Hudson	1609	Explored the Hudson River
For France		
Giovanni da Verrazano	1524	Explored the east coast of North America, including New York harbor
Jacques Cartier	1534-1542	Explored the St. Lawrence River
Samuel de Champlain	1603-1615	Explored the St. Lawrence River Founded Quebec
Jacques Marquette/ Louis Joliet	1673	Explored the Mississippi River
Robert de La Salle	1666-1682	Explored the Great Lakes Founded Louisiana after reaching the mouth of the Mississippi River

Chart Study

Most European explorers reached the Western Hemisphere. **Which two countries explored the east coast of North America?**

▲ SAMUEL DE CHAMPLAIN

Founding Quebec

Champlain sailed to North America in 1603. He landed on the eastern coast of the present-day Canadian provinces of Nova Scotia, New Brunswick, and Prince Edward Island. The French called this region **Acadia.**

In 1608, Champlain established **Quebec**—the first permanent French settlement—near the mouth of the St. Lawrence River. Here, he and a small group of 24 settlers built a wooden fort to prepare for the first winter. The winter was bitterly cold and only 8 settlers survived.

The French and the Native Americans

Champlain saw the importance of maintaining peace with the Native Americans. He sent out young men to learn their languages and to study the customs of the Algonquin and Huron.

Unlike the Spaniards, who tried to change Native American cultures, most French settlers—beginning with Champlain—tried to accept Native American ways. Because of this attitude, some Native Americans became strong allies of the French.

Champlain explored and mapped Lake Ontario and Lake Huron, two of the five **Great Lakes** located at the western end of the St. Lawrence River. He also traveled to present-day northern New York. There he came to another lake which he named after himself—**Lake Champlain.** Champlain became known as "the Father of New France." Just as the Spaniards called their North American empire New Spain, the French called theirs New France.

The French Fur Trade

The economy of New France was based on the fur trade. Traders sent a steady supply of beaver, otter, and fox skins back to France. These skins, especially beaver skins, were highly prized for making hats and coats. Beaver hats were very fashionable in Europe, and upper-class Europeans were eager to buy them.

French traders and trappers traveled across New France using the rivers and lakes as highways. They set up trading posts along the way and became friendly with some Native Americans who supplied them with furs.

Exploring the Mississippi

As explorers, missionaries, and fur traders moved west into the interior of North America, they claimed more land for France. Native Americans they met along the way told them of a great river that lay south of the area the French had settled.

A trader, named **Louis Joliet,** and a priest, Father **Jacques Marquette,** heard the stories of the mighty river and hoped it was the trade route to Asia that everyone had been looking for. In 1673 the two men set out to find the waterway. They traveled by canoe south along Lake Michigan and down the Fox and Wisconsin Rivers.

Finally, Joliet and Marquette reached the Mississippi River. For several weeks, they paddled more than 1,000 miles (1,600 km) downriver. At length, they realized that the Mississippi River flowed south and was not a western route to the Pacific Ocean.

Ten years later, **Robert de La Salle** was determined to find out how far the Mississippi flowed. In 1682 he reached the mouth of the Mississippi, where it empties into the Gulf of Mexico. He and his men erected a stone column that claimed all the lands of the Mississippi Valley for France. He named the area **Louisiana** in honor of King Louis XIV.

★ The Boundaries of the French Empire

By 1700 New France took in a huge portion of North America. It included Acadia, Canada, and Louisiana. Canada was everything west of Acadia to the Great

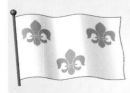

★★★ AMERICA'S FLAGS ★★★

Flag of New France Settlers in New France flew this French flag, which was based on the French Royal Banner, until 1763. White was the French royal color of the time.

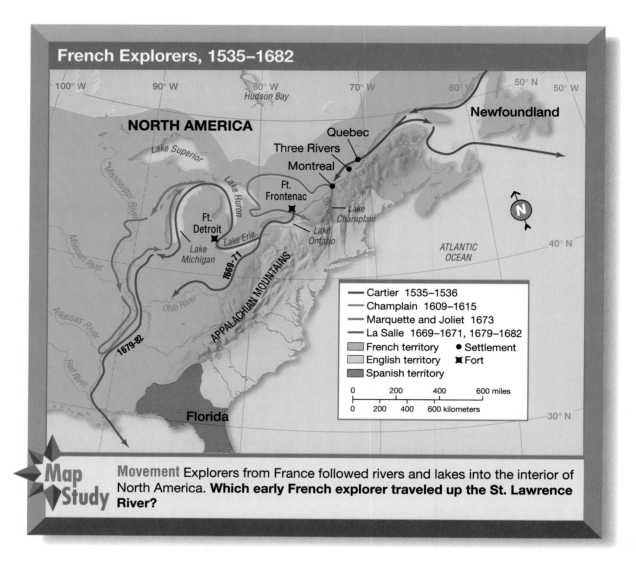

French Explorers, 1535–1682

NORTH AMERICA

Hudson Bay

Newfoundland

Lake Superior

Quebec
Three Rivers
Montreal
Ft. Frontenac

Lake Huron
Ft. Detroit
Lake Erie
Lake Michigan
Lake Ontario
Lake Champlain
St. Lawrence River

Mississippi River
Missouri River
Ohio River
Arkansas River
Red River

APPALACHIAN MOUNTAINS

ATLANTIC OCEAN

Florida

1669-71
1679-82

N

50° N
100° W   90° W   80° W   70° W   60° W   50° W
40° N
30° N

— Cartier 1535–1536
— Champlain 1609–1615
— Marquette and Joliet 1673
— La Salle 1669–1671, 1679–1682
▢ French territory   ● Settlement
▢ English territory   ✖ Fort
▢ Spanish territory

0   200   400   600 miles
0   200   400   600 kilometers

Map Study **Movement** Explorers from France followed rivers and lakes into the interior of North America. **Which early French explorer traveled up the St. Lawrence River?**

Lakes. Louisiana was the southern colony that stretched through central North America, along the Mississippi River, to the Gulf of Mexico.

Trappers, traders, priests, and soldiers continued to move into the lands that France claimed and built many trading posts and forts. Today's cities of Detroit, St. Louis, and New Orleans stand on the sites of earlier French trading posts.

★ Attracting French Settlers

While New France eventually prospered, it did so without many French settlers. Reports of cold weather and attacks by the Iroquois kept many people from leaving France. Also, the government and economy of France was stable and people had no reason to leave.

Footnotes to History

The Wall in Wall Street   The Dutch in New Amsterdam built a wall across the southern end of Manhattan to keep Native Americans out of their settlement. Wall Street, world-renowned center of finance in present-day New York City, takes its name from this wall.

In 1625 fewer than 60 people lived in Quebec. By 1665 there were only about 2,500 French settlers, mostly men, in all of New France. To encourage settlement, King Louis XIV set up a land grant system. It gave land to French nobles in return for bringing settlers from France to farm the land.

Despite its slow population growth, New France eventually had enough people to establish several important towns along the banks of the St. Lawrence River.

The French government set up a network of military forts that connected Canada with Louisiana and its claims along the Mississippi River. The forts, combined with close ties between French settlers and many Native American groups, put France in a strong position. It could easily defend its empire against Spain and other European countries.

★ Arrival of the Dutch and Swedes

By the 1600s Europe's hopes of finding a Northwest Passage to Asia were fading. Dutch merchants began to wonder if ships could reach Asia by going *northeast* around Europe, through the Arctic Ocean.

In 1609 Dutch sailors aboard a ship called the *Half Moon* attempted to find such a route. After waiting a month for ice in the Arctic Ocean to thaw, their captain—an English sailor named **Henry Hudson**—decided to turn around and sail west across the Atlantic Ocean. The *Half Moon* landed along the North American coast. Hudson claimed the area for the Dutch.

The Dutch quickly became interested in the North American fur trade. They built a post for trading with the Native Americans at present-day Albany, New York. They also started the settlement of **New Amsterdam** on Manhattan Island. Eventually the Dutch colony, called New Netherland, spread to include parts of present-day New York, New Jersey, Connecticut, and Delaware.

In the late 1630s, Sweden began sending people to North America. The Swedes settled just south of New Netherland on the Delaware in an area they called New Sweden. Though small, New Sweden troubled the Dutch in New Amsterdam. The Dutch did not want to compete with other European countries for fur trade. Conflict between the two groups would soon arise.

★ SECTION 3 REVIEW ★

Checking for Understanding

1. **Identify** Samuel de Champlain, Louis Joliet, Jacques Marquette, Robert de La Salle, Quebec, Great Lakes, Louisiana, New Amsterdam.

2. **How** did most French settlers choose to make their living?

3. **What** kinds of settlements did the French build in Louisiana?

4. **Why** did the Dutch become interested in North American settlements?

Critical Thinking

5. **Drawing Conclusions** Why do you think the Native Americans might have considered the fur traders to be less of a threat than farmers were?

ACTIVITY

6. Create a newspaper advertisement for fashionable beaver hats that would appeal to wealthy Europeans of the 1600s.

Using Key Vocabulary

Match the numbered items in Column A with their definitions in Column B.

1. **conquistador**
2. **mission**
3. **mestizo**
4. **presidio**
5. **creole**

a. person of mixed Spanish and Native American background
b. Spanish military fort
c. Spanish conqueror
d. religious community where Native Americans learned about Christianity
e. person of Spanish descent born in America

Reviewing Facts

1. **Name** two things that aided the Spanish in their attack on the Aztec.
2. **Describe** the position of Native Americans in Spanish colonial society.
3. **Describe** the main duty of viceroys in the Spanish colonies.
4. **List** the three areas of New France.
5. **Who** made Dutch claims in North America?

Understanding Concepts

Economic Development

1. How did the gold and silver from the Americas contribute to Spain's power?
2. What was the main economic activity of the French and Dutch in North America?
3. What role did Native Americans play in the economy of New France?

Conflict and Cooperation

4. Why did Native Americans cooperate more with French settlers than with the Spanish?
5. Why was it helpful for the French to make allies of the Native Americans?

Critical Thinking

1. **Drawing Conclusions** Based on evidence in this chapter, do you think the Spanish or French government did a better job of governing their colonies?
2. **Making Inferences** Why do you think the French had trouble attracting settlers to New France?

History and Geography

Missions in New Spain

Study the map showing Spanish missions in northern Mexico and the borderlands. Then answer the following questions.

1. **Place** In what present-day states were the Spanish missions located?
2. **Location** Near what city was the northernmost Spanish mission located?
3. **Place** Along which river did the Spaniards build a line of presidios?

Missions in New Spain by the 1700s

San Francisco · CA · UT · CO · Santa Barbara · Los Angeles · San Diego · AZ · NM · Santa Fe · El Paso · TX · San Antonio · *Rio Grande* · PACIFIC OCEAN · **MEXICO** · Gulf of Mexico · Mexico City

‡ Mission   ■ Presidio   • City
0   200   400   600   800 miles
0 200 400 600 800 kilometers

4. **Region** Between what two major bodies of water did the lands of new Spain lie?

5. **Location** Around what city were most missions located?

6. **Movement** In what direction would a priest travel to go from a Sante Fe mission to a mission near Los Angeles?

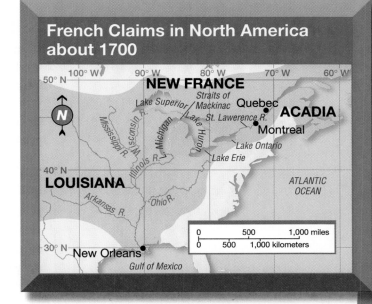

French Claims in North America about 1700

NEW FRANCE
Straits of Mackinac
Lake Superior
Quebec
ACADIA
St. Lawerence R.
Montreal
Wisconsin R.
Lake Michigan
Lake Huron
Lake Ontario
Lake Erie
Mississippi R.
Illinois R.
LOUISIANA
ATLANTIC OCEAN
Arkansas R.
Ohio R.
New Orleans
Gulf of Mexico

0   500   1,000 miles
0   500   1,000 kilometers

50° N 100° W 90° W 80° W 70° W 60° W
40° N
30° N

Interdisciplinary Activity: Language Arts

Cooperative Learning

Working in a group, research the influence of Spanish, French, or Dutch colonization on American culture. Choose one group and decide how words in our language, styles of architecture, and foods were influenced by them. Other areas of influence might include clothing styles, traditions, and holidays. Present your findings in an illustrated brochure. Photographs from old magazines and maps could be used to add information to your brochure. Personal experiences of classmates might also add details. Include information about locations in the United States where the cultural influence is particularly strong.

6. Between what lines of latitude on the map does Lake Ontario lie?

7. Along what river that connects to the Atlantic Ocean does Montreal lie?

8. In what direction would you travel to reach New Orleans from Montreal?

Practicing Skills

Understanding Latitude and Longitude

Use the map showing the area of French settlement to answer the following questions.

1. What are the latitude and longitude coordinates of New Orleans?

2. Between what lines of longitude do four of the five Great Lakes lie?

3. Between which Great Lakes are the Straits of Mackinac located?

4. Which rivers meet at 33°N, 91°W and flow south to the Gulf of Mexico?

5. What line of longitude lies closest to Quebec on the east?

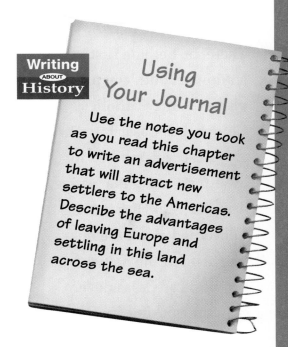

Writing ABOUT History

Using Your Journal

Use the notes you took as you read this chapter to write an advertisement that will attract new settlers to the Americas. Describe the advantages of leaving Europe and settling in this land across the sea.

Bartolomé de Las Casas was born in Spain but moved to Hispaniola around the age of 26. There, he became first a landowner and later a bishop in the Catholic Church. Las Casas is probably best remembered for his efforts to aid the Native Americans in Hispaniola. Concerned about the mistreatment of the native peoples, Las Casas never gave up working for laws to end their oppression.

Read to Discover

In this selection from *History of the Indies,* Las Casas writes about the opponents of Christopher Columbus and the arguments against his voyages. As you read, think of how you might have reacted to Columbus's plans in the 1400s. Would you have supported or opposed him?

Reader's Dictionary

Ptolemy	ancient Greek astronomer
sages	wise people
vaunted	boasted about
proponents	people who are in favor of something
subtle	not strong
antipodes	lands on the opposite side of the earth
adduced	gave examples
refrain	a repeated phrase
contradict	argue against
convened	met

from History of the Indies

by Bartolomé de Las Casas (1474–1566)

Some said that it was impossible that after so many thousands of years these Indies should be unknown, if there were such places in the world, for surely Ptolemy and the many other astronomers, geographers, and sages that had lived would have known something of them, and would have left some reference to them in writing, since they had written of many other matters; hence, they said, to affirm what Columbus affirmed was to claim to know or divine more than anyone else. Others argued this way: The world is infinitely large, and therefore in many years of navigation it would be impossible to reach the end of Asia, as Christopher Columbus proposed to do by sailing westward. . . .

Still others, who vaunted their mathematical learning, talked about astronomy and geography, saying that only a very small part of this inferior sphere is land, all the rest being entirely covered with water, and therefore it could only be navigated by sailing along the shores or coasts, as the Portuguese did along the coasts of Guinea; the proponents of this view had read precious few books on navigation, and had done even less sailing themselves. They added that whoever sailed directly west, as Christopher Columbus proposed to do, could never return, for supposing that the world was round, and that going westward you went downhill, then once you had left the hemisphere described by Ptolemy, on your return you must go uphill, which ships could not do— truly a subtle and profound reason, and proof that the matter was well understood! Others cited Saint Augustine, who . . . denied the existence of antipodes . . . and their refrain was: "Saint Augustine doubts." Then someone had to bring up the business of the five zones, of which three, according to many are totally uninhabitable; this was a commonly held opinion among the ancients, who, after all, did not know very much. Others adduced still other reasons, not worth mentioning here since they came from the kind of people who disagree with everybody—who find any statement illogical, no matter how sound. . . .

And so Christopher Columbus could give little satisfaction to those gentlemen whom the monarchs had convened, and therefore they pronounced his offers and promises impossible and vain and worthy of rejection. . . . Finally the monarchs sent a reply to Columbus, dismissing him for the time being, though not entirely depriving him of the hope of a return to the subject when their Highnesses should be less occupied with important business, as they were at that time by the War of Granada.

▲ Map of Hispaniola

Responding to Literature

1. How did Las Casas answer those people who thought the seas could be navigated only by sailing along the shores or coasts?

2. According to Las Casas, why did some people believe a ship could never return from a westward voyage?

3. St. Augustine is said to deny the existence of antipodes. What reasons can you think of for his belief?

4. According to the ancients, how many zones existed in the world?

ACTIVITY

5. Imagine that you are a friend and supporter of Christopher Columbus. Think of three reasons that his voyage should be financed. Using note cards, outline these reasons. Then prepare a short speech to convince a monarch or businessperson to grant Columbus the money and supplies he needs.

Chapter 1

The Geography of the Americas

Geographers organize the study of the earth and its people around five themes. A globe, an important tool of geographers, shows the earth in its true shape as a sphere. A map, another tool of geography, is a drawing of the earth on a flat surface. Some maps in this book are special-purpose maps; they give information on specific topics, such as physical regions, climate, or human activities.

The eight major physical regions of the United States are the Hawaiian Islands, the Pacific Coast, the Intermountain region, the Rocky Mountains, the Interior Plains, the Canadian Shield, the Appalachian Mountains, and the Coastal Plains. The largest climate regions include the highland, steppe, humid continental, and humid subtropical.

Chapter 2

The First Americans

The first Americans came from Asia across a land bridge to the Americas during the Ice Age. Their descendants were the Native Americans, who developed many different cultures. The Anasazi and the Mound Builders were the major early cultures in North America. Later cultures are divided into 10 groups according to geographic location: the Arctic, Subarctic, Northeast Woodlands, Southeast, Plains, Southwest, Northwest Coast, Plateau, Great Basin, and California. In Mexico, Central America, and South America, the Maya, Aztec, and Inca developed advanced civilizations.

▲ CANOE BY HAIDA CARVER

CAUSES

- Introduction of new Asian trade goods in Europe
- Strong national rulers make travel safe for merchants in Europe
- Europeans improve shipbuilding and apply navigational tools such as the compass and astrolabe

• The Age of Exploration

EFFECTS

- Europeans make voyages to the Americas
- Rise of large European empires in North and South America
- Destruction of many Native American populations and cultures
- Competition among European countries for control in the Americas

Chapter 3

Explorers Reach the Americas

Northern sea traders briefly settled in North America in the early 1000s, while the rest of Europe was still living in the isolation of the Middle Ages. Beginning in the late 1000s, Western Europeans fought a series of religious wars called the Crusades in Southwest Asia. The demand for new trade goods brought to Europe by the Crusaders led to the Age of Exploration.

▲ PONCE DE LEÓN

Portugal led the way as Europe sought a sea route to Asia. Spain, which supported the voyages of Christopher Columbus, was the first to reach the Americas, however. Spain quickly set up colonies in the Caribbean. Other European countries made a number of voyages of exploration to the Americas after Columbus first landed in 1492.

Chapter 4

European Empires in the Americas

After arriving in the Caribbean, Spain went on to conquer the Aztec and Inca civilizations. It used the wealth gained from these conquests to build up its military strength and to finance more explorations in the Americas. During the 1500s, it built the American empire of New Spain that included Central and South America, Mexico, and the northern borderlands. New Spain was divided into large estates, where landowners relied on Native Americans and enslaved Africans to do the work of mining and farming. Spain also sent many missionaries to the Americas to teach Christianity and Spanish culture to the Native Americans.

The French and Dutch, who made settlements in the Americas after the late 1500s, were mainly interested in profits to be made from the fur trade. Instead of trying to change the Native Americans, they often made allies of them.

Understanding Unit Themes

1. **Geography and the Environment** What role did the environment of North America play in the development of diverse Native American cultures?

2. **Influence of Technology** How did improved navigational technology advance the Age of Exploration? What specific advancements were most important?

3. **Conflict and Cooperation** Describe the friendly and unfriendly dealings that different European settlers had with Native Americans. How did these dealings affect the settling of North America?

UNIT 2
COLONIAL SETTLEMENT
1587–1775

★★

CHAPTER
5
The 13 English Colonies
1607–1733

CHAPTER
6
Life in the 13 Colonies
1620–1763

CHAPTER
7
The Road to Revolution
1754–1775

◄ MORTAR AND PESTLE

History AND ART

**Mayflower and Speedwell
in Dartmouth Harbor**
by Leslie A. Wilcox, c. 1971

The Puritans' voyage in search of religious freedom began in Dartmouth Harbor and ended off
the coast of present-day Massachusetts.

SETTING THE SCENE

Between 1607 and 1733, the British set up thirteen colonies along the East Coast. Despite their diverse backgrounds, English colonists placed a high value on the rights and freedoms they had under British law. When the king and Parliament threatened these rights, the colonists rebelled against British rule.

Themes

★ Beliefs, Ideas, and Institutions
★ Conflict and Cooperation
★ Civil Rights and Liberties

Key Events

★ English settlement of Jamestown, Virginia
★ Founding of the New England, Middle, and Southern Colonies
★ British win French and Indian War
★ Meeting of Stamp Act Congress
★ Boston Tea Party
★ Fighting between British and Americans at Lexington and Concord

Major Issues

★ Desire for religious freedom brought many settlers to the English colonies.
★ Native Americans and colonists clashed over Native American lands.
★ New British policies after the French and Indian War led to protest and revolution.

► THE BOSTON MASSACRE

▲ NEW ENGLAND HOME

◄ CEREMONIAL BOW

Portfolio Project

Use library resources to learn about daily life and customs in the New England, Middle, or Southern Colonies. Use the information to help you write a story about a young person who might have lived in the colonies. Illustrate your story with drawings based on your research.

There's No Place Like Home

Background

Jamestown, the first permanent English settlement, was not an easy place in which to carve out a living. Colonists had to work very hard just to stay alive. Almost every minute of the day was spent building houses, hunting or growing food, making tools, sewing clothing, or nursing the sick. In this activity you will create a model of the Jamestown fort and the surrounding colony.

Believe It OR NOT!

Did you know that the Pilgrims are not responsible for our official celebration of Thanksgiving? Thanks go to Sara Josepha Hale, a nineteenth-century magazine editor. She enlisted hundreds of people to write letters to politicians and ministers asking them to make the last Thursday in November a day of thanksgiving. President Abraham Lincoln proclaimed it a national holiday in 1863.

Materials

- cardboard boxes: enough to make one large piece of cardboard at least 2 feet by 3 feet and 20–30 smaller pieces in a variety of sizes
- assorted colored markers
- colored construction paper
- popped popcorn
- 3–4 cups of soil
- tea bags
- scissors
- glue
- tape
- string
- ruler

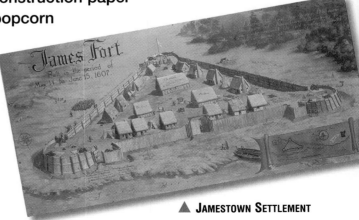

▲ JAMESTOWN SETTLEMENT

What To Do

A. Make a flat cardboard base for your model of Jamestown. Cut one large piece of cardboard to make the base at least 2 feet by 3 feet.

B. On your base mark in pencil where the bay, river, fort, houses, and farms will be placed. Use the illustration on the previous page as a guide.

C. Create the bay and the river that surrounded Jamestown using markers or construction paper.

D. Cut small pieces of cardboard to create the fort, houses, outbuildings, and fences for your model. Build each structure by connecting the cardboard pieces with tape.

E Attach the buildings and fences to the base with glue.

F. Use string to outline several plots of farmland behind the homes that surround the fort. Glue tea leaves (from tea bags) on some plots to represent tobacco crops. Glue popcorn on some plots to represent corn crops.

G. Apply a layer of glue and sprinkle it with dirt to create a road system.

H. Use the remaining cardboard and construction paper to make models of boats, docks, a church, a school, or other community buildings. Use markers and construction paper to add forests, bushes, and other details to the landscape.

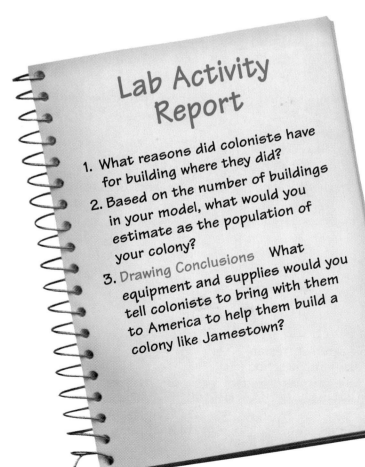

Lab Activity Report

1. What reasons did colonists have for building where they did?

2. Based on the number of buildings in your model, what would you estimate as the population of your colony?

3. *Drawing Conclusions* What equipment and supplies would you tell colonists to bring with them to America to help them build a colony like Jamestown?

GO A STEP FURTHER

ACTIVITY

Some British companies ran advertisements to encourage people to settle in America. Write an advertisement to attract settlers to your colony of Jamestown.

CHAPTER 5

★★

The 13 English Colonies
1607–1733

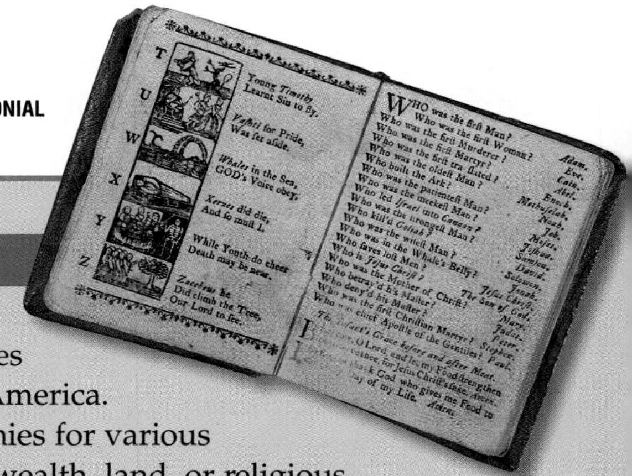

▶ **EARLY COLONIAL TEXTBOOK**

SETTING THE SCENE

Focus

In the 1600s and early 1700s, the English established thirteen colonies along the Atlantic coast of North America. People came to the American colonies for various reasons—including the pursuit of wealth, land, or religious freedom. Settlers brought their values and beliefs with them, including the idea of self-government. Some colonies welcomed people of different backgrounds, making America a land of diversity from its earliest beginnings.

Journal Notes

What were the reasons for establishing each of the American colonies? Why did different colonies attract different groups of settlers? Keep a record of these as you read the chapter.

Concepts to Understand

★ What **beliefs, ideas, and institutions** the colonists brought to America

★ How different ways of life created **cultural diversity** in the colonies

Read to Discover . . .

★ the reasons people migrated to the American colonies.

★ the ways that each of the thirteen colonies grew and developed.

Americas

1607 English found Jamestown
1620 Mayflower Compact signed

1647 Massachusetts establishes elementary schools

| 1600–1624 | 1625–1649 | 1650–1674 |

1608 Samuel de Champlain founds Quebec

1660 England passes Navigation Acts

World

NOVA BRITANNIA.
OFFERING MOST
Excellent fruites by Planting in
VIRGINIA.

Exciting all such as be well affected
to further the same.

LONDON
Printed for SAMUEL MACHAM, and are to befold at
his Shop in Pauls Church-yard, at the
Signe of the Bul-head.
1609.

◄ ENGLISH AD TO
ENTICE PLANTERS

History AND ART

Signing of the Compact on the Mayflower
by Edward Percy Moran, c. 1900

The leaders of the Mayflower composed and signed the Mayflower Compact, establishing a government for the new colony. The Puritans elected John Carver to serve as their governor.

1690 *New England Primer*, first elementary textbook, is published

1701 French establish Fort Detroit

1733 Georgia, last of the 13 colonies, is founded

1675–1699

1700–1724

1725–1749

1689 William and Mary sign English Bill of Rights

1700s Age of Enlightenment begins

1725 English Quakers speak out against slavery

★★★

English Settlers in Virginia

SETTING THE SCENE

Read to Learn . . .

★ what happened to the first American settlement at Roanoke.
★ how investors raised money to start colonies in North America.
★ what problems the colonists at Jamestown faced.

Terms to Know

★ joint-stock company
★ charter
★ plantation
★ indentured servant
★ burgesses
★ royal colony

People to Meet

★ John Smith
★ Pocahontas
★ Powhatan
★ John Rolfe

Places to Locate

★ Roanoke Island
★ Virginia
★ Chesapeake Bay
★ James River
★ Jamestown

◀ ENGLISH TOBACCO AD

The English established their first permanent settlement in the Americas in 1607. However, English merchants and adventurers had been engaged in failed efforts since the late 1500s.

With the permission of Queen Elizabeth, Sir Walter Raleigh raised money to establish a colony, and in 1585 a small group of men sailed for the Americas. They landed on **Roanoke Island** near the coast of present-day North Carolina. In less than a year, they had run short of food, and when an English ship unexpectedly arrived, all the colonists boarded and returned to England.

★ Lost Colony at Roanoke

Raleigh tried again in 1587, sending an expedition of 91 men, 17 women, and 2 children under the leadership of John White. Raleigh hoped this group would form the nucleus of a farming community. Shortly after arriving, one of the women gave birth to Virginia Dare, the first American-born child of English parents. Virginia was White's grandchild.

White left his daughter, granddaughter, and the rest of the colonists after several weeks to return to England for supplies and more settlers. He hoped to return in a few months, but hostilities between England and Spain prevented his return.

When he did return in 1590, he found the island completely deserted with no trace of the settlers. The only clue was the word CROATOAN—the name of a Native American group on a nearby island—carved on a post.

No trace of the colonists has been found. The fate of the the "Lost Colony" remains a mystery.

★ Staking a Claim in the Americas

The possibility of riches in America commanded the attention of the English. By 1600 Spain had gained a fortune from the gold and silver in its American colonies in western North America, present-day Florida, South America, and the Caribbean. The English king, James I, could not afford to send ships and supplies to America, and English nobles were unwilling to risk their private wealth.

English merchants, however, were eager for a share in the rich new continent. In 1606 merchants in the cities of London and Plymouth came up with a new way to share the costs of starting a colony.

The Virginia Companies

The merchants formed two companies, the **Virginia Company of Plymouth** and the **Virginia Company of London.** Each was a joint-stock company that sold shares to investors. Each investor contributed only a small part of the cost. If the company's project succeeded, investors shared the profits. If it failed, they lost only as much money as they had put in.

Upon receiving official permission from King James I, each company received a charter—a document that let them settle and trade in a certain area in the Americas. The London group's charter permitted it to settle land between present-day North Carolina and the Potomac River. The land was named **Virginia.** The charter granted colonists of Virginia the same rights as English citizens.

★ The Settlement of Jamestown

In December 1606 the London Company sent three ships—the *Discovery,* the *Susan Constant,* and the *Godspeed*—to start a colony in North America. The 144 men—no women were sent—faced a rough, stormy voyage. More than 40 died at sea. Finally, in April 1607 the ships reached Virginia.

They sailed into **Chesapeake Bay** and up a wide river that the colonists named the **James River** after their king. They landed on a peninsula 60 miles (96 km) up the river, and established their settlement, named **Jamestown.**

Jamestown Faces Problems

Jamestown's location was a good spot to keep a lookout for Spanish ships. It was also a good spot to trade with nearby Native Americans. It had serious drawbacks, however. The swampy land was

▲ **RECONSTRUCTION OF JAMESTOWN SETTLEMENT**

Picturing History

▲ LANDING AT JAMESTOWN In 1607 the Virginia Company of London established Jamestown, the second attempt at establishing an English colony in America. **What was the name of England's first colony in America?**

filled with mosquitoes and lacked good drinking water. As a result, many colonists died of malaria or typhoid fever.

Jamestown faced another serious problem. Its colonists knew nothing about living in a wilderness. Many of them were gentlemen from wealthy English families. They had never worked and had no practical skills. They had come to America for gold and adventure, not to cut wood, build homes, or plant crops. By September 1607 about half the colonists had died from the hard life, and by the next January only 38 were still alive.

John Smith Takes Charge

Governing Jamestown was perhaps the biggest problem colonists faced. The London Company had originally set up a board of 13 to rule the settlers. The board members quarreled and some quit. Many of the colonists refused to plant crops and only searched for gold. Without a strong leader, Jamestown's future was in danger.

Captain **John Smith,** a brave adventurer, stepped forward to take charge. Smith had no patience with the colonists' complaints. He promptly ordered the people—including the idle gentlemen—to build houses and fortifications, dig wells, clear fields, and plant crops. He made it clear that "he that will not work shall not eat."

Smith also bargained for supplies with the local Native Americans, members of the Powhatan confederacy. Smith claimed to have been captured by the Powhatans but was later released. He said that **Pocahontas**—daughter of the chief called **Powhatan**—had begged for his life. Later Pocahontas married colonist **John Rolfe.**

The "Starving Time"

Corn and freshwater from the Native Americans helped the colony survive. Under John Smith's leadership, conditions in Jamestown improved. About 500 new settlers—this time including women—came from England to join the colony in 1609. Unfortunately, Smith was hurt in a gunpowder explosion and had to return to England for medical treatment.

Once again, the colony faced hardship. That winter the food supply ran low and people fought one another for roots, acorns, and even insects. Only 60 settlers survived the "starving time," the winter of 1609–1610.

★ The Growth of Jamestown

Even with its painful beginnings, Jamestown became more stable and new settlers continued to arrive. Investors and the English government, however, still demanded a profit.

A Plantation Economy

The colony's economy did not flourish until the settlers began growing a new crop—tobacco. John Rolfe began planting tobacco in 1612. He had seen the Native Americans smoking it in pipes. Because the native tobacco was bitter and harsh, Rolfe experimented with seeds from a milder plant from the West Indies.

Within a few years, colonists shipped thousands of pounds of Virginia tobacco to England and earned huge profits. The habit of smoking rapidly spread throughout Europe. King James I, however, condemned it as "a custom loathsome to the eye, hateful to the nose, harmful to the brain, dangerous to the lungs."

Tobacco growing changed farming in Virginia. Planters set up large farms, or plantations, along the coastal rivers. Growing tobacco was hard, backbreaking work. Planters in Virginia hired indentured servants, people who agreed to work a certain number of years—usually from 3 to 7—in exchange for their passage to America. When the agreed upon time was up, indentured servants were free citizens. Between 100,000 and 150,000 men and women came to America as indentured servants in the 1600s.

Newcomers From Africa

In 1619 a Dutch ship from the West Indies brought the first Africans—20 of them—to Jamestown. The first child of African descent born in the English colonies was a boy named William, born in 1624.

These colonial African workers were probably treated as indentured servants by the tobacco planters. Some of these servants later became free citizens.

Encouraging Family Life

The hardships of the early years discouraged many people, especially women, from coming to Virginia. A few women came voluntarily or as indentured servants. London Company officials knew, however, that families were needed to make the colony stable.

In 1620 about 100 women sailed into Jamestown following promises they would have a place to live and freedom to choose their own husbands. The company charged each man who married one of these women 150 pounds (68 kg) of tobacco. Jamestown eventually became a community with families and a growing population.

Native American Neighbors

At first, mainly through the efforts of John Smith, English settlers and Native Americans were on good terms. Pocahontas married planter John Rolfe in 1614 and went with him to England where she was introduced to London society. In 1617, on her way home to America, Pocahontas caught smallpox and died.

Pocahontas's father, Powhatan, died the next year and relations between settlers

▼ AD FOR SERVANTS AND WORKERS

Picturing History

▲ BRIDE SHIP ARRIVING IN JAMESTOWN Several years after the founding of Jamestown, bride ships from England arrived to help balance the population of men and women. **What did it cost to marry one of these women?**

▲ THE HOUSE OF BURGESSES In July 1619, the House of Burgesses became the first elected lawmaking body in the colonies. **Who had the authority to refuse laws passed by the House of Burgesses?**

★ The Beginning of Self-Government

Under Jamestown's charter, the London Company controlled the colony and named a council to run it. Settlers worked for the company, which owned the land. In 1619 the company sent a governor to rule Jamestown and began granting land to individuals. It also gave colonists a voice in running the colony's government. Thus, the first form of representative government began in the English colonies.

Adult freemen could elect representatives, or burgesses, to a lawmaking body, the **House of Burgesses.** This assembly could make laws to govern the colony, although the governor of the London Company could refuse to approve them. The House of Burgesses met for the first time in a Jamestown church in July 1619.

Although by 1624 Jamestown was beginning to prosper, King James I was unhappy with the way officials were running the Virginia colony. Problems with colonists and the lack of profits caused the king to take back the charter. He then made Virginia a royal colony, a colony under the control of the king. He appointed a royal governor but did not abolish the House of Burgesses.

and Native Americans declined. The Native Americans resented the amount of land the colonists were taking, and the chief who succeeded Powhatan mistrusted the English.

Mistrust led to violence. In 1622 some Native Americans made surprise attacks on colonists. The attackers killed nearly 350 people, including John Rolfe. The colonists in turn attacked the local Native American villages and burned their crops. After many battles, the English gained control of the area.

★ SECTION 1 REVIEW ★

Checking for Understanding

1. **Identify** John Smith, Pocahontas, Powhatan, John Rolfe, Roanoke Island, Virginia, Chesapeake Bay, James River, Jamestown.

2. **Define** joint-stock company, charter, plantation, indentured servant, burgesses, royal colony.

3. **What** hardships did the first settlers in Jamestown face?

4. **What** was important about Virginia's House of Burgesses?

Critical Thinking

5. **Determining Relevance** Why did the English want a colony in North America? How successful was Jamestown in meeting England's needs?

ACTIVITY

6. Imagine that you are a shareholder in the London Company in 1619, trying to attract new settlers. Create a poster to persuade people in England to move to Jamestown.

Rippling Highways

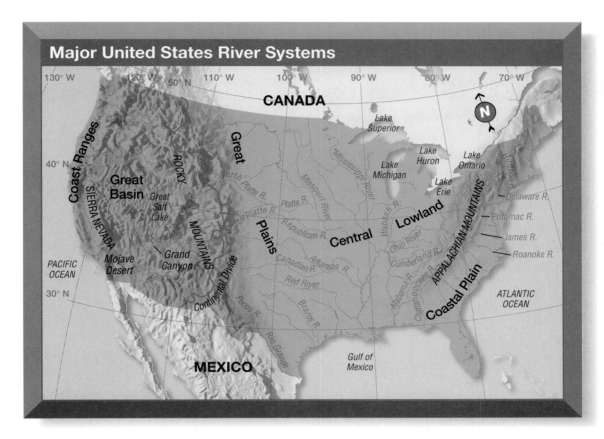

Major United States River Systems

When European explorers landed in eastern North America they did not find a system of roads into the interior of the continent. They faced an almost unbroken thick, dark wall of trees. The sparkling waters of the broad eastern rivers were the only roads to be found.

Explorers, settlers, fur traders, and missionaries all traveled America's great rivers. Nearly all the earliest colonial cities, from Boston and New York south to Savannah, were built on good harbors at the mouths of rivers. Farmers in the Middle and Southern Colonies built their farms along the banks of the Delaware, James, and the Ashley Rivers. They loaded barrels of wheat or tobacco at their own docks to be taken downriver to seaport cities. These settlers also built their homes with the front doors facing the river, ready to welcome travelers.

Making the Geography Connection

1. How were America's rivers used by early explorers and settlers?

2. Why were early American towns built along rivers?

ACTIVITY

3. Create a poster that would convince America's early eastern settlers to travel west by flatboat. Use artwork and description to tell people the advantages of this type of travel.

127

★★★

Pilgrims Found Plymouth Colony

SETTING THE SCENE

Read to Learn . . .

★ why the Pilgrims wanted to leave England.
★ why the Pilgrims signed the Mayflower Compact.
★ how Native Americans helped the colonists at Plymouth.

Terms to Know

★ Puritans
★ Separatists
★ Pilgrims
★ Mayflower Compact
★ Thanksgiving

People to Meet

★ John Carver
★ Samoset
★ Massasoit
★ Squanto

Places to Locate

★ Netherlands
★ Cape Cod
★ Massachusetts
★ Plymouth

▶ WILLIAM BRADFORD'S SILVER CUP

The hope of a new start in life brought most people to England's American colonies. A new start, however, had different meanings for different people. The people who settled Jamestown hoped to find gold and make profits. Other groups looked for a place where they could freely follow their religious beliefs.

★ Religious Disagreement in England

England had been a Protestant country since 1534, when King Henry VIII broke away from the Roman Catholic Church and formed the Anglican Church. Not everyone in England was happy with the new church, however. Many wanted to return to the Roman Catholic belief and rituals.

Puritans and Separatists

Other critics of the Anglican Church wanted to "purify" the church by getting rid of all Roman Catholic influences. Known as Puritans, most of these people stayed in the Anglican Church and tried to change it from within.

A small group of Puritans, however, disapproved so strongly of the Anglican Church that they would not worship there. They left the church and as Separatists, worshiped by themselves. This practice enraged the English government. These Separatists were attacked often for their beliefs and shut out of their communities.

Life in England became so difficult for Separatists that in 1608 one group moved to the city of Leyden in the **Netherlands,** a country known for its religious tolerance. They called themselves Pilgrims, a term for travelers with a religious goal.

After a few years, the Pilgrims still felt out of place in the Netherlands. It was more difficult to earn a living there. They also worried about their children being influenced too much by the Dutch. Despite the hazards of crossing the Atlantic, some of the Leyden Pilgrims decided to move to America. There they hoped to establish a community based on religious freedom.

★ Starting the Plymouth Colony

Organizing the voyage was difficult because most of the Pilgrims had little money. Eventually they joined with other English Separatists who also wanted to leave England, and gained a charter from the London Company to set up a colony in Virginia. One prosperous businessman, **John Carver,** arranged financial backing and found the group a small but seaworthy ship, the *Mayflower.*

Journey to America

In September 1620, after several delays the *Mayflower* set sail from Plymouth, England. It carried about 100 men, women, and children including Separatists from Leyden and England.

The Atlantic crossing was stormy, and winds blew the ship off course. Finally, on November 9, 1620, the *Mayflower* came to rest at the tip of **Cape Cod,** off the coast of present-day **Massachusetts.**

The Mayflower Compact

The Pilgrims had not reached Virginia, but rather the New England region named and mapped by John Smith in

▼ MODERN-DAY BUTTER CHURN

Linking Past and Present

★★★★★★★★★★★ ★★★ ★

Cream to Butter

Colonists could take nothing for granted. Almost everything they needed had to be made.

Then

A Job for Everyone

With no supermarkets, running water, or refrigeration, the people of Plymouth Colony had to grow or make everything

they needed. The men grew the crops and hunted for game. Food products were cooked or preserved mostly by women. Bringing in firewood and churning the butter were common chores for children. All tasks were time-consuming and done by hand.

Now

Machines Do the Work

Today milk products are processed in modern dairies that have clean, refrigerated

equipment. Continuously churning, stainless steel machines can make cream into butter in three minutes or less.

► COLONIAL BUTTER CHURN

1614. They were outside the area of their charter and its laws. To establish some kind of law and discipline, Pilgrim leaders decided that they must make an agreement before they went ashore.

The 41 men aboard signed a document setting up a form of self-government and agreeing to obey laws passed by the majority. This pact became known as the Mayflower Compact. John Carver was chosen governor of the new colony.

Landing at Plymouth

The Pilgrims searched for nearly a month before they found **Plymouth** harbor. In late December they stepped ashore and settled on cleared land that had once been a Native American village.

In the bleak, cold winter, the Pilgrims, like the Virginia colonists, had their "starving time." By spring almost half of them had died. Those that survived managed to keep the colony alive. **William Bradford,** the second governor of Plymouth, later wrote in his history:

❝ . . . [I]n two or three months' time half of their company died, especially in January and February, being the depth of winter, and wanting houses and other comforts; being infected with the scurvy and other diseases which this long voyage . . . had brought upon them. ❞

★ Native Americans and the Pilgrims

The colonists who survived the winter were surprised one March day when a

 ▲ *THE FIRST THANKSGIVING* by Jennie A. Brownscombe, c. 1914 This traditional depiction of the first Thanksgiving shows Pilgrims sharing their bountiful harvest with Native Americans. **What Native American group helped the Pilgrims survive at Plymouth?**

tall Native American named **Samoset** appeared and greeted them in English. Samoset introduced them to **Massasoit** (MAS•uh•soit), chief of the Wampanoags (wahm•puh•NOH•AGS), the group that controlled present-day southeastern Massachusetts.

One of the Wampanoags, **Squanto,** taught the Pilgrims how to survive in their new home. He taught them how to hunt in the forests, how to plant corn, and where to catch fish. Squanto also acted as their interpreter, helping to maintain peace between the colonists and Native Americans. The Pilgrims, grateful for Squanto's help, called him "a special instrument sent of God."

Plymouth Survives

Thanks to the help of the nearby Wampanoags, the Pilgrims had an abundant harvest in 1621. They shared their bounty with the Native Americans in a festival usually thought to be the first Thanksgiving in the English colonies. The meal probably included corn bread, wild game birds, greens, venison, and shellfish.

In 1621 the Council for New England officially granted the Pilgrims a charter for their settlement at Plymouth. A few

new settlers arrived, but Plymouth Colony grew slowly. It had only 300 settlers by 1630 and 3,000 by 1660.

The Pilgrims were always a poor community. As late as the 1640s, they had only one plow among them. However, they clung to their belief that God had put them in America to live as a truly Christian community. On the whole, the Pilgrims were content to live their lives in what they considered godly ways.

At times the Pilgrims spoke of serving as a model for other Christians. Governor Bradford wrote:

 As one small candle may light a thousand, so the light here kindled hath shone to many, yea in some sort to our whole nation. 🙾

★ **SECTION 2 REVIEW** ★

★★★★★★★★★★★★★★★★★   ★★★★★★★★★★★★★★★★★

Checking for Understanding

1. **Identify** John Carver, Samoset, Massasoit, Squanto, Netherlands, Cape Cod, Massachusetts, Plymouth.

2. **Define** Puritans, Separatists, Pilgrims, Mayflower Compact, Thanksgiving.

3. **Why** did the Pilgrims leave England?

4. **How** did Native Americans help the Pilgrims at Plymouth survive?

Critical Thinking

5. **Making Comparisons** How were the settlements of Jamestown and Plymouth similar? How were they different?

ACTIVITY

6. Working alone or with a partner, create a cartoon strip that tells the story of the Pilgrims' journey from England to the Plymouth Colony.

★★

Settling the New England Colonies

SETTING THE SCENE

Read to Learn . . .

★ why the Puritans founded the Massachusetts Bay Colony.

★ why settlers moved from Massachusetts Bay to Rhode Island and Connecticut.

★ why conflicts arose between the Native Americans and the colonists.

Terms to Know

★ Great Migration
★ Massachusetts Bay Company
★ commonwealth
★ toleration
★ Fundamental Orders of Connecticut
★ constitution

People to Meet

★ John Winthrop
★ Roger Williams
★ Anne Hutchinson
★ Thomas Hooker
★ Metacomet

Places to Locate

★ New England Colonies
★ Boston
★ Providence
★ Rhode Island
★ Connecticut
★ New Hampshire
★ Maine

▶ **PURITAN BIBLE BOX**

Interest in the American colonies continued to grow in England. Political issues and church conflicts made many groups seriously consider crossing the Atlantic in search of new opportunities. The New England described by John Smith attracted many who wanted personal or economic freedom. They settled the **New England Colonies.**

★ Puritans in Massachusetts

The Separatists who founded Plymouth in America were a tiny group compared

with the number of Puritans in England. These Puritans were under continuous attack and punishment for criticizing the Anglican Church. This pressure forced many Puritans to seek religious freedom in the American colonies. There they hoped to freely follow their beliefs. News of possible wealth and success in the new lands also drew the Puritans.

The year 1630 marked the beginning of what is called the Great Migration. Ten years after Plymouth Colony was founded, 1,000 people crossed the stormy Atlantic to New England. In the next 10 years, some 16,000 people would journey to this part of America.

The Massachusetts Bay Company

In 1625 Charles I succeeded his father, James I, as king of England. The new king despised the Puritans and put more pressure on them to follow the Anglican Church. Represented by **John Winthrop,** a well-to-do lawyer and landowner, the Puritans requested a colonial charter from the king. In 1629 the Puritans received their charter and formed the Massachusetts Bay Company.

Settling the Colony

In 1630, 17 ships with more than 1,000 Puritan settlers left England to establish the Massachusetts Bay Colony just north of Plymouth. It was the largest single migration of this type in the seventeenth century. The expedition was better organized than the Jamestown or Plymouth trips. Settlers brought large stores of food, clothing, tools, and livestock with them.

"A City Upon a Hill"

In Massachusetts Bay, the Puritans hoped to build a Christian society that would be a model for the rest of the world. As John Winthrop, who became the colony's first governor, wrote: "For we must consider that we shall be like a City upon a Hill; the eyes of all people are on us."

The new colony overcame harsh weather and disease, and prospered. By the early 1640s some 16,000 colonists were living in **Boston,** the capital, and in smaller neighboring towns such as Watertown and Charlestown. Good access to rivers and other waterways made Boston a successful trading center.

Using the Bible as their guide, the Puritans practiced the kind of religion they had wanted in England. Instead of being ruled by a bishop or other distant leader, each church was run by its congregation. This meant that church members chose their own minister. They also transformed the Massachusetts Bay Company from a trading company into a commonwealth, a self-governing political unit. It was the first of its kind in America.

The General Court

The **General Court,** which made the laws, at first included only the Puritans who were investors in the Massachusetts Bay Company. Later all adult freemen became members of the company, provided they were church members. They elected the governor and members of the General Court.

Many of the colony's laws enforced Puritan ways of thinking. Everyone, even nonmembers, had to attend long Sunday church services. The rest of the day was to be spent praying and reading the Bible. Dancing and sports or games were strictly forbidden.

★ A New Colony in Rhode Island

Although the Puritans came to Massachusetts to find freedom for their own beliefs, they did not believe in religious toleration—the acceptance of different beliefs. The Puritans treated those who disagreed with them harshly. Some were driven from the colony; others left to start their own new settlements.

Roger Williams Speaks Out

In Salem, a town north of Boston, the young minister **Roger Williams** preached ideas that angered Puritan leaders.

Williams believed the church had too much power in governing the colony. Civil officials, he said, should not punish people for following their consciences. Nor should people have to belong to the church to vote. Williams said the church and the government should be separate. This idea shocked the Puritans. This **separation of church and state** would later become a basic principle of American government.

Williams also questioned the Massachusetts Bay charter. He said that colonists could not legally settle on the land unless they bought it from the Native Americans.

Angered by Williams's ideas, in 1635 the General Court banished him from the colony. In the dead of winter, he and a few friends fled south to Narragansett Bay. There they spent the winter with the Native Americans, the Wampanoags, who trusted Williams as a friend.

A Place for Religious Tolerance

True to his principles, Williams bargained with the Narragansetts for a piece of land to start a community. He named it **Providence.** People who were unhappy with the strict laws of Massachusetts Bay Colony were welcome in Providence. Williams also accepted people who held beliefs other than his own even if he disagreed with the beliefs. Quakers and Jews eventually found a home in his new colony.

Providence prospered because it had better farmland than much of Massachusetts. Puritan laws drove many people to this neighboring island of religious tolerance, and three other towns were started. Eventually these towns joined together as the colony of **Rhode Island** under a charter that Williams obtained from the English Parliament in 1644. The smallest of the English colonies, Rhode Island held on to the ideas that set it apart from its neighbors.

Hutchinson Challenges Church Leaders

One Puritan who found refuge in Rhode Island was **Anne Hutchinson,** a gentle but brilliant and outspoken woman. Born Anne Marbury, in England in 1591, she married William Hutchinson, a merchant, in 1612. Even in England, Hutchinson had firm ideas about her religious faith and her church.

▲ ANNE HUTCHINSON

In 1634 the Hutchinsons, a strong Puritan family, moved to Boston. Hutchinson became the center of a group of women who met to discuss the Bible as well as other somewhat new ideas. At these gatherings, Hutchinson announced her belief that people should speak to God themselves, not through ministers or the church. She did not believe that church leaders should be so powerful. Her claims that she herself had communicated directly to God threatened the control ministers had over church members. Hutchinson spoke boldly that a more powerful place in society should be given to women. These ideas outraged Puritan leaders. They could not let her statements go unchallenged.

The arguments over Hutchinson split the colony. In 1637 she was put on trial for her beliefs. Hutchinson defended herself by quoting the Bible and law, but the General Court found her "a woman unfit for our society" and banished her.

Along with her family and friends, she founded the town of Portsmouth south of Providence. When her husband died in 1642, she moved to the Dutch colony of New Netherland. Hutchinson was killed the next year during a war between the Dutch and Native Americans. ★★★

★ West to Connecticut

Some faithful Puritans left Massachusetts by their own choice. By the middle of the 1630s, many colonists believed that Massachusetts was becoming too crowded. Looking for better farmland, several groups traveled west along trails cut through the wilderness by Native Americans. In the valley of the Connecticut River they started the towns of Windsor and Wethersfield.

In 1636 the minister **Thomas Hooker** led his congregation from Massachusetts to **Connecticut,** where they built a town they called Hartford. Hooker had his own ideas about running a colony and limiting the powers of government. Massachusetts laws that allowed only church members to vote, for example, disturbed him.

With leaders from the other towns, Hooker worked out a plan of government known as the Fundamental Orders of Connecticut. This document was the first American constitution, or plan of government, to be written. It provided for an assembly and an elected governor. Under these orders, all men who were property owners could vote. In 1662 Connecticut became a separate colony when it was granted a separate charter by the king.

★ New Hampshire and Maine

No one knows for sure who were the first European settlers in New Hampshire. But in 1622 John Mason and Sir Ferdinando Gorges received a grant in the area that is today **New Hampshire** and **Maine.** Massachusetts claimed the settled areas in both Maine and New Hampshire. New Hampshire became a royal colony in 1680, while Maine remained part of Massachusetts until 1820.

▲ *HOOKER AND COMPANY JOURNEY THROUGH THE WILDERNESS FROM PLYMOUTH TO HARTFORD IN 1636* by Frederic Edwin Church, 1846 A Congregationalist minister, Thomas Hooker led his followers to Connecticut to form a less restrictive government. **What is the name of the first American constitution?**

★ Colonists and Native Americans Clash

As more settlers arrived in New England, they took over Native American lands. They cleared forests for farming, thus driving away much of the wild game the Native Americans depended on for food. The settlers often let their livestock run wild, and the animals frequently destroyed the Indians' crops. The Native American population in the area had been declining for years as a result of epidemic diseases. Now land and food shortages worsened their plight.

The Puritans also tried to convert the Native Americans to Christianity and change their way of life. Hoping to stop the English invasion and save their heritage, Native Americans fought back.

The Pequot Wars

As the Connecticut colonists moved westward and built more towns, they pushed the Pequot Indians from their lands. Clashes broke out and colonists were killed in Indian raids. Puritan leaders took revenge, destroying Native American crops and villages.

In 1637 English settlers and their Native American allies surprised the Pequots with an attack on their main fort. Some 500 Pequot men, women, and children were killed. This nearly wiped out the Pequot nation and allowed the English to take over their land.

King Philip's War

Distrust and tension between settlers and Native Americans again erupted into war in 1675. The Wampanoag chief **Metacomet,** whom the English called **King Philip,** brought together his allies throughout southern New England. Native Americans continued to protest the English moving onto their lands. They also resented the colonial government that tried to make them obey English laws. For three years the Native Americans burned towns and farms and killed or kidnapped settlers.

In turn, the English struck back, destroying villages and killing or wounding thousands of Native Americans. Some, including Metacomet's wife and son, were captured and sold into slavery in the West Indies. In 1676, Metacomet was killed, and King Philip's War came to an end.

★ SECTION 3 REVIEW ★

Checking for Understanding

1. **Identify** John Winthrop, Roger Williams, Anne Hutchinson, Thomas Hooker, Metacomet, New England Colonies, Boston, Providence, Rhode Island, Connecticut, New Hampshire, Maine.

2. **Define** Great Migration, Massachusetts Bay Colony, commonwealth, toleration, Fundamental Orders of Connecticut, constitution.

3. **What** were the reasons for the founding of Rhode Island and Connecticut?

4. **Why** was King Philip's War fought?

Critical Thinking

5. **Recognizing Ideas** How important was religious freedom to the Puritans at Massachusetts Bay Colony? What was their attitude toward other religions?

ACTIVITY

6. Choose one event from this chapter, such as the founding of Rhode Island or Anne Hutchinson's journey. Use a small box to create a scene illustrating that event. Use small objects and paint to represent buildings, trees, and other scene details.

★★★

Settling the Middle Colonies

SETTING THE SCENE

Read to Learn . . .

★ who the first settlers were in New York, Pennsylvania, New Jersey, and Delaware.
★ how the English gained control of the Middle Colonies.

Terms to Know

★ patroon
★ proprietor
★ proprietary colony
★ Quakers

People to Meet

★ Henry Hudson
★ Peter Minuit
★ Peter Stuyvesant
★ King Charles II
★ James, Duke of York
★ William Penn

Places to Locate

★ Hudson River
★ New York
★ New Jersey
★ Pennsylvania
★ Delaware

◀ COLONIAL GRINDSTONE

A land of wide river valleys, thick forests, and excellent harbors lay between New England and Virginia. By the early 1600s, the Dutch and the Swedes already had settlements here. Eventually the English would acquire all of this region, which became known as the **Middle Colonies.**

★ New Netherland Becomes New York

The Dutch showed an early interest in developing trade routes with Asia. In 1609 on a voyage for the Dutch government,

Henry Hudson sailed up a beautiful, wide river, which is now named for him. Like other explorers in North America, Hudson was looking for a Northwest Passage—a sea route to Asia. The **Hudson River** was not the hoped-for route, but Hudson's voyage gave the Dutch a claim to the lands along it.

The Beginning of New Netherland

Although the Netherlands was a small country, its large fleet of trading ships sailed all over the world. In 1621 the Dutch West India Company set up a trading colony—New Netherland—in the area

Hudson had explored. In 1624 the company sent 30 families to settle the area.

The center of the new colony was **New Amsterdam,** located on the tip of Manhattan Island where the Hudson River enters New York Harbor. In 1626 **Peter Minuit** (MIHN•yuh•wuht), the governor of the colony, paid the Native Americans 60 Dutch guilders—about $24—in beads, knives, and other trading goods in exchange for the island.

Compared with the New England Colonies, New Netherland grew very slowly. Most Dutch people had no real reason to migrate to a frontier colony. Their country was prosperous and tolerant of different religions. To encourage more settlers, the Dutch West India Company let it be known that the colony welcomed all people, including those who had fled New England for religious reasons.

The company also gave huge tracts of Hudson riverfront land to anyone who would bring 50 new settlers to New Amsterdam. These landowners, or patroons, ran their large estates as they wished, enforcing their own laws. The people who worked on a patroon's estate had little voice in their government.

New Sweden Established

The fur trade brought settlers from Sweden. In 1638 the Swedes built Fort Christina in the Delaware River valley at present-day Wilmington, Delaware. The population of New Sweden—as it was called—remained small.

The Dutch, however, saw New Sweden as a rival for trade. In 1655 **Peter Stuyvesant** (STY•vuh•suhnt), the Dutch governor of

New Netherland, seized the colony and made it part of New Netherland.

The Swedish colonists who stayed on under Dutch rule brought the American colonies an important new skill. As they had done in Sweden's thick forests, the people cut trees and notched the logs to build log cabins. Quick and easy to build using only an ax, the log cabin became the most common kind of frontier home.

A New English King Takes Over

While English colonies in North America were growing, political events had exploded in England. In 1642 civil war broke out between Parliament, which was dominated by Puritans, and supporters of King Charles I. To the shock of many people, the king was beheaded for treason.

For 11 years, Puritan leaders ran England. Then in 1660, the monarchy returned to power under the popular **King Charles II.** The new king turned his attention to his American empire. Only New Netherland kept him from holding all the Atlantic coast. In 1664 Charles sent his younger brother, **James, Duke of York,** to seize the Dutch colony.

In August 1664 the people of New Amsterdam were surprised to see four English warships anchored in their harbor. Governor Stuyvesant tried to get the colonists to arm themselves and fight, but they were tired of the bad-tempered governor and his arbitrary rule. Without a fight, New Netherland surrendered to the English. New Amsterdam was renamed **New York** in honor of the king's brother, the Duke of York.

• •

Footnotes to History

Delivering the Mail on Horseback   The first mounted postal delivery route in America was established in 1673. Connecting Boston and New York City, a horse rider took three weeks to deliver the mail from one city to the other.

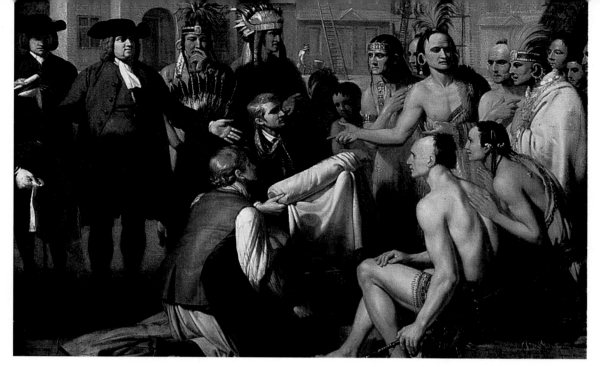

PENN'S TREATY WITH THE INDIANS by Benjamin West, 1771 William Penn's strong religious beliefs, such as all people are equal in the sight of God, led him to sign a fair treaty with Native Americans. **William Penn belonged to what religious group?**

Colonial Government

Charles II made James the proprietor, or owner, of the colony of New York. This type of colony, a proprietary colony, was awarded to one person or a group of people by the king. James let the Dutch settlers keep their lands, religion, and customs. As before, the colony allowed religious freedom to all. New York colonists had no say in their government, however. James appointed a governor and a council to rule the colony.

Many English people did not settle in New York because of its controlled government. On the other hand, the colony attracted settlers seeking religious freedom from Scotland, France, and other European countries.

★ New Jersey

The Duke of York hoped to make a profit from his land, but his property was so large he could not manage it all. He gave some of his land, between the Hudson and Delaware Rivers, to two friends, Lord John Berkeley and Sir George Carteret. The area was named **New Jersey** after Carteret's birthplace.

Neither proprietor actively worked to develop a colony, but they kept up York's policy of religious freedom. East and West Jersey developed separately until 1702, when they became a royal colony.

★ William Penn's Colonies

Soon the Middle Colonies were home to another group that believed in religious tolerance. South of New Jersey, **William Penn** founded a colony as home to his religious community, the Quakers. Penn was a strong champion of tolerance for all people.

Quakers were persecuted because their beliefs angered authorities. For example, Quakers believed that all people—whether wealthy or poor—were equal in the sight of God. They refused to take oaths, and women were allowed to speak in their meetinghouses. They opposed war and would not serve in the army. Quakers also refused to pay taxes. They were the first religious group in the colonies to take a stand against slavery. Like other Quakers, Penn went to jail several times for expressing his beliefs. It was unusual for someone of Penn's social class to be a Quaker. His wealth and influence, however, allowed him to create a haven for other Quakers in America.

The Founding of Pennsylvania

Penn's father had once loaned King Charles a large sum of money. To repay the loan, in 1681 the king made the younger Penn the proprietor of a large grant of land in America. Penn named it **Pennsylvania**—Penn's woods—to honor his father.

To attract settlers, he distributed pamphlets that described the colony's beauty and richness. One pamphlet described Pennsylvania as a land where "the Air is sweet and clear, the Heavens serene, like the South-parts of France, rarely Overcast."

Penn's plan of government was based on religious freedom and popular support of the government. He treated the Native Americans fairly, paying them for their land. Pennsylvania's farms quickly became prosperous. In addition to English Quakers, the colony drew many other European settlers.

One large group of settlers were German farmers fleeing religious wars. They settled on the rich farmland along the Delaware and Susquehanna Rivers in tight-knit communities that kept alive their customs. These people became known as the **Pennsylvania Dutch,** from the word *Deutsch,* meaning "German."

Delaware

One problem that landlocked Pennsylvania faced was the lack of seaports from which to ship its farm products. Farmers produced large quantities of wheat, barley, and rye for export. In 1682 Penn received a grant from James, Duke of York, for three counties along the Delaware River, once part of New Sweden. This gave the colony access to the Atlantic Ocean and shipping to England.

Trying to unite Pennsylvania with these lower counties, called **Delaware,** caused trouble among the settlers. As proprietor, Penn later allowed the area to elect their own assembly, although he remained its governor. The counties later broke away to form the separate colony of Delaware.

★ SECTION 4 REVIEW ★

Checking for Understanding

1. **Identify** Henry Hudson; Peter Minuit; Peter Stuyvesant; King Charles II; James, Duke of York; William Penn; Hudson River; New York; New Jersey; Pennsylvania; Delaware.
2. **Define** patroon, proprietor, proprietary colony, Quakers.
3. **Why** did the English want the Dutch settlement of New Netherland?
4. **What** were William Penn's goals for the colony of Pennsylvania?

Critical Thinking

5. **Identifying Alternatives**   What different reasons did New York and Pennsylvania have for welcoming people of various religions and nationalities?

ACTIVITY

6. You have been asked to create a flag for one of the Middle Colonies. Choose one colony; then decide what symbols and colors you will use to represent it.

★★

Settling the Southern Colonies

SETTING THE SCENE

Read to Learn . . .

★ why Maryland was founded.
★ why Carolina became two colonies.
★ what Georgia's proprietor hoped to achieve.

Terms to Know

★ Toleration Act
★ naval stores
★ indigo

People to Meet

★ Lord Baltimore
★ James Oglethorpe
★ King George II

Places to Locate

★ Maryland
★ Potomac River
★ Carolina
★ Charles Town
★ Georgia
★ Savannah River

◀ LORD BALTIMORE SHILLING

Wealthy English people continued to see colonial America as a good long-term investment. By 1630 they had given up the idea of quick riches such as gold or silver being found. Huge profits were being made by Virginia's tobacco planters and farmers. Between 1632 and 1732 proprietors established four new colonies south of the Delaware River. Together with Virginia, this region became the **Southern Colonies.**

★ Maryland, a Religious Refuge

After the Church of England was established, the English who remained Roman Catholic often faced persecution or dis-

crimination. Like other groups, they sought a safe place in America.

Lord Baltimore Starts a Colony

George Calvert, a Catholic whose title was **Lord Baltimore,** made several unsuccessful tries to start a colony where he and other people could safely practice Roman Catholicism. After being turned away from Jamestown, he returned to England, where he died in 1632 while waiting for a new land grant.

A month later Calvert's son Cecil, the second Lord Baltimore, was granted a charter for the colony of **Maryland.** To attract settlers, he announced a generous land plan. Settlers would receive land for themselves plus extra acres for each child

Founding the Thirteen Colonies

Colony	Date Founded	Reasons Founded	Founders or Leaders
New England Colonies			
Massachusetts Plymouth Mass. Bay Colony	1620 1630	Religious freedom Religious freedom	John Carver, William Bradford, John Winthrop
New Hampshire	1622	Profit from trade and fishing	Ferdinando Gorges, John Mason
Rhode Island	1636	Religious freedom	Roger Williams
Connecticut	1636	Profit from fur trade, farming; religious and political freedom	Thomas Hooker
Middle Colonies			
New York	1624	Expand trade	Dutch settlers
Delaware	1638	Expand trade	Swedish settlers
New Jersey	1664	Profit from selling land	John Berkeley, George Carteret
Pennsylvania	1681	Profit from selling land; religious freedom	William Penn
Southern Colonies			
Virginia	1607	Expand trade	John Smith
Maryland	1632	Profit from selling land; religious freedom	Cecil Calvert
North Carolina	1663	Profit from trade and selling land	Group of eight aristocrats
South Carolina	1663	Profit from trade and selling land	Group of eight aristocrats
Georgia	1732	Religious freedom; protection against Spanish Florida; safe home for debtors	James Oglethorpe

Chart Study

The 13 colonies were founded over a span of 125 years. **What were the two most common reasons for founding these colonies?**

▲ GEORGE CALVERT

and each servant with them. A person with a large family could receive a huge estate and pay only a small tax to the proprietor.

In 1633, Lord Baltimore sent two ships, the *Ark* and the *Dove,* to Maryland. They carried more than 200 settlers, both Protestants and Roman Catholics. The settlers bought land from the Native Americans, paying with goods such as axes, hoes, and clothing. They built a fort, a chapel, and small cabins in their first settlement at a site they called St. Mary's.

Prosperity and Conflict

With a warm climate and good soil for farming, Maryland prospered. Its excellent waterways, such as the **Potomac**

River, made it easy to ship goods to and from England. Rivers were also a source of fish, oysters, and crabs. Maryland farmers grew a variety of crops. As in Virginia, tobacco was the most profitable.

At first the colony's Catholics and Protestants lived in peace, but within a few years the Protestants outnumbered the Catholics. To protect both groups, Lord Baltimore issued the Toleration Act in 1649. This law guaranteed all Christians the right to worship as they pleased. It did not include tolerance for other religious groups such as Jews, however.

★ The Two Carolinas

The profits made by tobacco planters in Virginia and Maryland encouraged English aristocrats to become proprietors of southern colonies. In 1663 King Charles II granted eight English nobles a large tract of land along the Atlantic coast south of Virginia. In thanks, the new proprietors named the colony **Carolina,** from the Latin form of Charles.

The Carolina proprietors were eager to attract settlers. They advertised their colony in pamphlets:

> **Carolina is a fair and spacious province on the continent of America. . . . That which lies near the sea is sandy and barren. . . . The woods are stored with deer and wild turkeys, of a great magnitude. . . .**

Despite this advertising, Carolina grew slowly at first. The climate was humid and, as in Virginia, the swampy coastal land caused fever and malaria. The proprietors' plan of offering large amounts of land to a few titled nobles was another problem affecting Carolina's growth. They did not open the land to less wealthy settlers. This prevented the colony from attracting large groups of settlers.

Northern and Southern Regions

From the beginning, Carolina divided naturally into two regions. The northern part was settled mostly by people from Virginia. They moved southward looking for new farmland to grow tobacco and corn. From the thick pine forests, they could supply the English navy with lumber and naval stores. This term includes products such as tar, pitch, and turpentine that are used in shipbuilding.

Settlement of the British Colonies, 1607–1760

Before 1660
Between 1660 and 1700
Between 1700 and 1760
Regional boundary
● Town or city

Map Study

Region The British Colonies offered new opportunities and new freedom to settlers from Europe. **Where were most settlements before 1660 located?**

South Carolina attracted other groups—settlers from the West Indies, England, and other parts of Europe. English colonists from the island of Barbados founded the major port city of **Charles Town**—present-day Charleston.

Some settlers from the West Indies introduced the growing of indigo, a plant that produces a blue dye. Others grew rich by planting rice on large plantations, which demanded many workers. Most plantation owners in South Carolina used enslaved Africans, who brought their knowledge of rice-growing from Africa. They also tended cattle, which were slaughtered for their meat that was exported.

★ Georgia, a Colony for the Poor

The last English colony founded in America—**Georgia**—was also very unique. It was established for completely different reasons than any other colony. Georgia's proprietor, General **James Oglethorpe,** became interested in helping London's poor while investigating the conditions in debtors' prisons. Thousands of English men, women, and children were in prison, most for owing small amounts of money. They could not be released until they had paid their debt, yet had no way to earn any money. Oglethorpe decided to start a colony to give such people a second chance.

In 1732 Oglethorpe and some friends received a charter from **King George II** for land between the **Savannah River** and the border of Spanish Florida. While Oglethorpe was worried about the poor, the king wanted a buffer between South Carolina and Spanish troops in Florida.

A Slow Start

The colony, Georgia, was named in honor of the king. After setting up a fortified town at the mouth of the Savannah River in 1733, Georgia grew slowly. To Oglethorpe's disappointment, many debtors did not want to come to the colony when they heard they might have to risk their lives fighting the well-trained Spanish. Oglethorpe's own rules also discouraged settlers. He set strict limits on how much land they could own, forbade the use of African slave labor, and outlawed the sale or use of liquor. Later, a more liberal landholding policy and removal of the slaveholding prohibition contributed to Georgia's growth and prosperity.

★ SECTION 5 REVIEW ★

★★★★★★★★★★★★★★★★★★★★★★★★★★★★★★★★★★★★★★

Checking for Understanding

1. **Identify** Lord Baltimore, James Oglethorpe, King George II, Maryland, Potomac River, Carolina, Charles Town, Georgia, Savannah River.

2. **Define** Toleration Act, naval stores, indigo.

3. **Why** did George Calvert want to start the colony of Maryland?

4. **Who** was the colony of Georgia intended to help?

Critical Thinking

5. **Analyzing Primary Sources** Read the quotation from the advertisement for Carolina on page 143. What was the writer's purpose?

ACTIVITY

6. Work with a small group to create a bulletin-board display titled "The Southern Colonies." Include slogans and pictures to show the colonies' origins, climate, land, and products.

BUILDING SKILLS
Social Studies Skills

Reading a Bar Graph

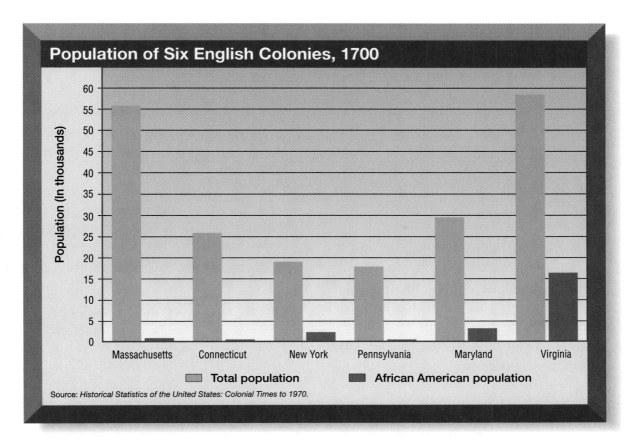

Population of Six English Colonies, 1700

Population (In thousands)

Massachusetts — Connecticut — New York — Pennsylvania — Maryland — Virginia

☐ Total population   ■ African American population

Source: *Historical Statistics of the United States: Colonial Times to 1970.*

Graphs are a way of showing numbers or statistics in a clear, easy-to-read way. One type of graph often used to compare statistics is a bar graph.

Learning the Skill

A bar graph provides information along two sides or axes. The **horizontal axis** is the line across the bottom of the graph. The **vertical axis** is the line along the side. Both have labels to tell you what kind of information they are showing. Bars on the graph run horizontally or vertically along these axes. A double bar graph, such as the one on this page, shows a comparison of information. A key tells you what each bar represents.

Practicing the Skill

1. What two kinds of populations are shown on this graph?

2. Which colonies are included on the graph?

3. Which two colonies had the largest total population in 1700?

4. Which New England colony had the highest African American population in 1700?

APPLYING THE SKILL

5. Gather information about the number of students in each class in your school and create a bar graph to represent what you find.

Using Key Vocabulary

Use the following vocabulary words to complete the sentences below.

toleration   Mayflower Compact
proprietor   indigo
charter

1. To settle in a certain area, people had to be granted a _____ by the ruler of England.

2. A grant of land from King Charles made William Penn the _____ of the colony of Pennsylvania.

3. A source for blue dye is the plant called _____.

4. Before they landed at Plymouth, the Pilgrims signed the _____ to establish a form of self-government.

5. To accept a person who has a different religious faith means to show _____.

Reviewing Facts

1. **Explain** how the Virginia Company of London raised money to finance the costs of a new colony.

2. **Identify** Squanto and explain what he did for the colonists at Plymouth.

3. **Describe** the events that led to the founding of Rhode Island.

4. **Explain** why William Penn wanted to start the colony of Pennsylvania.

5. **List** the Southern Colonies that were founded after Virginia was successful.

Understanding Concepts

Beliefs, Ideas, and Institutions

1. Why did Puritans, Quakers, and Roman Catholics all want to leave England?

2. Why is the House of Burgesses important to the history of the United States?

3. Besides England, what countries established colonies around the Hudson and Delaware Rivers?

Cultural Diversity

4. Why did Roger Williams found Rhode Island?

5. Why did the colony of New York have a greater variety of people than the colony of Massachusetts Bay?

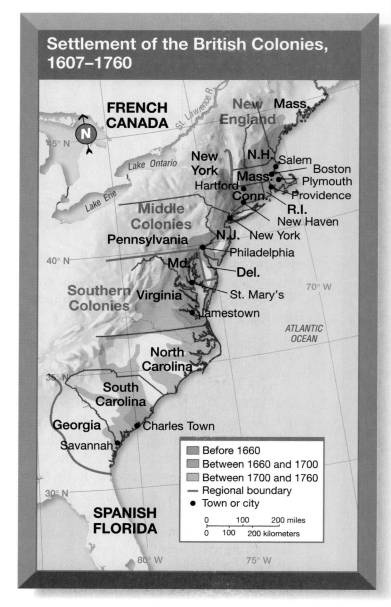

Settlement of the British Colonies, 1607–1760

FRENCH CANADA
St. Lawrence R.
New England
New Mass.
45° N
Lake Ontario
New York
N.H.
Salem
Mass.
Boston
Hartford
Conn.
Plymouth
Providence
Lake Erie
R.I.
New Haven
Middle Colonies
Pennsylvania
N.J. New York
Philadelphia
40° N
Md.
Del.
70° W
Southern Colonies
Virginia
St. Mary's
Jamestown
ATLANTIC OCEAN
North Carolina
35° N
South Carolina
Georgia
Charles Town
Savannah
30° N
SPANISH FLORIDA
80° W
75° W

■ Before 1660
■ Between 1660 and 1700
■ Between 1700 and 1760
— Regional boundary
● Town or city

0   100   200 miles
0   100   200 kilometers

History and Geography

Settlement of the British Colonies

Study the map on page 146. Then answer the questions below.

1. **Location**   Which colonies had the largest areas of settlement before 1660?

2. **Region**   In which group of colonies did most of the settlement occur after 1700?

Critical Thinking

1. **Determining Cause and Effect**   Explain how a family's religion would most likely affect its decision on where to settle in the American colonies.

2. **Understanding Points of View**   If you had lived in Puritan Massachusetts, which group of settlers who left to start their own colonies might you have joined? Why?

Cooperative Learning Interdisciplinary Activity: The Arts

Work with a group to write a two-act play about the establishment of one of the colonies described in this chapter. One act should take place in England or Europe, and the other act in America. Some members of the group can design costumes and sets while others work on writing the play.

Practicing Skills

Reading a Bar Graph

Study the bar graph. Then answer the questions below.

1. What do the numbers on the vertical axis represent?

2. What was the approximate value of exports to England in 1700?

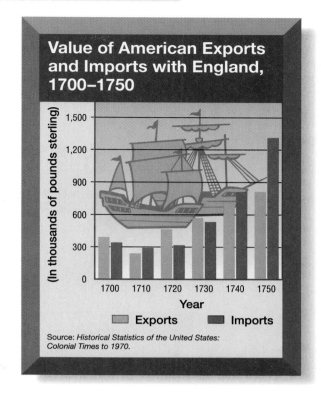

Value of American Exports and Imports with England, 1700–1750

(In thousands of pounds sterling)

Exports ■ Imports

Source: *Historical Statistics of the United States: Colonial Times to 1970.*

3. What was the first year in which the value of exports and of imports were both more than 500,000 pounds sterling?

4. In which years were there more exports than imports?

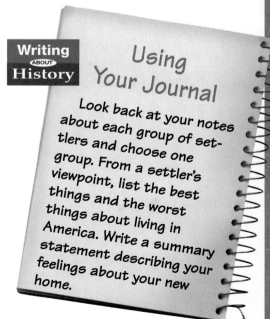

Writing ABOUT History

Using Your Journal

Look back at your notes about each group of settlers and choose one group. From a settler's viewpoint, list the best things and the worst things about living in America. Write a summary statement describing your feelings about your new home.

CHAPTER 6

★★

Life in the 13 Colonies
1620–1763

SETTING THE SCENE

Focus

Colonists brought traditions from their home countries and developed new ways of life in America. While lifestyles varied from region to region, in time the colonists found that they shared many concerns.

Concepts to Understand

★ How **diverse populations and cultures** led to different ways of life in the thirteen colonies

★ How **American democracy** took root and grew in the colonies

Read to Discover . . .

★ the reasons that particular ways of life developed in different regions of the colonies.

★ how events in England helped to strengthen democracy in the colonies.

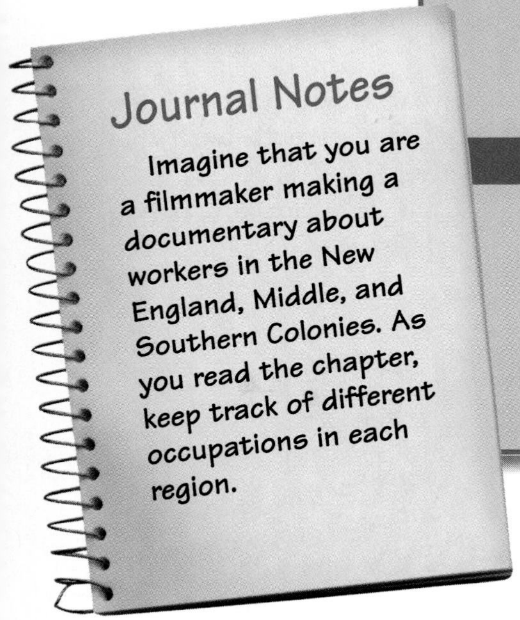

Journal Notes

Imagine that you are a filmmaker making a documentary about workers in the New England, Middle, and Southern Colonies. As you read the chapter, keep track of different occupations in each region.

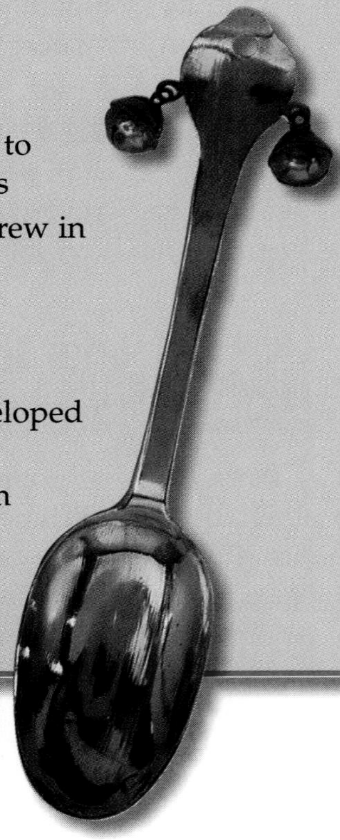

▶ COLONIAL BABY'S SPOON

Americas	1607 Jamestown founded	1654 First Jewish settlers arrive in New
	1647 Massachusetts establishes public schools	Amsterdam from Brazil

1600–1649	1650–1699

World   1660 England passes Navigation Acts

History AND ART

Dame's School
by Thomas Webster

Nineteenth-century artist Thomas Webster painted this scene of a dame school in New England. Dame schools were a popular means of education in the 1700s.

◀ HORNBOOK FROM COLONIAL SCHOOL

1700s Thousands of Africans are brought to America and enslaved

1750 New England merchants lead colonial trade
1763 British begin to enforce Navigation Acts

1700–1749

1750–1799

1725 English Quakers speak out against slavery
1748 France and England compete for trade with India

★★

The New England Colonies

SETTING THE SCENE

Read to Learn . . .

★ what ways New England colonists made a living.
★ how much New Englanders valued education.
★ how community life was organized in New England.

Terms to Know

★ subsistence farming
★ export
★ import
★ artisan
★ triangular trade routes

Places to Locate

★ West Indies
★ Nantucket
★ Martha's Vineyard
★ Boston
★ Newport

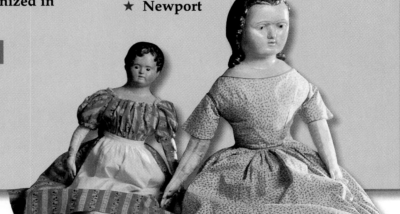

► CHILDREN'S DOLLS

T he newcomers' wagon rolled along the dusty New England road and stopped at the grassy common in the center of town. After weeks of rocking in a ship across the Atlantic, the travelers were happy to be on land. This place did not look much different than their home in England. Would life in America be as they imagined?

In the late 1600s the New England Colonies welcomed many settlers. What they found was a way of life based on the Puritan ethic of work and strict rules. Many qualities that people think of as typically American began with these thrifty, hardworking New Englanders.

★ Making a Living

With a harsh climate and poorer land than other parts of the colonies, New England developed an economy based on more than farming. The region did have valuable natural resources and drew more and more settlers, mainly from England. These people made their living from the environment around them—the land and the sea.

Farming

Farming in New England was not an easy life. Much of the land was hilly or too rocky and hard to plow. Before they could plant, farmers had to spend days picking rocks out of the soil. They piled up stones to make fences between the fields or to build house foundations and fireplaces. Many of these stone fences are still standing in New England today.

The growing season in these northern colonies was short. Farmers could plant and harvest only one crop—such as corn—before the ground froze and winter set in. Most farms were small and all family members worked together. They produced just enough for the family's own needs. This type of farming is called sub-sistence farming. Sometimes farm families produced extra food—apples from the orchard, honey from their beehives—that they could sell.

Harvesting the Sea

The cold waters of the Atlantic were a richer source of food than the thin New England soil. New England harbors were within easy sailing distance of the great fishing grounds in the Atlantic Ocean. Fishing fleets sailed regularly from the ports of Gloucester and Portsmouth.

Fishing was a backbreaking, dangerous way to make a living. The most important catch was codfish, which New Englanders dried or salted to store, cooked in chowders, and pressed to make cod-liver oil. Fishing boats also brought back halibut, herring, and mackerel.

Fishing became an important part of the New England economy. Fishers caught enough fish to export it, or sell it elsewhere. They sent some to other colonies. They packed large quantities of salted or dried fish in barrels to ship to markets in Europe and the islands of the West Indies. With the profits from exports, New Englanders could import, or buy goods brought in from Europe.

The more adventurous sailors took up whaling, which held the promise of better pay. They hunted whales for their valuable oil, which was used in oil lamps. Other parts of the whale such as the bones

and spermaceti—a waxy substance used in candle making—were also valued.

The islands of **Nantucket** and **Martha's Vineyard,** along with New Bedford on the mainland, were important whaling centers. Many whalers' crews included Native Americans. This is how St. John de Crevecoeur, a French writer who settled in America, described the crew of a whaling ship and the dangers they faced:

> ❝ . . . [T]hey always man them with thirteen hands [sailors] in order that they may row two whale-boats, the crews of which must necessarily consist of six, four at the oars, one standing on the bows with the harpoon, and the other at the helm. It is also necessary that there should be two of these boats, that if one should be destroyed in attacking the whale, the other . . . may be ready to save the hands. ❞

Living From the Forest

When Europeans arrived, thick forests covered most of eastern North America. Colonists cut down trees to clear land, supply firewood, and build houses and furniture. Like the Native Americans, settlers hunted in the forests for deer, squirrel, or wild turkeys to feed their families.

Timber from the forests also proved valuable for shipbuilding. Cedar, oak, and white pine all made excellent ship timber. Starting with fishing boats, New England shipbuilders went on to make ocean-going ships for the transatlantic and Caribbean trade. While there were shipyards in most American port cities, more than half the ships built in the colonies came from Massachusetts, New Hampshire, and Rhode Island. England encouraged colonial shipbuilding because its own forests had been cut years earlier.

Business and Trade

Shipbuilders provided jobs for many artisans, or craft workers, and other laborers. Carpenters and coopers—barrel makers—found steady work in shipyards. Other artisans made sails, rope, and nails. Small factories produced naval stores from the white pines of New Hampshire. Naval stores were products such as turpentine or rosin used to maintain wooden ships. Some colonists found jobs on ships while others worked on the docks, loading and unloading goods.

Women in the Economy

Women played an important role in the development of the economy of New England. On family farms, most wives worked side by side with their husbands. Many New Englanders became merchants. Women whose husbands were away at sea often opened shops. Others produced goods for sale such as cloth, garments, candles, soap, or furniture.

Triangular Trade Routes

Trading ships were constantly sailing in and out of the harbors of **Boston** and **Newport.** They brought in luxuries such as tea, English-made cloth, and furniture, as well as books and news from Europe. By 1740 New England's trading center was Boston, the largest city in the colonies with 17,000 people.

Colonial merchant ships followed regular trading routes. Some ships went directly from the colonies to England and back. Others followed what came to be called the triangular trade routes because the routes formed a triangle. On one leg of such a route, ships took fish, grain, meat, and lumber to the West Indies. There the ship's captain traded for sugar, molasses—a syrup made from sugarcane—and fruit, which he then took back to New England. Colonists used the molasses and sugar to make rum.

The rum, along with manufactured goods, was then shipped on the next leg of the route—to West Africa. It was traded for Africans who had been captured by slave traders. On the final leg of the route, the ships carried the Africans back to the West Indies, where planters were always in need of workers. With the profits, the captain bought more molasses and sugar to sell in the colonies. A later route brought enslaved West Africans directly to the American colonies.

★ A Belief in Education

In the 1600s, many people could not read. The Puritans believed that people needed enough education to read the Bible and understand laws. Those parents who could read taught their children at home, along with instructing them about religious beliefs and practical skills. A common scene in New England was a group of

- -

Footnotes to History

Female Attorney in Maryland   The first female barrister, or lawyer, in America was Margaret Brent. She was the colonial attorney for the Lord Proprietor of Maryland, Cecilius Calvert. Brent was also the first American woman to be denied the right to vote. Brent attempted to vote in the Maryland General Assembly in 1648. At that time, Maryland's law limited the vote to landowners. Despite the fact that Brent was a wealthy landowner, she was denied the right to vote based on her gender. Women were denied the right to vote until 1920, when the Nineteenth Amendment was passed.

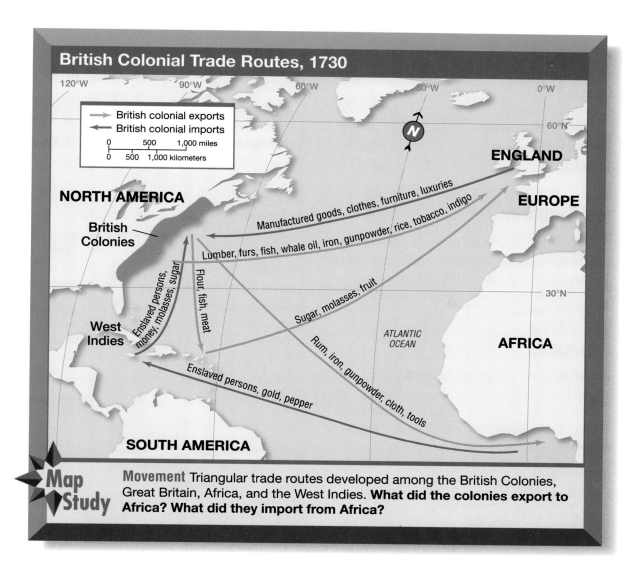

British Colonial Trade Routes, 1730

British colonial exports
British colonial imports

0   500   1,000 miles
0   500   1,000 kilometers

NORTH AMERICA

British Colonies

ENGLAND

EUROPE

Manufactured goods, clothes, furniture, luxuries

Lumber, furs, fish, whale oil, iron, gunpowder, rice, tobacco, indigo

West Indies

Enslaved persons, money, molasses, sugar

Flour, fish, meat

Sugar, molasses, fruit

ATLANTIC OCEAN

AFRICA

Rum, iron, gunpowder, cloth, tools

Enslaved persons, gold, pepper

SOUTH AMERICA

Map Study

Movement Triangular trade routes developed among the British Colonies, Great Britain, Africa, and the West Indies. **What did the colonies export to Africa? What did they import from Africa?**

children sitting around a fireplace reading aloud from a shared book. This took place at private **dame schools.** Here women taught the alphabet, reading, verses from the Bible, and perhaps simple arithmetic. For colonial girls, this was probably their only chance at formal schooling.

Books were scarce in the colonies. Instead of textbooks, dame schools usually had a hornbook, a flat wooden board shaped like a paddle. It held a sheet of paper printed with the alphabet and the Lord's Prayer, covered by a thin sheet of transparent horn.

By about 1690, Boston printers began to publish the *New England Primer.* Soon this book of illustrated alphabet verses and simple religious texts appeared in most New England homes and schools.

The First Public Schools

Because of the Puritans' concern for education, Massachusetts laws required all towns to teach their children to read. In 1647, the colony set up the first public school system under the **Massachusetts School Law.** The law provided that every township with more than 50 households must hire someone to teach its children to read and write. This law marked a step toward universal education.

The first college in the colonies was Harvard, founded in Cambridge, Massachusetts, in 1636. The first colonial colleges mainly trained ministers. By the 1700s, some young men were studying to be lawyers. Most who wanted to be lawyers or doctors, however, got their training by working alongside professionals.

★ Community Life

From the beginning, towns were the center of New England life. Colonists believed that issues of religion and government should be settled within their own communities.

The Town

In a typical New England town, settlers built two rows of houses facing an open field called the green or the common. The church, or **meetinghouse** as it was often called, stood on one side of the

green. As the town grew, more rows of houses and streets were built around the green. Most houses had a small garden and orchard.

At first, cattle and sheep grazed on the green. Later on, pastures were fenced behind the village. The common became the social center of the town. Many New England towns today still have a town green.

One typical New England house style had two stories in front and one in back, with a long sloping roof. Because it resembled the shape of boxes in which salt was stored in colonial kitchens, this style of house was often called a saltbox. Most houses were built around a large central chimney, with fireplaces for both heating and cooking.

▶ **WILLIAM BRADFORD'S BIBLE**

▲ *PILGRIMS GOING TO CHURCH* by George H. Boughton, 1867 Religion was an important part of Pilgrim life. **What evidence shown in this picture suggests that the settlers did not yet feel safe?**

Family Life

The family was important in New England. Puritan children, like their parents, had to work hard and follow the strict ideas of discipline. Still, many families were close and devoted to each other.

Even with chores and religious duties, children had time to play, and parents found time to tell stories and make toys. Puritan children played jacks, marbles, hide-and-seek, and other familiar games.

Observing the Sabbath

In a community centered on religion, Sunday, or the Sabbath, was a high point of the week. Farm and household chores were set aside because Puritan laws forbade most kinds of work on Sunday. People put on their best clothes—which might be of rich fabric even if plainly cut—to go to the meetinghouse.

Inside, men sat on one side of the center aisle, women on the other. Servants or African slaves stayed in the back or in the balcony. In winter churchgoers shivered through long services in unheated buildings. A Sunday morning service included several hours of intense preaching by the minister. There was another service in the afternoon. To make sure that people stayed awake, a "tithingman" walked up and down the aisle carrying a long pole with a feather at one end and a knob on the other. Drowsy churchgoers were either tickled gently or rapped on the head.

Town Meetings

The meetinghouse was also where New Englanders met to deal with community problems and other issues. At the yearly **town meeting,** all the free men of the town discussed and voted on important community questions. Town meetings were limited at first to landowning church members but later included all white male property owners. This democratic tradition is still carried out today throughout New England and across America. Now women also attend.

Town meetings were never dull and often noisy. Should a citizen be allowed to build a fence? Could a new road cut through the field of another citizen? People brought up every detail of community life for discussion and elected the town leaders, called selectmen.

Although not every community member could vote, town meetings were an important step toward democracy. Thomas Jefferson called them "the wisest invention ever devised by the wit of man for the perfect exercise of self-government and for its preservation."

★ SECTION 1 REVIEW ★

Checking for Understanding

1. **Identify** West Indies, Nantucket, Martha's Vineyard, Boston, Newport.
2. **Define** subsistence farming, export, import, artisan, triangular trade routes.
3. **What** were three of the ways in which New Englanders made a living?
4. **Why** was the Massachusetts School Law of 1647 important?

Critical Thinking

5. **Analyzing Information** Why were the town meetings not completely democratic?

ACTIVITY

6. Learn more about whaling and the products that were obtained from whales. Make an illustrated poster showing these products and the parts of the whale that were used in producing them.

QUILTING

Quilts are pieces of history. Their very names suggest long-ago times and traditions—Rising Sun, Wild Goose Chase, Star of Bethlehem. For colonial women, quilts were something more. They were a chance to create works of art. The tiny scraps of fabric that were sewn into quilt patterns told a family's story, using pieces of a favorite shirt or baby's dress. In practical terms, warm quilts were useful and necessary in cold colonial houses.

Geometric Shapes Form Patterns

By the middle of the 1700s, inexpensive cotton fabrics in many colors and patterns were available from India, another British colony. To show off the beautiful colors and designs, quilters sewed square blocks from smaller patches cut into geometric shapes such as triangles or diamonds. Every small scrap of material could be used, including leftovers from larger projects such as shirts or dresses.

A quilter worked hard to create lively and imaginative block patterns or put her special touch on a traditional design such as "Double Wedding Ring." New patterns were named for familiar objects, events, and occasions. Some included designs of a family home, a special flower, even people. Sometimes quilts were patterned after patriotic or religious themes. A quilter sometimes signed and dated the finished quilt.

Finished quilt blocks were sewn together, creating a design of repeated patterns over the quilt top. The top was sewed to a layer of padding and then to the quilt bottom. Few colonial homes had paintings or much decoration; their quilts provided both color and beauty.

▲ COLONIAL QUILT

Making the Arts Connection

1. Where did quilters get the fabrics to make quilts?

2. What kinds of shapes were used in the quilt blocks?

3. How did quilts let the maker express individual artistic talent?

ACTIVITY

4. Create a geometric pattern for a quilt block using cut scraps of fabric or colored paper. Use squares, triangles, and diamonds in your pattern. Glue your scraps to a piece of paper to make a quilt block.

★★★★★★★★★★★★★★★★★★★★★★★★★★★★★★★★★★★★★

The Middle Colonies

SETTING THE SCENE

Read to Learn . . .

★ why the Middle Colonies were known as breadbasket colonies.
★ which groups of people settled in the Middle Colonies.
★ what life was like on the frontier.

Terms to Know

★ cash crop
★ Conestoga wagon
★ patroon
★ apprentice
★ frontier

Places to Locate

★ Philadelphia
★ New York City
★ Delaware River
★ Baltimore
★ Appalachian Mountains

◄ PINE TREE SHILLING, 1652

Sailing into New York Harbor in the early 1700s made most sea captains smile. They could see a bustling harbor, a growing community, and profits to be made. Growth and prosperity were evident throughout the Middle Colonies of New York, Pennsylvania, New Jersey, and Delaware. Here the land was gentler, and the people were more varied in background than in New England.

★ The Breadbasket Colonies

For farmers, the Middle Colonies had many advantages—rich soil, a generally mild climate, and a long growing season.

The region also included several long, deep rivers that made it easy to transport produce from inland farms to the sea.

Crops for Sale

Because of the good climate and soil, farmers in the Middle Colonies could produce more food—especially meat and grains—than they needed to feed themselves. People in other colonies, in the West Indies, and in Europe were eager to buy the wheat and other grains they grew. These became cash crops, food crops grown to be sold. Beef and pork were also exported.

The Middle Colonies produced so much grain that they became known as the "breadbasket colonies." Millers ground the grain into flour and the corn into meal.

From this, colonists baked wheat or rye bread or made cornmeal puddings. European settlers introduced new foods—Dutch cooks baked waffles, while the Germans made pretzels and noodles.

Taking Farm Goods to Market

Most farmers in the Middle Colonies shipped their grain through two port cities—**Philadelphia** and **New York City.** They loaded barrels of grain and flour and shipped them by boat along the **Delaware River** to Philadelphia and along the Hudson River to New York City. Farmers in central Pennsylvania shipped their products along the Susquehanna River to the Chesapeake Bay. All three rivers flowed through the rich farmlands of the Middle Colonies.

Many Pennsylvania Dutch farmers had settled farther west, away from these rivers. To get their crops to market by road, they developed a new vehicle named the Conestoga wagon after a nearby valley. The Conestoga wagon

was large and very sturdy, more than 20 feet (6 m) long with a curved, boat-shaped body. Above the wagon bed, a homespun cloth cover was stretched over an arched framework. Because its wheels did not easily sink into mud, it was well suited to the poor roads.

A team of four to six horses pulled a single Conestoga wagon, which could hold a ton or more of farm produce. A traveler through Pennsylvania noted, "In the months of September and October, it is no uncommon thing, on the Lancaster and Reading roads, to meet in one day from fifty to one hundred of these wagons. . . . " In later years, pioneers would use a wagon similar to the Conestoga wagon to travel west.

New York Farms

Owning their own land was important to colonists. In parts of New York State, however, the old Dutch patroon system of land ownership continued. Five wealthy families ran their huge estates like small kingdoms. The Van Rensselaer family manor—owned into the 1700s—covered nearly 2 million acres (810,000 ha). Its thousands of farmer tenants had to pay rent to the patroon, or owner family. Unhappy tenants rebelled several times but failed to change the system.

▲ FLOUR MILL Farmers from the surrounding area brought their wheat to be ground at this water-powered mill. **What other farm crop was usually ground into meal?**

★ Business, Trade, and Cities

Besides the farmers themselves, other people in the Middle Colonies prospered from agriculture. Millers ground grain, and many people worked on ships or built ships that transported farm goods. An upper class of wealthy merchant families grew up in New York and Philadelphia.

Other businesses and small crafts industries developed too. Many families in the 1700s spun thread, wove linen, or knit wool at home. Artisans, such as iron-makers, tailors, glassblowers, and silversmiths, had workshops attached to their homes.

In cities, small shops sold goods such as hats, books, and tea brought by ship from England. In smaller towns, a general store sold everything that people did not make for themselves. At sawmills workers cut wooden boards and lumber. Using local clay, brickmakers baked bricks for building houses or paving streets.

Cities Grow Quickly

By the mid-1700s Philadelphia and New York had passed Boston as the largest cities in the colonies. Philadelphia, with more than 23,000 people in 1760, was bigger than most cities in Great Britain. It was a major center for shipping exports. The city of **Baltimore** also grew quickly.

Busy port cities were a contrast to the quiet countryside. City streets were paved with bricks or cobblestones and lined with shops and inns. There was the noise and clatter of horses' hooves and cartwheels. Crowds of people spoke many languages.

Many settlers in the Middle Colonies built houses like those they had known in Europe. Dutch influence, for instance, was strong in New York. Neat Dutch houses were built of red brick, usually 1½ stories high, with steep roofs. Each had a

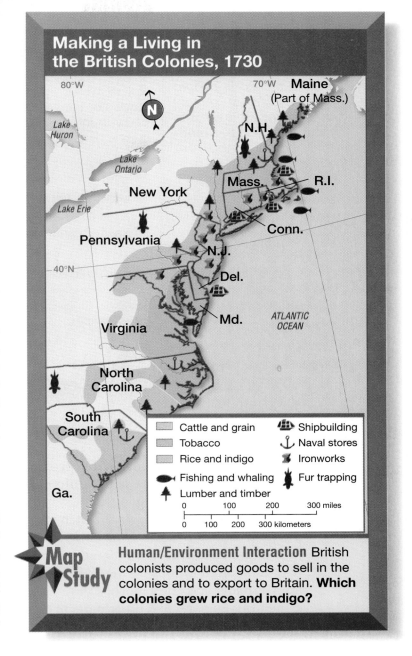

Making a Living in the British Colonies, 1730

Key:
- Cattle and grain
- Tobacco
- Rice and indigo
- Fishing and whaling
- Lumber and timber
- Shipbuilding
- Naval stores
- Ironworks
- Fur trapping

0 100 200 300 miles
0 100 200 300 kilometers

Map Study **Human/Environment Interaction** British colonists produced goods to sell in the colonies and to export to Britain. **Which colonies grew rice and indigo?**

Dutch door divided into upper and lower sections. The upper part could be opened to see visitors, while the lower was closed to keep out animals.

★ A Different Kind of Community

The people of the Middle Colonies were different than their northern New England neighbors who were mostly English. The

★★★★★★★★★★★★★★★★★★   ★★★★★★★★★★★★★★★★

The Fear of Smallpox

Throughout history, people have feared certain deadly diseases. Today, at least one of those diseases—small-pox—has been wiped out worldwide.

Then_____

A Dreaded Disease

Europeans brought smallpox to the Americas. This disease killed or scarred millions of people. Smallpox was as contagious, or easy to catch, as the common cold. If a victim coughed the virus into the air, anyone nearby might catch it. Native Americans had no resistance to the virus and easily became infected. Whole populations died.

Now_____

A Dead Disease

In 1796 English doctor Edward Jenner introduced a

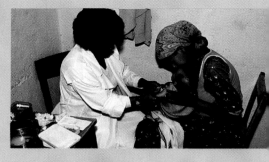

▲ A MODERN VACCINATION

vaccine that prevented smallpox. By the 1940s, smallpox had been wiped out in Europe and North America. By 1980 smallpox was officially declared dead throughout the world.

► COLONIAL DOCTOR

★★★★★★★★★★★★★★★★★★   ★★★★★★★★★★★★★★★★

Middle Colonies were settled by people from many countries, with different beliefs, customs, and languages.

Descendants of the original Dutch and Swedish settlers lived in New York, New Jersey, and Delaware. Other large groups who came from Europe by the 1700s were the Germans and the French. Many also came from England and other parts of the British Isles. Some were Scotch-Irish, Welsh, or Scottish.

Many Religions

Unlike the New England Colonies, the Middle Colonies did not have a single religion that was more powerful than any other. People who came from one country usually shared the same religious beliefs. Most belonged to one of several Protestant denominations, or groups, that had faced persecution in Europe. A minority of the people were Roman Catholics or Jews.

Many Germans followed the Lutheran religion, as did the Swedes. Others belonged to smaller groups with distinctive beliefs, such as the Amish and the Mennonites. One Mennonite leader who came to Pennsylvania in 1683 described his trip as traveling on a "Noah's Ark" of religious faiths. He arrived with Roman Catholics, Lutherans, Quakers, and Calvinists as well as his own group of German Mennonites.

Quakers came to the Middle Colonies from England, while the Scots and Scotch-Irish were mostly Presbyterian. Most French settlers were *Huguenots,* a term for French Protestants. The Dutch were mainly Dutch Reformed, another Protestant group. The Jews in New York, Rhode Island, and Pennsylvania came from Spain and Portugal.

Country Customs and Fun

As soon as Pennsylvania was founded in 1681, groups of immigrants poured into its Delaware River valley. Newcomers worked together to clear land and establish communities. One German custom that soon spread throughout the region was barn raising. Neighbors gathered to help raise the frame of the barn, then relaxed with a huge outdoor feast with music and dancing. Sheepshearing, cornhusking, and butchering were other chores that settlers often shared. Any community gathering might end with footraces and jumping contests. Women also gathered in one another's farmhouses to spin or make quilts together.

★ Education and Training

While many colonists respected education, the Middle Colonies did not set up public schools. Children were taught by private tutors or in church or private schools. Merchants in some cities funded charity schools for those who could not afford private school fees.

Not all young people continued their schooling. Any ambitious 12- or 13-year-old could learn a craft by becoming an apprentice, or trainee, to a master craft worker. The apprentice would work without wages for several years while learning the craft. Everything from shoeing horses to making wigs was taught in this way.

The master was required to provide the apprentice with food, board, and clothing. Sometimes the master also gave instruction in religion and basic reading and writing. At the end of training, an apprentice might become a paid assistant in the same shop or go to work for another artisan.

★ The Frontier

Early colonists settled in a band along the Atlantic coast and the banks of a few large rivers. As more and more people

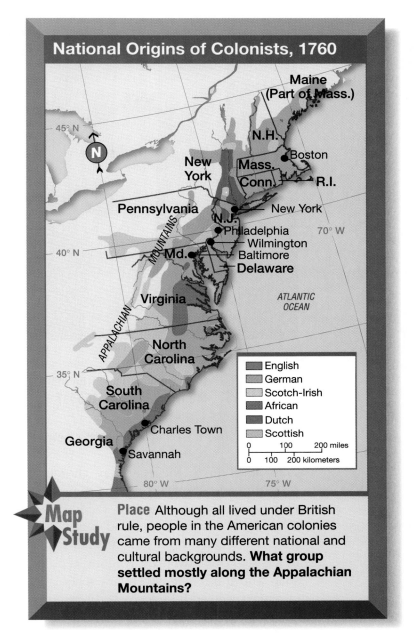

National Origins of Colonists, 1760

English
German
Scotch-Irish
African
Dutch
Scottish

Map Study — **Place** Although all lived under British rule, people in the American colonies came from many different national and cultural backgrounds. **What group settled mostly along the Appalachian Mountains?**

arrived, some moved farther inland to the frontier, a thinly settled area on the outer limits of the colonies. In the 1600s, the frontier of the Middle Colonies was the eastern foothills of the **Appalachian Mountains.** By the 1700s the frontier extended west into the Ohio Valley.

The frontier drew an assortment of people. Many—including young married couples, recent immigrants, and former indentured servants—wanted cheap land and a new start in life. Some young single men wanted adventure and freedom from

▲ COLONISTS GATHER TO WORK Settlers used wooden paddles to separate fibers from the flax plant. The fibers were then spun into cloth. **What area was called the frontier in the 1600s?**

the laws and restrictions in the settled colonies.

In addition to the everyday chores of farming and housekeeping, men and women on the frontier had to do many other jobs. They cut trees to build their homes—usually one-room cabins. They made their own furniture, wagons, candles, soap, and shoes. There were few schools, so children received little formal education.

Because frontier families all faced the same dangers and hardships, they developed a spirit of independence and equality. Women worked alongside men and carried equal responsibility for the well-being of the frontier family. People of different culture groups shared and mixed their traditions and beliefs. Few of the social class distinctions were common in these settled regions far from cities.

★ **SECTION 2 REVIEW** ★

★★★★★★★★★★★★★★★★★

Checking for Understanding

1. **Identify** Philadelphia, New York City, Delaware River, Baltimore, Appalachian Mountains.
2. **Define** cash crop, Conestoga wagon, patroon, apprentice, frontier.
3. **Why** were the Middle Colonies called the breadbasket colonies?
4. **What** groups of people settled in the Middle Colonies?

Critical Thinking

5. **Predicting Consequences** How do you think the Native Americans who lived on the frontier would have reacted to the movement of settlers into the area?

ACTIVITY

6. Illustrate a colonial street scene in New York or Philadelphia. Label shops and buildings.

★★★

The Southern Colonies

SETTING THE SCENE

Read to Learn . . .

★ what the economy of the Southern Colonies was based on.
★ how Southern planters came to depend on enslaved labor.
★ what life was like on a plantation.

Terms to Know

★ urban
★ rural
★ Tidewater
★ Middle Passage
★ slave codes

Places to Locate

★ Chesapeake Bay
★ Potomac River
★ James River
★ Savannah River
★ West Africa

◀ INDIGO PLANT

Life in the Southern Colonies of Virginia, Maryland, North and South Carolina, and Georgia differed in several ways from that in the other regions. City, or urban, life was important in the Middle Colonies. In contrast, the South was mainly rural—mostly farms, with few towns and only one large city, Charles Town.

As in New England, the first settlers in the Southern Colonies were English. Many, however, were wealthy aristocrats and friends of the king. They belonged to the Anglican Church. Later settlers came from other parts of Britain—Scotland and Ireland—and from France.

★ An Agricultural Economy

Most settlers in the Southern Colonies made their livings from the land, but they belonged to two very different groups. A few wealthy planters owned thousands of acres. They made up a rich, upper class. The rest were farmers—the lower class—who owned small farms or worked for a large planter. Their lives were more like those of small farmers in the other colonies.

The land along the region's southern coast had long, hot, humid summers, mild winters, and heavy rainfall. Besides

▲ SHIPPING TOBACCO Planters shipped barrels of tobacco to Europe and the West Indies. **Along what tidal rivers was most tobacco shipped?**

raising corn and cattle for their tables, farmers grew three cash crops—tobacco, rice, and indigo. All three required the hard work of many people. As a result, planters came to depend on the labor of enslaved Africans who were an important part of the colonial population.

Tobacco Growing

Tobacco was the first crop grown in Virginia to bring farmers a profit. Later the crop spread to North Carolina and Maryland. A few Southern planters who owned thousands of acres grew half of all the tobacco shipped to England each year. Families with smaller farms of 100 or 200 acres (41 or 81 ha) grew the rest.

Large plantations covered acres of land along **Chesapeake Bay.** They hugged the banks of slow-flowing tidal rivers, including the **Potomac,** the **James,** and the **York.** This part of Virginia came to be called the Tidewater, because ocean tides affected the rivers for miles upstream. Most plantations had their own docks on the rivers. Planters could ship barrels of tobacco downstream to the coast and then directly to England. For this reason, the Southern Colonies had fewer major port cities than the New England or Middle Colonies.

Rice and Indigo

Around 1680 a ship captain brought some rice seed to South Carolina from the African island of Madagascar. Planters in South Carolina and Georgia found that the swampy coastal lands near the **Savannah River** were perfect for growing rice. By the 1720s, some rice planters introduced an irrigation system that increased the size of their crops.

Another important crop in South Carolina was indigo, a plant used to produce a rich blue dye. One planter who promoted this crop was Eliza Lucas. Her father, governor of the West Indies island of Antigua, left Eliza Lucas to manage the family plantation in South Carolina. Experimenting with growing indigo, she found that it would grow well in the highlands where rice would not.

Indigo was harvested while the rice was still growing, which made it a profitable second crop for Carolina planters. It was a valuable export to England, where textile manufacturers used indigo to dye cloth.

To make a profit from the kind of crops grown in the Southern Colonies, planters needed many laborers. At first planters used indentured servants, both African and European, to work in the fields. Soon, however, most of the workers were Africans brought from the West Indies. Many already had experience growing rice in Africa. About this time planters began to treat Africans as slaves for life—as property that could be owned—rather than as servants who would be free after several years.

★ The African Population

By 1760 there were about a quarter of a million Africans in the colonies. Enslaved Africans were shipped directly from **West Africa** to the American colonies. Most enslaved Africans—more than 200,000—worked in the fields and houses of the

Southern Colonies. Smaller numbers of Africans and people of African descent lived in New England and the Middle Colonies. Some were enslaved, working as household servants or on farms. Others were free people who worked as artisans or sailors.

The Slave Trade

As soon as European settlers built plantations in the Americas and the Caribbean islands, they began to depend on workers brought by force from Africa. Most came from West Africa. By the 1700s slave traders, often armed with European guns, reached deeper into the African continent. They raided villages and kidnapped men, women, and children to satisfy the demand for workers.

The Africans were brought to America or the West Indies in small, overcrowded ships. Africans later told their story of the horrors and brutality of the Middle Passage, the route between Africa and America. Slave traders viewed the people as cargo, not human beings, packing in as many as possible to increase the profits from the trip. People were chained and packed together in dark, filthy, cramped compartments. Sometimes there was not room enough to stand or even sit up. Many died from ill treatment and lack of fresh food and water.

Many colonists did not think that slavery was wrong. The need for laborers was more important than the welfare of the Africans. Some believed that they were doing Africans a favor by teaching them Christianity and forcing them to forget African culture.

Around the early 1700s, some colonies made these attitudes law. They passed slave codes, laws that denied enslaved

▲ *SLAVES BELOW DECK OF ALBANEZ* by Francis Maynell, 1846 From 1600 to 1850, nearly 15 million enslaved Africans were brought to the Americas on ships. **What laws denied Africans most of their rights?**

Africans most of their rights. Under the codes enslaved people were looked on as both persons and property. Under some slave codes, enslaved people could not carry weapons or hold meetings. In most places, it was against the law for them to learn to read and write.

Reactions to Slavery

Some enslaved Africans tried to run away from slaveholders, and a few found refuge with local Native Americans. Most runaways, however, were later caught and returned to their slaveholders. Those who were not caught had little chance of making a life for themselves. European colonists were suspicious of any African they did not know. Rebellions and resistance by the enslaved occurred both on slave ships and on plantations.

Free Africans

Some enslaved Africans became skilled workers, such as carpenters or seamstresses. Generous slaveholders might allow them to work for other families and keep part of the money. Sometimes a worker earned enough money to buy his or her freedom and perhaps that of a spouse or child. Some slaveholders gave trusted servants their freedom. Eventually, small communities of free Africans grew up in towns and cities throughout the colonies.

★ The Southern Plantation

Every American colony had a wealthy upper class. The rich planters of the South developed their own way of life on their plantations.

A plantation centered on the "big house," or the family mansion. Often it stood on a hill, overlooking a river. A typical plantation house had two stories and was built of brick. Through its tall windows could be seen a graceful staircase in the entrance hall. To avoid the danger of fire, the kitchen was in a separate building. Other small buildings clustered around the mansion, including barns, laundries, and stables. At some distance away were the small cabins of the slave quarters.

Most of the plantation workers were enslaved men and women. Many were field-workers who planted and tended crops. Others were artisans such as blacksmiths and shoemakers, while still others worked as servants in the mansion. These workers made the plantation self-sufficient, supplying almost all its needs.

★ SECTION 3 REVIEW ★

Checking for Understanding

1. **Identify** Chesapeake Bay, Potomac River, James River, Savannah River, West Africa.

2. **Define** urban, rural, Tidewater, Middle Passage, slave codes.

3. **What** were the three important cash crops of the Southern Colonies? Why were enslaved Africans important to farmers?

4. **Describe** how enslaved Africans could gain their freedom.

Critical Thinking

5. **Making Comparisons** What were some major ways in which the Southern Colonies were different from New England? How were these two regions alike?

ACTIVITY

6. Imagine that you are someone from New England visiting your cousins on a farm in the Carolinas. Write a letter to a friend at home describing your visit.

BUILDING SKILLS
Study and Writing Skills

Writing a Topic Sentence

▲ NEW ENGLAND FARM

Learning the Skill

In an essay or explanation, a paragraph is a group of sentences centered on a single idea or topic. The **topic sentence** summarizes the main idea of the whole paragraph. The other sentences further explain the main idea. The topic sentence often appears at the beginning of the paragraph. It can also be in the middle or at the end.

In the paragraph below, the topic sentence is in darker type.

Geography affected the economies of the different regions of American colonies. In New England, a cool climate and rocky soil made farming difficult. The many harbors and rich fishing grounds nearby, however, encouraged trade and fishing. In the Southern Colonies, a warm climate and flat, moist land encouraged the growth of plantations.

Practicing the Skill

Write a topic sentence for each paragraph below.

1. Although the Puritans left England to follow their religious beliefs, Puritan colonies did not grant that freedom to others. Rhode Island, on the other hand, allowed people of all faiths to worship as they pleased. Quakers in Pennsylvania accepted many different religious beliefs.

2. Most indentured servants were people who wanted to come to America but could not afford to pay the passage. In exchange for their fare, they promised to work for a certain number of years for someone else. When the term of service ended, the servant was free to work anywhere.

APPLYING THE SKILL

3. Look at a recent edition of your daily newspaper. Choose one story on the front page and underline the topic sentence in each paragraph.

★★★★★★★★★★★★★★★★★★★★★★★★★★★★★★★★★★★★★★

Democracy Takes Root

SETTING THE SCENE

Read to Learn . . .

★ how the Glorious Revolution in England affected the colonies.
★ why England passed the Navigation Acts.
★ how the colonists tried to establish their rights as citizens.

Terms to Know

★ bill of rights
★ libel
★ mercantilism
★ Navigation Acts
★ legislature

People to Meet

★ James II
★ Sir Edmund Andros
★ Nathaniel Bacon
★ John Peter Zenger

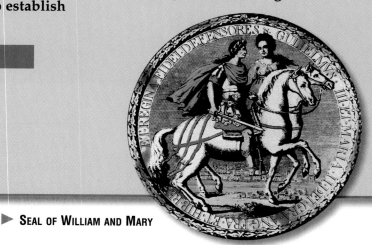

▶ SEAL OF WILLIAM AND MARY

During much of the time that the American colonies were being settled, civil war and political changes were causing turmoil in England. As a result, the faraway colonies were generally left alone to handle their own affairs. When the English monarchy was restored in 1660, it again turned its attention to America.

★ Changes in Colonial Governments

Charles II, the new king, wanted more control over the colonies and their profitable trade. Founded by different groups and proprietors, the American colonies were spread out along the Atlantic coast. Charles chartered new royal colonies in which he chose the governor and council. Later he changed the charters of Massachusetts and New Hampshire, making them royal colonies.

The Dominion of New England

When Charles died in 1685, his brother, the Duke of York, became king as **James II.** He immediately tried to unite New England, New York, and New Jersey as "the Dominion of New England." James appointed a single governor and council for the dominion and abolished the colonial assemblies elected by the colonists.

The dominion's royal governor, **Sir Edmund Andros,** set up new rules. He placed restrictions on New England town meetings, schools, and the press. Because the rights of the colonists did not seem important to Andros, he was widely hated. Andros was especially unpopular in Massachusetts, where he tried to replace the Puritans' Congregational Church with the Anglican Church.

The Glorious Revolution

Neither James II nor the Dominion of New England lasted very long. The English people feared the king would try to make their country Roman Catholic. So, in 1688, the English Parliament unseated James and gave the throne to James's daughter Mary, a Protestant, and her husband, William of Orange.

People were so pleased by this peaceful change that it became known as the **Glorious Revolution.** The next year the new king and queen agreed to a bill of rights that put limits on their power. At the same time it listed "true, ancient . . . rights and liberties of the people."

When people in Boston heard about the changes in England, they moved quickly against Governor Andros. He tried to escape but was caught, imprisoned, and sent back to England. That ended the Dominion of New England.

William and Mary restored elected assemblies in the individual colonies. The assemblies did not have a great deal of power, however. Royal governors still had the final authority over colonial assemblies and courts.

★ Bacon's Rebellion

The revolt against Andros was not the first protest against colonial governors. In 1676 **Nathaniel Bacon,** a planter on the Virginia frontier, charged that Governor William Berkeley was not doing his job.

Bacon claimed the Virginia governor was not protecting the frontier from raids by Native Americans and was more interested in the profitable fur trade. Bacon soon took action in what was called **Bacon's Rebellion.** He led 300 small farmers and servants in a raid against the Native Americans.

Then civil war broke out between Bacon's volunteers and the governor's troops. The farmers marched on Jamestown, demanded other reforms, and later burned the town. The governor fled. Bacon's Rebellion was gaining popular support when Bacon suddenly became ill and died. Without him, the rebellion collapsed.

Bacon's Rebellion was by no means a failure. Charles II ordered Governor Berkeley back to England to explain how he had allowed such disorders to arise in Virginia. Berkeley died before he had a

Picturing History ▲ BACON'S REBELLION The raid against Native Americans by Bacon's mob showed Governor Berkeley to be a weak governor. **How did King Charles II react to the rebellion in Berkeley's colony?**

chance to report to the king, but governors who came after him ruled in a much different manner. They relaxed their personal control over the colony and allowed Virginians more voice in their own government.

Zenger Fights for Freedom of the Press

Armed revolts were not the only way to protest against colonial governors. One man who protested with the printed word was **John Peter Zenger.** Born in Germany in 1697, he came to America at age 13 and became an apprentice printer. In 1726 he started his own print shop. In 1733, Zenger began to publish the *New York Weekly Journal,* a newspaper that openly opposed Governor William Cosby.

The paper criticized the governor for a year, until Zenger finally was arrested and copies of the newspaper were burned in public. Zenger was tried for libel, the act of publishing harmful statements. Zenger's lawyer, Andrew Hamilton, defended Zenger saying the printer should be found not guilty because his criticisms of the governor were true. Hamilton asked the jurors to stand up for freedom against the governor claiming, "It is the best cause. It is the cause of liberty." Spectators cheered as the jury agreed and found Zenger not guilty. Zenger's case was the first one in America to protect freedom of the press.

▲ ZENGER'S NEWSPAPER

★★★

★ Controls on Colonial Trade

England wanted its colonies to be profitable. The American colonies were valuable for their natural resources and their trade of goods. As early as 1650 Parliament passed laws to regulate trade. These laws had both helpful and harmful effects.

Most European countries with colonies followed a policy called mercantilism. This policy meant that to gain wealth, a country had to sell more goods than it bought. The English colonies were

Restrictions on Colonial Trade, 1650–1750

Acts	Restrictions
Navigation Acts 1650, 1651, 1660–1661, 1696	Only English or English-built ships could carry on colonial trade. Tobacco, cotton, indigo, and other colonial products could only be sent to England. Colonial trade laws had to agree with the Navigation Acts.
Woolen Act 1699	Prohibited the colonial exports of wool or wool products.
Hat Act 1732	Prohibited the exporting of hats from one colony to another.
Molasses Act 1733	Levied a large duty on foreign sugar, molasses, and rum.
Iron Act 1750	Prohibited building of new colonial iron plants. Prohibited colonial import duties on iron bought from Britain.

Chart Study

British trade acts affected many American products. **Which trade act dealt with food products?**

important because of this policy. First, they provided raw materials to the home country. Second, the colonists were a ready-made market for products from the home country.

To make mercantilism work, England passed laws to control colonial trade. These laws were known as the Navigation Acts. The first of these laws, passed in 1660, said that the colonists must use English-built ships for all their trade. In addition, certain colonial products, including tobacco, cotton, and indigo, could be sold only in England or in an English possession. Later laws said that colonists could buy only English-made goods. Any crops or products bought or sold elsewhere had to be shipped through England and be taxed. As a last measure, England imposed duties on the coastal trade among the English colonies.

★ Moving Toward Self-Government

Restoration of colonial assemblies had been an important result of the Glorious Revolution. It supported the colonists' belief that the English Parliament, even though far away, ought to listen to them. Americans actually had a lot of freedom to run local affairs through their assemblies.

Rights of the Colonists

The colonists were proud of the rights they had as English citizens. These rights included the right to a fair trial by a jury of equals, and the right to be taxed by law-makers elected by the people.

Local governments in each colony were shaped by the founders, by royal officials, and by the settlers themselves. Not surprisingly, colonial governments were organized somewhat like the government of England. Most colonies had an appointed governor and a legislature, or law-making body, with two houses—the council and the assembly. This was the same organization followed in the English Parliament.

Members of the assembly, or lower house, were elected by the voters of the colony. Slowly, the assembly gained the power to pass tax bills and to decide how tax money would be spent. The assembly also ran the colony's military affairs.

Compared with people in Europe, the American colonists had an unusual chance to take part in their government. A limited number of them had the right to vote. Generally, however, voters were white men over the age of 21 who owned property. Women generally could not vote even if they owned property. Other adults who could not vote included indentured servants, slaves, and Native Americans.

★ SECTION 4 REVIEW ★

Checking for Understanding

1. **Identify** James II, Sir Edmund Andros, Nathaniel Bacon, John Peter Zenger.

2. **Define** bill of rights, libel, mercantilism, Navigation Acts, legislature.

3. **Why** were colonies important to England's policy of mercantilism?

4. **How** were most colonial governments organized?

Critical Thinking

5. **Supporting an Opinion** Why do you think that the colonists wanted to be taxed by representatives that they had elected themselves?

ACTIVITY

6. Imagine that you are a merchant in one of the thirteen colonies. Write and illustrate a newspaper ad that shows your opinion of the Navigation Acts.

Using Key Vocabulary

Match each word in Column A with the correct definition in Column B.

Column A
1. subsistence farming
2. cash crop
3. urban
4. slave codes
5. legislature

Column B
a. laws that denied rights to enslaved Africans
b. farming that produces little more than the farm family needs
c. official body that makes laws
d. living in or related to cities
e. farm product grown to be sold

Reviewing Facts

1. **Explain** how people in New England used natural resources to make a living.

2. **Tell** how and why education in New England was different from that in the Middle Colonies.

3. **List** at least one important product exported by each region of the colonies: New England, Middle, Southern.

4. **Describe** how enslaved Africans were a part of the colonies' "triangular trade routes."

5. **Explain** how most colonial governments were organized and how officials were chosen.

Understanding Concepts

Diverse Populations and Cultures

1. Which group of colonies had the most varied populations in terms of religion and nationality? Why was this so?

2. What generalization can you make about the people in the Southern Colonies and the social classes they belonged to?

3. What basic rights were denied the enslaved Africans in the Southern Colonies?

American Democracy

4. How were town meetings in the New England Colonies an important step toward democracy in America?

5. What effect did the Glorious Revolution in England have on colonists' attitudes toward their rights as citizens?

History and Geography

Eastern North America in 1700

Study the map of eastern North America in 1700. Then answer the following questions.

1. **Place** Which town is located furthest inland from the Atlantic Ocean?

2. **Region** What part of the region was forested?

3. **Human/Environment Interaction** Near what physical features were most of the colonial settlements established?

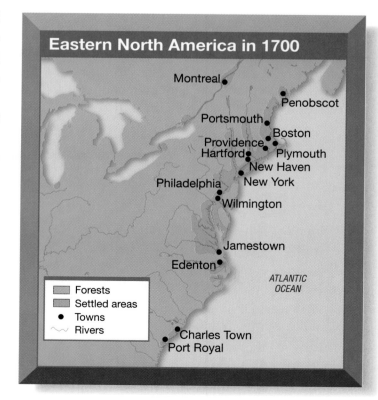

Eastern North America in 1700

Montreal
Penobscot
Portsmouth
Boston
Providence
Hartford
Plymouth
New Haven
Philadelphia
New York
Wilmington
Jamestown
Edenton
ATLANTIC OCEAN
Charles Town
Port Royal

☐ Forests
☐ Settled areas
● Towns
〜 Rivers

CHAPTER 6 ★ REVIEW

Critical Thinking

1. **Determining Cause and Effect** How did the agriculture that developed in the Southern Colonies affect the lives of workers there?

2. **Understanding Point of View** Why did the English monarch and Parliament treat the colonists differently from English citizens in England? How did the colonists react?

3. **Analyzing Illustrations** What can you tell from the illustration below about treatment of Africans in the colonies?

Cooperative Learning Interdisciplinary Activity: Speech

Work in a small group to prepare an interview show with the following list of colonists as guests: New England town resident, Philadelphia merchant, enslaved person, Southern plantation family member, and someone from the frontier. Work together to develop a list of questions to ask the guests to find out about their lives. One group member acts as host; others are the colonists.

Practicing Skills

Writing a Topic Sentence

1. Read the paragraph below and identify its topic sentence.

Nowhere in the colonies could you find more diversity than in the Middle Colonies. The first settlers in New York and New Jersey had been the Swedes and the Dutch. Then came English Quakers in Pennsylvania, followed by German and Scotch-Irish settlers. Africans, both enslaved and free, added to the mixture.

2. The following paragraph lacks a topic sentence. Read the paragraph and write a topic sentence that expresses the main idea.

On the passage to America, enslaved Africans were given little food or water. Crammed into hot, stuffy holds below the decks, they often had no room to lie down. They were chained to keep them from jumping overboard or rebelling against their captors.

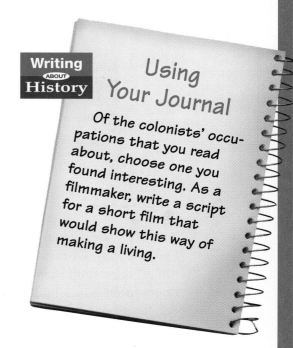

Writing About History **Using Your Journal** Of the colonists' occupations that you read about, choose one you found interesting. As a filmmaker, write a script for a short film that would show this way of making a living.

Cultural Kaleidoscope

Colonial Styles and Fashions

*F*ashion trends in Britain's thirteen colonies started in Europe. Wealthy colonists might buy imported clothing made in England. Colonial tailors and seamstresses often followed patterns or pictures from Europe.

Men's Hat Styles

Colonial men's headgear might call for an embroidered cap or a tricornered hat—one worn with a point in front and one on each side.

Colonial Hairstyles

Men and women alike often wore wigs for festive or formal occasions. Women's styles called for hair swept high on top. Men's styles were more flowing, often with hair tied in back. Powdering the wigs made them white.

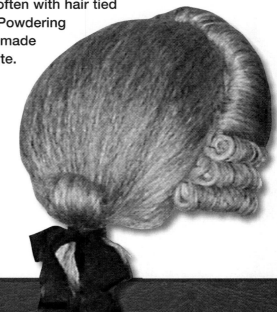

Bonnets

For everyday, women and girls wore ruffled caps both indoors and outdoors. More formal outings might call for a bonnet—plain or fancy.

Fashion Accessories

To complete her wardrobe, the colonial woman might carry a lovely fan to accent her gown. The wealthy gentleman might carry a finely crafted walking stick.

Dresses for Women and Girls

Colonial women wore dresses with long skirts and fitted waists. A shawl over the shoulders might add a touch of warmth or decoration.

On the Streets in Towns

A typical day in a colonial town found people going about their business.

CHAPTER 7

★★★

The Road to Revolution
1754–1775

SETTING THE SCENE

Focus

In 1760 most people in the thirteen colonies thought of themselves as British citizens, loyal to the king. Ten years later, however, those feelings of loyalty were changing. In 1763 Great Britain defeated France in a war fought in both America and Europe. This war not only made the colonists more self-reliant, but it also made the British want tighter control of its colonies.

Concepts to Understand

★ How **beliefs, ideas, and institutions** affected people living in the American colonies

★ What steps the colonists took to protect **American democracy** against British policies

Read to Discover . . .

★ why British policies changed after the French and Indian War.

★ why the colonists protested the Stamp Act and other new laws.

Journal Notes

Imagine you are a British journalist observing the protests taking place in the American colonies in the 1760s. Make notes of the different ways the colonists express their opposition to certain laws.

New-York, May 8, 1775.

Extract of a Letter From Philadelphia,

To a Gentleman in this City, dated the 6th inſt.

YESTERDAY evening Dr. FRANKLIN arrived here from London in ſix weeks, which he left the 20th of March, which has given great joy to this town, he ſays we have no favours to expect from the Miniſtry, nothing but ſubmiſſion will ſatiſfy them, they expect little or no oppoſition will be made to their troops, thoſe that are now coming are for New-York, where it is expected they will be received with cordiality. As near as we can learn there are about four thouſand troops coming in this fleet, the men of war and tranſports are in a great meaſure loaded with dry goods, to ſupply New-York, and the country round it, agents are coming over with them. Dr. Franklin is highly pleaſed to find us arming and preparing for the worſt events, he thinks nothing elſe can ſave us from the moſt abject ſlavery and deſtruction, at the ſame time encourages us to believe a ſpirited oppoſition, will be the means of our ſalvation. The Miniſtry are alarmed at every oppoſition, and lifted up again at every thing which appears the leaſt in their favour, every letter and every paper from hence, are read by them.

NEW-YORK: Printed by JOHN ANDERSON, at Beekman's-Slip.

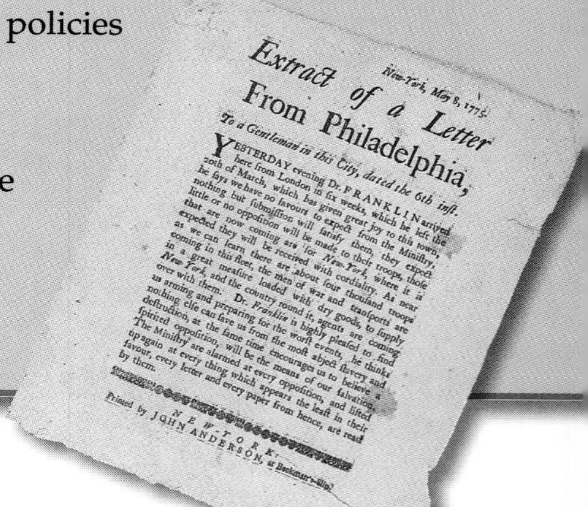

► COLONIAL NEWSPAPER

	1750–1754	1755–1759	1760–1764
United States	1754 French and Indian War begins		1763 French and Indian War ends
World		1756 Seven Years' War begins in Europe	1763 Treaty of Paris signed

Patrick Henry Before the Virginia House of Burgesses
by Peter Frederick Rothermel, 1851

This painting is typical of the historical works completed by this American artist. Rothermel combines sharp details with shadowy forms to provide contrast.

◀ CRISPUS ATTUCKS

1765 Stamp Act passed
1767 Townshend Acts passed

1770 Boston Massacre occurs
1774 First Continental Congress meets

1775 American Revolution begins
1775 Second Continental Congress meets

1765–1769

1770–1774

1775–1779

1773 Captain James Cook crosses Antarctic Circle

★★

An American Way of Life Develops

SETTING THE SCENE

Read to Learn . . .

★ what social classes existed in the American colonies by the mid-1700s.
★ how the Great Awakening affected the colonies.
★ how the Enlightenment influenced ideas in the colonies.

Terms to Know

★ gentry
★ social mobility
★ Great Awakening
★ revival
★ Enlightenment

People to Meet

★ George Whitefield
★ Jonathan Edwards
★ John Locke
★ Benjamin Franklin
★ Anne Dudley Bradstreet
★ Phillis Wheatley

Places to Locate

★ Philadelphia

▶ JONATHAN EDWARDS'S PAMPHLET

A Faithful NARRATIVE OF THE Surprizing Work of God IN THE CONVERSION OF Many HUNDRED Souls in *Northampton*, and the Neighbouring Towns and Villages of *New-Hampshire* in *New-England*. In a LETTER to the Revd. Dr. BENJAMIN COLMAN of *Boston*. Written by the Revd. Mr. EDWARDS, Minister of *Northampton*, on *Nov.* 6. 1736. With a Large PREFACE, By Dr. WATTS and Dr. GUYSE. And Published. LONDON, Printed for JOHN OSWALD, at the *Rose* and *Crown*, in the *Poultry*, near *Stocks-Market*. M.DCC.XXXVII. Price Stitch'd 1*s.* Bound in Calf-Leather, 1*s.* 6*d.*

P hilip Syng looked proudly at the beautiful silver inkstand he had just made for the Pennsylvania assembly, or legislature. Such fine work helped to give silversmiths a special place in the colonies. In **Philadelphia,** however, Syng was not just a talented artisan. He was now a member of the upper class, along with wealthy merchants and landowners.

This could never have happened in Great Britain. As an artisan there, he would have been considered part of a lower social class. Syng, like his friend, the printer Benjamin Franklin, had found that Americans looked at social status in a very different way.

This was just one aspect of the developing American way of life that helped to unite the colonists.

★ Colonial Society

By the mid-1700s, many families could trace their American roots back for several generations. People were no longer coming to the colonies with hopes of making money quickly and then returning home. Most of those who came to America now saw themselves as part of a unique culture, with few ties to their former homelands. The influence of Great Britain was still strong in many ways, but as America more clearly formed its own identity, that influence became less and less important.

Social Classes

The Europeans who settled in America had come from different countries and from varied social classes. They were lawyers, ministers, skilled artisans, farmers, and servants. Some were even criminals. In Great Britain, where many colonists came from, a person's social standing was based on family and tradition. In the colonies, however, social status depended mainly on wealth and occupation, not on birth.

The highest social class in the colonies was known as the gentry. It included church officials, wealthy landowners and planters, and successful merchants. In the middle class were skilled artisans, shopkeepers, and professional people such as doctors and lawyers. Next were poor farmers, free servants, and unskilled laborers. The lowest social class was made up of indentured servants and slaves.

Moving Up

What made American colonial society unique was social mobility, or the possibility for a person to move from one social class to another. In Great Britain and across Europe, a person stayed in the same class for life. Moving up in society was almost impossible.

This was not true in America. Here, people in the lower classes could improve their social standing. For example, a shopkeeper with a profitable business might buy a ship and become a well-to-do merchant, one of the gentry. An ordinary farmer could become a large landowner. Indentured servants, once they finished their service, could move into the middle class as artisans. Only slaves had no chance of improving their social standing.

★ The Great Awakening

Just as people came to America with different social backgrounds, they came, as well, with various religious beliefs. Religious freedom had been important to many colonists, and some had fled to America to escape religious persecution.

These men and women were fiercely dedicated to the practice of their religion. By the 1700s, however, religious leaders saw their congregations becoming interested in attaining wealth and success. They feared the people were drifting away from religion.

This changed in the 1730s and 1740s, when a movement known as the Great Awakening swept through the colonies. This revival, or renewed interest in religion, was characterized by preachers' fiery sermons warning people of the dangers of God's anger.

Traveling preachers were popular. They held outdoor revival services throughout the colonies, encouraging people to follow the Bible. The leading revivalist preacher was **George Whitefield** from Great Britain. He drew huge crowds as he traveled from Georgia to New England.

Influence of the Great Awakening

The Great Awakening affected the way people thought about religion. More than that, it affected the way people looked at one another and at their society. Massachusetts preacher **Jonathan Edwards** said the Great Awakening touched all people, "sober and vicious, high and low, rich and poor, wise and unwise. . . ."

Free persons stood side by side with those who were enslaved. Each one believed the message of the Great Awakening was for all people, regardless of their social standing. United in this belief, the colonists were more closely drawn together. The principles they came to believe in would help them to shape the direction of their lives—and the colonies.

▲ JOHN LOCKE

★ Enlightenment Ideas in America

While the Great Awakening provoked intense emotion, another movement emphasized science and reason as the guides to life. Followers of this movement thought that reason would help them see the world more clearly. Because of this belief, the movement became known as the Enlightenment, or the "Age of Reason."

John Locke and Natural Rights

One Enlightenment thinker was **John Locke,** an English writer. Locke wrote about the social contract that people made with their government. He determined that the purpose of government was to protect people's natural rights—life, liberty, and ownership of property. If a ruler or government failed to ensure these rights, then, in Locke's opinion, the government should be changed.

Locke's philosophy would prove to be of great importance to the colonial Americans. Although most had probably never heard of Locke himself, the idea of natural rights and responsible government became the basis of protest and revolt in the colonies.

Scientific Thinking

In addition to its emphasis on reason, the Enlightenment was marked by a respect for science and curiosity about the natural world. Scientists such as Italy's **Galileo** and England's **Sir Isaac Newton** introduced the idea that people could understand the world by observation and by experimentation.

As these ideas came to the colonies, people's interest in science grew. Colleges began to teach science, calling it natural philosophy. Many individuals carried on their own experiments, too.

An important figure in the development of American science was **Benjamin Franklin,** a Philadelphia printer, writer, diplomat, and inventor. Honored in many countries, Franklin was one of the most admired people in colonial America.

In 1752 Franklin conducted his best-known experiment—flying a kite during a thunderstorm to prove that lightning is a huge electrical charge. He used this new knowledge to invent the lightning rod.

★ Colonial Writers

Literature, too, was developing in the colonies. At first, American literature was made up of pioneer histories and travel journals, such as John Smith's description of Jamestown and William Bradford's account of the Plymouth Colony. Both were written as useful information for financial backers in England. Other early writing was religious, such as the *Bay Psalm Book,* which was the first book printed in the colonies.

Two women in the colonies became well-known poets. **Anne Dudley Bradstreet,** an early settler in Massachusetts Bay, at first wrote poetry reflecting her Puritan faith. Later, she wrote more personal poetry. In

1650 a book of her poems was printed in London—the first American poetry to be published.

Biography ★★★

Phillis Wheatley, the Poet

Phillis Wheatley was the second American woman to win fame for her poetry. Born in Africa in 1753, Wheatley was taken to America and enslaved at about the age of 8. In the household of the Wheatleys, a Boston merchant family, Phillis was treated like a family member. She was educated with the Wheatley children and learned to read both Latin and English. As a teenager, she began to write poems about current events or the deaths of famous people.

In 1772 she went to London with a Wheatley family member. There, a book of her poems was published. Later her work appeared in magazines throughout the colonies. Wheatley gained recognition for her talent and became popular with readers and critics alike. ★★★

▲ PHILLIS WHEATLEY

★ Newspapers and Political Writing

Newspapers, almanacs, books, and circulating libraries all helped raise the level of public awareness in the colonies. Because many of the newspapers carried political opinions, the growth of newspapers meant an increase in political activity, too.

Villagers at the local inn passed newspapers from person to person. European travelers were often amazed at the lively political discussions in American inns and surprised by how much ordinary farmers and workers knew about current events.

Benjamin Franklin—Printer, Publisher, and Political Writer

Benjamin Franklin was himself a printer, publisher, and political writer. For years, starting in 1732, he published his opinions in *Poor Richard's Almanack,* a colonial best-seller. Besides the calendars and forecasts that most almanacs contained, Poor Richard gave advice that is still quoted today:

❝ **Early to Bed, and early to rise, makes a Man healthy, wealthy and wise.** ❞

❝ **The sleeping Fox catches no Poultry.** ❞

❝ **There are no gains without pains.** ❞

Poor Richard's Almanack reinforced the growing American belief that anyone could be a success with hard work.

Libraries and Book Collections

By the mid-1700s, many colonists were well read and well educated. Every colony had a few libraries, booksellers, and book collectors.

▲ **FRANKLIN'S PRINT SHOP** As a young man, Benjamin Franklin worked in his brother's printing office. **What did Franklin later publish that became a best-seller?**

Most people could not afford to own many books, but colonists were quite eager to read and learn. To meet the demand for knowledge, in 1731 Ben Franklin organized the **Library Company of Philadelphia.** Any gentleman could read books when the library was open, but only paying members could borrow books. Lending libraries soon spread to other colonial cities.

★ Travel and Communication

With little spare time, most colonists never went far from home, except to take goods to market. The roads they used generally followed existing Native American foot trails. Eventually these were widened to let wagons pass. By 1760, stagecoaches were traveling on the roads that linked major cities.

For most of the 1600s mail service among the colonies had been poor and inefficient. Great improvements were made after 1753 by Ben Franklin, who had already been running Philadelphia's mail service. Letters were now carried by people on horseback. Riding day and night, they could carry a letter between Philadelphia and Boston in as little as six days.

Now it was possible for colonists to communicate with one another much more quickly than in the past. With the new roads came greater opportunities for spreading ideas, including the idea of revolution.

★ SECTION 1 REVIEW ★

Checking for Understanding

1. **Identify** George Whitefield, Jonathan Edwards, John Locke, Benjamin Franklin, Anne Dudley Bradstreet, Phillis Wheatley, Philadelphia.
2. **Define** gentry, social mobility, Great Awakening, revival, Enlightenment.
3. **What** social classes existed in the American colonies?
4. **How** did Benjamin Franklin reflect the spirit of the Enlightenment?

Critical Thinking

5. **Determining Cause and Effect** How did newspapers and transportation improvements affect colonial thinking?

ACTIVITY

6. Reread Benjamin Franklin's quotes from *Poor Richard's Almanack* on page 181. Select one of Poor Richard's sayings and write it in language you would use and understand today.

The French and Indian War

★★

SETTING THE SCENE

Read to Learn . . .

★ what nations claimed land in North America in the mid-1700s.
★ why France and England both wanted the land in the Ohio Valley.
★ how the outcome of the French and Indian War affected North America.

Terms to Know

★ French and Indian War
★ Iroquois League
★ Albany Plan of Union
★ Treaty of Paris

People to Meet

★ George Washington
★ General Edward Braddock
★ William Pitt
★ General James Wolfe
★ Marquis de Montcalm

Places to Locate

★ New France
★ St. Lawrence River
★ Mississippi River valley
★ Ohio Valley
★ Quebec

◀ FRENCH INFANTRYMAN, 1754

By the early 1700s, France and Great Britain were competing to be the richest and most powerful nation in Europe. Both had established empires around the world, with colonies in North America and the Caribbean islands. Both also maintained trading outposts in Africa and India.

The contest for power led to four wars in Europe and North America. King William's War (1689–1697), Queen Anne's War (1702–1713), and King George's War (1744–1748) all ended in an uneasy peace. When these wars were over, neither France nor Great Britain had won a clear victory, and by the 1750s yet another war was on the way.

The outcome of this war would change the map of North America. This struggle, known as the French and Indian War in the colonies and the **Seven Years' War** in Europe, resulted in the French losing all their holdings on the North American mainland.

★ European Claims in America

Although they were the most powerful, France and Great Britain were not the world's only empire-building nations. Two others—Russia and Spain—also claimed lands in North America.

Russia and Spain

Both Russia and Spain controlled territory in the West. Russia's fur-trading posts were located on the Pacific coast in the region that is Alaska and Canada today. Spain claimed a large part of the Southwest as New Spain. Included were Mexico and parts of present-day New Mexico, Arizona, Texas, and California.

Spain also held islands in the Caribbean and claimed the land that is now Florida. The border between Georgia and Spanish Florida was often a source of conflict between Britain and Spain.

France and Britain were the European powers that clashed most often. French settlements, known as **New France,** lay north and west of the English colonies, on the Atlantic coast and inland along the **St. Lawrence River.** The French also claimed land in the **Mississippi River valley.**

Both the French and the English claimed the land extending westward from the thirteen colonies. Until the 1750s, however, the Native Americans who lived there still controlled that land. French and English traders competed for the profitable fur trade. It was not long before their nations would clash over the land itself.

★ Trouble in the Ohio Valley

The center of the land quarrel was the **Ohio Valley,** located west of the Appalachian Mountains and south of the **Great Lakes.** The Ohio Valley was crossed by the Ohio River, which wound westward to the Mississippi River. Parts of Ohio, Kentucky, Indiana, Pennsylvania, West Virginia, and Illinois make up this region today.

Both France and England claimed the Ohio Valley, but the French moved into it first. At the beginning of the 1700s, French fur trappers roamed the valley in search of mink, beaver, and otter. By the 1740s, however, trappers from Virginia and Pennsylvania crossed into the Ohio Valley as well. This competition for fur trade upset the government leaders of New France.

English Colonists Move Into Ohio

Tensions grew when pioneer families from the English colonies moved west. Land companies owned vast areas of land that they had been granted by the colonial governments. Company owners hoped to make a profit by selling this frontier land and developing new settlements. Wealthy Virginia planters bought the land and backed these companies.

Land Claims in North America, 1754

Alaska

Arctic Circle

PACIFIC OCEAN

Hudson Bay

New France

Louisiana

Missouri R.

Colorado R.

Rio Grande

Mississippi R.

Ohio R.

13 British Colonies

ATLANTIC OCEAN

New Spain

Gulf of Mexico

Florida

West Indies

Caribbean Sea

Haiti

British
French
Spanish
Russian

0   300   600 miles
0   600 kilometers

Map Study

Location Four European countries claimed to own land in North America by the mid-1700s. **Which country's claims lay farthest south?**

Both the British government and the leaders of New France were determined to protect their claims to the Ohio Valley. The French wanted the land because it lay between Canada and their settlements in the Mississippi River valley. British settlers wanted to move west. By 1750 a struggle was under way for control of the Ohio region.

★ Native Americans Take Sides

Control of the Ohio Valley depended mainly on people who were generally ignored in colonial politics—the Native Americans who lived there. Their decision to support one side or the other was crucial in determining the outcome of the conflict in their region.

British traders, richer than the French, could offer the Native Americans more and better goods. The French, however, offered them something more important—respect. Unlike the British, the French tried to understand the Native American lifestyle. By the mid-1700s, the French had proved more successful than the British in forming good relations with most of the eastern Native Americans.

The six nations of the Iroquois League, however, sided with the British. The Iroquois League was a powerful Native American confederation. The Iroquois lived mainly in western New York and along the St. Lawrence River. The Iroquois controlled the fur trade in their territory and all boat travel on the Great Lakes.

★ First Steps Toward War

The rivalry between the British and the French grew. That rivalry and tensions among Native Americans set the stage for clashes in the Ohio Valley. These were the first steps toward a conflict known as the French and Indian War. It was part of a larger conflict known as the Seven Years' War, which was fought in Europe and Asia as well as in North America.

French Forts in the Ohio Valley

To strengthen their claims in the Ohio Valley, in 1752 the French began to build a string of military forts. These extended from Lake Erie in the northwest to as far south as the Ohio River.

The Virginians and other colonial leaders were furious. In 1753 Robert Dinwiddie, governor of Virginia, sent the French a warning. He accused the French of trespassing on Virginia's territory and ordered them to leave. A young major in the Virginia militia, 21-year-old **George Washington,** delivered the message.

The French commander treated Washington politely, but he refused to leave, saying that "no Englishman had a Right to trade upon those Waters (the Ohio River)."

The First Battles

When he returned, Washington was promoted and sent out once again. This time he led 150 soldiers from Virginia to the "forks of the Ohio," where present-day Pittsburgh stands. Their mission was to build a fort where the Allegheny and the Monongahela Rivers meet to form the Ohio River. Washington soon learned, however, that the French were building Fort Duquesne (doo•KAYN) on that site.

As Washington and his small army marched into Pennsylvania, they met a French scouting party near Great Meadows, about 50 miles (80 km) from Fort Duquesne. Washington ordered an attack, and 10 French soldiers were killed.

Under pressure, Washington's men quickly built a makeshift fort that they called **Fort Necessity.** As quickly as the fort was built, however, French forces surrounded it. Outnumbered and forced to surrender, the Virginians were taken prisoner. Most, including Washington, were later set free.

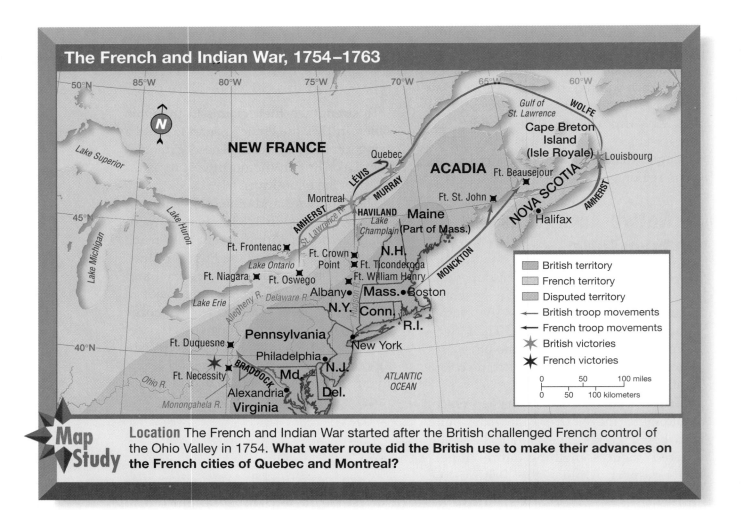

The French and Indian War, 1754–1763

Map Study

Location The French and Indian War started after the British challenged French control of the Ohio Valley in 1754. **What water route did the British use to make their advances on the French cities of Quebec and Montreal?**

★ Attempts at Colonial Unity

Delegates from seven colonies met in June 1754, in Albany, New York, with representatives of the Iroquois League. The colonists aimed to make sure the Iroquois would support the British colonists against the French.

The Albany Plan

The Iroquois and the colonists discussed issues of trade and resolved some of their differences. After the Iroquois left, colonial delegates turned toward other plans for working together, especially on defense. They finally agreed on a plan based largely on an idea presented by Benjamin Franklin, the delegate from Pennsylvania.

This Albany Plan of Union called for a council made up of delegates from each colony, with a leader appointed by the British king. Acting for all the colonies, the council would manage relations with Native Americans. It would have the authority to raise and equip an army and navy. To pay for these projects, the council would be able to tax the colonists.

When the plan was sent to the thirteen colonial assemblies, none approved it. Each colony wanted to control its own taxes and make its own decisions on military affairs.

★ Fighting the War

Several more small battles took place in the Ohio Valley before war was officially declared. In 1755 an army of about 2,000

British soldiers and 450 colonial troops set out to capture Fort Duquesne. **General Edward Braddock** commanded the expedition. Among his aides was George Washington.

Though Braddock was a brave and experienced soldier, he was used to European battle tactics, where soldiers lined up in neat rows and fought in open fields. Washington warned Braddock that this style of fighting would not work well in the forests against the French and their Native American allies.

Braddock did not listen. He even insisted on dragging heavy cannons along the muddy trails. The results were disastrous for the British. On July 9, 1755, the red-coated British were ambushed near Turtle Creek. As the French fired from the woods and hills, many British soldiers panicked. About 1,000 soldiers were killed. Braddock himself was wounded and died a few days later.

William Pitt Takes Charge

France and Great Britain declared war in 1756. By the summer of 1757, French and Native American troops had captured Fort Oswego on Lake Ontario and Fort William Henry on Lake George.

Great Britain's King George II was unhappy about the defeats and appointed **William Pitt** minister of war. Pitt took control and showed great skill for planning troop movements and strategy.

The war was being fought in Europe and India as well as in North America. Pitt, however, believed it would be won or

◄ **BRITISH WAR MEDAL**

▲ **BATTLE OF QUEBEC** British troops met French soldiers on the Plains of Abraham. **Who led the British troops? The French troops?**

Picturing History

lost in America. That is where he sent troops and the powerful British navy. This decision changed the course of the war.

During the next year, 1758, Great Britain won several important victories. One resulted in the fall of **Louisbourg,** a major French fort on Cape Breton Island. Another was the capture of Fort Duquesne, bringing the entire upper Ohio Valley under British control.

The Battle of Quebec

In 1759 Pitt gave **General James Wolfe** the most difficult task of the war—capturing **Quebec,** the capital of New France. Quebec supplied the other French forts farther up the St. Lawrence River. Taking the city would cut off French supplies and weaken New France.

Footnotes to History

A Name for Pittsburgh Fort Pitt, now Pittsburgh, Pennsylvania, was named in honor of William Pitt, who was the British war minister during the French and Indian War. Pitt was never in present-day Pennsylvania, however, and never saw the fort or the major Midwestern city that bears his name.

Quebec was a walled city built on top of steep cliffs that rise above the St. Lawrence River. Wolfe brought his fleet up the river—more than 200 ships carrying over 9,000 British and colonial soldiers, ready to attack. The cliffs, however, enabled Quebec to resist the siege for several months. Any enemy who tried to scale the cliffs was easily seen and fired upon.

Finally, Wolfe found a rough, unguarded path winding up the cliffs a few miles away. In the dead of night, General Wolfe and some 4,000 troops inched their way upward along the path. By the next day, they had reached their destination—the **Plains of Abraham,** a grassy field outside the city.

Battle on the Plains of Abraham

French commander **Marquis de Montcalm** marched his troops to meet the British. Montcalm and his men could not hold out against Wolfe's men. The British were victorious in the battle. The French were forced to surrender. Both General Wolfe and General Montcalm, however, were killed in the battle. As a soldier held the dying Wolfe, a message came that the French troops were retreating.

The capture of Quebec marked the end of French power in North America. The fighting continued though until 1760,

when General Jeffrey Amherst took Montreal, the other major city in New France. With this victory, the French and Indian War was finally over.

★ The Treaty of Paris

In 1763 the British and French officially ended the war by signing the Treaty of Paris. The peace negotiations had also involved Spain. Britain had declared war on Spain in 1762 and had taken control of some Spanish possessions. With the treaty, Great Britain now ruled New France (Canada), the Ohio Valley, and all French lands east of the Mississippi River, with the exception of New Orleans. France kept only its sugar colonies in the Caribbean and two small fishing islands near Canada. Spain, which had entered the war on the French side, had to give Florida to Great Britain. To repay Spain for its losses, France transferred the Louisiana Territory—including New Orleans—to Spain.

For the French, defeat was bitter. France was left with no land on the North American continent. There was only one small crumb of comfort—the thirteen colonies might revolt. A French leader likened them to a "ripe fruit," ready to drop off the branch.

★ SECTION 2 REVIEW ★

Checking for Understanding

1. **Identify** George Washington, General Edward Braddock, William Pitt, General James Wolfe, Marquis de Montcalm, New France, St. Lawrence River, Mississippi River valley, Ohio Valley, Quebec.

2. **Define** French and Indian War, Iroquois League, Albany Plan of Union, Treaty of Paris.

3. **What** issues caused the French and the British to go to war over the Ohio Valley?

Critical Thinking

4. **Predicting Outcomes** What might have happened in North America had France won the French and Indian War?

ACTIVITY

5. Choose one of the events in the French and Indian War, such as Braddock's defeat or the Battle of Quebec. Draw a cartoon strip showing the story of this event.

BUILDING SKILLS
Critical Thinking Skills

Making Generalizations

A generalization is a conclusion we draw from the facts that we have. It is a general statement that may or may not represent a true picture of the facts. We make generalizations every day about people, events, or situations.

► BENJAMIN FRANKLIN

Learning the Skill

Often, generalizations are made before all the facts have been presented or are available. To make a generalization that really works, you need sufficient information.

Practicing the Skill

The passage below was written by Benjamin Franklin about General Edward Braddock, whom he met before the disastrous expedition to Fort Duquesne. Read Franklin's account of the meeting. Then read the generalizations that follow it. Decide whether each one is valid based on what Franklin wrote.

❝ This general was, I think, a brave man, and might probably have made a figure as a good officer in some European war. But he had too much self-confidence, too high an opinion of the . . . regular troops, and too mean a one of both Americans and Indians. . . .

'After taking Fort Duquesne,' says he, 'I am to proceed to [Fort] Niagara; and having taken that, to [Fort] Frontenac, if the season will allow time; and I suppose it will, for Duquesne can hardly detain me above three or four days. . . . These [Indians] may, indeed, be a formidable enemy to your raw American militia, but upon the King's regular and disciplined troops, sir, it is impossible they should make any impression.' ❞

Generalizations

1. Braddock had an attitude of superiority toward Americans.

2. Braddock was confident about himself and his soldiers.

3. Braddock was a bad commander.

4. All British officers felt superior toward the Americans.

APPLYING THE SKILL

5. From what you have read in this chapter and elsewhere, write a generalization about the French and Indian War. Have at least three facts to back up your generalization. Exchange statements with a friend. Decide whether each of you has written a valid generalization.

SECTION 3

★★★★★★★★★★★★★★★★★★★★★★★★★★★★★★★★★★★★★★★

Taxes and Boycotts

SETTING THE SCENE

Read to Learn . . .

- ★ how the British government hoped to end its money problems after the French and Indian War.
- ★ why the colonists objected to the Stamp Act and the Townshend Acts.
- ★ how the British government reacted to the Boston Tea Party.

Terms to Know

- ★ Proclamation of 1763
- ★ quartering
- ★ Stamp Act
- ★ boycott
- ★ Townshend Acts
- ★ writs of assistance
- ★ Committees of Correspondence

People to Meet

- ★ Pontiac
- ★ George Grenville
- ★ Patrick Henry
- ★ Samuel Adams
- ★ Lord North

Places to Locate

- ★ Fort Detroit
- ★ Boston

The TIMES are Dreadful Doleful Dismal Dolorous, and DOLLAR-LESS.

NUMB 1195

Thursday, October 31. 1765

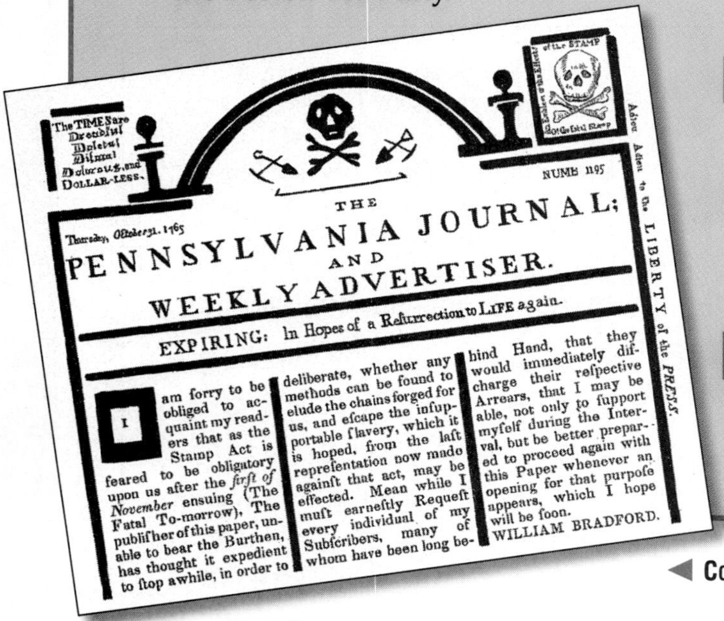

THE PENNSYLVANIA JOURNAL; AND WEEKLY ADVERTISER.

EXPIRING: In Hopes of a Reſurrection to LIFE again.

Adieu, Adieu to the LIBERTY of the PRESS.

I am ſorry to be obliged to acquaint my readers that as the Stamp Act is feared to be obligatory upon us after the *firſt of November* ensuing (The Fatal To-morrow), The publiſher of this paper, unable to bear the Burthen, has thought it expedient to ſtop awhile, in order to deliberate, whether any methods can be found to elude the chains forged for us, and eſcape the inſupportable ſlavery, which it is hoped, from the laſt repreſentation now made againſt that act, may be effected. Mean while I muſt earneſtly Requeſt every individual of my Subſcribers, many of whom have been long behind Hand, that they would immediately diſcharge their reſpective Arrears, that I may be able, not only to ſupport myſelf during the Interval, but be better prepared to proceed again with this Paper whenever an opening for that purpoſe appears, which I hope will be ſoon.
WILLIAM BRADFORD.

◀ COLONIAL NEWSPAPER ATTACKING STAMP ACT

The Treaty of Paris that ended the French and Indian War doubled the size of Great Britain's North American empire. The huge new territory, however, brought problems, as well as promise, to the British. The territory was expensive to support and to defend. When Great Britain tried to make the colonies pay for the services they received, the colonists grew furious. Angry protests made the situation worse.

★ Trouble on the Frontier

During the war, most Native Americans in the Ohio Valley supported the French. By 1760, though, the British had driven the French from that area. British traders took over where the French had been and more and more colonists settled in the region.

An Ottawa leader, **Pontiac,** sent out messengers to the Miami, Chippewa, and others encouraging them to join against the British takeover. Soon Pontiac's alliance included almost every group from Lake Superior to the lower Mississippi River valley.

In May 1763 the united Native American nations began a long attack of **Fort Detroit,** a British military outpost in the Great Lakes region. This uprising, called **Pontiac's Rebellion,** took the British forces by surprise. The Native Americans captured several forts and frontier settlements. When Pontiac learned that the French had signed the Treaty of Paris, and he could no longer depend on French aid, his forces stopped fighting.

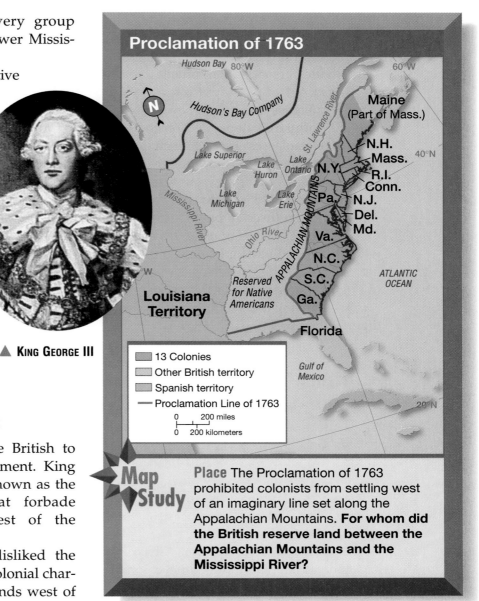

Proclamation of 1763

▲ KING GEORGE III

The Proclamation of 1763

Pontiac's Rebellion led the British to close western lands to settlement. King George III issued an order, known as the Proclamation of 1763, that forbade colonists from settling west of the Appalachian Mountains.

The American colonists disliked the proclamation. Some of their colonial charters promised them all the lands west of the Appalachians. They wanted a chance to settle the rich Ohio Valley. Some colonists simply ignored the proclamation and moved west.

To enforce the proclamation, the British government stationed troops in frontier forts. This further angered Americans who disliked the idea of supporting military troops during times of peace.

★ Money Problems

Of the many postwar problems facing Great Britain, the most pressing was the problem of money. Parliament looked

Map Study

Place The Proclamation of 1763 prohibited colonists from settling west of an imaginary line set along the Appalachian Mountains. **For whom did the British reserve land between the Appalachian Mountains and the Mississippi River?**

toward the colonies for a solution. The war had made the colonists safe from attack by the French and had cost them very little. Now, British citizens thought, the colonists ought to help pay the costs of the war.

Most colonists saw it differently. From their point of view, the war had not been fought to protect them, but rather to protect British trade. In addition, the colonists thought it seemed only right that the parent country should take responsibility for defending its empire.

The overwhelming job of solving Great Britain's financial problems went to a new prime minister, **George Grenville.** He began by enforcing existing laws and then went on to introduce some new policies.

Grenville persuaded Parliament to pass the **Sugar Act of 1764,** putting a tax on foreign molasses and sugar. Several New England industries depended on the less expensive molasses from French sugar colonies rather than the higher-priced British molasses. This new tax was lower than an older 1733 sugar tax, but the colonists still refused to pay it.

Another new law annoyed Americans who objected to having British soldiers in the colonies. The **Quartering Act,** passed in 1765, required colonists to pay for quartering—housing and feeding—British soldiers in their area.

★ Stamp Act Controversy

In 1765 Parliament passed the Stamp Act. This law forced people to pay a special tax on certain items that were then stamped to show the tax had been paid. Things people used every day, such as newspapers, playing cards, and legal documents like diplomas or licenses, were taxed under the Stamp Act.

The colonists believed that Grenville had gone too far. Up to this time, colonial assemblies had made the important decisions about taxes and expenses. Now, for the first time, Parliament was trying to tax the colonists directly.

The colonists knew that one basic right of British citizens was to be taxed only by the representatives they had elected. Yet no American voted in elections to Parliament. The Stamp Act, then, clearly violated the cherished idea of *no taxation without representation.*

Angry colonial lawyers, merchants, and newspaper printers organized their friends, neighbors, and workers to oppose the Stamp Act. Soon, protests against the hated Stamp Act erupted throughout the colonies. In some cities, crowds rioted in the streets and threatened agents of the British government. A small band of angry colonists formed a protest group called the **Sons of Liberty.** They seized and burned piles of the stamps.

Colonial merchants also acted together to fight the Stamp Act. By the end of 1765 more than 1,000 merchants had signed agreements to not buy or sell any British goods. This type of agreement later became known as a boycott.

Virginians took the lead in protests against the Stamp Act. In the House of Burgesses, a hot-tempered young lawyer named **Patrick Henry** called the Stamp Act illegal and proposed several resolutions against it. One resolution declared that the power to tax lay with the House of Burgesses alone. Other resolutions such as this were reprinted by newspapers throughout the colonies.

The Stamp Act Congress

The Massachusetts assembly suggested a meeting of representatives from all the colonies, to draw up a written protest. In October 1765, delegates from nine colonies met in New York City at the **Stamp Act Congress.**

In spite of the regional differences that separated them, the delegates were able to compose a petition and resolutions to send to King George III. These were carefully and respectfully worded. After all, the congressional delegates were still loyal British subjects—they simply wanted the government to recognize their rights under the British law.

Repeal of the Stamp Act

Grenville and others in England were astonished when they read about the colonists' reaction to the Stamp Act. In their opinion, Parliament had every right to tax Americans, as well as British subjects everywhere. Many members of Parliament were strongly against repealing the Stamp

▲ REPEAL OF THE STAMP ACT The colonists celebrated the British repeal of the Stamp Act as shown in this political cartoon. **What act did Parliament pass in place of the Stamp Act?**

Act, believing that such an action would weaken their ability to govern the empire.

On the other hand, British merchants who wanted to sell goods in America were pressuring Grenville to repeal the Stamp Act. The law was by now useless anyway, they reasoned, because no one obeyed it.

In March 1766 Parliament finally repealed the Stamp Act. At the same time, however, it passed another act meant to warn the colonists against any future protests. The **Declaratory Act** stated that Parliament had the right to rule and tax the colonies.

★ More Conflicts With Parliament

Parliament still intended to raise money from the colonies. In 1767 it passed another set of laws designed to do just that. Called the Townshend Acts after the finance official who wrote them, these laws placed import taxes on paint, glass, lead, paper, and tea coming into America.

The money would be used to pay British colonial officials. The acts even allowed officials to obtain writs of assistance, or blank search warrants. With these laws, officials could search anywhere for suspected smuggled goods.

Boycott of British Imports

The colonists once again protested. They sent petitions to Parliament. Merchants and planters throughout the colonies signed **nonimportation agreements** in which they agreed to not import the items that were taxable.

The Sons of Liberty saw to it that the intended boycott was carried out. At the same time, concerned colonial women organized as the **Daughters of Liberty.** They signed pledges against drinking tea and published notices in the local newspapers promising they would not buy British-made cloth.

To keep the pledge and still get fabric for clothes, the Daughters of Liberty met at spinning clubs to spin, weave, or knit

▲ BOSTON TEA PARTY Patriot Samuel Adams led the Boston protestors who destroyed a ship's cargo of East Indian tea. **What group was responsible for dumping the tea in the harbor?**

their own cloth. Wearing homespun fabric became an important symbol of American resistance against tyranny.

★ Talk of Independence

Tensions grew in the colonies, especially in the cities. New Yorkers were outraged when Parliament closed their colonial assembly. In **Boston,** riots against customs officials broke out on the waterfront. Boston citizens were angry at the sight of red-coated soldiers on the streets. **Samuel Adams,** an outspoken leader of the Sons of Liberty, kept the public anger simmering with his speeches and newsletters warning that Parliament was a threat to American rights and liberties.

The Boston Massacre

Finally the tensions exploded. On the night of March 5, 1770, a group of Boston youths and dockworkers began insulting and throwing snowballs at a British guard on duty. When more soldiers arrived, an angry mob surrounded them. The British captain, Thomas Preston, tried to calm his men and the crowd. In the confusion the soldiers began to fire their guns into the crowd. When the shooting stopped, five people lay dead in the street. One was **Crispus Attucks,** an African American sailor.

Captain Preston denied that he gave the order to fire, and he was later cleared of that charge. Samuel Adams, however, spoke for many colonists when he called the incident the **Boston Massacre.**

In April 1770 a new prime minister, **Lord North,** tried to improve relations with the colonies. The Townshend Acts were repealed, with the exception of the tax on tea. This tax remained to remind the colonists of Parliament's authority, for tea was a very popular drink.

★ The Conflicts Increase

During the next few years, tensions between the colonists and the British seemed to ease and colonial businesses recovered. Still, some colonial leaders were suspicious of Parliament and kept the idea of opposition alive.

One of these leaders was Samuel Adams. Along with a few others, he encouraged the colonists to remain watchful and aware of what the British were doing.

In 1772 Adams organized Committees of Correspondence in the towns of Massachusetts. In a time when there was no radio or telephone, these committees were a network for passing along news. Soon Committees of Correspondence formed in other colonies as well.

Trouble Over Tea

The next crisis in the colonies brewed over taxes on tea. In early 1773, the directors of the British East India Company asked Lord North for help with their financial troubles. To rescue the company, the government agreed to the **Tea Act.** It gave the East India Company exclusive rights to sell tea directly to the Americans without paying the British import tax. The company carried tea in its own ships and used its own sellers. This cut out business for colonial sea captains and merchants.

Lord North expected colonists to be pleased by the low prices under the Tea Act. Once again, however, the government had not understood the colonists. Merchants and shippers joined radicals like Samuel Adams to protest the act. Drinking tea became a symbol for giving in to Parliament's laws.

The Boston Tea Party

In the fall of 1773, ships carrying 500,000 pounds (227,000 kg) of East India Company tea were on their way to Boston, New York, Philadelphia, and Charles Town. Merchants protested and the Sons of Liberty made plans. In **Boston** more than 300 chests of valuable tea were waiting on board ship. Colonists were determined to send the ships and cargoes away. The governor of Massachusetts was equally determined to see the tea unloaded.

As the ship lay in the harbor, a band of people disguised as Mohawks ran silently down the docks. The group boarded the ships and dumped the tea into the harbor. Easily recognizable under the disguises were the faces of Boston's Sons of Liberty.

The news of the **Boston Tea Party,** as the incident became known, enraged Parliament. The response would push the colonists still further away, until tensions exploded into war.

★ SECTION 3 REVIEW ★

Checking for Understanding

1. **Identify** Pontiac, George Grenville, Patrick Henry, Samuel Adams, Lord North, Fort Detroit, Boston.
2. **Define** Proclamation of 1763, quartering, Stamp Act, boycott, Townshend Acts, writs of assistance, Committees of Correspondence.
3. **How** did the British government hope to solve Great Britain's financial problems after the French and Indian War?
4. **What** caused the meeting of the Stamp Act Congress? What did it accomplish?

Critical Thinking

5. **Identifying Alternatives**   If Parliament and the king had followed different policies, could they have prevented the moves toward independence? Why or why not?

ACTIVITY

6. Design a poster that encourages colonists to stop buying British goods.

★★

On the Brink of War

SETTING THE SCENE

Read to Learn . . .

★ why the colonists formed the Continental Congress.
★ what events led to the outbreak of the American Revolution.

Terms to Know

★ Intolerable Acts
★ First Continental Congress
★ militia
★ minutemen
★ Second Continental Congress

People to Meet

★ Paul Revere
★ John Hancock
★ William Dawes
★ George Washington

Places to Locate

★ Concord
★ Lexington

▶ BRITISH MUSKET, 1747

Benjamin Franklin called the Boston Tea Party "an act of violent injustice," and some Boston merchants were willing to start a collection to pay for the damage. To the British government, however, it was as act of lawlessness that deserved swift and severe punishment.

★ Punishing the Colonies

In March 1774 Parliament passed a series of laws known as the **Coercive Acts.** One of the acts closed the port of Boston until payment was made for the tea. Another act provided that British officials accused of a crime were to be tried in English rather than American courts. Still another act provided that

British troops could be quartered in any town in Massachusetts—even in private homes. Finally, the Massachusetts charter was amended to greatly reduce the colony's right of self-government.

The end result was that Boston and the colony of Massachusetts were to suffer for the actions of a handful of unknown persons who had staged the protest. The provisions of the Coercive Acts were so harsh that they were called the Intolerable Acts throughout the colonies.

At the same time Parliament passed the **Quebec Act.** This act extended the Canadian province of Quebec south to the Ohio River. It also allowed French Canadians to keep their laws, language, and Roman Catholic religion. Colonists saw the act as the first step toward doing away with jury trials and Protestantism in the colonies. They also believed the boundary changes were made to keep American settlers out of the western lands.

Colonists Take Charge

The Coercive Acts made many colonists want to fight back. **George Washington** expressed this feeling when he said "the cause of Boston now is and ever will be the cause of America." The Committees of Correspondence united the colonists more than ever before. A call went out for delegates from each colony to meet and discuss their common concerns. In September 1774, 56 delegates from every colony except Georgia met in Philadelphia to form what became known as the First Continental Congress.

★ The First Continental Congress

Discussions were difficult because each colony had its own needs and viewpoints. The right to control trade was an especially bitter point of debate. Even those who accepted Parliament's right to regulate trade objected to the Coercive Acts.

The most outspoken criticisms of Parliament came from Massachusetts and Virginia. As the congress got under way, a Boston silversmith named **Paul Revere** arrived with a set of resolutions passed at a meeting in Boston. In harsh, angry words, he delivered the **Suffolk Resolves.** They called the Coercive Acts "the attempts of a wicked administration to enslave Americans." The resolves also demanded the return of constitutional government and an end to trade with Great Britain and its West Indian colonies.

Not all of the delegates shared Revere's strong views. The resolutions passed by the congress were a compromise—a middle ground—between their points of view.

The congress did, however, approve most of the Massachusetts ideas for resistance. It even approved Massachusetts's plan for arming and training a militia—a group of citizens who would be ready to fight in any emergency.

The Continental Congress Takes a Stand

The congress based its final position on the colonists' natural rights (as John Locke had said) and the colonists' rights as British citizens. It issued a statement that

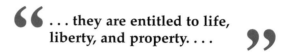

" ... they are entitled to life, liberty, and property. . . . "

The statement went on to declare that the colonists would never give up one of these rights against their will.

For the time being, the congress took only peaceful actions. It seemed to agree that Parliament could make laws about trade. On the other hand, it approved a ban on trade—both exports and imports—with Great Britain until the Coercive Acts were repealed.

One of the congress's statements was a direct appeal to the king. It asked him to make peace between Parliament and the Americans. The congress insisted that they, and the people they represented, were loyal subjects of George III. Most of the delegates had little hope that Parliament would listen to them. They arranged to meet again in a second congress in May 1775.

★ Moving Toward a Crisis

During the winter of 1774, Parliament debated ways to respond to the colonists. Some members were sympathetic to the colonists and hoped for a friendly solution. **Edmund Burke,** a writer, made several speeches asking for compromise. William Pitt, now a member of the House

▼ **MODERN-DAY MARCHING BAND**

A Song for the Times

Once, red-coated British soldiers sang "Yankee Doodle" to make fun of the roughly dressed colonial troops. Now it is one of America's favorite patriotic songs.

Richard Shuckburg, a British army surgeon in the French and Indian War, wrote the scornful new words of "Yankee Doodle" to make fun of the colonial soldiers. *Yankee* was a nickname for New Englanders, *doodle* a slang word for a fool or half-wit.

Then

A Teasing Tune

Both colonial Americans and the British knew the tune of the 1775 song— "Yankee Doodle."

Now

Familiar Favorite

Practically every American today can still whistle or sing "Yankee Doodle." As in colonial times, it is a favorite with

marching bands because it is lively and easy to play. Modern bands, however, have many more instruments than fifes and drums.

◄ **COLONIAL FIFE AND DRUM CORPS**

---

of Lords, argued that British troops should be withdrawn from America.

George III and his advisers, however, would not listen. They saw the colonies as disobedient children. The royal advisers wanted to keep British soldiers in America to enforce Parliament's laws.

The Colonists Take Arms

Several colonies were now moving toward open rebellion. Radical leaders were pushing for a break with Great Britain. Daily tensions between the colonists and British soldiers grew.

All through the winter of 1774–1775, British troops were being sent to the Boston area. At the same time, the Massachusetts militia drilled on village greens. The farmers and artisans in the militia were called minutemen because they could be ready to fight at a minute's notice.

Both the Americans and the British seemed to expect bloodshed. Speaking in

the Virginia House of Burgesses, Patrick Henry challenged the assembly:

❝ **The next gale that sweeps from the north [Massachusetts] will bring to our ears the clash of resounding arms! . . . Is life so dear, or peace so sweet, as to be purchased at the price of chains and slavery? . . . I know not what course others may take; but as for me, give me liberty, or give me death!** ❞

A Warning for the Minutemen

In the spring of 1775, American spies heard that the British were making plans against the militia. General Thomas Gage, they heard, was sending soldiers to take their supply of guns and gunpowder stored in **Concord,** a few miles from Boston. Gage had also been ordered to arrest two colonial leaders—Samuel Adams and Boston merchant **John Hancock.**

On the night of April 18, 1775, the American spy network in Boston waited to discover the route the British soldiers would take. Their plan of action was clear. Boston's North Church would serve as the signal tower. Dr. Joseph Warren planned to flash one light from the church bell tower if the British were approaching by land, and two lights if they came by sea.

As soon as Dr. Warren spotted British troops, he signaled the two waiting riders —**William Dawes** and **Paul Revere.** Immediately the men jumped on their horses and galloped to **Lexington,** with the urgent news that the redcoats were coming.

Battles at Lexington and Concord

About 700 British soldiers marched toward Concord. They reached Lexing-ton, a town on the way to Concord, soon after dawn on April 19. To their surprise, about 70 minutemen armed with muskets and pitchforks were waiting for them on Lexington Green.

No one knows who fired the first shot. According to one account, a British officer rode onto the green and called out to the militia: "Disperse, ye rebels!" Someone fired a shot. Then, more shots were fired, and 8 colonists fell dead and 10 were wounded. One British soldier was wounded.

The British redcoats continued on to Concord. They burned what little gunpowder the colonists had not used. At North Bridge, just outside of Concord,

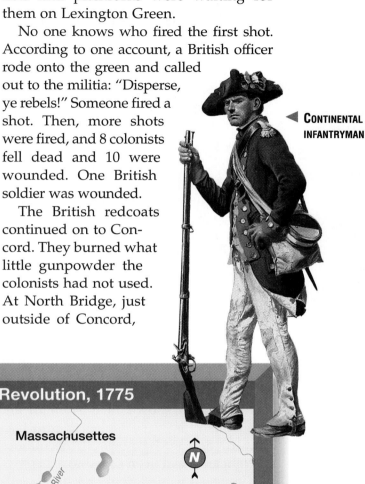

◀ **CONTINENTAL INFANTRYMAN**

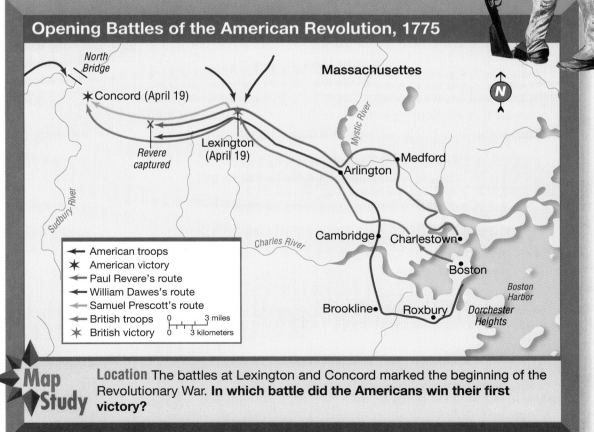

Opening Battles of the American Revolution, 1775

North Bridge

Concord (April 19)

Massachusettes

Mystic River

Revere captured

Lexington (April 19)

Medford

Arlington

Sudbury River

Charles River

Cambridge

Charlestown

Boston

Boston Harbor

Brookline

Roxbury

Dorchester Heights

Legend:
- ← American troops
- ✱ American victory
- ← Paul Revere's route
- ← William Dawes's route
- ← Samuel Prescott's route
- ← British troops
- ✱ British victory

0   3 miles
0   3 kilometers

Map Study

Location The battles at Lexington and Concord marked the beginning of the Revolutionary War. **In which battle did the Americans win their first victory?**

three redcoats and two minutemen were killed in a brief battle. Years later American poet Ralph Waldo Emerson wrote:

> **By the rude bridge that
>   arched the flood,
> Their flag to April's breeze
>   unfurl'd,
> Here once the embattled
>   farmers stood,
> And fired the shot heard
>   round the world.**

The fighting ended by noon. The colonists had shown their strength and the British had been forced to turn back toward Boston. By now, all the minutemen nearby had been called to arms.

Crouched behind trees and stone walls, they fired at the British. The march became a wild retreat. In the end, British casualties, those wounded or killed, were nearly three times those of the Americans. More important, the battle marked a turning point—the start of the American Revolution.

★ The Second Continental Congress

When the Second Continental Congress met in May 1775, things had changed dramatically. Now delegates from all thirteen colonies met to appoint a military commander and to raise an army. The congress chose **George Washington** to build a Continental Army. Washington was a veteran of the French and Indian War. This gave him the military experience that New Englanders respected.

Even while building an army and defying Parliament, the congress was still trying to avoid war. In July 1775 they sent the king an **Olive Branch Petition** hoping he would act to protect his loyal American subjects and remove British troops from American soil. The petition begged the king to stop the war and make peace with the colonists.

Their efforts failed. George III declared the Americans to be rebels. The Second Continental Congress would lead the American colonies directly into war.

★ SECTION 4 REVIEW ★

Checking for Understanding

1. **Identify** Paul Revere, John Hancock, William Dawes, George Washington, Concord, Lexington.

2. **Define** Intolerable Acts, First Continental Congress, militia, minutemen, Second Continental Congress.

3. **How** did the colonists respond to the Intolerable Acts?

4. **What** events led up to the first battle of the American Revolution?

Critical Thinking

5. **Recognizing Points of View** Why did some colonists support actions to hold on to their ties with Britain and the king?

ACTIVITY

6. Imagine you are a television news reporter covering Patrick Henry's speech to the House of Burgesses. Write an introduction as you interview Henry and quote his speech.

Paul Revere, Silversmith

Patriot, colonial leader, silversmith—all these words describe Paul Revere. Revere is best remembered for his daring ride to warn Americans about the British attack in 1775. His real career, however, was as one of Boston's most talented silversmiths. He learned the craft from his father, who had come from France. Paul took over the family business at the age of 21. He immediately made a name for himself as an honest and highly skilled artisan.

Revere was famous for the graceful balance and elegant style of his silverware. He made tea sets—teapot, cream pitcher, sugar bowl—in many shapes. In one set, the pieces might be oval with fluted sides. Another might be gracefully curved like pears, while another might have the look of classical Greek urns. Revere also made trays and bowls both round and oval. Similar bowls, made by modern silversmiths, are still called Revere bowls.

Revere the Engraver

Silversmiths of colonial times worked like sculptors to fashion each piece. Revere also enjoyed engraving pieces with rich decorations. Engraved designs are carved into a metal surface with a sharp tool. Such work had to be done very carefully because silver was a valuable metal. He might carve a large medallion with fancy letters in the middle of a tray, or cover the sides of a teapot with crisscrossing lines that formed the stems, leaves, and buds of flowers.

Revere used his engraving skill in other ways, as well. One of his most famous works was the printing plate that showed the patriots' version of the Boston Massacre. As a

▲ PAUL REVERE

serious patriot, he engraved plates to print colonial money. Revere's works can be seen in museums throughout the United States.

Making the Arts Connection

1. For what two careers is Paul Revere famous?

2. What kinds of silverware did Revere make?

3. What details made Revere's work outstanding?

ACTIVITY

4. Take a large piece of aluminum foil, fold it over, and lay it on a flat surface. Using a blunt pencil, etch or draw a decorative design for a tray or bowl onto the foil as Revere might have done.

Using Key Vocabulary

Use the following vocabulary words to complete the sentences that follow.

social mobility   quartering
Iroquois League   militia
Proclamation of 1763

1. King George issued the _____ to keep colonists from moving across the Appalachians.

2. Because _____ was possible in the American colonies, ordinary workers or farmers could rise to a higher class.

3. Colonial delegates met in Albany in an effort to make a trade agreement with the _____.

4. The First Continental Congress approved Massachusetts's resolution to arm and train its _____.

5. To make colonists share the cost of defense, a new law required the _____ of soldiers in their houses and barns.

Reviewing Facts

1. **Explain** how the Great Awakening affected people in the American colonies.

2. **Identify** the sites of major battles that ended the French and Indian War.

3. **Describe** the changes that took place in 1763 in the territories held by European countries in North America.

4. **Explain** why the British government passed new colonial trade laws after 1763.

5. **List** three of the actions taken by the First Continental Congress.

Understanding Concepts

Beliefs, Ideas, and Institutions

1. How did the Great Awakening affect the colonists' view of society?

2. How were the social class divisions in the American colonies different from those in British society?

American Democracy

3. Why did American colonists oppose laws such as the Stamp Act and the Townshend Acts?

4. What were Parliament's goals in passing the Intolerable Acts?

History and Geography

The Quebec Act, 1774

Study the map that shows the changes in North America after Great Britain passed the Quebec Act. Then answer the questions on page 203.

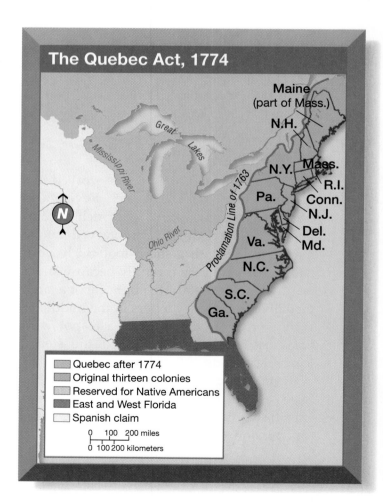

The Quebec Act, 1774

Maine (part of Mass.)
N.H.
Great Lakes
Mississippi River
N.Y.
Mass.
R.I.
Conn.
Pa.
N.J.
Proclamation Line of 1763
Del.
Va.
Md.
Ohio River
N.C.
S.C.
Ga.

N

☐ Quebec after 1774
☐ Original thirteen colonies
☐ Reserved for Native Americans
☐ East and West Florida
☐ Spanish claim

0   100   200 miles
0   100 200 kilometers

CHAPTER 7 ★ REVIEW

1. **Place** What bodies of water were part of Quebec after the Quebec Act?

2. **Location** What country claimed the land to the west of Quebec?

3. **Movement** What inland waterways marked the southern and western boundaries of Quebec's new territory?

Critical Thinking

1. **Understanding Cause and Effect** How was Pontiac's Rebellion related to the outcome of the French and Indian War?

2. **Making Comparisons** How were the First and Second Continental Congresses different from each other? How were they similar?

Cooperative Learning Interdisciplinary Activity: Citizenship

Form a small group and have each member research and play one of the following roles—a colonist whose home has been searched for smuggled goods, a colonist who has had a trial with no jury, a merchant whose business has been hurt by the Sugar Act, and a printer who was ruined by the Stamp Act. Work with your group to write a letter to George Grenville telling why you do not approve of his policy. Have one person from your group read the finished letter to the class.

Practicing Skills

Making Generalizations

Write a generalization based on the facts in each group of statements that follow.

1. **a.** Social classes in America depended on wealth and occupation.

   b. A colonial shopkeeper could earn enough to buy a ship.

   c. Indentured servants could earn freedom and start businesses.

2. **a.** Britain had huge war debts after the French and Indian War.

   b. Parliament passed the Sugar Act to make the colonists pay taxes on imported sugar and molasses.

   c. Parliament passed the Quartering Act to make colonists help pay for housing and feeding British troops.

3. **a.** To oppose the Stamp Act, colonists refused to buy goods from Britain.

   b. The Sons of Liberty burned shipments of stamped paper and attacked Stamp Act agents.

   c. To oppose the Tea Act, Bostonians dumped chests full of tea into Boston Harbor.

4. **a.** In 1770 British soldiers and street gangs clashed in the Boston Massacre.

   b. The Boston Tea Party was a protest act by Boston's Sons of Liberty.

   c. In 1775 the battles of Lexington and Concord were fought near Boston.

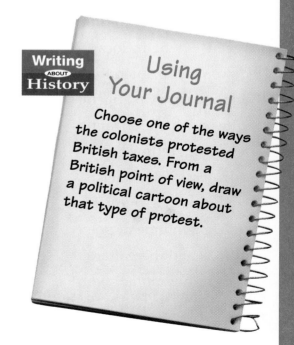

Writing ABOUT History

Using Your Journal

Choose one of the ways the colonists protested British taxes. From a British point of view, draw a political cartoon about that type of protest.

Read to Discover

Longfellow wrote *Paul Revere's Ride* many years after the American Revolution, yet he makes the legendary Paul Revere come to life. As you read this selection, look for feelings of suspense and patriotism that have made this poem popular for so many years. What mental pictures do Longfellow's words create?

Reader's Dictionary

muster	to gather
grenadiers	soldiers
girth	band that fits around the body of an animal
spectral	like a ghost

from *Paul Revere's Ride*

by Henry Wadsworth Longfellow (1807-1882)

Listen, my children, and you shall hear
Of the midnight ride of Paul Revere,
On the eighteenth of April, in Seventy-five;
Hardly a man is now alive
Who remembers that famous day and year.

He said to his friend, "If the British march
By land or sea from the town tonight,
Hang a lantern aloft in the belfry arch
Of the North Church tower as a signal light —
One, if by land, and two, if by sea;
And I on the opposite shore will be,
Ready to ride and spread the alarm
Through every Middlesex village and farm,
For the country folk to be up and to arm."

Meanwhile, his friend, through alley and street,
Wanders and watches, with eager ears,
Till in the silence around him he hears
The muster of men at the barrack door,
And the measured tread of the grenadiers,
Marching down to their boats on the shore.

Henry Wadsworth Longfellow, born in present-day Portland, Maine, began his literary career at the age of 13 when a local newspaper printed the young teen's first poem. After graduating from college, Longfellow became a professor of modern languages. He published his first volume of poetry in 1839 and thereafter became a popular favorite among both American and European readers.

Meanwhile, impatient to mount and ride,
Booted and spurred, with a heavy stride
On the opposite shore walked Paul Revere.
Now he patted his horse's side,
Now gazed at the landscape far and near,
Then, impetuous, stamped the earth,
And, turned and tightened his saddle girth;
But mostly he watched with eager search
The belfry tower of the Old North Church,
As it rose above the graves on the hill,
Lonely and spectral and somber and still.

And lo! As he looks, on the belfry's height
A glimmer, and then a gleam of light!
He springs to the saddle, the bridle he turns,
But lingers and gazes, till full on his sight
A second lamp in the belfry burns!

A hurry of hoofs in a village street,
A shape in the moonlight, a bulk in the dark,
And beneath, from the pebbles, in passing, a spark
Struck out by a steed flying fearless and fleet:
That was all! And yet, through the gloom and the light,
The fate of a nation was riding that night;
And the spark struck out by that steed, in his flight,
Kindled the land into flame with its heat.

So throughout the night rode Paul Revere;
And so through the night went his cry of alarm
To every Middlesex village and farm—
A cry of defiance and not of fear,
A voice in the darkness, a knock at the door,
And a word that shall echo for evermore!
For, borne on the night-wind of the Past,
Through all our history, to the last,
In the hour of darkness and peril and need,
The people will awaken and listen to hear
The hurrying hoof-beats of that steed,
And the midnight message of Paul Revere.

▲ PAUL REVERE'S RIDE

Responding to Literature

1. What was the midnight message of Paul Revere?

2. Do you think Paul Revere would have delivered his message the same way today? Explain your answer.

3. How does this poem make you feel about Paul Revere? Why?

ACTIVITY

4. Think about the scenes that Longfellow portrayed in this poem. Choose one scene and draw a picture of it as you think it would have appeared.

Chapter 5

The 13 English Colonies

The English founded their first permanent colony at **Jamestown, Virginia,** in 1607. The early settlers suffered many hardships. The colony began to flourish, however, after John Rolfe introduced tobacco growing in 1612. In 1619 the first Africans arrived in Virginia. In the same year the colonists created the **House of Burgesses.** They elected their own representatives to this lawmaking body.

Puritans fleeing religious persecution in England founded the colony of **Plymouth, Massachusetts,** in 1620. The Pilgrims, as the Plymouth settlers came to be known, signed the **Mayflower Compact.** This document outlined a system of self-government for the colony. Massachusetts grew rapidly as more Puritans arrived during the 1630s. Expanding population and lack of religious toleration in Massachusetts led to the founding of Rhode Island and Connecticut.

▲ **THE FIRST AMERICAN THANKSGIVING** BY JENNIE A. BROWNSCOMBE, C. 1914

By 1733 thirteen English colonies lined the Atlantic coast. They formed three regions—**New England,** the **Middle Colonies,** and the **Southern Colonies.** Individual proprietors from England founded the Middle and Southern Colonies under land grants from the king. The Southern Colonies included Maryland, the Carolinas, and Georgia. The Middle Colonies took in Pennsylvania, New Jersey, Delaware, and New York.

CAUSES

- Quebec Act allows French settlers in Ohio Valley
- British quarter soldiers in Boston colonists' homes
- Committees of Correspondence unite colonial opinion
- Coercive Acts close the port of Boston

• Meeting of First Continental Congress

EFFECTS

- Colonies approve protests in Boston
- Colonies ban trade with Great Britain
- Congress appeals directly to King George III for relief
- Delegates agree to meet again the next year

Chapter 6

Life in the 13 Colonies

Differences in natural resources and backgrounds of the settlers helped shape the development of the New England, Middle, and Southern Colonies. Because the New England environment lacked fertile soil, large-scale farming was not possible. Fishing, shipping, and trade—encouraged by ocean and forest resources—became the basis for wealth in New England. In the Middle and Southern Colonies, agriculture thrived in an environment of fertile soil and long growing seasons. Business and trade also developed in the cities of the Middle Colonies.

Education and the role of women varied among the regions. Education made the strongest gains in New England under the influence of the Puritans. The first college, Harvard, opened in 1636, and the first public school opened in 1647. New England women often operated shops. Women in agricultural colonies worked with their husbands on farms.

The African population grew during the 1700s. Although there were free Africans in all the colonies, most were brought from West Africa or the West Indies as enslaved workers. The largest number of enslaved Africans lived in the Southern Colonies.

Throughout the 1600s, England left the colonies mostly free to go their own way. The king chose royal governors, but the colonists elected their own representatives to the legislatures.

▲ THE BOSTON TEA PARTY

Chapter 7

The Road to Revolution

Unlike English society, social status in colonial America depended on the hard work of individuals. Democratic influences of the Great Awakening and the scientific thinking of the Enlightenment strengthened this social ideal. All three forces helped steer Americans toward a sense of independence.

Unique American attitudes turned into action after the **Treaty of Paris** in 1763. When the British imposed taxes to help pay for the **French and Indian War,** the colonists objected. Protests in Boston led to the **Boston Massacre** in 1770 and the **Boston Tea Party** in 1773.

In 1774 the colonies called the **First Continental Congress** to appeal to King George III. The British government, however, refused to change the tax laws or remove British troops from the colonies. In the spring of 1775, colonial minutemen clashed with British troops at Lexington and Concord. The **American Revolution** had begun. After the failure of a last-minute appeal to Britain, the **Second Continental Congress** began preparing for war.

Understanding Unit Themes

1. **Ideas, Beliefs, and Institutions**   How did religious beliefs lead to the founding of English colonies in North America? How did religion influence the lives and thinking of the British colonists?

2. **Conflict and Cooperation**   What conflicts arose between the British and the French in America? What role did Native Americans play in those conflicts? Why did conflicts arise between the colonies and Great Britain after the French and Indian War? How did the colonists at first try to solve their differences with Great Britain?

3. **Civil Rights and Liberties**   Why did the colonists feel that the British government was denying their civil rights? Why did colonists think they were automatically entitled to certain basic civil rights?

UNIT THREE
A NEW NATION
1776–1791

★★

CHAPTER
8
The American Revolution
1776–1783

CHAPTER
9
Creating a Nation
1776–1791

CITIZENSHIP HANDBOOK
AND
UNITED STATES
CONSTITUTION

► QUILL PEN
AND INK
HOLDER

History AND ART

Molly Pitcher at the Battle of Monmouth
by Dennis Malone Carter, 1854

Women helped in the fighting of the Revolutionary War. Molly Pitcher took the cannon from her fallen husband at the Battle of Monmouth, New Jersey, in 1778.

SETTING THE SCENE

Colonial objections to British laws could no longer be settled by protests or petitions to the king. Colonists in Massachusetts had already rebelled. War and the thirteen colonies' final break with Britain soon followed. When the fighting ended, a ragtag band of rebels claimed victory. From there, the new United States went on to build a representative government that became a lasting model for democracy and freedom.

▼ STATEHOUSE, PHILADELPHIA

Themes

★ American Democracy
★ Conflict and Cooperation
★ Civil Rights and Liberties
★ The Individual and Family Life

Key Events

★ Revolutionary War
★ Colonists declare independence from Great Britain
★ Treaty of Paris
★ Constitutional Convention
★ Ratification of United States Constitution

Major Issues

★ British government refuses to answer colonial complaints
★ Declaration of Independence divides Patriots and Loyalists
★ Weaknesses in the Articles of Confederation prevent Congress from handling national problems
★ Ratification of the Constitution divides opinion on the issue of a strong central government

▲ UNITED STATES CONSTITUTION

◄ GEORGE WASHINGTON AT YORKTOWN

Portfolio Project

Imagine yourself in George Washington's place during the Revolutionary War, the Confederation, and the years when the Constitution was written and ratified. Write a diary that you might have kept. Record your opinions and feelings about the major events of the time.

The Paper It's Printed On

Background

The American colonists had many uses for paper, but what was paper like in the 1700s? Government documents were written on parchment while newspapers, pamphlets, and personal letters were written on paper of lesser quality. Fibers from linen and cotton rags were pounded and pressed together to make this paper used by early Americans. Modern paper is made from wood pulp. You can make your own paper and recycle at the same time.

Believe It OR NOT!

Important government documents, including the Declaration of Independence, were written on parchment. Parchment was made from the skins of animals. A high-quality parchment called vellum was produced in Europe after the 1400s; it was made from the skins of calves, goat kids, or lambs.

Materials

- 2 full pages of newspaper torn into small pieces
- 2 to 3 cups of water
- kitchen blender or electric mixer (Safety Note: Do not take lid off blender while it is operating or put hands near blades.)
- 2 tablespoons of school glue
- dishpan
- one woman's nylon stocking
- wire clothes hanger
- bowl (if using a mixer)
- pen or pencil

What To Do

A. Untwist the clothes hanger and form it into a 6-inch square.

B. Carefully slip the wire square into the nylon stocking. Make sure the stocking is tight and flat. Tie each end of the stocking in a knot.

C. Put some torn paper and water into the blender (or bowl). Close the lid and turn it on high. Add more paper and water until the paper disappears and the mixture turns into a large ball of pulp. Then let the blender (or mixer) run for two or more minutes.

D. Put about 4 inches of water into the dishpan and add the glue.

E. Add the pulp to the water and mix well. While stirring, quickly slip the wire frame under the pulp and let it rest on the bottom of the dishpan. Then lift the frame slowly as you count to 20.

F. Let the pulp on the frame dry completely. When it is totally dry, pull the paper sheet from the frame.

G. If possible, use a hot iron to steam your paper as flat as possible. With a pen or pencil, try signing your name on your paper.

▲ HANDMADE PAPER

Lab Activity Report

1. About how long did you have to mix the paper and water before it formed a ball of pulp?

2. Describe the texture of the pulp before you added it to the dishpan.

3. How easy or difficult was it to write on your paper?

4. Drawing Conclusions How do you think your paper compares to the paper made out of cloth rags by the colonists? Which type of paper would be easier to use?

GO A STEP FURTHER

ACTIVITY

The signers of the Declaration of Independence risked being charged with treason when they put their names on the document. Who were these brave men? Who was the oldest signer? Why was Robert Treat Paine known as the "Objection Maker"? Find out more about the signers of this document. Make a chart showing their names, where they came from, and any other information, such as their occupations, that you can discover.

CHAPTER 8

★★★

The American Revolution
1776–1783

SETTING THE SCENE

Focus

In 1776 many Americans already saw the colonies as independent states. Now, after years of bickering with King George III and the British Parliament, they were determined to establish their independence. Declaring independence would be easy. Achieving it would be much more difficult.

Concepts to Understand

★ What steps the colonists took to secure and protect **American democracy**

★ How **conflict and cooperation** contributed to the success of the American Revolution

Read to Discover . . .

★ the weaknesses and strengths of the British and American military forces.

★ the outcome of the American Revolution.

Journal Notes

Imagine you are responsible for raising money to help the American troops in the Revolution. As you read this chapter, record what you think the soldiers might need to help them get through the war.

▲ WARNING TO THE BRITISH

United States	1775 Congress names George Washington commander of Continental Army	1776 Declaration of Independence is signed
		1777 Battles at Princeton and Saratoga
	1773–1775	**1776–1778**
World	1774 Joseph Priestley discovers oxygen	1776 James Watt improves the steam engine

Washington Crossing the Delaware
by Emanuel Gottlieb Leutze, 1851

Painted in Dusseldorf, Germany, this memorable painting shows General Washington and his troops crossing the Delaware River. Washington's surprise attack allowed the Continental Army to have an easy victory over the British.

◀ LIBERTY BELL

1779 John Paul Jones defeats British naval fleet

1781 British General Cornwallis surrenders at Yorktown

1779–1781

1780 India's first newspaper is published

1783 Treaty of Paris signed

1782–1784

1783 Spain, Sweden, and Denmark recognize the independence of the United States of America

★★★

Declaring Independence

SETTING THE SCENE

Read to Learn . . .

★ why the Second Continental Congress is considered to be the first government of the colonies.
★ how one person's writing moved Americans to support independence.
★ how the Declaration of Independence divided the nation.

Terms to Know

★ Olive Branch Petition
★ Continental Army
★ *Common Sense*
★ Declaration of Independence
★ preamble
★ Loyalist
★ Patriot

People to Meet

★ Ethan Allen
★ Benedict Arnold
★ Thomas Paine
★ Thomas Jefferson

Places to Locate

★ Lake Champlain
★ Bunker Hill

◄ REVOLUTIONARY WAR DRUM

Mud-spattered and tired, Caesar Rodney returned to Philadelphia on the afternoon of July 2, 1776. He arrived just in time for the vote. When the roll call reached his Delaware delegation, Rodney stood up and said:

❝ As I believe the voice of my constituents [voters] and of all sensible and honest men is in favor of independence and my own judgment concurs [agrees] with them, I vote for independence. ❞

★ The Second Continental Congress

Caesar Rodney had been elected a delegate to the **Second Continental Congress.** The First Continental Congress had met in 1774 to protest the Intolerable Acts and other British policies that the colonists disliked. Then the delegates had hoped that King George would receive their protests. They agreed, however, that if he did not respond, a second congress would meet the next spring. This congress would act as a central government and put together an army for the colonies' defense.

The Olive Branch Petition

As the colonists had feared, King George ignored their protests. The Second Continental Congress gathered according to plan in Philadelphia in May 1775. Most colonists and most members of the congress wanted the colonies to remain part of Great Britain. They wanted to rule themselves through their own legislatures, however.

With very little optimism left, the delegates drafted another letter to the king in one last attempt for peace. The letter, called the Olive Branch Petition, assured the king that most of the American colonists were still loyal to Great Britain and to him.

As they waited for a reply, the congress went about the business of governing. They understood now that their only option might be war with Great Britain. With this in mind, they organized an army. This was something new for the colonies. Up to this time, they had relied on local militias that defended their own small regions.

The new army, called the Continental Army, would represent and defend all the colonies. The delegates named George Washington, himself a member of the congress, commander of the army. Washington left Philadelphia to take charge of the colonial forces around Boston.

Washington's Army

Washington's newly formed Continental Army lacked discipline and training. Washington also had trouble finding recruits for the army. Most soldiers wanted to stay with local militias to protect their own homes, families, and land. Those who did join had to enlist for several years. The pay was not always regular, and there were often shortages of food and clothing. At its largest, the Continental Army included about 15,000 to 20,000 soldiers.

While the American forces were poorly equipped compared to the British, they did have some significant advantages over their opponents. They were well acquainted with the countryside. They knew how to survive in the wilderness, and they believed in their cause of freedom. Most important, Washington was a brilliant leader. He was America's greatest asset, even though he lost more battles than he won.

The British Army

Great Britain had an army of nearly 50,000 soldiers and the most powerful navy in the world. Its soldiers were well trained and led by officers with battle experience. To add to the strength of its army, the British hired professional German soldiers, called **Hessians,** to fight for them.

The British did suffer some disadvantages. In America, the British troops would be far from home and in unfamiliar territory. They would have to travel 3,000 miles (4,827 km) across the Atlantic Ocean to reach the colonies. They would be fighting an army hiding in the wilderness. The swamps, thick forested hills, and rapidly flowing rivers would be additional obstacles that the British troops did not expect.

★ The Green Mountain Boys

While the congress organized the new army and discussed military plans, small bands of rebel colonists attacked British outposts. **Ethan Allen,** a Vermont blacksmith, led one well-known group of rebels, the **Green Mountain Boys.**

On May 10, 1775, Allen and his followers joined forces with **Benedict Arnold** and his band of 400 soldiers from Boston. Together, they attacked **Fort Ticonderoga** (TY•kahn•duhr•OH•gah), a British outpost on New York's **Lake Champlain.**

DEATH OF GENERAL WARREN AT THE BATTLE OF BUNKER HILL by John Trumbull, 1786
A moral victory, the Battle of Bunker Hill showed that the untrained American militia could stand up against the professional British army. **Where did most of the fighting take place for the Battle of Bunker Hill?**

Arnold and Allen wanted to take the enemy by surprise. Their strategy called for them to work quietly, without being seen or heard. While the British soldiers slept, Allen and his group crawled through a broken wall and entered the British fort. The victory gave the rebels a valuable supply of ammunition and 50 cannons. They tied the cannons, which weighed 2 to 6 tons (1.8 to 5.4 t) each, to sleds and dragged them by oxen about 200 miles (322 km) to Boston.

★ The Battle of Bunker Hill

Even before Washington reached Boston, militia from all parts of New England began to surround the city. They wanted to keep a close watch on British troops there. British General **Thomas Gage** ordered his troops to set up cannons on Dorchester Heights, a high point just outside of Boston. Gage aimed to drive out the rebel forces.

After learning of the British plan, American Colonel **William Prescott** led 1,200 soldiers to fortify the area. His troops marched to **Breed's Hill** and nearby **Bunker Hill.** There they dug trenches and prepared their defense.

On June 17, 1775, about 2,000 British soldiers, dressed in full uniform and carrying heavy packs, struggled up Breed's Hill. The Americans had very little ammunition. They knew that every shot must be accurate. They could not waste a single one. With this in mind, American commanders gave the orders, "Don't fire until you see the whites of their eyes."

The British fell by the hundreds in two unsuccessful attacks. Finally, on the third charge, the Americans ran out of gunpowder and retreated.

Although most of the fighting took place on Breed's Hill, this battle later became known as the **Battle of Bunker Hill.** More than 1,000 British were killed or wounded. The Americans suffered only about 400 casualties. The British claimed victory as the Americans retreated. The battle, however, stood out as a moral victory for the Americans because the untrained militia had stood up to the British army.

Washington reached Boston by midsummer and began to train his army. When the cannons from Fort Ticonderoga arrived that winter, his soldiers placed them on Dorchester Heights. In March 1776, the British left Boston.

★ Declaring Independence

As the colonists had feared, King George III refused to honor their protests. The king saw the colonists as troublemakers and sent more troops to stop their rebellion. This action, along with the continued fighting in the colonies, led more and more Americans to favor breaking ties with Great Britain. Encouraging the move toward freedom was the writer and journalist **Thomas Paine.**

Common Sense

Paine had been in America only a few years when he wrote the pamphlet *Common Sense.* Published in January 1776, it declared that the American colonies received no benefits from their mother country, which was intent on exploiting them. Paine questioned some of the ideas that were basic to British society, such as the concept of a king and queen. He even referred to King George III as "the Royal Brute of Great Britain." Paine called on colonists to use common sense and become independent of Great Britain.

" The period of debate is closed. Arms, as a last resort, must decide the contest. . . . Everything that is right or reasonable pleads for separation. "

Almost half a million copies flooded the colonies. As Paine intended, his words stirred the colonists to action. *Common Sense* showed them that the time had come to formally declare independence. In Paine's words, "The sun never shined on a cause more just."

Lee's Resolution

The desire for independence grew. The congressional delegates, perhaps most of all, sensed the mood of the people and knew the time was right. On June 7, 1776, delegate **Richard Henry Lee** introduced a resolution to declare independence from Great Britain:

" . . . [T]hese United Colonies are, and of right ought to be, free and independent states. "

Picturing History

▲ THOMAS PAINE Thomas Paine's *Common Sense* was significant in persuading colonists towards the idea of breaking away from Great Britain. **How did Paine refer to King George III in his pamphlet?**

▲ *DRAFTING THE DECLARATION OF INDEPENDENCE* by J.L.G. Ferris **Thomas Jefferson prepared the first draft of the Declaration of Independence, while Benjamin Franklin and John Adams made suggestions. Who introduced the resolution to declare independence?**

Lee's dramatic and important words demonstrated the seriousness of the resolution. The congressional delegates had to consider it carefully. If it passed, there would be no turning back. If they agreed, each one would be a traitor in Great Britain's eyes. The penalty for treason was death. Was independence worth such a horrible price?

Supporters of Lee's resolution believed that it was. They formed a committee to prepare a formal declaration of independence. The members of the committee were **Thomas Jefferson** (Virginia), **Benjamin Franklin** (Pennsylvania), **John Adams** (Massachusetts), **Robert Liv-**

ingston (New York), and **Roger Sherman** (Connecticut).

After some debate the delegates chose Thomas Jefferson to write the declaration. Although shy by nature and a poor public speaker, Jefferson was well-known as an able writer. Jefferson gave his first draft to Benjamin Franklin. After a few changes, they submitted it to Congress.

The Final Decision

On July 2, 1776, more than a year after the first battle of the American Revolution, the Second Continental Congress adopted Lee's resolution. Two days later, on July 4, 1776, the delegates officially approved the Declaration of Independence.

John Hancock, president of the Second Continental Congress, signed the document first. As he did, he purposely wrote in large, bold letters, saying King George

> 66 **. . . can read my name without spectacles, and may now double his reward of £500 for my head.** 99

Word of the new declaration spread slowly through the colonies. As the news reached them, people gathered to listen. Crowds cheered, rang bells, and—although gunpowder was in short supply—fired guns in celebration.

The Declaration of Independence

In the Declaration of Independence, Jefferson wrote about a new, representative form of government to be put in place and carried out by the nation's people. Jefferson was influenced by the philosophy of Great Britain's **John Locke.**

The Declaration included four parts. The first part is called the preamble. It is an introduction that explains why the Continental Congress drew up the Declaration. The members thought that when a colony breaks its ties with the mother country, its reasons should be explained.

The second part, the Declaration of Rights, lists the rights of the citizens. Jefferson wrote:

> " We hold these truths to be self-evident, that all men are created equal, that they are endowed by their Creator with certain unalienable Rights, that among these are Life, Liberty, and the pursuit of Happiness. "

The Declaration goes on to explain that in a republic, people form a government to protect their rights. Jefferson wrote that a government should be based "on the consent of the governed." Like Locke, Jefferson believed that if a government takes away the rights of the people, it is the people's responsibility to overthrow that government.

The third part of the Declaration lists the colonists' complaints against the British government. The final section declares that the colonies are "free and independent states" with the full power to make war, to form alliances, and to trade with other countries.

The colonists promised to fight to defend their freedom. Now, however, the colonists no longer fought for their rights as British citizens. They fought as the citizens of a new nation.

JOIN, or DIE.

◀ EDITORIAL CARTOON PROMOTING COLONIAL UNITY, C. 1754

Loyalists and Patriots

Americans throughout the colonies faced a choice. Would they support the move toward independence or continued rule by Great Britain?

The nation was divided. The Loyalists supported ties with Great Britain. On the other side were Patriots, who favored separation from Great Britain. Both groups included dedicated men and women eager to support their positions and to change the minds of their opponents. The struggle between the Patriots and Loyalists grew as bitter as the struggle between the rebels and the British.

After seeing the success of the pamphlet *Common Sense*, some Loyalists wrote and distributed pamphlets of their own. Other Loyalists, called **Tories,** concentrated on preparing for the fight that was sure to come. Emotions ran high among colonists on both sides. Yet, a large number of men and women took neither side, content to wait and see what would happen.

★ SECTION 1 REVIEW ★

Checking for Understanding

1. **Identify** Ethan Allen, Benedict Arnold, Thomas Paine, Thomas Jefferson, Lake Champlain, Bunker Hill.

2. **Define** Olive Branch Petition, Continental Army, *Common Sense*, Declaration of Independence, preamble, Loyalist, Patriot.

3. **What** did the Second Continental Congress do to prepare the colonists for war?

4. **Name** the two groups who had opposite views about colonial independence.

Critical Thinking

5. **Drawing Conclusions** Why did it take a full year of fighting before the Declaration of Independence was written?

ACTIVITY

6. Design a poster that encourages colonists to support the Patriots' cause.

The Declaration of Independence

*D*elegates at the Second Continental Congress faced an enormous task. The war against Great Britain had begun, but to many colonists the purpose for fighting was unclear. As sentiment increased for a complete break with Britain, Congress decided to act. A committee was appointed to prepare a document that declared the thirteen colonies free and independent from Britain. More important, the committee needed to explain why separation was the only fitting solution to long-standing disputes with Parliament and the British Crown. Thomas Jefferson was assigned to prepare a working draft of this document, which was then revised. It was officially adopted on July 4, 1776. More than any other action of Congress, the Declaration of Independence served to make the American colonists one people.

★★★

The printed text of the document shows the spelling and punctuation of the parchment original. To aid in comprehension, selected words and their definitions appear in the side margin, along with other explanatory notes.

impel *force*

endowed *provided*

People create governments to ensure that their natural rights are protected.

If a government does not serve its purpose, the people have a right to abolish it. Then the people have the right and duty to create a new government that will safeguard their security.

Despotism
unlimited power

In Congress, July 4, 1776. The unanimous Declaration of the thirteen united States of America,

Preamble

When in the Course of human events, it becomes necessary for one people to dissolve the political bands which have connected them with another, and to assume among the powers of the earth, the separate and equal station to which the Laws of Nature and Nature's God entitle them, a decent respect to the opinions of mankind requires that they should declare the causes which impel them to the separation.—

Declaration of Natural Rights

We hold these truths to be self-evident, that all men are created equal, that they are endowed by their Creator with certain unalienable Rights, that among these are Life, Liberty, and the pursuit of Happiness.—

That to secure these rights, Governments are instituted among Men, deriving their just powers from the consent of the governed,—

That whenever any Form of Government becomes destructive of these ends, it is the Right of the People to alter or to abolish it, and to institute new Government, laying its foundation on such principles and organizing its powers in such form, as to them shall seem most likely to effect their Safety and Happiness. Prudence, indeed, will dictate that Governments long established should not be changed for light and transient causes; and accordingly all experience hath shewn, that mankind are more disposed to suffer, while evils are sufferable, than to right themselves by abolishing the forms to which they are accustomed. But when a long train of abuses and usurpations, pursuing invariably the same Object evinces a design to reduce them under absolute Despotism, it is their right, it is their duty, to throw off such Government, and to provide new Guards for their future security.—

▲ *DECLARATION OF INDEPENDENCE IN CONGRESS* by John Trumbull, 1824 ★★★★★★★★★★★★★★★★★★★★★★★★★★★★★★

List of Grievances

Such has been the patient sufferance of these Colonies; and such is now the necessity which constrains them to alter their former Systems of Government. The history of the present King of Great Britain is a history of repeated injuries and usurpations, all having in direct object the establishment of an absolute Tyranny over these States. To prove this, let Facts be submitted to a candid world.—

He has refused his Assent to Laws, the most wholesome and necessary for the public good.—

He has forbidden his Governors to pass Laws of immediate and pressing importance, unless suspended in their operation till his Assent should be obtained; and when so suspended, he has utterly neglected to attend to them.—

He has refused to pass other Laws for the accommodation of large districts of people, unless those people would relinquish the right of Representation in the Legislature, a right inestimable to them and formidable to tyrants only.—

He has called together legislative bodies at places unusual, uncomfortable, and distant from the depository of their public Records, for the sole purpose of fatiguing them into compliance with his measures.—

He has dissolved Representative Houses repeatedly, for opposing with manly firmness his invasions on the rights of the people.—

He has refused for a long time, after such dissolutions, to cause others to be elected; whereby the Legislative powers, incapable of Annihilation, have returned to the People at large for their exercise; the State remaining in the meantime exposed to all the dangers of invasion from without, and convulsions within.—

He has endeavoured to prevent the population of these States; for

usurpations
unjust uses of power

Each paragraph lists alleged injustices of George III.

relinquish *give up*
inestimable *priceless*

Annihilation *destruction*

convulsions
violent disturbances

The Declaration of Independence **221**

Naturalization of Foreigners *process by which foreign-born persons become citizens*

tenure *term*

Refers to the British troops sent to the colonies after the French and Indian War.

Refers to the 1766 Declaratory Act.

quartering *lodging*

Refers to the 1774 Quebec Act.

render *make*

abdicated *given up*

perfidy *violation of trust*

insurrections *rebellions*

Petitioned for Redress *asked formally for a correction of wrongs*

that purpose obstructing the Laws for Naturalization of Foreigners; refusing to pass others to encourage their migrations hither, and raising the conditions of new Appropriations of Lands.—

He has obstructed the Administration of Justice, by refusing his Assent to Laws for establishing Judiciary powers.—

He has made Judges dependent on his Will alone, for the tenure of their offices, and the amount and payment of their salaries.—

He has erected a multitude of New Offices, and sent hither swarms of Officers to harass our people, and eat out their substance.—

He has kept among us, in times of peace, Standing Armies without the Consent of our legislatures.—

He has affected to render the Military independent of and superior to the Civil power.—

He has combined with others to subject us to a jurisdiction foreign to our constitution, and unacknowledged by our laws; giving his Assent to their Acts of pretended Legislation:—

For quartering large bodies of troops among us:—

For protecting them, by a mock Trial, from punishment for any Murders which they should commit on the Inhabitants of these States:—

For cutting off our Trade with all parts of the world:—

For imposing Taxes on us without our Consent:—

For depriving us in many cases, of the benefits of Trial by Jury:—

For transporting us beyond Seas to be tried for pretended offences:—

For abolishing the free System of English Laws in a neighbouring Province, establishing therein an Arbitrary government, and enlarging its Boundaries so as to render it at once an example and fit instrument for introducing the same absolute rule into these Colonies:—

For taking away our Charters, abolishing our most valuable Laws, and altering fundamentally the Forms of our Governments:—

For suspending our own Legislatures, and declaring themselves invested with power to legislate for us in all cases whatsoever.—

He has abdicated Government here, by declaring us out of his Protection and waging War against us.—

He has plundered our seas, ravaged our Coasts, burnt our towns, and destroyed the Lives of our people.—

He is at this time transporting large Armies of foreign Mercenaries to compleat the works of death, desolation and tyranny, already begun with circumstances of Cruelty & perfidy scarcely paralleled in the most barbarous ages, and totally unworthy the Head of a civilized nation.—

He has constrained our fellow Citizens taken Captive on the high Seas to bear Arms against their Country, to become the executioners of their friends and Brethren, or to fall themselves by their Hands.—

He has excited domestic insurrections amongst us, and has endeavoured to bring on the inhabitants of our frontiers, the merciless Indian Savages, whose known rule of warfare, is an undistinguished destruction of all ages, sexes and conditions.

In every stage of these Oppressions We have Petitioned for Redress in the most humble terms: Our repeated Petitions have been answered only by repeated injury. A Prince, whose character is thus marked by every act which may define a Tyrant, is unfit to be the ruler of a free people.

Nor have We been wanting in attentions to our British brethren. We have warned them from time to time of attempts by their legislature to extend an unwarrantable jurisdiction over us. We have reminded them of the circumstances of our emigration and settlement here. We have appealed to their native justice and magnanimity, and we have conjured them by the ties of our common kindred to disavow these usurpations, which would inevitably interrupt our connections and correspondence. They too have been deaf to the voice of justice and of consanguinity. We must, therefore, acquiesce in the necessity, which denounces our Separation, and hold them, as we hold the rest of mankind, Enemies in War, in Peace Friends.—

unwarrantable jurisdiction *unjustified authority*

Resolution of Independence by the United States

We, therefore, the Representatives of the united States of America, in General Congress, Assembled, appealing to the Supreme Judge of the world for the rectitude of our intentions, do, in the Name, and by Authority of the good People of these Colonies, solemnly publish and declare, That these United Colonies are, and of Right ought to be Free and Independent States; that they are Absolved from all Allegiance to the British Crown, and that all political connection between them and the State of Great Britain, is and ought to be totally dissolved; and that as Free and Independent States, they have full Power to levy War, conclude Peace, contract Alliances, establish Commerce, and to do all other Acts and Things which Independent States may of right do.—

consanguinity *originating from the same ancestor*

rectitude *rightness*

And for the support of this Declaration, with a firm reliance on the protection of divine Providence, we mutually pledge to each other our Lives, our Fortunes and our sacred Honour.

The signers, as representatives of the American people, declared the colonies independent from Great Britain. Most members signed the document on August 2, 1776.

John Hancock
    President from
    Massachusetts

Georgia
Button Gwinnett
Lyman Hall
George Walton

North Carolina
William Hooper
Joseph Hewes
John Penn

South Carolina
Edward Rutledge
Thomas Heyward, Jr.
Thomas Lynch, Jr.
Arthur Middleton

Maryland
Samuel Chase
William Paca
Thomas Stone
Charles Carroll
    of Carrollton

Virginia
George Wythe
Richard Henry Lee
Thomas Jefferson
Benjamin Harrison
Thomas Nelson Jr.
Francis Lightfoot Lee
Carter Braxton

Pennsylvania
Robert Morris
Benjamin Rush
Benjamin Franklin
John Morton
George Clymer
James Smith
George Taylor
James Wilson
George Ross

Delaware
Caesar Rodney
George Read
Thomas McKean

New York
William Floyd
Philip Livingston
Francis Lewis
Lewis Morris

New Jersey
Richard Stockton
John Witherspoon
Francis Hopkinson
John Hart
Abraham Clark

New Hampshire
Josiah Bartlett
William Whipple
Matthew Thornton

Massachusetts
Samuel Adams
John Adams
Robert Treat Paine
Elbridge Gerry

Rhode Island
Stephen Hopkins
William Ellery

Connecticut
Samuel Huntington
William Williams
Oliver Wolcott
Roger Sherman

★★★★★★★★★★★★★★★★★★★★★★★★★★★★★★★★★★★★★★

The Colonies at War

SETTING THE SCENE

Read to Learn . . .

★ how Washington defeated the Hessians at Trenton and the British at Princeton.
★ why the American victory at Saratoga was a turning point in the war.
★ how European allies helped the Continental Army.

Terms to Know

★ blockade
★ Battle of Saratoga
★ Treaty of Alliance
★ privateer

People to Meet

★ Nathan Hale
★ General Charles Cornwallis
★ Marquis de Lafayette
★ George Rogers Clark
★ John Paul Jones

Places to Locate

★ Long Island
★ Valley Forge
★ Vincennes

► CONTINENTAL ARMY
RECRUITMENT POSTER

TO ALL BRAVE, HEALTHY, ABLE BODIED, AND WELL
DISPOSED YOUNG MEN,
IN THIS NEIGHBOURHOOD, WHO HAVE ANY INCLINATION TO JOIN THE TROOPS,
NOW RAISING UNDER
GENERAL WASHINGTON,
FOR THE DEFENCE OF THE
LIBERTIES AND INDEPENDENCE
OF THE UNITED STATES,
Against the hostile designs of foreign enemies,

TAKE NOTICE,

GOD SAVE THE UNITED STATES.

In a letter to King George III about the colonial rebellion, General Thomas Gage wrote, "They are now spirited up by a rage and enthusiasm as great as ever people were possessed of. . . ." Although the British were impressed with the colonists' determination, they did not believe that a ragtag, badly equipped group of rebels could beat a world power such as Great Britain. George Washington and his Continental Army would prove them wrong.

★ The War in the North

In the fall of 1775, the Continental Army moved into Canada hoping to win support from the French Canadians.

Richard Montgomery's forces marched from Fort Ticonderoga into Canada and captured Montreal in November 1775.

Meanwhile, **Benedict Arnold** led his troops through the wilderness of Maine, where they encountered blizzards and freezing temperatures. Supplies were short and they survived by eating anything they could find—bark, candles, and even shoe leather. Still, they continued on to Quebec and stormed the walled city on New Year's Eve, 1775.

The attack proved unsuccessful. Montgomery was killed, and Arnold was wounded. Not willing to give up the siege, Arnold's troops remained outside Quebec for the next few months. While the harsh winter continued, many soldiers died of starvation and disease. When the long winter ended and spring arrived at last, Arnold's soldiers were tired, hungry, sick, and depressed. When British reinforcements arrived in May, the troops admitted defeat. Canada would remain in British hands.

Dorchester Heights

The Battle of Bunker Hill left the British short of forces and supplies. To wait for fresh supplies and reinforcement troops, the British decided to stay in Boston during the summer of 1775.

Washington reached Boston in midsummer in 1775 and began to train his troops. On March 4, 1776, he placed the cannons from Fort Ticonderoga on Dorchester Heights and aimed them at the city. British **General William Howe** realized he could not force the Americans to leave. Two weeks later, the entire British army and 1,500 Loyalists evacuated Boston by ship. General Howe moved his troops north to Halifax, Canada, leaving Boston under American control.

After the British retreated to Canada, King George set up a blockade of all the ports in the colonies, to prevent goods and people from moving in and out of the area.

★ The New York Campaign

In June 1776, General Howe and his troops returned from Canada. This time they moved into New York City, which Howe viewed as an ideal location. From here he could easily march troops south to Philadelphia or north into New England. By overtaking New York City, he also could split the Northern and Southern colonies.

The Battle of Long Island

In an effort to defend New York, Washington moved about 19,000 troops south to **Long Island.** The untrained recruits proved no match for Howe's professional soldiers. To make matters worse, Washington had no navy to challenge the British in New York Harbor.

Washington tried to predict where the British troops would come ashore. He divided his army, sending 10,000 soldiers to Long Island and the rest to Manhattan. In August of 1776, Howe chose to land at Long Island.

During the Battle of Long Island, Washington's troops fought bravely, but at least 1,500 were killed, injured, or taken prisoner. The Americans were not able to hold New York, and for many weeks, Washington himself was in danger of being captured. Washington told his troops, "I will not ask any man go further than I do. I will fight so long as I have a leg or an arm."

Finally, Washington led his army on a retreat into New Jersey. He then crossed the Delaware River into Pennsylvania. In

★★★ AMERICA'S FLAGS ★★★

First Stars and Stripes, 1777–1795 After the Declaration of Independence, the British flag lost its meaning as a part of the United States flag. Thus the Continental Congress on June 14, 1777, designed the first Stars and Stripes. It determined that "the Flag of the United States be 13 stripes, alternate red and white; that the Union be 13 stars, white in a blue field representing a new constellation."

For Americans past and present, the color red symbolizes courage, white purity of ideals, and blue, strength and unity of the states.

★★★★★★★★★★★★★★★★★★★★

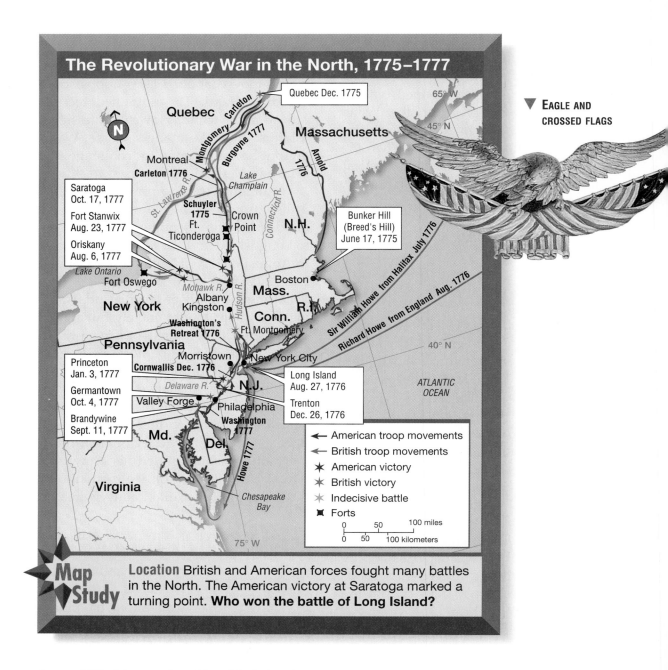

The Revolutionary War in the North, 1775–1777

Quebec Dec. 1775

Quebec

Massachusetts

Montreal
Carleton 1776

Saratoga
Oct. 17, 1777

Fort Stanwix
Aug. 23, 1777

Oriskany
Aug. 6, 1777

Schuyler 1775

Ft. Ticonderoga

Crown Point

Lake Champlain

N.H.

Bunker Hill (Breed's Hill)
June 17, 1775

Fort Oswego

Lake Ontario

Mohawk R.

Albany
Kingston

Mass.

Boston

Conn.

R.I.

New York

Washington's Retreat 1776

Ft. Montgomery

Pennsylvania

Morristown
Cornwallis Dec. 1776

New York City

Sir William Howe from Halifax July 1776

Richard Howe from England Aug. 1776

40° N

Princeton
Jan. 3, 1777

Germantown
Oct. 4, 1777

Brandywine
Sept. 11, 1777

Delaware R.

Valley Forge

N.J.

Long Island
Aug. 27, 1776

Trenton
Dec. 26, 1776

ATLANTIC OCEAN

Philadelphia

Washington 1777

Md.

Del.

Virginia

Chesapeake Bay

Howe 1777

←— American troop movements
←— British troop movements
★ American victory
★ British victory
★ Indecisive battle
▮ Forts

0   50   100 miles
0 50 100 kilometers

75° W

65° W

45° N

St. Lawrence R.

Montgomery

Burgoyne 1777

Carleton

Arnold 1776

Connecticut R.

Hudson R.

Map Study

Location British and American forces fought many battles in the North. The American victory at Saratoga marked a turning point. **Who won the battle of Long Island?**

▼ EAGLE AND CROSSED FLAGS

the end Washington lost New York, but he managed to escape the British. The British held New York City until the war ended seven years later.

Spying on the Enemy

Spying was common during the war. When captured, spies were labeled as traitors and typically sentenced to death by hanging. The threat of death, as horrible as it was, did not prevent some dedicated Patriots from spying for their country.

Nathan Hale, a 24-year-old American lieutenant, spied for George Washington during the New York campaign. He disguised himself, slipped behind enemy lines, and returned with information. Soon after, the British caught him. They swiftly condemned him to death. Hale's reported last words reflect his patriotic spirit:

❝ I only regret that I have but one life to lose for my country.❞

★ Victories at Trenton and Princeton

When Washington and his troops retreated from New York and crossed the Delaware into Pennsylvania, they were in desperate shape. Washington was so depressed that he wrote to his brother, "I think the game is pretty near up." His soldiers were tired and hungry. Some, sensing defeat, gave up and left for home.

The Continental soldiers never seemed to have enough food. The meat was often rotten, so they sprinkled it with salt to cover the bad taste. Hard, dried peas and moldy, stale bread were common.

In his despair, Washington came up with a daring strategy. He planned to launch a surprise attack on the British camp at **Trenton,** New Jersey. As his troops prepared for battle, Washington ordered Thomas Paine's new pamphlet *The Crisis* to be read to them. It offered these words of encouragement:

> **These are the times that try men's souls. The summer soldier and the sunshine patriot will, in this crisis, shrink from the service of their country; but he that stands it now, deserves the love and thanks of every man and woman.**

Surprise Attack

On December 25, 1776, the British soldiers, consisting mostly of Hessians, had gathered in their camps at Trenton to celebrate the Christmas holiday. That cold and stormy night Washington led 2,400 soldiers across the icy Delaware River. Under cover of darkness, all 2,400 managed to cross unseen. The next morning, Washington and his troops swept down on the sleeping Hessians. Within an hour and a half, the Hessians surrendered.

When British General Howe learned of the defeat at Trenton, he sent **General Charles Cornwallis** to pursue Washington and his troops. Washington, however, turned the situation to his advantage and defeated the British at **Princeton,** New Jersey, on January 3, 1777. Achieving another victory gave the Continental Army hope and confidence.

★ Turning the Tide

Great Britain's losses left that country's officials puzzled. Embarrassed by its mistakes, the British military asked **General John Burgoyne** to stop the Americans. He drew up a plan to gain control of the Hudson River valley in New York. If successful, the strategy would benefit the British by cutting New England off from the rest of the colonies.

The Battle of Saratoga

According to the plan, three armies would move on Albany, New York, at the same time. General Burgoyne would lead an army south from Montreal, Canada, into New York. General Howe's army would sail up the Hudson River from New York City. **Colonel Barry St. Leger** would move his forces from Lake Ontario eastward across the Mohawk Valley.

Although well-planned, the British campaign failed miserably, largely because the three commanders neglected to notify each other of changes in the original attack strategy. British General Howe decided to attack Philadelphia rather than meet Burgoyne at Albany. Benedict Arnold and his men stopped St. Leger at Fort Stanwix and turned him back. Burgoyne's troops were the only British forces to reach the Hudson River valley near Albany.

On the way, Burgoyne recaptured **Fort Ticonderoga** and fought other small battles, losing close to 1,000 soldiers. Not until Burgoyne reached the town of Saratoga, New York, did he learn that the other commanders would not be there to assist him.

Three weeks later, the Americans attacked Burgoyne in the Battle of Saratoga. The British army lost hundreds of soldiers. When they tried to retreat to Canada, Americans surrounded them. The Americans blocked every possible path to safety. On October 17, 1777, Burgoyne was forced to surrender, reporting the first major defeat of the British army. The Americans took at least 6,000 British soldiers as prisoners.

The Treaty of Alliance

Until the American victory at Saratoga, neither France nor any other country had been willing to openly support the colonists. The victory made clear that it was possible for the Americans to succeed. In February 1778, French King Louis XVI signed the Treaty of Alliance, assuring the Americans of the support they desperately needed.

Brutal Winter at Valley Forge

Before French aid reached America, Washington's army had to endure the harsh winter of 1777–78 at Valley Forge, Pennsylvania. The American soldiers had little protection from the freezing temperatures. Shoeless and dressed in rags, they huddled together inside flimsy tents until they could build small log huts. When complete, each dirt-floor hut measured about 14 feet by 16 feet. In spite of the small size, about 12 soldiers lived in each hut.

The soldiers slept on either the cold muddy hut floors or the straw mattresses that were usually crawling with lice. Food consisted mostly of firecakes, which were thin strips of dough made from a mixture of flour and water. Soldiers suffered from disease and frostbite. One soldier commented that the barefoot troops "might be tracked by their blood upon the rough, frozen ground." By spring, as many as 2,500 American soldiers had died from disease, exposure to the cold, and lack of food.

The long winter finally came to an end, and by spring, the troops were in better spirits. French aid had arrived, the streams and rivers ran with fish, and many soldiers who had left the camp sick returned healthy. Once again Washington began making battle plans.

★ Help From Europe

Throughout the American Revolution, Europeans provided help in the form of money and military expertise.

Baron Friedrich von Steuben, a Prussian soldier, spent the winter at Valley Forge helping Washington train the troops. He used his military experience to teach the Continental soldiers how to work together as a unit. From him, the soldiers learned how to make advances, how to retreat, how to carry their weapons, and how to use their bayonets. Von Steuben's great sense of humor helped keep the troops in good spirits.

- -

Footnotes to History

General Burgoyne's Second Career   General John Burgoyne was fired from his post after being defeated at the Battle of Saratoga. Fortunately, he had another career to fall back on; Burgoyne was a successful playwright. His comedy, *The Heiress*, was very popular in England and was translated into several foreign languages as well.

▲ *THE MARCH TO VALLEY FORGE* by William B.J. Trego, 1883 While waiting for French aid, American soldiers spent a brutal winter at Valley Forge, Pennsylvania. The long winter was costly, causing the death of many American soldiers. **What were the conditions of the living quarters at Valley Forge?**

The **Marquis de Lafayette** (LAH•fee•EHT), a young French soldier, fought with Washington in Pennsylvania. He became an American general at the age of 19. Lafayette enthusiastically supported the American cause. He received no payment for his military service, but fought out of love for America.

Others throughout Europe felt the same desire to fight for the American cause. **Thaddeus Kosciuszko** (kawsh•CHUSH•KOH) came from Poland and used his experience as an engineer to build trenches and forts for the Americans. **Casimir Pulaski,** also from Poland, trained and organized the first American cavalry—troops on horseback.

Bernardo de Gálvez, governor of Spanish Louisiana, helped the Americans even before Spain entered the war. He secretly provided supplies during the early years of the Revolution. After Spain entered the war in 1779, Gálvez's troops defeated the British at Baton Rouge and Natchez. His army then marched throughout the Gulf Coast area, capturing British forts at Mobile in 1780 and Pensacola in 1781. His campaigns diverted British troops from other war fronts.

★ The War in the West

The war continued to rage throughout the colonies. While Washington and his troops fought in the East, the British recruited Native Americans to help them in their frontier campaign farther west. At first, Native Americans did not want to take sides. Later, however, most joined the British, believing an alliance with them would help to turn back the white settlers moving onto their land.

Fighting broke out in the Ohio Valley as British and Native American forces began their invasion of frontier settlements. In 1778 **George Rogers Clark** of Virginia led volunteers on a raid against the British in the Ohio Valley. He captured British forts at Kaskaskia and Cahokia with the help of

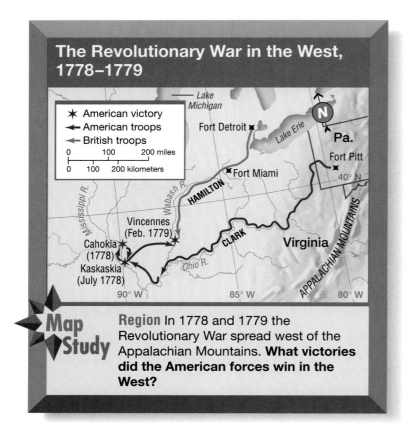

The Revolutionary War in the West, 1778–1779

* American victory
← American troops
← British troops

0   100   200 miles
0   100   200 kilometers

Lake Michigan

Lake Erie

Fort Detroit ×

Pa.

Fort Pitt ×

40° N

Fort Miami ×

HAMILTON

Wabash R.

Mississippi R.

Vincennes (Feb. 1779)

Cahokia (1778)

CLARK

Virginia

Kaskaskia (July 1778)

Ohio R.

APPALACHIAN MOUNTAINS

90° W   85° W   80° W

Map Study **Region** In 1778 and 1779 the Revolutionary War spread west of the Appalachian Mountains. **What victories did the American forces win in the West?**

★ The War at Sea

Congress established the Continental Navy in 1775. Its few ships, however, had little effect on the outcome of the war. To protect their ports, the colonists were forced to rely on armed private ships called **privateers.**

John Paul Jones

In 1779 an American warship, the *Bonhomme Richard,* won a surprising victory in one of the war's most famous sea battles. The conflict began when the ship's daring captain, **John Paul Jones,** sailed to the coast of Great Britain and attacked the British warship *Serapis* in the North Sea.

For awhile it looked as though Jones and his crew would be lost. In the fierce battle, cannonballs tore through the *Bonhomme Richard.* Seeing that the heavily damaged ship had caught fire, the British commander demanded that Jones surrender. The American captain's reply was strong and determined. "I have not yet begun to fight!" With that, his sailors boarded the *Serapis* and, fighting one-on-one, defeated the British.

Later John Paul Jones became known as the "Father of the American Navy." His heroism in the face of a bigger and better-equipped British fleet inspired Americans.

a group of Native Americans known as the **Miami.** Then Clark made a surprise attack on the British fort at **Vincennes,** in present-day Indiana. In February 1779, after marching more than 100 miles (161 km) through rain and icy weather, Clark's forces captured Vincennes. The loss weakened the British in the Ohio Valley.

★ SECTION 2 REVIEW ★

Checking for Understanding

1. **Identify** Nathan Hale, General Charles Cornwallis, Marquis de Lafayette, George Rogers Clark, John Paul Jones, Long Island, Valley Forge, Vincennes.

2. **Define** blockade, Battle of Saratoga, Treaty of Alliance, privateer.

3. **Why** did General Howe base his troops in New York City in June 1776?

4. **How** did the American victory at Saratoga help the Continental Army?

Critical Thinking

5. **Understanding Point of View** Why would Native Americans be interested in the outcome of the American Revolution?

ACTIVITY

6. Imagine that you had friends at Valley Forge during the winter of 1777–1778. Make a list of five things you would send to them to help them get through the winter.

Financing the War

The Continental Congress did not have the power to tax either the people or the individual colonial governments. Colonial leaders wondered how they would pay soldiers and buy food and supplies.

In 1775 the congress began to print large amounts of paper money called **Continental dollars.** So many were issued that they soon became worthless because there was no gold or silver to back them in the colonial treasury.

The congress turned to Great Britain's enemy, France. As ambassador to France, **Benjamin Franklin** convinced young King Louis XVI that the Americans could not lose the war. Secretly at first, then openly later, the French government gave huge sums of money to the Americans. France not only helped the colonies but it also encouraged Spain and the Netherlands to give financial aid to the colonies.

A few wealthy American businesspeople also dug deep in their pockets to save the Revolution with loans. Citizens loaned the congress money in exchange for bonds, or certificates that could later be cashed in for the full amount of the loan plus interest.

▲ BEN FRANKLIN AT THE COURT OF LOUIS XVI

Making the Economics Connection

1. Why did the Continental Congress have trouble raising money in the colonies?

2. Why was France willing to help the Americans finance the war?

3. What are bonds and why were they important?

ACTIVITY

4. Design a poster encouraging Patriots to buy bonds to support the war effort.

★★★

The War Moves South

SETTING THE SCENE

Read to Learn . . .

★ why the British shifted their focus to the South.

★ why the British had trouble defeating the small bands of Patriot raiders.

★ what role African Americans and women played in the war.

Terms to Know

★ Battle of Cowpens
★ pension

People to Meet

★ Frances Marion
★ Peter Francisco
★ Salem Poor

Places to Locate

★ Kings Mountain
★ Moore's Creek Bridge
★ Savannah
★ Charleston

◀ BENEDICT ARNOLD

About 1,200 Loyalists were killed, injured, or taken prisoner during the fierce fighting on top of **Kings Mountain,** in South Carolina in 1780. James Collins, a 16-year-old Patriot soldier, recalled the attack this way:

❝ **We soon attempted to climb the hill, but were fiercely charged upon and forced to fall back. . . . We tried a second time. . . . We took to the hill a third time. The enemy gave way.** ❞

With the capture of Kings Mountain, the Patriots scored a needed victory for the Americans in the South.

★ War in the South

Until 1778 only a few isolated conflicts had broken out between Patriots and Loyalists in the South. In one battle on February 27, 1776, Patriot forces crushed a Loyalist uprising at **Moore's Creek Bridge,** North Carolina. Although a small battle, its impact was great. Loyalists found the defeat discouraging, while the Patriot cause gained strength and popularity.

The British turned their attention to the Southern colonies when France entered the war in 1778. The British believed they had more support in the South and thought that support would help them to win more battles there. For almost three years the British marched through Georgia, the Carolinas, and Virginia without suffering a major defeat. On December 29, 1778, they captured the port city of **Savannah,** Georgia. **Charleston,** South Carolina, fell to the British on May 12, 1780.

Arnold Joins the British

General Washington became disheartened by the heavy losses in the South. At the same time, news of another loss added to his despair. **Benedict Arnold,** one of Washington's most trusted generals, had been caught spying for the British.

In 1780 Arnold tried to turn the American fort at West Point over to the British. When Arnold tried to deliver a message to the British, three Patriots intercepted it. They gave Washington the evidence in Arnold's own handwriting. Arnold became a general in the British army.

Patriot Raids

Here and there throughout the South, American victories helped to brighten the outlook for the colonists. South Carolina Patriots felt angry about the defeat at Charleston. Looking for revenge, many of them took the situation into their own hands by forming bands and raiding British camps in the countryside. Hit-and-run raids, similar to the Patriots' attack on Kings Mountain, worked well for them in the South. The Patriot raiders were skilled hunters, trained since childhood to use their rifles. They knew the land and could easily survive in the wilderness.

The "Swamp Fox"

Francis Marion, known as the "Swamp Fox," led one band of organized raiders. A quiet man, Marion was known for his imaginative war tactics and for his success in battle. Marion led his troops in quick strikes, cutting off enemy supplies and supply routes, and

▲ *THE "SWAMP FOX" AND HIS MEN* by William Ranney, c. 1850 Francis Marion, known as the "Swamp Fox," kept the British guessing by leading his troops on quick surprise raids. This painting shows Swamp Fox and his men setting out on an attack. **What are two possible reasons Francis Marion was called "Swamp Fox"?**

then running away. Marion usually struck at night, taking advantage of the darkness to surprise unsuspecting British troops.

Marion never stayed at the same camp more than once. His scouts perched in treetops and signaled the troops with shrill whistles. Whenever Marion and his troops came to a bridge near enemy lines, they covered the bridge with blankets to soften the sound of the horses' hooves as they crossed. Marion's raids helped keep the British off balance.

The Battle of Cowpens

Two other daring generals, **Daniel Morgan** and **Nathaniel Greene,** won battles for the Patriots in the South. On January 17, 1781, Morgan defeated the British in South Carolina at the Battle of Cowpens.

Greene used tactics similar to Marion. His hit-and-run raids kept the British off guard. Greene, considered by some to be Washington's best general, wrote of his experiences, "We fight, get beat, rise, and fight again." Following the Patriot victory at Cowpens, Greene's forces joined Mor-

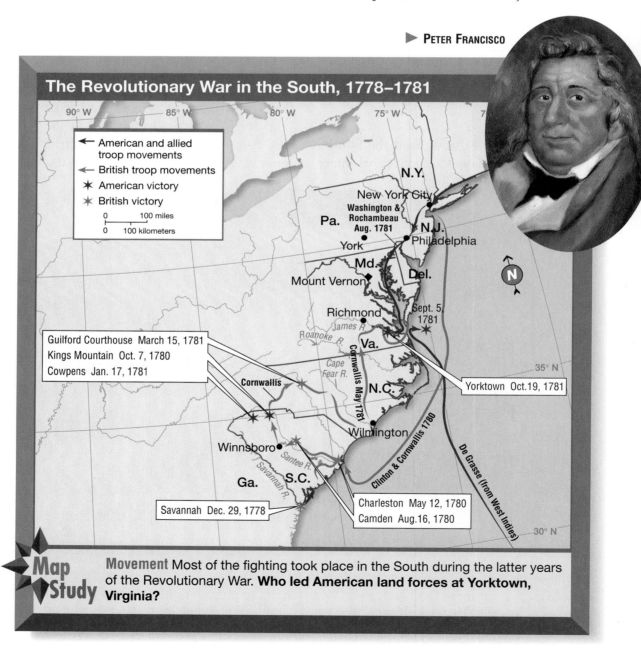

▶ PETER FRANCISCO

The Revolutionary War in the South, 1778–1781

← American and allied troop movements
→ British troop movements
★ American victory
★ British victory

Guilford Courthouse March 15, 1781
Kings Mountain Oct. 7, 1780
Cowpens Jan. 17, 1781

Yorktown Oct.19, 1781

Savannah Dec. 29, 1778

Charleston May 12, 1780
Camden Aug.16, 1780

Map Study

Movement Most of the fighting took place in the South during the latter years of the Revolutionary War. **Who led American land forces at Yorktown, Virginia?**

gan's, with hopes of crushing Cornwallis's weakened force. On March 15, 1781, the armies met in a bloody battle known as the **Battle of Guilford Courthouse** in North Carolina. Although Cornwallis drove the Patriots from the battlefield, the Americans badly battered his troops.

Biography ★★★

Peter Francisco, Hero at Guilford Courthouse

A monument at Guilford Courthouse marks the site of a charge made during a famous battle. The monument is known as the Francisco Monument. Born in the Portuguese Azores, as a young child **Peter Francisco** was taken from his family and abandoned on a dock in Virginia.

When the Revolution began, 16-year-old Francisco joined the Virginia militia and fought in many battles. Most accounts indicate that he was quite large, standing 6-feet 6-inches tall and weighing 260 pounds. Armed with a huge sword at Guilford Courthouse, Francisco killed 11 British soldiers.

Seriously wounded by a British bayonet, Francisco collapsed and was left for dead on the battlefield. He recovered and rejoined the troops for the Yorktown campaign. Francisco had earned a reputation for bravery and dedication to the revolutionary cause. ★★★

★ African Americans and the War

When the American Revolution began, the population of the colonies was approximately 2.5 million. More than a half million were African Americans. Slaveholders were afraid to give guns to either enslaved or free African Americans. In November 1775 orders went out to discharge all African American soldiers in the Continental Army.

 Picturing History

▲ **BATTLE OF COWPENS** Led by General Greene and General Morgan, American forces defeated the British at the Battle of Cowpens. **What fighting tactics did General Greene use against the British?**

Both Sides Encourage Enlistment

Soon after, the British offered enslaved persons their freedom in return for military service. Enslaved African Americans signed up in great numbers. According to one estimate, nearly 1,000 enslaved persons joined the British and gained their freedom.

The Americans, meanwhile, found themselves in need of troops. Realizing that great numbers of African Americans were fighting for the British, American policy changed to encourage the enlistment of those who were free or enslaved.

In reality, African Americans had been involved in the Revolution from the beginning. One of the first Americans to die for the revolutionary cause was African American **Crispus Attucks,** who was killed at the Boston Massacre on March 5, 1770. Many more would follow in his footsteps.

In all about 5,000 African Americans served as soldiers, minutemen, scouts,

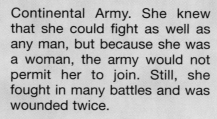

Women in War

During the American Revolution, women often served as secret agents, or accompanied troops as cooks, medics, laundresses, and guides. Some also fought in combat. Today, women have more active roles in the military.

Then

Soldier Without Her Name

In 1782 **Deborah Sampson** dressed in men's clothing, borrowed the name of her brother Robert, and joined the Continental Army. She knew that she could fight as well as any man, but because she was a woman, the army would not permit her to join. Still, she fought in many battles and was wounded twice.

Now

On Land, On Sea, In the Air

Today, women no longer have to disguise themselves in men's clothes in order to serve their country in the armed forces. They can enlist in any of the armed forces and move up the ranks just like their male counterparts. Women now make up almost one-fifth of the United States military forces. They serve on warships, fly jet fighters, and command their own units. Although women still do not fight in hand-to-hand combat, about 90 percent of today's military jobs are open to women.

▲ **U.S. NAVY OFFICERS**

◄ **DEBORAH SAMPSON**

guards, sailors, spies, laborers, fifers, and drummers in the Continental Army. **Jack Sisson** participated in a bold raid on British military headquarters in Newport, Rhode Island. **James Armistad** served valiantly as an American spy, working out of the headquarters of General Lafayette.

At least 12 African Americans, including **Caesar Bacon, Cuff Whittemore, Peter Salem,** and **Salem Poor,** fought at the Battle of Bunker Hill. American commanders singled out Salem Poor for his skill and valor. Fellow soldiers reported that he "behaved like an experienced officer, as well as an excellent soldier." They recommended that the Continental Congress recognize and honor him for his bravery.

Fighting for Freedom

The idea of fighting for freedom was particularly meaningful to the colonial African Americans. By the end of the war, some enslaved African Americans had gained their freedom. As a result of the war efforts of African Americans, Northern states such as Vermont, New Hampshire, Massachusetts, and Pennsylvania attempted to end slavery in their states.

The African Americans who returned to the South after serving in the Continental Army did not find an end to enslavement, however. Even though Virginia and other states passed laws giving freedom to ex-soldiers, most slaveholders did not free them.

★ Women and the War

Women also contributed to the war effort. With the men away on the battlefield, many women took on the responsibility of running the family farms and businesses. Other women followed their husbands to the army camps. There they cooked, sewed, carried ammunition, or served as nurses.

Some supported the war effort by making soap, gathering rags for bandages, and making coats and shirts to keep the soldiers warm through the winter. Because of a shortage of metal, many women melted down their pewter pitchers and cups for bullets.

A few women took part in battles. Mary Ludwig Hays McCauley spent seven years at her husband's side in battle. The soldiers called her "Moll of the Pitcher," or **Molly Pitcher,** because she carried water pitchers to the soldiers. She also helped the wounded and assisted the men at the cannons.

During the New Jersey Battle of Monmouth in 1778, McCauley's husband was wounded. She took his place on the battlefield, operating the cannon and firing at the British. The American government recognized her valiant service more than 40 years later and granted her a $50 per year pension, or payment for the military service she had performed. One year later Mary McCauley died.

Picturing History ▲ AFRICAN AMERICANS FIGHTING IN THE WAR Many African Americans fought for the Continental Army and gave their lives during the Revolutionary War. **Why did the American policy change, allowing African Americans to fight in the war?**

Women played other roles, as well. Lydia Darragh worked as a spy for the Continental Army. Mercy Otis Warren helped the war effort by writing newspaper articles in support of the Revolution.

★ SECTION 3 REVIEW ★

Checking for Understanding

1. **Identify** Francis Marion, Peter Francisco, Salem Poor, Kings Mountain, Moore's Creek Bridge, Savannah, Charleston.
2. **Define** Battle of Cowpens, pension.
3. **What** skills helped the Patriot raiders to defeat the British?
4. **How** did women contribute to the war effort?

Critical Thinking

5. **Determining Cause and Effect** Why did the Continental Army stop enlisting African Americans and then change its policy?

ACTIVITY

6. Design a symbol or logo that captures the spirit and determination of the Patriot raiders in the South.

★★★

Victory at Yorktown

SETTING THE SCENE

Read to Learn . . .

★ how France helped to end the war.
★ how General Washington defeated the British at Yorktown.
★ the terms of the Treaty of Paris.

Terms to Know

★ compromise
★ Treaty of Paris

People to Meet

★ Admiral François de Grasse

Places to Locate

★ Yorktown
★ Chesapeake Bay

▶ **AMERICAN MILITIAMAN**

In 1781 the British generals were confused and in disagreement over their next move. France's entry into the war had complicated matters for them. After a series of victories over the British navy, the French had won command of America's Atlantic coast. The British saw France's presence there as a challenge to their control of the sea.

★ The Final Battle

Following the Patriots' hit-and-run attacks in the South, General Cornwallis led his 7,500 troops north to **Yorktown, Virginia.** Yorktown was on a peninsula formed by the James River and **Chesapeake Bay.** Cornwallis thought this would be an excellent location. From here, he could receive supplies from British ships. In addition, he thought the site provided a safe haven for his army.

Cornwallis, though, was unprepared for the confrontation that would soon occur. On August 29, 1781, the commander of the French fleet, **Admiral François de Grasse,** anchored 29 warships in Chesapeake Bay. His fleet blocked the entrance and prevented Cornwallis from getting supplies. The blockade also kept Cornwallis from escaping by sea. At the same time, Washington's army and 7,000 French troops led by **General Jean de Rochambeau** (ROH•SHAM•BOH) hurried from New York to Virginia. By September 14 they had reached the peninsula. Meanwhile, additional forces led by Anthony Wayne and the Marquis de Lafayette converged on Yorktown.

The armies and the French navy trapped Cornwallis. Every route of escape by land and by sea had been blocked. British forces tried to rescue Cornwallis's army but could not penetrate the French and American lines. On October 17, 1781, Cornwallis wrote to General Washington, requesting a cease-fire. Two days later the British officially surrendered.

Surrender at Yorktown

On October 19, British and American troops met outside of Yorktown, along the river. The drums grew quiet as the two sides faced each other. General Washington waited to accept General Cornwallis's sword in the gesture of surrender. Cornwallis, however, was not there. Instead, he had named General Charles O'Hara to act in his place.

Learning of the substitution, Washington selected General Benjamin Lincoln to represent the Americans. This was a generous tribute to Lincoln, whose troops had been defeated in the battle at Charleston. Lincoln accepted O'Hara's sword and then directed the British troops to stack their weapons and return to Yorktown.

As the 7,000 British soldiers turned over their weapons to the Americans, the British band played a sad tune titled "The World Turn'd Upside Down." The British were dismayed. The Americans were jubilant. Washington's ragtag army had beaten King George's mighty forces. Although the war was not quite over, a major battle had been won, and the Americans knew victory was theirs.

★ The Road to Peace

When news of the surrender reached London, British prime minister Lord North exclaimed, "It is all over!" Parliament voted North out of office. Next, the two sides had to sit down and negotiate a peace agreement.

History AND ART

▲ *Surrender of Lord Cornwallis at Yorktown* by John Trumbull 1824 Trapped by American and French forces, General Charles Cornwallis surrendered at Yorktown. The victory would guarantee America's freedom from Great Britain. **Who represented the American forces at the surrender?**

Treaty of Paris

Delegates from the Continental Congress, including John Jay, Benjamin Franklin, and John Adams, traveled to Paris to meet with the British and work out the details of the treaty. It took almost two years for American and British peacemakers to reach a compromise, or an agreement acceptable to both sides. Finally, on September 3, 1783, the two sides signed the Treaty of Paris.

The treaty stated that Great Britain would acknowledge the independence of the colonists and remove its troops from American soil immediately. In addition, the treaty set new boundaries for the United States. The new territory included all the land west of the Appalachian Mountains to the Mississippi River. It extended from Canada in the north to Florida in the south. Great Britain returned Florida to Spain.

According to the treaty, the Americans agreed to ask state legislatures to pay Loyalists for property they lost in the war. Most states ignored the claims.

Washington's Farewell

With good reason Patriots throughout the colonies celebrated their victory as the last of the British troops left New York. General Washington, at the head of his troops, rode triumphantly into the city. The nation owed a great debt to Washington. His unwavering dedication, discipline, and superior judgment helped to win the American Revolution.

In December of 1783, Washington addressed his troops in a final farewell at Fraunces Tavern in New York City. Colonel Benjamin Tallmadge recorded Washington's words:

> **With a heart full of love and gratitude, I now take leave of you. . . . I cannot come to each of you, but shall feel obliged if each of you will come and take me by the hand.**

Tallmadge said every officer in the room marched up to the departing general. "Such a scene of sorrow and weeping I had never before witnessed."

When the war ended, Washington returned to his home at Mount Vernon, Virginia, where he planned to live quietly with his family. The war was over and independence had been won. Still, Washington knew there would be great challenges ahead for the young and promising country.

★ SECTION 4 REVIEW ★

Checking for Understanding

1. **Identify** Admiral François de Grasse, Yorktown, Chesapeake Bay.
2. **Define** compromise, Treaty of Paris.
3. **How** did France help the Americans defeat the British at Yorktown?
4. **How** did the land boundaries of the colonies change as a result of the Treaty of Paris?

Critical Thinking

5. **Predicting Consequences** What do you think would have happened if France had not entered the war?

ACTIVITY

6. Draw a picture of a gift that you think the Continental Congress might have sent to the French government in appreciation for its help in ending the war.

BUILDING SKILLS
Study and Writing Skills

Preparing an Outline

▲ SURRENDER OF GENERAL BURGOYNE AT SARATOGA

When the nation's Founders composed important letters or documents, they were sure to include important points and main ideas that conveyed the message they wanted to send. We do not know each step they followed in doing this, but chances are good that they followed an outline.

Learning the Skill

An **outline** helps identify important ideas and organize them in a way that makes them easy to understand and remember.

Before you begin an outline, identify the main idea and the details that support your idea. Suppose you want to write an essay on the battles of the American Revolution. Begin by creating an outline. You will need to decide which battles to include. Then decide what information is important about each of these battles. Your outline might look something like the partial outline above.

Battles of the American Revolution

I. The Battle of Saratoga
   A. Commanders
      1. American General Gates
      2. British General Burgoyne
   B. Casualties
      1. 450 Patriots
      2. 1,200 British
   C. Outcome
      1. First major victory for Patriots
         a. Morale boost for soldiers
         b. More support from France
      2. British strength in Northern colonies weakens
II. The Battle of Yorktown
   A. Commanders
      1. American General Washington
      2. British General Cornwallis
   B. Casualties
      1. 100 Patriots
      2. 600 British

Practicing the Skill

Use the sample outline above to answer these questions.

1. What are the two main topics in this outline?

2. If you wanted to add two facts about General Washington's appearance and age, where would you put them in the outline? Would you use numbers or letters to label the facts?

3. Would you use letters or numbers if you wanted to create a subtopic under "b. More support from France"?

APPLYING THE SKILL

4. Prepare an outline for one of the sections in Chapter 8.

Using Key Vocabulary

Use the vocabulary words below to complete the following sentences.

> **compromise**
> **Patriots**
> **Loyalists**
> **blockade**
> **privateers**

1. During the American Revolution, British ships set up a _____ of colonial ports.

2. Owners of American merchant ships who volunteered to go up against the British navy were called _____.

3. Colonists who sided with the British were given the name _____.

4. The Continental Army was made up of _____.

5. After much discussion, American and British representatives reached a _____ and signed the Treaty of Paris.

Reviewing Facts

1. **Describe** how the Declaration of Independence divided the nation.

2. **Tell** what actions the Second Continental Congress took to prepare the colonists for war.

3. **Identify** the battle that was the turning point for the Americans in the war.

4. **Name** the country that helped Washington defeat the British at Yorktown.

5. **List** the main terms of the Treaty of Paris.

Understanding Concepts

American Democracy

1. Describe the four parts of the Declaration of Independence.

2. Why did colonists have to break their ties with Britain in order to create a democracy?

Conflict and Cooperation

3. What advantages did the Continental Army have that the British army did not?

4. In what roles did African Americans serve in helping the American war effort?

5. How did European aid help the Americans to win the war?

History and Geography

Study the map showing the new territory gained as a result of the terms in the 1783 Treaty of Paris. Then answer the questions on page 243.

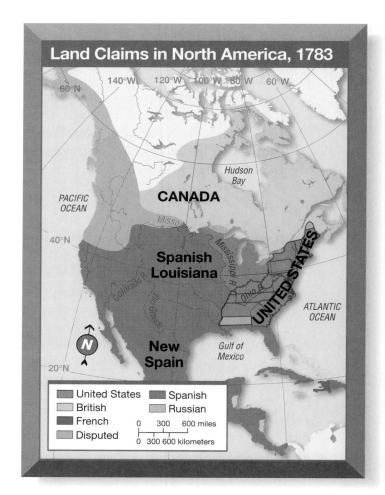

Land Claims in North America, 1783

Legend:
- United States
- British
- French
- Disputed
- Spanish
- Russian

0   300   600 miles
0   300 600 kilometers

1. **Location** What natural landmark formed the new western boundary of America?

2. **Region** What country claimed the most land in North America in 1783? What country claimed the least land?

3. **Movement** What country claimed the land north of America?

4. **Location** What country's land claims lay farthest north?

Critical Thinking

1. **Analyzing Information** If the phrase in the Declaration of Independence, "all men are created equal," had applied to all African Americans, how would their lives have been different after the war?

2. **Drawing Conclusions** After the American victory at Yorktown, the British played "The World Turn'd Upside Down." Two lines of the song are "If ponies rode men and grass ate cows; And cats should be chased to holes by the mouse." What do you think the British soldiers were trying to express by playing this song?

Interdisciplinary Activity: Language Arts

Cooperative Learning

Do library research to learn more about the lives of American soldiers during the Revolutionary War. From your research, select either an American soldier or an American regiment. Then organize your group into two smaller groups. One group will write a biography of an American soldier or a description of an American regiment. The other group will make a poster-size, illustrated map displaying the names and geographic locations where your soldier or regiment fought. Share your work with other members of the class.

Practicing Skills

Writing an Outline

Review the Declaration of Independence on pages 220–223. Then complete this outline.

The Declaration of Independence
  I. Preamble
 II. Declaration of Natural Rights
III. List of Grievances
 IV. Statement of Independence
  A. Rights of colonies
    1. To be free and independent states
    2. To not have to answer to the British monarchy
    3. _____
  B. Powers of colonies
    1. To levy war
    2. _____
    3. _____
    4. _____
  C. _____
    1. To sacrifice our lives
    2. _____
    3. To sacrifice our sacred honor

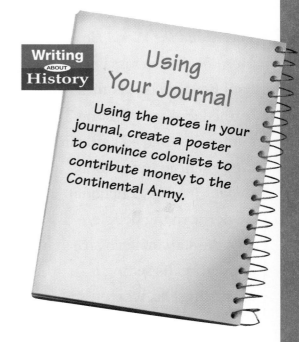

Writing ABOUT History

Using Your Journal

Using the notes in your journal, create a poster to convince colonists to contribute money to the Continental Army.

Author Esther Forbes wrote a number of books, among them the prize-winning biography *Paul Revere and the World He Lived In.* **As she researched Paul Revere's life, Forbes learned that many young apprentices played a role in the American Revolution.** *Johnny Tremain,* **a fictional work for young people, tells the story of such an apprentice. Its setting is Massachusetts, where Forbes was born.**

Read to Discover

In this passage from *Johnny Tremain*, English ships are docked in the harbor of Boston, unable to leave and unable to unload their tea cargo. What brought about this situation? How did the people of Boston react?

Reader's Dictionary

henchmen	helpers
Rab	Johnny's apprentice friend
bade	commanded
forthwith	happening now
disperse	break up
men-of-war	battle ships

from *Johnny Tremain*

by Esther Forbes (1891–1967)

Almost every day and sometimes all day, the mass meetings at Old South Church went on. Tempers grew higher and higher. Boston was swept with a passion it had not known since the Boston Massacre three years before. Riding this wild storm was Sam Adams and his trusty henchmen, directing it, building up the anger until, although the matter was not publicly mentioned, they would all see the only thing left for them to do was to destroy the tea.

Sometimes Rab and Johnny went to these meetings. It happened they were there when the sheriff arrived and bade the meeting forthwith to disperse. He said it was lawless and treasonable. This proclamation from Governor Hutchinson was met with howls and hisses. They voted to disobey the order.

Sometimes the boys slipped over to Griffin's Wharf. By the eighth of December the *Eleanor* had joined the *Dartmouth.* These were strange ships. They had unloaded their cargoes—except the tea. The Town of Boston had ordered them not to unload the tea and the law stated they could not leave until they had unloaded. Nor would the Governor give them a pass

▲ Boston, 1774

to return to England. At Castle Island the British Colonel Leslie had orders to fire upon them if they attempted to sneak out of the harbor. The *Active* and the *Kingfisher,* British men-of-war, stood by ready to blast them out of the water if they obeyed the Town and returned to London with the tea. The ships were held at Griffin's Wharf as though under an enchantment.

Here was none of the usual hustle and bustle. Few of the crew were in sight, but hundreds of spectators gathered every day merely to stare at them. Johnny saw Rotch, the twenty-three-year-old Quaker who owned the *Dartmouth,* running about in despair. The Governor would not let him leave. The Town would not let him unload. Between them he was a ruined man. He feared a mob would burn his ship. There was no mob, and night and day armed citizens guarded the ships. They would see to it that no tea was smuggled ashore and that no harm was done to the ships. Back and forth paced the guards. Many of their faces were familiar to Johnny. One day, even John Hancock took his turn with a musket on his shoulder, and the next night he saw Paul Revere.

Responding to Literature

1. Why were the ships so closely guarded?

2. Why was Rotch in despair?

3. How do you think the people of Boston felt about Governor Hutchinson? Explain.

ACTIVITY

4. Imagine you lived in Boston during this time. Your town's government will not let the tea ships unload their cargo. Create a poster either supporting this position or opposing it.

Cultural Kaleidoscope

Transportation and Communication

For the most part, folks stayed close to home during colonial and Revolutionary times. When they took a trip, they packed bags or trunks and planned to be away for some time. There was no other way. Speed and efficiency were not part of the transportation and communication scene.

Coaches, Passengers, and Inns

Horse-drawn coaches carried passengers between towns and cities. Many journeys lasted two days or more. The coaches stopped at inns at night and completed trips in stages. As a result, people called the coaches "stagecoaches."

Special Delivery?

Working for the British government, colonial riders on horseback and ship captains sailing along the coast carried the mail. To link the Northern colonies with the Southern colonies, a ship carried mail between New York City and Charleston, South Carolina, once a month. At the beginning of the Revolution, the Continental Congress created a similar postal system, headed by Ben Franklin.

Starting to Pave the Way

Before and during the Revolution, travel by land meant roadways clogged with ruts, tree roots, rocks, fallen trees, and mud. After the war, Americans made their first hard-surfaced roads out of crushed stone or wood planks. Private citizens built most of the roads and charged travelers a fee for using them. By 1789 land travel had improved enough that a New York publisher printed the nation's first road maps.

Getting the Word Around

Speechmaking was one way to reach the public with a message. The other way was to print the message in a newspaper. Whether colonist, Patriot, or citizen of the New Republic, Americans eagerly read and shared their newspapers. The *Pennsylvania Evening Post* was the first American newspaper printed daily. This issue is dated Friday, May 30, 1783.

Smooth Sailing

Whether the ship sailed along the coast or crossed the oceans, water travel was the best way to travel. Compared with land travel, cargo arrived in half the time and passengers arrived with fewer bruises. Americans had only a small navy. This huge British warship easily captured four American merchant ships near the end of the Revolutionary War.

CHAPTER 9

★★★

Creating a Nation
1776–1791

SETTING THE SCENE

Focus

Americans successfully met the challenge of establishing state governments and a national government under the Articles of Confederation. It soon became apparent, however, that weaknesses of the new national government might break it apart. America's leaders sought new solutions.

Concepts to Understand

★ How the Articles of Confederation and Constitution formed a foundation for **American democracy**
★ Why **civil rights and liberties** were so important to the people of the United States

Read to Discover . . .

★ the strengths and weaknesses of the Articles of Confederation.
★ the importance of compromises in creating the Constitution.

Journal Notes

As you read this chapter take notes on the things that Benjamin Franklin said and did during the Constitutional Convention.

► CONTINENTAL CURRENCY

United States		
	1776 Declaration of Independence signed	1781 Articles of Confederation ratified 1783 Treaty of Paris formally ends American Revolution
	1775–1779	**1780–1784**
World		1783 Spain, Denmark, Sweden recognize United States

THE
FEDERALIST:
ADDRESSED TO THE
PEOPLE OF THE STATE OF
NEW-YORK.

NUMBER I.

Introduction.

AFTER an unequivocal experience of the inefficacy of the fubfifting federal government, you are called upon to deliberate on a new conftitution for the United States of America. The fubject fpeaks its own importance ; comprehending in its confequences, nothing lefs than the exiftence of the UNION, the fafety and welfare of the parts of which it is compofed, the fate of an empire, in many refpects, the moft interefting in the world. It has been frequently remarked, that it feems to have been referved to the people of this country, by their conduct and example, to decide the important queftion, whether focieties of men are really capable or not, of eftablifhing good government from reflection and choice, or whether they are forever deftined to depend, for their political conftitutions, on accident and force. If there be any truth in the remark, the crifis, at which we are arrived, may with propriety be regarded as the æra in which
A   that

◀ **THE FEDERALIST**

History AND ART

Signing of the Constitution of the United States
by Howard Chandler Cristy

Delegates to the Constitutional Convention signed the final draft of the Constitution in Independence Hall.

1785 Land Ordinance passed
1788 U.S. Constitution ratified
1789 George Washington inaugurated
 as first President

1791 Bill of Rights ratified

1785–1789

1790–1794

1787 Turkey declares war on Russia
1789 French Revolution begins

1791 Haitians revolt against French
 colonial rule

★★★★★★★★★★★★★★★★★★★★★★★★★★★★★★★★

Forming a Union

SETTING THE SCENE

Read to Learn . . .

★ how the Articles of Confederation gave state governments more power than the national government.
★ the strengths and weaknesses of the Articles of Confederation.

Terms to Know

★ constitution
★ legislative branch
★ bicameral
★ executive branch
★ bill of rights
★ Articles of Confederation
★ ratify

People to Meet

★ John Dickinson

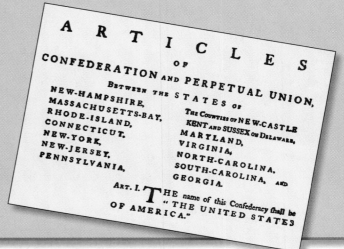

▲ THE ARTICLES OF CONFEDERATION

As fighting spread from Massachusetts in 1775, royal governors throughout the colonies watched their authority collapse. At first a few governors tried to organize Loyalist resistance, but eventually all royal governors abandoned their offices and fled.

In May 1776 Congress urged the colonies to replace their colonial charters with new constitutions, or plans of government. Colonists considered written constitutions important because they would spell out the rights of all citizens. They would also set limits on the power of government.

★ State Constitutions

Most states established governments similar to the colonial governments they replaced. Colonists felt concerned about giving too much power to a few people. As a result, they divided power between two branches. The legislative branch became the lawmaking branch. It included representatives elected by the states' voters. All states except Pennsylvania and Georgia created bicameral, or two-house, legislatures. Members of each house represented geographic districts. In nearly all states, voters directly elected the legislative members.

The second branch of government carried out the laws that this legislature made. This branch became known as the **executive branch.** A state governor headed the executive branch. Because many Americans had come to distrust strong executive power, most state governors were elected to one-year terms by their legislatures, and they had no power to reject bills.

Rights of Citizens

Although Americans considered individual rights to be important, the expression of American freedoms varied from state to state. For the most part, laws restricted citizenship to white male property owners. Neither women nor African Americans could vote in most states. New Jersey extended the right to vote to "all free inhabitants," so women could vote there. In 1807, however, the state legislature took the right away.

▲ **SLAVE SHACKLES**

Although the Revolution did not win full equality for all Americans, it began to move America in that direction. It became difficult to claim that "all men are created equal" in a society with enslaved people. Americans began to question the institution of slavery. Some states passed laws prohibiting the importation of slaves, and by 1804 every state north of Maryland had passed laws freeing enslaved African Americans.

Although states discriminated against their residents on the basis of race, sex, religion, and economic standing, most state constitutions included a **bill of**

Picturing History

▲ **SELF-GOVERNMENT** In the late 1700s Americans, such as these citizens of Boston, gathered to discuss their state governments. **How did most state constitutions divide the governing power at this time?**

rights that spelled out certain rights the states had to recognize and protect. These rights included trial by jury and freedom of the press.

★ The Articles of Confederation

Even as the 13 states began to write their constitutions, the Congress drew up its own blueprint for a national government. Writing a national constitution, though, proved difficult. In 1776 few Americans considered themselves citizens of one nation. Instead, they felt loyalty to their own states.

Although the states seemed unwilling to turn over power to the national government, the Congress finally drafted a constitution. On November 15, 1777, the Continental Congress completed and passed the Articles of Confederation and proposed that it go into effect after every state had approved it.

Claims in the West

Not until 1781, however, did all of the states ratify, or approve, the Articles. A delay in the ratification process occurred because of a dispute among the states. Several states claimed large tracts of western land. Based mainly on colonial charters that had granted land "from sea to sea," these claims often overlapped. In addition the six states without western land claims argued that the West should become public land, land belonging to the national government.

Although most states ratified the Articles, Maryland would not ratify it until all lands between the Appalachian Mountains and the Mississippi River became public land. Virginia, which had huge claims—the present-day states of Kentucky, West Virginia, Ohio, Indiana, Illinois, Michigan, and Wisconsin— refused to comply. Maryland worried that states like Virginia would become too powerful if allowed to keep their western lands.

 Picturing History ▲ RELIGION, CHURCHES, AND THE COLONIES This scene shows Virginia's Old Bruton Church. Religious freedom was important to most Americans in the late 1700s. **What part of state constitutions spelled out certain rights for citizens?**

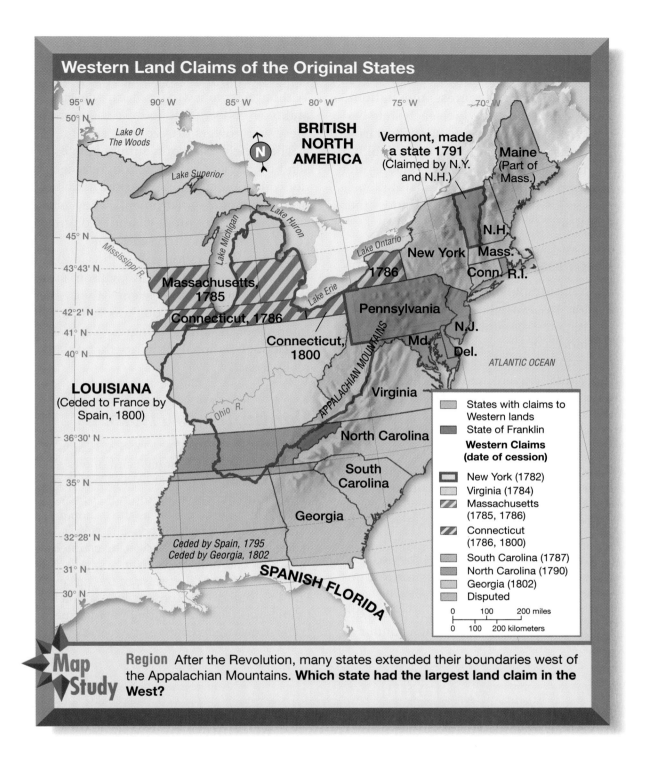

Western Land Claims of the Original States

BRITISH NORTH AMERICA

Vermont, made a state 1791 (Claimed by N.Y. and N.H.)

Maine (Part of Mass.)

Lake Of The Woods

Lake Superior

Lake Michigan

Lake Huron

Mississippi R.

Lake Ontario

Lake Erie

Massachusetts, 1785

Connecticut, 1786

Connecticut, 1800

New York 1786

N.H.

Mass.

Conn. R.I.

Pennsylvania

N.J.

Md.

Del.

ATLANTIC OCEAN

LOUISIANA (Ceded to France by Spain, 1800)

Ohio R.

APPALACHIAN MOUNTAINS

Virginia

North Carolina

South Carolina

Georgia

Ceded by Spain, 1795
Ceded by Georgia, 1802

SPANISH FLORIDA

Legend:
- States with claims to Western lands
- State of Franklin

Western Claims (date of cession)
- New York (1782)
- Virginia (1784)
- Massachusetts (1785, 1786)
- Connecticut (1786, 1800)
- South Carolina (1787)
- North Carolina (1790)
- Georgia (1802)
- Disputed

0   100   200 miles
0   100   200 kilometers

Map Study

Region After the Revolution, many states extended their boundaries west of the Appalachian Mountains. **Which state had the largest land claim in the West?**

Articles Ratified

Finally in 1781, with Lord Cornwallis and the British army moving toward Virginia, the state agreed to give up its land claims. Maryland ratified the Articles, and at last the states became united.

The Articles became the first constitution of the United States. The main author of the

Articles, **John Dickinson,** called it a "firm league of friendship" among the states. It established a loose alliance of states rather than a strong central government. Dickinson and the other writers feared a strong central government because of their experience with the British monarchy and Parliament. They purposefully created a weak national government under the Articles of Confederation.

The Articles of Confederation made the Continental Congress the national lawmaking body in which each state had one vote. Its powers included declaring war, raising an army and navy, making treaties, borrowing money, establishing a postal system, and conducting business with Native Americans and other countries.

Weaknesses of the Articles

The list of powers sounded impressive. Under the Articles of Confederation, though, the national government really remained much weaker than the state governments. It had no authority over individual citizens and very little control over state governments. The Continental Congress, now called the Confederation Congress, could make laws, but the writers provided no measures to carry out those laws. The Articles left it to the states to enforce laws passed by Congress. The Articles also made no provision for a court system. If states disagreed, they had no place to resolve their differences.

The Articles had other weaknesses, too. Every state could send delegates to Congress, but each state, whatever its size, had only one vote. The larger states did not like this policy, viewing it as unfair to them. Congress did hold all the powers connected to war and peace. These powers, however, actually meant very little. Without the money to finance a war or the ability to collect taxes to raise the money, these war powers proved useless.

The Articles did not require the states to send money to Congress. Congress could not collect money to pay for the activities of the national government. The states sent very little money, and Congress could not force them to send more.

George Washington called the Confederation Congress "a shadow without substance." It became clear that the Continental Congress could do little in the interests of the states. Congress kept talking about a national authority that did not really exist.

• •

Footnotes to History

Ben Franklin's Choice   The bald eagle became America's national symbol when it was placed on the Great Seal in 1782. Benjamin Franklin, however, did not approve and suggested the turkey as the national bird. He was strongly opposed to the American bald eagle that was, he claimed, "a bird of bad moral character . . . and often [full of lice]." In praise of the turkey, Franklin stated, "The turkey is . . . a much more respectable bird, withal [in addition, it is] a true original native of America."

★ **SECTION 1 REVIEW** ★

★★

Checking for Understanding

1. **Identify** John Dickinson.

2. **Define** constitution, legislative branch, bicameral, executive branch, bill of rights, Articles of Confederation, ratify.

3. **Why** were written constitutions important to the colonists?

4. **What** were three weaknesses of the Articles of Confederation?

Critical Thinking

5. **Distinguishing Fact From Opinion**   What do you think George Washington meant when he called the Confederation Congress "a shadow without substance"? Did he state a fact or an opinion?

ACTIVITY

6. Create a bumper sticker supporting ratification of the Articles of Confederation.

★★

The Confederation Era

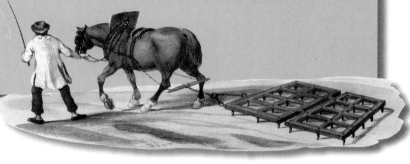

SETTING THE SCENE

Read to Learn . . .

★ the problems the new nation faced under the Articles of Confederation.
★ how the Northwest Ordinance provided for growth in the West.

Terms to Know

★ republic
★ economic depression

People to Meet

★ Daniel Shays

Places to Locate

★ Appalachian Mountains

▶ FARMER HARROWING FIELDS

U nder the Articles of Confederation, the United States was an unstable nation. Even as America expanded westward, it continued to have problems with other nations. Constant bickering among the states disrupted the government, and many groups within society became discontented. Americans had good reason to doubt whether their new nation would survive.

★ Settling the West

Until the end of the 1800s, "the West" was not a specific geographic region of the United States. Instead, the West described the next area of settlement as pioneers invaded the territories of Native Americans and removed them from their land. During the Confederation period,

the West lay just beyond the **Appalachian Mountains.** Between 1780 and 1790 the western population grew from about 2,000 to about 100,000.

Congress proved powerless to meet the needs of the westerners. It could not dislodge the British from their forts in the North. Without money, Congress could not purchase Native American land nor provide troops to protect the settlers.

The Land Ordinance of 1785

Prior to 1783, settlers claimed land in the West just by settling on it. Disputes among settlers became common and sometimes grew violent. As a result of this, and to raise money, Congress passed the **Land Ordinance of 1785.** This law provided a more orderly method for settling land north of the Ohio River.

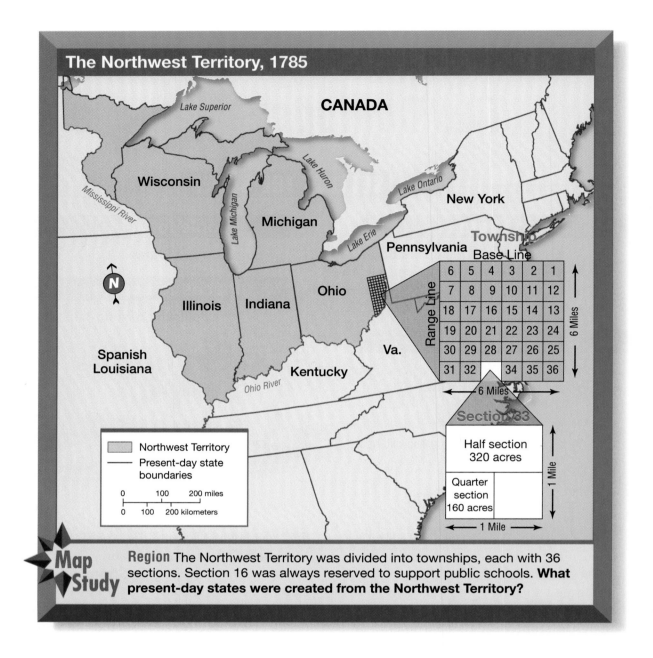

The Northwest Territory, 1785

CANADA

Lake Superior

Wisconsin

Lake Huron

Lake Ontario

New York

Mississippi River

Lake Michigan

Michigan

Lake Erie

Pennsylvania

Township

Ohio

Base Line

6	5	4	3	2	1
7	8	9	10	11	12
18	17	16	15	14	13
19	20	21	22	23	24
30	29	28	27	26	25
31	32	33	34	35	36

Range Line

6 Miles

Illinois

Indiana

Va.

Spanish Louisiana

Kentucky

Ohio River

6 Miles

Section 33

Half section 320 acres

1 Mile

Quarter section 160 acres

1 Mile

Northwest Territory

Present-day state boundaries

| 0 | 100 | 200 miles |
| 0 | 100 | 200 kilometers |

Map Study

Region The Northwest Territory was divided into townships, each with 36 sections. Section 16 was always reserved to support public schools. **What present-day states were created from the Northwest Territory?**

The ordinance stated that land would be surveyed and divided into townships 6 miles square (16 sq. km). Each township would contain 36 sections. A section consisted of 1 square mile (2.6 sq. km) and contained 640 acres (259 ha). Congress planned to sell the land at auctions for no less than $1 per acre. Revenue from the sale of one section in every township supported the creation of a public school. This is the first example of federal aid to education.

To attract land speculators, the law required that buyers take at least one whole section. Speculators could then divide their sections into smaller rectangular tracts and sell the tracts to settlers at a profit.

The Northwest Ordinance

While the Land Ordinance of 1785 dealt with the sale of land in the Northwest Territory, the **Northwest Ordinance,** passed in 1787, made provisions for governing the new territory. It stated that no less than three and no more than five territories could be carved out of the Northwest Territory. Congress would appoint a governor and three judges for each territory until it became populous enough to form its own government and become a state.

As soon as 5,000 adult white males settled a territory, it could elect a territorial legislature. The territory then could send a nonvoting delegate to represent it in Congress. When the population reached 60,000, the people of the territory could write a constitution and apply for statehood. If Congress approved the constitution, the territory became a state with the same rights as the existing states.

The ordinance placed only a few restrictions on the territories. First, their new government had to be a republic. A republic is a type of government in which representatives are elected to govern on behalf of the people. Second, the ordinance required territories to ensure freedom of religion and to guarantee trial by jury for those accused of crimes. Third, the ordinance prohibited slaveholding in the territory. The Northwest Ordinance became the first law in United States history to restrict the practice of slaveholding.

The Land Ordinance of 1785 and the Northwest Ordinance of 1787 became important achievements for the national government under the Articles of Confederation. For the first time, a nation had provided an orderly way for its colonies to become political equals. These laws became models for developing other lands into new states. Eventually five states arose from the Northwest Territory: **Ohio** (1803), **Indiana** (1816), **Illinois** (1818), **Michigan** (1837), and **Wisconsin** (1848).

▲ *DANIEL BOONE ESCORTING PIONEERS THROUGH THE CUMBERLAND GAP* by George Caleb Bingham, 1851–1852 In many of his paintings, George Caleb Bingham depicted the pioneer spirit and life in new territories. **What requirement existed to elect a territorial legislature?**

Picturing
(H)istory

▲ SHAYS'S REBELLION Daniel Shays's rebellion led people to believe that the United States could not form or run an effective government. **What set of laws governed the nation at the time of Shays's Rebellion?**

★ A Failing Economy

America in the 1770s and 1780s was a divided and often troubled nation. Just four years after the war, the new nation moved dangerously close to bankruptcy. Business slowed down, and many people could hardly pay their debts.

Worthless Money

The new nation's financial situation looked bleak. After the Revolution, the United States owed millions of dollars—money borrowed from foreign governments, states, and private citizens to pay for the war. Now the United States had to pay that money back. Because the national government did not have the power to collect taxes, it had to rely on the individual states to give it money. Between 1781 and 1789 the states gave Congress only about one-sixth of the money it requested.

During the Revolution, the Congress had printed Continental dollars. Without gold or silver to back it up, this paper money had very little value. Americans soon began to describe any worthless item as "not worth a Continental." To make matters worse, each state printed money of its own, too. The system caused much confusion. How much money was a Virginia dollar worth? Was a dollar in Rhode Island equal to a dollar in Maryland? Some states refused to accept money from other states, while some claimed that their money was more valuable than anyone else's.

Trade Among the States

Because of the unsettling financial situation, trade among the states became difficult. Arguments arose among states that refused to trade with one another. Some people resorted to a system of barter, exchanging goods for other goods instead of money. In North Carolina, for example, whiskey became a type of currency. Virginians used tobacco to repay debts.

Some states taxed goods that came from other states. This encouraged people to buy their own state's products and discouraged them from buying goods from other states. New York placed taxes on firewood from Connecticut and cabbage from New Jersey. Naturally, this policy enraged farmers and merchants who produced and sold the goods.

Economic Depression

American merchants saw their businesses decline. After the war, they still stocked many British goods that they could not sell. The nation had entered an **economic depression.** In an economic depression, business activity slows down and unemployment increases.

To add to the problem, Great Britain had passed laws making it difficult for American merchant ships to enter its ports. Great Britain also made the British West Indies off limits to any American traders. As a result, many American merchants went into debt. Shipbuilders and the shipping industry suffered as well.

Difficult Times for Farmers

Farmers experienced extreme hardships during this time. Throughout the war, demand for food had increased. To keep up, many farmers borrowed money from banks to buy more land and equipment. After the war, though, demand for farm products decreased. Farmers grew more food than they could sell and then could not repay the money they had borrowed. The banks began taking the farmers' lands away to pay their debts. When Spain closed its port of New Orleans at the mouth of the Mississippi River, farmers could no longer ship their goods south to the Gulf of Mexico for export to Europe.

Shays's Rebellion

In Massachusetts the economic situation became explosive. Because some farmers could not repay their debts, government authorities jailed them or seized their property. These farmers viewed the new government as just another variety of tyranny.

In September 1786, the farmers' discontent ignited a rebellion. Led by former Continental Army captain **Daniel Shays,** the farmers attacked and closed the courts in two Massachusetts counties, stopping land confiscations. In early 1787 Shays led more than 1,000 disgruntled farmers against the Springfield arsenal. Through donations from wealthy merchants, Massachusetts raised a militia force strong enough to meet Shays at Springfield.

Although the militia easily defeated the ragged group of farmers, **Shays's Rebellion** caused great alarm, and people who believed in orderly government became fearful. It seemed that the prophecies of those who said the United States could not form an effective system of government were coming true. Many people thought the Articles of Confederation did not work and should be rewritten. Some thought the Articles should be scrapped altogether. The United States did not seem to be united. State leaders called for a convention to discuss ways of revising the Articles of Confederation.

★ SECTION 2 REVIEW ★

Checking for Understanding

1. **Identify** Daniel Shays, Appalachian Mountains.
2. **Define** republic, economic depression.
3. **What** problems did the new nation face under the Articles of Confederation? Why did some feel the Articles should be rewritten?
4. **What** were the reasons behind Shays's Rebellion?

Critical Thinking

5. **Identifying Cause and Effect** How did the Northwest Ordinance encourage settlement of the western frontier?

ACTIVITY

6. Imagine you are a United States citizen in 1787. Write an editorial either defending the current government or citing reasons a new government is needed.

Planning Washington, D.C.

"Here," said Pierre Charles L'Enfant, "is where the two most important buildings in your new capital city should be built." The French engineer pointed to the west end of Jenkins Heights. The land was high ground. Standing there a few days before, L'Enfant and President George Washington could see all the way to the Potomac River. "[It] stands as a pedestal waiting for a monument," L'Enfant said.

The young engineer presented his final plans for the city of Washington, D.C., the new capital city for the new United States of America, in 1791. The blueprints showed a large rectangular grid broken by large "wheels."

The Capitol and the President's home (later called the White House) were the hub of the city. From the foot of the Capitol stretched the Mall. A large, L-shaped grassy

▲ L'ENFANT'S DRAWING OF WASHINGTON, D.C.

area, the Mall was about 400 feet (122 m) wide and about 1 mile (1.6 km) long.

L'Enfant carefully positioned other important government buildings around the hub. He connected the buildings to each other and to the hub with broad diagonal avenues, like the spokes of a wheel. All other streets of the city were based on the rectangular grid, running north to south and east to west.

Making the Math Connection

1. Around what buildings did L'Enfant plan the city of Washington, D.C.?

2. What geometric shapes did L'Enfant use in his plans?

3. What is the Mall?

▲ THE CAPITOL, WASHINGTON, D.C., 1824

ACTIVITY

4. L'Enfant planned diagonal avenues to shorten the distances between places. Draw a simple map of a route you take regularly. Include diagonal lines to shorten the distance you must travel.

★★★

The Constitutional Convention

SETTING THE SCENE

Read to Learn . . .

★ why large and small states argued over plans for the new Constitution.
★ what compromises make up the United States Constitution.

Terms to Know

★ Constitutional Convention
★ veto
★ compromise

People to Meet

★ Benjamin Franklin
★ James Madison
★ Edmund Randolph
★ William Paterson

▲ BENJAMIN FRANKLIN'S EYEGLASSES

Cannons fired and church bells rang as thousands of people lined the cobblestone streets of Philadelphia in May 1787. They stood expectantly, waiting for a glimpse of war hero George Washington and the other delegates as they rode by.

Philadelphia, the most modern city in the United States, hosted the convention that would give birth to the Constitution. It became known as the Constitutional Convention. Washington and other leaders, though, arrived in Philadelphia with one goal in mind—to revise the Articles of Confederation.

★ The Constitutional Convention

State leaders set the date for the meeting in Philadelphia as May 14, 1787, but the delegates did not arrive until May 24.

Eventually delegates arrived to represent 12 of the 13 states. Only Rhode Island did not send a delegate. Its state leaders wanted nothing to do with creating a stronger central government.

The Delegates

Fifty-five men attended one or more sessions of the convention, which lasted from May to September. These "Founding Fathers," as they have come to be known, included many of the most able political leaders in the United States. The delegates, though, did not truly represent the people of the United States. Most of the white male delegates made their livings as lawyers or judges. Twenty-one had college degrees, a high number for this time since few people had formal educations. Nearly all of the delegates had practical experience in government. Most had

▲ JAMES MADISON

helped write their state constitutions, and more than half had participated in the Continental Congress. They had witnessed the unhappy consequences of a weak central government.

Many of the delegates had been activists during the Revolution and their names were well known. Some of the most prominent figures of the time, however, did not attend the convention. **Thomas Jefferson, John Adams,** and **Thomas Paine** had duties in Europe at the time and could not attend. **Patrick Henry** had been selected as a delegate from Virginia, but he refused to go. He feared the move toward a strong central government and wanted no part of the proceedings. Henry stayed away, saying that he "smelled a rat in Philadelphia, tending toward monarchy."

Most of the delegates were in their 30s or 40s. **Benjamin Franklin,** the oldest delegate at 81, suffered from poor health and could not attend regularly. The convention unanimously chose **George Washington** to preside over the proceedings. First to arrive at the convention was **James Madison,** a Virginian; he brought elaborate plans and research. He came to Philadelphia with a draft of a completely new framework of government.

James Madison, a Key Player

Madison brought an impressive background to the convention. He had been a part of the Virginia government and had helped to write that state's constitution. Madison knew about the complicated issues of forming a republic. He also brought a well-defined political philosophy. He considered the main purpose of government to be "to act upon and for the individual citizen."

Right from the start, Madison favored writing a new constitution instead of revising the Articles of Confederation. Aware that his ideas might be unpopular, Madison prepared for the convention by arming himself with all the knowledge he could. From Europe, Thomas Jefferson helped by sending boxes of books on history and political thought. Madison's notebooks overflowed with information. A Georgia delegate at the convention said of Madison:

> ❝ [Of] the affairs of the United States, he perhaps, has the most correct knowledge of any man in the Union. . . . ❞

By the time he arrived in Philadelphia, Madison was ready to defend his beliefs.

Madison played an active role at the convention. He attended every session, sitting near the front so he would not miss a thing. His careful notes show that, in fact, he missed very little. They provide a detailed record of this very important event and

Footnotes to History

The Constitutional Convention Notes

Madison worked out a personal system of shorthand and then wrote a full account from these notes immediately following each session of the Constitutional Convention. Madison was very careful to keep his notes out of the public eye. His notes were finally published in 1840.

remain the best source of information on who said what during the meetings.

In addition to writing notes, Madison contributed greatly to the formation of the new constitution. Many of his ideas became woven into the document. Madison's contributions became so significant that they earned him the nickname "Father of the Constitution."

Madison's role in American history did not end with the Constitutional Convention. He became a political party leader, a member of the first House of Representatives, a secretary of state and, eventually, President of the United States. ★★★

★ The Convention Begins

At the beginning of the convention the delegates agreed that "nothing spoken in this House be printed or otherwise published." The delegates had to decide on a government for free people. Why, then, did they think the proceedings should be secret?

The delegates expected intense debate and knew that arguments would erupt. They hoped to keep these disagreements private so the distractions would not influence the people who would eventually either accept or reject the finished document.

To ensure their privacy, the delegates agreed to sit, day by day, in a room with closed windows and guards posted at the doors. Temperatures soared that summer, making the delegates even more uncomfortable. Still, they would continue to debate, argue, and compromise until they completed their job.

Besides agreeing to secrecy, the delegates agreed on other procedures. The delegates wanted to be able to change their minds. At the Constitutional Convention any subject could be brought up and voted on as many times as needed. The delegates also agreed to vote by states, with each state having one vote.

It did not take long for the delegates to realize that they could not amend the Articles of Confederation. Even those who most opposed a strong central government had to agree that the Articles were far too weak and could never hold a nation together. The country needed a new constitution.

★ The Virginia Plan

On May 29, Virginia governor **Edmund Randolph**—a more forceful speaker than Madison—presented Madison's proposal, now known as the **Virginia Plan.** The Virginia Plan called for a strong national government with three branches: legislative, executive, and judicial. The **legislative branch** of government makes laws, the **executive branch** carries out the laws, and the **judicial branch** determines if the laws are carried out fairly.

The Virginia Plan also called for a two-house legislature. In both houses the number of members would be based on

Picturing History ▲ EDMUND RANDOLPH Randolph's Virginia Plan called for a strong national government with three branches of government and a two-house legislature based on population. **Why did the Virginia Plan upset the smaller states?**

▲ GEORGE WASHINGTON

population. Thus, large states would have more representation than small ones. This differed from the Articles of Confederation, which gave each state one vote in Congress regardless of population.

Concern Over Representation

The first provision of the Virginia Plan upset the small states. If the plan based representation on population, all lawmaking would be controlled by the large states. Small states would retain little power. Not only that, the small states would be subject to laws they would have very little voice in creating.

On the other hand, delegates from large states such as Virginia, Massachusetts, and Pennsylvania asked why a state like Delaware with only about 59,000 people should have the same power as Virginia with almost 700,000 people.

The debate went back and forth. Delegates from Delaware, Maryland, and New Jersey, which had few people, argued that they would never give up the equal power they had enjoyed under the Articles of Confederation. In fact, **William Paterson** from New Jersey exclaimed that his state would "rather submit to a monarch, . . . than to such a fate."

Weakened State Power

The second provision of the Virginia Plan threatened to take some power away from the states. It declared that if two or more states could not settle their differences, the national legislature would step in and do it for them. Furthermore, the Virginia Plan suggested that Congress, not the people, should choose the President and national judges. The plan stated that the President and courts would have the power to veto, or reject, laws passed by Congress. The two houses of Congress, however, could turn around and override that veto.

The Virginia Plan provided a blueprint for a very powerful centralized government. It appeared much too extreme for many delegates who still remembered the shackles of British rule. No one is certain why James Madison wrote a plan that concentrated so much power in the national government. One theory is that Shays's Rebellion and the other revolts going on in the states led him to advocate a strong government that could deal effectively with any threat to the country.

★ The New Jersey Plan

The small states wasted no time in responding to the Virginia Plan. On June 15, New Jersey delegate William Paterson presented a counterproposal called the **New Jersey Plan.** It, too, provided for three branches of government. It kept the single-body Congress, though, as set forth in the Articles of Confederation. No matter how large, each state would have one vote in the legislature. Congress would keep the powers it had in the Articles, but would gain new powers to tax and to regulate trade among the states.

Most large-state delegates favored Madison's Virginia Plan and its national government with separate executive, legislative, and judicial branches and states subordinate to the national government. Most small-state delegates favored the New Jersey Plan, which continued the Confederation and left the states supreme.

Bitter debate raged over these differences for two weeks. Lacking a middle ground where the two sides could meet, the convention seemed in danger of collapsing. Washington wrote a friend, remarking

 I find but little ground on which the hope of a good establishment can be formed. . . . I almost despair of seeing a favorable issue [end] to the proceedings of our Convention. . . . 🙰

Washington continued the letter, adding that he regretted having anything to do with the convention. Franklin, also feeling downhearted, proposed that each session be opened with prayer, asking divine guidance in finding an acceptable compromise.

★ The Great Compromise

On July 2, the convention selected a "grand committee" made up of one delegate from each state to work toward a solution. Franklin agreed to chair the committee. The committee struggled through even more debate and negotiation before agreeing on a compromise. A compromise is an agreement in which each side agrees to give up something to gain something more important. The committee's compromise became known as the **Great Compromise.**

The plan called for Congress to be made up of two houses. Members of the upper house, called the Senate, would be chosen by state legislatures. Each state,

large or small, would have two senators. When presented with this part of the plan, the small states approved, pleased that they would keep as much power as they had under the Articles of Confederation.

The large states liked the second part of the plan. This stated that in the lower house, called the House of Representatives, the number of seats available to each state would be based on population. Voters in each state would directly choose each member. This idea closely resembled the one presented in the Virginia Plan. The Great Compromise passed in a very close vote on July 16, 1787.

With this matter settled, the delegates could turn their attention to another, perhaps more complicated, issue. This, too, centered around representation. If a state's population would determine the number of votes it had in the House of Representatives, could enslaved persons be counted as part of that population?

★ The Three-Fifths Compromise

Delegates disagreed bitterly on this issue. States from the North had economies that differed greatly from those in the South. Manufacturing and trade made up the economy in the North, where workers were mostly free men and women. The South was primarily agricultural. Enslaved African American men and women worked on its plantations.

The Southern states wanted to count enslaved persons as part of their population. By doing this, they could have more representatives in Congress. They did not want to count enslaved persons as a basis for paying taxes to the national government, though. This would make their taxes higher. The Northern states, on the other hand, thought enslaved persons should be counted for tax purposes, but not for representation in the House.

A Solution

To solve the problem, the delegates finally agreed to the **Three-Fifths Compromise.** According to the terms of this compromise, only three-fifths of the enslaved people in Southern states would be counted for both representation and taxation. The Northern states agreed, even though the Confederation Congress had earlier banned slavery in the Northwest Territory. The Northern states did not want to risk stalling the convention again.

Other compromises on slavery occurred at the convention. Northerners agreed that Congress could not outlaw the slave trade for 20 years. They also agreed that no state could stop an escaped slave from being returned to a slaveholder. Although some delegates criticized these compromises, their desire to establish an effective national government outweighed their desire to act against slavery.

★ Signing the Constitution

After four months of hard work, the delegates completed the new Constitution. Thirteen delegates had returned home; the remaining 42 named a committee to write the final draft. On September 17, 1787, 39 delegates signed the document.

Three refused to sign: George Mason of Virginia, who opposed the Constitution until his death; Edmund Randolph from Virginia, who eventually supported its approval by the states; and Elbridge Gerry from Massachusetts. Now the new Constitution would go to the states, where at least 9 of the 13 states would have to ratify it before it could become the law of the land.

Their work concluded, the delegates reviewed their efforts. No one seemed completely happy with the final plan, but most agreed it presented a vast improvement on the Articles they hoped it would replace. Madison recorded the reaction of the United States's most eminent citizen, Benjamin Franklin:

Doctor Franklin, looking toward the President's chair, at the back of which a rising sun happened to be painted . . . 'I have,' said he, 'often and often in the course of the Session . . . looked at that [sun] behind the President without being able to tell whether it was rising or setting; but now, at length I have the happiness to know it is a rising and not a setting Sun.'

★ SECTION 3 REVIEW ★

Checking for Understanding

1. **Identify** Benjamin Franklin, James Madison, Edmund Randolph, William Paterson.
2. **Define** Constitutional Convention, veto, compromise.
3. **What** was the major difference between the Virginia Plan and the New Jersey Plan?
4. **What** compromises did the Northern and Southern states agree to at the Constitutional Convention? Why did the delegates think these compromises were necessary?

Critical Thinking

5. **Drawing Conclusions** The delegates at the Constitutional Convention were careful to keep the proceedings private. Why?

ACTIVITY

6. Imagine you are a delegate at the Constitutional Convention. Write a firsthand account of a compromise at the convention. Remember to keep in mind whether you are from a large or small state or from a Northern or Southern state.

★★★

A More Perfect Union

SETTING THE SCENE

Read to Learn . . .

★ how the Constitution divides power between federal and state governments.
★ how ideas from the Enlightenment helped shape the Constitution.

Terms to Know

★ separation of powers
★ federalism
★ electoral college
★ checks and balances
★ impeachment
★ amendment

People to Meet

★ John Locke
★ Baron de Montesquieu

► CELEBRATING THE CONSTITUTION

The delegates at the Constitutional Convention laid down the principles of government that have served Americans for generations. The document they created has outlived every other constitution in the world, clearly standing the test of time.

★ Ideas Behind the Constitution

As the delegates began to write the new Constitution, they drew from a variety of sources—from the governments of other nations, British law, European thinkers, and from their own state constitutions.

The Iroquois League

One model for the Constitution originated close to home. Around 1570, the various nations of Iroquois united. In the **Iroquois League,** member nations each governed their own affairs but joined together for defense.

Europe's Influence

Ideas from Europe also influenced the Framers of the Constitution. The idea of limiting the power of a ruler was taken from England's **Magna Carta** of 1215. The idea of representative government also came from England. Its Parliament had made laws for the country since the mid-1200s.

The Articles of Confederation and the United States Constitution

Powers of Federal Government	Articles of Confederation	United States Constitution
Declare war; make peace	●	●
Coin money	●	●
Manage foreign affairs	●	●
Establish a postal system	●	●
Impose taxes		●
Regulate trade		●
Organize a court system		●
Call state militia for service		●
Protect copyrights		●
Take other necessary actions to run the federal government		●

Chart Study

The Constitution extended federal powers beyond those granted under the Articles of Confederation. **Which document allowed the government to organize state militias?**

The Framers also looked to Enlightenment philosophers for ideas. Enlightenment thinkers believed that people could improve society by using reason. Some of the Framers had read the works of **John Locke** and the **Baron de Montesquieu** (MAHN•tuhs•KYOO).

In 1690 Locke had outlined his ideas in *Two Treatises on Government.* He believed all people had natural rights to life, liberty, and property. He also believed that government should function as a contract between the ruler and the ruled. If a ruler should violate the rights of the people, the people had a right to rebel, Locke thought.

Years later, Montesquieu had proposed another revolutionary concept. In 1748 he published *The Spirit of Laws,* in which he suggested limiting the power of government by separating the governing bodies. This concept is known as the separation of powers. Montesquieu thought a government's power should be shared among three branches—legislative, executive, and judicial. He believed in clearly defining rules of law. This would prevent individuals or groups from using the government for their own purposes.

★ A Stronger National Government

The division of power proved to be one of the biggest differences between the Articles of Confederation and the new Constitution. The debate over who should retain the most power—the national or state governments had been carried on for a long time. Basic economic and social issues were at stake. Under the Articles, the states had more power than the national government. Under the new Constitution, the states delegated, or gave up, some of those powers to the national government. At the same time, the states reserved, or kept, other powers.

The division of power between the national government and the states is called federalism, leading some people to refer to the national government as the **federal** government. Federalism gives the United States a flexible system of government. Citizens elect both state and national officials. The national government has the power to act for the country as a whole, and states have power over many local matters.

Powers of the Federal Government

Under the Articles of Confederation, the balance of power had been lopsided. The states had so much power that the national government became ineffective. To help keep the government's power in check, the Constitution outlines the powers of the federal government. These powers include the power to declare war, to issue money, to regulate trade with other countries and among the states, and to make treaties.

Powers of the State Governments

The Constitution provides that powers not specifically given to the federal government nor denied to the states are reserved to the states or the people. States have the power to regulate trade within their borders; to establish local governments; to conduct local elections and determine qualifications of voters in state elections; to establish public schools; and to provide for the safety, health, and welfare of their citizens.

Powers That Overlap

Under the Constitution, the state and federal governments share some powers. Both have the power to tax, to try criminals in court, and to build roads.

Supreme Law of the Land

When states and the federal government disagree, the Constitution is considered the supreme law of the land. This means that the national government has more power than the state governments when there is a conflict between the two.

★ Separation of Powers

The Constitution provided for a strong federal government. To keep it from becoming too powerful, the Framers found it necessary to separate the powers into three different branches. They did not believe a single body should make the laws, enforce the laws, and interpret the laws. They created three branches of government—the legislative, the executive, and the judicial—and defined the powers of each.

The Legislative Branch

The legislative branch of the national government is called the **United States Congress.** It is made up of the **Senate** and the **House of Representatives.** The main responsibility of this branch is to make laws. It also has the power to declare war and form armies, collect taxes, and set guidelines for trade among states and with other countries. Article I of the Constitution lists these powers.

Members of the House, called **representatives,** are elected by the people. The number of representatives in each state is based on that state's population. Representatives serve two-year terms. Members of the Senate, called **senators,** were once selected by the state legislatures. That changed in 1913, and now both representatives and senators are elected by voters. Each state has two senators who serve six-year terms.

The Executive Branch

Article II of the Constitution calls for an executive branch to carry out the laws passed by the legislative branch. This branch includes the Chief Executive—the **President**—and also the **Vice President** and any advisers. The President is commander in chief of the armed forces and is responsible for relations with other countries.

The Judicial Branch

Article III provides for the judicial branch. This branch includes the Supreme Court, the highest court of the land. The Supreme Court and other federal courts hear cases that involve constitutional rights, disputes between states, and laws passed by Congress.

★ Electing the President

Instead of allowing the people to elect the President directly, the writers of the Constitution developed the idea of an electoral college.

The electoral college is made up of people called **electors** who represent the voters in each state. The number of electors is the same as the total number of senators and representatives in that state. According to the Constitution, the electors met every four years to vote on a President. The candidate who received the most votes was elected President. The person who received the second highest number became Vice President.

We still use the electoral college today. In 1804, however, the Constitution was changed to allow the electors to vote separately for the President and Vice President.

★ Checks and Balances

The writers built safeguards into the Constitution to keep each branch from assuming too much authority. This system of safeguards is called checks and balances. It gives each branch control over the other branches.

For example, after Congress passes a bill, that bill cannot go into effect until the President signs it into law. This gives the executive branch a check on the legislative branch. The President can either sign the bill or veto it. If it is vetoed the Congress can override the veto with a two-thirds vote by both houses of Congress.

Besides overriding a veto, the Congress can check the President's power in other ways. The President possesses the power to make treaties with other countries, but the Senate must approve the treaty with a two-thirds vote. If a President behaves irre-

sponsibly or breaks a law while serving in office, the Congress can take the President to court. This process is called impeachment. An impeachment charge may lead to the removal of the President from office.

Both the President and Congress have ways to check the powers of the courts. The President is responsible for appointing all the federal judges, but the judges must then be approved by the Senate. Like the President, the judges can be removed from office by Congress if they break a law or behave in an irresponsible way.

★ Ratifying the Constitution

The Framers of the Constitution anticipated that ratification would be difficult. Rhode Island, which had boycotted the convention, certainly would not approve the document. It seemed foolish to insist on unanimous approval. Instead, the Constitution provided that ratification by 9 of the 13 states would be sufficient.

Heated debates soon spread throughout the states. Americans divided into two groups. **Federalists** favored the Constitution and the strong national government it created. **Anti-Federalists** did not want the Constitution to replace the Articles of Confederation.

Federalists and Anti-Federalists

James Madison, Alexander Hamilton, and **John Jay** became the best-known Federalists. Using pen names, they wrote a series of essays, called *The Federalist* papers, defending the Constitution and urging others to support it.

▶ CHAIR USED BY WASHINGTON AT THE CONSTITUTIONAL CONVENTION

Linking Past and Present

Dancing

From rural farms to urban mansions, dance in colonial America was often a common recreation.

▶ **DANCING THE MINUET**

Then

Colonial Dance

During the colonial period, the minuet, a gliding dance in 3/4 time, dominated European social dancing. Couples performed line dances such as the reel to the accompaniment of a fiddler. The reel soon gave way to a more daring dance called the cotillion, a dance imported from the courts of France. This dance was the forerunner of modern square dancing.

Now

Modern Forms

During the twentieth century, American popular music incorporated African American, Cuban, and South American rhythms to create new dances. Just as the minuet characterized its era, such dances as the Charleston, the tango, the samba, and the bossa nova dominated different eras during the twentieth century. Eventually, the new forms combined to produce today's highly individualized and free-moving dancing.

▶ **MODERN DANCERS**

Federalists pointed out that the weaknesses of the Articles of Confederation actually weakened the entire country. They stressed that only unity among the states would ensure protection against threats to peace from inside as well as outside the country.

Anti-Federalists included **John Hancock, Samuel Adams,** and **Patrick Henry.** They attacked almost everything about the Constitution and complained that it failed to protect basic liberties. Because of this, they reasoned, the government under the Constitution could easily take these rights away. In addition, they argued that the delegates had been charged with repairing the Articles of Confederation, not writing an entirely new document. The delegates had done far more than they had had a right to do.

Responding to one of the Anti-Federalist objections, Federalists promised that if the states ratified the Constitution, **amendments,** or additions and changes, would be made to provide a bill of rights to protect the people.

The Vote

Ratification was to be decided by special conventions to be called in each state. This process was supported by the Declaration of Independence which stated that governments "derive their just powers from the consent of the governed."

As the doors of the state conventions opened in the fall of 1787, the debates began. By the year's end, Delaware, Pennsylvania, and New Jersey had ratified the Constitution. The next three states, Georgia, Connecticut, and Massachusetts, gave their votes of approval early in 1788. Within months Maryland and South Carolina also approved the Constitution.

New Hampshire ratified the Constitution in June 1788—the ninth state to do so.

The Ninth PILLAR erected !
"The Ratification of the Conventions of nine States, shall be sufficient for the establishment of this Constitution, between the States so ratifying the same." Art. vii.
INCIPIENT MAGNI PROCEDERE MENSES.

If it is not up it will rise.

The Attraction must be irresistible

Picturing History

▲ SUPPORT FOR RATIFICATION A Pro-Federalist cartoon celebrates Virginia and New York's becoming the tenth and eleventh states to ratify the Constitution in 1788. **From the cartoon, which state was first to ratify the Constitution?**

The Constitution could now go into effect. The new government could not hope to succeed, however, without the participation of its two largest states—Virginia and New York. By the end of June, both had ratified the document by narrow margins.

By the end of 1788, only two states had yet to ratify the Constitution. Both North Carolina and Rhode Island waited until the new government began to function before they voted for ratification. North Carolina voted in 1789. Rhode Island, which had also refused to participate in the convention, became the very last state to ratify in 1790.

★ Adding a Bill of Rights

The first Congress served in many ways as a continuation of the Constitutional Convention. Its most important task was adding a bill of rights to the Constitution. Congress approved 12 amendments on September 25, 1789. Ten of them were ratified by the states by the end of 1791. We know these amendments today as the **Bill of Rights.**

You will learn more about the Bill of Rights, the Constitution, and the rights and responsibilities of citizens in the *Citizenship Handbook* that follows this chapter.

★ SECTION 4 REVIEW ★

Checking for Understanding

1. **Identify** John Locke, Baron de Montesquieu.

2. **Define** separation of powers, federalism, electoral college, checks and balances, impeachment, amendment.

3. **What** ideas influenced the Framers and shaped the Constitution?

4. **How** does the Constitution divide power between the national and state governments?

Critical Thinking

5. **Making Inferences** Why was it important that New York and Virginia ratify the Constitution even though it had already been approved by nine states?

ACTIVITY

6. Create a chart comparing the Articles of Confederation with the Constitution of the United States.

BUILDING SKILLS
Critical Thinking Skills

Distinguishing Fact From Opinion

Suppose a friend says, "Our school's basketball team is awesome. That's a fact." Actually, it is not a fact; it is an opinion. Can you tell the difference?

▼ HIGH SCHOOL BASKETBALL TEAM

Learning the Skill

If your friend had said, "We have the highest-ranking team in the state," that could be a fact. Facts answer specific questions such as what happened, who did it, when and where did it happen, and why did it happen? Statements of fact can be checked for accuracy and proven. The first statement about the basketball team cannot be proven. We can look up the rankings of state teams, though, and determine whether the second statement is a fact.

Opinions express beliefs and feelings. Although they may truly reflect someone's thoughts, we cannot prove or disprove them. Opinions often begin with phrases such as *I believe, I think, probably, it seems to me,* or *in my opinion.* They often contain words such as *might, could, should,* and *ought* and superlatives such as *best, worst,* and *greatest.*

If you confuse opinions and facts, the information you gather or convey to others may be inaccurate. To distinguish between the two, ask yourself these questions: Does this statement give specific information about an event? Can I check the accuracy of this statement? Does this statement express someone's feelings or beliefs? Does it include words such as *I believe* or superlatives such as *the greatest?*

Facts and opinions can both contribute valuable information about history. Facts provide specific information about events. Opinions reflect how people feel about these events.

Practicing the Skill

Read each statement below. Write **F** for each fact and explain how you could check its accuracy. Write **O** for each opinion and identify words and phrases that indicate it is an opinion.

1. The Articles of Confederation set up a one-house legislature in which each state had a single vote.

2. During the Confederation period, the national government could not raise money through taxes.

3. The Articles of Confederation was a total disaster for the new American states.

4. The central government should be weak so that states have more power.

5. We ought to scrap the Articles of Confederation and make a new plan for the government.

APPLYING THE SKILL

6. Create a sales pitch for a product or service. Use an actual product or service or create one of your own. Include at least five facts and five opinions in your sales pitch and present it to the class. Have students identify the facts and opinions.

273

Using Key Vocabulary

Use the vocabulary words below to complete the following sentences.

> veto
> Anti-Federalists
> economic depression
> federalism
> ratify

1. At least 9 of the 13 states had to _____ the Constitution before it could go into effect.

2. After the American Revolution, the states experienced a(n) _____.

3. The President can _____ decisions made by the legislature.

4. The division of power between national and state governments is called _____.

5. The _____ tried to keep the states from ratifying the Constitution.

Reviewing Facts

1. **Why** was the Northwest Ordinance necessary?

2. **What** caused Shays's Rebellion?

3. **What** was the Three-Fifths Compromise?

4. **Why** did the Constitution divide the federal government into three branches?

5. **What** powers are given to both federal and state governments?

Understanding Concepts

American Democracy

1. Why were many Americans afraid of a strong central government?

2. What was the main difference between the Articles of Confederation and the Constitution regarding the amount of power granted to state governments and to the national government?

3. What is a republic?

Civil Rights and Liberties

4. In what ways were the delegates to the Constitutional Convention representative of the people? In what ways were they not representative?

5. What powers does the Supreme Court have to protect the rights of citizens?

Critical Thinking

1. **Hypothesizing** Why was a powerful national government necessary to unite the 13 states?

2. **Drawing Conclusions** Why did the Northern states agree to the Three-Fifths Compromise and other compromises on slavery?

3. **Analyzing Information** Why did the Framers of the Constitution call for ratification by only 9 of 13 states, and not all? Do you think this was wise or foolish? Why?

4. **Predicting Consequences** If the Baron de Montesquieu read the new Constitution of the United States, what do you think he would say about it? Would he have signed it? Why or why not?

History and Geography

Communication

By 1790 Philadelphia was one of the information capitals of the United States. The map on page 275 shows the number of days it took for newspapers in Philadelphia to publish events that occurred elsewhere. Study the map and then answer the questions that follow.

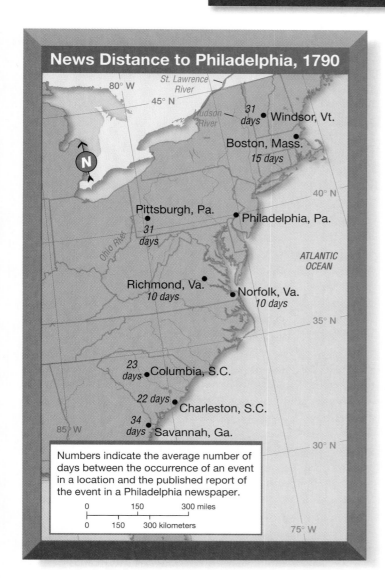

News Distance to Philadelphia, 1790

Windsor, Vt. 31 days

Boston, Mass. 15 days

Pittsburgh, Pa. 31 days

Philadelphia, Pa.

Richmond, Va. 10 days

Norfolk, Va. 10 days

Columbia, S.C. 23 days

Charleston, S.C. 22 days

Savannah, Ga. 34 days

ATLANTIC OCEAN

Numbers indicate the average number of days between the occurrence of an event in a location and the published report of the event in a Philadelphia newspaper.

0   150   300 miles
0   150   300 kilometers

research to come up with interview questions focusing on the new Constitution. Have one student be the host who asks questions and makes comments. The other students should play the roles of a wealthy merchant, a poor farmer, a Southern plantation owner, a Native American, and an enslaved African American.

Practicing Skills

Distinguishing Fact From Opinion

The sentences below are taken from a speech by Patrick Henry in 1788 opposing the adoption of the Constitution. For each numbered sentence, write *F* if it is a fact and *O* if it is an opinion.

[1] ". . . you ought to be extremely cautious, watchful, jealous of your liberty; [2] for instead of securing your rights, you may lose them forever. [3] If a wrong step be now made, the republic may be lost forever. . . . [4] I have the highest respect for those gentlemen who formed the convention. . . . [5] That they exceeded their power is perfectly clear."

1. **Movement** How long, on average, did it take information from Pittsburgh to reach Philadelphia? From Savannah? From Windsor?

2. **Region** What effect do you think this information time lag might have had on different regions of the country?

Cooperative Learning Interdisciplinary Activity: Language Arts

In a small group write a script for a television newsmagazine called "You Are There." Do

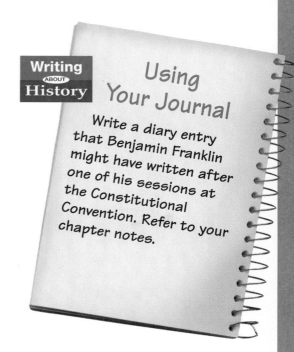

Writing ABOUT History

Using Your Journal

Write a diary entry that Benjamin Franklin might have written after one of his sessions at the Constitutional Convention. Refer to your chapter notes.

Citizenship Handbook
and
United States Constitution

For more than 200 years, the United States has flourished. As citizens we enjoy the rewards of our system of government, but we also have certain responsibilities. Through our participation, this system will continue to provide the blessings of life, liberty, and the pursuit of happiness.

★★★

A Lasting Plan of Government

SETTING THE SCENE

Read to Learn . . .

★ what goals shape the Constitution.
★ how the Constitution is organized.
★ how amendments to the Constitution have expanded American democracy.

Terms to Know

★ Preamble
★ article
★ checks and balances
★ amendment
★ federalism

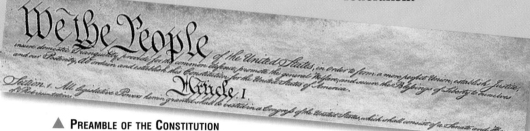

▲ PREAMBLE OF THE CONSTITUTION

The Constitution is the nation's most important document. Written in 1787, it set up a system of government that has weathered crisis and change for more than 200 years. Its priceless heritage is its ability to adapt, or change, while preserving the basic form of American government.

★ The Constitution

The Constitution is the basic law of the United States. Although it is a relatively short document, it manages to accomplish a great deal in very few words.

The Constitution's most obvious purpose was to provide a framework for the United States government. The Constitution does more than outline the structure of our government, however. As the highest authority of the nation, it has legal and political force. The power of all the branches of government and all elected officials, even the President, comes from the Constitution.

The Preamble

The Constitution begins with an introduction, or Preamble. The Preamble identifies ideas that the government stands for and states the purpose of the Constitution.

❝ We, the people of the United States, in Order to form a more perfect Union, establish Justice, insure domestic Tranquility, provide for the common defence, promote the general Welfare, and secure the Blessings of Liberty to ourselves and our Posterity, do ordain and establish this Constitution for the United States of America. ❞

▲ **STUDENTS VIEW ORIGINAL CONSTITUTION**

The Goals

The middle of the Preamble lists six goals for the United States government:

1. To "form a more perfect Union"—to allow the states to operate as a single country, for the benefit of all

2. To "establish Justice"—to make certain that all citizens are treated fairly and equally

3. To "insure domestic Tranquility"—to keep peace among the people

4. To "provide for the common defense"—to maintain armed forces to protect the country and its citizens from attack

5. To "promote the general Welfare"—to ensure, as much as possible, that citizens will be free from poverty, hunger, and disease

6. To "secure the Blessings of Liberty to ourselves and our Posterity"—to guarantee that no American's basic rights will be taken away, now or in the future (*Posterity* means generations not yet born.)

The Articles

Following the Preamble, the Constitution is broken into seven parts, or articles. The Founders saw the Constitution as a contract between people and their government. The seven articles set forth the terms of the contract. The first three articles describe the powers and responsibilities of the three branches of government.

Article I

Article I states that a Congress made up of two houses—the Senate and the House of Representatives—will carry out the legislative duties of government. The article then describes how each house will be organized and how its members will be chosen.

The article also lists the powers given to Congress, including the power to tax, to regulate trade, to coin money, and to declare war. Following this list is another that tells what powers are denied to Congress.

Article II

Article II deals with the executive branch and provides for a President and Vice President to carry out the duties of this branch. The article explains how these two leaders are to be chosen. It then goes on to list the President's powers, including the power to command the armed forces, to make treaties with other nations, and to pardon criminals. The President also has the power to appoint certain government officials. Under the system of checks and balances, however, the Senate must approve these appointments. The system of checks and balances is explained in detail in the next section of the *Handbook.*

Article III

Article III gives the judicial powers of government to a Supreme Court and other federal courts. The President appoints the judges of these courts. These judges serve for life or, in the words of the Constitution, "during good behavior." Article III states that the courts will have the power to judge "all cases . . . arising under this Constitution." This statement allows the Supreme Court to prevent the other branches from violating the Constitution.

Articles IV–VII

Article IV explains the relationship between the states and the national government. Article V specifies how the Constitution can be changed. Article VI discusses general provisions about the government. Article VII states that the Constitution will go into effect after nine states ratify it.

★ Amending the Constitution

Any change in the Constitution is called an amendment. Article V of the Constitution explains the two steps in the amendment process: An amendment must first be proposed, and then it must be ratified.

An amendment may be proposed in either of two ways: by vote of two-thirds of the members of both houses of Congress or by a national convention. Two-thirds of the state legislatures must request a national convention. (Such a convention has never been called.)

Ratifying Amendments

Once an amendment has been proposed, three-fourths of the states must ratify it. The states have two ways to ratify an amendment: either by a vote in each state legislature or by calling special state conventions. Only one amendment, the Twenty-first Amendment, was ratified by means of state conventions. Since 1789 more than 9,000 amendments have been proposed. Only 27 have been ratified.

In addition to deciding which ratification method will be used, Congress also sets a time limit on ratification. Since the early 1900s, Congress has called for a

seven-year time limit. If three-fourths of the states have not approved an amendment by this time, it dies. Congress, however, can extend the time limit.

★ Bill of Rights

The Constitution describes the powers and authority of the national government. The first 10 amendments to the Constitution, known as the Bill of Rights, describe the powers and rights of American citizens. These amendments, ratified in 1791, reflect the belief of the Framers of the Constitution in the principle of limited government. The amendments place strict limits on how the national government can use its power over the people.

First Amendment

The First Amendment is probably the best known and most cherished part of the Bill of Rights. It protects five basic freedoms that are essential to the American way of life: freedom of religion, speech, the press, assembly, and to petition the government.

Second Amendment

The Second Amendment guarantees Americans the right to serve in a state militia and to bear arms.

Third Amendment

The Third Amendment limits the power of the national government to force Americans to quarter, or house, soldiers. In peacetime, soldiers may not move into private homes except with the owner's consent. In times of war, the practice is also prohibited unless people are requested to do so by law.

Fourth Amendment

The Fourth Amendment, sometimes known as the Privacy Amendment, protects Americans against unreasonable searches and seizures.

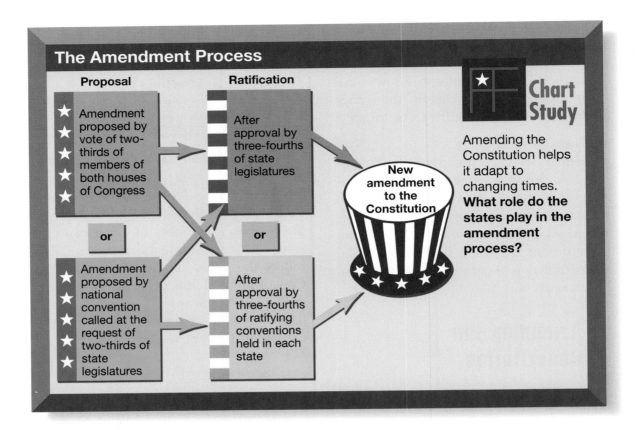

The Amendment Process

Proposal

★ Amendment proposed by vote of two-thirds of members of both houses of Congress

or

★ Amendment proposed by national convention called at the request of two-thirds of state legislatures

Ratification

After approval by three-fourths of state legislatures

or

After approval by three-fourths of ratifying conventions held in each state

New amendment to the Constitution

Chart Study

Amending the Constitution helps it adapt to changing times. **What role do the states play in the amendment process?**

Fifth Amendment

The Fifth Amendment protects the rights of people accused of a crime. The amendment states that no one can be put on trial without first being **indicted,** or formally accused, by a group of citizens called a grand jury.

The Fifth Amendment also protects people from **double jeopardy.** This means that people who are accused of a crime and judged not guilty may not be put on trial again for the same crime.

In addition, the Fifth Amendment protects an accused person's right to remain silent. It guarantees that people cannot be forced to testify against themselves.

The Fifth Amendment states that no one may be denied life, liberty, or property without **due process of law.** This means following procedures established by law and guaranteed by the Constitution.

Finally, the Fifth Amendment also protects a person's property rights. It limits the government's power of **eminent domain.** Eminent domain is the right of government to take private property (usually land) for public use.

Footnotes to History

The Latest Change   The most recent amendment to be added to the Constitution was the Twenty-seventh Amendment. It was proposed on September 25, 1789, but not ratified until May 7, 1992. This amendment prevents Congress from passing immediate salary increases for itself. It delays congressional pay raises until after the next election. Congress passed the amendment in 1789 and sent it to the states for ratification. Because no time limit was set for its ratification, the proposal did not become part of the Constitution until Michigan became the 38th state to ratify it, 202 years later.

Sixth Amendment

The Sixth Amendment guarantees additional rights to people accused of crimes. It requires that they be told the exact nature of the charges against them. It also requires that the accused be allowed a trial by jury. A person, though, may ask to be tried only by a judge.

Accused individuals must have the right to hear and question all witnesses against them. They must also be permitted to call witnesses in their own defense. Finally, they are entitled to have a lawyer. Since the amendment was written, the Supreme Court has ruled that if an accused person cannot afford to hire a lawyer, the government must provide one. The government will pay the fees of this court-appointed lawyer.

Seventh Amendment

The Seventh Amendment guarantees the right to a jury trial in civil cases if the amount of money involved is more than $20. It does not, however, require a trial. Both sides may decide to have their dispute settled by a judge instead.

Eighth Amendment

The Eighth Amendment forbids excessive bail—that is, an amount that is much too high. The Eighth Amendment also forbids "cruel and unusual punishments." For many years, Americans have debated what this really means. It is generally agreed that it means that punishment should be in proportion to the crime committed.

Ninth Amendment

The Ninth Amendment makes clear that the rights spelled out in the Constitution are not the only rights of the American people.

Tenth Amendment

The Tenth Amendment is also a reminder of what the Constitution does not say. In this case, it concerns the principle of federalism. Federalism is a system of government in which the power to govern is shared between the national government and the states. The Constitution talks about certain powers of national and state governments. Many other powers of government—such as the power to set up schools or to license lawyers—are not mentioned at all.

Under the Tenth Amendment, any powers the Constitution does not specifically give to the national government are reserved for the states or for the people.

★ SECTION 1 REVIEW ★

Checking for Understanding

1. **Define** Preamble, article, checks and balances, amendment, federalism.
2. **What** six goals of government are stated in the Preamble?
3. **How** is the Constitution organized?
4. **Why** have amendments been added to the Constitution?
5. **What** is the meaning of *double jeopardy* as it is used in the Fifth Amendment?

Critical Thinking

6. **Interpreting Primary Sources** Study the Preamble to the Constitution. Why might this sentence encourage good citizenship?

ACTIVITY

7. Photograph scenes in your community that show the freedoms guaranteed in the Bill of Rights. Put your photos on a poster entitled "The Face of Liberty."

★★★★★★★★★★★★★★★★★★★★★★★★★★★★★★★★★★★★

Five Principles of the Constitution

SETTING THE SCENE

Read to Learn . . .

★ what five principles guided the Framers of the Constitution.
★ how national and state governments share power.
★ how power is divided in the federal government.
★ how the system of checks and balances works.

Terms to Know

★ liberty
★ popular sovereignty
★ representative democracy
★ direct democracy
★ electoral college
★ tyranny
★ federalism
★ veto

▶ IOWA STATE CAPITOL

T he nation's Founders respected **lib-erty**, or the freedom of people to live as they choose. Experience had taught them, however, that people do not always choose wisely or fairly. Therefore, they wanted to create a government strong enough to control acts of selfishness or injustice.

To balance liberty with a strong government, the Founders relied on five principles, or rules. These principles include: **popular sovereignty, limited government, federalism, separation of powers,** and **checks and balances.**

★ Popular Sovereignty

The Declaration of Independence says government gets its power from "the con-sent of the governed." This idea is the basis for the principle of **popular sovereignty**. *Sovereignty* means "authority," and *popular* means "of the people." So popular sovereignty is the "authority of the people." In other words, the people hold the final authority, or ruling power, in government.

Indirect Rule

In 1787 popular sovereignty was a controversial idea. Even the Framers wanted to avoid giving the people too much power. They did not want to encourage mob rule, or rule by a lawless mass of people. The Framers also worried that smaller, less powerful groups might suffer. As a result, they established a **representative democracy**. In this type of government, people elect leaders or officials to make decisions for them.

A representative democracy allowed the government to grow. Even in the late 1700s, the United States had too many people for everyone to take part directly in decision making. As the nation grew, direct democracy—decision making by all the people—would have been even more impossible.

A Growing Voice

The Constitution as written by the Founders allowed the people to vote directly for members of the House of Representatives in Congress. State legislatures, however, chose members of the Senate. As a result, the people—who elected their state legislatures—voted indirectly for their senators.

The Founders also set up a system for indirect election of the President. Each state was to choose a group of officials called **electors** according to a method decided by the state legislature. The electors would meet to vote on the state's choice for President. This system of indirect election of the President is called the electoral college.

Over time, American voters demanded a greater role in government. In 1913, the Seventeenth Amendment ended the indirect election of senators. Now people vote directly for members of both houses of Congress. The electoral college, however, still chooses the President even though citizens also vote for this office.

Over the past 200 years, more people have won the right to vote. In the late 1700s, only white male property owners over age 21 could vote. Today all eligible citizens over age 18 can take part in elections.

★ Limited Government

While the Founders wanted a government stronger than the one under the Articles of Confederation, they also wanted to guard against tyranny, or cruel and unjust rule. To meet these aims, the

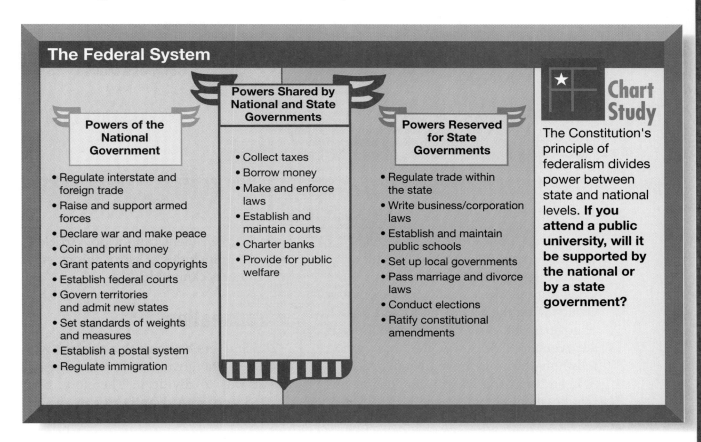

The Federal System

Powers of the National Government
- Regulate interstate and foreign trade
- Raise and support armed forces
- Declare war and make peace
- Coin and print money
- Grant patents and copyrights
- Establish federal courts
- Govern territories and admit new states
- Set standards of weights and measures
- Establish a postal system
- Regulate immigration

Powers Shared by National and State Governments
- Collect taxes
- Borrow money
- Make and enforce laws
- Establish and maintain courts
- Charter banks
- Provide for public welfare

Powers Reserved for State Governments
- Regulate trade within the state
- Write business/corporation laws
- Establish and maintain public schools
- Set up local governments
- Pass marriage and divorce laws
- Conduct elections
- Ratify constitutional amendments

Chart Study

The Constitution's principle of federalism divides power between state and national levels. **If you attend a public university, will it be supported by the national or by a state government?**

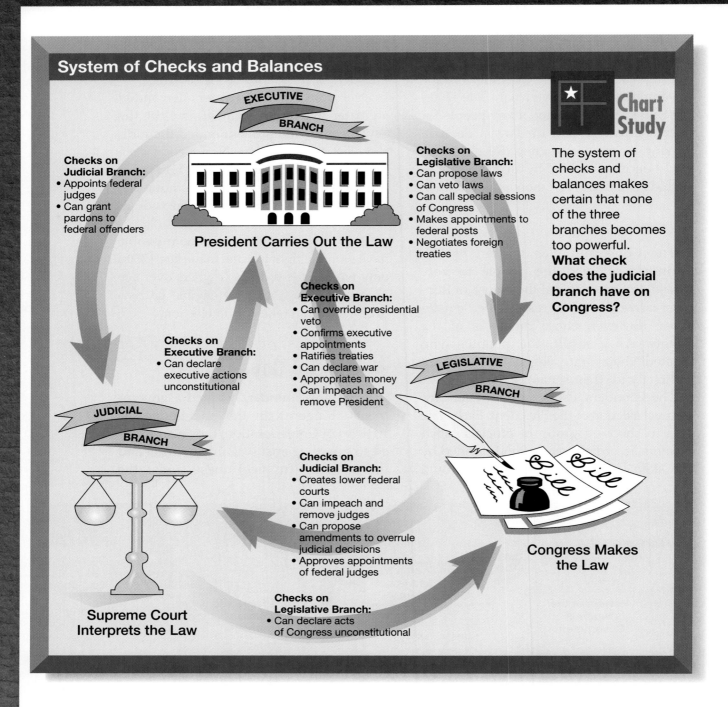

System of Checks and Balances

EXECUTIVE BRANCH

President Carries Out the Law

Checks on Judicial Branch:
• Appoints federal judges
• Can grant pardons to federal offenders

Checks on Legislative Branch:
• Can propose laws
• Can veto laws
• Can call special sessions of Congress
• Makes appointments to federal posts
• Negotiates foreign treaties

Checks on Executive Branch:
• Can override presidential veto
• Confirms executive appointments
• Ratifies treaties
• Can declare war
• Appropriates money
• Can impeach and remove President

Checks on Executive Branch:
• Can declare executive actions unconstitutional

JUDICIAL BRANCH

LEGISLATIVE BRANCH

Checks on Judicial Branch:
• Creates lower federal courts
• Can impeach and remove judges
• Can propose amendments to overrule judicial decisions
• Approves appointments of federal judges

Supreme Court Interprets the Law

Checks on Legislative Branch:
• Can declare acts of Congress unconstitutional

Congress Makes the Law

Chart Study

The system of checks and balances makes certain that none of the three branches becomes too powerful. **What check does the judicial branch have on Congress?**

Framers set up a limited government, or one that does not have absolute authority.

The biggest limit on government is the Constitution. The Constitution spells out clearly what the members of each branch of government can and cannot do. If leaders overstep their power, the Constitution tells how they may be removed.

In addition, the Constitution denies certain powers to government. Article I, Section 9, specifically names things the federal government cannot do. Article I, Section 10, includes a list of things state governments cannot do.

★ Federalism

The Framers believed that the best way to prevent the government from abusing power was to divide it. Therefore, they divided and spread authority in several different ways. One way was to divide authority between the national government and state governments. This sharing of power between different levels of governments is known as federalism.

Division of Powers

To prevent arguments between federal and state governments, the Framers **delegated,** or assigned, certain powers to the federal government. They also **reserved,** or saved, certain other powers to the states. Finally, they listed **concurrent,** or shared, powers that both the federal and state governments could exercise. The federal system chart identifies each of these powers.

The Supremacy Clause

In a federal system, the laws of a state and the laws of the national government may conflict. To deal with this possibility, the writers of the Constitution included the supremacy clause. Found in Article VI, the supremacy clause states that the Constitution and the laws of the national government are the "supreme law of the land." In any conflict between national law and state law, the national law has the higher authority.

★ Separation of Powers

Although the Framers took power from the states, they did not give it to the national government unchecked. To prevent the national government from abusing its power, the Framers divided it among three branches. Each branch holds part of the power of government. The legislative branch makes the laws. The executive branch, headed by the President, carries out the laws. The judicial branch, headed by the Supreme Court, interprets laws.

★ Checks and Balances

The Framers did not stop at merely separating the federal government into three branches. To keep any one of these three branches from becoming too powerful, the Constitution also set up a system of checks and balances. Under this system each branch of government is able to check, or limit, the power of the others.

The President has an important check on the power of Congress. The President can veto, or reject, a bill Congress proposes and keep it from becoming a law.

Congress can also check the Chief Executive's power. It has the power to **override,** or defeat, the President's veto. To do so, however, requires a vote by two-thirds of the members of both houses.

The judicial branch can check the power of both the legislative and executive branches. The Supreme Court has the power to decide the meaning of laws and to declare that a law goes against the Constitution.

★ **SECTION 2 REVIEW** ★

Checking for Understanding

1. **Define** liberty, popular sovereignty, representative democracy, direct democracy, electoral college, tyranny, federalism, veto.

2. **Name** the three types of powers found in the Constitution.

3. **What** is the main goal of the system of checks and balances?

Critical Thinking

4. **Predicting Consequences**   Suppose the Framers had set up a direct democracy. How might our history have been different?

ACTIVITY

5. **List the five major principles of the Constitution. Then create drawings or find magazine clippings that illustrate each.**

★★★

Government in Action

SETTING THE SCENE

Read to Learn . . .

★ what clauses in the Constitution have allowed government to change.

★ how a bill becomes a law.

★ the roles of the President of the United States.

Terms to Know

★ precedent
★ bureaucracy
★ diplomacy
★ executive agreement
★ constituent
★ impeach

◀ U.S. PRESIDENTIAL SEAL

In 1787 nobody knew if the Constitution would work. "This is to be a political experiment," said James Madison. The experiment—and the Constitution—succeeded. One reason for the Constitution's success is that the Framers did not write complicated laws to set up the government. Instead, they used very general language. They left it up to future generations to fill in the details of government.

★ A Flexible Document

How has the Constitution kept up with changing times? One way is through the day-to-day practices of government leaders and citizens. Over time, these practices have brought so-called informal, or nonwritten, changes to the Constitution.

Elastic Clause

The Framers gave Congress the power to make "all laws which shall be necessary and proper" for carrying out the tasks of government. This provision—found in Article I, Section 8, Clause 18—is known as the **elastic clause,** or **necessary and proper clause.**

What does "necessary and proper" mean? The Framers never said. This gave the government a lot of freedom to act. As a result, the federal government—through the passage of new laws—has expanded its power greatly since 1787.

Commerce Clause

Article I, Section 8, Clause 3 is another example of the Constitution's general language. This clause says that Congress has the power to "regulate Commerce with foreign Nations, and among the several States."

Over time, the government has used this clause to exercise authority in a number of different areas. It has banned **discrimination,** or unfair treatment, of different races. It has built a sprawling interstate highway system. In the 1990s, it used the commerce clause to pass laws governing information sent over computer networks.

Judicial Review

The power of the Supreme Court to review government acts and possibly declare them unconstitutional is known as **judicial review.** The Constitution never directly gave the courts this power. A strong-willed chief justice named **John Marshall,** however, believed that this was what the Founders meant. In 1803, Marshall called an act of Congress unconstitutional in a landmark case known as *Marbury* v. *Madison.* By doing this, he established a precedent, or example, for future courts to follow.

Practice and Tradition

Routine political practices have changed government, too. The Constitution, for example, did not call for the President to have a **cabinet,** or panel of advisers. President George Washington started the practice by relying on a group of trusted assistants.

★ The Role of the President

As defined by the Constitution, the President has four main duties.

Chief Executive

An executive is a manager. As Chief Executive of the United States, the President's job is to manage the government by carrying out its laws. A great many laws

Picturing History

▲ ROLES OF THE PRESIDENT The President's main roles are chief executive, chief of state, commander in chief, and chief legislator. **Which role allows the President to sign legislation into law?**

exist. Therefore, the President relies on a huge bureaucracy, or organization of government workers.

The federal bureaucracy includes the departments that make up the cabinet. It also includes more than 30 executive agencies. Each agency is in charge of some special task or program. The National Aeronautics and Space Administration (NASA), for example, manages the nation's space program.

Chief of State

As chief of state, the President directs national diplomacy, or relations with foreign countries. Three powers help the President to carry out this task. They include the power to appoint ambassadors who represent the United States in other countries, the power to make treaties with foreign countries, and the power to issue executive agreements. An executive agreement is an agreement that the President makes directly with the head of state from another country.

Commander in Chief

The President serves as the highest-ranking officer in the armed services. Only Congress can declare war. The President, however, can order troops to become involved in serious situations at home and abroad without the approval of Congress. The President also has the power to appoint and remove commanding officers from service.

Chief Legislator

The Constitution does not give law-making powers to the President. The President still influences the passage of laws in two important ways. First, the President suggests laws to Congress and works for their passage. Second, the President can use the veto to prevent the passage of laws that the President opposes.

★ The Role of Congress

The President has a great deal of power. Congress, however, is the branch of government that touches our lives most closely.

Structure of Congress

Congress is made up of two houses—the **House of Representatives** and the **Senate.** The House has 435 voting members and

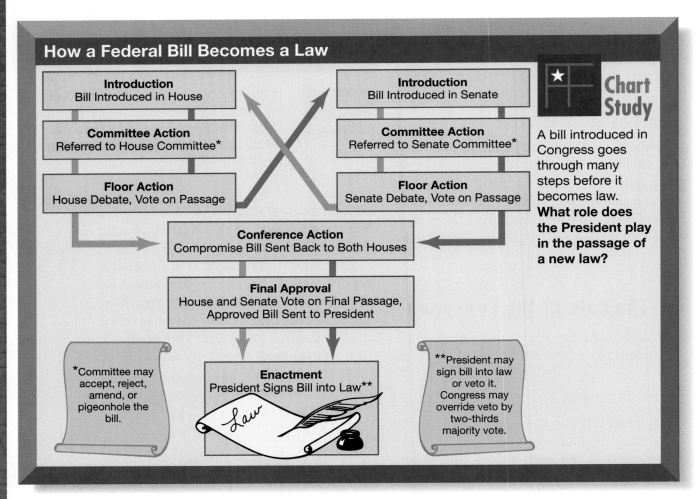

How a Federal Bill Becomes a Law

Introduction
Bill Introduced in House

Committee Action
Referred to House Committee*

Floor Action
House Debate, Vote on Passage

Introduction
Bill Introduced in Senate

Committee Action
Referred to Senate Committee*

Floor Action
Senate Debate, Vote on Passage

Conference Action
Compromise Bill Sent Back to Both Houses

Final Approval
House and Senate Vote on Final Passage, Approved Bill Sent to President

*Committee may accept, reject, amend, or pigeonhole the bill.

Enactment
President Signs Bill into Law**

Law

**President may sign bill into law or veto it. Congress may override veto by two-thirds majority vote.

★ **Chart Study**

A bill introduced in Congress goes through many steps before it becomes law. **What role does the President play in the passage of a new law?**

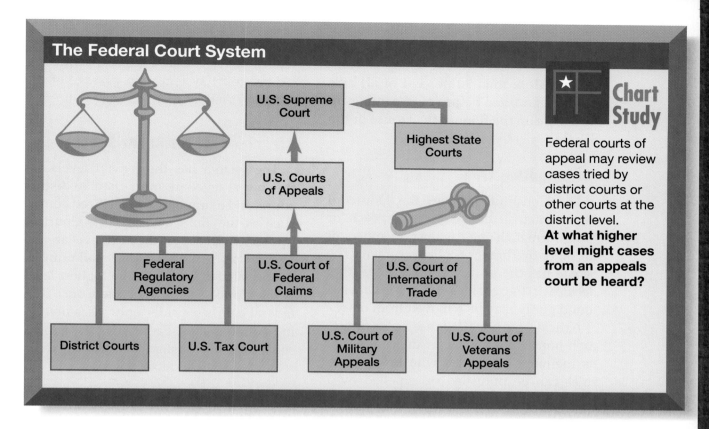

The Federal Court System

- U.S. Supreme Court
- Highest State Courts
- U.S. Courts of Appeals
- Federal Regulatory Agencies
- U.S. Court of Federal Claims
- U.S. Court of International Trade
- District Courts
- U.S. Tax Court
- U.S. Court of Military Appeals
- U.S. Court of Veterans Appeals

Chart Study

Federal courts of appeal may review cases tried by district courts or other courts at the district level. **At what higher level might cases from an appeals court be heard?**

5 nonvoting delegates from territories. The number of representatives from each state depends on a state's population. States with larger populations have more representatives. The Senate has 100 members—two for each state.

All representatives in the House serve two-year terms which begin and end at the same time. This means that every two years, the whole House comes up for reelection. Elections usually take place in even-numbered years. Senators serve six-year terms. Unlike the House, however, terms are staggered. About one-third of the Senate comes up for reelection every two years.

Representing Voters

The election schedules encourage members of Congress to keep in touch with their constituents. Constituents are the voters who elect public officials to represent them.

The election schedule of the House requires a representative seeking reelection to campaign among home con-

stituents at least every two years. The Senate's staggered election schedule means that one-third of the senators campaign at home every two years.

Lawmaking

Thousands of **bills,** or proposed laws, come before Congress each year. As the chart on page 288 shows, a bill must go through several steps to become law. All 535 members of Congress, therefore, cannot hope to consider all the bills presented to them.

To examine bills, Congress has committees in each house. **Standing committees,** or permanent committees, specialize in different areas, such as agriculture, trade, energy, or foreign affairs.

Both the Senate and the House must pass legislation in exactly the same language. Whenever they pass different versions of a bill, they create a **conference committee** of members of both houses to iron out their differences. The House and Senate must then approve the conference committee's version of the bill before it can be sent to the President.

Most bills never make it out of committee. More than 90 percent of all bills die in committee before ever coming up for a vote on the floor of the House or the Senate.

Investigating Wrongdoing

The Constitution gives the House of Representatives the power to impeach, or bring formal charges against, members of the other two branches of government. The Senate has the power to hold a trial that decides if the charges are true. Officials found guilty may be removed from office.

Article I, Section 3, Clause 2 also directs each house to set rules for the conduct of its members. Members who break these rules can be punished or expelled by a two-thirds vote of that house.

★ The Role of the Courts

The United States federal court system is only briefly described in the Constitution. However, it is one of the nation's most important institutions. Its function is to interpret the laws of the land and to preserve and protect the rights the Constitution guarantees. As such, it plays a vital role in the system of checks and balances that protects our democracy.

Article III of the Constitution called for the creation of a Supreme Court and a system of lower courts. Congress set up the federal court system with passage of the Judiciary Act of 1789.

Structure of the Court System

The system has three main levels. At the lowest level are more than 90 district courts and a number of specialized courts, such as the Tax Court and the Court of Military Appeals. At the next level are the 13 Courts of Appeals and a small number of specialized courts. At the highest level is the United States Supreme Court. The federal courts consider only cases involving national laws. Each state has its own separate court system for hearing cases related to state and local laws.

The Appeals Process

Most federal cases begin at the district level. In these courts, either a judge or a jury reaches a decision. Citizens unhappy with a district-level decision may appeal, or ask the next highest court to review the case.

The court of last appeal is the Supreme Court. Nine justices—including the chief justice—sit on the Court. Decisions of the Supreme Court are made by a simple majority, or a vote of at least five justices.

★ SECTION 3 REVIEW ★

Checking for Understanding

1. **Define** precedent, bureaucracy, diplomacy, executive agreement, constituent, impeach.
2. **How** does a bill become a law?
3. **Identify** the roles of the President of the United States.
4. **What** purpose do committees serve in Congress?

Critical Thinking

5. **Understanding Cause and Effect** How has the elastic clause helped government to change with the times?

ACTIVITY

6. Write a job description for one of the following officials: President, chief justice, member of the House or Senate.

Duties and Responsibilities of Citizens

★★★

SETTING THE SCENE

Read to Learn . . .

★ what major duties come with citizenship.
★ what the responsibilities of American citizens are.

Terms to Know

★ duties
★ responsibilities
★ toleration

◀ **VOTER AT THE POLLS**

As citizens of the United States, we are expected to carry out certain duties and responsibilities. Duties are things we are required to do; if we fail to perform them, we are subject to legal penalties, such as fines or imprisonment. Responsibilities, on the other hand, are things we should do; they are obligations that we fulfill voluntarily. Fulfilling both our duties and our responsibilities helps ensure that we have good government and that we continue to enjoy our rights.

★ Duties

Some countries require much from their citizens. In some countries, for example, citizens must serve in the armed forces for a period of time each year. In other countries, citizens are required to live in cities far away from their families and friends to work at jobs assigned to them by the government.

The United States government asks much less of its citizens than many other countries. Nevertheless, the government does require its citizens to perform the following duties.

Obey the Laws

This is a citizen's most important duty. If citizens do not obey the law, the government cannot maintain order and protect the health, safety, and property of its citizens. The laws we must obey, including criminal laws, traffic laws, and local laws, all have a purpose. Criminal laws are designed to prevent citizens from

Defend the Nation

All men aged 18 and over are required to register with the government in case the country needs to **draft,** or call up, men for military service. Since the end of the Vietnam War, there has been no draft, and American military service has been voluntary. Nevertheless, the government has the authority to use the draft if the country should suddenly have to go to war.

Serve in Court

The Constitution guarantees every citizen the right to a trial by jury. To ensure this, every citizen must be prepared to serve on a jury. People can ask to be excused from jury duty if they have a good reason, but it is better to serve if possible. People on trial depend on their fellow citizens to give a fair and just verdict at their trials. Another duty of citizens is to serve as witnesses at a trial, if called to do so.

Attend School

In most states, people are required to attend school until age 16. This is important both to you and to the government. School is where you acquire much of the knowledge and skills you will need to be a good citizen.

Picturing **History**

▲ NATURALIZATION Citizens from other nations become United States citizens through a process called naturalization. The process takes several years and involves many steps. **What are the duties of citizenship?**

harming one another; traffic laws prevent accidents; and local laws help people get along with one another.

Pay Taxes

Taxes pay for the government's activities. Without them, the federal government could not pay its employees, maintain an army and navy to defend its citizens, or help those in need. Your city could not hire police or firefighters, and your state could not pave roads or maintain prisons.

Citizens pay taxes in several ways. The federal government and some states and cities collect income taxes, a percentage of the wages people receive. Most states and some cities collect sales taxes. Your school district collects taxes on the residential and commercial property within the district.

★ Responsibilities

The responsibilities of citizenship are not as clear-cut as the duties. Because responsibilities are voluntary, people are not arrested or punished if they do not fulfill these obligations. The quality of our government and of our lives will diminish, however, if our responsibilities are not carried out.

Be Informed

Keep in mind that government exists to serve you. Therefore, one of your responsibilities as a citizen is to know what the government is doing and to voice your opinion about its actions. When the government learns that most people favor or oppose an action, it usually considers their wishes.

Vote

Voting is one of American citizens' most important responsibilities. By voting, people exercise their right of self-government. Voters choose the people who run the government, and in doing so, they give their consent to that government. If people do not like the way an elected official is doing the job, it is their responsibility to choose someone else for that job in the next election. Taking the responsibility to vote ensures that leadership is changed in a peaceful, orderly manner.

Participate in Government

Another responsibility of citizens is to participate in their community and in their government. Participating in your government and community is extremely important.

Think about what your community would be like if no one would serve as mayor, or no one would volunteer to fight fires or coach a baseball team, and if no one would ever speak out or do anything to help solve community problems.

Respect Rights of Others

To enjoy your rights to the fullest, you must be prepared to respect other people's rights as well. For example, if you live in an apartment building, you have an obligation to keep the volume on your radio or television down so that it does not disturb your

Picturing History

▲ CIVIC PARTICIPATION There are many ways for people to be responsible citizens. **What makes the responsibilities of citizenship different from the duties of citizenship?**

neighbors. You also expect them to do the same for you. Many of our laws have been enacted to encourage people to respect each other's rights. A person who continues to play a radio or television too loudly can be arrested for disturbing the peace.

Citizens have a responsibility to show the same respect for public property and for the property of others. Sometimes people who would not dream of breaking a neighbor's window will vandalize their school or a city bus because "no one owns it." Yet, such public property belongs to all of us, and we all pay if it is stolen or damaged.

Respect Diversity

Citizens have a responsibility to respect the rights of people with whom they disagree. Respecting and accepting others, regardless of their beliefs, practices, or other differences, is called toleration. It means giving people whose ideas you dislike a chance to express their opinions. Without toleration for the views of others, a real discussion or exchange of ideas is impossible.

One of America's great strengths has always been the diversity of its people. Immigrants have brought a variety of religions, traditions, and lifestyles to this country, and they continue to do so. As citizens, we all have a responsibility to respect the practices and traditions of others when they are different from our own, just as we expect others to respect our traditions.

Picturing History ▲ CONSTITUTION BICENTENNIAL One strength of the United States and its Constitution is respect for diversity. **What term describes accepting the beliefs of others?**

★ SECTION 4 REVIEW ★

Checking for Understanding

1. Define duties, responsibilities, toleration.
2. What are the major duties of American citizens?
3. What are the responsibilities of American citizens?
4. List three ways in which citizens might pay taxes.

Critical Thinking

5. Evaluating Information   Why are citizens' responsibilities to their communities such an important part of our democratic system?

ACTIVITY

6. Write a letter to the editor of your local newspaper expressing your opinion about an issue in your community.

HANDBOOK ★ REVIEW

Using Key Vocabulary

Match each item in Column A with the items in Column B.

Column A

1. Preamble
2. article
3. duties
4. federalism
5. representative democracy

Column B

a. things citizens are required to do
b. parts of a contract
c. decision making through elected officials
d. opening statement of Constitution
e. sharing of powers between national and state governments

Reviewing Facts

1. **Describe** the main parts of the Constitution.
2. **Describe** how power is divided in the federal government.
3. **Explain** the purpose of the electoral college and its membership.
4. **List** the five main principles of American government.
5. **State** some of the rights and duties of citizenship.

Understanding Concepts

Civil Rights and Liberties

1. What principles of government are reflected in the Bill of Rights?
2. How does due process of law protect individual rights?

American Democracy

3. Why is an educated population so important to maintaining the freedoms of a democratic society?

4. What clause in the Constitution allows the government to expand its powers?
5. Why is the principle of checks and balances important to American democracy?

Critical Thinking

1. **Analyzing Information** Review the six goals for the United States government as they are described in the Preamble to the Constitution. List them in order of importance as you think they should be carried out. Why did you select your first listed goal as most important? What goal would you eliminate if you had to? Why?

2. **Predicting Consequences** Suppose the Constitution had not provided for amendments. How might the history of our nation have been different?

3. **Comparing and Contrasting** Compare the powers of the federal government in 1787 with the powers of the federal government today. Do you think the Framers of the Constitution would approve of the changes? Why or why not?

Cooperative Learning Interdisciplinary Activity: Civics

Form a group to write a constitution for your school. Begin the document with a preamble that lists goals for school government. Next divide your group into smaller committees, each of which writes an article describing one branch of the school government. Be certain to list the functions of each branch. Meet again as a group to review and agree upon the articles.

As a group, decide if you think some powers should be denied to the school government and list these in another article. Finally, decide if you think a bill of rights is necessary. If so, list the rights you think should be added.

The Constitution of the United States

The Constitution of the United States is truly a remarkable document. It was one of the first written constitutions in modern history. The Framers wanted to devise a plan for a strong central government that would unify the country, as well as preserve the ideals of the Declaration of Independence. The document they wrote created a representative legislature, the office of President, a system of courts, and a process for adding amendments. For over 200 years, the flexibility and strength of the Constitution has guided the nation's political leaders. The document has become a symbol of pride and a force for national unity.

The entire text of the Constitution and its amendments follows. For easier study, those passages that have been set aside or changed by the adoption of amendments are printed in blue. Also included are explanatory notes that will help clarify the meaning of each article and section.

▲ INDEPENDENCE HALL, PHILADELPHIA

Preamble

We, the people of the United States, in Order to form a more perfect Union, establish Justice, insure domestic Tranquility, provide for the common defence, promote the general Welfare, and secure the Blessings of Liberty to ourselves and our Posterity, do ordain and establish this Constitution for the United States of America.

The Preamble introduces the Constitution and sets forth the general purposes for which the government was established. The Preamble also declares that the power of the government comes from the people.

The printed text of the document shows the spelling and punctuation of the parchment original.

Article I

Section 1

All legislative Powers herein granted shall be vested in a Congress of the United States, which shall consist of a Senate and House of Representatives.

Section 2

1. The House of Representatives shall be composed of Members chosen every second Year by the People of the several States, and the Electors in each State shall have the Qualifications requisite for Electors of the most numerous Branch of the State Legislature.

2. No Person shall be a Representative who shall not have attained to the Age of twenty-five Years, and been seven Years a Citizen of the United States, and who shall not, when elected, be an Inhabitant of that State in which he shall be chosen.

3. Representatives and direct Taxes shall be apportioned among the several states which may be included within this Union, according to the respective Numbers, which shall be determined by adding to the whole Number of free Persons, including those bound to Service for a Term of Years, and excluding Indians not taxed, three-fifths of all other Persons. The actual Enumeration shall be made within three Years after the first Meeting of the Congress of the United States, and within every subsequent Term of ten Years, in such Manner as they shall by Law direct. The Number of Representatives shall not exceed one for every thirty Thousand, but each state shall have at Least one Representative; and until such enumeration shall be made, the State of New Hampshire shall be entitled to chuse three; Massachusetts eight, Rhode Island and Providence Plantations one, Connecticut five, New York six, New Jersey four, Pennsylvania eight, Delaware one, Maryland six, Virginia ten; North Carolina five, South Carolina five, and Georgia three.

4. When vacancies happen in the Representation from any State, the Executive Authority thereof shall issue Writs of Election to fill such Vacancies.

5. The House of Representatives shall chuse their Speaker and other Officers; and shall have the sole Power of Impeachment.

Article I. The Legislative Branch

Section 1. Congress

The power to make laws is given to a Congress made up of two chambers to represent different interests: the Senate to represent the states; the House to be more responsive to the people's will.

Section 2. House of Representatives

1. Election and Term of Office

"Electors" means voters. Every two years the voters choose new Congress members to serve in the House of Representatives. The Constitution states that each state may specify who can vote. But the 15th, 19th, 24th, and 26th Amendments have established guidelines that all states must follow regarding the right to vote.

2. Qualifications

Representatives must be 25 years old, citizens of the United States for 7 years, and residents of the state they represent.

3. Division of Representatives Among the States

The number of representatives from each state is based on the size of the state's population. Each state is divided into congressional districts, with each district required to be equal in population. Each state is entitled to at least one representative. The number of representatives in the House was set at 435 in 1929. Since then, there has been a reapportionment of seats based on population shifts rather than on addition of seats.

Only three-fifths of a state's slave population was to be counted in determining the number of representatives elected by the state. Native Americans were not counted at all.

The "enumeration" referred to is the census, the population count taken every 10 years since 1790.

4. Vacancies

Vacancies in the House are filled through special elections called by the state's governor.

5. Officers

The speaker is the leader of the majority party in the House and is responsible for choosing the heads of various House committees. "Impeachment" means indictment, or bringing charges against an official.

Section 3. The Senate
1. Number of Members, Terms of Office, and Voting Procedure
Originally, senators were chosen by the state legislators of their own states. The 17th Amendment changed this, so that senators are now elected directly by the people. There are 100 senators, 2 from each state.

2. Staggered Elections; Vacancies
One-third of the Senate is elected every two years. The terms of the first Senate's membership was staggered: one group served two years, one four, and one six. All senators now serve a six-year term.

The 17th Amendment changed the method of filling vacancies in the Senate.

3. Qualifications
Qualifications for the Senate are more restrictive than those for the House. Senators must be at least 30 years old and they must have been citizens of the United States for at least 9 years. The Framers of the Constitution made the Senate a more elite body in order to produce a further check on the powers of the House of Representatives.

4. President of the Senate
The Vice President's only duty listed in the Constitution is to preside over the Senate. The only real power the Vice President has is to cast the deciding vote when there is a tie. However, modern Presidents have given their Vice Presidents new responsibilities.

5. Other Officers
The Senate selects its other officers, including a presiding officer (president pro tempore) who serves when the Vice President is absent or has become President of the United States.

6. Trial of Impeachments
When trying a case of impeachment brought by the House, the Senate convenes as a court. The chief justice of the United States acts as the presiding judge, and the Senate acts as the jury. A two-thirds vote of the members present is necessary to convict officials under impeachment charges.

7. Penalty for Conviction
If the Senate convicts an official, it may only remove the official from office and prevent that person from holding another federal position. However, the convicted official may still be tried for the same offense in a regular court of law.

Section 4. Elections and Meetings
1. Holding Elections
In 1842 Congress required members of the House to be elected from districts in states having more than one representative rather than at large. In 1845 it set the first Tuesday after the first Monday in November as the day for selecting presidential electors.

2. Meetings
The 20th Amendment, ratified in 1933, has changed the date of the opening of the regular session of Congress to January 3.

Section 3
1. The Senate of the United States shall be composed of two Senators from each State, chosen by the Legislature thereof; for six Years; and each Senator shall have one Vote.

2. Immediately after they shall be assembled in Consequence of the first Election, they shall be divided as equally as may be into three Classes. The Seats of the Senators of the first Class shall be vacated at the Expiration of the second Year, of the second Class at the Expiration of the fourth Year, and of the third Class at the Expiration of the sixth Year, so that one-third may be chosen every second Year; and if Vacancies happen by Resignations, or otherwise, during the Recess of the Legislature of any State, the Executive thereof may make temporary Appointments until the next Meeting of the Legislature, which shall then fill such Vacancies.

3. No person shall be a Senator who shall not have attained the Age of thirty Years, and been nine Years a Citizen of the United States, and who shall not, when elected, be an Inhabitant of that State in which he shall be chosen.

4. The Vice President of the United States shall be President of the Senate, but shall have no vote, unless they be equally divided.

5. The Senate shall chuse their Officers, and also a President pro tempore, in the absence of the Vice-President or when he shall exercise the Office of the President of the United States.

6. The Senate shall have the sole Power to try all impeachments. When sitting for that purpose they shall be on Oath or Affirmation. When the President of the United States is tried, the Chief Justice shall preside: And no person shall be convicted without the Concurrence of two-thirds of the Members present.

7. Judgment in Cases of Impeachment shall not extend further than to removal from Office, and disqualification to hold and enjoy any Office of Honor, Trust or Profit under the United States: but the Party convicted shall nevertheless be liable and subject to Indictment, Trial, Judgment and Punishment, according to Law.

Section 4
1. The Times, Places, and Manner of holding Elections for Senators and Representatives, shall be prescribed in each state by the Legislature thereof; but the Congress may at any time by Law make or alter such Regulations, except as to the Places of Chusing Senators.

2. The Congress shall assemble at least once in every Year, and such Meeting shall be on the first Monday in December, unless they shall by Law appoint a different Day.

Section 5

1. Each House shall be the Judge of the Elections, Returns and Qualifications of its own Members, and a Majority of each shall constitute a Quorum to do Business; but a smaller Number may adjourn from day to day, and may be authorized to compel the Attendance of absent Members, in such Manner, and under such Penalties as each House may provide.

2. Each House may determine the Rules of its Proceedings, punish its Members for disorderly Behaviour, and, with the Concurrence of two-thirds, expel a Member.

3. Each House shall keep a Journal of its Proceedings, and from time to time publish the same, excepting such Parts as may in their Judgment require Secrecy; and the Yeas and Nays of the Members of either House on any question shall, at the desire of one-fifth of those Present, be entered on the Journal.

4. Neither House during the Session of Congress, shall, without the Consent of the other, adjourn for more than three days, nor to any other Place than that in which the two Houses shall be sitting.

Section 6

1. The Senators and Representatives shall receive a Compensation for their Services, to be ascertained by Law, and paid out of the Treasury of the United States. They shall in all Cases, except Treason, Felony and Breach of the Peace be privileged from Arrest during their attendance at the Session of their respective Houses, and in going to and returning from the same; and for any Speech or Debate in either House, they shall not be questioned in any other place.

2. No Senator or Representative shall, during the Time for which he was elected, be appointed to any civil Office under the Authority of the United States, which shall have been created, or the Emoluments whereof shall have been encreased, during such time; and no Person holding any Office under the United States, shall be a Member of either House during his continuance in Office.

Section 7

1. All Bills for raising Revenue shall originate in the House of Representatives; but the Senate may propose or concur with Amendments as on other bills.

2. Every Bill which shall have passed the House of Representatives and the Senate, shall, before it become a Law, be presented to the President of the United States; If he approve he shall sign it, but if not he shall return it, with his Objections, to that House in which it shall have originated, who shall enter the Objections at large on their Journal, and proceed to reconsider it. If after such Reconsideration two-thirds of that House shall agree to pass the bill, it shall be sent, together with the objections, to the other House, by which it shall likewise be reconsidered, and if approved by two-thirds of that House, it shall

Section 5. Organization and Rules of Procedure

1. Organization

Until 1969 Congress acted as the sole judge of qualifications of its own members. In that year, the Supreme Court ruled that Congress could not legally exclude victorious candidates who met all the requirements listed in Article I, Section 2.

A "quorum" is the minimum number of members that must be present for the House or Senate to conduct sessions. For a regular House session, a quorum consists of the majority of the House, or 218 of the 435 members.

2. Rules

Each house sets its own rules, can punish its members for disorderly behavior, and can expel a member by a two-thirds vote.

3. Journals

In addition to the journals, a complete official record of everything said on the floor, as well as the roll call votes on all bills or issues, is available in the *Congressional Record*, published daily by the Government Printing Office.

4. Adjournment

Neither house may adjourn for more than three days or move to another location without the approval of the other house.

Section 6. Privileges and Restrictions

1. Pay and Privileges

To strengthen the federal government, the Founders set congressional salaries to be paid by the United States Treasury rather than by members' respective states. Originally, members were paid $6 per day. Salaries for senators and representatives are $129,500.

The "immunity" privilege means members cannot be sued or be prosecuted for anything they say in Congress. They cannot be arrested while Congress is in session, except for treason, major crimes, or breaking the peace.

2. Restrictions

"Emoluments" means salaries. The purpose of this clause is to prevent members of Congress from passing laws that would benefit them personally. It also prevents the President from promising them jobs in other branches of the federal government.

Section 7. Passing Laws

1. Revenue Bills

"Revenue" is income raised by the government. The chief source of government revenue is taxes. All tax laws must originate in the House of Representatives. This ensures that the branch of Congress which is elected by the people every two years has the major role in determining taxes. This clause does not prevent the Senate from amending tax bills.

2. How Bills Become Laws

A bill may become a law only by passing both houses of Congress and by being signed by the President. If the President disapproves, or vetoes, the bill, it is returned to the house where it originated, along with a written statement of the President's objections. If two-thirds of each house approves the bill after the President has vetoed it, it becomes law. In voting to override a President's veto, the votes of all members of Congress must be recorded in the journals or official records. If the President does not sign or veto a bill within 10 days (excluding Sundays), it becomes law. However, if Congress has adjourned during this 10-day period, the bill does not become law. This is known as a "pocket veto."

3. Presidential Approval or Veto

The Framers included this paragraph to prevent Congress from passing joint resolutions instead of bills to avoid the possibility of a presidential veto. A bill is a draft of a proposed law, whereas a resolution is the legislature's formal expression of opinion or intent on a matter.

Section 8. Powers Granted to Congress

1. Revenue

This clause gives Congress the power to raise and spend revenue. Taxes must be levied at the same rate throughout the nation.

2. Borrowing

The federal government borrows money by issuing bonds.

3. Commerce

The exact meaning of "commerce" has caused controversy. The trend has been to expand its meaning and, consequently, the extent of Congress's powers.

4. Naturalization and Bankruptcy

"Naturalization" refers to the procedure by which a citizen of a foreign nation becomes a citizen of the United States.

5. Currency

Control over money is an exclusive federal power; the states are forbidden to issue currency.

6. Counterfeiting

"Counterfeiting" means illegally imitating or forging.

7. Post Office

In 1970 the United States Postal Service replaced the Post Office Department.

8. Copyrights and Patents

Under this provision, Congress has passed copyright and patent laws.

9. Courts

This provision allows Congress to establish a federal court system.

10. Piracy

Congress has the power to protect American ships on the high seas.

11. Declare War

While the Constitution gives Congress the right to declare war, the United States has sent troops into combat without a congressional declaration.

become a Law. But in all such Cases the Votes of both Houses shall be determined by Yeas and Nays, and the Names of the Persons voting for and against the Bill shall be entered on the Journal of each House respectively. If any Bill shall not be returned by the President within ten Days (Sundays excepted) after it shall have been presented to him, the Same shall be a Law, in like Manner as if he had signed it, unless the Congress by their Adjournment prevent its Return, in which Case it shall not be a Law.

3. Every Order, Resolution, or Vote to which the Concurrence of the Senate and House of Representatives may be necessary (except on a question of Adjournment) shall be presented to the President of the United States; and before the Same shall take Effect, shall be approved by him, or, being disapproved by him, shall be repassed by two-thirds of the Senate and House of Representatives, according to the Rules and Limitations prescribed in the case of a Bill.

Section 8

The Congress shall have the Power

1. To lay and collect Taxes, Duties, Imposts and Excises, to pay the Debts and provide for the common Defence and general Welfare of the United States; but all Duties, Imposts and Excises shall be uniform throughout the United States;

2. To borrow money on the credit of the United States;

3. To regulate Commerce with foreign Nations, and among the several States, and with the Indian Tribes;

4. To establish an uniform Rule of Naturalization, and uniform Laws on the subject of Bankruptcies throughout the United States.

5. To coin Money, regulate the Value thereof, and of foreign Coin, and fix the Standard of Weights and Measures;

6. To provide for the Punishment of counterfeiting the Securities and current Coin of the United States;

7. To establish Post Offices and post Roads;

8. To promote the Progress of Science and useful Arts, by securing for limited Times to Authors and Inventors the exclusive Right to their respective Writings and Discoveries;

9. To constitute Tribunals inferior to the Supreme Court;

10. To define and punish Piracies and Felonies committed on the high Seas, and Offenses against the Law of Nations.

11. To declare War, grant Letters of Marque and Reprisal, and make Rules concerning Captures on Land and Water;

12. To raise and support Armies, but no Appropriation of Money to that Use shall be for a longer Term than two Years;

13. To provide and maintain a Navy;

14. To make Rules for the Government and Regulation of the land and naval forces;

15. To provide for calling forth the Militia to execute the Laws of the Union, suppress Insurrections, and repel Invasions;

16. To provide for organizing, arming, and disciplining, the Militia, and for governing such Part of them as may be employed in the Service of the United States, reserving to the States respectively, the Appointment of the Officers, and the Authority of training the Militia according to the discipline prescribed by Congress;

17. To exercise exclusive Legislation in all Cases whatsoever, over such District (not exceeding ten Miles square) as may, by Cession of particular States, and the acceptance of Congress, become the Seat of Government of the United States, and to exercise like Authority over all Places purchased by the Consent of the Legislature of the State in which the Same shall be, for the Erection of Forts, Magazines, Arsenals, dock-Yards, and other needful Buildings;—And

18. To make all Laws which shall be necessary and proper for carrying into Execution the foregoing Powers, and all other Powers vested by this Constitution in the Government of the United States, or in any Department or Officer thereof.

Section 9

1. The Migration or Importation of such Persons as any of the States now existing shall think proper to admit, shall not be prohibited by the Congress prior to the Year one thousand eight hundred and eight, but a tax or duty may be imposed on such importation, not exceeding ten dollars for each Person.

2. The privilege of the Writ of Habeas Corpus shall not be suspended, unless when in Cases of Rebellion or Invasion the public Safety may require it.

3. No Bill of Attainder or ex post facto Law shall be passed.

4. No capitation, or other direct, Tax shall be laid unless in Proportion to the Census or Enumeration herein before directed to be taken.

5. No Tax or Duty shall be laid on Articles exported from any State.

6. No Preference shall be given by any Regulation of Commerce or Revenue to the Ports of one State over those of another: nor shall Vessels bound to, or from, one State, be obliged to enter, clear, or pay Duties in another.

12. Army
This provision reveals the Framers' fears of a standing army.

13. Navy
This clause allows Congress to establish a navy.

14. Rules for Armed Forces
Congress may pass regulations that deal with military discipline.

15. Militia
The "militia" is now called the National Guard. It is organized by the states.

16. National Guard
Even though the National Guard is organized by the states, Congress has the authority to pass rules for governing its behavior.

17. Nation's Capital
This clause grants Congress the right to make laws for Washington, D.C.

18. Elastic Clause
This is the so-called "elastic clause" of the Constitution and one of its most important provisions. The "necessary and proper" laws must be related to one of the 17 enumerated powers.

Section 9. Powers Denied to the Federal Government

1. Slave Trade
This paragraph contains the compromise the Framers reached regarding regulation of the slave trade in exchange for Congress's exclusive control over interstate commerce.

2. Habeas Corpus
Habeas corpus is a Latin term meaning "you may have the body." A writ of habeas corpus issued by a judge requires a law official to bring a prisoner to court and show cause for holding the prisoner. The writ may be suspended only during wartime.

3. Bills of Attainder
A "bill of attainder" is a bill that punishes a person without a jury trial. An "ex post facto" law is one that makes an act a crime after the act has been committed.

4. Direct Taxes
The 16th Amendment allowed Congress to pass an income tax.

5. Tax on Exports
Congress may not tax goods that move from one state to another.

6. Uniformity of Treatment
This prohibition prevents Congress from favoring one state or region over another in the regulation of trade.

7. Appropriation Law

This clause protects against the misuse of funds. All of the President's expenditures must be made with the permission of Congress.

8. Titles of Nobility

This clause prevents the development of a nobility in the United States.

Section 10. Powers Denied to the States

1. Limitations on Power

The states are prohibited from conducting foreign affairs, carrying on a war, or controlling interstate and foreign commerce. States are also not allowed to pass laws that the federal government is prohibited from passing, such as enacting ex post facto laws or bills of attainder. These restrictions on the states were designed, in part, to prevent an overlapping in functions and authority with the federal government that could create conflict and chaos.

2. Export and Import Taxes

This clause prevents states from levying duties on exports and imports. If states were permitted to tax imports and exports, they could use their taxing power in a way that weakens or destroys Congress's power to control interstate and foreign commerce.

3. Duties, Armed Forces, War

This clause prohibits states from maintaining an army or navy and from going to war, except in cases where a state is directly attacked. It also forbids states from collecting fees from foreign vessels or from making treaties with other nations. All of these powers are reserved for the federal government.

Article II. The Executive Branch

Section 1. President and Vice President

1. Term of Office

The President is given power to enforce the laws passed by Congress. Both the President and the Vice President serve four-year terms. The 22nd Amendment limits the number of terms the President may serve to two.

2. Election

The Philadelphia Convention had trouble deciding how the President was to be chosen. The system finally agreed upon was indirect election by "electors" chosen for that purpose. The President and Vice President are not directly elected. Instead, the President and Vice President are elected by presidential electors from each state who form the electoral college. Each state has the number of presidential electors equal to the total number of its senators and representatives. State legislatures determine how the electors are chosen. Originally, the state legislatures chose the electors, but today they are nominated by political parties and elected by the voters. No senator, representative, or any other federal officeholder can serve as an elector.

7. No Money shall be drawn from the Treasury, but in Consequence of Appropriations made by Law; and a regular Statement and Account of the Receipts and Expenditures of all public Money shall be published from time to time.

8. No Title of Nobility shall be granted by the United States:—And no Person holding any Office of Profit or Trust under them, shall, without the Consent of the Congress, accept of any present, Emolument, Office, or Title, of any kind whatever, from any King, Prince, or foreign State.

Section 10

1. No State shall enter into any Treaty, Alliance, or Confederation; grant Letters of Marque and Reprisal; coin Money; emit Bills of Credit; make any Thing but gold and silver Coin a Tender in Payment of Debts; pass any Bill of Attainder; ex post facto Law, or Law impairing the Obligation of Contracts, or grant any Title of Nobility.

2. No State shall, without the Consent of the Congress, lay any Imposts or Duties on Imports or Exports, except what may be absolutely necessary for executing its inspection Laws: and the net Produce of all Duties and Imposts, laid by any State on Imports and Exports, shall be for the Use of the Treasury of the United States; and all such Laws shall be subject to the Revision and Controul of the Congress.

3. No State shall, without the Consent of Congress, lay any duty on Tonnage, keep Troops, or Ships of War in time of Peace, enter into any Agreement or Compact with another State, or with a foreign Power, or engage in War, unless actually invaded, or in such imminent Danger as will not admit of delay.

Article II

Section 1

1. The executive Power shall be vested in a President of the United States of America. He shall hold his Office during the Term of four years, and together with the Vice-President chosen for the same Term, be elected, as follows:

2. Each State shall appoint, in such Manner as the Legislature thereof may direct, a Number of Electors, equal to the whole Number of Senators and Representatives to which the State may be entitled in the Congress: but no Senator or Representative, or Person holding an Office of Trust or Profit under the United States, shall be appointed an Elector.

3. The Electors shall meet in their respective States, and vote by Ballot for two Persons, of whom one at least shall not be an Inhabitant of the same State with themselves. And they shall make a List of all the Persons voted for and of the Number of Votes for each; which List they shall sign and certify, and transmit sealed to the Seat of the Government of the United States, directed to the President of the Senate. The President of the Senate shall, in the Presence of the Senate and House of Representatives, open all the Certificates, and the Votes shall then be counted. The Person having the greatest Number of Votes shall be the President, if such Number be a Majority of the whole Number of Electors appointed; and if there be more than one who have such Majority, and have an equal Number of Votes, then the House of Representatives shall immediately chuse by Ballot one of them for President; and if no Person have a Majority, then from the five highest on the List the said House shall in like Manner chuse the President. But in chusing the President, the Votes shall be taken by States, the Representation from each State having one Vote; a quorum for this Purpose shall consist of a Member or Members from two-thirds of the States, and a Majority of all the States shall be necessary to a Choice. In every Case, after the Choice of the President, the Person having the greatest Number of Votes of the Electors shall be the Vice-President. But if there should remain two or more who have equal votes, the Senate shall chuse from them by Ballot the Vice President.

4. The Congress may determine the Time of chusing the Electors, and the Day on which they shall give their Votes; which Day shall be the same throughout the United States.

5. No person except a natural born Citizen, or a Citizen of the United States, at the time of the Adoption of this Constitution, shall be eligible to the Office of President; neither shall any Person be eligible to that Office who shall not have attained to the Age of thirty-five years, and been fourteen Years a Resident within the United States.

6. In Case of the Removal of the President from Office, or of his Death, Resignation, or Inability to discharge the Powers and Duties of the said Office, the same shall devolve on the Vice-President, and the Congress may by Law provide for the Case of Removal, Death, Resignation or Inability, both of the President and Vice-President, declaring what Officer shall then act as President, and such Officer shall act accordingly, until the disability be removed, or a President shall be elected.

7. The President shall, at stated Times, receive for his Services a Compensation, which shall neither be encreased nor diminished during the Period for which he shall have been elected, and he shall not receive within that Period any other Emolument from the United States, or any of them.

8. Before he enter on the execution of his office, he shall take the following Oath or Affirmation "I do solemnly swear (or affirm) that I will faithfully execute the Office of President of the United States, and will to the best of my Ability, preserve, protect and defend the Constitution of the United States."

3. Former Method of Election

This clause describes the original method of electing the President and Vice President. According to this method, each elector voted for two candidates. The candidate with the most votes (as long as it was a majority) became President. The candidate with the second highest number of votes became Vice President. In the election of 1800, the two top candidates received the same number of votes, making it necessary for the House of Representatives to decide the election. To prevent such a situation from recurring, the 12th Amendment was added in 1804.

4. Date of Elections

Congress selects the date when the presidential electors are chosen and when they vote for President and Vice President. All electors must vote on the same day. The first Tuesday after the first Monday in November has been set as the date for presidential elections. Electors cast their votes on the Monday after the second Wednesday in December.

5. Qualifications

The President must be a citizen of the United States by birth, at least 35 years old, and a resident of the United States for 14 years. See Amendment 22.

6. Vacancies

If the President dies, resigns, is removed from office by impeachment, or is unable to carry out the duties of the office, the Vice President becomes President. (Amendment 25 deals with presidential disability.) If both the President and Vice President are unable to serve, Congress has the power to declare by law who acts as President. Congress set the line of succession in the Presidential Succession Act of 1947.

7. Salary

Originally, the President's salary was $25,000 per year. The President's current salary of $200,000 plus a $50,000 taxable expense account per year was enacted in 1969. The President also receives numerous fringe benefits including a $120,000 nontaxable allowance for travel and entertainment, and living accommodations in two residences—the White House and Camp David. However, the President cannot receive any other income from the United States government or state governments while in office.

8. Oath of Office

The oath of office is generally administered by the chief justice, but can be administered by any official authorized to administer oaths. All Presidents-elect except Washington have been sworn into office by the chief justice. Only Vice Presidents John Tyler, Calvin Coolidge, and Lyndon Johnson in succeeding to the office have been sworn in by someone else.

Section 2. Powers of the President
1. Military, Cabinet, Pardons
Mention of "the principal officer in each of the executive departments" is the only suggestion of the President's cabinet to be found in the Constitution. The cabinet is a purely advisory body, and its power depends on the President. Each cabinet member is appointed by the President and must be confirmed by the Senate. This clause also makes the President, a civilian, the head of the armed services. This established the principle of civilian control of the military.

2. Treaties and Appointments
The President is the chief architect of American foreign policy. He or she is responsible for the conduct of foreign relations, or dealings with other countries. All treaties, however, require approval of two-thirds of the senators present. Most federal positions today are filled under the rules and regulations of the civil service system. Most presidential appointees serve at the pleasure of the President. Removal of an official by the President is not subject to congressional approval. But the power can be restricted by conditions set in creating the office.

3. Vacancies in Offices
The President can temporarily appoint officials to fill vacancies when the Senate is not in session.

Section 3. Duties of the President
Under this provision the President delivers annual State-of-the-Union messages. On occasion, Presidents have called Congress into special session to consider particular problems.

The President's duty to receive foreign diplomats also includes the power to ask a foreign country to withdraw its diplomatic officials from this country. This is called "breaking diplomatic relations" and often carries with it the implied threat of more drastic action, even war. The President likewise has the power of deciding whether or not to recognize foreign governments.

Section 4. Impeachment
This section states the reasons for which the President and Vice President may be impeached and removed from office. (See annotations of Article I, Section 3, Clauses 6 and 7.)

Article III. The Judicial Branch

Section 1. Federal Courts
The term *judicial* refers to courts. The Constitution set up only the Supreme Court but provided for the establishment of other federal courts. There are presently nine justices on the Supreme Court. Congress has created a system of federal district courts and courts of appeals, which review certain district court cases. Judges of these courts serve during "good behavior," which means that they usually serve for life or until they choose to retire.

Section 2
1. The President shall be Commander in Chief of the Army and Navy of the United States, and of the Militia of the several States, when called into the actual Service of the United States; he may require the Opinion, in writing, of the principal Officer in each of the executive Departments, upon any subject relating to the Duties of their respective Offices, and he shall have Power to Grant Reprieves and Pardons for Offences against the United States, except in Cases of Impeachment.

2. He shall have Power, by and with the Advice and Consent of the Senate, to make Treaties, provided two-thirds of the Senators present concur; and he shall nominate, and by and with the Advice and Consent of the Senate, shall appoint Ambassadors, other public Ministers and Consuls, Judges of the supreme Court, and all other Officers of the United States, whose Appointments are not herein otherwise provided for, and which shall be established by Law. But the Congress may by Law vest the Appointment of such inferior Officers, as they think proper, in the President alone, in the Courts of Law, or in the Heads of Departments.

3. The President shall have Power to fill up all Vacancies that may happen during the Recess of the Senate, by granting Commissions which shall expire at the End of their next Session.

Section 3
He shall from time to time give to Congress Information of the State of the Union, and recommend to their Consideration such Measures as he shall judge necessary and expedient; he may, on extraordinary occasions, convene both Houses, or either of them, and in Case of Disagreement between them, with respect to the Time of Adjournment, he may adjourn them to such Time as he shall think proper; he shall receive Ambassadors and other public Ministers; he shall take Care that the Laws be faithfully executed, and shall Commission all the Officers of the United States.

Section 4
The President, Vice-President and all civil Officers of the United States, shall be removed from Office on Impeachment for, and Conviction of, Treason, Bribery, or other high Crimes and Misdemeanors.

Article III

Section 1
The Judicial Power of the United States, shall be vested in one supreme Court, and in such inferior Courts as the Congress may from time to time ordain and establish. The Judges, both of the supreme and inferior Courts, shall hold their Offices during good Behaviour, and shall, at stated Times, receive for their Services, a Compensation, which shall not be diminished during their Continuance in Office.

Section 2

1. The judicial Power shall extend to all Cases, in Law and Equity, arising under this Constitution, the Laws of the United States, and treaties made, or which shall be made, under their Authority; to all Cases affecting ambassadors, other public ministers and consuls; to all cases of admiralty and maritime Jurisdiction; to Controversies to which the United States shall be a party; to Controversies between two or more states; between a State and Citizens of another State; between Citizens of different States; between Citizens of the same State claiming Lands under Grants of different States, and between a State, or the Citizens thereof, and foreign States, Citizens or Subjects.

2. In all Cases affecting Ambassadors, other public Ministers and Consuls, and those in which a State shall be Party, the supreme Court shall have original Jurisdiction. In all the other Cases before mentioned, the supreme Court shall have appellate Jurisdiction, both as to Law and Fact, with such Exceptions, and under such Regulations as the Congress shall make.

3. The trial of all Crimes, except in Cases of Impeachment, shall be by Jury; and such Trial shall be held in the State where the said Crimes shall have been committed; but when not committed within any State, the Trial shall be at such Place or Places as the Congress may by Law have directed.

Section 3

1. Treason against the United States, shall consist only in levying War against them, or in adhering to their Enemies, giving them Aid and Comfort. No Person shall be convicted of Treason unless on the Testimony of two Witnesses to the same overt Act, or on Confession in open Court.

2. The Congress shall have power to declare the Punishment of Treason, but no Attainder of Treason shall work Corruption of Blood, or Forfeiture except during the Life of the Person attainted.

Article IV

Section 1

Full Faith and Credit shall be given in each State to the public Acts, Records, and judicial Proceedings of every other State. And the Congress may by general Laws prescribe the Manner in which such Acts, Records, and Proceedings shall be proved, and the Effect thereof.

Section 2. Jurisdiction

1. General Jurisdiction

Use of the words *in law and equity* reflects the fact that American courts took over two kinds of traditional law from Great Britain. The basic law was the "common law," which was based on over five centuries of judicial decisions. "Equity" was a special branch of British law developed to handle cases where common law did not apply.

Federal courts deal mostly with "statute law," or laws passed by Congress, treaties, and cases involving the Constitution itself. "Admiralty and maritime jurisdiction" covers all sorts of cases involving ships and shipping on the high seas and on rivers, canals, and lakes.

2. The Supreme Court

When a court has "original jurisdiction" over certain kinds of cases, it means that the court has the authority to be the first court to hear a case. A court with "appellate jurisdiction" hears cases that have been appealed from lower courts. Most Supreme Court cases are heard on appeal from lower courts.

3. Jury Trials

Except in cases of impeachment, anyone accused of a crime has the right to a trial by jury. The trial must be held in the state where the crime was committed. Jury trial guarantees were strengthened in the 6th, 7th, 8th, and 9th Amendments.

Section 3. Treason

1. Definition

Knowing that the charge of treason often had been used by monarchs to get rid of people who opposed them, the Framers of the Constitution defined treason carefully, requiring that at least two witnesses be present to testify in court that a treasonable act was committed.

2. Punishment

Congress is given the power to determine the punishment for treason. The children of a person convicted of treason may not be punished nor may the convicted person's property be taken away from the children. Convictions for treason have been relatively rare in the nation's history.

Article IV. Relations Among the States

Section 1. Official Acts

This provision ensures that each state recognizes the laws, court decisions, and records of all other states. For example, a marriage license or corporation charter issued by one state must be accepted in other states.

Section 2. Mutual Duties of States

1. Privileges
The "privileges and immunities," or rights of citizens, guarantee each state's citizens equal treatment in all states.

2. Extradition
"Extradition" means that a person convicted of a crime or a person accused of a crime must be returned to the state where the crime was committed. Thus, a person cannot flee to another state hoping to escape the law.

3. Fugitive-Slave Clause
Formerly this clause meant that slaves could not become free persons by escaping to free states.

Section 3. New States and Territories

1. New States
Congress has the power to admit new states. It also determines the basic guidelines for applying for statehood. One state, Maine, was created within the original boundaries of another state (Massachusetts) with the consent of Congress and the state.

2. Territories
Congress has power over federal land. But neither in this clause nor anywhere else in the Constitution is the federal government explicitly empowered to acquire new territory.

Section 4. Federal Protection for States
This section allows the federal government to send troops into a state to guarantee law and order. The President may send in troops even without the consent of the state government involved.

Article V. The Amending Process
There are now 27 Amendments to the Constitution. The Framers of the Constitution deliberately made it difficult to amend or change the Constitution. Two methods of proposing and ratifying amendments are provided for. A two-thirds majority is needed in Congress to propose an amendment, and at least three-fourths of the states (38 states) must accept the amendment before it can become law. No amendment has yet been proposed by a national convention called by the states, though in the 1980s a convention to propose an amendment requiring a balanced budget had been approved by 32 states.

Section 2
1. The Citizens of each State shall be entitled to all Privileges and Immunities of Citizens in the several States.

2. A Person charged in any State with Treason, Felony, or other Crime, who shall flee from Justice, and be found in another State, shall on demand of the executive Authority of the State from which he fled, be delivered up, to be removed to the State having Jurisdiction of the crime.

3. No Person held to Service of Labour in one State, under the Laws thereof, escaping into another, shall, in Consequence of any Law or Regulation therein, be discharged from such Service or Labour, but shall be delivered up on Claim of the Party to whom such Service or Labour may be due.

Section 3
1. New States may be admitted by the Congress into this Union; but no new State shall be formed or erected within the Jurisdiction of any other State; nor any State be formed by the Junction of two or more States, or parts of States, without the Consent of the Legislatures of the States concerned as well as of the Congress.

2. The Congress shall have Power to dispose of and make all needful Rules and Regulations respecting the Territory of other Property belonging to the United States; and nothing in this Constitution shall be so construed as to Prejudice any Claims of the United States, or of any particular State.

Section 4
The United States shall guarantee to every State in this Union a Republican Form of Government, and shall protect each of them against Invasion; and on Application of the Legislature, or of the Executive (when the Legislature cannot be convened) against domestic Violence.

Article V
The Congress, whenever two-thirds of both Houses shall deem it necessary, shall propose Amendments to this Constitution, or, on the Application of the Legislatures of two-thirds of the several States, shall call a Convention for proposing Amendments, which, in either Case, shall be valid to all Intents and Purposes, as part of this Constitution, when ratified by the Legislatures of three-fourths of the several States, or by Conventions in three-fourths thereof, as the one or the other Mode of Ratification may be proposed by the Congress; Provided that no Amendment which may be made prior to the Year One thousand eight hundred and eight shall in any Manner affect the first and fourth clauses in the Ninth Section of the first Article; and that no State, without its Consent, shall be deprived of its equal Suffrage in the Senate.

Article VI

1. All Debts contracted and Engagements entered into, before the Adoption of this Constitution, shall be as valid against the United States under this Constitution as under the Confederation.

2. This Constitution, and the Laws of the United States which shall be made in Pursuance thereof; and all Treaties made, or which shall be made, under the Authority of the United States, shall be the supreme Law of the Land; and the Judges in every State shall be bound thereby, any Thing in the Constitution or Laws of any State to the Contrary notwithstanding.

3. The Senators and Representatives before mentioned, and the Members of the several State Legislatures, and all executive and judicial Officers, both of the United States and of the several States, shall be bound by Oath or Affirmation, to support this Constitution; but no religious Test shall ever be required as a Qualification to any Office or public Trust under the United States.

Article VII

The Ratification of the Conventions of nine States shall be sufficient for the Establishment of this Constitution between the States so ratifying the same.

Done in Convention, by the Unanimous Consent of the States present, the Seventeenth Day of September, in the Year of our Lord one thousand seven hundred and Eighty-seven, and of the Independence of the United States of America the Twelfth. In Witness whereof We have hereunto subscribed our Names.

Article VI. National Supremacy

1. Public Debts and Treaties

This section promised that all debts the colonies had incurred during the Revolution and under the Articles of Confederation would be honored by the new United States government.

2. The Supreme Law

The "supremacy clause" recognized the Constitution and federal laws as supreme when in conflict with those of the states. It was largely based on this clause that Chief Justice John Marshall wrote his historic decision in *McCulloch* v. *Maryland*. The 14th Amendment reinforced the supremacy of federal law over state laws.

3. Oaths of Office

This clause also declares that no religious test shall be required as a qualification for holding public office. This principle is also asserted in the First Amendment, which forbids Congress to set up an established church or to interfere with the religious freedom of Americans.

Article VII. Ratification of the Constitution

Unlike the Articles of Confederation, which required approval of all thirteen states for adoption, the Constitution required approval of only nine of thirteen states. Thirty-nine of the 55 delegates at the Constitutional Convention signed the Constitution. The Constitution went into effect in June 1788.

Signers

George Washington, **President and Deputy from Virginia**

New Hampshire
John Langdon
Nicholas Gilman

Massachusetts
Nathaniel Gorham
Rufus King

Connecticut
William Samuel Johnson
Roger Sherman

New York
Alexander Hamilton

New Jersey
William Livingston
David Brearley
William Paterson
Jonathan Dayton

Pennsylvania
Benjamin Franklin
Thomas Mifflin
Robert Morris
George Clymer
Thomas FitzSimons
Jared Ingersoll
James Wilson
Gouverneur Morris

Delaware
George Read
Gunning Bedford, Jr.
John Dickinson
Richard Bassett
Jacob Broom

Maryland
James McHenry
Daniel of St. Thomas Jenifer
Daniel Carroll

Virginia
John Blair
James Madison, Jr.

North Carolina
William Blount
Richard Dobbs Spaight
Hugh Williamson

South Carolina
John Rutledge
Charles Cotesworth Pinckney
Charles Pinckney
Pierce Butler

Georgia
William Few
Abraham Baldwin

Attest: William Jackson,
Secretary

Amendment 1.
Freedom of Religion, Speech, Press, and Assembly (1791)

The 1st Amendment protects the civil liberties of individuals in the United States. The 1st Amendment freedoms are not absolute, however. They are limited by the rights of other individuals.

Amendment 2.
Right to Bear Arms (1791)

The purpose of this amendment is to guarantee states the right to keep a militia.

Amendment 3.
Quartering Troops (1791)

This amendment is based on the principle that people have a right to privacy in their own homes. It also reflects the colonists' grievances against the British government before the Revolution. Britain had angered Americans by quartering (housing) troops in private homes.

Amendment 4.
Searches and Seizures (1791)

Like the 3rd Amendment, the 4th Amendment reflects the colonists' desire to protect their privacy. Britain had used writs of assistance (general search warrants) to seek out smuggled goods. Americans wanted to make sure that such searches and seizures would be conducted only when a judge felt that there was "reasonable cause" to conduct them. The Supreme Court has ruled that evidence seized illegally without a search warrant may not be used in court.

Amendment 5.
Rights of Accused Persons (1791)

To bring a "presentment" or "indictment" means to formally charge a person with committing a crime. It is the function of a grand jury to see whether there is enough evidence to bring the accused person to trial. A person may not be tried more than once for the same crime (double jeopardy).

Members of the armed services are subject to military law. They may be tried in a court martial. In times of war or a natural disaster, civilians may also be put under martial law.

The 5th Amendment also guarantees that persons may not be forced in any criminal case to be a witness against themselves. That is, accused persons may refuse to answer questions on the ground that the answers might tend to incriminate them.

Amendment I

Congress shall make no law respecting an establishment of religion, or prohibiting the free exercise thereof; or abridging the freedom of speech, or of the press; or the right of the people peaceably to assemble, and to petition the Government for a redress of grievances.

Amendment II

A well-regulated Militia, being necessary to the security of a free State, the right of the people to keep and bear Arms, shall not be infringed.

Amendment III

No soldier shall, in time of peace be quartered in any house, without the consent of the Owner, nor in time of war, but in a manner to be prescribed by law.

Amendment IV

The right of the people to be secure in their persons, houses, papers, and effects, against unreasonable searches and seizures, shall not be violated, and no Warrants shall issue, but upon probable cause, supported by Oath or affirmation, and particularly describing the place to be searched, and the persons or things to be seized.

Amendment V

No person shall be held to answer for a capital, or otherwise infamous crime, unless on a presentment or indictment of a Grand Jury, except in cases arising in the land or naval forces, or in the Militia, when in actual service in time of War or public danger; nor shall any person be subject for the same offence to be twice put in jeopardy of life or limb; nor shall be compelled in any criminal case to be a witness against himself, nor be deprived of life, liberty, or property, without due process of law; nor shall private property be taken for public use, without just compensation.

Amendment VI

In all criminal prosecutions, the accused shall enjoy the right to a speedy and public trial, by an impartial jury of the State and district wherein the crime shall have been committed, which district shall have been previously ascertained by law, and to be informed of the nature and cause of the accusation; to be confronted with the witnesses against him; to have compulsory process for obtaining witnesses in his favor, and to have the Assistance of Counsel for his defence.

Amendment VII

In suits at common law, where the value in controversy shall exceed twenty dollars, the right of trial by jury shall be preserved, and no fact tried by a jury, shall be otherwise reexamined in any Courts of the United States, than according to the rules of common law.

Amendment VIII

Excessive bail shall not be required, nor excessive fines imposed, nor cruel and unusual punishments inflicted.

Amendment IX

The enumeration in the Constitution, of certain rights, shall not be construed to deny or disparage others retained by the people.

Amendment X

The powers not delegated to the United States by the Constitution, nor prohibited by it to the States, are reserved to the States respectively, or to the people.

Amendment XI

The Judicial power of the United States shall not be construed to extend to any suit in law or equity, commenced or prosecuted against one of the United States by Citizens of another State, or by Citizens or Subjects of any Foreign State.

Amendment 6.
Right to Speedy, Fair Trial (1791)

The requirement of a "speedy" trial ensures that an accused person will not be held in jail for a lengthy period as a means of punishing the accused without a trial. A "fair" trial means that the trial must be open to the public and that a jury must hear witnesses and evidence on both sides before deciding the guilt or innocence of a person charged with a crime. This amendment also provides that legal counsel must be provided to a defendant. In 1963, the Supreme Court ruled, in *Gideon* v. *Wainwright*, that if a defendant cannot afford a lawyer, the government must provide one to defend the accused person.

Amendment 7.
Civil Suits (1791)

"Common law" means the law established by previous court decisions. In civil cases where one person sues another for more than $20, a jury trial is provided for. But customarily, federal courts do not hear civil cases unless they involve a good deal more money.

Amendment 8.
Bail and Punishment (1791)

"Bail" is money that an accused person provides to the court as a guarantee that he or she will be present for a trial. This amendment ensures that neither bail nor punishment for a crime shall be unreasonably severe.

Amendment 9.
Powers Reserved to the People (1791)

This amendment provides that the people's rights are not limited to those mentioned in the Constitution.

Amendment 10.
Powers Reserved to the States (1791)

This amendment protects the states and the people from an all-powerful federal government. It provides that the states or the people retain all powers except those denied them or those specifically granted to the federal government. This "reserved powers" provision is a check on the "necessary and proper" power of the federal government provided in the "elastic clause" in Article I, Section 8, Clause 18.

Amendment 11.
Suits Against States (1795)

This amendment provides that a lawsuit brought by a citizen of the United States or a foreign nation against a state must be tried in a state court, not in a federal court. This amendment was passed after the Supreme Court ruled that a federal court could try a lawsuit brought by citizens of South Carolina against a citizen of Georgia. This case, *Chisholm* v. *Georgia*, decided in 1793, was protested by many Americans, who insisted states would lose authority if they could be sued in federal courts.

Amendment 12.
Election of President and Vice President (1804)

This amendment changes the procedure for electing the President and Vice President as outlined in Article II, Section 1, Clause 3.

To prevent the recurrence of the election of 1800 whereby a candidate running for Vice President (Aaron Burr) could tie a candidate running for President (Thomas Jefferson) and thus force the election into the House of Representatives, the Twelfth Amendment specifies that the electors are to cast separate ballots for each office. The votes for each office are counted and listed separately. The results are signed, sealed, and sent to the president of the Senate. At a joint session of Congress, the votes are counted. The candidate who receives the most votes, providing it is a majority, is elected President. Other changes include: (1) a reduction from five to the three highest candidates receiving votes among whom the House is to choose if no candidate receives a majority of the electoral votes, and (2) provision for the Senate to choose the Vice President from the two highest candidates if neither has received a majority of the electoral votes.

The Twelfth Amendment does place one restriction on electors. It prohibits electors from voting for two candidates (President and Vice President) from their home state.

Amendment 13.
Abolition of Slavery (1865)

This amendment was the final act in ending slavery in the United States. It also prohibits the binding of a person to perform a personal service due to debt. In addition to imprisonment for crime, the Supreme Court has held that the draft is not a violation of the amendment.

This amendment is the first adopted to be divided into sections. It is also the first to contain specifically a provision granting Congress power to enforce it by appropriate legislation.

Amendment XII

The Electors shall meet in their respective States and vote by ballot for President and Vice-President, one of whom, at least, shall not be an inhabitant of the same State with themselves; they shall name in their ballots the person voted for as President, and in distinct ballots the person voted for as Vice-President, and they shall make distinct lists of all persons voted for as President, and of all persons voted for as Vice-President, and of the number of votes for each, which lists they shall sign and certify, and transmit sealed to the seat of the government of the United States, directed to the President of the Senate;—The President of the Senate shall, in the presence of the Senate and House of Representatives, open all the certificates and the votes shall then be counted;—The person having the greatest number of votes for President, shall be the President, if such number be a majority of the whole number of Electors appointed; and if no person have such majority, then from the persons having the highest numbers not exceeding three on the list of those voted for as President, the House of Representatives shall choose immediately, by ballot, the President. But in choosing the President, the votes shall be taken by states, the representation from each state having one vote; a quorum for this purpose shall consist of a member or members from two-thirds of the states, and a majority of all the states shall be necessary to a choice. And if the House of Representatives shall not choose a President whenever the right of choice shall devolve upon them, before the fourth day of March next following, then the Vice-President shall act as President, as in the case of the death or other constitutional disability of the President.—The person having the greatest number of votes as Vice-President, shall be the Vice-President, if such number be a majority of the whole number of Electors appointed, and if no person have a majority, then from the two highest numbers on the list, the Senate shall choose the Vice-President; a quorum for the purpose shall consist of two-thirds of the whole number of Senators, and a majority of the whole number shall be necessary to a choice. But no person constitutionally ineligible to the office of President shall be eligible to that of Vice-President of the United States.

Amendment XIII

Section 1

Neither slavery nor involuntary servitude, except as a punishment for crime whereof the party shall have been duly convicted, shall exist within the United States, or any place subject to their jurisdiction.

Section 2

Congress shall have power to enforce this article by appropriate legislation.

Amendment XIV

Section 1

All persons born or naturalized in the United States, and subject to the jurisdiction thereof, are citizens of the United States and of the State wherein they reside. No State shall make or enforce any law which shall abridge the privileges or immunities of citizens of the United States; nor shall any State deprive any person of life, liberty, or property, without due process of law, nor deny to any person within its jurisdiction the equal protection of the laws.

Section 2

Representatives shall be apportioned among the several States according to their respective numbers, counting the whole number of persons in each State, excluding Indians not taxed. But when the right to vote at any election for the choice of electors for President and Vice-President of the United States, Representatives in Congress, the Executive and Judicial officers of a State, or the members of the Legislature thereof, is denied to any of the male inhabitants of such State, being twenty-one years of age, and citizens of the United States, or in any way abridged, except for participation in rebellion, or other crime, the basis of representation therein shall be reduced in the proportion which the number of such male citizens shall bear to the whole number of male citizens twenty-one years of age in such State.

Section 3

No person shall be a Senator or Representative in Congress, or elector of President and Vice-President, or hold any office, civil or military, under the United States, or under any State, who, having previously taken an oath, as a member of Congress, or as an officer of the United States, or as a member of any State legislature, or as an executive or judicial officer of any State, to support the Constitution of the United States, shall have engaged in insurrection or rebellion against the same, or given aid or comfort to the enemies thereof. But Congress may by a vote of two-thirds of each House, remove such disability.

Section 4

The validity of the public debt of the United States incurred for payment of pensions and bounties for service, authorized by law, including debts in suppressing insurrections or rebellion, shall not be questioned. But neither the United States nor any State shall assume or pay any debt or obligation incurred in aid of insurrection or rebellion against the United States, or any claim for the loss or emancipation of any slave; but all such debts, obligations and claims shall be held illegal and void.

Amendment 14.
Rights of Citizens (1868)

The clauses of this amendment were intended (1) to penalize Southern states that refused to grant African Americans the vote, (2) to keep former Confederate leaders from serving in government, (3) to forbid payment of the Confederacy's debt by the federal government, and (4) to ensure payment of the war debts owed the federal government.

Section 1. Citizenship Defined By granting citizenship to all persons born in the United States, this amendment granted citizenship to former slaves. The amendment also guaranteed "due process of law." By the 1950s, Supreme Court rulings used the due process clause to protect civil liberties. The last part of Section 1 establishes the doctrine that all citizens are entitled to equal protection of the laws. In 1954 the Supreme Court ruled, in *Brown* v. *Board of Education of Topeka,* that segregation in public schools was unconstitutional because it denied equal protection.

Section 2. Representation in Congress This section reduced the number of members a state had in the House of Representatives if it denied its citizens the right to vote. This section was not implemented, however. Later civil rights laws and the 24th Amendment guaranteed the vote to African Americans.

Section 3. Penalty for Engaging in Insurrection The leaders of the Confederacy were barred from state or federal offices unless Congress agreed to revoke this ban. By the end of Reconstruction all but a few Confederate leaders were allowed to return to public life.

Section 4. Public Debt The public debt incurred by the federal government during the Civil War was valid and could not be questioned by the South. However, the debts of the Confederacy were declared to be illegal. And former slaveholders could not collect compensation for the loss of their slaves.

Section 5. Enforcement Congress was empowered to pass civil rights bills to guarantee the provisions of the amendment.

Amendment 15.
The Right to Vote (1870)
Section 1. Suffrage for African Americans The 15th Amendment replaced Section 2 of the 14th Amendment in guaranteeing African Americans the right to vote; that is, the right of African Americans to vote was not to be left to the states. Yet, despite this prohibition, African Americans were denied the right to vote by many states by such means as poll taxes, literacy tests, and white primaries.
Section 2. Enforcement Congress was given the power to enforce this amendment. During the 1950s and 1960s, it passed successively stronger laws to end racial discrimination in voting rights.

Amendment 16.
Income Tax (1913)
The origins of this amendment went back to 1895, when the Supreme Court declared a federal income tax unconstitutional. To overcome this Supreme Court decision, this amendment authorized an income tax that was levied on a direct basis.

Amendment 17.
Direct Election of Senators (1913)

Section 1. Method of Election The right to elect senators was given directly to the people of each state. It replaced Article I, Section 3, Clause 1, which empowered state legislatures to elect senators. This amendment was designed not only to make the choice of senators more democratic but also to cut down on corruption and to improve state government.

Section 2. Vacancies A state must order an election to fill a Senate vacancy. A state may empower its governor to appoint a person to fill a Senate seat if a vacancy occurs until an election can be held.

Section 3. Time in Effect This amendment was not to affect any Senate election or temporary appointment until it was in effect.

Section 5
The Congress shall have power to enforce, by appropriate legislation, the provisions of this article.

Amendment XV

Section 1
The right of citizens of the United States to vote shall not be denied or abridged by the United States or by any State on account of race, color, or previous condition of servitude.

Section 2
The Congress shall have power to enforce this article by appropriate legislation.

Amendment XVI
The Congress shall have power to lay and collect taxes on incomes, from whatever source derived, without apportionment among several States, and without regard to any census or enumeration.

Amendment XVII

Section 1
The Senate of the United States shall be composed of two Senators from each State, elected by the people thereof, for six years; and each Senator shall have one vote. The electors in each state shall have the qualifications requisite for electors of the most numerous branch of the state legislatures.

Section 2
When vacancies happen in the representation of any State in the Senate, the executive authority of such State shall issue writs of election to fill such vacancies: *Provided*, that the legislature of any State may empower the executive thereof to make temporary appointments until the people fill the vacancies by election as the legislature may direct.

Section 3
This amendment shall not be so construed as to affect the election or term of any Senator chosen before it becomes valid as part of the Constitution.

Amendment XVIII

Section 1
After one year from ratification of this article the manufacture, sale, or transportation of intoxicating liquors within, the importation thereof into, or the exportation thereof from the United States and all territory subject to the jurisdiction thereof for beverage purposes is hereby prohibited.

Section 2
The Congress and the several states shall have concurrent power to enforce this article by appropriate legislation.

Section 3
This article shall be inoperative unless it shall have been ratified as an amendment to the Constitution by the legislatures of the several States, as provided in the Constitution, within seven years from the date of the submission hereof to the states of the Congress.

Amendment XIX

Section 1
The right of citizens of the United States to vote shall not be denied or abridged by the United States or by any state on account of sex.

Section 2
Congress shall have power to enforce this article by appropriate legislation.

Amendment XX

Section 1
The terms of the President and Vice President shall end at noon on the 20th day of January, and the terms of the Senators and Representatives at noon on the 3rd day of January, of the years in which such terms would have ended if this article had not been ratified; and the terms of their successors shall then begin.

Section 2
The Congress shall assemble at least once in every year, and such meeting shall begin at noon on the 3rd day of January, unless they shall by law appoint a different day.

Amendment 18.
Prohibition of Alcoholic Beverages (1919)
This amendment prohibited the production, sale, or transportation of alcoholic beverages in the United States. Prohibition proved to be difficult to enforce, especially in states with large urban populations. This amendment was later repealed by the 21st Amendment.

Amendment 19.
Woman Suffrage (1920)
This amendment, extending the vote to all qualified women in federal and state elections, was a landmark victory for the woman suffrage movement, which had worked to achieve this goal for many years. The women's movement had earlier gained full voting rights for women in four Western states in the late nineteenth century.

Amendment 20.
"Lame-Duck" Amendment (1933)
Section 1. New Dates of Terms This amendment had two major purposes: (1) to shorten the time between the President's and Vice President's election and inauguration, and (2) to end "lame-duck" sessions of Congress.

When the Constitution first went into effect, transportation and communication were slow and uncertain. It often took many months after the election in November for the President and Vice President to travel to Washington, D.C., and prepare for their inauguration on March 4. This amendment ended this long wait for a new administration by fixing January 20 as Inauguration Day.

Section 2. Meeting Time of Congress "Lame-duck" sessions occurred every two years, after the November congressional election. That is, the Congress that held its session in December of an election year was not the newly elected Congress but the old Congress that had been elected two years earlier. This Congress continued to serve for several more months, usually until March of the next year. Often many of its members had failed to be reelected and were called "lame-ducks." The 20th Amendment abolished this lame-duck session, and provided that the new Congress hold its first session soon after the November election, on January 3.

Section 3. Succession of President and Vice President This amendment provides that if the President-elect dies before taking office, the Vice President-elect becomes President. In the cases described, Congress will decide on a temporary President.

Section 4. Filling Presidential Vacancy If a presidential candidate dies while an election is being decided in the House, Congress may pass legislation to deal with the situation. Congress has similar power if this occurs when the Senate is deciding a vice-presidential election.

Section 5. Beginning the New Dates Sections 1 and 2 affected the Congress elected in 1934 and President Roosevelt, elected in 1936.

Section 6. Time Limit on Ratification The period for ratification by the states was limited to seven years.

Amendment 21.
Repeal of Prohibition Amendment (1933)
This amendment nullified the 18th Amendment. It is the only amendment ever passed to overturn an earlier amendment. It remained unlawful to transport alcoholic beverages into states that forbade their use. It is the only amendment ratified by special state conventions instead of state legislatures.

Section 3
If, at the time fixed for the beginning of the term of the President, the President elect shall have died, the Vice President elect shall become President. If a President shall not have been chosen before the time fixed for the beginning of his term, or if the President elect shall have failed to qualify, then the Vice President elect shall act as President until a President shall have qualified; and the Congress may by law provide for the case wherein neither a President elect nor a Vice President elect shall have qualified, declaring who shall then act as President, or the manner in which one who is to act shall be selected, and such person shall act accordingly until a President or Vice President shall have qualified.

Section 4
The Congress may by law provide for the case of the death of any of the persons from whom the House of Representatives may choose a President whenever the right of choice shall have devolved upon them, and for the case of the death of any of the persons from whom the Senate may choose a Vice President whenever the right of choice shall have devolved upon them.

Section 5
Sections 1 and 2 shall take effect on the 15th day of October following the ratification of this article.

Section 6
This article shall be inoperative unless it shall have been ratified as an amendment to the Constitution by the legislatures of three-fourths of the several States within seven years from the date of its submission.

Amendment XXI

Section 1
The eighteenth article of amendment to the Constitution of the United States is hereby repealed.

Section 2
The transportation or importation into any State, Territory, or possession of the United States for delivery or use therein of intoxicating liquors, in violation of the laws thereof, is hereby prohibited.

Section 3
This article shall be inoperative unless it shall have been ratified as an amendment to the Constitution by conventions in the several States, as provided in the Constitution, within seven years from the date of the submission hereof to the States by the Congress.

Amendment XXII

Section 1

No person shall be elected to the office of the President more than twice, and no person who had held the office of President, or acted as President, for more than two years of a term to which some other person was elected President shall be elected to the office of the President more than once.

But this Article shall not apply to any person holding the office of President when this Article was proposed by the Congress, and shall not prevent any person who may be holding the office of President, or acting as President, during the term within which this Article becomes operative from holding the office of President or acting as President during the remainder of such term.

Section 2

This article shall be inoperative unless it shall have been ratified as an amendment to the Constitution by the legislatures of three-fourths of the several States within seven years from the date of its submission to the States by the Congress.

Amendment XXIII

Section 1

The District constituting the seat of Government of the United States shall appoint in such manner as the Congress may direct:

A number of electors of President and Vice President equal to the whole number of Senators and Representatives in Congress to which the District would be entitled if it were a State, but in no event more than the least populous State; they shall be in addition to those appointed by the States, but they shall be considered, for the purposes of the election of President and Vice President, to be electors appointed by a State; and they shall meet in the District and perform such duties as provided by the twelfth article of amendment.

Section 2

The Congress shall have power to enforce this article by appropriate legislation.

Amendment 22.
Limit on Presidential Terms (1951)

This amendment wrote into the Constitution a custom started by Washington, Jefferson, and Madison, whereby Presidents limited themselves to two terms in office. Although both Ulysses S. Grant and Theodore Roosevelt sought third terms, the two-term precedent was not broken until Franklin D. Roosevelt was elected to a third term in 1940 and then a fourth term in 1944. The passage of the 22nd Amendment ensures that no President is to be considered indispensable. It also provides that anyone who succeeds to the presidency and serves for more than two years of the term may not be elected more than one more time.

Amendment 23.
Presidential Electors for the District of Columbia (1961)

This amendment granted people living in the District of Columbia the right to vote in presidential elections. The District casts three electoral votes. The people of Washington, D.C., still are without representation in Congress.

Amendment 24.
Abolition of the Poll Tax (1964)

A "poll tax" was a fee that persons were required to pay in order to vote in a number of Southern states. This amendment ended poll taxes as a requirement to vote in any presidential or congressional election. In 1966 the Supreme Court voided poll taxes in state elections as well.

Amendment 25.
Presidential Disability and Succession (1967)
Section 1. Replacing the President The Vice President becomes President if the President dies, resigns, or is removed from office.

Section 2. Replacing the Vice President
The President is to appoint a new Vice President in case of a vacancy in that office, with the approval of the Congress.

The 25th Amendment is unusually precise and explicit because it was intended to solve a serious constitutional problem. Sixteen times in American history, before passage of this amendment, the office of Vice President was vacant, but fortunately in none of these cases did the President die or resign.

This amendment was used in 1973, when Vice President Spiro Agnew resigned from office after being charged with accepting bribes. President Richard Nixon then appointed Gerald R. Ford as Vice President in accordance with the provisions of the 25th Amendment. A year later, President Nixon resigned during the Watergate scandal, and Ford became President. President Ford then had to fill the vice presidency, which he had left vacant upon assuming the presidency. He named Nelson A. Rockefeller as Vice President. Thus both the presidency and vice presidency were held by men who had not been elected to their offices.

Section 3. Replacing the President With Consent If the President informs Congress, in writing, that he or she cannot carry out the duties of the office of President, the Vice President becomes Acting President.

Section 4. Replacing the President Without Consent If the President is unable to carry out the duties of the office but is unable or unwilling to so notify Congress, the cabinet and the Vice President are to inform Congress of this fact. The Vice President then becomes Acting President. The procedure by which the President may regain the office if he or she recovers is also spelled out in this amendment.

Amendment XXIV

Section 1
The right of citizens of the United States to vote in any primary or other election for President or Vice President, for electors for President or Vice President, or for Senator or Representative in Congress, shall not be denied or abridged by the United States or any State by reason of failure to pay any poll tax or other tax.

Section 2
The Congress shall have power to enforce this article by appropriate legislation.

Amendment XXV

Section 1
In case of the removal of the President from office or his death or resignation, the Vice President shall become President.

Section 2
Whenever there is a vacancy in the office of the Vice President, the President shall nominate a Vice President who shall take the office upon confirmation by a majority vote of both houses of Congress.

Section 3
Whenever the President transmits to the President pro tempore of the Senate and the Speaker of the House of Representatives his written declaration that he is unable to discharge the powers and duties of his office, and until he transmits to them a written declaration to the contrary, such powers and duties shall be discharged by the Vice President as Acting President.

Section 4
Whenever the Vice President and a majority of either the principal officers of the executive departments or of such other body as Congress may by law provide, transmit to the President pro tempore of the Senate and the Speaker of the House of Representatives their written declaration that the President is unable to discharge the powers and duties of his office, the Vice President shall immediately assume the power and duties of the office of Acting President.

Thereafter, when the President transmits to the President pro tempore of the Senate and the Speaker of the House of Representatives his written declaration that no inability exists, he shall resume the powers and duties of his office unless the Vice President and a majority of either the principal officers of the executive departments or of such other body as Congress may by law provide, transmit within four days to the President pro tempore of the Senate and the Speaker of the House of Representatives their written declaration that the President is unable to discharge the powers and duties of his office. Thereupon Congress shall decide the issue, assembling within forty-eight hours for that purpose if not in session. If the Congress within twenty-one days after receipt of the latter written declaration, or, if Congress is not in session, within twenty-one days after Congress is required to assemble, determines by two-thirds vote of both houses that the President is unable to discharge the powers and duties of his office, the Vice President shall continue to discharge the same as Acting President; otherwise, the President shall resume the power and duties of his office.

Amendment XXVI

Section 1

The right of citizens of the United States, who are eighteen years of age or older, to vote shall not be denied or abridged by the United States or by any State on account of age.

Section 2

The Congress shall have power to enforce this article by appropriate legislation.

Amendment XXVII

No law, varying the compensation for the services of Senators and Representatives, shall take effect, until an election of Representatives shall have intervened.

Amendment 26.
Eighteen-Year-Old Vote (1971)
This amendment made 18-year-olds eligible to vote in all federal, state, and local elections. Until then, the minimum age had been 21 in most states.

Amendment 27.
Restraint on Congressional Salaries (1992)
Any increase in the salaries of members of Congress will take effect in the subsequent session of Congress.

▲ THE CAPITOL, WASHINGTON, D.C.

Chapter 8

The American Revolution

As the fighting around Boston spread in the spring of 1775, delegates to the **Second Continental Congress** met in Philadelphia. They made a last appeal—the **Olive Branch Petition**—for peace. Britain denied the appeal. Preparing for the war now bound to come, the Congress formed the **Continental Army.** It placed George Washington in command of the army.

At first the Americans fought only for their rights as British subjects. By July of 1776, however,

Congress chose complete separation from Britain by adopting the **Declaration of Independence.** From then on, American Patriots fought for the right to form their own country.

▲ *DRAFTING THE DECLARATION OF INDEPENDENCE* BY **J.L.G. FERRIS**

CAUSES

- **Failure of the Olive Branch Petition**
- **Ethan Allen and Benedict Arnold capture Fort Ticonderoga**
- **British soldiers clash with colonists in Battle of Bunker Hill**
- **Publication of Thomas Paine's** *Common Sense*

The Thirteen Colonies Declare Independence

EFFECTS

- **Foundations laid for democratic government**
- **Colonial purpose shifts from fighting for British rights to fighting for a new nation**
- **Colonists forced to choose between Patriot and Loyalist causes**
- **Americans set up their own government during and after the Revolution**

The Patriots won some early victories at Ticonderoga, Trenton, and Princeton. The British—headquartered in New York—held the upper hand, however, until the American victory at **Saratoga** in 1777. A few months later France agreed to help the Patriots. By early 1779, the Americans under the leadership of George Rogers Clark controlled the **Ohio Valley.** By the spring of 1781, Patriots in the South had pursued and weakened the forces of British General Cornwallis. Combined American and French forces trapped Cornwallis and forced him to surrender at **Yorktown, Virginia,** in October 1781. Within two years, Britain recognized American independence in the **Treaty of Paris.**

Chapter 9

Creating a Nation

After declaring their independence in 1776, the colonies set about writing new state constitutions to replace their old colonial charters. Most of the new state governments provided for a bicameral legislature, a governor with limited authority, and a bill of rights. The Second Continental Congress drafted the Articles of Confederation. Adopted in 1781, the **Articles of Confederation** allowed for a league of friendship among powerful state governments and a weak central government.

The **Confederation Congress** successfully settled western land issues after the end of the war. It could not, however, solve the new nation's problems with worthless money, debt, trade, economic depression, and citizen uprisings. Thoughtful Americans called for a government better able to deal with important national issues.

In 1787 political leaders met in the **Constitutional Convention** at Philadelphia. Instead of revising the Articles of Confederation, they wrote the **United States Constitution**—an entirely new plan of government. Under the new government, the states retained a number of important powers. The national government, however, was the supreme law of the land. Federalists and Anti-Federalists debated the Constitution for months. **Federalists** were people who favored a strong central government. **Anti-Federalists** opposed strong central government. By June 1788, nine states had ratified the Constitution. The new government could

begin. One of its first duties, as promised during the ratification debate, would be to add a bill of rights. These amendments would guarantee personal rights and freedoms.

Citizenship Handbook and United States Constitution

The Founders set down six goals of government in the **Preamble** to the Constitution. Then they outlined the government in the Constitution's seven **articles.** They based the government on five principles: 1) popular sovereignty, 2) limited government, 3) federalism, 4) separation of powers, and 5) checks and balances.

They separated federal power among the **legislative, executive,** and **judicial** branches. Through measures such as the legislature's power of impeachment, the executive veto, and judicial interpretation, they permitted the three branches to check one another and keep a balance of power among them.

The Constitution's flexible language and amendment provisions have enabled it to change with the times. Americans, though, still must live up to certain duties and responsibilities as citizens in order to preserve good government and personal rights.

Understanding Unit Themes

1. **American Democracy** What two ideas in the Declaration of Independence support the principle of popular sovereignty? How did the Magna Carta and French philosopher Montesquieu influence the Founders?

2. **Conflict and Cooperation** What division did the Declaration of Independence cause among Americans? How did the question of representation in Congress challenge the Constitutional Convention? How was the problem solved?

3. **Civil Rights and Liberties** Why did Anti-Federalists insist upon adding the first 10 amendments to the new Constitution?

4. **The Individual and Family Life** How can individual Americans help assure good government and the protection of citizens' rights?

▲ INDEPENDENCE HALL, PHILADELPHIA

UNIT FOUR
EARLY YEARS OF THE REPUBLIC
1789–1830

★★

CHAPTER **10**	CHAPTER **11**	CHAPTER **12**
The Federalist Era 1789–1800	The Age of Jefferson 1800–1815	The Nation Grows 1815–1830

▲ COTTON GIN

History AND ART

The Constitution and Guerriere, War of 1812
unknown artist

There is speculation over who painted this battle scene from the War of 1812. It is usually attributed to Thomas Birch, who lived from 1779 to 1851.

SETTING THE SCENE

During the formative years of the new Republic the government put its finances in order, witnessed the birth of political parties, improved the transportation system, and more than doubled the territory within its borders.

▲ FOUNDRY IN NEW ENGLAND

Themes

★ Conflict and Cooperation
★ United States's Role in World Affairs
★ Economic Development
★ Influence of Technology
★ Beliefs, Ideas, and Institutions

Key Events

★ George Washington inaugurated as first President
★ Louisiana Territory purchased
★ War of 1812
★ Missouri Compromise of 1820
★ Monroe Doctrine declared

▲ CAPITOL, WASHINGTON, D.C., 1830

Major Issues

★ Native Americans resist new settlement in Ohio and the Northwest Territory.
★ Disagreements over a strong federal government lead to the first political parties and the doctrine of states' rights.
★ Sectional divisions develop.
★ Missouri's application for statehood sparks debate about the practice of slavery.

◀ BILL OF RIGHTS

Portfolio Project

Prepare a report on one of the 10 states admitted to the Union between 1791 and 1821. Describe its admission to statehood and details of the first legislature, governor, and state capital.

HANDS-ON HISTORY
LAB ACTIVITY

All Aboard!

Background

The ships crowding American harbors in the late 1700s and 1800s were versions of the earliest European sailing ships. The galleon, from the mid-1500s, was a large double-masted ship used to carry cargo and as a warship. The East Indiamen carried on trade between Europe and Asia during the 1600s. Trade between Europe and the United States in the 1700s flowed on smaller packet ships. By the mid-1880s trim, speedy clipper ships filled America's harbors. Try building three different styles of sailing ships to see which design is speedier.

Believe It OR NOT! The USS *Constitution* is the oldest sailing warship in the world still afloat. Launched in 1797, the *Constitution* served in many battles, including those of the War of 1812. It was nicknamed "Old Ironsides" because a sailor said he saw gunshots bouncing off its strong, oak hull as if it were made of iron. Today the *Constitution* is docked in Boston.

▲ THE *SAVANNAH*

Materials

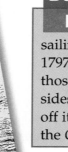

- 8-inch square of Styrofoam, ½–1 inch thick
- plastic knife
- scissors
- colored construction paper
- tape
- drinking straws
- ruler
- deep rectangular baking pan
- electric fan

What To Do

A. Cut 3 sailboat hulls of different shapes from Styrofoam—each about 3 inches long and 2 inches wide.

B. Cut straw masts to the lengths you think will perform best in wind.

C. Cut sails of different shapes and sizes from construction paper. Plan to use more than one sail per boat if you think it will increase speed.

D. Use tape to attach the sails to the masts.

E. Push the masts into the hulls, being careful not to go all the way through.

F. Give each boat a name and write the name on its sail.

G. Record the names of your boats on a sheet of paper.

H. Fill the baking pan with water.

I. Put the fan directly behind one of the narrow ends of the pan. Turn the fan on low and check to make sure that the air blows across the water evenly. Move the fan closer or farther away from the pan as needed. Then turn the fan off.

J. Place your three boats in the water at the end of the pan nearest the fan. Turn on the fan.

K. Record how each of your boats performs in the wind.

Lab Activity Report

1. Which of your sailing vessels moved the fastest?

2. Which vessel held the straightest course?

3. How do you think you could improve the design of your fastest boat to make it sail even faster?

4. Drawing Conclusions In the 1850s, sailing ships were replaced by ships with steam-driven engines. What advantages would a constant source of power, such as steam, provide to a ship captain?

GO A STEP FURTHER

ACTIVITY

Use library sources to learn the names of some of the most famous clipper ships. Create a sketch of your favorite one and list interesting facts about it under your sketch.

CHAPTER 10

★★

The Federalist Era
1789–1800

SETTING THE SCENE

Focus

The Constitution set up a completely new framework of government that was meant to be flexible and lasting. Along with the excitement of a new nation came challenges and growing pains. Many people, both Americans and foreigners, wondered: Could this new kind of government last?

Concepts to Understand

★ How the **beliefs and ideas** of the nation's leaders influenced the development of government
★ How the new government defined **its role in world affairs**

Read to Discover . . .

★ the organization of the new national government.
★ the causes and effects of internal and foreign challenges to the United States government.
★ the competing political views that led to the growth of party politics.

Journal Notes

The 1790s were the beginning of a fundamental split in political ideas in the United States. Make two columns in your journal. As you read the chapter, note the differing points of view about each issue on which people were divided.

▶ BIBLE USED AT WASHINGTON'S INAUGURATION

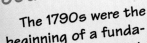
United States

1781 Articles of Confederation ratified

1788 Constitution ratified
1789 George Washington becomes President
1789 First Congress meets

| 1780–1784 | 1785–1789 |

1789 French Revolution begins

World

History AND ART

Washington's Inauguration
by Hy Hintermeister

Hintermeister's twentieth-century painting shows George Washington being sworn in as the first President of the United States. Having defeated the British, the United States set out to establish a new government.

1791 Bill of Rights ratified
1794 Whiskey Rebellion
1796 John Adams elected President

1800 United States capital moves to Washington, D.C.

1790–1799

1800–1804

1791 Toussaint-Louverture leads slave revolt in Saint Domingue (Haiti)
1799 Rosetta Stone found in Egypt

1800 Napoleon Bonaparte becomes ruler of France

★★

Establishing the New Government

SETTING THE SCENE

Read to Learn . . .

★ how Congress organized the legislative branch of the government.
★ how the executive and judicial branches were organized.
★ what plans the new government made to pay the United States's debts.

Terms to Know

★ ratification
★ Bill of Rights
★ cabinet
★ unconstitutional
★ national debt
★ excise tax
★ tariff

People to Meet

★ George Washington
★ John Adams
★ Thomas Jefferson
★ Alexander Hamilton
★ John Jay

Places to Locate

★ District of Columbia

▶ **WASHINGTON'S CARRIAGE**

Some people expected the occasion to be as elaborate as the crowning of a king. Instead, the central figure wore a plainly cut suit of brown, American-made broadcloth, with knee breeches and white silk hose. His hair, pulled back and tied with a ribbon, was powdered white for the occasion. Standing on the small balcony of Federal Hall in downtown New York City, **George Washington** took the oath of office on April 30, 1789:

> **I do solemnly swear that I will faithfully execute the office of President of the United States and will, to the best of my ability, preserve, protect, and defend the Constitution of the United States.**

Washington then added the words, "So help me God."

The crowds filling the streets cheered as America's first national hero became the United States's first President. This was just one of many firsts for this new government, which now faced its first challenges.

★ Shaping a New Government

Americans and foreigners alike eagerly waited to view the first actions of the unique new government in the United States of America. Was the Constitution strong enough to withstand the challenges that would confront it?

Soon after the ratification, or vote of approval, of the Constitution, elections were held for the members of the new government. Then, as the Constitution provided, members of the **electoral college**—a group of presidential electors chosen by the states—voted for two people. The person with the most electoral votes became President. The person with the next largest number became Vice President.

Electors Select Washington

The electors unanimously chose George Washington as President. Americans and foreigners alike respected, trusted, and admired him. He had earned this respect as a military hero and as president of the Constitutional Convention. **John Adams,** a lawyer and patriot leader from Massachusetts, received the next largest vote and became the first Vice President.

In those first federal elections, members of Congress were also elected. Members of the House of Representatives were elected by the people, as they are elected today. Senators, however, were chosen by the state legislatures—a practice that continued until the Constitution was amended in 1913.

With the first elections, the new government was under way. The newly elected officials—and the new nation—faced many challenges. The United States was a weak country. Its army was small, and it had no navy. Frontier settlements were under attack by Native Americans. Pirates constantly threatened American trade. The United States owed money, with no way to raise it. President Washington and the government would need to meet all these challenges.

The Reluctant President

Washington, who had spent much of his life as a soldier, reluctantly accepted the job as the first President. In a letter to a friend early in 1789, he expressed his doubts:

 ... so unwilling am I, ... to quit a peaceful abode for an ocean of difficulties, without that competency of political skill, abilities, and inclination, which are necessary to manage the helm ....

While Washington was a cautious President, he proved a capable leader who used his integrity and firmness in making sound decisions. He had no models to follow in his new job. It was his responsibility to establish the President's role in the United States government as well as to organize the executive department. Nearly everything Washington did in his first term of office established a model that later Presidents followed.

★★★ AMERICA'S FLAGS ★★★

Betsy Ross Flag, 1790 Legend holds that it was Philadelphia seamstress Betsy Ross who stitched the first Stars and Stripes. Supposedly, George Washington gave her the design and asked her to make the flag in 1776. Historical fact does not support this account, however. The popular "Betsy Ross flag," with 13 stars arranged in a circle, did not appear until the early 1790s. Its creator is unknown.

★★★★★★★★★★★★★★★★★★★★★★★★

★ The Branches of Government

Before facing these challenges, the new government had to organize itself. The Constitution had set up a framework of government with three branches that both supported and limited one another's powers. Now officials had to build a working government on that framework.

The Legislative Branch

The United States Congress, the legislative branch, met for the first time in New York City in March 1789. As the Constitution required, both houses chose leaders. Members of the House of Representatives chose as speaker Frederick Muhlenberg, a Lutheran minister from Pennsylvania. According to the Constitution, the Vice President is the official leader and president of the Senate. The first Senate chose a *president pro tempore,* who would temporarily take charge when Vice President John Adams had other duties.

Congress Passes Bill of Rights

The first session of Congress passed much important legislation. The most important was the addition of a Bill of Rights, the first 10 amendments to the Constitution. These amendments describe the powers and rights of American citizens. This answered many complaints made during the struggle for ratification of the Constitution.

Many people feared a strong central government unless citizens were specifically promised certain civil rights. To ensure ratification, the Federalists had promised to add these rights later. **James Madison,** elected to the House of Representatives in 1789, sponsored the first 10 amendments. The amendments guaranteed such rights as freedom of speech and religion and the right to trial by jury.

The necessary two-thirds majority of Congress passed the Bill of Rights in September 1789. Before the amendments could become law, however, the legislatures of three-fourths of the states had to ratify them. The Bill of Rights was not ratified until 1791. Congress passed 12 amendments, but only 10 were originally approved by the states. One of the 12 was ratified in 1992 and became the Twenty-seventh Amendment.

The Executive Branch and Cabinet

Article II of the Constitution mentions "executive departments" but does not name them. In 1789 Congress established the first three departments: State, War, and Treasury. A few months later, in the **Judiciary Act of 1789,** Congress created the office of attorney general.

As President, Washington chose the heads of the executive departments, who were called secretaries. He met with these advisers, known as the cabinet, to discuss actions and policies. This was one of the many ways that the United States was taking a different road from European governments. There, the heads of cabinet departments were chosen from members of the legislature.

The first cabinet included several outstanding men. Washington appointed the many-talented **Thomas Jefferson** of Virginia as secretary of state, in charge of foreign affairs. The first secretary of war was Henry Knox, who had been chief of artillery during the Revolution. **Alexander Hamilton,** a lawyer who had worked hard for ratification of the Constitution, became secretary of the treasury. Another respected lawyer, **Edmund Randolph** of Virginia, was named attorney general.

The Judicial Branch

The third, or judicial, branch interprets the nation's laws. The Constitution establishes only the Supreme Court as the

▲ THE FIRST CABINET Though he did not hold regular meetings with his cabinet, President Washington relied on their expert advice to help run the government. Henry Knox is seated at left. Next to him are Thomas Jefferson, Edmund Randolf (back turned), Alexander Hamilton, and Washington himself. **Who was the first secretary of state?**

▲ **MEMORIAL TANKARD**

highest court in the land. The details of organizing the rest of a court system were left to Congress.

Congress organized the federal court system with the passage of the Judiciary Act of 1789. This act stated that the Supreme Court should be made up of 1 chief justice and 5 associate justices. Today the Supreme Court has 9 members (a chief justice and 8 associate justices). The Judiciary Act of 1789 also set up lower federal courts—3 circuit courts and 13 district courts.

The Judiciary Act of 1789 made clear the Supreme Court's power over state courts. It gave the Supreme Court the power to rule on the decisions of state courts about whether state laws were unconstitutional—that is, contrary to what is written in the Constitution.

Washington appointed **John Jay** as the first chief justice. Jay was a successful New York lawyer who had been one of the writers of *The Federalist,* which argued for the ratification of the Constitution. According to the Constitution, Supreme Court justices are appointed by the President with the advice and consent of Congress.

★ A Nation in Debt

The new United States faced many financial challenges in the early 1790s, but probably the most serious of these was the large debt from the Revolutionary War. The total amount a government owes on money it has borrowed is called the national debt. The government had borrowed millions of dollars from foreign governments and individual citizens to finance the American Revolution. Many states were also in debt from the war.

Alexander Hamilton Develops Economic Plan

Alexander Hamilton was born on the island of Nevis in the West Indies in 1755. He worked with a trading company in the Caribbean until his employers, impressed by his skills and ambition, sent him to school in New York.

As a student, Hamilton wrote fiery pamphlets for independence. At 22, he became an aide to General George Washington early in the Revolution. In 1782 he became a lawyer and was one of New York's delegates to the Continental Congress. Working hard to ratify the Constitution, he wrote letters to newspapers as well as essays that were part of *The Federalist*.

Hamilton had a strong, clear vision of the United States's future. As he tried to build a strong federal government, he disagreed openly with members of Congress and others—especially Thomas Jefferson—who favored strong state governments.

As secretary of the treasury, he developed an economic plan to deal with the nation's debts and provide a secure base of credit for the country. His plan called for the federal government to pay the debts owed by both the nation and the states.

Opposition to Hamilton's Plan

Many Southerners, notably James Madison, did not like Hamilton's plan. Most states in the South had paid off their debts. Also, many Southern farmers had sold their government bonds to Northern merchants at very low prices because they needed cash. According to Hamilton's plan, federal funds would pay the new owners of the bonds, so tax money from the South would end up in Northern hands. Southerners, led by Jefferson, opposed the plan also because they did

▲ **ALEXANDER HAMILTON**

not want to see the power of the state governments weakened by being dependent on the federal government.

Compromise

Together Madison and Jefferson reached a compromise with Hamilton. Jefferson and his Southern followers agreed to the payment of state debts in return for a promise to locate the new national capital in the South. It would be built along the Potomac River between Maryland and Virginia. A special territory, the **District of Columbia,** was created so that no one state could claim the capital city. While waiting for the new Capitol to be built, Congress made Philadelphia the capital city.

In 1795 Hamilton resigned as secretary of the treasury. President Washington reluctantly accepted his resignation and wrote him an appreciative letter: "In every relation that you have borne to me, I have found that my confidence in your talents, exertions, and integrity has been well placed." Hamilton remained a trusted friend to Washington and one of the most influential people in government.   ★★★

★ The Bank of the United States

Another important part of Hamilton's financial plan was a national bank. He proposed four duties for the bank. The bank would handle the federal government's money. It would also help collect tax money, issue paper money, and give out loans to help the growth of businesses.

Many people in the country thought a national bank was a bad idea. Since the Constitution did not establish a national bank, they argued, the government did not have the power to set it up. Southerners, including Jefferson and Madison, argued that the bank would create a wealthy upper class. They pointed out that Hamilton was helping wealthy Northern merchants at the expense of Southern farmers. Bankers, investors, and Congress, however, favored Hamilton's plan. In 1791, Congress passed a bill creating the Bank of the United States.

Taxes and Rebellions

Once the government had agreed to pay the war debts, Hamilton needed a plan to raise money. The national government also needed money for improvements such as bridges and highways. Hamilton wanted to levy an excise tax—a tax placed on goods made, sold, and used within the country. He also wanted to set import tariffs, or taxes placed on certain manufactured goods brought into the country. Besides raising money, the tax on imports would make foreign goods expensive to buy. That would encourage the growth of American industries, another of Hamilton's goals. Congress passed these taxes in 1791 and 1792.

The Whiskey Rebellion

The new excise tax on whiskey, however, angered farmers on the Western frontier. Because bad roads made it hard for them to ship grains such as rye and corn to market, they turned their crops into whiskey, which was used almost like cash on the frontier. The whiskey tax, they felt, was as unfair as British taxes had been. In 1794, government agents clashed with farmers in western Pennsylvania who refused to pay the tax. Fighting broke out, and several people were killed.

The so-called **Whiskey Rebellion** was a test of the new federal government's power. President Washington responded angrily. He sent in the militia, and the revolt was over.

★ SECTION 1 REVIEW ★

Checking for Understanding

1. **Identify** George Washington, John Adams, Thomas Jefferson, Alexander Hamilton, John Jay, District of Columbia.
2. **Define** ratification, Bill of Rights, cabinet, unconstitutional, national debt, excise tax, tariff.
3. **What** were some challenges facing the United States when George Washington became the first President?
4. **What** did Hamilton see as the duties of the Bank of the United States?

Critical Thinking

5. **Recognizing Points of View** Why did Hamilton believe that the federal government should pay the states' war debts as well as its own? Why did some states object?

ACTIVITY

6. Put yourself in the place of President Washington choosing his first cabinet members. Write a Help Wanted advertisement for one of these official positions: chief justice, secretary of the treasury, secretary of state.

Gilbert Stuart, Portrait Painter

"Only Gilbert Stuart, you know, can paint a true portrait," claimed art lovers of the late 1700s. "He doesn't just paint a face; he shows character!"

Perhaps it was Stuart's single-minded interest in faces that allowed him to capture a personality on canvas. After establishing his career in Britain, he came back to America in 1793.

As the leading American portrait painter during the Federalist period, Stuart ignored a number of art techniques used by other artists. He rarely painted full-length portraits or detailed backgrounds. Instead, he concentrated on the face, placing the subject in light that shone directly on his or her features, while leaving the background dark or cloudy.

Faces—Stuart was interested primarily in faces. With quick, broad strokes he first created an indistinct, cloudy image on the canvas. Then gradually, with more quick strokes, he brought the face "into focus" as he saw it. While Stuart painted, he talked, laughed, and told stories and jokes to be sure that his model's face was lively and full of expression.

Stuart began painting when he was 13, and his popularity as a portrait painter lasted throughout his life. Many people wanted to be painted in his unique style, though he sometimes disappointed people with unfinished pictures. While successful, he was often in debt because he enjoyed living well. One of his most famous paintings is this unfinished portrait of George Washington, one of several paintings he made of the first President.

▲ UNFINISHED PORTRAIT OF GEORGE WASHINGTON

Making the Arts Connection

1. For what kind of paintings was Gilbert Stuart most famous?

2. What techniques did Stuart use to focus on his subjects' faces?

3. What were some techniques used by other artists during the Federalist period?

ACTIVITY

4. Gilbert Stuart was particularly well-known for his remarkable skill in capturing the skin's various tones. To do so, he used a combination of colors. Trace around your hand on a sheet of paper. Then, using crayons, pencils, or paints, experiment to see how close you can come to reproducing the tones of your skin.

Dealing With Other Nations

Read to Learn . . .

★ why the United States tried to remain neutral in European wars.
★ how the Jay Treaty with Britain affected the new nation.
★ why Washington decided not to seek a third term as President.

Terms to Know

★ tribute
★ neutral
★ impress

People to Meet

★ John Jay
★ Thomas Pinckney

Places to Locate

★ Appalachian Mountains
★ Northwest Territory
★ Mediterranean Sea
★ Barbary Coast

◀ HOOKED RUG, 1790s

As a newcomer to world politics, the United States in the 1790s was weak compared with the powerful European nations—Great Britain, France, and Spain. The United States had only a small army and no navy. It had to work hard to gain the respect of other countries.

★ Challenges From Other Nations

The United States was not yet strong enough to risk getting involved in world conflicts. It found other ways to settle disputes with the nations that challenged it both in North America and overseas.

Conflicts in the Northwest Territory

The Treaty of Paris in 1783 was supposed to settle arguments about the land west of the **Appalachian Mountains.** On paper this land belonged to the United States. The British had agreed to leave their forts in the **Northwest Territory**—a region bounded by the Ohio River, the Great Lakes, and the Mississippi River—and stop trading with Native Americans.

In the 1790s, however, Great Britain still had forts in the Ohio Valley and Great Lakes region. They continued to trade with their Native American allies and stir them up against settlers. As American settlers moved West, Native Americans attempted

▲ TREATY OF GREENVILLE After the loss at the Battle of Fallen Timbers, the Shawnee lost any hope of keeping their land. **Who led the Shawnee at the Battle of Fallen Timbers?**

to defend their lands. With weapons and encouragement from the British, the Miami and other groups attacked American frontier settlements in the Ohio Valley, driving some settlers away.

President Washington hoped to end the bloodshed. In 1790 and 1791, Washington sent troops into the Northwest Territory. The federal troops were badly defeated by Native Americans led by Miami Chief Little Turtle. An alliance of the Miami, Shawnee, and Delaware continued to resist the takeover of their lands.

As the violence spread, Washington ordered the governor of the Northwest Territory, General Arthur St. Clair, to the region with a huge American army to defeat the Native Americans. St. Clair moved north from Cincinnati and into Native American territory. His army, badly weakened by disease and desertion, was attacked in November 1791 near the present-day Ohio-Indiana border. Only 500 American soldiers survived one of the worst defeats in American military history.

The Native Americans demanded that all settlers north of the Ohio River leave the territory. Washington sent another army headed by Anthony Wayne, a former Revolutionary War general, to challenge their

demands. In August 1794, Wayne's army defeated 800 Native Americans under Shawnee Chief Blue Jacket at the **Battle of Fallen Timbers** (near present-day Toledo). The Battle of Fallen Timbers crushed the Native Americans' hopes of keeping their land. In the **Treaty of Greenville** (1795), the Native Americans agreed to surrender most of the land in present-day Ohio.

Spain Controls the Mississippi

Spain held the Louisiana Territory, located west of the Mississippi River. Spain had gained this territory during the French and Indian War. For years Spain and the United States had argued about boundaries and Americans' right to use the Mississippi River and the port of New Orleans for trade. This route was especially important for people living west of the Appalachians. They shipped their crops by flatboat down the Ohio and Mississippi Rivers. Spanish officials often made trouble for foreigners in Louisiana.

Pirates in the Mediterranean

Americans trading abroad met a different enemy. In the **Mediterranean Sea,** traders faced pirates from the states of the **Barbary Coast** of North Africa—Morocco, Algiers, Tunis, and Tripoli. Pirates stole cargoes, seized American ships, and imprisoned American sailors. The Barbary pirates ignored the protests of the United States, knowing it was powerless without a navy. To sail safely, the United States had to pay tribute, or protection money, to local rulers.

★ Choosing Neutrality

The most serious challenge from abroad came with the beginning of the French Revolution. In 1789 many French people rebelled against the high taxes and oppressive rule of the monarchy and set up a republic. Over several years of bloody fighting, the king and queen of France and many aristocrats were arrested and beheaded on the guillotine.

Monarchs in other European countries worried that the fight for liberty and equality in France might spill over into their countries. In 1793 Great Britain and several other nations went to war against the revolutionary government of France.

France now called on the United States to abide by the Treaty of Alliance of 1778. According to this treaty, the two nations would provide aid to each other in war. President Washington, however, wanted the United States to stay neutral, or not take sides. He believed the country was not prepared to go to war. In particular, he did not want to challenge the British navy. He sought the advice of his two chief cabinet officers, Thomas Jefferson and Alexander Hamilton.

Hamilton and Jefferson Disagree

As they did on many other issues, Hamilton and Jefferson disagreed on a policy toward France. Hamilton supported Washington's decision for a number of reasons. Like many other Americans, he was horrified when the French Revolution turned to violence and bloodshed. For practical reasons, too, Hamilton believed that the United States should stay on good terms with Great Britain. After all, three-fourths of America's trade was with Britain. Tariffs on British goods brought in a great deal of money. Besides, the British had asked only for neutrality, not help.

Jefferson thought the Treaty of Alliance with France was still binding. Jefferson believed in the democratic ideals of the revolution in France. He and many Americans supported the French revolutionaries who were demanding the same rights that Americans had won a few years earlier. He believed that an alliance with France gave the United States more power to bargain with Great Britain.

Washington Makes a Decision

Washington decided to recognize the new French Republic. He explained to the French, however, that the 1778 treaty had been made with King Louis XVI, who had been executed. The United States had no treaty with the new French government. In April 1793, Washington issued a **Proclamation of Neutrality,** stating that the United States would continue to trade with both France and Great Britain. He declared that the United States would be "friendly and impartial." He warned that Americans who helped either side would be denied the protection of the government and would be subject to punishment.

The Genet Affair

Many Americans, however, still felt sympathy for the French revolutionaries. They welcomed a French diplomat, Edmond Genet (zhuh•NAY), who came seeking financial help. Although he won much popular support, Genet went too far. He plotted to ignore Washington's neutrality order and equip ships to fight the British. This put Washington's neutrality proclamation to the test.

Challenges to Neutrality

As Genet had shown, staying neutral was not easy. When Americans tried to trade with both Great Britain and France, the result was an undeclared war at sea. Both the French and the British seized hundreds of American ships. The powerful British navy, however, caused the most harm to American merchant shipping.

Late in 1793 the British government passed a series of rules limiting the rights of neutral ships at sea. The British ships not only stopped and seized American ships, they also impressed, or kidnapped, American sailors to serve in the British navy. The British claimed that these sailors were really British citizens who had "jumped ship," or moved to America from Britain.

★ Agreement With Great Britain

The President's principal advisers, Jefferson and Hamilton, again disagreed on how to act toward Britain. Jefferson advised a ban, or embargo, on imports of British goods, but Hamilton said that such a ban would hurt the American economy as well. Instead, he suggested that Washington send a peace mission to London to meet with British officials. Chief Justice **John Jay** led the mission.

Although Great Britain was far more powerful than the United States, British officials were willing to listen to Jay's proposals. They did not want to lose American trade or see the United States allied with France. Great Britain's former colonies were still its most profitable market. As a result, they agreed to a treaty.

The **Jay Treaty,** signed late in 1794, dealt with several troublesome issues. Britain agreed to withdraw from its forts in the Northwest Territory. It also allowed American merchant ships to trade in the British West Indies. Commissions were to settle the disputed boundaries between Canada and the United States. The United States agreed to see that private debts would be repaid.

The Jay Treaty disappointed many Americans. The British had not promised to stop seizing American ships or kidnapping American sailors. Many people were

 ▲ OUTRAGE OVER THE JAY TREATY Americans symbolically burned Chief Justice John Jay because his treaty did not stop the seizing of American ships by Great Britain. **What effect did the Jay Treaty have on the relationship between the United States and Spain?**

also upset at the idea of paying debts to Britain for the American Revolution.

Washington agreed to the treaty and asked the Senate to ratify it. The treaty passed by a slim margin and provided peace. This gave the young nation time to become stronger and more prosperous.

• •

Footnotes to History

The "First President"   The first person to be addressed "President of the United States" was not George Washington. In 1781 Maryland finally ratified the Articles of Confederation, and the union among the 13 states went into effect. John Hanson, the man who signed the Articles for Maryland, was immediately elected president of the assembly. His formal title was President of the United States in Congress Assembled.

When Washington won his great victory at Yorktown during the American Revolution, Hanson sent him a letter to congratulate him. Washington wrote back to Hanson, addressing his letter to the President of the United States. There was no executive branch under the Articles. Hanson's position was comparable to that of the speaker of the House today.

★ Agreement With Spain

The Jay Treaty caused Spain to rethink its foreign policy with the United States. Spanish leaders now realized that the United States and Great Britain might work together against the Spanish Empire in North America.

This alarmed Spanish leaders and led them to make a treaty with the American envoy, **Thomas Pinckney,** in October 1795. According to Pinckney's Treaty, American ships were allowed to use the lower Mississippi and to trade through the port of New Orleans. Spain recognized the 31st parallel as the southern boundary of the United States and the Mississippi River as the western boundary.

★ Washington Leaves Office

During Washington's two terms of office, he established a firm foundation for the new national government. He made the presidency a stronger office than had been expected. By deciding not to seek reelection in 1796, he set a standard. Until 1941 no American President served more than two terms.

Many people encouraged Washington to seek another term, but he was tired of public office. In his mid-sixties, he wanted to retire to his estate at Mount Vernon.

Washington's Farewell Address

As was his time in office, the words of Washington's Farewell Address were a guide to future leaders. He urged them to be independent in dealing with other nations:

> The great rule of conduct for us, in regard to foreign Nations, is . . . to have with them as little Political connection as possible. . . .
>
> 'Tis our true policy to steer clear of permanent alliances, with any portion of the foreign world;—so far, I mean, as we are now at liberty to do it. . . .

Washington cautioned the nation to guard against threats to its unity. In his address, Washington warned against the development of divisive political parties and rivalries between the Northern and Southern interests in the country.

★ SECTION 2 REVIEW ★

Checking for Understanding

1. **Identify** John Jay, Thomas Pinckney, Appalachian Mountains, Northwest Territory, Mediterranean Sea, Barbary Coast.

2. **Define** tribute, neutral, impress.

3. **What** other powers in North America were a challenge to the United States in the 1790s?

4. **How** did the French Revolution affect American foreign affairs?

5. **What** troublesome issues did the Jay Treaty deal with?

Critical Thinking

6. **Drawing Conclusions** Why did Washington warn against making alliances with foreign nations? What characteristics of the United States in the 1790s would make this good advice?

ACTIVITY

7. Make a map showing possible trade routes that might take American ships along the Barbary Coast. Label the nations of Morocco, Algiers, Tunis, and Tripoli.

★★★

Political Parties Develop

SETTING THE SCENE

Read to Learn . . .

★ what caused political parties to form in the United States.
★ who were the leaders of the first political parties.
★ what issues were important in the election of 1796.

Terms to Know

★ Federalists
★ Democratic-Republicans
★ political party
★ loose construction
★ strict construction
★ caucus

People to Meet

★ John Fenno
★ Philip Freneau
★ Thomas Pinckney
★ Aaron Burr

February 22nd, 1732
December 14th, 1799

▲ WASHINGTON BANNER

When George Washington took office for his first term, the country had no political parties. By the end of his second term that had changed. He worried that the nation's unity would be threatened by leaders with differing views. He feared that these differences would split the nation.

Washington had reason to worry. He had seen his closest advisers, Alexander Hamilton and Thomas Jefferson, disagree so bitterly about government policies that both had resigned from the cabinet. They were brilliant leaders who had the support of many citizens who held the same beliefs and viewpoints.

★ Dividing Into Parties

On most issues, Hamilton and Jefferson disagreed too sharply for any kind of compromise. Even before Washington's second term ended, their followers had split to form two groups. The group led by Hamilton, which supported most of the decisions made by the government, were known as Federalists. Jefferson and James Madison led an opposition group known as the Democratic-Republicans (sometimes called Republicans, but not related to the modern Republican party).

The two parties reflected their leaders' personalities in many ways. Hamilton was sharp, focused, and ambitious, an active political leader. Jefferson, more a country gentleman, appeared more relaxed, although his mind was constantly working on new ideas. He expressed his democratic ideals but tried to avoid actual politics.

The First Parties

The Federalists and the Democratic-Republicans were the nation's first political parties. A political party is a group of people with similar ideas and beliefs about government. The members of a political party usually agree on the way to run the government and on the policies that should be carried out. Members of political parties work together to get their leaders elected and to influence government decisions.

The Constitution made no provisions for political parties. The authors of the Constitution actually had hoped that political parties would not form. They did not like what they saw as the results of political parties in other countries. During the fight over ratification of the Constitution,

those who favored a central government—all the new national leaders—were known as Federalists.

★ Conflicting Party Viewpoints

The Framers of the Constitution shared many of the same ideas and beliefs about government. Still, they had to make some compromises over issues that seriously divided them. Conflict over some of these issues later returned to destroy the unity of the country.

Differing Views

As you have read, Hamilton, rather than Jefferson, influenced many of President Washington's decisions. Like Hamilton, Washington wanted to ensure the strength of the central government. Jefferson, on the other hand, wanted a weak central government. Even though Washington tried to stand apart from opposing groups and be a symbol of national unity, he was thought of as a Federalist.

Trying to keep a balance, however, Washington had tried to get the two men

Differences Between the First Political Parties

Federalists	Democratic-Republicans	Chart Study
Leader: Alexander Hamilton	**Leader:** Thomas Jefferson	Hamilton and Jefferson represented the beliefs of opposition parties. **Which leader would have encouraged trade with France?**
Favored: • Rule by the wealthy and educated class • Strong federal government • Emphasis on manufactured products • Loose interpretation of Constitution • Pro-British, anti-French positions • National bank • Protective tariffs	**Favored:** • Rule by the people • Strong state governments • Emphasis on agricultural products • Strict interpretation of the Constitution • Pro-French, anti-British positions • State banks • Free trade	

Japanese Imports

Using products made in Japan is nothing new for Americans. Two hundred years ago, however, the imports were not electronic chips or luxury cars.

▶ LACQUER PLATE

Then

Lacquer Boxes and Woven Mats

For most of the 1700s, Japan was largely closed to traders from the West. Yet in May of 1799, Captain James Devereaux brought his ship *Franklin* back to Boston from a voyage to the Dutch East Indies and Japan. Landing in Japan had not been on the captain's original schedule, but he was given a chance to make a run into Nagasaki harbor. There he traded sugar, tin, elephant tusks, cotton goods, pepper, and cloves for shiny lacquer boxes and trays, Japanese mats, and pans.

Now

Cameras and Cars

Today the United States is Japan's main trading partner. From Japanese factories to American stores come automobiles, televisions, VCRs, stereos, cameras, and computers. Look around you. What Japanese products are part of your everyday life?

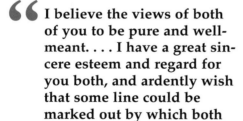

▶ JAPANESE CAR

to work out their differences. Knowing Jefferson was discontented, Washington wrote him this note:

> 66 I believe the views of both of you to be pure and well-meant. . . . I have a great sincere esteem and regard for you both, and ardently wish that some line could be marked out by which both [of] you could walk. 99

Nevertheless, by 1793 Jefferson was so unhappy that he resigned as secretary of state. The rival groups and their points of view moved further apart.

Federalist Viewpoints

Federalists represented mainly the interests of the gentry—wealthy Americans such as manufacturers, bankers, and business owners. Much of their support was in the big cities of the Northeast such as Philadelphia, New York, and Boston.

Some plantation owners in the South also agreed with Federalist views. Hamilton and his followers wanted to see the government run by wealthy, successful people. They found popular democracy a disturbing idea.

The Federalists supported a strong national government that they believed would hold the states together in a firm union. They wanted the government to support the growth of cities, trade, businesses, and industries. In foreign policy, they supported the country's chief trading partner—Great Britain.

Federalists worked to increase the power of the national government, based on what the Constitution allowed. Because the Constitution was a very general framework, however, it did not answer some specific problems. The Federalists, therefore, looked at the meaning behind the words in the Constitution and interpreted them to allow the government to do more. This is called following a loose construction of the Constitution.

The Democratic-Republican View

In contrast, the Democratic-Republicans favored the interests of artisans, shopkeepers, and small farmers. The party drew much of its support from the South. Jefferson and other members of the party believed in the ability of ordinary people to govern themselves. He wanted power to be shared by all the people, not limited to a small, select group.

The United States in the 1790s was overwhelmingly a farming nation. Small farmers made up about 90 percent of the population. Jefferson loved the country and believed that farm families who owned and worked their land were the nation's strength. According to Jefferson, "Those who labour in the earth are the chosen people of God." He wanted to establish a system of public education to help farmers better understand and defend their rights and freedoms.

Jefferson took a dim view of the growth of cities and manufacturing—the opposite of the Federalists' support for them. Like many people in rural areas, he saw cities as evil. "The mobs of great cities," he said, "add so much to the support of pure government, as sores do to the strength of the human body."

In foreign policy, the Democratic-Republicans supported the new French Republic rather than Great Britain. They looked on France as an ally.

Rather than work for a strong central government, Democratic-Republicans worked to increase the power and independence of state governments. They believed in limiting the authority of the federal government to the powers specifically granted to it in the Constitution. This is called a strict construction of the Constitution.

The Political Press Widens the Gap

Since colonial times, American newspapers had been very political. In the 1790s the number of newspapers more than doubled, drawing still more readers. The new political parties quickly sponsored newspapers that followed their viewpoints. Both Jefferson and Hamilton probably wrote anonymously for their respective papers, even though both were still in the government.

The Federalists' newspaper for shaping public opinion was the *Gazette of the United States.* Its editor and publisher was **John Fenno.** The *Gazette* praised the decisions of Washington's administration, many of which followed Hamilton's advice.

In 1791, Jefferson and Madison chose the poet **Philip Freneau** to start a rival newspaper, the *National Gazette.* Many articles and editorials in the paper criticized Washington's administration. Freneau was a skillful writer who attacked Hamilton in print as an enemy of true republican government while praising Jefferson as "that illustrious Patriot, Statesman, and Philosopher."

▲ *THE RESIDENCE OF DAVID TWINNING* by Edward Hicks, 1787 Jefferson and the Democratic-Republicans believed that farming families and ordinary people were the strength of the United States. **What percentage of the population were farmers in the 1790s?**

Throughout 1793 Hamilton and Jefferson and their supporters engaged in a nasty battle of words in the two newspapers, calling each other names and accusing the other of all kinds of dishonorable actions that were harmful to the nation. Writing under the pen name "T.L.," Hamilton accused Jefferson of encouraging division in the United States, "which, unless soon checked, may involve the country in all the horrors of anarchy."

★ Politics Dominate the Election of 1796

The rivalries between the Federalists and the Democratic-Republicans spread into Congress. Both parties tried to gain control of Congress. During Washington's second term, the Democratic-Republicans won a majority of seats in the House of Representatives.

For the first time, political parties chose the candidates for the presidential election of 1796. The Federalists supported **John Adams** for President and **Thomas Pinckney** for Vice President. The Democratic-Republican candidate for President was **Thomas Jefferson.** Their candidate for Vice President was **Aaron Burr,** a well-known lawyer who was a senator from New York.

Party Caucus

The four candidates were chosen by each political party at a caucus, or private meeting, held by congressional leaders. Because the Constitution did not mention political parties or ways of nominating candidates for President, party leaders developed the caucus.

The Constitution provided that the presidency and vice presidency would go to the two candidates with the highest number of electoral votes. Each elector voted for two candidates, without specifying which was for President or which was for Vice President. In 1796 this brought political rivals together in office.

When the electoral votes were counted, the Federalist candidate John Adams received the highest number of votes—71. Jefferson, the Democratic-Republican leader, received the second-highest number of votes—68. This meant that the President and Vice President came from opposing political parties. Would this bring balance to the executive branch and unite the two parties? Or would the differences between the two parties grow wider?

★ SECTION 3 REVIEW ★

Checking for Understanding

1. **Identify** John Fenno, Philip Freneau, Thomas Pinckney, Aaron Burr.

2. **Define** Federalists, Democratic-Republicans, political party, loose construction, strict construction, caucus.

3. **What** were the major differences between the Federalist and Democratic-Republican parties?

4. **What** was the outcome of the presidential election of 1796?

Critical Thinking

5. **Identifying Alternatives** Why did political parties form in the United States? Could they have been avoided?

ACTIVITY

6. Create a political cartoon that reflects the views of the editor of either the *National Gazette*, which supported Jefferson and the Democratic-Republicans, or the *Gazette of the United States*, which supported Hamilton and the Federalists.

Writing a Paragraph

Paragraphs are the building blocks of an essay or other composition. Each *paragraph* is a unit, a group of sentences about a single topic or idea. The shortest story and the longest book are each made up of paragraphs carefully arranged in logical order.

Learning the Skill

Most well-written paragraphs share four characteristics. Learning how to put a paragraph together gives you a flexible and useful tool in writing.

• First, a paragraph expresses one main idea or is about one subject. Especially in informative writing, a *topic sentence* states that main idea. The topic sentence may be located at the beginning, the middle, or the end of a paragraph.

▲ BENJAMIN BANNEKER

• Second, the rest of the sentences in a paragraph support the main idea. The main idea may be developed by facts and definition, by examples or incidents, or by reasons.

• Third, the sentences are arranged in a logical order.

• Fourth, transitional words or phrases link sentences within the paragraph. These words can also link one paragraph with the next. Examples include *next, then, finally, also, because, however,* and *as a result.*

Practicing the Skill

Use the sentences below to build a paragraph containing a topic sentence and other sentences that give supporting details. Arrange the sentences in a logical order and add transitional words if you need to. Underline your topic sentence.

1. Because of his talent, George Washington made him part of the team planning the new federal district.

2. In 1789 he correctly predicted an eclipse.

3. He became the first African American appointed to a job by a President of the United States.

4. Benjamin Banneker, an African American from Maryland, had an unusual career.

5. In 1771 he began to study astronomy.

APPLYING THE SKILL

6. Choose a topic that interests you—a place, a hobby, a sport—and write two explanatory paragraphs about it. Organize the paragraphs differently, if possible. Then exchange papers with a classmate. Can he or she find the topic sentence in your paragraph? Does it work logically?

★★

Troubled Times for John Adams

SETTING THE SCENE

Read to Learn . . .

★ how problems with France divided the nation.
★ what laws the Federalists passed to hurt the Democratic-Republicans.
★ how the Federalist party lost power.

Terms to Know

★ XYZ Affair
★ alien
★ deport
★ sedition
★ nullify
★ states' rights

People to Meet

★ John Adams
★ Charles C. Pinckney
★ Charles Maurice de Talleyrand
★ Abigail Adams

Places to Locate

★ Washington, D.C.

◀ JOHN ADAMS

The first election dominated by political parties had a strange outcome—the President and Vice President belonged to different parties. The division between their points of view, complicated by problems with France, would make President **John Adams**'s term in office a stormy time for the country.

★ Adams in Office

Adams had served the American colonies and the United States in many ways before he became President. One of Massachusetts's most active Patriots, he later became ambassador to France, to the Netherlands, and to Great Britain. He helped to negotiate the Treaty of Paris with the British in 1783 that ended the Revolution.

In the first presidential election in the United States, Adams became Washington's Vice President. He described that post as "the most insignificant office that ever the invention of man contrived. . . ." Still, as a dedicated Federalist, he backed the policies followed by Washington and Hamilton. Adams was a testy, stubborn man whose personality may have kept him from getting the respect he deserved.

Problems With France

As the United States tried to stay neutral during Washington's second term, relations with France grew worse. The French were unhappy with the Jay Treaty, which protected trade with Great Britain. French ships stopped American ships in the Caribbean and seized their cargoes. The French also tried to influence the 1796 election in favor of Jefferson, who sympathized with France.

When Adams began his presidency, anti-French feelings ran high. Americans were furious that the French were interfering with both trade and politics. Adams knew this might be his biggest challenge. Early in 1797, he wrote to Henry Knox, former secretary of war:

> **I have it much at heart to settle all disputes with France, and nothing shall be wanting on my part to accomplish it, excepting a violation of our faith and a sacrifice of our honor. But old as I am, war is, even to me, less dreadful than iniquity [wickedness] or deserved disgrace.**

To avoid war with France, Adams sent a three-person peace commission to Paris. The diplomats were prominent political figures—**John Marshall, Charles C. Pinckney,** and **Elbridge Gerry.**

The meeting with the French, however, made relations even worse. The French foreign minister, **Charles Maurice de Talleyrand,** sent three agents to meet with the Americans. The French agents offered the Americans a treaty with France—at a price. The French agents demanded that a bribe of $250,000 and a loan of about $10 million be paid to Talleyrand. Outraged at being asked for a bribe, Pinckney replied, "No! Not a sixpence!"

The XYZ Affair

The event soon became public, with the French agents known only as X, Y, and Z. The so-called XYZ Affair made many people even angrier with France, bringing the two countries closer to war. A popular slogan was "Millions for defense, but not one cent for tribute!"

Congress quickly voted to enlarge the United States army and navy. Soon American warships were waging an undeclared naval war with France.

Winning the Peace

The XYZ Affair forced President Adams to seriously consider asking Congress to declare war on France to preserve American honor. He angrily blamed not only the French but also Americans who showed "unqualified devotion to the

Footnotes to History

Not One Cent for Tribute?   For many years Americans took pride in their popular slogan, "Millions for defense, but not one cent for tribute." Historically, however, the statement was not really true. In the early years of the Republic, the United States often paid tribute to other countries to avoid war. In 1786 the United States gave $10,000 to Morocco, in 1795 it began giving a yearly tribute of $21,600 to Algiers. In 1805 the United States paid Tripoli $60,000 for the return of captured American citizens. As you will learn in Chapter 11, the United States eventually went to war to end this practice.

Picturing History

▲ THE XYZ AFFAIR This political cartoon shows Americans resisting threats and demands for money from French officials. **What did the French agents demand in return for a treaty with France?**

French Republic." This accusation, of course, was aimed at Jefferson and the Democratic-Republicans.

Before publicly asking Congress to declare war, Adams decided to wait. He hoped that either France would negotiate or the American people would unite against France. Soon Talleyrand did want to meet again with American diplomats. France's new leader, **Napoleon Bonaparte,** was at war with Britain and did not want the United States as an enemy too.

Adams once again sent an American peace commission. In the **Convention of 1800,** France and the United States agreed on terms for peace.

Losing Federalist Support

Many historians consider that making peace with France was Adams's greatest achievement as President. At the time, though, many Federalists were angry

about the treaty. They vigorously opposed friendship with France. Many were eager for war as a way to strengthen the federal government. Hamilton himself hoped to lead the army. Making peace divided the Federalists and lost Adams the support of his own party. Adams, however, was very proud of his accomplishment. He wrote that he wanted the following words on his gravestone: "Here lies John Adams who took upon himself the responsibility of the peace with France in the year 1800."

★ Alien and Sedition Acts

Beginning in 1798, the Federalist-controlled Congress passed four laws that stirred up a storm of debate. The new laws were aimed at stopping the growth of the Democratic-Republican party. Three of the laws, known collectively as the Alien Acts, were supposedly to protect the country from aliens, or foreigners living in the United States.

The **Naturalization Act** increased the time required to become a United States citizen from 5 to 14 years. Federalists wanted to make citizenship more difficult for newcomers. Most new immigrants coming from France and Ireland joined the Democratic-Republican party.

The **Alien Act** gave the President power to imprison or deport—send out of the country—any foreigner. This applied to people from both friendly and enemy nations, if they were considered dangerous. The Federalists hoped this law would silence the French refugees who opposed Federalist calls for war.

The **Alien Enemies Act** allowed the United States government to arrest and deport all aliens who were citizens of foreign nations at war with the United States.

The final law in this group was the **Sedition Act.** Sedition means to act or speak out against the government in a way that causes unrest. This law made it a crime to speak or write critically about the President, members of Congress, the federal government, or federal laws. Its purpose was to silence criticism.

Under the Sedition Act, about 25 Democratic-Republican newspaper editors and others were arrested and 10 were convicted for printing criticisms of President Adams. No aliens were ever deported under these laws. The Alien and Sedition acts brought a quick, angry response from Jefferson and other Democratic-Republicans.

Madison and Jefferson Respond

To Jefferson, James Madison, and others, the Sedition Act looked like a direct attack on the Bill of Rights and the liberties of Americans. It violated the First Amendment to the Constitution, which protects freedom of speech and of the press. Free speech includes the right to criticize the President and other government leaders.

To challenge the Sedition Act, Madison and Jefferson wrote two statements, or resolutions, that were approved by the state legislatures of Virginia and of Kentucky.

The Kentucky and Virginia Resolutions

The Kentucky and Virginia Resolutions of 1798 claimed that the Alien and Sedition acts could not be put into action because they were in violation of the Constitution.

Moreover, the resolutions said, the people of each state had the right to nullify, or cancel, a federal law within that state. Each state could determine whether the federal government had gone beyond its constitutional powers. It could then decide whether or not to obey such laws. This was the states' rights theory. It was one of the principles that anti-Federalists, who opposed a strong federal government, had always held.

The Federalists, believers in a strong federal government, rejected the states' rights theory. They argued that the people of the United States had formed the federal government and that only the Supreme Court could declare a law unconstitutional. No other state legislature agreed with the Kentucky and Virginia Resolutions. The resolutions, however, did raise questions about whether the states or the federal government had the final say over the constitutionality of laws.

These questions were not resolved during Jefferson's lifetime. The issue over states' rights would reappear in the 1830s.

★ Federalists Lose Power

The Federalists remained the major political power in 1798, although a rival party was quickly growing. The Federalists controlled Congress and the presidency. The Sedition Act and the harsh way it was enforced, however, made the Federalists and John Adams look high-handed and tyrannical. Many people still feared the idea of a king or a government with too much power. By 1800 the Federalists had lost the support of many people.

John Adams also had other problems when he sought reelection to the presidency in 1800. His stand on making peace with France had split his own party. Hamilton and other Federalists refused to support Adams as their presidential candidate.

At the same time, Jefferson and the Democratic-Republicans were gaining support in every state. In many people's minds, Jefferson stood for more liberty and less government.

Thomas Jefferson was the obvious choice as the Democratic-Republican candidate for President. Aaron Burr, a well-known New York lawyer and former senator, was their candidate for Vice President. Burr had helped organize the

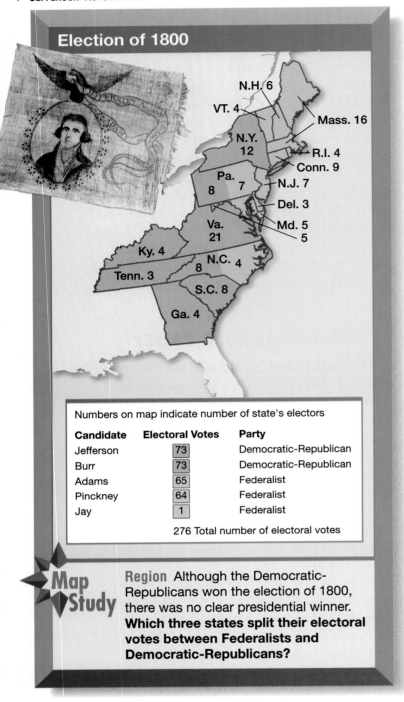

Election of 1800

Numbers on map indicate number of state's electors

Candidate	Electoral Votes	Party
Jefferson	73	Democratic-Republican
Burr	73	Democratic-Republican
Adams	65	Federalist
Pinckney	64	Federalist
Jay	1	Federalist

276 Total number of electoral votes

Map Study

Region Although the Democratic-Republicans won the election of 1800, there was no clear presidential winner. **Which three states split their electoral votes between Federalists and Democratic-Republicans?**

as a force that would destroy the nation. The final voting came closer than expected and produced a strange result. The Federalist candidates, John Adams and Charles C. Pinckney (brother of Thomas Pinckney), received 65 and 64 electoral votes, respectively. *Both* Democratic-Republican candidates (Jefferson and Burr), however, received 73 votes.

The Democratic-Republicans had won. But who was President, Jefferson or Burr? The party had meant Jefferson to be President, but the voting method did not make this clear. The ambitious Burr would not step aside, and the battle for the presidency became a personal struggle between Burr and Jefferson. According to the Constitution, the tie-breaking vote now went to the House of Representatives.

Hamilton Swings the Vote

For this vote, each state had one vote in the House. At first most Federalists voted for Burr, whom they disliked somewhat less than the hated Jefferson. Then the Federalist leader Alexander Hamilton decided to use his influence in support of Jefferson.

Despite his long history of disagreeing with Jefferson, Hamilton was more dismayed by the idea of Burr as President. He called Burr "as unprincipled and dangerous a man as any country can boast." After 35 rounds of votes, the House elected Thomas Jefferson as the third President of the United States. Burr became Vice President.

party in New York, where he and Hamilton had long been bitter political enemies. Jefferson mistrusted Burr, but he needed his help to win Northern votes.

★ The Election of 1800

The election of 1800 was vicious and hard-fought. Each side pictured the other

Amending the Constitution

The tie vote made it clear that the election method set down in the Constitution had flaws. To avoid another tie, the Twelfth Amendment to the Constitution was passed in 1804. This amendment calls for electors to vote on separate ballots to elect the President and the Vice President.

★ The Federalist Legacy

Along with losing the election of 1800, the Federalist party lost much of its power. Federalists, depending on strict laws and an elite group of leaders, distrusted the common people who were gaining a voice in government. The party never again gained national power.

The Federalists, nevertheless, had guided the new United States through a crucial time. They made the government work and gave it a solid financial base. They also won respect from other nations of the world. In addition, the United States had expanded with three new states—Vermont, Kentucky, and Tennessee.

Adams took one last opportunity to preserve the Federalist view of the Constitution. Until his last night in office, Adams wrote out appointments for many federal judges who would hold office for their lifetimes. The most important of these "midnight judges" was **John Marshall,** named as chief justice. Marshall led the Supreme Court from 1801 until his death in 1835. You will learn more about Adams's midnight appointments in Chapter 11.

A New Capital

Another Federalist legacy was the new capital city, named for George Washington after his death in 1799. Bills passed by Congress created the District of Columbia, or **Washington, D.C.,** on a tract of land given by Maryland and Virginia. As President, Washington had named a commission to plan the city. Although denied the right of citizenship, **Benjamin Banneker,** a highly skilled African American scientist and mathematician, was chosen as a member.

The city plan was drawn by a French-born architect, **Pierre Charles L'Enfant.** It was to have broad avenues, a long, tree-lined mall, and impressive classical-style buildings.

Although George Washington lay the cornerstone of the United States Capitol in 1793, only one wing of the building had been finished in 1800 when Congress moved in. John and **Abigail Adams** were the first presidential family to live in the not-quite-finished President's House, later called the White House. The rest of the city consisted of few other buildings, surrounded by woods and wilderness.

★ SECTION 4 REVIEW ★

Checking for Understanding

1. **Identify** John Adams, Charles C. Pinckney, Charles Maurice de Talleyrand, Abigail Adams, Washington, D.C.

2. **Define** XYZ Affair, alien, deport, sedition, nullify, states' rights.

3. **What** incidents brought France and the United States close to war in 1797–98?

4. **What** four laws made up the Alien and Sedition acts?

5. **How** did the Federalists try to stop the growth of the Democratic-Republican party?

Critical Thinking

6. **Identifying Cause and Effect**   The Federalists wanted a strong central government and healthy trade. Why would this lead them to want war with France and good relations with Britain?

ACTIVITY

7. The Sedition Act was aimed at newspapers that supported the Democratic-Republicans but had little effect on those that supported Federalists. Choose a side in this debate and make a poster advertising your newspaper.

Using Key Vocabulary

Use the following vocabulary terms to complete the sentences that follow.

> **Bill of Rights**
> **neutral**
> **political party**
> **sedition**
> **loose construction**

1. To give the federal government more powers, Federalists looked for a _____ of what the Constitution said.

2. To protect people's liberties, Congress amended the Constitution to add a _____.

3. The United States tried to remain _____ instead of getting involved in wars between European nations.

4. In the 1790s, differences between political goals led groups of people to form a _____.

5. Federalists angered many Americans by making criticism of the government, or _____, a serious crime.

Reviewing Facts

1. **Identify** the three branches of the United States government and at least one step taken to organize each one in 1789.

2. **List** three reasons why relations between the United States and Great Britain became strained in l793.

3. **Name** the two political parties that formed in the United States in the 1790s and each one's chief leader.

4. **Describe** the events leading to and following the XYZ Affair.

5. **Tell** why the Federalist Congress passed the Alien and Sedition acts.

Understanding Concepts

Beliefs and Ideas

1. How did George Washington influence the development of the executive branch of government?

2. What were Hamilton's economic plans for the United States?

3. What did Jefferson and Madison do in response to the Alien and Sedition acts?

4. Why was it necessary to amend the Constitution after the election of 1800?

U.S. Role in World Affairs

5. Why did Presidents Washington and Adams think it was important to keep the country neutral? What nations made this difficult?

Critical Thinking

1. **Drawing Conclusions**   Most early American leaders disliked the idea of political parties, yet they formed them anyway. Why do you think this occurred?

2. **Understanding Ideologies**   What was Thomas Jefferson's view of how the United States should be governed? What was Alexander Hamilton's view? Do some politicians today still hold a similar point of view?

3. **Identifying Central Issues**   What do you think was the most important principle for people who opposed the Sedition Act? What other principle did Jefferson and Madison try to uphold in their reaction?

History and Geography

British Forts in the 1790s

The British held on to their frontier outposts until the Jay Treaty. Study the map on page 351. Then answer the questions that follow.

British Forts Held Until 1796

British posts held until 1796

U.S. posts

0   150   300 miles

0   150   300 kilometers

1. **Location** What two British forts were located in New York?

2. **Region** What is similar about the location of those two forts?

3. **Movement** Along what natural transportation route were British forts located? Why would this matter to the Americans?

4. **Location** About how many miles apart were the easternmost and westernmost U.S. posts?

Cooperative Learning Interdisciplinary Activity: Civics

As a group, plan a campaign to recruit new members for your political party in 1798. Begin by deciding whether you are part of the Federalist party or the Democratic-Republican party. Divide up these tasks among the people in your group: research party issues, draw up a party platform, create slogans and logos, design posters, write newspaper editorials supporting your view or attacking your opponents', draw political cartoons about your rivals.

Practicing Skills

Writing a Paragraph

Write a short paragraph for each of the topic sentences below. Each paragraph must have at least three sentences supporting the topic and arranged in a logical way. Use transitional words or phrases to connect your ideas smoothly.

1. As secretary of the treasury, Alexander Hamilton set up a program to solve the new nation's financial problems.

2. George Washington made every effort to keep the United States neutral.

3. Congress and President Washington took several steps to organize the judicial branch of the government.

4. The Federalists and the Democratic-Republicans were the nation's first political parties.

5. The tie vote in the election of 1800 made it clear that the Constitution had flaws.

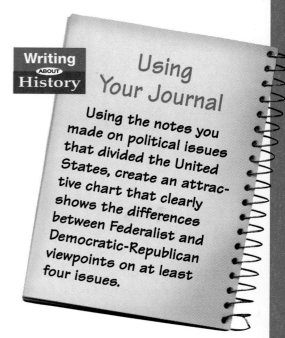

Writing ABOUT History

Using Your Journal

Using the notes you made on political issues that divided the United States, create an attractive chart that clearly shows the differences between Federalist and Democratic-Republican viewpoints on at least four issues.

Cultural Kaleidoscope

Schools and Education

Going to school in the new Republic could mean cold log cabins and frozen ink, dirt floors, and drafty windows. Comfortable or not, education mattered to Americans.

No Ballpoints

Most children used slate boards and chalk for doing their lessons. If paper was available, students used charcoal or quill pens for writing. Families made ink at home, which children brought to school.

Class in Session

Most schoolhouses had one room and one teacher for all subjects and all students. In geography class, students memorized the names of countries, rivers, and lakes. In reading class, they read stories that taught them proper behavior. At the end of the week, they might take part in a lively spelling match.

Words and Texts

Noah Webster's *American Dictionary* listed American spellings and expressions in a dictionary for the first time. Webster—a Hartford, Connecticut, schoolmaster—also published a spelling book and a reader used in the schools.

College Days

Religion and classic studies such as Latin continued to be on the subject list at institutions such as Amherst College. Thanks to earlier Americans like Ben Franklin, science was also part of the college course of study.

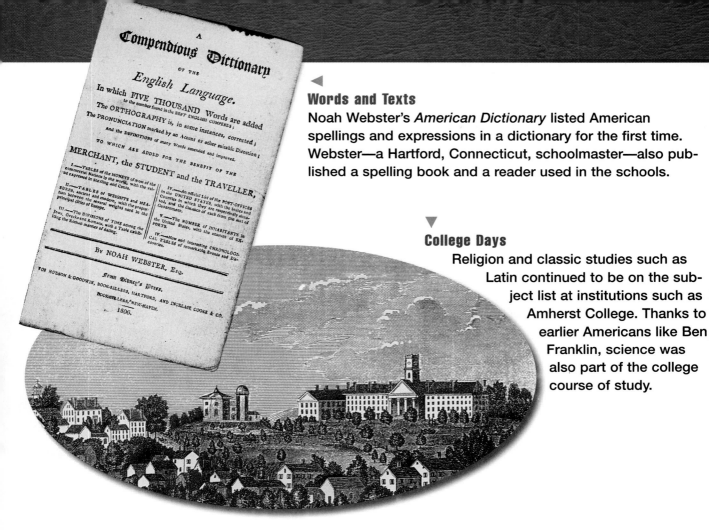

Secondary Education

As in colonial days, only well-to-do young men could expect to go to college. Secondary schools known as academies, however, became widespread during the early years of the Republic. In academies the young sons and sometimes the daughters of middle-class Americans studied history, art, literature, mathematics, and French.

Students, Take Your Seats

Desks in schoolhouses might be log tables built into the walls of the schoolhouse. Seats could be long benches with no backs.

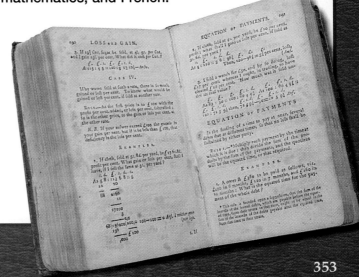

CHAPTER 11

★★

The Age of Jefferson
1800–1815

SETTING THE SCENE

Focus

The election of 1800 was one of the turning points in American history. For the first time in modern history, the political power of a country transferred peacefully from one political party to another. The presidency of Thomas Jefferson launched a new era, a time of far-reaching change and rapid growth for the new nation.

Concepts to Understand

★ How Jefferson's policies affected the **economic development** of the United States

★ How the United States gained a respected **role in world affairs**

Read to Discover . . .

★ the opportunities that the Louisiana Purchase brought the United States.

★ the events leading up to and during the War of 1812.

▶ **HUNTING SHIRT**

Journal Notes

Young Americans had many chances for adventure—at home, at sea, and on the frontier—in the years between 1800 and 1815. As you read the chapter, keep a record of those opportunities and the ways each of them appeals to you.

United States

1801 Thomas Jefferson becomes President
1804 Lewis and Clark explore Louisiana Territory

1807 Embargo Act goes into effect
1808 James Madison elected President

1800–1804	1805–1809

1800 Napoleon Bonaparte becomes ruler of France
1804 Haiti becomes an independent nation

1805 Modern-day Egypt is founded

World

GEORGE CLARK'S COMPASS

Perry's Victory on Lake Erie, 1813
by William Birch

During the War of 1812, a young naval officer, Oliver Hazard Perry, led 10 small ships on an attack against the British. The victory on Lake Erie gave Americans hope of winning the war.

1812 Congress declares war on Great Britain
1814 War of 1812 ends

1810–1814

1815 Battle of New Orleans
1815 Treaty of Ghent ratified

1815–1819

1815 Napoleon defeated at Battle of Waterloo

★★★

Jefferson Takes Control

SETTING THE SCENE

Read to Learn . . .

★ how Republican views on government policies differed from Federalist views.
★ how the Supreme Court increased its power and influence.

Terms to Know

★ democratic
★ laissez-faire
★ impeachment
★ *Marbury* v. *Madison*
★ judicial review
★ precedent

People to Meet

★ Thomas Jefferson
★ John Marshall
★ Albert Gallatin
★ William Marbury
★ James Madison

Places to Locate

★ Washington, D.C.

◀ THOMAS JEFFERSON

The tall, red-haired Virginian was gifted in many fields. One of the country's best architects, he designed the classical red brick buildings of the University of Virginia, the Virginia Capitol, and his own home at Monticello. He was a good musician, too, and enjoyed playing the violin.

As an inventor—still another talent—he designed a special music stand for the friends with whom he played chamber music. He was a gardener, a linguist—a person who speaks many languages—and an inspiring writer. With all those talents, it may be surprising that **Thomas Jefferson** is remembered mainly as a political thinker and the third President of the United States.

★ The Jeffersonian "Revolution"

Two days after his inauguration, Thomas Jefferson wrote a letter to a fellow Republican. (Originally called Democratic-Republicans, the Jeffersonians were now commonly called Republicans. They were not, however, related to the present-day Republican party.) In the letter, he referred to his election victory as the "revolution of 1800 . . . as real a revolution in the principles of our government as that of 1776 was in form." By using the word *revolution*, Jefferson meant that the American people had voted for changes as great as those they had fought for in the Revolutionary War.

The peaceful revolution of 1800 proved to the world that the young republic could make political changes without violence—something very unusual at the time. Even though the Federalists were in despair at losing the presidency, they peacefully turned over control of the federal government. This was the first time in modern history that the political control of a country passed from one political party to another through a democratic election.

Jefferson's Inauguration

On March 4, 1801, Thomas Jefferson became the first President to take the oath of office in the new capital of **Washington, D.C.** Jefferson was sworn in by Chief Justice **John Marshall,** a Federalist who was one of John Adams's last appointees. At the time, the city was still unfinished. Its streets were unpaved, and few buildings were completed.

If Washington was an odd sort of national capital, Jefferson was in many ways an odd sort of man to be the founder of a political party and head of state. He hated crowds, avoided making speeches, and was too thin-skinned to enjoy rough-and-tumble politics, that is, politics involving much fighting between people and parties.

A Call for Unity

The change in leadership brought great political and philosophical change to the presidency. Jefferson believed the people were the source of a government's power. He wanted to make government more democratic, providing all people with equal rights. Pleading for national harmony after the bitter election, Jefferson encouraged all citizens to work together, stating: "All, too, will bear in mind this sacred principle . . . that the minority possess their equal rights, which equal law must protect, . . . Let us, then, fellow-citizens, unite with one heart and one mind. . . . We are all Republicans, we are all Federalists."

By this he meant that despite their distrust of democracy, Federalists recognized that problems are finally settled by the will of the people, and that despite their distrust of centralized power, the Republicans did not propose to destroy the federal government.

★ Simplifying Government

Federalists supported a strong central government and rule by an elite, or a wealthier, better-educated small class of people. Jefferson believed in states' rights

 ▲ MONTICELLO Thomas Jefferson had many talents including being a skilled architect. He designed buildings at the University of Virginia and his home at Monticello. **What other talents did Jefferson have?**

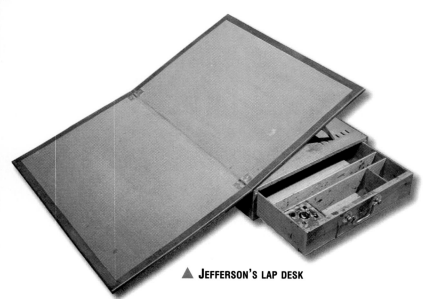

▲ JEFFERSON'S LAP DESK

from injuring one another, shall leave them otherwise free to regulate their own pursuits of industry and improvement, and shall not take from the mouth of labor the bread it has earned. "

When George Washington was President, Jefferson had opposed many of Hamilton's economic plans. As President, though, Jefferson did promise to pay off the national debt, encourage agriculture and trade, and preserve the country's credit.

To help cut spending, he appointed **Albert Gallatin** as secretary of the treasury. An immigrant from Switzerland, Gallatin was a brilliant financier who had been an outstanding member of the House of Representatives.

Gallatin worked to simplify government and avoid the high costs of war and defense. He and Jefferson greatly cut military spending. They cut the army from 4,000 to 2,500 men and made similar cuts in the number of sailors and naval officers. These actions reduced the United States's naval fleet from 25 to 7 ships.

Gallatin also cut the staff of the executive branch to reduce government spending. These measures together helped cut the national debt from $83 million to about $45 million. Though Jefferson had opposed the formation of a national bank, Gallatin convinced him to keep the Bank of the United States intact, or untouched.

and rule by the majority. He thought state governments were closer to the people than the national government. In contrast to Alexander Hamilton's idea that the government should actively promote banking, commerce, and industry, Jefferson advocated a hands-off policy called laissez-faire (LEH•SAY•FEHR). This French term means generally, "let people do as they choose."

Jefferson and the Republicans believed the federal government's role should be to keep people from injuring each other. The citizens should be "free to regulate their own pursuits."

"A Wise and Frugal Government"

Besides limiting the power of the federal government, Jefferson wanted to cut the federal budget and lower taxes. He summed up his vision of government in his Inaugural Address when he said,

" A wise and frugal [economical] Government, which shall restrain [prevent] men

No Internal Taxes

With these savings, Jefferson and the Republican-controlled Congress could

Footnotes to History

Jefferson Walks to His Inauguration Historians often tell how Jefferson walked to his own inauguration wearing a simple gray homespun suit. The simplicity of the third President, though, was completely unintended. Jefferson walked to the inauguration and wore plain clothes only because bad weather had delayed the arrival of a new $6,000 carriage and an expensive velvet suit.

repeal the unpopular excise taxes on whiskey and other products. They actually ended all internal taxes. The federal government's only sources of money were now tariffs on imports and revenue from the sale of Western lands.

Proudly, Jefferson said that those revenues—without the addition of taxes—would be great enough to pay for roads, education, arts, and other public works. Beginning his second term, he pointed out that it was

> ❝ . . . the pride and pleasure of an American to ask, what farmer, what mechanic, what laborer, ever sees a tax gatherer of the United States? ❞

Out With the Alien and Sedition Acts

The hated Alien and Sedition acts instituted by the Federalists expired at the end of 1801. Jefferson did not renew them. Instead, he pardoned those who had been convicted under the acts, even refunding the fines that had been paid.

Congress passed a new naturalization act. It went back to the 5-year residency requirement for citizenship, instead of the 14 years required by the Alien Acts.

★ Conflict With the Judicial Branch

The Republicans had gained control of Congress and the presidency in 1800. Between the election and Jefferson's inauguration, Federalists in Congress passed the **Judiciary Act of 1801.** This act increased the number of federal judges. Outgoing President John Adams then filled many positions with members of his own party. These judges were known as **"midnight judges"** because Adams supposedly signed appointments for judges until midnight on his last day in office.

▲ **CHIEF JUSTICE JOHN MARSHALL**

Impeaching the Judges

Republicans argued that this way of packing the courts with Federalists was unfair. One of the first acts of Congress after Jefferson took office was to repeal the Judiciary Act. After doing away with the midnight judges by abolishing their positions, the Republicans tried to remove other Federalist judges by impeachment.

Impeachment means bringing charges of wrongdoing against a public official. According to the Constitution, a majority of the House of Representatives can vote to bring such charges against any government official. The Senate then acts as a court to put the impeached official on trial. If two-thirds of the Senate finds the official guilty, he or she is dismissed from office.

In March 1804, Republicans in Congress managed to impeach and dismiss a district judge and critic of Republicans, John Pickering of New Hampshire. They next targeted Supreme Court Justice Samuel Chase, a harsh critic of the Republicans. The House impeached Chase, but there were not enough Senate votes to convict him. This ended the campaign to impeach Federalist judges.

★ A Stronger Supreme Court

Jefferson soon clashed with Chief Justice John Marshall, his distant cousin. The case, which became famous as *Marbury v. Madison,* involved one of Adams's last-minute judicial appointments.

As one of his midnight judges, Adams had named **William Marbury** as justice of the peace in the District of Columbia. Marbury's official commission, however, was not delivered to him before Jefferson took office. Because Marbury was a Federalist, Jefferson ordered the new secretary of state, **James Madison,** not to send Marbury his papers.

Marbury then petitioned the Supreme Court to order Madison to carry out his duties and deliver the commission. The **Judiciary Act of 1789** gave the Court the power to issue such an order. After all, said Marbury, a President had signed and sealed the commission.

The Supreme Court voted unanimously in the case of *Marbury* v. *Madison.* They decided that Marbury had the right to his commission but that the Court would not force Madison to hand it over to him. The reason, Chief Justice Marshall explained, was that part of the Judiciary Act of 1789 was unconstitutional. Under the Constitution, Congress could not give the Supreme Court such power.

Judicial Review

The case of *Marbury* v. *Madison* was the first time that the Supreme Court claimed that it could declare that a law passed by Congress was unconstitutional. This power is called judicial review.

This Supreme Court ruling on *Marbury* v. *Madison* set a precedent—a model that later lawyers and judges would follow. From then on, the Supreme Court could use the power of judicial review as a check against the other branches of government. This gave the Supreme Court more power than it had ever had.

Jefferson and the Republicans disliked the decision because Federalists still controlled the Supreme Court. In addition, Jefferson believed in a strict construction of the Constitution—limiting the authority of the federal government to the powers specifically granted to it by the Constitution. He pointed out that the Constitution says nothing about judicial review of federal laws. Nevertheless, Jefferson and the Congress accepted the ruling.

★ SECTION 1 REVIEW ★

Checking for Understanding

1. **Identify** Thomas Jefferson, John Marshall, Albert Gallatin, William Marbury, James Madison, Washington, D.C.

2. **Define** democratic, laissez-faire, impeachment, *Marbury* v. *Madison,* judicial review, precedent.

3. **What** did Jefferson and Gallatin do to cut government spending? Where did the government get its revenue?

4. **What** precedent did the Supreme Court establish in the case of *Marbury* v. *Madison?*

Critical Thinking

5. **Determining Relevance** Write a short list of the principles and ideas about government that Thomas Jefferson believed in. Then show how those ideas related to the actions he took in his first term.

ACTIVITY

6. Draw a picture of what you think the city of Washington, D.C., looked like on the day of Jefferson's inauguration.

The Louisiana Purchase

SETTING THE SCENE

Read to Learn . . .

★ why President Jefferson wanted control of the Mississippi River and New Orleans.
★ how the United States doubled in size in the early 1800s.
★ how explorations of the West helped the United States to grow.

Terms to Know

★ cede

People to Meet

★ Robert Livingston
★ James Monroe
★ Meriwether Lewis
★ William Clark
★ Sacajawea
★ Zebulon Pike

Places to Locate

★ Saint Domingue
★ Missouri River
★ Rocky Mountains
★ St. Louis
★ Columbia River
★ Oregon Country

◀ THE LOUISIANA PURCHASE TREATY

Although Americans moved westward even before the American Revolution, in the 1790s most of the population of the United States still clung close to the Atlantic coast. To people at this time, the West was the land west of the Appalachian Mountains, extending to the Mississippi River.

In the early 1800s, this notion began to change as settlers moved west of the Mississippi River in search of new land and new opportunities. The United States was beginning to grow rapidly.

★ Making a Deal With Napoleon

In 1800 the western border of the United States was the Mississippi River. Spain controlled both the lower Mississippi and the important port city of New Orleans. Spanish control often caused problems for Americans west of the Appalachian Mountains. Americans depended on the river to ship their flour, pork, apples, and other products downriver for export to the East and to the West Indies.

Despite treaties, Spanish officials made trouble for American shippers. They occasionally stopped them from using the lower Mississippi River or imposed a tax on goods sent through New Orleans.

The Louisiana Territory

The land from the Mississippi River west to the Rocky Mountains—the **Louisiana Territory**—had changed hands between France and Spain several times in the past 100 years. In a secret treaty in 1800, Spain ceded, or granted, the Louisiana Territory to France.

When Jefferson learned of this treaty in 1801, he recognized that it held possible dangers for the United States. France's ambitious general, **Napoleon Bonaparte,** now a dictator, had plans to conquer Europe. Jefferson feared that Napoleon would also want to build an empire in North America. Spain might give him even more of its American colonies, including the Floridas.

Jefferson also feared that French rule over the Louisiana Territory would be even more of a threat to American trade and travel along the Mississippi River and through New Orleans. This would disrupt the growth and development of the western United States.

▶ **NAPOLEON BONAPARTE**

Jefferson was unwilling to see more land in North America in European hands. He authorized **Robert Livingston,** ambassador to France, to offer to buy New Orleans and West Florida. He sent **James Monroe,** a diplomat and former Virginia governor, as a special envoy, or agent, to negotiate the purchase. The House of Representatives voted $2 million for the purchase, but Jefferson authorized Monroe to offer up to $10 million.

A Revolution in the Caribbean

While French and American officials were negotiating, the French were distracted by events in the Caribbean. Inspired by the ideals of the French Revolution, in 1791 enslaved Africans and other laborers in the French colony of **Saint Domingue** had revolted against French plantation owners. After fierce and bitter fighting, the rebels, led by **Toussaint-Louverture** (TOO•SAN LOO•vuhr•TUR), declared the colony an independent republic. Toussaint set up a new government.

In 1801 Napoleon sent an army to recapture it. Toussaint was captured and imprisoned in France. Only a few years later, however, England and France once again were at war. Napoleon needed his army elsewhere. In 1804 the rebels regained their freedom and set up the republic of Haiti.

★ The Louisiana Purchase

The rebellion in Saint Domingue, combined with his war with Britain, ended Napoleon's interest in a French empire in North America. Instead of sending troops to Louisiana, Napoleon needed his troops to fight wars in Europe.

Napoleon preferred to sell the Louisiana Territory to the United States rather than see the British obtain it. Besides, he could use money from the sale to pay for the war with Britain. He ordered his foreign minister, Talleyrand, to ask Livingston how much the United States was willing to pay for all of the Louisiana Territory.

Surprised by the offer, Livingston replied that he had the authority to buy New Orleans and Florida, not all the Louisiana Territory. How could he make such a decision? Luckily, Monroe arrived the next day. After discussing the matter, he and Livingston agreed to purchase the Louisiana Territory.

The United States and France signed a treaty in May of 1803. It gave the United States the Louisiana Territory for $15 million. The addition almost doubled the size of the United States.

★ Controversy Over the Purchase

Considering the territory to be gained, it may be hard to see why anyone would hesitate. Yet, Jefferson faced a difficult decision. The **Louisiana Purchase** soon became the center of debate.

Jefferson and other Republicans were **strict constructionists.** That is, they believed that the federal government can do only what the Constitution says—and nothing more. Yet the Constitution does not specifically give the federal government the power to purchase territory from another country.

On the other hand, the huge territory, much of it unexplored, was an unexpected prize. Owning it would end all the problems with using the Mississippi River. Jefferson himself had always been interested in the West and had sent out expeditions to map parts of it. He had studied Native American cultures.

One way out of the dilemma was to pass a constitutional amendment that authorized the purchase of the Louisiana Territory. Jefferson's advisers, however, worried that waiting to act on the treaty might give Napoleon time to change his

Picturing History

▲ TRANSFER OF LOUISIANA The French flag was lowered and the United States flag was raised over the Louisiana Territory. **How much did the United States pay for the territory?**

mind. They pointed out that the President did have the power to make treaties.

Jefferson, therefore, sent the treaty to the Senate for ratification in October of 1803. In his message to Congress, he explained its importance:

    ❝ While the property and sovereignty of the Mississippi and its waters secure an independent outlet for the produce of the western States . . . the fertility of the country, its climate, and extent, promise in due season important aids to our treasury. . . . ❞

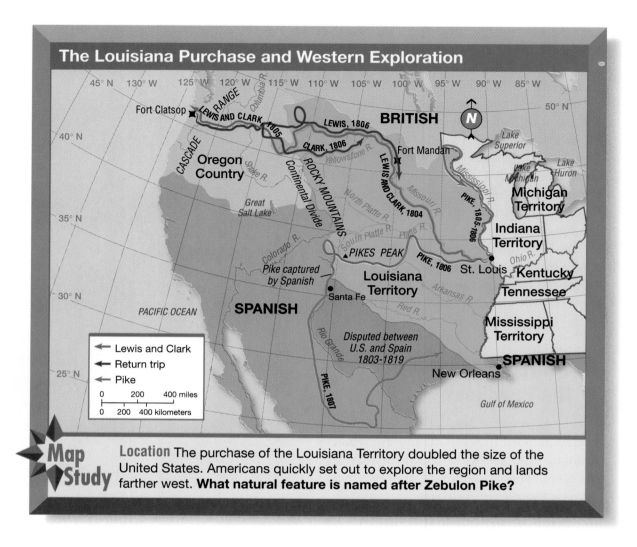

The Louisiana Purchase and Western Exploration

Map Study

Location The purchase of the Louisiana Territory doubled the size of the United States. Americans quickly set out to explore the region and lands farther west. **What natural feature is named after Zebulon Pike?**

Federalist Opposition

For the unhappy Federalists, the Louisiana Purchase was just one more Jeffersonian action to dislike. They feared that this would increase the power of the South by adding more states to the Union that supported slavery and favored Southern policies.

Federalist newspapers also cried out against the cost. They wrote that if the $15 million purchase price were stacked up in silver dollars, the stack would be three miles high! Twenty-five ships would be needed to transport this money to France.

The idea of so much new, open land, however, appealed to most Americans as much as it did to Jefferson. The Federalists' opposition harmed their own cause more than it endangered passage of the treaty.

The Senate quickly approved the treaty, thus doubling the size of the United States and opening the way for westward expansion.

★ The Lewis and Clark Expedition

Much of the land west of the Mississippi River was unknown to Americans. Jefferson eagerly organized an expedition to learn more about the area. To lead it, he appointed **Meriwether Lewis** and **William Clark,** a fellow Virginian. Both men were knowledgeable amateur scientists, and had done business with Native Americans. Lewis was a captain in the army. Clark reenlisted in the army with the rank of lieutenant. Although Lewis outranked Clark, both men agreed to lead the expedition jointly.

The expedition was the first scientific project in the nation's history to receive federal money. Jefferson gave Lewis and Clark specific instructions. He told them to find the sources of the **Missouri River,** to try to find a usable route across the **Rocky Mountains** to the Pacific Ocean, and to observe the customs of the Native Americans they met.

They were also to note carefully the features of the land, the weather, and the plants and animals they saw. Jefferson asked for detailed maps of the area.

Starting Out

In the spring of 1804, the Lewis and Clark expedition set out from **St. Louis, Missouri,** following the Missouri River. Three boats carried the four dozen members of the expedition and extensive supplies, including gifts for the Native Americans such as plumed hats, beads, paints, and knives.

Lewis and Clark recorded their data in great detail. They even sent packages back to Jefferson with samples of items from the Louisiana Territory. One package contained a stuffed antelope, a weasel, three squirrels, a prairie dog, the horns of a mountain goat, elk horns, a buffalo skin, and a number of Native American items.

Shortly before winter, the expedition reached the homeland of the Mandans, a Native American nation located in what is now North Dakota. The explorers built Fort Mandan and settled in for the winter.

Crossing the Rocky Mountains

The next spring, April 1805, the expedition organized their equipment and supplies and set out for the Rocky Mountains. They had a new guide and interpreter, a Shoshone woman named **Sacajawea** (SA•kuh•juh•WEE•uh) who had married

▲ **WILLIAM CLARK'S JOURNAL**

a French trader. Sacajawea had lived in the Rocky Mountains, so she became an invaluable addition to the expedition team.

When they reached an area known as the Black Hills, the landscape changed from flatland to hills, to "large irregular masses of rocks and stones." From the top of these hills, Lewis glimpsed the Rocky Mountains, "the object of all our hopes, and the reward of all our ambition."

Sacajawea guided the expedition to Shoshone country in Idaho where she had been born and raised. As the terrain became more rugged, the explorers lost many horses loaded with supplies. Sacajawea and her people helped Lewis and Clark get more horses to continue their journey across the Rocky Mountains.

To the Pacific Coast

Sacajawea and six other Shoshone guides led the expedition through the rugged Rocky Mountains and down into the valley of the great **Columbia River.** They reached the Pacific Ocean in the late autumn of 1805 and spent the winter in the **Oregon Country.** The next spring they started back toward St. Louis. On September 23, 1806, the Lewis and Clark expedition reached St. Louis two years and four months and almost 8,000 miles (12,900 km) after the start of their journey.

The expedition fully satisfied Jefferson's hopes. It did not find an all-water route across North America, for there was none.

Lewis and Clark did, however, find and map several passes through the Rockies.

They established friendly relations with many Native American nations and brought back a wealth of information about the Louisiana Territory and its wildlife and resources. The expedition strengthened the United States's claim to the Oregon Country.

★ The Discovery of Pikes Peak

At the same time Lewis and Clark were exploring the Louisiana Territory, Lieutenant **Zebulon Pike** was leading a smaller expedition to the upper Mississippi River.

Pike did not find the source of the Mississippi, although he did learn much about the land and about British trade there. Later, in 1806–1807, Pike explored the Colorado region and sighted the tall mountain now known as **Pikes Peak.**

★ The Election of 1804

At the end of Jefferson's first term, the United States was prosperous and at peace. Its size had just doubled as a result of the Louisiana Purchase. Jefferson easily won reelection in 1804. In this election, though, Jefferson had a new running mate. George Clinton replaced Aaron Burr as the Vice President.

The Burr Conspiracy

In 1804 Burr left the Republican party to run for governor of New York as an independent. He sought Federalist support for his candidacy, but Alexander Hamilton, still a Federalist leader, forcefully campaigned against him. Even after Burr lost the race by a large margin, Hamilton continued to criticize Burr's integrity, or moral values.

Burr angrily challenged Hamilton to a duel, a gunfight. Hamilton reluctantly agreed. On a July morning in 1804, Burr and Hamilton met. At the signal, Burr fired and shot a bullet into Hamilton's body. Hamilton died the next day. Burr became a political outcast. Later the United States government tried him for treason for attempting to establish an empire for himself on the Western frontier. Although Burr was acquitted, he soon left the country.

★ SECTION 2 REVIEW ★

Checking for Understanding

1. **Identify** Robert Livingston, James Monroe, Meriwether Lewis, William Clark, Sacajawea, Zebulon Pike, Saint Domingue, Missouri River, Rocky Mountains, St. Louis, Columbia River, Oregon Country.

2. **Define** cede.

3. **Why** were the Mississippi River and New Orleans important to the United States?

4. **What** was Jefferson's dilemma about buying the Louisiana Territory? How did he resolve it?

Critical Thinking

5. **Cause and Effect** How do you think the Lewis and Clark expedition encouraged people to move west in the early 1800s?

ACTIVITY

6. Create a want ad for people to join the Lewis and Clark expedition. Your ad should include the skills and abilities that the people would need for the expedition and what the job would entail.

The Lewis and Clark Expedition—A New Frontier

As the Lewis and Clark expedition set off from St. Louis on May 14, 1804, its goals were both scientific and political. Captains Meriwether Lewis and William Clark, along with about 40 experienced soldiers, hunters, and lumberers, set out to explore the vast Louisiana Territory—its plants, animals, geology, climate, and terrain. Their trip would also establish a claim to the rich Oregon Territory.

With a flat-bottomed keelboat and two dugouts, they traveled up the Missouri River, crossed the Rocky Mountains, then paddled down the Columbia River to the Pacific coast. The two explorers carefully mapped the entire trip, which covered about 8,000 miles (12,900 km). As Jefferson had asked, they noted the latitude and longitude of natural features such as rapids and islands. They packed their journals with descriptions and sketches of all they saw. One amazing sight was huge herds of buffalo on the prairies. "I do not think I exaggerate," Lewis wrote, saying he could see 3,000 animals at one time.

Many of the local plants and animals were new to Lewis and Clark. They collected and preserved specimens, such as a prairie dog, jackrabbit, black-tailed deer, pronghorn, and mountain sheep. Huge grizzly bears were a frequent threat to the party. The annoyed explorers gave the bear its scientific name: *Ursus arctos horribilis,* or "terrible bear." They also found some huge bones that may have been those of a dinosaur.

By the time the team returned to St. Louis in 1806, they had filled many journals with fascinating information about the new territory. A narrative of the journey published in 1814 tempted other adventurous Americans to pack up and go west to settle and live.

◄ MERIWETHER LEWIS

► WILLIAM CLARK

Making the Science Connection

1. What were the purposes of Lewis and Clark's expedition?

2. How did the explorers study plants and animals in Louisiana Territory?

3. How did they record details about the land and climate?

ACTIVITY

4. Accurate descriptions and drawings made Lewis and Clark's observations valuable. Look out the window now and choose an example of flora (plants) or fauna (animals). Draw and describe it so exactly that someone who had never seen it would be able to recognize it.

★★★

Troubles With France and Britain

SETTING THE SCENE

Read to Learn . . .

★ how Barbary pirates interfered with American trade.

★ how France and Great Britain challenged the United States's neutrality.

★ what steps President Jefferson took to avoid war with France and Britain.

Terms to Know

★ blockade
★ impressment
★ deserter
★ embargo

People to Meet

★ Edward Preble
★ Stephen Decatur

Places to Locate

★ Barbary Coast States
★ Mediterranean Sea

▶ AMERICAN SAILORS

Thomas Jefferson had entered the presidency committed to Washington's policy of neutrality. Yet, the United States and Europe were dependent upon each other. When Great Britain and France each tried to manipulate trade with the United States as a weapon against the other, the United States sought ways to fight back.

★ Piracy in the Mediterranean

In the early 1800s, trade between the United States, the West Indies, and Europe grew. American traders found new ports as well, trading as far away as China, Africa, and Argentina. An old problem, however, threatened trade—the pirates of the **Barbary Coast States.**

For years pirates from the Barbary Coast states of North Africa—Morocco, Algeria, Tunisia, and Tripoli—had harassed ships in the **Mediterranean Sea.** They captured crews and cargoes, demanding tribute, or payment for protection. Between 1789 and 1801, the United States paid several million dollars in such tributes.

War With Tripoli

In 1801 the pasha, or ruler, of Tripoli (part of present-day Libya) increased the amount of tribute he wanted from the United States. When Jefferson refused to pay this tribute, Tripoli declared war on the United States.

Jefferson hesitated to declare war because the Constitution did not specifically allow it. Instead, he quickly received from Congress the authority to send warships to the Mediterranean Sea. He ordered the navy to blockade, or close off, the port of Tripoli.

One American ship, the *Philadelphia*, ran aground off Tripoli. Pirates captured its captain and crew. To keep the pasha from using the ship, Commodore **Edward Preble** ordered the *Philadelphia* destroyed.

A daring young American officer, Lieutenant **Stephen Decatur,** led a raiding party into the harbor of Tripoli at night, boarded the ship, and set it on fire. Admiringly, the British naval hero Lord Horatio Nelson called the raid "the most daring act of the age."

The war with Tripoli ended in 1805 when the pasha signed a peace agreement ending the payment of tribute. The United States did pay a $60,000 ransom for its captured sailors. Even so, all payments to the Barbary Coast States did not end until 1815 when the United States signed a treaty with Algiers.

The war against the Barbary pirates was popular at home. It demonstrated the need for the United States to maintain a navy. It also proved to other countries that the United States would fight to protect its interests.

★ American Neutrality Challenged

Since coming to power in France, Napoleon Bonaparte had been steadily expanding his empire. He was a threat to British trade and sea power, and in 1803 France and Great Britain were at war again. Other European nations joined the fight against Napoleon, but it was the conflict between France and Britain that affected the United States.

Jefferson declared the United States's neutrality in the Napoleonic Wars, just as Washington and Adams had in earlier European wars. Both France and Britain, however, announced that they would stop American ships headed for the other side's ports. Each hoped to hurt the other country's trade and deprive it of needed food and supplies.

French and British warships did seize some American trade ships. Although hundreds of American ships were seized between 1805 and 1807, neutrality was profitable for American traders. Ships that maneuvered through the blockades established by France and Great Britain made great profits—making it worth the risks of being caught.

Seizing American Sailors

The British also continued to take sailors from American ships and force them to serve on British ships. This practice, called impressment, was common in Great Britain. The British navy claimed that the American sailors were the king's

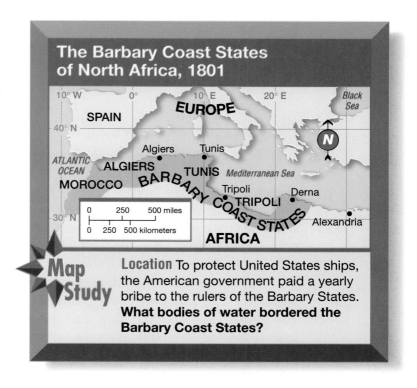

The Barbary Coast States of North Africa, 1801

Map Study

Location To protect United States ships, the American government paid a yearly bribe to the rulers of the Barbary States. **What bodies of water bordered the Barbary Coast States?**

Linking Past and Present

The American Diet

Most Americans eat a lot. But do they eat well? Apparently not much has changed in nearly 200 years.

Then_____

Too Much Fat

French visitors to the United States in 1807 complained that Americans ate too much butter, lard, salt pork, and greasy puddings. Indeed, one visitor said that American eating habits were so bad that a day didn't pass in this country without "heaping indigestions upon one another" from one meal to the next.

▲ EARLY AMERICAN MARKET

Now_____

Too Much Fat!

In July 1988 the surgeon general of the United States reported that most nutritional health problems are caused by poor eating habits. Americans, the report said, eat too many foods that are high in fat, salt, and sugar.

---

subjects. Some were in fact deserters from the British navy, sailors who had left British warships to sail on American ships.

The British, however, seized even British-born sailors who had become American citizens (which British law did not recognize). Despite the government's protests, the British continued impressment.

The Chesapeake-Leopard Affair

In June 1807, the American warship *Chesapeake* had just left its base in Virginia. British sailors on the *Leopard* ordered it to stop so they could search for British deserters. When the commander of the *Chesapeake* refused, the *Leopard*'s guns opened fire.

Taken by surprise, three of the crew of the *Chesapeake* were killed and others wounded. The ship was badly damaged. The British boarded the ship and took four suspected deserters, three of whom were Americans.

The damaged *Chesapeake* limped back to its home port. Americans in both parties were outraged and demanded war with Great Britain. President Jefferson remarked, "This country has never been in such a state of excitement since the battle of Lexington."

Jefferson, however, knew that the United States was not ready for war with the greatest sea power in the world. He looked for other ways to stop the interference with America's trade and end the insults to America's pride.

★ A Ban on Foreign Trade

Jefferson's decision was to place an embargo, an official government ban, on trade with both Great Britain and France. He hoped to hurt their war efforts enough to force them to stop seizing American ships and sailors.

The Embargo Act

Congress passed the **Embargo Act** in December of 1807, prohibiting all American ships and their cargo from leaving the United States for foreign ports. The act was a disaster for American trade and for Jefferson's own popularity. Great Britain was hurt only a little, whereas France was hardly hurt at all by the act.

American harbors were crowded with ships and cargo with no place to go. It is estimated that as many as 50,000 sailors were out of work, and as many as 100,000 other workers lost their jobs. Businesses failed, and many people were imprisoned for debt. Prices of goods dropped because there was a surplus. Even the government, which depended on import tariffs, lost millions of dollars. Smuggling goods across the Canadian border to get around the embargo became common.

The Embargo Act caused the greatest hardship for merchants and shipowners in the Northeast—mostly Federalists. Some of these Federalists suggested that Jefferson had acted unconstitutionally. Farmers and planters also suffered because they lost markets in other countries for their surplus crops.

On the one-year anniversary of the Embargo Act, sailors and shipbuilders in port towns of the Northeast protested the act by marching to funeral music. Ships in the harbors flew their flags at half-mast to protest the act.

Softening the Embargo Act

Like George Washington before him, Thomas Jefferson had decided not to run for a third term. In the election of 1808, Jefferson's secretary of state and fellow Republican, **James Madison,** won the presidency. Although Madison easily defeated the Federalist candidate, Charles C. Pinckney, the Federalists finished stronger than they had in the last election.

A few days before Jefferson left office, Congress repealed, or canceled, the Embargo Act. Jefferson approved a replacement act—the **Non-Intercourse Act.**

The Non-Intercourse Act allowed Americans to trade with any nation except France and Great Britain. Although less harmful to American trade than the Embargo Act, the Non-Intercourse Act was no more successful in forcing France and Great Britain to respect the rights of the United States. In 1810 Congress replaced it with Macon's Bill No. 2, which stated that if either France or Great Britain agreed to respect neutral rights, the United States would cut off trade with the other nation.

★ SECTION 3 REVIEW ★

★★★★★★★★★★★★★★★★★★ ★★★★★★★★★★★★★★★★★★

Checking for Understanding

1. **Identify** Edward Preble, Stephen Decatur, Barbary Coast States, Mediterranean Sea.

2. **Define** blockade, impressment, deserter, embargo.

3. **How** did President Jefferson respond to Tripoli's declaration of war?

4. **Why** was British interference with American ships more serious than that by the French?

Critical Thinking

5. **Identifying Alternatives** What other steps might the United States have taken instead of establishing the Embargo Act?

ACTIVITY

6. Use *Historical Statistics of the United States* to find the value of the United States's imports and exports from 1800 to 1810. Make a double line graph showing this information.

★★★★★★★★★★★★★★★★★★★★★★★★★★★★★

The War Hawks

SETTING THE SCENE

Read to Learn . . .

★ why President Madison stopped American trade with Great Britain.
★ how conflicts grew between Native Americans and settlers on the frontier.
★ which Americans wanted war with Great Britain.

Terms to Know

★ shaman
★ war hawk

People to Meet

★ James Madison
★ Tecumseh
★ The Prophet
★ William Henry Harrison

Places to Locate

★ Indiana Territory
★ Tippecanoe River
★ Wabash River
★ Prophetstown

British Barbarity and Piracy!!

The Federalists say that Mr. Christopher Gore ought to be supported as Governor—for his *attachment to Britain.*—If British influence is to effect the suffrages of a free people, let them read the following melancholy and outrageous conduct of British Piracy, and judge for themselves.

The "LEOPARD OUTSPOTTED" or Chesapeak Outrage outdone.

▶ NEWSPAPER CONDEMNING BRITISH PIRACY

A fter two terms as President, Thomas Jefferson retired to his beloved home at Monticello. In a letter to Pierre Du Pont de Nemours, a friend, Jefferson wrote how happy he was to retire to "my family, my books and farms. . . . Never did a prisoner, released from his chains, feel such relief as I shall on shaking off the shackles of power."

In writing the epitaph for his own tombstone, Jefferson chose to be remembered for accomplishments other than for being President. The short epitaph reads:

❝ **Author of the Declaration of Independence, of the Statute of Virginia for Religious Freedom, and Father of the University of Virginia.** ❞

★ James Madison Takes Over

Jefferson's handpicked successor as President was his political ally, friend, fellow Virginian, and secretary of state— **James Madison.** Madison's running mate was George Clinton, a former governor of New York. The Federalist candidates were the same as in 1804, Charles C. Pinckney and Rufus King.

In spite of Americans' anger over the Embargo Act, the Republicans won the election of 1808 decisively. Madison owed his victory mainly to support in the South and the West. All the New England states except Vermont voted Federalist.

Madison, a man known for his brilliant mind, had played a large part in writing the Constitution and passing the Bill of Rights. He and Jefferson shared the same ideas about government. Madison planned to follow Jefferson's policy of neutrality, but events forced him to change those plans.

More Trouble With Britain

With the Non-Intercourse Act, the United States's economy began to recover somewhat from the Embargo Act. Yet the law did little to force France and Britain to respect the neutral rights of the United States.

In 1810 Congress passed a new law that reopened trade with all nations. It also allowed the President to reinstate the embargo if France or Britain again interfered with American ships. Finally, if either country lifted its restrictions on American trade, the United States would cut off trade with the other one.

Napoleon saw a chance to hurt Britain and so agreed that France would end its restrictions on American trade. Madison gave Britain a last chance to do the same, but British ships continued to attack American merchant ships and seize American sailors. In March 1811, President Madison cut off trade with Great Britain. The two countries moved closer to war.

★ Native American Resistance

The British-American struggle on the seas was linked to continuing conflicts in the Ohio Valley and the Northwest Territory. As more Americans moved west of the Appalachians, they displaced the Native Americans who lived there.

As Native Americans realized that they were losing their way of life, they fought back. Often the British helped. Settlers on the frontier knew that it was the British in

Picturing History ▲ JAMES MADISON During the election of 1808, Thomas Jefferson endorsed his secretary of state, James Madison, for the presidency. **Who was Madison's running mate in 1808?**

Canada who supplied the Native Americans with guns. They resented the British and the Native Americans equally.

New Native American Leaders

During these difficult times, a remarkable Native American leader emerged to lead the resistance. In about 1808, a Shawnee chief named **Tecumseh** (tuh•KUHM•suh) began to form a confederation of all the Native Americans east of the Mississippi River. Tecumseh knew that a united front was necessary for effective resistance. He rejected the idea that any one tribe could sell land that belonged to all the Native Americans. He pointed out that the Treaty of Greenville signed after the Battle of Fallen Timbers granted the victorious white settlers only a limited territory.

Tecumseh worked with his brother, a shaman, or religious leader. Tecumseh's brother, Tenskwatawa, was known as **The Prophet.** They founded a settlement in the **Indiana Territory,** where the **Tippecanoe River** and the **Wabash River** meet (near present-day Lafayette, Indiana). Known as **Prophetstown,** it became the center of the confederation.

◀ TECUMSEH

Biography ★★★★

Tecumseh Seeks Unity

The name *Tecumseh,* or *Tikamthi,* means "Shooting Star." This name suited the Shawnee leader born in Ohio in 1768. He stressed to the Native American nations that there was strength through unity. He urged them to think of themselves first as "red people" and second as members of a certain nation. He tried to give them a feeling of pride and an identity beyond loyalties to their nations.

His brother, The Prophet, called on the people to retain their own ways and reject those of white settlers. He impressed his followers with dreams, chants, and an accurate prediction of an eclipse of the sun.

In August 1810 Tecumseh asked for a meeting with **William Henry Harrison,** the governor and military commander in the Indian territory. Tecumseh urged that the United States give up some recently "purchased" territory on the grounds that the chiefs who signed the treaty had no authority to do so. Harrison replied that only the President could answer such a request. Tecumseh answered:

> ❝ Well, as the great chief is to decide the matter, I hope the Great Spirit will put sense enough into his head to induce him to give up this land. It is true, he is so far off he will not be injured by the war; he may sit still in his town . . . while you and I will have to fight it out. ❞

Tecumseh had threatened the Americans with war, but he hoped to delay until his forces were stronger. In the fall of 1811, he left Prophetstown to seek alliances with the Creek Nation and others in the Southeast. He told The Prophet to avoid any confrontations with the army.

Harrison feared the growing strength of the Indian confederation. Aware that Tecumseh was away, he decided to attack Prophetstown. When he and about 1,000 soldiers arrived at the settlement, The Prophet panicked and led his warriors into what is known as the **Battle of Tippecanoe,** near present-day West Lafayette, Indiana. Many soldiers and warriors died, and Prophetstown was burned. In revenge, some Native Americans raided frontier settlements. The Battle of Tippecanoe was only the beginning of a long, deadly war between Native Americans and white settlers on the frontier.

Tecumseh died in 1813. His death destroyed the dream of a Native American confederation. Afterward, several Native American nations made peace with Harrison. ★★★

★ A Call for War

Americans now had two reasons to be angry at Britain. The continuing trouble at sea insulted American pride and hurt trade. The conflicts on the frontier, with the British supporting Native Americans, hurt westward expansion.

People who urged war with Britain became known as war hawks. As troubles on the frontier and at sea continued, the number of war hawks increased.

Anti-British feelings were strongest in the West and South. Members of Congress from the West said there could be no peace on the frontier until the British were pushed out of North America. They wanted to conquer British Canada as well as safeguard the frontier.

Members of Congress from the South joined in the calls for a strong stand against Great Britain. Many Southerners wanted to obtain Florida from Spain, Britain's ally. It was a haven for runaway slaves and Native American raiding parties. Acquiring Florida also appealed to those who wanted to add more land to the United States.

War Is Declared

The harsh winter of 1811–1812, along with the American embargo, caused great

Picturing History

▲ BATTLE OF TIPPECANOE The Battle of Tippecanoe began a series of battles between Native Americans and white settlers. **Who led the Native Americans at the Battle of Tippecanoe?**

hardship for the British. Food was scarce, and British-made factory goods piled up on docks and in warehouses. Britain's war with Napoleon continued. The British, desperate for help, repealed the orders for interference in American shipping.

Before President Madison learned that the British government had changed its policy, he gave in to the demands of the war hawks. On June 18, 1812, he asked Congress to declare war against Great Britain.

★ SECTION 4 REVIEW ★

Checking for Understanding

1. **Identify** James Madison, Tecumseh, The Prophet, William Henry Harrison, Indiana Territory, Tippecanoe River, Wabash River, Prophetstown.

2. **Define** shaman, war hawk.

3. **Why** was support for war against Great Britain strongest in the West and South?

4. **What** events led to the failure of Tecumseh's confederation?

Critical Thinking

5. **Identifying Cause and Effect** What effect did frontier battles with Native Americans have on Americans' feelings about declaring war on Great Britain?

ACTIVITY

6. Choose a side in the argument about war with Great Britain. Then draw a political cartoon supporting your point of view.

BUILDING SKILLS
Critical Thinking Skills

Comparing Points of View

Learning the Skill

Much of history is the story of opposing viewpoints and how the differences between them were resolved. To really understand history, you must learn to compare points of view on an issue. To do so, first look for the basic differences between the viewpoints. Also, identify what aspect of the issue each viewpoint stresses. Then ask yourself: "How does this point of view reflect the general attitudes of this person or group?"

One issue that divided Americans in the early 1800s was the acquisition of the Louisiana Territory. The two passages reflect different points of view about this issue. Read these excerpts and answer the questions.

A. "... [T]he fertility of the country, its climate and extent, promise in due season important aids to our treasury, an ample provision for our posterity, and a widespread field for the blessings of freedom and equal laws. . . . With the wisdom of Congress it will rest to take those . . . measures which may be necessary for the immediate occupation and temporary government of the country; for its incorporation into our Union. . . ."
—President Thomas Jefferson (1803)

B. "But as to Louisiana, this new, immense, unbounded world, if it should ever be incorporated into this Union . . . I believe it will be the greatest curse that could at present befall us. . . . Gentlemen on all sides, with very few exceptions, agree that the settlement of this country will be highly injurious and dangerous to the United States. . . . Thus our citizens will be removed to the immense distance of two or three thousand miles from the

▶ PRESIDENT JEFFERSON

◀ SENATOR WHITE

capital of the Union, where they will scarcely ever feel the rays of the General Government. . . ."
—Senator Samuel White (1803)

Practicing the Skill

1. Who are the writers of each passage?

2. What does Jefferson think about the future importance of Louisiana?

3. What is Senator White's point of view on the issue of acquiring Louisiana?

4. What can you conclude is each writer's general attitude toward the expansion of the United States?

APPLYING THE SKILL

5. On the editorial page of your local newspaper, find two letters to the editor that express different viewpoints on the same issue or topic. Read the letters and identify the main differences between their points of view.

★★★★★★★★★★★★★★★★★★★★★★★★★★★★★★

The War of 1812

SETTING THE SCENE

Read to Learn

★ what challenges the United States faced when the War of 1812 began.
★ about the major campaigns of the War of 1812.
★ how the War of 1812 affected the United States.

Terms to Know

★ privateer
★ national anthem

People to Meet

★ Oliver Hazard Perry
★ Dolley Madison
★ Francis Scott Key
★ Andrew Jackson

Places to Locate

★ Detroit
★ Fort Michilimackinac
★ Fort Dearborn
★ Lake Erie
★ Fort McHenry

▶ AMERICAN MILITIA COAT, 1812

When President James Madison sent his war message to Congress, he gave several reasons for declaring war. He accused the British government of acts "hostile to the United States as an independent and neutral nation." He declared that "our commerce has been plundered in every sea. . . ." and he blamed the British for frontier warfare with Native Americans.

★ Lack of Preparation for War

The United States entered the war at a great disadvantage. The military was weak and unprepared. The regular army had a small force of soldiers led by inexperienced officers. It had to depend on help from state militias.

To challenge the powerful British navy, the United States navy in 1812 had fewer than 20 oceangoing ships. In the first year of the war, Congress failed to authorize the building of more warships. The United States paid privateers, or armed ships owned by individuals, to fight. Although privateers could not stand up to British warships, they were able to capture more than 1,300 British merchant ships. The British in turn blockaded the coast, stopping American shipping.

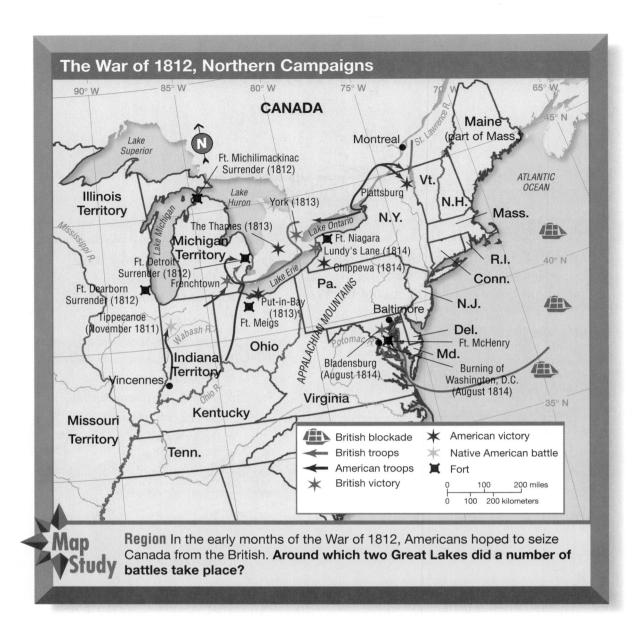

The War of 1812, Northern Campaigns

CANADA

Lake Superior

Ft. Michilimackinac Surrender (1812)

Lake Huron

York (1813)

Montreal

St. Lawrence R.

Maine (part of Mass.)

ATLANTIC OCEAN

Illinois Territory

Lake Michigan

The Thames (1813)

Michigan Territory

Ft. Detroit Surrender (1812)

Frenchtown

Ft. Dearborn Surrender (1812)

Mississippi R.

Plattsburg

Vt.

N.H.

N.Y.

Lake Ontario

Ft. Niagara

Lundy's Lane (1814)

Chippewa (1814)

Mass.

R.I.

Conn.

N.J.

Lake Erie

Pa.

Put-in-Bay (1813)

Ft. Meigs

Tippecanoe (November 1811)

Wabash R.

Ohio

APPALACHIAN MOUNTAINS

Baltimore

Del.

Ft. McHenry

Md.

Bladensburg (August 1814)

Burning of Washington, D.C. (August 1814)

Potomac R.

Vincennes

Indiana Territory

Ohio R.

Kentucky

Virginia

Missouri Territory

Tenn.

British blockade	American victory
British troops	Native American battle
American troops	Fort
British victory	

0   100   200 miles
0   100   200 kilometers

Map Study

Region In the early months of the War of 1812, Americans hoped to seize Canada from the British. **Around which two Great Lakes did a number of battles take place?**

★ The Campaign for Canada

One major goal of the war was the conquest of Canada, Britain's last holding in North America. Henry Clay, a war hawk from Kentucky and speaker of the House, bragged in Congress that the United States could easily win a war in Canada. He said that the militia of Kentucky by itself could "place Montreal and Upper Canada at your feet."

The First Invasions

Clay was too optimistic, however. The first plan was a three-way invasion of Canada from **Detroit,** from Fort Niagara on Lake Ontario, and from Lake Champlain in New York. All three campaigns failed.

The most embarrassing was the loss of Detroit. General **William Hull,** governor of the Michigan Territory, led his troops across the Detroit River into Canada but was forced to retreat by the British and their Native American allies. Soon after, Hull surrendered Detroit to the British, who held it for more than a year.

The invasions from Fort Niagara and Lake Champlain were almost as unsuccessful. The British defeated and captured the American forces when the state militias refused to help or to fight outside their states.

Still more United States defeats came in the West. Combined British and Native American forces captured both **Fort Michilimackinac** in northern Michigan and **Fort Dearborn** (present-day Chicago). With these victories, the British had control of much of the Northwest Territory.

At sea, the tiny United States navy had little chance against the British fleet. A few individual ships, however, fought boldly. One famous sea battle in August 1812 was between the frigate *Constitution*, captained by Isaac Hull, and the British ship *Guerriere*. During fierce combat Hull won a decisive battle. The *Constitution*'s crew, proud that the ship's oak hull resisted British guns, called it Old Ironsides.

Victory on the Great Lakes

During 1813 matters improved in the western end of the war zone and brought American victories. In April, United States troops captured the city of York (present-day Toronto), the capital of Upper Canada, and burned some official buildings.

A few months later, **Oliver Hazard Perry,** a young naval officer, assembled a fleet of 10 small ships that daringly attacked British warships on **Lake Erie.** Perry triumphantly reported: "We have met the enemy and they are ours." The victory forced the British to leave Detroit and made Perry a hero. It also won back control of Michigan and gave Americans a much-needed boost in spirits.

Battle of the Thames River

The **Battle of Lake Erie** cleared the way for another invasion of Canada. In October 1813, General William Henry Harrison took an army of about 3,500 across Lake Erie in pursuit of the British forces fleeing from Detroit. In the **Battle of the Thames River,** they defeated a smaller force of about 600 British and 1,000 Native Americans led by Tecumseh.

Tecumseh, who held the rank of brigadier general in the British army, was killed in the fighting. His death ended the British-Shawnee alliance. However, fighting continued back and forth on the Canada–New York border.

★ The British Invasion

By the spring of 1814, Britain and its allies had defeated Napoleon in Europe. Britain could now send thousands of its best troops to fight the United States. While fighting continued on the New York–Canada border, another British army arrived in the Chesapeake Bay.

The British Burn Washington

On August 24, 1814, Americans were shocked when British troops captured Washington, D.C. Only about 1,000 badly equipped Americans defended the capital against a British force of 6,000.

President Madison and his cabinet fled the city to avoid capture. There was barely time to save historic government

★★★ AMERICA'S FLAGS ★★★

The First Star-Spangled Banner, 1795–1818 The Stars and Stripes flag gained two more stars and two more stripes in 1795, after Kentucky and Vermont had joined the Union. This flag flew over Fort McHenry during the War of 1812 and inspired Francis Scott Key to write "The Star-Spangled Banner."

Congress realized that the flag would become too large if a stripe were added for every new state. It decided to keep the stripes at 13—for the thirteen original colonies—and to add a star for each new state.

★★★★★★★★★★★★★★★★★★★★★★★

DOLLEY MADISON

Picturing History

THE BURNING OF WASHINGTON, D.C. After sailing up Chesapeake Bay, British troops captured and burned the United States capital. **Why did the British burn Washington, D.C.?**

papers such as the original Declaration of Independence. **Dolley Madison,** the wife of the President, is credited with saving many important papers along with a famous portrait of George Washington.

To avenge the burning of the Canadian capital of York, the British set Washington on fire. Fire gutted the Capitol, the President's House (later called the White House), and other buildings.

"The Rockets' Red Glare"

The British celebrated the burning of Washington, regarding it as a decisive end to the war. They moved on to attack the harbor at Baltimore in early September. The troops at **Fort McHenry,** who protected the city and the harbor, held off the British bombardment for 25 hours, finally forcing the British army to retreat.

Francis Scott Key, a Washington lawyer, watched the fierce battle from the deck of a prisoner-of-war exchange ship. He was so moved by what he saw that he scribbled a few lines of poetry on an envelope. Set to the tune of a traditional English song, it became popular throughout the country. In 1931 Congress adopted it

as the national anthem, an official song of praise and patriotism.

★ The Battle of New Orleans

Late in 1814, British forces planned to invade the United States from the south, at New Orleans. General **Andrew Jackson** and his backwoods—rural—sharpshooters were ready for them, however. Jackson's soldiers were confident they would win. Admiringly, they called Jackson "Old Hickory," because they knew of no wood tougher than hickory. Jackson had earned his name leading the Tennessee militia against Creek warriors in 1813.

The Battle of New Orleans on January 8, 1815, was the greatest victory of the war. Jackson's sharpshooters patiently hid behind bales of cotton, their guns aimed at the 8,000 British soldiers sent to capture the city. In the battle that followed, more than 2,000 British soldiers were killed or wounded. American casualties were only about 20.

What neither side knew was that the **Battle of New Orleans** was needless. Because communications were slow, neither side knew that more than two weeks earlier, the United States and Britain had signed a peace treaty in Ghent, Belgium.

★ The War Ends

The war had deeply divided the nation. Many people in New England had been opposed to the war. These people, mostly Federalists, saw that the war would ruin their local economies. In December 1814, delegates from New England met in secret at Hartford, Connecticut. The **Hartford Convention** talked of forming a confederacy of New England states.

Before the delegates could meet with the President to press their demands, news of the victory at New Orleans and the end of the war forced them to abandon their demands. Not much more was heard from the Federalist party.

The Aftermath of the War

The **Treaty of Ghent,** signed on Christmas Eve of 1814, ended the fighting but actually settled nothing. It did not deal with the rights of American ships or the impressment of American sailors. Neither side gained or lost territory.

Most Americans felt proud and self-confident at the end of the War of 1812. The young nation had gained new respect from other nations in the world. Americans felt a new sense of patriotism and a strong national identity.

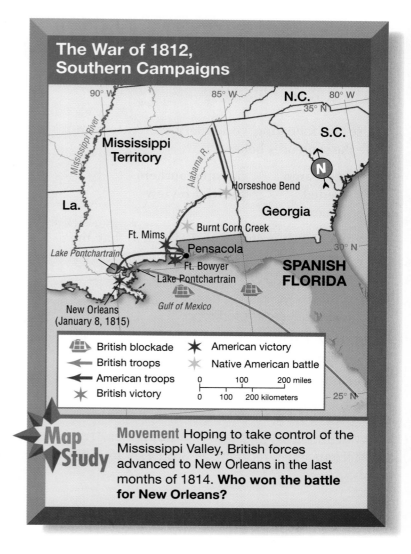

The War of 1812, Southern Campaigns

Mississippi River · 90° W · 85° W · N.C. · 80° W · 35° N · S.C. · **Mississippi Territory** · Alabama R. · Horseshoe Bend · N · **La.** · **Georgia** · Ft. Mims · Burnt Corn Creek · Lake Pontchartrain · Pensacola · 30° N · Ft. Bowyer · Lake Pontchartrain · **SPANISH FLORIDA** · New Orleans (January 8, 1815) · Gulf of Mexico · 25° N

British blockade — American victory
British troops — Native American battle
American troops — 0 · 100 · 200 miles
British victory — 0 · 100 · 200 kilometers

Map Study

Movement Hoping to take control of the Mississippi Valley, British forces advanced to New Orleans in the last months of 1814. **Who won the battle for New Orleans?**

★ SECTION 5 REVIEW ★

Checking for Understanding

1. **Identify** Oliver Hazard Perry, Dolley Madison, Francis Scott Key, Andrew Jackson, Detroit, Fort Michilimackinac, Fort Dearborn, Lake Erie, Fort McHenry.

2. **Define** privateer, national anthem.

3. **What** were the disadvantages of the United States in the War of 1812?

4. **Why** was Perry's victory on Lake Erie important for the United States?

Critical Thinking

5. **Determining Relevance** Describe the impact the Battle of New Orleans had on the outcome of the war. What action by the Federalists did it stop?

ACTIVITY

6. Read the words of "The Star-Spangled Banner" and imagine that you are Francis Scott Key. Draw a picture to illustrate a scene from the song.

Using Key Vocabulary

Use the following vocabulary words to complete the sentences below.

embargo   national anthem
ceded   judicial review
shaman

1. When the Supreme Court decided that the Judiciary Act was unconstitutional, it set a precedent for using the power of _____.

2. In an 1800 treaty, Spain _____ the Louisiana Territory to France.

3. In 1807 Congress ordered an _____ on American trade with Great Britain and France.

4. Tecumseh's brother, The Prophet, was a _____ who urged his followers to return to traditional ways of life.

5. Watching the American flag flying over Fort McHenry inspired Francis Scott Key to write the _____.

Reviewing Facts

1. **Describe** the changes that Jefferson's administration made in the government built up by the Federalists.

2. **Identify** the goals of the Lewis and Clark expedition to the Louisiana Territory.

3. **Trace** the actions taken by President Jefferson in the war against the Barbary States.

4. **Explain** Tecumseh's reasons for forming a confederation of eastern Native Americans.

5. **List** the reasons why the United States was at a disadvantage at the beginning of the War of 1812.

Understanding Concepts

Economic Development

1. Why was control of the Mississippi River and New Orleans important to the United States?

2. What were Jefferson's main economic goals for the United States when he became President?

U.S. Role in World Affairs

3. How did the War of 1812 affect Americans' attitude toward their nation?

4. How did the War of 1812 affect Great Britain's attitude toward the United States?

History and Geography

Congress Votes on the War of 1812

Study the map. Then answer the questions.

1. **Region**   In what states was there no opposition to the war? What regions are they in?

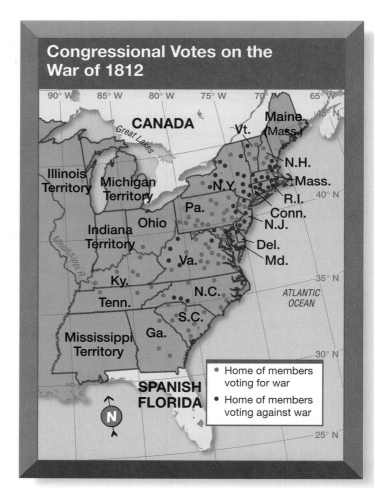

Congressional Votes on the War of 1812

- Home of members voting for war
- Home of members voting against war

2. **Location** What was the southernmost state in which members of Congress were opposed to the war against Britain?

Critical Thinking

1. **Identifying Central Issues** What did the Republican victory in 1800 show about the strength of the Constitution and the new United States government?

2. **Making Comparisons** In what ways did Jefferson's election bring a "revolution" in American politics? What were some significant differences between his administration and those of Adams and Washington? How were they alike?

Cooperative Learning Interdisciplinary Activity: Debate

Have each member of your group choose to be one of the following people: Thomas Jefferson, Tecumseh, Henry Clay, William Henry Harrison, John Adams, or Andrew Jackson. Prepare and present a debate on the pros and cons of declaring war on Great Britain in 1812.

Practicing Skills

Comparing Points of View

The two passages represent different viewpoints about the Embargo Act. Read the passages and then answer the questions.

A. "I have always understood that there were two objects contemplated by the embargo laws. . . . Precautionary, in saving our seamen, our ships and our merchandize from the plunder of our enemies and avoiding the calamities of war. Coercive, by addressing strong appeals to the interests of both the belligerents. The first object has been answered beyond my most [hopeful] expec-

tations. . . . But, Sir, these are not the only good effects of the embargo. It has preserved our peace—it has saved our honor—it has saved our national independence."
—Senator W.B. Giles, 1808

B. "[The embargo] prostrated the whole commerce of America and produced a degree of distress in the New England States greater than that which followed upon the War. I always thought that it was a measure of doubtful policy, but I sustained it. . . [to give it] a fair experiment. A year passed away, and the evils, which it inflicted upon ourselves, were daily increasing in magnitude and extent; and in the meantime . . . Great Britain was enjoying a triumphant monopoly of the commerce of the world."
—Justice Joseph Story, 1831

1. Which passage supports the embargo? Which indicates it was a bad idea?

2. What reasons does Senator Giles give for his opinion on the embargo?

3. What economic effects of the embargo does Justice Story mention?

Writing ABOUT History

Using Your Journal

Imagine that you have had the chance to take part in an American adventure—for instance, accompanying Lewis and Clark or fighting Barbary pirates. Write a letter home describing what you have done and seen.

CHAPTER 12

★★

The Nation Grows
1815–1830

SETTING THE SCENE

Focus

The War of 1812 brought sweeping changes in the way Americans viewed themselves and the world in which they lived. They developed intense feelings of patriotism—pride, loyalty, and devotion to the country. At the same time, however, competition among the regions grew greater. The North, the West, and the South each cultivated an identity and tried to improve its own economic and political interests.

Concepts to Understand

★ How **economic development** during the Industrial Revolution brought changes to the United States

★ Why nationalism in the United States encouraged western expansion and helped define the **United States's role in world affairs**

Read to Discover . . .

★ the impact of the growth of industry on the American way of life.

★ why the United States began to emerge as a world power.

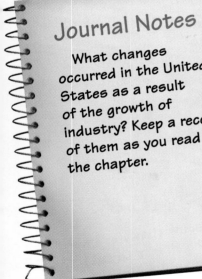

Journal Notes

What changes occurred in the United States as a result of the growth of industry? Keep a record of them as you read the chapter.

▶ SPINDLE OF THREAD

United States

1813 Francis Cabot Lowell builds power loom in Waltham, Massachusetts
1814 War of 1812 ends

1816 James Monroe elected President
1818 National Road reaches Wheeling
1819 Adams-Onís Treaty

1810–1814	1815–1819

World

1815 Napoleon defeated at Waterloo
1816 Argentina wins independence

Fourth of July in Center Square, Philadelphia
by John Lewis Krimmel, 1819

Less than 50 years after the signing of the Declaration of Independence, Fourth of July celebrations had become a national tradition.

▲ PATTENS, WOODEN-SOLED SANDALS, C. 1830S

1820 James Monroe reelected President
1820 Missouri Compromise is passed
1823 Monroe Doctrine proclaimed

1825 John Quincy Adams becomes President
1825 Erie Canal completed

1820–1824	1825–1829

1821 Venezuela gains independence
1821 Mexico expels colonial rulers
1824 Simón Bolívar frees Peru from colonial rule

1825 Bolivia declares its independence
1826 Pan-American Peace Conference held

★★★

Industries Take Root

SETTING THE SCENE

Read to Learn . . .

★ how industrial development began in the United States.

★ which inventions helped the growth of American industry.

★ what working conditions were like in factories.

★ why cities grew rapidly.

Terms to Know

★ Industrial Revolution
★ textile
★ factory system
★ interchangeable parts
★ division of labor
★ mass production

People to Meet

★ James Hargreaves
★ Richard Arkwright
★ Eli Whitney
★ James Watt
★ Oliver Evans
★ Samuel Slater
★ Moses Brown
★ Francis Cabot Lowell

Places to Locate

★ Pawtucket, Rhode Island
★ Waltham, Massachusetts

◀ SAMUEL SLATER

At the time of the American Revolution, agriculture dominated the American economy. In the nineteenth century, a new revolution would take place. The invention of new machines and the development of new economic practices would upset Thomas Jefferson's vision of the United States as a simple agricultural society.

★ A Revolution in Industry

The rise of factories that used machines to produce goods caused great changes in the United States. The changes affected where and how people lived, how they earned their living, and what kinds of goods they could buy. The growth of industry eventually produced changes so great that this time in history is called the Industrial Revolution.

The Industrial Revolution in Britain

The Industrial Revolution began in Great Britain in the middle of the 1700s. British inventors developed new machinery and new sources of power—water, steam, and coal. New machines made possible whole new ways to produce goods. Power-driven tools slowly replaced hand tools.

The Industrial Revolution in Britain affected the textile, or cloth, industry first. New machines made thread or yarn and wove it into cloth. Before the Industrial Revolution, families and artisans had completed these processes at home or in small shops. Now owners built factories to house these new, large machines and hired large groups of workers.

Factory owners began to organize factory work so that it was completed as rapidly and efficiently as possible. The factory system—using machinery and workers together—made it possible for workers to produce large quantities of goods.

The British marketed their goods throughout the world. Low prices helped investors in the factories make huge profits. Knowing that they had the secret of manufacturing, the British carefully guarded their inventions. The British Parliament passed laws making it illegal for any machines, plans for machines, or skilled workers to leave Britain. Disobeying these laws brought severe punishment.

Revolutionary Inventions

Both British and American inventors contributed to the Industrial Revolution. Several early inventions propelled the growth of the textile industry.

In 1764 an Englishman, **James Hargreaves,** invented the spinning jenny. This machine spun many threads at one time, unlike the handheld spinning wheel that could only spin one thread.

In 1769 another Englishman, **Richard Arkwright,** took the spinning jenny one step further, inventing the water frame, a water-powered device that held many more spindles and produced thread faster. In 1786 **Edmund Cartwright** developed a steam-powered loom for weaving cotton.

British industries used cotton imported from the United States. In 1793 an American inventor, **Eli Whitney,** invented the **cotton gin,** a machine that removed the seeds from cotton. With this machine, workers could prepare cotton for shipment to textile mills more quickly than ever before. A worker using the cotton gin could clean as much cotton as 50 people could by hand.

The first factories depended on the energy generated by running water and had to be built near rivers. In 1796 British manufacturers began to use a new source of energy—steam. **James Watt** of Scotland improved the design of steam engines and made their use practical. A few years later, in 1802, an American inventor, **Oliver Evans** of Delaware, built the first high-pressure steam engine for powering machinery. As a result of Evans's steam engine, factories no longer had to be built near streams or rivers.

★ Industry in the United States

The Industrial Revolution did not get started in the United States until the early 1800s. Before then, the United States produced mainly raw materials such as cotton, lumber, iron, and wheat.

Picturing History

▲ EARLY TEXTILE MILL Products made in factories were turned out more efficiently and at a lower cost than those made at home. **The first factories depended on what energy source?**

Linking Past and Present

★★★★★★★★★★★★★★★★★★★★★★ ★★★★★★

The Pencil

Even an object as common as a pencil was unknown before the Industrial Revolution. Who had the bright idea to create the pencil?

◄ **DIXON PENCIL FACTORY, 1800s**

Then

Wooden Case, Graphite Core

The first American-made pencils came from the factory of Joseph Dixon in Salem, Massachusetts. Dixon founded his factory to make pencils in 1827. Dixon made several products using the smooth, but greasy, black mineral graphite. Each pencil had a wooden "wrapper" around a core of clay and graphite. Graphite is often mistaken for lead, so many people called the handy writing tool a "lead pencil."

Now

Wooden Case, Graphite Core

Pencils are now the most widely used writing tool in the world—and in space as well, for astronauts have found that pencils (unlike most pens) work well in conditions of weightlessness. Ordinary pencils are still made with wooden cases and cores of clay and graphite. And many of the 2 billion pencils made in the United States each year still come from Dixon's factories.

★★

Artisans, such as blacksmiths, weavers, and carpenters, used hand tools to make their products. Although mills powered by water ground corn and wheat into flour and meal, almost everything else was made by hand, including shoes, saddles, glass, hats, wagons, nails, and books.

Before the American Revolution, the colonies had depended on Britain for manufactured goods. British regulations, in fact, had discouraged American industry from competing.

After independence, however, Americans were free to share in the profits of the Industrial Revolution. Some states offered rewards to people from Britain who would bring their knowledge of machines and industry to America.

Sharing the Secrets

The rewards offered drew some clever and adventurous inventors. In 1789 **Samuel Slater,** a 21-year-old apprentice in Arkwright's textile mill in England, mem-orized the design of the machinery. Knowing that he would not be allowed to leave Britain, he traveled in disguise to the United States. Once in New York, Slater offered his services to **Moses Brown,** a wealthy Quaker who owned an inefficient cotton mill in **Pawtucket, Rhode Island.**

Within a year, Slater re-created from memory Arkwright's cotton mill. The Pawtucket mill housed 72 spindles powered by the falling water of the nearby river. It was the first factory in the United States. By 1800, seven similar mills had been built in New England. The Industrial Revolution had come to America.

Thanks in part to the region's many swift-running rivers, the Northeast soon became the industrial center of the United States. Waterpower turned the waterwheels that ran the machines of the new factories. In addition, a number of New England traders, realizing the profit they could make from factories, invested their money in them.

The Lowell Landmark

At first, American textile factories produced only yarn and thread. Families working at home still used hand looms to weave yarn and thread into cloth. In 1813 a young Bostonian, **Francis Cabot Lowell,** took another step in industrialization.

After seeing power looms in Britain, Lowell built one himself. He then placed the looms along with thread-spinning spindles in a new factory at **Waltham, Massachusetts.** Now, for the first time, the entire process of converting cotton into cloth took place in one building.

New Methods of Working

In 1798 Eli Whitney, who had invented the cotton gin while working in Georgia, came up with another idea that spurred the Industrial Revolution. He thought of a new way to manufacture guns.

He invented a machine that made it possible for workers to cut pieces of metal in exactly the same shape every time. With such a device, each part of a gun could be made in large numbers—all exactly alike. Each part could then be used in making guns that were also exactly alike. As a result, it also became easy to replace broken parts.

This system of making interchangeable parts, or parts that are exactly alike, revolutionized gun making. While some workers cut metal with patterns, others put the gun parts together. Dividing up the work in this way and giving each worker one or two simple jobs to do is called division of labor. This system was soon used in other types of factories.

Interchangeable parts, division of labor, and other new manufacturing methods made mass production of goods possible. This meant that goods could be made in large quantities, in a short time, for less cost. Before long, other factories were producing such items as wagon wheels, stoves, axes, and other tools.

Picturing History
▲ SLATER'S MILL Technology from Great Britain's Industrial Revolution helped Samuel Slater build a mill in Pawtucket, Rhode Island, in 1790. **Why did Slater have to travel in disguise to America?**

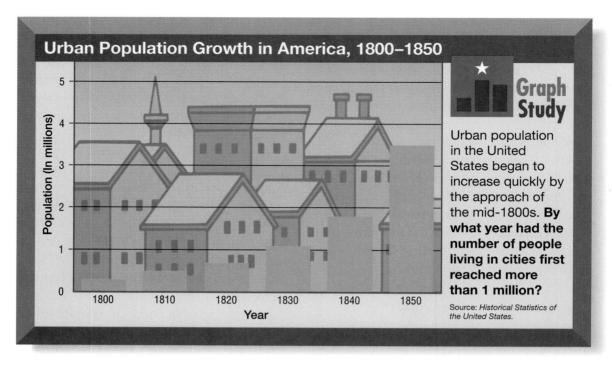

Urban Population Growth in America, 1800–1850

Population (In millions)

5
4
3
2
1
0

1800 1810 1820 1830 1840 1850

Year

Graph Study

Urban population in the United States began to increase quickly by the approach of the mid-1800s. **By what year had the number of people living in cities first reached more than 1 million?**

Source: *Historical Statistics of the United States.*

★ Industrial Working Conditions

The Industrial Revolution changed people's lives. Artisans who made goods in their homes now had to compete with factory-made goods. Many people left family farms and shops to work in the new factories. For some it meant new opportunities, but for many it meant a new kind of drudgery.

Women and children made up a large percentage of workers in factories because they could be paid less than men. Because wages were low, entire families sometimes had to go to work in a factory.

Factory workers put in long hours—12 to 14 hours a day, 6 days a week—often in unsafe and unhealthy working conditions. Bad lighting and poor ventilation harmed the workers' health. Poor working conditions were typical of American industry throughout much of the nineteenth century.

As machines replaced hand tools, jobs for skilled craft workers became scarce. Before industrialization, there had been enjoyment in skilled work and pride in good handicraft. Now, workers tended to machines, performed the same tasks over and over, and took little pride in the completed product.

In an effort to improve their working conditions, workers organized into **labor unions.** Labor unions demanded higher wages and better working conditions. Skilled artisans, such as carpenters, shoemakers, and printers, formed the first labor unions in the United States. Later unskilled laborers and female workers began to organize.

Growing Cities

In 1810 about 90 percent of the American population still lived on farms. The spread of the factory system and mass production caused cities to grow as more people moved to be near new factories. New York City ranked as the United States's largest city in 1810. Its population doubled from about 96,000 to about 203,000 between 1810 and 1830. Philadelphia's population went from about 91,000 in 1810 to about 161,000 in 1830.

Cities offered more job opportunities and better chances for education, as well as libraries, theaters, and other kinds of entertainment. Even in colonial times, however, cities had been troubled by problems with clean water, fire protection, and public health.

As cities grew rapidly, these problems worsened and new ones developed. Large groups of newcomers from the country settled in factory areas. Housing around factories became overcrowded, run-down, and unhealthy to live in. Crime also became a problem.

Biography ★★★

Mother Elizabeth Seton Champions Education

The problem of poverty in great industrial cities inspired a number of people to try to help. Elizabeth Ann Seton (1774–1821) was left a widow at the age of 29. Although she had five children to raise alone, she saw the need for free education for the poor. A convert to Roman Catholicism, she put her efforts into opening a free Catholic elementary school in Baltimore, Maryland. Her children attended the school along with the children of recent immigrants.

A few years later in 1809, Seton founded a religious order called the Sisters of Charity, the first such order founded in the United States. Now called Mother Seton, she led this group of nuns in helping the sick and establishing orphanages.

Mother Seton is the founder of the Catholic parochial, or private church-sponsored, school system in the United States. In 1975 she became the first native-born American canonized—made a saint—by the Roman Catholic Church. ★★★

◀ **ELIZABETH ANN SETON**

★ SECTION 1 REVIEW ★

★★★★★★★★★★★★★★★★★

Checking for Understanding

1. **Identify** James Hargreaves, Richard Arkwright, Eli Whitney, James Watt, Oliver Evans, Samuel Slater, Moses Brown, Francis Cabot Lowell, Pawtucket, Waltham.

2. **Define** Industrial Revolution, textile, factory system, interchangeable parts, division of labor, mass production.

3. **What** inventions helped the growth of the textile industry?

4. **What** factors made the Northeast the first industrial region of the United States?

Critical Thinking

5. **Forming Opinions** By leaving Britain with his knowledge of manufacturing, Samuel Slater broke the law, yet he helped start the textile industry in America. Do you think he was right or wrong to do this? Explain your answer.

ACTIVITY

6. Think of an example of division of labor in making or building something. Draw a diagram showing the process.

★★★★★★★★★★★★★★★★★★★★★★★★★

Moving West

SETTING THE SCENE

Read to Learn . . .

★ why Americans moved west in the early 1800s.

★ how transportation systems improved in the United States in the early 1800s.

Terms to Know

★ Wilderness Road
★ turnpike
★ toll
★ National Road
★ canal

People to Meet

★ Daniel Boone
★ John Fitch
★ Robert Fulton
★ De Witt Clinton

Places to Locate

★ Cumberland Gap
★ Lake Erie
★ Hudson River
★ Erie Canal
★ Buffalo, New York

◀ NATIONAL ROAD MILE MARKER

130
TO
WHEELING
to
Frostburgh
10

During the early history of the United States, the frontier continually moved westward. As the Atlantic coastal area became crowded, people packed their belongings and moved to unsettled land in the West.

To one observer in 1817, "Old America seemed to be breaking up and moving westward." George Flower, who migrated to Illinois from England in the same year, recorded the following observation of Americans on the move:

> ❝ Some came in wagons and light carriages, overland; some on horseback; some in arks; some in skiffs [small boats]; and some by steamboat, by New Orleans. ❞

★ Land!

Why did so many Americans and newcomers from Europe move to the frontier? Pioneers in general shared a dream of new opportunities on the frontier. Most important was the chance to own inexpensive land with rich soil.

In addition to new settlers from Europe, many Americans also moved west, lured by rich soil and cheap land. They came from all sections of the country. Cotton planters from the South, cattle and sheep ranchers from New England, and merchants and storekeepers from the East all moved west looking for new economic opportunities.

Moreover, some American pioneers moved westward because they had worn out the soil on their land and needed to find new, fertile land. Farmers then knew little about the soil, preserving nutrients, or preventing erosion. When the soil became thin, these farm families simply packed up, moved west, and started another farm.

Conestoga wagons, developed by Pennsylvania's German Americans during the colonial era, carried everything the families owned on their journey west. These sturdy, canvas-topped wagons were pulled by yoked oxen or teams of horses on the long, slow journey.

Once the pioneers arrived, their survival depended upon the long-handled ax and the rifle. With the ax, farmers cleared trees from the land so it could be planted and built cabins and furniture for their families. The rifle was indispensable for hunting and protection.

★ Pathways to the West

In 1775 **Daniel Boone** led a group of 30 lumberers from Virginia through the Powell River valley and across the **Cumberland Gap,** a natural pass through the Appalachian Mountains. (It is near where the states of Virginia, Tennessee, and Kentucky meet.) With mighty blows from their axes, Boone's party cleared a trail to central Kentucky. It became the main road west. By 1800 about 20,000 settlers traveled this rocky, primitive trail, known as the Wilderness Road, to settle south of the Ohio River.

Pioneer settlers moved west by many routes besides the Wilderness Road. Some made their way to the **Northwest Territory** over rough wagon roads. Then they loaded their belongings onto flatboats and floated down the Ohio River. New Yorkers usually took the route across the Mohawk River valley to **Lake Erie.** Other settlers from the Northeast crossed the mountains in western Pennsylvania and followed trails to Pittsburgh, at the head of the Ohio River.

Biography ★★★

The Lincoln Family on the Move

The Lincolns of Virginia, like many other families, heard Daniel Boone's tales of the rich black soil, blue-green grass, and clear streams of Kentucky.

Like many people with small farms, the family of Abraham Lincoln worked hard to make ends meet. They listened eagerly as Boone explained that they could buy all the land they wanted for 40 cents an acre. The family decided to take its chances in the West. In 1782 they followed the Wilderness Road into Kentucky and settled along the Green River on more than 2,000 acres.

Although the Lincolns worked hard on their land in Kentucky, a dispute over the ownership encouraged them to move once again. Because they had heard stories of good land farther west, late in 1816 the Lincolns packed up all their household goods, their four horses, and their children—Sarah and Abraham. Crossing the Ohio River to the north, they settled at Little Pigeon Creek in Indiana, a lonesome country with two or three miles (3.2 to 4.8 km) between settlers. Abraham

Picturing History

▲ THE WILDERNESS ROAD Travel across the Appalachian Mountains to the Ohio Valley could take several weeks. **What is the name of the natural pass through the Appalachian Mountains?**

Lincoln, who later became the nation's 16th President, wrote:

> 66 **It was a wild region, with many bears and other wild animals still in the woods . . . the panther's scream filled [the] night with fear . . . bears preyed on the swine . . . [There was] about one human being to each square mile.** 99

In search of richer farmland, in 1830 the Lincolns again moved farther west to Illinois. According to Abraham, the uneven muddy trail made the journey "slow and tiresome," and they often had to wade through rivers and creeks. ★★★

★ Transportation Systems Improve

Westward travel on roads, trails, and waterways increased dramatically in the early 1800s. The increasing numbers of pioneers moving west made it clear that Americans were on the move and needed reliable transportation systems. The rise of industry and an increase in agricultural production also encouraged improvements in transportation. People wanted cheap, speedy transportation to get raw materials to factories and goods to market.

Between 1800 and 1830, several private companies decided to go into the road-building business. In New York and Pennsylvania these companies constructed many private roads called turnpikes, with the approval of state governments. These roads had spiked poles, or pikes, that blocked the roads like gates. When travelers on the roads paid a toll, the charge for using the road, the tollkeepers turned the pikes aside to let them continue.

The toll money paid for building the roads. Within a short time, turnpikes connected a number of cities in the East and led to major rivers of the West.

The National Road

Settlers moving west demanded a better land route to help their region grow more rapidly. Many settlers wanted parts of the West to gain statehood. Better transportation would surely increase the population in the West and at the same time make moving goods quicker and less costly.

In 1806 Congress approved government funds to finance building the National Road, which led to the West. Work on the road did not begin immediately, however, because of President Jefferson's concern that the Constitution did not provide for the government to build roads. Finally, construction began in 1811. The $7 million project took seven years to complete. The road, with a crushed stone surface and large stone bridges, connected Cumberland, Maryland, with Wheeling, Virginia (present-day West Virginia).

From the day the National Road opened, it was crowded with people moving west. One observer noted, "We are seldom out of sight, as we travel on this grand track towards the Ohio, of family groups, behind and before us."

The National Road moved westward with the pioneers. In 1830 Congress voted to lengthen the new road to Columbus, Ohio, and later to Indianapolis, Indiana. By 1852 the road stretched to Vandalia, Illinois.

The National Road made it possible for people to travel in all kinds of weather. The crushed stone allowed water to drain, so that wagon wheels did not get stuck in ruts and potholes. Travelers on the National Road had fewer problems with dust and mud. Taverns and inns along the road provided food and rest for travelers.

★ Depending on Waterways

Even though the number of roads increased during the early 1800s, rivers remained the nation's main means of transportation. Before the 1820s most travelers sailed, floated, or poled their way downriver on flatboats and rafts. Getting back upriver against the current, however, proved challenging. Teams of horses slowly pulled boats upstream, often against strong currents. They moved so slowly that travelers could leave the boats and walk along the shoreline.

Steam Replaces Sails

John Fitch, another ingenious American inventor, designed a steamboat in 1785 but could not find financial backing to carry out his ideas. In 1807 **Robert Fulton** incorporated some of Fitch's design for a steamboat and built the *Clermont.*

Fulton launched his steamboat on the **Hudson River.** It traveled 150 miles (241 km) upriver from New York to Albany in an amazing 32 hours. The return trip downriver took only 30 hours. The *Clermont* became an immediate success. Before long, steamboats carried people and goods along the Mississippi River and the Great Lakes. These water systems became important trade routes to the interior.

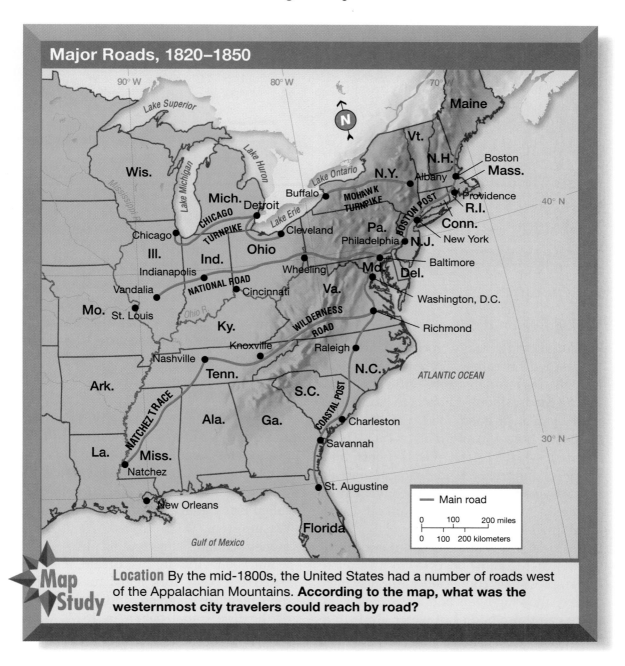

Major Roads, 1820–1850

Map Study

Location By the mid-1800s, the United States had a number of roads west of the Appalachian Mountains. **According to the map, what was the westernmost city travelers could reach by road?**

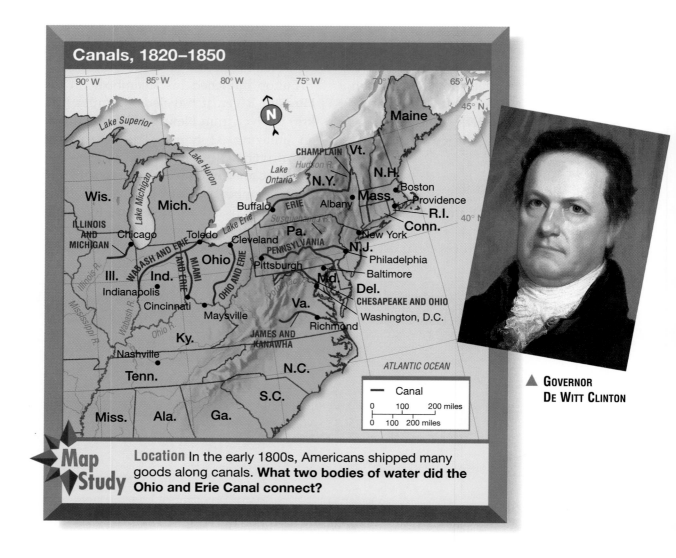

Canals, 1820–1850

Canal

0   100   200 miles

0   100   200 miles

Map Study Location In the early 1800s, Americans shipped many goods along canals. **What two bodies of water did the Ohio and Erie Canal connect?**

▲ GOVERNOR DE WITT CLINTON

Canal Connections

For moving heavy goods, Americans depended on canals. Shipping goods on canals was much more efficient than using roads. It took 4 horses to haul a 1.5-ton load on a good road. On the other hand, 2 horses could pull a canal boat loaded with 50 tons. While boats and barges could carry large loads at a small cost, rivers were not always conveniently located. As a result, a period of canal building began.

A canal is a channel dug out and filled with water to allow boats to cross a stretch of land. Canals connected natural waterways, allowing boats and barges to travel between those bodies of water. By 1815 a number of short canals had been built.

The canal-building craze did not really begin, though, until the **Erie Canal** was completed in 1825.

"Clinton's Ditch"

New York's governor, **De Witt Clinton,** and other New Yorkers dreamed of connecting the Great Lakes with the Mohawk and Hudson Rivers and, finally, New York City. Clinton drew up plans for the so-called Erie Canal and took his proposal to Washington, D.C., to ask for federal money. Congress rejected his idea.

Still believing in his dream, Clinton asked the New York legislature to fund the canal. They agreed, and construction of the Erie Canal began in 1817. Many people laughed at the idea of Clinton's "big ditch"—sure that a canal about 363 miles (584 km) long and 4 feet (1.2 m) deep would fail. But others disagreed.

John Williams, a Detroit merchant, believed in Clinton's dream. In a letter he wrote to a friend in 1817, he described what he believed the Erie Canal would bring:

 The projected canal to connect the waters of Lake Erie with those of the Hudson [River] will no doubt greatly accelerate the population and prosperity of this country. . . .

In 1825 a freight barge named the *Seneca Chief* traveled the Erie Canal from **Buffalo,** at the eastern end of Lake Erie, to Albany, on the upper Hudson River. From Albany, the *Seneca Chief* continued its journey down the Hudson River to New York City. There, De Witt Clinton proudly poured a kegful of water from Lake Erie into the Atlantic Ocean to celebrate.

By 1830 New York stood to make a huge profit from canal tolls—even after paying for the cost of building and maintaining the canal. The canal lowered the cost of moving a ton of goods from 30 cents to less than 2 cents per mile. It also dramatically cut travel time.

▲ THE ERIE CANAL

The Erie Canal opened a continuous water route linking the Great Lakes with New York City's harbor on the Atlantic coast. It speeded up settlement of the Great Lakes region and created the easiest, quickest, and cheapest way to send goods from the Northeast to the West. As a result, New York City became the major center for goods being shipped to the Great Lakes ports.

The success of the Erie Canal inspired others. Pennsylvania had a system of waterways connecting Philadelphia with other parts of the state. In Ohio and Indiana, canals linked the Great Lakes ports with the Ohio and Mississippi rivers. In New Jersey canals connected the Delaware and Raritan rivers.

★ SECTION 2 REVIEW ★

★★★★★★★★★★★★★★★★★

Checking for Understanding

1. **Identify** Daniel Boone, John Fitch, Robert Fulton, De Witt Clinton, Cumberland Gap, Lake Erie, Hudson River, Erie Canal, Buffalo.

2. **Define** Wilderness Road, turnpike, toll, National Road, canal.

3. **What** methods of transportation did pioneers use to move to the West?

4. **Why** did canals seem to be the answer to the country's transportation problems?

★★★★★★★★★★★★★★★★★

Critical Thinking

5. **Determining Cause and Effect** How did the Erie Canal affect the Great Lakes region?

ACTIVITY

6. Create a chart with sketches illustrating the major means of transportation that helped the United States grow. Write a caption under each sketch explaining how this mode of transportation helped the country develop.

BUILDING SKILLS

Social Studies Skills

Understanding Line Graphs

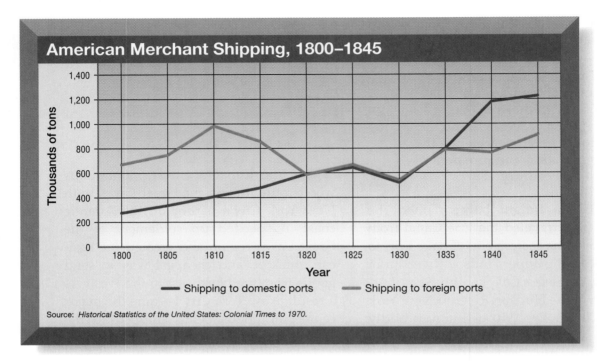

American Merchant Shipping, 1800–1845
Thousands of tons
1,400
1,200
1,000
800
600
400
200
0
1800
1805
1810
1815
1820
1825
1830
1835
1840
1845
Year
Shipping to domestic ports
Shipping to foreign ports
Source: *Historical Statistics of the United States: Colonial Times to 1970.*

Learning the Skill

Graphs are a way of showing numbers visually, making them easier to read and understand. **Line graphs** are often used to show changes in number or quantity over time. They show information along two dimensions. The **horizontal axis** (or x-axis) is the line along the bottom of the graph. If the graph shows information over time, this axis usually shows the time period. The **vertical axis** (y-axis) is the line that runs up the side of the graph.

Sometimes a graph—a double-line graph—shows more than one line, recording two related quantities. For instance, you and a friend might both record your running speeds for footraces over a period of time on one graph, using a line of a different color for each of you. Before trying to understand any graph, be sure to read the labels on both axes and the key for each line.

Practicing the Skill

Study the line graph and answer the following questions. Remember to start by reading the title of the graph and the labels on each axis. Read the key to see what each colored line represents.

1. What kind of information does the graph give?
2. What are the time intervals on the horizontal axis?
3. What quantity is measured on the vertical axis?
4. What trend seems to be beginning in 1835?

APPLYING THE SKILL

5. **Measure changes in temperature or rainfall for a two-week period. Record your data every day. At the end of two weeks, plot the information on a line graph. Be sure to label each axis in the graph and give it a title.**

★★★

Nationalism and Sectionalism

SETTING THE SCENE

Read to Learn . . .

★ why feelings of national pride and loyalty increased among Americans in the early 1800s.
★ why rivalries between sections of the country increased.

Terms to Know

★ nationalism
★ American System
★ protective tariff
★ monopoly
★ interstate commerce
★ sectionalism
★ Missouri Compromise

People to Meet

★ James Monroe
★ Henry Clay
★ James Tallmadge, Jr.
★ John Quincy Adams
★ Andrew Jackson

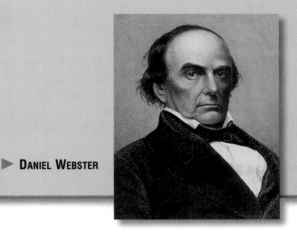

► DANIEL WEBSTER

Americans celebrated the Fourth of July with special joy in 1815. Proud patriots rang bells and waved banners. Marching bands paraded to the sounds of fifes and drums. Lively crowds sang patriotic songs and listened to rousing speeches.

★ National Unity

The War of 1812 stirred strong feelings of nationalism, or feelings of pride and devotion, among Americans everywhere. Americans thought more than ever about their nation's interests, needs, and goals. They wanted the nation to be independent and self-sufficient.

The Era of Good Feelings

In 1816 citizens in all parts of the United States supported the Republican party. A Republican President, James Madison, and a Republican majority in Congress firmly controlled the nation. Former Federalists such as John Quincy Adams (son of President John Adams) joined the Republican party.

Election of 1816

James Monroe of Virginia and William Crawford of Georgia competed to be the Republican candidate in the election of 1816. Monroe won by a narrow vote. He then easily won the presidential election with 183 electoral votes. His competitor, Federalist candidate Rufus King, won only 34 electoral votes.

The United States was enjoying great prosperity in March 1817 when Monroe gave his Inaugural Address. The new President spoke of national unity and general agreement on national issues. He proclaimed that

> **66** **National Honor is National property of the highest value.** **99**

For a brief time in American history, political rivalry had seemed to fade away. The editor of a Boston newspaper wrote that an "Era of Good Feelings" had begun. Nationalism and unity seemed stronger than sectional feelings or party loyalties. By 1820 Federalists had vanished from national politics and President Monroe was reelected without opposition.

Outgoing President Madison's last message to Congress in 1817 expressed America's growing mood of nationalism. The War of 1812 had clearly demonstrated that Jefferson's ideal of a central government with limited functions could not meet the needs of a nation in times of crisis. Sounding more like a Federalist than a Republican, Madison urged the federal government to guide the growth of trade and industry. The large Republican majority in Congress agreed. The Republican party made a change from favoring states' rights to championing federal power.

★ The American System

Henry Clay, a Republican and speaker of the House, proposed a nationalist program to improve the nation. Clay's "American System" aimed to help the economy of each section of the country and increase the power of the federal government. Clay called for higher tariffs, a Bank of the United States, and internal improvements, such as the building of roads, bridges, and canals.

Clay designed the American System to halt the growing sectionalism that he saw in the country. Not all congressional leaders agreed with Clay, though, and they did not accept all of his proposals. Although Congress did not spend much money on internal improvements, other parts of the American System did become law.

▲ HENRY CLAY

Footnotes to History

A Ceremony Outdoors   The fifth President of the United States, James Monroe, was the first President to be inaugurated outdoors. Usually the President took the oath of office in the House of Representatives, but when senators insisted on bringing fancy red armchairs to the ceremony, the House refused. Instead of arguing over the situation, someone decided to hold the inauguration outdoors.

Another National Bank

In 1816 the Republican majority in Congress brought back the national bank, which had been allowed to end in 1811. In 1791 as a member of Congress, Madison had criticized Hamilton's national banking system. In 1816, however, President Madison signed a bill creating the Second Bank of the United States.

Republican leaders changed their minds about the national bank when they saw the confusion that resulted after the first bank closed in 1811. Many officials of state banks acted unwisely. They made too many loans and allowed too much money into circulation.

The result was **inflation**—rapid rises in the prices of goods. Prices rose faster than incomes, so that American families could buy less and less with each dollar. Also, without a national bank, the federal government had no safe place to keep its funds. The Second Bank of the United States restored order to the money supply, helping American businesses to grow.

Trade Protection

Another problem with the economy was a flood of goods from Britain following the War of 1812. British factories, often more advanced, turned out goods of higher quality and at a cheaper cost than goods made in America.

By flooding the United States with their goods, the British hoped to keep American businesses from competing. American manufacturers called for high tariffs to protect their growing industries.

The Republicans followed another of Hamilton's Federalist ideas when they passed a bill in 1816 to impose a protective tariff. The new tariff taxed imports, thus raising the prices of imported goods. Merchants added the tariff to the price of imported goods. This made them more expensive and encouraged people to buy cheaper American-made goods.

★★★ AMERICA'S FLAGS ★★★

Flag of 1818 By 1818 the number of states had reached 20. In April President Monroe signed a bill that set the basic design of the flag. Each newly admitted state added a star to the field of blue. The addition of a new star took place on the Fourth of July following the state's year of entry. The 13 stripes symbolizing the original states remained unchanged.

The Great Star Flag Congress did not state how the stars should be arranged, so flag-makers used various designs. The Great Star Flag placed the stars in the form of a five-pointed star.

★★★★★★★★★★★★★★★★★★★★★★★★

★ Nationalism and the Supreme Court

In three of its decisions in the early 1800s, the Supreme Court, led by Chief Justice John Marshall, supported the powers of the national government. In the case of *Fletcher* v. *Peck* in 1810, the Supreme Court ruled that acts of a state government could be declared void if they violated provisions of the Constitution.

In 1819 the Court decided *McCullough* v. *Maryland.* It said that the state of Maryland could not tax the local office of the Bank of the United States because it was the property of the national government. Being able to impose such a tax, the Court said, would give states power to destroy the national government.

The Court also ruled that the national bank was constitutional, even though the Constitution did not specifically give Congress the power to create one. Marshall observed that the Constitution specifically permitted Congress to issue money, borrow money, and collect taxes. Therefore, he concluded that the federal government could choose any method that was "necessary and proper" to exercise the powers the Constitution had given it.

In 1824 the Court again ruled in favor of federal government power. In *Gibbons v. Ogden,* the state of New York had granted a monopoly to a steamship operator running ships between New York and New Jersey. This meant no competitors could run steamboats on the same route. The Supreme Court, however, said that only Congress had the power to make laws governing interstate commerce, or trade between states.

★ A Split Into Sections

Different regions of the country had maintained different interests and priorities since colonial times. In the early 1800s, three distinct sections developed in the United States—the North, the South, and the West.

The North included the Northeast, New England, and the Middle Atlantic states. The South covered what is now the Southeast. The West included the area between the Appalachian Mountains and the Mississippi River. Geography, economics, and history all contributed to sectional differences and distinct ways of life in these sections.

Divisions grew deeper. Many people began to wonder whether sectionalism—rivalry based on the special interests of different areas—might divide the nation.

Clay, Calhoun, and Webster

Three young members of Congress played powerful roles in national politics in the first half of the 1800s. **Henry Clay** of Kentucky represented the West. **John C. Calhoun** of South Carolina spoke for Southern interests. **Daniel Webster** of Massachusetts protected the interests of New England. Each leader, although nationalist, remained concerned with protecting the interests of his own section of the country.

▼ IRON LADLES

Picturing History ▲ THE TARIFF QUESTION Tariffs protected many of the North's industries. However, the passage of protective tariffs increased sectional tension between the North and South in the 1800s. **Why did protective tariffs anger Southerners?**

Sectional Disagreements

In 1818 and 1824 Congress passed protective tariffs that were even higher than the one passed in 1816. Some Americans protested. Southerners were especially angry, thinking that the tariff protected Northern manufacturers at their expense.

Prior to the protective tariffs, Southerners had been able to buy cheaper goods from Britain. The high protective tariffs made them buy costly manufactured goods made in Northern factories.

Statehood for Missouri?

Westward expansion brought a serious clash between sectional interests in 1819. In that year the **Missouri Territory** asked Congress to be admitted as a state. Most Missouri settlers had come from Kentucky and Tennessee, where slavery was allowed. They believed, therefore, that slavery ought to be legal in the new state of Missouri. A majority in the House of Representatives disagreed.

James Tallmadge, Jr., of New York added an amendment to the Missouri statehood bill. It proposed that Missouri gradually abolish slavery in order to be admitted to the Union. The issue of slavery created bitter debates in Congress. The House passed the Tallmadge Amendment, but the Senate blocked it.

Slavery was not the only sectional issue raised by Missouri's statehood. Southerners also feared that they would lose power in the federal government. At the time the population in the North was slightly larger than in the South. In 1819 the North's population was more than 5 million people. This gave the North 105 members in the House of Representatives.

The slave states of the South had about 4.5 million people, giving them 81 members in the House. Representation of slave states in the Senate was balanced, for there were 11 slave states and 11 free states. The

The Missouri Compromise, 1820

Missouri Compromise Line (36° 30′ N)

Maine, 1820

Missouri, 1821

PACIFIC OCEAN

ATLANTIC OCEAN

Gulf of Mexico

- Free state
- Free territory
- Slave state
- Slave territory
- Non-United States territory

0   200   400 miles
0 200 400 kilometers

Map Study

Region After 1820 all new states north of the Missouri Compromise line were to enter the Union as free states. **Did Missouri enter the Union as a free state or a slave state?**

addition of Missouri as a free state would swing the balance in favor of the North.

★ The Missouri Compromise

Debates in Congress heated to the boiling point. Fearing a split in the Union, Henry Clay proposed the Missouri Compromise. It narrowly passed only because Maine had also requested admission as a state.

Clay proposed that Maine enter the Union as a free state. Missouri could then enter as a slave state. This would keep an even balance of power in the Senate—12 free states and 12 slave states.

The Missouri Compromise also settled the question of slavery in the rest of the Louisiana Territory. Slavery would be prohibited north of the parallel 36°30′, a line running west from the southern boundary of Missouri.

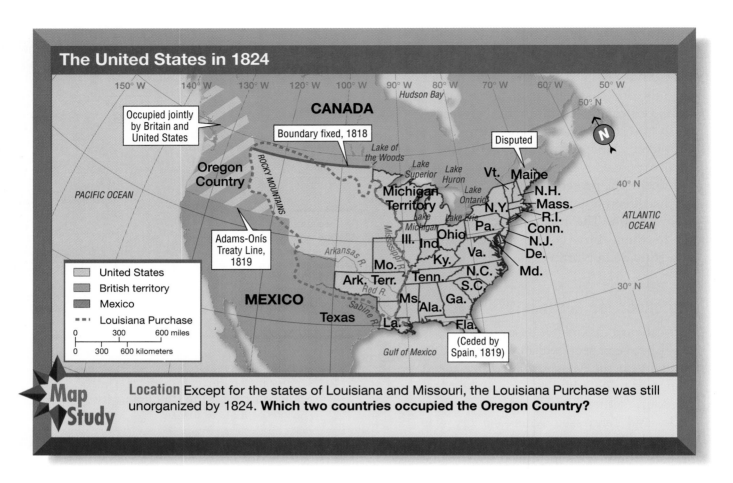

The United States in 1824

Occupied jointly by Britain and United States

Boundary fixed, 1818

Disputed

CANADA

Hudson Bay

Lake of the Woods

Lake Superior

Lake Huron

Lake Ontario

Lake Michigan

Lake Erie

Oregon Country

ROCKY MOUNTAINS

Adams-Onís Treaty Line, 1819

PACIFIC OCEAN

Michigan Territory

Vt. Maine

N.H.

Mass.

N.Y.

R.I.

Conn.

Pa.

N.J.

De.

Md.

Ill. Ind. Ohio

Va.

Ky.

N.C.

S.C.

ATLANTIC OCEAN

Mo.

Arkansas R.

Ark. Terr.

Red R.

Tenn.

Mississippi R.

MEXICO

Sabine R.

Texas

La.

Ms. Ala. Ga.

Fla.

Gulf of Mexico

(Ceded by Spain, 1819)

Legend:
- United States
- British territory
- Mexico
- - - Louisiana Purchase

0   300   600 miles
0   300   600 kilometers

150° W 140° W 130° W 120° W 110° W 100° W 90° W 80° W 70° W 60° W 50° W

50° N 40° N 30° N

Map Study

Location Except for the states of Louisiana and Missouri, the Louisiana Purchase was still unorganized by 1824. **Which two countries occupied the Oregon Country?**

The Missouri Compromise promised a temporary solution to this sectional conflict. It did nothing to solve the basic problem, however. Americans moving west took their different ways of life with them—one based on slavery, the other based on free or hired labor.

★ Sectionalism and the Election of 1824

Sectional differences, and not political parties, influenced the election of 1824. The presidential candidates, though all Republicans, came from different sections of the country. **John Quincy Adams** of Massachusetts, Monroe's secretary of state, represented the Northeast. Wealthy merchants and factory owners of the cities backed him. **William Crawford** of Georgia, Monroe's secretary of the treasury, won support from Southern states along the Atlantic coast. In the West, Kentucky and the new states bordering the Great Lakes campaigned for **Henry Clay.** Settlers of the Old Southwest backed **Andrew Jackson.**

Not surprisingly, no candidate won a majority of the votes in the election. As the Constitution provides, the House of Representatives decided the outcome. Clay, with the fewest electoral votes, was out of the running. Crawford was President Monroe's favorite, but illness took him out of the running. The choice would be between Jackson and Adams. Jackson had won both the most popular votes and the most electoral votes. He felt confident that he would gain a majority in the House.

As speaker of the House, Clay was in a position to influence the outcome. Not wanting to aid a rival Westerner, he threw his support to Adams. Clay's influence swayed the members of the House to vote for Adams. Adams won easily on the first ballot on February 9, 1825. The tally was 13 states for Adams, 7 for Jackson, and 4 for Crawford.

Charges of a "Corrupt Bargain"

When Adams named his cabinet he appointed Clay secretary of state. An anonymous letter to newspapers charged that Clay was given the job as a result of a secret agreement, or a "corrupt bargain." It was claimed that Adams had promised Clay the position in return for his support. Although no proof was ever found, the charges hurt the Adams administration.

★ New Party Politics

The election of 1824 ended the Era of Good Feelings. Differences among the Republicans deepened. Instead of one party influencing the nation, two rival parties again challenged each other.

Andrew Jackson now aimed to win the presidential election in 1828. His supporters, emphasizing their ties to the common people, formed a new version of the Democratic-Republican party and soon became known as Democrats. Today's Democratic party traces its roots to the Democratic-Republican party. Adams and Clay led the political group called the National Republicans.

Election of 1824

Candidate	Electoral Vote	Popular Vote	House Vote
Jackson	99	153,544	7
Adams	84	108,740	13
Crawford	41	46,618	4
Clay	37	47,136	–

Chart Study

The presidential election of 1824 was decided in the House of Representatives. **How many more popular votes did Jackson have than Adams?**

The two parties' policies differed. The National Republicans favored a strong federal government, while the Democrats supported states' rights. National Republicans tended to be from the Northeast, with support coming from owners of businesses and banks. Democratic-Republicans came mostly from the South and West. They had the support of farmers and factory workers.

The National Republicans and the Democratic-Republicans later became well-organized political parties. Never again would an election not be influenced by political parties.

★ SECTION 3 REVIEW ★

Checking for Understanding

1. **Identify** James Monroe, Henry Clay, James Tallmadge, Jr., John Quincy Adams, Andrew Jackson.
2. **Define** nationalism, American System, protective tariff, monopoly, interstate commerce, sectionalism, Missouri Compromise.
3. **Name** three distinct sections of the United States that developed in the early 1800s.
4. **Tell** why John Q. Adams was accused of making a corrupt bargain with Henry Clay.

Critical Thinking

5. **Drawing Conclusions** How did the Missouri Compromise temporarily solve the sectional conflict over slavery?

ACTIVITY

6. Imagine you are living in the United States in 1815. Create a banner for your community's Fourth of July celebration that expresses your feelings about the United States.

Industrialization

▲ *ON THE RIVER* BY GEORGE CATLIN

Beginning in the 1830s, factories in the United States seemed to multiply overnight. Power-driven machines hummed in textile mills and coal mines and along American railroad tracks. Statistics and percentages are some of the best ways to show the pace of industrialization.

Between the 1830s and the mid-1850s, manufacturing went from 17 percent of the nation's total production to 32 percent. The remainder, of course, came from agriculture.

The growth of industry depended on—and encouraged—rapid growth in new ways of transportation. Railroads, canals, and roads all had a part in carrying raw materials to factories and manufactured goods to market. From 9,000 miles (14,481 km) of railroad track in 1850, a boom in railroad building created nearly 30,000 miles (48,270 km) of shining rails crossing the eastern half of the United States. The costs of transportation fell to 6 percent of what they were in 1815.

Making the Math Connection

1. If you expressed the growth of the manufacturing sector in this period—17 percent to 32 percent—as fractions, which statement would be correct?
   a. Manufacturing accounted for less than a fifth of the United States's production in the 1830s but was nearly a third in the 1850s.
   b. Manufacturing was one-quarter of the United States's total production in the 1830s, growing to about one-half in the 1850s.

2. If shipping a bushel of wheat cost 50 cents in 1815, what did it cost in 1850?

ACTIVITY

3. Using figures from the article, draw a circle graph showing how the United States's production was divided between manufacturing and agriculture in 1856.

Monroe and Foreign Affairs

★★

SETTING THE SCENE

Read to Learn . . .

★ how Canada gained self-rule.
★ why people in Latin American countries fought wars for independence.
★ how the Monroe Doctrine affected American foreign policy.

Terms to Know

★ ultimatum
★ diplomatic recognition
★ Monroe Doctrine

People to Meet

★ James Monroe
★ John Quincy Adams

Places to Locate

★ Canada
★ Mexico

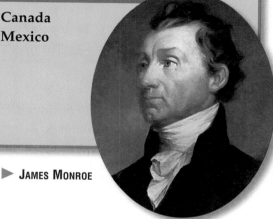

▶ JAMES MONROE

As the United States expanded and faced its internal differences, great changes were also taking place in neighboring countries.

★ Canada Becomes a Nation

Although the French first settled Canada, Britain had controlled it as a colony since 1763. In 1791 Britain decided to divide Canada into two parts. Upper Canada included an area settled mainly by English-speaking people. Mostly French people lived in Lower Canada.

In the 1800s, however, Canadians united to rebel against British rule. **Lord Durham,** the governor of Canada,

advised Parliament to unite Upper and Lower Canada and allow Canadians to control local affairs. Parliament agreed.

In 1867 the provinces of Nova Scotia, New Brunswick, Ontario, and Quebec joined the **Dominion of Canada.** Other provinces soon followed. Slowly and peacefully, America's northern neighbor became a nation.

★ Agreement Over Florida

For years, American leaders had wanted to own Spanish Florida. In 1810 President Madison claimed West Florida, a strip of land along the Gulf of Mexico to New Orleans. The Spanish also claimed this land, as well as the peninsula then called **East Florida** (present-day Florida).

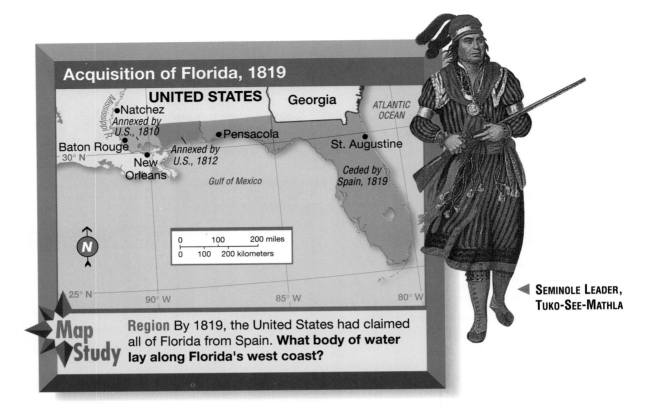

Acquisition of Florida, 1819

UNITED STATES

Georgia

Natchez
*Annexed by
U.S., 1810*

Baton Rouge
30° N

New Orleans

Pensacola
Annexed by U.S., 1812

St. Augustine

Ceded by Spain, 1819

Gulf of Mexico

ATLANTIC OCEAN

Mississippi River

N

| 0 | 100 | 200 miles |
| 0 | 100 | 200 kilometers |

25° N   90° W   85° W   80° W

SEMINOLE LEADER, TUKO-SEE-MATHLA

Map Study

Region By 1819, the United States had claimed all of Florida from Spain. **What body of water lay along Florida's west coast?**

East Florida continued to be a problem for the United States. Runaway slaves hid there. Creeks and Seminoles who lived in East Florida often raided nearby American settlements. In 1818 Andrew Jackson and his soldiers chased the Seminoles across the border into East Florida, seized the Spanish forts at St. Marks and Pensacola, and raised the American flag.

Fearing war with Spain, but knowing that Americans embraced Jackson as a popular hero, President **James Monroe** asked his cabinet for advice on the matter. Secretary of State **John Quincy Adams** saw it as a chance to acquire Florida. He persuaded Monroe to issue an ultimatum, a demand that could have serious consequences if ignored. Adams demanded that Spain either govern Florida properly or sell it to the United States.

The Spanish army, too weak to fight the United States, gave into Adams's demands. In 1819 Spain ceded Florida to the United States in the **Adams-Onís Treaty.** In return the United States paid $5 million to American citizens who had claims against Spain for property damage.

★ Independence in Latin America

In 1800 the United States was the only independent country in the Americas. European powers such as Great Britain, France, the Netherlands, Portugal, and particularly Spain ruled the rest of the hemisphere. Over the next two decades, however, many Latin American colonies revolted against Spain and declared their independence.

The Mexican Revolution began in 1810. **Mexico** finally won its freedom from Spain in 1821. Other Latin American colonies also fought for their independence, and by 1825 Spain had lost all of its colonies in Latin America except Puerto Rico and Cuba.

★ The Monroe Doctrine

The United States quickly granted diplomatic recognition, an official acknowledgment, to the new nations of Latin America. Spain, however, planned to recapture its colonies with the help of its European allies. In 1822 Austria, Prussia, Russia, and France agreed to help Spain retake Latin America.

The leaders of the United States would not allow this to happen. In 1823 Secretary of State John Quincy Adams advised the President to make clear to the world the power of the United States in the Western Hemisphere. He wanted to warn European nations to keep out of affairs in the hemisphere.

The British also opposed a European invasion of Latin America because they had developed a profitable trade with the newly founded Latin American nations. British merchants feared losing this market if Spain regained its colonies in Latin America. As a result, the British welcomed the United States's stand.

British Proposal

British leaders suggested to the Americans that the two nations issue a joint statement about Latin American independence. Adams determinedly objected to the British proposal of cooperation. Distrusting the British, he urged the United States to act on its own. The President agreed.

When President Monroe gave his yearly address to Congress in 1823, he included a bold statement on United States foreign affairs that has become known as the Monroe Doctrine. He said the United States would not interfere in the internal concerns of any European nation. He also declared that

> ❝ [the] American continents . . . are henceforth not to be considered as subjects for future colonization by any European powers. ❞

He went on to say that any move on the part of a European country "to extend their system to any portion of the hemisphere" would be determined by the United States as an act, "dangerous to our peace and safety."

Reactions to the Monroe Doctrine

Except for Britain the Monroe Doctrine startled Europe. Europeans were surprised at the boldness of the new nation. They did not challenge it, though, for no nation wanted to confront a United States that had the backing of Britain and its powerful navy.

Americans felt proud of the Monroe Doctrine. It showed the political independence of the United States and its growing nationalism. The Monroe Doctrine would become especially important when the United States became a major sea power.

★ SECTION 4 REVIEW ★

Checking for Understanding

1. **Identify** James Monroe, John Quincy Adams.
2. **Define** ultimatum, diplomatic recognition, Monroe Doctrine.
3. **What** were the advantages of the addition of Florida to the United States?
4. **Why** did John Quincy Adams urge President Monroe to issue the Monroe Doctrine?

Critical Thinking

5. **Hypothesizing** What do you think might have happened to the Western Hemisphere if there had not been a Monroe Doctrine?

ACTIVITY

6. Write a newspaper editorial supporting or rejecting the ideas of the Monroe Doctrine.

Using Key Vocabulary

Use the following vocabulary words to complete the sentences below.

diplomatic recognition
mass production
turnpikes
ultimatum
sectionalism

1. _____ of goods in factories made more things available at lower prices.

2. During the early 1800s private companies built roads called _____ that charged users a fee, or toll.

3. Economic differences increased _____ in the United States in the early 1800s.

4. After the revolutions in Latin America, the United States granted the new countries _____.

5. President Monroe's _____ to Spain led to Spain ceding Florida to the United States.

Reviewing the Facts

1. **List** the major inventions and inventors that revolutionized the textile industry in Britain and the United States.

2. **Describe** the improvements made in the transportation systems in the United States in the early 1800s.

3. **Identify** the main point of President Monroe's Inaugural Address in 1817.

4. **Identify** the broad categories that contributed to sectional differences and distinct ways of life in the United States in the early 1800s.

5. **Explain** the issues and outcomes of the Missouri Compromise of 1820.

6. **Name** the two major outcomes of the Adams-Onís Treaty.

Understanding Concepts

Economic Development

1. How did the Industrial Revolution change the way in which goods were produced and the way people worked?

2. How was the transportation system in the United States affected by the rise of industry?

3. What effect did changes in transportation have on westward expansion?

U.S. Role in World Affairs

4. How did conflicts between Britain and the United States lead to increased nationalism?

5. In what way did the Monroe Doctrine encourage nationalism in the United States?

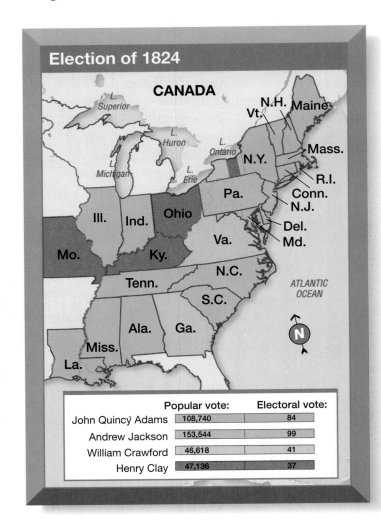

Election of 1824

	Popular vote:	Electoral vote:
John Quincy Adams	108,740	84
Andrew Jackson	153,544	99
William Crawford	46,618	41
Henry Clay	47,136	37

History and Geography

The Election of 1824

Study the map of the 1824 election on page 410. Then answer the questions that follow.

1. **Region** In which part of the country did Andrew Jackson have the most support?
2. **Region** In which region did Henry Clay receive support?
3. **Location** What was the southernmost state in which John Quincy Adams had support?

Practicing Skills

Understanding a Line Graph

The line graph below plots the number of patents issued between 1810 and 1840. Use the graph to answer the following questions.

1. In what year were the most patents issued?
2. In what years did the number of patents drop?
3. In general, what kind of trend does this line graph follow?

Cooperative Learning
Interdisciplinary Activity: Language Arts

With a group, do library research to find first-hand reports about pioneers in the West in the early 1800s. Then divide into two smaller groups to produce a skit about traveling and living in the West during this time. One small group can write the skit, another small group can make props and scenery for the skit. The skit should have enough parts for everyone in the group. Share your skit with other members of your class.

Critical Thinking

1. **Determining Cause and Effect** How did the protective tariff help American industries? What was its effect on sectionalism?
2. **Linking Past and Present** Roads, canals, and railroads were early transportation links between East and West. What major links tie different sections of the country together today?

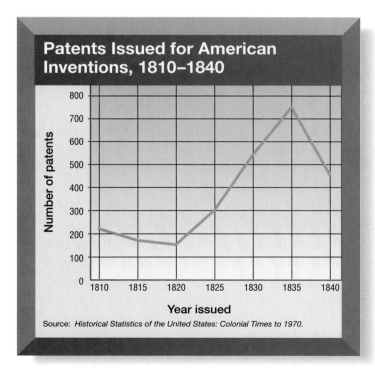

Patents Issued for American Inventions, 1810–1840

Source: *Historical Statistics of the United States: Colonial Times to 1970.*

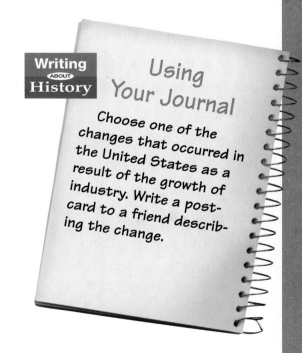

Writing ABOUT History

Using Your Journal

Choose one of the changes that occurred in the United States as a result of the growth of industry. Write a postcard to a friend describing the change.

Read to Discover

Night Flying Woman tells the story of Oona, Ignatia Broker's great-great-grandmother. Oona was still a child when the Ojibway were forced to leave their land and find a new home. As you read, look for the ways in which Oona overcomes her fears. What gives the Ojibway faith that they will continue as a people?

Reader's Dictionary

Anishinabe   Ojibway name for "people"
Gitchi Manito   Great Spirit

from Night Flying Woman

by Ignatia Broker (1919–1987)

On this, the fifth night of their travels, after the people had given thanks and eaten the evening meal, there was a firelight council. The people decided to stay on this small lake for two days while three of the men went deep into the forest to look for the new place.

The next morning, very early, Grandfather, Oldest Uncle, and Father walked into the thick forest. Oona did not see them leave, for she was sleeping soundly. When Mother told her that they were gone, Oona looked at the forest fearfully. It seemed very unfriendly. She thought, "It has swallowed up my grandfather and father." She became fretful.

Mother said, "Daughter, look at the forest again but do not look and see only the dark and shadows. Instead, look at the trees, each one, as many as you can. Then tell me what you think."

Oona looked at the trees. Then she walked to the forest's edge to see them better. There were many, many kinds of trees. Some were tall, so tall that they must surely touch the sky, thought Oona. Instead of leaves they had needles that were long and pointed like porcupine quills. Beneath these tall trees smaller ones reached up, as if in friendship. As Oona looked at the trees, she heard the si-si-gwa-d—the murmuring

Born on the White Earth Ojibway Reservation in Minnesota, Ignatia Broker grew up hearing the stories of her people. She decided that one day she would tell others about Ojibway traditions. Through her writing, Broker passed on many Ojibway tales about "the purity of man and nature and keeping them in balance."

that the trees do when they brush their branches together. It was a friendly sound, and the sun sent sparkles through the si-si-gwa-d that chased the shadows. Suddenly the forest seemed different to Oona, and she knew that Grandfather, Oldest Uncle, and Father had gone into a friendly place.

"Mother," said Oona, "I have the feeling now that the trees are glad we are here. The forest is happy and I know that we will be happy, too."

"That is good, my daughter, for I also have the feeling that this will be a good and happy place." A-wa-sa-si and Grandmother, who had been listening, nodded their heads in agreement.

A-wa-sa-si said, "The forests have never failed the Ojibway. The trees are the glory of the Gitchi Manito. The trees, for as long as they shall stand, will give shelter and life to the Anishinabe and the Animal Brothers. They are a gift. As long as the Ojibway are beneath, the trees will murmur with contentment. When the Ojibway and the Animal Brothers are gone, the forest will weep and this will be reflected in the sound of the si-si-gwa-d. My grandmother told me this is so, and her grandmother told her. When the forest weeps, the Anishinabe who listen will look back at the years. In each generation of Ojibway there will be a person who will hear the si-si-gwa-d, who will listen and remember and pass it on to the children. Remembering our past and acting accordingly will ensure that we, the Ojibway, will always people the earth. The trees have patience and so they have stood and have seen many generations of Ojibway. Yet will there be more, and yet will they see more."

▲ CONIFER FOREST

Responding to Literature

1. Why did Oona's father, uncle, and grandfather go into the forest?

2. What caused Oona's feelings about the forest to change?

3. What was the important message that Oona was given?

ACTIVITY

4. Create a painting or drawing that pictures the forest as Oona saw it.

DIGEST

The Federalist Era

The new government met for the first time in April 1789 in New York City. As promised during the ratification process, Congress passed the Bill of Rights during its first session and sent the amendments to the states for ratification.

Though reluctant, **George Washington** accepted the office of President and guided the Republic through its early, uncertain days. His secretary of the treasury, **Alexander Hamilton,** put the nation's finances in order by paying its debts, raising taxes, and establishing a national bank. Disagreements between Hamilton and **Thomas Jefferson**—also a cabinet member—led to the first political parties. Hamilton's party, the Federalists, favored a strong central government. Jefferson's party, the Democratic-Republicans favored stronger state governments.

▲ TREATY OF GREENVILLE

Washington tried to keep the nation neutral when the French Revolution brought about war in Europe. Problems with France continued to grow, however. Federalist **John Adams**—the second President—signed an unpopular treaty with France to avoid war. Attempts by Adams's supporters to silence criticism resulted in a weakened Federalist party.

The Democratic-Republicans won the election of 1800, denying Adams a second term. Due to voting methods at that time, the House of Representatives cast the final vote for the Democratic-Republican presidential candidate. In a close vote, they chose Thomas Jefferson as the next President.

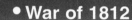

CAUSES

- British attacks on American ships and impressment of American sailors
- British support for Native Americans in the West
- American trade suffers from British interference with shipping
- Possibility of acquiring Florida from Spain, a British ally

• War of 1812

EFFECTS

- United States wins respect of Great Britain and other foreign countries
- American ships enjoy freedom of the seas
- Americans experience increased pride and sense of national identity
- Native Americans forced to give up land in Ohio Valley and Northwest Territory
- Settlement of West increases

Chapter 11

The Age of Jefferson

President Jefferson brought a new philosophy to the presidency. He hoped to enlarge democracy by supporting states' rights, cutting government spending and taxing, and reducing the role of government. Jefferson ran into conflict with the

▲ TRANSFER OF LOUISIANA

judiciary when courts took actions not clearly stated in the Constitution. Nevertheless, Chief Justice **John Marshall** strengthened the role of the Supreme Court in the federal government.

Although questioning his authority to purchase territory, Jefferson bought Louisiana from France. The **Louisiana Purchase** doubled the size of the United States. It also ended conflict with Spain over shipping rights on the Mississippi River.

Britain and France interfered with American shipping at sea. The British often impressed American sailors in their attacks. In addition, the British gave aid to **Tecumseh** and other Native Americans. War with Britain was declared in 1812. Although the **War of 1812** ended without a clear victory or defeat, the young nation gained the respect of foreign powers and felt a new surge of pride and patriotism.

Chapter 12

The Nation Grows

By 1800 the United States had joined the Industrial Revolution. **Samuel Slater,** a British mill worker, provided the plans for the first American

factory—in Pawtucket, Rhode Island. Business leaders of the Northeast quickly built more factories. This **industrialization** spurred the growth of cities in the Northeast.

American settlers streamed into the Western frontier. Three different sections soon appeared— the **North,** the **South,** and the **West.** Sectionalism sparked arguments over the spread of slavery. The **Missouri Compromise** of 1820 calmed the debate in Congress.

Spanish and Portuguese colonies in Latin America fought for independence. The United States quickly recognized the new nations. In 1823 it issued the **Monroe Doctrine,** warning European powers to stay out of the Western Hemisphere.

▲ THE ERIE CANAL

Understanding Unit Themes

1. **Economic Development** How did Alexander Hamilton plan to help the nation's economy grow?

2. **Conflict and Cooperation** How did Congress settle the dispute over whether Missouri would be a free or a slave state?

3. **United States's Role in World Affairs** Why did the United States by 1823 have the confidence to issue the Monroe Doctrine?

4. **Influence of Technology** How did the Industrial Revolution change where people lived and how they worked?

5. **Ideas, Beliefs, and Institutions** Why did Congress pass the Alien and Sedition Acts? Why did Democrats disagree with them?

UNIT FIVE
THE NATION EXPANDS
1820–1860

★★

CHAPTER **13**	CHAPTER **14**	CHAPTER **15**
The Age of Jackson 1824–1842	Manifest Destiny 1820–1860	The Spirit of Reform 1820–1860

▲ CHEROKEE BEADED BAG

History AND ART

Verdict of the People
by George Caleb Bingham, 1854–1855

The spirit of democracy was a common theme in the paintings of this artist. Bingham's paintings often showed what he considered examples of good citizenship.

416

SETTING THE SCENE

America grew stronger as the nation approached the mid-1800s. As the nation expanded its borders, adventurers, pioneers, and gold seekers headed West. At the same time, many reformers sought to improve society.

▼ **WAGON TRAIN**

Themes

★ American Democracy
★ Conflict and Cooperation
★ Beliefs, Ideas, and Institutions
★ The Individual and Family Life
★ Civil Rights and Liberties

Key Events

★ Andrew Jackson's presidency broadens American democracy
★ Native American removal in the East
★ United States acquires Oregon Country
★ Texas War for Independence
★ Mexican War
★ California Gold Rush
★ Beginning of the Underground Railroad
★ Seneca Falls Convention

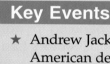

▲ **WOMEN'S RIGHTS MEETING**

Major Issues

★ Disagreements over the tariff and states' rights threaten the Union.
★ Jackson's war against the Bank of the United States results in economic depression and bank failures.
★ Belief in Manifest Destiny brings war with Mexico and further loss of land for Native Americans.
★ Abolitionists' demands to end slavery anger both Northerners and Southerners.

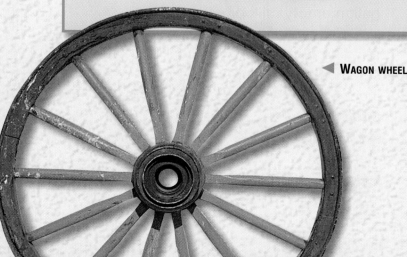

◄ **WAGON WHEEL**

Portfolio Project

Keep a list of leading Americans from the early to mid-1800s. Select a person that you think is especially interesting. After researching that person's contributions, prepare a television script that reviews the person's life.

Go For the Gold!

Background

In the mid-1800s a call echoed across the United States. "There's gold in California!" People found gold in the hills, in the mountains, and in the streams. Gold nuggets to stuff into pockets and knapsacks were there for the taking. Prospectors and adventurers by the thousands headed west hoping to make their fortunes. Teachers, farmers, businesspeople, and merchants armed themselves with picks and shovels. They attacked streambeds and gravel beds, searching for shiny gold dust, flakes, and nuggets. Because much of this valuable mineral washed down from California's mountains, panning for gold in rivers became a common choice for prospecting. Prospectors had to sort through soil and other surface materials for the gold to become visible. Some hopeful prospectors built simple machines, such as the sluice box, to help them. You can build a simple model sluice box to see the process they used.

▲ CALIFORNIA GOLD MINERS

Believe It OR NOT!

Stories of gold in California were not new. In 1842 a rancher in southern California found gold dust on the roots of a wild onion he dug up for lunch. No one paid much attention until James Marshall found gold while building a sawmill on John Sutter's property in 1848.

Materials

- ½ gallon empty milk or juice carton
- sand, dirt, gravel, with 3 or 4 heavy metal screw nuts (gold nuggets)
- 3 small dowel rods about 6 inches long
- modeling clay
- large baking pan
- water
- scissors

What To Do

A. Use the clay to form a ridge about 1 inch high at one end of the baking pan.

B. Cut off the top and one side of the empty milk or juice carton.

C. At the flat end of the carton, cut a U-shaped opening. Leave about ½ inch around 3 sides.

D. Turn the carton so that the cut-away side is up, forming a trough. Make 2 small holes near the bottom of the trough about 2 inches away from the U-shaped end for the water to drain.

E. Using scissors; poke 3 holes about 1 inch apart at the bottom of both sides of the carton. Push the dowel rods through the holes. (See diagram)

F. Place the trough in the cake pan with the open end on the clay ridge.

G. Place a handful of sand, dirt, gravel, and metal screw nuts at the upper end of your trough. Pour water down your trough and look for "gold nuggets." Repeat the process several times. Now you are sluicing for "gold."

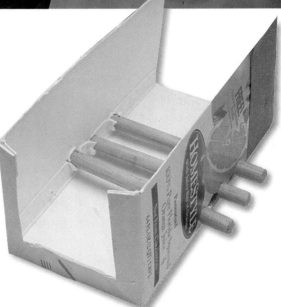

Lab Activity Report

1. Which materials tended to wash all the way down the trough?

2. What happened to the heavier "gold nuggets"?

3. How efficient do you think sluicing was as a mining method?

4. *Drawing Conclusions* How much mining experience and money for equipment do you think the average Forty-Niner brought to the gold fields?

GO A STEP FURTHER

ACTIVITY

Find out more about the discovery of gold at Sutter's Mill near Sacramento in 1848. Write a series of diary entries that you think John Sutter might have made about the discovery of gold and the arrival of miners.

CHAPTER 13

★★★

The Age of Jackson
1824–1842

► OSCEOLA, SEMINOLE LEADER

SETTING THE SCENE

Focus

By the early 1820s, most of the leaders of the American Revolution had died or lay near death. A new generation of leaders stepped forward to take their place. Many Americans demanded that these leaders guide the nation toward greater democracy. Andrew Jackson heeded their call. In 1828 voters sent Jackson to the White House. This rough-and-tumble President from the frontier breathed a new spirit of equality into American politics.

Journal Notes

Imagine that you are a newspaper reporter assigned to cover Andrew Jackson. Keep a record of your thoughts about this strong-minded President.

Concepts to Understand

★ How **American democracy** expanded during the early 1800s
★ What federal actions brought **conflict and cooperation** among Americans in the North, South, and West

Read to Discover . . .

★ the groups that gained or lost rights in the 1820s.
★ the new political practices that emerged in the Jackson era.

United States			
1824 John Q. Adams chosen President by House of Representatives	**1828** Andrew Jackson elected President	**1832** Jackson challenges the Bank of the United States	
1820–1824	**1825–1829**	**1830–1834**	
1821 Greece begins war of independence	**1825** First public railroad opens in Britain	**1830** Revolutions occur in France, Belgium, and Poland	
World			

▲ JACKSON CAMPAIGN BOX

History AND ART

Stump Speaking
by George Caleb Bingham, 1854–1855

Paintings by George Bingham in the 1850s expressed the growth of public participation in the democratic process. For nearly five years, Bingham explored and depicted the human aspect of politics.

1836 Martin Van Buren elected President
1838 Cherokee begin Trail of Tears

1840 William Henry Harrison elected President
1841 President Harrison dies

1835–1839	1840–1844	1845–1849

1838 Guatemala, Costa Rica, Honduras, and Nicaragua gain independence

1840 Upper and Lower Canada united
1842 Britain defeats China in Opium War

1845 Potato famine begins in Ireland

★★

The People's President

SETTING THE SCENE

Read to Learn . . .

★ why some Americans wanted a greater voice in government.
★ how the election of 1824 divided Americans.
★ why the election of 1828 marked a turning point in politics.

Terms to Know

★ suffrage
★ caucus
★ nominating convention

People to Meet

★ Henry Clay
★ Andrew Jackson
★ John Quincy Adams
★ William Crawford

Places to Locate

★ Appalachian Mountains
★ Mississippi River

◀ JACKSON'S WHITE BEAVER HAT

On the evening of July 3, 1826, a small group of people stood quietly in a darkened bedroom at Monticello, a home in Virginia. They watched as 83-year-old Thomas Jefferson struggled to breathe. Another group gathered in a darkened bedroom of a house in Quincy, Massachusetts. This group stayed near the bed of 91-year-old John Adams.

In the early dawn hours, Jefferson asked weakly if it was July 4. His friends assured him it was. "Just as I wished," murmured Jefferson. A few hours later, on the 50th anniversary of the approval of the Declaration of Independence, Jefferson died. John Adams followed several hours later.

The deaths of these two giants from the American Revolution left people stunned. Clearly, Americans stood on the threshold of a new era. They looked around for leaders to guide the nation on its journey toward greater democracy.

★ Broadening Political Power

The Declaration of Independence held out a great promise. "All men are created equal," declared the document. In fact, however, only a select group of people—white male property owners—made decisions about government.

New Voices From the West

As new states entered the Union, the rules of leadership began to change. Settlers who carved out states in lands between the **Appalachian Mountains** and the **Mississippi River** judged leaders by new standards. Westerners respected self-made leaders—people who succeeded on their own rather than on inherited wealth or family name. The hardships of frontier life had taught people the value of cooperation and hard work.

When new Western states wrote constitutions, they gave suffrage, or the right to vote, to all white men. States in the East soon followed the example of the West. One by one, they eliminated voting restrictions based on property, payment of taxes, or religion. By the 1830s, the number of qualified voters in the United States had skyrocketed.

Limits on the Vote

While large numbers of free white men won the right to vote, many free African American men lost it. Most northern states had allowed them to vote early in the 1800s. However, these states took the vote away or restricted it during the 1820s and 1830s.

Other groups in the United States also had no voice in politics. Women, Native Americans, and enslaved African Americans were still denied the right to vote.

An End to "King Caucus"

The white men who did win the right to vote in the 1820s and 1830s made sure leaders heard their voices. In addition to voting at the polls, they wanted a say in choosing who would run for President.

Under the political practices of the time, a handful of party officials gathered in private meetings to nominate people for office. Such a closed political meeting is called a caucus. Because only party leaders took part in nominating caucuses, people called this method of choosing candidates "King Caucus." Critics said the process limited democracy. People demanded an end to "King Caucus."

In the 1830s, party officials bowed to public pressure. They began to hold nominating conventions instead of party caucuses. At the nominating conventions, delegates from each state cast their votes for political candidates.

Expansion of the vote and the death of "King Caucus" created an air of excitement. More and more people felt the drama of politics. As a result, voter turnout increased sharply. In the presidential election of 1824, fewer than 27 percent of qualified voters took part. By 1840, voter turnout was more than 80 percent. By contrast, voter turnout has been less than 60 percent in recent present-day presidential elections.

★ The Disputed Election of 1824

In 1824 Western voters saw a chance to elect one of their own "favorite sons," or regional candidates, to office. That year, two Westerners competed for the presidency—**Henry Clay** of Kentucky and **Andrew Jackson** of Tennessee. An Easterner—**John Quincy Adams** of Massachusetts—and a Southerner—**William Crawford** of Georgia—also ran. All candidates ran as Democratic-Republicans, the only political party at that time.

The Candidates

John Quincy Adams, the son of President John Adams, had spent his life studying national politics. As former secretary of state under President Monroe, he had also learned much about foreign affairs. Adams, however, was not well liked. Many people found him cold.

Henry Clay, on the other hand, won people over almost immediately with his quick wit and charm. These traits had helped Clay earn respect for his skill at compromise in the House of Representatives. His ability to negotiate deals had led Clay to become speaker of the House.

Like Clay, William Crawford enjoyed national fame as a longtime member of Congress. People knew him best as President Monroe's secretary of the treasury.

The fourth candidate, Andrew Jackson, captured popular attention as the hero of the Battle of New Orleans. Even more important, people saw him as the symbol of a self-made man of the Western frontier. Although Jackson owned land and held enslaved persons, he constantly reminded people of his humble origins. Many ordinary Americans looking to expand democracy saw Jackson as very much like themselves.

Picturing History ▲ JOHN QUINCY ADAMS Without a majority of the popular vote, John Quincy Adams won the presidential election of 1824. **Who received the majority of the popular vote in the election of 1824?**

The "Corrupt Bargain"

In the election of 1824, Jackson won far more popular votes than any of the other candidates. Neither Jackson nor any other candidate, however, won a majority of the electoral votes. For the second time in United States history, the House of Representatives would choose the President. Henry Clay received the fewest electoral votes and so was out of the race. Ill health forced Crawford to withdraw. By the time the vote was to begin, the House had only two candidates to choose from—Adams and Jackson.

People waited in suspense as the House began voting. As speaker of the House, Henry Clay was in a position to influence the final count. At Clay's urging, most of his supporters threw their votes to Adams. Clay's action gave Adams enough votes to win the presidency. A short time later Adams named Clay his secretary of state.

Enraged supporters of Jackson charged Adams and Clay with reaching a "corrupt bargain." "[Clay] shines and stinks like a rotten mackerel by moonlight," declared John Randolph of Virginia.

★ New Political Parties

Following the 1824 election, the old Democratic-Republican party began to split apart. People who supported Adams and Clay called themselves National Republicans. The National Republicans included Eastern business owners, Southern planters, and former Federalists. Supporters of Jackson were determined that Adams should not succeed. They branded the National Republicans enemies of the common people. They then formed a new version of the Democratic-Republican party to challenge them. The name would later be shortened to Democratic party. Today's Democratic party traces its roots to the time of Jackson.

The Election of 1828

A new face of politics showed itself in 1828. No longer did people choose among heroes of the American Revolution. They now watched as Adams and Jackson, again running for President, bitterly attacked each other.

Jackson labeled Adams an aristocrat, or a member of the upper class. Jackson also pointed to funds that Adams had spent on national projects such as roads and canals. He claimed that by supporting such projects, Adams had shown he favored a powerful federal government. Jackson hoped to turn voters who feared federal power away from Adams.

Adams struck back. He went so far as to call Jackson "a barbarian and savage who could scarcely spell his own name." Adams's backers painted Jackson as a ruffian with a furious temper.

President From the West

On Election Day, Jackson won by a landslide. His support came from people newly armed with the vote—urban Eastern workers, farmers in the South, and people from the new Western states. Upon learning of Jackson's victory, Massachusetts senator Daniel Webster wrote:

Picturing History

▲ ANDREW JACKSON In 1828, Jackson campaigned as a man of the people, while trying to depict John Quincy Adams as an aristocrat. **What group from the South voted largely for Jackson?**

> ❝ My opinion is that when he comes [to office] he will bring a breeze with him. Which way it will blow, I cannot tell. . . . My *fear* is stronger than my hope. ❞

Jackson's supporters believed that he represented the "common man." He became the symbol of the growing power of democracy.

★ SECTION 1 REVIEW ★

★★★★★★★★★★★★★★★★★★ ★★★★★★★★★★★★★★★★★★

Checking for Understanding

1. **Identify** Henry Clay, Andrew Jackson, John Quincy Adams, William Crawford, Appalachian Mountains, Mississippi River.

2. **Define** suffrage, caucus, nominating convention.

3. **What** changes took place in voter qualifications in the early 1800s?

4. **How** did these changes benefit Andrew Jackson?

Critical Thinking

5. **Determining Cause and Effect** How did the election of 1824 give rise to new political parties?

ACTIVITY

6. Choose one of the candidates in the election of 1824, and create a campaign poster that reflects your candidate's strengths.

★★★

A New Spirit in the White House

SETTING THE SCENE

Read to Learn . . .

★ how the spoils system operated under President Jackson.
★ why President Jackson battled the Bank of the United States.

Terms to Know

★ spoils system
★ kitchen cabinet
★ pet bank

People to Meet

★ Nicholas Biddle
★ Roger Taney

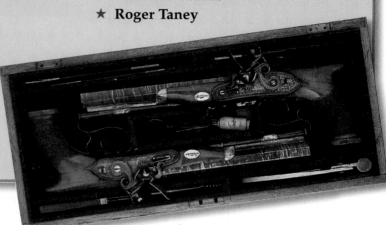

▲ ANDREW JACKSON'S DUELING PISTOLS

A short time before his inauguration, Jackson's beloved wife Rachel died. The grief-stricken Jackson hardly looked like the person to lead the United States into a new era. Jackson, however, set aside his mourning in the name of the people.

In keeping with the new spirit of democracy, Jackson gave a giant inaugural party. Rugged country folk and enthusiastic townspeople poured into the White House. One onlooker described the scene:

> ❝ Ladies fainted, men were seen with bloody noses, and such a scene of confusion took place as is impossible to describe. . . . Ladies and gentlemen had only been expected at this Levee [reception]. . . . But it was the People's day, and the People's President, and the People would rule. ❞

★ The Spoils System

Some Americans viewed the events of Jackson's Inauguration Day as a bad sign. Supreme Court Justice Joseph Story claimed that "the reign of King Mob seemed triumphant." Jackson, however, saw the day as a signal of changes to come. He intended to involve his supporters in far more than White House parties.

Rewards for Victory

Shortly after his inauguration, Jackson fired many government employees. He then replaced them with his own loyal supporters. Politicians had quietly followed this practice for years. Jackson, however, openly defended it. "To the victor belong the spoils of the enemy," declared Jackson.

In war, spoils mean riches that a victorious army seizes from its enemy. For Jackson, the spoils of political victory meant taking government jobs from opponents and giving them to the victor's own supporters. Jackson handed out more political jobs to his supporters than any President before him. Thereafter, the practice became known as the spoils system.

Jackson believed the spoils system expanded democracy. He felt any intelligent person could fill a government position. Changing officeholders, argued Jackson, gave more people a chance to take part in governing.

An Unofficial Cabinet

Jackson angered many people by relying upon a group of his own personal advisers, nicknamed the kitchen cabinet. Critics believed Jackson should seek the advice of the cabinet members approved by Congress. Jackson, however, turned a deaf ear to critics. "I care nothing about clamors," he once remarked. "I do precisely what I think just and right."

★ War With the Bank

In 1832 Jackson felt it "just and right" to do battle with the Bank of the United States. Debate had surrounded the Bank ever since its creation in 1816. The federal government deposited all of its money in the Bank. As a result, the Bank had complete control over credit. It also decided how much money state banks received. Farmers and merchants hated the Bank. So did Andrew Jackson.

▲ POLITICAL CARTOON, "THE SPOILS SYSTEM"

Jackson focused his anger at **Nicholas Biddle,** president of the Bank since 1823. In Jackson's mind, Biddle represented the power of wealthy Easterners. Biddle, who came from a well-to-do Philadelphia family, viewed Jackson with equal distaste.

The two headstrong leaders finally tangled in 1832. That year, Biddle asked Congress to renew the Bank's charter, although the charter was not due to run out until 1836.

Henry Clay ran against Jackson for President. He saw the Bank as a way to unseat Jackson. If Jackson signed a congressional bill to renew the Bank, he would lose votes in the South and West. A veto of the Bank bill, on the other hand, would cost Jackson votes in the North.

Clay skillfully pushed the Bank bill through Congress. Jackson lay ill in his bed when the news reached him. He

· ·

Footnotes to History

Log Cabin President   Andrew Jackson was the first President born in a log cabin. Earlier Presidents came from wealthy families. He was also the first President in office to ride a train.

Picturing History

▲ "THE BANK WAR" This 1833 cartoon illustrates the disorder that followed President Jackson's transfer of federal funds from the Bank of the United States into state banks. **How did Nicholas Biddle attempt to stop President Jackson?**

found the strength, however, to veto the Bank renewal bill and charged that the Bank was corrupt and anti-American.

Shutting Down the Bank

Biddle said the President's charges had "all the fury of a chained panther biting at the bars of his cage." Biddle, however, soon found the "panther" on the loose. In the 1832 election, the common people handed Jackson a sweeping victory.

Jackson promptly ordered Secretary of the Treasury **Roger Taney** (TAW•nee) to put federal funds into certain state banks, known as pet banks, instead of into the Bank of the United States. Biddle struck back by restricting the flow of money out of the Bank of the United States. Paper money became so scarce that a financial crisis seemed likely.

The loss of federal funds crippled the Bank. In 1836 when its charter ran out, it went out of business.

★ SECTION 2 REVIEW ★

Checking for Understanding

1. **Identify** Nicholas Biddle, Roger Taney.
2. **Define** spoils system, kitchen cabinet, pet bank.
3. **What** arguments did Jackson use to defend the spoils system?
4. **What** methods did Jackson use to destroy the Bank of the United States?

Critical Thinking

5. **Forming Opinions** Tell why you would agree or disagree with Jackson's use of the spoils system.

ACTIVITY

6. Create a political cartoon that makes a point about Jackson's reelection in 1832.

Interpreting a Political Cartoon

You probably recognize the figure of Uncle Sam right away. Uncle Sam has been a popular symbol for the United States for more than 100 years. Recognizing different kinds of symbols increases your skill in interpreting political cartoons.

Learning the Skill

A political cartoon is a drawing that expresses a point of view about a certain issue or topic. The creator of the cartoon hopes to influence people's opinions.

Political cartoonists use a number of tools to make their point. They often use symbols like Uncle Sam to represent something else.

A symbol can represent an idea, a concept, or a feeling. Symbols are often used in political cartoons to stand for a variety of ideas about United States government. A donkey, for example, is a symbol commonly used to represent the Democratic party. Political cartoonists use the elephant to stand for the Republican party.

Cartoonists also make use of caricature. A caricature is a drawing that exaggerates or changes a person's physical features. A person who talks a great deal, for example, might have a caricature that shows him or her with a very large mouth. A caricature can be positive or negative, depending on the artist's point of view.

Sometimes cartoonists help readers interpret their message by adding labels or captions. The cartoon below has a title that tells you the subject is a race between Henry Clay, on the right, and President Jackson and Vice President Van Buren, on the left. The race concerns the Bank war. Another label tells you the race is occurring "over Uncle Sam's course," meaning in American politics. Clay wanted to keep the Bank of the United States. Jackson wanted to kill it.

Race over Uncle Sam's Course

Practicing the Skill

1. How does the cartoonist represent the Bank of the United States?

2. What does the club in Jackson's hand mean?

3. Which figure or figures are drawn in negative caricature?

4. Do you think the cartoonist is for or against the Bank of the United States? Why?

APPLYING THE SKILL

5. Find a cartoon about a present-day political figure in a newspaper or magazine. Explain the cartoonist's point of view and the tools used to make the point.

★★★★★★★★★★★★★★★★★★★★★★★★★★★★★★★★★★★★★

Crisis and Conflict

SETTING THE SCENE

Read to Learn . . .

★ how the debate over tariffs created a crisis for the Union.
★ how Native Americans lost their ancestral lands in the Southeast.

Terms to Know

★ tariff
★ sovereign
★ states' rights
★ nullification
★ secede
★ Trail of Tears

People to Meet

★ John C. Calhoun
★ Daniel Webster
★ Robert Hayne
★ Sequoya
★ John Marshall
★ John and Quatie Ross
★ Osceola

Places to Locate

★ South Carolina
★ Georgia
★ Florida

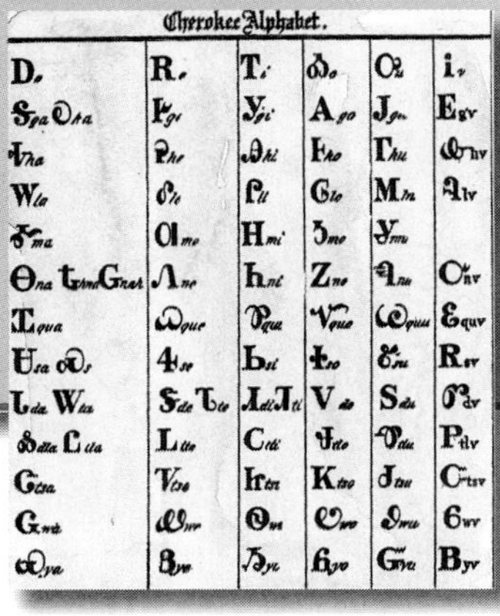

◀ **CHEROKEE ALPHABET**

By the time Jackson reached the White House, he had learned to control his famous temper. Jackson sometimes enjoyed using his popular image as a firebrand, however, to make opponents back down. Early in his second term, Jackson needed all his control and skill to deal with one of the biggest crises of his administration.

★ The Tariff of Abominations

Jackson's crisis grew out of a tariff, or tax on imported goods, passed by Congress in 1828, just before he came into office. As a result of the tariff, the price of foreign goods sold in the United States increased. Northern manufacturers and Western farmers liked the tariff. High prices on foreign goods made it easier for them to sell their products to American buyers. Southern planters, however, hated the tariff. Because the South used many imported goods, the tariff raised the price of nearly everything Southerners purchased.

Unhappy Southerners nicknamed the protective tariff the **Tariff of Abominations.** An abomination is something disgusting or hateful. They turned to **John C. Calhoun,** Jackson's Vice President, to battle against it.

The Argument for States' Rights

In 1828 Calhoun stated that the Union was an agreement among sovereign, or independent, states. Each state government, said Calhoun, had the right to nullify, or cancel, any federal law—such as the tariff—that it considered unconstitutional.

Calhoun had raised a serious issue. Did the states have the right to limit the power of the federal government? Or did the federal government have the final say in differences with the states? Calhoun favored states' rights—the belief that an individual state may restrict federal authority.

The Argument in Favor of the Union

In January of 1830, Senator **Daniel Webster** of Massachusetts delivered a scorching attack on states' rights. He saw states' rights as a threat to the Union. Webster stood on the floor of the Senate to challenge a speech given by Senator **Robert Hayne** of **South Carolina.** Hayne had defended the idea of nullification, or the right of states to declare federal laws illegal.

In a two-day speech, Webster defended the Constitution and the Union. Near the end of his speech he cried, "Liberty and Union, now and forever, one and inseparable!"

★ Jackson vs. Calhoun

Nobody knew exactly where Jackson stood on the issue of states' rights. Many Southerners dared to hope that Jackson—a planter and slaveholder—might side with them. In the spring of 1830, supporters of states' rights invited the President to a dinner party.

At the dinner, several guests gave toasts in favor of states' rights. Finally, Jackson rose. The President locked eyes with Vice President John Calhoun and declared: "Our Federal Union—it must be preserved!"

Calhoun did not flinch. With his eyes firmly fixed on Jackson, Calhoun stood to deliver his own toast. "The Union—next to our liberty, the most dear!" With these simple words, Calhoun placed the liberty of a state above the Union.

In December 1832, Calhoun resigned before his term as Vice President ended. He sought and won election as a senator from South Carolina. Martin Van Buren, who had run with Jackson in Jackson's successful reelection in the fall of 1832, became the next Vice President.

★ Nullification Crisis

Questions of states' rights continued to arise. In 1832 Southern anger boiled over when Congress passed a new tariff on imports. This tariff lowered earlier rates slightly, but the South had wanted it removed completely. South Carolina lashed out by passing the **Nullification Act.** This law declared the tariff "null, void, and no law." The people of South Carolina also threatened to secede, or leave the Union, if the federal government challenged the state law.

When Jackson heard the news, he vowed to use force if needed to uphold the federal law. South Carolina had hoped other states would follow its lead. No state did, however. In March 1833, Congress passed a compromise tariff proposed by Henry Clay. Although the tariff lowered rates only slightly, South Carolina accepted the proposal. The state legislature repealed the Nullification Act. However, the idea of secession remained firmly planted in the minds of many Southerners.

★ A Tragic Policy for Native Americans

President Jackson took a firm stand against Southerners on the tariff and on nullification. He sided with them, however, on another key issue of the 1830s. This issue involved the resettlement of Native Americans on lands west of the Mississippi River.

When Jackson entered the White House, the federal government already had a long-standing policy of backing white settlers moving onto Native American lands. Jackson campaigned for office by promising to continue this policy. He strongly believed that Native Americans should give up their lands to settlers. He also believed that Native Americans could live more freely in Indian Territory—or present-day Oklahoma.

By the 1820s, only about 120,000 Native Americans remained east of the Mississippi. Many of those belonged to the

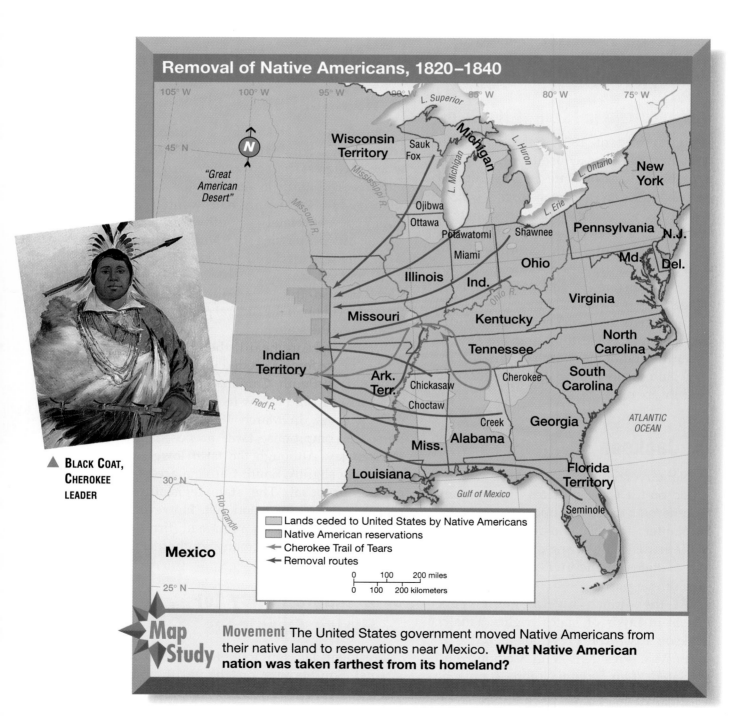

Removal of Native Americans, 1820–1840

Lands ceded to United States by Native Americans
Native American reservations
Cherokee Trail of Tears
Removal routes

0   100   200 miles
0   100   200 kilometers

▲ BLACK COAT, CHEROKEE LEADER

Map Study

Movement The United States government moved Native Americans from their native land to reservations near Mexico. **What Native American nation was taken farthest from its homeland?**

▲ THE TRAIL OF TEARS The United States government forced Native Americans from their lands in the 1830s, relocating them to reservations west of the Mississippi River. **Why did the Cherokee call the forced march "The Trail of Tears"?**

Choctaw, Chickasaw, Creek, Seminole, and Cherokee Nations of the Southeast. Southern cotton planters looked hungrily at their rich lands and pressured Native American leaders to exchange their traditional lands for territory in the West.

Resistance

In 1828, the year Jackson first won the presidency, the Cherokee asked the Supreme Court to defend the rights of Native Americans in the Southeast. The state of **Georgia** had claimed the right to make laws for the Cherokee. The Cherokee claimed that federal treaties protected Native Americans as sovereign, self-ruling nations.

The Cherokee presented a strong defense. Most Cherokee had adopted the customs of white settlers. A leader named **Sequoya** had developed a written alphabet for the Cherokee. Using these letters, the Cherokee learned to read and write.

They published a newspaper called the *Cherokee Phoenix*. They also wrote a constitution that set up a representative form of government.

Chief Justice **John Marshall** sided with the Cherokee in their complaints against Georgia. In 1832 the Supreme Court declared Georgia's actions against this Native American group unconstitutional. President Jackson, however, sided with Georgia. He ignored the Court's decision.

The Trail of Tears

While the Supreme Court debated Cherokee claims, Jackson convinced his supporters in Congress to pass the **Indian Removal Act of 1830.** This act provided funds for the federal government to remove Native Americans from the eastern United States.

At first Native Americans refused to sign treaties recognizing the law. Jackson, however, used his power as President to send federal troops onto Native American lands. At gunpoint, Native Americans signed new treaties.

The Cherokee held out until 1838. Then, they too agreed to move west. That fall Cherokee leader **John Ross** led his people on a forced march to Indian Territory. The brutal weather of the Great Plains claimed thousands of lives. Wrote one observer: "Even aged females . . . were traveling with heavy burdens attached to their backs, sometimes on frozen ground . . . with no covering on their feet."

By the time John Ross arrived in Indian Territory, about one-eighth of his people had fallen. Among those who died was his wife **Quatie Ross.** The Cherokee called their sorrowful trek "The Trail Where They Cried." History knows it as the Trail of Tears.

Biography ★★★

Osceola Makes War

In southern **Florida,** a Seminole leader refused to listen to soldiers who asked the Seminole to give up their land. The leader was **Osceola,** a Creek from present-day Alabama. Osceola had moved to Florida in the early 1800s while he was in his teens.

Living among the Seminole, he soon became a respected hunter and warrior.

Soldiers presented Osceola with a treaty to sign. The treaty called for the Seminole to move to Indian Territory within 3 years. Osceola spoke for all his Seminole followers. "I love my land and will not go from it!" he vowed. It is said that he then drove a knife through the treaty. In so doing, Osceola and the Seminole declared war against the federal government.

The Seminole had fought the government once before. A large group of runaway slaves lived with the Seminole and helped them in their fight. Jackson now used federal troops to fight Osceola in the Second Seminole War. The war lasted seven years, from 1835 to 1842. Federal troops in 1837 captured Osceola. They then put him in a prison near Charleston, South Carolina. Less than a year later, in January 1838, Osceola died in his prison cell.

Osceola's people continued to fight after his death. The federal government rounded up many Seminole and sent them west. Some Seminole, however, slipped far into the Florida swamps known as the Everglades. Their descendants still live there today.   ★★★

★ SECTION 3 REVIEW ★

Checking for Understanding

1. **Identify** John C. Calhoun, Daniel Webster, Robert Hayne, Sequoya, John Marshall, John and Quatie Ross, Osceola, South Carolina, Georgia, Florida.

2. **Define** tariff, sovereign, states' rights, nullification, secede, Trail of Tears.

3. **Why** did the Tariff of Abominations create a crisis for the Union?

4. **How** did Native Americans resist efforts to remove them from their lands?

Critical Thinking

5. **Interpreting Primary Sources** In an appeal to the American people, the Cherokee wrote: "We wish to remain on the land of our fathers. We have a perfect and original right to remain." On what basis did the Cherokee claim ownership of land in the South?

ACTIVITY

6. Create a newspaper drawing to illustrate the Indian Removal from the Native Americans' point of view for a special issue of the *Cherokee Phoenix.*

★★

The End of the Jacksonian Era

SETTING THE SCENE

Read to Learn . . .

★ what problems Jackson's successor faced.
★ why an economic crisis developed in 1837.
★ how the Whigs came to power.

Terms to Know

★ specie

People to Meet

★ Martin Van Buren
★ William Henry Harrison
★ John Tyler

Places to Locate

★ Tennessee
★ New York

► HARRISON CAMPAIGN FLAG

On March 4, 1837, popular President Jackson turned over the reins of government to **Martin Van Buren.** After Van Buren delivered his Inaugural Address, Jackson rose to leave for his home in **Tennessee.** As he headed for his carriage, the crowd raised its voice in one great cheer of love and admiration.

★ The Election of 1836

While he was still in office, Jackson was so popular that one observer suggested he could remain President for life. In 1836, however, Jackson used his influence to win the Democratic nomination for his hand-picked successor, Martin Van Buren.

The Whigs, the political party that included the National Republicans by this time, ran three candidates against Van Buren. They hoped to split the popular vote and force the election into the House of Representatives. Van Buren stunned the Whigs by claiming a sweeping victory. Van Buren promised to walk "in the footsteps of President Jackson."

People from Van Buren's home state of **New York** hailed the new President for his skill in dealing with voters and other political leaders. Within two months of taking office, however, Van Buren ran into problems that overwhelmed his skills. The cause of his trouble reached back to Jackson's war on the Bank of the United States.

★ Problems Left to Van Buren

In 1836, the last full year of Jackson's presidency and the year before Van Buren took office, the charter for the Bank of the United States ran out. Left free of controls from the Bank, individual banks all over the country set their own rules for operating. Many state banks began to loan money freely. They also printed many paper notes as money, more than they could back up by specie. Specie is hard cash in the form of gold or silver.

Easy credit and the large amount of paper money from banks helped increase prices, especially the price of land. As land prices went up and up, speculators bought more and more land. As long as prices continued to rise, the speculators could hope to resell their purchases quickly for more than they had paid for them. Americans of all classes, from low-paid clerks to wealthy bankers, became speculators. Most used credit or borrowed paper money to pay for the land.

▲ Martin Van Buren

An Economic Crisis

The rush to buy government land at rising prices had alarmed Jackson during his last year in office. He tried to stop the land speculators in 1836 by issuing a much-disputed paper called the *Specie Circular*. The paper stated that government land could be purchased only with specie.

Because most speculators did not have enough gold or silver to purchase land, sales of land quickly fell. Reduced sales lowered prices. As a result, many Americans who planned to pay off their loans by selling their land at higher prices could not pay their debts. Banks took over many properties. The banks, however, could not sell the land for enough money to recover the loans they had made to speculators.

Problems for Banks and Business

With banks facing cash money problems, people began to fear that banknotes would lose their value. People rushed to exchange their paper money for gold or silver coins. As a result, more and more banks had trouble doing business.

The economic crisis worsened when the price of cotton dropped in the South. Lacking cash, many Southerners failed to repay their bank loans. A similar situation developed in the West when bad weather wiped out wheat crops in 1836.

Because many people had less money to spend, the demand for factory goods dropped. Factory owners cut back on the amount of goods they produced and laid off workers. In some Northeastern cities, jobless and homeless workers and families huddled together for comfort on cold streets.

The Panic of 1837

Within three months after Van Buren took office, the economic crisis reached its peak. The so-called **Panic of 1837** set in. Several important banks in the East closed

Two Wheelers

Before the 1800s, Americans usually turned to wagons, coaches, and horses for transportation. The two wheeler, however, was on its way.

Then

The Boneshaker

By about 1840, a few Americans were riding two wheelers called velocipedes. With no pedals or chains, the velocipede had to be moved along by the rider's feet pushing on the ground. Then pedals were added to the front wheels, and the early bicycle was born. The wheels themselves were wooden. They made the ride so bumpy that people called the early bicycles "boneshakers."

Now

Chains, Gears, and More

Today's cyclists ride in style and comfort. They speed along

on slim tires and have gears, chains, and hand brakes to aid them. If they are wise, they wear helmets for safety. Perhaps boneshaker riders would have liked a little padding too.

---

their doors and went out of business. Banks all over the country quickly did the same.

The new President was not responsible for the panic, but he did little to relieve it. He felt, as did many members of the Democratic party, that the government should not interfere in the economy.

Van Buren did, however, persuade Congress to establish an independent federal treasury in 1840. The government would no longer deposit its money with private individual banks as it had started to do during President Jackson's war with the Bank of the United States. Instead, the government would store its money in the federal treasury. The private banks had used government funds to back their banknotes. The new treasury system would prevent banks from using government funds in this way and so help guard against further bank crises.

★ The Election of 1840

Before the Panic of 1837, Americans saw the Whigs as the party of the rich. The Whigs wanted to change this image. With the economic crisis spreading, the Whigs searched in the late 1830s to find a candidate who would appeal to the common people. In 1839 they chose General **William Henry Harrison,** the hero of the 1811 Battle of Tippecanoe.

Log Cabin Campaign

Harrison came from a well-to-do Virginia family. He enjoyed a good education and lived in a 16-room mansion on 3,000 acres (1,215 ha) of land. Most Americans had no way of knowing about Harrison's background. The Whigs, therefore, bombarded the nation with advertisements

▲ THE LOG CABIN CAMPAIGN William Henry Harrison's 1840 election campaign was full of slogans, banners, rallies, and parades. **What was the Whigs' campaign plan?**

and posters that presented Harrison as a humble Ohio farmer born in a log cabin.

The Whigs used the log cabin as the symbol of the 1840 campaign. The Whigs selected **John Tyler** of Virginia as Harrison's running mate. They coined a catchy slogan to capture the public's imagination: "Tippecanoe and Tyler Too."

The Whigs took the campaign on the road. In towns all over the United States, they organized rallies, parades, and barbecues. The strategy paid off. In 1840 a huge voter turnout gave Harrison a sweeping victory. Harrison walked away with 234 electoral votes, compared to only 60 electoral votes received by Van Buren.

Death of President Harrison

Harrison had little time to enjoy his victory. While giving his inaugural speech, he caught a cold. Harrison died of pneumonia a month later.

Harrison's death thrust Tyler into the presidency. Tyler would change the course of history by following a policy of westward expansion that even Jackson would have approved.

John Tyler was the first Vice President to become President upon the death of an elected President. Since Tyler in 1841, six other Vice Presidents have become President because a President died in office.

★ SECTION 4 REVIEW ★

Checking for Understanding

1. **Identify** Martin Van Buren, William Henry Harrison, John Tyler.

2. **Define** specie.

3. **What** caused the Panic of 1837?

4. **How** did Van Buren respond to the economic crisis?

5. **How** did the Whigs win the 1840 election?

Critical Thinking

6. **Determining Cause and Effect** How was Jackson's war with the Bank linked to the Panic of 1837?

ACTIVITY

7. Write a campaign slogan for the election of 1840. Design a campaign button and write your slogan on it.

Bank Panics

▲ **BANKNOTE ISSUED IN 1856**

▼ **NATIONAL BANKNOTE**

Bank panics, such as the **Panic of 1837,** have much to do with fear. The fear comes when people see signs that the banks or businesses in which they have placed their money might fail. Fear becomes panic when many people suddenly begin to withdraw bank deposits or sell their investments.

The results of a panic can be widespread and severe, as in 1837. Banks collapse. Loans are hard to get. Businesses slump into a depression, and workers lose jobs.

Causes of Bank Panics

Panics have a number of different causes. Most often, however, conditions are very much like those leading up to the Panic of 1837. People have plenty of money to spend. Banks are willing to take risks. Speculators are active. The worst panic in United States history, known as the Great Depression, struck in 1929.

One of the biggest causes of bank panics in the early 1800s was that each bank printed its own money. Hundreds of different kinds of banknotes caused much confusion. In addition, there was no way to control how much or how little money the banks would print.

The economic picture improved in the 1860s when the federal government set up national banks. The national banks printed common banknotes that gradually replaced the many different state banknotes.

Today a system of 12 Federal Reserve Banks, set up by the federal government, regulates all banks. It also controls the amount of money in use. In addition, most banks have federal insurance to protect depositors' money. These measures help strengthen the economy and give people confidence in the banking system. Panics are thus unlikely.

Making the Economics Connection

1. How does fear relate to bank panics?
2. What are some causes of panics?
3. Why are panics unlikely now?

ACTIVITY

4. Design and create banknotes for your own imaginary bank. Work with a partner to plan how to use your notes to make a large purchase.

Using Key Vocabulary

Use the following vocabulary words to complete the sentences below.

specie   sovereign
caucus   kitchen cabinet
spoils system

1. A _____ was a closed meeting at which presidential candidates were chosen by a small group of people.

2. President Jackson worked with an unofficial group of advisers known as his _____.

3. The _____ involved replacing government workers with one's own supporters.

4. John C. Calhoun believed that the states were _____ and so could nullify any federal law within their borders.

5. In 1836 many banks printed paper money not backed up by gold or silver _____.

Reviewing Facts

1. **Name** the two new political parties created after the election of 1824.

2. **List** the powers the Bank of the United States had over the nation's money.

3. **Tell** how the Tariff of 1828 divided the North and the South.

4. **Describe** how Jackson stopped land speculation in 1836.

5. **Tell** how William Henry Harrison won the election of 1840.

Understanding Concepts

American Democracy

1. What groups gradually won voting rights during the early 1800s?

2. What groups still did not share in government in the early 1800s?

Conflict and Cooperation

3. How did the tariff and nullification issue develop into a crisis? How did Jackson handle the nullification crisis in 1832?

4. Why did Jackson's battle with the Bank create an economic crisis for the nation?

5. What actions did Native Americans take to resist resettlement in the West?

History and Geography

The Election of 1828

Study the 1828 election map. Then answer the questions that follow.

1. **Region** Which general areas of the United States voted for Andrew Jackson in the election of 1828?

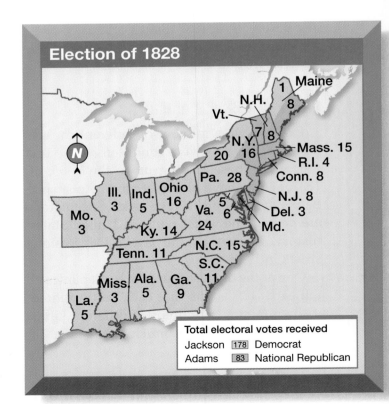

Election of 1828

Maine 1
N.H. 8
Vt.
N.Y. 7 8
20 16
Mass. 15
R.I. 4
Pa. 28
Conn. 8
Ill. 3   Ind. 5   Ohio 16
N.J. 8
Va. 5 6
Del. 3
Mo. 3
Ky. 14   24
Md.
Tenn. 11
N.C. 15
S.C.
Miss. 3   Ala. 5   Ga. 11 9
La. 5

Total electoral votes received
Jackson 178 Democrat
Adams   83   National Republican

2. **Location** Which candidate won more votes in Adams's home state of Massachusetts?

3. **Place** Which three states divided their total electoral count between the two candidates?

Critical Thinking

1. **Understanding Point of View** Why did Jackson think the spoils system helped further the rights of ordinary citizens?

2. **Drawing Conclusions** Based on evidence in this chapter, what conclusions can you draw about Jackson's view of presidential power?

Interdisciplinary Activity: Civics

In groups of three or four students, do library research to determine the popular vote in the elections of 1824, 1832, 1836, and 1840. Show the results of your research in the form of election maps similar to the one on page 440. Write five questions that explore trends shown on the maps. Challenge other students to answer these questions.

Practicing Skills

Interpreting a Political Cartoon

Some people called Andrew Jackson a "man of the people." Others called him a power-hungry ruler. Use the following questions to help you decide how the cartoonist who drew this cartoon viewed President Jackson.

1. What symbols does the cartoonist use to suggest kings and queens?

2. What symbols are used to represent the United States?

3. How does the cartoonist use labels and captions?

4. What does the cartoonist want readers to think of President Jackson?

▲ "KING ANDREW THE FIRST" CARTOON

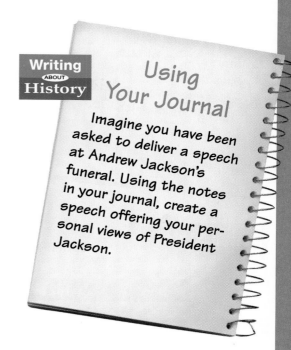

Writing ABOUT History

Using Your Journal

Imagine you have been asked to deliver a speech at Andrew Jackson's funeral. Using the notes in your journal, create a speech offering your personal views of President Jackson.

CHAPTER 14

★★★★★★★★★★★★★★★★★★★★★★★★★★★★★★

Manifest Destiny
1820–1860

▶ MINING TOOLS

SETTING THE SCENE

Focus

The drive to expand the boundaries of the United States became a goal for many Americans in the 1830s. American journalist John L. O'Sullivan declared: "It is . . . our manifest destiny to overspread the whole continent." Eventually the United States government would acquire land in present-day Oregon, Texas, California, Utah, and the remainder of the Southwest.

Concepts to Understand

★ How the **beliefs and ideas** of Americans led to westward expansion
★ Why **individuals and families** migrated to the West and shaped political events in Oregon, Texas, and California

Read to Discover . . .

★ the reasons Americans moved westward.
★ why Texans declared independence from Mexico.
★ what caused war between Mexico and the United States.
★ how the Gold Rush of 1848 changed the history of California.

Journal Notes

Put yourself in the position of Native Americans on lands west of the Mississippi River. Record your impressions of the wave of settlers who crossed into your lands during the mid-1800s.

United States

1821 Stephen Austin founds colony in Texas

1836 Battle of the Alamo fought
1836 Texas wins independence

| 1821–1830 | 1831–1840 |

World

1821 Mexico wins independence from Spain
1825 Egyptian troops invade Greece

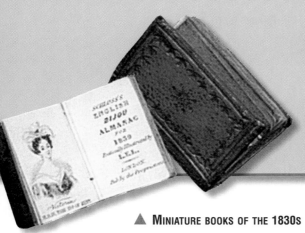

▲ MINIATURE BOOKS OF THE 1830S

History AND ART

Among the Sierra Nevada Mountains
by Albert Bierstadt, 1868

Albert Bierstadt was an artist from the Hudson River School. Bierstadt specialized in painting grand pictures of awesome mountain scenery.

1846 Mexican War begins
1848 California Gold Rush begins
1848 Mexican War ends

1853 United States makes Gadsden Purchase

1841–1850

1851–1860

1842 Treaty of Nanking ends Opium War in China

1853 United States begins trade with Japan

★★★

The Oregon Country

SETTING THE SCENE

Read to Learn . . .

★ what nations had conflicting claims to the Oregon Country.
★ how traders and trappers paved the way for western expansion.

Terms to Know

★ rendezvous
★ pass
★ emigrate
★ prairie schooner
★ annex

People to Meet

★ Robert Gray
★ John Jacob Astor
★ mountain men
★ James Beckwourth
★ Jedediah Smith
★ Marcus and Narcissa Whitman

Places to Locate

★ Oregon Country
★ Oregon Trail
★ Independence, Missouri

◀ PRAIRIE HUNTER

The grizzly bear stood so close Hugh Glass could smell it. Sweat rolled off Glass's brow, nearly blinding him. With a steady finger, the fur trapper squeezed back the hammer on his musket. As the bullet struck the animal, the bear hurled itself into Glass. Another trapper described what happened next:

❝ . . . [T]he bear caught him and hauled him to the ground, tearing and lacerating [cutting up] his body [at a] fearful rate. ❞

Glass not only survived, he continued to hunt grizzly bear and other animals in the **Oregon Country.** The adventures of fur trappers like Glass soon caught the attention of other people—people who wanted to claim more than the region's fur-bearing animals. They came to capture the land itself.

★ Settlers Move West

The Oregon Country included the present-day states of Oregon, Washington, Idaho, and parts of Wyoming, Montana, and Canada. The Rocky Mountains bounded the region on the east, while the Pacific Ocean hemmed it on the west.

Within the Oregon Country climates and vegetation varied. Lands west of the coastal mountains, called the Cascades, enjoyed mild temperatures and abundant rainfall. On the east side of the mountains, however, the landscape changed dramatically. The Cascades prevented the rain-bearing clouds that rolled off the Pacific from heading inland. As a result, a dry plateau sprawled eastward from the Cascades to the Rockies.

For the non-Native Americans who first set foot in the Oregon Country, its wealth lay in fur-bearing animals. For centuries, fashionable Europeans and North Americans wore hats made of beaver pelts. To meet the demand, fur trappers exhausted the supply of beaver in one stream after another. By the early 1800s, a few adventurous trappers plunged across the Mississippi River in search of new forests to hunt.

Trappers often traveled trails blazed by the Native Americans. Groups that lived in the Oregon Country included the Cayuses, Yakimas, Chinooks, Nez Perce, and Blackfeet. Most had deep ancestral roots in the region, even as Europeans and Americans refused to recognize Native American rights to the land. Instead, they labeled the lands a "wilderness" and freely staked their claims.

★ Conflicting Claims

Four nations—Russia, Spain, Great Britain, and the United States—tried to take control of the Oregon Country. Of these nations, Great Britain and the United States pursued their claims most actively.

The British based their claims in Oregon Country on the explorations of Sir Francis Drake and George Vancouver. Drake visited the coast of Oregon in 1579. A member of Vancouver's crew navigated a river part of the way through Oregon in 1792. Fort Vancouver, the only permanent British outpost in Oregon, took its name from this expedition.

The United States based its claim on the voyages of **Robert Gray.** In 1792 this New England sea captain gave the Columbia River its name. In 1805 the Lewis and Clark expedition reached the mouth of this river and strengthened the United States's claims to the area. By 1807 American fur traders had set up scattered trading posts along Lewis and Clark's route. They had to compete with British traders who pushed into Oregon from Canada.

American fur trader **John Jacob Astor** sent a shipload of supplies and workers around the tip of South America in 1811. The workers built a trading post near the mouth of the Columbia River. Here they set up Astoria, the first American settlement on the Pacific coast. Although Astoria lasted only a short time, it gave Americans another claim to Oregon.

Agreement With Great Britain

In 1818 Great Britain and the United States agreed to share the Oregon Country for 10 years. Under the agreement, British and American citizens would enjoy equal rights. With few settlers in the region, Spain and Russia gave up their claims in 1825.

★ The Mountain Men

Both British and American fur-trading companies rushed to secure their claims to the Oregon Country. In 1822 one American company advertised for "ENTERPRISING YOUNG MEN" to sign up for work. More than 100 people—Scots, Germans, Spaniards, New Englanders, Southerners, and African Americans—responded to the ad. Some hired on as camp keepers, people who cooked and guarded the camp. Others took jobs as trappers. From their ranks came a rough-and-tumble group of explorers known as the **mountain men.**

▲ *THE WHITE TRAPPER* by Frederic Remington
Mountain men depended on trapping and the fur trade in order to survive. **Where did trappers meet to sell their furs and buy supplies?**

Life of a Mountain Man

The mountain man lived a tough, lonely life. Aside from the clothes on his back, he traveled with little more than a "possibles sack." Inside this small leather pouch, a mountain man carried all he might possibly need—an awl for stitching leather, a mold for making lead musket balls, and a surgeon's lance for digging out bullets.

During the spring trapping season, a mountain man might haul 6 to 8 heavy iron traps on his back. To set the traps, he waded into bone-chilling streams. When game was in short supply, he went to bed hungry. One band of trappers ate nothing but roots for 10 days. Mountain men learned many of their trapping skills and survival methods from Native Americans, especially from the Native American women they married.

In the summer, trappers' spirits soared as they headed to a meeting place called the rendezvous (RAHN•dih•voo). There they relaxed and met traders from Missouri who bought their furs and sold supplies. The rendezvous saved mountain men from traveling long distances for supplies. They also came looking for fun.

"These men are chock full of brag and fight," chuckled mountain man Joe Meek.

Because mountain streams froze between October and March, trappers gathered in winter camps of up to 60 men. During the day they hunted. In the evening, they huddled around fires in buffalo-hide lodges "spinning long yarns [tales] until midnight. . . ."

Blazing a Path for Others

The epic journeys of the mountain men opened the door for settlement of the West. An African American mountain man, **James Beckwourth,** discovered a pass, or opening, through the Sierra Nevada mountains into California. **Jim Bridger** and a friend strode across the South Pass of the Rocky Mountains. **Jedediah Smith** brought back colorful accounts of the geysers and boiling springs of what is now Yellowstone National Park. **Manuel Lisa,** a Spanish American trapper, led a trip up the Missouri River in 1807. He founded Fort Manuel, the first outpost on the upper Missouri River.

"To explore unknown regions was . . . [their] chief delight," wrote a clerk in one fur-trading company. By exploring unknown regions, the mountain men surveyed paths for the pioneers who would soon follow.

End of an Era

The mountain men recognized changes were coming when covered wagons began showing up in their camps. In 1836 two missionary couples—**Marcus and Narcissa Whitman** and Henry and Eliza Spalding—arrived at the annual rendezvous. Narcissa and Eliza became the first non-Native American women to cross the Rocky Mountains.

The two couples came to set up missions among the Cayuses. The Whitmans chose to build their settlement at a site where the Snake and Columbia Rivers meet. In letters to friends and family, the Whitmans encouraged others to emigrate, or move, to Oregon.

Troubles with Native Americans, though, cost the Whitmans their lives. In 1847 measles spread to Cayuse children at the mission. The epidemic claimed the lives of both non-Native American and Cayuse children. The Cayuses blamed the intruders for the disease. They attacked and killed the Whitmans and 12 others. News of the Whitmans' deaths, however, did not stop settlers from pouring into the region.

As settlers arrived, a change in fashion ended a way of life for the mountain men. In the late 1830s and 1840s, people stopped wearing beaver hats. Within a few years the mountain men found themselves out of work. Some turned to farming in the rich valleys of the Pacific Northwest. Others became guides for wagon trains. The route they knew best—the **Oregon Trail**—soon became a major highway across the continent. The Oregon Trail extended from **Independence, Missouri,** to the Columbia River in Oregon.

★ Oregon Fever

Emigrants only trickled into Oregon until reports made their way back east and stories grew into tall tales. One rumor claimed that pigs "roamed about precooked . . . [for] anyone who might be hungry." Other rumors described turnips 5 feet in diameter and wheat 6 feet tall. Stories like these sparked an outbreak of "Oregon fever." Between 1840 and 1860, more than 60,000 people traveled the Oregon Trail. Even today, the ruts carved by their wagons scar parts of the Great Plains.

Traveling the Oregon Trail

The journey west began at jumping-off places like Independence, Missouri. Here families stocked their lightweight covered wagons, known as prairie schooners, and hitched them to teams of oxen. Several

families then formed a wagon train. Each wagon train elected a leader to make decisions on the trail.

Most wagon trains left Independence in May. By then, enough spring grass covered the plains to feed the oxen. The emigrants had five months to cross the Rockies. If they arrived later, they might freeze to death in blinding blizzards.

Once on the trail, the wagons rolled each day at dawn. As the oxen crawled along at 2 miles an hour, the leader cried out, "Catch up! Catch up!" Near dusk the men began scouting for water and grass. When they found both, they drew the wagons into a circle. While the livestock grazed and the men stood guard, the women fried bacon and baked biscuits over fires fueled with buffalo chips (dried manure).

When the wagons hit deep rivers or steep mountains, families had to lighten their loads. So they dumped barrels, ploughs, clothing, trunks, spades, and anything else that slowed them down. Other emigrants helped themselves to the discards. One man "camped beside an old stove and baked some bread." Others picked up books, read them, and

▲ PRAIRIE SCHOONERS Traveling west was long and difficult. Families in wagon trains relied on each other to survive the journey. **Why did wagon trains leave Independence, Missouri, in May?**

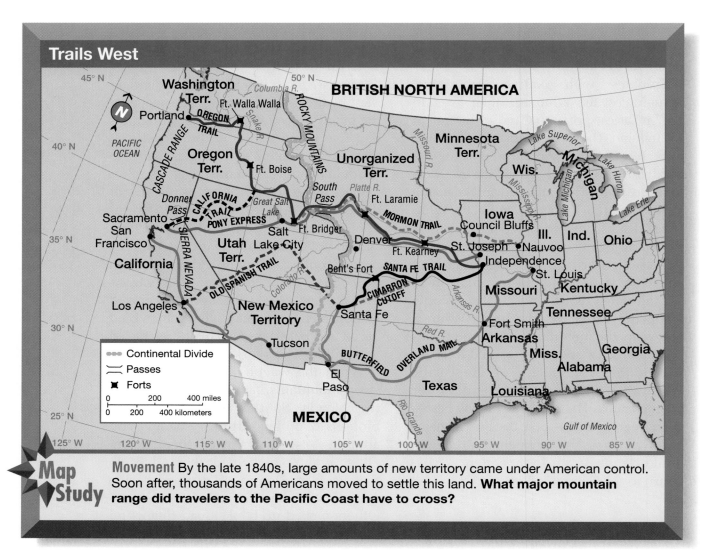

Trails West

BRITISH NORTH AMERICA

Continental Divide
Passes
Forts

0   200   400 miles
0   200   400 kilometers

Map Study

Movement By the late 1840s, large amounts of new territory came under American control. Soon after, thousands of Americans moved to settle this land. **What major mountain range did travelers to the Pacific Coast have to cross?**

tossed them back on the ground, into the "prairie library."

The travelers helped one another by using the "roadside telegraph," messages left on boards, rocks, tree trunks, and even animal skulls beside the trail. Many emigrants owed their lives to these warnings about dead-end shortcuts or poison water holes.

Hardships and Heartaches

Hundreds of travelers never reached Oregon. Some turned back or settled on the plains. Many died of diseases such as cholera and smallpox. Still others drowned in swollen rivers or died in accidents. Graves and the carcasses of dead animals lined the trail. Wrote one weary traveler:

❝ **It is a hardship without glory, to be sick without a home, to die and be buried like a dog on the Plains.** ❞

Native Americans

For the most part, Native Americans traded with the travelers and tried to lessen their misery. Native Americans provided travelers with horses, clothing, and fresh food. Some Native Americans fed hungry wagon trains or guided them over difficult stretches along the trail. Settlers had been led to believe that Native American groups posed a threat to those crossing the plains. In reality, there were few incidents of violence between wagon trains and Native

Americans. But eventually relations soured. Conflicts developed in the 1850s. Until then diseases such as cholera proved far more dangerous to settlers.

Governing Oregon

Despite peaceful relations with the British, American settlers wanted to annex, or add, Oregon to the United States. Many other Americans felt the same way. In Congress Tennessee representative Davy Crockett compared joint occupancy—shared ownership—to the time he shared a tree branch with a panther. "The place war [was] big enough for us both," said Crockett, "but we couldn't agree to stay there together."

★ Fifty-Four Forty or Fight!

James K. Polk agreed with Americans who wanted to annex Oregon. As a presidential candidate in 1844, Polk declared that all of Oregon should belong to the United States. This was dramatized by the campaign slogan "Fifty-four forty or fight!" This meant he demanded that the United States expand its territory to the parallel 54°40', the southern boundary of Alaska.

Polk won the election by a slim margin and began negotiations with Great Britain.

▲ JAMES K. POLK

In 1848 the two nations decided to extend the boundary between Canada and the United States to the forty-ninth parallel. This line already formed much of the United States-Canadian border.

Oregon became a territory in 1848 and a state in 1859. The transfer of territory occurred without bloodshed. The acquisition of Texas, though, would not be as peaceful.

★ SECTION 1 REVIEW ★

Checking for Understanding

1. **Identify** Robert Gray, John Jacob Astor, mountain men, James Beckwourth, Jedediah Smith, Marcus and Narcissa Whitman, Oregon Country, Oregon Trail, Independence.

2. **Define** rendezvous, pass, emigrate, prairie schooner, annex.

3. **How** did Great Britain and the United States come to share Oregon jointly?

4. **What** hardships did emigrants face on the Oregon Trail?

Critical Thinking

5. **Determining Cause and Effect** What effect did the mountain men have on the exploration of western mountains and on relations with the Native Americans who lived there?

ACTIVITY

6. Create an enlarged version of the map on page 448. Then add illustrations that show in pictures the story of the Oregon Trail.

Analyzing a Primary Source

▲ *SPIRIT OF THE FRONTIER* BY JOHN GAST, 1872

How do historians figure out what happened in the past? They do some detective work. They comb through bits of evidence from the past to reconstruct events. These bits of historical evidence—both written and illustrated—are called *primary sources.*

Learning the Skill

Primary sources are records of events by the people who witnessed them. They include letters, diaries, photographs and pictures, news articles, legal documents, and so on.

Primary sources yield several important kinds of information. Often, they give detailed accounts of events. The people who created these sources rarely guessed that their work would be so important. Here lies a problem with using primary sources. They reflect only one perspective on the past. For this reason, a historian must examine as many perspectives as possible before drawing any conclusions about the past.

Practicing the Skill

The primary source below comes from the diary of a woman who traveled the Oregon Trail in 1853. Read the document and answer the questions that follow.

"Tuesday, May 17th We had a dreadful storm of rain and hail last night and very sharp lightning. It killed two oxen for one man. We have just encamped on a large flat prairie, when the storm commenced in all its fury. . . . I never saw such a storm. The wind was so high I thought it would tear the wagons to pieces. Nothing but the stoutest covers could stand it. The rain beat into the wagons so that everything was wet. As we could have no tents pitched, all had to crowd into the wagons and sleep in wet beds with their wet clothes on, without supper. The wind blew hard all night and this morning presents a dreary prospect surrounded by water, and our saddles have been soaking in it all night and are almost spoiled! . . ."

—Amelia Stewart Knight

1. Who wrote this document?

2. What event does the author describe?

3. What happened to the people and their equipment?

4. From this account, explain why weather was so important to pioneers moving west.

APPLYING THE SKILL

5. Find a primary source from your past—a photo, a report card, an old newspaper clipping, your first baseball card, and so on. Bring this source to class and explain what it shows about the time from which the item comes.

★★

Texas Independence

SETTING THE SCENE

Read to Learn . . .

★ how conflict developed between Mexico and settlers in Texas.
★ how Texas won its independence from Mexico.

Terms to Know

★ Tejanos
★ empresario
★ reform

People to Meet

★ Stephen F. Austin
★ Antonio López de Santa Anna
★ Sam Houston
★ Juan Seguin

Places to Locate

★ San Antonio
★ Goliad

TEXAS!!

Emigrants who are desirious of assisting Texas at this important crisis of her affairs may have a free passage and equipments, by applying at the NEW-YORK and PHILADELPHIA HOTEL, On the Old Levee, near the Blue Stores.

Now is the time to ensure a fortune in Land: To all who remain in Texas during the War will be allowed 1280 Acres. To all who remain Six Months, 640 Acres. To all who remain Three Months, 320 Acres. And as Colonists, 4600 Acres for a family and 1470 Acres for a Single Man.

New Orleans, April 23d, 1836.

▲ ADVERTISEMENT FOR TEXAS SETTLERS

Mexican cannons boomed outside the Alamo's walls. Colonel William Travis put his face in his hands and tried to think. His co-commander, Jim Bowie, lay sick with pneumonia. His small force would not hold out for long. Travis picked up a quill pen and wrote a plea for help.

❝ To the people of Texas & all Americans in the world. . . . I call on you in the name of liberty, of patriotism & everything dear to the American character, to come to our aid. . . . ❞

Soon people all over the United States learned about the desperate situation at the Alamo. The road to the Alamo started in the 1820s with the arrival of the first United States settlers in a Spanish-owned colony called Texas.

★ Colonizing Texas

In 1820 Texas included a handful of Americans and about 3,000 Tejanos. Tejanos are people of Mexican heritage who consider Texas their home. Most of the region belonged to Native Americans—

▲ STEPHEN F. AUSTIN

Comanche, Apache, and others—who fiercely resisted colonial settlement. Spanish officials believed they might lose control of Texas unless they lured more settlers into the territory.

The First Texas Empresarios

In the early 1800s, the Spaniards decided to offer large tracts of land to empresarios—people who agreed to recruit settlers. News of the offer caught the attention of Missouri businessman Moses Austin. In 1821 Austin convinced the Spanish government to give him a huge tract of land along the Brazos River. In exchange, Austin promised to bring 300 families to his colony.

Moses Austin died before he could organize his colony. His son, **Stephen F. Austin,** carried out his plans. In 1821 he established the first settlements along the Brazos and Colorado Rivers. About this same time, Mexico won its independence from Spain. Mexico soon issued new land grants to Austin and extended the boundaries of his colony.

American Colonists in Texas

The Mexican government granted each settler in Texas large tracts of land. In exchange, the colonists promised to become citizens of Mexico, obey Mexico's laws, and accept the Roman Catholic faith.

Austin chose the first group of settlers carefully. He frowned on lying, using foul language, or drinking alcohol. He wanted only "civilized and industrious" settlers for his new colony. Austin issued land titles to almost 300 families. These hand-picked pioneers later became known as the Old Three Hundred.

Although other empresarios founded other colonies, Austin's settlement proved the most successful. By 1831, about 5,665 people lived in his colony.

Growing Conflicts

The Mexican government used the empresario system to ensure loyalty. Meanwhile thousands of United States settlers moved into Texas without Mexico's permission. Unlike Austin's colonists, they never promised to uphold Mexican

• •

Footnotes to History

Father of Texas   Stephen F. Austin earned the name "Father of Texas" because of his leadership in populating the Mexican Territory of Texas. By doing this, Austin fulfilled his father's dying request to colonize Texas. After Texas won its independence, Austin lost the presidential election to Sam Houston. Houston appointed him secretary of state.

laws or accept the Roman Catholic faith. Instead, they wanted to keep their own culture, or ways of living.

Even the Old Three Hundred had scattered clashes with the government. Colonists on the Brazos were using slaves to grow cotton in 1829 when the Mexican government prohibited slavery. The cotton growers protested so vigorously that the government decided to permit slavery in Texas, at least temporarily. Slaveholders balked at the idea that the government might deprive them of their human "property."

Settlers from the United States also had quarrels with the form of government in Mexico. They wanted to have the same voice in government that they had enjoyed in the United States. Mexican officials, however, insisted on tight political control.

Mexican Fears

By 1830 more than five times as many Anglos, or United States settlers, lived in Texas as Tejanos. Manuel Mier y Teran, a Mexican general assigned to Texas, warned:

The North Americans have conquered whatever territory adjoins them. In less than a half century, they have become masters of extensive colonies which formerly belonged to Spain and France and of . . . territories from which have disappeared the former owners, the Indian tribes.

Mexican officials heeded the warning. In 1830 the Mexican Congress banned further Anglo immigration. It also ordered construction of five new army posts in Texas to enforce Mexican laws.

These actions brought furious protests from Anglo settlers. Many people talked about defending their rights. A few even talked of splitting Texas off from the Mexican state to which it belonged.

In 1833 Stephen F. Austin traveled to Mexico City with a petition. The petition listed reforms, or improvements, demanded by both Anglos and Tejanos. The reforms included repeal of the ban against immigration and creation of a separate Texas state.

★ The Fight for Independence

Austin waited for months to present his petition to General **Antonio López de Santa Anna,** the new head of the Mexican government. When they finally met, Santa Anna insisted that Texas remain part of Mexico. Austin wrote a letter urging Texans to go ahead with statehood. When the letter fell into government hands, Santa Anna threw Austin in prison.

Austin secured his release eight months later. By this time, Santa Anna had suspended the Mexican constitution and assumed the powers of a dictator. Many Texans believed the time had come to break away from Mexico.

"Come and Take It"

News of unrest in Texas reached Santa Anna. In October 1835, he ordered soldiers to seize a cannon at the Texas town

★★★ AMERICA'S FLAGS ★★★

Texas Republic, 1839 For its first six years, this Lone Star flag symbolized the independent nation of the Republic of Texas. Texans kept the Lone Star banner as their official state flag after joining the Union in 1845.

★★★★★★★★★★★★★★★★★★★★★★

Picturing History

▲ THE BATTLE OF THE ALAMO Outnumbered by the Mexican army, the Texans fought heroically to defend the Alamo. **Where is the Alamo located?**

of Gonzales. When Mexican troops arrived, they faced dozens of Texas volunteers. Over the cannon, the Texans had defiantly hung a flag that read "Come and Take It."

After a brief skirmish, the soldiers left without the cannon. Today many Texans consider the fight at Gonzales "the Lexington of Texas," or the first battle in the Texas war for independence.

Santa Anna did not intend to surrender Texas without a fight. He soon ordered Mexican troops to occupy the Texas town of **San Antonio.** In early December hundreds of Texas volunteers attacked the city. After five days they drove out the Mexicans. The Texas Revolution had begun.

Defense of the Alamo

On March 2, 1836, Texans met at Washington-on-the-Brazos. At this meeting, they announced the creation of the Republic of Texas. They placed **Sam Houston,** a former governor of Tennessee, in command of the army.

Meanwhile, in San Antonio, less than 200 Texas soldiers took cover in and defended an empty mission called the Alamo. The defenders, both Anglos and Tejanos, included **William Travis, Jim Bowie,** and **Davy Crockett.**

For 12 days Santa Anna's forces shelled the mission. Defenders inside the Alamo held out against overwhelming odds. Finally, on March 6, Santa Anna ordered an all-out attack. The first wave of Mexican soldiers faced the long rifles of Davy Crockett and his Tennessee sharpshooters. These riflemen picked off soldiers 200 yards (183 m) away. For every Mexican soldier that fell, however, another moved forward.

Mexican troops swarmed over the walls of the Alamo. The defenders fought on in furious hand-to-hand combat. A bullet killed Travis. Bowie died fighting from his sickbed. Mexican soldiers captured and executed Crockett. By 9 A.M., all the Alamo defenders had died. Only a handful of women, children, and slaves survived.

The Goliad Massacre

The fight at the Alamo angered and inspired Texans. To learn firsthand about the Alamo, Sam Houston met with Susanna Dickinson, one of the survivors, in Gonzales. After hearing Dickinson's account of the final battle, Houston vowed to prevent other Alamos. He sent word to James Fannin, the commander in **Goliad,** to abandon the fort there.

Fannin waited several days before obeying the order. When he finally led troops from the town, they ran into a Mexican army on the Texas prairie. After a short fight, Fannin surrendered his force. A week later, the Mexicans began to execute the prisoners. Many escaped, including Fannin, but some 350 others fell before Mexican firing squads.

The Battle of San Jacinto

News of events at the Alamo and Goliad spread like wildfire among Texans. About 1,400 volunteers rushed to join Sam Houston, who did not strike immediately. He took time to build an army.

He also stayed informed of the movements of the Mexican army with the help of two spies—Deaf Smith and Smith's African American son-in-law Hendrick Arnold.

In April 1836, Sam Houston decided to strike. He moved his troops onto the prairie just west of the San Jacinto River. On April 21, the Mexican soldiers settled down for an afternoon siesta, or nap. At that moment, Houston ordered the attack. Texas volunteers raced into battle, screaming "Remember the Alamo" and "Remember Goliad."

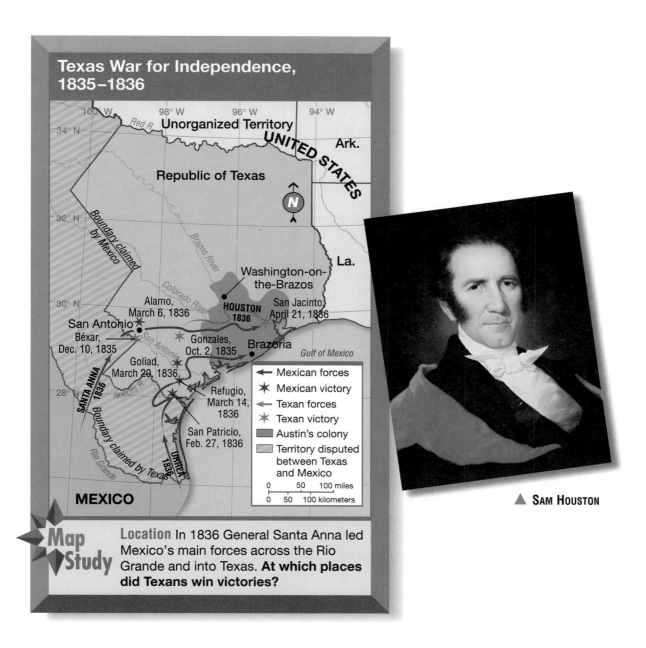

Texas War for Independence, 1835–1836

Legend:
→ Mexican forces
✳ Mexican victory
← Texan forces
✳ Texan victory
■ Austin's colony
▨ Territory disputed between Texas and Mexico

0   50   100 miles
0   50   100 kilometers

▲ SAM HOUSTON

Map Study

Location In 1836 General Santa Anna led Mexico's main forces across the Rio Grande and into Texas. **At which places did Texans win victories?**

▲ JUAN SEGUIN

Biography ★★★★

Juan Seguin, A Texas Hero

Juan Seguin grew up on his family's ranch along the San Antonio River. He disliked the arrogant Santa Anna. Like many Tejanos, Seguin believed Santa Anna would use the army to crush all opposition.

Seguin became one of the first volunteers to join the Texas Revolution. He commanded a company of Tejanos in San Antonio. He and eight members of his company fought at the Alamo. Seguin risked his life to slip through Mexican lines to find reinforcements. When he returned on March 6, he saw the Alamo in flames.

At the Battle of San Jacinto, Houston was not sure the Tejanos should participate. He feared Anglos might mistake them for the enemy. Seguin and his followers refused such protection, declaring that they had joined the army and wanted to face the enemy. Houston admired the courage of Seguin and the Tejanos and changed his mind.

The battle of San Jacinto lasted only 18 minutes. It became the most intense battle of the Texas Revolution. More than 600 Mexican soldiers died. Hundreds more were wounded or captured. Mexican soldiers shot two horses from under Houston before a musket ball finally shattered his ankle. When the battle ended, only nine Texans had died.

Santa Anna had disappeared during the fighting. The next day Texas soldiers found him hiding in tall grass and took him prisoner.   ★★★

The Republic of Texas

The war had ended. On May 14 Texans forced Santa Anna to sign a peace treaty. He also signed a secret treaty promising to support Texas independence. In September 1836, Texans elected Sam Houston president of the new independent nation—the Republic of Texas.

★ SECTION 2 REVIEW ★

★★★★★★★★★★★★★★★★★   ★★★★★★★★★★★★★★★★★

Checking for Understanding

1. **Identify** Stephen F. Austin, Antonio López de Santa Anna, Sam Houston, Juan Seguin, San Antonio, Goliad.

2. **Define** Tejanos, empresario, reform.

3. **How** did the Mexican government attempt to control United States settlers who moved into Texas?

4. **What** were some of the causes of the Texas Revolution?

Critical Thinking

5. **Making Predictions**   How do you think people in the United States responded to news of Texas's independence?

ACTIVITY

6. Imagine you are Stephen F. Austin and you need to recruit settlers to colonize Texas. Draw an advertisement or create a catchy slogan that would attract American colonists to Texas.

★★★★★★★★★★★★★★★★★★★★★★★★★ ★★★★★★★

War With Mexico

SETTING THE SCENE

Read to Learn . . .

★ how the Mexican War began and why some Americans opposed the war.

★ how the United States obtained New Mexico and California.

Terms to Know

★ Bear Flag Republic
★ cede

People to Meet

★ Zachary Taylor
★ Winfield Scott
★ Stephen Kearny

Places to Locate

★ Santa Fe
★ Mexican Cession
★ Gadsden Purchase

▶ OIL LAMP, 1840S

The United States officially recognized the Republic of Texas as an independent nation in 1837. However, Congress did not immediately annex it. Because many people in the northern United States opposed entry of another slave state into the Union, Texas continued to exist as an independent country.

Peace between Texas and Mexico remained uneasy from the start. Mexico never recognized Texas's independence. The two governments quarreled over borders and territory. Twice in 1842 Mexican troops seized San Antonio. Texans responded by marching to Laredo, a border town on the Rio Grande, and then into

Mexico. Tensions increased when Texas passed a resolution claiming land all the way to present-day California. A showdown seemed inevitable.

★ From Sea to Shining Sea

People in the United States who favored expansion watched events in Texas intently. Texas already had signed several agreements with Great Britain. If Texas went to war with Mexico, it might form an alliance with the British. With British help, Texas could expand its reach all the way to the Pacific.

By the mid-1840s, a group of Americans wanted to see the United States claim that honor for itself. They believed the nation had a "manifest destiny." *Manifest* means clear or obvious. *Destiny* means something that is sure to happen. Some Americans thought the nation was obviously meant to expand and spread across the continent. They gave little thought to the Native Americans and Mexicans who would lose their lands in the process.

Annexation of Texas

After gaining independence from Mexico, Texans immediately voted to seek admission to the United States. Most Southerners strongly supported extending the cotton-growing area by annexing Texas. Northern abolitionists, however, opposed adding another slave state to the Union.

Presidents Andrew Jackson and Martin Van Buren had refused to recommend annexation. The issue soon arose again. As the 1844 election approached, territorial expansion took center stage. The Democrats nominated **James K. Polk** of Tennessee as their presidential candidate. As you read earlier in the chapter, Polk campaigned with the slogan "Fifty-four forty or fight!" and made manifest destiny the main issue in the campaign.

Polk won in a close election. Outgoing President John Tyler considered Polk's victory a mandate for the annexation of Texas. In February 1845, at Tyler's urging both houses of Congress passed a joint resolution to annex Texas. In December 1845, Texas became the twenty-eighth state to enter the Union; however, some problems still had to be resolved. The boundary between Texas and Mexico remained undetermined, and the Mexican government threatened war.

President Polk responded by sending agent John Slidell to resolve differences. Polk instructed Slidell to convince Mexico to accept the Rio Grande as the southern border of Texas. He also told Slidell to offer Mexico $25 million for California and $5 million for New Mexico.

Mexican officials exploded in outrage. They considered such a low sum of money an insult and refused to even speak with Slidell.

★ The Brink of War

President Polk wanted to move against Mexico. He knew most Americans backed expansion but was not sure they would back it to the point of war.

Polk decided to press the question by sending troops into Texas. Soldiers under the command of General **Zachary Taylor** crossed the Nueces (nu•AY•suhs) River and set up posts just north of the Rio Grande. Although Texas claimed this as its southern boundary, Mexico considered it Mexican territory. Colonel Ethan Allen Hitchcock, one of Taylor's aides, observed:

> **We have not one particle of right to be here. . . . It looks as if the government sent a small force on purpose to bring on a war, so as to have a pretext for taking California and as much of this country as it chooses.**

In April 1846, Mexican soldiers attacked a United States cavalry patrol and killed 11 Americans. Taylor quickly notified Polk. On May 9 President Polk announced that "Mexico has . . . shed American blood on American soil." He then asked Congress for an official declaration of war. On May 13 both houses of Congress voted by a large majority to declare war on Mexico.

Opposition to the War

Fourteen antislavery representatives in the House voted against the war. Ohio representative Joshua Giddings called the

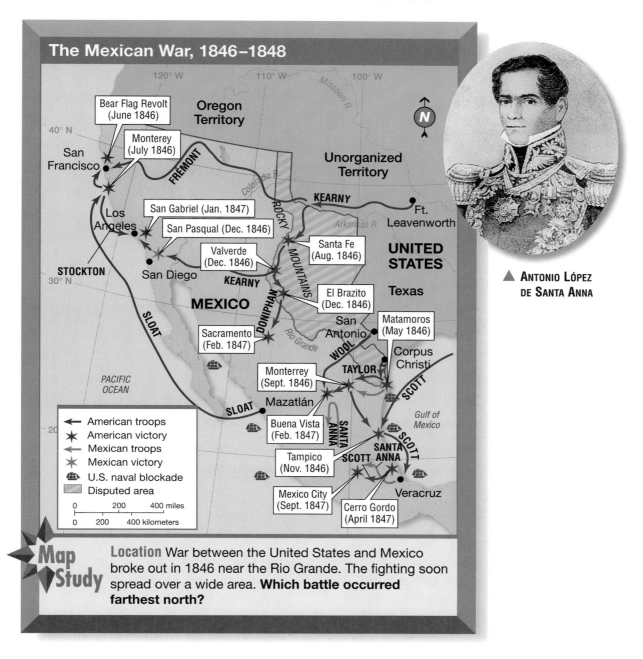

The Mexican War, 1846–1848

Bear Flag Revolt (June 1846)
Oregon Territory
Monterey (July 1846)
San Francisco
FRÉMONT
KEARNY
Ft. Leavenworth
Unorganized Territory
San Gabriel (Jan. 1847)
Los Angeles
San Pasqual (Dec. 1846)
Santa Fe (Aug. 1846)
UNITED STATES
ROCKY MOUNTAINS
STOCKTON
Valverde (Dec. 1846)
San Diego
KEARNY
MEXICO
El Brazito (Dec. 1846)
Texas
SLOAT
DONIPHAN
Sacramento (Feb. 1847)
San Antonio
Matamoros (May 1846)
Rio Grande
WOOL
Corpus Christi
Monterrey (Sept. 1846)
TAYLOR
PACIFIC OCEAN
SLOAT
Mazatlán
SANTA ANNA
SCOTT
Buena Vista (Feb. 1847)
Gulf of Mexico
Tampico (Nov. 1846)
SCOTT
SANTA ANNA
SCOTT
Mexico City (Sept. 1847)
Cerro Gordo (April 1847)
Veracruz

Legend:
← American troops
★ American victory
← Mexican troops
★ Mexican victory
U.S. naval blockade
Disputed area

0   200   400 miles
0   200   400 kilometers

▲ Antonio López de Santa Anna

Map Study

Location War between the United States and Mexico broke out in 1846 near the Rio Grande. The fighting soon spread over a wide area. **Which battle occurred farthest north?**

war "aggressive, unholy, and unjust." Illinois representative Abraham Lincoln challenged Polk to name the spot where Mexicans "shed American blood on American soil."

People outside of Congress also criticized "Mr. Polk's War." New England poet John Greenleaf Whittier wrote, "[I am] heartsick with this miserably wicked Mexican War." Abolitionists considered the war a Southern plot to add more slave states to the Union. They called it a scheme to steal "bigger pens to cram in slaves." Most American newspapers, though, rallied behind the President.

Major Battles

Even before Congress declared war, General Taylor's soldiers fought north of the Rio Grande at Palo Alto and Resaca de la Palma. In May of 1846, Taylor and his army crossed the Rio Grande into Mexico. By September they captured Monterrey.

In late 1846 Santa Anna rallied his forces. He personally led an army

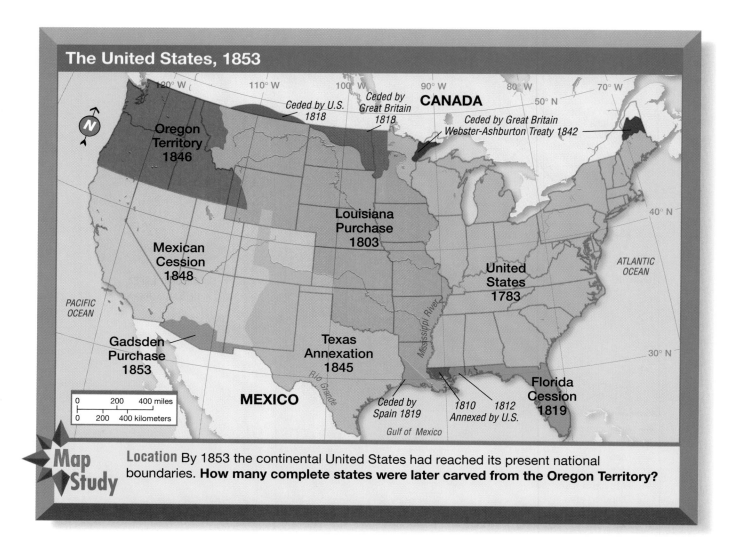

The United States, 1853

Oregon Territory 1846

Ceded by U.S. 1818

Ceded by Great Britain 1818

CANADA

Ceded by Great Britain
Webster-Ashburton Treaty 1842

Louisiana Purchase 1803

Mexican Cession 1848

United States 1783

ATLANTIC OCEAN

PACIFIC OCEAN

Gadsden Purchase 1853

Texas Annexation 1845

MEXICO

Rio Grande

Mississippi River

Ceded by Spain 1819

1810 · 1812 Annexed by U.S.

Florida Cession 1819

Gulf of Mexico

0   200   400 miles
0   200   400 kilometers

Map Study

Location By 1853 the continental United States had reached its present national boundaries. **How many complete states were later carved from the Oregon Territory?**

---

against Taylor. In February 1847, however, Taylor regained the upper hand after defeating Santa Anna at the Battle of Buena Vista.

As armies clashed in Mexico, General **Winfield Scott** landed troops on the Gulf Coast near Veracruz. Scott's army won victory after victory as it marched west. In September 1847, after Mexicans made a heroic last stand at Chapultepec (chuh•POOL•tuh•PEHK), Scott took over Mexico City.

The Bear Flag Republic

Soon after the war began, General **Stephen Kearny** marched his army to **Santa Fe,** the capital of present-day New Mexico. The Mexican governor, along with Mexican troops, fled without firing a shot. From Santa Fe, Kearny led about 300 soldiers to California.

In 1846 some 500 Americans lived in California. Captain **John C. Frémont,** an American army officer and explorer, urged Americans to revolt against their Mexican rulers. In the summer of 1846, rebels hoisted a handmade flag emblazoned with a grizzly bear. With this act, they announced the creation of the independent Bear Flag Republic.

When General Kearny arrived, the rebels replaced the Bear Flag with the Stars and Stripes. Frémont joined United States forces in fighting the Mexican War. In January 1847, Mexicans in California surrendered, and the United States took possession of the territory.

Making Peace

On February 2, 1848, the Mexicans signed the **Treaty of Guadalupe Hidalgo.** Under its terms, Mexico ceded, or gave up, all of California and New Mexico. This territory has since become known as the **Mexican Cession.** It included the present-day states of California, Nevada, Utah, and parts of Arizona, Colorado, Wyoming, and New Mexico. The United States agreed to pay $15 million for these lands and agreed to pay the claims of American citizens against Mexico up to $3.25 million. Mexico agreed to recognize Texas as part of the United States. The Mexican government also accepted the Rio Grande as the border between Texas and Mexico.

★ Gadsden Purchase

Americans, however, wanted still more territory claimed by Mexico. Railroad owners envisioned a southern route to the Pacific that ran over a strip of land just south of the Gila River. To fulfill this dream, James Gadsden, the minister to Mexico, arranged to buy this land for $10 million. The **Gadsden Purchase** completed the boundary between Mexico and the United States and the expansion of the United States across the continent.

★ New Citizens

The acquisition of Mexican land brought thousands of Mexican citizens into the United States. The Mexican government worried about the fate of these people. To protect their rights, Mexican negotiators insisted that the Treaty of Guadalupe Hidalgo include provisions allowing Mexicans to freely relocate to Mexico. For Mexicans who remained on their land, the treaty promised them "all the rights of citizens of the United States according to the principles of the Constitution."

A difficult choice faced Mexicans. About 2,000 people headed south into Mexico. A far larger number, however, chose to stay in the United States. Mexicans who remained in the United States contributed to a rich culture that blended Spanish and Native American traditions. When English-speaking settlers moved to the Southwest, they brought their own ideas and culture with them. The settlers, though, learned much from the Mexican Americans. Mexican Americans taught the newcomers how to irrigate the soil and mine minerals.

Many settlers, however, did not treat Mexican Americans and Native Americans fairly. These two groups struggled to protect their cultures and rights against the newcomers.

★ SECTION 3 REVIEW ★

Checking for Understanding

1. **Identify** Zachary Taylor, Winfield Scott, Stephen Kearny, Santa Fe, Mexican Cession, Gadsden Purchase.

2. **Define** Bear Flag Republic, cede.

3. **What** were the causes of the war between Mexico and the United States?

4. **Who** urged Americans living in present-day California to revolt against Mexican rule?

5. **What** were the terms of the Mexican Cession?

Critical Thinking

6. **Analyzing Information** Why do you think the Texas voters approved annexation to the United States by a great majority?

ACTIVITY

7. Imagine you were a Mexican living on lands acquired in the Mexican Cession. Write diary entries in which you record your feelings on learning the terms of the Treaty of Guadalupe Hidalgo.

★★★

Spanning a Continent

SETTING THE SCENE

Read to Learn . . .

★ why the Mormons settled in what is now Utah.
★ how California's population boomed in 1849.

Terms to Know

★ forty-niner
★ prospector
★ vigilante

People to Meet

★ Brigham Young
★ John Sutter
★ Biddy Mason

Places to Locate

★ Salt Lake City
★ San Francisco
★ Isthmus of Panama

◄ GOLD RUSH TRAVEL ADVERTISEMENT

In July 1847, **Brigham Young** stood on a hill overlooking Utah's Salt Lake Valley. According to legend, Young saw a vision of a great city. He turned to the people who had followed him into the desert. "This is the right place!" Young declared confidently.

★ The Mormons

Young's view of Salt Lake Valley marked the end of a 1,300-mile (2,092-km) journey from Iowa. Young and his followers had walked the entire distance, hauling

their possessions behind them in two-wheeled carts. They came to the desert for the same reason countless settlers had first traveled to North America—for religious freedom.

A New Church

The settlers of Utah belonged to the Church of Jesus Christ of Latter-day Saints. They referred to themselves as "Saints." Most people, though, knew them as **Mormons.**

The Mormons owed their origins to **Joseph Smith,** a farmer in upstate New

York. In the 1820s Smith had a vision that convinced him to found a new Christian sect, or religious group. Smith's faith and enthusiasm won converts. Several of his beliefs, however, won even more enemies.

Smith believed that property should be held in common. He also supported polygamy, the idea that a man could have more than one wife. This angered a large number of people in the 1800s. Mormons eventually gave up this practice.

Journey Into the Desert

Harassed by neighbors suspicious of their beliefs, the Mormons moved from New York to Ohio to Missouri and then to Illinois. In 1844 a mob attacked and killed Smith. His successor, Brigham Young, decided to lead the Mormons to shelter in the Far West.

In 1847 about 150 Mormons began their long trek. Eventually more than 15,000 people made the difficult journey, following Young to Utah Territory. Over the next decade, the Mormons built 1,043 miles (1,678 km) of canals and irrigated 154,000 acres (62,370 ha) of formerly arid, or dry, land. In 1850 Congress recognized Young as the governor of the Utah Territory. By 1860 about 30,000 Mormons lived in **Salt Lake City** and more than 90 other towns in present-day Utah. Utah eventually entered the Union in 1896 as the forty-fifth state.

◀ JOSEPH SMITH

Picturing History ▲ MORMONS MOVE WEST Using handcarts, oxen, and wagons, the Mormons traveled west across the Great Plains and Rocky Mountains to the Utah Territory in search of religious freedom. **Who led the Mormons to Utah?**

★ Rushing to California

As the Mormons built houses in the desert, Swiss immigrant **John Sutter** ordered a crew of workers to build a sawmill along the American River in northern California. On January 24, 1848, a golden glint in the river caught the eye of John Marshall, the supervisor of the job. Marshall reached into the water and pulled out a lump of ore. A single word slipped through Marshall's lips: "Gold."

Marshall tried to keep his discovery a secret, but word spread quickly to nearby towns. The mayor of Monterey, California, described the reaction of townspeople:

      [T]he farmers have thrown aside their plows, the lawyers their briefs, the doctors their pills, the priests their prayerbooks, and all are now digging for gold. ”

Picturing History

▲ GOLD MINING Thousands of people went to California during the Gold Rush searching for great wealth. **What term did people use for gold seekers in California?**

Forty-Niners by the Shipload

The gold seekers who stampeded into California became known as the forty-niners for the year, 1849, in which many of them came. Thousands of forty-niners sailed to **San Francisco** from New York, Boston, and Galveston. Most traveled around the southern tip of South America. Some more adventurous—or impatient—travelers sailed to the **Isthmus of Panama.** They climbed on mules and rode through the steamy jungle to reach the Pacific coast. At the coast, they caught ships bound for California.

The people who departed from the ships in San Francisco came from nearly every corner of the earth. During the first half of 1849, 5,000 miners arrived from Chile alone. Others came from as far away as China.

Traveling Overland

By far the greatest number of gold seekers traveled to California on overland trails. Guided by former mountain men, many traveled over a southern spur of the Oregon Trail, called the California Trail. Still others headed over the Mormon Trail. In 1849 alone, more than 80,000 people poured across the continent.

★ Life in the Mining Towns

When the forty-niners reached California, they threw up temporary towns overnight with names such as Shinbone Peak and You Bet. Most townspeople lived in tents. The lucky ones owned cabins, most of which lacked windows or chimneys.

Some women staked claims, but more made money by opening boardinghouses or laundries. One laundress along the Feather River earned $1,000 a week— more money than some miners.

Mining towns had no police or prisons, so robbers posed a real threat to business owners and miners, also called

464   **UNIT 5** The Nation Expands: 1820–1860

Jeans

One of the most enduring made-in-the-USA fashions came out of the mining camps of California.

Then

Only for Gold Miners

Levi Strauss listened as miners complained about how fast their clothes wore out. Strauss had an idea. He stitched up a pair of pants made from a tough easy-to-care-for fabric called denim. To make sure the pants were extra tough, Strauss folded the seams and reinforced the corners with small copper tacks called rivets. The pants did not tear when miners hung their tools or bags of gold from their belts or pockets, and the dark blue color did not show dirt! Strauss had a fashion hit. In 1873 his company began producing the first Levi's.

Now

A World Favorite

Today people call Levi's by a variety of names—dungarees, denims, blue jeans, jeans, or by the name of the designer who makes them. Regardless of the name, miner's pants are the top sportswear choice of people around the world. Imagine standing in a market in the middle of Nairobi, Kenya, or Kathmandu, Nepal. Your blue jeans may be a hotter trading item than your American dollars. How many pairs of jeans do you own?

▲ TEENAGERS IN JEANS

◀ EARLY LEVI PANTS AD

---

prospectors. Townspeople took law into their own hands, forming vigilance committees. The committee members, or vigilantes, drove petty thieves out of town and hanged murderers. Such hasty justice became known as vigilante justice—law without judge or jury.

★ Dreams of Freedom

In 1849 California delegates drafted a constitution that prohibited slavery. The next year California entered the Union as a free state. Hoping to find riches and freedom, a number of African Americans headed west.

By 1852 more than 2,000 African Americans lived in California. Some struck it rich in the mines. Others succeeded at business enterprises. **Biddy Mason,** for example, worked as a nurse. She then invested her savings in real estate until she built up a fortune. Mason used some of her money to found Los Angeles's first elementary school for African American children.

As a group, African Americans in California boasted savings of more than $2.3 million by 1855. The shadow of prejudice, however, still produced huge inequalities. The California legislature denied African Americans the right to vote. Black laws barred African Americans from testifying in court and prohibited integrated schools.

Led by African American journalists such as San Francisco newspaper owner **Mifflin Gibbs,** African Americans forced the repeal of the black laws. But they did not win the vote until passage of the Fifteenth Amendment in 1870.

Freedom Lost

For Native Americans, the migration of thousands of settlers to California proved disastrous. Tens of thousands of prospectors forced Native Americans to work. Native American men toiled in the mines while Native American women worked in households. Disease and forced labor reduced the Native American population in California from about 150,000 in 1848 to 35,000 by 1860.

The national government had created the Bureau of Indian Affairs in 1824. The bureau attempted to reduce Native American land claims. In the 1850s the government advocated confining Native Americans on reservations, or lands set aside for Native Americans. Despite Native Americans' fierce resistance to this policy, by 1858 the bureau had created eight reservations in California.

The Search for the Gold Mountain

Immigrants from China also felt the heavy hand of prejudice. Lured by tales of the American's *Gam San,* or "Gold Mountain," hundreds of Chinese peasants poured into California from 1849 to 1851. By 1852 their numbers had swelled into the thousands.

The rising tide of immigration from Asia alarmed the miners in the United States. In 1852 they convinced state lawmakers to tax foreign-born miners who did not plan to become citizens. Federal law limited citizenship to whites, so Chinese miners had to pay the tax or quit mining. Under the law, the government took a total of $5 million from the pockets of Chinese prospectors.

Forced out of mining, the Chinese opened other businesses. Chinese laundries, restaurants, and boardinghouses became familiar sights in the mining towns. In San Francisco these shops made up a city within a city called Chinatown.

The End of the Gold Rush

Although the Gold Rush continued into the 1850s, latecomers found little gold left in rivers and streams. After a few years, large companies took over most of the mining in California. Many forty-niners settled down as farmers, shopkeepers, or city workers in towns like San Francisco. When the mines ran dry, smaller towns went bust and people moved on. Many towns became abandoned ghost towns. Some people continued the search for gold, however. Their search carried them north to British Columbia, east to Colorado, and across the Pacific Ocean to Australia.

★ SECTION 4 REVIEW ★

Checking for Understanding

1. **Identify** Brigham Young, John Sutter, Biddy Mason, Salt Lake City, San Francisco, Isthmus of Panama.
2. **Define** forty-niner, prospector, vigilante.
3. **Why** did the Mormons settle in the deserts of Utah?
4. **How** did the Gold Rush help California grow?

Critical Thinking

5. **Making Comparisons** How was the establishment of a settlement in Utah in the 1840s similar to the founding of the Massachusetts Bay Colony in the 1620s?

ACTIVITY

6. Draw or create a scene of a California mining town.

The Giant Sequoia

The first non-Native Americans to see the soaring giant sequoias of California could scarcely believe their eyes. The trees seemed to have no crowns, or tops. Their cinnamon-colored trunks just climbed up, up, and up.

Equally impressive were the trees' circumferences. Circumference is the measurement around the tree's base, or trunk. The trunks of some trees are more than 100 feet (30 m) in diameter. In 1858 cattle herder Hale Tharp set up a temporary home in a giant sequoia hollowed out by a fire.

▲ GIANT SEQUOIA TREE

Many of the giant sequoias living today are several thousand years old. It is estimated that the General Sherman Tree, in Sequoia National Park, is between 2,200 and 2,500 years old. It is the world's largest tree in volume of wood. The tree is 275 feet (83.8 m) tall and its base has a circumference of 103 feet (31.4 m).

One of the oldest and largest of the trees was cut down before laws were passed to protect them. Scientists have determined that this tree had been growing since 1305 B.C.—when ancient Egypt was at the height of its power.

Giant sequoias grow only on the western slopes of the Sierra Nevada mountains in California. These evergreen trees are very durable. Scientists do not believe any have ever died from old age, disease, or insect attack. Their extremely thick bark protects them from injury by fire. Lightning has destroyed or damaged the tops of many of the trees.

Making the Science Connection

1. What are the giant sequoias?
2. Where do they grow?

ACTIVITY

3. The General Sherman Tree is the largest plant on Earth. Create an illustrated chart to explain just how large it is to a younger student. Illustrate the General Sherman on your chart, labeling its height and circumference. Then add pictures or illustrations of familiar things that are about the same height or size for comparison. For example, you might picture two school buses, one on top of the other, to represent the circumference of the huge sequoia.

Using Key Vocabulary

Use the listed words to complete the following sentences.

annex	reforms
cede	vigilante
emigrate	

1. In the Treaty of Guadalupe Hidalgo, Mexico agreed to _____ California to the United States.

2. Many settlers used the Oregon Trail to _____ to the Far West.

3. President Polk wanted to _____ Texas to the United States.

4. A _____ kept order in a California mining town.

5. An independent state and an end to the ban on American immigration were two _____ requested by Texans in 1835.

Reviewing Facts

1. **Describe** the life of mountain men in the Oregon Country.

2. **What** role did the idea of manifest destiny play in the presidential election of 1844?

3. **Identify** two issues that the Mexican government and American Texans disagreed about.

4. **List** two ways the United States obtained territory from Mexico.

5. **Describe** how the discovery of gold fueled California's population growth.

Understanding Concepts

Beliefs and Ideas

1. What belief fueled Americans' desire to push across the Mississippi?

2. What desire brought Brigham Young and his followers to Utah's Salt Lake Valley?

Individual and Family Life

3. Why did Brigham Young and the Mormons travel such a great distance to settle in Utah in the 1840s?

4. What was the link between slavery and opposition to the Mexican War?

5. Why were many American settlers attracted to the Oregon Country and California?

History and Geography

The Oregon and California Trails

Study the routes of the western trails shown on the map. Then answer the following questions.

1. **Region** Which mountains did settlers have to cross to reach Oregon's Pacific coast? To reach California's Pacific coast?

The Oregon and California Trails

2. **Location** In what city did the Oregon Trail begin? In what city did it end?

3. **Movement** How do you think the use of these trails helped settle the plains as well as the West?

Critical Thinking

1. **Comparing and Contrasting** In what sense did the mountain men and missionaries of the early 1800s play a similar role to that of the European explorers of the 1500s?

2. **Drawing Conclusions** Why do you think forty-niners risked their lives and savings to travel to California and search for gold? Do people today take great risks to make a fortune?

Cooperative Learning Interdisciplinary Activity: Geography

With three classmates, find out more about mountain men at the library. Choose a name for a mountain man and select a route for him to follow through the West. Then organize your group into two pairs. Have one pair write a diary in which your mountain man describes his experiences. Have the other pair make a poster-size, illustrated map of the route your mountain man travels. Share the diary and map with the rest of the class. (For a twist, make one of the mountain men a woman.)

Practicing Skills

Analyzing a Primary Source

The primary source on this page is part of a letter to Henry Clay, an influential national leader, in 1837. Read the document and then answer the questions.

"... I proceed now to a consideration of what is to me the strongest argument against annexing Texas to the United States. This measure will extend and perpetuate slavery. ...

By this act, slavery will be perpetuated in the old states as well as spread over new. It is well known that the soil of some of the old states has become exhausted by slave cultivation. ... They now adhere to slavery, not on account of the wealth which it extracts from the soil, but because it furnishes men and women to be sold in newly settled and more southern districts. It is by slave breeding and slave selling that these states subsist. Take away from them a foreign market, and slavery would die. ... By annexing Texas, we shall not only create it where it does not exist, but breathe new life into it, where its end seemed to be near. ..."

—Reverend William Ellery Channing

1. Who is the author of this letter?

2. What is the general topic of this letter?

3. Does the author support or reject the annexation of Texas?

4. What is the author's main reason for this viewpoint?

5. According to this letter, why did the annexation of Texas produce strong conflicts among Americans in the 1830s and 1840s?

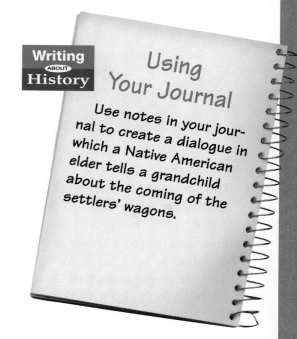

Writing ABOUT History

Using Your Journal

Use notes in your journal to create a dialogue in which a Native American elder tells a grandchild about the coming of the settlers' wagons.

Cultural Kaleidoscope

Sports and Recreation

In the early 1800s, Americans began to find new ways to relax and enjoy themselves. Some popular sports and games of today first made their appearance during this time. Of course, these sports looked much different then.

▲
Strike?
Americans everywhere took up bowling, a favorite sport of New Englanders since colonial days.

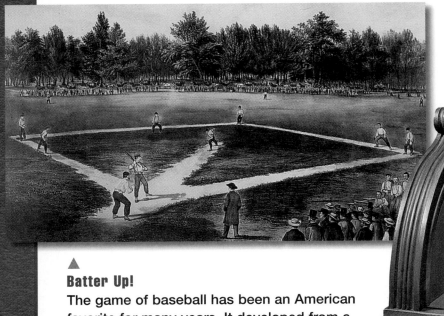

▲
Batter Up!
The game of baseball has been an American favorite for many years. It developed from a game called "rounders" that New England colonists played as early as the 1600s. Baseball as we know it today began with the Knickerbocker Base Ball Club of New York, formed in 1845. This baseball (right) from 1839 is one of the first ever made. It is now on display at the Baseball Hall of Fame in Cooperstown, New York.

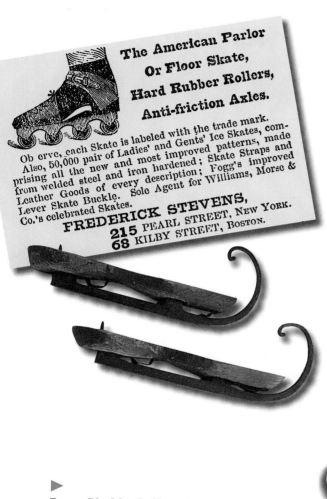

The American Parlor
Or Floor Skate,
Hard Rubber Rollers,
Anti-friction Axles.

Ob erve, each Skate is labeled with the trade mark. Also, 50,000 pair of Ladies' and Gents' Ice Skates, comprising all the new and most improved patterns, made from welded steel and iron hardened; Skate Straps and Leather Goods of every description; Fogg's improved Lever Skate Buckle. Sole Agent for Williams, Morse & Co.'s celebrated Skates.

FREDERICK STEVENS,
215 PEARL STREET, NEW YORK.
68 KILBY STREET, BOSTON.

► Gliding on Ice and Wheels

Ice skating took on new life and grace when E.W. Bushnell of Philadelphia made the first all-steel ice skates in 1850. His new skates made the sport more popular and led to the creation of skating clubs throughout the country. For warmer seasons, skaters could also enjoy roller skates.

► From Bladderball to Football

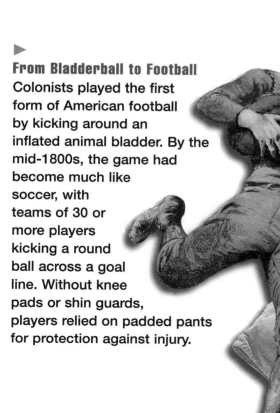

Colonists played the first form of American football by kicking around an inflated animal bladder. By the mid-1800s, the game had become much like soccer, with teams of 30 or more players kicking a round ball across a goal line. Without knee pads or shin guards, players relied on padded pants for protection against injury.

CHAPTER 15

★★

The Spirit of Reform
1820–1860

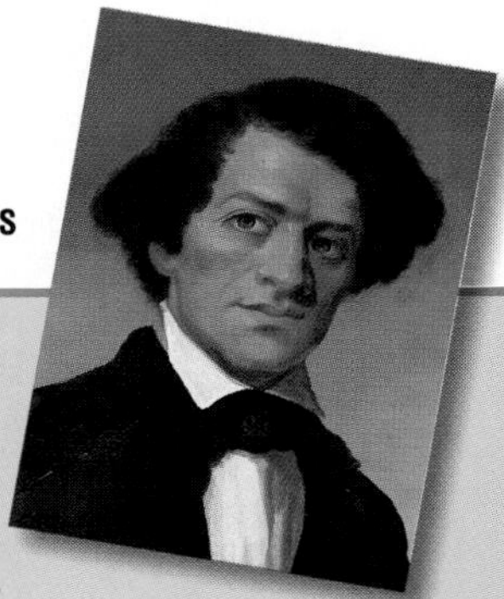

► FREDERICK DOUGLASS

SETTING THE SCENE

Focus

During the 1800s Americans worked to improve their lives. A spirit of reform swept across the nation. Cultural reformers broke free from European art forms and created an American style. Social reformers crusaded against what they viewed as the evils of their day. From about 1820 to 1860, the reform movements reshaped the cultural and social landscape of the United States.

Concepts to Understand

★ How new **beliefs, ideas, and institutions** influenced educators, artists, and writers
★ Which reforms of the era had the most lasting effect on **civil rights and liberties** in the United States

Read to Discover . . .

★ how American art and literature changed during the nineteenth century.
★ what reform movements began during this period.

Journal Notes

How did the social and cultural movements during this period get started? Record facts that answer when, where, how, and who about their beginnings.

United States

1825 John Quincy Adams becomes sixth United States President
1826 American Temperance Society forms in Boston

1832 William Lloyd Garrison starts the New England Anti-Slavery Society
1837 Massachusetts forms the first state board of education

1820–1829	1830–1839

World

1822 The American Colonization Society founds the west African nation of Liberia

1830 Greece becomes an independent nation
1839 Opium War begins in China

The Pic-Nic
by Thomas Cole, 1846

Thomas Cole helped inspire many of the Hudson River artists. He is also America's first notable landscape painter.

◄ THE TEMPERANCE MOVEMENT

1846 United States and Mexico go to war
1848 First women's rights convention opens in Seneca Falls, New York

1840–1849	1850–1859

1845 Irish potato famine spurs immigration to the United States
1848 Europe erupts in revolutions

1854 Crimean War begins

★★★

Literature, Art, and Science

SETTING THE SCENE

Read to Learn . . .

★ what European critics said about American art in the 1820s.
★ how American writers and artists created a uniquely American style.
★ what scientific achievements Americans contributed to the world.

Terms to Know

★ poll tax

People to Meet

★ Washington Irving
★ James Fenimore Cooper
★ Nathaniel Hawthorne
★ Edgar Allan Poe
★ Henry Wadsworth Longfellow
★ Walt Whitman
★ Emily Dickinson
★ Ralph Waldo Emerson
★ Henry David Thoreau

Places to Locate

★ Hudson River valley

◀ EDGAR ALLAN POE

In 1820 British critic Sydney Smith summed up American culture this way:

  ❝ In the four quarters of the globe, who reads an American book? Or goes to an American play? Or looks at an American picture or statue? . . . Literature the Americans have none—no native literature, we mean. It is all imported. ❞

Smith's evaluation came close to the truth. Many American writers and artists did indeed copy European themes, characters, and settings. Americans complained that the short history of the United States failed to provide adequate material for stories, novels, and paintings. After 1820 this began to change and Americans started writing stories with American themes.

★ Creating an American Literature

In the late 1820s, Andrew Jackson declared himself champion of the "common people." Suddenly, the ordinary American seemed worthy of attention. More and more American authors turned away from European characters and used American types in their work.

Even before Jackson became President, a few American writers had begun to create American literature. These writers served as models for others who broke away from European traditions.

Early Writers of American Literature

Readers received their first taste of the new American literature in 1820 when **Washington Irving** published a collection of tales called the *Sketch Book.* Irving's stories opened readers' eyes to the richness of American folklore.

The *Sketch Book* included "Rip Van Winkle" and "The Legend of Sleepy Hollow." Both tales were set in New York's **Hudson River valley** and had American characters. Rip Van Winkle was a colonial farmer who fell asleep for 20 years and completely missed the American Revolution. Ichabod Crane arrived in Sleepy Hollow to teach school but soon fled under mysterious circumstances.

Soon after in 1823, **James Fenimore Cooper** created Natty Bumpo—the first great American fictional hero. A tough pioneer in deerskin leggings, Bumpo appeared in several Cooper novels, including *The Pioneers, The Deerslayer,* and *The Last of the Mohicans.* These novels had nothing to do with the sophisticated world of Europe. Instead, they paid tribute to the beauty and danger of the American frontier.

Poet and editor **William Cullen Bryant** carried on a personal crusade for American literature. Bryant traveled the country urging authors to abandon Europe and celebrate America. He displayed his own national pride in "The Prairies":

66 **These are the gardens of the
   Desert, these
   The unshorn fields,
      boundless and beautiful,
   For which the speech of
      England has no name.** 99

Later American Writers

Author **Nathaniel Hawthorne** was descended from the Puritans who had settled Salem, Massachusetts, almost 200 years before his birth. The Puritan traditions fascinated Hawthorne and provided a natural focus for his fiction. His most famous novels, *The Scarlet Letter* and *The House of Seven Gables,* explored Puritan views of guilt and innocence, and good and evil. As a result, Hawthorne's books presented a distinctly American outlook.

Hawthorne's friend **Herman Melville** also employed the voices of distinctly American characters—New England whalers. Melville once said that a whaling ship was "my Yale College and my Harvard." He used his experiences at sea to create *Moby Dick,* his masterpiece. *Moby*

Picturing History ▲ RIP VAN WINKLE Washington Irving depicted American folklore in many of his stories, such as "Rip Van Winkle."
What other story helped give Irving his fame?

Dick tells of the hunt for a white whale and examines Americans' materialism and idealism. When *Moby Dick* was published in 1851, most critics harshly criticized it, and readers ignored it. Today, though, many consider *Moby Dick* one of the greatest of all American novels.

William Wells Brown wrote the first published fiction by an African American. Brown's novel *Clotel* came out in 1853 and described the life of America's enslaved people. Years earlier he also had written the story of his own life in slavery and of his escape to freedom.

Edgar Allan Poe may have been the most eccentric American author of the 1800s. Poe abused drugs and worried constantly about money. His poetry, essays, and short stories seemed to reflect his troubled life. They reeked of death, evil, and horror. Yet Americans became fascinated with Poe's work. Readers still enjoy Poe classics such as "The Raven" and "The Tell-Tale Heart."

Women Writers

By the mid-1800s many women had contributed to American literature. **Margaret Fuller**'s *Woman in the Nineteenth Century* had great influence on the movement for women's rights.

Dozens of women writers, including **Catharine Sedgwick** and **Fanny Fern,** wrote serials for newspapers and magazines. Their fiction became known as "the domestic novel." Women wrote many of the best-selling novels and earned far more money than male authors of the time.

Poets Sing of America

Nineteenth-century poetry also reflected the new enthusiasm for American themes. Among all the poets of the 1800s, Americans loved **Henry Wadsworth Longfellow** best. His poems were easy to understand and full of optimism. They revived American legends for generations of children who memorized "Paul Revere's Ride" and *The Song of Hiawatha.*

By writing about the American past, Longfellow created a sense of identity for Americans. In "Paul Revere's Ride," Longfellow gives life to an American legend.

> " Listen, my children, and
>   you shall hear
> Of the midnight ride of
>   Paul Revere,
> On the eighteenth of April,
>   in Seventy-five;
> Hardly a man is now alive
> Who remembers that
>   famous day and year. "

Longfellow also found material for his stories in the lives of common people.

Other poets explored the dark side of American culture. New Hampshire's **John Greenleaf Whittier,** for example, cried out against slavery in many of his works. He referred to slaveholders and their government allies in 1856 when he wrote: "The age is dull and mean. Men creep, Not walk."

New Yorker **Walt Whitman** attempted to speak for all Americans. His verses glorified women, sailors, pioneers, city dwellers, and Presidents. "The United States themselves are essentially the greatest poem," Whitman wrote in *Leaves of Grass,* his collection of poems that appeared in 1855. For almost 40 years, Whitman remained absorbed in America. He continued to revise and reissue *Leaves of Grass* until his death in 1892.

New England's **Emily Dickinson** seemed as eccentric as Edgar Allan Poe. She always dressed in white and lived in seclusion. She composed many poems about loneliness, love, and death but published only seven during her lifetime.

Dickinson's poetry became so widely read after her death that several lines have become American truisms. For instance, most people have heard "There is no

Frigate like a Book" or "If I can stop one heart from breaking, I shall not live in vain." Today Dickinson is regarded as a leading poet of the 1800s.

The Influence of Emerson

Many people considered **Ralph Waldo Emerson** of Boston, Massachusetts, the conscience of nineteenth-century America. Emerson urged Americans to discard corrupt European thinking. In an address at Harvard University, Emerson declared Americans ready for intellectual independence.

> **We will walk on our own feet; we will work with our own hands; we will speak our own minds.**

Emerson scorned materialism and valued individualism and harmony between human beings and nature. Soon Emerson became a well-known lecturer and won many supporters.

In addition to lecturing, Emerson wrote widely read poetry and essays. Emerson celebrated Andrew Jackson's idea of common people in many of his writings. He wrote: "I embrace the common, I explore and sit at the feet of the familiar and low."

Another Massachusetts writer, **Henry David Thoreau** (thuh•ROH), regarded Emerson as his spiritual father. Thoreau put into practice the ideas that Emerson preached. Thoreau moved to a small cabin at Walden Pond in northeast Massachusetts. There he spent two years thinking and writing about nature.

Thoreau often voiced dissent in a world that worshiped material progress and expansion. To protest slavery and the Mexican War, Thoreau refused to pay a poll tax—a sum of money paid in exchange for the right to vote—and consequently served time in jail. Afterward, he wrote the essay "Civil Disobedience" in which he encouraged others to disobey unjust laws. Later his best-known work, *Walden*, popularized his ideas about living a simple life.

★ New American Painters

Early American painters, such as John Singleton Copley, Benjamin West, and Gilbert Stuart, studied abroad and learned

History AND ART

▲ *PLAINS AND PLATEAU INDIANS* by George Catlin, c. 1830 George Catlin's fascination and appreciation for Native Americans caused him to paint many different groups. **What American artist was among the first to paint African Americans?**

Footnotes to History

Familiar Face   Gilbert Stuart's portraits of George Washington are probably very familiar to you. You see a Stuart painting almost every time you buy something. Why? Stuart's portrait of the first President is on the $1 bill.

a formal style of painting. Their pictures portrayed neatly cultivated fields and countrysides and great men and women of society. Inspired by Jacksonian democracy and thinkers such as Emerson, later American artists developed a different style. Their paintings showed America's vast wilderness and the variety of its people.

American Schools of Art

In 1819 young **Thomas Cole** came to the United States from his native England. By the late 1820s, Cole became famous for his paintings of American landscapes. Poet William Cullen Bryant called Cole's paintings "scenes of wild grandeur peculiar to our country."

Around 1825 a group of artists including Cole and Asher Durand, called the **Hudson River School,** painted landscapes of the Hudson River and Catskill Mountains in New York.

Another school of painting known as genre art developed during the 1830s. Genre artists depicted everyday subjects, such as men negotiating for a horse and children playing on an abandoned stagecoach. Famous genre painters included **George Caleb Bingham** of Missouri and **William Sidney Mount** of New York. Mount was one of the first American artists to paint African American people.

Around 1830 Pennsylvania's **George Catlin** set out to paint every group of Native Americans in North America. By the end of the decade, he had more than 40 groups represented on canvas.

★ Scientific Advances

American men and women also won international fame in the field of science. **Maria Mitchell** taught herself astronomy—the study of objects outside the earth's atmosphere—and discovered a comet in 1847. **Joseph Henry** invented an electromagnetic motor and aided in the research of accurate weather prediction.

Matthew Maury, an officer in the United States Navy, developed ways to predict winds and ocean tides. This research reduced the time it took ships to sail from port to port. Thirteen nations honored Maury for his research.

Dr. Crawford Long of Georgia and **Dr. William Morton** of Boston developed a method of using ether as an anesthetic—a substance that produces numbness—during surgery.

The American achievements in literature, art, and science in the 1800s had long-lasting effects. These pioneers created an American voice and made Americans proud of the richness of their land and past.

★ SECTION 1 REVIEW ★

Checking for Understanding

1. **Identify** Washington Irving, James Fenimore Cooper, Nathaniel Hawthorne, Edgar Allan Poe, Henry Wadsworth Longfellow, Walt Whitman, Emily Dickinson, Ralph Waldo Emerson, Henry David Thoreau, Hudson River valley.

2. **Define** poll tax.

3. **What** did Ralph Waldo Emerson contribute to American art and literature?

Critical Thinking

4. **Drawing Conclusions** Why do you think an American style of painting and writing was not developed until the 1800s?

ACTIVITY

5. Imagine you are a poet, writer, or painter. If you were going to depict an important event in American history, which event would you choose? Why?

Medical Treatments

Imagine having a tooth pulled and feeling every tug and pang! Before the mid-1840s patients faced this ordeal whenever they underwent surgery. Few drugs were available to dull the pain and shock of operations. Then two Americans, Crawford Long, a doctor, and William Thomas Morton, a dentist, discovered that a gas called ether safely put patients to sleep during surgery. In 1846 Morton publicly demonstrated his discovery for the first time at a Massachusetts hospital. Soon other doctors were performing operations thought impossible before the use of ether as a painkiller.

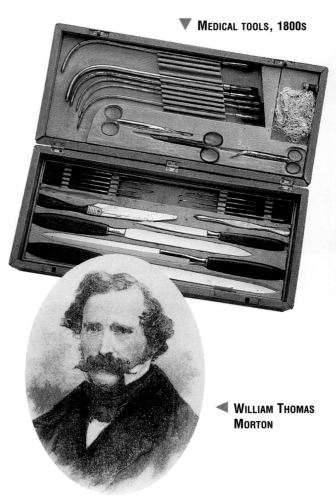

▼ MEDICAL TOOLS, 1800S

◄ WILLIAM THOMAS MORTON

Surgery in the 1800s

Even after early surgeons had ether, the operations they performed were vastly different from modern ones. Today doctors and nurses dress in gowns and masks and sterilize instruments before performing surgery. These precautions help prevent germs from infecting the incisions, or cuts, that surgeons make. Such safeguards were unknown in the mid-1800s. Doctors operated in their street clothes and seldom cleaned their instruments between operations. They had few if any trained nurses to assist them. Half of all patients who had operations died because their incisions became infected.

Patients in the 1800s seldom felt much confidence in their doctors. Doctors usually treated illnesses by letting blood, applying herbal remedies, or prescribing rest and fresh air. They received little formal education and learned to practice simply by watching older doctors. Often a sick person consulted a minister or barber before—or instead of—a doctor.

Making the Science Connection

1. Why was the discovery of ether important?

2. Under what conditions were operations performed in the 1800s?

3. What were common treatments for illness at that time?

ACTIVITY

4. Invent a device to reduce the pain or discomfort from illness. Draw your invention and use labels and captions to explain how it works.

★★★

Calls for Widespread Education

SETTING THE SCENE

Read to Learn . . .

★ why reformers thought American education needed to be changed.
★ how American reformers changed education.
★ why women and minorities had difficulty obtaining an education.

Terms to Know

★ common school movement

People to Meet

★ Horace Mann
★ Emma Willard
★ Elizabeth Blackwell
★ Prudence Crandall
★ Thomas Gallaudet
★ Samuel Gridley Howe

► PAGE FROM *McGuffey's Reader*

Tom huddled in a corner of the schoolroom, his toes and fingers stinging from the cold. According to school rules, Tom had to sit farthest from the stove because his father had not contributed any firewood. Tom could hardly hear the teacher and had no book with which to follow the lesson.

★ Early Education in the United States

Tom's day at school was typical for most students in the United States during the early 1800s. Some children did not even have the opportunity to get a meager education like Tom's. Few African Americans, for example, were allowed to attend school at all.

Sectional Differences in Schools

American schools varied from section to section across the country. As early as 1647, Massachusetts passed a law requiring towns to provide schools for their children. The rest of New England adopted similar laws. The towns, not the states, paid for the schools.

Early on, the Middle Atlantic states also took responsibility for education. New York, for instance, organized a school system in 1784. Private societies, though, had to raise the money to fund the schools. From 1805 to 1852, the Free School Society of New York City supported the city's school system. In 1827 Philadelphians organized a similar society in their city.

The federal government mandated education for people in the lands west of New York and north of the Ohio River. In the

Northwest Ordinance of 1787, Congress set aside a section of land in each township for the support of schools.

Public schools in the North and West seldom had enough money to furnish good educations. Few people made donations to the societies that supported city schools, and the land grants brought little income.

Southern schools had even less support. In the South families had to work so hard to make a living that little time or money was left for schooling. The South was made up of small farms and plantations. Few towns existed to provide schools. Often a local minister taught children from neighboring farms in a school built on an unused field.

Well-to-do people in all sections of the country managed to give their children good educations. Many paid for privately operated schools rather than sending their children to public schools supported by a school society or land grants. In the South wealthy planters hired private tutors for their children and later sent them to Europe to finish their education.

★ Educational Reform

During the 1830s more Americans qualified to vote than ever before. Educational reformers argued that voters needed good educations to make sound decisions about their government. The reformers proposed raising the standards of schools across the nation and supporting them with taxes. To accomplish these goals, they started the common school movement.

Voices For and Against Change

Not everyone favored common schools, also referred to as free, or tax-supported, public schools. In the 1830s few people paid state or federal taxes. As a result, many strongly objected to paying taxes for public schools.

Horace Mann of Massachusetts spearheaded the campaign for common schools. Mann was especially concerned about poor children. Their families could not afford to send them to private schools or to contribute to the support of schools in their district. Mann won over taxpayers

▲ *THE COUNTRY SCHOOL* by Winslow Homer, 1871 By the mid-1800s, free public school had gained acceptance. Horace Mann led a campaign for state-supported schools, establishing the first state board of education in 1837. **What state had the first state board of education?**

to his way of thinking by pointing out the benefits to society. He explained that education "does better than to disarm the poor of their hostility toward the rich, it prevents them being poor."

Common Schools in the 1800s

In 1837 Mann helped Massachusetts form the first state board of education in the United States. Under his leadership, the board raised teachers' salaries, established statewide standards of education, set up the first schools for teacher training, and extended the school year to six months. After many years, the efforts of Mann and other reformers resulted in common schools in most states.

During the 1840s and 1850s, the flood of immigrants into the United States helped free public schools gain general acceptance. Many Americans realized that schools were the ideal agents to teach American values to the new arrivals.

The schoolbooks already in use were ideal for introducing American values. The popular *McGuffey's Reader,* for example, focused as often on morals as on reading skills. A typical McGuffey exercise read:

> **Beautiful hands are they that do**
> **Deeds that are noble good and true;**
> **Beautiful feet are they that go**
> **Swiftly to lighten another's woe.**

Despite advances in public education between 1830 and 1860, schools needed more improvements. School buildings remained inadequate. During the late 1830s in one Connecticut county, the average school housed 30 students at a time. Yet it measured only 7 feet (2.3 m) by 18 feet (6 m). In 1842 Mann compared these cramped quarters for children with the neat buildings complete with walkways that New England farmers built for their hogs.

Other areas of education also had not changed or had not changed enough. Most states did not require that students attend school. Others required attendance for only 12 weeks a year. And most students' education ended with the eighth grade. By 1860 only about 40 public high schools existed across the nation. As late as 1900, only about 4 percent of the population between the ages of 17 and 22 went on to higher education.

★ Women, Minorities, and Schools

Even with reforms, for many Americans getting into any kind of school remained a struggle. Most areas of the country neglected the education of women, African Americans, and the physically challenged. Bold and far-sighted reformers, however, took up their cause.

Education of American Women

By the end of the Revolutionary War, most elementary schools admitted girls. Girls, however, received only a basic education. Even private schools taught girls morals and manners rather than science and mathematics.

In 1819 reformer **Emma Willard** pointed out to the New York legislature that the education of women had "been too exclusively directed to fit them for displaying . . . [their] charms. . . ." Two years later Willard remedied the situation by starting the Troy Female Seminary in New York. Parents of students there were shocked to find their daughters studying, among other subjects, anatomy. In 1824 **Catharine Beecher** founded a similar school in Connecticut. And in 1837 Mary Lyon established Mount Holyoke Seminary in Massachusetts.

Oberlin College in Ohio, founded in 1833, admitted women on the college level in 1837. Professional schools continued to reject women applicants until Geneva College admitted **Elizabeth**

Blackwell. In 1849 Blackwell became the first woman in the United States to earn a medical degree. For most women, though, higher education remained out of reach.

African American Schooling

Few places offered any kind of education to African Americans in the early 1800s. Salem, Boston, and New York City were among the exceptions.

In the 1830s Quaker **Prudence Crandall** opened her school in Connecticut to African American girls from all over the Northeast. Soon after, Connecticut passed a law forbidding schools from accepting out-of-state African American students. Crandall was arrested, tried, and convicted for breaking the law, but a higher court freed her. When Crandall reopened her school in 1834, a mob closed it down.

Almost all institutions of higher learning barred African Americans from attending. Two exceptions were Amherst College in Massachusetts and Bowdoin College in Maine. They produced the first African American college graduates in 1826.

Pennsylvania opened Lincoln University in 1854. It was the first college in the United States exclusively for African Americans. Little progress was made in higher education for African Americans until years after the Civil War.

The Hearing and Visually Impaired

Some reformers concentrated on improving the education of the hearing and visually impaired. Reverend **Thomas Gallaudet** went all the way to France to find a teacher for the hearing impaired in the United States. Two years later in 1817, Gallaudet opened the first free school for hearing-impaired students in **Hartford, Connecticut.**

Massachusetts hired **Samuel Gridley Howe** to organize the Perkins Institution for the Blind in 1831. Howe ran the Boston school for 44 years. While there he developed a raised alphabet that enabled the visually impaired to read. He also instructed teachers who eventually taught in other schools for the visually impaired. Horace Mann admired Howe's work so much that he admitted, "I should rather have built up the Blind Asylum than to have written Hamlet. . . ."

The nation made headway in the field of education in the 1800s. The words of Thomas Jefferson in 1816 reminded Americans how important it was to continue the progress.

If a nation expects to be ignorant and free, it expects what never was and never will be.

★ SECTION 2 REVIEW ★

Checking for Understanding

1. **Identify** Horace Mann, Emma Willard, Elizabeth Blackwell, Prudence Crandall, Thomas Gallaudet, Samuel Gridley Howe.

2. **Define** common school movement.

3. **What** problems existed in American education before 1830 and how were some of them resolved?

4. **Why** did many Americans object to common schools?

Critical Thinking

5. **Predicting Consequences** What would be the consequences for the nation if states today did away with their public school systems? Explain your predictions.

ACTIVITY

6. Ask your grandparents or other adults who are more than 50 years old what they remember about their public school days.

★★★

Social and Cultural Change

SETTING THE SCENE

Read to Learn . . .

★ why the treatment of the mentally ill changed in the mid-1800s.
★ what techniques temperance societies used to win people over to their beliefs.
★ how the Second Great Awakening affected reform movements.

Terms to Know

★ House of Refuge
★ temperance movement
★ prohibition
★ Second Great Awakening
★ socialism

People to Meet

★ Dorothea Dix
★ Josiah Quincy
★ John Cocke
★ Robert Owen

Places to Locate

★ Syracuse
★ Philadelphia

► DOROTHEA DIX

With pity and horror on her face, **Dorothea Dix** stared into a cell at a poorhouse—a public house for people who could not live on their own—in Danvers, Massachusetts. Inside, a young woman was beating on the cell bars. Her hair looked matted and dirty, and her clothes hung in rags. Dix stayed to observe as long as she could. But the bad smell from the cell soon forced her to leave.

★ Reforming Prisons

At the beginning of the nineteenth century, Americans viewed the United States as a land of unlimited opportunity. Many believed that those who failed did so because they had bad characters.

As a result, debtors, children who were offenders, and the mentally ill were often locked up in jails with murderers and thieves. Dorothea Dix and other reformers worked to change Americans' ways of thinking about these institutions and their inmates.

New Prison Systems

During the early 1800s, some Americans realized that mistreatment of prisoners did little to improve the characters of criminals. Worse, it warped the characters of children and debtors. After all, these prisoners were more victims of society than dangerous lawbreakers.

In response to these new ideas, states shifted their focus from punishment to rebuilding character. Beginning in 1816 New York and Pennsylvania built new prison systems near **Syracuse** and **Philadelphia.** The authorities there attempted to change prisoners through work, Bible study, and meditation.

Josiah Quincy became a vocal prison reformer in Massachusetts. During the 1820s he led a pamphlet crusade against cruelty in New England prisons. He also spoke out against locking up children with hardened criminals. In 1823 Quincy became mayor of Boston. During his administration, he helped form the Prison Discipline Society and started making changes in prisons.

Due to the efforts of reformers like Quincy, Boston and other places in the United States opened Houses of Refuge during the 1820s. These institutions took in only very young offenders. The children there attended classes, learned trades, and received religious instruction.

Rescuing Mentally Ill Prisoners

Dorothea Dix first observed prison conditions while teaching Sunday school at a Boston prison for women in 1841. She wanted to find out if all the prisons in the state were as appalling. Over a two-year period, Dix investigated 18 state penitentiaries, 300 county jails, and more than 500 poorhouses.

Dix decided to appeal to the Massachusetts government for help. In 1843 she addressed the following report to the state legislature:

❝ **I proceed, gentlemen, briefly to call your attention to the present state of Insane Persons confined . . . , in cages, closets, cellars, stalls, pens! Chained, naked, beaten with rods, and lashed into obedience. . . .** ❞

As a result of Dix's report, Massachusetts passed a law to build mental hospitals where mental illness could be treated as a disease rather than a crime. Dix continued her appeals in New England and other parts of the nation. By 1852 she had persuaded 11 states to open hospitals for persons with mental illness.

★ Crusading for Temperance

Reformers considered alcoholism—the excessive and continued use of alcoholic drinks—a major cause of crime. After the American Revolution, rum, beer, whiskey, and hard cider became cheap and easy to get. As a result, the number of American alcoholics increased. Crime, poverty, and the abuse of wives and children increased right along with it.

Alcohol abuse was widespread during this time. Employers often paid part of workers' wages in rum or whiskey. Workers took rum breaks similar to today's coffee breaks.

Reformers felt the widespread use and abuse of alcohol undermined American society. Most of the reform leaders were religious leaders interested in doing away with the social evils of poverty and crime, often brought about by heavy drinking.

The reformers began a campaign against drinking. The campaign is known as the temperance movement. In 1826 concerned citizens in Boston formed the American Temperance Society, and in a few years about 1,000 local organizations sprang up across the nation. Some temperance groups took a moderate approach and asked people to drink less alcohol. Other groups insisted that the sale of alcohol be banned altogether.

The Campaign Against Alcohol

Southerners turned out to be especially zealous temperance workers. Well-to-do planter Joseph Flourney toured Georgia collecting signatures on a petition requesting the statewide prohibition, or banning, of liquor. Another wealthy planter, **John Cocke** of Virginia, led the crusade for a nationwide prohibition of alcohol. In 1836 Cocke became the president of the American Temperance Union.

Northern and Southern temperance societies used propaganda to win support for their cause. They held meetings, gave speeches, and distributed pamphlets. They even sang songs such as "Drink Nothing, Boys, but Water," and "Father, Bring Home Your Money Tonight."

State legislators took the reformers' message to heart. In 1838 Massachusetts passed the "Fifteen-Gallon Law." This act banned the sale of less than 15 gallons of liquor at a time, unless doctors prescribed it as medicine. In 1851 Maine became the first state to ban the manufacture and sale of alcoholic drinks.

By 1857 several states had passed prohibition laws. Many Americans protested the laws, and most of the laws were later repealed. The temperance movement stayed alive, though, and found renewed support later in the century.

▲ TEMPERANCE BANNERS

★ The Second Great Awakening

A revival, or reawakening, of religious faith and social feeling occurred in the early 1800s. During this period ministers went from town to town preaching to large crowds. Preachers urged listeners to renew their faith and cure the evils of society. This movement, called the Second Great Awakening, filled many Americans with determination to make social reforms.

Ideal Communities

Some religious reformers wished to reorganize American society. These reformers attempted to organize societies that ensured an ideal life for all members. Such societies practiced communal living. Communal living means that all members of a community live together and are considered equal.

A new European idea called socialism influenced the founders of these societies. Socialism means that a community of people own all property together, not as individuals. Socialists tried to do away with poverty and inequality.

A famous English socialist, **Robert Owen,** started such a community at New Harmony, Indiana. All adults were expected to work eight hours a day, while children received free educations. Many of the community members, though, found it hard to follow Owen's strict policies. By 1827 the community had failed.

Religious Communal Groups

Joseph Smith attempted to build a religious communal society by founding the Church of Jesus Christ of Latter-day Saints, or the Mormon Church. Smith's movement, called Mormonism, enjoyed rapid growth and established communal living at Kirtland, Ohio. Later, persecution drove the Mormons west to Utah.

▲ **THE SERMON** by Julius Gari Melchers, 1886 Religion regained importance in the early 1800s. Revival meetings, communal groups, and ideal social communities were abundant during this time. **What European idea helped shape the beliefs of people trying to form ideal communities?**

The Shakers, founded by Ann Lee in 1772, also established communal living. They isolated themselves from the rest of the world and supported themselves by working in small industries. The Shakers led simple lives. Although few Shakers are left, their handiwork, especially furniture, is highly valued by collectors today.

The growth of religious groups, revival meetings, the building of thousands of new churches, and the founding of scores of colleges and universities characterized the Second Great Awakening. Although most of those caught up in the Second Great Awakening were white, free African Americans established their own churches at this time. These Baptist and Methodist churches proclaimed a message of spiritual salvation. This message had special meaning for those who suffered from the bonds of slavery.

★ SECTION 3 REVIEW ★

★★★★★★★★★★★★★★★★★★★   ★★★★★★★★★★★★★★★★★★★

Checking for Understanding

1. **Identify** Dorothea Dix, Josiah Quincy, John Cocke, Robert Owen, Syracuse, Philadelphia.

2. **Define** House of Refuge, temperance movement, prohibition, Second Great Awakening, socialism.

3. **How** did temperance societies win people over to their beliefs?

4. **How** did the Second Great Awakening influence reform movements?

Critical Thinking

5. **Determining Cause and Effect** What effect did Dorothea Dix's appeals on behalf of mentally ill persons have on state legislatures?

ACTIVITY

6. Compose and record a song designed to win supporters for one of the reform movements discussed in the section.

★★

The Antislavery Movement

SETTING THE SCENE

Read to Learn . . .

★ who led the fight against slavery.
★ what techniques antislavery leaders used to further their cause.
★ how Americans responded to abolitionists.

Terms to Know

★ abolitionist
★ emancipation
★ Underground Railroad

People to Meet

★ David Walker
★ William Lloyd Garrison
★ Angelina and Sarah Grimké
★ Elijah Lovejoy
★ Frederick Douglass
★ Harriet Tubman

ATTENTION
SOUTHERN MEN!
DOWN WITH
THE ABOLITION PRESS
MEET AT
SCHNEIDER'S
A N o'clock This Night
DECEMBER 26, 1860

◀ POSTER AGAINST ABOLITION

M r. Johnson and his servant quietly waited to board the northbound steamboat. The other passengers could not make out Johnson's face because a handkerchief was tied around his head as if he had a toothache. Johnson and his servant appeared very anxious.

They had good reason to be nervous. Johnson was actually Ellen Craft, the servant was her husband William, and they were fugitive slaves headed for freedom.

★ The Antislavery Movement

Ellen and William escaped from a Southern plantation. Planters depended on enslaved persons to work their cotton and tobacco fields. By 1840 nearly 2.5 million enslaved people lived in the South.

At one time the North also had slavery. By 1804 every Northern state legislature had passed laws to eliminate it. The Southern economy, though, depended on slave labor. That is why Ellen and William headed north. They were part of an ever-growing number of enslaved African Americans who fled to free territory. Many of these men and women were aided by abolitionists—people who wanted to end slavery.

Antislavery Societies

Although a few American colonists had opposed slavery, an organized antislavery movement did not begin until after the

Revolutionary War. A religious group called Quakers started the antislavery movement. Quakers had opposed slavery since colonial times. In 1775 the Quakers organized the first antislavery society.

Other groups wished to end slavery for political reasons. The Declaration of Independence stated that "all men are created equal." Yet many Americans did not apply this statement to African Americans. Reformers felt this situation had to change. By 1792 antislavery groups had sprung up in every state from Massachusetts to Virginia.

The American Colonization Society

Meanwhile the **American Colonization Society** stated it could help free African Americans. Founded in 1817, the society set up a colony for free African Americans. In 1822 President James Monroe helped the society establish a colony, **Liberia,** in western Africa.

At first the society recruited African Americans to settle in Liberia. Many African Americans, though, wished to remain in the United States, their home. African Americans feared that the society aimed to strengthen slavery. By getting rid of free African Americans, slaveholders could build up the institution of slavery without opposition.

Abolitionist Leaders

Free African Americans joined mostly upper-class whites and became the backbone of the fight to end slavery. In 1827 two African Americans, **John Russwurm** and **Samuel Cornish,** began the first African American newspaper, an antislavery newspaper called *Freedom's Journal.* Each issue exposed the horrors of slavery and criticized slaveholders. African American **David Walker** also stood out among early abolitionists. He lectured against slavery and contributed articles to *Freedom's Journal.*

In 1829 Walker published *An Appeal to the Coloured Citizens of the World.* Instead of speaking to would-be abolitionists, Walker's pamphlet directly addressed enslaved persons. In his *Appeal* Walker called on enslaved men and women to fight for their freedom. He also cautioned and encouraged them.

66 **Never make an attempt to gain [your] freedom . . . until you see your way clear— when that hour arrives and you move, be not afraid or dismayed. . . . Our sufferings will come to an end, in spite of all the Americans this side of eternity.** 99

Walker's powerful messages helped give rise to a new, more militant wave of abolitionists.

Picturing History ▲ AMERICAN SLAVE MARKET Abolitionists tried to expose the horrors of enslavement, such as slave auctions, in antislavery newspapers. **Who started the first African American newspaper?**

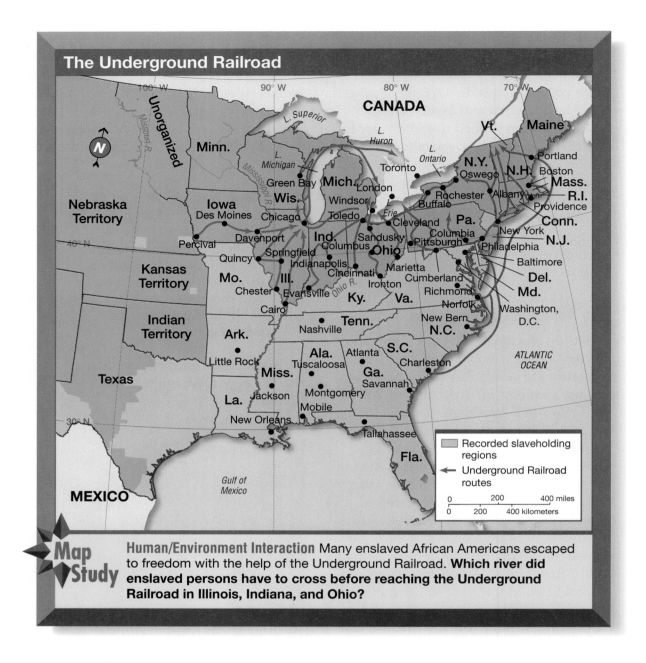

The Underground Railroad

Recorded slaveholding regions

← Underground Railroad routes

Map Study **Human/Environment Interaction** Many enslaved African Americans escaped to freedom with the help of the Underground Railroad. **Which river did enslaved persons have to cross before reaching the Underground Railroad in Illinois, Indiana, and Ohio?**

★ Abolitionists Call for Immediate Action

In 1831 white abolitionist **William Lloyd Garrison** founded *The Liberator,* a Boston antislavery newspaper. In the first issue, Garrison demanded the immediate emancipation, or freeing, of all enslaved persons. He urged abolitionists to take action without delay. "The success of any great moral enterprise," he once wrote, "does not depend upon numbers." Garrison denounced both Northerners who refused to be shocked by slavery and Southerners who held enslaved persons.

The Fight Against Slavery Expands

In 1833 Garrison founded the New England Anti-Slavery Society. Two years later abolitionists formed the American Anti-Slavery Society. Sixty-three delegates from 11 states attended the society's first meeting. This new, broader organization gave the antislavery cause greater strength and fresh hope. By 1836 abolitionists had formed 500 local chapters around the country, and by 1840 membership had risen to more than 150,000. Abolitionist societies included both African American and white members.

Unlike early antislavery societies, those formed in the 1830s demanded immediate and unconditional emancipation.

Supporters of the Antislavery Movement

Abolitionists came from all sections of the country. Sisters **Angelina** and **Sarah Grimké,** born on a plantation in South Carolina, moved to Philadelphia to speak out against the horrors of slavery that they had witnessed firsthand. Journalist **Elijah Lovejoy** campaigned for abolition in the West. Editor **Horace Greeley** lobbied for emancipation in the *New York Tribune,* and New Englander **Wendell Phillips** spoke so eloquently against slavery that people called him "abolition's golden trumpet."

The North also had many prominent African American abolitionists, such as writer William Nell and minister Henry Highland Garnet. Garnet became famous for his impassioned challenge to enslaved people: "Rather die free men than live to be slaves."

Isabella Baumfree, although born into slavery in New York, gained her freedom when New York abolished slavery. She changed her name to **Sojourner Truth** and vowed to tell the world about the cruelty of slavery. She began a tireless crusade against injustice.

The most articulate African American spokesperson for the cause was **Frederick Douglass.** Born into slavery, Douglass secretly taught himself to read, although Southern laws prohibited it. Douglass escaped from slavery in Maryland in 1838 and settled in Massachusetts. By 1842, speaking as "a recent graduate from the institution of slavery with his diploma on his back," he captivated audiences by talking about his life in bondage. Dou-

glass also spoke out against the injustices faced by free African Americans.

In addition to his public speaking, Douglass edited a widely read abolitionist journal called the *North Star.* Douglass's speaking and writing abilities so impressed audiences that opponents refused to believe he had been a slave. They alleged he was an impostor put in place by the abolitionists. In reply, he wrote three very moving autobiographies.

The Underground Railroad

Many abolitionists, like Douglass, did more than lecture and write. They became "conductors" on the Underground Railroad. The Underground Railroad began around 1817. It was not an actual railroad but a series of houses where conductors hid runaway enslaved persons and helped them reach the next "station," or safe house, on the railroad. Enslaved African Americans made their way to the North or Canada on the railroad.

Harriet Tubman became the most famous African American conductor on the Underground Railroad. Tubman fled from slavery in 1849. Later she explained why she risked her life to escape:

 There was one of two things I had a right to, liberty or death; if I could not have the one, I would have the other.

Afterward, Tubman helped others escape. She returned to the South 19 times and led more than 300 enslaved people— including her own parents—to freedom. Slaveholders offered a reward of $40,000 for her, dead or alive. But she managed to avoid discovery time after time.

★ Response to the Antislavery Movement

Abolitionists, such as William Lloyd Garrison, soon became unpopular in the North and South. Garrison's fiery declarations against slavery raised tensions between Northerners and Southerners. He chose as his motto, "No union with slaveholders," and supported the peaceful separation of the free states from the slave states.

Northern Workers React Against Abolitionists

Many Northerners disapproved of the antislavery movement. These Northerners included mostly mill owners and bankers who depended on cotton from the South. They viewed the abolitionists' attacks on slavery as threats to their businesses and wealth. Other Northerners feared that free African Americans would come to the North and take their jobs.

Northerners snubbed abolitionists and excluded them from social gatherings. They pelted antislavery speakers with eggs and stones. Some abolitionists even lost their jobs because of their beliefs.

One abolitionist, Elijah Lovejoy, lost his life because of his beliefs. He made some Northerners angry by writing antislavery editorials in his Illinois journal, the *Alton Observer*. Three times a mob destroyed his printing presses. Lovejoy continued to attack slavery. On November 7, 1837, attackers set fire to his presses and then shot Lovejoy. His death shocked many Northerners and caused them to join the antislavery movement.

Southerners Defend Slavery

The movement to end slavery made many Southerners uneasy. They accused abolitionists of encouraging violence. Southern clergy argued that the Bible condoned slavery. Others contended slaveholders treated the enslaved well. Southerners who favored abolition usually remained quiet or moved north.

The antislavery movement deepened the division between the North and the South. The South threatened to leave the Union unless government authorities agreed to suppress abolitionist materials. Southern postal workers refused to deliver abolitionist newspapers.

The antislavery movement threatened the Southern way of life and Southern hostility to abolition continued to grow. In 1836 under Southern pressure, the House of Representatives passed a gag rule providing that all abolitionist proposals should be set aside without debate.

Despite the tensions, the antislavery movement affected national politics very little at first. The Missouri Compromise had fixed boundaries between slave and free states. At this time no prominent politician wished to endanger the Union by attacking slavery in the South.

★ SECTION 4 REVIEW ★

Checking for Understanding

1. **Identify** David Walker, William Lloyd Garrison, Angelina and Sarah Grimké, Elijah Lovejoy, Frederick Douglass, Harriet Tubman.
2. **Define** abolitionist, emancipation, Underground Railroad.
3. **What** techniques did abolitionists use to further their cause?
4. **How** did many Americans react to abolitionists?

Critical Thinking

5. **Making Inferences** Why did the Grimkés move from South Carolina to Philadelphia?

ACTIVITY

6. Find a political cartoon that depicts abolitionists or expresses an abolitionist sentiment. Use it as a model to create your own cartoon about the antislavery movement.

★★

The Women's Rights Movement

SETTING THE SCENE

Read to Learn . . .

★ why women became unhappy with their positions in the mid-1800s.

★ how working in the antislavery movement prepared women to fight for their own rights.

★ what traits leaders of the women's rights movement shared.

Terms to Know

★ suffrage

People to Meet

★ Margaret Fuller
★ Lucretia Coffin Mott
★ Elizabeth Cady Stanton
★ Lucy Stone
★ Susan B. Anthony

Places to Locate

★ London
★ Seneca Falls

► ELIZABETH CADY STANTON

Women took a special interest in the antislavery movement. As they fought for social reform for African Americans, they realized that they also lacked full social and political rights. When women such as Angelina and Sarah Grimké tried to participate actively in the antislavery movement, they often met resistance. As a result, many abolitionists became crusaders for women's rights.

Equal rights for women would require major reform. In the 1800s women actually had fewer rights than in colonial times. They had few political or legal rights. Women could not vote. They could not hold public office. A woman's husband owned all of her property.

★ Antislavery Movement Gives Women a Boost

Women from New England to Ohio joined the antislavery societies. They worked hard, gathering signatures on thousands of petitions to send to Congress. They also read about and discussed the abuses of slavery. Many saw similarities between the treatment of enslaved persons and women.

In her book *Woman in the Nineteenth Century*, journalist **Margaret Fuller** observed that "there exists in the minds of men a tone of feeling toward women as towards slaves." Abolitionists Angelina and Sarah Grimké confronted this feeling when they spoke to antislavery groups. Audiences did not criticize their stand on slavery. They did, though, question their right to speak in public.

As a result, the Grimkés soon found themselves in the midst of "an entirely new contest—a contest for the rights of woman." Sarah wrote that "all I ask . . . is that [men] will take their feet from off our necks and permit us to stand upright."

★ The Women's Rights Movement

Their involvement in the antislavery movement and other reform movements gave women roles outside their homes and families. They learned valuable skills, such as organizing, working together, and speaking in public. Eventually they used these skills to further their own cause— the women's rights movement.

In 1840 nine women from the United States attended the World Anti-Slavery Convention in **London.** When the women arrived at the convention, however, the male delegates barred them from participating. The women and some male allies protested. On the first day of the convention, delegates debated the situation.

Clergy at the convention considered it improper for women to participate. Other male delegates declared women "unfit for public or business meetings." In the end, the majority of delegates decided that women could not take part in discussions. Instead, the women delegates would have to sit in the gallery behind a curtain.

Humiliated and angry, two of the women, **Lucretia Coffin Mott** and **Elizabeth Cady Stanton,** spent hours after the meetings talking about women's position in society. They realized that they could not bring about social change if they themselves lacked social and political rights. Stanton and Mott "resolved to hold a convention as soon as we returned home, and form a society to advocate the rights of women."

Linking Past and Present

Pants for Women

At one time a woman who wore pants created a public scandal.

Then

Ladies' Legwear Creates Scandal

In the early 1850s, women's rights worker Amelia Jenks Bloomer thought that huge hoops and long skirts kept women from moving about easily and naturally. She began wearing her solution to the problem of women's clothing—a pair of loose trousers gathered at the ankles. The trousers—invented by Elizabeth Miller but commonly called "bloomers"— caused quite a sensation. Bloomer stopped wearing bloomers after a time because she believed that they distracted attention from the more important features of the women's rights movement.

◀ BLOOMERS UNDER A SKIRT

Now

Pants in Every Woman's Wardrobe

Bloomers were about 80 years ahead of the times. Women wearing pants became commonplace in the 1930s, and pants outfits became popular in the 1940s. Today women wear pants of all lengths and styles, for any and every occasion.

▲ MODERN PANTSUIT

The Seneca Falls Convention

Eight years passed before the two friends organized their convention. On July 19, 1848, the first women's rights convention opened in **Seneca Falls, New York.** Both male and female delegates attended the convention. The delegates issued the Seneca Falls Declaration, which proclaimed that "all men and women are created equal."

Then the declaration listed several resolutions. One of them demanded **suffrage,** or the right to vote, for women. Even supporters of women's rights hesitated to pass this bold demand. Mott exclaimed, "Oh, Lizzie, thou will make us ridiculous! We must go slowly." But Stanton refused to withdraw the resolution. After much heated debate, it passed by a narrow margin.

The Seneca Falls Convention marked the beginning of an organized women's rights movement. Following the convention, women did not achieve all of their demands. They did, however, overcome some obstacles. Many states passed laws permitting women to own their own property and keep their earnings. Many men and women, though, continued to oppose the movement. Most politicians ignored or acted hostile to the issue of women's rights.

▲ **LUCY STONE**

Biography ★★★

Lucy Stone Speaks Out

The work of dedicated women like **Lucy Stone** kept the "Woman Question" from fading away. Born in 1818 on a Massachusetts farm, Stone had to plead with her father to let her go to school. Her brothers had been sent to college, but Stone's father, like many people, thought that girls needed only an elementary education.

At 16 Stone became a teacher and resolved to attend college. At age 25 Stone entered Oberlin College in Ohio. Despite a lack of money, she was determined to graduate. She worked three jobs at once but could pay for only two years of schooling. After much hesitation her father lent her enough money to finish her education.

At graduation time Oberlin teachers invited Stone to write an address for the graduation ceremonies. Stone, though, could not give her own speech. Women were barred from speaking publicly. A man would have to read her speech. So Stone refused to write it.

Over the years Stone experienced unfair treatment many times. As a teacher she earned less than men doing the same work. As a student she struggled to pay for her education while her father readily paid her brothers' way. When she became a public speaker after earning her degree, she faced disapproval and worse. During Stone's lectures critics attacked her in mobs, doused her with water, and hit her with a book.

Despite people's hostility Stone persevered. She felt constantly reminded of the inferiority of women in her society. This became a common theme in the lives of women who participated in the women's rights movement.

Stone began speaking publicly for women's rights in 1847. She defiantly asserted her goal:

> **I expect to plead not for the slave only, but for suffering humanity everywhere. Especially do I mean to labor for the elevation of my sex.**

Audiences likened her voice to "a silver bell." Years later she became known as "the morning star of the women's rights movement." ★★★

Susan B. Anthony Enters the Movement

Susan B. Anthony, a powerful organizer, soon joined the women's rights movement. Anthony grew up as a Quaker. Her father encouraged her to get an education and so she became a teacher. A dedicated reformer, Anthony joined the temperance movement and worked for the American Anti-Slavery Society.

In the spring of 1851, Anthony met Elizabeth Cady Stanton, and the two formed a lifelong friendship. Anthony later became president of the American Woman Suffrage Association and worked tirelessly to win other rights for women. Anthony also became one of the first to urge full participation of African Americans in the woman suffrage movement.

Through her efforts the state of New York agreed to grant married women the guardianship of their children and control of their own wages. Today Anthony is one of the early movement's best-remembered leaders.

African American Women Join the Struggle

African American women were inspired to fight for women's rights as they had fought for the rights of African Americans.

Sojourner Truth, a former slave, spoke out against slavery and in defense of women's rights. No African American woman attended the Seneca Falls Convention and only a few other women's rights conventions because abolition remained a more urgent concern. Truth, however, often attended the meetings to remind women that their African American sisters had a place in the movement for women's rights.

As African American women fought to end slavery, they inspired women with their tremendous achievements. Harriet Brent Jacobs wrote *Incidents in the Life of a Slave Girl* and reminded women they could influence their own lives.

★ SECTION 5 REVIEW ★

Checking for Understanding

1. **Identify** Margaret Fuller, Lucretia Coffin Mott, Elizabeth Cady Stanton, Lucy Stone, Susan B. Anthony, London, Seneca Falls.

2. **Define** suffrage.

3. **Why** did women become unhappy with their position in the mid-1800s? About what areas of their daily lives were they most concerned?

4. **How** did women's work in the antislavery movement prepare them to fight for their own rights?

Critical Thinking

5. **Comparing and Contrasting** Compare the personalities of the two founders of the women's rights movement, Lucretia Coffin Mott and Elizabeth Cady Stanton.

ACTIVITY

6. Are women today denied any rights that men have? Draw up an agenda for a new Seneca Falls Convention listing topics for discussion and items to be put up for a vote.

BUILDING SKILLS
Critical Thinking Skills

Drawing Conclusions

Letitia places a package of frozen meat on the kitchen counter to defrost and leaves the house. When she returns, the empty meat package is lying on the floor next to her dog Prudence. What has happened?

Learning the Skill

Letitia uses what she knows about her dog to **draw a conclusion:** Prudence snatched the meat and ate it. Next Letitia searches the house for the meat. When she fails to find it, she feels certain that her conclusion is correct.

You can use the same process Letitia used whenever you read. It can help you understand facts that are stated indirectly. You can also exercise this skill to make a judgment. For example, as a member of a jury, you would weigh evidence and your knowledge of human behavior to draw a conclusion about a defendant's guilt or innocence.

Here are some steps to follow when drawing a conclusion:

- **Review** the facts that are stated directly.
- **Add** your knowledge and insight to develop a conclusion.
- **Look** for information to check the accuracy of your conclusion.

Practicing the Skill

Read these letters from Susan B. Anthony to Elizabeth Cady Stanton. Then answer the questions that follow.

> Rochester, May 26, 1856
>
> Dear Mrs. Stanton,
>
> I am now . . . ready to commence operations on that report [to the New York Teacher's Convention]. Don't you think it would be a good plan to first state *what* we mean by educating the sexes together, then go on to show how the few institutions that profess to give *equal* education fail? . . . [P]lease mark out a plan and give [it to] me as soon as you can.

▲ SUSAN B. ANTHONY

> Thursday night, June 5, 1856
>
> . . . And, Mrs. Stanton, not a *word written* on that Address for Teacher's Convention. . . . I beg you . . . set yourself about the work. It is of but small moment *who writes* the Address, but of *vast moment* that it be well done. . . . [D]on't say *No* nor *don't delay* it a moment. . . .

1. What is the subject of the speech referred to in the letters?

2. Which statements support your conclusion?

3. Who wrote the speech? Who delivered it?

4. Which statements support these conclusions?

5. What evidence could help prove your conclusions?

APPLYING THE SKILL

6. Read a newspaper article about a criminal court case. Use the facts in the article to draw a conclusion about the innocence or guilt of the accused.

Using Key Vocabulary

Use the vocabulary words below to complete the following sentences.

emancipation
temperance movement
Second Great Awakening
abolitionists
Underground Railroad

1. Reformers who worked to limit the manufacture and sale of alcoholic beverages belonged to the _____.

2. People who demanded an end to slavery were called _____.

3. The _____ helped enslaved people escape to the North.

4. William Lloyd Garrison demanded the immediate _____ of all enslaved persons in *The Liberator*.

5. The religious revival that swept the nation in the 1800s was called the _____.

Reviewing Facts

1. **List** three novels from the 1800s with American characters and settings.

2. **Describe** changes in education after 1830.

3. **Explain** how the Second Great Awakening affected reform movements between 1830 and 1860.

4. **List** four leaders in the antislavery movement.

5. **Identify** five rights that men denied women in the 1800s.

History and Geography

Higher Education

Use the numbers on the map to answer the following questions.

1. **Location**   Based on the information on the map, which two states had the most colleges and universities in 1830?

2. **Location**   Which two states had the most colleges and universities in 1860?

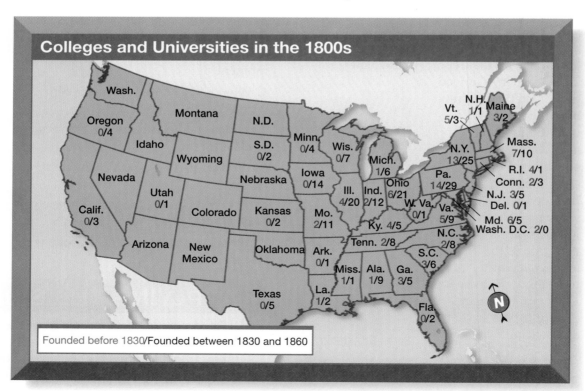

Colleges and Universities in the 1800s

Wash.
Oregon 0/4
Montana
N.D.
N.H. 1/1
Vt. 5/3
Maine 3/2
Idaho
S.D. 0/2
Minn. 0/4
Wis. 0/7
N.Y. 13/25
Mass. 7/10
Wyoming
Mich. 1/6
Pa. 14/29
R.I. 4/1
Conn. 2/3
Nevada
Nebraska
Iowa 0/14
Ohio 6/21
N.J. 3/5
Utah 0/1
Ill. 4/20
Ind. 2/12
W. Va. 0/1
Va. 5/9
Del. 0/1
Calif. 0/3
Colorado
Kansas 0/2
Mo. 2/11
Ky. 4/5
Md. 6/5
Wash. D.C. 2/0
Arizona
New Mexico
Oklahoma
Ark. 0/1
Tenn. 2/8
N.C. 2/8
S.C. 3/6
Texas 0/5
La. 1/2
Miss. 1/1
Ala. 1/9
Ga. 3/5
Fla. 0/2
N

Founded before 1830/Founded between 1830 and 1860

CHAPTER 15 ★ REVIEW

Understanding Concepts

Beliefs, Ideas, and Institutions

1. How did Jacksonian democracy help change American literature?

2. Why did reformers argue that more Americans should be better educated in the 1800s?

Civil Rights and Liberties

3. Why did Dorothea Dix have to appeal to state legislatures on the behalf of the mentally ill?

4. How did early antislavery societies differ from the New England Anti-Slavery Society?

5. What was the relationship between the abolitionist and the women's rights movements?

Critical Thinking

1. **Interpreting Primary Sources** In 1838 one observer commented:

> " A peaceable man can hardly venture to eat or drink, or to go to bed or to get up, to correct his children or to kiss his wife, without obtaining the permission and direction of some . . . society. "

How does the speaker feel about reformers?

2. **Drawing Conclusions** How did poet Henry Wadsworth Longfellow feel about America's people?

3. **Summarizing** Summarize the goals of reformers between 1830 and 1860.

Cooperative Learning Interdisciplinary Activity: Language Arts

In small groups plan an escape on the Underground Railroad. Have each group member plan a part of your escape, such as what route you will take and what supplies are needed. Write your plan and include a map or diagram of your route.

Practicing Skills

Drawing Conclusions

Read the passage and answer the questions below. Remember to review the information and add your own knowledge before drawing any conclusions.

> " Master Thomas at length said he would stand it no longer. I had lived with him nine months, during which time he had given me a number of severe whippings, all to no good purpose. He resolved to put me out, as he said, to be broken; and, for this purpose, he let me for one year to a man named Edward Covey. . . . "

—Frederick Douglass, 1845

1. How long had Douglass lived with Thomas?

2. Why did Thomas send Douglass to Covey's place for a year?

3. Which statements from the passage support your conclusion?

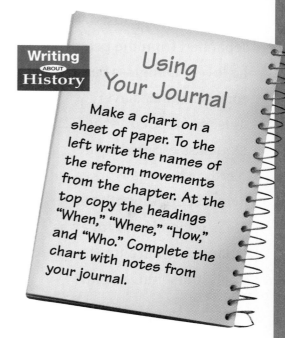

Writing ABOUT History

Using Your Journal

Make a chart on a sheet of paper. To the left write the names of the reform movements from the chapter. At the top copy the headings "When," "Where," "How," and "Who." Complete the chart with notes from your journal.

Frederick Douglass's childhood in the South was typical of slaves. He was neglected, abused, and separated from the people he loved. Douglass became convinced that slavery must be stopped. At age 21, Douglass escaped to the North, where he worked to gain freedom for others. He is remembered today as a powerful voice for the abolitionist movement.

Read to Discover

In this passage from his autobiography, Frederick Douglass begins to teach himself to write. How did he show off his accomplishments among other boys? What risks did he take to teach himself? After reading this passage, why do you think Douglass was later considered a well-educated adult?

Reader's Dictionary

scow	type of boat
ballast	something carried on a ship to make it sail evenly
treacherous	dishonest
hewing	cutting down
elicited	brought about
flogging	beating

from *My Bondage and My Freedom*

by Frederick Douglass (1818–1895)

I went, one day, on the wharf . . . and seeing two Irishmen unloading a large scow of stone, or ballast, I went on board, unasked, and helped them. When we had finished the work, one of the men . . . asked . . . if I were [a] slave. I told him "I was a slave for life.". . . They both had much to say about the matter, and expressed the deepest sympathy with me. . . . They went so far as to tell me that I ought to run away, and go to the [N]orth; that I should find friends there, and that I should then be as free as anybody. I, however, pretended not to be interested in what they said, for I feared they might be treacherous. White men have been known to encourage slaves to escape, and then—to get the reward—they have kidnapped them, and returned them to their masters. . . . I was too young to think of running away immediately; besides, I wished to learn to write before going. . . .

After this manner I began to learn to write: I was much in the ship yard, . . . and I observed that the carpenters, after hewing and getting a piece of timber ready for use, wrote on it the initials of the name of that part of the ship for which it was intended. . . . I soon learned these letters, and for what they were placed on the timbers.

My work now, was to keep fire under the steam box, and to watch the ship yard while the carpenters had gone to dinner. This interval gave me a fine opportunity for copying the letters named . . . and the thought was soon present, "if I can make four [letters] I can make more.". . . [W]hen I met boys about the Bethel Church, or on any of our playgrounds, I . . . would make the letters which I had been so fortunate as to learn, and ask them to "beat that if they could." With playmates for my teachers, fences and pavements for my copy books, and chalk for my pen and ink, I learned the art of writing. . . . By this time, my little "Master Tommy" had grown to be a big boy, and had written over a number of copy books and brought them home. They had been shown to the neighbors, had elicited due praise, and were now laid carefully away. . . . When my mistress left me in charge of the house, I had a grand time; I got Master Tommy's copy books and a pen and ink, and, in the ample spaces between the lines, I wrote other lines as nearly like his as possible. The process was a tedious one, and I ran the risk of getting a flogging for marring the highly prized copy books of the oldest son. . . . [S]leeping as I did in the kitchen loft—a room seldom visited by any of the family—I got a flour barrel up there, and a chair; and upon the head of that barrel I have written, (or endeavored to write,) copying from the [B]ible and the Methodist hymn book, and other books

▲ SOUTHERN PLANTATION SLAVE QUARTERS

which had accumulated on my hands, till late at night, and when all the family were in bed and asleep.

Responding to Literature

1. Why did young Douglass pretend to be uninterested in what the Irishmen on the wharf said?

2. How did Douglass learn to make letters and write words?

3. How did the location of Douglass's sleeping space help him learn to write?

ACTIVITY

4. Create a comic strip with four or five panels. In the panels, illustrate the story of how Frederick Douglass learned to write. Include "word balloons" to show some thoughts you think he might have had.

Chapter 13

The Age of Jackson

In the early 1800s, white males received the right to vote without restrictions based on wealth, religion, or property. During the same years, **nominating conventions** replaced caucuses as methods of choosing candidates for public office. These changes broadened American democracy. Women, African Americans, and Native Americans, however, were still denied suffrage.

Democrat **Andrew Jackson** won the presidency in 1828 as the hero of the common people. He made wide use of the **spoils system** and fought the Bank of the United States.

Debate over import tariffs brought conflict between the North and South. Led by **John C. Calhoun,** Southern members of Congress defended the idea of nullification. In 1832 South Carolina threatened to secede. Jackson opposed Southern states' rights claims. He sided with the South, however, when he enforced the tragic removal of Native Americans from their homes in the East.

▲ THE TRAIL OF TEARS

Democratic Vice President **Martin Van Buren** easily won the presidency after Jackson's second term. Economic hard times and the **Panic of 1837,** however, made Van Buren's presidency difficult. In 1840 **William Henry Harrison** and **John Tyler** swept into office. Vice President Tyler stepped into the presidency after Harrison's death.

CAUSES

- Easy bank loans encourage land speculation
- Jackson requires specie for government land purchases
- Speculators lose money and cannot repay bank loans

• Bank Panic of 1837

EFFECTS

- Economic crisis deepens throughout the land
- Federal government ends deposits in private banks
- Government creates federal treasury to store its funds

Chapter 14

Manifest Destiny

By 1800 both the United States and Great Britain had a foothold in the Oregon Country. This area included present-day Oregon, Washington, Idaho, and parts of Wyoming and Montana. The Lewis and Clark expedition, fur traders, missionaries, and early settlers strengthened United States claims to Oregon. In 1848 the United States annexed Oregon in a peaceful border settlement with Britain.

While wagon trains rolled along the Oregon Trail in the north, other American settlers were moving into Texas. **Stephen F. Austin,** under a grant from the Mexican government, founded the first and most successful colony in 1825. Disagreements over slavery and Mexican laws led Texans to declare independence from Mexico in 1836. By this time, the spirit of Manifest Destiny had overtaken the country, and many Americans wanted to annex Texas. Annexation took place in 1844.

Two years later, the United States declared war against Mexico. Under the 1848 **Treaty of Guadalupe Hidalgo,** the United States acquired the Mexican Cession. This territory took in present-day California, Nevada, Utah, and parts of Arizona, Colorado, Wyoming, and New Mexico. The nation now stretched from sea to sea.

Mormon settlers, arriving in 1847, had already started an American settlement in Utah. News of gold finds in California brought a rush of settlers to the territory in 1849. In 1850 California became a state.

Chapter 15

The Spirit of Reform

Early American artists and writers copied the styles and themes popular in Europe. During the 1800s, however, American artists and writers turned to American subjects.

▲ ESCAPING ON THE UNDERGROUND RAILROAD

From the early to mid-1800s, reformers worked to improve American society. Some reforms resulted in better treatment of prisoners and mentally handicapped persons. Others checked alcohol abuse. Although opposed by Southern planters and some Northerners, the antislavery movement gained strength. **Abolitionists** spoke publicly and wrote boldly in favor of an immediate end to slavery. After 1840 women leaders started a movement of their own to gain equal rights with men. Women's status throughout the 1800s, however, remained inferior to men's.

▲ AMONG THE SIERRA NEVADA MOUNTAINS
BY ALBERT BIERSTADT, 1868

Understanding Unit Themes

1. **American Democracy** How did the philosophy of President Andrew Jackson help enlarge democracy? How did the use of nominating conventions affect democracy?

2. **Conflict and Cooperation** Why did the United States declare war on Mexico?

3. **Ideas, Beliefs, and Institutions** How did American art and literature change after 1800?

4. **The Individual and Family Life** How did the efforts of Dorothea Dix, Harriet Tubman, William Lloyd Garrison, and Susan B. Anthony influence America's history?

5. **Civil Rights and Liberties** How did the activities of reformers during this period affect American education today?

UNIT SIX
RIFT AND REUNION
1820-1877

★★

▲ CIVIL WAR
OIL LAMP

History AND ART

The Last Salute
by Don Troiani, 1988

Present-day painter Don Troiani shows the South surrendering at the end of the Civil War. Generals from the North and South salute one another at the beginning of the ceremony.

SETTING THE SCENE

In the mid-1800s, differences between the North and the South grew so strong that compromise no longer seemed possible. Tragically, Americans turned to civil war to settle their disagreements.

▶ *THE LIBERATOR* NEWSPAPER

Themes

★ Economic Development
★ Influence of Technology
★ Conflict and Cooperation
★ Civil Rights and Liberties

Key Events

★ Compromise of 1850
★ Southern secession
★ Emancipation Proclamation
★ General Lee surrenders to General Grant
★ Passage of the Thirteenth, Fourteenth, and Fifteenth Amendments
★ Election of 1876 and the end of Reconstruction

Major Issues

★ Texas annexation and Mexican Cession territories reopen debates over slavery
★ Enforcement of the Fugitive Slave Act increases abuse of African Americans
★ *Dred Scott* decision reverses the Missouri Compromise
★ Southerners decide on secession
★ Emancipation Proclamation shifts Northern aim in Civil War

▲ AFRICAN AMERICANS IN COTTON FIELD

▲ FREEDMEN'S SCHOOL

Portfolio Project

Create a scrapbook for the Civil War period of history. Use your own original drawings and photocopies of maps, pictures, and other illustrations from library sources. Arrange your collection around different subjects and write a short explanation of each subject.

A Morse Code Message

Background

Armies in the Civil War made use of the newest communication system—the telegraph. Samuel Morse sent the first long distance message in 1844, using a code of short and long electrical signals. Telegraph operators over the world began using this code to send messages. Make your own simple telegraph sender using a battery-powered circuit and try sending a message in Morse code.

▲ DEMONSTRATION OF EARLY TELEGRAPH

Believe It
OR
NOT!   The fastest speed recorded for a hand-key transmission of Morse code is 175 symbols a minute. A member of the United States Army Signal corps accomplished this feat in 1942.

Materials

■ size D battery
■ tape
■ 2 feet of insulated wire, cut into 3 pieces
■ paper clips
■ thumbtacks
■ flashlight-sized light bulb and holder
■ piece of thick cardboard or soft wood about 1 foot square
■ copy of the Morse code

What To Do

A. Trap the end of one piece of wire under a thumbtack and tape the other end to one terminal of the battery.

B. Connect another piece of wire to the other battery terminal and the light bulb holder.

C. Connect a third piece of wire to the light bulb holder and a second tack about 1 inch from the first one.

D. Trap a paper clip under the first thumbtack and bend the end up at an angle. The paper clip will act as a telegraph key. Tap the bent paper clip down on the second thumbtack and observe what happens.

E. Try tapping the paper clip to the thumbtack in short and long connections as shown on the dots and dashes of the Morse code.

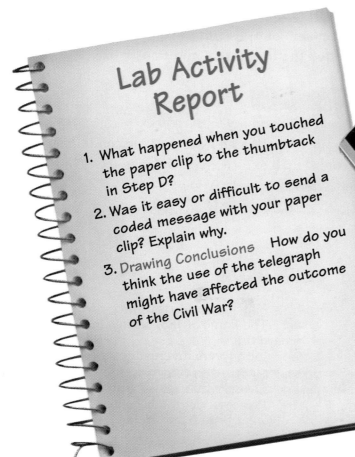

Lab Activity Report

1. What happened when you touched the paper clip to the thumbtack in Step D?

2. Was it easy or difficult to send a coded message with your paper clip? Explain why.

3. Drawing Conclusions How do you think the use of the telegraph might have affected the outcome of the Civil War?

GO A STEP FURTHER

ACTIVITY

Find out more about Samuel Morse and his telegraph and its success as a communication system. Create a chart showing the advantages and disadvantages of using the telegraph compared to modern communication systems such as the telephone.

CHAPTER 16

★★★

Sectional Differences
1820–1860

SETTING THE SCENE

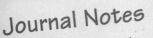

◄ JOHN DEERE'S PLOW, 1838

Focus

By the 1850s the North and South had developed distinctly different ways of life. By 1860 cities had multiplied, and the North had developed a manufacturing economy that rivaled industrial Europe. The South experienced remarkable growth, too, but in agriculture instead of manufacturing. Southerners increased cotton production dramatically and spread their plantations to the south and west.

Journal Notes

How did the societies and economies of the North and South differ? List the differences as you read the chapter.

Concepts to Understand

★ Why **economic development** of the North and South differed
★ How economics affected **the individual and family life**

Read to Discover . . .

★ how inventions changed the economy in the North.
★ why Northern immigrants experienced poor working conditions.
★ why the cotton gin contributed to increased slavery in the South.
★ how Southern society was structured.

United States	1820 Missouri Compromise creates balance between slave and free states	1831 Nat Turner leads a slave revolt 1837 The Panic of 1837 brings economic hard times 1837 John Deere invents the steel plow
	1820–1829	**1830–1839**
World	1821 Peru wins independence from Spain	1837 Princess Victoria becomes queen of Great Britain and Ireland

History AND ART

Where Cotton Is King
by Konstantin Rodko, 1908

This painting demonstrates a style of art known as "folk art." Folk art tries to depict the lives and surroundings of common people.

◀ SINGER SEWING MACHINE, 1851

1844 Samuel Morse sends first long distance telegraph message
1846 Elias Howe patents his sewing machine

1854 Nativists form the American party

1840–1849

1850–1859

1840 Union Act unites Upper and Lower Canada
1840 World Anti-Slavery Convention held in London

★★★

The Changing North

SETTING THE SCENE

Read to Learn . . .

★ what advances in transportation and communications occurred between 1820 and 1860.
★ what inventions changed farming and other kinds of work in the United States.

Terms to Know

★ clipper
★ telegraph
★ seamstress
★ patent
★ royalty

People to Meet

★ Robert Fulton
★ Oliver Evans
★ Samuel F.B. Morse
★ John Deere
★ Cyrus McCormick
★ Elias Howe

Places to Locate

★ Hudson River
★ New Orleans, Louisiana
★ Mississippi River

◀ TELEGRAPH SOUNDER

On July 28, 1855, the captain of the *Henry Clay* navigated down the **Hudson River.** The steamboat's passengers strolled on deck or sampled food in the luxurious dining room. Then the captain spotted the steamer *Armenia*. With grim determination he ordered his crew to stoke the boiler. When the captain of the *Armenia* saw the *Henry Clay*, he too demanded more fuel. The race was on! Passengers on both boats shouted with excitement, but their excitement soon turned to panic. The *Henry Clay* caught fire, and its passengers scrambled for their lives. By the end of the day, 90 people had drowned or burned to death.

★ River Transportation

Before steamboats Americans had depended on flatboats to carry passengers and goods downriver. Flatboats amounted to little more than hastily assembled rafts moved along by the current. Going upstream required poles, sails, and plenty of time and labor. Once most travelers reached their destination, they tore apart their flatboats and used the timber for shelter or fuel. In **New Orleans** at the mouth of the **Mississippi River,** builders eagerly bought up flatboats and used them as lumber for houses and sidewalks.

In 1787 American **John Fitch** built a steam-powered boat that could move against the current. Unfortunately it proved impractical for carrying goods and passengers. Not until **Robert Fulton** developed the *Clermont* did steamboats begin to take over American waterways.

In 1807 Fulton launched the *Clermont* on the Hudson River. Scoffers called it Fulton's Folly and a "floating sawmill caught on fire." But it went upstream from New York City to Albany in 32 hours and proved that a steamboat could carry goods and passengers long distances. From then on New Yorkers traveled upstream and down with equal ease.

Steam travel also flourished on the Mississippi River and its tributaries. Other inventors adapted Fulton's design for these fast, shallow western rivers. **Henry M. Shreve** built a shallow-hulled riverboat that one observer claimed "could float on a heavy dew." **Oliver Evans** of Delaware added a high-pressure engine. It was lighter and cheaper than the low-pressure engine on the *Clermont*. Despite the hazards, steamboats linked Western waterways with the Southern and Eastern Coasts and helped unite the nation.

★ Ocean Travel

In 1842 China opened several major ports to Western nations. American merchants sent trading ships to acquire Chinese goods such as silk, cinnamon, and firecrackers. They especially wanted Chinese tea. Because the freshest tea fetched the highest prices, merchants with the fastest ships made the largest profits.

Oceangoing steamers already traveled to Europe. No steamship, however, could carry enough coal to keep going around the tip of Africa and on to East Asia. Swift sailing ships called **packets** made the trip from China to the United States in six months—long enough for delicate teas to spoil. Tea merchants demanded even faster sailing ships.

Clipper Ships

In 1841 Virginian **John Griffiths** designed a new kind of ship. He claimed that its knifelike bow would slice through the water and its extra sails would catch every gust of wind. Two New York merchants had the ship built and named it the *Rainbow*.

The *Rainbow* was launched in 1845. It traveled to and from China in the time it took a packet to sail one way. Merchants sold the tea that the *Rainbow* carried for twice what the ship cost to build. Pleased by the ship's success, the merchants ordered a similar ship called the *Sea Witch*.

The *Sea Witch* measured 170 feet (52 m) long, and its main mast rose 14 stories. It made good time on its first and second voyages. On its third voyage, the *Sea Witch* set a record that no sailing ship the same size has ever broken. In 1849 it completed the passage from China to New York in 74 days and 14 hours.

In American slang of the 1800s a good clip meant "a fast pace." Therefore, Americans called sailing ships like the *Rainbow* and *Sea Witch* clippers. In 1849 clipper ships began running between New York and San Francisco as well as to China. In 1851 **Donald McKay,** builder of

Picturing
History

STEAMBOATS ON THE MISSISSIPPI RIVER Steam-powered boats became a common sight on the Mississippi River in the mid-1800s. **Who improved the steamboat built by John Fitch?**

the fastest clipper ships, launched the *Flying Cloud*, which set a new record by sailing from New York to California in less than 90 days.

The era of the clipper ships lasted only about 20 years. In the mid-1850s California started producing its own goods and depended less and less on trade with the East Coast. As the shipping business to San Francisco slowed down, traders demanded fewer clippers.

In 1869 the **Suez Canal** connected the Mediterranean and Red Seas for the first time. The canal made the voyage between New York and China 4,000 miles (6,436 km) shorter. Too narrow and shallow for most sailing ships, the canal was well suited for oceangoing steamships. Thus, steamships soon replaced clippers on the trade routes.

★ American Railroads

The reign of the riverboat proved almost as short-lived as the rule of the clipper. Steamboats traveled fast, but trains went faster. In two or three days, a train covered the same distance that it took a steamboat one week to cover. In addition, railroads could go almost anywhere while boats had to follow the waterways. As a result, many travelers opted to ride the rails rather than the riverboats.

The first successful use of the steam locomotive in the United States occurred on the

• •
Footnotes to History

Machine Versus Horse   Some people once laughed at trains. Many believed that horse-drawn carriages were safer and faster. A huge crowd watched in Baltimore as a steam-powered engine, the *Tom Thumb*, raced a horse-drawn carriage. Although the horse at first struggled to keep up, the *Tom Thumb* suddenly broke down. The defeat of *Tom Thumb*, however, did not mean the end of the steam engine.

Charleston and Hamburg railroad line in South Carolina in 1831. Other railroads began to operate almost simultaneously.

Not only did the railroads offer speedy transportation, they could be built quickly as well. By 1840 the United States boasted more than 400 railroad companies and more miles of rails than all of Europe. By 1860 the total miles covered by American railroads numbered 30,000 (48,270 km)—enough to cross the country 10 times.

Despite technological advances, passengers found train travel troublesome and dangerous. Schedules changed without notice. The cars were stuffy and sooty. Cinders even set fire to passengers' clothes. Accidents occurred on a regular basis because of fast speeds or faulty construction. Yet Americans continued to board trains at every stop. As engineers developed better rails and engines, railroads became the most important means of transportation. By the 1850s Americans demanded a coast-to-coast railroad.

★ Faster Communications

Americans proved as inventive with communications as with transportation. In 1832 talk of discoveries in Europe inspired American painter **Samuel F.B. Morse.** European scientists had proven that wires could transmit electricity. Morse reasoned that electricity might be used to carry long-distance messages along the wires. He also concluded that if electricity could travel along a wire "ten miles without stopping, I can make it go around the globe."

Morse Invents the Telegraph

Morse spent the next three years working on the telegraph, a device used to send messages across a wire. He and Alfred Vail developed the dot-dash communication system. Later this system became known as **Morse code.**

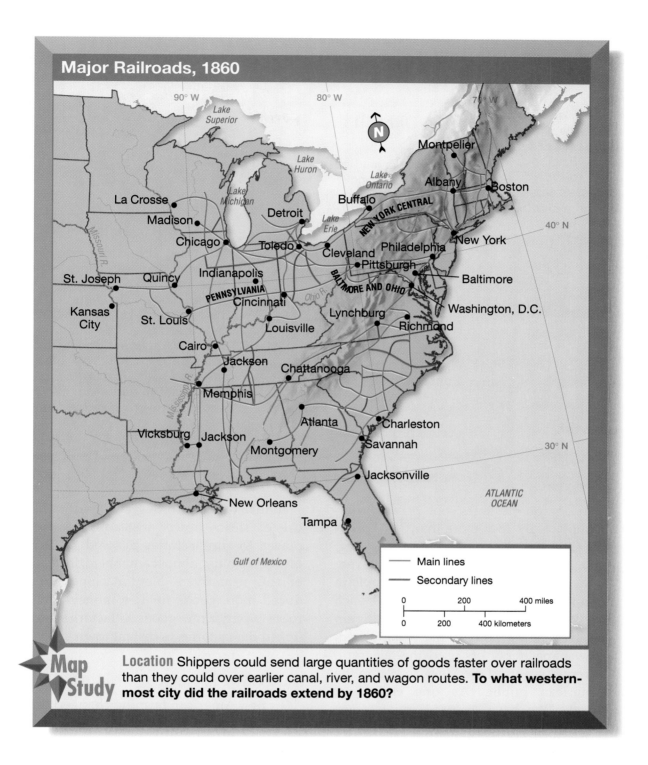

Major Railroads, 1860

Main lines
Secondary lines

Map Study

Location Shippers could send large quantities of goods faster over railroads than they could over earlier canal, river, and wagon routes. **To what western-most city did the railroads extend by 1860?**

Not until 1843, however, did Congress fund an experimental telegraph line between Washington, D.C., and Baltimore. On May 24, 1844, Morse demonstrated the telegraph by sending the first message: "What hath God wrought!" A few seconds later the operator in Baltimore tapped back the same message.

Americans were astonished. Boston lawyer Richard Henry Dana wrote:

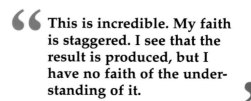

This is incredible. My faith is staggered. I see that the result is produced, but I have no faith of the understanding of it.

Linking Past and Present

Baseball

Experts today disagree over where baseball was invented. The idea for baseball originated either in England, in a game called rounders, or in the United States when it was created by Abner Doubleday.

◀ **BASEBALL IN THE 1800s**

Then

The Old Ball Game

"How many bases?" "Where's second?" "How far to third?" These baseball questions had no set answers in the early 1800s. The game's rules varied from town to town. Fields came in all sizes, and teams had no set number of players.

In 1845 Alexander Cartwright founded the Knickerbocker Base Ball Club of New York and drew up a set of rules for his team. His rules quickly caught on, and soon teams everywhere were playing organized baseball.

Now

Modern Baseball

Players still follow many of Cartwright's rules. Other rules have been added through the years. Since Cartwright's day the number of innings, pitching distance, procedures for making outs, and rules for strikes and walks have changed. All baseball teams today play by the same set of rules—no matter who they are or where they play.

Telegraph messages soon became commonplace. By 1846 more than 5,000 miles (8,045 km) of telegraph wire were strung, and 3,000 more miles (4,827 km) were under construction. As a result, people in remote country towns and big cities such as Boston, New York, and Washington received news the day that it happened. Newspaper reporters used the telegraph to report events of the Mexican War to the American public. As one enthusiast noted, "We have every morning news from all parts of the Union."

★ The Northern Economy Expands

From 1840 to 1860 rapid growth became the dominant characteristic of the Northern economy. The growth was largely due to new methods of farming, inventions, and the expanding transportation system.

Industry in the North grew rapidly. The use of steam power instead of waterpower to run factories allowed factory owners to build almost anywhere, instead of only near rivers. New machines produced more goods for less money. Railroads brought raw goods to factories and linked the factories to distant towns.

New Ways to Farm

At first American farming changed little. After the Industrial Revolution reached America, however, inventors created ways to produce more crops with less work. For example, since the 1700s farmers had been using heavy iron plows. In 1837 Vermont blacksmith **John Deere** fashioned a lightweight plow from polished steel. It sliced through the soil more cleanly than an iron plow and even "sang," or vibrated, as it tilled the earth.

Another invention allowed farmers to produce more because it helped them work faster. Farmers had been cutting grain with scythes since ancient times. In July 1831, Virginian **Cyrus McCormick** demonstrated what observers called "a right smart curious" machine. McCormick's reaper harvested 14 times more grain than 2 men with scythes could cut in the same amount of time.

Ingenious Inventions

As the century unfolded, inventors came up with innovation after innovation—the safety pin, barbed wire, and the revolver were just some of the marvelous new inventions. Others found ways to improve existing products. These improved products, such as stoves, butter churns, screws, nails, sulfur matches, and rubber, became just as impressive as the new inventions.

In the early 1830s, New Yorker **Walter Hunt,** inventor of the safety pin, developed the first machine to sew interlocking stitches. Hunt feared, though, that his invention would take work away from seamstresses, or women who sewed for a living. So he abandoned the sewing machine without getting a patent—the exclusive right to use, make, or sell the invention.

More than 10 years later, **Elias Howe** of Massachusetts produced a similar machine. Howe filed a patent in 1846 and went to England to market his invention. When he returned to the United States, Isaac Singer had already produced and sold a version of Howe's machine. Howe took Singer to court and won a royalty, or payment, for every sewing machine built in the United States.

Later Singer struck a deal with Howe and two other inventors who had improved Howe's invention. They agreed to combine their innovations in one machine, mass-produce it, and share the profits.

Out of the Home, Into the Factory

As Hunt had feared, the sewing machine proved disastrous for seamstresses. A worker using a sewing machine produced dozens of shirts in the time it took a seamstress to sew a few seams by hand. The cost of clothing dropped. Many seamstresses had to find new ways to earn a living.

The sewing machine helped factory workers turn out many garments quickly. Cheap ready-made clothing became widely available for the first time. The sewing machine became another invention that changed life in the North.

★ SECTION 1 REVIEW ★

Checking for Understanding

1. **Identify** Robert Fulton, Oliver Evans, Samuel F.B. Morse, John Deere, Cyrus McCormick, Elias Howe, Hudson River, New Orleans, Mississippi River.
2. **Define** clipper, telegraph, seamstress, patent, royalty.
3. **How** did steamboats improve river travel?
4. **Why** did American merchants trading in East Asia use clipper ships instead of packets and steamers?

Critical Thinking

5. **Determining Cause and Effect** How did the sewing machine affect families and seamstresses?

ACTIVITY

6. Research the number of acres of grain harvested in the United States before and after McCormick introduced his reaper. Then create a chart or graph to illustrate your findings.

★★★★★★★★★★★★★★★★★★★★★★★★★★★★★★★

Life in the North

Read to Learn . . .

★ what conditions existed in Northern factories during the mid-1800s.

★ how workers responded to those conditions.

★ how increased immigration affected life in the North.

Terms to Know

★ labor union
★ strike
★ immigrant
★ assimilate
★ nativist
★ discrimination

People to Meet

★ Terence Powderly
★ Mary Harris

Places to Locate

★ Lawrence, Massachusetts
★ Lynn, Massachusetts

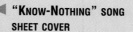

◀ "KNOW-NOTHING" SONG SHEET COVER

In January 1860 workers went about their jobs at the Pemberton textile mill in **Lawrence, Massachusetts.** Factory work was often unhealthful as well as dangerous. Cotton lint flew in workers' eyes. The drone of machinery filled their ears. No one saw or heard the telltale signs of a tragedy about to happen.

Suddenly the Pemberton Mill collapsed, trapping 900 people inside. Alarms rang throughout the city. The people of Lawrence rushed to dig through the rubble in a frantic search for survivors. The accident killed 88 mill workers and severely injured 116, most of whom later died.

★ Working Conditions Before 1860

The Pemberton Mill typified many Northern factories in the mid-1800s. Workers flocked to factories for jobs, despite low pay and hazardous working conditions. Factory owners cared little about workers' safety or welfare. Factory owners, though, had not always been like this.

Conditions in Early Textile Mills

The first factories and mills in the nation opened in New England. The region provided plenty of streams to run machinery.

It also provided big-city markets where manufacturers could sell their goods.

Factory owners liked to hire young women. Women would work for lower wages than men because the women planned to work only until they married. Then they would stay home, raise children, and manage their households.

To attract women workers, owners offered clean, supervised boardinghouses. They even allowed free time for reading, gardening, or attending lectures. Women worked 12 to 15 hours a day—about the same amount of time they had spent on housework or farming. Factory work seemed easier, however, and workers had Sundays off.

Conditions Decline

At one time employers knew all their workers by their first names. Then employers felt some responsibility for their workers' welfare. As the demand for goods increased, factories multiplied. The mushrooming factories of the early to mid-1800s employed thousands of workers. Bosses cared less and less about the workers' well-being. New factory owners built shabby housing near the noise and dirt of the factory. Factory managers cut wages and extended working hours.

In 1851 most workers received between $4 and $6 a week. Yet the average family of 5 needed at least $10.37 a week for rent, food, fuel, and clothing. This amount allowed for no luxuries and no money to pay medical bills.

Just to make ends meet, many children also had to work. In 1832 children made up about one-third of the nation's factory workers. They worked 12-hour days for 6 days a week. Often they made as little as 11 cents a day. Many suffered crippling or fatal accidents while on the job.

Profits alone motivated the owners of the new factories. Workers suffered as a result. Most factories were poorly lit and not well ventilated. In addition, employers expected workers to operate more machines at a faster pace. As a result, many exhausted or hurried workers caught their hair or fingers in the machinery.

★ Workers Organize

Workers began to resist poor working conditions. During the mid-1800s, workers started to organize labor unions, or organizations that try to improve the working conditions and wages of their members. Then the Panic of 1837 caused some businesses to close and made jobs scarce. Workers wanted to hang on to their jobs no matter how harsh the conditions. As a result, labor unions made little progress for more than 10 years.

In the 1850s labor unions reemerged, mostly among skilled workers such as printers, stonecutters, and blacksmiths. These unions of skilled workers became known as trade societies. They wanted to protect their high wages. Many also demanded a 10-hour day.

Unskilled factory workers soon began to organize and demand higher wages and shorter working hours. To achieve

Picturing History ▲ CHILD LABOR Children working in factories faced horrible conditions while trying to help their families. **How many hours a day did children work?**

▲ ARRIVAL OF IMMIGRANTS Immigration in the 1800s dramatically increased the population of the United States. **Why did employers hire immigrants?**

these goals, some unions called strikes. A strike means that workers refuse to do their jobs until employers meet their demands. Most early strikes failed. Because strikes were illegal, strikers faced fines and jail sentences.

Women Workers Organize

Women workers faced special challenges. They earned less money than men and most union leaders would not allow women to join. In 1824 the first women's strike occurred. In 1833 a union for female factory workers formed.

In 1860 Massachusetts shoemakers went on strike for higher wages. One thousand women joined 5,000 men and paraded through a snowstorm in **Lynn,**

Massachusetts, marching and carrying banners. The women's banners proclaimed "American ladies will not be slaves" and "Give us a fair compensation and we will labor cheerfully." After several weeks, the strikers finally won higher wages. But the factory owners refused to recognize the union.

Some unions did make gains during the late 1840s and 1850s. In response to union demands, Pennsylvania, Massachusetts, New Hampshire, and other states legislated 10-hour workdays. They also required schooling for children to prevent them from working long hours. In 1842 a Massachusetts court declared that workers even had a legal right to strike. This acceptance of labor unions, though, had force only in Massachusetts. Many years went by before unions made a nationwide impact.

★ Workers From Across the Ocean

Most of the workers at the Pemberton Mill had been Irish immigrants. An immigrant is a person who comes to a country with the intention of living there permanently. Millions of Europeans had come to the United States during the first half of the 1800s. The nation's industrial growth required a large labor supply. Employers discovered that immigrants would work long hours for low wages with few complaints.

Immigration Between 1830 and 1860

In the 1830s nearly 600,000 immigrants entered the United States. For the next 2 decades, the tide of immigration rose sharply. As a result, about 4.2 million immigrants arrived between 1840 and 1860. By 1860 one out of every eight Americans had been born elsewhere. Most came from Europe. One European mayor could not resist commenting on the phenomenon to an American visitor: "I welcome you in the name of our city's 4,000 people, 3,000 of whom are now in your country."

German Immigrants

Why did Europeans leave their native countries? In 1848 German academics and skilled workers led a movement to unite 38 states into one nation. When their revolution failed, they fled to avoid harm from government authorities. Thousands came to the United States. Soon after, many German peasants followed them across the ocean.

In all about 1.3 million Germans immigrated to the United States before 1860. Many stayed in New York City, where they had entered the country, while others continued inland. There they settled on farms near the Ohio River and Great Lakes.

Irish Immigrants

An even larger group—about 40 percent of all the immigrants—came from Ireland. In the 1800s poor Irish farmers depended on potatoes for food. Between 1845 and 1854, a disastrous blight, or disease, ruined several potato crops. By 1855 1 million peasants had died from famine—severe food shortages—or sickness. Rather than starve, many survivors chose to leave. One and a half million Irish sold their belongings and bought passage to the United States.

Once in the United States, most Irish immigrants settled in or near eastern cities such as Boston and New York. They lived in crowded, unhealthy conditions and took whatever jobs they could find.

The immigrants supplied much of the unskilled labor needed to build the North's growing industries. The men mined coal, dug canals, and built railroads. The women worked as servants and in factories. By 1852 half the factory workers in New England mills had come from foreign countries. Most of these workers were Irish.

Immigrants and the American Way

Over time immigrants assimilated, or adopted the manners and language of their new country. They also made contributions to American society. Germans taught Americans **horticulture,** or the science of growing fruits, vegetables, and flowers.

The Irish furnished leaders for the labor movement. Irish American **Terence Powderly** headed a labor union called the Knights of Labor in 1879. And Irish-born **Mary Harris**—better known as Mother Jones—led a campaign to end child labor in 1903.

America had become a nation of immigrants. As author Herman Melville noted:

> **Our blood is as the flood of the Amazon, made up of a thousand noble currents all pouring into one. We are not a nation, so much as a world.**

★ Immigrants Face Resentment

Some native-born Americans distrusted anyone different from themselves. They did not welcome the immigrants. They resented and feared their different languages, customs, and religions. These Americans especially mistrusted Catholics, many of whom were Irish and German immigrants. Americans who felt this way became known as nativists.

Nativists wanted to discourage immigrants from coming to the United States. They also wanted to stop those already here from becoming citizens or participating in politics. Some nativists proposed that immigrants wait 21 years to qualify for citizenship. Others demanded laws barring Catholics and immigrants from public office.

Know-Nothing Party

To get what they wanted, nativists formed a new political party, the American party. Their critics called it the Know-Nothing party because members always responded "I know nothing" when asked about the organization's secret activities. The party became so powerful that in 1856 Know-Nothing candidates won 48 seats in Congress. Soon after, though, the party collapsed.

In spite of hardships, immigrants continued to flock to the United States and participate in American democracy. Once the Irish gained the vote, they quickly learned to use it for their benefit. They organized political machines in big cities such as Boston and New York to help elect their candidates. In 1880, for instance, Irish voters elected **William R. Grace** as the first Irish Catholic mayor of New York City.

★ African Americans in the North

Slavery had once been legal in the North. By the early decades of the 1800s, though, all Northern and New England states had passed emancipation laws to abolish slavery. Thousands of African Americans lived in the North.

Although they had been freed, many African Americans faced discrimination in the northern states. Discrimination occurs when certain groups of people are not treated fairly.

In no state could an African American serve on a jury or be elected to Congress. In most areas, African Americans could not ride in the same carriage or work in the same building with a white person. Good jobs were seldom open to them. African Americans most often faced complete social and economic separation from whites.

Despite the overwhelming obstacles they faced, some free African Americans established successful careers. **James Forten,** a leading abolitionist speaker, began his career as a sailmaker and became wealthy as the owner of a Philadelphia sail factory. **Frederick Douglass** and **Harriet Tubman** became powerful and influential Northerners while fighting against slavery.

Although denied voting rights, African Americans fought bravely in every American war, published their own newspapers, and founded their own churches. Many also contributed time and money to the antislavery movement.

★ SECTION 2 REVIEW ★

★★★★★★★★★★★★★★★★★

Checking for Understanding

1. **Identify** Terence Powderly, Mary Harris, Lawrence, Lynn.
2. **Define** labor union, strike, immigrant, assimilate, nativist, discrimination.
3. **How** did bosses treat factory workers in the mid-1800s?
4. **Why** did immigrants come to the United States in the mid-1800s?

★★★★★★★★★★★★★★★★★

Critical Thinking

5. **Making Predictions** What do you think Irish immigrants might have said to other Americans who wanted immigrants to wait 21 years to become citizens?

ACTIVITY

6. Imagine you are a journalist reporting on the collapse of the Pemberton Mill. Record your report on tape.

The Cotton Kingdom

SETTING THE SCENE

Read to Learn . . .

★ how the North and South differed before 1860.
★ what effect the cotton gin had on the lives of Southerners.

Terms to Know

★ yeomanry
★ cotton gin

People to Meet

★ Eli Whitney
★ Catherine Greene

Places to Locate

★ New Orleans, Louisiana

▶ ELI WHITNEY

Plantation mistress Louisa McCord and her two daughters eagerly rifled through the trunk that had just arrived from Philadelphia. It contained the newest styles of dresses.

Soon after, Louisa wrote to thank her sister Mary Middleton who had sent the trunk. Without Mary's gifts from the North, Louisa admitted, she felt "sadly behind hand in my fashions and am often tempted to turn quaker—just because their fashions I believe never change."

★ The Southern Economy

Life in Louisa McCord's South differed greatly from life in Mary Middleton's North. Between 1820 and 1860, the North became increasingly urban and industrialized. Meanwhile, the South remained largely agricultural with few large cities. As a result, the South had to purchase most of its manufactured goods from the North.

Southern Conservatism

While Northerners bragged about their go-ahead spirit, Southerners prided themselves on their love of tradition. Life in the South moved at a leisurely pace. One Alabama politician summed up the Southerners' point of view this way:

 We want no manufactures;
we desire no trading, no
mechanical or manufacturing

classes. As long as we have our rice, our sugar, our tobacco and our cotton, we can command wealth to purchase all we want. **"**

This outlook encouraged the growth of plantations but prevented the growth of cities. The South had 7 cities with populations of more than 8,000 in 1820. By 1850 just 12 cities had more than 10,000 people. Only **New Orleans,** with 150,000 people, compared to Northern cities in size. Smaller communities proved just as rare. One British visitor to the South in 1856 noted that "towns and villages are few and far between."

Southern Manufacturing

Before 1860 Southerners still produced much of their cloth and clothing at home. During the 1850s traveler Frederick Law Olmstead noted:

" In Ohio the spinning-wheel and hand-loom are curiosities, and homespun would be a conspicuous and noticeable material of clothing, [but] half the white population of Mississippi still dress in homespun, and at every second house the wheel and the loom are found in operation. **"**

When Olmstead referred to the white population, he meant the **yeomanry,** or families on small Southern farms. Plantation owners wore factory-made cloth from England and, increasingly, from the North.

Some Southerners willingly tried manufacturing. They built a few factories in the South during the 1850s. These factories made mostly flour, tobacco products, and cotton cloth. They never produced as

Picturing History ▲ VIEW OF ROME, GEORGIA Unlike industrial cities in the North, Southern towns depended mostly on agriculture to support their economies. **What did Southern factories produce in the 1850s?**

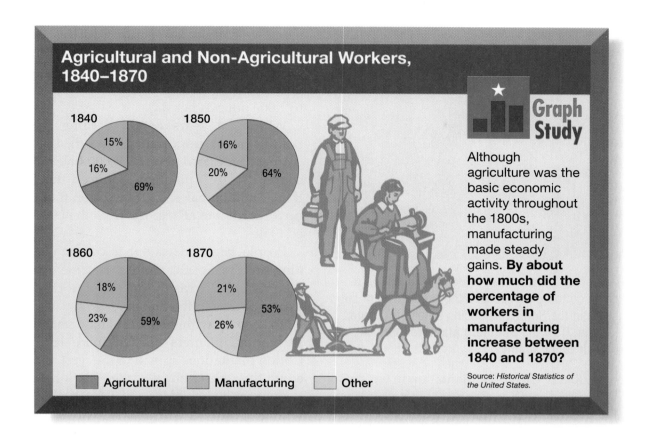

Agricultural and Non-Agricultural Workers, 1840–1870

1840
15%
16%
69%

1850
16%
20%
64%

1860
18%
23%
59%

1870
21%
26%
53%

☐ Agricultural ☐ Manufacturing ☐ Other

Graph Study

Although agriculture was the basic economic activity throughout the 1800s, manufacturing made steady gains. **By about how much did the percentage of workers in manufacturing increase between 1840 and 1870?**

Source: *Historical Statistics of the United States.*

much as similar Northern factories. The South remained a land of small farms and large plantations. In 1851 one Alabama newspaper sized up the situation this way:

 We purchase all our luxuries and necessities from the North. Our slaves are clothed with Northern manufactured goods, . . . work with Northern hoes, plows, and other implements. The slaveholder dresses in Northern goods, rides in a Northern saddle, sports his Northern carriage, reads Northern books. In Northern vessels his products are carried to market, his cotton is ginned with Northern gins, his sugar is crushed and preserved with Northern machinery, his rivers are navigated by Northern steamboats. 99

★ The Cotton Gin

In colonial times rice, indigo, and tobacco made up the South's main crops. After the American Revolution, demand for these crops decreased. European mills, however, wanted Southern cotton. But cotton took time and labor to produce. A worker spent a full day removing seeds from just one pound of cotton. The entire South produced only 1.5 million pounds (681,000 kg) of cotton in 1790. At this rate cotton planters could not turn a profit.

The demand for cotton increased in Great Britain and the northern United States as a result of the Industrial Revolution. As textile mills produced cheaper goods faster, they needed more cotton. To provide more cotton, the South required a faster way of removing the seeds.

Eli Whitney Invents Cotton Gin

In 1793 a Yale graduate named **Eli Whitney** visited **Catherine Greene** at

▲ THE COTTON GIN AT WORK The invention of the cotton gin increased the production of cotton in the South, producing a need for more labor. **How did Southern planters increase their labor supply?**

Mulberry Grove—a plantation in Georgia. Whitney came to Georgia to be a tutor on a plantation.

Impressed by Whitney's ingenuity, Greene and her manager, Phineas Miller, asked him to build a device to remove the seeds from cotton pods. Whitney developed a revolving cylinder with wooden teeth projecting through thin slots. As the cylinder turned, the teeth were supposed to pull cotton fibers through the slots and leave the seeds behind.

When Whitney tried out his invention, it failed to work. Greene suggested that he use wire teeth instead of wooden ones. The wire did the trick.

Whitney called the machine the cotton gin, "gin" being short for engine. Greene gave him the money to produce more cotton gins, but neither Whitney nor Greene made much profit. Others simply observed how the machine worked and built their own gins. By the time Whitney took out a patent in 1794, planters across the South already had copies of his invention.

Cotton Is King

Although a simple machine, the cotton gin produced large results. A worker using a cotton gin could process 50 pounds of cotton, rather than 1 pound, per day. If a worker operated the cotton gin by waterpower, production increased to 1,000 pounds per day.

Within 10 years cotton became the South's most important crop. In 1820 planters produced about 335,000 bales of cotton. By 1850 planters produced more than 2 million bales. In 1860 cotton made up 57 percent of all exports from the United States.

People began to say that cotton was king in the South. Cotton became the South's biggest cash crop and the chief export of the United States.

To keep up with the increasing demand for cotton, planters needed more land. Cotton plantations spread to the west and south throughout the so-called black belt, known for its rich black soil. Cotton plantations sprang up in southern Tennessee, Alabama, Mississippi, Louisiana, and Texas.

The invention of the cotton gin made a tremendous impact on the nation. It happened just as Northerners started to build textile mills. The factories created demand for cotton and the cotton gin allowed the South to meet that demand.

Northerners profited from the cotton boom, too. The South shipped much of its raw cotton to the North. There Northerners used it to manufacture cloth and often sold the cloth back to the South. This exchange helped fuel industrial growth in New England.

Slavery Revived

Different relationships between workers and owners characterized the Northern and Southern economies. In the South enslaved African Americans made up most of the labor supply.

Before the Industrial Revolution, some Southern planters had profited greatly from slave labor. At that time rice, indigo, and tobacco crops brought great

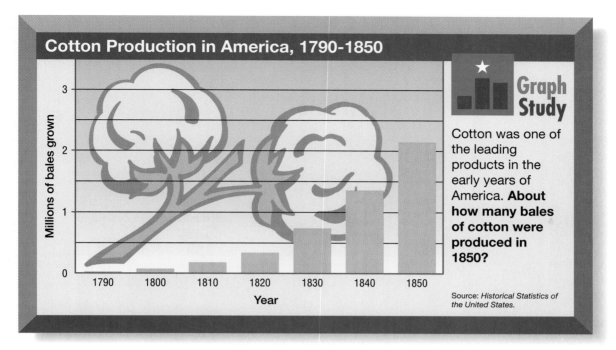

Cotton Production in America, 1790–1850

Millions of bales grown

Year

★ **Graph Study**

Cotton was one of the leading products in the early years of America. **About how many bales of cotton were produced in 1850?**

Source: *Historical Statistics of the United States.*

profits. When demand for these crops decreased, demand for slave labor also decreased.

With Eli Whitney's invention of the cotton gin, slave labor became profitable again throughout the South. As a result of the ever-larger cotton crops, the demand for slave labor increased. The United States had banned the slave trade with Africa in 1808. When cotton production rose, the demand for enslaved persons outstripped the supply, and the prices for the enslaved spiraled. In 1790 a field hand cost between $300 and $350. By 1860 the average cost was $1,500.

Slave traders began to smuggle enslaved people from the West Indies.

Sometimes they even kidnapped free African Americans in the North and sold them into slavery. Between 1790 and 1850, the number of Southern slaves increased from 500,000 to more than 3 million. By 1860 slaves in the South numbered 4 million.

Slave traders made tremendous profits. A typical dealer in Memphis earned $96,000 in a year. A slave trading company took in more than $500,000 per partner. These figures reflect the large investment Southern slaveholders made in enslaved persons. The Southern plantation owners had no intention of freeing what they considered their most valuable pieces of property.

★ SECTION 3 REVIEW ★

★★★★★★★★★★★★★★★★★★

Checking for Understanding

1. **Identify** Eli Whitney, Catherine Greene, New Orleans.

2. **Define** yeomanry, cotton gin.

3. **How** did the North and South differ between 1830 and 1860?

4. **Why** did Southerners say cotton was king?

Critical Thinking

5. **Determining Cause and Effect** What effect did the cotton gin have on Southern slavery?

ACTIVITY

6. Use copies of pictures showing life in the North and South between 1830 and 1860 to make contrasting posters.

Spirituals

▲ MUSIC ON THE PLANTATION

**When Israel was in Egypt's land:
Let my people go,
Oppressed so hard they could not stand
Let my people go.**
—from "Go Down, Moses"

Enslaved African Americans often sang **spirituals,** or religious folk songs such as "Go Down, Moses." Filled with strong emotions, spirituals were based on stories and characters from the Bible. Old Testament accounts of Hebrews in captivity especially appealed to enslaved African Americans.

Often enslaved African Americans created spirituals while working in the fields. No single person made up a song. One worker introduced a few words or a melody, then another would change or add to them.

Singing spirituals became a group effort. One worker sang a verse, and the rest of the workers sang the chorus. Or one person called out a line, and the others responded with the next line. During religious services, the whole congregation clapped their hands to the rhythm of the music.

The words and melodies of spirituals differed, but the emotions they expressed stayed constant. Enslaved men and women poured their hope for a better life after death and their longing for freedom into almost every song.

Making the Arts Connection

1. What is a spiritual?

2. What emotions do spirituals express?

3. Why do you think enslaved African Americans especially liked the Old Testament stories of Hebrews in captivity?

ACTIVITY

4. Find a recording of spirituals at the library and listen to the words and music.

526

★★★★★★★★★★★★★★★★★★★★★★★★★★★★

Life in the South

SETTING THE SCENE

Read to Learn . . .

★ what classes made up Southern society.
★ how African Americans lived in the South.

Terms to Know

★ overseer
★ slave codes
★ extended family

People to Meet

★ Solomon Northup
★ Denmark Vesey
★ Nat Turner

Places to Locate

★ Charleston, South Carolina

$1200 TO 1250 DOLLARS! FOR NEGROES!!

THE undersigned wishes to purchase a large lot of NEGROES for the New Orleans market. I will pay $1200 to $1250 for No. 1 young men, and $850 to $1000 for No. 1 young women. In fact I will pay more for likely

NEGROES,

Than any other trader in Kentucky. My office is adjoining the Broadway Hotel, on Broadway, Lexington, Ky., where I or my Agent can always be found.

WM. F. TALBOTT.

LEXINGTON, JULY 2, 1853.

The New Orleans slave market, one of the busiest in the South, often sent traders to other cities for new stock.

◀ **AD TO PURCHASE SLAVES**

A crowd gathered in the bright Savannah sunshine. A man with a loud voice was asking for bids. On a platform stood an enslaved African American, his head held high. Fear and grief clouded his face because he had been forced to leave his wife and children. Within minutes, the man had a new owner. Afterward he wrote this letter to his family:

> **❝ My Dear wife I [write] . . . with much regret to inform you that I am Sold to a man by the name of Peterson. . . . Give my love to my father & mother and tell them good Bye for me. And if we Shall not meet in this world I hope to meet in heaven. My Dear wife for you and my Children my pen cannot Express the [grief] I feel to be parted from you all. ❞**

★ Southern Class Structure

The presence of slavery affected all aspects of Southern life. Yet only about one-fourth of all white Southerners held slaves. Most of these held 20 slaves or fewer. Just a few plantations were large enough to have hundreds of enslaved persons living and working there. Most Southerners, even those who were not slaveholders, respected large slaveholders and admired their way of life. Because of their great wealth slaveholders greatly influenced Southern politics, society, and economy.

The Planters

The owners of large plantations held the highest positions in Southern society. Southerners considered land and slaves as badges of wealth and prestige. The more land and slaves Southerners acquired, the higher their standing rose. Wealthy planters cultivated the best land and enslaved 50 to 200 or more people.

A visit to a grand Southern plantation before 1860 left a memorable impression. A long, stately drive wound past a series of small buildings. These included the stable, the cotton gin shed, a corn mill, a church, a school, a blacksmith shop, and the slaves' quarters. At the end of the drive stood what the slaves called "the big house"—generally a white-columned mansion. Magnolia trees and other plants dotted the carefully tended grounds around the big house.

Plantation owners included both men and women, but most plantations had male owners. Each day the plantation owner either gave instructions to the overseer or personally directed the slaves. The overseer supervised the slaves at work. The plantation owner made decisions about planting and harvesting the crops. Plantation owners often participated in politics and promoted laws that upheld slavery.

The planter's wife managed the household. She usually sewed, supervised the house servants, cared for the sick, and often educated her young children. The mistress also entertained and attended parties at nearby plantations.

The Yeomanry

The yeomanry ranked just below the planters in Southern society. This class of farmers and ranchers made up a large part of the South's population. They usually owned hundreds, rather than thousands, of acres and held between 10 and 40 slaves. Some held no slaves at all. Instead, they worked their farms themselves or had hired hands to help.

The yeomanry enjoyed the company of their neighbors. They gathered for logrolling, corn shucking, and wood burning. On occasion they even came together for a house-raising, which according to one historian seemed "more like a good natured social gathering than . . . hard work." The women of the community always prepared food to serve the workers. After the work was finished, a square dance usually followed.

Poor Whites

Poor whites stood at the bottom of white society in the South. Poor whites made up a small percentage of the Southern population. Most lived in the mountains and pine woods, areas some called the "land of do without." They rented their land, often paying the rent with part of their crops.

Farmers had forced poor whites off fertile land into the rugged frontier area of the South. For food they hunted, trapped, and grew peas, corn, beans, cabbage, sweet potatoes, and other vegetables. Many poor whites barely kept their families from starving. Yet they enjoyed rights denied to enslaved and free African Americans.

Free African Americans

Free African Americans occupied a position in Southern society lower than poor whites. About 200,000 free African Americans lived in the South around 1850. Most of them were runaway slaves or were descended from slaves freed during and after the American Revolution. Others bought their freedom. Free African Americans, in both the North and South, suffered harsh treatment at the hands of whites.

Many laws restricted African Americans' freedom. In the South they had to register, wear special badges, pay special taxes, and live in separate areas from whites. By the 1850s some Southern states had passed laws that ordered African Americans to leave or be re-enslaved. Even without such laws, free African Americans did not feel secure. Many feared being kidnapped and sold into slavery just as Solomon Northup was.

Solomon Northup Writes *Twelve Years a Slave*

Solomon Northup's parents had been slaves in the North. They became free when their slaveholder died. After being freed, they moved to Minerva, New York, where Northup was born in 1808.

Later Northup lived in Glens Falls, New York, with his wife and three children. Northup worked on the Champlain Canal as a lumber contractor and saved enough money to buy a farm. Northup considered his life "happy and prosperous." Then the Northups moved to Saratoga Springs, New York, in 1834.

Seven years later events took a disastrous turn. Two white stage performers hired Northup to play the fiddle in their act. They went to Albany and then New York City. Then they persuaded Northup to go with them to Washington, D.C. Once there they drugged Northup and sold him into slavery.

Northup awoke alone in a dark cellar. After several hours two strangers appeared. Northup later learned that one of them was slave dealer James Burch. Burch claimed that he had just purchased Northup. Northup insisted that he was free and could not be sold. For this Burch beat him severely. The slave dealer threatened to kill Northup if he said such a thing again.

Burch shipped Northup from Washington to New Orleans, where planter William Ford bought him. Ford proved a kind master, but he experienced financial hard times and had to sell Northup after less than a year. This time Northup found himself in the hands of a cruel slaveholder.

After 12 years in captivity, Northup managed to send a letter to the white family that had held his parents. They produced evidence that Northup was a free man, and his slaveholder released him. Northup wrote *Twelve Years a Slave*, a book about his ordeal. The book gave Northerners a firsthand look at the slave system and became a best-seller.   ★★★

★ The Life of an Enslaved Person

Many enslaved persons worked in the big house or the plantation owner's stables. Some became skilled carpenters or blacksmiths. Those with skills sometimes worked in a nearby city. All or most of their wages went to the slaveholder.

Most enslaved persons, however, labored in the fields tending tobacco, cutting sugarcane, or picking cotton. The overseer punished the field hands when he wanted them to work harder. Most were punished with a lash, which was usually made of rawhide or cowhide.

▼ **AFRICAN AMERICAN BLACKSMITH**

▲ ENSLAVED AFRICAN AMERICANS Family members provided strength and security for one another. **Why did Southern law not recognize slave marriages as permanent?**

Even young children had to work. Enslaved girls as young as four or five helped with child care and other chores. If children did their tasks incorrectly, overseers punished them.

Some slaveholders provided food, clothing, and decent housing for enslaved people. Others gave their workers little to eat and shacks to live in. Josiah Henson described his slave quarters this way:

> We lodged in long huts, and on the bare ground. . . . In a single room were huddled . . . ten or a dozen persons, men, women, and children. . . . Our beds were collections of straw and old rags, . . . The wind whistled and the rain and snow blew through the cracks, and the damp earth soaked in the moisture till the floor was miry as a pig-sty.

Slave Codes

Across the South legislatures passed laws called slave codes, to control enslaved people. Slave codes denied slaves basic human rights. For instance, an enslaved person had no standing in a court of law and could not testify against a white person. Enslaved people could not own property or strike a white person, even in self-defense.

In addition, enslaved people could not leave their plantations without permission. They could not own guns. They could not hire themselves out or buy and sell goods. The law barred them from assembling unless a white person was present. In most Southern states, teaching an African American to read or write was against the law.

The Auction Block

All enslaved persons dreaded being sold because their new masters might be

Despite the severe limitations placed on them, many enslaved African Americans made valuable contributions to the United States. Henry Blair, for example, patented two corn harvesters. Benjamin Montgomery invented a boat propeller.

The Treatment of Slaves

In *Twelve Years a Slave*, Northup described the life of a field hand on a Southern plantation:

> The hands are required to be in the cotton fields as soon as it is light in the morning, and, with exception of ten or fifteen minutes, which is given them at noon to swallow their allowance of cold bacon, they are not permitted to be a moment idle until it is too dark to see, and when the moon is full, they often times labor till the middle of night.

crueler than the last. They also shuddered at the thought of a slave auction. One former slave described such an auction this way:

> **They would stand the slaves up on the block and talk about what a fine-looking specimen . . . they was, tell how healthy they was, look in their mouth and examine their teeth just like they was a horse, and talk about the kind of work they would be fit for and could do.**

This treatment humiliated the persons being sold. Worse, however, was the anguish families went through when different buyers separated them. For some the grief proved unbearable. Solomon Northup met a young mother named Eliza at a slave auction. Later her two young children were taken from her on the auction block. After years of mourning, the tormented woman died.

Families, Religion, and Resistance

Southern law did not recognize slave marriages as permanent because husbands and wives were separated so often. Preachers who presided at slave marriages even changed the wedding vows to "until death or distance do you part." In some places slaveholders forbade enslaved persons to call one another "mother," "father," or "sister." Some slaveholders tried to erase all family feeling among slaves.

Nevertheless, enslaved persons clung to their families as long as possible. Grandparents, aunts, uncles, and cousins stuck together. This extended family provided strength, pride, and love. The women in a family gathered to do laundry, make quilts, and share stories about their day. Fathers and mothers taught their children stories and songs. Many

African cultures used these folktales to pass on their history. They also passed on skills, such as dancing, playing music, and using herbs as medicine.

On Sundays several families gathered for worship. When planters introduced enslaved persons to Christianity, African Americans adapted what they heard to fit their needs. They identified with the Bible's message of hope for the downtrodden and despised. Many spirituals expressed a message of salvation like this one:

> **Didn't my Lord deliver Daniel
> Deliver Daniel,
> Deliver Daniel,
> Didn't my Lord deliver Daniel,
> And why not every man?**

African Americans often resisted the slaveholders. Some ran away, but others used more subtle methods. One Northerner saw women workers in the field raise their hoes and stop working after the overseer passed. They did not lower the hoes again until the overseer turned around. Some enslaved African Americans learned

Picturing History ▲ **NAT TURNER'S REVOLT** Nat Turner tried to lead African slaves to freedom by revolting against slavery. **What was one result of Turner's revolt?**

to read and write even though doing so violated the law. They referred to this as "stealing" learning. A house servant might "accidentally" break a mistress's favorite vase. Others pretended not to hear the master's orders. They alluded to their passive resistance when they sang, "Got one mind for the boss to see; Got another mind for what I know is me."

Armed Resistance

African Americans rarely took up arms against whites. Slave codes ensured that African Americans seldom obtained guns. Because the well-armed whites worked hard to prevent them, revolts had almost no chance of success. Some defiant African Americans, however, revolted and terrorized Southern whites.

Denmark Vesey, an enslaved African American, won money in a street lottery and bought his freedom. Afterward he lived in **Charleston, South Carolina,** and worked as a carpenter.

In the summer of 1822, Vesey organized a revolt. Before the uprising took place, however, the authorities discovered his plan. They executed Vesey and 35 other African Americans.

Nine years later an African American named **Nat Turner** led a revolt in Virginia. Turner, a popular religious leader among his fellow slaves, believed that God had chosen him to lead his people to freedom.

On August 21, 1831, Turner and his followers killed his master and his family. Others joined Turner and, for 24 hours, murdered family after family until about 60 whites were dead. State and federal troops hunted the countryside for Turner, killing more than 100 African Americans in the process. After 4 days they managed to find and arrest most of the rebels. The authorities did not capture and execute Turner, though, for another 6 weeks. As a result of Turner's revolt, Southerners imposed even stricter slave codes to discourage further rebellion.

Some abolitionists disapproved of Turner's uprising. They feared it set back efforts to end slavery. But one Southerner put their misgivings to rest:

> **If your course was wholly different—If you distilled sweet nectar from your lips and discoursed sweetest music. . . . [D]o you imagine you could prevail on us to give up a thousand millions of dollars in the value of our slaves?**

★ SECTION 4 REVIEW ★

Checking for Understanding

1. **Identify** Solomon Northup, Denmark Vesey, Nat Turner, Charleston.

2. **Define** overseer, slave codes, extended family.

3. **What** were the levels of society in the South before 1860?

4. **How** did enslaved African Americans respond to the conditions of slavery in the South?

Critical Thinking

5. **Drawing Conclusions** Few Southerners maintained plantations with large numbers of slaves. Why do you think this small group was able to dominate the political, economic, and social life of the South?

ACTIVITY

6. Draw scenes that illustrate differences between planters and enslaved people in the 1800s.

Interpreting a Circle Graph

Interpreting a Circle Graph

Suppose you have to report on your city's schools. You find a circle graph in the local newspaper about students' favorite school activities. You want to use it in your report. But what does the graph mean?

Learning the Skill

Circle graphs are used to compare parts of a whole. The whole circle stands for the entire amount of something. The sections stand for the parts that make up the whole.

In the graph below, the circle stands for all the city's students, or 100 percent. Each section of the circle stands for a percentage, or part, of the students. The labels tell you that 50 percent of the students prefer sports, 12.5 percent prefer music, and so on. The percentages in a circle graph always add up to 100 percent.

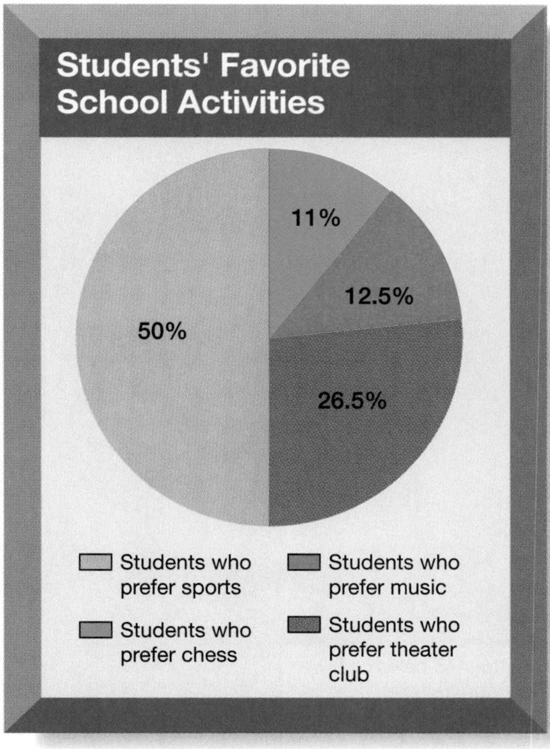

To interpret the graph, compare the sections. You can see that the section labeled "sports" is larger than any other. So the graph shows that sports are the most popular activities.

When two circle graphs appear together, read their titles and labels. Then compare the graphs for similarities and differences.

Students' Favorite School Activities

- 11%
- 12.5%
- 50%
- 26.5%

Legend:
- Students who prefer sports
- Students who prefer music
- Students who prefer chess
- Students who prefer theater club

Practicing the Skill

Use these graphs to answer the following questions.

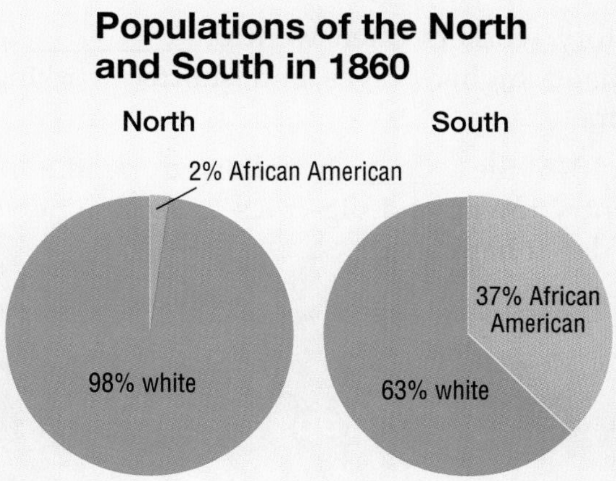

Populations of the North and South in 1860

North
- 2% African American
- 98% white

South
- 37% African American
- 63% white

1. What do the two graphs represent?
2. What percentage of the population in the North was white in 1860?
3. Where did African Americans make up over one-third of the population?
4. What can you conclude from the graphs about the total population of the North and South?

APPLYING THE SKILL

5. Find a circle graph related to the economy in a newspaper or magazine. Compare its sections, and then draw a conclusion about the economy.

Using Key Vocabulary

Use the listed vocabulary words to complete the following sentences.

telegraph	cotton gin
strike	slave codes
immigrants	

1. The _____ made it possible for the South to meet the North's growing demand for cotton.

2. Millions of European _____ came to the United States in the 1800s and became industrial workers.

3. _____ barred enslaved African Americans from learning how to read and write in most Southern states.

4. Factory workers often went on _____ to demand higher wages and shorter working hours.

5. By 1846 the _____ allowed people in country towns and big cities to receive news the day it happened.

Reviewing Facts

1. **List** the hardships Northern factory workers suffered.

2. **Name** five inventors from the North.

3. **Explain** the difficulties free African Americans faced in the North and in the South.

4. **Identify** two effects of the cotton gin in the South.

5. **Describe** how enslaved African Americans in the South resisted the slaveholders.

History and Geography

Products of the South

Study the map symbols on the maps below and then answer the following questions.

1. **Region** Which region do you think had the cooler climate—the largest tobacco-growing areas or the cotton-growing areas that produced 46 or more bales of cotton per square mile (2.6 per sq. km)?

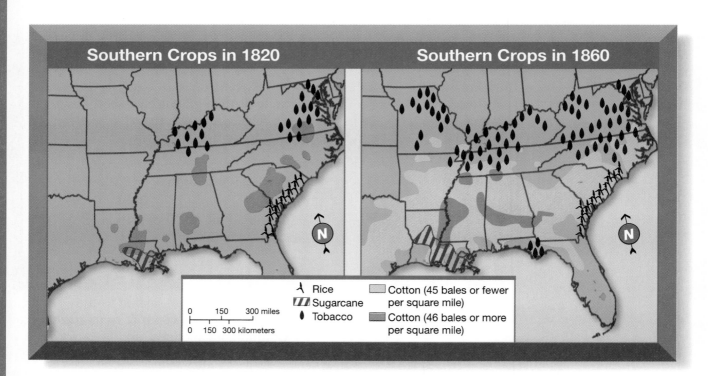

Southern Crops in 1820   Southern Crops in 1860

0   150   300 miles
0   150   300 kilometers

Rice
Sugarcane
Tobacco
Cotton (45 bales or fewer per square mile)
Cotton (46 bales or more per square mile)

2. **Location** Where was sugarcane grown in 1860?

3. **Movement** Which Southern crop on the map failed to move south or west between 1820 and 1860?

Understanding Concepts

Economic Development

1. How did the economies of the North and South differ?

2. What did Southerners mean by cotton was king?

The Individual and Family Life

3. How did labor unions try to help workers?

4. Why were enslaved families torn apart?

5. How did industrialization affect the daily lives of Northerners?

Critical Thinking

1. **Comparing and Contrasting** Point out similarities and differences in the lives of Northern workers and Southern yeomanry.

2. **Making Predictions** How do you think Southerners in the mid-1800s would have reacted if Northerners threatened the cotton industry and slavery?

Cooperative Learning ## Interdisciplinary Activity: Technology

Pass around a sheet of paper on which each member of your group writes a clue to the identity of an inventor or invention discussed in the chapter. For example, a clue might read: "I built a shallow-hulled riverboat" or "I produced garments five times faster than a seamstress." After each member has written a clue, join another group to exchange clues and answers.

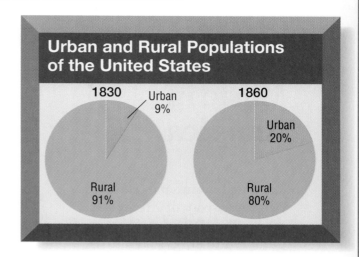

Urban and Rural Populations of the United States

1830 Urban 9%
Rural 91%

1860 Urban 20%
Rural 80%

Practicing Skills

Interpreting a Circle Graph

Study the circle graphs on this page. Then answer the following questions.

1. In which year did more than 90 percent of all Americans live in rural areas?

2. How large was the urban population in each year?

3. What change in the American population do the two graphs show?

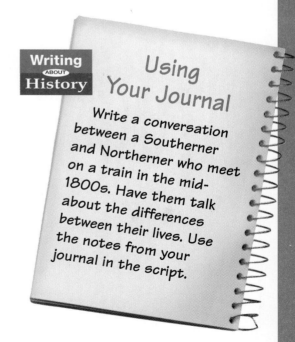

Writing ABOUT History

Using Your Journal

Write a conversation between a Southerner and Northerner who meet on a train in the mid-1800s. Have them talk about the differences between their lives. Use the notes from your journal in the script.

Cultural Kaleidoscope

Music in America

Music became part of the American way of life in the mid-1800s. Often, neighbors gathered to sing, play musical instruments, or dance for the evening's entertainment.

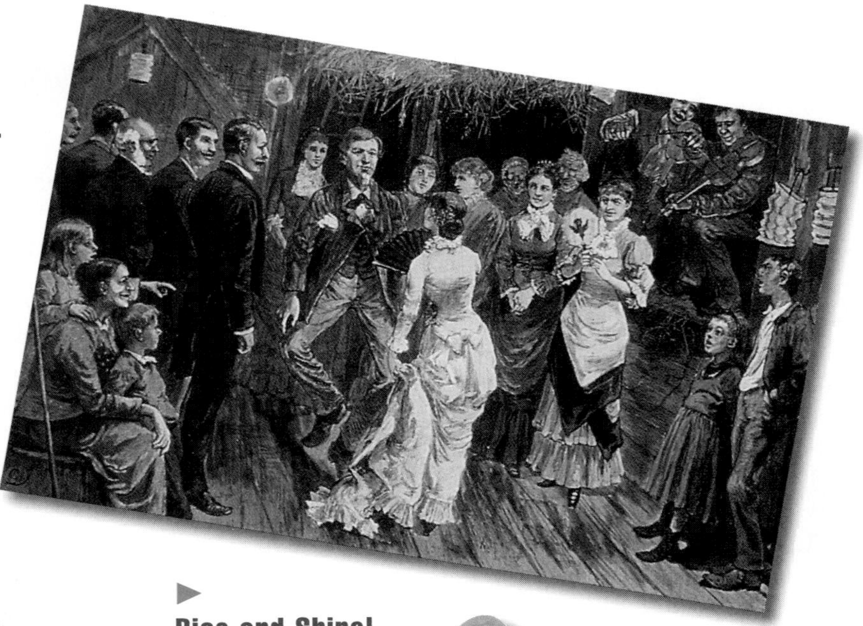

▼
The Popular Violin
From fashionable parlor to rustic frontier, Americans all across the continent enjoyed violin music.

▼
Country Barn Dance
No country barn dance was complete without a violin, better known then as a "fiddle." Spectators helped out by singing and clapping while the fiddler fiddled and the dancers danced.

▶
Rise and Shine!
Civil War musicians became important—though not always popular—members of their military units. The harsh blare of the bugle told soldiers when to advance or retreat in battle, when to awaken, and even when to eat. One poem "honoring" buglers complained:

No matter, be it rain or snow,
That bugler still is bound to blow.

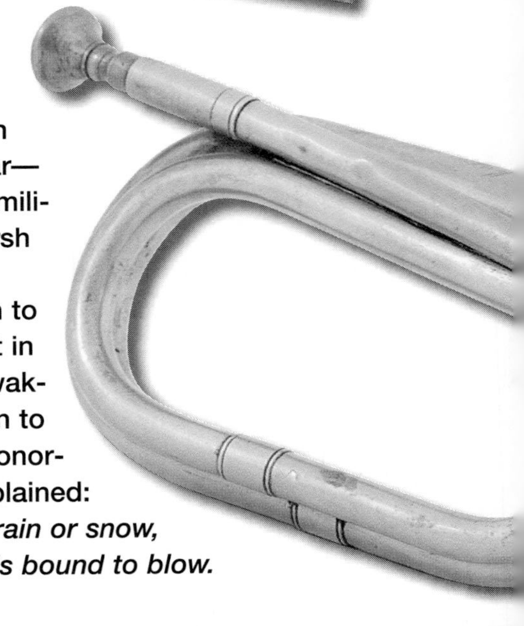

Strings Across the Country

Stringed instruments were popular with people around the country. Western travelers liked the banjo because it was light and easy to carry along rugged wagon trails. At the same time, the mountain dulcimer was a favorite in the Appalachian region of the United States.

African American Spirituals

Enslaved African Americans created and sang spirituals, or inspirational songs with religious themes. Many spirituals pointed the way to freedom. For example, "I am Bound for the Land of Canaan" told of going North. Groups such as the Fisk Jubilee Singers helped to popularize spirituals in the late 1800s.

Singing for Fun

Americans often joined in singing around the piano. Some songs, like *Dixie* in the South, expressed loyalty to a cause. Others, like "Oh! Susanna," told a story.

I WISH I WAS IN
DIXIE'S LAND

Written and Composed expressly for
Bryant's Minstrels
DAN. D. EMMETT.

Arranged for the Pianoforte by
W. L. HOBBS.

NEW-YORK;
Published by FIRTH, POND & CO., No. 547 Broadway.

Guitars in the Southwest

Spanish priests played guitars in the Southwest as early as the 1500s. By the mid-1800s, ranchers and cowboys strummed guitars throughout the West. They often sang along to amuse themselves and to help calm restless cattle.

CHAPTER 17

★★★

Road to Civil War
1850–1860

▶ **PUBLIC NOTICE ABOUT** *DRED SCOTT* **CASE**

SETTING THE SCENE

Focus

Until the mid-1800s the North and South handled their differences peaceably. The disagreements focused on one main question: What would be the status of slavery in new western states? A series of compromises kept an uneasy truce through the 1850s. With the election of Abraham Lincoln in 1860, however, the South believed it had no choice but to leave the Union.

Concepts to Understand

★ How expansion was influenced by **geography and the environment**
★ How **conflict and cooperation** over slavery led to secession

Read to Discover . . .

★ the major differences between the North and the South.
★ the events that led seven Southern states to secede from the Union.

Journal Notes

Events during the 1850s were influenced by a number of outstanding political figures. As you encounter these men and women, make a note of their names and your first impressions of their personalities and motivations.

United States	1848 Zachary Taylor elected President	
	1848 Free-Soil party formed	1850 Compromise of 1850 passed
	1846–1849	**1850–1853**
World		1852 The South African Republic is established
		1853 The Crimean War begins between Turkey and Russia

View of Harpers Ferry
by Ferdinand Richardt, 1858

John Brown, an abolitionist, targeted the armory at Harpers Ferry for his attack. Yet Danish painter Ferdinand Richardt depicts a peaceful view of the town.

▲ LINCOLN CAMPAIGN POSTER

1854 Kansas-Nebraska Act passed
1857 Supreme Court makes *Dred Scott* decision

1859 John Brown raids Harpers Ferry
1860 Abraham Lincoln elected President
1860 South Carolina secedes

1854–1857

1857 Indian soldiers revolt against British rule in the Sepoy Rebellion

1858–1861

1861 Czar Alexander II abolishes serfdom in Russia

★★★★★★★★★★★★★★★★★★★★★★★★★★★★★★★

Settling Differences

SETTING THE SCENE

Read to Learn . . .

★ why the Mexican Cession divided the North and the South.

★ how Northerners and Southerners tried to settle their differences.

Terms to Know

★ sectionalism
★ popular sovereignty
★ Free-Soil party
★ secede
★ Compromise of 1850

People to Meet

★ Daniel Webster
★ John C. Calhoun
★ Henry Clay
★ Stephen A. Douglas

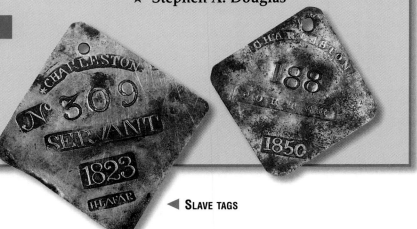

◀ SLAVE TAGS

Daniel Webster fixed his dark gaze on the other senators as he began his speech on March 7, 1850:

> ❝ I wish to speak today, not as a Massachusetts man, nor as a Northern man, but as an American. . . . I speak today for the preservation of the Union. . . . [F]or the restoration to the country of that quiet and that harmony which make the blessings of this Union so rich and so dear to us all. . . . ❞

Many of Webster's listeners shared his anxiety about the country's future, but the Senate was as divided as the rest of the nation. What developments had robbed the country of harmony and threatened the Union?

★ Regions Grow Further Apart

While the addition of new territories gave the country room to grow and expand, it also raised questions that brought deep divisions. In the mid-1800s, the United States gained vast new territories in the West. Eventually, those territories would become states. Would they be slave or free states? The issue of slavery in the West would set the North against the South.

The issue of slavery in new states was not new. You read in Chapter 12 that the **Missouri Compromise of 1820** kept the number of slave states and free states equal. The Missouri Compromise applied only to those states carved out of the Louisiana Purchase. The Mexican Cession in 1848 added a vast stretch of western lands not covered by the Missouri Compromise. Once again, the question of slavery in the territories became an issue.

Dispute Over Slavery in the West

Even before the war with Mexico had ended, growing antislavery feelings in the North led the House of Representatives, with its Northern majority, to pass the **Wilmot Proviso.** An antislavery Democrat, David Wilmot, introduced this measure. It would outlaw slavery in all territory acquired from Mexico. The bill was defeated in the Senate, where the North and South were equally represented.

The debate over slavery in the territories strengthened feelings of sectionalism. Sectionalism means that people are *more* loyal to their state or region than to the country as a whole. Southerners united in their support for slavery and accused the North of threatening their way of life. Northern abolitionists believed slavery to be morally wrong and demanded that the national government outlaw it.

Some politicians suggested other ways to settle the question of slavery in the territories. Senator **Lewis Cass** of Michigan recommended that the voters who lived in a territory should decide whether the states they formed would be slave or free. This idea supported popular sovereignty, or the notion that people should have the right to rule themselves.

★ The Election of 1848

There seemed to be no way of reconciling the opposing views on slavery in the new territories. In the election of 1848, both Northerners and Southerners tried to play down any discussion of slavery. The Democrats, although controlled by their Southern wing, nominated Northern Senator Lewis Cass of Michigan as their presidential candidate. The Whigs, who enjoyed strong support in the North, nominated **Zachary Taylor,** a hero of the Mexican War who owned a plantation in Louisiana with more than 100 slaves. His running mate, Millard Fillmore, was a moderate New York politician.

The Free-Soil Party

Many Northern Whigs backed Taylor because he seemed a sure winner, but "conscience Whigs" rebelled. They refused to back a slaveholder or risk opening the West to slavery. They broke with the Whigs and united with Northern Democrats to form their own party. The Free-Soil party chose former President **Martin Van Buren** as their candidate and campaigned with the slogan, "Free soil, free speech, free labor, and free men."

Although Taylor became President, the Free-Soil party received an impressive number of votes. Clearly, the slavery issue hurt both major parties.

▲ ZACHARY TAYLOR

Picturing History

▲ SENATE DEBATE An intense debate raged in the Senate over the admission of California as a free state. **What bill did Congress pass to help resolve the problem?**

★ The California Question

The California Gold Rush in 1848 intensified questions about slavery in the new territories. By the end of 1849, an estimated 95,000 forty-niners from all over the world had settled in California. Along with this tremendous growth came an urgent need for government.

President Taylor believed statehood could become a solution to the issue of slavery in the territories. As long as lands remained territories, the federal government decided the issue of slavery. Once the territories became states, their own governments could settle the slavery question.

At the suggestion of President Taylor, a convention met in Monterey, California, in the fall of 1849 and adopted a constitution that prohibited slavery. The newly created government immediately applied for admission to the Union as a free state. California's application for statehood touched off a long and bitter debate.

Admission of California would tip the balance of power in the Senate in favor of free states, which already held a majority in the House. Southern leaders threatened to leave the Union if it admitted California as a free state.

★ Threats to the Union

In January 1849, South Carolina Senator **John C. Calhoun** acted against what he saw as a threat to the Southern way of life. Calling a caucus, or private meeting, of the Southern members of Congress, he denounced the Ordinance of 1787 and the Missouri Compromise of 1820 as attacks on the South.

Calhoun claimed that any more similar Northern-sponsored measures would bring an end to slavery, start a race war, and lead to rule by African Americans. Calhoun warned that the South would secede, or leave the United States.

Calhoun's views seemed too extreme for many people. Even slaveholding senators, including Sam Houston of Texas and Thomas Hart Benton of Missouri, opposed him. Many Southern newspapers also declared their loyalty to the Union. Some Southern members of Congress, however, agreed with Calhoun. In the Southern states, some state legislatures, local conventions, and newspaper editors adopted his ideas.

In Congress debate over California's statehood dragged on for a year. When Calhoun first talked of seceding, Representative Robert Toombs of Georgia loudly opposed any such move. Before 1849 ended, however, Toombs stood in the House and declared, "I am for disunion."

★ Compromise of 1850

To resolve the crisis, Congress turned to Senator **Henry Clay.** Clay had earned the nickname the "Great Compromiser" for working out the details of the Missouri Compromise of 1820. Now, 30 years later, the 73-year-old Clay used all his charm and eloquence to persuade Congress to compromise one more time.

Clay's Proposal

In January 1850 Clay presented a bill in Congress with the following provisions: (1) admission of California as a free state; (2) organization of New Mexico and Utah as territories with popular sovereignty; (3) payment to Texas for giving up some territory in New Mexico; (4) an end to the slave trade, but not slavery, in the District of Columbia; and (5) passage of a strict federal law enforcing the return of runaway, or fugitive, slaves. Clay designed the proposals to give both sides some of their demands. Eventually the proposals would become the Compromise of 1850.

Opposition and Support

Senator Calhoun—so ill that he had to sit grimly in his seat while another senator read his speech for him—rejected any compromise as unfair to the South. His speech stated that some of "the cords which bind these states together in one common Union" had already been broken or weakened by the North's hostility. He warned that continued unrest over slavery "will snap every cord" so that "nothing will be left to hold the states together except force."

Three days later, Senator Daniel Webster delivered a speech in favor of the compromise. Although he had been Clay's rival for decades, Webster supported Clay's attempt to save the Union. Like many Northerners he disagreed with the institution of slavery. Breaking up the Union, however, seemed even worse.

Linking Past and Present

★★★★★★★★★★★★★★★

Paper Bags

The world seemed a different place without the common paper bag. It was once a challenge to carry home groceries, and people could not "brown-bag" lunches, either.

Then_____

Baskets and Boxes

In 1852 shoppers in West Dennis, on Massachusetts's Cape Cod,

◀ SHOPPING IN THE 1800S

smiled in delight as they made their rounds of the shops. Instead of carrying a clumsy shopping basket or juggling many small parcels, they added purchase after purchase to the same brown paper bag. Inventor Luther C. Crowell had come up with a bag of stiff brown paper folded and sealed at one end. It could be made in many handy sizes.

Now_____

Not Just Brown Any More

Shoppers today use billions of paper bags, not only brown but many different colors—sometimes prettier than the items they

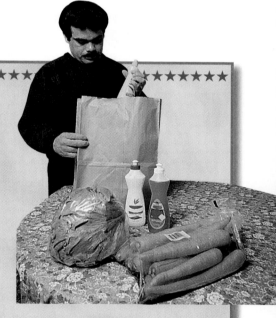

▲ SHOPPING IN THE 1990S

hold! Many bags are printed with store symbols. No matter what hue, however, each is still folded and sealed at one end, much like Crowell's original design.

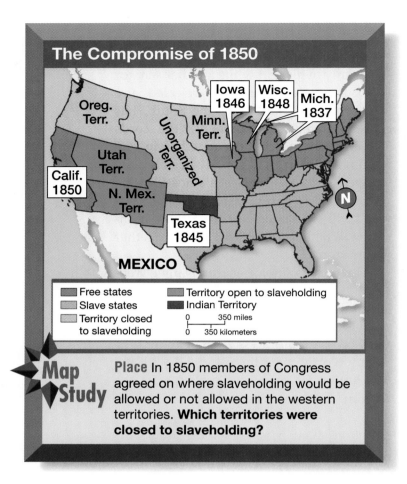

The Compromise of 1850

Oreg. Terr.

Iowa 1846

Wisc. 1848

Mich. 1837

Minn. Terr.

Unorganized Terr.

Utah Terr.

Calif. 1850

N. Mex. Terr.

Texas 1845

MEXICO

N

- ■ Free states
- ■ Slave states
- ■ Territory closed to slaveholding
- ■ Territory open to slaveholding
- ■ Indian Territory

0   350 miles
0   350 kilometers

Map Study

Place In 1850 members of Congress agreed on where slaveholding would be allowed or not allowed in the western territories. **Which territories were closed to slaveholding?**

August Clay realized his five proposals would have a better chance of passing separately. At this point **Stephen A. Douglas,** a young senator from Illinois, hammered five bills out of Clay's proposal. Douglas guided each bill through and won Senate approval for all of them.

The Compromise Is Passed

In September 1850 Congress passed the bills. Together, they closely resembled Clay's original compromise proposals. President Taylor—who might have vetoed them—had died in July. His successor, Millard Fillmore, signed the bills into law.

Webster wrote a friend shortly after passage of the bills:

> ❝ I can now sleep of nights. We have gone through the most important crisis that has occurred since the founding of the government, and whatever party may prevail, hereafter the Union stands firm. ❞

Webster was willing to compromise and support the South's demand that fugitive slaves be returned if doing so would save the Union.

The angry debates continued. Even with Webster's support, Clay had to plead for his compromise again and again. By

For a time, the compromise patched up the North-South quarrel. Yet basic differences persisted. Many Southerners agreed with Calhoun's charges that the North had wronged the South. They also remembered his remedy—secession.

★ SECTION 1 REVIEW ★

Checking for Understanding

1. **Identify** Daniel Webster, John C. Calhoun, Henry Clay, Stephen A. Douglas.

2. **Define** sectionalism, popular sovereignty, Free-Soil party, secede, Compromise of 1850.

3. Why did Northern Whigs form the Free-Soil party?

4. What did Southerners give up in the Compromise of 1850? What did they gain?

Critical Thinking

5. **Drawing Conclusions** Do you think the Compromise of 1850 was fair to both sides? Why or why not?

ACTIVITY

6. Create a campaign poster for one of the candidates in the 1848 election. Include slogans or symbols to gain popular support.

★★

Moving Closer to Conflict

SETTING THE SCENE

Read to Learn . . .

★ how Northerners reacted to the Fugitive Slave Act.
★ why the Kansas-Nebraska Act caused bloodshed.
★ how the *Dred Scott* decision affected slavery in the territories.

Terms to Know

★ Fugitive Slave Act
★ Kansas-Nebraska Act

People to Meet

★ Harriet Tubman
★ Sojourner Truth
★ Harriet Beecher Stowe
★ John Brown
★ Dred Scott
★ Roger B. Taney

Places to Locate

★ Lawrence, Kansas

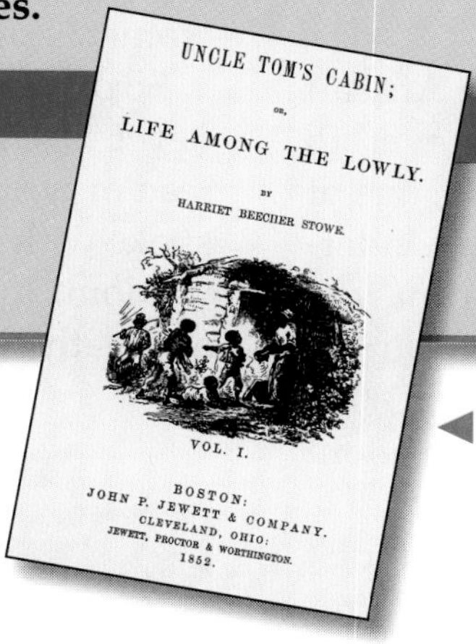

UNCLE TOM'S CABIN;
OR,
LIFE AMONG THE LOWLY.
BY
HARRIET BEECHER STOWE.

VOL. I.

BOSTON;
JOHN P. JEWETT & COMPANY.
CLEVELAND, OHIO;
JEWETT, PROCTOR & WORTHINGTON.
1852.

◄ HARRIET BEECHER STOWE'S *UNCLE TOM'S CABIN*

The crowd in Syracuse, New York, fell silent as Reverend J. W. Loguen stood to speak. Years before, Loguen had escaped to freedom on his master's horse. He had gone to college and become a minister. Now his audience waited to hear what he had to say about the Fugitive Slave Act:

> ❝The time has come to change the tones of submission into tones of defiance—and to tell Mr. Fillmore and Mr. Webster, if they propose to execute this measure upon us, to send on their bloodhounds. . . . I don't respect this law—I don't fear it—I won't obey it! It outlaws me, and I outlaw it.❞

Although the Compromise of 1850 kept peace for a few years, the provisions of the Fugitive Slave Act aroused deep anger in the North. It aroused new calls for an end to slavery.

★ Growing Support for Abolition

A Fugitive Slave Act had been in effect since 1793, making it a crime to help runaway enslaved persons. The new Fugitive Slave Act, passed as part of the Compromise of 1850, however, set up harsher punishments. Now anyone caught aiding fugitive slaves could be fined $1,000 and be jailed for six months.

With the new law, slaveholders hunted fiercely for runaways, whom they thought of as valuable lost property. They sent agents, offered rewards, or traveled north themselves to hunt down those who had run away. Agents even caught free African Americans and claimed they were fugitives. Free or enslaved African Americans could not testify in their own defense to prove that they were not fugitives.

Abolitionist Protests

Watching fugitives being brutally seized and driven back into slavery convinced more people of the evils of slavery. Despite the penalties, many Northerners openly assisted runaways.

Former slaves and free-born African Americans worked harder than ever to help their people. **Harriet Tubman,** one of the best-known conductors on the Underground Railroad, began guiding runaway slaves all the way to Canada. In Ohio Elijah Anderson led more than 1,000 enslaved African Americans to freedom between 1850 and 1855.

To win support for the abolitionist movement, **Frederick Douglass** and others who had gained freedom spoke at meetings and church services. Some wrote their life stories, known as "slave narratives." One of these books, *Narrative of Sojourner Truth: A Northern Slave,* was published in 1850 by the well-known abolitionist editor William Lloyd Garrison. The book depicted the effects of slavery in the North.

Sojourner Truth, Striving for Truth

"I was born a slave in Ulster County, New York," Isabella Baumfree began when she told her story to audiences. Called "Belle," she lived in the cellar of her master's mansion house. Born around 1797 Belle's life changed drastically when she became free in 1828 under a New York law that banned slavery.

In 1843 Belle chose a new name. "**Sojourner Truth** is my name," she said, "because from this day I will walk in the light of [God's] truth." She began to work in the movements both for abolition and for women's rights.

Sojourner Truth had never been taught to read or write, but she spoke with wit and wisdom. In 1852 at a gathering

▲ SOJOURNER TRUTH

Footnotes to History

Freedom Packages   Many Northerners defied the Fugitive Slave Act and helped slaves escape. Henry Brown, a slave in Richmond, Virginia, had a friend build a box to send through the mail. Brown poked three breathing holes in it and placed himself inside. The trip to freedom was rough. At one point the box was thrown so hard that Brown's neck was almost broken. Brown reached Philadelphia, though, and when his Northern friends opened the box, the former slave stood up and fainted.

of Ohioans, a rowdy farmer challenged her: The Constitution did not oppose slavery. Was she against the Constitution?

In answer, Sojourner used an example the farmer could understand. She knew that insects called weevils had eaten that year's wheat crop in Ohio. So she described walking near a wheat field and touching the tall, healthy-looking stalks but finding no grain there. "I says, 'God, what's the matter with this wheat?' And he says to me, 'Sojourner, there's a little weevil in it.'"

The farmer started to interrupt but she went on: "I hears talk about the Constitution and rights of man. I come up and I takes hold of this Constitution. It looks mighty big. And I feels for my rights. But they not there. Then I says, 'God, what ails this Constitution?' And you know what he says to me? . . . 'Sojourner, there's a little weevil in it.'" ★★★

A New Picture of Slavery

Many of the people who read slave narratives and listened to the stories told by freed African Americans already believed in abolition. A new novel published in 1852, though, brought the cruel story of slavery to a wider audience, moving them to tears and anger.

Harriet Beecher Stowe came from a family of well-known educators and clergy. After moving from Connecticut to Ohio, she heard stories about slavery from those escaping by the Underground Railroad. She also visited plantations in nearby Kentucky. After the passage of the Fugitive Slave Act, Stowe used her experiences to write the novel *Uncle Tom's Cabin*—portraying a kindly plantation family, the brutal overseer Simon Legree, and a saintly enslaved man, Uncle Tom.

First printed as a series in an abolitionist newspaper, *Uncle Tom's Cabin* came out as a book in 1852. In the first week, it sold 10,000 copies. Later it was reprinted in 37 languages, sold more than 1 million

▲ WARNING TO AFRICAN AMERICANS

copies in the British Empire, and became a hit play. While Stowe portrayed some Southerners sympathetically, her descriptions of a suffering slave and heartless slaveholder swayed more Northerners than ever against slavery.

Uncle Tom's Cabin also turned Southerners against the North. In South Carolina, Mary Chesnut spoke for many slaveholders when she complained in her diary about Stowe and other Northern abolitionists. She believed that they did not know what they were talking about. Their antislavery opinions, she said, were an "obsession with other decent people's customs" and a "self-serving" way to make money.

★ Kansas-Nebraska Act

In 1854 the political truce over slavery ended with the passage of the Kansas-Nebraska Act. Senator Stephen A. Douglas of Illinois proposed the act to set up territorial governments in the Nebraska Territory and to encourage rapid settlement of the region. Douglas and other Northern leaders also hoped to build a transcontinental railroad through their states rather than through the Southern part of the country.

The Nebraska Territory stretched from Texas to Canada and from Missouri west to the Rocky Mountains. Douglas knew that the South did not want to add another free state to the Union. He, therefore, proposed dividing the region into two territories, Nebraska and Kansas. In each territory settlers would decide the issue of slavery by popular sovereignty.

Leaders throughout the South supported the proposal. They believed slaveholders in Missouri would move across the border into Kansas. Eventually, Kansas would become a slave state. President Franklin Pierce, a Democrat elected in 1852, also supported Douglas's proposal. With the President's help, Douglas pushed the bill through Congress.

Northerners became outraged. They felt betrayed. Popular sovereignty in Kansas and Nebraska, in effect, canceled the Missouri Compromise. The Kansas-Nebraska Act opened the possibility of new slave states in the West—an area that had been free for more than 30 years.

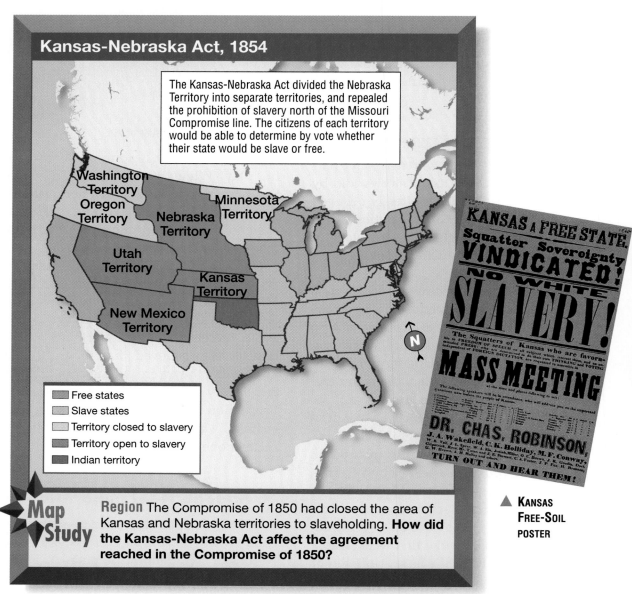

Kansas-Nebraska Act, 1854

The Kansas-Nebraska Act divided the Nebraska Territory into separate territories, and repealed the prohibition of slavery north of the Missouri Compromise line. The citizens of each territory would be able to determine by vote whether their state would be slave or free.

Washington Territory
Oregon Territory
Minnesota Territory
Nebraska Territory
Utah Territory
Kansas Territory
New Mexico Territory

N

- Free states
- Slave states
- Territory closed to slavery
- Territory open to slavery
- Indian territory

Map Study

Region The Compromise of 1850 had closed the area of Kansas and Nebraska territories to slaveholding. **How did the Kansas-Nebraska Act affect the agreement reached in the Compromise of 1850?**

▲ KANSAS FREE-SOIL POSTER

Bleeding Kansas

The passage of the Kansas-Nebraska Act started a race to win Kansas for one side or the other. Backers of slavery from Missouri and other slave states moved to the territory. Under popular sovereignty, they could vote for Kansas to enter the Union as a slave state.

To counter the proslavery groups, the New England Emigrant Aid Society helped Free-Soilers, members of the Free-Soil party, to migrate to Kansas and "vote to make it free." The settlers built the town of **Lawrence, Kansas,** which became a Free-Soil stronghold. Other emigrant aid societies in Free-Soil states also sent settlers and weapons.

Antislavery settlers soon outnumbered proslavery ones. In 1855 Kansas held elections to choose its lawmakers. Hundreds of drifters known as **border ruffians** crossed the border from Missouri. They harassed antislavery settlers in Kansas and voted illegally for a proslavery government.

As a result, Kansas elected a proslavery legislature. Its members passed what the Free-Soilers called "black laws." One law punished antislavery talk with 5 years in prison. Another law gave 10 years in jail to anyone caught helping escaped slaves. Antislavery forces refused to obey the new government in Kansas. They drafted a free-state constitution and elected their own representative to Congress.

Violence increased. Shootings and barn-burnings became common. On April 23, 1856, a proslavery sheriff was shot outside the town of Lawrence. Proslavery newspapers blamed the town's Free-Soilers and cried for war. In May an army of border ruffians and proslavery Kansans looted and burned Lawrence, killing five abolitionists in the process.

John Brown, a fanatical abolitionist from the Northeast, had come to Kansas with his 5 sons to join the antislavery forces. When Brown heard of the murders at Lawrence, he decided he had to avenge the crime. On the night of May 24, Brown and some followers murdered 5 proslavery settlers at Pottawatomie Creek. More fighting and killing followed. By late 1856, more than 200 people had been killed. Americans began to call the territory Bleeding Kansas.

★ Violence in the Senate

The violence extended to the nation's capital, where anger over the issue of slavery exploded in the Senate. Senator **Charles Sumner** of Massachusetts made a long speech viciously denouncing Southern slaveholders and Senator **Andrew Butler** of South Carolina as supporters of the crime of slavery in Kansas. The speech enraged Butler's nephew, South Carolina representative **Preston Brooks.**

Two days later—the day after the burning of Lawrence, Kansas—Brooks approached Sumner at his desk on the Senate floor and beat him with a heavy cane, splintering the wood. Bleeding and half-conscious, Sumner was helped out of the Senate. Shocked Northerners viewed Sumner as a martyr and held protest meetings against the violence. For some Southerners, however, Brooks became a hero. Admirers sent him more canes. One cane bore the inscription "Hit him again." Meanwhile in Kansas the struggle over slavery continued. Antislavery settlers eventually won the fight because of their great numbers. In 1861 Kansas entered the Union as a free state.

★ The *Dred Scott* Decision

During the 1850s Southerners often criticized the federal government for treating them unfairly. In 1857, however, the Supreme Court took their side on the question of slavery and pushed the North and South further apart.

▲ DRED SCOTT The Supreme Court ruled that as an African American, Dred Scott could not sue for his freedom because he was not a citizen. **What did the Supreme Court rule unconstitutional in the *Dred Scott* case?**

In the 1830s an army doctor in Missouri bought an enslaved man, **Dred Scott.** The doctor then moved with his household to Illinois, a free state, and next to Wisconsin Territory, where slavery was banned by the Missouri Compromise. Later the family returned to Missouri, where the doctor died. In 1846 Dred Scott decided to sue for freedom for himself and his family. He claimed that living in free territory had made him a free person.

With the help of antislavery lawyers, Scott's case eventually reached the Supreme Court. Many of the justices, however, favored slavery. The Court voted 7 to 2 against him. On March 6, 1857, Chief Justice **Roger B. Taney** (TAW•nee) delivered an opinion that upheld the Southern view that Scott had no right to sue in a federal court. The Court ruled against Scott because the founders of the United States did not intend for African Americans to be citizens. In addition, Scott's travels to free territory had not affected his status as a slave. Slaves were property, said Taney, and the Fifth Amendment prohibited Congress from taking property without "due process of law." He also said that the Missouri Compromise ban on slavery north of the 36°30′ line was unconstitutional because Congress had no right to prohibit slavery in the territories. In effect, the decision meant that the Constitution protected slavery. Abolishing slavery would require a constitutional amendment.

Rather than settling the issue, the *Dred Scott* decision aroused bitterness among the abolitionists and increased tensions between the North and South. Many Southerners now happily considered all territories open to slavery. Stunned Northerners vowed to fight the decision.

★ SECTION 2 REVIEW ★

Checking for Understanding

1. **Identify** Harriet Tubman, Sojourner Truth, Harriet Beecher Stowe, John Brown, Dred Scott, Roger B. Taney, Lawrence, Kansas.
2. **Define** Fugitive Slave Act, Kansas-Nebraska Act.
3. **How** did the Fugitive Slave Act affect the abolitionist movement?
4. **What** events led to violence and bloodshed in Kansas?

Critical Thinking

5. **Making Comparisons** *Uncle Tom's Cabin* sparked high tensions between the North and South. How was it similar to Thomas Paine's *Common Sense?*

ACTIVITY

6. Find a slave narrative at the library and choose one incident in it. Turn the incident into a brief first-person monologue that you can present in class or record on tape.

King Cotton

▲ *Cotton Pickers*, by Ethel Magafan, 1940

▲ **Cotton carding paddles**

How did cotton become the "king" crop in the southern United States? Europeans and Americans of the 1700s and 1800s called cotton a miracle fiber. It was light, cool, soft, durable, and easy to dye, sew, and care for. Cotton had been one of the first products brought from India by British explorers and merchants in the late 1600s. Employees of the British East India Company, suffering in India's hot climate, thankfully exchanged their heavy woolen clothes for light cotton clothing. They also began sending supplies of the wondrous fabric back to England. The material quickly became immensely popular.

Planters in the southern American colonies found that cotton would thrive in the hot, humid climate, though it took the hard work of many people. The South's growing season was long enough for a cotton crop to ripen each year.

With the invention of the cotton gin in the 1790s, cotton production and exports increased astoundingly. By 1840 the United States produced more than 60 percent of the world's cotton. By 1860 Southern plantations produced more than 1 billion pounds (454,000,000 kg) yearly. The greatest amount was still being shipped to England. At the same time, however, new American textile factories began to increase the demand for cotton.

Making the Geography Connection

1. How did cotton growing become a part of the British and American way of life?

2. What geographic factors made it possible for Southern states to base their economy on cotton?

ACTIVITY

3. Using an encyclopedia, make a list of products using cotton or cottonseed (for example, clothing, towels, oils). Make a list of ways you use cotton, in as many different categories as possible.

★★★

A New Political Party

SETTING THE SCENE

Read to Learn . . .

★ how the Republican party formed.
★ the issues and results of the Lincoln-Douglas debates.

Terms to Know

★ Republicans
★ debate
★ Freeport Doctrine

People to Meet

★ John C. Frémont
★ James Buchanan
★ Abraham Lincoln

► JOHN C. FRÉMONT

Disagreement over the Kansas-Nebraska Act split the old Whig party and brought about new political alliances. The Whigs had refused to take a stand on slavery in the territories. As a result, proslavery Whigs drifted into the Democratic party. Meanwhile Whigs and Democrats opposed to the Kansas-Nebraska Act joined Free-Soilers in loosely organized anti-Nebraska groups.

Gradually, the anti-Nebraska groups united. They organized first on the state level. In Wisconsin they met in the town of Ripon on February 24, 1854. The chairman suggested that they call themselves Republicans. Eventually the Republicans became a new national party.

The first national convention of the Republican party took place in Pittsburgh, Pennsylvania, in February 1856. It brought together fragmented groups of state-level Republicans, abolitionists, Free-Soilers, and anti-Nebraska Whigs and Democrats. Members of the new party accused Southerners of forcing slavery on the territories. Some thought that the institution of slavery kept wages low for white workers. Others considered slavery immoral. All Republicans agreed that Congress should keep slavery out of the western territories. Most Republicans did not expect to eliminate slavery in the South.

★ The Election of 1856

Members of the new Republican party met in June in Philadelphia to nominate a presidential candidate. They chose **John C. Frémont,** a western explorer and leader of the California uprising against Mexico in 1846. Republicans rallied around their candidate with the cry "Free Men, Free Soil, Frémont."

By 1856 the Democratic party was made up mostly of Southerners. Meeting in Cincinnati, Ohio, they nominated **James Buchanan** of Pennsylvania, an experienced diplomat and former member of Congress. They endorsed the notion of popular sovereignty.

The American party, or Know-Nothing party, had grown quickly between 1853 and 1856 by attacking immigrants and promoting temperance. The Know-Nothings nominated former President **Millard Fillmore.** This new party lost support quickly because it ignored the issue of slavery in the territories.

Due to large support in the South, Buchanan won the election. With only a minority of the popular vote, he won all of the Southern states except Maryland and received 174 electoral votes against 114 for Frémont and 8 for Fillmore. Frémont carried 11 of the 16 free states. The election of 1856 made it quite clear that sectionalism now played a critical role in American politics.

★ Abraham Lincoln Becomes a National Figure

As a young man **Abraham Lincoln** moved to New Salem, Illinois, where he purchased a country store. He entered

Picturing History ▲ JAMES BUCHANAN James Buchanan defeated John C. Frémont and Millard Fillmore in the election of 1856. **What helped Buchanan win the election?**

politics in 1832, losing the race for state legislator. In 1834 he again ran for the legislature and won. During this time he began studying law and received his attorney license in 1836.

Lincoln had belonged to the Whig party for more than 20 years. From 1834 to 1841 he served in the Illinois state legislature and in 1846 voters elected him to the House of Representatives. Republicans and not Whigs, though, addressed the spread of slavery—one of Lincoln's

Footnotes to History

A Humble Start Two Presidents, Millard Fillmore and Andrew Johnson, were once indentured servants. An indentured servant, unlike a slave, was under a contract to a master for a certain length of time. Like slaves, though, indentured servants did not have many rights.

Andrew Johnson ran away from his master. Fillmore served his master for several years and then bought his freedom for $30.

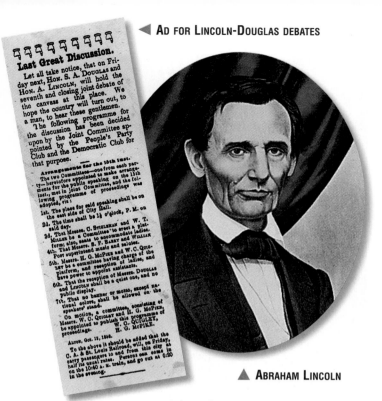

▲ ABRAHAM LINCOLN

concerns. After the Whig party collapsed, he joined the Republicans. Lincoln campaigned vigorously for Frémont. As Illinois voters listened to him speak, they enjoyed the way he made complex arguments easy to understand.

People admired Lincoln's honesty, wit, and soft-spoken manner. He served one term in the United States House of Representatives. Ten years later, in 1858, he decided to challenge Senator **Stephen A. Douglas** for his seat in the Senate. When accepting the nomination, Lincoln delivered a stirring speech to a cheering crowd at the Illinois Republican convention. As he began to speak, he seemed afraid and stiff, but soon he energetically swung his long arms and rose up on his toes to stress each point:

> ❝ **A house divided against itself cannot stand. I believe this government cannot endure permanently half slave and half free. I do not expect the Union to be dissolved—I do not expect the house to fall—but I do expect it will cease to be divided. . . .** ❞

★ The Lincoln-Douglas Campaign

The next month, Douglas kicked off his campaign in Chicago. He exclaimed to a throng of excited Democrats that Lincoln's "house divided" speech called for war between the North and South. Douglas attacked the idea of African American equality. The American government, Douglas claimed, "was made by the white man, for the benefit of the white man, to be administered by white men."

Speaking the following night, Lincoln denied Douglas's charge of wanting war. Whereas Douglas thought of slavery as a political concern, Lincoln raised the moral question of slavery. Lincoln considered slavery an evil that must be limited so that it would die out. "Let us discard all this quibbling about . . . this race and that race and the other race being inferior." He urged his listeners to "once more stand up declaring that all men are created equal."

Lincoln knew he could not attract the large crowds that Douglas did. Therefore, he followed Douglas across the state, often traveling on the same train. Douglas relaxed in a private car while Lincoln rode in a public coach.

The Great Debates

In late July Lincoln challenged Douglas to a series of debates, or public discussions, on slavery. After some hesitation, Douglas accepted the challenge. During the campaign, the men debated seven times. The debates centered on the extension of slavery into the free territories.

Lincoln and Douglas held their first debate in Ottawa, Illinois, before a crowd of 10,000 people. The two rivals sat side by side on the speakers' platform. Douglas—short but powerfully built, with a large head—looked the part of his nickname, "Little Giant." He dressed smartly, sometimes wearing a ruffled shirt and broad-brimmed plantation hat. Tall, thin Lincoln, on the other hand, wore a baggy suit and kept his carpetbag of notes beside him.

Douglas spoke in a deep voice and gestured with clenched fists. Knowing that many voters disliked abolitionists, he labeled Lincoln and his party "Black Republicans." In a shrill but forceful voice, Lincoln accused Douglas of having a "don't care" attitude toward the spread of slavery into the territories. Douglas often ridiculed Lincoln for declaring African Americans equal to whites.

As the debates continued, Lincoln devised a way to discredit Douglas within his own party. During the debate at Freeport, Illinois, Lincoln asked Douglas if the people of a territory could exclude slavery prior to the formation of a state constitution. In other words, was popular sovereignty still workable despite the *Dred Scott* decision?

Lincoln had trapped Douglas. If he answered "yes," Douglas would appear to support popular sovereignty, thereby opposing the *Dred Scott* decision. Such an answer would improve his chances for reelection as a senator but cost him Southern support for the presidential race in 1860. A "no" answer would make it seem as if he had abandoned popular sovereignty, on which he had based his political career. This answer would be welcomed in the South, but it might cost him the senatorial election.

To solve the dilemma, Douglas stated that the decision did not necessarily void popular sovereignty in the territories. Yes, he admitted that the Supreme Court had said that neither Congress nor the governments of the territories could prohibit slavery by law. On the other hand, in places where Free-Soilers made up the majority, they could destroy slavery simply by refusing to pass laws that protected it. Douglas's explanation later became known as the Freeport Doctrine.

Lincoln continued to stress this fundamental difference between himself and Douglas. Douglas ignored the moral question of slavery, while Lincoln regarded it as morally, socially, and politically evil.

An End . . . and a Beginning

Douglas won the 1858 election by a narrow margin and kept his place in the Senate. Still, he lost the support of many Democrats outside Illinois. Lincoln won an impressive popular vote in the state, and the election debates made him a national figure. At the time, however, a disappointed Lincoln predicted that he would "now sink out of view."

★ **SECTION 3 REVIEW** ★

Checking for Understanding

1. **Identify** John C. Frémont, James Buchanan, Abraham Lincoln.

2. **Define** Republicans, debate, Freeport Doctrine.

3. **What** groups of people came together to form the Republican party?

4. **How** did Abraham Lincoln become a national figure in politics?

Critical Thinking

5. **Interpreting Primary Sources** Why did Douglas and other Democrats charge that Lincoln's "house divided" speech was a call for war between the North and South?

ACTIVITY

6. Choose an idea from one of Lincoln's speeches and design a bulletin board display around it.

Election of 1860 and Secession

SETTING THE SCENE

Read to Learn . . .

★ why John Brown invaded Harpers Ferry.
★ how Southern states tried to form a separate nation.

Terms to Know

★ homestead act
★ armory
★ Crittenden Plan

People to Meet

★ John C. Breckinridge
★ John Bell
★ Alexander H. Stephens

Places to Locate

★ Springfield, Illinois
★ Harpers Ferry, Virginia
★ Charleston, South Carolina

◀ LINCOLN-HAMLIN
CAMPAIGN FLAG

The people of **Springfield, Illinois,** began to jump in the streets, singing and shouting. Some threw their hats in the air. Still others climbed to their rooftops to cheer. In the statehouse, dignified politicians rolled on the carpet. Everywhere, people sang:

> ❝ Ain't I glad I joined the
> Republicans,
> Joined the Republicans,
> Joined the Republicans,
> Ain't I glad I joined the
> Republicans,
> Down in Illinois. ❞

The wild election-night celebration of Abraham Lincoln's victory in the 1860 presidential election echoed in other places in the North. In the South, however, the news brought confusion, anger, and despair.

★ An Uneasy Decade

The United States had little to celebrate during the 1850s. Year after year, relations between the North and South grew worse. A serious depression, or economic downturn, hit the North in 1857. To help businesses and poor farmers, Northerners pressed for higher tariffs and free land. Southerners in Congress would not act to raise tariffs, however. Congress passed a homestead act offering free land to settlers, but President Buchanan vetoed it.

Violence over slavery continued to rage in Kansas. Then in October 1859, abolitionist **John Brown** brought his war against slavery into Virginia, not far from the nation's capital.

John Brown's Raid

Now almost 60 years old, with a long white beard, Brown thought of himself as an avenging angel doing God's will by destroying slavery, even if it meant killing people. Brown had formed a small army of 18 followers. On the night of October 16, 1859, Brown and his men invaded **Harpers Ferry, Virginia** (now West Virginia). They occupied a federal armory, or storehouse for weapons. Then they seized a nearby rifle factory and took several hostages. They hoped to use captured guns and rifles to arm all the enslaved persons in the area and ignite a slave revolt that would end in freedom for all enslaved African Americans.

By morning, local farmers and militia had rushed to town in a panic, fearing a slave rebellion. Brown and his followers probably could have escaped, but Brown refused. No others tried to escape until it was too late. By the time Brown tried to negotiate with the militia, they had trapped him.

Rumors spread in Washington of a huge slave rebellion. President Buchanan sent in army troops and a company of United States Marines, commanded by Colonel **Robert E. Lee.** On the second morning, the marines—plus a huge crowd—surrounded Brown. When Brown refused to surrender, the soldiers battered down the door and attacked with bayonets. One of the officers wounded and captured Brown.

John Brown's raid on the arsenal had lasted 36 hours. No local people had joined his cause. Ten of Brown's men, including two of his sons, had been killed. Brown's raiders had killed 4 civilians, 1 marine, and 2 slaves.

Reactions in the North and South

Northerners had mixed reactions to the raid. Was John Brown a courageous martyr to the cause of freedom or a madman? At his trial, Brown testified in a moving and dignified manner. Northern abolitionists especially admired his hatred for slavery, and many believed that his execution would give their cause a martyr and hero.

▲ John Brown

In the South people's reactions to the raid consisted of fear, anger, and hatred for the North. Southerners became convinced that they could not live safely in the Union. Northern support for Brown horrified Southerners as much as the raid itself. Many Southerners feared the possibility of a slave rebellion, and they became convinced that the North hoped to produce one.

Southern towns organized militias and declared martial law. Rumors of plots and revolts spread like wildfire. Planters enforced harsh discipline, threatening to whip or hang any enslaved persons who acted at all rebellious.

Government authorities convicted John Brown of treason and murder and sentenced him to hang on December 2, 1859. On the way to the gallows, riding in a wagon with his own coffin, he looked around at the Virginia fields and the Blue Ridge Mountains. "This is a beautiful country," he said. "I never had the pleasure of really seeing it before." Then he walked resolutely to the scaffold.

★ The Election of 1860

John Brown's raid became a major theme in the presidential election campaigns of

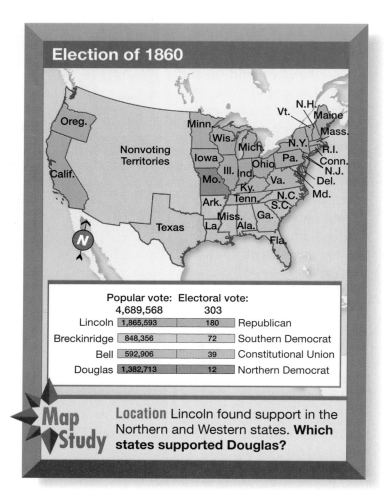

Election of 1860

Oreg.

Calif.

Nonvoting
Territories

Texas

Minn.

Wis.

Iowa

Mich.

Ill. Ind. Ohio

Mo.

Ark.

La.

Miss. Ala.

Ga.

Fla.

Ky.

Tenn.

S.C.

N.C.

Va.

Md.

Del.

N.J.

Pa.

N.Y.

Conn.

R.I.

Mass.

Vt. N.H. Maine

	Popular vote: 4,689,568	Electoral vote: 303	
Lincoln	1,865,593	180	Republican
Breckinridge	848,356	72	Southern Democrat
Bell	592,906	39	Constitutional Union
Douglas	1,382,713	12	Northern Democrat

Map Study **Location** Lincoln found support in the Northern and Western states. **Which states supported Douglas?**

1860. Democrats grabbed the chance to hurt Republicans. They branded the raid a "Black Republican" plot and accused party leaders of plotting with Brown.

The issue distressed Republicans. Many admired Brown's ideals but not his actions, which they saw as crimes. "John Brown was no Republican," Lincoln protested. Still, Southerners remained suspicious of Republicans and anyone who refused to support slavery.

Parties and Their Candidates

The issue that splintered the nation also broke apart parties. In 1860 **Stephen A. Douglas** tried to hold onto his leadership in the Democratic party. However, he insisted that as President he would not annul laws that discouraged slavery in the territories.

This stand lost Douglas the support of Southern delegates at the Democratic convention in **Charleston, South Carolina.** It split the Democratic party. Northern Democrats nominated Douglas for President and supported popular sovereignty. Southern Democrats chose **John C. Breckinridge** of Kentucky, supporting the ideals of the *Dred Scott* decision.

Alarmed by sectional divisions, a group of former Whigs put together the Constitutional Union party. They nominated Senator **John Bell** of Tennessee and championed the Union and the Constitution, attempting to avoid the slavery issue.

Before John Brown's raid, Republicans considered William H. Seward their first choice for President. Many voters, however, considered Seward's views against slavery too extreme. Democrats blamed him for inspiring the raid on Harpers Ferry. **Abraham Lincoln,** who had fewer enemies and remained popular outside the Northeast, seemed a safer choice. Although he opposed extending slavery into the territories, he conceded Southerners' right to have slavery in the South.

Republican Platform

The Republican platform also called for a homestead act, a transcontinental railroad, and a protective tariff. These goals appealed to farmers, Westerners, and manufacturers. Southerners, however, detested the Republicans' platform and their candidate. Many Southerners thought of Lincoln as an abolitionist and believed the Republicans wanted to make war upon the South. They feared that if Lincoln became President, they would lose their voice in the national government. Lincoln's name did not even appear on the ballot in 10 Southern states. A newspaper in Atlanta, Georgia, insisted that the South "would never submit to . . . the inauguration of Abraham Lincoln." It predicted the South would secede rather than accept Lincoln as President.

Election Results

On November 6, 1860—Election Day—telegraph wires flashed the results from the nation's polls to Springfield, Illinois. Lincoln and his friends celebrated victories in New England, the Northwest, and Pennsylvania. Then the news came that New York voted Republican. Those votes won Lincoln the presidency.

The final tally showed Lincoln carried every free state except New Jersey. This gave him a majority of the electoral votes. Yet, because of the three-way race, he received only 40 percent—less than a majority—of the popular vote.

★ Moving Toward Secession

Southerners reacted differently to Lincoln's election. In Charleston, South Carolina, people set off fireworks and fired cannons to salute the South Carolina flag. Southerners were certain that a new nation would be born in South Carolina. A Charleston newspaper editorial proclaimed, "The tea has been thrown overboard, the revolution of 1860 has been initiated." A few days later, the United States senators from South Carolina resigned from Congress, and the state

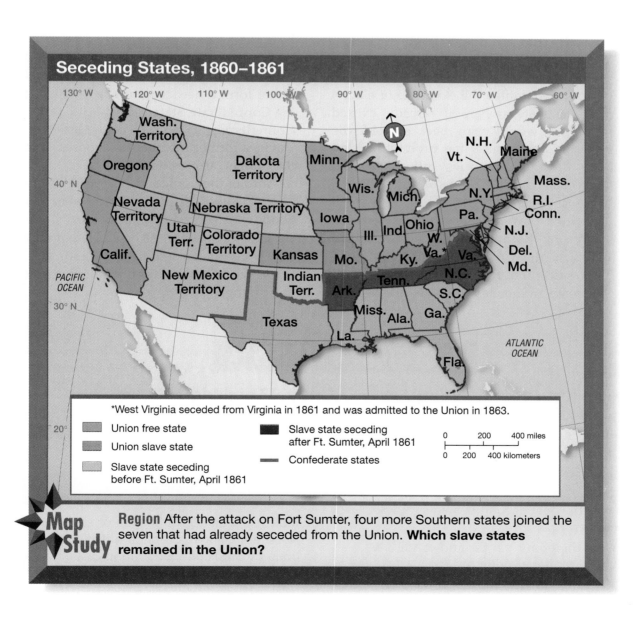

Seceding States, 1860–1861

*West Virginia seceded from Virginia in 1861 and was admitted to the Union in 1863.

- Union free state
- Union slave state
- Slave state seceding before Ft. Sumter, April 1861
- Slave state seceding after Ft. Sumter, April 1861
- Confederate states

Map Study — **Region** After the attack on Fort Sumter, four more Southern states joined the seven that had already seceded from the Union. **Which slave states remained in the Union?**

legislature called a convention to decide what steps to take. For South Carolina, the time to secede had come.

Dissenting Southerners

Not all Southerners seemed as eager to leave the Union as the people in Charleston. **Alexander H. Stephens** implored the Georgia legislature not to act unless the federal government moved against the South. He thought the South could defend its rights better within the Union. Stephens said, however, that if Georgians decided to secede, he would support his state: "Their cause is my cause, and their destiny is my destiny."

Senator **John Crittenden** of Kentucky also tried to save the Union by proposing his Crittenden Plan, which involved several amendments to the Constitution. One would guarantee the existence of slavery in the states where it already existed. Another would bring back the old Missouri Compromise line prohibiting slavery in the territories but allowing a popular vote at the time of statehood.

Although not yet in office, Lincoln wielded power as head of his party. He advised Republicans in Congress to oppose the Crittenden Plan. Otherwise, he said, the Republican party would become "a mere sucked egg, all shell and no meat—the principle all sucked out." Republicans voted down the plan.

Secession!

On December 20, 1860, before Lincoln was sworn in as President, delegates at the South Carolina convention voted unanimously to secede from the United States. By February 1861, Mississippi, Florida, Alabama, Georgia, Louisiana, and Texas had also voted to leave the Union. These states based their right to secede on the theory of states' rights. They defined the Constitution as a contract among sovereign states. The Northern states had broken that contract by refusing to enforce the Fugitive Slave Act and by denying the Southern states their equal rights in the territories.

On February 4, delegates met in Alabama to form a new nation. They named it the **Confederate States of America**, or the Confederacy. They elected Jefferson Davis, a former member of Congress and the cabinet, as president.

Word of the Confederacy spread fast. In Galena, Illinois, a man ran into a leather goods store owned by a former army officer Ulysses S. Grant. As he blurted out the news, Grant turned to him and said, "Davis and the whole gang of them ought to be hung!"

★ SECTION 4 REVIEW ★

Checking for Understanding

1. **Identify** John C. Breckinridge, John Bell, Alexander H. Stephens, Springfield, Harpers Ferry, Charleston.
2. **Define** homestead act, armory, Crittenden Plan.
3. **What** was the goal of John Brown's raid on Harpers Ferry?
4. **Why** were there four parties and candidates in the presidential election of 1860?

Critical Thinking

5. **Making Comparisons** How did people in the North and the South react to John Brown's raid?

ACTIVITY

6. Make up a campaign slogan or song for Abraham Lincoln, Stephen A. Douglas, John C. Breckinridge, or John Bell in the 1860 presidential election.

BUILDING SKILLS
Social Studies Skills

Interpreting an Election Map

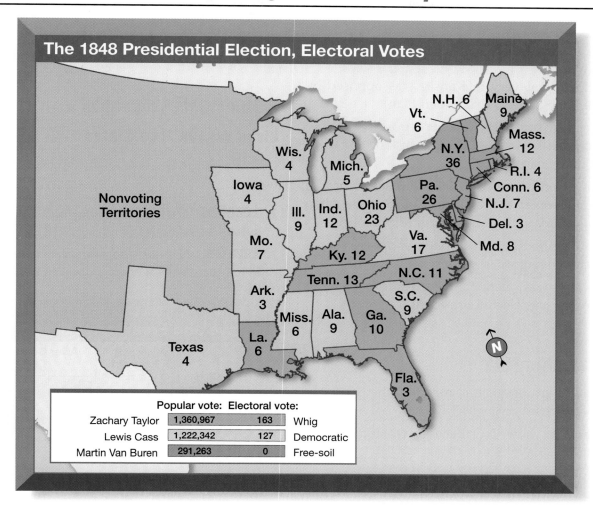

The 1848 Presidential Election, Electoral Votes

Nonvoting Territories

Wis. 4
Iowa 4
Mo. 7
Ark. 3
Texas 4
La. 6
Miss. 6
Ala. 9
Mich. 5
Ill. 9
Ind. 12
Ky. 12
Tenn. 13
Ga. 10
Fla. 3
Ohio 23
Va. 17
N.C. 11
S.C. 9
Vt. 6
N.H. 6
Maine 9
N.Y. 36
Pa. 26
Mass. 12
R.I. 4
Conn. 6
N.J. 7
Del. 3
Md. 8

N

	Popular vote:	Electoral vote:	
Zachary Taylor	1,360,967	163	Whig
Lewis Cass	1,222,342	127	Democratic
Martin Van Buren	291,263	0	Free-soil

Learning the Skill

An election map shows the support for candidates in different areas. For example, a presidential candidate might win many votes in western states but very few in the East.

A presidential election has two kinds of results: the **popular vote** and the **electoral vote.** The candidate with the most popular votes in a state wins all that state's electoral votes. (The number of electors from each state equals the combined number of its senators and representatives in Congress.)

Practicing the Skill

1. What color represents the Democratic party?

2. What was the popular vote for Cass? How many electoral votes did he win?

3. How many electoral votes did New York have in this election?

APPLYING THE SKILL

4. In an almanac, newspaper, or other reference work, find the results of a recent city, state, or national election. Draw an election map to present those results. Include a key.

Using Key Vocabulary

Choose the term in each pair that best completes the sentence.

1. Allowing slavery in Kansas was opposed by the (Free-Soilers/Crittenden Plan).
2. The (Wilmot Proviso/Freeport Doctrine) would have banned slavery in land obtained from Mexico.
3. The (Compromise of 1850/Kansas-Nebraska Act) reversed the Missouri Compromise's ban on slavery in the lands north of Missouri.
4. In 1860 the Republican party supported (popular sovereignty/a homestead act).
5. Southerners planned to (debate/secede) if Lincoln was elected President.

Reviewing Facts

1. **List** the proposals that made up the Compromise of 1850.
2. **Describe** how Northerners reacted to the Fugitive Slave Act of 1850.
3. **Explain** how the Kansas-Nebraska Act led to violence in Kansas.
4. **Identify** the groups who came together to form the Republican party in 1854 and 1856.
5. **Name** the seceding Southern states that formed the Confederate States of America in February 1861.

Understanding Concepts

Geography and the Environment

1. How did the idea of popular sovereignty in the territories contradict the Missouri Compromise?
2. How did the *Dred Scott* decision affect the civil rights of African Americans?

Conflict and Cooperation

3. What caused the Democratic party to split in 1860?
4. Why did Republicans reject the Crittenden Plan?

History and Geography

Slave Versus Free States

Study the maps below and answer the questions.

1. **Location** After the Compromise of 1850, what territories were left open to slavery?
2. **Location** Under the Kansas-Nebraska Act what territories were left open to slavery?

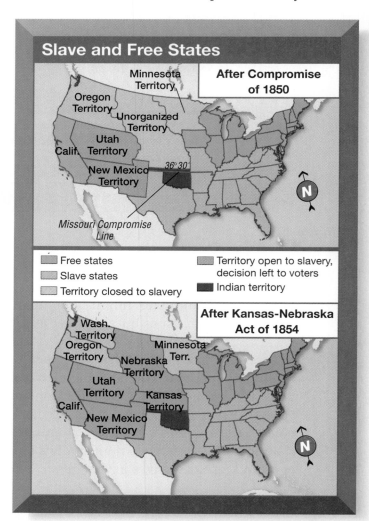

Slave and Free States

After Compromise of 1850

Minnesota Territory
Oregon Territory
Unorganized Territory
Utah Territory
Calif.
New Mexico Territory
36° 30'
Missouri Compromise Line

Free states
Slave states
Territory closed to slavery
Territory open to slavery, decision left to voters
Indian territory

After Kansas-Nebraska Act of 1854

Wash. Territory
Oregon Territory
Minnesota Terr.
Nebraska Territory
Utah Territory
Kansas Territory
Calif.
New Mexico Territory

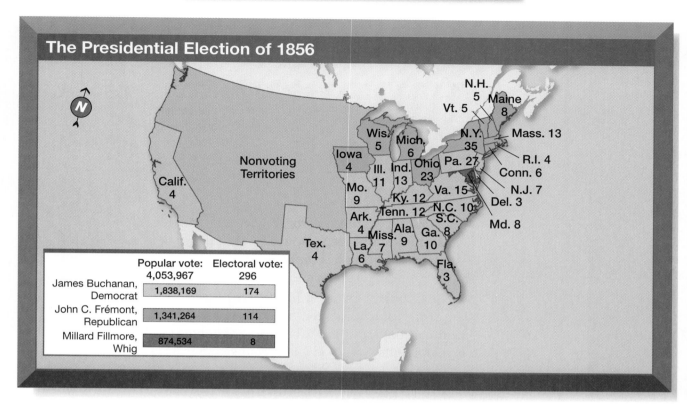

The Presidential Election of 1856

	Popular vote: 4,053,967	Electoral vote: 296
James Buchanan, Democrat	1,838,169	174
John C. Frémont, Republican	1,341,264	114
Millard Fillmore, Whig	874,534	8

Practicing Skills

Interpreting an Election Map

1. Which candidate and party won the electoral vote in Illinois?

2. Where did Buchanan have the strongest support?

Critical Thinking

1. **Drawing Conclusions** Do you think popular sovereignty was the best way to decide the slavery issue in new territories? Explain.

2. **Determining Cause and Effect** How did John Brown's raid turn Southerners against both Douglas and Lincoln?

Cooperative Learning Interdisciplinary Activity: Debate

With three other classmates, decide which person will take each of these roles: Henry Clay, Daniel Webster, John C. Calhoun, or William Seward. In the library, find the speeches these senators gave about the Compromise of 1850. Then update the language of your senator's speech. Use the revised speeches to stage a debate for the class.

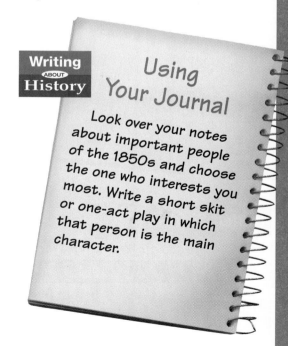

Writing ABOUT History

Using Your Journal

Look over your notes about important people of the 1850s and choose the one who interests you most. Write a short skit or one-act play in which that person is the main character.

CHAPTER 18

★★★

The Civil War
1861–1865

► **CONFEDERATE OFFICER'S COAT**

SETTING THE SCENE

Focus

In 1861 the Civil War erupted because Americans could not peacefully resolve their differences. In some families brothers would fight brothers and cousins would fight cousins.

The Civil War changed the course of warfare. The armies still employed muskets, horses, and drummer boys, but they also took advantage of the latest developments—railroads, telegraphs, and ironclad ships.

Concepts to Understand

★ How the **influence of technology** played a role in the Civil War
★ How **civil rights and liberties** were restricted and expanded during the Civil War

Read to Discover . . .

★ how major battles affected the outcome of the war.
★ how the border states influenced President Lincoln's decisions.
★ what role transportation systems played in the Civil War.

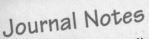

Journal Notes

When and where did the major battles of the Civil War take place? Keep a record of the battles and their outcomes as you read the chapter.

United States			
	1861 Civil War begins	1862 Emancipation Proclamation issued	1863 Emancipation Proclamation goes into effect
	1861	**1862**	**1863**
World	1861 Benito Juárez becomes president of Mexico	1862 Independence of African nation of Zanzibar recognized	1863 International Red Cross founded in Switzerland

Fight for the Colors
by Don Troiani, 1985

Don Troiani has painted several dramatic Civil War scenes such as this one of the Battle of Gettysburg. His works show the feelings of soldiers during battle.

◀ UNION SOLDIER'S GLOVE AND REVOLVER

▶ CIVIL WAR SOLDIERS

1864 Abraham Lincoln reelected President

1864

1864 Prussia defeats Denmark in war

1865 Thirteenth Amendment abolishes slavery
1865 Civil War ends

1865

SECTION 1

★★★★★★★★★★★★★★★★★★★★★★★★★★★★★★

The War Begins

SETTING THE SCENE

Read to Learn . . .

★ what war strategies developed in the North and the South.
★ what advantages the North and the South held in the war.
★ how the Union secured the border states.

Terms to Know

★ border states
★ martial law
★ strategy

People to Meet

★ Robert Anderson
★ P.G.T. Beauregard
★ Winfield Scott
★ Ulysses S. Grant
★ Albert S. Johnston
★ Robert E. Lee

Places to Locate

★ Fort Sumter
★ Richmond, Virginia
★ Baltimore, Maryland

◄ BATTLEFIELD CANNON

On March 4, 1861, Abraham Lincoln took the presidential oath of office. In his Inaugural Address, Lincoln insisted that the Union was indivisible and that secession was unconstitutional. He called Southerners his "fellow countrymen" and begged all Americans to listen to "the better angels of our nature." He also warned that the federal government would "hold, occupy, and possess" all its property in the states that had seceded.

When Lincoln spoke of federal property, he meant the post offices, forts, and military supply houses that the federal government controlled in each state. In 1861 many of the seceding states took over these federal operations. They said

they did not want a government of outsiders conducting business on their soil.

★ The Path to War

The federal government still held two federal forts in the South. One of them, **Fort Sumter,** stood on a rocky island in the harbor at Charleston, South Carolina. When the fort ran short of supplies, its commander, Major **Robert Anderson,** informed President Lincoln that he needed more soldiers and provisions.

Meanwhile, a general in the Confederacy's new army, **P.G.T. Beauregard,** surrounded the harbor with cannons. He intended to stop any federal reinforcements from reaching the fort. The Confederates waited for Major Anderson to surrender.

Four weeks after his inauguration, Lincoln sent a fleet with supplies to the fort. He decided against sending soldiers knowing it would only anger the Southerners more. Southerners, though, viewed Lincoln's orders to send supply ships as an act of war. When the Confederacy learned of the approaching fleet, Beauregard began to bombard the fort on April 12.

From inside the fort Captain Abner Doubleday described the attack:

66 Showers of balls . . . and shells . . . poured into the fort in one incessant stream, causing great flakes of masonry to fall in all directions. 99

Anderson Surrenders

On the second day of bombardment, a stout man carrying a white flag stumbled through the rubble at the fort. He came straight to the point:

66 Major Anderson, . . . It is time to put a stop to this, sir. The flames are raging all around you and you have defended your flag gallantly. Will you evacuate, sir? 99

Anderson reluctantly agreed. After 34 hours of bombardment, but with no loss of life, Fort Sumter surrendered. The Confederates hoisted their flag over the fort, and all the guns in the harbor sounded a triumphant salute. Almost immediately Lincoln began mobilizing the North for war. The Civil War had begun.

▲ *SUNSET AT FORT SUMTER* by Conrad Wise Chapman, 1864 Chapman, an enlisted soldier, produced some of the most striking paintings of the Civil War. This piece demonstrates Chapman's use of strong light and contrasting shades. **How did the United States react to the capture of Fort Sumter?**

Preparing for War

News of the attack on Fort Sumter stirred nationalist feelings in the North. When Lincoln requested 75,000 volunteers for 90 days to help restore order in the South, more people responded than could be equipped or trained. One Bostonian wrote a friend in England, "I never knew what popular excitement could be. The whole population, men, women, and children, seem to be in the streets with Union flags. . . ."

Although the Confederate states had hoped for a peaceful withdrawal from the Union, the news of the skirmish at Fort Sumter aroused intense emotions. Jefferson Davis called for 100,000 volunteers. A visitor to the South found "revolutionary fever in full sway. . . . Young men are dying to fight." Both sides expected to win and to win quickly.

★ Securing the Border States

President Lincoln wanted to reunite the country. He wanted to avoid making the abolition of slavery a goal of the war, though. In the first place, not all Northerners agreed on abolition. In the second place, Lincoln wanted to hold on to the border states.

More Southern States Secede

The border states lay directly north and south of the line that divided the Union and Confederacy. All of them permitted slavery. The border states on the south side of the line—Virginia, North Carolina, Arkansas, and Tennessee seceded soon after the attack on Fort Sumter. Western Virginians did not want to secede with their government. In 1863 they organized the state of **West Virginia** and sided with the Union. The border states to the north—Delaware, Maryland, Kentucky, and Missouri supported the Union but not the abolitionist cause.

An Iron Fist in Maryland

Virginia's secession put the federal capital, Washington, D.C., in danger. To its south lay **Richmond, Virginia,** where Jefferson Davis had relocated the capital of the Confederacy. To its north lay Maryland, where many people held slaves and supported the Confederacy. If Maryland seceded, the Union capital would be in enemy territory. Lincoln determined to hold Maryland at all costs.

Some Maryland citizens turned to violence, burning railroad bridges and even taking over the mail. Only a week after the fall of Fort Sumter, a mob sympathetic to the Southern cause attacked Union troops as they passed through **Baltimore, Maryland,** on their way to Washington. Soldiers and civilians opened fire and killed about 16 people. The first fatalities, or deaths, of the Civil War had occurred.

Lincoln responded by placing Baltimore under martial law, a form of military rule that includes suspending Bill of Rights freedoms. Government authorities arrested people who advocated secession or otherwise openly supported the Confederacy and held them without trials. Although tensions remained high throughout the war, Lincoln's action kept Maryland in the Union.

• •

Footnotes to History

Johnny Reb and Billy Yank   Northern troops called the Southern soldier *Johnny Reb* or *Reb,* after the term *rebel.* Southerners called the Northerners *Billy Yank, Yank,* or *Yankees.*

Holding Missouri and Kentucky

Lincoln considered the border states of Missouri and Kentucky important to the Union because these states controlled the Mississippi and Ohio Rivers. Kentucky had elected a pro-Union government, by a very narrow margin. Although it declared its neutrality at first, Kentucky remained in the Union. In Missouri, where slaveholders controlled the state, Lincoln supported rebellion against the pro-Confederate elected state government. Although partisan warfare plagued the state for the rest of the war, Missouri did not leave the Union.

★ A Divided Nation

At the beginning of the war, neither the North nor the South seemed prepared to fight. Each side had advantages and disadvantages.

The South

The Confederacy considered itself an independent nation. The Southerners, fighting for independence on home soil, could win simply by holding out against Union attacks. Davis believed there would be no war unless the Union forced one. Southerners fought to preserve their way of life—the cotton economy and the plantation culture dependent on slave labor.

Southerners, skilled with rifles and horses, had a tradition of military service that made them excellent soldiers. As an agricultural region with poor communications and few big cities, the South could not be paralyzed by a blow at a vital center.

The South proved ill-equipped to wage war, however. The South faced difficulties in producing weapons and other military supplies because it had few factories. The South also possessed few railroads to move troops and supplies. The South's population was much smaller than the North's,

▲ **UNION SOLDIER**

and more than one-third of the population included enslaved African Americans. Reluctant to use slaves as soldiers, the South would find it difficult to raise a large army. The Confederacy remained open to attack along its border with the Union and along its extensive coastline.

The North

Whereas Southerners had a clear, emotional picture of what they fought for, Northerners fought to reestablish the Union. Many Northerners did not consider the elimination of slavery important. The North would need to invade the South to bring it back into the Union. It could lose the war if its people lost the desire to wage war.

The North enjoyed superiority in resources of every sort—population, money, transportation, food, and manufacturing. Industry in the North proved a decisive advantage for the Union army. Factories quickly went from producing peacetime goods to making war supplies. Its vast railroad system provided the means for moving men and supplies.

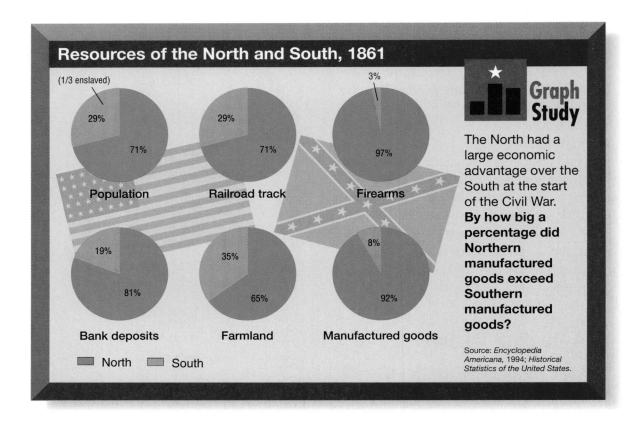

Resources of the North and South, 1861

(1/3 enslaved)
- Population: 29% / 71%
- Railroad track: 29% / 71%
- Firearms: 3% / 97%
- Bank deposits: 19% / 81%
- Farmland: 35% / 65%
- Manufactured goods: 8% / 92%

■ North   ■ South

Graph Study

The North had a large economic advantage over the South at the start of the Civil War. **By how big a percentage did Northern manufactured goods exceed Southern manufactured goods?**

Source: *Encyclopedia Americana*, 1994; *Historical Statistics of the United States.*

★ Military Strategies

When Fort Sumter fell, the Union army included about 16,000 soldiers—too few to win a war. After Lincoln's call to arms, so many Northerners tried to join the militia that recruiters had to turn volunteers away. Those who joined the troops organized into regiments and headed to Washington. For the most part, amateurs led amateurs in the Union army. Few, if any, of the soldiers and officers had much fighting experience.

The Union's Three-Pronged Strategy

The most experienced American general was **Winfield Scott.** Lincoln put Scott in charge of the Union armies. Scott devised a three-step plan, or strategy, to defeat the South. Scott planned to: **1)** blockade Confederate ports to ruin the South's economy and cut off supplies from Europe, **2)** take control of the Mississippi River to split the South and prevent the Confederacy from using the river to supply troops, and **3)** capture the capital at Richmond to seize the Confederate government.

There would be two main fronts. The Eastern front extended from the Appalachian Mountains to the Atlantic Ocean. The Western front lay between the Appalachian Mountains and the Mississippi River.

The Confederacy's Defensive Strategy

The Confederate army practiced a very simple strategy—fight a defensive war. To win, the South did not have to do anything except hold out against enemy attacks. Because European nations bought most of their cotton, Southerners were counting on Europeans to provide war materials and other supplies.

★ Military Leadership

To have any chance of winning the war, each side would have to rely on strong leaders who could make difficult decisions. The Constitution of the United States made President Lincoln the commander in chief of the military. The constitution of the Confederate States also gave the top command post to its president, Jefferson Davis.

During the early years of the war, the South had the better army. Many of its officers had attended the United States Military Academy at West Point before the war began. Most of the top officers in the Union army resigned to fight for the South.

Lincoln and His Generals

President Lincoln had little fighting experience, but he would prove to be a strong leader for the Union. Most Americans considered him cool-headed and fair.

General Scott, the commander of the Union army, earned the nickname "Old Fuss and Feathers" because of his extraordinary neatness and strict adherence to military rules. The elderly Scott would not last as commander of the Union forces. It became evident that Scott felt unprepared to handle the inexperienced recruits, and Lincoln replaced him as the war progressed. Unfortunately, Lincoln would have to go through several leaders before he found one that he could put his faith in.

Eventually Lincoln discovered his best leader, **Ulysses S. Grant.** Grant, born in Ohio, graduated from West Point and fought in the Mexican War. When the Civil War began, Grant was a colonel in the Illinois infantry. By 1863, after several victories in the Western states, President Lincoln finally recognized Grant as an able military leader and rewarded him with the rank of three-star general. Many military experts claim that Grant's strength lay in his ability to move quickly and outmaneuver the enemy. He would play a major role in winning the war for the North.

Davis and His Generals

Davis chose **Albert S. Johnston** to lead the battles in the West and **Robert E. Lee** in the East. Lee understood the battlefield as well as anyone in the military. He seemed able to predict the movements of the Union and knew its weak points. Willing to take risks, Lee did not wait to be attacked. Often he would make the first move.

Lee had rejected Lincoln's offer to lead the Union armies and took command of Confederate forces in Virginia. Although Lee disagreed with slavery and secession, he decided that he could not "raise my hand against my relatives, my children, my home."

★ SECTION 1 REVIEW ★

Checking for Understanding

1. **Identify** Robert Anderson, P.G.T. Beauregard, Winfield Scott, Ulysses S. Grant, Albert S. Johnston, Robert E. Lee.

2. **Define** border states, martial law, strategy.

3. **How** did the goals of the North and the South differ in the Civil War?

4. **What** was the Union's three-step strategy to win the war?

Critical Thinking

5. **Predicting Consequences** If you had lived in 1861, would you have said the North or the South would win the war? Why?

ACTIVITY

6. Imagine that you are a Northerner or a Southerner in 1861. Write a journal entry that explains your reasons for joining the Union or the Confederate army.

★★★

The War in the East

SETTING THE SCENE

Read to Learn . . .

★ how the Emancipation Proclamation changed Northerners' view of the war.
★ why the Battle of Gettysburg was a turning point in the war.

Terms to Know

★ Rebels
★ Yankees
★ commandeer
★ blockade-runner
★ ironclad
★ Emancipation Proclamation

People to Meet

★ Thomas "Stonewall" Jackson
★ George McClellan
★ Ambrose Burnside
★ Joseph Hooker
★ George Meade

Places to Locate

★ Bull Run (Manassas, Virginia)
★ Antietam, Maryland
★ Fredericksburg, Virginia
★ Chancellorsville, Virginia
★ Gettysburg, Pennsylvania

◄ BANNER FOR UNION
AFRICAN AMERICAN
TROOP

In the summer of 1861, hundreds of people on horseback or in carriages filled the roads leading to **Manassas, Virginia,** from Washington. They made the 25-mile (40-km) journey to see Union and Confederate troops in the first battle of the Civil War.

They carried picnic baskets and champagne. A feeling of anticipation and excitement filled the air. Many people brought binoculars to view the action more closely. They were sure the battle would not last long. They had no doubt that the Northern army would easily overpower the Rebels, or Confederate army.

★ The Fighting Begins

Confederate troops under the command of General P.G.T. Beauregard had camped along a Virginia stream called **Bull Run.** Both President Lincoln and General Scott agreed that the enemy's army had moved much too close to Washington, D.C. They wanted to drive the enemy farther from the nation's capital. Union leaders also believed that if the Northern army could destroy the Confederate army, the war might end at once. Hopes were high for the Yankees, or Union army, as the battle approached.

▲ GENERAL THOMAS "STONEWALL" JACKSON

The First Battle of Bull Run

On July 21, 1861, Union General Irvin McDowell moved 31,000 Union troops across Bull Run. At first Union troops pushed the 35,000 Confederates back. Then, when they ran up against General Thomas Jackson and his group of Virginians, the tables turned. General Jackson stood coolly at the head of his brigade amid a shower of Union bullets. Inspired by their general, the Southern troops held their ground. One Confederate general stated that Jackson stood "like a stone wall." From that day on the general was known as **Thomas "Stonewall" Jackson.**

Union troops fought well at first, but the Confederates were better organized. Using the railroad and telegraph, Confederate officers quickly supplied reinforcements. Union forces, tired from the long, hot battle, suddenly retreated.

Although the retreat started slowly and orderly, the hundreds of onlookers from Washington soon got in the way. When masses of grimy, bloody men headed their way, the picnickers panicked and rushed to the road. Together, panic-stricken soldiers and civilians started running and stopped only when they reached the Potomac River.

The Confederates proved as disorganized by victory as the Union forces were by defeat. Short on supplies and transportation, they did not pursue the fleeing troops.

The battle demonstrated that both armies needed training. It also suggested that the war would be long and bloody. Bull Run struck a severe blow to Union morale and to Lincoln's confidence in his officers. Scott retired and Lincoln summoned General **George McClellan** to build up the Union's armies.

McClellan immediately began training and organizing his troops. Although a superb trainer of men, he often appeared reluctant to commit troops to battle.

★ More Southern Victories

Only 100 miles separated the Confederate capital of Richmond from the national capital of Washington, D.C. Union leaders determined that if they could capture Richmond and take over the Confederate government, they could quickly end the fighting.

After spending the winter of 1861–62 training his forces, McClellan finally attempted to capture Richmond. Instead of heading directly toward Richmond, he

Footnotes to History

Different Names, Same Battle Many Civil War battles have two names. The Union named battles after the nearest body of water. The Confederacy named them after the nearest settlement. Therefore, the battle called the **Battle of Bull Run** (a creek) in the North was known as the **Battle of Manassas** (a settlement) in the South.

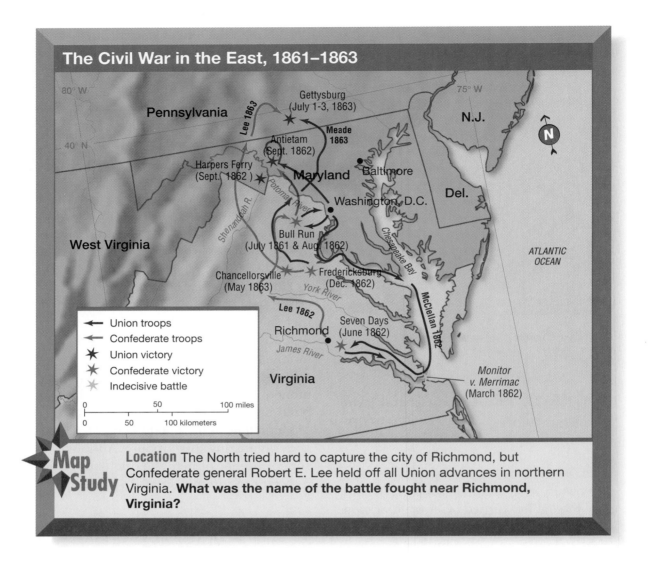

The Civil War in the East, 1861–1863

Pennsylvania
Gettysburg
(July 1-3, 1863)
Lee 1863
Meade 1863
N.J.
Antietam
(Sept. 1862)
Harpers Ferry
(Sept. 1862)
Maryland
Baltimore
Del.
Washington, D.C.
Potomac River
West Virginia
Shenandoah R.
Bull Run
(July 1861 & Aug. 1862)
Chesapeake Bay
ATLANTIC OCEAN
Chancellorsville
(May 1863)
Fredericksburg
(Dec. 1862)
York River
Lee 1862
McClellan 1862
Richmond
Seven Days
(June 1862)
James River
Virginia
Monitor
v. Merrimac
(March 1862)

N

Legend:
← Union troops
← Confederate troops
✶ Union victory
✶ Confederate victory
✶ Indecisive battle

0   50   100 miles
0   50   100 kilometers

Map Study

Location The North tried hard to capture the city of Richmond, but Confederate general Robert E. Lee held off all Union advances in northern Virginia. **What was the name of the battle fought near Richmond, Virginia?**

chose a complicated and cautious route that he thought would avoid Confederate forces. He sent 100,000 troops by boat to a peninsula between the York and James Rivers in Virginia. He planned to move into Richmond from the south. After winning several small battles, McClellan's troops marched to within 6 miles (10 km) of Richmond. Then, in the **Battles of the Seven Days** in June of 1862, Southern armies overwhelmed McClellan's troops. The South's largest army of 95,000—the Army of Northern Virginia—led by Robert E. Lee encountered McClellan's forces. Lee began a series of counterattacks and forced McClellan to retreat.

Although McClellan, only 25 miles (40 km) from Richmond, occupied a good

position to resume the campaign, time and time again he found reason to delay. Instead of replacing him with a more aggressive general, Lincoln ordered McClellan to northern Virginia to unite with forces under General John Pope at Bull Run. The President hoped to begin a new offensive against Richmond on a direct overland route.

Lee's troops moved quickly to the north, wanting to reach Pope's army before McClellan could join forces with him. On August 29, 1862, Pope attacked the approaching Confederates. General Lee's forces overcame the Union army in the **Second Battle of Bull Run.** The Union soldiers once again retreated to Washington, D.C.

★ The War at Sea

Although Union troops continued to lose battles on land, the Union navy controlled the seas. To blockade the Southern coast, the Union navy seized, or **commandeered,** tugboats, ferries, whalers, and fishing schooners.

The blockade stopped much of the South's trade with other countries. Southern **blockade-runners**—fast ships that outran the federal ships—often slipped through the blockade. They could not supply all the goods the South needed, however.

The *Merrimack* and the *Monitor*

The small Confederate navy aimed to break the blockade. The most daring attempt came when they captured a Union warship named the *Merrimack.* They fitted the ship with thick iron armor and renamed it the *Virginia.* Called an ironclad, this new iron-plated ship staged the South's greatest challenge to the North.

On March 8, 1862, the *Virginia* attacked Northern wooden warships at Hampton Roads in Virginia. The Northern cannons hit the *Virginia* time after time but could not sink it. The *Virginia*, on the other hand, destroyed two Northern vessels and drove three others ashore.

That evening a Northern ironclad called the *Monitor* reached Hampton Roads. When the *Virginia* appeared the next day, the *Monitor* came to meet it. For the first time in naval history, ironclad fought ironclad. The *Monitor* was easier to handle than the *Virginia,* and its guns were mounted on a revolving turret. The two ships pounded each other for four hours.

Neither ship suffered much damage, but the *Monitor* stopped the *Virginia* from threatening the Union navy again. The battle between the *Virginia* and *Monitor*

Picturing History **IRONCLAD SHIPS** The Union's *Monitor* defeated the Confederate's *Merrimack* off the coast of Virginia, preserving the Union's blockade. The battle would mark the end of wooden warships. **What did the Confederates rename the *Merrimack?***

Picturing History

▲ PRESIDENT LINCOLN AND GENERAL McCLELLAN
This photo shows President Lincoln and General McClellan conferring at Antietam. **Why didn't McClellan follow the retreating Confederates?**

marked a turning point in naval history. From then on ironclads replaced older wooden warships in sea battles.

★ The Battle of Antietam

General Lee's victory at the Second Battle of Bull Run encouraged him to invade the Union. He planned to surprise Washington, D.C., from the north and destroy Northern morale. A victory on Northern soil might also help the South win British and French support. British and French leaders favored the South over the North because Southern farms supplied British and French textile industries with cotton. The Europeans, however, wanted to be certain that the South could win before sending money and materials to the Confederacy.

In September 1862, Lee and his force of 45,000 soldiers slipped into Maryland and disappeared into the mountains. He split his forces, sending Stonewall Jackson to seize the arsenal at Harpers Ferry. Unluckily, one of his officers lost the orders describing his army's movements. Union soldiers found the orders wrapped around three cigars at an abandoned campsite and brought them to McClellan. McClellan now knew that Lee had divided his army.

Even with this knowledge, McClellan did not immediately attack.

Lee learned of the information leak, and realizing that he no longer had the advantage of surprise, prepared to fight anyway. McClellan finally attacked on September 17, 1862, along **Antietam** (an•TEE•tuhm) Creek near Sharpsburg, Maryland. In the bloodiest single day of fighting in the entire war, McClellan's 90,000-man army repeatedly attacked Lee's forces producing enormous casualties on both sides. More than 26,000 soldiers were killed or wounded. On the night of September 18, the Confederates slipped off to Virginia.

McClellan's army suffered too much damage to pursue the retreating Rebels. Lee missed his chance for a victory in the North. The battle ended in a draw. Because Lee and his army retreated, however, the North claimed it a victory for the Union.

★ The Emancipation Proclamation

The victory at Antietam also helped President Lincoln issue the Emancipation Proclamation. In 1860 and 1861 the 11 states of the Confederacy seceded mainly because they feared Lincoln would interfere in their rights and the institution of slavery. The North had entered the war only to reunite the Union, not to end slavery. Lincoln made this clear when he stated, "If I could save the Union without freeing any slave, I would do it; and if I could save it by freeing all the slaves, I would do it. . . ."

By the middle of 1862, Lincoln came to believe that he needed to broaden the goals of the war. In the face of Southern victories on land, the North's spirits sank, and he realized he needed the full support of antislavery groups. Lincoln made a decision to end slavery. He chose to wait until Union armies won a major battle to announce his decision. He feared that if he did not wait critics might view his action as a desperate attempt to gather support in the face of defeat.

When the news of Antietam was telegraphed to Lincoln, he called his cabinet together and told them:

> [S]everal weeks ago, I read to you an Order I had prepared. . . . I think the time has come now. I wish it were a better time. . . . The action of the army against the Rebels has not been quite what I should have best liked. But they have been driven out of Maryland.

On September 22 Lincoln issued a preliminary proclamation, or official public announcement. It declared all slaves in seceded states "forever free" unless the states returned to the Union by January 1, 1863. The new year came and went and no Confederate states reentered the Union. The Emancipation Proclamation went into effect on January 1, 1863.

The proclamation did not actually free a single slave. It excluded the more than 800,000 slaves in the border states that remained in the Union or in Union-occupied areas. It applied only to lands outside federal control. Thus, it weakened the Confederacy without angering slaveholders in the Union.

Lincoln's action gave the war meaning for many Northerners. It transformed the war into a struggle against slavery. The proclamation also discouraged foreign powers from aiding the South. Many European countries that had laws banning slavery refused to take sides against a government fighting to end slavery.

Lincoln later supported the Thirteenth Amendment of the Constitution, which was ratified on December 18, 1865. The amendment abolished slavery in every state of the Union.

▲ *FIRST READING OF THE EMANCIPATION PROCLAMATION* by Francis Bicknell Carpenter
Following the Union victory at Antietam, President Lincoln issued the Emancipation Proclamation. The proclamation did not apply to Union or Union-occupied states.
What amendment to the Constitution ended slavery?

COME AND JOIN US BROTHERS.
PUBLISHED BY THE SUPERVISORY COMMITTEE FOR RECRUITING COLORED REGIMENTS
1210 CHESTNUT ST. PHILADELPHIA

Picturing History

▲ AFRICAN AMERICAN RECRUITMENT ADVERTISEMENT
The Emancipation Proclamation included President Lincoln's decision to allow African Americans to join the Union army. **Why had Lincoln been opposed to enlisting African Americans?**

★ African American Soldiers

Until the very end of the war, the South refused to let African Americans join the military. Confederate armies often used enslaved persons to dig fortifications, cook, drive wagons, and perform other labors. Widespread opposition to arming them for combat existed in the South.

The Emancipation Proclamation announced Lincoln's decision to permit African Americans to join the Union army. Earlier in the war, Lincoln had opposed enlisting African Americans as soldiers. He feared the border states would object. Some officers in the field, though, wanted and needed their help.

About 20,000 African Americans served in the Union navy. At least 180,000 African Americans served in the Union army. Two-thirds of them had been slaves when they fled the South. African American troops formed 166 all-African American regiments, most of which had white commanders. Only about 100 African Americans

became officers. African American soldiers faced other types of discrimination, too. For example, most Union commanders used African American soldiers as laborers rather than sending them into combat.

On the Battlefield

Eventually African American soldiers fought in all major battles and hundreds of skirmishes. Many of the African American regiments distinguished themselves in combat. Twenty-three African American men earned the military's Medal of Honor for their bravery.

The 54th Massachusetts Volunteers became the best-known African American regiment. Its soldiers assaulted Fort Wagner in Charleston Harbor on July 18, 1863. Under heavy fire, the soldiers forced their way into the fort. The commander and many of the troops died in fierce hand-to-hand combat. The soldiers' bravery inspired other African Americans to enlist.

★ Confederate Victories at Fredericksburg and Chancellorsville

After Lee retreated at Antietam, McClellan hesitated six weeks before pursuing him. Then he began a slow advance toward Richmond. Lincoln lost patience with McClellan and replaced him with General **Ambrose Burnside.**

In late 1862 Burnside led his troops east to **Fredericksburg, Virginia,** on the Rappahannock River. By the time the Union troops crossed the river, Lee had amassed 73,000 soldiers. The Confederates held off the Union forces for several weeks. Then Burnside retreated.

Admitting his failure, Burnside resigned. Lincoln replaced him with General **Joseph Hooker.** Lee outmaneuvered Hooker, too. On May 4, 1863, the Confederates defeated Hooker's forces at **Chancellorsville, Virginia.**

Although Southerners had won the battle at Chancellorsville, they suffered a great loss. During a night skirmish, edgy Confederates accidentally shot one of their own—Stonewall Jackson. His left arm had to be amputated. Lee told Jackson's chaplain: "He has lost his left arm; but I have lost my right arm." By May 10 Jackson, suffering from delirium, shouted orders from his sickbed. Suddenly he grew calm and said, "No, let us cross over the river and rest under the shade of the trees." Then he died.

★ The Battle of Gettysburg

Encouraged by almost destroying Hooker's army of 138,000 at Chancellorsville and wanting to end the war as soon as possible, Lee decided to invade the North once again.

In June 1863, Lee's army moved north into southern Pennsylvania. Just before the battle broke out, Lincoln replaced Hooker with Pennsylvanian General **George Meade.** An accidental clash between small units at **Gettysburg** developed into a bloody battle that marked the turning point of the war. On July 1–3, 1863, Meade's Northern army of about 85,000 clashed with Lee's Confederate forces of about 65,000 in the most celebrated battle of the war—the Battle of Gettysburg.

The first shots exploded on July 1 when a Confederate brigade searching for supplies encountered Union soldiers just outside of Gettysburg. By the end of the day, Meade's forces had been pushed south of town. They took a strong defensive position on high ground. The front ran about 3 miles (5 km) along Cemetery Ridge, with Culp's Hill and Cemetery Hill at one end, and hills called Round Top and Little Round Top at the other.

A confident Lee ordered flanking attacks at both ends of the Union position on July 2. After a full day of battle, Union forces still held their positions. On July 3

Picturing History

▲ THE BATTLE OF GETTYSBURG The Battle of Gettysburg lasted three days. The Union won the battle, but both sides had heavy casualties. **Who led the famous charge against Union troops during the battle?**

Lee decided to attack the Union center in what has become known as Pickett's Charge. Led by General **George E. Pickett**, about 13,000 Confederates marched almost 1 mile (1 km) across an open field and ran up the slopes of Cemetery Ridge under heavy enemy fire. Only a few troops reached the top of the ridge, and Union forces quickly killed or captured them. Pickett's gallant charge had failed.

After three days of fighting, Union casualties numbered nearly 23,000. More than 22,000 Confederates were killed or wounded, about 7,000 of them in Pickett's charge. "Don't let the enemy escape," Lincoln wired the victorious Meade.

On July 4 Lee retreated into Virginia. Once again, the Union army failed to pursue him. "Our army held the war in the hollow of its hand," lamented Lincoln. "We had only to stretch forth our hands and they were ours. And nothing I could say or do could make the Army move."

Gettysburg was a victory for the North and the turning point of the war. Never again would the weakened Confederate forces be strong enough to seriously threaten the Union.

★ The Gettysburg Address

The burial sites of the soldiers who lost their lives at Gettysburg stretched for miles. Northerners built a cemetery at Gettysburg to honor the dead. President Lincoln attended the dedication ceremony on November 19, 1863. He sat with his arms folded while Edward Everett, one of the most famous speakers of the time, gave the two-hour dedication speech. Lincoln then rose and spoke for only three minutes. His brief remarks are now recognized as one of the finest speeches ever made.

In a few words, Lincoln made clear why Union soldiers died. He reminded Americans that their nation was ". . . conceived in Liberty, and dedicated to the proposition that all men are created equal." He concluded his short remarks by saying:

> [W]e here highly resolve that these dead shall not have died in vain . . . and that government of the people, by the people, for the people, shall not perish from the earth.

★ SECTION 2 REVIEW ★

Checking for Understanding

1. **Identify** Thomas "Stonewall" Jackson, George McClellan, Ambrose Burnside, Joseph Hooker, George Meade.

2. **Define** Rebels, Yankees, commandeer, blockade-runner, ironclad, Emancipation Proclamation.

3. **In** what state did the bloody battle of Antietam take place?

4. **Why** did Lincoln issue the Emancipation Proclamation?

5. **Why** was Gettysburg a turning point in the war?

Critical Thinking

6. **Interpreting Primary Sources** In Lincoln's Gettysburg Address he said the cemetery was "a final resting place for those who here gave their lives that the nation might live." What did he mean by "the nation might live"?

ACTIVITY

7. General Robert E. Lee commanded the Army of Northern Virginia. General Ulysses S. Grant led the Army of the Potomac. Design a flag for either Lee or Grant's regiment.

The Telegraph

◄ SAMUEL F.B. MORSE

Samuel F.B. Morse invented the telegraph receiver and developed a type of code consisting of short pulses, or dots and dashes. The code is called the Morse code.

The dots and dashes of the Morse code became an important instrument in the Civil War, especially for the North. At the height of the war, the North sent as many as 3,000 messages a day by telegraph.

To send a message over the wires, the telegraph operators set up battery wagons near the battlefields. Operators used a switch or key to create short pulses of electric current that would travel through the wire. Heavy, 150-volt batteries supplied the power to send the signal. Many telegraph operators were killed in the Civil War because they worked so close to the action.

Coded Messages

Lincoln and his chief military advisers gathered in a telegraph office at the War Department to await information from the battlefronts. Messengers on horseback raced messages from the battlefields to battery wagons. Telegraph operators relayed information about the movement of troops, the numbers of dead and injured, and requests for more food and supplies. To prevent the enemy from intercepting their messages, the North and South made up their own special codes called **ciphers.**

Journalists who followed the armies used the telegraph to relay information to their newspapers. Families of soldiers relied on the newspapers to learn the latest news from the front.

During the war, the North ran 15,000 miles of new telegraph wire. The South added only about 1,000 miles. The earliest telegraph wire was not insulated, or wrapped, so it had to be strung on poles. Later wires were laid on the ground and could withstand foot and wagon traffic.

Making the Science Connection

1. How did the President and military leaders make use of the telegraph during the war?

2. Why was the telegraph important to the families of soldiers?

3. Did the North or the South use telegraphs more during the war?

ACTIVITY

4. Write the title of your favorite song or movie using International Morse Code. The code is listed in most dictionaries and encyclopedias. Give your coded message to another person to decipher.

★★

The War in the West

SETTING THE SCENE

Read to Learn . . .

★ the importance of rivers in the war in the West.
★ why the Union wanted to take over Vicksburg and Chattanooga.

Terms to Know

★ siege

People to Meet

★ Ulysses S. Grant
★ Albert Sidney Johnston
★ William Tecumseh Sherman

Places to Locate

★ Shiloh, Tennessee
★ Vicksburg, Mississippi
★ Chattanooga, Tennessee

► BATTLE OF SHILOH

Although the Union armies lost battles in the West, they won every major campaign. In little more than two years, they cut the Confederacy in two.

In 1861 the war in the West was devoted to a struggle for control of the border states. In spite of strong pro-Confederate minorities, both Kentucky and Missouri were cleared of Confederate troops.

★ Taking the Mississippi Valley

In the following year, the Confederacy was squeezed from both the north and the south as both sides fought to control the Mississippi River. The Union advance began when General **Ulysses S. Grant** attacked two Confederate forts on the Kentucky-Tennessee border.

Confederates had built Fort Henry on the Tennessee River and Fort Donelson on the Cumberland River, hoping to stop Union troops from using the rivers to travel south. In February 1862, Grant amassed 15,000 soldiers and a squadron of ironclad gunboats and captured Fort Henry. Most of the Confederate troops fled to Fort Donelson. Grant and his troops pursued them.

On February 14, 1862, Union gunboats shelled the fort. The next day the Yankees attacked and surrounded the fort. On

February 16, the fort's commander, realizing that the fort would soon fall, asked for the best terms of surrender that Grant would accept. Grant replied, "No terms except unconditional and immediate surrender can be accepted." In other words the Rebels had to give up everything. The fort commander agreed, and about 13,000 Confederate soldiers surrendered. The Union victory broke the Confederates' first line of defense in the Mississippi Valley and opened the South for invasion. When Northerners heard the news, they celebrated and nicknamed their new hero "Unconditional Surrender" Grant.

★ Surprise at Shiloh

The fall of Fort Donelson opened the way for a Union advance south toward a railroad center at Corinth, Mississippi. From there Grant planned to move west along the railroad to capture Memphis, Tennessee.

The bloody two-day battle of **Shiloh** on the Tennessee-Mississippi border in April 1862, though, slowed the Union advance. General **Albert Sidney Johnston** planned to surprise and attack Grant's troops. The size of Johnston's army equaled the Union forces. Therefore, Johnston chose to attack before Union reinforcements arrived. He told his troops, "Tonight we will water our horses in the Tennessee River."

Early on April 6, Grant heard guns but thought little of it. Scouts who went to investigate reported, "The Johnnies are there thicker than Spanish needles in a fence corner." Soon after, the Rebels overran the camp and pushed the Yankees toward the river.

The Northern Troops Rally

Some Union troops refused to fall back, obeying Grant's order to "maintain that position at all costs." A handful of soldiers from the 53rd Ohio regiment stood their

Picturing History

▲ **GENERAL GRANT AND HIS STAFF** General Ulysses S. Grant often met with members of his staff to discuss battle strategy. **What did the Union accomplish by defeating the Confederates at Fort Donelson?**

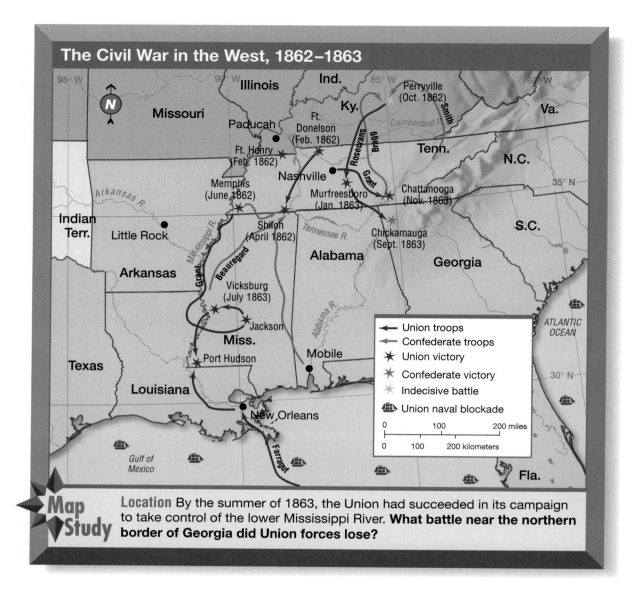

The Civil War in the West, 1862–1863

Illinois
Ind.
Missouri
Perryville (Oct. 1862)
Va.
Paducah
Ft. Donelson (Feb. 1862)
Ky.
Cumberland R.
Smith
Ft. Henry (Feb. 1862)
Rosecrans
Bragg
Tenn.
N.C.
Memphis (June 1862)
Nashville
Grant
Murfreesboro (Jan. 1863)
Chattanooga (Nov. 1863)
35° N
Indian Terr.
Arkansas R.
Little Rock
Shiloh (April 1862)
Tennessee R.
Chickamauga (Sept. 1863)
S.C.
Mississippi R.
Beauregard
Alabama
Georgia
Arkansas
Grant
Vicksburg (July 1863)
Jackson
Alabama R.
Miss.
Mobile
Texas
Port Hudson
Louisiana
New Orleans
30° N
ATLANTIC OCEAN
Farragut
Gulf of Mexico
Fla.

Legend:
— Union troops
— Confederate troops
★ Union victory
✴ Confederate victory
✴ Indecisive battle
⛨ Union naval blockade

0   100   200 miles
0   100   200 kilometers

Map Study

Location By the summer of 1863, the Union had succeeded in its campaign to take control of the lower Mississippi River. **What battle near the northern border of Georgia did Union forces lose?**

---

ground, along with General Benjamin Prentiss and his division. Prentiss's soldiers repelled wave after wave of Southerners and even killed General Johnston. Union soldiers fired so fast and hard that the Confederates dubbed the area the "Hornets' Nest."

By nightfall, 25,000 Union reinforcements reached the tired and beaten troops holding out at Shiloh. The next day Grant used his much larger force to defeat the Confederates. The Rebels limped back to Corinth.

Grant's forces had stopped the Confederates from retaking western Tennessee. Grant suffered 13,000 casualties. The South lost nearly 11,000. When Grant looked at

the battlefield littered with bodies he said, "It would have been possible to walk across the clearing in any direction stepping on dead bodies without a foot touching the ground." When Northern critics urged Lincoln to replace Grant because of the heavy Union losses, Lincoln refused, saying, "I can't spare this man—he fights." Lincoln perceived that Grant represented the best hope for the Union cause.

★ Capturing the South's Highways

By the end of 1862, Union armies occupied all of western Tennessee and moved south into Mississippi. Only the strategically important city of **Vicksburg, Mississippi,** blocked Union control of the Mississippi River and success of the Union's western strategy. A stream of food, cotton, and other supplies poured into Vicksburg and the rest of the South from the West on the Mississippi River. These supplies kept Southern soldiers alive and fighting. If Grant and his army cut that supply line, the South would suffer greatly. Admiral David Farragut and his fleet of Union gunboats already had captured New Orleans at the river's mouth. Once Vicksburg fell, the Union would control the Mississippi River.

The Vicksburg Campaign

Grant hoped to seize the city quickly, but acres of impassable swampland lay between his army and Vicksburg. In late 1862 and early 1863 Grant made several attempts to capture the city but failed. Finally in May 1863, Grant embarked on one of the most daring campaigns in military history. He planned to go around the swamp. His army would march east deep into enemy territory and capture Jackson, Mississippi, to stop Confederates there from interfering. This way he could get to Vicksburg on dry ground.

After transporting his forces down the Mississippi River to just below Vicksburg, he started inland. Against the established rules of military science and the advice of his staff, Grant cut loose from his base of supplies. Grant permitted the Union soldiers only as much food as they could carry or get along the way.

The Confederate commander of Vicksburg at first stayed behind his fortifications,

Linking Past and Present

★★★★★★★★★★★★★

Through the Camera's Eye

Mathew Brady captured the Civil War forever on film. He was one of America's first photojournalists—photographers who record the news in photographs.

By war's end, he and his many assistants had recorded the battles, the camps, and the lives and deaths of Union soldiers in more than 10,000 photos. Brady called the camera "the eye of history."

▲ **MODERN PHOTOJOURNALISTS**

Then

Moved by a Spirit

Mathew Brady claimed that when the Civil War broke out, "A spirit in my feet said go and I went." He packed photographic and developing equipment in an old delivery wagon and traveled with the Union army.

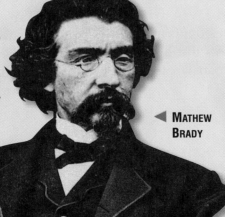

◄ **MATHEW BRADY**

Now

Every Picture Tells a Story

Today photojournalists travel all over the world to cover news and sporting events. They zoom their photos back to newspapers and magazines via computers. Many risk their lives to cover wars and natural disasters. Much of our view of the world is based on their photographs.

★★★★★★★★★★★★★★★★★★★★★★★★★★★★★

> " We are utterly cut off from the world, surrounded by a circle of fire. . . . The fiery shower of shells goes on day and night. . . . A shell came tearing through the roof, burst upstairs, tore up that room; . . . the pieces coming through both floors down into the cellar. . . . "

Hungry and battered, the Confederates surrendered on July 4, 1863, the day after the Southern defeat at Gettysburg. The Union split the South in half and now controlled the Mississippi River. The collapse of the Confederacy would soon follow.

Chickamauga and Chattanooga

Union forces now attempted to cut the Confederacy again—through eastern Tennessee and Georgia. They aimed to capture **Chattanooga,** a rail center on the Tennessee-Georgia border. While Grant's army began to occupy Vicksburg, other Union troops chased General Braxton Bragg and his Confederates from Chattanooga. By mid-September, though, the Confederates rallied and beat the Yankees in a bloody battle at nearby **Chickamauga Creek.** This would prove to be the Confederates' last important victory in the Civil War.

The Union army pulled back to Chattanooga. The Confederates boxed them in and waited for them to surrender. Inside Chattanooga the Union soldiers, without

thinking Grant was trying to trick him into taking to the field. Moving quickly, Union forces reached Jackson almost without opposition. Then Grant turned and fought his way back west to the outskirts of Vicksburg. In 17 days his troops had marched 180 miles (290 km) and won five battles against larger forces.

Grant tried to take the city by storm but failed. He then began a siege, or a blockade of the city. The siege would force Confederate soldiers and citizens to stay in the city while cutting off all their food and supplies. They would have to surrender or starve.

Federal gunboats and artillery shelled the city day and night for more than six weeks. The terrified population of Vicksburg dug in and hid in caves to escape Union shells. Starving residents ate horses, mules, and dogs. As the bombardment continued, a woman wrote in her diary:

Footnotes to History

A Soldier's ID Heavy death tolls in battle led Civil War soldiers to devise the first dog tags for identification if they were killed. Soldiers printed their names and addresses on handkerchiefs or paper, which they pinned to their clothing before going into battle.

food, began to starve. An Indiana private described their rations as "One cracker for each meal. We generally eat them up in three days and starve the other two."

The Union could not afford to lose an army regiment. Trains carrying relief troops sped from the East, and Grant's troops arrived from the West to bolster the forces. To feed the trapped army, Grant opened up a "cracker line"—the soldiers' name for a supply route. Then he turned his attention to defeating the Confederates.

The Rebels held the hills and ridges around Chattanooga. On November 24, Union troops under General Hooker scrambled up a ridge called Lookout Mountain and routed a small Confederate force. The next morning the Union soldiers cheered to see the Stars and Stripes waving from the mountaintop.

Meanwhile, General **William Tecumseh Sherman** and his Union troops attacked the flank of the main Confederate force on Missionary Ridge. Grant wanted to divert the enemy's attention away from Sherman. He ordered soldiers to charge halfway up the steep Missionary Ridge. The soldiers, frustrated and angry from their defeat at Chickamauga, did not stop halfway as ordered. They continued up the steep slopes in one of the most remarkable charges in military history. Chanting "Chickamauga! Chick-

★★★ AMERICA'S FLAGS ★★★

Seventeenth Flag of the Union, 1863 The Union flag of 1863 held 35 stars. Like all the Union flags of the Civil War, it retained stars for the seceded Southern states. Thus it supported Lincoln and the North's claim that the Union could not be broken.

★★★★★★★★★★★★★★★★★★★★★★★

amauga!" they reached the top and scattered the confused Confederates.

★ Success in the West

The Confederate army retreated to Georgia. The Union had achieved two of its three goals. First, their naval blockade had cut off European supplies to the South. Second, by taking control of the Mississippi River, the Union had split the Confederacy. Southerners had lost the rivers and railways that carried food from western farms to eastern troops. The South had lost the war in the West. In addition, the North had cut the Confederacy through Tennessee. Now Northerners could carry out the final step of the plan that General Scott proposed years ago—invading the Deep South.

★ SECTION 3 REVIEW ★

★★★★★★★★★★★★★★★★★   ★★★★★★★★★★★★★★★★★

Checking for Understanding

1. **Identify** Ulysses S. Grant, Albert Sidney Johnston, William Tecumseh Sherman.

2. **Define** siege.

3. Why were rivers important to Confederate and Union armies in the West?

4. What war goals had the North achieved after the Battle of Chattanooga?

Critical Thinking

5. **Drawing Conclusions** Would the North and South have gone to war if they had known how many soldiers would be killed?

ACTIVITY

6. Imagine you are General Grant. Write a letter to the family of a Union soldier who died during battle.

Interpreting a Battle Map

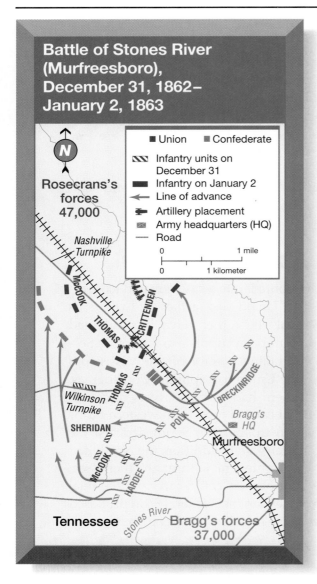

Battle of Stones River (Murfreesboro), December 31, 1862– January 2, 1863

- ■ Union ■ Confederate
- ⬚⬚ Infantry units on December 31
- ▬ Infantry on January 2
- ← Line of advance
- Artillery placement
- Army headquarters (HQ)
- — Road

0   1 mile

0   1 kilometer

Rosecrans's forces 47,000

Nashville Turnpike

McCOOK

THOMAS

CRITTENDEN

Wilkinson Turnpike

THOMAS

SHERIDAN

POLK

BRECKINRIDGE

Bragg's HQ

Murfreesboro

McCOOK

HARDEE

Tennessee

Stones River

Bragg's forces 37,000

In a war each army tries to gain control of land. Maps can help us understand the strategy used by each side to win a battle.

Learning the Skill

Battle maps use colors and symbols to tell the story of a battle. Look at the map on this page showing the Battle of Stones River (Murfreesboro) in Tennessee. It includes four kinds of information.

First, the map uses colors to identify the opposing sides. Blue represents the Union army, red represents the Confederate army. The map includes the names of commanding officers, total troop numbers for each side, and important dates.

Second, symbols represent troops and equipment. A blue bar represents one Union infantry unit. Other symbols stand for artillery and troop headquarters.

Third, the map shows important landscape features such as rivers, railroads, and roads. Because these features may help or hinder an army's movements, they strongly affect the outcome of the battle.

Fourth, battles involve troop movements over a period of time. On this map striped and solid bars represent the troops and arrows show where they moved during battle.

Practicing the Skill

Use the map of the Battle of Stones River to answer these questions.

1. Who were the Union and Confederate commanders and officers?

2. Where was the Union's artillery located?

3. Which group of Confederate troops broke through McCook's line on December 31?

4. Where were McCook's troops on January 2? Did they advance or retreat to this location?

5. Which side gained the most ground in this battle? Explain your answer.

APPLYING THE SKILL

6. Create a three-dimensional model of the Battle of Stones River. Use movable pieces to represent troops. Then demonstrate troop movements over the course of the battle.

★★★★★★★★★★★★★★★★★★★★★★★★★★★★

Behind the Lines

SETTING THE SCENE

Read to Learn . . .

★ why some Northerners and Southerners opposed their governments.

★ how the North and the South raised armies and paid for war.

★ how the war changed the roles of women in society.

Terms to Know

★ Copperheads
★ habeas corpus
★ conscription
★ quota
★ bounty
★ greenbacks

People to Meet

★ Clara Barton
★ Mary Ann Bickerdyke

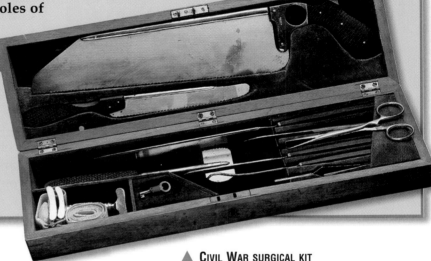

▲ CIVIL WAR SURGICAL KIT

The Civil War was the largest war ever fought on the North American continent. Of the 1.5 million Southern white males of fighting age, about 900,000 served in the Confederate armies. Of 4 million such males in the North, about half fought in the war. In addition, more than 200,000 African Americans fought and served in the Union military, and thousands more performed manual labor.

More Americans lost their lives in the Civil War than in any other conflict in the history of the United States. Even in the early battles, soldiers died at a shockingly high rate. As the war dragged on, the Union suffered terrible casualties but grew stronger. Confederate losses, however, gradually weakened the South's will to fight.

★ Wartime Government

In a long war fought on a vast scale, victors are decided as much by government policies behind the lines as on the battlefield. Both Union and Confederate government leaders greatly increased their powers to raise and supply the armies, finance the war, and suppress antiwar opinions.

▲ PRESIDENT ABRAHAM LINCOLN

Growing Discontent in the North

Many Northerners criticized the government during the war. Irate abolitionists condemned Lincoln's accommodating attitude toward slavery and his refusal to make the end of slavery a goal of the war. Members of Lincoln's own party in Congress, a faction called the Radical Republicans, joined the opposition. Radical Republicans opposed Lincoln's view that the war was about preserving the Union.

At the other extreme stood a faction of Democrats, or Peace Democrats, who called for ending the war at any price, even if that meant welcoming the South and slavery back into the Union, or letting the slave states separate in peace. Republican newspapers compared these Democrats to the poisonous copperhead snake. The term caught on and Peace Democrats came to be known as Copperheads. Some Copperheads encouraged Northerners to resist the war and others openly supported the South.

The Issue of Rights

Many of the measures Lincoln used to quiet opposition violated constitutional guarantees of free speech, press, and assembly. He prevented a state legislature from meeting. He denied some opposition newspapers use of the mails and used the army to shut other newspapers down. He suspended the right of habeas corpus and jailed thousands of suspected Confederate sympathizers. Habeas corpus guarantees a person who is arrested the right to appear before a judge in a court of law. Lincoln agonized over these decisions, but he believed that the survival of the Union during an emergency overrode the Constitution.

Trouble in the South

The South, too, had its share of problems. In some areas, white citizens opposed the war, as did enslaved African Americans. Some people, especially those in areas that limited slavery, refused to recognize the Confederate government or to serve in the Southern army.

In addition, Jefferson Davis encountered opposition to creating a strong central government. Davis had to turn rebels into citizens and create loyalty to a new government out of disloyalty to an old one. Many Southerners strongly supported states' rights, resisted paying taxes to a central government, and did not fully support the military.

★ Raising the Armies

In the beginning, both the North and the South relied on volunteers to build up their armies. The rising number of casualties, though, reduced enthusiasm for the war, and enlistments decreased.

Both the North and South enforced conscription, or the drafting of men for military service. In April 1862 the South, with less than one-half the population of the North, began drafting men aged 18 to 35. These men had to serve as long as the war lasted. Later, as the need to maintain its armies increased, the Confederate congress raised the upper age limit to 50.

Conscription in the North began in 1863. The Enrollment Act decreed that men between 20 and 45 join the military for three years. When the federal government needed soldiers, it specified a quota, or fixed number, from each state. A man could excuse himself by paying $300, or by hiring a substitute to take his place. This law favored the wealthy over the poor. Such substitutions aroused criticism that the war appeared "a rich man's war and a poor man's fight."

The draft was unpopular in the North and the South. In the South some state govenors helped their citizens evade the draft. In the North, opposition led to riots in several cities.

The Bounty System

To encourage volunteers, many states in the North offered a bounty, or payments of money to a person for entering the armed services. Under this system, a volunteer could collect $1,000 or more by enlisting for three years. This led to the practice of "bounty jumping," whereby a man would enlist, collect his bounty, and then desert, only to reenlist somewhere else.

★ Wartime Economies

The North's economy grew stronger during the war. Northern farmers began to use the new industrial machines to harvest crops. Farm production increased. The war produced great demands for shoes, clothes, and other Northern products.

As the North's economy boomed, the South grew weaker from invasion and destruction. Confederate President Davis

and his government faced severe economic challenges. The South, with less money and industry than the North, required the use of all available human and economic resources to defend it. The Confederate government seized control of the economy and snatched rail lines from private owners. It determined how much wool or cotton and how many boots factories would produce. The Union blockade soon strangled the Southern economy.

Paying for the War

The North proved far more successful than the South in financing the war. About one-fourth of the $4 billion the North needed came from taxation, and the rest from borrowing and issuing paper money. Congress established the first income tax in 1861. The government also asked people to loan it money by buying government bonds. The government promised to pay the money back with interest after the war.

▲ RECRUITMENT POSTER FOR UNION ARMY

The federal government also printed $400 million worth of greenbacks, paper money not backed by gold or silver. Issuing more money caused the prices of goods to go up because each dollar became worth less. Most wages stayed the same, so people could not buy as much.

Like the North, the South also tried to raise money with taxes and bonds, but its already strained economy could not meet wartime needs. People in the South became less willing to cooperate. When the South tried printing more paper money, it drastically increased the prices of everyday goods. Near the war's end, flour cost up to $300 a barrel and shoes cost $200 a pair.

Supplying the Armies

The Confederacy faced an uphill struggle in carrying out its war effort. Its government encouraged factories to supply troops with arms and ammunition, but the South lacked the industrial capacity to provide other necessities.

The North, on the other hand, had a strong industrial base, but overcharging and corruption plagued the efforts of the Union government to supply its troops. Army contractors sometimes supplied shoddy clothing, rotten meat, and defective shoes. In spite of this, Union armies proved better equipped than their enemy.

★ Hardships of War

Wounded soldiers faced the horrors of crude medical care. Few doctors of the time knew that germs spread infection. Army surgeons never boiled their instruments. If the wounded survived their operations, recuperating patients and volunteers nursed them back to health. More than half of the people who died in the Civil War died from disease, not injuries from battle. Malaria, typhoid, and dysentery spread quickly through the troops.

In both the North and the South, women played a vital role in the care of wounded and dying soldiers. **Dorothea Dix,** who had campaigned for the rights of the mentally ill, volunteered after the shelling of Fort Sumter. She supervised all the female nurses for the Union forces. **Sojourner Truth,** a leader in the antislavery movement, worked as a nurse and also cared for freed slaves. **Clara Barton** served in numerous Union field hospitals and later founded the American Red Cross. **Mary Ann Bickerdyke** worked on the front lines of battle caring for wounded Union troops.

Although the South had fewer aid societies, many women volunteered as nurses. Others gathered to knit socks, make clothing, and prepare food for soldiers. Many women moved to the cities from farms to make their lives easier and to find jobs. During the war the population of Richmond, for example, tripled.

★ SECTION 4 REVIEW ★

Checking for Understanding

1. **Identify** Clara Barton, Mary Ann Bickerdyke.
2. **Define** Copperheads, habeas corpus, conscription, quota, bounty, greenbacks.
3. **Why** did President Lincoln suspend the writ of habeas corpus during the war?
4. **How** did the war affect the economies of the North and the South?

Critical Thinking

5. **Analyzing Information** Do you think Lincoln acted in the country's best interest when he suspended the writ of habeas corpus? Explain.

ACTIVITY

6. Draw a cartoon about the conscription laws in the North or the South.

★★★

Surrender at Appomattox

SETTING THE SCENE

Read to Learn . . .

★ why Sherman's march to the sea caused so much destruction.

★ how the Civil War came to an end.

Terms to Know

★ total war

People to Meet

★ **William Tecumseh Sherman**

★ **Philip Henry Sheridan**

★ George McClellan

Places to Locate

★ Atlanta, Georgia

★ Columbia, South Carolina

★ Petersburg, Virginia

★ Appomattox Court House, Virginia

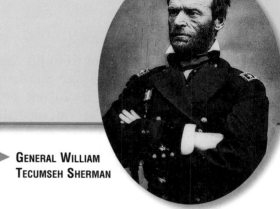

▶ GENERAL WILLIAM TECUMSEH SHERMAN

After the Southern defeats of 1863, Northern troops occupied large areas of the Confederacy and controlled the Mississippi River. The Southern railroad system lay in ruins and Southern armies suffered from lack of supplies. The Northern armies readied to deal the final blow. On March 9, 1864, Lincoln promoted Grant to lieutenant general and gave him command of all Northern armies. Grant declared to Lincoln, "Whatever happens, there will be no turning back."

★ Wearing Down the South

As commander in chief, Grant planned to wage total war against the Confeder-

ates, destroying their armies as well as their resources. The total war policy also meant that Southern citizens suffered as much as Confederate soldiers. Grant targeted Richmond and Atlanta, the last two major rail links between Southern troops and their food and supplies. Grant set out for Richmond and ordered General **William Tecumseh Sherman** to Atlanta.

Meanwhile Grant ordered **Philip Henry Sheridan** to destroy the rich farmlands that fed the Confederate army. He instructed Sheridan to devastate the area so completely that a crow flying over the area would need to carry its own rations. Sheridan did just that in the Shenandoah Valley of Virginia.

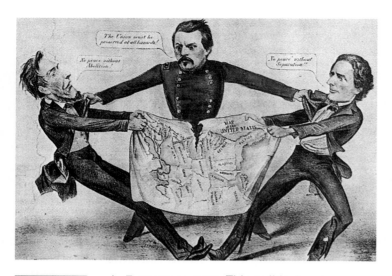

▲ ELECTION OF 1864 This political cartoon, drawn during the election of 1864, shows George McClellan trying to save the Union at any cost. **What party nominated McClellan for President?**

The March to the Sea

Sherman also set out to fulfill Grant's orders. He wanted to show Southerners that their government could not protect them. In May 1864, he set out for **Atlanta** from Chattanooga with 100,000 soldiers. Sherman captured Atlanta in September, defeating a Confederate army of about 62,000. After several battles, much of Atlanta burned to the ground and Sherman destroyed the main railroad line. One Indiana soldier wrote, "We have utterly destroyed Atlanta. I don't think any people will want to try and live there now."

In November Sherman began a campaign that would make him one of the generals directly responsible for Northern victory and the most hated man in the South. Sherman's troops began a march to the Georgia coast. Sherman planned to march his men across Georgia to Savannah and the sea. His troops would forage for food, or live off the land. Sherman's forces left a 60-mile-wide (96 km) strip of burned crops, barns, and warehouses in their path. They destroyed everything they could not use, aiming to destroy Southern morale and will to continue the fight.

Sherman's Reception

Slaves greeted Sherman's troops wherever they went. Sherman described them as "simply frantic with joy." One woman pointed at the general and cried, "There's the man that rules the world!"

White Southerners viewed Sherman differently. A Georgia newspaper called him "the Attila of the West" and his soldiers "hell-hounds." Some Georgians burned bridges and shot at soldiers to slow them down. Others fled their homes in fear.

Sherman reached the Atlantic coast at Savannah, Georgia, in December 1864 and sent Lincoln the following wire: "I beg to present you as a Christmas gift the city of Savannah. . . ." Next Sherman's army marched north. After the Union rampage through **Columbia,** the state capital, the city lay in ruins.

★ The Election of 1864

In the midst of war a presidential election took place. In the North the war divided both major parties—Republicans and Democrats—into peace and war factions. The Republican party temporarily changed its name to the Union party to attract Democrats who supported the war.

Now known as Unionists, the Republicans nominated Lincoln and chose a war Democrat for Vice President, Andrew Johnson of Tennessee. The largely antiwar Democrats nominated **George McClellan,** the popular general whom Lincoln had twice removed from command.

Lincoln did not expect to win reelection. A New York politician exclaimed, "The people are wild for peace. Lincoln's reelection is an impossibility." Sherman's capture of Atlanta, coupled with McClellan's refusal to support his party's peace platform, though, gave Lincoln a decisive victory. The Republican victory signaled a continuation of the war until the South surrendered and slavery ended.

★ Ending the War

While Sherman marched to Atlanta, Grant's forces fought Lee's army at three sites in Virginia—the **Wilderness, Spotsylvania Court House,** and **Cold Harbor.** In all three battles, both sides suffered enormous losses. The battles, though, took the heaviest toll on Grant's soldiers. Lee expected Grant to retreat, as other Union generals had after being defeated. Grant, however, refused to admit defeat.

On to Richmond

Grant moved his army closer to Richmond after each battle. Lee's army followed and tried to prevent the Yankees from reaching the capital. Part of Grant's army slipped past Lee and reached **Petersburg, Virginia.**

All railroads supplying Richmond ran through Petersburg. If Union troops took Petersburg, Richmond would also fall. The soldiers stormed the town but failed to capture it. Soon Lee and his army arrived and dug in to defend Petersburg. Grant's forces attacked Lee's defenses again and again but made little headway.

In June 1864, Grant realized that only a siege could destroy Lee's army. He would force Lee's troops to stay in the trenches at Petersburg until they ran out of supplies and soldiers. The siege lasted nine months. Grant's troops suffered severe losses, but so did Lee's forces. Grant could get new troops, while Lee ran out of soldiers.

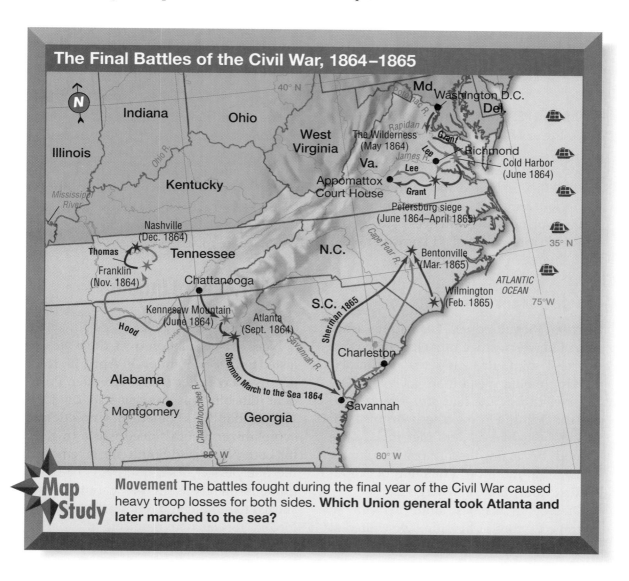

The Final Battles of the Civil War, 1864–1865

Map Study — **Movement** The battles fought during the final year of the Civil War caused heavy troop losses for both sides. **Which Union general took Atlanta and later marched to the sea?**

▲ LEE SURRENDERS TO GRANT Grant offered generous terms of surrender and ordered his troops not to celebrate. "The rebels are our countrymen again," he said. **What did Grant agree the Confederate soldiers could keep?**

On April 2, Grant finally broke through Lee's lines. That same day the Confederate government evacuated Richmond. Union troops entered the city on April 3. When Lincoln visited the captured capital, thousands of African Americans turned out, cheering him every step of the way. One man shouted, "I know I am free for I have seen Father Abraham."

Lee and Grant at Appomattox

When Richmond fell, Lee and his army retreated westward. Grant chased Lee and overtook him. Realizing that continued fighting would mean more lives lost, Lee dispatched a white flag and a request to cease fighting. On the afternoon of April 9, 1865, the two leaders met in a house owned by a Southern farmer, Wilmer McLean, in the little settlement of **Appomattox Court House** in Virginia.

Dressed in his best uniform with an engraved sword at his side, Lee waited at McLean's two-story brick house. He

explained to an aide, "I have probably to be General Grant's prisoner and thought I must make my best appearance." Grant showed up wearing a rumpled coat and muddy boots. He had no sword. They greeted each other and talked. Then Grant offered generous terms of surrender. As Lee read the terms, he mentioned that his soldiers owned their horses. Grant agreed to let the men keep the horses for spring plowing. In the terms, Confederate soldiers also received a day's rations. Grant permitted the Confederate officers to keep their side arms and released them on parole. Lee agreed to the terms, and the generals shook hands.

Lee gazed sadly toward the valley where his defeated army waited. Then he mounted his horse, Traveler, returned Grant's salute, and rode off. Later Grant heard his soldiers firing victory salutes. He knew how humiliated the Confederates felt and ordered the noise stopped. "The war is over," he said. "The Rebels are our countrymen again."

Within a short time, all other Confederate generals also surrendered. Although Confederate President Jefferson Davis fled, Union forces eventually captured him in Georgia. On May 26, 1865, the long, bitter struggle that split the nation finally came to an end.

★ Abraham Lincoln Assassinated

Northerners' elation over their victory lasted only a brief time. On April 14, 1865, just five days after Lee's surrender, President Lincoln was assassinated by John Wilkes Booth, a fanatical Confederate sympathizer. Booth's deed was a tragedy for both North and South, for it removed the one person best equipped to resolve immense tensions in the country as it started to rebuild and reunite. Lincoln had looked forward to reuniting the nation from the outset of the war.

Lincoln in the White House

When Abraham Lincoln and his family first arrived at the White House they stood in the East Room, astonished at its immense size. Their simple home in Springfield, Illinois, could fit easily into this room alone!

A simple family man, Lincoln loved to frolic with his youngest sons, Tad and Willie. Family fun provided a happy diversion for Lincoln as he grappled with the horrors and difficulties of the Civil War. The issues of war forced the President to rise early and toil late into the night. He ended his days by visiting the War Department's telegraph office to read dispatches from the battlefield. President Lincoln often told stories and jokes, not only to illustrate important points, but also to dissolve tensions during the war. His sense of humor, though, could not transcend the national—or Lincoln's personal—despair.

Lincoln's family lived in constant fear that the capital would be attacked by Confederates. They worried over threats to the President's life. In February 1862, both Tad and Willie fell sick to typhoid fever. Although Tad recovered, Willie died.

As Lincoln's wife Mary became overwhelmed with grief, Lincoln recovered to lead the shattered nation. The anguish in

▲ ABRAHAM LINCOLN AND HIS SON TAD

the White House reflected the anguish of the nation. Knowing that he bore responsibility for so much suffering, Lincoln once asked a friend if it did not seem strange that he "who couldn't cut the head off a chicken, and who was sick at the sight of blood, should be cast into the middle of a great war, with blood flowing all about me?"

Not until General Lee surrendered the Confederate forces could Lincoln allow himself to relax. On April 14, 1865, he joined his wife for a carriage ride and a play. That evening an assassin took his life. No other President had faced such a national crisis, or endured such personal tragedies, yet the President dealt with both with compassion and greatness. ★★★

★ SECTION 5 REVIEW ★

★★★★★★★★★★★★★★★★★★★★   ★★★★★★★★★★★★★★★★★★★★

Checking for Understanding

1. **Identify** William Tecumseh Sherman, Philip Henry Sheridan, George McClellan, Appomattox Court House.

2. **Define** total war.

3. **How** did Sherman's march to the sea help end the war?

4. **How** did siege warfare defeat Lee's army?

Critical Thinking

5. **Drawing Conclusions** Why do you think Lincoln considered Grant to be a good general?

ACTIVITY

6. Write a poem that a Civil War soldier might have written after hearing that the war was over.

Using Key Vocabulary

Match each word with the correct description.

a. strategy
b. ironclad
c. conscription
d. bounty
e. Copperheads

_____ 1. draft
_____ 2. *Monitor*
_____ 3. payment for enlisting
_____ 4. plan
_____ 5. Northerners against the war

Reviewing Facts

1. **Name** the three steps in Scott's plan to defeat the South.

2. **List** the advantages each side held over the other in the war.

3. **Identify** the reasons Gettysburg and Vicksburg were important battles.

4. **Describe** ways in which the North and South raised money to finance their war efforts.

5. **Explain** why Sherman's march to the sea is called total war.

Understanding Concepts

Influence of Technology

1. How did the North's industrial strength help it in the war?

2. How did the North use railroads and ships to its advantage in the war?

Civil Rights and Liberties

3. Why did Lincoln avoid the issue of slavery when the war began?

4. Why did Lincoln at first oppose allowing African Americans to enlist in the Union army? Why did he change his mind?

5. Describe how the Emancipation Proclamation changed the war for many Northerners.

Critical Thinking

1. **Determining Cause and Effect** What caused riots in the North during the war?

2. **Predicting Outcomes** How might the war have been affected if Lincoln had lost the presidential election of 1864?

3. **Forming Opinions** Many Southerners called Grant and Sherman barbaric for waging total war. Do you think civilian property should be intentionally destroyed in a war? What is your opinion of total war?

History and Geography

The Battle of Shiloh

The map on page 599 shows troop locations and movement during the Battle of Shiloh, April 6–7, 1862. Examine the positions of Union and Confederate forces over the two-day period. Then answer the following questions.

1. **Location** Compare the location of the Union troops on April 6 morning and evening. In what direction had they moved? Why?

2. **Location** Describe the location of Confederate generals Hardee, Polk, Bragg, and Breckinridge on the evening of April 6.

3. **Movement** What action did Grant's Union forces take on the morning of April 7?

4. **Place** What change in the number of troops allowed Grant to take action on April 7?

5. **Place** A huge number of soldiers died at the Battle of Shiloh. What about the place's geography might have contributed to this?

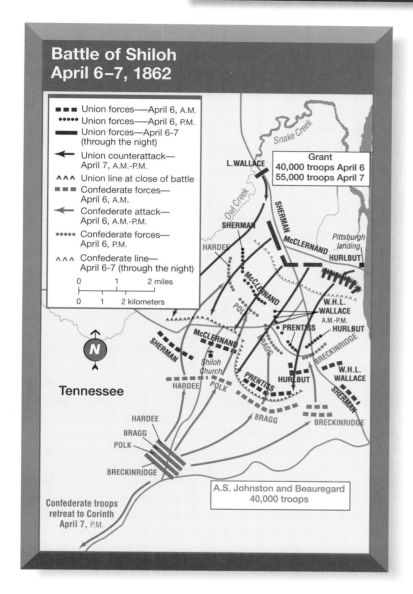

Battle of Shiloh
April 6–7, 1862

- ▪▪▪ Union forces—April 6, A.M.
- •••• Union forces—April 6, P.M.
- ▬▬▬ Union forces—April 6-7 (through the night)
- ← Union counterattack—April 7, A.M.-P.M.
- ʌʌʌ Union line at close of battle
- ▪▪▪ Confederate forces—April 6, A.M.
- ← Confederate attack—April 6, A.M.-P.M.
- •••• Confederate forces—April 6, P.M.
- ʌʌʌ Confederate line—April 6-7 (through the night)

0   1   2 miles
0   1   2 kilometers

Snake Creek

Owl Creek

L. WALLACE

Grant
40,000 troops April 6
55,000 troops April 7

SHERMAN
SHERMAN
McCLERNAND
HARDEE
Pittsburg Landing
HURLBUT
McCLERNAND
POLK
W.H.L. WALLACE
A.M.-P.M.
PRENTISS
HURLBUT
BRAGG
BRECKINRIDGE
McCLERNAND
SHERMAN
Shiloh Church
PRENTISS
HARDEE POLK
HURLBUT
W.H.L. WALLACE
SHERMAN

N

Tennessee

HARDEE
BRAGG
POLK
BRECKINRIDGE
BRAGG
BRECKINRIDGE

A.S. Johnston and Beauregard
40,000 troops

Confederate troops
retreat to Corinth
April 7, P.M.

Interdisciplinary Activity: Language Arts

Join with three or four other students to form a group. Choose one of the following topics for your group: spies, nurses, or soldiers. Find the names of women from the Civil War who fit into your group's category. Assign one name to each group member. Have that member do library research on that woman. Discover as much as possible about her life, family, and activities during the war. Then use the research to write a story about the woman's contribution to the war. Arrange a time with your teacher to read your group's story to the rest of the class. Bind your group's stories, make a cover, and title your book.

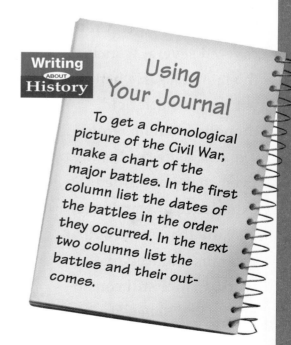

Writing ABOUT **History**

Using Your Journal

To get a chronological picture of the Civil War, make a chart of the major battles. In the first column list the dates of the battles in the order they occurred. In the next two columns list the battles and their outcomes.

Practicing Skills

Interpreting a Battle Map

Study the battle map above. Then answer the questions that follow.

1. Where and when did this battle take place?

2. Which army attacked and which defended its position?

3. Where did the Confederate army begin this battle and which way did it move?

4. Where were Hardee's troops located just before the battle?

Read to Discover

What is it like to be a soldier facing battle for the first time? Henry Fleming, the young recruit in *The Red Badge of Courage*, offers some answers as he thinks about his role in the war. What battle does Henry fight with himself before he fights in an actual Civil War battle?

Reader's Dictionary

veterans	experienced soldiers
Huns	soldiers known for their fierce fighting
haversack	bag soldiers used to carry personal items
tumult	uproar

Stephen Crane began his career in journalism while still in his teens. Later, as a reporter, Crane covered several wars in the late 1890s. He had not yet seen a battlefield, though, when he wrote *The Red Badge of Courage.* Even so, he described the experience of war so realistically that even combat veterans admired his work. Critics still consider *The Red Badge of Courage* a masterpiece.

from *The Red Badge of Courage*

by Stephen Crane (1871–1900)

Various veterans had told him tales. Some talked of gray, bewhiskered hordes who were advancing with relentless curses, and chewing tobacco with unspeakable valor—tremendous bodies of fierce soldiery who were sweeping along like the Huns. Others spoke of tattered and eternally hungry men who fired despondent powders. "They'll charge through hell's fire an' brimstone t'git a holt on a haversack, an' sech stomachs ain't a-lastin' long," he was told. From the stories, the youth imagined the red, live bones sticking out through slits in the faded uniforms.

Still, he could not put a whole faith in veterans' tales, for recruits were their prey. They talked much of smoke, fire, and blood, but he could not tell how much might be lies. . . .

However, he perceived now that it did not greatly matter what kind of soldiers he was going to fight, so long as they fought, which fact no one disputed. There was a more serious problem. He lay in his bunk pondering upon it. He tried to mathematically prove to himself that he would not run from a battle.

Previously he had never felt obliged to wrestle too seriously with this question. In his life he had taken certain things for granted, never challenging his belief in ultimate success, and bothering little about means and roads. But here he was confronted with a thing of moment. It had suddenly appeared to him that perhaps in a battle he might run. He was forced to admit that as far as war was concerned he knew nothing of himself. . . .

A little panic-fear grew in his mind. As his imagination went forward to a fight, he saw hideous possibilities. He contemplated the lurking menaces of the future, and failed in an effort to see himself standing stoutly in the midst of them. He recalled his visions of broken-bladed glory, but in the shadow of the impending tumult he suspected them to be impossible pictures.

He sprang from the bunk and began to pace nervously to and fro. "Good Lord, what's th' matter with me?" he said aloud.

He felt that in this crisis his laws of life were useless. Whatever he had learned of himself was here of no avail. He was an unknown quantity. He saw that he would again be obliged to experiment as he had in early youth. He must accumulate information of himself, and meanwhile he resolved to remain close upon his guard lest those qualities of which he knew nothing should everlastingly disgrace him. "Good Lord!" he repeated in dismay.

▲ UNION SOLDIERS

Responding to Literature

1. How did Henry view the veterans and their war tales?

2. Why did Henry express doubts about his belief in himself?

3. What feelings do you think you might have just before participating in a military battle?

ACTIVITY

4. Draw pictures of items you think a young Civil War recruit would carry in a soldier's haversack. Include an item or two that you think might give the soldier courage.

CHAPTER 19

★★★

Reconstruction
1865–1877

► **TICKET TO IMPEACHMENT TRIAL**

SETTING THE SCENE

Focus

The Civil War had ended. Readmitting the Southern states to the Union became the first order of business. Leaders agonized and argued over how to reunite the shattered nation. Few periods in the history of the United States have produced as much bitterness or created as much controversy as this era known as Reconstruction.

Concepts to Understand

★ How Reconstruction policies affected the **civil rights and liberties** of freed African Americans and white Southerners

★ How government policies redefined **American democracy** during Reconstruction

Read to Discover . . .

★ the Reconstruction plans of Lincoln and the Radical Republicans.
★ what caused the clash between Congress and President Johnson.
★ what obstacles African Americans in the South faced.
★ how Reconstruction ended.

Journal Notes

As you read the chapter, make notes of the challenges and problems facing both white and African American Southerners after the war.

United States	
1865 Civil War ends	**1868** President Andrew Johnson impeached
1865 Abraham Lincoln assassinated	
1865 Thirteenth Amendment ratified	**1868** Fourteenth Amendment ratified
	1870 Fifteenth Amendment ratified

1864–1867	**1868–1871**

World	
1867 The Dominion of Canada established	**1869** Suez Canal completed in Egypt
	1871 Unification of Germany completed

Southern Plantation
by William Aiken Walker, 1885

Artist William Aiken Walker depicts life for African Americans on a Southern plantation during Reconstruction.

◄ BADGE WORN BY FREED AFRICAN AMERICANS

1872 Yellowstone National Park created
1872 President Ulysses S. Grant reelected

1876 Rutherford B. Hayes elected President
1877 Compromise of 1877 ends military occupation of the South

1872–1875

1876–1879

1876 Korea becomes an independent nation
1876 Serbia declares war on Turkey

★★

Restoring the Union

SETTING THE SCENE

Read to Learn . . .

★ how President Lincoln and Radical Republicans disagreed on Reconstruction plans for the South.
★ why President Lincoln wanted to pass the Thirteenth Amendment.

Terms to Know

★ Reconstruction
★ amnesty
★ Radical Republicans
★ pocket veto
★ Thirteenth Amendment

People to Meet

★ Abraham Lincoln
★ Frederick Douglass
★ John Wilkes Booth

► REPORT OF JOHN WILKES BOOTH'S TRIAL

At the close of the Civil War, the federal government turned its attention to restoring the Union. Readmitting the Southern states proved difficult. The President and Congress had different opinions about the best way to deal with the defeated South.

War had left the cities and farms of the South in ruins. In 1865 the South needed to rebuild its devastated communities and to reconstruct its entire way of life. States and towns had to reestablish their governments, while Southern society had to transform itself by including nearly 4 million freed African Americans, most of whom had no jobs, land, or education. Northerners and Southerners and whites and African Americans disagreed over how to meet these challenges.

★ Planning for Reconstruction

In the 12-year period following the Civil War, known as Reconstruction, Americans struggled to rebuild the South and to reunite their war-torn nation. The term *Reconstruction* also refers to the government program by which the Union restored relations with the Confederate states after their defeat.

Reconstruction lasted from 1865 to 1877. Although the Reconstruction era started after the Civil War, plans for it began earlier. President **Abraham Lincoln**, considering Reconstruction his responsibility, formed a plan for reconstructing the South after hearing news of Northern military successes in 1863.

Lincoln's Reconstruction Plan

Before the end of the war, Lincoln and Congress frequently clashed over plans for the South. Some people believed the South should be punished. Lincoln thought that he needed to restore the Union gently. He wanted the Southern states to rejoin the Union as quickly as possible.

Lincoln announced his plan, known as the **Ten Percent Plan,** in December 1863. He offered amnesty, or official forgiveness of crimes, to Southerners who pledged an oath of loyalty to the United States and accepted the elimination of slavery. This amnesty applied to everyone except a few high-ranking Confederate officials. Lincoln hoped this amnesty would persuade many Confederates to renew their allegiance to the Union. Once 10 percent of the number of voters in the 1860 election had taken the loyalty oath, those loyal voters could set up a state government. Congress would then readmit the state to the Union. Lincoln believed that once the new government began to function, the spirit of loyalty to the Union would spread throughout the state.

The Union-occupied areas of Louisiana, Arkansas, and Tennessee quickly took advantage of this plan and applied for admission to the Union in 1864. Congress, however, refused to seat the newly elected representatives from these states. Under the Constitution, only Congress had the power to admit territories or states to the Union. For this reason, Congress believed that the legislature, not the President, should control Reconstruction.

Lincoln's plan did not address the plight of the newly freed African Americans. Therefore, he strongly supported adding a constitutional amendment to

Picturing History

▲ RADICAL REPUBLICANS Radical Republicans maintained the authority of Congress over Reconstruction. **What Radical Republican bill did Lincoln pocket veto?**

permanently abolish slavery. He also urged that African Americans who could read and write and those who had served in the Union army be allowed to vote. His plan, however, did not force the Southern states to give full citizenship to African Americans.

Objections From Congress

Some Republican members of Congress, along with other Northerners, wanted to punish the rebellious Southern states and destroy all Southern economic and political powers. Many bitterly opposed slavery and saw the war as a chance to use federal power to force major changes in the South and protect the rights of African Americans. Since many considered these ideas extreme, or *radical,* their supporters became known as Radical Republicans, or Radicals.

Elevators and Skyscrapers

Architects in the 1800s could build taller and taller buildings, but one thing limited them—the number of stories that people could climb by way of stairs. Without the invention of the elevator, skyscrapers would never have been practical.

▲ MODERN EXTERIOR ELEVATOR

Then

Rising to the Top

In 1868 a news story from New York City caught the attention of the entire country. Some New York architects proposed to construct a building *five stories high*—a towering 130 feet! The building had been especially designed to use Elisha Otis's "safety" elevator, invented about 10 years earlier. Otis's invention was the first elevator that had an automatic safety device to keep the car from falling if the ropes or cables broke. If the steam-powered elevators proved successful, the architects promised even taller skyscrapers would appear.

Now

How High Can It Go?

Today's elevators climb 10 or more times as high as Otis's first elevator. The 87 elevators in the Sears Tower in Chicago, for example, rise to about 1,400 feet in the 110-story building.

◀ OTIS ELEVATOR WITH SAFETY HOIST

The Radicals considered Lincoln's Reconstruction plan too mild. Ignoring the President, Congress passed its own tough Reconstruction bill in July 1864. The **Wade-Davis Bill,** sponsored by Senator Benjamin Wade of Ohio and Representative Henry Winter Davis of Maryland, proposed putting the South under military rule. This bill required a majority of a state's electorate to take the loyalty oath, and required the new state constitutions to abolish slavery. When a majority of the white males (not 10 percent) of the state pledged their allegiance to the Union, the governor could call a state constitutional convention. Delegates would be elected by those who took an "ironclad oath" swearing that they had never willingly aided or fought for the Confederacy. Few Southerners could make this claim. The bill made it almost impossible for Southerners to shape new state governments.

Lincoln refused to sign the bill because he considered it too harsh. He used the pocket veto to let it die. A pocket veto is the President's power to kill a bill by not signing it for 10 days, when Congress is not in session.

The Thirteenth Amendment

Lincoln wanted to ensure that slavery would never divide the nation again. He worried that the courts might declare the Emancipation Proclamation unconstitutional. In April 1864 the Senate approved the Thirteenth Amendment, but the House of Representatives rejected it. The Thirteenth Amendment would abolish slavery throughout the United States.

Lincoln decided to take the issue to the people. During the 1864 presidential campaign, he gave his wholehearted support to the amendment. Following his decisive victory in the November election, Lincoln urged the House to pass the amendment. On January 31, 1865, 119 representatives voted for the amendment—three more votes than the two-thirds majority needed to pass it. When Republicans in the House heard the results, they jumped to their feet and cheered. In the galleries African American onlookers embraced each other with joy. The states quickly ratified the amendment, and it became law in December 1865. The institution that had divided and tormented the nation existed no more.

★ Extending the Olive Branch

In 1864 Abraham Lincoln became the first President since Andrew Jackson to win a second term in office. Lincoln welcomed the chance to end the conflict for which many Southerners blamed him.

With Malice Toward None

On March 4, 1865, dark clouds hung over the Capitol as Lincoln arrived to take the oath of office. In the crowd waited many well-known people, including the abolitionist editor **Frederick Douglass** and the dashing young actor **John Wilkes Booth.** When Lincoln rose to speak, the clouds parted and the sun shone briefly.

In his speech Lincoln shared his thoughts about the meaning of the war. He observed that both sides "read the same Bible, and pray to the same God; and each invokes His aid against the other." Lincoln explained that both prayers could not be answered. Finally, in words that many would remember, Lincoln concluded:

66 **With malice toward none; with charity for all; . . . let**

us strive on to finish the work we are in; to bind up the nation's wounds; . . . to do all which may achieve and cherish a just and a lasting peace, among ourselves, and with all nations. 99

Listeners cheered the speech and later lined up by the hundreds at a White House reception. Frederick Douglass tried to join them but police barred him because he was African American. As soon as Lincoln heard that Douglass stood at the door, however, he invited him in. Douglass later described the scene:

66 **I could not have been more than ten feet from him when Mr. Lincoln saw me; his countenance lighted up and he said in a voice which was heard all around: 'Here comes my friend Douglass.'** 99

Lincoln shook Douglass's hand and said, "I saw you in the crowd today listening to my address. There is no man's opinion that I value more than yours: what did you think of it?" Douglass hesitated to hold up the reception line, but Lincoln repeated his question.

"Mr. Lincoln, it was a sacred effort," Douglass said. "I am glad you liked it," Lincoln replied. Never before, Douglass wrote later, had an African American attended an inaugural reception and exchanged opinions with the President.

★ The Assassination

About a month later, on the night of April 14, 1865, Lincoln and his wife relaxed by attending the play *Our American Cousin* at Ford's Theater in Washington, D.C. As they sat in the presidential box, John Wilkes Booth, an actor obsessed with aiding the South, entered the box from the rear and shot Lincoln in the head.

▲ LINCOLN ASSASSINATED This newspaper sketch shows the scene at Ford's Theater the night Lincoln was shot. **Why did some Radical Republicans view Lincoln's death with relief?**

▲ JOHN WILKES BOOTH

The audience stood stunned. Mary Lincoln held her husband and wept. An army doctor rushed into the box and tried to revive the President. Another doctor joined him. Although they restored Lincoln's breathing, it became clear that his head wound would prove fatal.

The doctors carried Lincoln to a boardinghouse across the street. Government officials and military officers crowded into the small bedroom. With Lincoln's wife and son, they watched and grieved through the night. At 7:22 on the morning of April 15, Lincoln died. As a doctor covered the dead President's face and a pastor uttered a prayer, Secretary of War Edwin Stanton murmured, "Now he belongs to the ages."

Reactions to Lincoln's Death

Some Radical Republicans viewed the President's death with relief. They had feared that former Southern leaders would regain power under Lincoln's generous Reconstruction terms. Now they could enforce their own harsher policies.

Most others viewed Lincoln's death as a tragedy. The shocked country deeply mourned. General Ulysses S. Grant wept openly at the funeral. On April 21 a funeral train carrying Lincoln's body began its journey from Washington, D.C., to his home of Springfield, Illinois. All along the route, thousands of men, women, and children silently watched and wept as the train rode by. The President became one of the final casualties of the war.

★ SECTION 1 REVIEW ★

Checking for Understanding

1. **Identify** Abraham Lincoln, Frederick Douglass, John Wilkes Booth.

2. **Define** Reconstruction, amnesty, Radical Republicans, pocket veto, Thirteenth Amendment.

3. **Why** did Radical Republicans disapprove of Lincoln's Ten Percent Plan?

4. **How** did Lincoln help ensure the abolition of slavery in the United States?

Critical Thinking

5. **Identifying Central Issues** What was radical about the plans of the Radical Republicans?

ACTIVITY

6. Imagine you are a cartoonist who sides with the Radical Republicans. Draw a political cartoon critical of Lincoln's Reconstruction plans.

★★★

President and Congress Clash

SETTING THE SCENE

Read to Learn . . .

★ how Congress and the President disagreed on Reconstruction policies.
★ why Radical Republicans called for President Johnson's impeachment.

Terms to Know

★ black codes
★ Fourteenth Amendment
★ impeach

People to Meet

★ Andrew Johnson
★ Charles Sumner
★ Thaddeus Stevens
★ Edwin Stanton
★ Ulysses S. Grant

◀ THADDEUS STEVENS

As the nation mourned the death of President Lincoln in April 1865, a very different man took office. His battles with Congress over policies toward the South would end in bitterness, anger, and a historic confrontation.

★ The New President

On April 15 Vice President **Andrew Johnson** took the presidential oath of office. Although a Southerner and a Democrat, Republicans had chosen him as Lincoln's running mate because they thought he would appeal to War Democrats and voters in the border states. Johnson had strongly supported the Union. As a senator from Tennessee, he stayed in Congress when his state seceded. He denounced his fellow Tennesseans for choosing secession.

Northerners felt anger as well as sorrow in the weeks following Lincoln's assassination. They cried for vengeance against all Confederate leaders. The new President, though, pledged that his policies essentially "would be the same as that of the late President."

The President and the Radicals

Johnson became hampered in his efforts because, as an unelected President, he enjoyed little popular support. Radical Republicans at first hoped that Johnson would support a strict Reconstruction plan. After all, Johnson had often exclaimed that "traitors must be punished."

▲ ANDREW JOHNSON

Radical Republicans and Andrew Johnson, though, had little in common. The Radicals wanted to keep Southerners, especially conservative Democrats, out of Congress to strengthen their party's influence. Without Southern interference, they could extend African Americans' civil rights. As a former slaveholder, Johnson cared little for the rights of African Americans and insisted that "White men alone must manage the South."

On the other hand, the new President and the Radical Republicans both hated the wealthy planters who had ruled the South before the war. A self-educated man, Johnson came from a poor rural background. He represented the interests of small farmers and mountaineers. Early in his political career, Johnson had promised to "show the stuck-up aristocrats who is running this country." Now he had the chance.

★ Johnson's Plan for Reconstruction

True to his word, Johnson went along with much of Lincoln's policy. He, too, believed that the President should take the lead on Reconstruction. Johnson began his work on Reconstruction while Congress was not in session.

On May 29, 1865, Johnson issued two proclamations. The first offered amnesty and the return of property—except slaves—to all who would take an oath of loyalty to the Union. Like Lincoln, Johnson barred certain groups from taking the oath. One group included supporters of the Confederacy who owned property worth $20,000 or more. These wealthy landowners, however, could appeal to the President for special pardons.

The second proclamation dealt with the organization of loyal state governments in the South. In each state, Johnson would appoint a temporary governor. He would call a state convention and oversee the election of convention delegates. Only those who had taken the loyalty oath could vote or serve as delegates.

The state conventions would write new constitutions and decide who qualified to vote or hold office. Next, the voters could elect a governor, state lawmakers, and members of Congress. In addition, the states had to ratify the Thirteenth Amendment, declare secession illegal, and agree not to pay Confederate debts.

Radical Opposition

By the end of 1865 all the seceded states had formed new governments—some under Lincoln's plan, some under Johnson's. When Congress reconvened, Johnson declared these states restored to the Union. He called on Congress to seat the newly elected Southern senators and representatives.

The Radicals in Congress protested the leniency of Johnson's plan. It allowed the return of Confederate leadership in the Southern states. For example, Mississippians elected a former Confederate general as governor. In Georgia voters chose Alexander Stephens, once vice president of the Confederacy, as a United States senator. Clearly, these officials could not qualify for the loyalty oath. Johnson might have stopped these Confederates from assuming office and called for new elections, but to do so would be admitting that his plan had failed. Instead, he granted presidential pardons to nearly every former Confederate official who requested it.

★ The Black Codes

African Americans suffered under Johnson's reconstructed governments. Although Southern governments had to abolish slavery, they still seized the chance to deny African Americans the right to vote, an opportunity to learn, and freedom to work. The new Southern state governments passed black codes—restrictive laws that applied only to African Americans. Southern legislatures designed these laws to reestablish white control over African Americans.

In South Carolina, for example, African Americans had to have licenses to do any jobs other than farm work. A Mississippi law prevented them from buying or even renting farmland. Vagrancy laws in many states imposed fines on unemployed African Americans. The state government auctioned off those who could not pay to white landowners who paid their fines.

Although many Northerners also treated African Americans unfairly, the black codes outraged them. These laws made a mockery of the Thirteenth Amendment, but the President did nothing to help African Americans.

★ Congress Against the President

Senator **Charles Sumner** of Massachusetts and Representative **Thaddeus Stevens** of Pennsylvania, the leaders of the Radicals in Congress, fought untiringly for the rights of African Americans and to build a new Southern society. Even before Congress met in December 1865, Sumner and Stevens began to formulate a plan to undo Johnson's program

Stevens persuaded Congress to deny seats to the newly elected members from the South. Congress also created the Joint Committee on Reconstruction. The committee studied and reported on the situation in the South, particularly the conditions for newly freed African Americans.

Civil Rights Laws

The Radical Republicans continued to take steps to protect Southern African Americans. They pushed through a bill to strengthen and lengthen the life of the **Freedmen's Bureau,** created in March 1865. The Freedmen's Bureau worked to provide education, housing, and other improvements for African Americans in the South. Johnson vetoed the bill.

The Radicals responded by passing the **Civil Rights Act of 1866.** It guaranteed African Americans some basic rights of citizens, such as owning property and bringing lawsuits. Johnson vetoed it, denouncing the Radical Republicans as traitors who did not wish to restore the Union.

The President's actions drove moderate Republicans to rally behind the Radicals and helped override Johnson's veto of the civil rights bill—the first time in United States history that Congress had overridden a presidential veto on a significant matter. Then Congress passed the Freedmen's Bureau bill over the President's veto as well.

Under the Civil Rights Act of 1866, for the first time the Bill of Rights of the Constitution applied to all Americans, except Native Americans. Opponents of the act claimed that it gave the federal government expanded powers and violated states' rights. Sumner, however, insisted, "There can be no state rights against human rights."

The Fourteenth Amendment

Fearing that the Civil Rights Act might be overturned in court, the Joint Committee on Reconstruction drafted the Fourteenth Amendment. It defined citizenship to include African Americans and required that no state deny any person "the equal protection of the laws." It also denied the vote to most former Confederate leaders and prohibited any state from paying Confederate war debts.

Johnson Fights Back

Once the enemy of Southern leaders, Johnson now acted as their ally against Congress. Claiming that the absence of Southern representation in Congress made the Fourteenth Amendment unconstitutional, Johnson urged Southerners to reject it. As the 1866 congressional elections neared, it became clear that they would reveal whether the President or Congress would control the direction of Reconstruction.

The election provided an overwhelming victory for the Radicals, who gained control of both the House and Senate. They now had enough strength to override any presidential veto.

★ Radical Reconstruction

Now firmly in control, the Radical Republicans began implementing their policies for Reconstruction. They wanted to sweep away the new state governments in the South to ensure that former Confederate leaders would have no role in governing the South and to protect the freed African Americans' right to vote. Inspired by self-interest as well as by concern for the freed African Americans,

Radicals wanted to punish the South. The Radicals expected that African Americans would express their gratitude for freedom by voting Republican.

Reconstruction Legislation

In March 1867, Congress passed a Reconstruction Act that abolished the South's new state governments and placed the states under military rule. The revolutionary act divided the former Confederacy, except Tennessee, into five military districts. The army, or martial law, would govern the districts. Congress readmitted Tennessee to the Union because it had already met all of the requirements of the legislation.

To be restored to the Union, each of the states had to frame and ratify a state constitution that gave African Americans the right to vote. If Congress approved the constitution, if the state legislature ratified the Fourteenth Amendment, and if the amendment became a part of the Constitution, then the state would be readmitted to the Union. By 1868 Louisiana, Alabama, Arkansas, Florida, North Carolina, and South Carolina had met these requirements and regained statehood. The Fourteenth Amendment also became part of the Constitution. Although Johnson vetoed the Reconstruction Act, Congress easily overrode his veto.

★ The Radicals in Power

The Radicals became determined to reduce the presidential power that Lincoln had assumed during the Civil War and to remove Johnson as an obstacle to their plans. In March 1867, Congress passed the Command of the Army Act, which severely limited the President's power as commander in chief. The Tenure of Office Act accompanied this legislation. It required Senate approval for the

President to remove any government official, including cabinet members whose appointment had required its consent.

Johnson had long wanted to remove Secretary of War **Edwin Stanton,** the only cabinet member who openly sided with the Radicals. While Congress remained in recess, Johnson dismissed him.

Stanton barricaded himself in his office and refused to be fired. Congress supported Stanton and claimed that, under the 1867 Tenure of Office Act, the President could not fire any official the Senate had approved. Johnson proclaimed the recent act unconstitutional and demanded that the Supreme Court settle the issue.

★ Johnson Impeached

Ignoring the President's argument, Thaddeus Stevens seized the opportunity. He called on the House of Representatives to impeach Johnson, or charge the President with misconduct. On February 24, 1868, for the first time in American history the House voted 126 to 47 to impeach a President.

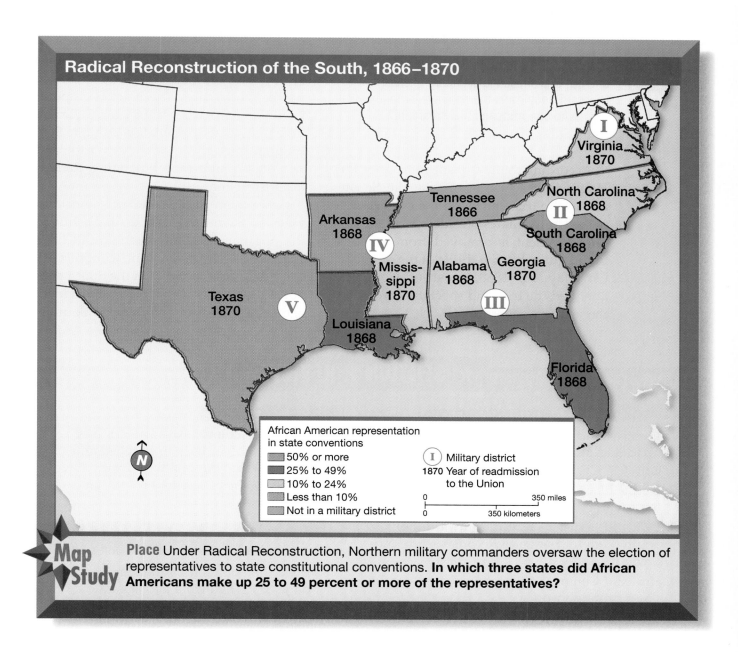

Radical Reconstruction of the South, 1866–1870

Virginia 1870
Tennessee 1866
North Carolina 1868
Arkansas 1868
South Carolina 1868
Mississippi 1870
Alabama 1868
Georgia 1870
Texas 1870
Louisiana 1868
Florida 1868

African American representation in state conventions
- 50% or more
- 25% to 49%
- 10% to 24%
- Less than 10%
- Not in a military district

Ⅰ Military district
1870 Year of readmission to the Union

0 ———— 350 miles
0 ———— 350 kilometers

Map Study

Place Under Radical Reconstruction, Northern military commanders oversaw the election of representatives to state constitutional conventions. **In which three states did African Americans make up 25 to 49 percent or more of the representatives?**

▲ IMPEACHMENT TRIAL President Johnson's attempt to dismiss his secretary of war gave Radical Republicans the opportunity to impeach him. **Who can impeach the President?**

Many senators relished the chance to get rid of Johnson, but some felt uneasy about what seemed a clearly political charge. Some senators believed that the Constitution did not intend for a President to be removed if he disagreed with Congress.

The final vote was 35 to 19, one ballot shy of the two-thirds needed to convict. Andrew Johnson remained President. The balance of powers among the three branches of government survived.

★ The Election of 1868

The Radical Republicans sought a candidate in the 1868 election who could sweep the country and keep them in power. They chose the North's popular Civil War hero, General **Ulysses S. Grant.** The Democrats nominated Horatio Seymour, former governor of New York, and ran on a platform condemning Radical Reconstruction.

Grant won easily, with 214 electoral votes to Seymour's 80. A small shift in the popular vote, however, would have changed the results. Grant won because carpetbag governments in the South supported him and despite terrorist tactics against Republican voters in the South.

According to the Constitution, after the House impeaches an official, the Senate acts as the trial court and the chief justice of the United States presides over the trial. The President is removed from office if found guilty by two-thirds of the senators. On May 16, 1868, most of Congress attended the trial and spectators crowded the visitors' gallery.

★ SECTION 2 REVIEW ★

Checking for Understanding

1. **Identify** Andrew Johnson, Charles Sumner, Thaddeus Stevens, Edwin Stanton, Ulysses S. Grant.
2. **Define** black codes, Fourteenth Amendment, impeach.
3. **How** did Johnson's attitudes toward the South seem to change as Reconstruction proceeded?
4. **How** did Congress's plans for Reconstruction differ from Johnson's?

Critical Thinking

5. **Making Predictions** No United States President has ever been impeached and convicted. What do you think would have happened if the Senate had convicted Johnson?

ACTIVITY

6. Read the Fourteenth Amendment on page 311. Then write and illustrate a picture book for new voters about the rights the amendment guarantees.

★★

The South During Reconstruction

SETTING THE SCENE

Read to Learn . . .

★ how the Freedmen's Bureau helped African Americans.
★ why Congress passed the Civil Rights Act of 1871.

Terms to Know

★ tenant farmers
★ sharecroppers
★ Ku Klux Klan
★ Fifteenth Amendment
★ scalawags
★ carpetbaggers

People to Meet

★ Oliver O. Howard
★ Robert Smalls
★ Alexander Stephens

▲ CARPETBAG, 1870S

When the Civil War ended, Confederate soldiers returned home tired, ragged, and hungry. They returned to a land much different from the one they left behind. They returned to a ravaged land in ruins. In the absence of government rule, roaming bands of army deserters had robbed defenseless homes. Thousands of African Americans and Southern whites suffered from disease and hunger.

★ New Ways of Life

The devastation of war and Reconstruction policies affected all levels of Southern society. In Mississippi a woman remembered her father's homecoming:

❝ He had come home to a house stripped of every article of furniture. The plantation was stripped of the means of cultivating any but a small portion of it. A few mules and one cow made up the stock. ❞

Southerners who had invested heavily in Confederate currency lost everything when the funds became worthless after the war. Many lost their land because they could not pay taxes or other debts. Throughout the South, on both plantations and small farms, war widows struggled to hold on to their property and keep it producing.

The Plight of Workers

Poor African Americans and whites realized that to have social and economic status in the South they needed land. One African American soldier returning from the war exclaimed, "Every colored man will be a slave, and feel himself a slave until he can raise [his] own bale of cotton . . . and say [this] is mine!"

Few African Americans had money to buy land, though, despite the low prices. As a result, some became tenant farmers, farming land that they rented. Even this sometimes proved beyond the means of many poor Southerners. The chronic shortage of cash in the war-torn South made payment of wages difficult. Many Southerners became sharecroppers, persons who worked the owner's land and received a share of the crops in return.

★ The Freedmen's Bureau

African Americans faced immense dangers and hostility in winning their rights after the Civil War. The war had devastated the South's land and resources. Both

▲ FREEDMEN'S BUREAU OFFICER Officers from the Freedmen's Bureau tried to relieve tensions between whites and African Americans. **Who was the first director of the Freedmen's Bureau?**

whites and African Americans lost their crops and often their homes. African Americans worried about losing their new freedom, especially after Lincoln's death.

In March 1865, Congress established the **Freedmen's Bureau,** an agency of the army directed by General **Oliver O. Howard.** The Bureau distributed food to millions of former slaves. It made efforts to settle African Americans on their own land. In addition, the Bureau provided medical help. By 1867 it had started 46 hospitals and staffed them with doctors and nurses. At first the Bureau gave food and clothing to all families in the war-ravaged South, including poor whites. The founders of the Bureau, though, viewed its primary mission as helping African Americans adjust to their new freedom.

The Bureau tried to find jobs for African Americans. It encouraged them to sign labor contracts with planters to provide work in return for wages or a share of the crops. Because most of the former slaves could neither read nor write, Bureau agents tried to prevent planters from cheating the freed African Americans.

The Bureau settled thousands of freed men and women on plantations that owners had abandoned or that the army had seized. In some states, the Bureau paid the settlers for harvesting corn and cotton on the plantations.

Many setbacks plagued the Bureau's work. The first Freedmen's Bureau Act provided for the sale of land to freed people. African Americans began working the land and hoped to buy it. President Johnson's Reconstruction program, however, ordered this land returned to its original owners. Though the settlers tried to resist, the army that once liberated them now moved in and evicted them from their farms.

New Chances for Education

The Bureau's greatest achievements lay in education. It started free public schools for African American men, women, and

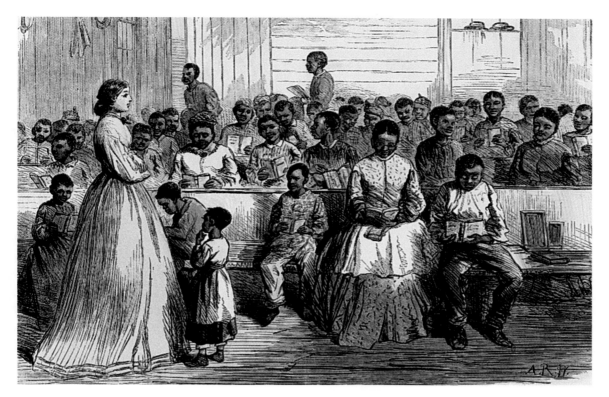

▲ SCHOOL FOR FREEDMEN The Freedmen's Bureau set up hundreds of schools attended by African American adults and children. **What colleges did the Freedmen's Bureau establish for African Americans?**

children. Private organizations such as missionary societies supplied teachers and books. Many white Southerners violently opposed education for freed people. Their threats and violence made life dangerous for teachers and students. Still, by 1869 about 9,500 white and African American teachers worked in Freedmen's Bureau schools. By 1870, more than 247,000 students attended 4,329 schools.

For those who wanted to go on to higher education, the Freedmen's Bureau established colleges. They included Howard University (named for Oliver Howard), Fisk University, and Hampton Institute.

Congress decided to end the Freedmen's Bureau in 1872. The agency had started as an emergency measure and members of Congress decided the emergency had ended. Without the Bureau, however, Congress lost the best way of protecting the rights of African Americans in the South.

★ White Southerners Resist Change

Despite immense hardships, newly freed people reveled in the small details of freedom. Before the Civil War, some laws banned African Americans from wearing hats, or carrying canes, or looking white people in the eye. In the summer of 1865, some freed people began donning hats, twirling canes, and refusing to yield the right of way to whites on sidewalks.

Not accustomed to change, white Southerners found the African Americans' new behavior "intolerably insolent and overbearing." White families that had given their servants freedom became confused and frightened by the changes in their society. The military occupation troops made them feel powerless. They felt relieved when Johnson's plan gave Southern leaders control of reconstructed governments.

▲ TERRORIST GROUP The Ku Klux Klan used violence and threats to prevent African Americans from acting independently or voting. **Under what law did President Grant arrest Klan members?**

Terrorism and the Ku Klux Klan

While Southern legislatures enacted black codes, terrorist bands formed to defend white Southerners' old way of life. These groups viewed themselves as protective societies. They took names like the Regulators, the Knights of the White Camelia, and the Ku Klux Klan.

In Pulaski, Tennessee, former Confederate cavalry leader Nathan Bedford Forrest organized the Ku Klux Klan in 1866. By recruiting members from all classes of white Southern society, it became the most powerful of the protective societies.

To hide their identities, Klan members wore hoods over their heads. By padding their horses' hooves, they approached their victims silently. At first Klansmen claimed that they wanted only to scare African Americans who acted too independently. Soon they resorted to violence to intimidate or eliminate African Americans and overthrow Republican rule in the South. They launched a reign of terror and began whipping and murdering those who refused to be scared, especially Republican leaders and voters.

During the Reconstruction years, the Klan and other groups killed thousands of African Americans and their white friends. They beat and wounded many more and burned homes, schools, and churches.

President Grant used the **Civil Rights Act of 1871** to arrest 5,000 Klansmen across the South. He wished to destroy the Klan and restore law and order in the South. For a while at least, the Klan and other secret societies disbanded.

★ African Americans in Politics

Voting became one of proud Southern African Americans' new freedoms. In the 1868 presidential election, they turned out 700,000 strong for the Republican party and greatly contributed to Grant's victory. The election made Republicans realize that if African Americans could vote throughout the country, they could help Republicans win elections.

Grant came into office determined to enforce the Reconstruction Act and gave

* * *

Footnotes to History

Equal Rights   The first racially mixed jury in the history of the United States was selected after the Civil War to try Confederate President Jefferson Davis for treason. The government allowed Davis to go free, though, before the trial began.

firm support to protecting African Americans' rights. In his Inaugural Address, the President urged Congress to pass the Fifteenth Amendment.

This amendment would extend the right to vote to all American males over age 21, regardless of race. Many African Americans in the North and West still did not have that right.

The unevenness of voting laws angered whites in the South and African Americans in the North. It seemed to show that Republicans cared more about defeating Southern Democrats than helping African Americans. With Grant's backing, the amendment became part of the Constitution on March 30, 1870.

Grant also appointed two African American justices of the peace in the District of Columbia. A French statesman observed that Grant was "not only preaching, but also practising the doctrine of the equality of the races," as "the first President who has dared give a black man a post in the administration."

African Americans in Government

Although African Americans held no more than 15 or 20 percent of the political offices at the height of Reconstruction, some became outstanding leaders. During Reconstruction African Americans served as lieutenant governors, secretaries of state, and treasurers in the state governments of South Carolina, Florida, Mississippi, and Louisiana. Voters elected them to state legislatures and as delegates to constitutional conventions.

African American voters made an impact at the national level, too. Mississippi elected two African Americans—Hiram Revels and Blanche K. Bruce—to the Senate. All together the Southern states sent 20 African Americans to the House of Representatives. South Carolina alone elected eight African Americans to Congress, including **Robert Smalls.**

Biography ★★★★

Robert Smalls, A National Leader

Robert Smalls became an unexpected hero during the Civil War when he seized the Confederate steamer *Planter* in Charleston harbor, sailed it through the Confederate defenses, and turned it over to the Union navy. Born in Beaufort, South Carolina, in 1839, Smalls began life in slavery and learned to be a skillful sailor. He later captained the stolen ship for the Union navy.

After the war, the mainly African American citizens of Beaufort elected their hero to the state constitutional convention and then the legislature. Next they helped send him to the United States House of Representatives. A man questioning why Smalls became so popular with voters declared, "Smalls ain't God!"

"That's true, that's true," an old man replied, "but Smalls' young yet."

Smalls's skill as a politician and speaker kept him in Congress until 1887, longer than any other African American from South Carolina. ★★★

▲ ROBERT SMALLS

★ Reconstruction Governments

Although African Americans exercised their right to vote, whites dominated Southern governments. Many former Whigs, or Southerners interested in the economic development of the South, joined Republican governments. Southerners insultingly nicknamed these people scalawags. Most Southerners considered scalawags disloyal.

Some Northerners moved to the South after the war looking for business opportunities. Southerners called them carpetbaggers because they carried inexpensive suitcases made of carpet fabric. Southerners ridiculed carpetbaggers and portrayed them as penniless adventurers who arrived with all their possessions in carpetbags. Although many carpetbaggers and scalawags truly wanted to help the South, Southerners bitterly resented them and viewed them as greedy opportunists eager to gain power and wealth.

★ Civil Rights Showdown

In 1870 Senator Charles Sumner introduced a bill to limit racial discrimination in public places such as streetcars, hotels, churches, and cemeteries. Sumner and his supporters hoped to "remove the last lingering taint of slavery" from the country. Again and again, the bill failed to pass.

In 1874 Sumner's bill came before the House. **Alexander Stephens** of Georgia, once vice president of the Confederacy, led the opposition to the bill. Compared with many Southern whites, Stephens held liberal views. He had opposed secession, black codes, and the Klan. He supported the right of African Americans to vote, but thought the civil rights bill violated states' rights.

Robert Elliot, a representative from South Carolina, stood up to answer Stephens's arguments. Elliot argued eloquently for the bill, saying it would be the "capstone of that temple of liberty." While the war had brought African Americans political freedom, this bill offered civil freedom as well.

The fight to pass the bill dragged on, weakening the already ailing Sumner. The Senate passed the bill in May 1874—about two months after Sumner's death. Almost a year later, in February 1875, the **Civil Rights Act of 1875** passed both houses and went into effect. The Justice Department, though, made little effort to enforce the bill and the Supreme Court ruled it unconstitutional in 1883. African Americans' struggle for equality would continue into the twentieth century.

★ SECTION 3 REVIEW ★

Checking for Understanding

1. **Identify** Oliver O. Howard, Robert Smalls, Alexander Stephens.
2. **Define** tenant farmers, sharecroppers, Ku Klux Klan, Fifteenth Amendment, scalawags, carpetbaggers.
3. **What** did the Freedmen's Bureau do to help African Americans?
4. **How** did the federal government control terrorist groups in the South?

Critical Thinking

5. **Determining Relevance** Why was getting an education so important for newly freed people?

ACTIVITY

6. Imagine yourself as a reporter on the scene at one of the events in this section. Tape-record an eyewitness account.

THE NEW SOUTH

After the Civil War ended, the South had little money. The South also had a large need for new business and industry. Northerners and Southerners recognized the South's lack of manufacturing had been a major reason for its defeat. Yet the South had plentiful resources of coal and water power, which attracted Northern factory owners. Plenty of cheap labor was available, too, from war-weary veterans and newly freed African Americans.

During Reconstruction, however, most new Southern state governments rejected factory owners and industrialists from the North. They returned instead to cotton production. Worldwide demand for cotton remained high, and many plantations started producing crops almost immediately after the war. By the end of Reconstruction, cotton production was almost as high as before the war.

When the Reconstruction governments changed, another group of Southerners—business owners—took over the rule of states from carpetbaggers and opponents of manufacturing. These business leaders willingly cooperated with Northern industrialists in building a new South. In the 1880s and 1890s, new lumber and mining projects, the tobacco industry, and the railroads appeared in the South.

The railroads led the way in the early years of Reconstruction. Far behind the North in miles of track in 1860, 10 years later the South had 2,500 miles (4,022 km) of new track that carried passengers, goods, and raw materials. In 1876 the railroads bought federal lands in the South and laid track to open up coalfields in Virginia and West Virginia and iron ore mines in Georgia. A new South—less cotton, more industry—headed toward the twentieth century.

▲ FOUNDRY IN BIRMINGHAM, ALABAMA

Making the Economics Connection

1. What factors in the South attracted Northern manufacturers after the Civil War?

2. How did the railroads help the growth of Southern industry?

3. What natural resources helped support the new Southern industries?

ACTIVITY

4. Choose a new business you would like to bring to your town or city. Draw a map showing where you would locate your store or factory. Write a short caption explaining why your town is a good location for this business.

621

★★★★★★★★★★★★★★★★★★★★★★★★★★★★★★★★★★★★★★★

Reconstruction Ends

SETTING THE SCENE

Read to Learn . . .

★ the consequences of pardons for former Confederates.

★ why conservative Democrats helped a Republican become President in 1877.

Terms to Know

★ filibuster
★ segregation

People to Meet

★ Charles Caldwell
★ Rutherford B. Hayes
★ Samuel J. Tilden

► PRESIDENT ULYSSES S. GRANT

In April 1870, the *New York Tribune* pleaded, "Let us have done with Reconstruction. The country is tired and sick of it. . . . LET US HAVE PEACE." Reconstruction did not end suddenly, though, when the last federal troops withdrew from Southern states. It fell apart gradually and violently.

★ Amnesty and Its Effects

Beginning in 1869, a series of changes in state and federal laws made it easier for former Confederates to regain their right to vote. In 1872 Congress issued a general amnesty to all but about 600 former Confederate officials.

The increase in white Southern voters allowed the Democratic party to make a comeback. In 1870 border states began electing more conservative Democrats. Democrats also outnumbered the African Americans, scalawags, and carpetbaggers in the Virginia and North Carolina governments.

All across the South, conservative Democrats regained political power. Success made them work even harder. For many white Southerners, destroying the Republican party became a crusade.

Violence in Mississippi

As politics grew more violent, Republicans grew tired and lost the will to carry out Reconstruction. In the fall of 1875, white Mississippians wanted to be sure that Republicans lost in elections for the state legislature. Hundreds of white Democrats, many from neighboring Alabama, roamed the Mississippi countryside.

When Republicans gathered for meetings, armed Democrats would provoke a riot and open fire, killing mostly African Americans. They shot or lynched African Americans whom they suspected would vote Republican.

Governor Adelbert Ames asked for federal troops to help stop the murders, but President Grant refused. Ames recruited a militia of white and African American soldiers. **Charles Caldwell,** a former African American state senator, led the effort to distribute weapons.

Until Election Day, the bloody struggle continued between the militia and bands of angry whites. Not surprisingly, Democrats won by a landslide. Mississippi's Republican party lost its power. A few months later, Democrat attackers murdered Caldwell.

Terrorism at the Polls

Violence did not occur only in Mississippi. In other Southern states, conservative Democrats terrorized African Americans to prevent them from voting. Carrying rifles, whites watched the polls to ensure that voters chose Democratic candidates. If African Americans dared to vote Republican, whites destroyed their crops, burned their barns and houses, beat them, and sometimes murdered them.

Democrats used other kinds of tactics, too. They published the names of Republican voters—both African American and white—in the newspapers, so that employers would know whom to fire or not hire. More and more African Americans stayed away from the polls. Democrats defeated Republicans again and again.

★ Problems Among Republicans

Pardons for former Confederates, along with terrorism against African American voters, weakened the Republican party in the South. Abuses of power in the party itself also helped undo the gains of Reconstruction.

Corruption in the Grant administration hurt the Republican party. The President appointed many of his friends to office. Some of them used their jobs to profit illegally. In addition, Democrats investigated and found Republican state officials guilty of bribery, misuse of funds, and other crimes.

The Republicans then in Congress no longer cared about the same issues as Radical Republicans at the beginning of Reconstruction. Thaddeus Stevens, Charles Sumner, Joshua Giddings, and other champions of African American rights no longer influenced Congress. Newer Republican politicians wrestled with inflation, tariffs, and corrupt government. A depression in 1873 made most Republicans focus on the economy instead of civil rights.

Picturing History ▲ THE GRANT ADMINISTRATION Numerous problems in the Grant administration hurt the Republican party. **What happened in 1873 to make Republicans focus on the economy?**

▲ RIBBON FROM
RUTHERFORD B. HAYES
CAMPAIGN

★ The Election of 1876

The election of 1876 produced a violent struggle between the parties. Republicans and Democrats competed for control of the South as well as the White House. The major parties nominated two state governors for President: **Rutherford B. Hayes** of Ohio for the Republicans and **Samuel J. Tilden** of New York for the Democrats.

Showdown in South Carolina

By 1876 in the South, Republicans remained in power only in South Carolina, Florida, and Louisiana. Democrats became determined to take all three states.

In South Carolina the campaign resembled a war rather than a political contest. Armed white Democrats terrorized both white and African American Republicans. Democrats formed political societies called rifle clubs that distributed rifles and knives to their members. They broke up Republican meetings and murdered African American officials. In Charleston, some Republicans fought back, burning buildings and smashing shop windows.

Alarmed, President Grant ordered the armed Democrats to disband. When they refused, the President sent in federal troops. Despite their presence, terror and fraud dominated Election Day in South Carolina. Depending on who held power in the county, armed Republicans or Democrats rode from poll to poll, voting again and again. In addition, hundreds of Georgians and North Carolinians crossed into South Carolina and voted illegally.

A Disputed Vote

Republicans still headed the election boards that counted votes. They declared Hayes the presidential winner; however, disputed returns in Oregon, South Carolina, Louisiana, and Florida threw the election in doubt and Democrats protested. Republicans charged that Democrats had won votes only by intimidating African American voters. The national vote proved so close that these states' votes would decide the presidency.

The Constitution provided no method to resolve the disputed votes. Tensions in the country rose to an intense level. Rumors spread that the South intended on inaugurating Tilden by force if necessary. Citizens feared that a new civil war might erupt. Almost no one, though, wanted another war.

In December Congress created an electoral commission to resolve the disputed vote. The commission accepted the Republican votes, giving the disputed states to Hayes. Southern Democrats then began a filibuster, a long speech meant to delay congressional action. It prevented the House from counting electoral votes.

Inauguration Day approached, yet the country still had no new President. At last, Southern Democrats worked out a private compromise with Hayes. In return for their accepting him as President, Hayes would withdraw federal troops from the South, appoint a Southerner to his cabinet, and grant economic help.

On March 5, 1877, Hayes became the nineteenth President. By the end of April the last federal troops had left the South. Reconstruction had ended.

Aftermath of Reconstruction

Reconstruction had proved to be a moderate program that fell far short of providing the newly freed African Americans with the protection and rights they needed. When Reconstruction came to an end, African Americans found themselves abandoned again.

With troop withdrawals and the end of Reconstruction governments, African Americans lost most of the gains they had made. The new majority in Congress revoked much of the legislation passed during Reconstruction and stopped federal help in supervising elections. Southern state governments implemented tests, taxes, and other methods to keep African Americans from voting. New state governments closed schools and ended other programs that helped both poor whites and African Americans.

The Supreme Court also tore down protections for African Americans. In 1883 it declared the Civil Rights Act of 1875 unconstitutional. States could now enforce segregation, or separate people by race, in places such as theaters and trains. Southern states passed laws, called "Jim Crow" laws, that separated African Americans from whites. In 1896 the Supreme Court

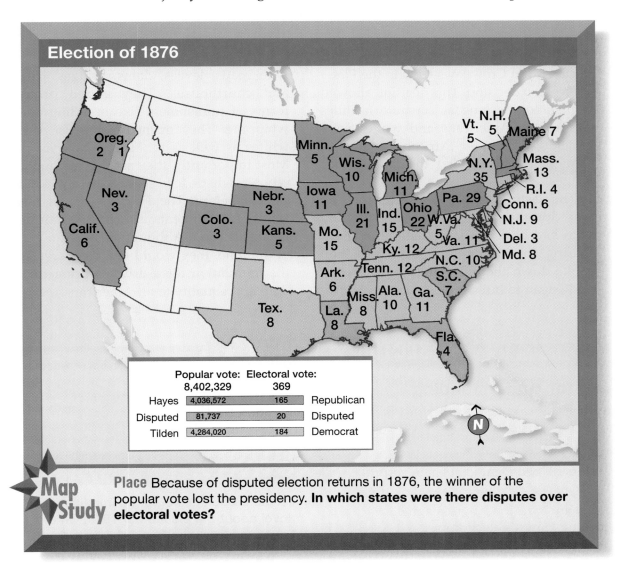

Election of 1876

	Popular vote: 8,402,329	Electoral vote: 369	
Hayes	4,036,572	165	Republican
Disputed	81,737	20	Disputed
Tilden	4,284,020	184	Democrat

Map Study **Place** Because of disputed election returns in 1876, the winner of the popular vote lost the presidency. **In which states were there disputes over electoral votes?**

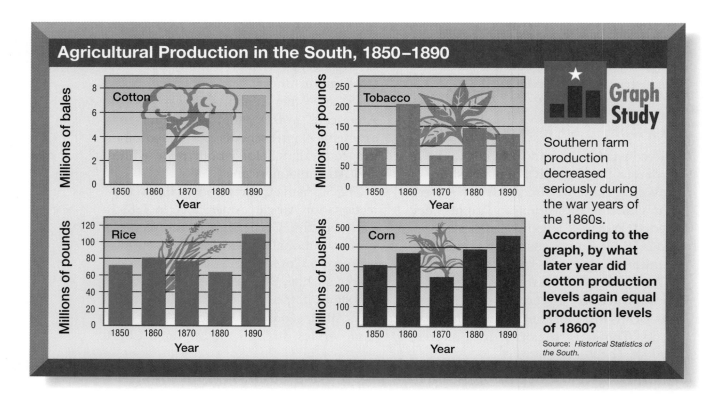

Agricultural Production in the South, 1850–1890

Cotton — Millions of bales (vertical axis: 0, 2, 4, 6, 8); Year (horizontal axis: 1850, 1860, 1870, 1880, 1890)

Tobacco — Millions of pounds (vertical axis: 0, 50, 100, 150, 200, 250); Year (horizontal axis: 1850, 1860, 1870, 1880, 1890)

Rice — Millions of pounds (vertical axis: 0, 20, 40, 60, 80, 100, 120); Year (horizontal axis: 1850, 1860, 1870, 1880, 1890)

Corn — Millions of bushels (vertical axis: 0, 100, 200, 300, 400, 500); Year (horizontal axis: 1850, 1860, 1870, 1880, 1890)

Graph Study

Southern farm production decreased seriously during the war years of the 1860s. **According to the graph, by what later year did cotton production levels again equal production levels of 1860?**

Source: *Historical Statistics of the South.*

declared Jim Crow laws legal in the *Plessy v. Ferguson* decision. This decision allowed segregation as long as separate facilities for African Americans and whites were equal. Facilities for African Americans, though, rarely equaled the facilities for whites.

The lasting legacy of Reconstruction was due mainly to Radical Republicans who had been state and federal officials. During their brief time in office, they broke down the old plantation economy and began to build a new, modern South, with roads, levees, dams, bridges, jails, and courthouses. They ended brutal forms of punishment like branding and whipping. They opened voting to poor whites as well as to African Americans. Most importantly, they set up free public schools where few schools of any kind existed before. The Fourteenth and Fifteenth Amendments also passed during Reconstruction. Although largely ignored at the time, they would one day serve as the foundation for a drive to bring freedom and equality to all Americans.

★ SECTION 4 REVIEW ★

Checking for Understanding

1. **Identify** Charles Caldwell, Rutherford B. Hayes, Samuel J. Tilden.

2. **Define** filibuster, segregation.

3. **What** factors helped Democrats gain control of Southern states?

4. **Why** did Democrats in Congress agree to stop blocking Hayes's election?

Critical Thinking

5. **Cause and Effect** What effects of Reconstruction can you identify today?

ACTIVITY

6. Create a book jacket for an imaginary novel about the election of 1876. On the front, draw a scene from the book. On the back, write a story summary.

BUILDING SKILLS
Critical Thinking Skills

Identifying Central Issues

If you read the headlines on a newspaper's front page or listen to a five-minute news broadcast, you will quickly learn the main news items of the day. These are the central issues, the main questions that concern people today.

Learning the Skill

History tells about the central issues of other times and places—how people dealt with the important questions of their day.

How do we find the central issues in a historical document? To get started, first be sure you know the setting of the article or document: the time, the place, and who the writer is. Second, think about past events that occurred there.

Finally, you would read the article carefully and look for statements that refer to those issues. Remember that past events determine the central issues of any time period.

▲ W.E.B. Du Bois

Practicing the Skill

The passage below is from a history of Reconstruction by W.E.B. Du Bois, an African American scholar. In it he describes the attitudes of people in Charleston, South Carolina, just after the Civil War. Read the passage and answer the questions.

> "The economic loss which came through war was great, but not nearly as influential as the psychological change, the change in habit and thought. . . .
>
> The hatred of the Yankee was increased. The defeated Southern leaders were popular heroes. Numbers of Southerners planned to leave the country, and go to South America or Mexico. . . .
>
> The labor situation, the prospect of free Negroes, caused great apprehension [fear]. It was accepted as absolutely true by most planters that the Negro could not and would not work without a white master."

1. Du Bois begins by naming two kinds of losses from the war. What are they? Which does he say was greater?

2. Is Du Bois mainly describing the reactions of whites or African Americans?

3. Identify some central issues that concerned the white residents of Charleston.

APPLYING THE SKILL

4. Identify a central issue of history today. Bring a news article about this issue to class. Be ready to identify the central issue and explain why it is important to people today and what they are doing about it.

Using Key Vocabulary

Use each term below in a newspaper headline that might have appeared during the Reconstruction period.

> Radical Republicans
> carpetbagger
> Ku Klux Klan
> Fifteenth Amendment
> amnesty

Reviewing Facts

1. **List** the objections Congress had to President Lincoln's plans for Reconstruction.

2. **Name** the central ideas of the Thirteenth, Fourteenth, and Fifteenth Amendments.

3. **Explain** why Radical Republicans wanted to remove President Andrew Johnson from office.

4. **Describe** the work of the Freedmen's Bureau.

5. **Identify** the factors that weakened the Republican party in the 1870s.

History and Geography

Reestablishment of Conservative Governments in the South

Study the map and then answer the following questions.

1. **Location**   In which states did Reconstruction governments last the longest?

2. **Region**   Which state was readmitted first? What geographic reason can you find to explain this?

3. **Movement**   Do you think Virginia's nearness to Washington, D.C., was a reason for its reestablishing a conservative government sooner than other states? Explain your answer.

Reestablishment of Conservative Governments in the South

- Va. 1869/1868
- N.C. 1868/1870
- Tennessee 1866/1869
- Arkansas 1868/1874
- S.C. 1868/1876
- Alabama 1868/1874
- Georgia 1868/1871
- Miss. 1870/1876
- La. 1868/1876
- Texas 1869/1873
- Fla. 1868/1876

Legend:
- Former Confederate states
- **1868** Date readmitted to Union
- 1873 Date of takeover by conservative government

CHAPTER 19 ★ REVIEW

Understanding Concepts

Civil Rights and Liberties

1. How did the election of 1868 illustrate the importance of African American votes to the Republican party?

2. What civil and political rights did African Americans gain under the Constitution during Reconstruction?

3. What were the goals of the first civil rights laws? What happened to those laws?

American Democracy

4. What postwar changes were hard for most white Southerners to accept? What were their responses?

5. In what ways, if any, did Radical Republican policies benefit white Southerners during Reconstruction?

Critical Thinking

1. **Identifying Cause and Effect** What kind of relationship did President Johnson and Radical Republicans have when he first became President? Why did it change?

2. **Understanding Point of View** How do you think African Americans in the South felt when President Hayes ended Reconstruction? Explain your answer.

Cooperative Learning Interdisciplinary Activity: Language Arts

With two other students, choose one African American who held a state or national office during Reconstruction and research that person's biography. You may want to focus on a dramatic political event or give an overview of life events. Then collaborate on a skit highlighting that person's career. Present the skit to the class.

Practicing Skills

Identifying Central Issues

The excerpt below was written by a carpetbagger—a person from New York who moved to South Carolina in 1870. Read the passage and answer the questions.

"... [T]he fact is still evident that the 'black code' of South Carolina was essentially a slave code, and that it was intended so to be. Its adaptation of the old terms, 'master' and 'servant,' to white employer and Negro freedman under contract ... would alone go far to stamp it as reactionary. ... Add the fact that it [the code] was made by masters for freedmen; add the further fact that in all their mutual relations it was to be interpreted and enforced by masters for freedmen...."

1. According to this writer, why were the black codes passed?

2. What details does he give to support this view?

3. What central issue of Reconstruction is this passage about?

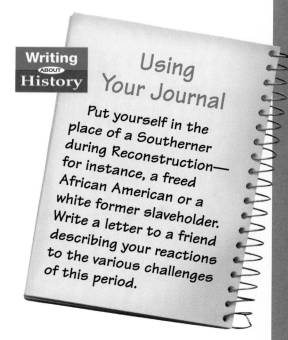

Writing ABOUT History

Using Your Journal

Put yourself in the place of a Southerner during Reconstruction—for instance, a freed African American or a white former slaveholder. Write a letter to a friend describing your reactions to the various challenges of this period.

Chapter 16

Sectional Differences

Steam engines of the **Industrial Revolution** brought about many changes, especially in the North, by the mid-1800s. First, steamboats replaced flatboats on rivers. Then steam locomotives replaced river travel with **railroads.** Railroads and the **telegraph** both helped link distant places.

Steam-driven factory machines increased the number of manufacturing plants, workers, and cities. The new industrial factories also greatly increased the amount of goods workers could produce. Workers, though, received low wages and faced dangerous working conditions.

The South bought clothing, machinery, and other goods produced in Northern factories. Its own economy centered on agriculture. Its population, mostly rural, included yeoman farmers, large planters, poor whites, and African Americans.

▲ STEAMBOATS ON THE MISSISSIPPI RIVER

Most African Americans were enslaved. They provided the labor for producing the South's cash crops—especially cotton, which Southerners sold to Northern textile mills. **Slaveholding,** however, caused untold misery among African Americans.

CAUSES

- Disagreements over slaveholding
- Kansas-Nebraska Act brings violence in Kansas
- *Dred Scott* decision cancels Missouri Compromise
- John Brown raids Harpers Ferry arsenal
- South secedes
- Confederates attack Fort Sumter

- Civil War

EFFECTS

- United States outlaws slavery
- South rebuilds its economy
- Constitution grants African Americans citizenship and the right to vote
- United States passes first civil rights legislation

Chapter 17

Road to Civil War

Northerners and Southerners disagreed sharply on allowing slavery in the lands acquired from Mexico in the 1840s. After intense debate and threats of Southern secession, Congress passed provisions known as the **Compromise of 1850.** This set of laws agreed to some of the demands made by abolitionists, **Free-Soilers,** and proslavery groups but completely satisfied none of them.

Enforcement of the **Fugitive Slave Act** and the *Dred Scott* decision enraged Northerners and strengthened the abolitionist movement during the 1850s. During the same decade, **popular sovereignty** brought bloodshed in Kansas. Finally, in 1859, abolitionist John Brown seized weapons at Harpers Ferry, hoping to start a slave rebellion. Frightened Southerners became shocked when some people in the North supported Brown's actions.

Antislavery and proslavery strife caused the Whig party to collapse. The new **Republican** party, the Free-Soil party, supported Abraham Lincoln for President. Voters elected Lincoln to the presidential office in 1860. As a result, seven Southern states seceded and formed the **Confederacy**.

Chapter 18

The Civil War

The Civil War began in April 1861, when Confederates bombarded the federal arsenal at **Fort Sumter,** South Carolina. The Union's navy successfully blockaded Southern seaports. The Union's land forces, though, could not stand up to Confederate General Robert E. Lee in Virginia during the first years of the fighting. Lincoln, in 1863, put the **Emancipation Proclamation** into effect. He hoped the measure would strengthen Northern support for the war.

Union forces, under the direction of General Ulysses S. Grant, proved more successful in the West. At Shiloh, Tennessee, and other battle sites, both sides suffered enormous losses. In July of 1863, however, the Union gained control of the Mississippi River—a vital supply route for the South. The following year, Union General William Sherman's army cut a path of destruction through the Deep South. General Grant, now in the East, led a costly but steady advance toward the Southern capital of Richmond. He entered the city on April 2, 1865. Lee surrendered a week later, and the war was officially over by the end of May.

Chapter 19

Reconstruction

Looking ahead to the end of the war, Lincoln proposed to deal generously with most Southerners. After Lincoln's assassination,

▲ CARPETBAG, 1870S

President Johnson put a similar **Reconstruction** plan into place. Southern leadership and abuses of African Americans changed little, however, under Johnson's plan. After bitter quarrels with Johnson and an **impeachment** attempt against him, Congress took over Reconstruction.

Under Republican governments during Radical Reconstruction, African Americans won the right to vote. Voters elected many African Americans to public office. Many more received education in the **Freedmen's Bureau** schools. Southern Democrats resisted the changes in Southern politics and society. They used political tactics and terror to try to regain control. By 1877, they succeeded, and Reconstruction ended.

▲ FIGHT FOR THE COLORS, BY DON TROIANI, 1985

Understanding Unit Themes

1. **Economic Development** What effects did the Industrial Revolution have on the economies of the North and the South?

2. **Influence of Technology** How did steam power and electricity change transportation and communication? How did new methods of production change the ways people worked and lived?

3. **Conflict and Cooperation** Why did the Compromise of 1850 create further strife at the same time that it calmed arguments?

4. **Civil Rights and Liberties** How did laws and amendments passed during Reconstruction extend the rights of African Americans?

UNIT SEVEN
MODERN AMERICA EMERGES
1877–PRESENT

★★

CHAPTER
20
Reshaping the Nation
1877–1900

CHAPTER
21
The Twentieth Century
1900–Present

► TELEGRAPHIC TICKER

 History AND ART

Three Flags
by Jasper Johns, 1958

Paintings by Jasper Johns typically feature two-dimensional objects. For example, Johns has painted pictures that consist entirely of flags, maps, numbers, and letters.

After the Civil War, new technology and industries thrust the United States into the modern era. With economic strength came increasing responsibility in the world.

Themes

★ Influence of Technology
★ The Individual and Family Life
★ Civil Rights and Liberties
★ U.S. Role in World Affairs

Key Events

★ Farmers form the Populist party
★ Spanish-American War
★ United States builds Panama Canal
★ World War I
★ Great Depression
★ World War II
★ Civil Rights movement
★ Vietnam War
★ End of the cold war

Major Issues

★ The United States becomes an industrial giant.
★ The United States fights the spread of communism.
★ Civil Rights movement gains momentum.
★ The United States takes on new global responsibilities at the end of the cold war.

▲ FIRST LUNAR LANDING, 1969

▲ VIETNAM WAR PROTEST

◄ EDDIE RICKENBACKER AND WORLD WAR I PLANE

Portfolio Project

Create a time line of events for this unit. Illustrate each event with an original drawing or a photocopy of an illustration. For current events, you may cut cartoons or photos from recent newspapers or magazines.

A Popping Population Map

Background

The population of the United States has reached 260,800,000 according to the latest government figures. That means that there is a population density—or number of people per square mile—of about 74 people per square mile (28 people per sq. km) in the United States. Where do most of these people live? What factors influence where the most people live? To better understand the distribution of population in the United States, use popcorn to create your own population map of your country.

▲ BUSY NEW YORK CITY STREET

Believe It OR NOT!

Canada, the United States's neighbor to the north, has an area about 500,000 square miles (1,295,000 sq. km) larger than that of the United States, but a population density of only 8 people per square mile (3 people per sq. km).

Materials

- population density map of the United States
- piece of large posterboard
- newspaper
- popcorn kernels
- hot-air popper
- food coloring
- water
- 6 small transparent cups or jars
- white household glue
- colored pencils or markers
- 6 large mixing bowls
- 6 spoons

What To Do

A. Using the population density map of the United States as a reference, trace an outline of the United States onto the posterboard. Be sure to include Alaska and Hawaii.

B. Add lines marking the different levels of population density that you see on the map.

C. Add a key to your map. Most maps include 6 density levels, from uninhabited to more than 250 people per square mile. You will need 6 shades of colored popped corn, one for each level, to complete your map.

D. Pop your popcorn, *carefully* following directions for your popper. Divide the popped corn into 6 bowls.

E. Color your popcorn. Mix food coloring with a small amount of water, each in a different cup. Then stir the colored water into the popcorn, mixing well to coat each piece.

F. Spread the colored popcorn on newspaper to dry.

G. Glue the colored popcorn onto your map to represent the different population densities. Color code your key.

Lab Activity Report

1. What regions of the United States are the most densely populated?

2. What regions are the most sparsely populated?

3. Look at the levels of population densities along coastlines. What similarities and differences do you see?

4. Drawing Conclusions What areas of the United States do you think will grow in population over the next 20 years? Why?

GO A STEP FURTHER

ACTIVITY

Compare your population density map of the United States to a physical map of the country. List the major physical features that you think could have caused low and high population density areas.

CHAPTER 20

★★★

Reshaping the Nation
1877–1900

► **RAILROAD POSTER**

SETTING THE SCENE

Focus

The United States changed greatly in the years after the Civil War. Americans, eager to claim the last "unsettled" lands, migrated to the prairies. At the same time, industrialization altered the face of the country. Once a nation of farmers, the United States rapidly became a nation of cities. In addition, this land of new opportunities attracted immigrants from all over the world.

Journal Notes

How did America change in the late 1800s? Keep a record of the changes as you read the chapter.

Concepts to Understand

★ How the **influence of technology** transformed the United States from a farming to an industrial nation

★ Why the changes the nation experienced in the late 1800s reshaped **individual and family life**

Read to Discover . . .

★ the changes that took place in America in the late 1800s.

★ how these changes affected American lives.

United States	1869 First transcontinental railroad completed	1876 The Sioux defeat Custer at Little Bighorn River	1886 Statue of Liberty completed
	1868–1874	**1875–1881**	**1882–1888**
World			1882 Germany, Austria, and Italy form the Triple Alliance

◄ "CANDLESTICK" TELEPHONE

History AND ART

The Cliff Dweller
by George Wesley Bellows, 1913

Bellows's work often demonstrated humor and adventure. Some of his most popular themes included athletic events and landscapes.

1891 Farmers form the
Populist party
1892 Grover Cleveland
elected President

1896 William McKinley
elected President
1901 Theodore Roosevelt
becomes President

1889–1895

1894 Sino-Japanese War
begins

1896–1902

1900 Boxer rebellion in
China begins
1901 First transatlantic
wireless message sent

★★

Westward Expansion

SETTING THE SCENE

Read to Learn . . .

★ why railroads greatly influenced the opening of the last American frontier.
★ how miners and ranchers helped settle the West.
★ how life for Native Americans changed in the late 1800s.

Terms to Know

★ subsidy
★ boomtown
★ ghost town
★ open range
★ cow town
★ homesteader
★ reservation

People to Meet

★ Cornelius Vanderbilt
★ Jay Gould
★ J.P. Morgan
★ Buffalo Bill
★ Sitting Bull
★ Crazy Horse
★ George Custer

Places to Locate

★ Great Plains
★ Black Hills, South Dakota
★ Wounded Knee, South Dakota

◀ SIOUX GHOST DANCE SHIRT

Americans built railroads in the West at a furious pace during and after the Civil War. By 1890 almost 200,000 miles (124,200 km) of railroad crisscrossed the country. These railroads led the way west and opened up America's last frontier—the **Great Plains**—to settlement.

★ Building Railroads

On May 10, 1869, builders completed the first transcontinental railroad line at Promontory Point, Utah. The president of the Central Pacific Railroad Company, Leland Stanford, raised a silver sledgehammer and drove a golden spike into the final railroad tie. The whole country celebrated as telegraph wires flashed the news. Railroad lines now spanned the continent.

Railroad Tycoons

A few Americans grew rich and powerful from the construction of railroads. Railroad tycoons **Cornelius Vanderbilt** and **Jay Gould,** for example, made millions of dollars. They might not have succeeded, however, without government help. Both Vanderbilt and Gould often bribed government officials to arrange cash subsidies—grants of money to assist a company—and choice land grants. Railroad heads also cooperated with bankers to gain more profits. New York banker **J.P. Morgan** formed a compact with major railroad owners to eliminate competition from smaller railroads.

Meanwhile, thousands of workers involved in the day-to-day construction of the railroads received only $1 or $2 a day. Most workers came from Ireland and China, and many had fought in the Civil War. Their backbreaking work seemed never ending. They dug, chiseled, and dynamited their way across the United States. Many lost their lives. In 1889 alone 22,000 railroad workers were injured or killed.

★ The Rush to the Mines

People started to move to the Rockies and Great Plains even before the railroads reached those areas. After 1849 miners flocked to California looking for gold and silver and hoping to make quick fortunes. Mining continued to attract settlers to the West throughout the late 1800s.

Towns sprang up wherever people discovered gold or silver. Americans called these communities boomtowns because of their rapid growth. When miners exhausted the veins of ore, they quickly moved on. These communities dwindled into ghost towns—empty towns where no one lived.

★ Cattle Kingdoms Spread

After the Civil War, the demand for beef encouraged cattle raisers to ranch in the open range—the broad grasslands in the West. On the open range, ranchers grazed their herds free of charge and unrestrained by boundaries. Eastern demand created opportunities for great profits.

In 1866 dozens of Texas ranchers drove a quarter of a million cattle along the old Shawnee Trail to the closest railroad station in Sedalia, Missouri. That same year Texans **Charles Goodnight** and **Oliver Loving** drove their cattle along an old mail route to mining camps in Colorado. Soon Texas became a major beef supplier and the Goodnight-Loving Trail became the main artery for cattle drives to the Rockies.

In 1867 the Kansas Pacific Railroad completed a rail line that ran as far west as Abilene, Kansas. Cattle merchant **Joseph McCoy** built pens at the railroad station to hold herds waiting for shipment east. Between 1867 and 1871, freight trains carried 1.5 million cattle from Abilene to meatpacking plants in Chicago and Kansas City. Then the Santa Fe Railroad

Picturing History

▲ MINING TOWNS The discovery of gold started a mass migration of people to the West. People flocked into "boomtowns" hoping to become rich. **What name was given to a boomtown after everyone left?**

built lines through Wichita, Ellsworth, and Dodge City. It grabbed the majority of the cattle market and sent an additional 2.5 million cattle east. These Kansas railroad centers became known as cow towns because their main business became shipping cattle.

Decline of the Cattle Industry

The open-range cattle industry collapsed even more quickly than it had risen. Too many animals on open ranges resulted in overgrazing, depriving all livestock and wild animals of food. Overproduction drove prices down, and sheepherders and farmers competed with ranchers for land. Finally, two severe winters in 1885–1886 and 1886–1887 killed thousands of animals. The cattle industry survived, but the day of large herds on the open range ended. From then on, ranchers raised herds on fenced-in ranches.

★ Farmers on the Plains

In the 1870s and 1880s, farmers poured onto the land between the Mississippi River and the Rocky Mountains. Pioneers before them had passed through on their way to the Far West. They considered this land too dry to farm. The new pioneers, however, eagerly settled the nation's last frontier.

Congress encouraged farmers to move to the West by passing the **Homestead Act** of 1862. The federal government designed this legislation as a form of government aid—helping to create new markets for the nation's growing economy. The law granted 160 acres (64.8 ha) of land to the heads of families for $10—the cost of filing a deed. The homesteaders, or persons granted land under the Homestead Act, had to improve the land and live on it for five years. Then they could apply for full ownership. The act, though, did not prove a complete success. Many homesteaders, unable to make a decent living, abandoned their lands before the end of five years. Others used fraud and trickery to gain land for business interests.

Challenges of Frontier Life

The men and women who traveled west faced a hard life on the Great Plains. Blizzards, spring floods, and summer droughts made survival difficult. Clouds of grasshoppers sometimes ate entire crops. Hailstorms posed still another threat to farmers. Sometimes the summer sky sent a rain of hailstones as big as hens' eggs that could destroy everything a family had struggled months to produce.

Over time, pioneer families developed ways to handle the challenges of frontier life. They became experts at dry farming, or planting crops in a way that keeps the soil moist longer. They also came up with solutions to living in a region with few trees. They built their homes using squares of hard sod, piled one on top of another. An Illinois farmer, **Joseph Glidden,** even found a way to build fences on the treeless prairie. His invention of barbed wire made him a wealthy man.

★ Native Americans on the Plains

Long before the first settlers arrived, other people called the plains and prairies home. Native American groups, including the Sioux, Cheyenne, Comanche, Arapaho, Kiowa, and Pawnee, lived on the Great Plains. Many of these groups hunted the great herds of buffalo that moved across the grasslands. The hunters and their families used the meat for food, the horns for spoons, the bones for knives and arrow tips, and the hides for robes, blankets, shoes, and tepees. "Buffalo chips"—dried manure—provided fuel. Buffalo tendons formed the strings of bows.

Newcomers to the plains killed off the great herds that the Native Americans depended on for survival. In the 1860s railroad companies hired sharpshooters such as William Frederick Cody to furnish buffalo meat to western railroad workers. Cody once claimed that he killed more than 4,000 buffalo in less than 18 months and earned the nickname **Buffalo Bill.** Then in 1871 leather factories started offering $3 apiece for buffalo hides. Gangs of hunters swarmed over the plains, shooting the animals, taking their hides, and leaving the rest to rot in the sun. Other hunters slaughtered buffalo merely for the sport of the chase. Over the next decade, hunters killed more than 1 million buffalo each year. In 1865 at least 15 million buffalo had roamed the land; by 1875 fewer than 1,000 buffalo survived.

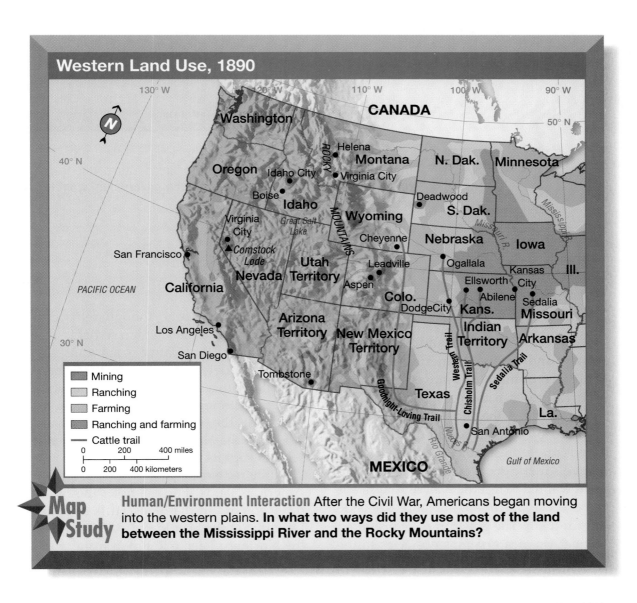

Western Land Use, 1890

Mining
Ranching
Farming
Ranching and farming
Cattle trail

0   200   400 miles
0   200   400 kilometers

Map Study **Human/Environment Interaction** After the Civil War, Americans began moving into the western plains. **In what two ways did they use most of the land between the Mississippi River and the Rocky Mountains?**

▲ *LAST STAND OF THE PATRIARCH* by Henry Francis Farny, 1905 The movement of white settlers to the West forced Native Americans to change where they lived. **Where did the government want to resettle Native Americans?**

◀ CHEYENNE SHIELD OF PAINTED BUFFALO HIDE

Trouble on the Frontier

Between the 1850s and the 1880s, whites and Native Americans fought almost constantly as Native Americans tried to preserve their civilizations. This fighting, called the Indian Wars, usually occurred on a small scale but sometimes flared up to resemble a war. Ignoring Native American sovereignty, the government wanted to resettle Native Americans on reservations, or special lands set aside just for them. The government considered Native American nations obstacles to the spread of white society. Groups like the Kiowa and Comanche, though, refused to abandon their homelands to settlers.

Eventually the Native Americans lost their lands, defeated largely by the technological resources and diseases of the white settlers. Although the government promised that the reservation lands would belong to the Native Americans forever, it seldom kept its promises.

White settlers began to want the Native American lands. For example, the Sioux received land in the **Black Hills** of South Dakota. Yet they could not stop crews for the Northern Pacific Railroad from crossing reservation lands while surveying for the railroad. When settlers discovered gold in the Black Hills, miners swarmed onto the reservation.

The government reduced the size of most reservations or moved the Native Americans to lands undesirable to whites. The Sioux decided they had suffered enough. **Sitting Bull** and **Crazy Horse** led their people off the reservation. Near the Little Bighorn River in southern Montana Territory, they joined forces with several thousand other Sioux and Cheyenne.

In June 1876, they overwhelmed Colonel **George Custer** and more than 200 troops sent to round up the Sioux. In the ensuing battle, the Native Americans killed Custer and all of his troops. The Sioux and Cheyenne won the battle, but within months government soldiers found them and forced them to surrender.

A group of Apaches, led by Geronimo, became the last Native American nation to hold out. By the time the Americans captured Geronimo in 1886, American troops had confined every Native American group to reservations.

The Dawes Act

Life on the reservations grew more difficult. Some government agents in charge of the reservations cheated and abused the Native Americans. Native Americans felt disheartened because they could no longer follow their ways of life.

In 1887 Congress passed the **Dawes Act.** This law abolished collective land ownership and offered each Native American family 160 acres of land. After a probation period of 25 years, Native Americans would be granted ownership of the land and United States citizenship. In this way, Congress hoped to force Native Americans to abandon their collective societies and to take up farming like other Americans in the West.

Some Native American groups—the Plains peoples, for example—based their way of life on the buffalo hunt, moving from place to place following the buffalo. They did not understand the legal technicalities of land ownership, knew little about farming, and became demoralized by reservation life.

The final defeat of the Native Americans occurred on December 29, 1890. The American army rounded up cold and starving Sioux men, women, and children at **Wounded Knee, South Dakota.** Suddenly a shot fired, and the American soldiers massacred the defenseless Native Americans, darkening the December snow.

★ SECTION 1 REVIEW ★

Checking for Understanding

1. **Identify** Cornelius Vanderbilt, Jay Gould, J.P. Morgan, Buffalo Bill, Sitting Bull, Crazy Horse, George Custer, Great Plains, Black Hills, Wounded Knee.

2. **Define** subsidy, boomtown, ghost town, open range, cow town, homesteader, reservation.

3. **How** did railroads help open the West to settlement?

4. **What** challenges did settlers on the plains face?

Critical Thinking

5. **Recognizing Point of View** Many Americans in the 1800s imagined the West as free, open land awaiting civilization by white people. Assume the role of a Native American and respond to this view.

ACTIVITY

6. Create a poster that the United States government might have used to encourage farmers to move west.

★★

New American Industries

SETTING THE SCENE

Read to Learn . . .

★ what rich natural and human resources helped change America from a nation of farmers to an industrial power.
★ how big business affected workers.

Terms to Know

★ heavy industry
★ patent
★ entrepreneur
★ corporation
★ capital
★ monopoly
★ laissez-faire

People to Meet

★ Cyrus W. Field
★ Thomas Alva Edison
★ John D. Rockefeller
★ Andrew Carnegie
★ Gustavus Swift

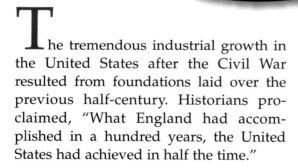

◄ EDISON'S LIGHT BULB

The tremendous industrial growth in the United States after the Civil War resulted from foundations laid over the previous half-century. Historians proclaimed, "What England had accomplished in a hundred years, the United States had achieved in half the time."

★ Reinventing the United States

Even as settlers moved west to farm the last American frontier, farmers in other parts of the country moved to the cities. They took jobs in the new urban industries that recent inventions made possible. The United States changed from a nation of farmers to a modern, industrial nation.

Rich Natural Resources

The country's rich farmlands, great forests, and mighty rivers helped the early colonists develop a strong agricultural economy. As the nation grew, Americans developed resources of a different kind. In addition to talented inventors, they had eager investors, willing workers, and a pro-business government. These new resources made the expansion of American industry possible.

The United States also possessed other necessary ingredients for industry—plenty of natural resources. The world's largest deposits of coal lay in western Pennsylvania, the Mississippi Valley, and Appalachia. The shores of Lake Superior held major supplies of iron ore. Mines in western states contained gold, silver, lead, zinc, copper, and bauxite—the ore used to make aluminum.

These minerals formed the base of heavy industry in the United States. A heavy industry produces materials such as coal, iron, or steel. Out of these materials, Americans built railroads, bridges, skyscrapers, and machinery for the factories that transformed the nation. By the late 1800s, the United States had become the world's number one manufacturing nation.

Wizards of Wonder

During the late 1800s, an invention boom spurred the growth of industry. The government granted so many patents—licenses protecting people's rights to make, sell, or use their inventions—that one Washington official thought nothing else could be invented. He even recommended that the government close the patent office. Many inventions led to the creation of new industries. Other inventions helped produce goods more cheaply or quickly.

Some of the most important inventions appeared in communications. The telegraph had already brought rapid changes in the communications industry in the 1840s. Then in 1866, **Cyrus W. Field** laid a transatlantic telegraph cable. Now a message sent to someone in Europe arrived in minutes instead of weeks. During the next

▲ *By Industry We Thrive,* A Lithograph by Kimmel and Voigt The abundance and variety of natural resources helped to build strong industries in the United States. **What types of materials does heavy industry produce?**

▲ Long Distance Call
Alexander Graham Bell is shown opening the New York-to-Chicago long distance line in 1892. **Who laid the first transatlantic telegraph cable?**

decade, **Alexander Graham Bell** developed the telephone. By the 1890s a nationwide telephone company installed nearly half a million telephones in cities across the United States.

Americans also developed new sources of power. **Thomas Alva Edison** led others in building the first large power plants to furnish electricity to entire cities. By the turn of the century, electric power lit homes and offices and ran streetcars, elevators, and factories.

In 1859 **Edwin L. Drake** drilled the first oil well to extract petroleum from the ground. Then people turned petroleum into kerosene, a fuel used in lamps, stoves, and heaters. In the early 1900s, though, Americans discovered other uses for petroleum when inventors developed the automobile.

★ Growth of Big Business

As industry grew, so did opportunities for success. The nation's great economic power became concentrated in individual hands. For example, **John D. Rockefeller, Andrew Carnegie,** and **Gustavus Swift** created business empires in the oil, steel, and meatpacking industries. These large and powerful business empires became known as "big business." The leaders of these businesses became known as entrepreneurs because they took risks to start new businesses and developed new ways of doing business. Although some entrepreneurs went from rags to riches, this proved rare. Most business empires survived by eliminating competition—fairly or unfairly.

★ Corporations and Monopolies

Entrepreneurs such as Carnegie, Rockefeller, and Swift organized their businesses into corporations. A corporation is a business in which investors own shares. New factories and machinery cost large amounts of money, more than any individual possessed. By letting investors buy shares, corporations could raise capital, or the money needed to start and run a business.

• •

Footnotes to History

Another Invention   In 1889 John Styth Pemberton invented a new brew from the coca plant. He labeled it Coca-Cola and billed it "the intellectual beverage." He also claimed that it cured headaches and upset stomachs and "lifted the spirits."

Some American businesses, such as Rockefeller's Standard Oil Company, grew large enough to force almost all the other companies that competed with them out of business. When one company gains control over an industry, it becomes a monopoly. Rockefeller's Standard Oil Company, for example, controlled 90 percent of the oil business in the United States by 1878.

A Hands-Off Government

The government followed a laissez-faire (lehs•ay•FEHR) or "hands-off," policy toward big business and industry. Americans who supported laissez-faire believed that they could best help business by leaving it alone. Congress passed no guidelines or regulations for the activities of business giants such as Rockefeller or Carnegie. It passed no income taxes that might lower profits. It passed no laws guaranteeing a minimum wage or workers' safety. Businesses operated as they wished.

Many Americans strongly supported their government's hands-off policy. They believed that the growth of business and industry brought progress that everyone shared. As industrial giants like Rockefeller relentlessly gained economic power, the gap between the rich and the poor widened. Some people began to question their government's policy.

Willing Workers

The nation achieved industrial growth based largely on the labor of ordinary men and women. Although workers benefited from industrial growth, they had to endure difficult working conditions and diminishing control over their own lives.

Some workers joined together in unions to bargain for better working conditions. Union members hoped to raise wages and improve working conditions. The **Knights of Labor** became the first national union to include skilled and unskilled

---

Linking Past and Present

Recording History

Amazing new technology produced the phonograph in 1877. More than a century later, even more amazing new technology totally replaced it.

Then_____

In the Groove

On a December day in 1877, Thomas Edison demonstrated a new machine to his staff

▼ EARLY PHONOGRAPH

that seemed to do the impossible. It "captured" sound and then played it back. The new invention had two needles. One needle recorded the sounds by etching grooves on a cylinder wrapped in tin foil. The other needle played back the sounds by retracing the grooves. The machine was the first phonograph, and the foil-wrapped cylinder became the first record.

Now_____

On the Beam

In 1983 the compact disc (CD) and the CD player replaced the phonograph. The shiny aluminum CD and its needleless

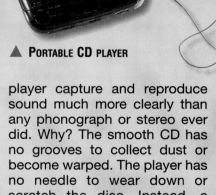

▲ PORTABLE CD PLAYER

player capture and reproduce sound much more clearly than any phonograph or stereo ever did. Why? The smooth CD has no grooves to collect dust or become warped. The player has no needle to wear down or scratch the disc. Instead, a highly concentrated light beam, called a laser, releases the sound from the CD.

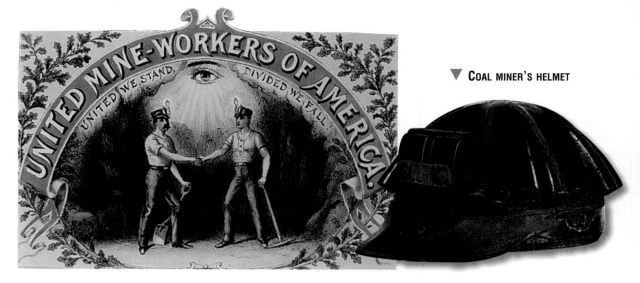

▼ COAL MINER'S HELMET

Picturing History ▲ LABOR UNIONS Union members joined in hoping for higher wages and better working conditions. **What labor union was the first to include skilled and unskilled workers?**

workers in the 1870s. In 1886 the **American Federation of Labor (AFL)** was formed by several labor organizations. It became the most successful labor organization in the country.

Many workers used strikes to achieve their goals. They refused to do their jobs until their employers agreed to certain demands. In 1877 a national railroad strike became the first of many violent confrontations between workers and employers. Few strikes succeeded between 1865 and 1900, however. Employers usually hired other workers or waited until the strikers ran out of money and returned to work. In general, the public viewed labor unions in a negative manner and government authorities usually sided with employers against strikers.

By the end of the 1800s most workers found themselves with less political power and control of the workplace. Meanwhile, the big businesses managed to protect their interests and wealth.

★ **SECTION 2 REVIEW** ★

Checking for Understanding

1. **Identify** Cyrus W. Field, Thomas Alva Edison, John D. Rockefeller, Andrew Carnegie, Gustavus Swift.

2. **Define** heavy industry, patent, entrepreneur, corporation, capital, monopoly, laissez-faire.

3. **What** natural and human resources helped change the United States into an industrial nation?

4. **How** did industrialization change American life?

Critical Thinking

5. **Making Inferences** Many people called entrepreneurs such as Cornelius Vanderbilt and John D. Rockefeller "robber barons." Infer from your reading why people used this name.

ACTIVITY

6. Design a board game in which players can experience the ups and downs of factory work in the late 1800s. Include spaces such as "Workday extended to 12 hours, miss a turn," and "Your union wins a pay hike. Collect $5."

BUILDING SKILLS
Social Studies Skills

Reading a Time Zone Map

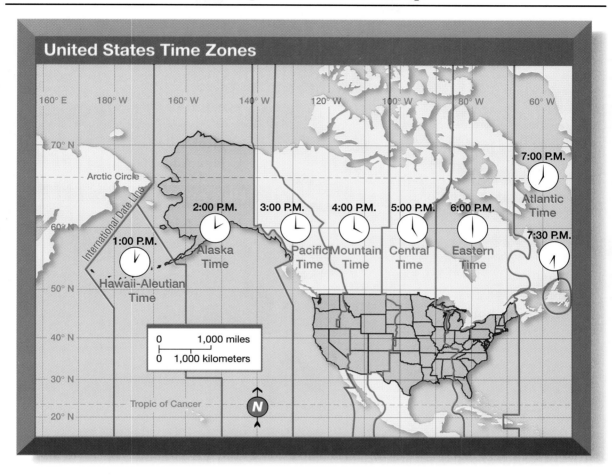

United States Time Zones

Learning the Skill

In the 1800s few Americans could agree on the time of day because every community determined its own time by the position of the sun. Then in the late 1800s the new railroads required a single standard time for scheduling and routing. In 1883 the railroad companies divided the United States into four standard time zones. Not until 1918, though, did Congress pass official standardized time zones.

In 1884 an international conference fixed worldwide time zones. Under this system, the world was divided into 24 different time zones with the Prime Meridian—0° longitude—as the starting point.

Practicing the Skill

1. What United States time zone lies farthest west?

2. If it is 6 P.M. in Washington, D.C., what time is it in San Diego, California?

3. Which United States time zone will celebrate the beginning of the year 2000 last?

APPLYING THE SKILL

4. It takes two hours to fly from Denver, Colorado, to Chicago, Illinois. If you leave Denver at 2 A.M. Friday, what time will it be in Chicago when you arrive?

★★★

New Immigrants, Modern Cities

SETTING THE SCENE

Read to Learn . . .

★ the struggles of immigrants in the United States.

★ how American cities had changed at the turn of the century.

Terms to Know

★ tenement
★ slum
★ settlement house

People to Meet

★ Jacob Riis
★ Jane Addams

Places to Locate

★ Ellis Island
★ Harlem

◄ STATUE OF LIBERTY

The woman smiled as she recalled her arrival in the United States:

> 66 My first day in America I went with my aunt to buy some American clothes. . . . I took my old brown dress and shawl and threw them away! . . . When I looked in the mirror, I couldn't get over it. I said, boy, Sophie, look at you now. Just like an American. 99

★ Starting Over

Like Sophie, many courageous immigrants came to the United States in search of a new start. They left their native countries to escape hunger, poverty, and political oppression. In the 1880s almost half a million immigrants arrived at the docks in New York City each year.

Immigrants in the Late 1800s

Most immigrants before 1870 came from the northern and western nations of Europe. They included Irish, Germans, Scots, and English. After 1870 the pattern of immigration changed. Large numbers of immigrants from eastern and southern Europe also came to the United States. More than one-half of the new immigrants came from Italy, Russia, Austria, and Hungary. They included many Catholics, as well as Jews fleeing persecution in Europe.

Most new immigrants from Europe arrived in New York. After 1886 as the newcomers approached the shores of their new home they viewed the majestic Statue of Liberty, their first sight of America. The statue stood on a small island in New York Harbor and held up a glowing torch as if lighting the newcomers' way. By 1892 the federal government had set up an official immigration center on **Ellis Island** near the statue.

Thousands of immigrants also reached America through other ports. Many Asian immigrants entered the country at San Francisco. Most of them came from China and Japan. Although the immigrants faced many struggles in their new country, they helped build the new nation.

★ Immigrants Face Discrimination

Not all Americans welcomed newcomers to their country. The immigrants' languages and customs seemed strange to some Americans and aroused distrust and discrimination.

Immigrants usually lived in their own neighborhoods, practiced their own customs, and spoke their own languages to ease the pain of separation from their native lands. Many Americans wondered if immigrants could ever be assimilated into American life. Some people, especially workers, blamed immigrants for low wages. Employers found that immigrants would accept lower wages than native Americans.

◀ IMMIGRANTS, LATE 1800s

Immigration, 1860–1900

Immigrants (In thousands) vs. Year

★ Graph Study

Europeans made up the greatest number of immigrants in the late 1800s, but Latin American and Canadian immigration made large gains during the early 1900s. **What year on the graph saw the least number of immigrants?**

Source: *Historical Statistics of the United States.*

Others resented the different cultures and religions of the many immigrants.

In the late 1800s hostility grew toward many of the new racial and ethnic groups coming into the country. Some historians believe the rapid changes occurring in America because of industrialization influenced this reaction. Immigrants became easy targets of hostility for Americans uncertain or disturbed by the rapid social changes.

★ Strangers in the City

During the late 1800s and early 1900s, the city became a magnet that drew people and ideas and created new lifestyles. Most immigrants settled in American cities. African Americans from rural areas of the United States joined them there. Both groups came looking for jobs and housing, but most found city life difficult and confusing.

Community Life in Urban Areas

In big cities such as San Francisco, Chicago, and New York, immigrants found comfort in living close to others from their homelands and in retaining their old customs and ways. They clustered together in neighborhoods where they went to the same church or synagogue. They joined the same clubs. They read newspapers and magazines in their own languages. In this way they tried to recreate the feeling of being back home.

After 1900 African Americans from the Southern rural areas formed these same

 Picturing History ▲ URBAN PROBLEMS Overcrowding and poverty caused many social changes in cities throughout the United States. **Who shocked Americans with his photographs of New York City slums?**

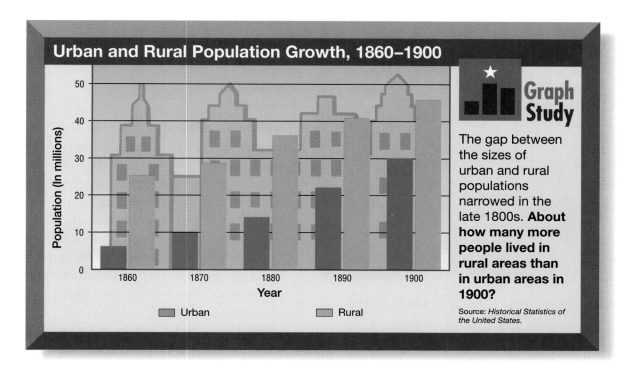

Urban and Rural Population Growth, 1860–1900

Population (In millions)

Year

☐ Urban   ☐ Rural

Source: *Historical Statistics of the United States.*

Graph Study

The gap between the sizes of urban and rural populations narrowed in the late 1800s. **About how many more people lived in rural areas than in urban areas in 1900?**

kinds of close-knit urban communities. In New York City, for example, they congregated by the thousands in an area called **Harlem.**

Challenges of City Life

Despite the sense of community in neighborhoods, city life demoralized many newcomers. Every day they faced crime and poverty. In addition, cities had expanded so fast that the growing population lacked enough housing and social services to meet its needs. Poor sewer and sanitation systems contributed to widespread death and disease. Great fires commonly destroyed entire city blocks.

Most newcomers to American cities could not afford to own houses. They stayed in city centers and rented from landlords who squeezed as many residents as possible into the smallest available spaces. Landlords proved unwilling to maintain good conditions at these overcrowded apartment buildings, or tenements. As more and more people crammed into tenements, poor, run-down areas developed, called slums. An entire family often lived in a single, small room in slums.

Urban Reformers

A Danish immigrant named **Jacob Riis** shocked many Americans with his photographs of New York slums. His pictures and articles introduced middle-class Americans to places with names like Bandits' Roost, Bottle Alley, and Kerosene Row. In 1890 he published his photographs and reports in a book entitled *How the Other Half Lives.* He challenged his readers to renew the face of the cities.

During the 1880s and 1890s, legions of middle-class reformers accepted Riis's challenge. They campaigned for clean water and better sewage systems and demanded better ventilation, plumbing in all new buildings, and mandatory vaccinations. These improvements meant that fewer people died of diseases like typhoid fever and smallpox.

Believing that poverty and desperate living conditions drove many of the urban poor to crime, many ministers worked to improve the quality of life in the

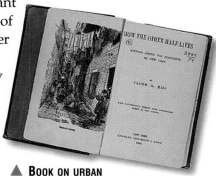

▲ **BOOK ON URBAN LIFE BY JACOB RIIS**

▲ JANE ADDAMS WITH CHILDREN FROM A CHICAGO SETTLEMENT HOUSE

Biography ★★★

Jane Addams—An American Social Worker

Jane Addams led the settlement-house movement. She and Ellen Gates Starr founded the Hull House in one of the poorest sections of Chicago in 1889. She recruited college students to live in slums and help the local residents to improve themselves and their environment. Settlement-house workers organized community activities such as clubs, classes, and day nurseries. Some even pressured city governments to improve schools, parks, and community services.

Addams hoped to foster democracy by breaking down barriers between the rich and the poor. Addams insisted that "the dependence of classes on each other is reciprocal [mutual]." Addams's settlement houses became "neighborhood centers," designed for people of every nation and ethnic group. Addams believed strongly in the need to research the causes of poverty and crime and in the importance of trained social workers to help the poor.

Most important, settlement-house workers, led by Addams, taught immigrant families about American customs and the American political system. In time, the immigrants would learn about America and make substantial contributions to society. ★★★

cities. Ministers demanded that the churches help slum dwellers in practical ways. They called this action to improve society's problems the "social gospel."

Social gospel ministers founded special schools for slum children. They included gyms, libraries, and social rooms in their church buildings. Some also furnished employment bureaus and summer outings. One religious group, the Salvation Army, offered food, ice, coal, and religious services to the poor.

Another group of reformers established settlement houses. Settlement houses, located in the slums, provided immigrant families with food, education, and health care.

★ SECTION 3 REVIEW ★

Checking for Understanding

1. **Identify** Jacob Riis, Jane Addams, Ellis Island, Harlem.

2. **Define** tenement, slum, settlement house.

3. **How** did reformers try to help the poor in the cities?

4. **Why** did some Americans feel and act hostile toward immigrants?

Critical Thinking

5. **Summarizing** What was life like for newcomers to American cities at the turn of the century?

ACTIVITY

6. Create a collage illustrating the origins of immigrants who came to the United States after 1870.

The Ashcan School

▲ *LUXEMBOURG GARDENS* BY WILLIAM JAMES GLACKENS, 1906

At the end of the nineteenth century, an art "rebellion" took place in the United States. Eight young artists began to paint in a new manner. The style and subject of their paintings shocked the leading art critics. To ridicule the young artists and their paintings, the critics called them the "Ashcan School."

Why did critics dislike Ashcan paintings so intensely? At the time leaders in the American art community considered only certain subjects suitable for painting. Ashcan artists, on the other hand, used parks, streets, alleys, city halls, and saloons as settings. They crowded each painting with everyday Americans doing everyday things. According to critics, the scenes in the paintings seemed as common as the ashcans used to collect garbage. No art museum, they insisted, would ever exhibit such ashcan art.

The critics proved wrong. Today the Ashcan School's paintings hang in leading American art galleries. These young artists introduced realism, a kind of painting that has remained one of the most popular forms of American art.

Making the Arts Connection

1. What did Ashcan School artists paint?

2. Why did critics of the time dislike Ashcan School paintings?

3. How might historians today use the paintings of the Ashcan School?

ACTIVITY

4. Create a diorama, collage, or painting depicting a city scene. Use the medium of your choice—paint, crayon, newspaper, or pictures from old magazines.

★★

Rural and Urban Reforms

SETTING THE SCENE

Read to Learn . . .

★ how farmers fought to improve their lives.
★ what reforms the Populists supported.
★ how Progressives changed American life.

Terms to Know

★ cooperative
★ nationalize
★ graduated income tax
★ gold standard

People to Meet

★ Oliver H. Kelley
★ Grover Cleveland
★ James B. Weaver
★ William Jennings Bryan
★ William McKinley
★ Theodore Roosevelt

◀ SILVER DOLLAR, 1879

For years after the Civil War, American farmers prospered. Farm machinery helped them grow more crops with fewer workers. Improved transportation opened up more markets for farm goods.

★ Hard Times for Farmers

In the late 1800s, though, farmers' luck changed. Prices for many farm products dropped sharply. At the same time, the farmers' costs kept rising. Unable to make a living, many farm families abandoned their farms and headed to cities in search of jobs.

Along with economic hardship, farmers faced another problem. At one time Americans respected farmers. They agreed with Thomas Jefferson who wrote: "The small land holders are the most precious part of a [country]." As the United States industrialized, however, Americans started to place greater value on urban life than on farm life. They began to ridicule farmers and the hard lives they led. City dwellers called farmers "hicks" and "hayseeds."

Farmers felt confused and bitter about the serious problems they faced. Life on the farm had always been difficult. Farm families, though, took comfort in realizing the importance of their work. Now other Americans pitied them. This, along with economic troubles, made the loneliness and rough work of farm life almost unbearable for some farmers. They blamed the banks, the railroads, and government leaders for their problems.

Farmers Organize

After national leaders proved unresponsive to the farmers' problems, **Oliver H. Kelley** founded the Patrons of Husbandry in 1867. Most people called the organization the Grange. Kelley organized the Grange to combat the poverty and loneliness of farm life. By 1875 farmers had formed more than 21,000 Grange lodges, or local branches, throughout the United States.

The Grange started as a social organization for farmers. It attempted to bring farm families together and help them develop a sense of community. Soon it developed into an economic and political force. Some lodges formed cooperatives in which the members carried on their business activities as a group. By doing this, they hoped to minimize their losses and increase their profits.

In 1891 the farmers decided to organize on a national level. They created their own political party called the People's, or Populist, party. The birth of the Populist party marked the beginning of a farmers' revolt.

The Farmers' Revolt

The Populist party wanted to help farmers solve their problems. The party urged the federal government to help keep prices for farmers' crops high. It also called on government to nationalize, or take over, public transportation and communication. Populists hoped that nationalization would finally end the railroads' high rates.

Although the Populist party included mostly farmers, Populists wanted to make government more responsive to the needs of all ordinary people. The Populists pushed for a graduated income tax—a federal tax that required wealthy people to pay a higher percentage of their income than poorer people—and the election of senators by popular vote rather than by state legislatures. The Populists also supported various demands of factory workers, including the eight-hour workday.

★ The Money Problem

Most important, the Populists demanded that the government expand the money supply by permitting silver to become, along with gold, the basis for money. At that time, America maintained the gold standard. This meant that the government did not print paper dollars unless it had enough gold to back each paper bill. This limited the amount of money available. Meanwhile the population increased. As each dollar gained in value, farmers earned less as prices for crops dropped and the value of their debts increased.

Railroads, bankers, and large businesses opposed these proposals. They welcomed the shortage of dollars. The money that bankers collected in mortgage payments from farmers bought more than it could have the year before! Bankers and wealthy business owners, now known as "goldbugs," pressured Congress to keep the gold standard.

◄ **GRANGE FARMER**

The Battle Heats Up

In the 1892 presidential election, Democrat **Grover Cleveland** defeated Republican

▲ PRESIDENTIAL CANDIDATE
William Jennings Bryan ran for the Populists in the presidential election of 1896. **Why did the Populist party choose Bryan?**

incumbent **Benjamin Harrison** and the Populist candidate, **James B. Weaver,** by a landslide. The farmers continued to revolt, though.

In 1893 the nation experienced its worst financial depression yet. Many Americans thought the gold standard had caused the crisis, and they turned against President Cleveland.

In the 1896 election, the Democrats replaced Cleveland as their presidential candidate. Instead they chose a young representative from Nebraska, **William Jennings Bryan.** The Populists, learning of Bryan's pro-silver platform, made him their presidential candidate, too.

In one of the most dramatic campaigns in history, Bryan crisscrossed the country, railing against the Republican party's goldbug candidate, **William McKinley.** An energetic campaigner, Bryan became famous for his speaking abilities. In the end, however, he lost to McKinley, the choice of wealthy supporters.

Bryan's defeat ended the Populist party. Many Populist ideas, though, went on to become law. During the early 1900s, the federal government established the graduated income tax. Americans began to elect their senators directly. Even later in the century, the federal government helped farmers control the prices of their crops.

★ The Progressive Era

Historians have named the years following the heyday of the Populist party the Progressive era. Americans became convinced that rapid industrialization and urbanization had created huge problems and chaos. They searched for ways to cure society's ills while maintaining progress. During this period from 1890 to 1917, the Progressive movement developed and spread across the United States. This movement profoundly changed American life and politics.

Improving the American Way

Progressives pressed for many of the same reforms that earlier groups had demanded. They wanted honest and democratic government, the regulation of big business, improvements in the job

Footnotes to History

Anything You Want   A farmers' cooperative launched a mail-order business to meet the needs of farmers. Montgomery Ward and Company was founded in 1872. The company offered such a large variety of merchandise that many people believed they could order anything they wanted. One farmer even wrote to the company asking for a wife.

▲ THE RIGHT TO VOTE Women gained the right to vote with the ratification of the Nineteenth Amendment in 1920. **What did the Eighteenth Amendment prohibit?**

conditions of factory workers, and better housing for the poor. The most militant progressives worked for woman suffrage, the prohibition of alcoholic drinks, and an end to child labor.

Eventually progressives organized on the national level. In the early 1900s, three Progressive Presidents sat in the White House. One of them, **Theodore Roosevelt,** who became President after McKinley's assassination, became hugely popular with American voters. He promised all Americans a "square deal," or an equal opportunity to succeed. He sided with the public against big business

and encouraged reforms to help children and women workers.

Even after the Progressive era ended, progressives won important victories, including the addition of two amendments to the Constitution. In 1919 the country adopted the **Eighteenth Amendment,** which made the manufacture, sale, and transportation of liquor illegal in the United States. And in 1920 Americans ratified the **Nineteenth Amendment,** which granted women the right to vote. The Twenty-first Amendment, ratified in 1933, later repealed the Eighteenth Amendment.

★ SECTION 4 REVIEW ★

Checking for Understanding

1. **Identify** Oliver H. Kelley, Grover Cleveland, James B. Weaver, William Jennings Bryan, William McKinley, Theodore Roosevelt.

2. **Define** cooperative, nationalize, graduated income tax, gold standard.

3. **What** problems did farmers face at the end of the 1800s?

4. **How** did the Populist party think the federal government should help the farmers and working people?

Critical Thinking

5. **Making Inferences** Progressives pressed for a number of reforms to give voters more power. Why do you think they wanted voters to have more power?

ACTIVITY

6. Come up with a slogan for the Progressive candidate for a local, state, or federal office. Use the slogan to create a campaign poster.

Using Key Vocabulary

Use the vocabulary words listed below to complete the following sentences.

entrepreneurs   monopolies
homesteaders   nationalize
slums

1. The federal government gave free land to _____ if they improved and lived on it for five years.

2. The Populists wanted to _____ the railroads so that the federal government could control the railroads' shipping rates.

3. _____ such as Rockefeller and Carnegie were willing to risk their fortunes for the chance to make more money.

4. Ordinary Americans mistrusted some big business because some companies organized _____, which raised the prices of goods.

5. Most immigrants lived in the cities' poorest sections called _____.

Reviewing Facts

1. **Explain** how railroads helped settle the West.

2. **List** the natural and human resources that made the United States an industrial nation.

3. **Describe** what life was like for immigrants in American cities during the late 1800s.

4. **Name** the presidential candidates the Democratic and Populist parties nominated in 1896.

5. **Identify** the goals of the Progressive movement.

Understanding Concepts

Influence of Technology

1. What role did the railroads play in developing the cattle industry?

2. Why were the nation's rich resources important to its industrial growth?

3. How did entrepreneurs such as Carnegie and Rockefeller encourage the growth of industry?

Individual and Family Life

4. Why did society's view of the farmer change in the late 1800s?

5. How did immigration in the second half of the 1800s affect the United States?

History and Geography

The Texas Cattle Trails

Study the cattle trails shown on the map. Then answer the questions on page 661.

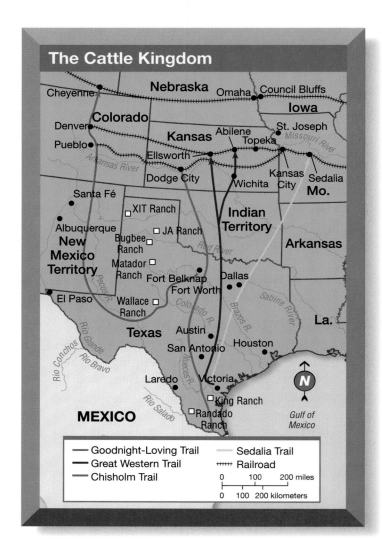

The Cattle Kingdom

— Goodnight-Loving Trail
— Great Western Trail
— Chisholm Trail
Sedalia Trail
++++ Railroad

0   100   200 miles
0 100 200 kilometers

1. **Region** In what part of Texas were most of the large cattle ranches found?

2. **Place** Along which trail did many major Texas cities develop?

3. **Human/Environment Interaction** Where did the trails end? Explain why.

Critical Thinking

1. **Making Inferences** How did American values change in the late 1800s?

2. **Identifying Alternatives** Describe how the federal government might have dealt with Native Americans more fairly.

Practicing Skills

Reading a Time Zone Chart

The chart below is a flight schedule for flights from New York City. The departure times are Eastern Standard times. The arrival times reflect the standard time of the destination city. Refer to the map of United States standard time zones on page 649 and the flight schedule to answer the following questions.

Flight Number	Departure Time	Arrival Time	Destination
527	8:00 A.M.	10:39 A.M.	Dallas, Texas
579	10:15 A.M.	12:24 P.M.	Atlanta, Georgia
4959	2:45 P.M.	3:55 P.M.	Baltimore, Maryland
1985	3:25 P.M.	6:45 P.M.	San Francisco, Calif.
1493	4:25 P.M.	8:55 P.M.	Seattle, Washington
1425	5:45 P.M.	8:40 P.M.	Salt Lake City, Utah

1. How long would it take you to reach Seattle, Washington, from New York on Flight 1493?

2. How long will the flight be if you fly from New York to Salt Lake City on Flight 1425?

3. Which flight on the schedule is the longest flight?

4. How many hours would be added to your day if you flew from New York City to Dallas, Texas, on Flight 527?

5. You are taking Flight 1425. Your parent has asked you to call home after you arrive in Salt Lake City. What time will the phone ring in New York City if you call home as soon as you reach your destination?

Cooperative Learning

Interdisciplinary Activity: Economics

In groups of three or four, research the cost of foods available during the 1890s. Share the information you have found with your group. Budget $6—half the weekly income of a factory worker's family—for food. As a group make a week's shopping list for the family. Then have each group member choose a day of the week and plan that day's menus for a family of four. Share your menus with the rest of the class.

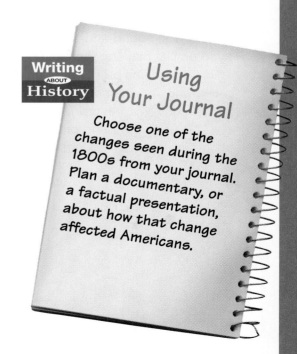

Writing ABOUT History

Using Your Journal

Choose one of the changes seen during the 1800s from your journal. Plan a documentary, or a factual presentation, about how that change affected Americans.

Cultural Kaleidoscope

Modern Technology for Modern Times

*T*wentieth-century Americans have witnessed greater advances in technology than most people could have imagined. As technology changed, so did the ways Americans lived, worked, traveled, studied, and entertained themselves.

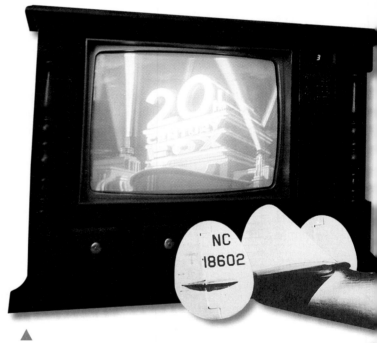

Have Ford, Will Travel
The automobile revolutionized travel and transportation. Henry Ford introduced his Model T in 1908. By 1924 he was mass-producing cars to sell for $290. This low price put working-class Americans behind the wheel.

The World of Sound
The CD, or compact disc, became the latest technology in sound and storage after 1983. Played on CD players, the plastic-and-metal discs produce far clearer music than did earlier tapes and records. CDs also store and play back different kinds of information, including books and video documents.

What's on Prime Time?
After World War II, television joined radio in bringing news and entertainment into every home. Beginning in 1954, screens carried images in living color.

Starstruck at the Movies

By 1915 projectors made it possible to show motion pictures to theater audiences. After World War I, Hollywood movies and movie stars began entertaining the nation.

Reaching for the Stars

Communications satellites made it possible to send and receive messages almost anywhere on Earth. In 1962, *Telstar I* became the first communications satellite to transmit television images.

The Information Age

Computers made space flights possible in the 1960s. By 1980, computers had entered businesses and homes. There they enabled users to reach and process huge amounts of information. Laptop computers of the 1990s made the information age portable.

Up and Away!

In 1933, just 30 years after the Wright brothers' famous flight, passenger airlines went into business. The planes carried 10 passengers. By 1970 jumbo jet airliners could carry more than 400 passengers.

No Need to Find a Pay Phone

Introduced in 1983, the cellular telephone made it possible to call anyone from almost anywhere.

CHAPTER 21

★★★

The Twentieth Century
1900–Present

▶ **1957 CHEVROLET**

SETTING THE SCENE

Focus

The twentieth century has witnessed profound changes in the United States. Technological and social advances altered the nation's destiny. Americans suffered through wars and economic and political turmoil. Today the United States faces great challenges as it continues to lead the charge for democracy.

Concepts to Understand

★ How the United States transformed its **role in world affairs** to become a world leader
★ Why the **civil rights and liberties** of Americans are different today than they were a century ago

Read to Discover . . .

★ the events that led to the emergence of the United States as the world's leader.
★ how the United States is changing to meet the needs of the future.

Journal Notes

What changes in the twentieth century have affected how Americans live? List the changes as you read the chapter.

United States

1914 Panama Canal opens
1917 United States enters World War I
1929 Stock market crashes, Great Depression begins
1941 Japanese attack Pearl Harbor
1950 American forces land in Korea

1901–1925	1926–1950

World

1911 Mexican Revolution
1914 World War I begins
1917 Russian Revolution
1918 World War I ends
1933 Adolf Hitler comes to power in Germany
1939 World War II begins
1945 World War II ends

History AND ART

The City From Greenwich Village
by John Sloan, 1922

John Sloan's paintings focus on social reform. Many of his works, such as this one, depict everyday life in New York City.

◀ THE VIETNAM WAR MEMORIAL

1963 President Kennedy assassinated
1969 Neil Armstrong walks on moon
1973 End of Vietnam War

1951–1975

1961 Communists build Berlin Wall

1991 Persian Gulf War begins
1992 Bill Clinton elected President
1996 Bill Clinton reelected President
1997 President Clinton and Congress
reach agreement to balance the budget

1976–2000

1991 Soviet Union collapses
1995 Dayton Peace Accord ends conflict in Bosnia

★★★★★★★★★★★★★★★★★★★★★★★★★★★★★★★

World War I Era

SETTING THE SCENE

Read to Learn . . .

★ how the United States became involved with lands outside its borders.
★ why the United States entered World War I.
★ why the United States became a world leader.

Terms to Know

★ nationalism
★ neutral
★ armistice
★ reparations

People to Meet

★ William McKinley
★ Theodore Roosevelt
★ Woodrow Wilson

Places to Locate

★ Hawaii
★ Cuba
★ Guam
★ Philippines
★ Puerto Rico
★ Panama

BOYS and GIRLS! You can Help your Uncle Sam Win the War

Save your Quarters BUY WAR SAVINGS STAMPS

▶ **POSTER FOR WAR SAVINGS STAMPS**

The news that events in the world's most powerful nations had exploded into war took Americans by surprise. Europeans had been at peace for more than 40 years. Little did they suspect that when the war ended, the United States would emerge as a world leader.

★ Becoming a World Power

Europe had always been the United States's major trading partner. In the second half of the 1800s, business and government leaders became interested in Asia and Latin America as a source of new markets.

Expansion in the Pacific

In 1898 during the presidency of **William McKinley,** the United States annexed the Hawaiian Islands. The islands provided a base for the American navy. From **Hawaii** the United States could oversee its trade in Japan and China.

The same year the United States went to war with Spain after the American press aroused intense American anger by reporting the brutal way that Spain crushed a rebellion in **Cuba.** Almost immediately, fighting extended to Spanish colonies in the Pacific Ocean as well as in Cuba. When the Spanish-American War ended, not only did Cuba gain its independence, but the United States also gained **Guam** and the **Philippines.**

Its new territories drew the United States even closer to Asia. Americans now had naval bases and refueling stations throughout the Pacific. These bases made trade with China, Japan, and Korea much easier for American ships.

Latin American Policies

The United States also took an active role in the affairs of Latin America. As a result of the Spanish-American War, the United States had acquired **Puerto Rico.** The Americans soon came to view themselves as guardians of the whole Western Hemisphere, not just the Caribbean.

Theodore Roosevelt, who became President after McKinley's assassination in 1901, liked to proclaim "Speak softly, but carry a big stick." He meant that he preferred peace, but that he would use force when necessary. Roosevelt used the "big stick" to gain control of the isthmus of **Panama.**

For years the United States and other countries had wanted to build a canal across Central America to connect the Atlantic and Pacific oceans. Then Colombia controlled Panama, and the Colombian legislature rejected the United States's offer to buy a strip of land across the isthmus. Roosevelt became determined to obtain the canal site. In 1903 he helped organize and finance a revolt in Panama. With the help of American marines, the Panamanian rebels over-threw their Colombian rulers and set up their own government.

Representatives of the United States and the new government of Panama quickly signed a canal treaty. For $10 million plus an annual fee, Panama granted Americans control of a strip across the isthmus. Finished in 1914, the **Panama Canal** ranks as one of the greatest engineering works of all time.

★ World War I

While the United States defined its relationship to the rest of the world, relationships among European nations changed. Competition for overseas empires, the building of military alliances, and nationalism—a people's pride in its country—increased. The growth of these forces led to the outbreak of World War I in 1914. On one side stood the **Central Powers**—Germany, the Ottoman Empire, and Austria-Hungary. On the other side were the

▼ **PRESIDENT T. ROOSEVELT AND THE "BIG STICK"**

Allies, including Great Britain, France, Italy, and Russia, as well as many smaller nations.

Between 1914 and 1917, the United States remained neutral. In other words, it did not choose sides in the war. Neutrality helped American business boom. Both the Central Powers and the Allies traded with the United States. They also borrowed money from American banks and businesses to buy war supplies. Most American aid, though, went to the Allied forces.

In an effort to stop American aid to the Allies, German submarines torpedoed American merchant ships. In 1915 the Germans sank the *Lusitania*, a British ship with 128 Americans aboard. In February 1917, the British gave President **Woodrow Wilson** a secret German message they had discovered. In it, Germany proposed an alliance between Germany and Mexico if the United States entered the war. The Germans promised to give Texas, New Mexico, and Arizona back to Mexico. Shortly after, in March, German submarines sank three American ships. On April 2, 1917, the President asked Congress to declare war on Germany. On April 6, 1917, America entered World War I.

Turning the Tide of Battle

American troops entered the war just when it seemed the Allies could not hold out against the Germans much longer. Germany prepared an offensive against British and French troops in the spring of 1918 to end the war. The arrival of the "Yanks," or Americans, changed their plans.

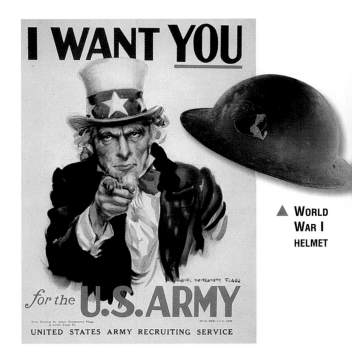

▲ WORLD WAR I HELMET

▲ WORLD WAR I RECRUITMENT POSTER

By October 1918, German troops had almost been forced out of France. The other Central Powers had surrendered or started to consider surrendering. On November 11, 1918, the Allies and the Germans signed an armistice, or an agreement to end the fighting.

★ War's Aftermath

By the end of the war, the United States had become a world leader in trade, industry, and finance. Other nations now looked to the United States for political, as well as economic, leadership.

President Wilson had prepared for peace early, even before the war ended. He thought hard about what America fought for in the war. Did it fight just to

· ·

Footnotes to History

The End World War I ended when German leaders agreed to an armistice, or an agreement to stop fighting. As the Germans agreed to the armistice, the warring guns fell silent on November 11, 1918, at 11:00 A.M.—the eleventh hour of the eleventh day of the eleventh month.

defeat the Central Powers, or to establish a new world order? What must be done to ensure lasting peace?

Wilson decided on a policy that came to be known as the **Fourteen Points.** The Fourteen Points aimed for peace based on justice for all the world's nations. The policy included demands for freedom of the seas, a reduction in military spending by all nations, and independence for Europe's overseas colonies and for minority ethnic groups. It also included a request for the creation of an international group, or a league of nations, to guarantee independence to "great and small states alike."

The Treaty of Versailles

President Wilson felt greatly disappointed at the peace conference, though. The Treaty of Versailles included the Fourteen Points, but other clauses weakened its impact. France, Italy, and Britain wanted to punish Germany. They demanded that Germany pay heavy reparations, or payments for losses they suffered during the war. The Europeans' treatment of Germany contradicted the spirit of Wilson's Fourteen Points.

Later, the United States Senate rejected the peace treaty. Many senators, especially Republicans, were suspicious of the

History AND ART

▲ *SIGNING OF THE TREATY OF VERSAILLES* by John Johansen, 1919 The Treaty of Versailles included President Wilson's Fourteen Points. **What provision in the treaty stopped United States senators from accepting it?**

League of Nations. They refused to give up the independence of the United States to control its own destiny in world affairs. They believed Americans must remain free to act in their own best interests.

★ SECTION 1 REVIEW ★

Checking for Understanding

1. **Identify** William McKinley, Theodore Roosevelt, Woodrow Wilson, Hawaii, Cuba, Guam, Philippines, Puerto Rico, Panama.
2. **Define** nationalism, neutral, armistice, reparations.
3. **How** did the United States obtain control of the Panama Canal?
4. **Why** did the United States enter World War I?

Critical Thinking

5. **Understanding Point of View** Why do you suppose the European Allies were more interested than the United States in collecting reparations from Germany?

ACTIVITY

6. Create a propaganda poster that the Allies may have used to persuade Americans to support them in World War I.

Aerial Warfare

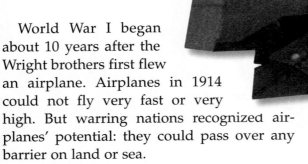

World War I began about 10 years after the Wright brothers first flew an airplane. Airplanes in 1914 could not fly very fast or very high. But warring nations recognized airplanes' potential: they could pass over any barrier on land or sea.

At the beginning of the war, armies used planes for scouting missions only. Soon, however, scientists and engineers on both sides designed planes with more powerful engines. These improved planes could carry bombs long distances and drop them on enemy targets. To stop enemy bombers, the rival armies developed fighter aircraft—small, fast, easy-to-maneuver planes armed with guns. Planes improved so much that they flew twice as fast and high at the end of World War I as they had at the start.

Modern Aircraft

Germany introduced jet planes late in World War II. The German jets could fly almost 550 miles per hour. By the 1960s American and Soviet jets roared through the skies at more than 1,000 miles per hour.

During the 1950s helicopters greatly improved and became widely used. By the 1960s they rivaled jeeps as the military's favorite all-purpose cross-country vehicles. Scientists adapted jet engines to helicopters so that the copters could fly faster and higher and carry heavier loads.

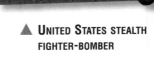

▲ **UNITED STATES STEALTH FIGHTER-BOMBER**

Today United States military aircraft includes fighters, helicopters, troop transports, survey aircraft, and bombers. One of the most advanced bombers is the F-117 stealth fighter. It is designed mainly to attack ground forces and ships. A winglike shape and flat surfaces that absorb radar energy make it difficult for enemy radar to detect.

Making the Science Connection

1. How does the military use aircraft against the enemy?

2. Draw a time line showing improvements in aircraft over the years. Use facts from the feature in the time line.

3. What types of aircraft does the United States use today?

ACTIVITY

4. Design a personal flying vehicle to replace the automobile. Label each part and briefly explain what advantage it has over an automobile.

SECTION 2

Between Two Wars

SETTING THE SCENE

Read to Learn . . .

- ★ how the American way of life changed after World War I.
- ★ about the hard times after the 1920s.
- ★ about the New Deal.

Terms to Know

- ★ stock
- ★ margin
- ★ depression
- ★ bread line

People to Meet

- ★ Henry Ford
- ★ Herbert Hoover
- ★ Franklin Delano Roosevelt

Places to Locate

- ★ Great Plains

Order Your Advts For Next Sunday's Globe Today

The Boston Daily Globe

BOSTON, FRIDAY MORNING, OCTOBER 25, 1929—FIFTY-SIX PAGES

Order Next Sunday's Globe From Your Dealer Today

TWO CENTS

BIG CRASH AND RALLY IN STOCKS

All Records for Severity of Decline Broken---12,894,650 Shares Traded In, a New High Mark---Tape 160 Minutes Behind at Close---Pool Formed at Morgan Office at Conference of Bankers Checks Headlong Break; Then Some Stocks Recover 10 to 20 Points---Banks and Brokers Sound

BALLOT PROBE IS STOPPED BY JUDGE

Defied by Curley and Ward Bolster Ends Hearing

$100,000 FIRE LOSS TO HOME IN HINGHAM

Thayer Estate Destroyed by Blaze of Undetermined Origin—House Closed Wednesday For Winter

TIPSY DRIVING CASE

TABLE SHOWING GYRATIONS OF SOME LEADING STOCKS

Wild Scenes on Exchange During Height of Selling Stampede, Extra Police Summoned

Thousands Ruined as Runaway Market Forces Brokers to Toss Their Holdings Over

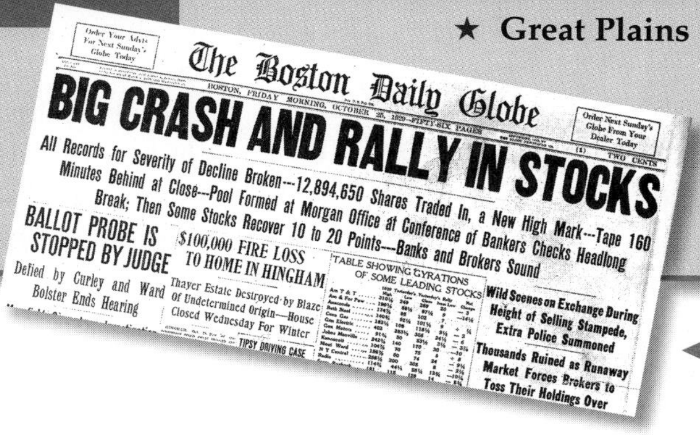

◀ NEWSPAPER SHOWING STOCK MARKET CHANGES

The decade after World War I became a time of significant and dramatic social, economic, and political changes. Americans discovered a booming market for consumer goods at home and a strong market for American products in the war-ravaged countries of Europe.

★ Postwar Prosperity

By 1921 American industries had changed to meet the needs of peacetime. More goods and services appeared on the market, and prices began to drop. For eight years some Americans enjoyed prosperity. Between 1921 and 1929, those Americans lived better than any people ever before in history.

During the 1920s the everyday life of American people changed in almost every way. Earlier inventions such as trolley cars, typewriters, and sewing machines granted Americans more free time. They spent this time enjoying new forms of entertainment, such as radio and talking movies. **Henry Ford** offered the first inexpensive automobile, the Model T. Vacations away from home became popular, too. The decade of the 1920s became known as the "roaring twenties" because of the boom in everything from business to entertainment.

Americans also experimented with prohibition—banning alcoholic drinks—in the 1920s. The Eighteenth Amendment, ratified in 1919, made it illegal to make or sell liquor. Prohibition did not last, though. People found and casually used ways to get around the law. Gangsters became millionaires by providing the

▲ BREAD LINE AT A SOUP KITCHEN, 1930S

population with alcohol. In 1933 the Twenty-first Amendment repealed the Eighteenth Amendment.

Problems Arise

Not all Americans enjoyed the good life, however. While some Americans enjoyed the roaring twenties, large segments of society lived through hard times. The gap between the rich and the poor grew enormous. Crop prices declined steadily. At the same time, the cost of fertilizer, farm machinery, and mortgages went up.

Social problems existed, too. The pressures of modern life weakened family ties. As a result juvenile crime and other antisocial behavior increased. Some Americans blamed the country's problems on people who seemed different—Jews, Roman Catholics, African Americans, and foreigners—and revived the Ku Klux Klan.

★ From Boom Times to Bad Times

In late October 1929, America's booming economy suddenly skidded to a halt. A prolonged slump in agricultural pro-duction, industrial overproduction, high tariffs, and a stock market crash combined to shatter the economy.

The Stock Market Crash

Businesses sold stock, or shares of ownership, in their companies to raise money. In the 1920s more Americans than ever invested in the stocks of corporations. The value of stocks soared. People began to buy stocks on margin, or with borrowed money, as stock values increased.

In October 1929, stock prices began to drop sharply. Investors panicked and sold their stocks for any price they could get. People who had bought stocks on margin expected to pay for them when they sold the stocks at higher prices. When people stampeded to sell their stocks, the stock market crashed, and these investors could not pay for their stock. They lost all their money and became ruined, along with hundreds of banks and companies.

The Great Depression

After the stock market crashed in 1929, Americans suffered the worst business depression, or economic downturn, in the nation's history. Called the **Great Depression,** it struck the United States severely and hit most countries worldwide. Between 1929 and 1933, many businesses and factories closed, and millions of workers lost their jobs.

The Great Depression hit American workers in cities especially hard. In some cities, such as Detroit and Chicago, more than half of the people lost their jobs. Many families used up their savings just to survive. When their money ran out, they were forced to accept handouts. Bread lines, or lines of people waiting for a free meal, stretched for blocks in every large city. Thousands of people searched through garbage cans for scraps of food or waited outside restaurant kitchens in the hopes of receiving a free meal.

American farmers suffered greatly, too. Farm prices dropped sharply. For many farmers, years of dry weather made the situation even worse. In parts of the **Great Plains** a long drought turned the "breadbasket of the world" into a "dust bowl." Many farmers had to give up their land.

After losing their jobs, their farms, and their savings, some Americans had to leave home to search for work. Nearly 2 million people rode freight trains from town to town looking for work. These jobless people often built shacks out of scraps of metal or wooden crates to live in and stayed there without running water or heat. People called these shantytowns Hoovervilles after **Herbert Hoover,** the President at the time.

As the Depression dragged on, many Americans lost faith in their government. They blamed President Hoover for their hard times because none of his policies eased the suffering of massive unemployment.

★ The New Deal Era

During the 1932 presidential campaign, **Franklin Delano Roosevelt** promised a "new deal for the American people." Most Americans desperately desired some new solution to the nation's problems. Roosevelt won the election. During his first three months in office—known as the "Hundred Days"—he pushed revolutionary laws through Congress to create new government agencies to help the needy and to aid economic recovery. He also took charge of the banks so that people no longer worried about losing their money when banks closed. Roosevelt, better known as FDR, permanently changed the federal government's relationship with society.

The New Deal Ends

Americans seemed better off in 1936 than they had been when FDR took office in 1933. Even so, when FDR began his second term, the Great Depression had not yet ended. He continued to effect new reforms. In 1937 business slowed and another recession hit the nation. This time Americans blamed Roosevelt and the New Deal. When FDR proposed numerous programs after this, Congress would not cooperate with the President.

Although reform under Roosevelt ended, the New Deal produced lasting effects. It greatly increased the power of the presidency and the size of the federal government. It also established the idea that the federal government is responsible for the welfare of needy Americans. Eventually the economic boom sparked by another world war would finally end the Great Depression.

★ SECTION 2 REVIEW ★

Checking for Understanding

1. **Identify** Henry Ford, Herbert Hoover, Franklin Delano Roosevelt, Great Plains.

2. **Define** stock, margin, depression, bread line.

3. **Why** did American business boom in the early 1920s?

4. **What** happened to the American economy after the stock market crash in 1929?

Critical Thinking

5. **Making Inferences** Why did the stock market crash in 1929 affect all Americans rather than only those who owned stocks?

ACTIVITY

6. Create a poster showing how your city or state has changed from the "roaring twenties" to today.

Writing an Essay

Learning the Skill

A well-written essay has three main parts—the **introduction,** the **body,** and the **conclusion.** The introduction, consisting of one or more paragraphs, states the topic of the essay and the author's viewpoint. Most important, the introduction should grab the reader's interest.

The body of the essay has several paragraphs that develop the subject and the writer's viewpoint. Each paragraph should advance the writer's argument and give evidence to support this argument. Finally, the conclusion restates and summarizes the writer's viewpoint.

Practicing the Skill

Read the essay. Then answer the questions that follow.

The nation's founders might not recognize American government if they were alive today. Government's role in people's lives has expanded over the last 220 years. The New Deal, especially, helped change what Americans expect from government.

Before Roosevelt entered office, the government assumed little responsibility for the jobless or the elderly. Americans had to depend on savings, families, or charity to get through hard times. The Great Depression wiped out savings, devastated whole families, and exhausted private charities. Americans learned the hard way that these resources made a flimsy safety net.

New Dealers tried to ensure that American workers could survive hard times. One way members of Congress did this was to pass laws that strengthened labor unions. Labor unions protected workers' rights against the greed of owners and bosses. New Dealers also began social insurance programs to help the jobless and those too old to work. The New Deal gave American workers a new slant on the role of government.

▼ GOVERNMENT JOBS

Many New Deal laws and programs still exist. For instance, Americans take for granted benefits such as unemployment insurance and Social Security. Today many people consider the protection of the jobless and the elderly an important role of government.

1. What argument is presented in the introduction?
2. Which paragraphs form the body of the essay?
3. What main points in the body support the argument?
4. What is the conclusion of the essay?

APPLYING THE SKILL

5. Identify a group in your community that needs help from the government. Write an essay that explains what kind of help the group needs and why the government should provide it.

★★★★★★★★★★★★★★★★★★★★★★★★★★★★★★★★★

World War II Era

SETTING THE SCENE

Read to Learn . . .

★ why the United States entered World War II.

★ what effects World War II had on the world.

Terms to Know

★ dictatorship
★ ultimatum
★ Holocaust

People to Meet

★ Franklin D. Roosevelt
★ Harry S Truman

Places to Locate

★ Pearl Harbor, Hawaii

▶ PEARL HARBOR, SINKING OF THE *ARIZONA*

▶ BRONZE STAR MEDAL FOR HEROISM

Early in the morning on December 7, 1941, Japanese planes attacked the United States fleet at **Pearl Harbor, Hawaii.** Within hours the bombers sank 21 ships and destroyed 300 aircraft. The toll in human lives amounted to more than 2,000 American soldiers and sailors. What led to this tragic event?

★ World War II

With the New Deal over, President **Franklin D. Roosevelt** turned his attention to the growing threat of war in Europe. Economic worries and feelings of bitterness remaining from World War I caused democratic governments to collapse in parts of Europe. In Italy, Germany, and Japan, powerful dictatorships had taken over the governments. In dictatorships the leaders hold complete authority over the people they rule. In Italy, Benito Mussolini and his Fascist party controlled the government. Adolf Hitler and the Nazi party came to power in Germany. A small group of military leaders held the reins of government in Japan.

The Axis Powers

The leaders of Italy, Germany, and Japan attempted to restore their nations to their former greatness through the use of

▲ **D-Day** American troops, under heavy fire, stormed the beaches of Normandy, France, on June 6, 1944. **When did Germany surrender to Allied forces, ending the war in Europe?**

the military. In 1935 Mussolini attacked and took control of Ethiopia in Africa. In 1937 Japan attacked China and conquered the eastern part of the country. In 1938 Hitler invaded Austria. Then, a year later, he conquered Czechoslovakia. Soon Germany joined forces with Italy and Japan to form the **Axis Powers.**

The world rapidly drifted toward another world war. On September 1, 1939, the German army invaded Poland. Two days later Britain and France declared war on Germany. Soon the Germans began a sweeping attack on western Europe.

Many Americans had considered involvement in World War I a mistake and wanted to stay out of this war. As the Germans continued to increase their power, Americans became willing to aid Britain

and the other **Allied Powers.** After the German army invaded France and forced it to surrender, the United States began to send aid to the Allies and the Soviet Union, which Hitler had invaded in 1941.

America Enters World War II

The Japanese attack on Pearl Harbor on December 7, 1941, united Americans. Congress declared war on Japan the following day. The British and Canadians quickly did the same. Germany and Italy joined Japan in declaring war on the United States. Americans now were fully involved in World War II on the side of the Allies.

The road to victory for the Allies proved long, hard, and bloody. The Allies stopped the Axis powers in North Africa by May 1943. Meanwhile, the Soviets fought desperately to turn back the German invaders. In February 1943 the Soviet army forced the Nazis to retreat. By mid-1943 American and British troops took the offensive and invaded Italy.

The Allies pushed to recapture countries lost to the Axis powers. After long, bitter fighting they drove the Germans out of Italy. On June 6, 1944, known as D-Day, the Allies crossed the English Channel to the beaches of Normandy, France. The invasion proved a success. In less than a month, more than 1 million Allied troops had moved across France. By late summer of 1944, the Allies stood at Germany's border.

The Allies Win the War

In late 1944 and early 1945, American and Soviet troops invaded Germany. The

・・・

Footnotes to History

Pearl Harbor Predicted   Beginning in 1931, 10 years before the Japanese surprise attack on Pearl Harbor, every student at the Japanese Naval Academy had to answer the following question to graduate: "How would you carry out a surprise attack on Pearl Harbor?" It is not known if Japanese military leaders used any of the students' answers to plan the real attack.

◀ AMERICAN MILITARY HELMET NICKNAMED THE "STEEL POT"

Germans suffered from a lack of supplies. Repeated bombings of their factories, military bases, and transportation systems made it impossible for the Germans to continue fighting. On May 7, 1945, the Germans surrendered. The Allies had won the war in Europe.

The war against Japan continued though. American generals feared that if the Allies invaded Japan, many American soldiers would die. **Harry S Truman,** who became President after Roosevelt died, issued the Japanese an ultimatum, or a last chance to surrender immediately. When Japanese leaders failed to surrender, the President decided to use the newly developed atomic bomb.

On August 6, 1945, the United States dropped an atomic bomb on Hiroshima, Japan. When the bomb exploded, a sheet of flame spread over the city. The bomb killed between 70,000 and 100,000 people. About 100,000 others died later from the effects of radiation. Three days later an American plane dropped another bomb on Nagasaki. This bomb killed nearly 40,000 people instantly and many more later. Japan finally admitted defeat on August 14, 1945.

★ On the Home Front

Americans became amazed at the speed with which industries turned to making war materials. Within weeks of the attack on Pearl Harbor, the government directed private companies to cut back or ban production of bicycles, beer cans, refrigerators, toothpaste tubes, and more than 300 other items and to produce war goods.

To raise funds for the war effort, the federal government increased taxes and sold war bonds in amounts ranging from $25 to $10,000. In 1942 the government extended the income tax to include middle- and lower-income people.

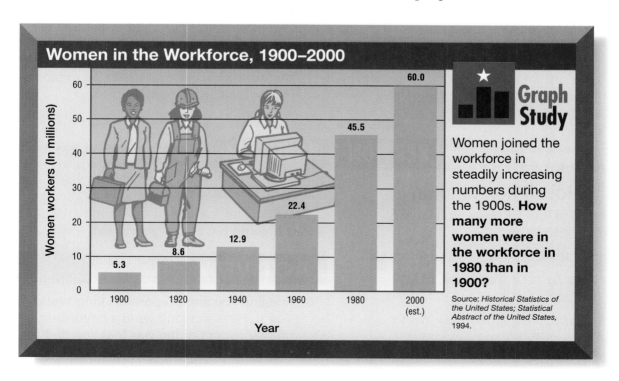

Women in the Workforce, 1900–2000

Women workers (in millions)

- 1900: 5.3
- 1920: 8.6
- 1940: 12.9
- 1960: 22.4
- 1980: 45.5
- 2000 (est.): 60.0

Year

★ **Graph Study**

Women joined the workforce in steadily increasing numbers during the 1900s. **How many more women were in the workforce in 1980 than in 1900?**

Source: *Historical Statistics of the United States; Statistical Abstract of the United States,* 1994.

◀ ROSIE THE RIVETER

The need for defense workers altered traditional patterns of American society. As millions of men joined the armed forces, more women than ever before entered the labor force. "If you can drive a car, you can run a machine," became an advertising slogan for industries.

The government, newspapers, radio, and newsreels encouraged women to take factory jobs as a patriotic duty. About 5 million women entered the workforce during the war. "Rosie the Riveter," who first appeared in overalls in a Lockheed Aircraft poster, became a national symbol of the vital contribution women made to the war effort.

The war brought about the mistreatment of some Americans. After the bombing of Pearl Harbor, the government, distrusting Japanese Americans, moved thousands of them to relocation camps even though they displayed no disloyalty to the nation. The government ruthlessly disregarded the rights of these Japanese Americans and forced them to suffer extreme and lasting hardships.

★ After the War

World War II became the costliest and most destructive war ever. At least 50 million people died as a result of the war—more than during any other war. The war devastated billions of dollars worth of property. Life in some countries would not return to normal for many years.

Hitler had appealed to national pride and racial hatred in Germany, using force to silence all opposition. Hitler's Nazi party blamed Germany's economic problems on its Jewish population and savagely killed nearly 6 million Jews in concentration camps. The Nazis also murdered about 6 million others. This mass murder is known as the Holocaust.

People from all over the globe looked for ways to prevent such a terrible conflict from happening again. They believed that an international organization dedicated to freedom and cooperation among peoples everywhere could ensure peace. In April 1945, delegates from 50 nations met in San Francisco to create just such an organization—the United Nations.

★ SECTION 3 REVIEW ★

★★★★★★★★★★★★★★★★★★   ★★★★★★★★★★★★★★★★★★

Checking for Understanding

1. **Identify** Franklin D. Roosevelt, Harry S Truman, Pearl Harbor.

2. **Define** dictatorship, ultimatum, Holocaust.

3. **What** events led to the outbreak of World War II?

4. **Why** did the United States enter World War II?

Critical Thinking

5. **Drawing Conclusions**   Do you think World War II could have been prevented? Explain.

ACTIVITY

6. Imagine you are a reporter during World War II. Research and write a news story on one aspect of the war that you find especially interesting or important.

★★★★★★★★★★★★★★★★★★★★★★★★★★★★★★★★★★★★★★

The Cold War Years

SETTING THE SCENE

Read to Learn . . .

★ why the United States fought in Korea.
★ why the Vietnam War divided America.
★ about the civil rights movement.
★ how Watergate shook Americans' confidence in government.

Terms to Know

★ cold war
★ free world
★ segregation

People to Meet

★ Dwight D. Eisenhower
★ John F. Kennedy
★ Lyndon B. Johnson
★ Richard Nixon
★ Martin Luther King, Jr.

Places to Locate

★ Soviet Union
★ Vietnam

◀ PEACE BUTTON

A powerful legacy of mistrust and competition shadowed the peace following World War II. The United States and the **Soviet Union** emerged from the war as the world's two most powerful nations and struggled for world leadership. This rivalry became known as the cold war because although great tensions divided them, the two countries did not actually fight each other.

★ The Cold War Begins

The cold war began when the Soviet Union took control of most of Eastern Europe after World War II. Soviet troops occupied Poland, Czechoslovakia, Hungary, Bulgaria, Romania, the eastern part of Germany, and other Eastern European countries. The Soviets forced these nations to set up Communist governments.

Leaders of the free world, or non-Communist nations, grew convinced that the Soviets planned to spread communism all over the world. The Soviet Union already backed Communists who attempted to take over Greece and Turkey. President **Harry S Truman** believed the United States had to stop Communist expansion and establish American influence through a show of strength. The United States sent aid to Greece and Turkey to restore order. Truman also greatly aided Western European countries.

Linking Past and Present

American Fads

Of the hundreds of fads that have come and gone in the United States, at least two have been good for Americans' health.

Then

Hula Hoops

In the late 1950s, people of all ages everywhere seemed to be spinning hula hoops around their middles. To keep the hoops aloft, hula hoopers had to move their hips in a circle quickly and continuously. By Halloween 1958, when the fad began dying down, 100 million hula hoops had been sold, and many Americans had improved their muscle tone.

Now

In-line Roller Skates

In the mid-1980s, in-line skates zoomed onto sidewalks and streets. The new skates had four wheels, like roller skates, lined up one after another. Skaters gave their hearts and legs a good workout while they enjoyed speeding along at up to 40 miles per hour (64 kmph).

▶ **IN-LINE SKATER**

◀ **HULA "HOOPER"**

In 1949 the United States joined the free nations of Europe and Canada to form a military alliance against the Soviets. The **North Atlantic Treaty Organization (NATO)** agreed that an attack against any one of them in Europe or North America would be considered an attack against all of them. In response to NATO, the Soviet Union formed the **Warsaw Pact,** a military alliance of the Soviet-controlled countries.

★ America Fights in Korea

Five years after World War II ended, the cold war turned hot. Since the end of World War II, Korea had been divided into two nations. A Soviet-influenced Communist government ruled **North Korea.** In June 1950, North Korea made a surprise attack on **South Korea.** By invading the south, the Communists hoped to unite the two Koreas into one Communist country.

Without formally declaring war, President Truman sent American troops to assist the South Koreans. The United Nations (UN) agreed to help the Americans and the South Koreans fight the North Koreans. Americans, though, made up about 90 percent of the UN forces.

Peace talks to end the war began in July 1951—barely a year after North Korea's invasion of South Korea. The talks—and the bloody fighting—dragged on for two more years. Finally, in July 1953, the participants signed a treaty. After years of fighting, Korea remained divided and tensions between North and South Korea persisted. By fighting in Korea, the United

States showed that it would willingly fight to halt Communist expansion.

★ The Vietnam War

Like Korea, **Vietnam** had been divided into separate countries. Communists governed **North Vietnam** but not **South Vietnam.** In South Vietnam Communist rebels known as the Vietcong began a civil war to gain control of the government. The Vietcong received strong support from North Vietnam.

The United States backed South Vietnam's government, although it ruled as an unpopular dictatorship. Presidents **Dwight D. Eisenhower** and **John F. Kennedy** both gave financial aid and military advice to South Vietnam's non-Communist government. Under President **Lyndon B. Johnson** the United States began sending troops in 1965. By 1969 more than 543,000 American soldiers fought in South Vietnam.

The War Divides America

Although the United States sent more and more troops to Vietnam, the Communists continued fighting. As the war dragged on, increasing numbers of American soldiers died. Americans began to question and criticize their country's involvement in the war. Night after night, they viewed vivid images of the suffering and bloodshed on their televisions. In the late 1960s, antiwar protests erupted, mainly on college campuses. Violence and chaos clouded American life. Meanwhile, the war was costing the United States thousands of young lives and billions of dollars.

The War Ends

In 1968 President Johnson announced that he would not seek reelection. He also indicated that he would seek a negotiated peace in Vietnam. Shortly after **Richard Nixon** took office in 1969, he announced a plan to end the war. Americans would train the South Vietnamese army to defend itself. Then American forces would gradually leave. Not until 1973, though, did both sides agree to a cease-fire. In 1975 North Vietnam took control of South Vietnam and united the two countries.

★ The Civil Rights Movement

Despite obstacles, African Americans pressed for equal rights. Their efforts became known as the civil rights movement. President Kennedy took office in 1961 and became a strong supporter of civil rights. He proposed laws to end segregation, or the separation of whites and African Americans. Segregation was practiced in all parts of the United States, although it was most dominant in the South. In the 1960s African Americans still lacked the opportunities to obtain good educations and good jobs. Several states even discouraged them from voting.

Picturing History

▲ THE WAR IN VIETNAM The Vietnam War proved to be one of the most controversial wars in United States history. **In what year did the United States agree to a cease-fire in Vietnam?**

Martin Luther King, Jr., Leads the Fight for Civil Rights

A young minister named Dr. **Martin Luther King, Jr.,** began a nonviolent struggle for civil rights in 1955. That year he led a bus boycott in Montgomery, Alabama. It started when African American Rosa Parks disregarded a local law and courageously refused to give up her seat on a bus to a white person. King urged African Americans not to ride the buses until the government repealed the unfair law. King's tactic worked. His success inspired others to join his nonviolent fight.

In 1963 King led a huge march to protest discrimination in Birmingham, Alabama. Police used fire hoses and dogs to drive back the protesters and jailed King. As a result of the events in Birmingham, President Kennedy urged Congress to pass laws that would abolish segregation in the United States.

King and other civil rights leaders then organized a march on Washington, D.C., in August 1963 to influence Congress to pass the new laws.

King received the Nobel Peace Prize in 1964. In 1968 an assassin shot and killed him. His dream lives on in Americans who still strive for justice and peace. ★★★

▲ MARTIN LUTHER KING, JR.

President Johnson and Civil Rights

President Kennedy did not live to see the passage of the civil rights laws he proposed. On November 22, 1963, the nation watched in horror as an assassin struck him down. This tragic event shocked and saddened Americans. Vice President Lyndon B. Johnson took over as President. Johnson worked hard to get Congress to enact the civil rights laws that Kennedy had wanted. As a result Congress passed the **Civil Rights Act of 1964.**

The new act banned segregation and discrimination in all public places. In addition, the law made it illegal to deny people jobs or to keep them from attending school because of their race or religion.

★ The Nixon Years

Even while the Vietnam War raged on, President Nixon attempted to improve American relations with the Communist world. To try to end the cold war, Nixon took the daring step of visiting both the People's Republic of China and the Soviet Union in 1972. The President's historic trip to China greatly improved relations between the Chinese and Americans.

Also during Nixon's first term, the United States became the leading nation in space exploration. In 1969 millions of Americans watched astronauts Neil Armstrong and Edwin Aldrin on their televisions as they walked on the moon.

Nixon won reelection in 1972 by a landslide. He received 18 million more votes than the Democratic candidate, George McGovern. Despite his huge election victory, Nixon faced serious problems in his second term of office.

Watergate Scandal

In June 1972, police arrested five men for breaking into the Democratic party's national headquarters in the Watergate building in Washington, D.C.

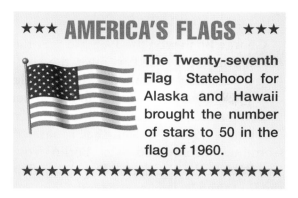

President Nixon denied newspaper reports implicating the involvement of members of his staff. In May 1973, the Senate Select Committee on Presidential Campaign Activities began public hearings on Watergate. Millions of Americans watched in fascination as a parade of witnesses testified about the illegal activities of members of Nixon's White House staff and by the Committee to Reelect the President (CREEP).

In July 1974, after months of hearings, the House Judiciary Committee recommended the impeachment of Nixon charging that the President had interfered with the Watergate investigation. It also charged that Nixon had broken his constitutional oath as President to uphold the law.

Nixon appeared before the American people on television and announced that he would resign the presidency. On August 9, 1974, Nixon officially left the office of President of the United States rather than face the likely possibility of impeachment. Nixon became the first American President ever to resign.

★ After Watergate

On the day Nixon left the presidency, Vice President **Gerald Ford** took the presidential oath of office. Ford had taken over as Nixon's Vice President when Spiro Agnew resigned after another Nixon White House scandal. As a result, Ford became the first President elected neither to the presidency nor the vice presidency.

While still reeling from the Watergate scandal, Americans elected **Jimmy Carter** President in 1976. Carter seemed honest and intelligent with a strong sense of morality. Many Americans believed they could trust him. He stressed over and over again that he was not part of the Washington establishment. As a Washington outsider, though, Carter often found working with Congress difficult.

The Reagan Years

In the 1980 election campaign, Republican **Ronald Reagan** promised economic growth and development and a strong military defense. The tide of conservatism that swept him into office also resulted in a Republican-controlled Senate. He quickly began to lower taxes and reduce government spending on social programs. Reagan also fought communism vigorously, especially in Latin America. His overwhelming reelection in 1984 demonstrated strong support for his policies.

Reagan began his second term intent on keeping the United States strong, defending it against possible aggression from the

Picturing History ▲ **REAGAN AND GORBACHEV** President Reagan worked with Soviet leader Gorbachev in an attempt to better the relationship between the United States and the Soviet Union. **What did Gorbachev call his new economic program?**

Bush and the End of the Cold War

George Bush won the 1988 presidential election and promised to meet the challenges of what he called a new world order. The sweeping reforms in the Soviet Union affected Eastern Europe. In November 1989, the wall that separated Communist-controlled East Berlin from free West Berlin came tumbling down. For the first time in almost 30 years, Germans could travel freely between East and West Germany. In 1990 the two Germanys reunited. Poland, Czechoslovakia, Yugoslavia, Bulgaria, Hungary, Romania, and Albania—the Soviet-dominated countries in Eastern Europe—broke up along ethnic lines and discarded their Communist rulers, or at least made way for more democratic government.

The Soviet Union itself began moving toward democracy. Eventually it fell apart as its various republics proclaimed their independence. In December 1991, several of the nations formed a loose confederation called the **Commonwealth of Independent States.** By 1993 the cold war, which had determined international politics for more than 40 years, had ended.

Picturing History

▲ THE BERLIN WALL With the fall of the Berlin Wall, Germany was again a united nation. **What confederation today consists of former Communist-controlled republics?**

Soviet Union. The United States spent enormous amounts of money to build up its military.

The late 1980s and early 1990s were years of astonishing change. During Reagan's second term, Soviet leader **Mikhail Gorbachev** began changing his country's economy and society. He called his new program **perestroika,** which means "restructuring" in Russian. The program's policies encouraged free market enterprise and **glasnost,** or political openness.

★ SECTION 4 REVIEW ★

Checking for Understanding

1. **Identify** Dwight D. Eisenhower, John F. Kennedy, Lyndon B. Johnson, Richard Nixon, Martin Luther King, Jr., Soviet Union, Vietnam.

2. **Define** cold war, free world, segregation.

3. **What** was the purpose of NATO? What countries formed this organization?

4. **What** was the cause of the Korean War?

5. **Who** were the Vietcong and what was their goal?

6. **What** American practice did the civil rights laws proposed by President Kennedy aim to abolish, or end?

Critical Thinking

7. **Drawing Conclusions** Led by Martin Luther King, Jr., nonviolent protesters risked arrest by breaking segregation laws. Why do you think that King believed breaking these laws was necessary? Do you agree with him? Why or why not?

ACTIVITY

8. Create a time line of the civil rights movement. Research and clip pictures from magazines and newspapers of historic and present-day civil rights events and issues. Add captions that explain the issues.

Toward a New Century

Read to Learn . . .

★ how a coalition of nations won the Persian Gulf War.

★ how the role of the United States in world relations has changed in the 1990s.

★ about the challenges Americans face at home in the 1990s.

Terms to Know

★ multinational state

People to Meet

★ Saddam Hussein
★ George Bush
★ Bill Clinton
★ Yitzhak Rabin
★ Yasir Arafat
★ Bob Dole

Places to Locate

★ Kuwait
★ Somalia
★ Bosnia-Herzegovina

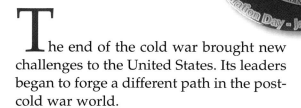

◄ MEMORIAL BUTTON, INAUGURATION DAY 1993

The end of the cold war brought new challenges to the United States. Its leaders began to forge a different path in the post-cold war world.

★ The Persian Gulf War

On August 2, 1990, Iraqi President **Saddam Hussein's** troops invaded and easily overwhelmed **Kuwait,** Iraq's oil-rich neighbor. Following the invasion Iraq controlled 20 percent of the world's oil reserves. President **George Bush,** with cooperation from more than 25 other nations, assembled a huge military coalition called Operation Desert Shield. The United Nations authorized military action to restore Kuwait's independence. Operation Desert Storm began January 16, 1991, when the U.S. and its allies launched a series of air strikes against Iraq. After a month of bombing, a lightning-swift ground assault freed Kuwait and ended the war. Since then, Saddam Hussein has remained a threat to the region's peace and stability, and the United States has had to take additional action against Iraq. Moreover, concern over the possibility that Iraq continues to develop chemical, biological, and nuclear weapons remains acute.

★ Demands for Change

In the early 1990s, the rapidly increasing size of the federal government worried many Americans. Americans were also concerned about the economic downturn that had occurred under President Bush. In 1992 they expressed a desire for change by electing Democrat **Bill Clinton** over Bush and third-party candidate H. Ross Perot.

During his first term, President Clinton sought to make sweeping reforms in the nation's health-care and welfare programs. Although Democrats held the majority in Congress, Republicans prevented most of Clinton's proposals from becoming law. They defeated Clinton's health-care proposal by presenting it as another "big government" program that would increase costs without improving the quality of national health care. In the 1994 congressional elections Republicans gained control of both houses of Congress for the first time in 40 years.

★ America in a Changing World

The struggle between communism and democracy had virtually ended by the time Clinton took office. Yet throughout the world, bloody wars erupted over ethnic hatreds, political boundaries, and religious views.

▲ PRESIDENT BILL CLINTON IN BOSNIA-HERZEGOVINA

Civil War in Somalia

A civil war in the east African nation of **Somalia** became one of the first crises to face President Clinton. President Bush had already sent more than 28,000 American troops there in 1992 to lead a United Nations humanitarian mission. Criticized for not providing adequate protection for them, Clinton withdrew American troops.

Civil Conflict in Bosnia-Herzegovina

Yugoslavia had been created in 1918 after Austria-Hungary was defeated in World War I. It was a multinational state, or a nation with many different ethnic groups. Six republics became part of the new nation—Serbia, Slovenia, Croatia, Bosnia-Herzegovina, Montenegro, and Macedonia. Each republic included a mix of ethnic groups.

Centuries-old differences based on ethnic, religious, and territorial issues divided the various people of Yugoslavia. In 1991 Slovenia, Croatia, Bosnia-Herzegovina, and Macedonia declared their independence. Croatia and Bosnia-Herzegovina were both plunged into war as minority Serbs in each country, fearing domination by majority governments, tried to seize control. Serbia (the largest of the republics) supported the Serb minorities. As a result of the war, about 300,000 people died and 2.7 million lost their homes.

In 1995 the leaders of Croatia, Bosnia-Herzegovina, and Serbia met with President Clinton in Dayton, Ohio. The meeting resulted in the signing of the Dayton Peace Accord, which divided Bosnia into two ethnic substates. The declared truce was shaky, however, and Clinton sent United States troops to Bosnia to help keep the peace.

Peace Agreement in the Middle East

Israel is the home of three major religions—Judaism, Christianity, and Islam—and two major ethnic groups—Arabs and

Picturing History

▲ **PEACE AGREEMENT** With President Clinton looking on, Israel's Prime Minister Yitzhak Rabin (left) and PLO leader Yasir Arafat (right) signed a peace agreement in 1993. **What did the PLO recognize by signing the peace agreement?**

Jews. Since early in this century, Arabs and Jews have fought over control of Israel, and relations between the two groups have been bitter. To try to resolve the conflict, President Clinton assembled a policy team to look for permanent solutions to the conflict.

On September 13, 1993, Israeli Prime Minister **Yitzhak Rabin** (EE•tsahk rah•BEEN) and Palestine Liberation Organization (PLO) leader **Yasir Arafat** (YAH•suhr AIR•uh•fat) reached an agreement. The PLO recognized Israel's right to exist, and Israel recognized the PLO as the representative of the Palestinians. In addition, the two sides agreed on a framework for limited Palestinian self-rule in the Gaza Strip and on the West Bank.

Two years later Israel's cabinet approved an agreement with the PLO that would grant self-rule to most of the 1 million Palestinians on the West Bank. The peace process suffered a jolt, however, when a right-wing Israeli student assassinated Rabin on November 4, 1995.

Since Rabin's assassination, progress toward peace has been slowed by actions on both sides. In the years since the 1993 agreement, Palestinian suicide bombers have killed or maimed hundreds of Israelis. In 1996 a new Israeli government under Prime Minister Benjamin Netanyahu came to power. It enraged the Arabs by continuing construction of Jewish settlements on the West Bank and in Jerusalem. Peace talks have continued, despite violent opposition, but the outlook for peace remains dim.

Peace Between Israel and Jordan

President Clinton also helped work out a peace agreement between Israel and Jordan. In July 1994 Prime Minister Rabin and Jordan's King Hussein signed a historic peace treaty officially ending the state of war that had existed between their countries for nearly half a century.

★ America and the World Economy

The United States worked hard to stay strong in a competitive world marketplace. In 1994 it used the **North American**

CHAPTER 21 The Twentieth Century: 1900–Present   **687**

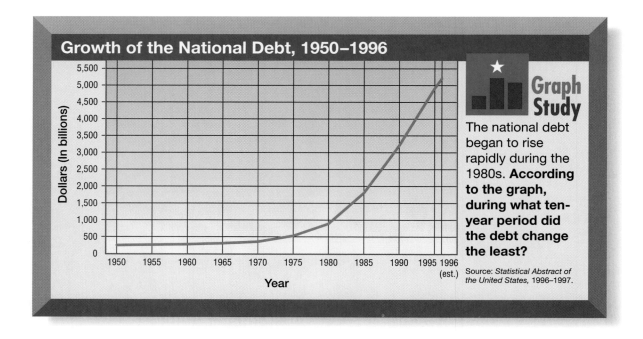

Growth of the National Debt, 1950–1996

Graph Study

The national debt began to rise rapidly during the 1980s. **According to the graph, during what ten-year period did the debt change the least?**

Source: *Statistical Abstract of the United States, 1996–1997.*

Free Trade Agreement (NAFTA) to create closer economic links with its North American neighbors. Under NAFTA, the United States, Canada, and Mexico would slowly end tariffs and other barriers to trade among the three countries.

The United States also worked to build trade with individual nations in Asia. In the 1990s it signed new trade agreements with Japan and kept trade open with China. In 1995 the United States decided to put the bitterness of the Vietnam War behind it and officially recognized the government of Communist Vietnam. This decision paved the way for all kinds of new business opportunities for American companies in Vietnam.

★ Changes and Challenges

American political leaders faced several key issues during the 1990s, all of which defied easy solutions. The issues involved balancing the federal budget, reducing the national debt, toughening standards for welfare, and determining the proper role of government in other social programs.

The Environment

Threats to the environment continued to trouble Americans. In 1995 the earth's surface temperature reached a record high. Scientists think this was caused by global warming—warming created as gases released by burning fuels, such as coal and natural gas, trap the sun's heat. Scientists predict that continued warming could lead to problems such as erratic weather patterns and the spread of tropical diseases.

Risks to Health

The increase in the number of cases of acquired immunodeficiency syndrome (AIDS) became a major concern for Americans in the late 1980s and 1990s. In 1996 new drugs caused the first drop in the number of Americans diagnosed with AIDS. Many Americans remain infected with the disease, however.

Cigarette smoking also concerned many Americans. In 1996 the government restricted cigarette advertising in an effort to reduce teen smoking. It also tightened enforcement of laws that make it illegal for teenagers to purchase cigarettes. In 1997 the government began negotiating a multi-billion dollar settlement requiring the tobacco industry to fund public health programs.

Welfare Reform

Both Democratic and Republican leaders called for reforming the welfare system. Twice President Clinton vetoed Republican-backed welfare legislation. Then, in 1996, President Clinton signed a bill that fulfilled his 1992 promise to "end welfare as we know it." The new law ended the main federal welfare program, turning welfare over to the states.

Federal Budgetary Issues

The Republican majorities in Congress engaged the President in a major battle over balancing the federal budget and reducing the national debt. Their inability to reach a compromise led to partial government shutdowns in 1995 and 1996. But in 1997, Clinton and Congress agreed on a plan to balance the budget in five years.

1996 Presidential Election

In the 1996 elections, President Clinton ran against Republican **Bob Dole,** the former Senate majority leader, and Reform Party candidate H. Ross Perot. Clinton appealed to many voters by promising to "build a bridge to the twenty-first century." His legislative record on the economy, welfare reform, and crime control made it difficult for his opponents to attack him on those issues, and he easily won reelection. Bill Clinton became the first Democrat to win reelection since Franklin D. Roosevelt had 60 years earlier.

★ Toward the Twenty-first Century

The movement toward democracy from Russia to South Africa and the rise of new trouble spots from Haiti to Bosnia presented the United States with new challenges as the twentieth century waned. Many worried about sending troops to intervene in other countries' disputes. Americans debated whether to continue as a world leader or to focus on domestic problems.

Americans also questioned whether they could continue to afford expensive national programs for health and welfare. Some argued that the states should handle these problems, while others believed that only federal programs would ensure adequate protection for all.

Whatever their views though, Americans approached the twenty-first century as a free nation committed to the truths expressed in the Declaration of Independence: that all are created equal and "endowed by their Creator with certain unalienable Rights . . . Life, Liberty, and the pursuit of Happiness," and that to secure these rights government would continue to draw its powers from "the consent of the governed."

★ SECTION 5 REVIEW ★

Checking for Understanding

1. **Identify** Saddam Hussein, George Bush, Bill Clinton, Yitzhak Rabin, Yasir Arafat, Bob Dole, Kuwait, Somalia, Bosnia-Herzegovina.

2. **Define** multinational state.

3. **What** event sparked the Persian Gulf War?

4. **What** challenges do Americans face today?

Critical Thinking

5. **Analyzing Information** Why do you think the United States wants to establish peace in the Middle East?

ACTIVITY

6. Create an award to give to the ideal United States citizen in the year 2000.

Using Key Vocabulary

Match the listed vocabulary words with their correct definitions below.

depression
dictatorship
nationalism
segregation
neutral

_____ 1. a people's pride in their country

_____ 2. a government in which a leader, or group of leaders, have complete authority over the people they rule

_____ 3. the separation of whites and African Americans

_____ 4. a period of declining economic activity

_____ 5. choosing not to take sides in a dispute

Reviewing Facts

1. **Explain** how the United States became involved in World War I.

2. **Describe** the event that triggered the Great Depression.

3. **Describe** the role the United States played in the cold war.

4. **Tell** why many Americans opposed the Vietnam War.

5. **List** three ways the United States changed in the 1990s.

Understanding Concepts

U.S. Role in World Affairs

1. Why did the position of the United States in world affairs shift after World War I?

2. How did the role of the United States in the world change after World War II?

3. How did changes in the world affect the United States in the 1990s?

Civil Rights and Liberties

4. What strategies did Martin Luther King, Jr., use in his struggle for African Americans' civil rights?

5. What was the effect of the welfare reform legislation that President Clinton signed in 1996?

Critical Thinking

1. **Forming Opinions** FDR's policies under the New Deal greatly expanded the power and size of the federal government. Do you think this expansion was necessary? Why or why not?

2. **Making Inferences** Why was American opposition to the Vietnam War greater than American opposition to World War I?

3. **Analyzing Fine Art** Study the painting "In a Free Government" by artist Jacob Lawrence. Then answer the questions on page 691.

a. What can you conclude about the relationship between the people in this painting?

b. What do you think the artist is saying about government?

History and Geography

The War in Vietnam

Study the map of the Vietnam War. Then answer the questions.

1. **Regions** In which region of South Vietnam did Americans set up most of their bases—the interior, the coast, or the border along Cambodia and Laos?

2. **Location** On what line of latitude was the Demilitarized Zone located?

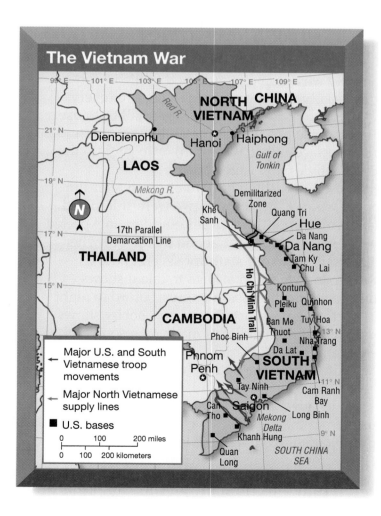

The Vietnam War

Major U.S. and South Vietnamese troop movements

Major North Vietnamese supply lines

U.S. bases

Interdisciplinary Activity: The Arts

Cooperative Learning

Develop an advertising campaign to promote a new image for the United States in the year 2000. As a group, decide on the general message that you want to communicate. Then organize your group into three smaller groups and have each group design an ad for a different medium—radio, television, or print. Share your ads with the class.

Practicing Skills

Writing an Essay

Choose one of the topics below, and write an essay. Remember to include an introduction, a body, and a conclusion.

1. The most serious challenge young people will face in the twenty-first century

2. What I would do if I were President

3. What schools should teach in the twenty-first century

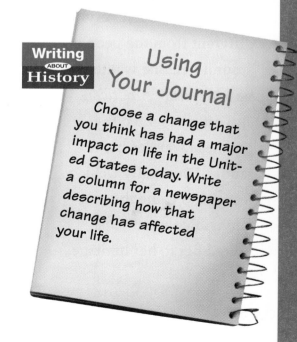

Writing ABOUT History

Using Your Journal

Choose a change that you think has had a major impact on life in the United States today. Write a column for a newspaper describing how that change has affected your life.

Read to Discover

Yoshiko Uchida's family, like many Japanese Americans, were patriotic citizens during World War II. Japanese Americans, however, were treated as enemies because of their heritage. The American government relocated them to camps during the war. How did Yoshiko and her sister, Kay, spend their time in the internment camp?

Reader's Dictionary

Tanforan	horse racing park used as a camp for Japanese Americans
mess hall	military-style dining area
contraband	forbidden items

from The Invisible Thread

by Yoshiko Uchida (1921–1992)

Gradually we became accustomed to life in Tanforan, especially to standing in long lines for everything. We lined up to get into the mess hall or to use a laundry tub or to buy something at the canteen (finding only shoelaces when we got in) or to get into the occasional movies that were shown.

We got used to rushing back to our stall after dinner for the 6:00 P.M. head count (we were still in bed for the morning count), and to the sudden unexpected campwide searches for contraband by the FBI when we were confined to our stalls for several hours.

For diversion we could also go to talent shows, recorded concerts, discussion groups, Saturday night dances, softball games, art classes, and hobby shows exhibiting beautiful handicraft made by resourceful residents from scrap material.

Soon visitors from the outside were allowed to come in as far as the grandstand, and many of our friends came laden with cakes, fruit, candy, cookies, and news from the outside.

Representatives from the university, the YMCA and YWCA, and various church groups also came to give us their support and help. They were working

Yoshiko Uchida grew up in California in the 1930s. As a Japanese American, she sometimes felt very different from the people around her. She wanted to be a "typical" American, and often resented the Japanese ways of her family. Eventually Uchida learned to value the "invisible thread" that linked her to her heritage.

on arrangements to get students out of camp and back into schools as soon as possible.

One day our neighbor Mrs. Harpainter came to see us, bringing all sorts of snacks along with flowers from her garden for Mama. Her boys, however, were not allowed inside because they were under sixteen.

When Kay and I heard they were waiting outside the gate, we hurried to the fence to talk to them.

"Teddy! Bobby!"

We ran to greet them, squeezing our fingers through the chain links to touch their hands.

But an armed guard quickly shouted, "Hey, you two! Get away from the fence!"

Kay and I stepped back immediately. We didn't want to tangle with anyone holding a gun. Bobby and Teddy watched us in total horror, and told us later that they thought we were going to be shot right before their eyes.

When my mother's good friend, Eleanor Knight, came to see us, we asked her to see how Laddie was getting along. Each day we wondered about him, but the boy who had promised to write hadn't even sent us a postcard. And then we learned why he had not written.

"I'm so sorry," Eleanor wrote, "but your dear Laddie died just a few weeks after you left Berkeley."

I was sure he had died of a broken heart, thinking we had abandoned him. I ran outside to find a place to cry, but there were people wherever I turned. I didn't want to see anybody, but there was no place to hide. There was no place to be alone—not in the latrine or the showers or anywhere in the entire camp.

▲ INTERNMENT OF JAPANESE AMERICANS

Responding to Literature

1. Why were Teddy and Bobby not allowed inside the camp?

2. Why did representatives from churches and other groups visit the camp?

3. How do you think you would feel in Uchida's place in the internment camp?

ACTIVITY

4. Draw plans for a community memorial suitable for remembering Japanese Americans treated unfairly during World War II.

Chapter 20

Reshaping the Nation

Railroads brought farmers, ranchers, and miners to the West in the last half of the 1800s. Native Americans, most of whom lived in the West by that time, fought against white settlement. Eventually they were forced onto **reservations.**

The eastern United States also experienced big changes. Thanks to modern inventors, Americans could talk to one another on telephones and light their cities with electric lamps. Industries and cities grew as never before.

A new wave of **immigrants** streamed into the cities to take factory jobs. Workers of all backgrounds tried to improve unsafe factory conditions. Owners, however, seldom changed wages or work rules.

Life proved difficult for both immigrant and African American families, who moved to cities looking for work. **Reformers** like Jacob Riis exposed dirty, overcrowded slums. Their work helped change some of the worst conditions.

▲ ARRIVAL OF IMMIGRANTS, 1887

Farmers throughout the country fell on hard times after the Civil War. Local groups succeeded in getting lower railroad rates for shipping their products to market. These groups later formed the **Populist** political party. The Populists and members of the **Progressive movement,** which came later, brought about a number of reforms. The graduated income tax, direct primaries, and direct election of senators were some of their reforms.

CAUSES

- Military dictatorships in Germany, Italy, and Japan
- Germany invades Poland and Western Europe
- Japan invades the Asian mainland and islands of the Pacific
- Japan attacks American naval base in Hawaii

• World War II

EFFECTS

- United Nations formed
- United States and the Soviet Union become world superpowers
- Cold war develops between Western democracies and Eastern Communist countries

---

Chapter 21

The Twentieth Century

By the time the United States entered the twentieth century, it had acquired Hawaii, the Philippines, Puerto Rico, and Guam. Theodore Roosevelt, who became President in 1901, started the building of the **Panama Canal.** He also established the United States as a police officer among Latin American nations.

From April of 1917 to November of 1918, the United States helped its European allies fight and win **World War I.** After the war, the United States became recognized as a leader among the world's most powerful nations.

▲ 1957 CHEVROLET

Americans celebrated a booming economy during the 1920s. The **Great Depression** replaced the good life, however, near the end of the 1920s. During the 1930s, President Franklin D. Roosevelt tried to fight the depression with his **New Deal** program. Laws passed during the New Deal introduced the belief that the federal government has the duty to help Americans in need.

From 1941 to 1945, Americans joined **World War II** to help stop Axis powers from overrunning Europe and the Pacific. After the war, the United States and the Soviet Union, a Communist country, emerged as the world's superpowers. Differences between the two superpowers and their allies created the **cold war.** Trying to stop the spread of communism, the United States took part in open warfare in Korea (1950-1953) and Vietnam (1965-1973). During the cold war era, Americans also started the **civil rights movement,** attacked poverty, and saw the first resignation of a President.

◄ MARTIN LUTHER KING, JR.

▲ THE VIETNAM WAR MEMORIAL

The collapse of the Soviet Union in 1991 ended the cold war. Now the only superpower, the United States had to decide what role it would play in keeping peace around the world. Near the end of the twentieth century, the nation participated in a global economy and tried to control government spending.

Understanding Unit Themes

1. **Influence of Technology** What effect did the industrial growth of the late 1800s have on urban living? What effect did it have on the West? How did the automobile boost the American economy?

2. **The Individual and Family Life** Why did farm families join Grange lodges and form the Populist party? What was life like for immigrant and African American families in the cities?

3. **Civil Rights and Liberties** What victories did African Americans win in the struggle toward equal rights? What peaceful strategies did African Americans use to win equal rights?

4. **U.S. Role in World Affairs** What new challenges did the United States face after the cold war?

Appendix Contents

Atlas Key

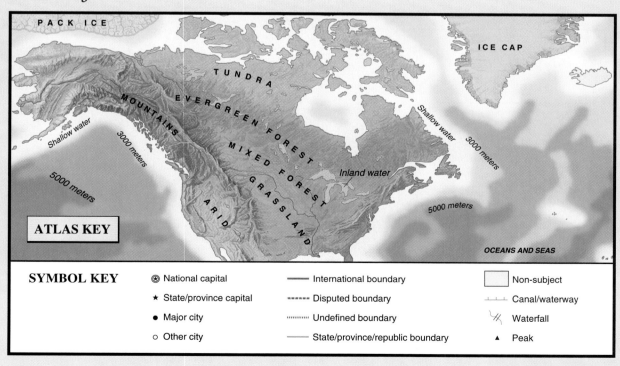

PACK ICE

ICE CAP

TUNDRA

EVERGREEN FOREST

MOUNTAINS

Shallow water

3000 meters

5000 meters

MIXED FOREST

Inland water

Shallow water

3000 meters

GRASSLAND

ARID

5000 meters

ATLAS KEY

OCEANS AND SEAS

SYMBOL KEY		
⊛ National capital	—— International boundary	▢ Non-subject
★ State/province capital	----- Disputed boundary	⊥⊤⊥ Canal/waterway
● Major city	.... Undefined boundary	↘ Waterfall
○ Other city	—— State/province/republic boundary	▲ Peak

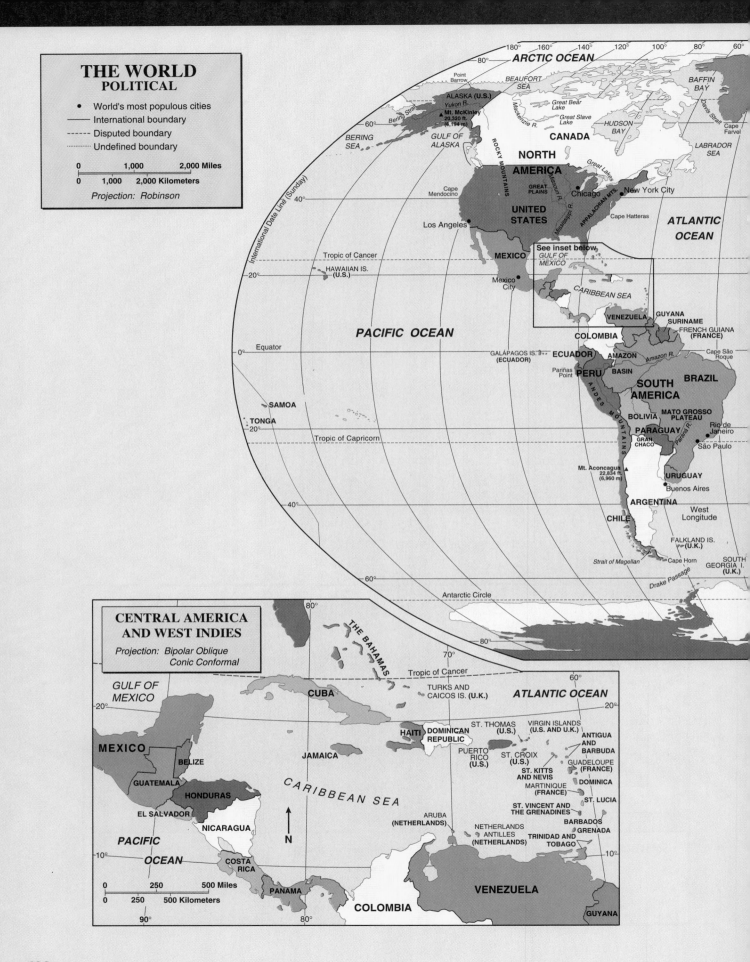

THE WORLD
POLITICAL

- • World's most populous cities
- — International boundary
- — — Disputed boundary
- ······· Undefined boundary

0   1,000   2,000 Miles
0   1,000   2,000 Kilometers

Projection: Robinson

ARCTIC OCEAN

Point Barrow
BEAUFORT SEA
BAFFIN BAY

ALASKA (U.S.)
Yukon R.
Mt. McKinley 20,320 ft. (6,194 m)
Bering Strait
BERING SEA
GULF OF ALASKA
Great Bear Lake
Mackenzie R.
Great Slave Lake
HUDSON BAY
Davis Strait
Cape Farvel
LABRADOR SEA

International Date Line (Sunday)

CANADA

NORTH AMERICA

ROCKY MOUNTAINS

Cape Mendocino

GREAT PLAINS
Missouri R.
Great Lakes
Chicago
New York City

UNITED STATES

Mississippi R.
APPALACHIAN MTS.
Cape Hatteras

ATLANTIC OCEAN

Los Angeles

Tropic of Cancer

See inset below
GULF OF MEXICO

MEXICO

HAWAIIAN IS. (U.S.)

20°

Mexico City

CARIBBEAN SEA

VENEZUELA
GUYANA
SURINAME
FRENCH GUIANA (FRANCE)

COLOMBIA

PACIFIC OCEAN

Equator   0°

GALÁPAGOS IS. (ECUADOR)
ECUADOR

AMAZON
Amazon R.
Cape São Roque

Pariñas Point
PERU
BASIN

SOUTH AMERICA

BRAZIL

SAMOA

MATO GROSSO PLATEAU

BOLIVIA

TONGA

20°

ANDES MOUNTAINS

PARAGUAY
GRAN CHACO
Paraná R.

Rio de Janeiro
São Paulo

Tropic of Capricorn

Mt. Aconcagua 22,834 ft. (6,960 m)

URUGUAY
Buenos Aires

40°

ARGENTINA

West Longitude

CHILE

FALKLAND IS. (U.K.)

Strait of Magellan
Cape Horn
Drake Passage

SOUTH GEORGIA I. (U.K.)

60°

Antarctic Circle

80°

CENTRAL AMERICA AND WEST INDIES

Projection: Bipolar Oblique Conic Conformal

GULF OF MEXICO

THE BAHAMAS

80°

CUBA

70°

Tropic of Cancer

TURKS AND CAICOS IS. (U.K.)

ATLANTIC OCEAN

60°

20°

20°

MEXICO

BELIZE

GUATEMALA

JAMAICA

HAITI
DOMINICAN REPUBLIC

ST. THOMAS (U.S.)
PUERTO RICO (U.S.)
ST. CROIX (U.S.)

VIRGIN ISLANDS (U.S. AND U.K.)
ANTIGUA AND BARBUDA
GUADELOUPE (FRANCE)
DOMINICA
MARTINIQUE (FRANCE)
ST. LUCIA

ST. KITTS AND NEVIS

HONDURAS

CARIBBEAN SEA

EL SALVADOR

NICARAGUA

PACIFIC OCEAN

ST. VINCENT AND THE GRENADINES

BARBADOS
GRENADA

ARUBA (NETHERLANDS)
NETHERLANDS ANTILLES (NETHERLANDS)

TRINIDAD AND TOBAGO

N

10°

COSTA RICA

PANAMA

10°

0   250   500 Miles
0   250   500 Kilometers

VENEZUELA

COLOMBIA

GUYANA

90°   80°

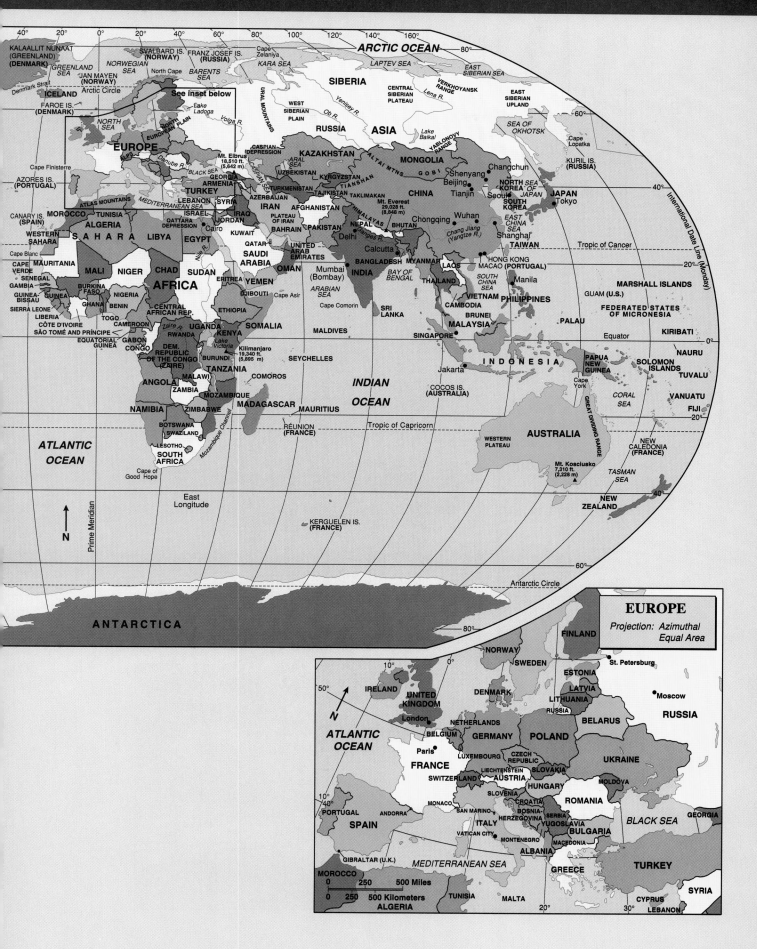

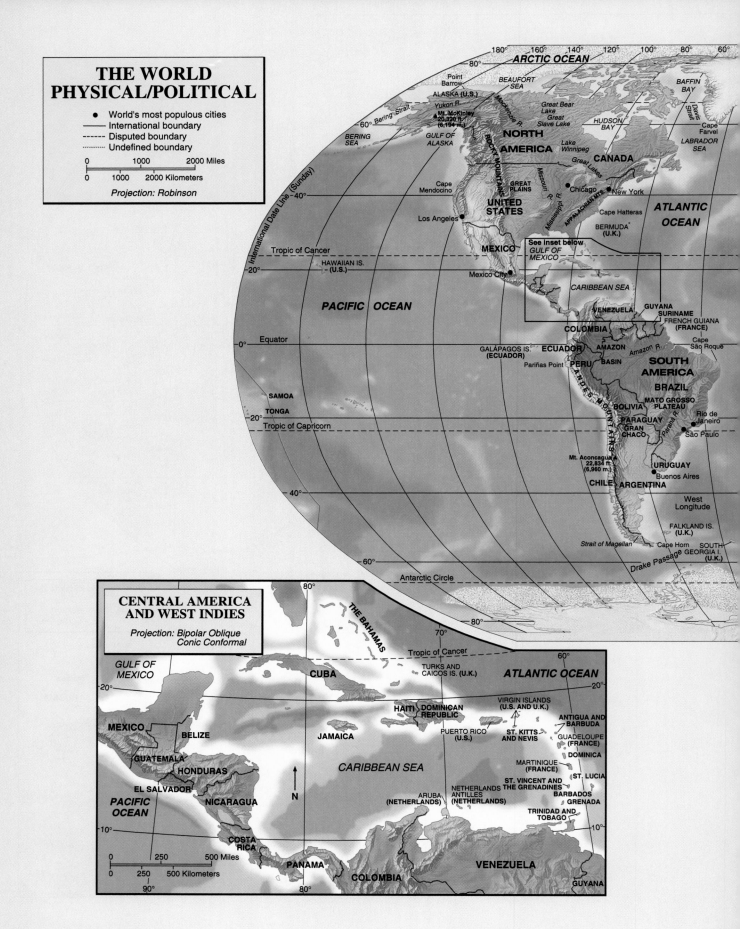

THE WORLD PHYSICAL/POLITICAL

- ● World's most populous cities
- —— International boundary
- ----- Disputed boundary
- ········· Undefined boundary

0   1000   2000 Miles

0   1000   2000 Kilometers

Projection: Robinson

ARCTIC OCEAN

BEAUFORT SEA

Point Barrow

BAFFIN BAY

Davis Strait

ALASKA (U.S.)

Yukon R.

Bering Strait

BERING SEA

Mt. McKinley 20,320 ft. (6,194 m.)

GULF OF ALASKA

Great Bear Lake

Great Slave Lake

HUDSON BAY

Cape Farvel

LABRADOR SEA

ROCKY MOUNTAINS

NORTH AMERICA

Lake Winnipeg

CANADA

Cape Mendocino

GREAT PLAINS

Missouri R.

Great Lakes

Chicago

New York

UNITED STATES

Mississippi R.

APPALACHIAN Mts.

Cape Hatteras

ATLANTIC OCEAN

Los Angeles

BERMUDA (U.K.)

International Date Line (Sunday)

Tropic of Cancer

MEXICO

See inset below

GULF OF MEXICO

HAWAIIAN IS. (U.S.)

Mexico City

CARIBBEAN SEA

GUYANA

SURINAME

FRENCH GUIANA (FRANCE)

VENEZUELA

PACIFIC OCEAN

Equator

COLOMBIA

GALÁPAGOS IS. (ECUADOR)

ECUADOR

AMAZON

Amazon R.

Cape São Roque

PERU

BASIN

SOUTH AMERICA

Pariñas Point

BRAZIL

MATO GROSSO PLATEAU

SAMOA

BOLIVIA

Rio de Janeiro

TONGA

PARAGUAY

Tropic of Capricorn

GRAN CHACO

Paraná R.

São Paulo

Mt. Aconcagua 22,834 ft. (6,960 m.)

URUGUAY

Buenos Aires

CHILE

ARGENTINA

West Longitude

FALKLAND IS. (U.K.)

Strait of Magellan

Cape Horn

SOUTH GEORGIA I. (U.K.)

Drake Passage

Antarctic Circle

CENTRAL AMERICA AND WEST INDIES

Projection: Bipolar Oblique Conic Conformal

THE BAHAMAS

GULF OF MEXICO

CUBA

Tropic of Cancer

TURKS AND CAICOS IS. (U.K.)

ATLANTIC OCEAN

MEXICO

BELIZE

HAITI

DOMINICAN REPUBLIC

VIRGIN ISLANDS (U.S. AND U.K.)

ANTIGUA AND BARBUDA

JAMAICA

PUERTO RICO (U.S.)

ST. KITTS AND NEVIS

GUADELOUPE (FRANCE)

GUATEMALA

HONDURAS

DOMINICA

CARIBBEAN SEA

MARTINIQUE (FRANCE)

ST. LUCIA

EL SALVADOR

N

ST. VINCENT AND THE GRENADINES

PACIFIC OCEAN

NICARAGUA

ARUBA (NETHERLANDS)

NETHERLANDS ANTILLES (NETHERLANDS)

BARBADOS

GRENADA

TRINIDAD AND TOBAGO

0   250   500 Miles

COSTA RICA

0   250   500 Kilometers

PANAMA

VENEZUELA

COLOMBIA

GUYANA

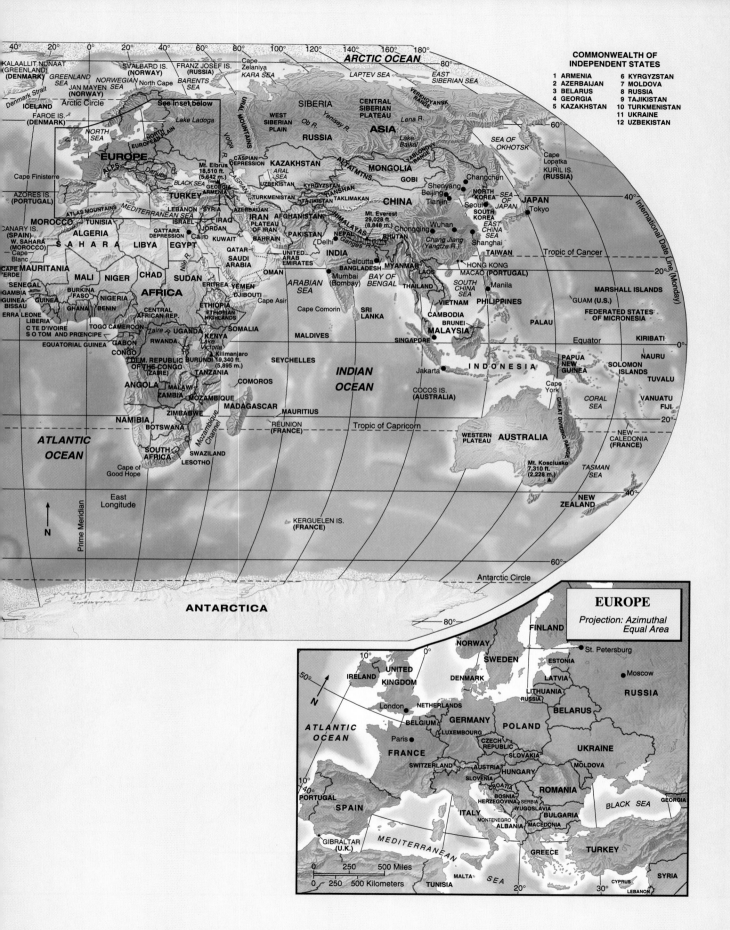

PACIFIC OCEAN

WASHINGTON
Seattle
Olympia
Portland Columbia River
Salem
OREGON

IDAHO
Boise
Snake River

MONTANA
Helena
Missouri River

WYOMING
Great
Salt
Lake

NORTH DAKOTA
Bismarck

SOUTH DAKOTA
Pierre
Missouri

NEVADA
Carson City
Sacramento
San Francisco Oakland
San Jose
CALIFORNIA

UTAH
Salt Lake
City

North Platte River

Cheyenne
South Platte River

NEBRASKA
Platte River

Denver
COLORADO
Arkansas River

KANSAS

Los Angeles
San Bernardino
Long Beach
San Diego

Las Vegas

Colorado River

ARIZONA
Phoenix
Gila River
Tucson

Rio Grande

Santa Fe

NEW
MEXICO

Pecos River

OKLAHOMA
Oklahoma City
Red River

Brazos River

Colorado River

Fort Worth
TEXAS

Austin

San Antonio

Rio Grande

GULF
OF
CALIFORNIA

Sacramento River

HAWAII
Honolulu
PACIFIC OCEAN
0   100 Miles
0   100 Kilometers

Arctic Circle
Bering Strait
Yukon River
ALASKA
BERING SEA
0   250   500 Miles
0   250   500 Kilometers

CANADA
Juneau
GULF OF
ALASKA

MEXICO

CANADA

MINNESOTA

MICHIGAN

Lake Superior

Lake Michigan

Lake Huron

MAINE
★ Augusta

Montpelier ★ N.H.
VT. ★ Concord

Minneapolis • ★ St. Paul

WISCONSIN

Mississippi River

Grand Rapids •

Lake Ontario

Albany ★

Hudson River

Boston ★
MASS.

Madison ★ • Milwaukee

Lansing ★
Detroit •

Rochester •
Buffalo •

Syracuse •

Hartford ★
Providence ★
CONN. R.I.

IOWA

Des Moines ★

Chicago •

Gary •
Hammond

Toledo •

NEW YORK

PENNSYLVANIA

Cleveland •
Akron •
Canton •
Youngstown • Harrisburg ★

Newark •
New York •
N.J.
Trenton ★
Bridgeport •

Omaha •

ILLINOIS

OHIO

Pittsburgh •

Philadelphia •
Camden •

Lincoln •

Springfield ★

Indianapolis ★

Dayton • • Columbus

Baltimore •

MD.
Annapolis ★
Washington ⊛

Dover ★
DEL.

Topeka ★

Kansas City •

INDIANA

Cincinnati •

Ohio River

WEST
VIRGINIA

D.C.

Kansas City
Jefferson City ★

St. Louis •
East
St. Louis •

Frankfort ★

Charleston ★

Richmond ★

ATLANTIC

OCEAN

MISSOURI

KENTUCKY

Louisville •

VIRGINIA

Newport News •
Norfolk •

Tulsa •

Mississippi River

Nashville ★

Raleigh ★

ARKANSAS

Memphis •

TENNESSEE

NORTH CAROLINA

Little Rock ★

Tennessee R.

Columbia •

SOUTH
CAROLINA

Birmingham •

Atlanta •

UNITED STATES

Dallas •

LOUISIANA

ALABAMA

Montgomery ★

GEORGIA

⊛ National capital

★ State capital

• Major city

International boundary

State boundary

MISSISSIPPI

Jackson •

Baton Rouge ★

Jacksonville •

Houston •

New Orleans •

★ Tallahassee

FLORIDA

0   150   300 Miles
0   150   300 Kilometers

GULF OF MEXICO

• Orlando

Tampa •

Projection: Albers Equal Area

St. Petersburg •

N

Miami •

THE
BAHAMAS

CUBA

CANADA

MINNESOTA
Lake of the Woods
Red Lake
Duluth
Minneapolis ★ St. Paul
Rochester

WISCONSIN
Green Bay
Appleton
Madison
Milwaukee
Racine

MICHIGAN
Lake Superior
Lake Michigan
Lake Huron

Grand Rapids
Flint
Lansing
Detroit
Ann Arbor

MAINE
Moosehead Lake
Bangor
Mt. Washington 6,288 ft. (1,905 m.)
Augusta
Lewiston
Portland
Lake Champlain
Burlington
Montpelier
N.H.
VT.
Concord
Manchester

St. Lawrence River

Lake Ontario
Utica
Rochester
Syracuse
Albany
MASS.
Springfield
Worcester
Boston
Cape Cod
Hartford
Providence
R.I.
CONN.
New Haven
Newark
Yonkers
New York
N.J.

Niagara Falls
Buffalo
Binghamton
Erie
Lake Erie

NEW YORK
Hudson R.
ADIRONDACK MTNS.

Sioux City
Dubuque
Cedar Rapids
Davenport
IOWA
Omaha
Council Bluffs
Lincoln

ILLINOIS
Rockford
Aurora
Joliet
Chicago
Gary
Hammond
South Bend
Peoria
Springfield
Decatur

INDIANA
Fort Wayne
Muncie
Indianapolis

OHIO
Toledo
Cleveland
Akron
Canton
Youngstown
Columbus
Dayton
Cincinnati
Parkersburg

Pittsburgh
Wheeling

PENNSYLVANIA
Susquehanna River
Harrisburg
Allentown
Philadelphia
Trenton
Camden
Wilmington
N.J.

CENTRAL LOWLAND

Kansas City
Topeka
Lawrence
Kansas City
Independence
Jefferson City
St. Louis
East St. Louis
Harry S. Truman Res.

MISSOURI
Springfield

WEST VIRGINIA
Charleston
Huntington

Arlington
Washington
D.C.
Annapolis
Baltimore
MD.
Dover
DEL.
DELAWARE BAY

VIRGINIA
Richmond
Newport News
Norfolk
CHESAPEAKE BAY

ATLANTIC OCEAN

Evansville
Louisville
Lexington
Frankfort
KENTUCKY
Owensboro
Ohio River
Wabash R.

Roanoke
Roanoke River

Greensboro
Durham
Raleigh
Winston-Salem
Cape Hatteras

Tulsa
OZARK PLATEAU
R.S. Kerr Res.
ARKANSAS
Fort Smith
Lake Eufaula
Lake Texoma

OZARK PLATEAU
Cumberland Plateau
Nashville
Knoxville
TENNESSEE
Mt. Mitchell 6,684 ft. (2,037 m.)
Charlotte
NORTH CAROLINA

Chattanooga
Huntsville
Tennessee R.
Memphis
North Little Rock
Little Rock
Hot Springs
Pine Bluff

Spartanburg
Greenville
Columbia
SOUTH CAROLINA
Charleston

Dallas
Shreveport
LOUISIANA
Toledo Bend Res.

Birmingham
Tuscaloosa
ALABAMA
Montgomery
Meridian
MISSISSIPPI
Jackson
Hattiesburg

Atlanta
Augusta
GEORGIA
Macon
Columbus
Albany
Savannah

APPALACHIAN MOUNTAINS
CUMBERLAND
Chattahoochee R.
Alabama R.

COASTAL PLAIN

Sam Rayburn Reservoir
Houston
Lake Charles
Lafayette
Baton Rouge
Lake Pontchartrain
New Orleans
Biloxi
Mobile
Pensacola

Jacksonville

Tallahassee
FLORIDA
Orlando
Cape Canaveral
Tampa
St. Petersburg
Lake Okeechobee
Palm Beach
Miami Beach
Miami

GULF OF MEXICO

N

Cape Sable
Key West
Straits of Florida

THE BAHAMAS

CUBA

UNITED STATES

⊛ National capital
★ State capital
● Major city
━━ International boundary
── State boundary

0 — 150 — 300 Miles
0 — 150 — 300 Kilometers

Projection: Albers Equal Area

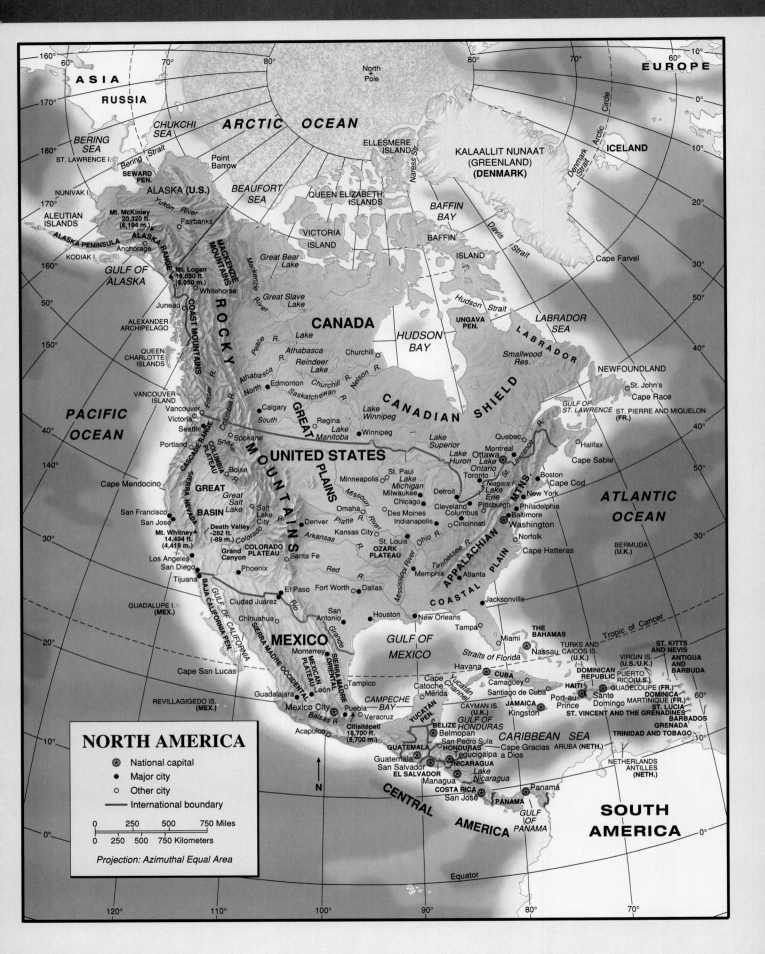

NORTH AMERICA

- ⊛ National capital
- ● Major city
- ○ Other city
- —— International boundary

| 0 | 250 | 500 | 750 Miles |
| 0 | 250 | 500 | 750 Kilometers |

Projection: Azimuthal Equal Area

LATIN AMERICA

⊛ National capital
● Major city
○ Other city
— International boundary

0	500	1000 Miles
0	500	1000 Kilometers

Projection: Miller Cylindrical

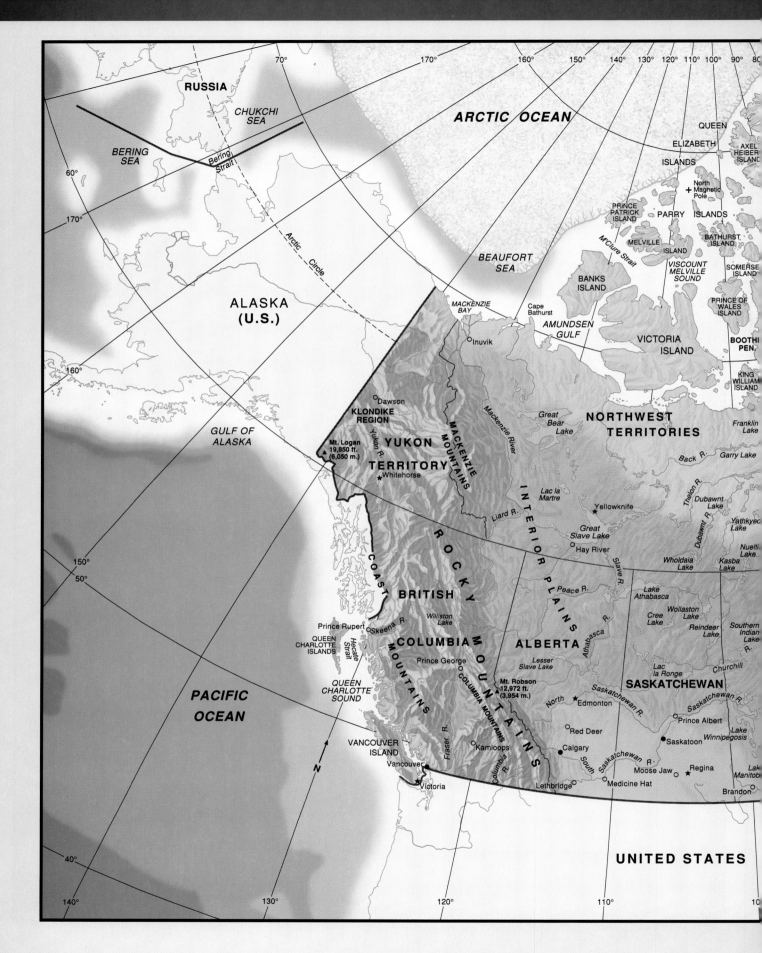

RUSSIA

CHUKCHI
SEA

ARCTIC OCEAN

QUEEN
ELIZABETH
ISLANDS

AXEL
HEIBER
ISLAND

BERING
SEA

Bering Strait

North
Magnetic
Pole

PRINCE
PATRICK
ISLAND

PARRY ISLANDS

MELVILLE
ISLAND

BATHURST
ISLAND

SOMERSET
ISLAND

Arctic Circle

McClure Strait

VISCOUNT
MELVILLE
SOUND

ALASKA
(U.S.)

BEAUFORT
SEA

MACKENZIE
BAY

Cape
Bathurst

AMUNDSEN
GULF

BANKS
ISLAND

VICTORIA
ISLAND

PRINCE
OF
WALES
ISLAND

BOOTHI
PEN.

Inuvik

KING
WILLIAM
ISLAND

GULF OF
ALASKA

Dawson

KLONDIKE
REGION

Mackenzie River

Great
Bear
Lake

NORTHWEST
TERRITORIES

Franklin
Lake

Mt. Logan
19,850 ft.
(6,050 m.)

YUKON
TERRITORY

Yukon R.

MACKENZIE MOUNTAINS

Back R.

Garry Lake

Whitehorse

Liard R.

Lac la
Martre

Yellowknife

Thelon R.

Dubawnt R.

Dubawnt
Lake

Yathkyed
Lake

INTERIOR PLAINS

Great
Slave Lake

Nuelti
Lake

Hay River

Slave R.

Wholdaia
Lake

Kasba
Lake

COAST

BRITISH

R O C K Y

Peace R.

Lake
Athabasca

Cree
Lake

Wollaston
Lake

Reindeer
Lake

Southern
Indian
Lake

Prince Rupert

Skeena R.

Williston
Lake

COLUMBIA
MOUNTAINS

Athabasca R.

Lac
la Ronge

Churchill R.

QUEEN
CHARLOTTE
ISLANDS

Hecate
Strait

Prince George

ALBERTA

Lesser
Slave Lake

SASKATCHEWAN

PACIFIC
OCEAN

QUEEN
CHARLOTTE
SOUND

M O U N T A I N S

Mt. Robson
12,972 ft.
(3,954 m.)

COLUMBIA MOUNTAINS

North

Edmonton

Saskatchewan R.

Saskatchewan R.

Prince Albert

Lake
Winnipegosis

Red Deer

Saskatoon

VANCOUVER
ISLAND

Fraser R.

Kamloops

Columbia R.

Calgary

South Saskatchewan R.

Moose Jaw

Regina

Lak
Manitob

Vancouver

Victoria

Lethbridge

Medicine Hat

Brandon

N

UNITED STATES

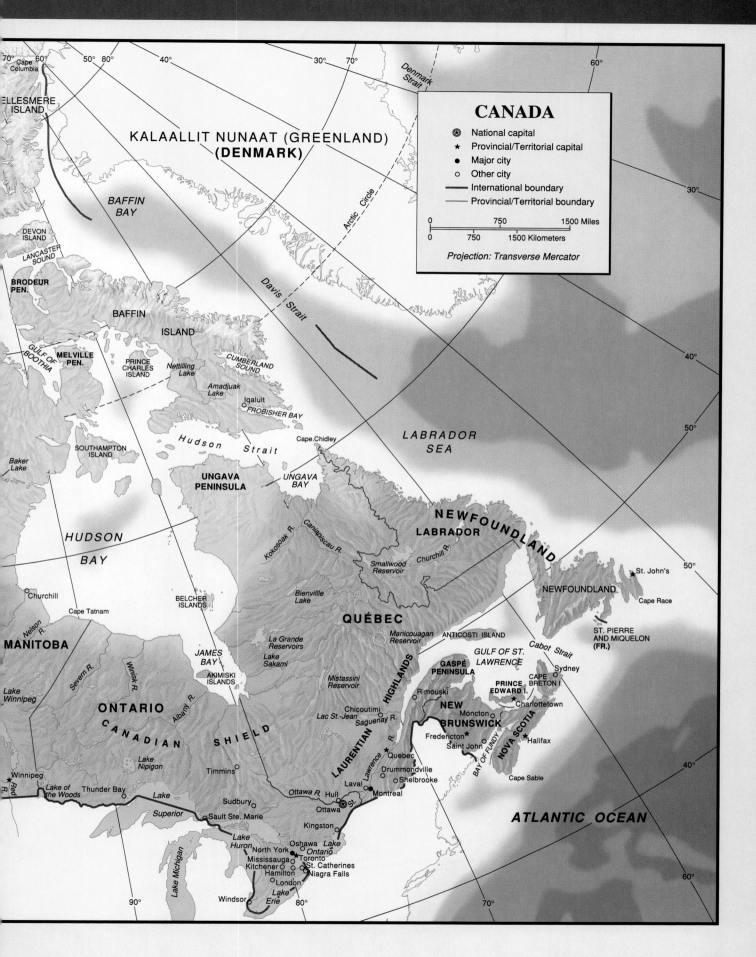

KALAALLIT NUNAAT (GREENLAND)
(DENMARK)

CANADA

⊚ National capital
★ Provincial/Territorial capital
● Major city
○ Other city
━━━ International boundary
──── Provincial/Territorial boundary

0   750   1500 Miles
0   750   1500 Kilometers

Projection: Transverse Mercator

Cape
Columbia

ELLESMERE
ISLAND

BAFFIN
BAY

DEVON
ISLAND

LANCASTER
SOUND

BRODEUR
PEN.

BAFFIN

ISLAND

GULF OF
BOOTHIA

MELVILLE
PEN.

PRINCE
CHARLES
ISLAND

Nettilling
Lake

Amadjuak
Lake

Iqaluit
FROBISHER BAY

CUMBERLAND
SOUND

Davis   Strait

Arctic   Circle

Denmark
Strait

LABRADOR
SEA

Hudson   Strait

Cape Chidley

SOUTHAMPTON
ISLAND

Baker
Lake

UNGAVA
PENINSULA

UNGAVA
BAY

NEWFOUNDLAND

LABRADOR

HUDSON

BAY

BELCHER
ISLANDS

Kokosoak R.

Caniapiscau R.

Smallwood
Reservoir

Churchill R.

St. John's

NEWFOUNDLAND

Cape Race

Churchill

Cape Tatnam

Bienville
Lake

ST. PIERRE
AND MIQUELON
(FR.)

MANITOBA

Nelson R.

JAMES
BAY

AKIMISKI
ISLANDS

La Grande
Reservoirs

Lake
Sakami

QUÉBEC

Manicouagan
Reservoir

ANTICOSTI ISLAND

Cabot Strait

Sydney

Lake
Winnipeg

ONTARIO

Severn R.

Winisk R.

Albany R.

Mistassini
Reservoir

GASPÉ
PENINSULA

GULF OF ST.
LAWRENCE

CAPE
BRETON I.

PRINCE
EDWARD I.

Charlottetown

CANADIAN   SHIELD

Chicoutimi
Lac St.-Jean
Saguenay R.

Rimouski

NEW

BRUNSWICK

Moncton

NOVA SCOTIA

Lake
Nipigon

Timmins

LAURENTIAN   HIGHLANDS

Fredericton

Saint John

Halifax

Winnipeg

Red R.

Lake of
the Woods

Thunder Bay

Lake

Superior

Sault Ste. Marie

Sudbury

Ottawa R.

St. Lawrence R.

Hull
Ottawa

St.

Laval

Montreal

Quebec

Drummondville

Shelbrooke

BAY OF FUNDY

Cape Sable

ATLANTIC   OCEAN

Kingston

Lake
Huron

Oshawa

Lake

Ontario

Toronto

North York

Mississauga

Kitchener

St. Catherines

Hamilton

Niagra Falls

London

Lake

Erie

Windsor

Lake Michigan

Atlas   709

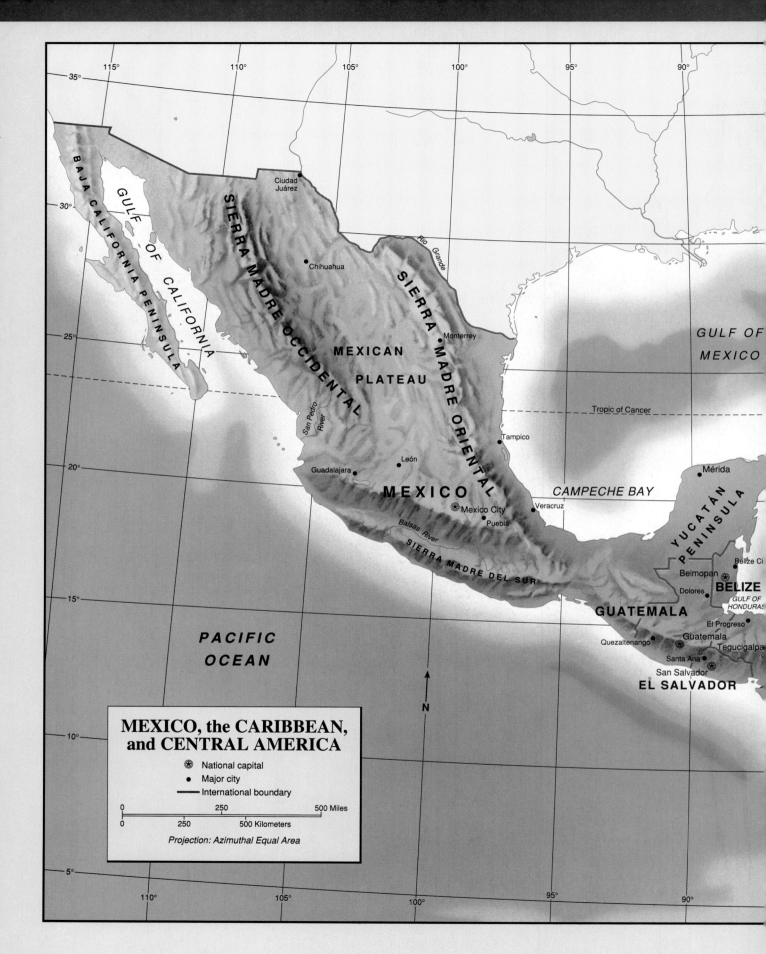

MEXICO, the CARIBBEAN, and CENTRAL AMERICA

⊛ National capital
● Major city
— International boundary

| 0 | | 250 | | 500 Miles |
| 0 | 250 | | 500 Kilometers | |

Projection: Azimuthal Equal Area

BAJA CALIFORNIA PENINSULA

GULF OF CALIFORNIA

SIERRA MADRE OCCIDENTAL

SIERRA MADRE ORIENTAL

MEXICAN PLATEAU

MEXICO

SIERRA MADRE DEL SUR

Balsas River

San Pedro River

Rio Grande

Tropic of Cancer

GULF OF MEXICO

CAMPECHE BAY

YUCATÁN PENINSULA

PACIFIC OCEAN

GUATEMALA

BELIZE

GULF OF HONDURAS

EL SALVADOR

N

Ciudad Juárez
Chihuahua
Monterrey
Tampico
León
Guadalajara
Mexico City
Puebla
Veracruz
Mérida
Belize Ci
Belmopan
Dolores
El Progreso
Quezaltenango
Guatemala
Tegucigalpa
Santa Ana
San Salvador

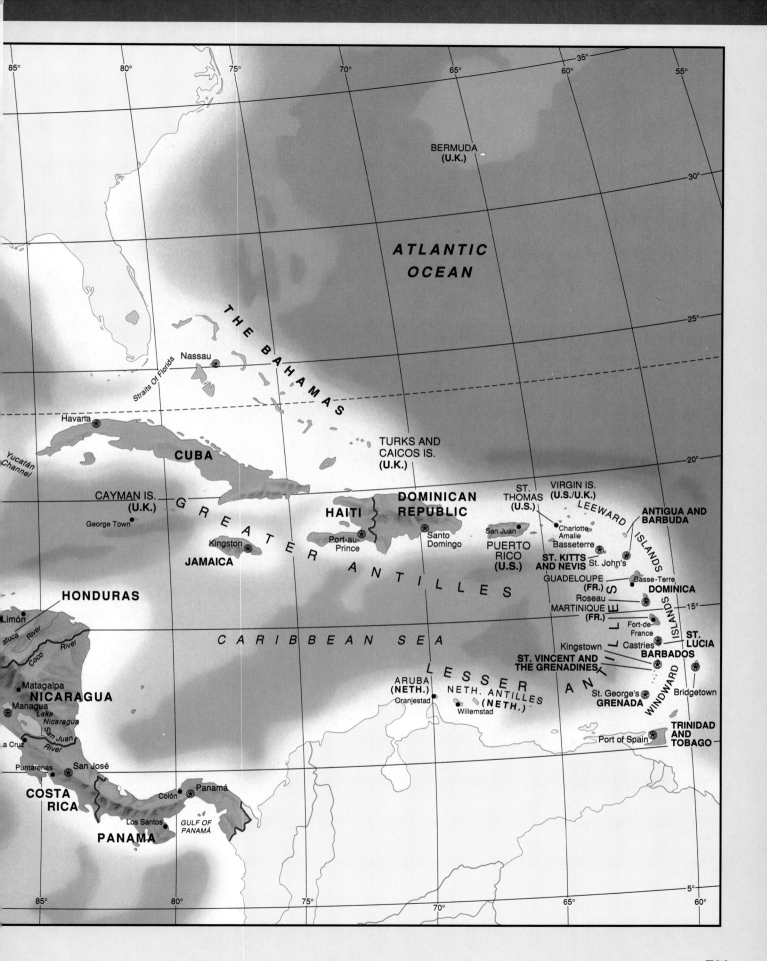

ATLANTIC
OCEAN

BERMUDA
(U.K.)

THE BAHAMAS

Straits Of Florida

Nassau

Havana

Yucatán Channel

CUBA

CAYMAN IS.
(U.K.)

George Town

Kingston

JAMAICA

GREATER ANTILLES

TURKS AND
CAICOS IS.
(U.K.)

HAITI

DOMINICAN
REPUBLIC

Port-au-Prince

Santo Domingo

PUERTO
RICO
(U.S.)

ST.
THOMAS
(U.S.)

San Juan

Charlotte Amalie

VIRGIN IS.
(U.S./U.K.)

LEEWARD ISLANDS

ANTIGUA AND
BARBUDA

St. John's

Basseterre

ST. KITTS
AND NEVIS

GUADELOUPE
(FR.)

Basse-Terre

DOMINICA

Roseau

MARTINIQUE
(FR.)

Fort-de-France

ST.
LUCIA

Castries

BARBADOS

HONDURAS

Limón

atuca River

Coco River

River

Matagalpa

NICARAGUA

Managua

Lake
Nicaragua

San Juan River

La Cruz

Puntarenas

San José

COSTA
RICA

Colón

Panamá

Los Santos

GULF OF
PANAMÁ

PANAMA

CARIBBEAN SEA

LESSER ANTILLES

ARUBA
(NETH.)

Oranjestad

NETH. ANTILLES
(NETH.)

Willemstad

ST. VINCENT AND
THE GRENADINES

Kingstown

St. George's

GRENADA

Bridgetown

WINDWARD ISLANDS

Port of Spain

TRINIDAD
AND
TOBAGO

EUROPE

- ⊛ National capital
- ● Major city
- ○ Other city
- ▬ International boundary
- ─ Republic boundary
- ⊣⊢ Canal

0   100   200   300 Miles
0 100 200 300 Kilometers

Projection: Azimuthal Equal Area

Reykjavik

ICELAND

Arctic Circle

FAROE IS.
(DEN.)

*NORWEGIAN
SEA*

Trondheim

GULF OF BOTHNIA

NORWAY

SCANDINAVIAN HIGHLANDS

Goldhöppiggen
8,097 ft.
(2,468 m.)

Bergen

Oslo

SWEDEN

Uppsala

ÅLAND IS.

SHETLAND IS.
(U.K.)

Lake
Vänern

Stockholm

HIIUMAA
SAAREMAA I.
GOTLAND IS.

Cape
Wrath

ORKNEY
ISLANDS

NORTH

Skagerrak

Göteborg

Lake
Vättern

ÖLAND I.

OUTER HEBRIDES IS.

NORTHERN
IRELAND
(U.K.)

SCOTLAND

Glasgow

Edinburgh

SEA

JUTLAND

Kattegat

Copenhagen
DENMARK

Odense

Malmö

BORNHOLM I.

BALTIC SEA

RUSSIA

Belfast

PENNINE RANGE

**UNITED
KINGDOM**

Kiel
Canal

Rostock

Gdańsk

Szczecin

NORTH

Dublin

IRELAND

ISLE
OF
MAN

*IRISH
SEA*

Manchester

Leeds

Sheffield

ENGLAND

Hamburg

Elbe R.

Bremen

Berlin

POLAND

Cork

Liverpool

Birmingham

Amsterdam

NETHERLANDS

Mittelland
Canal

Hannover

Magdeburg

Poznań

Warsaw

Vistula

Cape Clear

St. George's
Channel

WALES

Cardiff

Bristol

London

The Hague

Rotterdam

BELGIUM

Antwerp

Essen

Dortmund

Cologne

Leipzig

Dresden

Wrocław

Łódź

Katow

ATLANTIC   OCEAN

English Channel

Strait of Dover

GUERNSEY I. (U.K.)
JERSEY I. (U.K.)

Brussels

Liège

LUXEMBOURG

Bonn

Frankfurt

Chemnitz

**CZECH
REPUBLIC**

Prague

Ostrava

Brno

SLOVA

BRETON
PEN.

Le Havre

Seine
River

Paris

Luxembourg

GERMANY

Marne-Rhine
Canal

Rhine
R.

Stuttgart

Danube

River

Munich

Linz

Vienna

Bratislava

Miskolc

Kra

Nantes

Loire

River

Marne R.

Strasbourg

Bodensee

Salzburg

AUSTRIA

Budapest

HUNGARY

FRANCE

LIECHTENSTEIN

Vaduz

Innsbruck

Graz

L. Balaton

Pécs

Cape Finisterre

BAY OF BISCAY

Bordeaux

**CENTRAL
MASSIF**

Lyon

Lausanne
Geneva

SWITZERLAND

Bern

Zürich

L. Geneva

Mt. Rosa
12,203 ft.
(4,634 m.)

ALPS

Milan

Turin

**PO
VALLEY**

Venice

Po R.

SLOVENIA

Ljubljana

Zagreb

Tisza

Novi Sad

CROATIA

Sava R.

Belgrade

Porto

CANTABRIAN MTNS.

Bilbao

PYRENEES

Toulouse

Garonne R.

Midi
Canal

Mt. Blanc
15,771 ft.
(4,807 m.)

Rhône R.

Montpellier

Nice

Genoa

Bologna

SAN MARINO

San Marino

DINARIC ALPS

**BOSNIA &
HERZEGOVINA**

Split

Valladolid

Duero River

Zaragoza

Ebro River

Aneto Peak
11,168 ft.
(3,404 m.)

ANDORRA

Andorra
la Vella

Marseille

GULF OF LION

MONACO

Monaco

Florence

APENNINES

Sarajevo

ADRIATIC SEA

PORTUGAL

IBERIAN

Madrid

Tagus

River

Lisbon

Setúbal

Guadiana

River

PENINSULA

SPAIN

Barcelona

Valencia

CORSICA
(FR.)

VATICAN CITY

Rome

ITALY

SAN MARINO

MONTENEGRO

MACEDONIA

Cape St. Vincent

**SIERRA
MORENA**

Seville

Granada

Murcia

Palma

BALEARIC IS.
(SP.)

SARDINIA
(IT.)

*TYRRHENIAN
SEA*

Naples

ALBANIA

Bari

Tiranë

G. OF
TARANTO

Málaga

Strait of Gibraltar

GIBRALTAR
(U.K.)

Cagliari

MEDITERRANEAN

Strait of Sicily

Palermo

SICILY

Catania

*IONIAN
SEA*

KEFALLINIA I.

AFRICA

PANTELLERIA
(IT.)

MALTA

Valletta

SEA

North Cape

30° 40° 70° 50° 70° 60° 80°

BARENTS SEA

Murmansk

KOLA PENINSULA

TIMAN RIDGE

Pechora R.

URAL MOUNTAINS

60°

ASIA

WHITE SEA

Arkhangel'sk

White Sea-Baltic Waterway

N. Dvina River

Vychegda River

Sukhona River

Mt. Konzhakovskiy 5,147 ft. (1,569 m.)

Kama R.

70°

FINLAND

Lake Onega

Volga-Baltic Waterway

Perm

50°

Tampere
Lake Saimaa
Turku
Espoo Helsinki
GULF OF FINLAND
Tallinn
ESTONIA

Lake Ladoga

St. Petersburg

Chudskoye Lake

Rybinsk Reservoir

Yaroslavl

Kazan

Kama River

Ufa

Kuybyshev Reservoir

ASIA

GULF OF RIGA
LATVIA
Riga

BALTIC PLAIN
Dvina W.

EUROPEAN PLAIN

River

Volga River

Volga-Baltic Waterway

Moscow

Nizhniy Novgorod

Samara

Orenburg

LITHUANIA
Kaunas
Vilnius
Minsk

River

Oka
Tula

Smolensk

CENTRAL RUSSIAN UPLAND

RUSSIA

VOLGA UPLAND

Volga River

Saratov

Volgograd Reservoir

KAZAKHSTAN

ARAL SEA

BELARUS

Pripet River

Desna R.

Kursk

Don River

Voronezh

40°

Kiev

Kremenchug Reservoir

Kharkov

Lugansk

Volgograd

Tsimlyansk Reservoir

Volga River

DEPRESSION

60°

Lvov

UKRAINE

DNIEPER UPLAND

Dniester R.

Dnepropetrovsk
Krivoy Rog
Zaporozhye

Donetsk

Don River

Rostov

Astrakhan

CASPIAN

Delta of the Volga

CASPIAN SEA

CARPATHIAN MTNS.
MOLDOVA
Chisinau
Prut River

DNIEPER LOWLAND
Dniep River

Kakhovka Res.

SEA OF AZOV

Debrecen

Odessa

CRIMEA

Krasnodar

Grozny

Cluj-Napoca

ROMANIA

Timişoara
Braşov

WALLACHIA PLAIN
Danube
Bucharest
River

Constanta

CAUCASUS MTNS.

Mt. Elbrus 18,510 ft. (5,642 m.)

BLACK SEA

Ruse

Varna

SERBIA
Niš

BULGARIA

Sofia
Plovdiv
Skopje
Musala Peak 9,536 ft. (2,926 m.)
Burgas

Bosporus

PENINSULA TURKEY

Salonika

BALKAN

Dardanelles
SEA OF MARMARA

Larissa

AEGEAN SEA

ASIA

GREECE

Patras
Piraeus
Athens

PELOPONNESE PEN.

RHODES

30°

CRETE (GR.)
Iráklion

30° 40° 50°

EURASIA

- ⊛ National capital
- ● Major city
- ○ Other city
- —— International boundary
- ----- Disputed boundary
- ········ Undefined boundary

ALBAN.	—Albania
BAH.	—Bahrain
B.H.	—Bosnia and Herzegovina
CR.	—Croatia
ISR.	—Israel
KUW.	—Kuwait
LIECH.	—Liechtenstein
LITH.	—Lithuania
LUX.	—Luxembourg
MACE.	—Macedonia
MON.	—Monaco
MONT.	—Montenegro
S.M.	—San Marino
SL.	—Slovenia
SWITZ.	—Switzerland
U.A.E.	—United Arab Emirates

0   500   1000 Miles
0   500   1000 Kilometers

Projection: Robinson

N

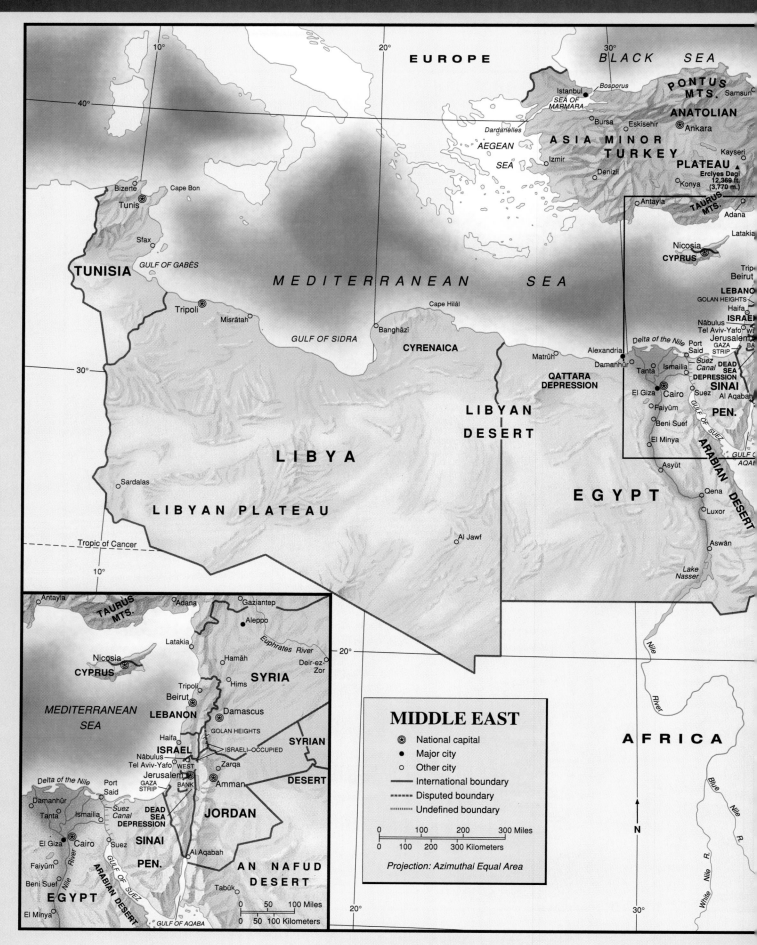

EUROPE

BLACK SEA

PONTUS MTS.

Istanbul
Bosporus
SEA OF MARMARA
Samsun
ANATOLIAN
Bursa
Eskisehir
Ankara
ASIA MINOR
Dardanelles
TURKEY
AEGEAN SEA
Izmir
Kayseri
Denizli
PLATEAU
Erciyes Dagi
12,369 ft.
(3,770 m.)
Konya
Antayla
TAURUS MTS.
Adana
Nicosia
Latakia
CYPRUS
Tripo
Beirut
Bizerte
Cape Bon
LEBANO
Tunis
GOLAN HEIGHTS
Haifa
ISRAEL
Sfax
Nâbulus
Tel Aviv-Yafo
WE
GULF OF GABÈS
Jerusalem
GAZA
BA
TUNISIA
STRIP
MEDITERRANEAN SEA
Cape Hilâl
Delta of the Nile
Port
Said
Tripoli
Alexandria
Misrâtah
Banghâzi
Matrûh
Damanhûr
Suez
Canal
DEAD
SEA
DEPRESSION
SINAI
GULF OF SIDRA
CYRENAICA
Tanta
Ismailia
QATTARA
DEPRESSION
El Giza
Cairo
Suez
PEN.
Al Aqaba
LIBYAN
Faiyûm
GULF OF SUEZ
ARABIAN
GULF O
AQA
DESERT
Beni Suef
30°
El Minya
LIBYA
Asyût
Sardalas
EGYPT
Qena
LIBYAN PLATEAU
Luxor
Aswân
Tropic of Cancer
10°
Al Jawf
Lake
Nasser

MEDITERRANEAN SEA

Antayla
TAURUS MTS.
Adana
Gaziantep
Aleppo
Latakia
Euphrates River
Nicosia
Hamâh
Deir-ez-Zor
CYPRUS
Tripoli
SYRIA
Hims
Beirut
20°
LEBANON
Damascus
MEDITERRANEAN
SEA
Haifa
GOLAN HEIGHTS
SYRIAN
ISRAEL
ISRAELI-OCCUPIED
Delta of the Nile
Nâbulus
Zarqa
DESERT
Damanhûr
Port
Said
Tel Aviv-Yafo
WEST
Tanta
Ismailia
Jerusalem
BANK
Amman
Suez
Canal
GAZA
STRIP
El Giza
Cairo
DEAD
SEA
JORDAN
Faiyûm
Suez
DEPRESSION
SINAI
Nile
River
Beni Suef
GULF OF SUEZ
ARABIAN
PEN.
AN NAFUD
El Minya
DESERT
Al Aqabah
EGYPT
Tabûk
DESERT
GULF OF AQABA

MIDDLE EAST

⊛ National capital
● Major city
○ Other city
—— International boundary
----- Disputed boundary
········ Undefined boundary

0   100   200   300 Miles
0 100 200 300 Kilometers

Projection: Azimuthal Equal Area

AFRICA

Nile
Blue
Nile
White
Nile
R.

N

0   50   100 Miles
0 50 100 Kilometers

716   Atlas

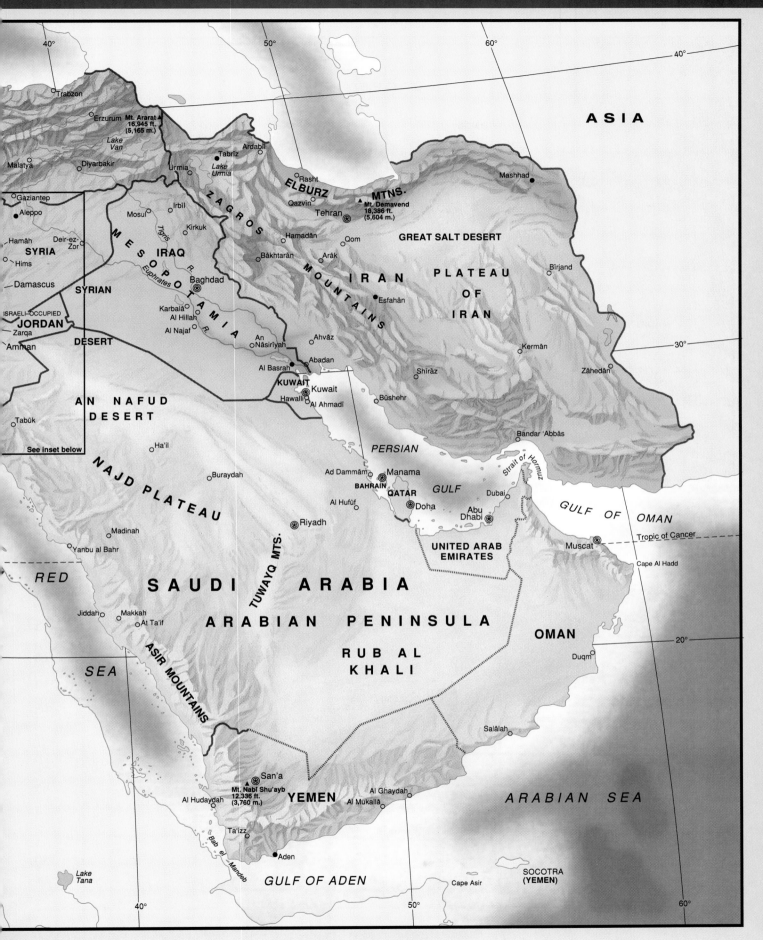

ASIA

Trabzon

Erzurum Mt. Ararat
16,945 ft.
(5,165 m.)
*Lake
Van*

Malatya   Diyarbakir   Tabrīz   Ardabīl
                              Urmia   *Lake
                                       Urmia*   Rasht   Mashhad
Gaziantep   Qazvin   ELBURZ   MTNS.
Aleppo   Mosul   Irbīl   Hamadān   Tehran   Mt. Demavend
                         Kirkuk   18,386 ft.
SYRIA   Hamāh   Deir-ez-   (5,604 m.)
         Hims   Zor   *Tigris R.*   Bākhtarān   Qom   GREAT SALT DESERT
Damascus   IRAQ   Euphrates R.   Arāk   Bīrjand
         SYRIAN   Baghdad   IRAN   PLATEAU
ISRAELI-OCCUPIED   Karbalā   Esfahān   OF
JORDAN   Al Hillah   IRAN
Zarqa   DESERT   Al Najaf   Ahvāz   Kermān   Zāhedān
Amman   An
                         Nāsirīyah   30°
                              Abadan
         AN   NAFUD   Al Basrah   Shīrāz
Tabūk   DESERT   KUWAIT Kuwait
                      Hawalli   Bandar ʻAbbās
                 See inset below   Al Ahmadī   Būshehr
                          Ha'il   PERSIAN   Strait of Hormuz
NAJD PLATEAU   GULF OF OMAN
                    Buraydah   Ad Dammām Manama   GULF   Dubai
Madinah   BAHRAIN QATAR   Abu
Yanbu al Bahr   Al Hufūf   Doha   Dhabi   Muscat   Tropic of Cancer
RED   Riyadh   UNITED ARAB   Cape Al Hadd
                                                  EMIRATES
Jiddah Makkah   SAUDI   ARABIA
        At Ta'if
        ASIR   ARABIAN   PENINSULA   OMAN   20°
SEA   MOUNTAINS   TUWAYQ MTS.
                      RUB AL   Duqm
                      KHALI
                                      Salālah
Al Hudaydah
            Mt. Nabī Shu'ayb   ARABIAN   SEA
            12,336 ft.   San'a   Al Ghaydah
Lake   (3,760 m.)   YEMEN   Al Mukallā
Tana   Ta'izz
            Aden   Cape Asir   SOCOTRA
         GULF OF ADEN   (YEMEN)

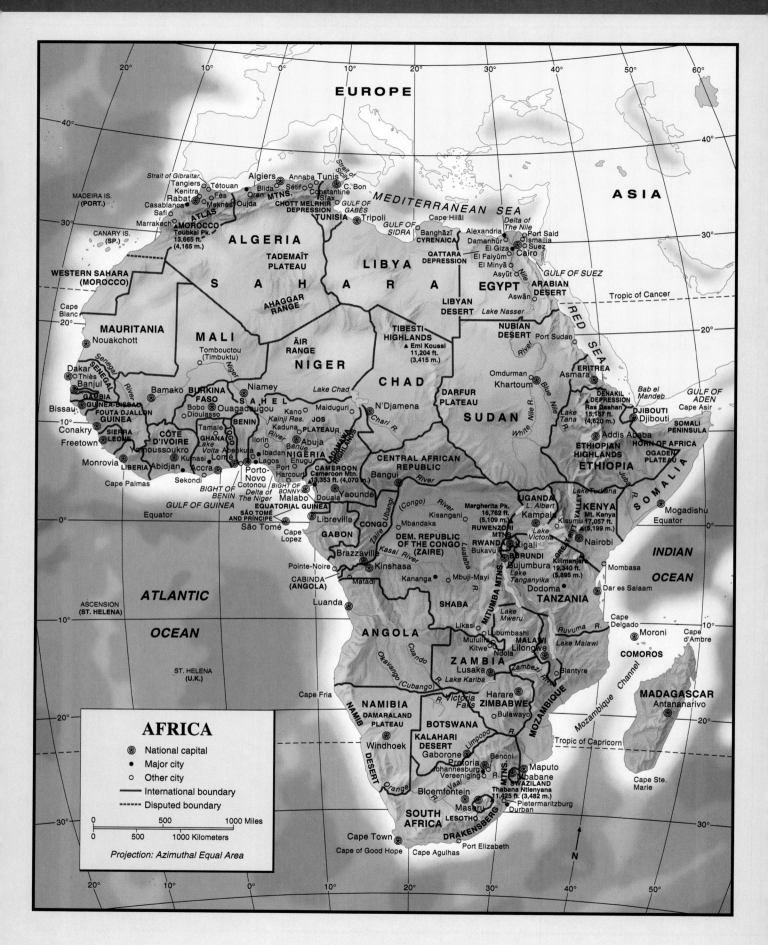

AFRICA

- ◉ National capital
- • Major city
- ○ Other city
- —— International boundary
- ---- Disputed boundary

0 ___ 500 ___ 1000 Miles
0 __ 500 __ 1000 Kilometers

Projection: Azimuthal Equal Area

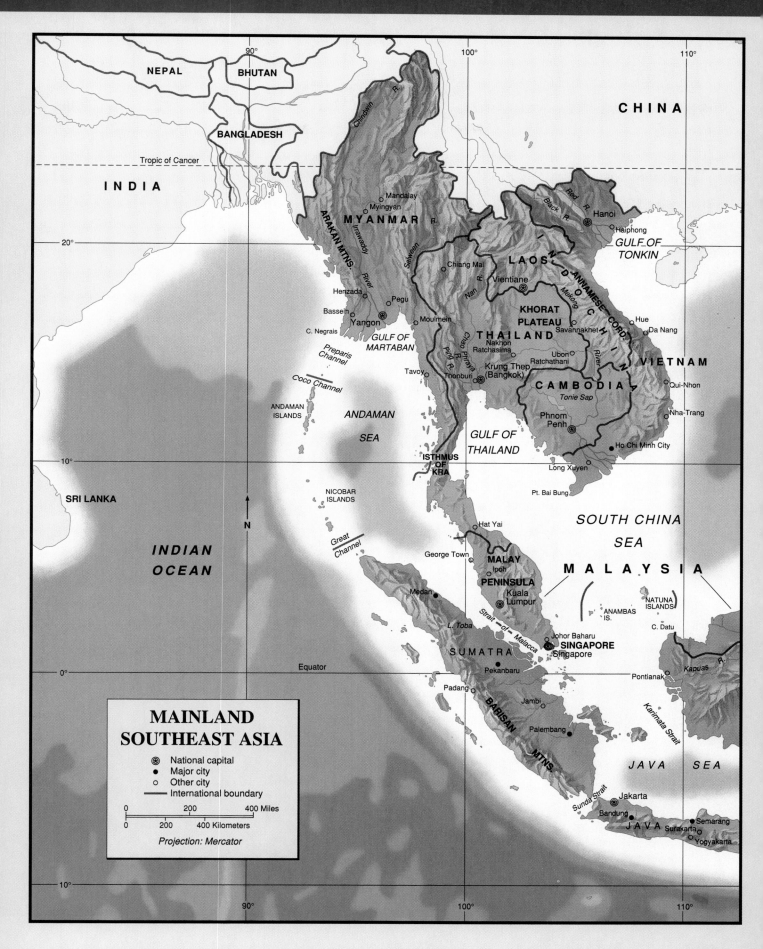

MAINLAND SOUTHEAST ASIA

- ⊛ National capital
- ● Major city
- ○ Other city
- —— International boundary

0   200   400 Miles

0   200   400 Kilometers

Projection: Mercator

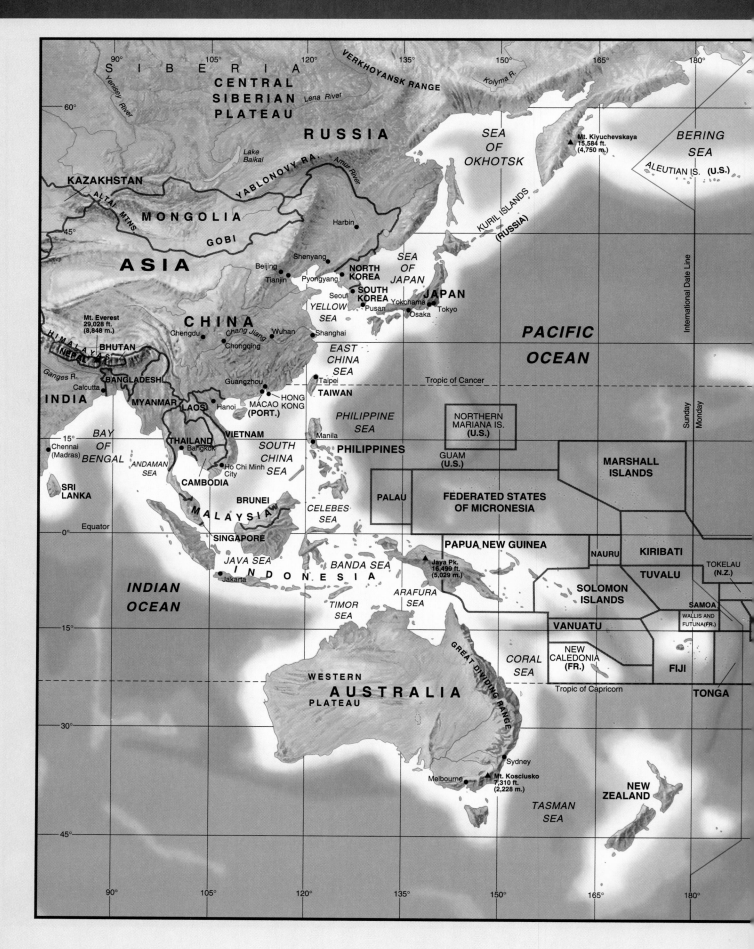

SIBERIA

CENTRAL SIBERIAN PLATEAU

Yenisey River

Lena River

VERKHOYANSK RANGE

Kolyma R.

RUSSIA

SEA OF OKHOTSK

▲ Mt. Klyuchevskaya 15,584 ft. (4,750 m.)

BERING SEA

KAZAKHSTAN

ALTAI MTNS

MONGOLIA

Lake Baikal

YABLONOVY RA.

Amur River

GOBI

ASIA

Harbin

CHINA

Shenyang

Beijing

Tianjin

Pyongyang

NORTH KOREA

SOUTH KOREA

Seoul

Pusan

SEA OF JAPAN

YELLOW SEA

Yokohama

Osaka

JAPAN

Tokyo

KURIL ISLANDS (RUSSIA)

ALEUTIAN IS. (U.S.)

PACIFIC OCEAN

Mt. Everest 29,028 ft. (8,848 m.)

HIMALAYAS

NEPAL

BHUTAN

Ganges R.

BANGLADESH

Calcutta

INDIA

MYANMAR

LAOS

Chengdu

Chang Jiang

Chongqing

Wuhan

Shanghai

Guangzhou

MACAO (PORT.)

HONG KONG

Hanoi

Taipei

TAIWAN

EAST CHINA SEA

Tropic of Cancer

PHILIPPINE SEA

NORTHERN MARIANA IS. (U.S.)

International Date Line

Sunday   Monday

Chennai (Madras)

BAY OF BENGAL

THAILAND

Bangkok

VIETNAM

ANDAMAN SEA

Ho Chi Minh City

CAMBODIA

SOUTH CHINA SEA

Manila

PHILIPPINES

GUAM (U.S.)

MARSHALL ISLANDS

SRI LANKA

BRUNEI

MALAYSIA

CELEBES SEA

PALAU

FEDERATED STATES OF MICRONESIA

Equator

SINGAPORE

JAVA SEA

Jakarta

INDONESIA

BANDA SEA

▲ Jaya Pk. 16,499 ft. (5,029 m.)

PAPUA NEW GUINEA

NAURU

KIRIBATI

TUVALU

TOKELAU (N.Z.)

INDIAN OCEAN

TIMOR SEA

ARAFURA SEA

SOLOMON ISLANDS

SAMOA

WALLIS AND FUTUNA(FR.)

VANUATU

NEW CALEDONIA (FR.)

CORAL SEA

FIJI

GREAT DIVIDING RANGE

WESTERN PLATEAU

AUSTRALIA

Tropic of Capricorn

TONGA

Sydney

Melbourne

▲ Mt. Kosciusko 7,310 ft. (2,228 m.)

NEW ZEALAND

TASMAN SEA

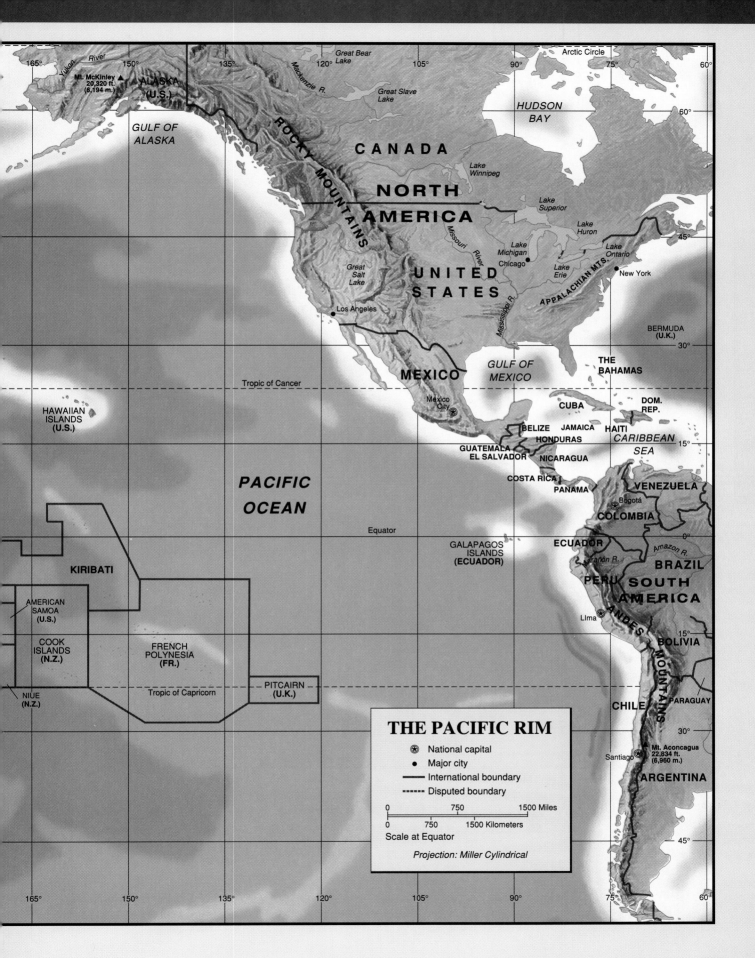

THE PACIFIC RIM

✵ National capital
● Major city
— International boundary
----- Disputed boundary

| 0 | 750 | 1500 Miles |
| 0 | 750 | 1500 Kilometers |

Scale at Equator

Projection: Miller Cylindrical

United States Databank

United States Climate Regions

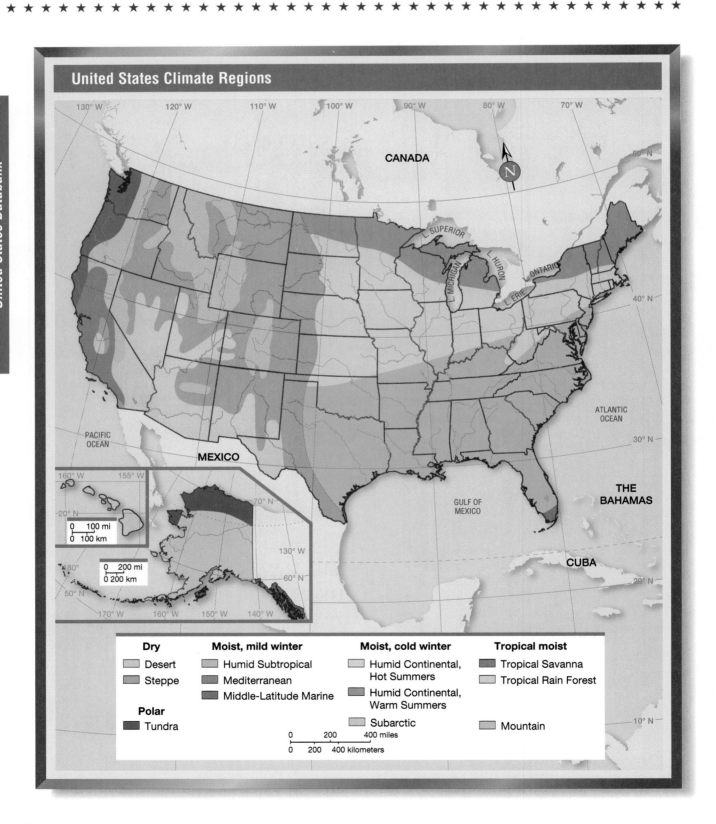

Dry
- Desert
- Steppe

Polar
- Tundra

Moist, mild winter
- Humid Subtropical
- Mediterranean
- Middle-Latitude Marine

Moist, cold winter
- Humid Continental, Hot Summers
- Humid Continental, Warm Summers
- Subarctic

Tropical moist
- Tropical Savanna
- Tropical Rain Forest
- Mountain

0   200   400 miles
0 200   400 kilometers

Population of the United States

Year	Population			Year	Population		
1790	3,929,214	4.5	–	1910	91,972,266	31.0	21.0
1800	5,308,483	6.1	35.1	1920	105,710,620	35.6	14.9
1810	7,239,881	4.3	36.4	1930	122,775,046	41.2	16.1
1820	9,638,453	5.5	33.1	1940	131,669,275	44.2	7.2
1830	12,866,020	7.4	33.5	1950	151,325,798	50.7	14.5
1840	17,069,453	9.8	32.7	1960	179,323,175	50.6	18.5
1850	23,191,876	7.9	35.9	1970	203,302,031	57.4	13.4
1860	31,443,321	10.6	35.6	1980	226,542,199	64.0	11.4
1870	39,818,449	13.4	26.6	1990	248,718,301	70.3	9.8
1880	50,155,783	16.9	26.0	1995*	262,755,000	74.3	5.6
1890	62,947,714	21.2	25.5	2000**	271,237,000	76.7	3.2
1900	75,994,575	25.6	20.7	2020**	288,807,000	81.7	6.5

Key:

☐ **Population per square mile of land**

☐ **Percentage increase over preceding census**

*estimated
**projected

Source: *Statistical Abstract of the United States*, 1996.

Population Distribution by Age

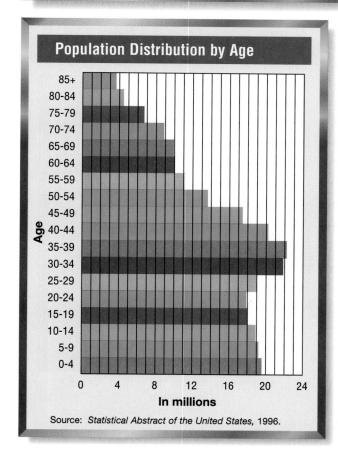

Source: *Statistical Abstract of the United States*, 1996.

Major Religions in the United States

Roman Catholic Church	60,190,605
Southern Baptist Convention	15,614,060
United Methodist Church	8,584,125
National Baptist Convention, U.S.A.	8,500,000
Jews	5,900,000
Church of God in Christ (Pentecostal)	5,499,875
Evangelical Lutheran Church in America	5,199,048
Muslims	5,100,000
Church of Jesus Christ of Latter-Day Saints (Mormon)	4,613,000
Presbyterian Church (U.S.A.)	3,698,136
African Methodist Episcopal Church	3,500,000
National Baptist Convention of America	3,500,000
Lutheran Church (Missouri Synod)	2,596,927
Episcopal Church	2,517,520
Assemblies of God	2,324,615
Orthodox Church in America	2,000,000
Churches of Christ	1,651,103
American Baptist Churches in the U.S.A.	1,507,934
United Church of Christ	1,501,310
Greek Orthodox Archdiocese of North and South America	1,500,000
African Methodist Episcopal Zion Church	1,230,842
Christian Churches and Churches of Christ	1,104,931

In thousands

Source: *World Year Book 1997*.

Political Parties in Power

George Washington, 1789–1797
John Adams, 1797–1801
Thomas Jefferson, 1801–1809
James Madison, 1809–1817
James Monroe, 1817–1825
John Quincy Adams, 1825–1829
Andrew Jackson, 1829–1837
Martin Van Buren, 1837–1841
William H. Harrison/John Tyler, 1841–1845
James K. Polk, 1845–1849
Zachary Taylor/Millard Fillmore, 1849–1853
Franklin Pierce, 1853–1857
James Buchanan, 1857–1861
Abraham Lincoln, 1861–1865
Andrew Johnson, 1865–1869
Ulysses S. Grant, 1869–1877
Rutherford B. Hayes, 1877–1881
James A. Garfield/Chester A. Arthur, 1881–1885
Grover Cleveland, 1885–1889
Benjamin Harrison, 1889–1893
Grover Cleveland, 1893–1897
William McKinley, 1897–1901
Theodore Roosevelt, 1901–1909
William H. Taft, 1909–1913
Woodrow Wilson, 1913–1921
Warren G. Harding, 1921–1923
Calvin Coolidge, 1923–1929
Herbert C. Hoover, 1929–1933
Franklin D. Roosevelt, 1933–1945
Harry S Truman, 1945–1953
Dwight D. Eisenhower, 1953–1961
John F. Kennedy, 1961–1963
Lyndon B. Johnson, 1963–1969
Richard M. Nixon, 1969–1974
Gerald R. Ford, 1974–1977
James E. Carter, Jr., 1977–1981
Ronald W. Reagan, 1981–1989
George H. W. Bush, 1989–1993
William J. Clinton, 1993–

▢ Federalist	▢ Democratic
▢ Democratic Republican	▢ Whig
	▢ Republican

Graduation Rates

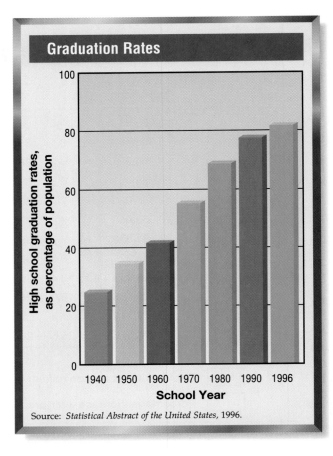

Source: *Statistical Abstract of the United States,* 1996.

Life Expectancy

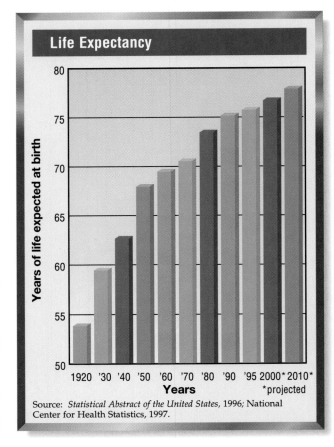

Source: *Statistical Abstract of the United States,* 1996; National Center for Health Statistics, 1997.

The United States

STATE*	YEAR ADMITTED	POPULATION (1996)	LAND AREA (sq mi)	CAPITAL	LARGEST CITY	HOUSE REP. (1996)**
1. Delaware	1787	724,842	1,954	Dover	Wilmington	1
2. Pennsylvania	1787	12,056,112	44,819	Harrisburg	Philadelphia	21
3. New Jersey	1787	7,987,933	7,418	Trenton	Newark	13
4. Georgia	1788	7,353,225	57,918	Atlanta	Atlanta	11
5. Connecticut	1788	3,274,238	4,845	Hartford	Bridgeport	6
6. Massachusetts	1788	6,092,352	7,838	Boston	Boston	10
7. Maryland	1788	5,071,604	9,774	Annapolis	Baltimore	8
8. South Carolina	1788	3,698,746	30,111	Columbia	Columbia	6
9. New Hampshire	1788	1,162,481	8,969	Concord	Manchester	2
10. Virginia	1788	6,675,451	39,597	Richmond	Virginia Beach	11
11. New York	1788	18,184,774	47,223	Albany	New York	31
12. North Carolina	1789	7,322,870	48,718	Raleigh	Charlotte	12
13. Rhode Island	1790	990,225	1,045	Providence	Providence	2
14. Vermont	1791	588,654	9,249	Montpelier	Burlington	1
15. Kentucky	1792	3,883,723	39,732	Frankfort	Louisville	6
16. Tennessee	1796	5,319,654	41,219	Nashville	Memphis	9
17. Ohio	1803	11,172,782	40,952	Columbus	Columbus	19
18. Louisiana	1812	4,350,579	43,566	Baton Rouge	New Orleans	7
19. Indiana	1816	5,840,528	35,870	Indianapolis	Indianapolis	10
20. Mississippi	1817	2,716,115	46,913	Jackson	Jackson	5
21. Illinois	1818	11,846,544	55,593	Springfield	Chicago	20
22. Alabama	1819	4,273,084	50,750	Montgomery	Birmingham	7
23. Maine	1820	1,243,316	30,864	Augusta	Portland	2
24. Missouri	1821	5,358,692	68,898	Jefferson City	Kansas City	9
25. Arkansas	1836	2,509,793	52,075	Little Rock	Little Rock	4
26. Michigan	1837	9,594,350	56,809	Lansing	Detroit	16
27. Florida	1845	14,399,985	53,997	Tallahassee	Jacksonville	23
28. Texas	1845	19,128,261	261,194	Austin	Houston	30
29. Iowa	1846	2,851,792	55,874	Des Moines	Des Moines	5
30. Wisconsin	1848	5,159,795	54,313	Madison	Milwaukee	9
31. California	1850	31,878,234	155,973	Sacramento	Los Angeles	52
32. Minnesota	1858	4,657,758	79,616	St. Paul	Minneapolis	8
33. Oregon	1859	3,203,735	96,002	Salem	Portland	5
34. Kansas	1861	2,572,150	81,823	Topeka	Wichita	4
35. West Virginia	1863	1,825,754	24,086	Charleston	Charleston	3
36. Nevada	1864	1,603,163	109,805	Carson City	Las Vegas	2
37. Nebraska	1867	1,652,093	76,877	Lincoln	Omaha	3
38. Colorado	1876	3,822,676	103,729	Denver	Denver	6
39. North Dakota	1889	643,539	68,994	Bismarck	Fargo	1
40. South Dakota	1889	732,405	75,897	Pierre	Sioux Falls	1
41. Montana	1889	879,372	145,556	Helena	Billings	1
42. Washington	1889	5,532,939	66,581	Olympia	Seattle	9
43. Idaho	1890	1,189,251	82,752	Boise	Boise	2
44. Wyoming	1890	481,400	97,104	Cheyenne	Cheyenne	1
45. Utah	1896	2,000,494	82,168	Salt Lake City	Salt Lake City	3
46. Oklahoma	1907	3,300,902	68,678	Oklahoma City	Oklahoma City	6
47. New Mexico	1912	1,713,407	121,364	Sante Fe	Albuquerque	3
48. Arizona	1912	4,428,068	113,642	Phoenix	Phoenix	6
49. Alaska	1959	607,007	570,373	Juneau	Anchorage	1
50. Hawaii	1959	1,183,723	6,423	Honolulu	Honolulu	2
District of Columbia (Washington, D.C.)	–	543,213	61	–	–	–
United States of America	–	265,283,783	3,536,341	Washington, D.C.	New York	435

* Numbers denote the order in which states were admitted.
** Number of members in House of Representatives
Source: *Population Estimates Program*, 1996.

United States Databank

Presidents of the United States

★ ★ ★ ★ ★ ★ ★ ★ ★ ★ ★ ★ ★ ★ ★

** The Republican party during this period developed into today's Democratic party. Today's Republican party originated in 1854.

George Washington

1

1789–1797

Born: 1732
Died: 1799
Born in: Virginia
Elected from: Virginia
Age when elected: 56
Occupations: Planter, Soldier
Party: None
Vice President: John Adams

John Adams

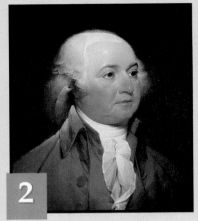

2

1797–1801

Born: 1735
Died: 1826
Born in: Massachusetts
Elected from: Massachusetts
Age when elected: 61
Occupations: Teacher, Lawyer
Party: Federalist
Vice President: Thomas Jefferson

Thomas Jefferson

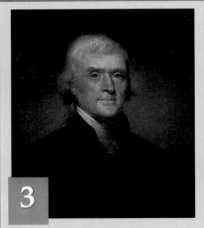

3

1801–1809

Born: 1743
Died: 1826
Born in: Virginia
Elected from: Virginia
Age when elected: 57
Occupations: Planter, Lawyer
Party: Republican**
Vice Presidents: Aaron Burr, George Clinton

James Madison

4

1809–1817

Born: 1751
Died: 1836
Born in: Virginia
Elected from: Virginia
Age when elected: 57
Occupation: Planter
Party: Republican**
Vice Presidents: George Clinton, Elbridge Gerry

James Monroe

5

1817–1825

Born: 1758
Died: 1831
Born in: Virginia
Elected from: Virginia
Age when elected: 58
Occupation: Lawyer
Party: Republican**
Vice President: Daniel D. Tompkins

John Quincy Adams

6

1825–1829

Born: 1767
Died: 1848
Born in: Massachusetts
Elected from: Massachusetts
Age when elected: 57
Occupation: Lawyer
Party: Republican**
Vice President: John C. Calhoun

Andrew Jackson

7

1829–1837

Born: 1767
Died: 1845
Born in: South Carolina
Elected from: Tennessee
Age when elected: 61
Occupations: Lawyer, Soldier
Party: Democratic
Vice Presidents: John C. Calhoun, Martin Van Buren

Martin Van Buren

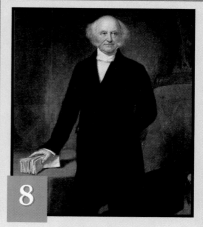

8

1837–1841

Born: 1782
Died: 1862
Born in: New York
Elected from: New York
Age when elected: 54
Occupation: Lawyer
Party: Democratic
Vice President: Richard M. Johnson

William H. Harrison

9

1841

Born: 1773
Died: 1841
Born in: Virginia
Elected from: Ohio
Age when elected: 67
Occupations: Soldier, Planter
Party: Whig
Vice President: John Tyler

John Tyler

10

1841–1845

Born: 1790
Died: 1862
Born in: Virginia
Elected as V.P. from: Virginia
Succeeded Harrison
Age when became President: 51
Occupation: Lawyer
Party: Whig
Vice President: None

James K. Polk

11

1845–1849

Born: 1795
Died: 1849
Born in: North Carolina
Elected from: Tennessee
Age when elected: 49
Occupation: Lawyer
Party: Democratic
Vice President: George M. Dallas

Presidents

Zachary Taylor

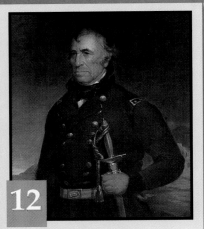

12

1849–1850

Born: 1784
Died: 1850
Born in: Virginia
Elected from: Louisiana
Age when elected: 63
Occupation: Soldier
Party: Whig
Vice President: Millard Fillmore

Millard Fillmore

13

1850–1853

Born: 1800
Died: 1874
Born in: New York
Elected as V.P. from: New York
Succeeded Taylor
Age when became President: 50
Occupation: Lawyer
Party: Whig
Vice President: None

Franklin Pierce

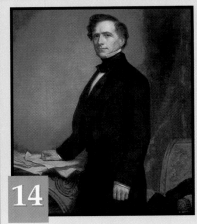

14

1853–1857

Born: 1804
Died: 1869
Born in: New Hampshire
Elected from: New Hampshire
Age when elected: 47
Occupation: Lawyer
Party: Democratic
Vice President: William R. King

James Buchanan

15

1857–1861

Born: 1791
Died: 1868
Born in: Pennsylvania
Elected from: Pennsylvania
Age when elected: 65
Occupation: Lawyer
Party: Democratic
Vice President: John C.
   Breckinridge

Abraham Lincoln

16

1861–1865

Born: 1809
Died: 1865
Born in: Kentucky
Elected from: Illinois
Age when elected: 51
Occupation: Lawyer
Party: Republican
Vice Presidents: Hannibal
   Hamlin, Andrew Johnson

Andrew Johnson

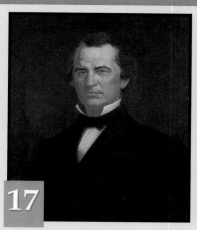

17

1865–1869

Born: 1808
Died: 1875
Born in: North Carolina
Elected as V.P. from: Tennessee
Age when became President: 56
Succeeded Lincoln
Occupation: Tailor
Party: Republican
Vice President: None

Ulysses S. Grant

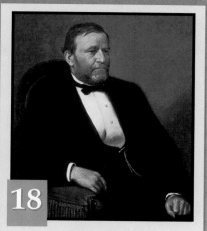

18

1869–1877

Born: 1822
Died: 1885
Born in: Ohio
Elected from: Illinois
Age when elected: 46
Occupations: Farmer, Soldier
Party: Republican
Vice Presidents: Schuyler Colfax,
Henry Wilson

Rutherford B. Hayes

19

1877–1881

Born: 1822
Died: 1893
Born in: Ohio
Elected from: Ohio
Age when elected: 54
Occupation: Lawyer
Party: Republican
Vice President: William A.
Wheeler

James A. Garfield

20

1881

Born: 1831
Died: 1881
Born in: Ohio
Elected from: Ohio
Age when elected: 49
Occupations: Laborer, Professor
Party: Republican
Vice President: Chester A. Arthur

Chester A. Arthur

21

1881–1885

Born: 1830
Died: 1886
Born in: Vermont
Elected as V.P. from: New York
Succeeded Garfield
Age when became President: 50
Occupations: Teacher, Lawyer
Party: Republican
Vice President: None

Presidents

Grover Cleveland

22 **24**

1885–89, 1893–97

Born: 1837
Died: 1908
Born in: New Jersey
Elected from: New York
Age when elected: 47; 55
Occupation: Lawyer
Party: Democratic
Vice Presidents: Thomas A.
   Hendricks, Adlai E. Stevenson

Benjamin Harrison

23

1889–1893

Born: 1833
Died: 1901
Born in: Ohio
Elected from: Indiana
Age when elected: 55
Occupation: Lawyer
Party: Republican
Vice President: Levi P. Morton

William McKinley

25

1897–1901

Born: 1843
Died: 1901
Born in: Ohio
Elected from: Ohio
Age when elected: 53
Occupations: Teacher, Lawyer
Party: Republican
Vice Presidents: Garret Hobart,
   Theodore Roosevelt

Theodore Roosevelt

26

1901–1909

Born: 1858
Died: 1919
Born in: New York
Elected as V.P. from: New York
Succeeded McKinley
Age when became President: 42
Occupations: Historian, Rancher
Party: Republican
Vice President: Charles W. Fairbanks

William H. Taft

27

1909–1913

Born: 1857
Died: 1930
Born in: Ohio
Elected from: Ohio
Age when elected: 51
Occupation: Lawyer
Party: Republican
Vice President: James S. Sherman

Presidents

Woodrow Wilson

28

1913–1921

Born: 1856
Died: 1924
Born in: Virginia
Elected from: New Jersey
Age when elected: 55
Occupation: College Professor
Party: Democratic
Vice President: Thomas R. Marshall

Warren G. Harding

29

1921–1923

Born: 1865
Died: 1923
Born in: Ohio
Elected from: Ohio
Age when elected: 55
Occupations: Newspaper Editor, Publisher
Party: Republican
Vice President: Calvin Coolidge

Calvin Coolidge

30

1923–1929

Born: 1872
Died: 1933
Born in: Vermont
Elected as V.P. from: Massachusetts
Succeeded Harding
Age when became President: 51
Occupation: Lawyer
Party: Republican
Vice President: Charles G. Dawes

Herbert C. Hoover

31

1929–1933

Born: 1874
Died: 1964
Born in: Iowa
Elected from: California
Age when elected: 54
Occupation: Engineer
Party: Republican
Vice President: Charles Curtis

Franklin D. Roosevelt

32

1933–1945

Born: 1882
Died: 1945
Born in: New York
Elected from: New York
Age when elected: 50
Occupation: Lawyer
Party: Democratic
Vice Presidents: John N. Garner, Henry A. Wallace, Harry S Truman

Presidents

Harry S Truman

33

1945–1953

Born: 1884
Died: 1972
Born in: Missouri
Elected as V.P. from: Missouri
Succeeded Roosevelt
Age when became President: 60
Occupations: Clerk, Farmer
Party: Democratic
Vice President: Alben W. Barkley

Dwight D. Eisenhower

34

1953–1961

Born: 1890
Died: 1969
Born in: Texas
Elected from: New York
Age when elected: 62
Occupation: Soldier
Party: Republican
Vice President: Richard M. Nixon

John F. Kennedy

35

1961–1963

Born: 1917
Died: 1963
Born in: Massachusetts
Elected from: Massachusetts
Age when elected: 43
Occupations: Author, Reporter
Party: Democratic
Vice President: Lyndon B. Johnson

Lyndon B. Johnson

36

1963–1969

Born: 1908
Died: 1973
Born in: Texas
Elected as V.P. from: Texas
Succeeded Kennedy
Age when became President: 55
Occupation: Teacher
Party: Democratic
Vice President: Hubert H. Humphrey

Richard M. Nixon

37

1969–1974

Born: 1913
Died: 1994
Born in: California
Elected from: New York
Age when elected: 55
Occupation: Lawyer
Party: Republican
Vice Presidents: Spiro T. Agnew,
Gerald R. Ford

Presidents

Gerald R. Ford

38

1974–1977

Born: 1913
Born in: Nebraska
Appointed by Nixon as V.P. upon Agnew's resignation; assumed presidency upon Nixon's resignation
Age when became President: 61
Occupation: Lawyer
Party: Republican
Vice President: Nelson A. Rockefeller

James E. Carter, Jr.

39

1977–1981

Born: 1924
Born in: Georgia
Elected from: Georgia
Age when elected: 52
Occupations: Business, Farmer
Party: Democratic
Vice President: Walter F. Mondale

Ronald W. Reagan

40

1981–1989

Born: 1911
Born in: Illinois
Elected from: California
Age when elected: 69
Occupations: Actor, Lecturer
Party: Republican
Vice President: George H.W. Bush

George H.W. Bush

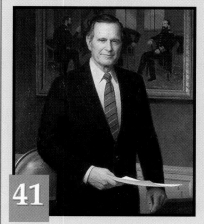

41

1989–1993

Born: 1924
Born in: Massachusetts
Elected from: Texas
Age when elected: 64
Occupation: Business
Party: Republican
Vice President: J. Danforth Quayle

William J. Clinton

42

1993–

Born: 1946
Born in: Arkansas
Elected from: Arkansas
Age when elected: 46
Occupation: Lawyer
Party: Democratic
Vice President: Albert Gore, Jr.

Presidents

When Am I Ever Going to Use This?

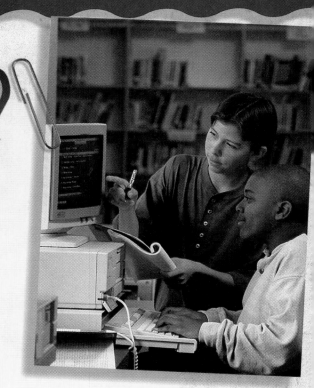

Although the world of work may seem far off, it is never too early to start thinking about what you will do when you finish your formal education. What you learn in this textbook will help you build a foundation of knowledge that will be extremely valuable to you when you start to work.

This handbook helps you start thinking about one of the most important decisions you will ever make—choosing a career. Over the past 20 years, the job market in the United States has changed dramatically. These changes will affect you. Many jobs that required little or no skills have disappeared, replaced with jobs that need a high level of many different skills. Increasingly, these new jobs need workers with good educational backgrounds, particularly in fields such as Social Studies.

Tomorrow's workers will need a broader educational background and better job skills. According to one senior executive, "The movement to a global economy means a very harsh, competitive environment. A degree of worry is legitimate, but not if you have world-class skills. You will be competing against Chinese, Russians, Poles, English, Brazilians, and Kenyans. You will have to do a better job and raise your skills."

PLANNING YOUR CAREER

You may have already started working a few hours a week while in middle school, or you may be planning to do so at some point while you are still at school. If so, you can get a head start on exploring your future career. Once you are finished with your education, work will be a major part of your life. As an adult you may spend most of your waking hours at your job, and you may work for 40 or 50 years. Having a job you enjoy becomes very important.

Identifying Your Aptitudes and Skills

Everyone has aptitudes and skills—things they naturally do well or things they have learned to do. Having good debating skills, for example, may indicate that you have an aptitude for the law. Being able to fix computers may indicate that you have an aptitude for electronics.

Different careers require different abilities. You will enjoy a career more—and probably be more successful at it—if you select an occupation that takes advantage of your skills and aptitudes. To do so, you need to think carefully about the abilities you have.

There are many different types of aptitudes. Some people have an aptitude for music; others have an aptitude for solving puzzles. Some of the types of aptitudes that may be relevant to your career are shown on the aptitude checklist.

APTITUDE CHECKLIST

✔ *General:* Ability to understand facts, opinions, and ideas

✔ *Verbal:* Ability to use words and ideas easily and clearly

✔ *Numerical:* Ability to solve math problems quickly and accurately

✔ *Spatial:* Ability to visualize shapes, heights, widths, and depths clearly

✔ *Observational:* Ability to notice details in objects and drawings

✔ *Motor:* Ability to coordinate movements of eyes, hands, and fingers

✔ *Social:* Ability to get along well with people

School to Work Activity: Assessing Your Aptitudes

On separate sheets of paper, list each of the seven types of aptitudes listed above. Then identify at least three things that you have done that reveal an aptitude in each category. If there are categories in which you feel you do not have an aptitude, omit that category. At the bottom of each page, write down at least three jobs that you think might make use of your aptitude in each category.

What Kind Career of Career Do You Want?

A career is a series of jobs related to a particular area of interest. To pursue a career, you will need to develop a set of skills. Thinking about the kind of career you might like to have will help you start obtaining these skills.

What Career Would You Be Suited For?

Choosing a career depends on many factors, including your interests and skills, your personality, your education and training, and job opportunities. Your first step in thinking about a career should be to identify what you like to do and what you are good at.

CAREER NEEDS CHECKLIST

✔ Am I a creative person? Do I want a job that will demand creativity?

✔ Do I like a regular routine, or do I prefer to perform a variety of tasks?

✔ Do I want to be involved in helping others?

✔ Do I want to make changes in society?

✔ Do I want to have power over decisions?

✔ Am I willing to work very long hours?

✔ How much do I value job security?

✔ How much do I value independence?

Career Explor

•CAREER EXPLORATIONS

Career Explorations

Researching Job Opportunities

Several sources can help you learn about different types of jobs. Three government publications are particularly helpful.

JOB RESOURCES

✔ *The Occupational Outlook Handbook* provides detailed information on 250 occupations. Included are job duties, working conditions, education and training requirements, advancement possibilities, job trends, and average earnings.

✔ *The Dictionary of Occupational Titles* lists 20,000 different jobs and is a good source for finding out about jobs you never knew about. The *Dictionary* provides detailed explanations of job responsibilities.

✔ *The Guide for Occupational Exploration* focuses on career interests and indicates the kind of jobs that match different interests. It also indicates how to prepare for a career and find a job in a particular field.

Other good sources of information are schools and libraries, which often have career resource centers, and the Internet, which has many useful Web sites. Many schools also have computerized guidance programs that you can use to find out about different careers.

Talking to people you know about their jobs is another valuable way of learning about different career opportunities. If you have friends or family who work in a field that interests you, you may want to conduct an informational interview with them.

INFORMATIONAL INTERVIEW CHECKLIST

✔ What do you do on a daily basis?
✔ What do you like most about your current job?
✔ What do you like least?
✔ What are the job qualifications for your position?
✔ What are the educational requirements?
✔ What specific skills are necessary?
✔ How did you get started in this field of work?
✔ What other kinds of organizations hire people in this field?
✔ What opportunities are there for career advancement?
✔ Does the job pay well?

School to Work Activity: Conducting an Informational Interview

Choose a job you think you would enjoy. Then try to locate someone who works in that field who would be willing to talk to you. Interview the person, using the checklist above. Then write a one-page report based on the results of your interview.

FUTURE CAREER TRENDS

The Changing Job Market

The job market has changed radically since the 1970s.

- Companies that once used American materials to produce goods exclusively for the American market now purchase materials abroad and sell their products all over the world—a trend known as globalization.
- Computerization and other technological innovations have changed the nature of the production process and the very way in which companies do business. Routine tasks, such as coding information or tightening screws, are now performed by computers or robots.
- Improvements in communications have made doing business internationally easier than ever before. Fax and Internet technologies allow firms separated by thousands of miles to communicate with each other as if they were in the same building. Overnight delivery services mean that goods can be shipped almost anywhere in the world within 24 hours.

These changes affect the United States job market in important ways:

- Many unskilled or semi-skilled manufacturing jobs are now performed abroad, where labor costs are much lower than they are in the United States. This decline in the manufacturing sector has meant that most new jobs are in the service sector. The service sector includes jobs in banking, insurance, communications, wholesaling and retailing, education, health care, engineering, architecture, construction, advertising, accounting, legal services, entertainment, tourism, and other industries in which services are provided.
- Good jobs in the United States now demand more education than they once did. Half of all new jobs created in the 1990s will require some education beyond high school, and almost a third of these jobs will require a college education.
- As many as 70 percent of the jobs created in 2010 will be jobs that do not exist today. To be ready to assume these new positions, workers will need to have broad-based educations and be flexible, innovative, and adaptable.

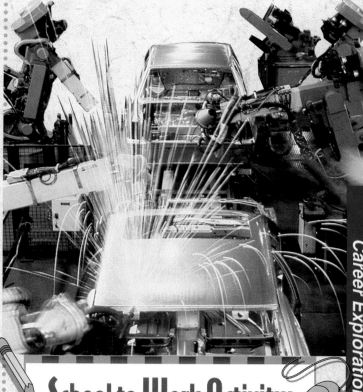

School to Work Activity: Using the Internet

Choose one of the following topics:

- Résumé writing
- Career opportunities
- Finding a job
- Interviewing for a job
- Job openings in your area

Use the Internet to research your topic. Once you have completed your research, write a one-page, paper on the topic including the Internet sites you used.

ANTIQUES DEALER

Job Description
Antiques dealers buy and sell antiques. Up to 40 percent of all antiques dealers eventually try opening and running their own shops.

Education/Training
Although specific degrees are not required, knowledge of history and art history is useful.

Salary and Outlook
Average salary: $18,500–$49,000. Job opportunities in the field are expected to remain steady.

Volunteer/Related Opportunities
Offer to help clean out the basement or storage area in your house or the house of a friend. With the aid of books and magazines, determine the age and value of the items you find there. Then prepare for and conduct a yard sale for your family.

School to Work Activity:
Visit a local antiques store, and choose one of the items on display. Ask the dealer to explain how to determine the age of the item you chose. Using a word processor, write a one-page report on the item you selected. Describe what the item is, what it was used for, where it came from, when it was created, and why it is valuable.

ARCHAEOLOGIST

Job Description
Archaeologists use scientific methods to recover and examine evidence of early human life. Some archaeologists work for museums or private corporations, but most work in universities, participating in archaeological digs when they are not teaching.

Education/Training
Archaeologists have doctoral degrees (Ph.D.s).

Salary and Outlook
Average salary: $15,000-$42,000. The number of jobs in archaeology is small, and new openings are expected only as archaeologists retire or leave the field.

Volunteer/Related Opportunities
Contact your local museum and offer to help clean displays for several Saturdays.

School to Work Activity:
Retrieve something from the garbage in your kitchen. Imagine that you are an archaeologist who discovers the item 1,000 years from now. Write a one-page paper describing what you think might be the archaeologist's insight into your culture and customs based on the item.

ARCHITECT

Job Description
Architects design buildings, ranging from houses to high-rises to hospitals and airports. Most architects work for private firms, with about a third self-employed. A few work for the government or for builders or real estate developers.

Education/Training
Architects must be licensed. To receive a license, an architect must receive a bachelor of architecture degree, complete an internship, and pass the architect registration examination.

Salary and Outlook
Average salary: $27,500–$100,000. Jobs in this field are expected to grow at an average rate through 2005.

Volunteer/Related Opportunities
Locate a local branch of a group, such as Habitat for Humanity, that rebuilds houses for the poor, and offer to help renovate a house in your neighborhood.

School to Work Activity:
Choose a building in your neighborhood or town that you find interesting. If you have a camera, take a picture of it. If you do not have a camera, sketch the building on a piece of paper. Present your photo or sketch to the class, and explain what about the building caught your eye.

ARCHIVIST

Job Description
Archivists collect and preserve documents—ranging from letters to blueprints to computer records to videotapes—for libraries, museums, and historical organizations. Archivists arrange displays and store documents electronically for use by researchers.

Education/Training
Archivists generally possess graduate degrees. Many receive dual master's degrees in subjects such as history and library science.

Salary and Outlook
Average salary: $28,300. Jobs in this field are expected to grow at an average rate through 2005. Turnover in the field is low.

Volunteer/Related Opportunities
Volunteer at your local historical society.

School to Work Activity:
Make a list of your family's important papers, such as birth certificates, adoption papers, death certificates, and passports. Create a folder, with a table of contents, for their safekeeping.

Career Explorations

ELECTED REPRESENTATIVE

Job Description
Elected representatives are chosen by voters to represent their interests in government forums. They work closely with their constituents, with interest groups, and with other members of government to identify areas of concern, establish goals for those areas, and implement plans to achieve those goals.

Education/Training
Although many legislators are lawyers, no specific educational background or degree is required to hold elected office. Many elected representatives begin working as volunteers.

Salary and Outlook
Pay varies, from nothing in some small communities to $200,000 for the President of the United States. Few new jobs will be created in this field. However, newcomers have a chance at a job every time an election is held.

Volunteer/Related Opportunities
Run for one of your class's elected offices yourself or offer to work on the campaign of another student.

School to Work Activity:
Look through your local newspaper to find four stories about local political decision making. For each issue, write a short paragraph summarizing where local politicians stand.

ENVIRONMENTALIST

Job Description
Environmentalists observe, research, and write about the state of the environment and use this information to promote legislation, protect the environment, and work toward change. Most environmentalists work for not-for-profit organizations and universities, where they aim to inform the public about environmental issues.

Education/Training
Most environmentalists have bachelor's degrees.

Salary and Outlook
Average salary: $28,500–$50,000. The number of jobs is expected to grow by 3,000 a year for the next 15 years.

Volunteer/Related Opportunities
Participate in the next clean-up day scheduled for your community.

School to Work Activity:
Call the local government agency or the private company in charge of trash removal in your area and ask for a list of items that can be recycled. Use what you learn to draw a poster encouraging recycling of all the recyclable items you have identified.

FASHION DESIGNER

Job Description
Fashion designers create new ideas and innovations for clothing. They must be knowledgeable about textiles and fashion trends, and they must be able to communicate their fashion ideas. Jobs can be found with fabric and clothing manufacturers.

Education/Training
Fashion designers usually have two- or four-year degrees in fashion design.

Salary and Outlook
Average salary: $13,500–$49,525. The number of jobs is expected to increase through 2005.

Volunteer/Related Opportunities
Volunteer to sort and exhibit donated clothing for your local thrift shop.

School to Work Activity:
Find a photograph that shows how people dressed during a particular historical period. Then write a paragraph explaining how fashion styles are different today than they were in the photograph you chose.

LAWYER

Job Description
Lawyers advise clients on legal concerns. Some lawyers handle civil matters, such as contracts and wills. Others practice criminal law, counseling clients who have been charged with crimes. Some lawyers eventually become partners in their firms or start their own businesses. Others become judges or run for public office.

Education/Training
Lawyers must receive law degrees from a law school accredited by the American Bar Association. They must also pass the bar examination of the state or states in which they plan to practice.

Salary and Outlook
Average starting salary: $29,200–$80,000; experienced lawyers average $115,000.

Since law schools continue to graduate more lawyers than there are new jobs, competition will remain stiff despite the fact that the number of jobs for lawyers is expected to rise dramatically.

Volunteer/Related Opportunities
Offer to help your school create a student review board hear cases and help determine punishments for minor student offenses.

School to Work Activity:
Attend a session of court in your area. Take notes on the proceedings. Summarize what you learn in a one-page paper.

Career Explorations

LIBRARIAN

Job Description
Librarians help people find and use information. They also select, purchase, and classify new library materials, and they manage libraries and their programs.

Education/Training
Librarians usually need master's degrees in library science. In addition, they must be familiar with computers.

Salary and Outlook
Average salary: $35,600. Slower than average growth of jobs in this field is expected through 2005.

Volunteer/Related Opportunities
Offer to work as a volunteer at your local library.

School to Work Activity:
Go to your local library and ask the librarian to help you find information on the successes and failures of President Clinton's second term. Then write a list of steps the librarian took to help you find that information.

MUSEUM STORE SALES ASSOCIATE

Job Description
Salespeople in museums stores are responsible for running the cash registers and stocking the shelves. They also may offer customers information on store items. For many, a job as a store sales associate is a first part-time or full-time job.

Education/Training
No formal education is required.

Salary and Outlook
Average salary: Minimum wage. The number of museum store sales associates will remain constant in the near future. However, the number of jobs for all sales associates will grow.

Volunteer/Related Opportunities
Volunteer to spend five lunch periods working at your school store.

School to Work Activity:
Write to a major museum and ask for a copy of its catalog. Identify one item sold by the museum and read the catalog's description. Now imagine you are a sales associate for that museum and a customer has asked you about that item. Write a paragraph explaining how you might respond.

PARK RANGER

Job Description
Park rangers perform a variety of duties at local, state, and national parks, including registering park guests, directing guests to sites and advising them regarding use of the park, and enforcing the park's laws. Park rangers also patrol the park, looking for campers in trouble or the beginnings of forest fires.

Education/Training
Park rangers usually have completed two to four years of college. Those wishing to work for the National Forest Service can apply with the U.S. Department of the Interior.

Salary and Outlook
Average salary: $18,000–$37,000. The limited number of park ranger jobs is expected to decrease, as a result of downsizing and budget cuts. Competition for these jobs will remain keen.

Volunteer/Related Opportunities
Spend a morning doing maintenance in the local park closest to your home.

School to Work Activity:
Use a map to identify one of your state's parks. Identify a site within the park to which you would direct visitors if you were a park ranger there. Then draw a poster encouraging guests to visit the site you have chosen.

POLICY ANALYST

Job Description
Policy analysts monitor state and national legislation to identify issues that may affect the organization or business for which they work. They then analyze the legislature's stand on these issues and report their analysis to their employers.

Education/Training
Policy analysts usually have bachelor's degrees. In addition, the job requires experience in legislative or policy research. Many people first work as interns before moving up to policy analysts.

Salary and Outlook
Average salary: $20,000–$40,000. Jobs in this field are expected to grow at an average rate through 2005.

Volunteer/Related Opportunities
Attend a meeting of the city council to identify issues currently affecting your area.

School to Work Activity:
Use the Internet or publications available from your local library to identify a bill recently introduced in Congress. Make a list of three groups or organizations that would be affected by this bill.

PRESERVATION SPECIALIST

Job Description
Preservation specialists preserve, repair, and catalog works of art and artifacts. They use technology such as x-rays, chemicals, and microscopes to determine an object's condition and need for repair.

Education/Training
Preservation specialists usually have master's degrees in preservation or a related field.

Salary and Outlook
Average salary for senior level: $48,900. The number of jobs for preservation specialists is expected to grow in the future, but competition will remain stiff.

Volunteer/Related Opportunities
Volunteer at your local museum and ask to see how preservation specialists perform their jobs.

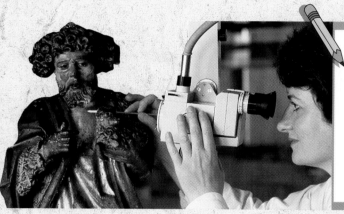

School to Work Activity:
Contact a professional cleaning company and ask how they remove stains from garments. Also ask them for tips on home remedies for removing stains. Share what you learn with the class.

PUBLIC RELATIONS SPECIALIST

Job Description
Public relations specialists attempt to influence public opinion in a positive way about a particular organization, such as a business, a hospital, a government agency, or a university.

Education/Training
Most public relations specialists hold bachelor's degrees, usually in public relations, communications, or journalism.

Salary and Outlook
Average salary: $23,000–$47,000. Jobs in this field are expected to grow at an average rate through 2005.

Volunteer/Related Opportunities
Offer to serve as public relations officer for one of your school's student government candidates.

School to Work Activity:
Look in the Sunday newspaper for advertisements for public relations specialists. Use the ads to determine what general qualifications are required for a job in the field of public relations. Then write your own imaginary response to the ad.

TEACHER (K-12)

Job Description
Kindergarten and elementary school teachers usually teach all subjects. Middle and high school instructors usually specialize in one or two subjects.

Education/Training
Teaching requires at least a bachelor's degree. In addition, to teach in a public

school an instructor must meet the teacher certification requirements in the state.

Salary and Outlook
Average salary: $36,500. Jobs for K–12 teachers are expected to increase at a faster than average rate through 2005.

Volunteer/Related Opportunities
Offer to help your history teacher prepare a lesson.

School to Work Activity:
Choose one of the historical events you have recently studied. Research and prepare a five-minute lesson on that topic. Then teach the lesson to your class.

TELEVISION REPORTER

Job Description
Television reporters follow leads, gather information, and write and present stories for television news shows.

Education/Training
Television reporters have bachelor's degrees, often in broadcast journalism, as well as some experience, frequently gained through internships.

Salary and Outlook
Average salary: $16,000–$62,000. The number of television reporter jobs is expected to remain fairly steady for the next ten years, and competition for these positions will be fierce.

Volunteer/Related Opportunities
Spend several hours volunteering at your local public access television station.

School to Work Activity:
Watch the evening news for three days, focusing on one television reporter. Keep a list of story topics covered by that reporter. Then list all the subjects that would need to be researched to present these stories.

The American Flag

★ ★

For Americans, the flag has always had a special meaning. It is a symbol of our nation's freedom and democracy.

The Flag of 1795

The flag of the United States symbolizes the nation's unity and independence. In addition, the flag stands for the hopes and ideas of the American people. Throughout its history, the American flag has undergone numerous changes. The flag of 1795 had 15 stripes, as well as 15 stars, to represent the 15 states.

Rules and Customs

Over the years, Americans have developed rules and customs concerning the use and display of the flag. One of the most important things every American should remember is to treat the flag with respect:

★ The flag should be raised and lowered by hand and displayed only from sunrise to sunset. On special occasions, it may be displayed at night.

★ The flag may be displayed on all days, weather permitting, particularly on national and state holidays and on historic and special occasions.

★ No flag should be flown above the American flag or to the right of it at the same height.

★ The flag may be flown at half-mast to mourn the death of public officials.

★ The flag should never touch the ground or floor beneath it.

★ The flag may be flown upside down only to signal distress.

★ When the flag becomes old and tattered, it should be destroyed by burning. According to an approved custom, the Union is first cut from the flag; and then the two pieces, which no longer form a flag, are burned.

Continental Colors
1775–1777

First Stars and Stripes
1777–1795

Betsy Ross Flag
c. 1790

15-Star Flag
1795–1818

20-Star Flag
1818

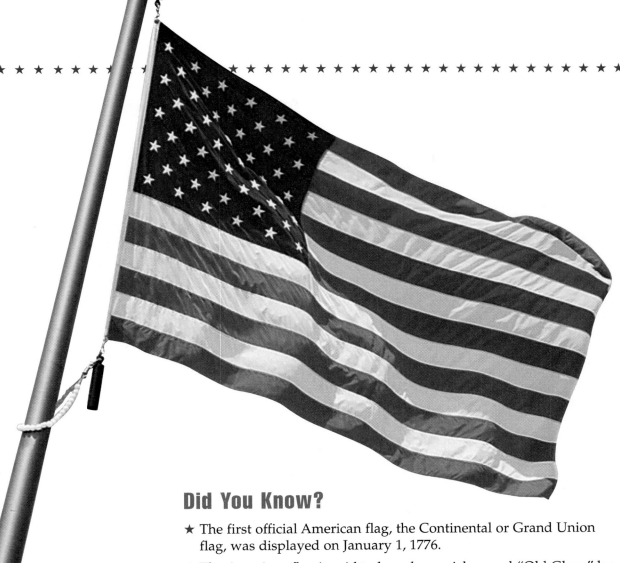

Did You Know?

★ The first official American flag, the Continental or Grand Union flag, was displayed on January 1, 1776.

★ The American flag is said to have been nicknamed "Old Glory" by William Driver, a Massachusetts sea captain.

★ The Stars and Stripes first flew around the world on the ship *Columbia of Boston* on its voyage from September 1787 to August 1790.

★ The flag was unfurled at the North Pole for the first time on April 6, 1909, by naval officer and Arctic explorer Robert Peary.

★ The flag was planted on the moon on July 20, 1969, after astronauts Neil Armstrong and Edwin Aldrin, Jr., piloted the lunar module *Eagle* to a landing on the moon's surface.

Great Star Flag
1818

35-Star Flag
1863–1865

38-Star Flag
1877–1890

48-Star Flag
1912–1959

50-Star Flag
1960

★ ★

The Magna Carta

The Magna Carta, signed by King John in 1215, marked a decisive step forward in the development of constitutional government in England. Later, it became a model for colonists who carried the Magna Carta's guarantees of legal and political rights to America.

1. That the English church shall be free, and shall have her rights entire, and her liberties inviolate; . . .

2. We also have granted to all the freemen of our kingdom, for us and for our heirs forever, all the underwritten liberties, to be had and holden by them and their heirs, of us and our heirs forever. . . .

39. No freeman shall be taken or imprisoned, or diseased, or outlawed, or banished, or in any way destroyed, nor will we pass upon him, nor will we send upon him, unless by the lawful judgment of his peers, or by the law of the land.

40. We will sell to no man, we will not deny to any man, either justice or right.

41. All merchants shall have safe and secure conduct to go out of, and to come into, England, and to stay there and to pass as well by land as by water, for buying and selling by the ancient and allowed customs, without any unjust tolls, except in time of war, or when they are of any nation at war with us. . . .

42. It shall be lawful, for the time to come, for any one to go out of our kingdom and return safely and securely by land or by water, saving his allegiance to us (unless in time of war, by some short space, for the common benefit of the realm).

60. All the aforesaid customs and liberties, which we have granted to be holden in our kingdom, as much as it belongs to us, all people of our kingdom, as well clergy as laity, shall observe, as far as they are concerned, towards their dependents.

63. . . . It is also sworn, as well on our part as on the part of the barons, that all the things aforesaid shall be observed in good faith, and without evil duplicity. Given under our hand, in the presence of the witnesses above named, and many others, in the meadow called Runnymede, between Windsor and Staines, the 15th day of June, in the 17th year of our reign.

Documents

The Mayflower Compact

On November 21, 1620, 41 colonists aboard the Mayflower *drafted this agreement. The Mayflower Compact was the first plan of self-government ever put in force in the English colonies.*

In ye name of God Amen. We whose names are underwritten, the loyall subjects of our dread soveraigne Lord King James, by ye grace of God, of Great Britaine, Franc, & Ireland king, defender of ye faith, &c. Haveing undertaken, for ye glorie of God, and advancemente of ye Christian faith and honour of our king & countrie, a voyage to plant ye first colonie in ye Northerne parts of Virginia, doe by these presents solemnly & mutualy in ye presence of God, and one of another, covenant, & combine ourselves togeather into a Civill body politick; for our better ordering, & preservation & furtherance of ye ends aforesaid; and by vertue hereof to enacte, constitute, and frame such just & equall Lawes, ordinances, Acts, constitutions, & offices, from time to time, as shall be thought most meete & convenient for ye generall good of ye colonie: unto which we promise all due submission and obedience. In witnes whereof we have hereunder subscribed our names at Cap-Codd ye -11- of November, in ye year of ye raigne of our soveraigne Lord King James of England, France, & Ireland ye eighteenth, and of Scotland ye fiftie fourth. Ano Dom. 1620.

Washington's Farewell Address

At the end of his second term as President, George Washington spoke of the dangers facing the young nation. He warned against the dangers of political parties and sectionalism, and he advised the nation against permanent alliances with other nations.

Citizens by birth or choice of a common country, that country has a right to concentrate your affections. The name of American, which belongs to you, in your national capacity, must always exalt the just pride of patriotism more than any appellation derived from local discriminations. With slight shades of difference, you have the same religion, manners, habits, and political principles. You have in a common cause fought and triumphed together. . . .

In contemplating the causes which may disturb our Union, it occurs as matter of serious concern that any ground should have been furnished for characterizing parties by geographical discriminations. . . .

No alliances, however strict between the parts, can be an adequate substitute. They must inevitably experience the infractions and interruptions which all alliances in all times have experienced. . . .

The great rule of conduct for us, in regard to foreign nations, is in extending our commercial relations to have with them as little political connection as possible. . . .

I anticipate with pleasing expectations that retreat in which I promise myself to realize . . . the sweet enjoyment of partaking, in the midst of my fellow citizens, the benign influence of good laws under a free government . . . the happy reward, as I trust, of our mutual cares, labors, and dangers.

The Star-Spangled Banner

During the British bombardment of Fort McHenry during the War of 1812, a young Baltimore lawyer named Francis Scott Key was inspired to write the words to "The Star-Spangled Banner." Although it became popular immediately, it was not until 1931 that Congress officially declared "The Star-Spangled Banner" as our national anthem.

O! say can you see, by the dawn's early light,
What so proudly we hail'd at the twilight's last gleaming,
Whose broad stripes and bright stars through the perilous fight,
O'er the ramparts we watched, were so gallantly streaming?
And the Rockets' red glare, the Bombs bursting in air,
Gave proof through the night that our Flag was still there;
O! say, does that star-spangled banner yet wave
O'er the Land of the free and the home of the brave!

The Monroe Doctrine

In an 1823 address to Congress, President James Monroe proclaimed what has become known as the Monroe Doctrine. The doctrine was designed to end European influence in the Western Hemisphere. In addition, it showed the world the American spirit of strength and unity, and became a cornerstone of United States foreign policy.

. . . With the existing colonies or dependencies of any European power we have not interfered and shall not interfere. But with the governments who have declared their independence and maintained it, and whose independence we have, on great consideration and on just principles, acknowledged, we could not view any interposition for the purpose of oppressing them, or controlling in any other manner their destiny, by any European power in any other light than as the manifestation of any unfriendly disposition toward the United States. . . .

Our policy in regard to Europe, which was adopted at an early stage of the wars which have so long agitated that quarter of the globe, nevertheless remains the same, which is not to interfere in the internal concerns of any of its powers; to consider the government de facto as the legitimate government for us; to cultivate friendly relations with it, and to preserve those relations by a frank, firm, and manly policy, meeting in all instances the just claims of every power, submitting to injuries from none. . . .

Memorial and Protest of the Cherokee Nation

While Native Americans were being forced from their homeland, Cherokee leaders put their protest before the United States Senate. Their call for justice went unheard.

It cannot be concealed that the situation of the Cherokees is peculiarly distressing. In adverting to that situation it is not done to arouse, at this late day, a useless sympathy, but only as matter of history, and from necessity in giving a fair and impartial illustration of their difficulties. It is well known to those who have paid any attention to their history for the last five years, that they have been contending for the faithful execution of treaties between their nation and the United States, and that their distresses have not been mitigated; their efforts seem to have increased their difficulties. It remains for them to seek an adjustment by treaty, and an equitable acknowledgement of their rights and claims, so far as circumstances will permit.

For this purpose, this delegation has been deputed, as the proper organ of the Cherokee people, to settle, by treaty, their difficulties; and they wish, in sincerity, to have them settled, for the good, peace, and harmony of the whole nation.

The Seneca Falls Declaration

One of the first documents to express the desire for equal rights for women is the Declaration of Sentiments and Resolutions, issued in 1848 at the Seneca Falls Convention in New York. Led by Lucretia Mott and Elizabeth Cady Stanton, the delegates adopted a set of resolutions that called for woman suffrage and opportunities in employment and education. Excerpts from the Declaration follow.

When, in the course of human events, it becomes necessary for one portion of the family of man to assume among the people of the earth a position different from that which they have hitherto occupied, but one to which the laws of nature and of nature's God entitle them, a decent respect to the opinions of mankind requires that they should declare the causes that impel them to such a course.

We hold these truths to be self-evident: that all men and women are created equal; that they are endowed by their Creator with certain inalienable rights; that among these are life, liberty, and the pursuit of happiness; that to secure these rights governments are instituted, deriving their just powers from the consent of the governed. Whenever any form of government becomes destructive of these ends, it is the right of those who suffer from it to refuse allegiance to it, and to insist upon the institution of a new government, laying its foundation on such principles, and organizing its powers in such form, as to them shall seem most likely to effect their safety and happiness. Prudence, indeed, will dictate that governments long established should not be changed for light and transient causes; . . . But when a long train of abuses and usurpations, pursuing invariably the same object, evinces a design to reduce them under absolute despotism, it is their duty to throw off such government and to provide new guards for their future security. . . .

The history of mankind is a history of repeated injuries and usurpations on the part of man toward woman, having in direct object the establishment of an absolute tyranny over her. To prove this, let facts be submitted to a candid world. . . .

Now, in view of the entire disfranchisement of one-half the people of this country, their social and religious degradation, in view of the unjust laws above mentioned, and because women do feel themselves aggrieved, oppressed, and fraudulently deprived of their most sacred rights, we insist that they have immediate admission to all the rights and privileges which belong to them as citizens of the United States. . . .

The Emancipation Proclamation

On January 1, 1863, President Abraham Lincoln issued the Emancipation Proclamation, which freed all slaves in states under Confederate control. The Proclamation was a significant step toward the Thirteenth Amendment (1865) that ended slavery in all of the United States.

Whereas on the 22d day of September, A.D. 1862, a proclamation was issued by the President of the United States, containing among other things, the following, to wit: That on the 1st day of January, in the year of our Lord 1863, all persons held as slaves within any state or designated part of a state, the people whereof shall then be in rebellion against the United States, shall be then, thenceforward, and forever free; and the executive government of the United States, including the military and naval authority thereof, will recognize and maintain the freedom of such persons and will do no act or acts to repress such persons, or any of them, in any efforts they may make for their actual freedom.

That the executive will, on the 1st day of January aforesaid, by proclamation, designate the states and parts of states, if any, in which the people thereof, respectively, shall then be in rebellion against the United States; and the fact that any state or the people thereof shall on that day be in good faith represented in the Congress of the United States by members chosen thereto at elections wherein a majority of the qualified voters of such states shall have participated shall, in the absence of strong countervailing testimony, be deemed conclusive evidence that such state and the people thereof are not then in rebellion against the United States. . . .

And, by virtue of the power and for the purpose aforesaid, I do order and declare that all persons held as slaves within said designated states and parts of states are, and henceforward shall be, free; and that the executive government of the United States, including the military and naval authorities thereof, will recognize and maintain the freedom of said persons.

And I hereby enjoin upon the people so declared to be free to abstain from all violence, unless in necessary self-defense; and I recommend to them that, in all cases when allowed, they labor faithfully for reasonable wages.

And I further declare and make known that such persons of suitable condition will be received into the armed service of the United States to garrison forts, positions, stations, and other places, and to man vessels of all sorts in said service. . . .

The Gettysburg Address

On November 19, 1863, President Abraham Lincoln gave a short speech at the dedication of a national cemetery on the battlefield of Gettysburg. His simple yet eloquent words expressed his hopes for a nation divided by civil war.

Four score and seven years ago our fathers brought forth on this continent a new nation, conceived in liberty, and dedicated to the proposition that all men are created equal.

Now we are engaged in a great civil war, testing whether that nation or any nation so conceived and so dedicated can long endure. We are met on a great battlefield of that war. We have come to dedicate a portion of that field as a final resting place for those who here gave their lives that that nation might live. It is altogether fitting and proper that we should do this.

But, in a larger sense, we can not dedicate—we can not consecrate—we can not hallow—this ground. The brave men, living and dead, who struggled here have consecrated it far beyond our poor power to add or detract. The world will little note nor long remember what we say here, but it can never forget what they did here. It is for us, the living, rather, to be dedicated here to the unfinished work which they who fought here have thus far so nobly advanced.

It is rather for us to be here dedicated to the great task remaining before us—that from these honored dead we take increased devotion to that cause for which they gave the last full measure of devotion; that we here highly resolve that these dead shall not have died in vain; that this nation, under God, shall have a new birth of freedom; and that government of the people, by the people, and for the people, shall not perish from the earth.

I Will Fight No More

In 1877 the Nez Perce Indians fought the government's attempt to move them to a smaller reservation. After a remarkable attempt to escape to Canada, Chief Joseph realized that resistance was hopeless and advised his people to surrender.

Tell General Howard I know his heart. What he told me before I have in my heart. I am tired of fighting. Our chiefs are killed. Looking Glass is dead. It is the young men who say yes or no. He who led the young men is dead. It is cold and we have no blankets. The little children are freezing to death. My people, some of them have run away to the hills and have no blankets, no food; no one knows where they are—perhaps freezing to death. I want to have time to look for my children and see how many I can find. Maybe I shall find them among the dead. Hear me my chiefs. I am tired; my heart is sick and sad. From where the sun now stands, I will fight no more forever.

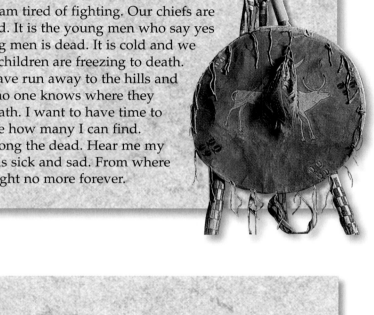

The Pledge of Allegiance

In 1892 the nation celebrated the 400th anniversary of Columbus's landing in America. In connection with this celebration, Francis Bellamy, a magazine editor, wrote and published the Pledge of Allegiance. The words "under God" were added by Congress in 1954 at the urging of President Dwight D. Eisenhower.

I pledge allegiance to the Flag of the United States of America and to the Republic for which it stands, one Nation under God, indivisible, with liberty and justice for all.

The Fourteen Points

On January 8, 1918, President Woodrow Wilson went before Congress to offer a statement of aims called the Fourteen Points. Wilson's plan called for freedom of the seas in peace and war, an end to secret alliances, and equal trading rights for all countries. The excerpt that follows is taken from the President's message.

. . . We entered this war because violations of right had occurred which touched us to the quick and made the life of our own people impossible unless they were corrected and the world secured once for all against their recurrence. What we demand in this war, therefore, is nothing peculiar to ourselves. It is that the world be made fit and safe to live in; and particularly that it be made safe for every peace-loving nation which, like our own, wishes to live its own life, determine its own institutions, be assured of justice and fair dealings by the other peoples of the world, as against force and selfish aggression. All the peoples of the world are in effect partners in this interest, and for our own part we see very clearly that unless justice be done to others it will not be done to us.

The program of the world's peace, therefore, is our program, and that program, the only possible program, as we see it, is this:

I. Open covenants of peace, openly arrived at, after which there shall be no private international understandings of any kind, but diplomacy shall proceed always frankly and in the public view.

II. Absolute freedom of navigation upon the seas, outside territorial waters, alike in peace and in war, except as the seas may be closed in whole or in part by international action for the enforcement of international covenants.

III. The removal, so far as possible, of all economic barriers and the establishment of an equality of trade conditions among all the nations consenting to the peace and associating themselves for its maintenance.

IV. Adequate guarantees given and taken that national armaments will be reduced to the lowest point consistent with domestic safety.

V. Free, open-minded, and absolutely impartial adjustment of all colonial claims, based upon a strict observance of the principle that in determining all such questions of sovereignty the interests of the population concerned must have equal weight with the equitable claims of the Government whose title is to be determined. . . .

XIV. A general association of nations must be formed under specific covenants for the purpose of affording mutual guarantees of political independence and territorial integrity to great and small states alike. . . .

Brown v. Board of Education

On May 17, 1954, the Supreme Court ruled in Brown *v.* Board of Education *that racial segregation in public schools was unconstitutional. This decision provided the legal basis for court challenges to segregation in every aspect of American life.*

The plaintiffs contend that segregated public schools are not "equal" and cannot be made "equal," and that hence they are deprived of the equal protection of the laws. Because of the obvious importance of the question presented, the Court took jurisdiction. . . .

Our decision . . . cannot turn on merely a comparison of these tangible factors in the Negro and white schools involved in each of the cases. We must look instead to the effect of segregation itself on public education.

In approaching this problem, we cannot turn the clock back to 1868 when the Amendment was adopted, or even to 1896 when *Plessy v. Ferguson* was written. We must consider public education in the light of its full development and its present place in American life throughout the nation. Only in this way can it be determined if segregation in public schools deprives these plaintiffs of the equal protection of the laws.

Today, education is perhaps the most important function of state and local governments. Compulsory school attendance laws and the great expenditures for education both demonstrate our recognition of the importance of education to our democratic society. . . . In these days, it is doubtful that any child may reasonably be expected to succeed in life if he is denied the opportunity of an education. Such an opportunity, where the state has undertaken to provide it, is a right which must be made available to all on equal terms.

We come then to the question presented: Does segregation of children in public schools solely on the basis of race, even though the physical facilities and other "tangible" factors may be equal, deprive the children of the minority group of equal educational opportunities? We believe that it does.

. . . .We conclude that in the field of public education the doctrine of "separate but equal" has no place. Separate educational facilities are inherently unequal. Therefore, we hold that the plaintiffs and others similarly situated for whom the actions have been brought are, by reason of the segregation complained of, deprived of the equal protection of the laws guaranteed by the Fourteenth Amendment. . . .

I Have a Dream

On August 28, 1963, while Congress debated wide-ranging civil rights legislation, Martin Luther King, Jr., led more than 200,000 people on a march on Washington, D.C. On the steps of the Lincoln Memorial he gave a stirring speech in which he eloquently spoke of his dreams for African Americans and for the United States. Excerpts of the speech follow.

. . . There are those who are asking the devotees of civil rights, "When will you be satisfied?"

We can never be satisfied as long as the Negro is the victim of the unspeakable horrors of police brutality. . . .We cannot be satisfied as long as the Negro's basic mobility is from a smaller ghetto to a larger one. We can never be satisfied as long as a Negro in Mississippi cannot vote and a Negro in New York believes he has nothing for which to vote. . . .

I say to you today, my friends, that in spite of the difficulties and frustrations of the moment I still have a dream. It is a dream deeply rooted in the American dream.

I have a dream that one day this nation will rise up and live out the true meaning of its creed, "We hold these truths to be self-evident, that all men are created equal."

I have a dream that one day on the red hills of Georgia the sons of former slaves and the sons of former slaveowners will be able to sit down together at the table of brotherhood.

I have a dream that one day even the state of Mississippi, a desert state sweltering with the heat of injustice and oppression, will be transformed into an oasis of freedom and justice.

I have a dream that my four little children will one day live in a nation where they will not be judged by the color of their skin, but by the content of their character. . . .

. . . When we let freedom ring, when we let it ring from every village and every hamlet, from every state and every city, we will be able to speed up that day when all of God's children, black men and white men, Jews and Gentiles, Protestants and Catholics, will be able to join hands and sing in the words of the old Negro spiritual: "Free at last! Free at last! Thank God Almighty, we are free at last!"

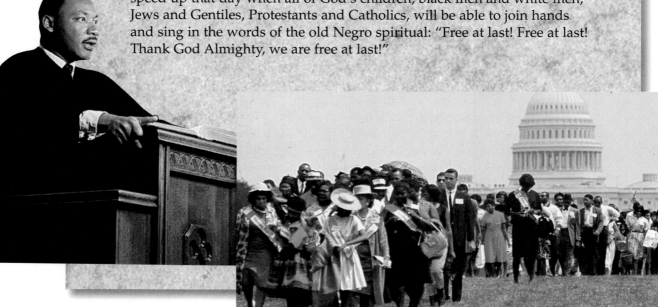

Gazetteer

★ ★

The gazetteer is a geographical dictionary that lists political divisions, natural features, and other places and locations. Following each entry is a description, its latitude and longitude, and a page reference that indicates where each entry may be found in this text.

A

Africa continent of the Eastern Hemisphere south of the Mediterranean Sea and adjoining Asia on its northeastern border (10°N/22°E) 70

Alabama state in the southeastern United States; 22nd state to enter the Union (32°45'N/87°30'W) 22

Alaska state in the United States, located in northwestern North America; territory purchased from Russia in 1867 (64°N/150°W) 22

Albany capital of New York located in the Hudson Valley; site where Albany Congress proposed first formal plan to unite the 13 colonies (40°45'N/73°45'W) 186

Allegheny River river in western Pennsylvania uniting with the Monongahela River at Pittsburgh to form the Ohio River (40°N/82°W) 186

Andes Mountains mountain system extending along western coast of South America (13°S/75°W) 53

Antarctica continent located around the South Pole (80°15'S/127°E) 15

Antietam Civil War battle site in western Maryland (39°45'N/77°30'W) 576

Appalachian Mountains chief mountain system in eastern North America extending from Quebec and New Brunswick to central Alabama (37°N/82°W) 22

Appomattox Court House site in central Virginia where Confederate forces surrendered ending the Civil War (37°N/77°W) 596

Arctic Ocean ocean in the northernmost part of the world (85°N/170°E) 22

Arizona state in the southwestern United States; 48th state to enter the Union (34°N/113°W) 110

Arkansas state in the south central United States; acquired as part of Louisiana Purchase (34°45'N/93°45'W) 22

Asia continent of the Eastern Hemisphere forming a single landmass with Europe (50°N/100°E) 15

Atlanta capital of Georgia located in the northwest central part of the state (33°45'N/84°30'W) 490

Atlantic Ocean ocean separating North and South America from Europe and Africa (5°S/25°W) 22

Australia continent and country southeast of Asia (25°S/125°E) 15

B

Baltimore city on the Chesapeake Bay in central Maryland (39°15'N/76°45'W) 161

Barbary Coast north coast of Africa between Morocco and Tunisia (36°45'N/3°E) 369

Baton Rouge capital of Louisiana located on the Mississippi River in the southeastern part of the state (30°30'N/91°15'W) 408

Black Hills mountains in southwestern South Dakota; site of conflict between the Sioux and white settlers during 1870s (44°15'N/103°45'W) 365

Boston capital of Massachusetts located in the eastern part of the state; founded by English Puritans in 1630 (42°15'N/71°W) 143

C

California state in the western United States; attracted thousands of miners during gold rush of 1849 (38°15'N/121°15'W) 110

Canada country in northern North America (50°N/100°W) 242

Charleston city in South Carolina on the Atlantic coast; original name Charles Town (32°45'N/80°W) 143

Chesapeake Bay inlet of the Atlantic Ocean in Virginia and Maryland (37°N/76°W) 226

Chicago largest city in Illinois; located in northeastern part of the state along Lake Michigan (41°45'N/87°30'W) 395

China country in eastern Asia; mainland (People's Republic of China) under communist control since 1949 (36°45'N/93°E) 66

Cincinnati city in southern Ohio on the Ohio River; grew as result of increasing steamship traffic during the mid-1800s (39°15'N/84°30'W) 395

Colorado state in the western United States (39°30'N/107°W) 110

Columbia River river flowing through southwest Canada and northwestern United States into the Pacific Ocean (46°15'N/124°W) 365

Concord village northwest of Boston, Massachusetts; site of early battle of the American Revolution on April 19, 1775 (42°N/71°W) 199

Connecticut state in the northeastern United States; one of the original 13 states (41°45'N/73°15'W) 143

Cuba country in the West Indies, North America (22°N/79°W) 77

D

Delaware state in the northeastern United States; one of the original 13 states (38°45'N/75°30'W) 143

Detroit city in southeastern Michigan; site of significant battles during the French and Indian War and the War of 1812 (42°15'N/82°15'W) 378

E

England division of the United Kingdom of Great Britain and Northern Ireland (56°30'N/1°45'W) 82

Erie Canal waterway connecting the Hudson River with Lake Erie through New York State (43°N/76°W) 396

Erie, Lake one of the Great Lakes between Canada and the United States (42°15'N/81°30'W) 108

Europe continent of the northern part of the Eastern Hemisphere between Asia and the Atlantic Ocean (50°N/15°E) 15

F

Florida state in the southeastern United States (30°30'N/84°45'W) 102

Fort Duquesne French fort on the site of Pittsburgh, Pennsylvania (40°30'N/80°W) 186

Fort Sumter Union fort on island near Charleston, South Carolina; site of first military engagement of Civil War (32°45'N/80°W) 567

France country in western Europe (49°45'N/0°45'E) 82

Fredericksburg city and Civil War battle site in northeast Virginia (38°15'N/77°30'W) 578

Freeport city in northern Illinois; site of 1858 Lincoln-Douglas debate (42°15'N/89°30'W) 555

G

Georgia state in the southeastern United States (32°45'N/83°45'W) 143

Germany country in central Europe; divided after World War II into East Germany and West Germany; unified in 1989 (50°N/10°E) 675

Gettysburg city and Civil War battle site in south central Pennsylvania; site where Lincoln delivered the Gettysburg Address (39°45'N/77°15'W) 579

Great Britain commonwealth comprising England, Scotland, and Wales (56°30'N/1°45'W) 178

Great Lakes chain of five lakes, Superior, Erie, Michigan, Ontario, and Huron, in central North America (45°N/87°W) 108

Great Plains flat grassland in the central United States (45°N/104°W) 22

Great Salt Lake lake in northern Utah with no outlet and strongly saline waters (41°15'N/112°45'W) 127

H

Harpers Ferry town in northern West Virginia on the Potomac River (39°15'N/77°45'W) 557

Hartford capital of Connecticut located on the Connecticut River in the central part of the state (41°45'N/72°45'W) 143

Hawaii state in the United States located in the Pacific Ocean (20°N/157°W) 22

Hiroshima city in southern Japan; site of first military use of atomic bomb, August 6, 1945 (34°15'N/132°30'E) 677

Hispaniola island in the West Indies in North America, where Haiti and the Dominican Republic are located (17°30'N/73°15'W) 77

Hudson Bay large bay in northern Canada (60°N/86°W) 108

Hudson River river flowing through New York State into the Atlantic Ocean at New York City (52°45'N/74°W) 226

Huron, Lake one of the Great Lakes between the United States and Canada in North America (45°15'N/82°45'W) 108

I

Illinois state in the north central United States; one of the states formed in the Northwest Territory (40°30'N/90°45'W) 22

Indian Territory land reserved by the United States government for Native Americans, now the state of Oklahoma (36°N/98°15'W) 490

Indiana state in the north central United States; one of the states formed in the Northwest Territory (39°45'N/86°45'W) 22

Iowa state in the north central United States acquired as part of the Louisiana Purchase (42°N/94°15'W) 22

Italy country in southern Europe along the Mediterranean Sea (44°N/11°15'E) 86

J

Jamestown first permanent English settlement in North America; located in southeastern Virginia (37°15'N/76°45'W) 143

Gazetteer

Japan island country in eastern Asia (36°30'N/133°30'E) 66

K

Kansas state in the central United States; fighting over slavery issue in 1850s gave territory the name "Bleeding Kansas" (38°30'N/98°45'W) 22

Kentucky state in the south central United States; border state that sided with the Union during the Civil War (37°30'N/87°30'W) 22

Kings Mountain Revolutionary War battle site in northern South Carolina (35°15'N/81°15'W) 234

Korea peninsula in eastern Asia between China, Russia, and the Sea of Japan, on which are located the countries of North Korea and South Korea (38°15'N/127°30'E) 680

Kuwait country of the Middle East in southwestern Asia between Iraq and Saudi Arabia (29°N/47°45'E) 685

L

Lexington Revolutionary War battle site in eastern Massachusetts; site of first clash between colonists and British, April 19, 1775 (42°26'N/71°13'W) 199

Little Rock capital of Arkansas located in the center of the state; site of 1957 conflict over public school integration (34°45'N/92°15'W) 490

London capital of United Kingdom located in the southeastern part of England (51°30'N/0°15'W) 181

Los Angeles city along the Pacific coast in southern California; industrial, financial, and trade center of western United States (34°N/118°15'W) 110

Louisiana state in the south central United States (30°45'N/92°45'W) 22

Louisiana Territory region of west central United States between the Mississippi River and the Rocky Mountains purchased from France in 1803 (40°N/95°W) 191

M

Maine state in the northeastern United States; 23rd state to enter the Union (45°30'N/69°45'W) 161

Maryland state in the eastern United States; one of the original 13 states (39°15'N/76°30'W) 143

Massachusetts state in the northeastern United States; one of the original 13 states (42°15'N/72°30'W) 143

Mediterranean Sea sea between Europe and Africa (36°15'N/13°30'E) 70

Mexico country in North America south of the United States (23°45'N/104°W) 53

Mexico, Gulf of gulf south of the United States and east of Mexico in North America (25°15'N/93°45'W) 53

Michigan state in the north central United States; one of the states formed in the Northwest Territory (45°N/85°W) 22

Michigan, Lake one of the five Great Lakes located in the north central United States (43°15'N/87°15'W) 108

Minnesota state in the north central United States; fur trade, good soil, and lumber attracted early settlers (46°15'N/96°15'W) 29

Mississippi state in the southeastern United States; became English territory after French and Indian War (32°30'N/89°45'W) 29

Mississippi River river flowing through the United States from Minnesota to the Gulf of Mexico; explored by French in 1600s (29°N/89°W) 184

Missouri state in the south central United States; petition for statehood resulted in sectional conflict and the Missouri Compromise (40°45'N/93°W) 29

Missouri River river flowing through the United States from the Rocky Mountains to the Mississippi River near St. Louis (38°45'N/90°15'W) 184

Montana state in the northwestern United States; cattle industry grew during 1850s (47°15'N/111°45'W) 29

Montgomery capital of Alabama; site of 1955 bus boycott to protest segregation (32°30'N/86°15'W) 490

Montreal city on the St. Lawrence River in southern Quebec, Canada (45°30'N/73°30'W) 108

N

Nashville capital of Tennessee located in the north central part of the state (36°15'N/86°45'W) 395

Natchez city in western Mississippi along the Mississippi River (31°30'N/91°15'W) 395

National Road road from Baltimore, Maryland, to Vandalia, Illinois (40°N/81°30'W) 395

Nebraska state in the central United States (41°45'N/101°30'W) 22

Netherlands country in northwestern Europe (53°N/4°E) 82

Nevada state in the western United States (39°30'N/117°W) 22

New Amsterdam town founded on Manhattan Island by Dutch settlers in 1625; renamed New York by British settlers (40°45'N/74°W) 109

New Hampshire state in northeastern United States; one of the original 13 states (44°N/71°45'W) 143

New Jersey state in the northeastern United States; one of the original 13 states (40°30'N/74°45'W) 143

New Mexico state in the southwestern United States; ceded to the United States by Mexico in 1848 (34°30'N/107°15'W) 110

New Orleans city in southern Louisiana in the Mississippi Delta (30°N/90°W) 364

New York state in the northeastern United States; one of the original 13 states (42°45'N/78°W) 143

New York City city in southeastern New York State at the mouth of the Hudson River; largest city in the United States (40°45'N/74°W) 143

Normandy region along French coast and site of D-Day invasion, June 6, 1944 (48°N/2°W) 676

North America continent in the northern part of the Western Hemisphere between the Atlantic and Pacific oceans (45°N/100°W) 40

North Carolina state in the southeastern United States; one of the original 13 states (35°45'N/81°30'W) 143

North Dakota state in the north central United States; Congress created Dakota Territory in 1861 (47°15'N/102°W) 22

Northwest Territory territorial division north of the Ohio River and east of the Mississippi River (47°30'N/87°30'W) 373

O

Ohio state in the north central United States; first state in Northwest Territory (40°30'N/83°15'W) 22

Ohio River river flowing from Allegheny and Monongahela rivers in western Pennsylvania into the Mississippi River (39°N/85°W) 134

Ohio Valley valley of the Ohio River, which flows from Pennsylvania to the Mississippi River at Cairo, Illinois (37°30'N/88°W) 373

Oklahoma state in the south central United States; Five Civilized Tribes moved to territory 1830–1842 (36°N/98°15'W) 22

Ontario, Lake one of the five Great Lakes between Canada and the United States (43°30'N/79°W) 108

Oregon state in the northwestern United States; adopted woman suffrage in 1912 (43°45'N/123°45'W) 22

Oregon Trail pioneer trail from Independence, Missouri, to the Oregon Territory (42°30'N/110°W) 464

P

Pacific Ocean world's largest ocean located between Asia and the Americas (0°/175°W) 22

Pearl Harbor naval base at Honolulu, Hawaii; site of 1941 Japanese attack, leading to United States entry into World War II (21°21'N/157°57'W) 675

Pennsylvania state in the northeastern United States (41°N/78°15'W) 143

Philadelphia city in eastern Pennsylvania on the Delaware River; Declaration of Independence and the Constitution both adopted in city's Independence Hall (40°N/75°W) 143

Pittsburgh city in western Pennsylvania; one of the great steelmaking centers of the world (40°30'N/80°W) 396

Plymouth town in eastern Massachusetts; first successful English colony in New England (42°N/70°45'W) 143

Portugal country in southwestern Europe (38°15'N/8°15'W) 82

Potomac River river flowing from West Virginia into Chesapeake Bay (38°N/77°W) 378

Promontory Point site in Utah where the first transcontinental railroad was completed (41°45'N/112°15'W) 638

Providence capital of Rhode Island; site of first English settlement in Rhode Island (41°45'N/71°30'W) 143

Puerto Rico United States possession in the West Indies (18°15'N/66°45'W) 77

Q

Quebec city in Canada, capital of Quebec Province, on the St. Lawrence River; first settlement in New France (46°45'N/71°15'W) 103

R

Raleigh capital of North Carolina located in the north central part of the state (35°45'N/78°45'W) 395

Rhode Island state in the northeastern United States; one of the original 13 states (41°30'N/71°45'W) 22

Richmond capital of Virginia located in the central part of the state; capital of the Confederacy during the Civil War (37°30'N/77°30'W) 234

Rio Grande river between the United States and Mexico in North America; forms the boundary between Texas and Mexico (26°N/97°30'W) 21

Roanoke island off the coast of present-day North Carolina that was site of early British colonizing efforts (35°N/75°39'W) 143

Rocky Mountains mountain range in western United States and Canada in North America (50°N/114°W) 22

Russia name of republic; former empire of eastern Europe and northern Asia coinciding with Soviet Union (60°30'N/64°E) 445

S

St. Augustine city in northeastern Florida on the Atlantic coast; oldest permanent existing European settlement in North America, founded in 1565 (30°N/81°15'W) 102

St. Lawrence River river flowing from Lake Ontario, between Canada and the United States, through Canada to the Atlantic Ocean (48°N/65°15'W) 378

St. Louis city in eastern Missouri on the Mississippi River (38°45'N/90°15'W) 364

Salt Lake City capital of Utah located in the northern part of the state; founded by Mormons in 1847 (40°45'N/111°45'W) 463

San Antonio city in south central Texas (29°30'N/98°30'W) 110

Santa Fe capital of New Mexico located in the north central part of the state (35°45'N/106°W) 102

Saratoga Revolutionary War battle site in the Hudson Valley of eastern New York State (43°N/73°51'W) 226

Seneca Falls town in New York State; site of 1848 woman's rights convention (43°N/77°W) 495

Sierra Nevada mountain range in eastern California (39°N/120°W) 127

South Africa country in southern Africa (28°S/24°45'E) 538

South Carolina state in the southeastern United States; one of the original 13 states (34°15'N/81°15'W) 143

South Dakota state in the north central United States; acquired through the Louisiana Purchase (44°15'N/102°W) 22

Soviet Union former country in northern Europe and Asia (60°30'N/64°E) 679

Spain country in southwestern Europe (40°15'N/4°30'W) 77

Superior, Lake one of the five Great Lakes between Canada and the United States in North America (47°45'N/89°15'W) 108

T

Tennessee state in the south central United States; first state readmitted to the Union after the Civil War (35°45'N/88°W) 22

Tenochtitlán Aztec capital on the site of present-day Mexico City (19°30'N/99°15'W) 53

Texas state in the south central United States; Mexican colony that became an independent republic before joining the United States (31°N/101°W) 22

Trenton capital of New Jersey located on the Delaware River; site of Revolutionary War battle in December 1776 (40°15'N/74°45'W) 226

U

Union of Soviet Socialist Republics *See* Soviet Union.

United States country in central North America; fourth largest country in the world in both area and population (38°N/110°W) 22

Utah state in the western United States; settled by Mormons in 1840s (39°30'N/112°45'W) 110

V

Valley Forge Revolutionary War winter camp northwest of Philadelphia (40°N/75°30'W) 226

Veracruz city in eastern Mexico on the Gulf of Mexico coast (19°15'N/96°W) 460

Vermont state in the northeastern United States; 14th state to enter the Union (43°45'N/72°45'W) 22

Vicksburg city and Civil War battle site in western Mississippi on the Mississippi River (32°21'N/90°52'W) 585

Vietnam country in southeastern Asia (16°N/108°E) 681

Virginia state in the eastern United States; colony in which first permanent English settlement in the Americas was established (37°N/78°W) 143

W

Washington state in the northwestern United States; territory reached by Lewis and Clark in 1805 (47°30'N/121°15'W) 22

Washington, D.C. capital of the United States located on the Potomac River at its confluence with the Anacostia River, between Maryland and Virginia; coinciding with the District of Columbia (38°53'N/77°02'W) 226

West Virginia state in the east central United States (39°N/80°45'W) 22

Wisconsin state in the north central United States; passed first state unemployment compensation act, 1932 (44°30'N/91°W) 22

Wyoming state in the western United States; territory provided women the right to vote, 1869 (42°45'N/108°30'W) 22

Y

Yorktown town in southeastern Virginia; site of final battle of Revolutionary War (37°15'N/76°30'W) 234

Glossary

★ ★

A

abolitionist person who wanted to end slavery (p. 488)

adobe building material made of earth and straw (p. 43)

Age of Exploration a period during the 1400s and 1500s during which many explorers sailed the oceans and mapped the world (p. 70)

Albany Plan of Union a plan proposed by Benjamin Franklin that called for a council of delegates from each colony with a leader appointed by the British king (p. 186)

alien foreigner living in the United States (p. 346)

amendment alteration, or written change, to a document (pp. 271, 279)

American System system proposed by Henry Clay that aimed to help the economy of each section of the country and increase the power of the federal government (p. 400)

amnesty act of a government by which pardon is granted to an individual or a group; official forgiveness of crimes (p. 605)

annex to add or make a part of (p. 449)

apprentice one who is bound to a master without pay to learn a craft or trade (p. 161)

aqueduct channel or pipe for flowing water (p. 55)

archaeologist scientist who searches for and studies the remains of people from the past (p. 39)

armistice an agreement to end fighting (p. 669)

armory place or building where arms and military equipment are stored (p. 557)

article section of a document (p. 278)

Articles of Confederation a constitution drafted by Congress on November 15, 1777 (p. 252)

artifact an object made by humans that represents a culture (p. 41)

artisan a person trained in a skill or labor (p. 152)

assimilate to adopt the manners and language of a country (p. 519)

B

Battle of Cowpens General Daniel Morgan defeated the British in South Carolina January 17, 1781 (p. 234)

Battle of Saratoga a turning point of the American Revolution in which the American militia defeated British forces (p. 228)

Bear Flag Republic the state of California that claimed independence from Mexico in 1846 (p. 460)

bicameral two houses of the legislative branch of government (p. 250)

bill of rights a document listing essential freedoms guaranteed to all citizens (p. 169)

Bill of Rights the first 10 amendments to the United States Constitution (pp. 169, 251)

black codes restrictive laws placed on newly freed African Americans following the Civil War (p. 611)

blockade something that prevents goods and people from moving in and out of an area (pp. 225, 369)

blockade-runner a fast ship that broke through a blocked port (p. 575)

boomtown town in the West in the 1800s that sprang up and grew quickly (p. 639)

border states the states along the line that divided the Union and Confederacy (p. 568)

borderlands the lands along the edge of a territory or claimed piece of land (p. 99)

bounty payment to soldiers for entering the armed services (p. 591)

boycott refusal to buy goods or have dealings with a country or other entity, usually to express disapproval or force acceptance of certain conditions (p. 192)

bread line lines of people waiting for a free meal during a depression (p. 672)

bureaucracy an organization of government workers (p. 287)

burgesses elected representatives to a lawmaking body in the English colonies (p. 126)

C

cabinet a group of advisers to the President (p. 328)

canal a channel dug out and filled with water to allow boats to cross a stretch of land (p. 396)

capital money and property needed to start and run a business (p. 647)

caravel small ship with a broad bow (p. 70)

carpetbaggers Northerners who moved to the South after the Civil War looking for business opportunities (p. 620)

cartographer a person who makes maps (p. 12)

cash crop food crop grown to be sold (p. 157)

caucus a closed, political meeting (p. 342)

causeway raised highway over water that connects islands to mainlands (p. 55)

cede to give up, as land (pp. 362, 461)

charter official document granting the right to settle and trade (p. 123)

checks and balances system set up in the Constitution where each branch of the government has some authority over the other (p. 270)

civilization highly developed culture, usually with organized religion and laws (p. 52)

cliff dwellers Native Americans who built houses in the walls of canyons (p. 43)

climate usual pattern of weather in an area over a long period of time (p. 26)

clipper ship of the 1800s designed for speed (p. 511)

cold war an uneasy peace after World War II marked by tensions between the United States and the Soviet Union (p. 679)

Columbian Exchange exchange of goods and ideas and people between Europe and the Americas (p. 82)

colony settlement made by a parent company (p. 79)

commandeer to take over or seize (p. 575)

Committees of Correspondence organized network for passing along news of British activity to the colonies (p. 195)

common school movement movement in support of raising standards in schools and supporting them with taxes (p. 481)

Common Sense a pamphlet written by Thomas Paine in 1776 to convince the colonists that it was time to become independent (p. 217)

commonwealth a self-governing political unit (p. 133)

compromise an agreement acceptable to both sides (p. 240)

Compromise of 1850 agreement that admitted California to the Union as a free state, allowed popular sovereignty in New Mexico and Utah, banned the slave trade in Washington, D.C., and passed a strict fugitive slave law (p. 543)

Conestoga wagon a type of horse-drawn covered wagon used to transport grain (p. 158)

conquistador Spanish adventurer in sixteenth-century America (p. 93)

conscription the drafting of men for military service (p. 590)

constituent voter who elects public officials to represent him or her (p. 289)

constitution a document presenting a plan of government (pp. 135, 250)

Constitutional Convention a 1787 meeting in Philadelphia during which the United States Constitution was written (p. 261)

Continental Army the army formed by the Second Continental Congress that would defend the colonies as a whole (p. 215)

cooperative group of individuals who join together to carry on business activities (p. 657)

coordinates degrees of latitude and longitude used to locate places on Earth (p. 13)

Copperheads the Peace Democrats who believed the Civil War should end at any cost (p. 590)

corporation a business in which investors own shares (p. 646)

cotton gin a machine that cleans the seeds from cotton fibers (p. 524)

cow town railroad center whose main business is shipping cattle to market (p. 640)

Creole mid-ranking person in Spanish colonial America born in New Spain of Spanish parents (p. 100)

Crittenden Plan proposed amendments to the Constitution guaranteeing slavery in the states where it already existed, and allowing popular vote when territories became states (p. 560)

Crusades a series of wars fought by European Christians between A.D. 1096 and 1270 (p. 65)

culture way of life of a group of people who share similar beliefs and customs (p. 41)

current constantly moving forces of air or water (p. 26)

D

debate public discussion where both sides of an issue are expressed (p. 554)

Declaration of Independence document stating the thirteen colonies were separate from Great Britain (p. 218)

democratic establishing that all people have equal rights (p. 357)

Democratic-Republicans those who believed in self-government and the sharing of power between all people (p. 341)

deport to send out of the country (p. 346)

depression a period of decline in economic activity and widespread unemployment (p. 672)

deserter soldier who abandons his or her military duty without permission (p. 370)

dictatorship political system in which the ruler has absolute authority over the government (p. 675)

diplomacy relations with foreign countries (p. 287)

diplomatic recognition an official acknowledgment (p. 408)

direct democracy government in which decisions are made by all the people (p. 283)

discrimination the practice of denying fair treatment to an individual (p. 520)

division of labor dividing up the work and giving each worker one or two simple jobs (p. 389)

duties tasks citizens are required to do (p. 291)

E

economic depression a period of time when business activity slows down and unemployment increases (p. 258)

electoral college representatives of voters in each state who select the President and Vice President (pp. 270, 283)

elevation the height of land above sea level (p. 20)

emancipation freeing of enslaved persons (p. 490)

Emancipation Proclamation President Abraham Lincoln's act that declared slavery illegal in the Confederacy (p. 576)

embargo an official government ban on trade (p. 371)

emigrate to leave one country to live in another (p. 447)

empresario person who agreed to recruit settlers to Texas for Spain in the early 1800s (p. 452)

Enlightenment a movement that emphasized science and reason as guides to help see the world more clearly (p. 180)

enslaved person a person without rights or privileges who is forced to serve another (p. 73)

entrepreneur an individual who takes risks to start new businesses or tries new ways of doing business (p. 646)

environment natural surroundings and resources (p. 10)

excise tax tax placed on goods made, sold, and used within a country (p. 331)

executive agreement an agreement that the President makes directly with the head of state of another country (p. 288)

executive branch the branch of government that carries out the laws made by the legislative branch (p. 251)

export a product that originates in one place and is sold in another (p. 151)

extended family a family that includes grandparents, aunts, uncles, cousins (p. 531)

F

factory system system that used machinery and workers together (p. 387)

federalism system of government in which power is distributed between national and state governments (pp. 268, 281)

Federalists those who supported the Constitution and a strong national government in the late 1700s (p. 338)

feudal system a system where the owner of the land managed both the land and its people (p. 64)

Fifteenth Amendment extends the right to vote to all American males over age 21 regardless of race (p. 619)

filibuster a lengthy speech used as a delaying tactic to prevent legislative action (p. 624)

First Continental Congress the first meeting of representatives from every colony, except Georgia, in September 1774 to discuss common concerns (p. 197)

foothills low hills at the base of a mountain (p. 20)

forty-niners gold seekers who went to California in 1849 (p. 464)

Fourteenth Amendment grants citizenship and equal protection of the laws to all persons born in the United States (p. 612)

free world non-Communist nations (p. 679)

Free-Soil party a political party founded in 1848 by antislavery Whigs and Democrats (p. 541)

Freeport Doctrine statement made by Senator Stephen A. Douglas that a territory could decide if it supported slavery (p. 555)

French and Indian War a war between the British and the French over claim to land in America; the British defeated both the French and the Indians in 1763 (p. 183)

frontier a thinly settled area on the outer limits of a colony (p. 161)

Fugitive Slave Act part of the Compromise of 1850; it mandated harsh penalties for those who assisted runaway slaves (p. 545)

Fundamental Orders of Connecticut the first American constitution or plan of government (p. 135)

G

gentry the highest social class of the American colonies (p. 179)

geography the study of the earth and its land, water, and plant and animal life (p. 8)

ghost town town in the West that was quickly abandoned after the Gold Rush (p. 639)

glacier large, thick body of slowly moving ice, found in mountains and polar regions (p. 39)

gold standard policy of printing money only when there is sufficient gold to back it up (p. 657)

graduated income tax a federal tax that requires wealthy people to pay a higher percentage of their income than poorer people pay (p. 657)

Great Awakening a movement in the 1730s and 1740s that was marked by renewed interest in religion (p. 179)

Great Migration the movement of English settlers to the American colonies from 1630 to 1640 (p. 132)

greenback paper money issued by the United States government that was not backed by gold or silver (p. 592)

interstate commerce trade between states (p. 402)

Intolerable Acts laws passed by England in 1774 to punish colonists for the Boston Tea Party (p. 196)

ironclad ironplated ships (p. 575)

Iroquois League a powerful Native American confederation (p. 185)

isthmus narrow piece of land connecting two larger pieces of land (p. 20)

H

habeas corpus legal principle that guarantees persons arrested the right to know charges brought against them and to appear before a judge in a court of law (p. 590)

heavy industry industry that produces materials such as coal, iron, or steel (p. 645)

hemisphere half of the earth; the Equator divides the earth into Northern and Southern hemispheres; the Prime Meridian divides it into Eastern and Western hemispheres (p. 15)

hieroglyphs ancient form of Egyptian writing using pictographs (p. 54)

Homestead Act a government offer of free land to settlers in 1862 (p. 640)

homesteader person granted land under the Homestead Act of 1862 (p. 640)

House of Refuge institution that took in and educated child offenders (p. 485)

I

immigrant person who moves from one place to make a permanent home in another place (pp. 11, 518)

impeach to bring formal charges against a federal or state public official with the intent of removing the official from office (pp. 270, 539)

import a trade product that is brought into a country (p. 151)

impressment act of forcing men to serve military duty (p. 369)

indentured servant person who agreed to work for a colonial employer for a specified time in exchange for passage to America (p. 125)

indigo a plant that produces a blue dye (p. 144)

Industrial Revolution a period of time marked by the rise of factories that used machines to produce goods (p. 386)

interchangeable parts system of making parts that are exactly alike (p. 389)

J

joint-stock company form of business organization; pooled funds of many investors or stockholders who can independently sell their shares of the company (p. 123)

judicial review the right of the Supreme Court to review laws passed by Congress (p. 360)

K

Kansas-Nebraska Act act in 1854 that divided the Nebraska Territory into two separate territories, and repealed the ban on slavery north of the Missouri Compromise line; the citizens of each territory would be able to determine whether their state would be slave or free (p. 547)

kitchen cabinet a group of personal advisers to President Andrew Jackson (p. 427)

Ku Klux Klan a secret group, first set up in the South after the Civil War, that terrorized African Americans and other minorities (p. 618)

L

labor union a group of workers who join together to convince management to improve working conditions and wages (p. 517)

laissez-faire a hands-off government policy concerning private businesses (pp. 358, 647)

latitude location north or south of the Equator measured by imaginary lines (parallels) numbered in degrees (p. 13)

legislative branch the lawmaking branch of government (p. 250)

legislature a lawmaking body (p. 171)

libel the act of publishing harmful statements (p. 170)

liberty freedom of people to live as they choose (p. 282)

Glossary

longitude location east and west of the Prime Meridian measured by imaginary lines (meridians) numbered in degrees (p. 13)

loose construction to increase the power of the national government based on the Constitution (p. 340)

Loyalist a colonist who sided with Great Britain during the American Revolution (p. 219)

M

maize a large-seeded grass cultivated by people in the central valley of Mexico which became the forerunner of corn (p. 40)

manor large estate owned by a noble on which peasants lived and were protected in exchange for their services (p. 63)

map projection a way of drawing the round earth on a flat map (p. 16)

Marbury v. *Madison* Supreme Court ruling that claimed a law passed by Congress was unconstitutional (p. 360)

margin buying stocks with borrowed money (p. 672)

martial law form of military rule that suspends Bill of Rights guarantees; laws administered by the military in an emergency situation when civilian law-enforcement agencies are not able to maintain order (p. 568)

mass production goods made in large quantities, in a short time, for less cost (p. 389)

Massachusetts Bay Colony a colony founded in 1630 by Puritans in the area around Massachusetts Bay (p. 133)

Massachusetts Bay Company company formed in 1629 by Puritans to start a colony in America (p. 133)

Mayflower Compact an agreement made by Pilgrim leaders that ensured self-government (p. 130)

mercantilism the theory that a state's power depends on its wealth (p. 170)

meridian lines of longitude (p. 13)

mesa area of raised land with steep sides; smaller than a plateau (p. 21)

mestizo person in the Spanish colonies of both Spanish and Native American parents (p. 100)

Middle Ages a period from A.D. 500 to 1500 during which feudalism replaced centralized government and the Roman Catholic church became a powerful force in Europe (p. 63)

Middle Passage the forced trip between Africa and America made by enslaved Africans (p. 165)

militia group of civilians declared by law to be called to military service and trained as soldiers to fight in emergencies (p. 197)

minutemen militia volunteers who could be ready to fight at a moment's notice during the American Revolution (p. 198)

mission religious community, often near a small town and surrounding a church (p. 99)

Missouri Compromise passed in 1820, it allowed all new states north of the Missouri Compromise line to enter the Union as free states; it would keep an even balance of power in the Senate—12 free states and 12 slave states (p. 403)

monarch a ruler or head of a country (p. 63)

monopoly exclusive control of a product or service in a particular market by a single company (pp. 402, 647)

Monroe Doctrine a policy that warned European nations not to interfere in the Americas (p. 409)

Mound Builders ancient Native American culture that built monuments of earth (p. 41)

multinational state a nation with many different ethnic groups (p. 686)

mutiny to seize control of a ship from the captain and officers (p. 77)

N

Nahuatl the language of the Aztec people (p. 93)

national anthem an official song of praise and patriotism (p. 380)

national debt the total amount a government owes (p. 329)

National Road a government-funded roadway that led to the West (p. 394)

nationalism feelings of pride and devotion to one's country (pp. 399, 667)

nationalize government action of taking over a business (p. 657)

nativist one who distrusts immigrants (p. 519)

naval stores products of pine forests used in wooden shipbuilding and maintenance (p. 143)

navigation the science of piloting ships or aircraft (p. 70)

Navigation Acts laws passed by England to control colonial trade (p. 171)

neutral choosing not to take sides in a dispute (p. 335)

nominating convention a meeting where delegates from each state cast their votes for political candidates (p. 423)

Northwest Passage water route to Asia through North America sought by European explorers (p. 85)

nullification right of states to declare a federal law illegal (p. 431)

nullify to declare a law invalid (p. 347)

O

Olive Branch Petition a letter of peace drafted by the Second Continental Congress to Great Britain (p. 215)

open range vast areas of unfenced lands in the West; used by ranchers for grazing cattle (p. 639)

overseer direct supervisor of enslaved workers (p. 528)

P

parallel lines of latitude (p. 13)

pass an opening between mountains (p. 446)

patent exclusive right to use, make, or sell an invention (p. 515)

Patriot one who supported independence from Great Britain for the thirteen colonies (p. 219)

patroon landowner in the Dutch colonies who received rent, taxes, and labor from tenant farmers (pp. 138, 158)

peninsulare government and church official in Spanish colonial America who had been born in Spain (p. 100)

pension payment for military service (p. 237)

pet bank a state bank (p. 428)

Pilgrim English settler seeking religious freedom in the Americas (p. 129)

plantation large farm worked by many laborers (pp. 81, 125)

pocket veto the President's power to retain a bill unsigned until Congress adjourns (p. 606)

political party a group of people who share the same viewpoints on governmental issues (p. 339)

poll tax a sum of money paid in exchange for the right to vote (p. 477)

popular sovereignty the belief that people should have the right to rule themselves (p. 282)

potlatch a feast held by wealthy Native American families of the Northwest where gifts were given to community members (p. 48)

prairie schooner lightweight, covered wagon (p. 447)

preamble the first part, or introduction, of a document (p. 218)

precedent a model to be used as a guide for future actions (p. 287)

precipitation moisture that falls as rain, snow, or sleet (p. 26)

presidio Spanish fort in the Americas built to protect mission settlements (p. 99)

privateer armed, private ship that protected colonial ports (pp. 230, 377)

Proclamation of 1763 official announcement from the British government that ended all settlement west of the Appalachian Mountains (p. 191)

prohibition banning of liquor (p. 486)

proprietary colony a colony given to an individual by the king of England (p. 139)

proprietor individual who received legal and exclusive right to a colony (p. 139)

prospector miner who explored areas for mineral deposits such as gold (p. 465)

protective tariff a tax on imports designed to protect American industries and goods (p. 401)

pueblo home built of adobe by Native Americans, or a community of these homes (p. 43)

Puritan member of the Anglican Church who wanted to "purify" the church (p. 128)

Q

Quaker Protestant reformer who believed in religious tolerance; also known as the Society of Friends (p. 139)

quartering housing and feeding (p. 192)

quota a fixed number limit (p. 591)

R

Radical Republicans representatives in Congress who supported rights for freedmen and held anti-Southern beliefs (p. 605)

ratification vote of approval (p. 327)

ratify to officially approve a proposal (p. 252)

Rebels members of the Confederate Army (p. 572)

Reconstruction period following the Civil War during which the South was rebuilt (p. 604)

reform improvement or change for the better (p. 453)

region parts of the earth that share common characteristics (p. 11)

relief differences in height in a landscape; how flat or rugged the surface is (p. 20)

Renaissance revival of interest in the arts, literature, culture, and learning of ancient Greece and Rome, c. 1400–1600 (p. 67)

rendezvous yearly meeting where mountain men traded furs for supplies (p. 446)

reparation payments made by a defeated nation as compensation for damages that occurred during a war (p. 669)

representative democracy government in which people elect leaders or officials to make decisions for them (p. 282)

Glossary

republic government in which people elect officials to represent them (p. 257)

Republicans a national political party started in 1854 (p. 552)

reservation special government land set aside for Native Americans (p. 642)

responsibilities tasks citizens should do (p. 291)

revival a period of religious awakening (p. 179)

royal colony a colony under control of the English king (p. 126)

royalty payment to make a patented device (p. 515)

rural to be outside a city, such as the countryside (p. 163)

S

saga unwritten legend or legacy (p. 63)

scalawags Southerners who joined the Republican party during Reconstruction and supported the economic development of the South (p. 620)

seamstress woman who sews for a living (p. 515)

secede withdraw from a large political body (p. 431)

Second Continental Congress the second meeting of all thirteen colonies in May 1775, to appoint a military leader and raise an army (p. 200)

Second Great Awakening revival of religious faith and social feeling during the early 1800s (p. 486)

sectionalism rivalry based on the special interests of different areas (p. 402)

sedition to act or speak out against the government to cause unrest (p. 346)

segregation enforced separation of racial groups in schooling, housing, and other public areas (p. 625)

separation of powers the division of power among the legislative, executive, and judicial branches of government (p. 268)

Separatists those who left the Anglican Church (p. 129)

serf peasant in the Middle Ages who was bound to the land (p. 64)

settlement house center located in city slum that provided immigrants with food, education, and health care (p. 654)

shaman a Native American religious leader (p. 46)

sharecroppers workers who farm the land owned by someone else and receive a share of the crops in return (p. 616)

siege the act of surrounding and attacking a fortified area over a period of time (p. 586)

slave codes laws that denied enslaved Africans most of their rights (p. 165)

slum poor, run-down area in the city (p. 653)

social mobility the opportunity for a person to move from one social class to another (p. 179)

socialism political system in which property is owned collectively (p. 486)

sovereign independent (p. 431)

specialized worker one who does only one kind of work (p. 52)

specie money in the form of gold and silver (p. 436)

spoils system practice of dismissing government job holders affiliated with a defeated party and replacing them with supporters of the winning party (p. 427)

Stamp Act law passed in 1765 by British Parliament that forced people to pay tax on items such as newspapers and legal documents (p. 192)

states' rights the belief that an individual state may restrict federal authority (p. 347)

stock shares of ownership in a company (p. 672)

strait narrow body of water lying between two pieces of land (p. 84)

strategy a plan (p. 570)

strict construction to limit the authority of the federal government to the powers specifically granted in the Constitution (p. 341)

subsidy grant of money given by the government to assist a company or other group (p. 639)

subsistence farming when farmers produce only enough to feed and maintain their families (p. 151)

suffrage right to vote (p. 423)

T

Taino Native American who lived in the Bahamas when Christopher Columbus first arrived there (p. 78)

tariff tax on imported goods (p. 331)

Tejanos people of Mexican heritage who consider Texas their home (p. 451)

telegraph device used to send messages by means of electrical impulses across a wire (p. 512)

temperance movement campaign against drinking started in the 1800s (p. 485)

tenant farmer worker who rents and farms land owned by another person and pays the rent either in cash or with a portion of the crop (p. 616)

tenement run-down, overcrowded apartment building in the city (p. 653)

tepee a Native American cone-shaped tent made from buffalo hides (p. 49)

terrace leveled off strips of land (p. 53)

textile fabric, especially woven or knitted (p. 387)

Thanksgiving a celebration of a bountiful harvest shared by the Pilgrims and Native Americans (p. 131)

Thirteenth Amendment abolished slavery in the United States (p. 606)

Tidewater the area around slow flowing rivers that are affected by the ocean tides (p. 164)

timberline elevation above which trees cannot grow (p. 30)

toleration the acceptance of different beliefs (p. 133)

Toleration Act a guarantee that all Christians had the right to worship as they please (p. 143)

toll a fee paid to use a road or turnpike (p. 394)

topography physical features of the earth's surface such as mountains (p. 20)

total war the destruction of armies as well as resources (p. 593)

totem pole a large wooden carving created by Native Americans (p. 48)

Townshend Acts laws passed by British Parliament that placed import duties on tea, paper, glass, and paint (p. 193)

Trail of Tears long journey made by the Cherokee to present-day Arkansas and Oklahoma after being forced from their land (p. 434)

Treaty of Alliance agreement in February 1778; the French army promised to support the American militia in their fight against the British (p. 228)

Treaty of Paris agreement reached by the British and French in 1763 that officially ended the French and Indian War (p. 188); also, a later agreement reached in 1783 in which Britain acknowledged the independence of the colonies (p. 240)

triangular trade route regular trading route that formed a triangle between West Indies, colonial America, Europe, and West Africa (p. 152)

tributary a small branch of a river (p. 21)

tribute payment for protection (p. 334)

turnpike private road blocked by pikes; required payment of a toll by travelers (p. 394)

tyranny cruel and unjust rule (p. 283)

U

ultimatum a demand that could have serious consequences if ignored (p. 408)

unconstitutional contrary to what is written in the Constitution (p. 329)

Underground Railroad series of houses where "conductors" hid runaway enslaved persons, helping them on their escape to freedom (p. 491)

urban relating to that within a city (p. 163)

V

veto action by which an executive rejects a bill submitted by a legislature; to refuse to approve (p. 264)

viceroy a governor of the Spanish empire ruling in the Americas (p. 99)

vigilante member of an organization of citizens who takes the law into his or her own hands (p. 465)

W

war hawk a person in 1812 who wanted the United States to go to war against Great Britain (p. 375)

weather condition of the earth's atmosphere over a short period of time (p. 26)

Wilderness Road rocky trail through the Appalachian Mountains; traveled by settlers heading south of the Ohio River (p. 393)

writs of assistance written orders that allowed officials to conduct unrestricted searches for suspected smuggled goods; blank search warrants (p. 193)

X

XYZ Affair event in 1797 in which French representatives demanded bribes from American ambassadors (p. 345)

Y

Yankee member of the Union Army in the Civil War (p. 572)

yeomanry families on small Southern farms (p. 522)

Glossary

Spanish Glossary

★ ★

A

abolitionist/abolicionista persona que quería dar fin a la esclavitud (p. 488)

adobe/adobe material de construcción hecho de tierra y paja (p. 43)

Age of Exploration/Época de las Exploraciones período que se extiende del Siglo XV al XVI, durante el cual muchos exploradores navegaron los mares y delinearon los mapas del mundo (p. 78)

Albany Plan of Union/Plan de Unión de Albany plan propuesto por Benjamín Franklin, que convocaba a un reunión de delegados de cada colonia con un líder designado por el rey británico (p. 186)

alien/extranjero forastero que vive en los Estados Unidos (p. 346)

amendment/enmienda alteración, o cambio escrito, en un documento (pp. 271, 279)

American System/Sistema Norteamericano sistema propuesto por Henry Clay que se proponía ayudar la economía de cada sector del país e incrementar el poder del gobierno federal (p. 400)

amnesty/amnistía acción de un gobierno por la cual se concede perdón a un individuo o grupo; perdón oficial de delitos (p. 605)

annex/anexar añadir o hacer una parte de algo (p. 449)

apprentice/aprendiz persona ligada a un patrono para aprender un arte u oficio sin recibir paga (p. 161)

aqueduct/acueducto canal o tubo grande para conducir las aguas (p. 55)

archaeologist/arqueólogo científico que busca y estudia los restos de personas del pasado (p. 39)

armistice/armisticio acuerdo para dar fin a una lucha (p. 669)

armory/arsenal lugar o edificio donde se almacenan armas y equipo militar (p. 557)

article/artículo secciones de un documento (p. 278)

Articles of Confederation/Artículos de la Confederación constitución redactada por el Congreso en noviembre 15, 1777 (p. 252)

artifact/artefacto objeto hecho por seres humanos representativo de una cultura (p. 41)

artisan/artesano persona entrenada en una destreza o trabajo (p. 152)

assimilate/asimilar adoptar las costumbres y el lenguaje de un país (p. 519)

B

Battle of Cowpens/Batalla de Cowpens en enero 17, 1781, el General Daniel Morgan derrotó a los británicos en South Carolina (p. 234)

Battle of Saratoga/Batalla de Saratoga momento decisivo en la Revolución Norteamericana en el cual la milicia norteamericana venció a las fuerzas británicas (p. 228)

Bear Flag Republic el estado de California que reclamó su independencia de Méjico en el año 1845 (p. 460)

bicameral/bicameral las dos cámaras de la rama legislativa del gobierno (p. 250)

Bill of Rights/Enmienda de los Derechos Civiles las primeras diez enmiendas a la Constitución de los Estados Unidos (pp. 169, 251)

black codes/códigos negros leyes restrictivas impuestas a los recién libertados afronorteamericanos después de la Guerra Civil (p. 611)

blockade/bloqueo alguna medida que evita que personas y productos entren y salgan de un área (pp. 225, 369)

blockade-runner embarcación rápida que se abría camino a través de un puerto bloqueado (p. 575)

boomtown/ciudad en auge pueblos en el Oeste en el siglo XIX que surgieron y se desarrollaron rápidamente (p. 639)

border states/estados limítrofes los estados a lo largo de la línea divisoria entre la Unión y la Confederación (p. 568)

borderlands/territorios fronterizos las tierras situadas en los bordes de un territorio o porciones de tierras reclamadas (p. 99)

bounty/paga sueldo de los soldados por unirse a las fuerzas armadas (p. 591)

boycott/boicot rechazo a comprar mercancías o a comerciar con un país u otra entidad, usualmente utilizado para expresar desaprobación o para forzar la aceptación de ciertas condiciones (p. 192)

bread line/fila del pan hilera de personas en espera de una comida gratis durante una depresión (p. 672)

bureaucracy/burocracia organización de empleados del gobierno (p. 287)

burgesses/diputados representantes elegidos al cuerpo legislativo en las colonias inglesas (p. 126)

C

cabinet/gabinete grupo de consejeros del Presidente (p. 328)

canal/canal cauce artificial excavado y llenado de agua que permite a los barcos cruzar una extensión de tierra (p. 396)

capital/capital el dinero y la propiedad necesarios para iniciar y dirigir una empresa (p. 647)

caravel/carabela pequeña nave con una proa ancha (p. 70)

carpetbaggers norteños que se mudaron al Sur después de la Guerra Civil en busca de oportunidades de negocio (p. 620)

cartographer/cartógrafo persona que dibuja mapas (p. 12)

cash crop/cultivo comercial cosecha de alimentos cultivada para la venta (p. 157)

caucus/concilio político reunión política a puertas cerradas (p. 342)

causeway/viaducto carreteras elevadas sobre el agua que unen las islas a tierra firme (p. 55)

cede/ceder renunciar, como por ejemplo, a tierras (pp. 362, 461)

charter/carta institucional documento oficial que concede el derecho de establecerse y comerciar (p. 123)

checks and balances/revisiones y comprobaciones sistema establecido en la Constitución por el cual cada rama del gobierno tiene alguna autoridad sobre las otras (p. 270)

civilization/civilización cultura altamente desarrollada que usualmente tiene religión y leyes organizadas (p. 52)

cliff dwellers/habitantes de los acantilados indígenas norteamericanos que construyeron casas en las paredes de los desfiladeros (p. 43)

climate/clima patrón constante en la temperatura de un área durante un largo período de tiempo (p. 26)

clippers/clípers barcos del siglo XVIII diseñados para alcanzar mayor velocidad (p. 511)

cold war/guerra fría paz inestable después de la Segunda Guerra Mundial, caracterizada por las tensiones entre Estados Unidos y la Unión Soviética (p. 679)

colony/colonia establecimiento fundado por una compañía madre (p. 79)

Columbian Exchange/intercambio colombino intercambio de mercancías, ideas y personas entre Europa y las Américas (p. 82)

commandeer/confiscar posesionarse o embargar (p. 575)

Committees of Correspondence/Comités de Correspondencia red organizada para transmitir noticias de la actividad británica a las colonias (p. 195)

common school movement/movimiento de las escuelas elementales movimiento que apoyaba la elevación de las normas (p. 481)

Common Sense/Sentido Común folleto escrito por Thomas Paine en 1776, para convencer a los colonos de que era hora de ser independientes (p. 217)

commonwealth/mancomunidad unidad política de gobierno propio (p. 133)

compromise/convenio acuerdo aceptable a ambas partes (p. 240)

Compromise of 1850/Convenio de 1850 acuerdo que admitía a California en la Unión como estado libre y que permitía la soberanía popular en Nuevo Méjico y en Utah, condenaba el comercio de esclavos en Washington D.C. y aprobaba una ley estricta para los esclavos fugitivos (p. 543)

Conestoga wagon/vagón Conestoga un tipo de vagón tirado por caballos para transportar el grano (p. 158)

conquistador/conquistador aventurero español del Siglo XVI en las Américas (p. 93)

conscription/reclutamiento alistamiento de los hombres para el servicio militar (p. 590)

constituent/elector votante que selecciona a los funcionarios públicos para sus cargos (p. 289)

constitution/constitución documento que contiene el plan de un gobierno (pp. 135, 250)

Constitutional Convention/Convención Constitucional reunión que tuvo lugar en Philadelphia en 1787 en la cual se redactó la Constitución (p. 261)

Continental Army/Ejército Continental ejército organizado por el Segundo Congreso Continental que debería defender las colonias como un todo (p. 215)

cooperative/cooperativa grupo de individuos que se asocian para desarrollar actividades comerciales (p. 657)

coordinates/coordenadas grados de latitud y longitud que se usan para localizar un lugar en la Tierra (p. 13)

Copperheads Demócratas de la Paz que creían que la Guerra Civil debía terminar a toda costa (p. 590)

corporation/corporación negocio en el cual los inversionistas poseen acciones (p. 646)

cotton gin/desmotadora de algodón máquina para quitar las semillas de las fibras de algodón (p. 524)

cow town/estación ganadera centro de ferrocarriles cuyo negocio principal es embarcar ganado al mercado (p. 640)

Creole/criollo persona de condición intermedia en la América colonial española, nacida en Nueva España de padres españoles (p. 100)

Crittenden Plan/Plan de Crittenden enmiendas propuestas a la Constitución garantizando la esclavitud en los estados donde ya ésta existía, y concediendo el voto popular a los territorios que se convertían en estados (p. 560)

Crusades/Cruzadas serie de expediciones militares realizadas por los cristianos europeos de los años 1096 al 1270 d.C. (p. 65)

culture/cultura modo de vida de un conjunto de personas que comparten creencias y costumbres (p. 41)

current/corriente fuerza de aire o de agua en constante movimiento que puede ser caliente o fría (p. 26)

D

debate/debate discusión pública en la cual se presentan dos aspectos de un asunto (p. 554)

Declaration of Independence/Declaración de Independencia documento que afirmaba que las colonias eran independientes de la Gran Bretaña (p. 218)

democratic/democrático que establece que todas las personas tienen los mismos derechos (p. 357)

Democratic-Republicans/republicanos democráticos aquéllos que creían en el gobierno propio y en la participación de todo el pueblo en el poder (p. 341)

deport/deportar expulsar del país (p. 346)

depression/depresión período de declinación en la actividad económica y de desempleo extendido por todas partes (p. 672)

deserters/desertores soldados que abandonan el servicio militar sin permiso (p. 370)

dictatorship/dictadura sistema político en el cual el jefe supremo tiene autoridad absoluta sobre el gobierno (p. 675)

diplomacy/diplomacia relaciones con países extranjeros (p. 287)

diplomatic recognition/reconocimiento diplomático aprobación oficial (p. 408)

direct democracy/democracia directa gobierno en el cual las decisiones son hechas por el pueblo (p. 283)

discrimination/discriminación la práctica de negar un trato justo a un grupo de individuos (p. 520)

division of labor/división del trabajo separación que da a cada uno de los trabajadores una o dos labores sencillas (p. 389)

duties/deberes tareas requeridas de los ciudadanos en una democracia (p. 291)

E

economic depression/depresión económica período de tiempo durante el cual la actividad comercial disminuye y aumenta el desempleo (p. 258)

electoral college/colegio electoral representantes o electores en cada estado que seleccionan al Presidente y al Vicepresidente (pp. 270, 283)

elevation/altitud altura de la tierra sobre el nivel del mar (p. 20)

emancipation/emancipación liberación de las personas esclavizadas (p. 490)

Emancipation Proclamation/Proclamación de la Emancipación ley del Presidente Lincoln que declaraba ilegal la esclavitud en la Confederación (p. 576)

embargo/embargo prohibición oficial del gobierno de comerciar (p. 371)

emigrate/emigrar abandonar un país para vivir en otro (p. 447)

empresario persona que aceptaban reclutar colonizadores para una zona fronteriza (p. 452)

Enlightenment/Iluminismo movimiento cultural que enfatizaba la ciencia y la razón como guías para ver el mundo más claramente (p. 180)

enslaved person/persona esclavizada persona sin derechos ni privilegios forzada a servir a otra (p. 73)

entrepreneur/empresario individuo que se arriesga a comenzar negocios o a hacerlos de modos distintos (p. 646)

environment/medio ambiente alrededores y recursos naturales (p. 10)

excise tax/impuesto sobre consumo impuesto que se paga sobre productos fabricados, vendidos y usados dentro de un país (p. 331)

executive agreement/acuerdo ejecutivo acuerdo que el Presidente toma directamente con el jefe de estado de otro país (p. 288)

executive branch/poder ejecutivo rama del gobierno que aplica las leyes hechas por el poder legislativo (p. 251)

export/mercancía exportada producto que proviene de un lugar y se vende en otro (p. 151)

extended family/familia completa grupo familiar que incluye a abuelos, tías, tíos y primos (p. 531)

F

factory system/sistema de fábrica sistema que utilizaba maquinaria y trabajadores a la vez (p. 387)

federalism/federalismo sistema de gobierno en el cual el poder se distribuye entre el gobierno nacional y los gobiernos estatales (pp. 268, 281)

Federalists/federalistas aquellos que apoyaban la Constitución y un gobierno nacional firme (p. 338)

feudal system/sistema feudal sistema en el cual el dueño de la tierra administraba tanto a ésta como a sus moradores (p. 64)

Fifteenth Amendment/Enmienda Décimoquinta extiende el derecho al voto a todos los hombres norteamericanos mayores de 21 años sin tomar en cuenta su raza (p. 619)

filibuster/filibusteo largo discurso usado como táctica dilatoria para prevenir una acción legislativa (p. 624)

First Continental Congress/Primer Congreso Continental primera reunión de representantes de todas las colonias, excepto Georgia, en septiembre de 1774, para discutir intereses comunes (p. 197)

foothills/cerros colinas de poca elevación al pie de una montaña (p. 20)

forty-niners buscadores de oro que fueron a California en 1849 (p. 464)

Fourteenth Amendment/Enmienda Décimocuarta concede la ciudadanía y la misma protección de las leyes a todas las personas nacidas en los Estados Unidos (p. 612)

Free-Soil party partido político fundado en 1848 por los Whigs antiesclavistas y los demócratas (p. 541)

free world/mundo libre naciones no comunistas (p. 679)

Freeport Doctrine/Doctrina Freeport declaración hecha por el Senador Stephen A. Douglas de que un territorio podía decidir si apoyaba o no la esclavitud (p. 555)

French and Indian War/Guerra contra los franceses y los indios guerra entre los británicos y los franceses para reclamar la tierra de América. Los británicos vencieron tanto a los franceses como a los indios en 1763 (p. 183)

frontier/frontera zona poco poblada en las afueras de una colonia (p. 161)

Fugitive Slave Act/Ley de los esclavos fugitivos parte del Convenio de 1850 que ordenaba fuertes castigos para quienes ayudaban a esclavos fugitivos (p. 545)

Fundamental Orders of Connecticut/Órdenanzas Fundamentales de Connecticut la primera constitución o plan de gobierno norteamericano (p. 135)

G

gentry la clase social más elevada en las colonias norteamericanas (p. 179)

geography/geografía el estudio del planeta Tierra: sus tierras, aguas y vida vegetal y animal (p. 8)

ghost town/pueblo fantasma pueblos del Oeste que fueron abandonados rápidamente después de la Fiebre del Oro (p. 639)

glazier/glaciar acumulación de hielo que se desliza lentamente, formada en las montañas y en las regiones polares (p. 39)

gold standard/patrón oro la política de imprimir dinero sólo cuando hay suficiente oro para respaldarlo (p. 657)

graduated income tax/impuesto graduado sobre la renta impuesto federal que requiere de personas ricas el pago de un porcentaje más elevado de sus entradas que de las personas pobres (p. 657)

Great Awakening/Gran Despertar movimiento de las décadas de 1730 y 1740 que se señaló por un interés renovado en la religión (p. 179)

Great Migration/La Gran Migración el movimiento de colonizadores ingleses hacia las colonias norteamericanas desde 1630 hasta 1840 (p. 132)

greenbacks/billetes greenback papel moneda emitido por el gobierno de los Estados Unidos que no estaba respaldado por oro ni plata (p. 592)

H

habeas corpus/hábeas corpus principio legal que garantiza a las personas detenidas el derecho de conocer los cargos hechos en su contra y de comparecer ante un juez o un tribunal de justicia (p. 590)

heavy industry/industria pesada industria que fabrica materiales como carbón, hierro o acero (p. 645)

hemisphere/hemisferio mitad de la Tierra. El ecuador divide a la Tierra en los hemisferios norte y sur. El primer meridiano la divide en los hemisferios oriental y occidental (p. 15)

hieroglyphs/jeroglíficos forma antigua de escritura egipcia mediante el uso de pictografías (p. 54)

Homestead Act/Ley de Repartición de Tierras oferta del gobierno de tierras gratuitas a los colonizadores en 1862 (p. 640)

homesteader persona a quien se concedió propiedad bajo la ley de Repartición de Tierras de 1862 (p. 640)

House of Refuge/Hogar de Refugio institución que recibía y educaba a abusadores de menores (p. 485)

I

immigrant/inmigrante persona que se muda de su país para hacer su residencia permanente en otro (pp. 11, 518)

impeach/impugnar formular cargos formales contra un funcionario público federal o estatal a fin de quitarlo de su cargo (pp. 270, 539)

import/mercancía importada producto comercial que se introduce en un país (p. 151)

impressment/leva forzosa acto de reclutar obligatoriamente hombres para el servicio militar (p. 369)

indentured servant/sirviente por contrato persona que aceptaba trabajar para un patrono de las colonias por un tiempo determinado a cambio del pasaje para América (p. 125)

indigo/añil planta que produce un colorante azul (p. 144)

Industrial Revolution/Revolución Industrial un período caracterizado por el surgimiento de fábricas que utilizaban máquinas para elaborar los productos (p. 386)

interchangeable parts/piezas intercambiables sistema de fabricar piezas exactamente iguales (p. 389)

interstate commerce/comercio interestatal comercio entre estados (p. 402)

Intolerable Acts/Leyes Intolerables leyes aprobadas por Inglaterra en 1774 para castigar a los colonos por el Motín del Té en Boston (p. 196)

ironclad/blindado buques revestidos con chapas metálicas (p. 575)

Iroquois League/Liga Iroquesa poderosa confederación de indígenas norteamericanos que fue la primera forma de gobierno representativo en Norteamérica (p. 185)

isthmus/istmo estrecha faja de terreno que une dos extensiones mayores de tierra (p. 20)

J

joint-stock company/compañía por acciones forma de organización de negocios en la cual se consolidan los fondos de muchos inversionistas o accionistas que pueden vender sus acciones independientemente (p. 123)

judicial review/revisión judicial derecho que tiene la Corte Suprema de revisar leyes aprobadas por el Congreso (p. 360)

K

Kansas-Nebraska Act/Ley Kansas-Nebraska esta ley, aprobada en 1854, abrió la posibilidad de estados esclavistas en el Oeste que previamente habían sido libres (p. 547)

kitchen cabinet/gabinete de cocina grupo de consejeros personales del Presidente Andrew Jackson (p. 427)

Ku Klux Klan/Ku Klux Klan un grupo secreto, establecido primeramente en el Sur después de la Guerra Civil, que aterrorizaba a los afronorteamericanos y a otras minorías (p. 618)

L

labor union/sindicato laboral grupo de trabajadores que se unen para convencer a la gerencia de que mejore las condiciones de trabajo y los salarios (p. 517)

laissez-faire/laissez-faire la política del "dejar hacer" del gobierno concerniente a las empresas privadas (pp. 358, 647)

latitude/latitud localización al norte o al sur del ecuador medida en grados por líneas imaginarias (paralelos) (p. 13)

legislative branch/poder legislativo la rama del gobierno que establece las leyes (p. 250)

legislature/legislatura cuerpo legislativo (p. 171)

libel/libelo acción de publicar afirmaciones infamatorias (p. 170)

longitude/longitud localización al este o al oeste del primer meridiano medida en grados por líneas imaginarias (meridianos) (p. 13)

loose construction/libre interpretación aumento del poder del gobierno nacional basándose en la Constitución (p. 340)

Loyalist/lealista colonos norteamericanos que apoyaban el gobierno inglés; alguien que es leal o permanece fiel a una causa política, partido o gobierno (p. 219)

M

maize/maíz hierba alta de granos, cultivada por los habitantes del valle central de México, que fue el precursor de nuestro maíz (p. 40)

manor/feudo finca grande perteneciente a un noble en la cual los labriegos vivían y recibían protección a cambio de sus servicios (p. 63)

map projection/proyección cartográfica manera de dibujar una superficie esférica de la Tierra en una superficie plana (p. 16)

Marbury v. Madison/Marbury v. Madison primer fallo de la Corte Suprema que declaró que una ley aprobada por el Congreso era inconstitucional (p. 360)

margin/margen la compra de acciones con dinero prestado (p. 672)

martial law/ley marcial forma de gobierno militar que suspende las garantías de los derechos civiles; leyes aplicadas por agencias militares en una situación de emergencia cuando las agencias civiles encargadas de aplicarlas no son capaces de mantener el orden (p. 568)

mass production/producción en masa artículos fabricados en grandes cantidades en corto tiempo y a un precio más bajo (p. 389)

Massachusetts Bay Colony/Colonia de la Bahía de Massachusetts colonia fundada en 1630 por los puritanos ingleses del área alrededor de la Bahía de Massachusetts (p. 133)

Massachusetts Bay Company/Compañía de la Bahía de Massachusetts compañía creada en 1629 por los puritanos para fundar una colonia en América (p. 133)

Mayflower Compact/Pacto del Mayflower acuerdo tomado por los líderes de los peregrinos, que aseguraba su gobierno propio (p. 130)

mercantilism/mercantilismo teoría que establece que el poder de un estado reside en su riqueza (p. 170)

meridian/meridiano líneas de longitud (p. 13)

mesa/meseta elevación de tierra de laderas escarpadas y más pequeña que una altiplanicie (p. 21)

mestizo/mestizo persona en las colonias españolas de padres españoles e indígenas americanos (p. 100)

Middle Ages/Edad Media período que se extiende desde el siglo VI al siglo XVI d.C., durante el cual el feudalismo reemplazó al gobierno centralizado y la Iglesia Católica Romana se convirtió en una fuerza poderosa en Europa (p. 63)

Middle Passage/Paso Central travesía forzada entre África y América que hacían los africanos esclavizados (p. 165)

militia/milicia grupo de civiles seleccionados por ley para ser llamados al servicio militar y entrenados como soldados para luchar en casos de emergencia (p. 197)

minutemen militia/milicia de los minutemen voluntarios listos a luchar en el acto (p. 198)

mission/misión comunidad religiosa, frecuentemente cerca de un pueblo pequeño y en los alrededores de una iglesia (p. 99)

Missouri Compromise/Pacto de Missouri aprobado en 1820, permitía a todos los nuevos estados al norte de la línea del Pacto de Missouri pertenecer a la Unión como estados libres; mantendría un constante equilibrio de poder en el Senado: 12 estados libres y 12 estados esclavistas (p. 403)

monarch/monarca gobernador o jefe de una nación (p. 63)

monopoly/monopolio control exclusivo de un producto o servicio en un mercado específico por una compañía única (pp. 402, 647)

Monroe Doctrine/Doctrina Monroe política que rechazaba la intervención de las naciones europeas en las Américas (p. 409)

Mound Builders/constructores de tierra antigua cultura indígena de Norteamérica que construyó monumentos de tierra (p. 41)

multinational state/estado multinacional nación con muchos grupos étnicos diferentes (p. 686)

mutiny/amotinar rebelarse para arrebatar la autoridad del capitán y oficiales de una nave (p. 77)

N

Nahuatl/náhuatl lenguaje de los aztecas (p. 93)

national anthem/himno nacional canto oficial de alabanza y patriotismo (p. 380)

national debt/deuda nacional cantidad total que un gobierno adeuda (p. 329)

National Road/Carretera Nacional una carretera mantenida con fondos públicos que conducía hacia el Oeste (p. 394)

nationalism/nacionalismo sentimientos de orgullo y devoción hacia la patria (pp. 399, 667)

nationalize/nacionalizar acción del gobierno de apoderarse de un negocio (p. 657)

nativist/nativista persona que desconfía de los inmigrantes (p. 519)

naval stores/establecimientos navales productos de bosques de pinos usados en la construcción y el mantenimiento de barcos de madera (p. 143)

navigation/navegación la ciencia de pilotar barcos o naves aéreas (p. 70)

Navigation Acts/Leyes de Navegación leyes aprobadas por Inglaterra para controlar el tráfico comercial de las colonias (p. 171)

neutral/neutral que prefiere no tomar partido en una disputa (p. 335)

nominating convention/convención de nominación una reunión en la cual los delegados de cada estado emiten sus votos por candidatos políticos (p. 423)

Northwest Passage/Paso del Noroeste ruta marítima al Asia a través de Norteamérica buscada por los exploradores europeos (p. 85)

nullification/anulación derecho de un estado a declarar nula una ley federal (p. 431)

nullify/anular declarar sin fuerza legal una ley (p. 347)

O

Olive Branch Petition/Petición de la Rama de Olivo carta de paz redactada por el Segundo Congreso Continental para Gran Bretaña (p. 215)

open range/espacio abierto vasta extensión de terrenos no cercados en el Oeste, usados por los granjeros para pasto del ganado (p. 639)

overseer/mayoral supervisor inmediato de obreros esclavizados (p. 528)

P

parallel/paralelo líneas de latitud (p. 13)

pass/paso desfiladero entre montañas (p. 446)

patent/patente derecho exclusivo a usar, construir o vender un invento (p. 515)

Patriot/Patriota los partidarios de la independencia de las 13 colonias de Gran Bretaña (p. 219)

patroon/encomendero dueño de tierras en las colonias holandesas que se beneficiaban de la renta, los impuestos y el trabajo de campesinos arrendatarios (pp. 138, 158)

peninsulare/peninsular oficial del gobierno y de la iglesia en la América colonial española nacido en España (p. 100)

pension/pensión pago por algún servicio militar (p. 237)

pet bank banco estatal (p. 428)

Pilgrims/peregrinos grupo de colonizadores ingleses que buscaban la libertad de religión en América (p. 129)

plantation/plantación granja de gran extensión cultivada por muchos jornaleros (pp. 81, 125)

pocket veto/veto de bolsillo opción del Presidente a retener un proyecto de ley sin firmarlo mientras que el Congreso no esté en sesión (p. 606)

political party/partido político grupo de personas que comparten los mismos puntos de vista en cuestiones gubernamentales (p. 339)

poll tax/impuesto sobre el voto cantidad de dinero que se pagaba a cambio del derecho al voto (p. 477)

popular sovereignty/soberanía popular la creencia de que un pueblo tiene el derecho de gobernarse a sí mismo (p. 282)

potlatch fiesta celebrada por las familias indígenas norteamericanas de la costa noroeste en las cual se hacían regalos a los miembros de la comunidad (p. 48)

prairie schooner/vagón de las praderas carruaje ligero cubierto (p. 447)

preamble/preámbulo la primera parte, o introducción, de un documento (p. 218)

precedent/precedente un modelo que podría ser usado como guía en casos futuros (p. 287)

precipitation/precipitación humedad que cae en forma de lluvia, nieve o aguanieve (p. 26)

presidio/presidio fuerte español en las Américas construido para proteger los establecimientos de las misiones (p. 99)

privateer/corsario navíos privados armados que protegían los puertos de las colonias (pp. 230, 377)

Proclamation of 1763/Proclamación de 1763 proclamación oficial del gobierno británico que dio fin a todos los establecimientos al oeste de las Montañas Apalaches (p. 191)

prohibition/prohibición mandato que prohibía el uso de bebidas alcohólicas en los Estados Unidos a principios del Siglo XX (p. 486)

proprietary colony/colonia de propietario colonia concedida a un individuo por el rey de Inglaterra (p. 139)

proprietor/propietario individuo que recibía el derecho legal y exclusivo sobre una colonia (p. 139)

prospectors/exploradores de minas mineros o dueños de negocios en pueblos mineros (p. 465)

protective tariff/arancel proteccionista impuesto sobre las importaciones destinado a proteger la industria norteamericana y sus productos (p. 401)

pueblo/pueblo casas hechas de adobe, fabricadas por americanos nativos; o una comunidad de las mismas (p. 43)

Puritans/puritanos miembros de la Iglesia Anglicana que se proponían "purificar" la iglesia (p. 128)

Q

Quaker/cuáquero reformadores protestantes que creían en la tolerancia religiosa; conocidos también como la Sociedad de los Amigos (p. 139)

quartering/alojar dar techo y alimento (p. 192)

quota/cuota cantidad que expresa un límite fijo de algo (p. 591)

Spanish Glossary

R

Radical Republicans/republicanos radicales miembros del Congreso que apoyaban los derechos de los esclavos emancipados y mantenían creencias antisureñas (p. 605)

ratification/ratificación voto de aprobación (p. 327)

ratify/ratificar aprobar oficialmente una proposición (p. 252)

Rebels/Rebeldes miembros del Ejército Confederado (p. 572)

Reconstruction/Reconstrucción período posterior a la Guerra Civil durante el cual fue reedificado el Sur (p. 604)

reform/reforma mejoras o cambios para mejorar (p. 453)

region/región partes de la Tierra que presentan características comunes (p. 11)

relief/relieve diferencias de altitud en una extensión de terreno; cuán llana o escabrosa es la superficie (p. 20)

Renaissance/Renacimiento renovación del interés por las artes, literatura, cultura y saber de las antiguas Grecia y Roma del siglo XV al XVII (p. 67)

rendezvous/rendezvous reunión anual en la cual los habitantes de las montañas intercambiaban pieles por alimentos (p. 446)

reparation/reparación pagos efectuados por la nación derrotada como compensación por daños causados durante una guerra (p. 669)

representative democracy/democracia representativa gobierno en el cual el pueblo elige a sus líderes o funcionarios para que tomen decisiones por él (p. 282)

republic/república gobierno sin rey, en el cual el pueblo elige delegados que los representen (p. 257)

Republicans/republicanos partido político nacional fundado en 1854 (p. 552)

reservation/reserva territorio especial del gobierno designado para residencia de indígenas norteamericanos (p. 642)

responsibilities/responsabilidades tareas que los ciudadanos deben realizar en una democracia (p. 291)

revival/renovación despertar religioso (p. 179)

royal colony/colonia real colonia bajo el dominio del rey de Inglaterra (p. 126)

royalty/regalía pago por patentar un proyecto (p. 515)

rural/rural fuera de la ciudad, así como el campo (p. 163)

S

saga/saga leyenda o legado no escrito (p. 63)

scalawags sureños que se unieron al Partido Republicano durante la Reconstrucción y que apoyaron el desarrollo económico del Sur (p. 620)

seamstress/costurera mujer que se gana la vida cosiendo (p. 515)

secede/separar abandonar una organización política grande a la cual se pertenecía (p. 431)

Second Continental Congress/Segundo Congreso Continental la segunda reunión de las trece colonias en mayo de 1775, para designar a un jefe militar y reclutar un ejército (p. 200)

Second Great Awakening/Segundo Gran Despertar renovación de la fe religiosa y del sentimiento de interés social en los primeros años del siglo XIX (p. 486)

sectionalism/regionalismo rivalidad basada en intereses particulares de diferentes áreas (p. 402)

sedition/sedición actuar o hablar contra el gobierno para causar inquietud (p. 346)

segregation/segregación separación forzada de grupos raciales en las áreas de instrucción, zonas de residencia y otras (p. 625)

separation of powers/separación de poderes la división del poder entre las ramas legislativa, ejecutiva y judicial del gobierno (p. 268)

Separatists/separatistas personas que se separaron de la Iglesia Anglicana (p. 129)

serf/siervo labriego de la Edad Media que estaba ligado a la tierra (p. 64)

settlement house/establecimiento benéfico centros usualmente situados en los barrios bajos, que ofrecían a los inmigrantes alimento, educación y cuidado de la salud (p. 654)

shaman líder religioso nativo de América (p. 46)

sharecroppers/aparceros granjeros que cultivan tierras que no les pertenecen, y que reciben a cambio de ello una participación en las cosechas (p. 616)

siege/sitio la acción de rodear y atacar una zona fortificada durante un período de tiempo (p. 586)

slave codes/códigos de esclavos leyes que negaban a los africanos esclavizados la mayoría de sus derechos (p. 165)

slum/barrio bajo área pobre en decadencia en una ciudad (p. 653)

social mobility/movilidad social la oportunidad que tiene una persona de pasar de una clase social a otra (p. 179)

socialism/socialismo sistema político en el cual la propiedad pertenece a la colectividad (p. 486)

Spanish Glossary

sovereign/soberano independiente (p. 431)

specialized worker/obrero especializado aquél que sólo realiza un tipo de trabajo (p. 52)

specie/especie dinero en forma de monedas de oro y plata (p. 436)

spoils system/sistema de acaparamiento la práctica de dejar fuera a empleados del gobierno afiliados al partido derrotado y reemplazarlos con simpatizadores del partido vencedor (p. 427)

Stamp Act/Ley del Timbre ley aprobada en 1765 por el Parlamento Británico que obligaba al pueblo a pagar impuestos sobre artículos tales como periódicos y documentos legales (p. 192)

states' rights/derechos de los estados la creencia de que un estado en particular puede restringir la autoridad federal (p. 347)

stock/valores acciones de propiedad en una compañía (p. 672)

strait/estrecho paso angosto de mar entre dos tierras (p. 84)

strategy/estrategia táctica (p. 570)

strict construction/interpretación estricta limitar la autoridad del gobierno federal a los poderes específicamente concedidos por la Constitución (p. 341)

subsidy/subsidio concesión de dinero hecha por el gobierno para ayudar a una compañía u otro grupo (p. 639)

subsistence farming/cultivo de supervivencia cuando los campesinos solamente producen lo suficiente para alimentar y mantener a sus familias (p. 151)

suffrage/sufragio derecho al voto (p. 423)

T

Taino/taíno indígenas norteamericanos que vivían en las Bahamas cuando Cristóbal Colón arribó a aquellas islas (p. 78)

tariff/arancel impuesto sobre productos importados (p. 331)

Tejanos/tejanos personas de ascendencia mexicana que consideraban a Texas como su patria (p. 451)

telegraph/telégrafo aparato usado para enviar mensajes mediante impulsos eléctricos a través de un hilo metálico (p. 512)

temperance movement/movimiento de moderación campaña en contra de las bebidas alcohólicas que comenzó a principios del siglo XIX (p. 485)

tenant farmer/campesino arrendatario agricultor que arrienda y cultiva tierras que pertenecen a otra persona y que pagan la renta en efectivo o con parte de la cosecha (p. 616)

tenement/casa de vecindad edificio de apartamentos deteriorado y superpoblado en la ciudad (p. 653)

tepee tienda en forma de cono de los indígenas norteamericanos, hecha de piel de bisonte (p. 49)

terrace/terraza fajas de tierra niveladas (p. 53)

textile/textil tela especialmente hilada o tejida (p. 387)

Thanksgiving/Acción de Gracias celebración en reconocimiento de la abundante cosecha compartida por los peregrinos y los indígenas norteamericanos (p. 131)

Thirteenth Amendment/Enmienda Décimotercera abolía la esclavitud en los Estados Unidos (p. 606)

Tidewater/agua de marea área que rodea a ríos de corrientes lentas que son afectados por las corriente oceánicas (p. 164)

timberline/límite de la vegetación elevación sobre la cual no pueden crecer los árboles (p. 30)

toleration/tolerancia aceptación de creencias diferentes a las propias (p. 133)

Toleration Act/Ley de Tolerancia la garantía de que todos los cristianos tenían el derecho de adorar a su modo (p. 143)

toll/peaje impuesto pagado por el uso de una carretera o camino público con portazgo (p. 394)

topography/topografía características físicas de la superficie de la Tierra, como las montañas (p. 20)

total war/guerra total destrucción de ejércitos así como de medios de subsistencia (p. 593)

totem pole/poste totémico poste alto de madera tallado creado por los indígenas norteamericanos (p. 48)

Townshend Acts/Leyes de Townshend ley aprobada por el Parlamento Británico que fijaba derechos de importación sobre el té, papel, vidrio y pintura (p. 193)

Trail of Tears/Sendero de las Lágrimas larga travesía realizada por los indios Cherokee a las actuales Arkansas y Oklahoma, después de haber sido expulsados de su tierra (p. 434)

Treaty of Alliance/Tratado de Alianza acuerdo por el cual el ejército francés prometió ayudar y unió sus fuerzas a la milicia americana el 17 de febrero de 1778 (p. 228)

Treaty of Paris/Tratado de París acuerdo logrado por los británicos y los franceses en 1763, que daba fin oficialmente a la Guerra contra los franceses y los indígenas (p. 188)

triangular trade/comercio triangular ruta comercial regular que formaba un triángulo entre las Indias Occidentales, la América colonial y África Occidental (p. 152)

tributary/tributario pequeña ramificación de un río (p. 21)

tribute/tributo pago a cambio de protección (p. 334)

turnpike/carretera de peaje carretera privada bloqueada por barreras de peaje; era requisito el pago de peaje a los viajeros (p. 394)

tyranny/tiranía gobierno cruel e injusto (p. 283)

U

ultimatum/ultimátum resolución terminante que podría tener serias consecuencias si no se tomara en cuenta (p. 408)

unconstitutional/inconstitucional contrario a lo que está escrito en la Constitución (p. 329)

Underground Railroad/Ferrocarril Subterráneo serie de casas donde guías escondían esclavos fugitivos y los ayudaban a escapar hacia la libertad (p. 491)

urban/urbano relativo a todo lo comprendido dentro de una ciudad (p. 163)

V

veto/veto acción por la cual un ejecutivo rechaza un proyecto de ley sometido por una legislatura. Renunciar a aprobar (p. 264)

viceroy/virrey gobernador del imperio español que regía en América (p. 99)

vigilante miembro de una organización de ciudadanos que toman la ley en sus propias manos (p. 465)

W

war hawk/halcón de guerra persona que en 1812 quería que los Estados Unidos fueran a la guerra contra de Gran Bretaña (p. 375)

weather/tiempo estado de la atmósfera de la Tierra durante un corto período de tiempo (p. 26)

Wilderness Road/Camino de la Selva senda rocosa a través de las Montañas Apalaches utilizada por los colonizadores que se dirigían hacia el sur del río Ohio (p. 393)

writs of assistance/ordenanzas de asistencia órdenes escritas que autorizaban a los oficiales a realizar registros ilimitados con el propósito de hallar mercancías de contrabando; órdenes de registro en blanco (p. 193)

X

XYZ Affair ocurrió en 1797 y en el cual los delegados de Francia sobornaban a los embajadores norteamericanos (p. 345)

Y

Yankees/Yankees miembros del Ejército de la Unión durante la Guerra Civil (p. 572)

yeomanry/pequeño propietario familias que residían en pequeñas fincas sureñas (p. 522)

Spanish Glossary

Italicized page numbers refer to illustrations. Preceding the page number, abbreviations refer to a map (m), chart (c), photograph or other picture (p), graph (g), cartoon (crt), or painting (ptg). Quoted material is referenced with the abbreviation (q) before the appropriate page number.

A

Abilene, Kansas, 639

abolition/abolitionists, 125, 144, 149, 166, 236, 251, 257, 266, 403–04, 453, 458–59, 472, 477, 488, 492, 493–94, 496, 546; John Brown and, *q557,* 549, 557; constitutional basis, 310; Kansas and, *m548, m562,* 548, 549, 552; leaders, 489–91; Abraham Lincoln's attitude toward, 568, 590. *See also* antislavery movement

Abraham, Plains of, 187–88

absolute location, 8–9, 32

academies, 353

Acadia, 106, 107

accused persons; rights of, 280, 281, 308, 309

Aconcagua, Mount, 20

acquired immunodeficiency syndrome (AIDS), 688

Adams, Abigail, 349

Adams, John, *p344, q344, q345, q346, q425,* 423; administration; France, relations with, 345–46; at Constitutional Convention, 262; death of, 422; Declaration of Independence, 218; 1800 election, 348–49; 1828 election, 425; election, 325, 342; Federalist party support for, 347; midnight judges, 359, 360; personality, 344; as Vice President, 327, 328; White House occupation, 349

Adams, John Quincy, *p424;* 1824 election, 420; election, 385, 404–05, 423–24, 472; political party, 399; as secretary of state, 408, 409, 425

Adams, Samuel, 194, 199, 271

Adams-Onís Treaty, 384, 408

Addams, Jane, *p654, q654,* 654

Adena culture, 42

adobe, 43

AFL. *See* American Federation of Labor

Africa; continent, 15; cultures, 61, 71–72; exploration of, 61, 70–71, 72–73; Ghana empire, 71, 72; immigration, 11; Mali empire, 71, 72; Slave Coast, 73; Songhai empire, 71, 72; trade, 71

African Americans; abolitionists, 546; after Civil War, 616–17; after Reconstruction, 625; in art, 478; Bill of Rights, coverage by, 611; black codes, 611; in California Gold Rush, 465–66; cities, movement to, 652–53; citizenship, 605; civil rights movement, 681–82; in Civil War, *p578,* 589; education,

p505, 483, 530, 532; education after Civil War, *p617,* 616–17; first, 125; free, in South, 528–29; in government, 619; immigration, 6; inventions by, 530; in the North, 520; religion, 487; in Revolutionary War, 235; urban planners, 343; voting rights, 618–19; voting rights, constitutional, 312; voting rights, loss of, 423; voting rights, Reconstruction, 623, 624; white reaction to freedom, 617–18; women's rights movement, involvement in, 496; writers, 476

Age of Enlightenment, 121

Age of Exploration, *c114,* 69–85, 114–15; motivation for, 74

Age of Reason, 180

Agnew, Spiro, 683

agriculture; cash crops, 157; dry farming, 640; economic conditions, 259; economic hardship, 656–57; farmers' organizations, 657; gold standard, 657; Grange, *p657;* on Great Plains, 640; labor, *g523;* Native American, 40; price controls, 658; sharecroppers, 616; subsistence farming, 151; tenant farmers, 616

AIDS. *See* acquired immunodeficiency syndrome

airplanes, *p662–63;* aerial warfare, 670; World War I, *p632*

Alabama; exploration of, 102; readmitted to Union, 612; secession, 560

Alamo, *p454,* 442, 451, 454–56, 455

Alaska, 103; climate, 28; highway system, 28; prehistory, 39; Russian control, 183; statehood, 683

Albania, 684

Albany, New York, 109; in Revolutionary War, 227

Albany Plan of Union, 186

alcohol drinking, 485

alcoholism, 485

Aleutian Islands, 47

Aleuts, 47

Alexander II, Czar, 539

Alexander, Lamar, 689

Algeria; U.S. relations with, 368, 369

Algiers; U.S. relations with, 345

Algonquin, 50, 89, 107

Alien Acts, 346

Alien Enemies Act, 346, 359

aliens, 346

Allegheny River, 185

Allen, Ethan, 215–16

Alliance, Treaty of, 228, 335

Allied Powers (World War II), 676–77

Allies (World War I), 668

alphabet; Cherokee, *p430,* 433

Alton Observer, 492

aluminum, 645

Amazon River, 21

amendments, 271; process, *c280,* 279, 306. *See also* Constitution of the United States

American Anti-Slavery Society, 490, 496

American colonies. *See* English colonies

American Colonization Society, 472, 489

American Federation of Labor (AFL), 648

American Red Cross, 592

American Revolution, 190–200; beginnings, 177; causes and effects, *c318;* citizens' rights, 219; Continental Army. *See* Continental Army; currency, 231; Declaration of Independence, 218–23; events leading to, 190–200, 207; first armed rebellion, 198; French support for, 228, 231, 232; independence, 214–19; music, 198; national debt, 329; Netherlands support for, 231; popular opinion, 215, 217, 219; Revolutionary War. *See* Revolutionary War; Spanish support for, 229, 231; summary, 318; women in, 236

American Temperance Society, 472, 485

American Temperance Union, 486

Ames, Adelbert, 623

Amherst, Jeffrey, 188

Amherst College, 483

Amish, 160

amnesty, 605, 622

Among the Sierra Nevada Mountains, ptg443

Amundsen, Roald, 85

Anasazi, 36, 41, 43, 101

Anderson, Elijah, 546

Anderson, Robert, 566–67

Andes Mountains, 20

Andros, Edmund, 169

Anglican Church, 133, 163, 169; Roman Catholicism, split from, 128

Anglos, 453

animals, prehistoric, 39

Antarctica; continent, 15; exploration, 177

Anthony, Susan B., 496

anti-Catholic sentiment, 519–20

Antietam, Battle of, 576

Anti-Federalists, 270, 271

anti-immigrant sentiment, 346, 519–20, 651–52

B

C

D

Index

Proclamation, 564, 576–577; families, *p530,* 531; freedom, 166; fugitives, 543, 544, 546; living conditions, 529–30; music, 526; Native Americans, 81–82; population, 488, 525; revolt in Saint Domingue, 362; revolts in U.S., 532, 557; status in Constitution, 265–66. *See also* slavery. *See also* slave trade

environment; development, 688; interaction with humans, 10; protection, 7, 31, 688

Environmental Protection Agency (EPA), 31

Equator, 8, 13, 15, 32, 97

Era of Good Feelings, 399, 405

Erie, Lake, Battle of, 379

Erie Canal, *p397,* 385, 396–97

Eriksson, Leif, *q62,* 62–63, 64

essays, 674

Esteban, 101

Ethiopia, 676

Europe, *m63, m66, m70, m77, m82, m83, m86, m102, m108, m698, m700, m712, m714;* American revolution and , 228–29; Civil War and, 577; in cold war, 679–80, 684; immigrants from, *p518, p651, p694,* 518–20, 650–53; Monroe Doctrine and, 408–09; World War I and, 667–69; World War II and, 675–77; in the twentieth century, 686, 689

Europe, continent, 15

Europeans Encountering Indians, ptg2

Evans, Oliver, 387, 511

Everett, Edward, 580

Everglades, 434

executive branch, 251, 269, 328; agreements, 288; constitutional authority, 278, 302–04. *See also* presidency

exploration. *See* individual countries

Exploration, Age of, *c114,* 69–85, 114–15

export, 151

F

factories. *See* manufacturing

Fallen Timbers, Battle of, 334, 373

families; extended, 531

famines, 519

Fannin, James, 454–55

farming. *See* agriculture

Farny, Henry Francis, 642

Farragut, David, 585

Fascist party, 675

Father of the Constitution, 263

Feathered Serpent, 92

federal government; branches of, 328–29; budget, 689; business, relations with, 647; citizens, relations with, 673; formation, 327–29; growth, 685–86; Native Americans, relations with, 642; powers, 269; simplification under Thomas Jefferson, 357–59; size, 673; state government, relations with. *See* states rights; states, relations with, 279, 431; strengthening power, 400; subsidies to railroads, 639

federalism, 268, 281; principles, 284–85

Federalist, The, 270, 329, 330

Federalist Era, 326–49

Federalist party, 338; John Adams, criticism of, 346; decline, 347; legacy, 349; Louisiana Purchase, opposition to, 364; philosophy, 339–40; War of 1812, opposition to, 381

Federalists, 270

Federal Reserve System, 439

Fenno, John, 341

Ferdinand, King of Spain, 76, 78

Fern, Fanny, 476

Ferris, J.L.G., 121, 218, 318

feudal system, 63–64

Field, Cyrus W., 646

Fifteen-Gallon Law, 486

Fifteenth Amendment, 312, 466, 602, 619, 626

Fifth Amendment, 280, 308, 550

Fifty-four forty or fight, 449, 458

Fifty-fourth Massachusetts Volunteers, 578

Fifty-third Ohio regiment, 583–84

Fight for the Colors, ptg565

filibusters, 624

Fillmore, Millard, 541, 544, 553; indentured servant, 553

First Amendment, 279, 308, 347

First American Thanksgiving, The, ptg206

First Crusade, 60, 65

First Reading of the Emancipation Proclamation, ptg577

First Thanksgiving, The, ptg130

First World War. *See* World War I

Fisk University, 617

Fitch, John, 395, 510–11

flags; Betsy Ross flag, *p327;* Confederate Battle flag, *p586;* Continental Colors, *p200;* Don't Tread on Me, *p212;* First Star-Spangled Banner, *p379;* First Stars and Stripes, *p225;* Flag of New England, *p131;* Flag of New France, *p107;* Flag of 1818, *p401;* Great Star flag, *p401;* Jefferson Victory flag, *p348;* Lincoln-Hamlin campaign flag, *p556;* Seventeenth flag of the Union, *p587;* Spanish flag, *p78;* Texas Republic (Lone Star flag), *p453;* Twentieth flag of the Union, *p640;* Twenty-fifth flag, *p667;* Twenty-seventh flag, *p683*

flatboats, 510

Fletcher v. Peck, 401

Florida; *m408,* 407–08; climate, 27; exploration of, 101–02; French settlement, 101; Great Britain acquisition of, 188; missions, 103; readmitted to Union, 612; secession, 560; Seminoles in, 434; Spanish control, 144, 184; U.S. acquisition of, *m408,* 407–08

Flower, George, *q392*

Flying Cloud, 512

Forbes, Esther, *p244*

Forbes, Steve, 689

Ford, Gerald, 683

Ford, Henry, 662, 671

Ford's Theater, 607

foreign affairs. *See* foreign policy

foreign policy; tribute, 345; U.S. role after communism, 686–88

Forrest, Nathan Bedford, 618

forty-niners, 464; population, 542

Founding Fathers, 261

foundry, *p320, p621*

Fourteen Points, 669

Fourteenth Amendment, 311–12, 602, 612, 626

Fourth Amendment, 279, 308

Fourth of July in Center Square, Philadelphia, ptg385

Fox River, 107

France; John Adams administration, relations with, 345–46; in American Civil War, 576; American Revolution, support for, 228, 231; exploration by, *c106, m82, m108,* 80, 85, 105–09; formation, 66; Germany, invasion by, 676; Germany, war against, 676; Great Britain, war against, 335; Great Britain, 1763 war against. *See* French and Indian War; immigrants, 160, 163; India, trade with, 149; land claims, *m184;* Latin America, involvement in, 409; Napoleonic wars, 362; Native Americans, relations with, 107, 109, 185; North American territory, *m111,* 188; reparations, demand for, after World War I, 669; revolution, 420; Revolutionary War, involvement in, 232, 238; U.S., trade with, 371, 373; George Washington administration, relations with, 335; in World War I, 668–69; XYZ Affair, 345

Francisco, Peter, 235

Franklin, Benjamin, *p189, q188, q196;* Albany Plan of Union, 186; ambassador to France, *p231;* at Constitutional Convention, 262, 266; Declaration of Independence, 218; eyeglasses, *p261;* mail, innovations in, 182, 246; national symbol, *q254;* as a printer, *p182;* as a scientist, 180; Treaty of Paris, 240; as a writer, 181

Fredericksburg, Virginia, 578

free enterprise, 646–47

Freedmen; school, *p505*

Freedmen's Bureau, *p616, p617,* 611, 616–17

freedom of speech; constitutional authority, 279; first court decision, 170; Sedition Act, 347

Freedom's Journal, 489

Freeport Doctrine, 555

Free School Society of New York City, 480

Free-Soil party, 538, 541, 549

free world, 679

Frémont, John C., *p552,* 460, 552–53

French and Indian War, *m186,* 183–88; Battle of Quebec, 187–88; beginning, 176; British debt, 191; colonial unity, 186; declared, 187; events leading to, 183–85; military aspects, 185, 186–88; Native Americans, 185; Ohio Valley, 184–85. *See also* Seven Years' War

Index

N

Index

Index

Index

X

Y

Z

Index

Acknowledgments

★ ★

Photo Credits

★ ★

Hillel Burger; **55** (t)Nawrocki Stock Photo, (b)Museum of Ethnology; **56** Library of Congress; **57** Loren McIntyre; **60** Michael Holford; **61** (l)Peabody Museum of Salem, (r)Shostal/SuperStock, Inc; **62** Werner Forman/Art Resource; **63** Ancient Art and Architecture Collection; **65** (l)Brown Brothers, (r)Candee Productions/Nawrocki Stock Photo; **67** Brown Brothers; **69** Stock Montage; **70** North Wind Picture Archive; **71** "Vue de Lisbonne" (detail, modified version) 17th centuryCollection of Museu do Arte, Antiga-Lisboa; **72** (t)Metropolitan Museum of Art, (b)Jean-Loup Charmet/Science Photo Library/Photo Researchers; **74** (l)Scala/Art Resource, (r)file photo; **75** Erich Lessing/Art Resource; **76** Archiv/Photo Researchers; **78** U. S. Architect of the Capitol; **79** Mary Evans Picture Library; **80** Scala/Art Resource; **81** City Art Gallery, Plymouth, England; **82** H. Armstrong Roberts; **84** Giraudon/Art Resource; **88** (t)Jerry Jacka, (b)Collection of the Montreal Museum of Fine Arts, Mary Fry Dawson Bequest; **89** (t)Stock Montage, (c)W. Bertsch/H. Armstrong Roberts, (b)North Wind Picture Archive; **90** Public Archives of Canada; **91** (t)SuperStock, Inc, (b)John Macionis; **92** Kunsthistoriches Museum, Vienna/Eric Lessing, Magnum; **94** Biblioteca Nacional, Madrid; **95** (t)R. B. Pickerinton/Nawrocki Stock Photo, (b)Stock Montage; **96** Bettmann Archive; **98** R. B. Pickerinton/Nawrocki Stock Photo; **99** file photo; **100** Laurie Platt Winfrey, Inc; **101 105** file photo; **106** Giraudon/Art Resource; **112** Bettmann Archive; **113** Robert Frerck/Tony Stone Images; **114** American Museum of Natural History; **115** (l)Archiv/Photo Researchers, (r)file photo; **116** Pilgrim Hall Museum; **117** (t)Bettmann Archive, (c)Frank & Marie-Therese Wood Print Collections, Alexandria, VA, (b)David McGlynn/FPG; **118** (l)Brent Turner/BLT Productions, (r)courtesy the Association for the Preservation of Virginia Antiquities; **119** Brent Turner/BLT Productions; **120** New York Public Library; **121** (t)The Pilgrim Society, Plymouth, MA (b) Nawrocki Stock Photo; **122** Frank & Marie-Therese Wood Print Collections, Alexandria, VA; **123** E. Cooper/H. Armstrong Roberts; **124** Bettmann Archive; **125** (t)Nawrocki Stock Photo, (b)North Wind Picture Archive; **126** Jamestown-Yorktown

Foundation; **128** Pilgrim Hall Museum; **129** (l)W. Sanders/Time LIFE Syndication, (r)John Colwell from Grant Heilman; **130** The Pilgrim Society, Plymouth, MA; **132** Pilgrim Hall Museum; **134** Stock Montage; **135** Wadsworth Atheneum, Hartford; **137** H. Armstrong Roberts; **139** Shostal/SuperStock, Inc; **141** Larry Stevens/Nawrocki Stock Photo; **142** Brown Brothers; **148** Eliot Elisofon/Time LIFE Syndication; **149** (t)Tate Gallery London/Lerner Fine Art Gallery/SuperStock, Inc, (b)Brown Brothers; **150** The Shelburne Museum, Shelburne, VT; **154** (t)courtesy The Pilgrim Society, Plymouth MA, (b)Bettmann Archive; **156** Henry Ford Museum and Greenfield Village; **157** Chase Manhattan Bank; **158** (t)H. Armstrong Roberts, (b)North Wind Picture Archive; **160** (t)SuperStock, Inc, (b)North Wind Picture Archive; **162** National Gallery of Art; **163** Nawrocki Stock Photo; **164** courtesy Duke University Library; **165** National Maritime Museum, London; **167** North Wind Picture Archive; **168** Bettmann Archive; **169** North Wind Picture Archive; **170** Frank & Marie-Therese Wood Print Collections, Alexandria, VA; **173** Bettmann Archive; **174** (tl)Bettmann Archive, (tr)Andy Levin/Photo Researchers, (bl)Lowell Georgia/Photo Researchers, (br)Archive Photos; **175** (tl)Archive Photos, (tr)(bl)Andy Levin/Photo Researchers, (br)SuperStock, Inc; **176** Herb Orth/Time LIFE Syndication; **177** (t)Red Hill/The Patrick Henry National Memorial, Brookneal, VA, (b)Archive Photos; **178** North Wind Picture Archive; **180** Bettmann Archive; **181** North Wind Picture Archive; **182** Sipley/H. Armstrong Roberts; **183** painting by Don Troiani, photo courtesy Historical Art Prints, Ltd; **187** (l)Frank & Marie-Therese Wood Print Collections, Alexandria, VA, (r)Nawrocki Stock Photo; **189 190** North Wind Picture Archive; **191** Bettmann Archive; **193** John Carter Brown Library, Brown University; **194** Frank & Marie-Therese Wood Print Collections, Alexandria, VA; **196** collection of Don Troiani, photo courtesy of Historical Art Prints, Ltd; **198** (l)H. Armstrong Roberts, (r)Mark Burnett; **199** Painting by Don Troiani, photo courtesy Historic Art Prints, Ltd; **201** Culver Pictures, Inc/SuperStock Inc; **204** Brown Brothers; **205** Frank & Marie-Therese Wood Print Collections, Alexandria, VA; **206,** The Pilgrim Society, Plymouth, MA; **207**

(t)Frank & Marie©Therese Wood Print Collections, Alexandria, VA, (b)painting by Don Troiani, photo courtesy Historical Art Prints, Ltd; **208** (t)Fraunces Tavern Museum, Gift of Herbert P. Whitlock, 1913, (b)Independence National Historic Park/National Park and Monument Association; **209** (t)North Wind Picture Archive, (c)file photo, (b)SuperStock, Inc; **210 211**(t)RMIP/Richard Haynes, (b)Mark Thayer; **212** Frank & Marie-Therese Wood Print Collections, Alexandria, VA; **213** (t)Metropolitan Museum of Art, Gift of John Stewart Kennedy, 1897 (97.34), (b)Reza Estakhrian/Tony Stone Images; **214** file photo; **216** SuperStock, Inc; **217** (l)Bettmann Archive, (r)Stock Montage; **218** (t)Archive Photos, (b)SuperStock, Inc; **219** Library of Congress; **221** Architect of the Capitol, Washington, DC; **224** Stock Montage; **226** National Gallery of Art, Washington, DC; **229** The Valley Forge Historical Society; **231** North Wind Picture Archive; **232** Devaney/SuperStock, Inc; **233** William T. Ranney, MARION CROSSING THE PEDEE, 1850, o/c,1983.126, Amon Carter Museum, Fort Worth, Texas; **234** courtesy J. Quintus Massie on behalf of descendants; **235** painting by Don Troiani, photo courtesy Historical Art Prints, Ltd; **236** (t)Earl Young/FPG, (b)courtesy Rhode Island Historical Society; **237** Stock Montage; **238** painting by Don Troiani, photo courtesy of Historical Art Prints, Ltd; **239** Architect of the Capitol, Washington, DC; **241** Frank & Marie-Therese Wood Print Collection, Alexandria, VA; **244** Bettmann Archive; **245** North Wind Picture Arc Picture Archive; **247** (t)Museum of Fine Arts, Boston, (c)Stock Montage, (b)Robert Harding Associates; **248** file photo; **249** (t)Art Resource, (b)North Wind Picture Archive; **250** Stock Montage; **251** (t)North Wind Picture Archive, (b)Archive Photos; **252** The Metropolitan Museum of Art, Gift of Mrs. A. WordsworthThompson, 1899 (99.28); **255** Bettmann Archive; **257** Washington University Gallery of Art, St. Louis, Missouri/SuperStock, Inc; **258** Bettmann Archive; **260** (t)The I. N. Phelps Stokes Collection of American Historical Prints, The New York Public Library/Laurie Platt Winfrey, Inc, (b)Bettmann Archive; **261** FPG; **262** North Wind Picture Archive; **263** Bettmann Archive; **264** White House Historical Association; **267** Aaron Haupt Photography; **270** Indepen-

York Public Library; **529** Jerry Pinkney, THE BLACKSMITH, courtesy of the Afro-American Historical and Cultural Museum; **530** Photo Researchers; **531** Stock Montage; **536** (t)Bettmann Archive, (bl)A. K. G. Berlin/SuperStock, Inc, (br)Chris Sorensen/State Historical Society of Wisconsin/Wisconsin Veterans Museum; **537** (tl)Edward Owen/Art Resource, (tr)courtesy Fisk University, Nashville, TN, (cl)Aldo Tutino/Art Resource, (cr)Bettmann Archive, (b)Nawrocki Stock Photo; **538** Stock Montage; **539** (t)courtesy Robert M. Hicklin, Jr., Inc, (b)Library of Congress; **540** courtesy The Charleston Museum; **541** White House Historical Assn; **542** National Portrait Gallery; **543** (l)Bettmann, (r)Brent Turner/BLT Productions; **545** New York Public Library; **546** Bettmann Archive; **547** Frank & Marie-Therese Wood Print Collections, Alexandria, VA; **548** North Wind Picture Archive; **550** Missouri State Historical Society; **551** (t)National Museum of American Art, Washington, DC/Art Resource, NY, (b)Bob Mullenix; **552** Bettmann Archive; **553** Smithsonian Institution; **554** (l)Stock Montage, (r)private collection/Bridgeman Collection/SuperStock, Inc; **556** Laurie Platt Winfrey, Inc; **557** H. Armstrong Roberts; **564** ECHOES OF GLORY: ARMS AND EQUIPMENT OF THE CONFEDERACY, photograph by Larry Sherer ©1991 Time-Life Books Inc; **565** (t)painting by Don Troiani, photo courtesy of Historical Art Prints, Ltd, (bl)Photo Network, (br)Culver Pictures, Inc; **566** James P. Rowan/Tony Stone Images; **567** Bettmann Archive; **569** The Burns Archive; **572** North Wind Picture Archive; **573** file photo; **575** Bettmann; **576** National Archives; **577** SuperStock, Inc; **578** Stock Montage; **579** Frank & Marie-Therese Wood Print Collections, Alexandria, VA; **581** Stock Montage; **582** Nawrocki Stock Photo, Art Brown Collection; **583** UPI/Bettmann; **585** (l)Motts Photographic Center/Warren Motts, (r)Aaron Haupt Photography; **589** Motts Photographic Center/Warren Motts; **590** Smithsonian Institution; **591** Collection of Don Troiani, Southbury, CT; **593** file photo; **594** Frank & Marie-Therese Wood Print Collections, Alexandria, VA; **596** Appomattox Court House National Historical Park; **597** North Wind Picture Archive; **600** Bettmann Archive; **601** Bettmann Archive; **602** file photo; **603** (t)David David Gallery, Philadelphia/SuperStock, Inc, (b)The American Numismatic Society; **604** Frank & Marie-Therese Wood Print Collections, Alexandria, VA; **605** North Wind Picture Archive; **606** (l)Stock Montage, (r)file photo; **608** (l)Frank & Marie-Therese Wood Print Collections, Alexandria, VA, (r)file photo; **609 610** file photo; **614** Bettmann Archive; **615** collection of Nancy Gewirz, Antique Textile Resource; **616** Stock Montage; **617** North Wind Picture Archive; **618** file photo; **619** Nawrocki Stock Photo; **621** Pembroke Herbert/Picture Research Consultants; **622** file photo; **623** Stock Montage; **624** courtesy Rutherford B. Hayes Presidental Center, Fremont, OH; **627** courtesy NAACP; **630** H. Armstrong Roberts; **631** (t)collection of Nancy Gewirz, Antique Textile Resource, (b)painting by Don Troiani, photo courtesy of Historical Art Prints, Ltd; **632** (t)collection of the Whitney Museum of American Art, 50th anniversary gift of the Gilman Foundation, Inc., The Lauder Foundation, A. Alfred Taubman, an anonymous donor and purchase, (b)Arthur Beck/Photo Researchers; **633** (t)NASA, (c)Archive Photo, (b)Motts Photographic Center; **634** (t)New York Convention and Visitor Bureau/Bart Barlow, (b)Matt Meadows; **635** Matt Meadows; **636** private collection/Bridgeman Collection/SuperStock, Inc; **637** (t)Los Angeles County Museum of Art, Los Angeles County Fund, CLIFF DWELLERS by George Bellows, (b)courtesy AT&T; **638** file photo; **639** Henry Ford Museum, The Edison Institute; **642** (t)Art Resource, (b)Denver Art Museum; **644** Culver Pictures, Inc; **645** collection of The New©York Historical Society; **646** file photo; **647** (l)Smithsonian Institution, (r)Studiohio; **648** (l)Bettmann, (r)Anthracite Museum Complex; **650** Tim Courlas; **651** Bettmann; **652** collection of The New©York Historical Society; **653** file photo; **654** Stock Montage; **655** William James Glackens, LUXEMBOURG GARDENS, 1906, oil on canvas, 23-3/4x32 in.(60.33x81.28 cm) In the Collection of the Corcoran Gallery of Art, museum purchase, William A. Clark Fund; **656** Mott's Photographic Center, Inc; **657** Library of Congress; **658** Bettmann Archive; **659** Schlesinger Library, Radcliffe College; **662** (t)B. McClurg/SuperStock, Inc, (c)Archive Photos, (b)SuperStock; **663** (t)(cl)(cr)Bettmann Archive, (bl)H. Armstrong Roberts, (br)Mark Burnett; **664** Robert Reif/FPG; **665** (t)National Gallery of Art, Washington, DC, (b)Tim Crosby/Gamma-Liaison; **666** Nawrocki Stock Photo; **667** Frank & Marie-Therese Wood Print Collections, Alexandria, VA; **668** (l)file photo, (r) Collection of Colonel Stuart S. Corning, photo by Rob Huntley/Lightstream; **669** National Portrait Gallery, Smithsonian Institution/Art Resource; **670** J. Novak/SuperStock, Inc; **671** Culver Pictures, Inc; **672** UPI/Bettmann; **674** FPG; **675** (l)UPI/Bettmann, (r)Warren Motts Photographic Center; **676** Wide World Photos; **677** Warren Motts Photographic Center; **678** National Archives; **679** file photo; **680** (l)Brown Brothers, (r)Lloyd Lemmerman; **681 682** Robert Ellison/Black Star; **683** Archive Photos/White House; **684** Peter Turnley/Black Star; **685** Mark Burnett; **686** AP/Wide World Photo, photo by Greg Gibson; **687** AP/Wide World Photos; **690** National Museum of American Art, Washington, DC/Art Resource; **692** Deborah Storms/Macmillan Publication Co; **693** Wide World Photo; **694** Bettmann Archive; **695** (tl)Robert Reif/FPG, (tr)Tim Crosby/Gamma-Liaison, (b)Flip Schulke/Black Star; **696** Larry Kunkel/FPG; **726** through **733** White House Historical Association; **734** David Young Wolff/Tony Stone Images; **735** Mimi Forsyth/Monkmeyer Press; **736** Lou Merrim/Monkmeyer Press; **737** Benelux/Photo Researchers; **738** Bob Thomason/Tony Stone Images; **739** Richard T. Nowitz/Photo Researchers; **740** Jonathon Nourok/Tony Stone Images; **741** Steven Peters/Tony Stone Images; **742** Jon Riley/Tony Stone Images; **743** D.J. Ball/Tony Stone Images; **744** Gaillarde/Gamma Liaison; **745** Bob Daemmrich/The Image Works; **748** North Wind Picture Archive; **749** Bettmann Archive; **752** National Portrait Gallery/Smithsonian Institution, Art Resource; **753** (l)Mark Burnett, (r)Smithsonian Institution; **754** (l)Photo Network, (r)Mark Burnett; **755** (t)Denver Art Museum, (b)Bettmann Archive; **756 757** UPI/Bettmann; **758** Flip Schulke/Black Star.